CALIFORNIA PLACE NAMES

DEL NORTE

SISKIYOU

MODOC

HUMBOLDT

TRINITY

SHASTA

LASSEN

TEHAMA

PLUMAS

MENDOCINO

GLENN

BUTTE

SIERRA

COLUSA

YUBA

NEVADA

LAKE

SUTTER

PLACER

YOLO

EL DORADO

ALPINE

NAPA

SACRAMENTO

AMADOR

SONOMA

SOLANO

CALAVERAS

MONO

MARIN

CONTRA COSTA

SAN JOAQUIN

TUOLUMNE

SAN FRANCISCO

ALAMEDA

STANISLAUS

MARIPOSA

SAN MATEO

SANTA CLARA

MERCED

MADERA

SANTA CRUZ

SAN BENITO

FRESNO

INYO

MONTEREY

TULARE

KINGS

SAN LUIS OBISPO

KERN

SAN BERNARDINO

SANTA BARBARA

VENTURA

LOS ANGELES

RIVERSIDE

ORANGE

SAN DIEGO

IMPERIAL

0 10 20 40 60 80 100 MILES

CALIFORNIA PLACE NAMES

The Origin and Etymology of Current Geographical Names

ERWIN G. GUDDE

*Revised and Enlarged Edition with Maps
and Reference List of Obsolete Names*

UNIVERSITY OF CALIFORNIA PRESS

Berkeley, Los Angeles, London

University of California Press
Berkeley and Los Angeles, California

University of California Press, Ltd.
London, England

ISBN: 0-520-01574-6
Library of Congress Catalog Card Number: 68-11311

Third Edition, 1969 revised and enlarged
Second Printing, 1974

Manufactured in the United States of America

Prefatory Note to Second Edition

SOME FRIENDLY critics, including the late Joseph Henry Jackson, literary editor of the San Francisco *Chronicle,* have called this book the definitive work on California geographical nomenclature. Actually, the word "definitive" cannot properly be applied to any historical account; it is especially unsuited when used for the history of the geographical nomenclature of a commonwealth which is still growing at a rapid pace.

An ideal etymological and geographical dictionary would include all place names of the State, either in individual entries or in summarizations of folk, group, or cluster names. Such an ideal work would necessarily have to be based on a geographical gazetteer of the entire State. About ten years ago, Olaf Jenkins, then chief of the California Division of Mines, and I did some preliminary work toward creating such a gazetteer, using the atlas sheets of the United States Geological Survey as a basis. We soon came to the realization that only a large subsidy would make such an undertaking feasible.

Until such a geographical gazetteer is published, no "definitive" dictionary of California geographical names can be produced. However, I believe that there is some justification in calling this book "basic." It contains most names in current use that seem to me to be of any importance or interest, and it gives complete or at least partial information about them. It is up to our onomatologists, historians, geographers, and philologists to fill the gaps gradually. The new edition is a step in this direction. Perhaps when one of my successors, about A.D. 2000, brings out the tenth edition of *California Place Names,* that volume may be a "definitive" work—at least on the day of its publication.

The present edition of this dictionary cannot be definitive for another reason. There are still sources which have not been tapped—manuscripts, maps, newspaper files, forgotten books. *California Place Names* probably provides all fundamental data, but additional research will add substance to many of the items and further round out the picture. To engage in such research would be a rewarding task for county and other local historical societies. Gertrude Steger's pioneer work on Shasta County and the more recent monograph by T. S. Palmer on Death Valley and that by Paul Schulz on Lassen National Park are a good beginning. Further field work and the searching of county records, great registers, newspaper files, and so forth may uncover new facts concerning the origin and meaning of the names of many settlements and topographical features.

Although the population of the State of California has about doubled since World War II, the number of new and original names that have been given to places in that period is insignificant. Most of the developers of new residential districts lack the imagination and the courage to bestow upon their subdivisions an unusual name. They simply add "Estates" or "Glorietta" or "Del Rey" or "Woodlands" to an already existing name; they append "town" or "burg" or "vale" to their personal name; or they call their developments "Forest Hills," "Glenhaven," or "Brookdale," or give them some fanciful Spanish name. When a number of towns amalgamated to establish a new and sizable city in 1956, they could find no better name than Fremont, a name borne by dozens of places in our western states. It is fortunate that the Post Office Department has laid down certain restrictions with respect to the naming of post offices and thus sometimes forces those who would give a place a trite name to find a new or distinctive one.

However, names of communities make up only a fraction of the new names in our growing State. Many of our topographic features are as yet unnamed; a hill which now seems to be too low and insignificant to have a name will be given one when economic development and denser population make it more important. The peculiar climatic conditions of our State make the creation of new reservoirs and artificial lakes necessary; these must have names. The U. S. Board on Geographical Names has begun to give individual names to hundreds of "forks," such as the West Fork of the South Fork of the North Fork of the San Joaquin River. Needless to say, the name-giving authorities show little imagination or originality. A California board on geographic names could be of great service in making future geographic nomenclature more varied and interesting by reviving Indian names, honoring deserving pioneers, and coining and creating entirely new names.

A few of our important names are still subjects of controversy—Marin and Tehama, Mount Saint Helena, and even California, our most important and most beautiful name. Many Southwestern place names—those of pre-Spanish Mexican origin, which form an extremely interesting linguistic group—are still awaiting a specialist who will establish their etymology. Native Indian names present a special problem. The original inhabitants had very few geographical names, and practically all of these were purely descriptive. That the name Natoma contains the Indian word for 'easterners' (i.e., the people who live upstream), that Carquinez is a Spanish version of the name of the original village of the *karquines*, 'traders,' that *monache* means 'the people whose stock in trade are flies (or larvae of flies),' and that Tahoe is derived from the Indian word for 'water' or 'sheet of water' are logical explanations of the origin of these names. The statements that Umunhum means 'dwelling place of the humming bird' and Inyo the 'abode of the Great Spirit' are also within reason. Mountains themselves were of no practical importance to the Indians and probably had no names, but many of them were associated with Indian mythology. But, until anthropologists and linguists show that the psychology of the Indians was consonant with giving places such names as 'knee pan' (Sespe), 'moon' (Ohai), and 'children of the mist that held their revels there on moonlit nights in times long past' (Paoha), such interpretations are extremely doubtful. In the original as well as in this revised edition of *California Place Names* I have included many such questionable interpretations; I leave the responsibility for them to students of California native languages.

The main criticisms of the original edition of this work have come from dictionary etymologists. It would be a hopeless task to try to refute them. If a Spanish dictionary gives *coche* as meaning 'carriage' or *monte* as meaning 'mountain,' these people will continue to insist that *Cañada de los Coches* means 'glen of the carriages,' not 'hog valley,' and that *Monte Diablo* means 'devil's mountain' and not 'devil's woods.' And nothing will convince them that neither the spelling nor the evolution of the name Putah Creek offers the slightest evidence that the term means 'whore creek.' In the well-known periodical *Atenea* (March, 1951) a Spanish scholar gives ten pages to a review of my book from the point of view of a dictionary etymologist. Cameron Creek was not named for a family named Cameron, he believes; since the country was once Spanish, the name is more likely a misspelling of *camarón,* 'shrimp'—even though there was no Spanish settlement for miles around. The name Aromas cannot refer to the odor of sulphur water, because "los olores sulfuroso no son 'aromas' en español." The reviewer graciously excuses me for not connecting Putah with 'whore': "El profesor Erwin Gudde para quien la razon historica vale mas que la razon de amor."

The comments of other critics have more justification. A British scholar speaks sarcastically of my statement that California is especially fortunate in having a rich and diversified nomenclature. Provincialisms of this kind will slip in when an author writes about a country dear to him. The nomenclature of California is actually no richer or more diversified than that of Scotland or Switzerland, or of Florida or Wisconsin. One might even be inclined to agree with Mark Twain and Walt Whitman that too many saints' names in California were applied in a purely mechanical manner and not because of any association with the natural, social, or political history of the places named. American men of letters of the nineteenth century were much more interested in applying geographical names in the West than is known. In 1850, when Frémont was still an influential person in California, Longfellow wrote to him, advising him concerning geographical names for the new country. It is unfortunate that this letter is lost.

The most common objection to the first edition was that it contained no obsolete names—a "geographical dictionary" should include vanished names as well as living ones. This criticism came from geographers and historians and even more often from natural scientists. To follow the well-meant advice to list obsolete names in the text or incorporate them in an appendix to the book was not practicable—there are too many of them. But the demand has been so insistent that I have finally decided to compile a gazetteer of vanished place names, which could serve as a supplement to this dictionary of living names.

Some critics complained of the lack of maps in the "geographical dictionary." To attach a folded modern map would serve no purpose—dozens of official and commercial maps are easily available. For this edition, however, I have provided a map of California showing the counties, and a chart (in four sheets) which shows graphically the evolution of geographical nomenclature in California. The county map will aid the reader in locating places which are usually identified by county in the text. The four sheets of the chart (which are not maps in the usual sense) identify the period in which the names or their roots originated.

My purpose in writing the book was not only to present the etymology and meaning of the place names but to bring out in the stories of these names the whole range of California history. I was gratified to learn that this was generally recognized and appreciated by readers of the original edition.

Another great satisfaction was the fact that the thousands of readers discovered only four errors of any consequence. Marysville was placed in the wrong county; the name of a mighty peak, Mount Humphreys, was lost somewhere between my desk and the linotype machine; my friend George Schrader of the Forest Service and I fell for the story of an "old-timer" concerning the name Peanut; and one important Mission source, Father Arroyo de la Cuesta's manuscripts of the grammar and vocabularies of a number of Indian dialects, was omitted from the Bibliography. It stands to reason that the revised edition, as well as the original, contains numerous minor errors. No book can be free of them, especially one which contains thousands of names and dates, and which involves many fields of study and dozens of languages and dialects. Fortunately, the majority of the readers of the first edition realized that only positive criticism is of any value; their corrections and suggestions were gratefully received and used for this new edition. If this voluntary coöperation continues, future editions will contain fewer errors and eventually, it is hoped, all will be eliminated.

Manuscript materials which have been examined since the publication of the first edition of *California Place Names* include the George Davidson papers, which Elisabeth K. Gudde sorted in the meantime, the papers of the Whitney Survey which Francis P. Farquhar presented to the Bancroft Library, and the beautiful collection of Western maps which Carl Wheat gave to that institution. Some additional Spanish manuscripts and land-grant papers were also examined; but Dorothy Huggins had done so thorough a job for the original edition that only a few additional items were brought to light. A few new books on California history in general and a number of articles on California names have been published; the names of those from which new information was drawn for this revised edition have been added to the Bibliography.

Of great importance for the study of California geographical names was the publication of Walter N. Frickstad's *A Century of California Post Offices.* When a post office is established and given the name of the community it serves, no new light is thrown on the origin and meaning of the name, but often a name which might otherwise have disappeared is thus perpetuated. If the name of the community is the same as or similar to that of an already existing post office, or if the post office is to serve several settlements and the local pride of any of them prevents the application of the name of one of the others, a new name must be found. Readers seeking additional information about current or obsolete post-office names are referred to Frickstad's excellent compilation.

Two other publications deserve special mention—Carl I. Wheat's monumental work on Western American cartography, the first volume of which appeared just as the revision was finished, and Robert F. Heizer's editions of "California Indian Linguistic Records" in *Anthropological Records,* published by the University of California Press.

Many of the old friends of *California Place Names* have liberally contributed to the revision: J. N. Bowman, Thomas P. Brown, Emanuel Fritz, Alfred L. Kroeber, B. H. Lehman, Yakov Malkiel, S. Griswold Morley, Fred B. Rogers, George R. Stewart, Elmer G. Still, Arturo Torres-Rioseco. In the U. S. Forest Service, the regional forester and his staff as well as its supervisors were as generous in supplying information for this as for the first edition. Again, many postmasters supplied important information; the staff of the Bancroft Library gave as valuable assistance for this as for the original edition; and Dorothy H. Huggins edited this revision with great care and eliminated many of the errors which my manuscript contained. August Frugé, Lucie Dobbie, John Goetz, Philip Lilienthal, Harold Small, and other members of the staff of the University of California Press were most helpful in giving the book its final shape.

For regional information the help of two men was especially valuable. Henry Mauldin of Lakeport supplied all the added information about Lake County names; his projected place-name book and his county history, models of painstaking local research, will be published in the near future. In J. D. Howard of Klamath Falls, Oregon, I had a unique informant who gave me valuable information about the names of Lava Beds National Monument which he himself had bestowed in his many years of exploring this interesting region.

There were others who supplied new information for this edition besides those given credit in the text: James de T. Abajian and Edwin H. Carpenter of the

California Historical Society; Frank Asbill, a grandson of the first settler in western Mendocino County; William E. Ashton, P. A. Bailey, Robert Becker, Stanley T. Borden; Sylvia Broadbent; Lelia Crouch; Ralph H. Cross; Donald C. Cutter; Sydney K. Gally; Carroll D. Hall, Assistant Historian of the California Park Commission; R. E. Hallawell, General Manager of the Southern Pacific; W. E. Hotelling; John K. Howard; Rockwell D. Hunt; Arthur E. Hutson; Olaf Jenkins, former Chief of the Division of Mines; George James; the late Joseph LeConte; John Lyman, Loye H. Miller, E. S. Morby; David F. Myrick; Paul Paine, A. L. Paulson; Howard Randolph; Paul Schulz; A. D. Shamel; Edwin F. Smith; Kenneth Smith; Irwin Solloway, cartographer of the California State Automobile Association; Justin G. Turner; Church Willburn. Professor Fritz Kramer drew the original sketch for the historical chart.

Elisabeth K. Gudde is the co-author of this revised edition, as she was of the first.

ERWIN G. GUDDE

Eichenloh, April 6, 1958

Prefatory Note to Third Edition

THE THIRD EDITION of *California Place Names* is considerably enlarged and improved over the third printing of the second edition. Fundamentally, however, the book remains unchanged, and the important items for which special research had been undertaken are essentially the same.

The rapid growth of the population of our commonwealth has naturally been paralleled by an increased number of names in the geographical alignment of the state — towns and subdivisions, post offices, state parks and beaches, redwood memorial groves, historic landmarks, dams and reservoirs. While their number is considerable, the etymological, or historical significance and importance of these new names, again, is not great. Most of these are simply taken from geographic features with established names which are already recorded in the book. Another large section of new names consists of commemorative names. Although all the men and women whose names have been put on the map of California doubtless deserve their place, this book does not include all of them. *California Place Names* is not a gazeteer which records all geographical names, regardless of their significance and importance.

A new feature of this edition is the reference list, or index, of obsolete, alternate, secondary, or variant names mentioned in the book and not otherwise alphabetized. It is not a list of *all* names that are now obsolete or forgotten. Such a roster would be valuable, but it does not fall within the scope of this book and would require a separate monograph.

Previous editions of *California Place Names* have been criticized by linguists because the pronunciation was not indicated by the International Phonetic Alphabet. We have nevertheless continued to use the symbols of Webster's dictionary wherever it is necessary to indicate the pronunciation. The International Phonetic Alphabet is of great importance for the science of linguistics. It does not belong, however, in a geographical, historical, etymological dictionary.

The science of California Indian languages and linguistics has received renewed attention in recent years, especially through the University of California *Publications in Linguistics*. With a few exceptions, we have not traced the place names (sometimes problematical) mentioned in these publications. These names, like many place names of Aztec derivation, require the pen of a competent scholar of Indian linguistics.

In spite of our efforts the new edition will again include many errors and omissions. Many minor interesting names will be lacking because we could not discover their origin and meaning. On the other hand, numerous unimportant or even obsolete names of places, like railroad stations, may still be included.

In addition to the long lists of contributors and helpers given in the first and second editions, we wish to express our appreciation to many new persons and agencies who have given voluntary, or solicited, information. Among these are Robert H. Becker, L. Burr Belden, Oscar Berland, Frances E. Bishop, L. J. Bowler, W. Harlan Boyd, Allen K. Brown, Earl E. Buie, Rupert Costo, Carl S. Dentzel, John B. DeWitt, Newton B. Drury, Arda Haenszel, Brother Henry, Robert T. Ives, J. R. R. Kantor, Addison S. Keeler, Fritz Kraemer, Oscar Lewis, Zelma B. Locker, Dale L. Morgan, Harry L. Nickerson, K. H. Patterson, Rodman W. Paul, Edward T. Planer, Sascha Schmidt, Genny Schumacher, Albert Shumate, Peter Tamony, J. B. Tompkins, Grant V. Wallace, Allen W. Welts, Walt Wheelock, and others mentioned in the text. Some government bureaus, like the U. S. Forest Service, the California State Mining Bureau, The California departments of Parks and of Water Resources, as well as many individual postmasters and other government officers supplied us with information; likewise the historical societies, the Save-the-Redwoods League, the California State Automobile Association, the Pacific Gas and Electric Company. The members of the staff of the University of California Press were again patient and efficient in producing the new edition, and the librarians at the Bancroft Library were as always helpful. We wish also to acknowledge the continued assistance of Fred D. Rogers, J. N. Bowman, and three members of the original advisory committee of *California Place Names*—George R. Stewart, Francis P. Farquhar, and S. Griswold Morley. George Stewart inspired the first edition of this book and has maintained an active interest through successive editions. We shall always remember those members of the advisory committee who are no longer with us, Aubrey Drury, Samuel T. Farquhar, and Edward W. Gifford. Sam Farquhar, who was manager of the University Press, took a special interest in the book and we are grateful for his generous assistance. The invaluable contributions of Dorothy Huggins Harding and Katherine Karpenstein, as well as the services of Henrietta Girgich, we also remember with gratitude. To Doris Sandford, our efficient secretary, we extend our thanks for her excellent work in the preparation of this revised dition.

Erwin G. Gudde
Elisabeth K. Gudde

Eichenloh, January 20, 1969

Contents

Maps

Introduction

THE PROBLEM. Names belong to the oldest elements of human speech. According to some authorities, they even antedate the verbs for eat, drink, sleep, or the nouns for hand, night, or child. Even in most primitive known societies people bore names—usually descriptive of their looks or their characteristics: "the redhead," "the bear killer," "the hunchback." Primitive people also gave names to places. Identifying locations by description was equally as important when humans were merely foragers and hunters as later when they settled down to agricultural pursuits. "Where the strawberries grow," "where the river can be crossed," "where the waters meet"—such primitive place naming we can easily associate with the earliest stages of culture. Descriptive names probably still outnumber all others in geographical nomenclature, although a diversification has been brought about by names arising from incidents, superstitious beliefs, the forming of landed estates, the desire to honor persons, and other causes.

In European countries the investigation into the origin and meaning of geographical names forms a recognized and assiduously studied branch of etymology. In this as in other fields of philology the Germans have been the pioneers and the teachers, although the classical treatise on geographical names, *Words and Places,* was written by an English scholar, Isaac Taylor. The study of place names has proved of greatest importance for the investigation of the primeval periods, which are thoughtlessly called "prehistoric" because their history cannot be studied on the basis of written documents. In 1821 Wilhelm von Humboldt, brother of the better-known Alexander (for whom our Humboldt Bay is named), succeeded in outlining the demarcations, which otherwise have completely disappeared, of an early stage of the settlement of Spain and Portugal solely on the basis of the place names. In many European geographical names we find apparent remnants of languages and dialects otherwise unrecorded, living witnesses of the onetime presence of people of whose language or culture no trace remains. Teutonic and Romanic languages have long since replaced most of the Celtic dialects once spoken in all western Europe, but the names of the Rhine and the Garonne and the Thames still demonstrate what languages were once spoken on their shores. The name Olympus designated a number of high peaks in Greece and Asia Minor, and simply meant "mountain" in whatever language was spoken in that part of the world before the invading Greeks swept down from the north.

Place-name study in the United States presents a slightly different aspect. The vast majority of our names have been bestowed upon the land within the last few hundred years by explorers, settlers, surveyors, officers of the government, railroad officials. Many of them are descriptive, many are transfer names, or honor our great, or preserve the names of the early settlers; still others owe their origin to an incident or to a misunderstanding, to their pleasant sound, or to artificial coining. With the exception of the names of Indian origin they generally offer few problems to the philologist. The origin, meaning, and application of most of them can be traced. This does not mean that they are less interesting. Our names are an essential part of our living presence, and in their stories are reflected all phases of the nature of the country and of the history of the people. This has been graphically shown in George Stewart's account, *Names on the Land.*

California is especially fortunate in having a rich and diversified nomenclature. Indians who lived here before the coming of the whites, Spanish navigators from aboard their ships, European cosmographers from the narrow confines of their studies, uncouth soldiers and preaching missionaries, Russians and Chinese, French Canadians and Pennsylvania Germans, bawdy miners and hard-working surveyors, postmasters and location engineers, settlers from all states of the Union and from every European country—all have contributed to the names on the California map.

NAMING THE LAND. To include in this Dictionary a full historical account of place naming in California was deemed impractical, but the following sketch will tell briefly how and when our map became dotted with names.

Our Indian place names, so far as they were genuine geographical terms, belong to a primitive, purely descriptive category. "The people who live south of us," "the people who have plenty of fish," "water" for a lake, perhaps modified when referring to a river—beyond that the nomenclature of the Indian languages of California had not progressed. A great many Indian place names, although actually Indian, were not bestowed upon features by the natives but by the white conquerors. Many others arose doubtless when Spanish or Americans misinterpreted Indian words as names of places, and these were then often accepted by the Indians.

The first period of European place naming extends from 1542, when Cabrillo sailed as the first navigator along the coast of what is now our State, until 1769, when the Spanish finally settled the country. In this period some of our coastal features were named by explorers and by European map makers, who used the vagueness of California as a geographic conception to indulge in fanciful nomenclature.

In 1769 the land route from Sonora and Lower California was opened up, and the Portolá and Anza expeditions named numerous places along their routes. The padres who accompanied these expeditions had a rather tedious way of applying the name of the saint on or near whose day a certain place was reached. Fortunately the soldiers often applied a name of their own, and many of these names, usually prompted by some incident, were preserved: El Trabuco because they lost a *trabuco* (blunderbuss); Carpinteria because they saw the natives build a boat; El Oso Flaco because they killed a 'lean bear.' In the colonization period which followed, most of the important physical features in Spanish-occupied territory were given names. The names of many of our cities and towns go back to missions, pueblos, and other localities named by civil or ecclesiastical authorities. The monotonous application of saints' names continued, but at the same time many of the Indian names, especially those of rancherias, were preserved. Of the greatest importance in this period were the Spanish and Mexican private land grants through whose *expedientes* and *diseños* hundreds of old names have survived to our day.

Spanish expeditions by sea after 1769, especially those of Bodega and Hezeta, also added to our geographical nomenclature, but these explorations practically ceased with the end of the eighteenth century. A number of exploring expeditions into the interior valley bestowed such important names as Sacramento and San Joaquin, Merced and Mariposa. Of the European and American expeditions, by land and sea, those of Vancouver (1792–1794), Beechey (1826–1827), and Frémont (1843–1847) were of considerable importance for place names. The reports and maps of La Pérouse, Humboldt, the two Kotzebue expeditions, Belcher, Jedediah Smith, Wilkes, and Duflot de Mofras were instrumental in fixing and transmitting many names.

After the American occupation no attempt was made to change the Spanish and Indian names. Some were translated, some were garbled, but on the whole the U. S. Coast Survey, the U. S. Land Office, and other mapping agencies conscientiously kept the names which were current or which were found on maps and in documents.

In the meantime the discovery of gold and the rapid infiltration of prospectors into regions of the State outside the old Spanish domain resulted in an entirely new class of names. Many of the Eastern states' names appeared on the map: Mississippi Bar, Virginia Creek, Michigan Bluff; the cosmopolitan composition was attested by the Yankee Hills, the Dutch Flats, the Chinese Camps, the Negro Bars. Colorful, unique, often bawdy names abounded: Henpeck City, Louseville, Petticoat Slide, Pinchemtight, Bloody Gulch, Raggedass Creek. As the settlement of the regions not frozen by the land grants progressed, there appeared the usual array of personal names for first settlers, descriptive names, and transfer names, especially those dear to the American heart like Washington, Lexington, Bunker Hill, Mohawk Valley, Arlington.

Greatly enriched was California geographical nomenclature by the Pacific Railroad Survey (1853–1854), the State Geological Survey (1861–1873), and the U. S. Geographical Explorations and Surveys West of the 100th Meridian (1875–1879). Many of the names of physical features owe their origin or their fixation to the men of these surveys.

Place naming in the subsequent decades followed the common pattern: new communities and subdivisions were named for a promoter, after a town "back East," after a physical feature if it seemed to have some publicity value, or were given a Spanish or supposedly Spanish name, or a manufactured name without any meaning but with a pleasant sound. The coming of the railroad brought new names into existence, often fantastic and farfetched names because the location engineers were not bound by any tradition when they established and named construction camps. The post office usually left the choice with the petitioners, provided they could find a name that would not be confused with one already in use. Our government agencies—Geological Survey, Park Service, Forest Service—in mapping the State depended (and still depend) mainly on local information, and in this manner placed many interesting names on the map; often they applied a descriptive name or created a cluster name by naming various features after one original place name.

To show when, how, and by whom these names were applied, to tell their meaning, their origin and their evolution, their connection with our national history, their relation to the California landscape and the California people—this is the purpose of the book.

Scope and Compass. This book is not a gazetteer. It does not contain all the names in the State, nor does it give the latitude and longitude, or the statistics of the places. The book is also no Baedeker which gives information to the tourist concerning our towns and physical features, our historical monuments and our spots of interest. It is restricted to information pertaining to the names and their application.

The term "place name" should be construed to mean the name of a geographic entity: a city or a railroad station, a lake or a river, a mountain range or a hill, a cape or an island. It has been used in this sense by most writers on geographical nomenclature and may be considered as definitely established. "Place name" is more convenient than "geographical name."

The names in this Dictionary have been drawn chiefly from a composite map of the State comprised of the following: the sheets of the topographical atlas of the U. S. Geological Survey as far as they were published and available on January 1, 1947; the atlas sheets made by the Corps of Engineers, U. S. Army, of quadrangles not covered by the Geological Survey, the charts of the Coast Survey, the maps of the Forest Service, and the best available county maps for other areas.

This composite map is the best available and the most official, but it does not present a perfect geographical picture of the State. A large number of names on the atlas sheets are "map names" created by the whim of surveyors or local enthusiasts. The oilmen of the Kettleman Hills would stare in amazement if they were asked what and where is El Hocico or La Canada Simada or El Arroyo Degollado. A large number of obsolete names are carried on these atlas sheets: the widely known Orinda crossroads in Contra Costa County are designated on the Concord atlas sheet, issued in 1942, as Bryant—a name that disappeared from common speech a generation ago. On the other hand, many locally current names were not recorded by the mapping agencies and many features were left nameless because no generally accepted local name was obtainable at the time the map was made. In spite of my attempt to make this a book of names which are alive and current, it will contain a number of names which are perhaps known only to the man who put them on a map or into a gazetteer. It will also contain a number of names which cannot be found on any map or which differ in location or in spelling. It was not always possible to be entirely consistent in deciding for one spelling or another. In general I followed the principle that misspellings on maps which have become time-honored and locally accepted, like Coleman instead of Kolmer Valley, should not be corrected. On the other hand, there was no reason to perpetuate obvious mistakes made by editors of topographical atlas sheets, like Hennerville instead of Hunewill. Wherever reliable local information was available, local usage took precedence over "official standing." Here, too, regional research could do much for California place names.

There are probably more than 150,000 place names in California, not counting street names in our cities. From these the most interesting and important names have been selected for individual treatment, and most of the frequently recurring names have been treated in a summary way. Since there is no absolute standard by which to judge the importance or interest of a name, the decision had to be left to the author and his advisers. As "important" are considered the names of all territorial units, such as counties and national domains; inhabited places of a sizable population, especially when connected with a post office or railroad station; the high peaks of our mountain ranges; other elevations which are landmarks or otherwise prominent; all rivers and the larger bays, creeks, and lakes; generally known valleys, canyons, islands, meadows, and gulches; prominent capes and promontories along the coast. In addition to these the book contains the names of numerous minor places and features interesting from the historical or philological point of view, or because their names hide a story of human interest. As important and interesting among folk names have been considered those of frequent recurrence, like Bear, Red, French, or names typically Californian, like Chinese, Fork, Bally. Here too a selection had to be made. Some common descriptive terms, like 'deep' or 'dark,' and some derivatives from fauna and flora, like 'frog' or 'poppy,' were not treated because no special significance is attached to them.

Since the book is primarily a dictionary of living names, it could not be burdened with the names of thousands of vanished mining camps, names of peaks and rivers and capes once well known, now lost or supplanted. A study of the obsolete and vanished names of the State would be extremely fascinating, but will have to be left for separate publication. Names no longer in use have been listed only if they are of historical, geographical, political, or anthropological interest, or if they honor a pioneer otherwise forgotten. The former name of many a place is mentioned under the entry of the present name.

Excluded are also the names of all streets and features within the areas of our cities, unless they are of more than local importance; also the names of railroads and highways, schools and churches, seamounts and submarine basins, except for a few which have some special geographical significance or could be listed in connection with a more important feature of the same name. A few new subdivisions are listed because they have unique names.

Included, on the other hand, are the names of Spanish and Mexican land grants. Strictly speaking, these are not "place names," but they have played so important a role in our political, legal, and economic history and have so much enriched the nomenclature of California that their inclusion seems justified. The majority of land-grant names will be found under group or folk names, or under the modern name preserving the land-grant name; a smaller number, unique or rare names, have been listed individually; some have been omitted because they are purely descriptive. There is considerable confusion in these land-grant names because they passed through a number of legal processes. They are given in this book as they are listed in Bowman's Index, that is, as he copied them from the *expedientes;* these sometimes differ from the names as they appear in the cases before the United States courts. Names of unclaimed and unconfirmed grants have been omitted.

STYLE AND METHOD OF PRESENTATION. The order of the entries is alphabetical as determined by the initial letters of the specific part: Pit River, see under Pit, but Point Arena, see Arena, Point; Mount Hilgard, see Hilgard, Mount; The Nipple, see Nipple, The. Descriptive adjectives are naturally considered a part of the specific term: North Bloomfield, see under N. For some places, especially towns, the generic term has become part of the specific name: Fort Bragg, see under F. In Spanish names, the preceding generic term, article, or other modifying particle has been treated as a part of the name: La Panza is listed under L, Santa Barbara under S. For frequently occurring Spanish names, however, all items are grouped together under the specific name: Los Coyotes will be found under C, Arroyo las Pozas under P. In names of land grants which are listed individually the Spanish definite article is entirely omitted, and the name is listed under the initial letter of the first noun, ordinarily the specific term. Cross references have been given when necessary.

For practical purposes several types of entry have been used besides the simple entry with one name only. The individual names of a "cluster name" are listed in chronological order, as far as is determinable, at the beginning of the entry. A cluster name signifies a number of names which were applied to various features in the same locality after one original name. (*See* Kaiser.) Where a number of features were named for the same reason or after one original feature, but at different times and in different districts, the story of each name is told separately but all are grouped together, again chronologically, in one paragraph. These may be called "group names." (*See* Golden Gate.) As for common names of frequent occurrence, the meaning, significance, and frequency of the name are given and added as separate entries, but in the same paragraph are those of special interest. (*See* Corral.) These are called "folk names" in this book—a term used by George R. Stewart.

The length of the entry naturally does not always correspond to the importance of the place or feature. A small hill with an etymologically interesting name may require many times the space given to the name of a majestic peak. Names applied in the broad daylight of history require less space than names whose origin is lost in the dusk before the coming of the white man.

For names which date back to former centuries, or went through a process of evolution, or were repeatedly changed, I have endeavored to give the first recording or mentioning of the name, variants important to the final version, and former names which lasted for some time or were officially applied.

Every attempt was made to treat uniformly all areas of the State, but a certain unevenness could not be avoided. Regions in which the names have already received special attention and territorial units whose officials supported the undertaking will naturally come closer to adequate presentation than others. A similar unevenness will be noticeable in the treatment of less important individual names. Big names for which special research was undertaken will be found treated in fairly even proportions. Many a small name, however, was included because information about it was available, whereas an equally important (or unimportant) name was omitted because the obscurity of its origin could not be penetrated.

Each entry was written as an entity. Failure to mention other interpretations or explanations of a name does not mean that I was unaware of them. Where different versions of the meaning and origin of a name seem plausible and logical or are supported by some evidence, they are naturally given, even if they do not sound entirely convincing. But notions of the believers in Indian princesses or products of dictionary etymologists are properly kept out.

The pronunciation given is that of the present day. Our place names are a part of our language, and the spoken idiom is a living thing which undergoes slight variations from generation to generation and changes perceptibly from century to century. Pronunciations, when given, represent actual usage of the present time. In other words, this dictionary records what people say, and does not presume to tell them what they should say. In frontier times the Grizzly Peaks were probably Grizzler Peaks since "grizzler" was the common designation for the animal; the name of the State must often have been pronounced Californy; but such pronunciations are not used today. The name Los Angeles had a fully Spanish pronunciation in Spanish and Mexican times, but it has long since become Americanized. Del Norte is a Spanish name, to be sure, but the people of Del Norte County say dĕl nôrt. There is often a marked difference in the pronunciation of a name by the older and by the younger generation—Tulare: tōō-lâr′-ė, tōō-lâr′. Names which are found in various sections of the State, like Canada or Coyote, differ naturally according to locality. Usually, names of Spanish origin will be found less Americanized in the southern counties than elsewhere. Sometimes two pronunciations are given, the first being the one most likely to win out. Where no pronunciation is indicated, it may usually be assumed that the common American way prevails. For some names, especially of out-of-the-way places, no pronunciation could be given because no information was obtainable, or because the information from different sources was too contradictory to permit a conclusion. Extensive field work will be required to establish the definite pronunciation of many California place names. The pronunciation of the names of land grants which have not otherwise survived as place names is not indicated.

In general, the location given in brackets after the name is the county, or a well-defined area such as San Francisco Bay. It was sometimes necessary, however, to refer to the topographical atlas sheet or to describe the place.

The spellings of Indian names are given as they are found in documents and on maps. Since the natives had no alphabet and could not spell out their names, the Spaniards and later the Americans wrote each name as it sounded to them. Spelling variants, of which there were often as many as a dozen, are given only where they have some bearing on the final evolution of the name, or where they are of etymological interest.

Older versions of Spanish names are likewise quoted as they appear in sources. Their spelling does not always correspond with present-day standards. Initial *Y* was almost invariably used for *I; s* was usually used instead of *z; v* and *b,* and often *ll* and *y,* were used interchangeably. The accent mark was used sporadically in documents, never on maps; on Costansó's *Carta Reducida* it was inserted by a later hand. In California place names of Spanish origin, ancient or modern, the accent mark is omitted in this book. Spanish personal names and words quoted bear the accent mark in accordance with modern Spanish orthography. This will account for the occurrence of the same name accented when it is a personal name and unaccented when it is a place name.

SUMMARY OF SOURCES. Rich manuscript material was at my disposal and was gratefully used: the compilations of the Northern California Writers' Project of the Work Projects Administration; the place-name files of the Atchison, Topeka and Sante Fe Railway System and of the Death Valley National Monument; the files of C. Hart Merriam, of Thomas B. Doyle, of Linnie Marsh Wolfe, of the State Geographic Board; the field copies of Farquhar's and Kroeber's monographs and of the first two editions of Davidson's Coast Pilot; the Bowman Index and the *diseños* of the land grants in the U. S. District Court; the George Davidson papers and correspondence; some of Charles Hoffmann's field notes; the originals or transcripts of numerous manuscripts in the Bancroft Library. These sources are described in the Glossary and Bibliography. At my disposal also were more than one thousand questionnaires containing local information gathered from rangers, surveyors, postmasters, librarians, teachers, county officials, and local historians.

In comparison with the abundance of unpublished material, the number of printed works dealing with place names is meager. The names in the larger part of the Sierra Nevada have been treated by Farquhar, the etymology of many of our Indian names is given by Kroeber, and Wagner's *Cartography* contains a wealth of information on the existing or obsolete names bestowed upon the coast by explorers before 1800. Nellie van de Grift Sanchez' *Spanish and Indian Place Names* is well known.

The only attempt to cover the entire State in a scholarly manner is Phil Townsend Hanna's *The Dictionary of California Land Names,* a broadly conceived work with much interesting information. There are other books, less comprehensive than Mr. Hanna's, which list the interesting and romantic names of the entire State: Thomas Brown, *Colorful California Names;* Laura McNary, *California Spanish and Indian Place Names;* Harry L. Wells, *California Names,* and others.

It seems strange that very few attempts have been made to investigate the names within the limits of a region. Gertrude A. Steger, however, has done an excellent piece of work with the geographical names of Shasta County, and Roscoe D. Wyatt has rendered a similar service to San Mateo County. William M. Maule has done first-class work on the names of the Carson, Walker, and Mono basins, Terry E. Stephenson on the names of Orange County, Elmer G. Still on those of the Livermore district, and Paul Parker on those of the Monterey district.

Among printed books not directly concerned with place names the most valuable as source material are the reports and diaries of the early explorers, and after the American occupation the reports of the various government agencies. The accounts and journals of travelers and a number of the county histories, particularly the older ones, yielded good material. However, for most of our entries, the information had to be pieced together from manuscripts and maps, local information and county histories, post-office directories and railroad reports, dictionaries and gazetteers.

Maps deserve a special note because they are a most valuable source for historical geography. They do not tell, at least not directly, the meaning and origin of a geographical name, but they are all-important for the application, evolution, and perpetuation of a name. In modern times, to be sure, the names of post offices, railroad stations, and incorporated towns are official and no map maker would undertake to change them. With the publication of the charts of the Coast Survey and the sheets of the topographical atlas by the Geological Survey the name of physical features, too, become fixed, and official if confirmed by decision of the Geographic Board. But as long as the geography of the country was, so to speak, in a liquid state, the fate of a name was more or less determined by the cartographers. No matter how solemnly and ceremoniously a mountain or a cape was christened, the name would not last unless an influential map maker recorded it.

For the earlier periods those maps were quoted which because of their influence and popularity were responsible for the application, fixation, and changing of names along the coast, especially those reproduced or described by Kohl, Nordenskiöld, and Wagner. The many local *planos,* mostly unpublished, which originated after 1769 in California directly, and most of the *diseños* of the land grants, were likewise examined. For the period of transition the most important general maps were those of European or American explorers: Vancouver, La Pérouse, Humboldt, Beechey, Wilkes, Duflot de Mofras, Frémont. After the American occupation the most influential maps in the fixing the nomenclature of the State were the charts of the Coast Survey, the maps of the Pacific Railroad Survey, Eddy's

official map of the State, the Land Office maps, some private maps like those of
Trask and Gibbes, and later those of Goddard and Bancroft. In the 1870's were
published the important though uncompleted maps of the State Geological (Whitney) Survey, and later those of the U. S. Survey West of the 100th Meridian
(Wheeler). In modern times it is the mapping of the U. S. Geological Survey, the
Forest Service, and the War Department, together with the continued activity of
the Coast Survey, which is mainly responsible for our geographical nomenclature—
if not for its origin, at least for its application.

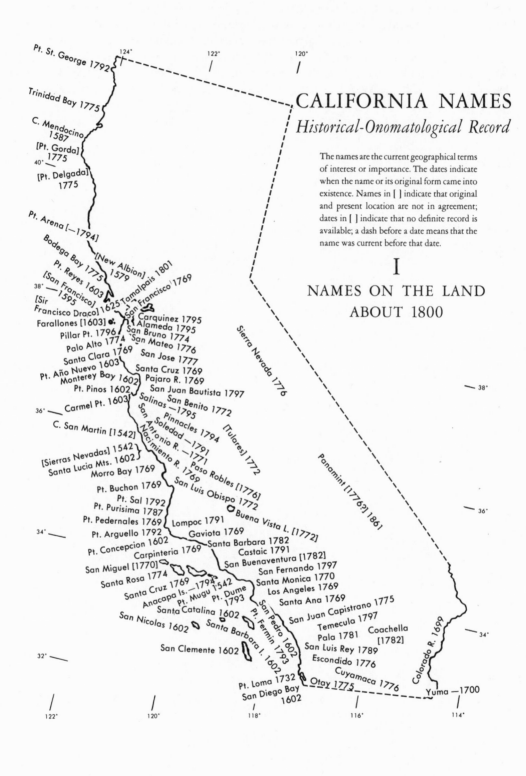

CALIFORNIA NAMES
Historical-Onomatological Record

The names are the current geographical terms of interest or importance. The dates indicate when the name or its original form came into existence. Names in [ ] indicate that original and present location are not in agreement; dates in [ ] indicate that no definite record is available; a dash before a date means that the name was current before that date.

I

NAMES ON THE LAND
ABOUT 1800

Pt. St. George 1792

Trinidad Bay 1775

C. Mendocino 1587
[Pt. Gorda] 1775
[Pt. Delgada] 1775

Pt. Arena [−1794]
Bodega Bay 1775
Pt. Reyes 1603
[San Francisco] −1595
[Sir Francisco Draco]
Farallones [1603]
Pillar Pt. 1796
Palo Alto 1774
Santa Clara 1769
Pt. Año Nuevo 1603
Monterey Bay 1602
Pt. Pinos 1602
Carmel Pt. 1603
C. San Martin [1542]
[Sierras Nevadas] 1542
Santa Lucia Mts. 1602
Morro Bay 1769
Pt. Buchon 1769
Pt. Sal 1792
Pt. Purisima 1787
Pt. Pedernales 1769
Pt. Arguello 1792
Pt. Concepcion 1602
Carpinteria 1769
San Miguel [1770]
Santa Rosa 1774
Santa Cruz 1769 −1794
Anacapa Is. 1542
Pt. Mugu
Santa Catalina 1602
San Nicolas 1602
San Clemente 1602

[New Albion] 1579
Tamalpais 1801
San Francisco 1769
Carquinez 1795
Alameda 1795
San Bruno 1774
San Mateo 1776
San Jose 1777
Santa Cruz 1769
Pajaro R. 1769
San Juan Bautista 1797
San Benito 1772
Salinas −1795
Pinnacles 1794
Soledad −1791
San Antonio R. −1771
Nacimiento R. 1769
Paso Robles [1776]
San Luis Obispo 1772
Buena Vista L. [1772]
Lompoc 1791
Gaviota 1769
Santa Barbara 1782
Castaic 1791
San Buenaventura [1782]
San Fernando 1797
Santa Monica 1770
Los Angeles 1769
Santa Ana 1769
Pt. Dume 1793
Santa Barbara I. 1602
Pt. Fermin 1602
San Pedro 1602

Sierra Nevada 1776

[Tulares] 1772

Panamint [1776?] 1861

San Juan Capistrano 1775
Temecula 1797
Pala 1781 Coachella [1782]
San Luis Rey 1789
Escondido 1776
Cuyamaca 1776
Colorado R. 1699
Pt. Loma 1732
Otay 1775
San Diego Bay 1602
Yuma −1700

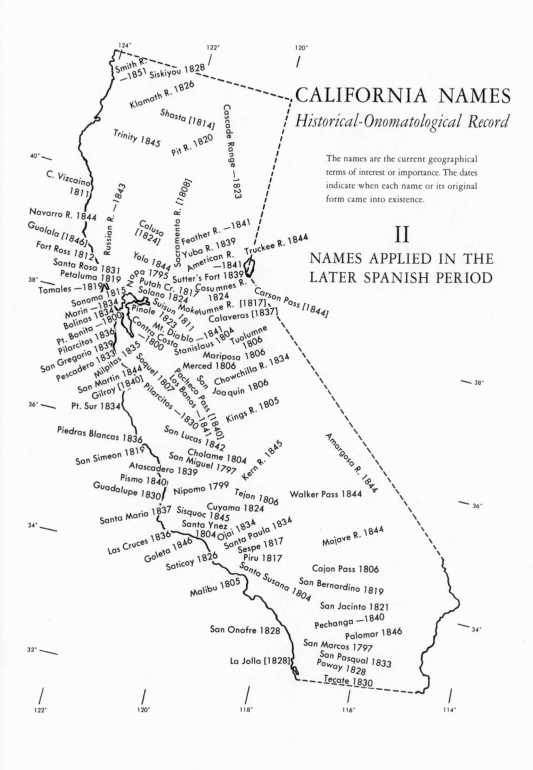

CALIFORNIA NAMES
Historical-Onomatological Record

The names are the current geographical
terms of interest or importance. The dates
indicate when each name or its original
form came into existence.

II

NAMES APPLIED IN THE
LATER SPANISH PERIOD

Smith R. —1851 Siskiyou 1828
Klamath R. 1826
Shasta [1814]
Trinity 1845   Pit R. 1820
Cascade Range —1823
C. Vizcaino 1811
Navarro R. 1844
Russian R. —1843
Sacramento R. [1808]
Gualala [1846]
Colusa [1824]
Fort Ross 1812
Yolo 1844   Feather R. —1841
Santa Rosa 1831   Napa 1795   Yuba R. 1839
Petaluma 1819   Putah Cr. 1817   American R. —1841   Truckee R. 1844
Tomales —1819   Solano 1824   Sutter's Fort 1839
Sonoma 1815   Cosumnes R. 1824
Marin —1834   Suisun 1811   Mokelumne R. [1817]   Carson Pass [1844]
Bolinas 1834   Pinole 1823   Calaveras [1837]
Pt. Bonita —1800   Mt. Diablo —1841
Pilarcitos 1836   Contra Costa —1800   Stanislaus 1804   Tuolumne 1806
San Gregorio 1839   Mariposa 1806
Pescadero 1833   Milpitas 1835   Merced 1806   Chowchilla R. 1834
San Martin 1844   Soquel 1807   Pacheco Pass [1840]   San Joaquin 1806
Gilroy [1840]   Los Banos
Pilarcitos —1830   Kings R. 1805
Pt. Sur 1834   —1841
Piedras Blancas 1836   San Lucas 1842
San Simeon 1819   Cholame 1804
Atascadero 1839   San Miguel 1797   Kern R. 1845
Pismo 1840   Amargosa R. 1844
Guadalupe 1830   Nipomo 1799   Tejon 1806   Walker Pass 1844
Cuyama 1824
Santa Maria 1837   Sisquoc 1845
Santa Ynez 1804   Ojai 1834
Las Cruces 1836   Santa Paula 1834   Mojave R. 1844
Goleta 1846   Sespe 1817
Saticoy 1826   Piru 1817
Santa Susana 1804   Cajon Pass 1806
Malibu 1805   San Bernardino 1819
San Jacinto 1821
Pechanga —1840   Palomar 1846
San Onofre 1828   San Marcos 1797
La Jolla [1828]   San Pasqual 1833
Poway 1828
Tecate 1830

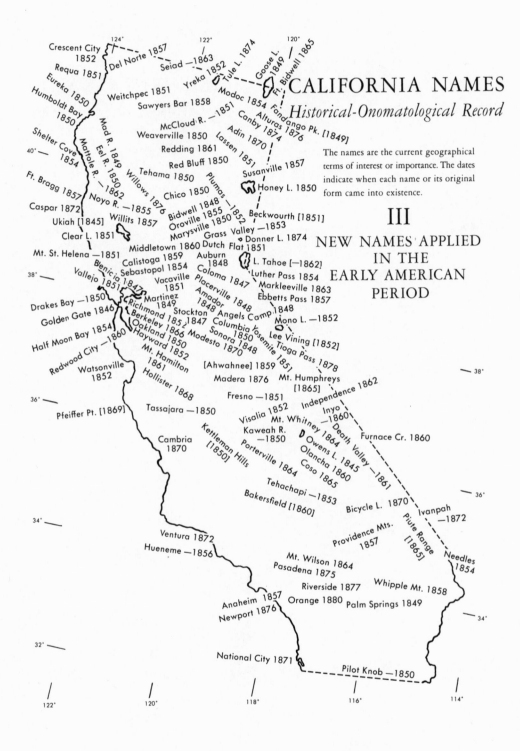

CALIFORNIA NAMES
Historical-Onomatological Record

The names are the current geographical terms of interest or importance. The dates indicate when each name or its original form came into existence.

III

NEW NAMES APPLIED
IN THE
EARLY AMERICAN
PERIOD

Crescent City 1852
Requa 1851
Eureka 1850
Humboldt Bay 1850
Shelter Cove —1854
Ft. Bragg 1857
Caspar 1872
Ukiah [1845]
Clear L. 1851
Mt. St. Helena —1851
Vallejo 1851
Drakes Bay —1850
Golden Gate 1846
Half Moon Bay 1854
Redwood City —1860
Watsonville 1852
Pfeiffer Pt. [1869]

Del Norte 1857
Seiad —1863
Yreka 1852
Weitchpec 1851
Sawyers Bar 1858
McCloud R. —1851
Weaverville 1850
Redding 1861
Red Bluff 1850
Tehama 1850
Mad R. 1849
Eel R. 1850
Mattole R. —1862
Noyo R. —1855
Willits 1857
Chico 1850
Bidwell 1848
Oroville 1855
Marysville 1850
Middletown 1860
Calistoga 1859
Benicia 1847
Sebastopol 1854
Vacaville 1851
Martinez 1849
Richmond 1852
Berkeley 1866
Oakland 1850
Hayward 1852
Mt. Hamilton 1861
Hollister 1868
Tassajara —1850
Cambria 1870

Tule L. 1874
Goose L. 1849
Ft. Bidwell 1865
Modoc 1854
Fandango Pk. [1849]
Alturas 1876
Canby 1874
Adin 1870
Lassen 1851
Susanville 1857
Honey L. 1850
Plumas —1852
Beckwourth [1851]
Grass Valley —1853
Dutch Flat 1851
Donner L. 1874
Auburn 1848
Coloma 1847
Placerville 1848
Amador 1848
Stockton 1847
Columbia 1850
Modesto 1870
Sonora 1848
[Ahwahnee] 1859
Madera 1876
Fresno —1851
Visalia 1852
Kaweah R. —1850
Kettleman Hills [1850]
Porterville 1864
Tehachapi —1853
Bakersfield [1860]

L. Tahoe [—1862]
Luther Pass 1854
Markleeville 1863
Ebbetts Pass 1857
Angels Camp 1848
Mono L. —1852
Lee Vining [1852]
Yosemite 1851
Tioga Pass 1878
Mt. Humphreys [1865]
Independence 1862
Inyo —1860
Mt. Whitney 1864
Owens L. 1845
Olancha 1860
Coso 1865
Death Valley —1861
Furnace Cr. 1860
Bicycle L. 1870

Ventura 1872
Hueneme —1856
Anaheim 1857
Newport 1876
National City 1871

Providence Mts. 1857
Piute Range [1865]
Ivanpah —1872
Needles 1854
Mt. Wilson 1864
Pasadena 1875
Riverside 1877
Whipple Mt. 1858
Orange 1880
Palm Springs 1849
Pilot Knob —1850

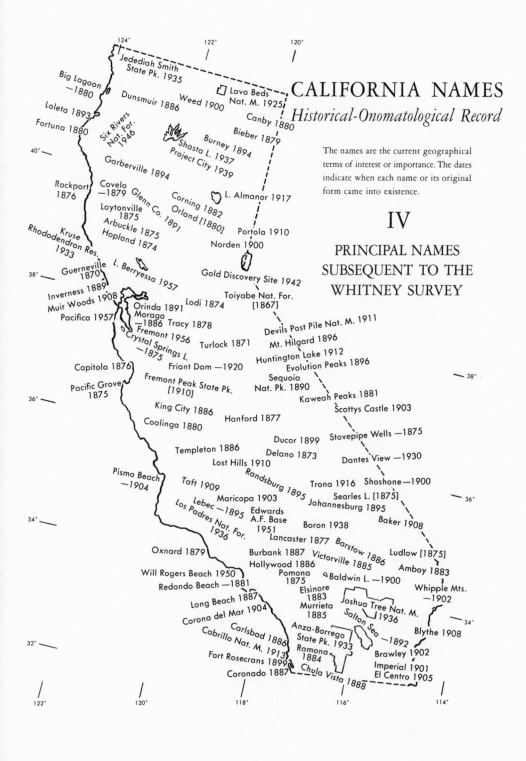

CALIFORNIA NAMES
Historical-Onomatological Record

The names are the current geographical
terms of interest or importance. The dates
indicate when each name or its original
form came into existence.

IV

PRINCIPAL NAMES
SUBSEQUENT TO THE
WHITNEY SURVEY

Jedediah Smith
State Pk. 1935

Big Lagoon
—1880

Loleta 1893

Fortuna 1880

Dunsmuir 1886

Weed 1900

Lava Beds
Nat. M. 1925

Canby 1880

Bieber 1879

Six Rivers
Nat. For.
1946

Burney 1894

Shasta L. 1937

Project City 1939

Garberville 1894

Rockport
1876

Covelo
—1879

Glenn Co. 1891

Corning 1882

Orland [1880]

L. Almanor 1917

Laytonville
1875

Arbuckle 1875

Hopland 1874

Rhododendron Res.
1933

Kruse

Guerneville
1870

L. Berryessa 1957

Portola 1910

Norden 1900

Gold Discovery Site 1942

Inverness 1889

Muir Woods 1908

Pacifica 1957

Orinda 1891

Moraga
—1886

Lodi 1874

Tracy 1878

Toiyabe Nat. For.
[1867]

Devils Post Pile Nat. M. 1911

Fremont 1956

Turlock 1871

Mt. Hilgard 1896

Crystal Springs L.
—1875

Friant Dam —1920

Huntington Lake 1912

Evolution Peaks 1896

Capitola 1876

Fremont Peak State Pk.
[1910]

Sequoia
Nat. Pk. 1890

Pacific Grove
1875

King City 1886

Hanford 1877

Kaweah Peaks 1881

Scottys Castle 1903

Coalinga 1880

Ducor 1899

Stovepipe Wells —1875

Templeton 1886

Delano 1873

Dantes View —1930

Lost Hills 1910

Pismo Beach
—1904

Taft 1909

Randsburg 1895

Trona 1916

Shoshone—1900

Maricopa 1903

Johannesburg 1895

Searles L. [1875]

Lebec —1895

Edwards
A.F. Base
1951

Boron 1938

Baker 1908

Los Padres Nat. For.
1936

Lancaster 1877

Barstow 1886

Ludlow [1875]

Oxnard 1879

Burbank 1887

Victorville 1885

Amboy 1883

Hollywood 1886

Pomona
1875

Baldwin L. —1900

Whipple Mts.
—1902

Will Rogers Beach 1950

Redondo Beach —1881

Elsinore
1883

Murrieta
1885

Joshua Tree Nat. M.
1936

Long Beach 1887

Corona del Mar 1904

Carlsbad 1886

Anza-Borrego
State Pk. 1933

Salton Sea —1892

Blythe 1908

Cabrillo Nat. M. 1913

Ramona
1884

Brawley 1902

Fort Rosecrans 1899

Chula Vista 1888

Imperial 1901

Coronado 1887

El Centro 1905

The Names

CALIFORNIA PLACE NAMES

Abalone, ăb-*à*-lō′-nĕ. The names of about ten points and coves along the coast testify to the presence of the large California mollusk, valued for its meat and for its shell lined with mother-of-pearl. The name originated probably in Rumsen territory of the Costanoan Indians, on the south shore of Monterey Bay, where Point Alones and Point Aulon still testify to the abundance of the mollusk of the genus *Haliotis.* The word is not listed by Henshaw, however, and the Rumsen word *aulun* for the red abalone, which Pinart recorded in 1878, is somewhat doubtful. The Indian word became in Spanish *aulone* and *avalone.* Both versions were used in early American times. Bayard Taylor, in 1849, gives a detailed description of the "avalones" near Point Pinos; an article in the Sacramento *Union,* November 21, 1856, is written as if "Aulone Shellfish" were the generally accepted name. The Coast Survey map of 1852 has a third version in Point Alones. *Aulinta* was the name of the Indian village at the site of modern Santa Cruz.

Abbot, Mount [Fresno]. Named by the Whitney Survey in honor of Henry Abbot (1831–1927), distinguished soldier and engineer, in the 1850's a member of the Pacific Railroad Survey. Sometimes erroneously spelled Abbott. (Farquhar.)

Absco [Ventura]. The name of the Southern Pacific station was coined from *A*merican *B*eet *S*ugar *Co*mpany in the 1920's.

Academy [Fresno]. The post office was so named because the Methodist Episcopal Church South erected here in 1874 an "academy" or secondary school. The place is shown on the Land Office map of 1879. The name has outlived the school; the academy building was razed years ago.

Acalanes, ä-ká-lä′-nēz [Contra Costa]. Indians dwelling south of San Pablo and Suisun bays, a division of the Costanoan family, were mentioned as *Sacalanes,* June 14, 1797 (PSP, XV, 13), and with various spellings in the baptismal records of Mission Dolores between 1794 and 1821 and in the reports of the first Kotzebue expedition, 1816. The present spelling was used in the Acalanes land grant, dated August 1, 1834. According to the testimony in land grant case 276 N.D., the rancheria *Sacalanes* was about a mile and a half northwest of modern Lafayette. A short-lived post office in 1854-1855 was spelled Acelanus.

Acampo [San Joaquin]. Applied to the station by the Southern Pacific when the Sacramento-Stockton section was built in the 1870's. *Acampo* is Spanish for a part of the commons used for pasture, but here as elsewhere it was applied because Americans associate *campo* with 'camp.'

"A" Canyon [Death Valley National Monument]. Local usage has given the name to a canyon which splits in a manner suggesting the letter "A." A small canyon near by is called "B" Canyon.

Acker Peak [Yosemite National Park]. Named by the Geological Survey in 1898 for William B. Acker, who for many years was in charge of matters concerning national parks in the Department of the Interior (Farquhar).

Acton [Los Angeles]. The name was applied to a station of the Saugus-Mojave section of the Southern Pacific, built 1873–1876, doubtless after one of the fifteen Actons then in existence in the East.

Adams Springs [Lake]. Named for Charles Adams, who settled there in 1869.

Adelanto, ăd-ê-lăn′-tō [San Bernardino]. The post office was established in 1917 and given the Spanish name, meaning 'progress' or 'advance.'

Adin, ā′-dĭn [Modoc]. Named by residents in 1870 for Adin McDowell, a native of Kentucky, who had settled in Big Valley in 1869.

Adobe, à-dō′-bĭ. Some twenty-five features in the State are so named because of the composition of the soil or the presence of an adobe house. The cluster name west of Mono Lake originated with Adobe Meadows, recorded on the von Leicht–Craven map of 1874. The name and the method of making sun-dried bricks were introduced into Spain by the

Arabs and became common in the American Southwest, where soil and climate are adapted to the adobe type of structure.

Aeroplane Canyon [Lake]. So named about 1944 after an Army airplane was lost south of Big Valley and the aviator bailed out in the canyon (Mauldin).

Aetna Springs [Napa]. Probably named in the 1880's, when John Lawley, owner of the Aetna Mine, discovered the hot mineral spring while mining quicksilver (Len Owens). Mount Aetna in Sicily doubtless suggested the original name.

Afton [San Bernardino]. The Union Pacific station was named when the railroad was constructed in 1904–1905, probably after one of the many other Aftons "back East." There is another Afton in Glenn County.

Agassiz, ăg′-á-sĕ, **Mount** [Kings Canyon National Park]. The name Agassiz Needle was applied by L. A. Winchell in 1879 for Louis Agassiz (1807–1873), famous Swiss-American scientist, probably to what is now Mount Winchell. The peak now bearing the name Agassiz is higher than Mount Winchell, but it is not a "needle." The 1940 edition of the Mount Goddard atlas sheet shows the old name, Agassiz Needle.

Agate Bay [Placer]. The bay on the north shore of Lake Tahoe was named by the Whitney Survey because of the presence of the variegated waxy quartz. The name appears on the von Leicht–Hoffmann Tahoe map of 1874.

Agate Creek [San Diego]. "I have marked the name Agate Creek ... as the abundance of this mineral in its bed was its distinguishing characteristic" (Blake, p. 67).

Agnew [Santa Clara]. Named for Abram Agnew and his family, who settled in the Santa Clara Valley in 1873. The original form, Agnew's, which referred to their seed farm, is retained in the name of Agnews State Hospital, but the shorter form was adopted for the railroad station and the post office.

Agnew: Meadow, Pass, Lake [Madera]. Named for Theodore C. Agnew, a miner, who settled here in 1877 and was of great service to the government by acting as a guide to troops on duty in Yosemite Park (Farquhar).

Agoura, ă-gōōr′-á [Los Angeles]. The community was first known as Picture City. When the post office was established in 1927 and the Post Office Department requested a single-word name, Agoura was chosen because the place was on the Agoura ranch. (E. W. Hutton.) The name may be a misspelling of Agoure, the family name of some stock

farmers of the 1890's.

Agua. The Spanish word for 'water' was a common generic geographical term for surface waters, mainly springs, and has survived in numerous place names. The word is now usually pronounced ä′-gwä, but ä′-gōō-ä and ä′-wä are also heard. Most frequently it is found with the modifying adjective *caliente*, 'warm' or 'hot.' This combination appeared in eleven land grants as the primary or secondary name and is preserved in some twenty places. **Agua Caliente Creek** [Alameda]. The name Agua Caliente appears on a *diseño* of 1835, and a land grant of that name is dated October 13, 1836. An *Arroyo del Agua Caliente* appears on Hoffmann's map of the Bay region (1873). On the San Jose atlas sheet the name is now Agua Caliente Creek, but a place called Warm Springs is on Agua Fria (cold water) Creek to the south. **Agua Caliente: Canyon**, town [Sonoma]. The origin of the name is found in the name of the land grant, first granted on May 7, 1836. The hot springs which gave the name to the grant are shown on the *diseño* of the regrant, dated July 13, 1840. **Agua Caliente Creek; Cañada Caliente** [San Diego]. The Indian rancheria *Jacopin* was called *El agua caliente* by the priests of San Diego Mission because of the near-by hot springs. June 4, 1840, the name appears in the title of the Valle de San Jose y Agua Caliente land grant, and it is shown on Gibbes' map of 1852. Less frequent is the combination with *fria*, 'cold.' **Agua Fria Creek** [Mariposa]. "This mine ... is called the 'Agua Fria Mine' from the circumstance of a stream of water gushing from the mountainside, which is so placed and sheltered as never to feel the heat of the sun, consequently the water is unusually cold as it springs from the rock ..." (Henry Huntly, 1850, quoted in *CHSQ*, XII, 75). The name of the town which developed around this mine was misspelled Agua Frio. In a number of other place names in California, the generic term *agua* has been combined with *buena* (good), *tibia* (tepid), *mansa* (quiet), *dulce* (sweet), *mala* (bad), *hedionda* (stinking), *puerca* (muddy), *amargosa* (bitter), *escondida* (hidden). Agua Hedionda [San Diego], August 10, 1842; Agua Puerca y las Trancas [Santa Cruz], October 31, 1843; Aguas Frias [Butte and Glenn], November 9, 1844; Aguas Nieves [Butte], December 22, 1844, were Mexican land grants. Agua Alta (high) Canyon [Riverside] and Agua Grande (great) Canyon [Montérey] sound like American applications. On several occasions the

Latin *aqua* has been used in place of the Spanish *agua,* probably in error. *See* Aqua.

Aguaje del Centinela [Los Angeles]. The name of this land grant, dated September 14, 1844, means 'spring of the sentinel.' *See* Centinela.

Aguajito, ä-gwä-hē'-tō: **Canyon** [Monterey]. The diminutive of *aguaje* (reservoir, spring, watering place) was used for the name of the Aguajito land grant, August 13, 1835. Another Aguajito grant, in Santa Cruz County, dated November 20, 1837, has not survived as a place name.

Aguanga, á-wäng'-gá: **Valley,** town [Riverside]; **Mountain** [San Diego]. The word is probably a Shoshonean Luiseño place name, with the locative case ending *-nga.* According to an Indian story (*AAE,* VIII, 151), the place was named *Picha Awanga* by a Temecula Indian. The present Canada Aguanga (Ramona atlas sheet) is shown as *Arroyo de Ahanga* on a *diseño* of the unconfirmed land grant Camajal y Palomar (1846). About 1850 the name appears in various spellings for an Indian village and a way station.

Aguerreberry, ăg'-ĕr-bĕr-ĭ: **Point** [Death Valley National Monument]. The original road to the point was built by "French Pete" Aguerreberry, who, with "Shorty" Harris, opened the Harrisburg mine in 1906. The name, spelled in various ways, was made "official" by Phil Townsend Hanna in the 1920's (Belden, January 8, 1861) .

Ahart Meadow [Fresno]. The meadow southeast of Huntington Lake was patented as a homestead to John Ahart about 1890 (Farquhar).

Ahpah: Creek, Ridge [Humboldt]. The name is derived from its Yurok designation, *o'hpo,* the etymology of which is unknown. According to Waterman (map 10), there is a large flat, *O'hpo,* near the creek; the name of the creek itself is given as *O'ho Wroi.*

Ahwahnee, ä-wä'-nē [Yosemite National Park]. The name was probably that of an Indian village in Yosemite Valley. According to Hodge, the name was *Awani* and the survivors of the original inhabitants designated the Yosemite Valley by this name. The word is probably Yokuts. When Indian agents called the tribe *Awalache* and *Awallache* in their reports of 1851, they were in Yokuts territory. The suffix *-che* means 'people' in the Yokuts language. Hittell in 1868 (*Yosemite,* p. 42) calls the tribe *Ahwahnachee.* It may be concluded, therefore, that the original name was 'Awala people' or 'Ahwahna people.' The specific term possibly means

'deep (or grassy) valley.' The version *Ahwahne* was apparently created by Bunnell in 1859 (*Hutch. Cal. Mag.,* III, 503). It was again taken up in the 1890's for advertising purposes, with another *e* added. **Ahwahnee** [Madera]. By decision of June 3, 1908, the Geographic Board changed the name of this station to Wassamma, doubtless upon the suggestion of Merriam, who believed that *Was-sa'-ma* was the original Indian name (*Mewan Stock,* p. 346). No attention seems to have been paid to the Board's decision.

Ahwiyah Point [Yosemite National Park]. The original name for Mirror Lake is preserved in the name of the northeast spur of Half Dome (David Brower). *See* Mirror Lake.

Alabama Hills [Inyo]. The name was given to the range by Southern sympathizers after the Confederate raider *Alabama* had sunk the Union man-of-war *Hatteras* off the coast of Texas, January 11, 1863. *See* Kearsarge.

Alabaster Cave [Placer]. The cave was discovered in 1860 and was so named because walls and ceilings were of limestone, a vein of which runs through the Sierra foothills (D. E. Cameron).

Alambique, á-lĕm'-bĭk: **Creek** [San Mateo]. The word is Spanish for a 'still' and is derived from the same Arabic stem as the English word alembic. Máximo Martínez testified in 1852 in the Pulgas land-grant case that he knew the creek first about 1839 and that "it took its name from a still placed there" (*WF,* VI, 374).

Alameda, ăl-á-mē'-dá: **Creek, city, County.** The word means 'grove of poplar trees' (*see* Alamo), but it is also used for groves of other shade trees. It is common as a place name in Spain. The general region of the southern part of the present county is called *la Alameda* in a letter of June 2, 1795 (Prov. Recs., VII, 54); it may have been so named earlier. In September of the same year the stream flowing through it is called *Rio de San Clemente* and *rio de la Alameda* (Arch. MSB, IV, 192 ff.). On August 8, 1842, the word appears in the name of the land grant Arroyo de la Alameda, and Alameda Creek is mentioned in the *Statutes* of 1850. The name was chosen for the city by popular vote in 1853; the county was created in the same year from parts of Contra Costa and Santa Clara counties.

Alamitos, ăl-á-mē'-tŏs. The Spanish word for 'little poplars (or cottonwoods)' was contained in the names of three land grants and has survived in **Alamitos Bay** [Los Angeles]

[5]

and the names of a number of creeks. **Los Alamitos** [Orange]. W. A. and J. R. Clark built a beet-sugar factory here in 1896 and named the place after Rancho Los Alamitos, part of the old Nieto grant.

Alamo, ăl'-à-mō. The Spanish word for 'poplar (or cottonwood) tree' was frequently used in Spanish times and has survived in a number of place names. The reason for naming was not necessarily an abundance of the trees; a single specimen sometimes gave rise to the name: "At this place [near the Salinas River] there was a poplar tree [*un álamo*] . . . within our camp, and for this reason the place was called Real del Alamo [Camp of the Poplar]" (Costansó, Sept. 27, 1769). The word Alamo appears in eight land grants or claims. There were two grants named Alamos y Agua Caliente (poplars and hot spring) in Los Angeles County, dated October 2, 1843, and May 27, 1846. **Alamo Pintado.** A grant in Santa Barbara County, dated August 16, 1843, was so called because of a tree painted with Indian symbols. Ballard, near Los Olivos, was formerly known as Alamo Pintado. The name of another grant in Santa Barbara County, dated March 9, 1839, is preserved in the name of **Los Alamos Valley** and the town **Los Alamos**. The latter was laid out and named by J. S. Bell and J. B. Shaw in 1876. Numerous were, and still are, the names in the desert regions where the Fremont cottonwood formed landmarks in the treeless plains and promised water to the wanderer: Alamo Solo, Alamo Mocho (trimmed cottonwood), Alamo Rancho, Alamo River, Alamorio (from *Alamo Rio*), Alamo Pintado. **Alamo: town, Creek, Ridge** [Contra Costa]. The town was settled in 1852, and is mentioned in the *Statutes* of 1854. *See* Cottonwood; Poplar.

Albany [Alameda]. The town, in former days jokingly known as O'Shean's View, was named Ocean View at its incorporation in 1908. The next year it was named Albany after the New York birthplace of Frank J. Roberts, the California town's first mayor. Albany Hill, *see* Cerrito.

Alberhill [Riverside]. Coined from the names of Albers and Hill, owners of the land on which the town was built about 1890.

Albion: River, town [Mendocino]. The ancient name of Britain was applied to the river, as well as to a land grant dated October 30, 1844, by William A. Richardson, captain of the port of San Francisco. Richardson, an Englishman, doubtless had in mind New Albion, the name bestowed upon northern

California by Drake. The town developed around the lumber mill built in 1853 by Dallas, Davidson, and MacPherson, and was named after the river. The post office was established June 29, 1859.

Alcatraz, ăl'-kà-trăz: **Island** [San Francisco Bay]. The name *Isla de Alcatraces* (pelican island) was given to what is now Yerba Buena Island on August 12, 1775, "on account of the abundance of those birds that were on it" (Eldredge, *Portolá,* p. 58). It thus appears on Ayala's chart of 1775 and on maps of San Francisco Bay in the following decades. Beechey, in 1826, transferred the name—as Alcatrazes Island—to the rock which is now the site of the Federal penitentiary. The plural form appeared on most maps until the Coast Survey created the present version in 1851. The Associated Oil Company owns, near Gaviota [Santa Barbara], a railroad siding and beach called Alcatraz.

Alcove Canyon [Lake]. First known as Elk Cove, because elk horns were numerous there. After the elk horns had disappeared, Elk Cove evolved into Alcove. In the early 1890's, this name was applied to the school district and thus became official. (Mauldin.)

Alder. The distribution of Alder Points, Creeks, Flats, and Hills from the northernmost section of the State to as far south as the Cuyamaca Mountains is a sign of the abundance of native alder—particularly white alder, but occasionally red alder and mountain alder. The name has been bestowed upon several communities: Alderpoint [Humboldt], Alder Springs [Glenn], Alder [Sacramento]. *See* Aliso.

Alessandro [Riverside]. The name was applied to the Santa Fe station in 1888 for the Indian hero in Helen Hunt Jackson's sentimental romance *Ramona,* then at the height of its popularity.

Alexander Grove [Humboldt]. Created as a memorial grove in Humboldt Redwoods State Park in 1929 and named for Charles B. Alexander (1848–1927), lawyer, banker, and businessman of New York and California, whose wife (the daughter of Charles Crocker, one of the Central Pacific "Big Four") had given half the property to the State.

Alexander Valley [Sonoma]. Named for Cyrus Alexander, a native of Pennsylvania, who came to California in 1832 or 1833 and in 1847 acquired two leagues of the Sotoyome land grant from Henry D. Fitch.

Alger, Lake [Mono]. Named in 1909 by R. B. Marshall for John Alger, a packer for the

Geological Survey (Farquhar).

Algodones, ăl-gŏ-dō′-něs [Imperial]. The place name preserves the name of a Yuman tribe which once dwelt on both sides of the Colorado; it is not from the Spanish word *algodón* (cotton). Venegas in 1758 (II, 185) spells the name *Achedomas,* and Garcés in 1774 (p. 383), *Jalchedunes.* The present spelling was not used until 1841 (Wilkes' map). Algootoon [Riverside], a now obsolete name mentioned by Bailey, was probably derived from the same root.

Algoso [Kern]. The place was known as Weed Patch because weeds grew there in profusion. When the Santa Fe branch line was built in 1922 the Spanish word *algoso,* meaning 'weedy,' was chosen as the name for the station, to distinguish it from another Weed Patch farther south.

Alhambra [Los Angeles]. The Alhambra tract was laid out in 1874 by George Hansen for the owners, "Don Benito" Wilson and his son-in-law, J. D. Shorb. The name of the Moorish fortress in Spain had been made popular by Washington Irving's book *The Alhambra.*

Alhambra: Valley, Creek [Contra Costa]. The original name *Cañada del Hambre* (valley of hunger) was doubtless applied because of some incident, although none of the popular stories current seems to be supported by documentary evidence. The name appears repeatedly on *diseños,* sometimes as *Paraje* [place] *de Ambre* and *Arroyo del Hambre;* May 8, 1842, it was applied to a land grant, Cañada del Hambre y las Bolsas del Hambre. Cronise mentions "The Hambre or Hungry Valley" in 1868, and Hoffmann (map of the Bay region) records Arroyo del Hambre in 1873. When Mrs. John Strentzel, John Muir's mother-in-law, settled there in the 1880's she renamed the valley because she disliked the old name.

Alice, Mount [Inyo]. This was the original name of Temple Crag. Now the name is applied to a lesser peak, two miles to the northeast. *See* Temple Crag.

Alisal. *See* Aliso.

Aliso, ă-lē′-sō. As alder (*aliso*) trees are native only where the source of water supply is permanent, their presence was particularly noted by early travelers. In the southern part of the State the Spanish form of the name for creeks and canyons still outnumbers the English form. Some of the names referred not to alders but to sycamores, which the Spaniards seem to have called, likewise, *aliso.* The mod-

ern Santa Fe station, **Aliso** [Orange], is situated on the land grant Cañada de los Alisos, dated June 18, 1841. The word *alisal* (alder or sycamore grove) was also repeatedly used in place names in Spanish times and is preserved in Alisal Creek [Santa Barbara] and Alisal Creek [Monterey]. The latter runs through the two Alisal land grants, which are dated December 19, 1833, and June 26, 1834. The name of another grant, Rincon del Alisal (corner of the alder grove) [Santa Clara], dated December 28, 1844, has not been preserved in California toponymy, but a little stream south of Mission San Jose [Alameda] is still called Cañada del Aliso. It was so called because of two very large sycamores, later cut down by a squatter named Fallon (*Century Magazine,* 1890, p. 190).

Alkali. The name appears often for surface waters in which the chemical is present. The best known are the lakes in Modoc County known locally as Surprise Valley Lakes, the lakes in Mono County, and the creek in Yosemite National Park.

All American Canal [Imperial]. The name, applied by the Imperial Irrigation District when the canal was proposed in 1916, was chosen to indicate that the new canal was entirely within the United States. The old canal which irrigated the Imperial Valley traversed Mexico for about sixty miles. (M. J. Dowd.)

Alleghany [Sierra]. The Alleghany tunnel, which gave the name to the settlement, was begun in April, 1853, and tapped the pay streak in October, 1855 (Co. Hist., 1882, pp. 473 f.). The post office was established and named in 1859. Like the many other Alleghanys, the name goes back to the Delaware Indian name for the Allegheny River.

Allensworth [Tulare]. Lieutenant Colonel Allen Allensworth founded the community about 1909 as part of a colonization scheme for Negroes. Unfortunately he was killed in an automobile accident in 1914 before his idea was completely carried out. (Mitchell.)

Alma [Santa Clara]. The settlement is shown in 1876 on the turnpike from which a branch road runs to the New *Alma*den Mine (p. 65 of *Historical Atlas Map of Santa Clara County*). The post office which had been established under the name Lexington, June 6, 1861, was changed to Alma, December 2, 1873.

Almaden, ăl-má-děn′ [Santa Clara]. The famous quicksilver deposit was identified by Andrés Castillero in 1845 and the mineral rights were granted him on December 30. The mine was known as the Santa Clara or Chaboya's mine. (Bowman Index.) The name New Almaden (after the famous Almaden quicksilver mine in Spain; *almadén,* in Spanish, means 'mine' or 'mineral') was used after 1848. The post office New Almaden was established July 5, 1861, and reëstablished December 23, 1873. It was again established January 4, 1934, under the name Almaden. Local pride forced the Post Office Department to restore the lost "New," December 1, 1953.

Almanor: Lake, post office [Plumas]. Coined from the names of *Alice, Martha,* and *Elinore,* the daughters of Guy C. Earl, president of the Great Western Power Company, which created the reservoir for the hydroelectric power project. The dam was completed in 1917, and the name was applied to the reservoir by Julius M. Howells, in charge of construction, in place of the older name, Big Meadows Reservoir.

Almonte, ăl-mŏn'-tĕ [Marin]. The old name, Mill Valley Junction, was changed in 1912 by the Southern Pacific upon petition of residents, to avoid confusion with Mill Valley. The proximity of Muir Woods may have suggested the name, which means 'at the woods.'

Alpaugh [Tulare]. Named in 1905 for John Alpaugh, one of the officers of the Home Extension Colony, which reclaimed the Tulare Lake "island," successively known as Hog Root, Root, and Atwell Island (Mitchell).

Alpha [Nevada]. Two early mining camps on the South Fork of Yuba River were called Hell-Out-for-Noon and Delirium Tremens ("The Knave," Sept. 15, 1946). In 1852 or 1853, when the country began to become respectable, these names were changed to Alpha and Omega, the first and the last letter of the Greek alphabet. Both are listed as post offices in 1858. Alpha is now a ghost town.

Alpine County. Formed and named by act of the legislature, March 6, 1864, from parts of Amador, El Dorado, Calaveras, and Tuolumne counties. The alpine character of the High Sierra region suggested the name. **Alpine: town, Heights, Creek** [San Diego]. The town was established in the 1880's by B. R. Arnold, and the name was proposed by an early resident because the district resembled her native Switzerland. Alpine Butte in Los Angeles County and several other features bear the name for the same reason.

Alta. The Spanish adjective for 'high' or 'upper' has always been a favorite in California place naming. It is sometimes used as a true specific geographical term: Piedras Altas [Monterey], Loma Alta [Monterey, Santa Barbara], Alta Vista [Sonoma], Agua Alta Canyon (high water canyon) [Riverside], Altacanyada [Los Angeles]. *Alta California* was the name of the Spanish (later Mexican) province, which is now our State, from 1772 to the American conquest. **Altaville** [Calaveras]. The old mining camp, variously known as Forks-of-the-Roads, Low Divide, and Cherokee Flat, adopted its present name at a town meeting in 1857. **Alta** [Placer]. The name, given to the station of the Central Pacific in 1866, is said to have been selected because the *Alta California,* a San Francisco newspaper, was favorable to the Central Pacific. **Altamont** [Alameda]. The station was named by the Central Pacific in 1869, probably because of its location at the highest point of Livermore Pass. There were several Altamonts in the eastern United States at that time. **Alta: Meadow, Peak** [Sequoia National Park]. In 1876 W. B. Wallace, Tom Witt, and N. B. Witt camped at the meadow and gave it this name because it was higher than any other meadow in the vicinity. The inhabitants of the Three Rivers settlement apparently extended the name to the mountain, on a slope of which the meadow is situated. It was formerly known as Tharp's Peak. (Farquhar.) **Altadena** [Los Angeles]. Coined from *alta* and the last part of Pasa*dena* and applied in 1887 to the community because of its position above Pasadena. Byron C. Clark had first used the name in 1886 for his nursery. **Alta Loma** [San Bernardino]. The name was applied in 1912 to a station on the line of the Pacific Electric Railway Company as the result of a popular vote. The next year the name was also given to the post office of Ioamosa, a name applied by farmers from Iowa. *See* Hermosa.

Altadena. *See* Alta.

Al Tahoe. *See* Tahoe.

Altamont. *See* Alta.

Altaville. *See* Alta.

Alton [Humboldt]. The place was named in 1862 by S. R. Perry after his home town in Illinois. In the 1880's the name was applied to the post office and to the station of the Eel River and Eureka Railroad.

Alturas, ăl-tōōr'-ăs [Modoc]. The place was first known as Dorris' Bridge, for Presley Dorris, who had built a bridge here across the Pit River. On the von Leicht–Craven map of 1874 it appears as Dorrisville. June 1, 1876, the legislature, upon petition, changed the name to the Spanish name, meaning 'heights.' *See* Dorris. Alturas is also the name of subdivisions and physical features in other parts of the State.

Alumine Peak [Shasta]. Named after an undeveloped alum mine at which beautiful alum crystals have been found (Steger).

Alum Rock: Park, Creek [Santa Clara]. Created as a park by act of the legislature in 1872 and called "The City Reservation"; later called by its present name because of the striking monolith in its center, on the sides and in the crevices of which alum dust is found.

Alvarado [Alameda]. The town was founded in 1851 by Henry C. Smith and named New Haven after the largest city of his home state, Connecticut. In March, 1853, it was made the seat of the newly formed Alameda County. In the meantime, two San Francisco attorneys, Strode and Jones, had laid out a town near by and named it in honor of Juan B. Alvarado, governor of California from 1836 to 1842. "The new county officials met in the upper story of Smith's store in Block 81 in New Haven; but the first minutes of their meeting are dated April 11, 1853, in Alvarado. By this date, then, New Haven had discarded its old name and taken that of the neighboring town." (*CHSQ*, XII, 173 f.) In the late 1830's, while Alvarado was governor, San Jose was called *Pueblo de Alvarado* and *San Jose de Alvarado* (DSP Mont., IV, 97; DSP San Jose, VI, 12). Several minor places in the State are named Alvarado for some of the numerous persons having that surname.

Alviso, ăl-vē′-sō: town, **Slough, Channel** [Santa Clara]. Named for Ignacio Alviso (1772–1848), who came to San Francisco from Mexico with the Anza expedition in 1776. February 10, 1838, he received the grant Rincon de los Esteros, on which was the landing place for Santa Clara and San Jose. Here the town was laid out in 1849 by Chester S. Lyman for three indefatigable promoters of the gold era, Peter H. Burnett, J. D. Hoppe, and Charles B. Marvin. The post office is listed in 1862.

Alvord: Mountains, Well [San Bernardino]. In 1860 or 1861 Charles Alvord with a party of prospectors went in search of the lost Gunsight silver lode in Death Valley. He discovered a black manganese ledge which contained "wire gold," but later attempts to find the place failed. Alvord was murdered in 1862. (Weight, pp. 48 ff.)

Amador, ăm′á-dôr: **Valley** [Alameda, Contra Costa]. José María Amador, a native of San Francisco, was a soldier in the San Francisco company from 1810 to 1827, then majordomo of Mission San Jose. He became the grantee of Rancho San Ramon, January 22, 1834. His name appears on Duflot de Mofras's map of 1844, and Amador Valley is mentioned in the *Statutes* of 1853. **Amador: Creek, County, City.** In 1848 Amador, with several Indians, established a mining camp near the site of the present town. The settlement and creek became known by his name. The county was created and named May 11, 1854. The post office was established under the name Amador City, August 19, 1863.

Amargosa: River, Desert, Range [Death Valley National Monument, Inyo, San Bernardino]. The name is recorded by Frémont in April, 1844: "It [the stream] is called by the Spaniards *Amargosa*—the bitter-water of the desert" (*Expl. Exp.*, 1853, p. 383). The Boundary Commission in 1861 records both the river and the range. Formerly, Death Valley was often called the Amargosa Desert because the Amargosa River flows through it as far as Badwater after making a **U** turn north of the Avawatz Mountains. What is now called the Amargosa Desert is mainly in Nevada. **Amargosa Creek** [Los Angeles] is doubtless also named for the bitterness of its water.

Amboy [San Bernardino]. Named by the Atlantic and Pacific Railroad (now Santa Fe) in 1883, apparently after one of the Amboys "back East." It was probably Lewis Kingman, a locating engineer of the railroad, who named the stations of the new line between this point and the Arizona border in alphabetical order: Amboy, Bristol, Cadiz, Danby, Edson, Fenner, and Goffs. All these names have counterparts elsewhere in the United States. It appears that, later, another railway official tried to continue the alphabet. In 1896 the station name Ibex (later Ibis) appears, and in 1904 a Homer, west of Ibex, and a Klinefelter, east of Ibex.

Americano Creek. *See* Creek.

American: River, Basin, Canyon, Canyon Creek, Flat, Hill [Placer, El Dorado, Sacramento]. The name for the river appears on Wilkes' map of 1841 and was doubtless supplied to Ringgold by Sutter: "I gave the name American River to the stream that now bears it from the fact that about three miles above the Fort was a pass [ford], where the Canadian trappers, who were called Americanos by the Spanish speaking Indians, crossed the stream. This place was called 'El Paso de los Americanos.' So I called this stream the

American River" (pp. 61 f.). *Rio de los Americanos* is shown on the *diseño* of the Arroyo Chico grant of 1843, and on October 1, 1844, the name was applied to the Leidesdorff grant. In the *Statutes* of 1850 the name American Fork, which had also been used by Sutter previously, is officially used, but in the early 1850's the present (and original) name came into current use. Jedediah Smith had given it the name Wild River in 1828, and in 1833 the river and a land grant were called Rio Ojotska. With a few exceptions in other western states, the use of the adjective, American, in place naming is apparently restricted to California, where it is found in several counties, mainly from the many gold camps called American during the gold rush. **American Valley** [Plumas]. The valley north of Quincy was named after Bradley's American Ranch, which was established in the 1850's.

Amphitheater. A favorite term for features which resemble the Roman open-air theater. The best known are the lake in Sequoia National Park, named in 1899 by W. F. Dean, the lake in Kings Canyon National Park, named in 1902 by J. N. LeConte, and the canyon near Saratoga Springs in San Bernardino County, named in 1922 by the Geological Survey.

Anacapa, ăn-á-kăp′-à: **Islands, Passage** [Ventura]. The Portolá expedition in January, 1770, called the westernmost island *Falsa Vela*, 'false sail,' because it looked like a ship, and the other two, *Las Mesitas*, 'small table hills' (Costansó, p. 152). Juan Pérez in March, 1774, named the group *Islotes de Santo Tomas*, a name which was sometimes used on European maps: Humboldt, 1811; Duflot de Mofras, 1844. Costansó (p. 148) had reported that *Anajup* was the native name for the island now called Santa Cruz. The name was probably later transferred to the westernmost of the Anacapa Islands. Vancouver in 1792 called all three islands *Eneeapah*, but spelled the name *Enecapa* on his maps. Gibbes has *Encapa*, the Coast Survey, *Anacape* in 1852. The Parke-Custer map gives the present spelling in 1854. The name is derived from Chumash Indian *Anyapah* (*AAE*, XII, 34), but its meaning is not known.

Anaheim, ăn′-à-hīm: city, **Landing, Creek, Bay, Canal** [Orange]. Coined from Santa *Ana*, the name of the river, plus the German suffix, *-heim* (home). The place was laid out by the Los Angeles Vineyard Society in 1857, and named by the stockholders on January 15,

1858, upon the suggestion of T. E. Schmidt. This German colony was the first large-scale agricultural settlement in the orbit of Los Angeles, and the present city still calls itself "the Mother Colony." The early local name was *Campo Aleman* (German field).

Analy, ăn′-à-lǐ: **Valley** [Sonoma]. Named after Annaly, Ireland, ruled by the O'Farrell family. Jasper O'Farrell came to California in 1843, bought the Rancho Estero Americano, and named the valley Annaly. When the township was formed in 1851, one "n" was omitted on the records and has never been restored. The name was applied to a post office, August 7, 1860.

Anaverde. *See* Verde.

Anderson [Shasta]. When the California and Oregon Railroad (now the Southern Pacific) reached the place in 1872, the station was named for Elias Anderson, owner of the American Ranch, who granted the right of way to the railroad.

Andersonia [Mendocino]. The place was named by and for Jeff Anderson, who built a sawmill there in 1903 (Borden). A post office was established July 26, 1904.

Anderson Ridge [Lake]. This ridge was named for Bob Anderson, a stockman in the region in the 1880's and 1890's (Mauldin).

Anderson Springs [Lake]. Named for Dr. A. Anderson, one of the discoverers of the springs in 1873.

Anderson Valley [Mendocino]. Named for Walter Anderson, who settled here in 1851. The Indian name of the valley was *Taa-bo-tah*. (Co. Hist., 1880, pp. 168, 360.)

Andesite: Peak, Ridge [Nevada]. Named by the Geological Survey because the chief component is the rock known as andesite. (Geographic Board, March, 1949.)

Andover [Placer]. Named by a division superintendent of the Southern Pacific after his home town in Massachusetts (*Grizzly Bear*, March, 1935).

Andrade, ăn-drä′-dě [Imperial]. Named by the Imperial Land Company for the Mexican general, Guillermo Andrade, who had sold the land for colonization to the California Development Company in 1900 (Tout). The post office was established and named in 1912. The name of the railroad station is Cantu.

Andreas, ăn-drä′-ăs: **Canyon** [Riverside]. Named for old "Captain Andreas," a chieftain of the Cahuilla tribe.

Andrews Creek [Shasta]. Named for Alexander R. Andrews, a member of the second California Constitutional Convention and an assemblyman from Shasta County at the 7th, 18th, and 19th sessions of the legislature, who (according to Steger) had mining claims on this creek.

Andrus Island [Sacramento]. Named for George Andrus, a settler of 1852.

Angela, Lake [Nevada]. Named in August, 1865, for Angela King, sister of Thomas Starr King, by a party of locating engineers for the Union Pacific Railroad (Maule).

Angeles National Forest. Created by combining the San Gabriel Forest Reserve and old San Bernardino National Forest and given the present name by proclamation of President Theodore Roosevelt in 1908 because the larger part of the forest is within the County of Los Angeles.

Angel Island [San Francisco Bay]. Named *Isla de los Angeles* by Ayala when the *San Carlos* anchored there in August, 1775. Beechey in 1826 translated it 'Angel Island.' Ringgold in 1851 tried to restore the Spanish version, but the charts of the Coast Survey kept the American form: 1850, Angel Island; 1851, Los Angeles Island; 1852, Angel Island. The Spanish version was sometimes used on later maps.

Angelo Creek [San Mateo]. Preserves the name of "Angelo," owner of a popular hotel at the Belmont crossroads in the 1850's.

Angels: Camp, Creek [Calaveras]. George or Henry Angel, said to have been a member of Stevenson's Volunteers, started mining at the creek in June, 1848. The place was described by Audubon and other diarists in the early 1850's. The post office was established May 27, 1853, and the place became well known as one of the richest gold diggings of the southern mines. It was incorporated as Angels in 1912, but popular usage prefers the name Angels Camp, which is still used by the post office and for Historic Landmark 287.

Angwin [Napa]. Named about 1874 for Edwin Angwin, who operated a summer resort on his property, which was a part of Rancho La Jota (C. D. Utt).

Animas [Santa Clara]. The name of a land grant dated November 28, 1808, and August 7, 1835. *Las Animas* (the souls) refers to All Souls' Day. The grant was also known as Carnadero and La Brea.

Anklin Meadows [Lassen National Park]. "These meadows were in the homestead entry of an early settler, named Anklin . . ." (Geographic Board, *Sixth Report*).

Anna Lake. *See* Emma Lake.

Annapolis [Sonoma]. The post office, established in the early 1900's, was not named directly after one of the many places of that name in the East, but after the Annapolis Orchards, established by Wetmore Brothers in the 1880's (Leland).

Annette [Kern]. Probably named for James L. Annette, who became head miller of the Kern River Mills in December, 1906.

Ano Nuevo, ăn'-ō noō-ā'-vō, **Point; Ano Nuevo: Bay, Creek, Island** [San Mateo]. The name *Punta de Año Nuevo* was given to the cape by Vizcaíno on January 3, 1603, because it was the first promontory sighted in the new year. It is one of the few names applied by early navigators which have lasted throughout the centuries for a point in the same general latitude. May 27, 1842, the name was used for the land grant Punta del Año Nuevo. On some American maps of the 1850's the translation, New Years Point, can be found. The first Coast Survey charts confused the genders: 1850, Pt. Anno Nueva; 1851, Pta. Año Nueva. Camacho's map of 1785 has two points called *Punta Falsa de Año Nuevo* (Wagner, p. 427), probably modern Pigeon and Franklin points. The Geological Survey and some modern maps preserve the spelling Año.

Antelope. About seventy-five places record the presence of the graceful animal which was once abundant in various parts of the State.

Antelope [Sacramento]. The name was applied to the settlement at Cross's brick warehouse by the Antelope Business Association in 1877. The post office was established June 19, 1877. The Spanish word for 'antelope,' *berrendo,* was repeatedly used for place names in Spanish times. None seem to have survived, unless the Southern Pacific stations Berendo [Los Angeles] and Berenda [Madera] were derived from the word. **Antelope Creek** [Tehama] is a translation of *Arroyo de los Berrendos* (Bidwell's map of 1844). **Antelope Bridge** [Lava Beds National Monument]. Named in January, 1917, by J. D. Howard because at its eastern entrance he found the pictograph of an antelope entering an enclosure.

Anthony: Ridge, Peak [Mendocino]. Named for the three Anthony brothers—James, Jesse, and George—who ran sheep on this mountain in the early 1890's (Forest Service). The oldest brother, James, was mentioned as a farmer in the Round Valley as early as 1874.

Anticline Ridge [Fresno]. The name is a geological term which designates the fold or arch of rock strata in which the layers dip in opposite directions from the crest.

Antimony Peak [Kern]. In 1854 W. P. Blake of the Pacific Railroad Survey (*Reports*, Vol. V, Pt. 2, pp. 291 ff.) identified the ore, which prospectors had hoped was silver, as "sulphuret of antimony, commonly known as Grey Antimony or Antimony-Glance," and traced the vein from the canyon high up the side of the mountain. **Antimony: Spring, Ridge, Canyon** [Death Valley National Monument]. Dr. S. G. George and his party were seeking the "lost" Gunsight Mine when they came upon an antimony deposit on December 25, 1860, which they first named "Christmas Gift." Wheeler atlas sheet 65-D records the name Antimony for a mine in the area. Deposits are found in other counties, including San Benito and Merced, where another peak is named Antimony.

Antioch [Contra Costa]. In 1849 the place was known as Smith's Landing for the first settlers, the twin brothers J. H. and W. W. Smith. In the following year the latter, a minister of the gospel, invited a group of New Englanders to settle on his property. At a picnic on the Fourth of July, 1851, the citizens chóse the new name, Antioch, the name of the Biblical city in Syria, in preference to Minton and Paradise, other names that had been suggested.

Antoine Cañon [Placer]. Named for a half-breed Indian called Antoine, who was a member of the Bronson prospecting party of 1850 (Co. Hist., 1882, p. 373).

Anvil: Spring, Canyon [Death Valley National Monument]. So named because Sergeant Neal, of the Bendire expedition of 1867, found at the spring an anvil, wagon rims, and a quantity of old iron. It is possible but not certain that these were the remnants of the blacksmith outfit which Asahel Bennett had brought into the valley in 1849. *See* Bennetts Well.

Anza Desert State Park [San Diego]. Established in 1933 and named in honor of Juan Bautista de Anza, leader of the famous Anza expedition, which crossed the park area in 1774. **Lake Anza** [Alameda]. Named in 1939 by the East Bay Regional Park Board in honor of the same explorer. The choice was the result of a local contest in which the winner was a twelve-year-old girl, Margaret Magnussen. (R. E. Walpole.) **Anza** [Riverside]. The name of the old post office Cahuilla was changed to Anza in 1926.

Anzar Lake [San Benito]. The name commemorates Juan Anzar, grantee of the land grant Aromitas y Agua Caliente, October 12, 1835.

Apache, á-păch'-ê. The name of the warlike Indian tribe which has left an indelible mark upon the geographical nomenclature of Arizona is represented in California by Apache Canyon and Potrero, in Ventura County.

Applegate [Placer]. The place was settled by Lisbon Applegate and was known as Bear River House. The post office was established in the 1870's, with George Applegate as postmaster.

Applesauce Creek [Siskiyou]. The name became known when in the 1890's mammoth quartz ledges were discovered in the vicinity. It is derived from the favorite exclamation of a Mr. Sullivan who had a cabin near the mouth of the creek. When he was lucky at card playing he was wont to exclaim, "That's the applesauce!" (Luddy.)

Apple Valley [San Bernardino]. The post office established April 16, 1949, at the resort city developed by Newt Bass, bears the name applied at the turn of the century by Mrs. Ursula M. Poates, a long-time resident of the Mojave Desert. To convince buyers that fruit could be grown in the desert, Mrs. Poates planted three apple trees in her greasewood-covered yard. Orchards were planted, but only a few of the trees remain today to recall Mrs. Poates's early land development scheme. (Corinne K. Flemings.)

Aptos, ăp'-tŏs: town, **Creek** [Santa Cruz]. A *Rancho de Aptos*, a sheep ranch of Mission Santa Cruz, is mentioned on July 5, 1807 (Arch. Arz. SF, II, 61). The name was applied to a provisional land grant, September 4, 1831. It was probably the Spanish rendering of the name of a Costanoan village or its chief.

Aqua. The Latin word for 'water' is found twice on the topographical maps: Aqua Escondida on the Branch Mountain atlas sheet, and Aqua Chinon Wash on the El Toro. In both, the word was probably meant to be the Spanish *agua*.

Arana Gulch [Santa Cruz]. The name commemorates José Arana, grantee of the land grant Potrero y Rincon de San Pedro Regalado, August 15, 1842.

Ararat, Mount. The mountain in Armenia, on which Noah's ark was grounded on the seventeenth day of the seventh month (2349 B.C., according to Archbishop Usher) after the remarkable voyage of a hundred and fifty days, has been a favorite name for peaks in various parts of the globe. California has four Mount Ararats—in Eldorado, Merced, Plumas, and San Diego counties.

Arboga [Yuba]. Named in 1911 by the Rev. N. M. Nelsien, pastor of the Swedish Mission Church, after his former home in Sweden (Paul Erickson).

Arbuckle [Colusa]. Named by surveyors of the Central Pacific Railroad when station and town were established in 1875 on the ranch of T. R. Arbuckle, who had settled there in 1866.

Arbuckle Mountain [Shasta]. Named for A. Arbuckle, a prospector of the early 1850's (Steger).

Arcadia [Los Angeles]. The city was platted and named by Herman A. Unruh, of the San Gabriel Valley Railroad, about 1888. Arcadia, the name of a district in Greece which became in pastoral poetry a locale of rural simplicity, is a favorite place name in the United States. The famous Arcadia Block in Los Angeles, built by Abel Stearns in 1858, was, however, named for his wife, Arcadia.

Arcane Meadow [Death Valley National Monument]. The high flat between Manly and Rogers peaks (formerly Baldy and Sugarloaf) was named by the Park Service in memory of J. B. Arcan, a member of the Bennett-Manly party of 1849 (Death Valley Survey).

Arcata, är-kǎ'-tà [Humboldt]. The town, an offspring of the Humboldt boom of 1850, was founded and named Union Town sometime before April 17 of that year by the Union Company. It appears on most maps as Union. To avoid confusion with Uniontown [El Dorado] the name was changed to Arcata in 1860: "... the town of Union ... is hereby changed to the name of the town of Arcata" (*Statutes*, 1860, p. 109). The new name is of uncertain origin. It had first been suggested in the Humboldt *Times* of January 20, 1855, its advocates asserting (through the process of wishful thinking) that it meant 'Union' in the local Indian dialect. The name of the Indian village at the site was *Kori*, mentioned in the Indian Report, September 21, 1851.

Arch. The word is often found along the coast for archlike formations. There are five Arch Rocks in the State, as well as an Arched Rock north of Tomales Bay, an Arch Beach south of Laguna Beach, and a Three Arch Bay south of Long Beach.

Arena, à-rē'-nà, **Point; Arena: Rock, Cove** [Mendocino]. The cape was first sighted by Ferrer in 1543 and called *Cabo de Fortunas*. It appears on the maps of the following two

hundred and fifty years under various names. The popular name among sailors in the latter part of the 18th century was apparently the descriptive term *Barra de Arena* (sand bar). Vancouver (1792) misspelled it *Barro de Arena,* and it appears thus on most American maps until 1851. Disturnell, 1847, has Punta Arena; Scholfield, 1851, Point Barro de Arena; Bancroft, 1858, Punta de Arena. The Americanized version, Pt. Arena, is recorded on the map accompanying the English translation (1849) of Schmölder's *Wegweiser* (Wheat, No. 83). It was used again by the Coast Survey in 1853 and won out when it was adopted for the maps of the Whitney Survey. The name Arena occurs in other parts of the State: Santa Barbara, Kern, and Merced counties, and Santa Cruz Island. Sand Point [Marin] is *Punta de Arenas* on a *plano* of 1776 (PSP Ben. Mil., I), and is mentioned by Font on March 27, 1776. Thomes Creek [Tehama] is labeled *Arroyo Arenoso,* 'sandy creek,' on the *diseño* of Los Saucos grant and on Bidwell's map of 1844.

Argos [San Bernardino]. The Santa Fe station was probably named after the city in Greece. Other classical names—Troy, Hector, Trojan—were applied to stations on the same part of the line and are shown on the Santa Fe maps after 1905.

Arguello, är-gwĕl'-ō, **Point** [Santa Barbara]. Vancouver named the point in 1792 for José Darío Argüello, at that time *comandante* at Monterey. It is called Pedernales on early Spanish maps. Both names refer obviously to the entire headland. The Coast Survey charts misspelled it Point Arguilla until 1874, though the 1858 edition of the Coast Pilot gave the proper spelling. *See* Pedernales. The station, Arguello, is named after the point; the near-by post office, Arlight, is a contraction of Point *Arguello light*house.

Argus: Peak, Range [Inyo, San Bernardino]. Like other characters from classical mythology, the many-eyed Argus has provided a convenient name for ships, periodicals, and places. An Argus mining district is shown on Farley's map of 1861; peak and range appear on sheet 65-D of the Wheeler atlas. The name was probably suggested because the peak seems to watch over the country to east, west, and south.

Arichi, Arroyo [Marin]. An *Arroyo de Arichi* (also spelled *Avichi*) is mentioned in the records of the Novato grant in the 1850's, and is shown on Hoffmann's map of the Bay region (1873). The meaning and origin of the name are not known.

Arlight. *See* Arguello.

Arlington. The name, of English derivation, has long been a favorite place name, increasing in popularity after the establishment of the National Cemeteries at Arlington, Virginia, at the close of the Civil War. In California more than ten places and features are named Arlington. **Arlington** [Riverside]. The place was developed by the Riverside Land and Irrigation Company in 1875 and named by popular vote. **Arlington Heights** [Alameda]. The tract was named by John H. Spring in 1911, after Arlington Avenue, Berkeley, which led to the subdivision.

Armada, är-mä'-då [Riverside]. The word is Spanish for 'fleet' or 'squadron'; but here, as in other places in the United States, it was chosen merely for its euphony, when a post office was established, September 25, 1895.

Armijo, är'-mĭ-ō [Solano]. The high school district preserves the name of José F. Armijo, in 1842 owner of the Tolenas rancho, northeast of Fairfield (D. A. Weir).

Armona [Kings]. The typical railroad name, possibly coined from Ramona by the construction engineer, was applied to a station of the Goshen-Huron branch line in the 1880's. When the San Joaquin branch of the Southern Pacific joined this branch east of the old station in June, 1891, the name was transferred to the new junction.

Armstrong Redwoods State Park [Sonoma]. The park was deeded by the county to the State, January 8, 1934, and named in memory of Colonel James B. Armstrong, the original owner, whose heirs had contributed toward its purchase by the county in 1917–1918.

Army Pass [Sequoia National Park]. So named because a trail was constructed over the pass by Troop K, Fourth Cavalry, in the 1890's (Farquhar).

Army Point [Solano]. Appears on Ringgold's map of 1850 as Navy Point. It was properly changed by the Coast Survey after the Army established a reservation there in 1851.

Arndt Lake [Tuolumne]. Named in 1896 by Lieutenant Harry C. Benson for Sergeant Alvin Arndt of the Fourth Cavalry, who had found a route from Matterhorn Canyon to Hetch Hetchy Valley in September, 1893 (Farquhar).

Arno [Sacramento]. The post office was established about 1890 and named after the river in Italy. Julio Valensin, an Italian, and Alice McCauley, daughter of the owner of the land, were married in Florence, which is situated on the Arno River.

Arnold [Calaveras]. The post office was established in 1934 and named for Bernice Arnold (now Mrs. McCallum), owner of the resort and first postmaster.

Arnot Peak [Alpine]. Named for Nathaniel D. Arnot, superior judge of Alpine County, 1879–1904 (Maule).

Aromas [Monterey]. The place was formerly known as Sand Cut because of the tunnel built by the Southern Pacific in the 1870's. The present name, applied to the post office about 1895, is derived from the land grant Aromitas y Agua Caliente (little odors and warm water), dated October 12, 1835. The *diseño* shows *Aromitas* as well as *Aromas;* both designations probably refer to the odors of sulphur water. The rancho is called Las Aromas in a report dated February 12, 1847 (Arch. Mont., XIII, 1).

Arrastre. A mining term derived from the Mexican *arrastrar,* meaning 'to drag along the ground,' applied in California gold-mining districts to the primitive milling apparatus used for drawing heavy weights over the ore in a circular pit by means of horse, mule, water, or hand power. The name is found in San Bernardino, Los Angeles, and Siskiyou counties. There is an Arrastra Flat south of Frazier Mountain [Ventura]. An Arastraville in Tuolumne County was once a rich gold mining camp. Arrastre Springs in the Avawatz Mountains in San Bernardino County was so named because in 1907 prospectors found an arrastre in an old Mexican gold camp.

Arrow. A number of features are so named either because of their shape or because arrowheads were found there. **Arrow: Peak, Ridge** [Kings Canyon National Park]. The peak was named in 1895 by Bolton C. Brown when he made the first ascent (Farquhar).

Arrowhead: Springs, Lake [San Bernardino]. Dr. David N. Smith settled near the hot springs in 1860. "The name given to the place is derived from a peculiar configuration resembling an arrow-head. . . . The springs are situated directly at the foot of the hill bearing this remarkable landmark" (Wilmington *Journal,* Oct. 27, 1866). The lake was originally called Little Bear Lake; a near-by post office, Arrowbear Lake, combines the old and the new name. There is an Arrowhead Mountain in Sonoma County, probably so named because Indian arrowheads were found there.

Arroyo, ă-roi'-ō. The word was used in Spanish California times for a watercourse—a creek or its bed. Sometimes the word *seco* (dry) was added to indicate the lack of water. *Arroyo* occurs in the principal or secondary names of thirty land grants. It has become a generic term in the southwestern United States and is frequently applied in place of "creek" or "canyon." In 1930 the Geological Survey considerably increased the number of Arroyos in the State by calling every gulch in the Kettleman Hills an arroyo. More than 150 waterways are now called Arroyos, chiefly in the San Francisco Bay region and the southern counties. Some have been hybridized: Big Arroyo [Tulare], once called Jenny Lind Creek; Dry Arroyo [Solano]; Surprise Arroyo [Fresno]. There are also some tautologies: Arroyo Grande Creek [San Luis Obispo]; Arroyo Seco Creek [Monterey]. **Arroyo Grande: Creek, Valley,** town [San Luis Obispo]. The name was preserved through the land grant Arroyo Grande or San Ramon, dated April 25, 1842. Parke-Custer record the name in 1855. The name of the town dates from 1867–1868, when a blacksmith shop and a schoolhouse were built.in the valley. **Arroyo Sanatorium** [Alameda] is named after the Arroyo Valle, on which it is situated. *See* Valle de San Jose. **Arroyo Paredon** [Santa Barbara]. The creek was known as Arroyo Parida or Parida Creek. In 1961 the Geographic Board restored what was apparently the original name, the Spanish word for 'thick wall.'

Arsenic Spring [Death Valley National Monument]. The amount of arsenic in the water— if there is any—is negligible; the effects of imbibing the water are not poisonous, but tonic, according to local Indians (Death Valley Survey).

Artesia [Los Angeles]. Named by the Artesia Company, which drilled artesian wells and established the town in the 1870's.

Arthur, Lake [Placer]. A power reservoir built in 1909 and named for W. R. Arthur, assistant manager of the water district.

Artois, är′-tois [Glenn]. The town (originally in Colusa County) was named Germantown by popular vote in 1876, most of the early settlers being German. The post office was established August 2, 1877. In 1918 the American name was replaced by the French *Artois,* after the district on the Western Front in World War I. The Post Office Department accepted the new name, May 22, 1918.

Artray Creek [Plumas, Lassen]. Coined in 1914 from the first names of *Ar*thur Barrett, a forest ranger, and *Ray*mond Orr, a timber reconnaissance man (Stewart).

Arvin [Kern]. Named for Arvin Richardson, the first storekeeper in the colony, which was established in 1910 (Santa Fe).

Asbill Creek [Lake]. The stream, also known as Conns Creek, was named for an old pioneer family. *See* Glossary.

Ash. In the United States, thousands of places and physical features include Ash in their names. Some of these are copied from English place names, but the greater number are for the tree. In California the tree is inconspicuous, of little value, and not common; hence, the number of places named for it is comparatively small. A few settlements, about ten creeks, and five peaks bear the name, and most of these are in the northern counties, where the name was probably given because the Oregon ash was found growing there. **Ash Meadows** and **Creek** [Inyo] were named for the leather-leaf ash: "The large valley was named on account of the presence of a small desert ash (*Fraxinus coriacea*) which was formerly abundant" (Palmer). *See* Fresno.

Ash Creek [Siskiyou]. So named because of the presence of volcanic ash. Shasta County has an Ashpan Butte.

Ashford: Canyon, Peak [Death Valley National Monument]. Named after the Ashford Mill, built in 1914. The Ashford brothers, of Shoshone, were prominent in the mining boom of that year.

Ash Hill [San Bernardino]. In 1883 the Southern Pacific Railroad named a siding on the newly constructed line (now Santa Fe) and erected a monument for Ben Ash, a surveyor who died of thirst while surveying there (Santa Fe).

Asilomar, ă-sĭl′-ŏ-mär, ă-sē′-lô-mär [Monterey]. The artificial name, coined from Spanish *asilo* (refuge) and *mar* (sea), was given by the National Board of the Y.W.C.A. to the meeting and vacation grounds which were established in 1913 for Y.W.C.A. groups and similar organizations (Mrs. B. B. Head). The post office is listed in 1915.

Aspen. The American aspen is found on the Sierra slopes at an elevation of 5,000 to 10,000 feet, from Mount Whitney to Oregon, and has given its name to about ten features, including the well-known Aspen Valley in Yosemite. The mountain in Shasta County called Aspen Butte should be Asperin Butte, according to a decision of the Geographic Board, Sept.-Dec., 1963.

Asphalt. California is one of the few regions in

which extensive deposits of asphaltum or bitumen are found. Their occurrence in the coastal counties from Santa Clara to Orange, and in Kern County, has given rise to a number of Asphalt, Tar, and Pitch Creeks, Springs, and Lakes. *See* Brea; Pismo.

Associated [Contra Costa]. The name was applied to the post office in 1913, when the Tidewater Associated Oil Company built the company town. The railroad station has the more melodious name Avon.

Asti [Sonoma]. Named after the city in Italy, a vineyard center. The place is a railroad station serving the wine-producing area of the Italian Swiss Colony, originally organized in 1881. The post office is listed in 1892.

Asuncion, ă-sŭn'-sĭ-ŏn [San Luis Obispo]. The Spanish word, referring to the Ascension of the Virgin Mary, is mentioned as a place name, *La Assumpcion,* by Font on March 4, 1776. Rancho de la Asuncion, near Mission San Luis Obispo, is mentioned November 26, 1827 (Registro, p. 17). June 18, 1845, the name was applied to a land grant. The von Leicht-Craven map (1874) shows the Anglicized form, Ascension, but when the station of the Southern Pacific was named the Spanish version was again used.

Atascadero, ă-tăs-ká-dâr'-ō: town, **Lake** [San Luis Obispo]. The name is shown on the von Leicht–Craven map (1874) and was applied to a station when the Southern Pacific was built in 1886. The modern community was developed in 1913 by the Atascadero Estates. The name was derived from that of the provisional land grant, Atascadero, dated December 21, 1839. A number of other geographic features called Atascadero were possibly named by Americans who liked the word and did not know that it means 'miry place.'

Atherton [San Mateo]. Named for Faxon D. Atherton, father-in-law of the novelist Gertrude Atherton. Atherton first visited California in 1836; in 1860 he acquired 500 acres of Rancho Las Pulgas, on which the town was built.

Athlone [Merced]. When the Central Pacific built through the valley in 1872, the station was named Plainsburg after the old settlement a few miles northeast. It appears that the Plainsburgers failed to make use of their chance to move to the new Plainsburg at the railroad, and the station was renamed, probably after the town in Ireland or the village in Michigan.

Atlanta [San Joaquin]. The name was applied in 1868 by William Dempsey, the first post-master, and by Lee Wilson, who came from Atlanta, Georgia (Tinkham).

Atlas Peak [Napa]. The peak was apparently not named after the classical mountain in Africa, but after the resort, Atlas, mentioned in the county history in 1881.

Atmore Meadows [Los Angeles]. Named by the Forest Service for Ted Atmore, an early settler.

Atolia [San Bernardino]. Applied by the Tungsten Mining Company in the early 1900's for two of its officers, *At*kins and De*Golia.* According to one source, DeGolia supplied only the *lia* and P. J. ("Pete") Osdick, of Osdick, the *o.*

Atwater [Merced]. The railroad station was built in the 1870's on the property of Marshall D. Atwater, a well-known wheat rancher, and named for him. The town was established by the Merced Land and Fruit Company in 1888 and named after the station.

Atwell Grove [Sequoia National Park]. The name commemorates A. J. Atwell of Visalia, sometime owner of the lumber mill which began operating here in 1879. In 1920, D. E. Skinner of Seattle bought the site and gave it to the Department of the Interior, thus supplying the nucleus for the present grove. In gratitude for the generous gift the grove was called Skinner Grove (Geographic Board, *Sixth Report*). Since the grove was locally better known as Atwell Grove, this name was recommended by the Park Service, and in April, 1946, the Board reversed its former decision and applied the new name.

Atwood [Orange]. Named in 1920 by the Santa Fe for W. J. Atwood, purchasing agent for the Chanslor-Canfield-Midway Oil Company. The former name, Richfield, which had been used during a brief boom in the early 1880's, was not accepted by the Post Office Department, because another Richfield had developed elsewhere. (Santa Fe.)

Auberry [Fresno]. Named for Al Yarborough, one of the four hunters who named Dinkey Creek in August, 1863. When the post office was established in the 1880's, the name was spelled as it was commonly pronounced.

Auburn: town, **Ravine** [Placer]. Gold was discovered in the ravine by Claude Chana, a Frenchman, in May, 1848. Among the miners who flocked to the place were former members of Stevenson's New York Volunteers. In August, 1849, the camp, known first as Rich Dry Diggings, then as North Fork Dry Diggings and Wood's Dry Diggings, was named after Auburn, New York, by Samuel W. Holladay: "By virtue of my august authority as Alcalde, in August, 1849, I named our diggings Auburn" (SCP:*P*, 1941, p. 34). As such the place is recorded on Butler's map, 1851. The post office was established July 21, 1853. Historic Landmark 404.

Audrain Lake [El Dorado]. Named for Thomas Audrain, whose way-station at Echo Summit was burned in 1865 in retaliation for his rejoicing openly at the news of Lincoln's assassination ("The Knave," January 20, 1959).

Aukum [El Dorado]. The post office was established September 23, 1895, and again April 9, 1920. The origin of the name is not known. Since October 28, 1861, the settlement and the post office have been known as Mount Aukum.

Aulon, Point [Monterey]. *See* Abalone.

Aumentos Rock [Monterey]. The name was applied to the rock near Point Pinos when the Coast Survey charted Monterey Bay, 1856–1857. Since José María Armenta was grantee of the Punta de Pinos grant, May 13, 1833, Armenta's was probably the original spelling.

Ausaymas [Santa Clara and San Benito]. The name of a land grant (also known as Cañada de los Osos, or Ausaymas y San Felipe), dated November 21, 1833, and February 6, 1836. *Ausayma*·was evidently a Costanoan village near San Juan Bautista (Kroeber).

Austin, Mount. *See* Mary Austin, Mount.

Austin Creek [Sonoma]. Probably named for Henry Austin, a pioneer settler in the region.

Austrian Gulch [Santa Clara]. Named for a group of Austrians who planted vineyards there in the 'seventies. It was a thriving colony until a cloudburst in 1889 undermined the foundations of the winery and swept thousands of gallons of wine into Los Gatos Creek. (Hoover, p. 539.)

Avalanche: Peak, Creek [Kings Canyon National Park]. The mountain was named by Muir in 1891, doubtless because of the marked course of avalanches. The name was subsequently transferred to Palmer Mountain, but it was restored on the Tehipite atlas sheet in 1939. There is another Avalanche Creek in Yosemite National Park.

Avalon: town, Bay [Santa Catalina Island]. The town was founded by George Shatto on property purchased from the Lick estate in 1887. "Mr. and Mrs. Shatto and myself were looking for a name for the new town, which in its significance should be appropriate . . . I found the name 'Avalon'" (Mrs. E. J. Whitney, quoted in HSSC:*P*, VI, 30). Avalon was the legendary elysium of King Arthur, a sort

of Celtic paradise. The name had been used repeatedly for places; the best known is the southeastern peninsula of Newfoundland. The former name of Avalon Bay, and perhaps the first name on California soil ever applied by an American, was Roussillon Bay: "As I was the first navigator who had ever visited and surveyed the place, I took the liberty of naming it after my much respected friend, M. De Roussillon" (William Shaler, 1803, in *American Register*, III, 147 f.). The Coast Survey left the bay nameless, but it became popularly known as Timms Cove for A. W. Timm. *See*·Timms Landing.

Avawatz: Mountains, Pass, Dry Lake [San Bernardino]. The name appears on the map of the Merriam expedition (1891) as Ivawatch, a name doubtless supplied by the Indians. It is derived from Southern Paiute *nä-hu-wätz*, 'mountain sheep'; the use of the prefix *iva-* ('white,' 'clear') in place of *nä-hu-* may imply that the word referred to 'white sheep' (O. J. Fisk). The name was commonly pronounced ä-vä-wäts' by the settlers, and the Geological Survey spelled it accordingly.

Avena, *ă-vē′-nà* [San Joaquin]. The Spanish word for 'oats' was applied to the railroad station when the line from Stockton to Merced was built in the early 1890's, presumably because fields of wild oats were noticeable near by.

Avenal, *ăv′-ė-năl*: **Creek, Ridge, Gap**, city [Kings]. The word is Spanish for 'oat field.' The creek is shown as Avenal on the Mining Bureau map of 1891; as Avendale, on the Land Office map of 1901. By decision of May 15, 1908, the Geographic Board adopted the former version. The community was named after the creek by the Standard Oil Company in 1929. There is an Avenaloca Mesa in Riverside County.

Avila, *ăv′-ĭ-là* [San Luis Obispo]. The town was laid out in 1867 and named in memory of Miguel Avila by his sons. Avila was a corporal at Mission San Luis Obispo and was the grantee of Rancho San Miguelito, April 8, 1839. By a decision of the Geographic Board, 1966 (July-Sept.), the place is now officially Avila Beach.

Avisadero, *ă-vē-zà-dâr′-ō*, **Point** [San Francisco]. The name for the tip of Hunters Point appears as *Pta. Avisadera* on Duflot de Mofras's *Plan* 16 (1844), possibly taken from an earlier map of Beechey. The Coast Survey has Avisada in 1850 and Avisadera in and after 1851. The present spelling is shown on Hoffmann's map of the Bay region, 1873. The word does not exist in Spanish; the term may have something to do with the verb *avisar,* 'to give warning,' or with *avistar,* 'to descry at a distance.' *See* Hunters Point.

Avon [Contra Costa]. Named after Shakespeare's Avon by the Southern Pacific when a station for shipping was established there in 1877–1878. The name of the post office is Associated.

Azul, á-zōōl'. The Spanish word for 'blue' is preserved in the names of several valleys, hills, mountains, and *sierras,* some of which may have been so named because ceanothus was observed blooming in spring. **Azule: Mountains, Springs** [Santa Clara]. A hybridization from *Sierra Azul,* which is recorded on a *diseño* of Cañada de los Capitancillos (1842) and elsewhere. On the New Almaden atlas sheet the range is still labeled Sierra Azul.

Azusa [Los Angeles]. The town was laid out in 1887, the "boom year," by J. S. Slauson and his associates, and named after the Azusa (Dalton) grant, on which it is situated. The origin of the name is found in the Indian name of the hill east of the present town, *Azuncsabit,* meaning probably 'skunk hill' or 'skunk place.' The Indian village, from which the name of the land grant is derived, was called *Asuksa-gna* in Gabrielino, or *Ashuksha-vit* in Serrano dialect (Kroeber), but in the *expedientes* of the Azusa land grants of May 10 and November 8, 1841, the modern spelling is used.

Babcock Lake [Yosemite National Park]. Named by Lieutenant N. F. McClure in 1895 for John P. Babcock, chief deputy, California State Board of Fish Commissioners (Farquhar).

Babel Slough [Yolo]. Named for Frederick Babel, a German who settled here May 15, 1849, and developed a fine stock farm.

Bachelor Valley [Lake]. Named for four early settlers who were bachelors: Richard Lawrence, Green Catran, Daniel Giles, and Benjamin Moore (Mauldin).

Backbone Creek [Shasta]. According to Grant Towendolly, folklorist of the Wintu, the natives' name for the creek was *Pa-sa-wei-weikit,* 'north cliff creek.' This, however, was unknown to a party of Germans who discovered a rich gold placer on the creek. "This creek is about fifteen miles north of the mountain heights known as the Back Bone, and as no name was known for it by the party making the discovery, they called it Back Bone Creek" (S.F. *Alta California,* June 7, 1852). The

mountains were originally named Devil's Backbone, because the trail across them was very narrow, steep, and rough (Steger). The name for the mountains does not appear on modern maps. **Jacks Backbone** [Shasta]. One day, when J. M. Simmons' hired man, Jack, was washing his clothes in the stream, his boss remarked: "When you're humped over like that, you look like yonder mountain." From then on the butte was known as Jacks Backbone. (Steger.) *See* Homers Nose. **Backbone: Mountain, Creek** [Fresno]. The name was applied to the ridge by the Geological Survey in 1904 because of its shape. Sonoma and San Bernardino counties each have a Devils Backbone.

Bacon Meadow [Fresno]. Named for Fielding Bacon, a pioneer stockman (Farquhar).

Baden [San Mateo]. Charles Lux (of Miller & Lux) had his Twelve Mile Farm here in the 1870's. Lux was born on the Rhine, opposite the Duchy of Baden. South San Francisco was called Baden until its incorporation in 1908.

Baden-Powell, Mount [Los Angeles]. The Geographic Board (*Sixth Report*) approved the present name for the eastern of the two North Baldys, which are within two miles of each other. The name honors Sir Robert S. S. Baden-Powell (1857–1941), founder of the Boy Scout organization in 1908.

Badger. Only a few places are named for this fur-bearing animal, which never was numerous in California and was almost exterminated before the American conquest. The best-known features are the mountains in Siskiyou County and in Lassen National Park, the ski area at Badger Pass, Yosemite, and the lake in Madera County. Badger Hill on the south bank of the Middle Yuba was a well-known mining town in the 1850's. The settlement Badger [Tulare] had a post office called Camp Badger as early as 1892. Some Badger names may be for a person so named, or for a person from Wisconsin, the "Badger State." *See* Tejon.

Badwater [Death Valley National Monument]. The name originated in a notation on the Furnace Creek atlas sheet published in 1910 that the water in the pool was not potable, i.e., it was "bad water." According to H. D. Curry, former Park naturalist, the water is full of common salt and Glauber's salts (Death Valley Survey).

Bagby [Mariposa]. Named for the owner of the hotel, B. A. Bagby, when the post office was established, June 30, 1897.

Bagdad [San Bernardino]. Named in 1883 by the Southern Pacific when the original line (now Santa Fe) was constructed. It was presumably nam_d after Bagdad, Iraq, because it is in the desert. In the 1850's there were two mining towns called Bagdad, one south of Oroville, the other on Trinity River.

Bagley: Flat, Mountain [Shasta]. Probably named for Alfred Bagley, who filed a claim for 160 acres, February 24, 1852 (Steger).

Baird Caves [Shasta]. The caves were named after the former Baird post office, which had been named in 1879 for Spencer E. Baird, U.S. fish commissioner in 1872 (Steger).

Bakeoven Meadow [Inyo National Forest]. The name originated from an old mud and stone oven constructed and used by early-day sheepherders for baking bread (J. T. Radel). *See* Hornitos.

Baker [San Bernardino]. The station was first known as Berry, for Joe Berry, an old prospector. To avoid confusion with other places of the same name, the Tonopah and Tidewater Railroad chose the present name in 1908 in honor of R. C. Baker, its president. The post office is listed in 1933.

Baker, Fort [Marin]. Named in 1897 by the War Department for Colonel Edward D. Baker, who commanded a Union regiment called, at first, the California regiment, early in the Civil War. He was killed in action at Ball's Bluff, October 21, 1861. In the 1850's, Baker, a native of England, had been a prominent lawyer and orator in San Francisco. Fort Baker was formerly called Lime Point Military Reservation.

Bakers Beach [San Francisco]. Named about 1866 for the Baker family whose dairy ranch was known as the Golden Gate ranch (State Library).

Bakersfield [Kern]. When in the early 1860's Colonel Thomas Baker, a civil and hydraulic engineer, undertook to develop a navigable waterway from Kern Lake to San Francisco Bay (a project which failed), he acquired a large parcel of land. A field enclosed by a fence and used as a corral became known as Baker's field; this name was transferred to the city in 1868.

Balance Rock [Tulare]. The name, which refers to the huge rock which balances on another at the entrance to the resort, was applied by a Mrs. Shively in 1900 (Ruth Squire). The post office is listed in 1936.

Balboa [Orange]. The subdivision was developed by the Newport Bay Investment Company in 1905 and named by E. J. Louis, Peruvian consul in Los Angeles, in honor of the discoverer of the Pacific Ocean. **Balboa Island.** The island was reclaimed by W. S. Collins in 1910–1912 and named after the older settlement across the channel.

Balch Park [Tulare]. The area known as Summer Home was acquired from the Southern California Edison Company by A. C. Balch of Los Angeles, who gave it to the county as a public park in 1923 (Mitchell).

Bald, Baldy. With the exception of black and red no other adjective is so frequently applied to hills and mountains. More than one hundred mountains, peaks, buttes, hills, rocks, and tops in all sections of the State are called Bald, and several Baldy, some of which are no longer bald. There is a Bald Jesse, an isolated peak, in Humboldt County. **Bald Mill Creek** [Fresno] was not so named because mill or creek was "bald," but because the Corlew Mill was on the creek which has its source on Bald Mountain. **Bald Rock** [Butte]. The bare landmark in the canyon of the Middle Fork of the Feather River was believed by the Indians to be the home of a monster. This might indicate that its original name was derived from a Wintun word. *See* Bally and Pelona.

Baldwin Lake [San Bernardino]. The lake was named for E. J. ("Lucky") Baldwin, one of the most spectacular promoters in the latter part of the 19th century, who invested much of his Alaska fortune here (O. J. Fisk). **Baldwin Park** [Los Angeles]. The city developed around the Pacific Electric station built in 1912 and was likewise named for "Lucky" Baldwin, former owner of the Puente de San Gabriel rancho, on which the city is situated.

Bale [Napa]. The name commemorates Dr. Edward F. Bale, a most spectacular character in the last decade of Mexican rule. He came to California from England in 1837, was probably the first practicing surgeon and druggist in the province, and was jailed for bootlegging in 1840 and for shooting at Salvador Vallejo in 1844. On March 14, 1841, he petitioned for a grant of the place called by the Indians *Calajomanas* or *Kolijolmanok*, which the doctor, with a gruesome sense of humor, twisted (in his petition) into Carne Humana. The name was officially accepted. On his "Human Flesh" ranch he erected the gristmill which was restored by the Native Sons of the Golden West in 1925.

Ball. Several mountains in the State, two granite pillars in Sierra National Forest, and a dome in Tulare County are so named because of their shape.

Ballarat [Inyo]. The place at the east end of Panamint Range was named after the gold mining center in Australia at the time of the gold boom in the 1890's. The post office was established June 21, 1897 and continued until 1917. Now the place is a ghost town, and the name is preserved only in a registered Historic Landmark and in a topographical quadrangle. The name of the place had been Post Office Springs and this name was kept for a mine until the twentieth century.

Ballard: settlement, **Creek** [Santa Barbara]. The place was named in 1881 by George W. Lewis in memory of his wife's first husband, W. N. Ballard. From 1862 to 1870 the latter had been the stage station agent at this place, then known as Alamo Pintado (Co. Hist., 1939, pp. 384 f.). See Alamo.

Ballast Point [San Diego Bay]. Probably Cabrillo's first landing place in what is now the State of California, September 28, 1542. The chroniclers of the Vizcaíno expedition of 1602–1603 noted that the stones at this point were suitable for ballast. González in 1734 calls it *la punta de los Guijarros* [cobblestones] *o Lastre* [ballast] (*Navegacion especulativa*, p. 305). The point was frequently called *Punta de Guijarros* in the years that followed, and until 1835 the fort at the site of Fort Rosecrans was also called *Guijarros* (Historic Landmark 69). When the Boston ships in the early part of the 19th century stopped at this point for taking on stones as ballast, the present name came into existence. In 1851, Ballast Point became the official name for it when the Coast Survey placed it on its sketch of San Diego Bay. **Ballast Point** [Catalina Island]. The name appears first in 1852 on the Coast Survey sketch of Catalina Harbor. It was doubtless applied for the same reason as that mentioned above. The outlines of the two points have a striking resemblance to each other.

Ballena. The Spanish word for 'whale' was repeatedly used in Spanish times as a place name along the coast. Indeed, it might have become the name of our State: early maps show the southernmost point of Lower California (now Punta de San Lucas, or Cabo San Lucas) as *Puerto* (or *Playa*) *Balenas* or *Punta de la California* (Wagner, pp. 410, 430). Had later cartographers and navigators taken a liking to the name, Ballenas might have spread further. **Ballena,** bă-lē'-nȧ: **Valley** [San Diego]. The valley was named

after the Indian *rancheria de la Ballena* mentioned by Padre José Sánchez in September, 1821 (Arch. MSB, IV, 211). The original name was suggested by a near-by hill shaped like a whale. Richardson's Bay [Marin] was formerly Whalers' Harbor, a translation of *Puerto de los Balleneros*. See Bolinas.

Ballona: Creek, Lagoon [Los Angeles]. The name is derived from the Ballona or Paso de las Carretas grant, dated November 27, 1839. According to a tradition of the Talamantes family, co-grantees of the rancho, the place was named after the city of Bayona in northern Spain, the home of one of their ancestors (W. W. Robinson, pp. 107 ff.). The letters "ll" and "y" in Mexican Spanish are both sounded like our consonant "y" and are frequently interchanged in writing.

Balloon Dome [Madera]. "A most remarkable dome, more perfect in form than any before seen in the State. It rises to the height of 1800 feet above the river, and presents exactly the appearance of the upper part of a sphere; or, as Professor Brewer says, 'of the top of a gigantic balloon struggling to get up through the rock.'" (Whitney, *Geology*, I, 401.) It was formerly known also as the Dome (or Great Dome).

Balloon Hill [San Mateo]. In 1898 or 1899 a captive balloon with several passengers escaped from San Francisco and landed on the top of this hill after drifting three days (A. K. Brown).

Bally, Bolly, Bully. One of the most interesting names in the State and unique because it is the only Indian name that has survived here as a generic geographical term. It is now used principally on the east side of the Trinity Mountains, which is north and central Wintun territory; originally, it was probably in common use throughout the Wintun area. There is an isolated Bally Peak about six miles east of Clear Lake; the *diseño* of the Los Putos grant [Solano, Napa] shows a mountain labeled *Buli;* that of the Cañada de Pogolimi grant [Sonoma] has a *Karsebalo,* apparently a mountain ridge, and a *tecabala.* Kroeber (*Place Names*, field copy) says there is no relation between the Wintun words *buli* (peak) and *bola* (spirit). Since, however, the name is (or was) found throughout the entire length of Wintun territory from Shasta to Solano counties, the assumption may be permitted that these Indians, like other primitive people, identified "spirit" with "mountain" and that both words are derived from the same stem and originally had the same meaning. The name survived locally in various spellings, and was occasionally found in literature. Cox in *Annals* of 1858 mentions on page 35 a "Baldy's or Bawly" north of Weaverville, and on page 110 a "Jollabollas." In Hutchings' *Illustrated California Magazine*, June, 1861, a Mount Balley between Shasta and Yreka is given. The name was rescued not long afterwards by the men of the Whitney Survey, who surveyed the region in the fall of 1862. The name is repeatedly discussed in Whitney's *Geology* (e.g., I, 323 ff.): "High mountains rise immediately north of Weaverville, the nearest considerable elevation being known as Mount Balley. 'Balley' appears to be the Indian term for a bare mountain, and the 'Shasta Balley' is to be distinguished from the 'Trinity Balley,' or the one near Weaverville; the orthography of the word is very doubtful." The fact that the men of the Whitney Survey assumed that *balley* means 'bare mountain' suggests that there may have been some confusion with the term "baldy." **Hayfork Bally** in Trinity National Forest is Hay Fork Baldy on the Big Bar atlas sheet. Other Baldys in the region, Indian Creek Baldy, Little Baldy, as well as Billys Peak, Ball Mountain, Bailey Hill, etc., may or may not have been derived from the same word by folk etymology. On page 325 Whitney discusses the name again: "[The peak] is known locally as 'Yalloballey,' an Indian name of which the orthography and meaning are doubtful. It is not unlikely that ... [it] is the same mountain that is indicated on the maps as 'Mount Linn,' a name which ... is not known to anyone in this part of the State." The map of the Survey (von Leicht–Craven, 1874) records Bullet [!] Chup, and North and South Yallo Balley. Today twelve or more peaks and hills in Shasta, Trinity, Tehama, and Lake counties are designated by the name. **Bully Choop: Mountain, Mountains** [Shasta, Trinity]. According to Helen Hogue, the Wintu version is *Bo-li Chu-ip* and the meaning 'high sharp peak.' **Shasta Bally, Shoemaker Bally** (for Simon Shoemaker), **Winnibulli, Bully Hill** (two) [Shasta]. Shasta Bally was *Bo-hem-bolly*, 'big mountain' (Towendolly). Winnibully (or Winibulli) preserves·the name of *Winimem*, a village on McCloud River. *Wini* is 'north,' according to Powers (p. 230); 'middle,' according to Hodge. **Yolla Bolly Mountains, Trinity Bally** [Trinity, Tehama]. The proper Wintu version is *Yo-la Bo-li*, which means 'high snow-covered peak' (Helen Hogue). The

Wintu name for Mount Shasta, as given by Towendolly, *Bo-lem-poi-yok,* may contain the same stem, although ordinarily the generic part stands last in the Wintu language. The name Bally is used sometimes as a true generic term and sometimes tautologically with Mountain or Hill, a confusion which existed already at the time of the Whitney Survey.

Baltic Peak [El Dorado]. The name of the Baltic Sea, between Scandinavia and Germany, was a favorite name for mines in the gold rush. The peak was named by the Forest Service after the Baltic Mine north of the mountain, which was in operation until 1907.

Baltimore Park [Marin]. Named after the Baltimore & Frederick Trading and Mining Company, which brought a sawmill round Cape Horn in 1849 and set it up at this place (Hoover, p. 194).

Bangor [Butte]. Named by the Lumbert brothers after their home town in Maine, when they settled here in 1855.

Banner: Canyon, Grade [San Diego]. The places were named after the gold mining camp Banner, which was established in 1870 (San Diego *Union*, March 29, 1935).

Banner Hill [Nevada]. The hill was named after the Banner mine (a favorite name for mines), which was located in 1860. In 1867 there was a Bannerville near the hill. (H. P. Davis.)

Banner Peak [Madera]. Named in 1883 by Willard D. Johnson, topographer of the Geological Survey, because he noticed cloud banners streaming from the summit (Farquhar).

Banner Ridge [Mono]. The elevation between Lake Crowley and Benton was named for the Banner Mine, which was situated on its slope (Wheelock).

Banning [Riverside]. The town, founded in 1884, was named by Welwood Murray for Phineas Banning, who with his brother Alexander operated the first regular stage line between Los Angeles and San Pedro in the 1850's. Until his death in 1885, Banning was the foremost promoter of improved transportation facilities in southern California and is remembered as one of the "grand old men" of the southern metropolis. *See* Wilmington.

Bannock [San Bernardino]. The name appears on the Santa Fe Railroad maps after 1903–1904. It was derived from the name of an Indian tribe in Idaho, the *Banak*, changed by folk etymology to "Bannock," after a kind of flapjack much used by early traders and settlers. The name is derived from the tribe's own name for themselves, *Panaiti*. (Leland, *CFQ*, V, 391.)

Banta [San Joaquin]. The name of Henry Banta, a pioneer settler, was applied to the station when the old Western Pacific Railroad from Oakland to Stockton was built in the 1860's.

Bar. The generic term referring to an obstruction in a river or creek became an important word in California geographical nomenclature during the gold rush. Gold washing at a bar soon developed into one of the principal methods of obtaining the precious metal, and maps of the gold district are dotted with mining camps named after a bar. Nine California communities and post offices are still designated as Bars and are listed under their specific names.

Barber Springs [Lassen]. So called for an Indian named Barber who, in 1857, was shot from ambush at the springs when he was returning from the Gold Run mines (Co. Hist., 1916, p. 94).

Barcroft, Mount [Mono]. The elevation south of White Mountain was named for Sir Joseph Barcroft (1872–1947), a British physiologist especially interested in the physiological effects of high altitude (Geographic Board, May, 1954).

Bard [Imperial]. The post office was established September 3, 1910, and was named for Thomas R. Bard, a director of the State Board of Agriculture, 1886–1887, U.S. senator, 1901–1905, in recognition of his promotion of the 13,000-acre irrigation district. A former post office, **Bardsdale** [Ventura], listed in 1892, was also named for him.

Barnard, Mount [Sequoia National Park]. Named for Edward E. Barnard (1857–1923), an astronomer at Lick Observatory, University of California, from 1888 to 1895, and then at Yerkes Observatory, University of Chicago, until his death; discoverer of the fifth satellite of Jupiter and many comets. The mountain was named at the first ascent, September 25, 1892, by C. Mulholland, W. L. Hunter, and their party (Farquhar).

Barney Lake [Mono]. Named for Barney Peeler, an old resident of Bridgeport (*SCB*, XII, 126).

Barranca Colorada [Tehama]. A Mexican land grant dated December 24, 1844. The name means 'red bank.' *See* Red.

Barrett Reservoir [San Diego]. In 1879 George W. Barrett and his sister homesteaded the land near the dam site, and his name was applied to the reservoir by the City of San Diego

in 1919 (B. B. Moore). The post office (now discontinued) for the settlement on Cottonwood Creek was named Barrett, February 4, 1915.

Barroso Mountain [Kern]. The Spanish word for 'pimpled' was applied because the alternate patches of barren ground and wooded areas have a spotted appearance when viewed from a distance (Crites, p. 268).

Barry, Fort [Marin]. The reservation was established by the War Department in 1904, from the part of Fort Baker known as Point Bonita, and named in honor of General William F. Barry (1818–1879), a veteran of the Mexican and Civil wars.

Barstow [San Bernardino]. Named in 1886 by the Santa Fe for William Barstow Strong, president of the railroad at that time. Since his name had already been commemorated in Strong City, his middle name was used for this junction on the line. In 1882, when the railroad was constructed by the Southern Pacific, the name was Waterman Junction, after the near-by mining community in which Robert W. Waterman, governor of California from 1887 to 1891, owned a silver mine. In the 1860's the place was known as Fishpond and was a stopping place for travelers.

Bartle [Siskiyou]; **Bartle Gap** [Shasta]. The name was applied to the station of the McCloud River Railroad in 1904. Abraham and Jerome Bartle ran cattle in the Shasta Valley and built a resort at what is now the McIntosh place. (Schrader.)

Bartlett: Springs, Creek, Flat, Mountain [Lake]. The health resort was named for Green Bartlett, a native of Kentucky, who drove cattle across the plains to California in 1856. In 1870 he discovered the spring and was cured by its waters, whereupon he bought the land around it and erected a hotel. (*CHSQ*, XXIII, 296.)

Bartolas [Kern]. The plateau in the High Sierra north of Onyx was named for a Frenchman who ran sheep there in early days (Crites, p. 268).

Bartolo Viejo, Paso de [Los Angeles]. A Mexican land grant dated June 12, 1835. On the *diseño* of the San Antonio grant (1838) *Paso de Bartolo* is shown where the *Camino Viejo* crosses the *Rio de San Gabriel*. Perhaps the name was different in its original form and meant 'Bartolo's Crossing on the old road.' One Bartolo Tapia is listed as the owner of a rancho in the Los Angeles district in 1816 (Bancroft, II, 353).

Barton Mound [Orange]. The name commemorates Sheriff James R. Barton, of Los Angeles, who was killed here in 1857 by a bandit, Juan Flores, and his band. *See* Sheriffs Spring; Flores Peak.

Barton: Peak, Creek [Kings Canyon National Park]. The name of the peak was proposed by the Sierra Club, for James Barton, a local cattleman. An earlier name was Mount Moraine. The creek was named after the peak in 1932.

Basin. The generic term seems to have been used in California more extensively than in other states: American, Blackcap, Big, Butte, Colusa, Sutter, and many minor Basins. Unlike the Great Basin, named by Frémont in 1843, most of these basins do not absorb waters which have no outlet to the sea. *See* Great Basin.

Bass Lake [Madera]. The impounded reservoir for electric-power generation was named after 1900, either for a person named Bass or for the fish. Fresh-water bass, not native to California, were planted in many lakes.

Bass Mountain [Shasta]. The older name, Saddleback Mountain, was changed by the Geological Survey in 1901 to honor John S. P. Bass, assemblyman from Shasta and Trinity counties in 1880 (Steger). Bass Station, seventeen miles from Shasta, was mentioned in Brewer's Notes, August 20, 1862.

Batavia [Solano]. The name was applied to a station of the California Pacific Railroad about 1870. It is the Latin name of the Netherlands and was first applied to a city in New York by early Dutch settlers.

Batequitos, bä-tä-kḗ'-tŏs: **Lagoon** [San Diego]. Font, on January 10, 1776, mentions "the place called *Los Batequitos*, a small watering place somewhat apart from the road on the side away from the sea," two leagues from "the village of Indians and the place called *San Alexos*" (*Compl. Diary*, pp. 190 f.). *See* San Elijo Lagoon. It was probably the place where the Portolá expedition had dug a *batequi* on May 27, 1769. The name is spelled Batiquitos on the San Luis Rey atlas sheet and Batiguitos by the Coast Survey. *Batequito* is the diminutive of *batequi*, which means 'water hole' in the Cahita language of Sinaloa (Peñafiel).

Battle. A favorite name for places where an engagement has been fought, the best-known of which is probably the name of the town in Sussex, England, said to have been named for the battle of Hastings (1066). In California the name appears about twelve times. **Battle Mountain** [San Diego] was named for

the near-by battlefield of San Pasqual, the scene of the engagement between Kearny's forces and the Californians, December 7, 1846. **Battle Island** [Clear Lake] was named because on its shore a detachment of soldiers under Captain Lyon (*see* Lyons Valley), in December, 1849, fought the Indians who had killed Andrew Kelsey (of Kelseyville) and Charles Stone. Gibbs mentions the name in 1851. **Battle Creek** [Tehama and Shasta]. This apparently is the creek called *Arroyo de la Campaña* on a *diseño* of Rancho Breisgau. It appears on the Frémont-Preuss map of 1848 as Noza Creek, but became known by the present name after a bloody engagement had been fought here between Indians and trappers in 1849 (Steger). Beckwith uses the present name in 1854. **Battle Rock** [Shasta]. Historic Landmark 116 commemorates a "battle" between Modocs and the miners whose operations interfered with the Indians' chief occupation, fishing. **Battle: Creek, Mountain** [Tulare]. So named because it was here that George Cahoon's burro "Barney" vanquished an unnamed mountain lion in a bloody skirmish (Farquhar).

Baulenes [Marin]. A Mexican land grant dated October 19, 1841, and November 29, 1845. *See* Bolinas; Tomales; Duxbury.

Baxter, Mount; Baxter Creek [Kings Canyon National Park]. Probably named for John Baxter, a rancher in Owens Valley (Farquhar).

Bay. A convenient name for a locality near a bay, usually in combination with -shore, -side, -view, etc. Five places are named after San Francisco Bay, two after Humboldt Bay, one each after Morro and Newport bays, and one after the nameless bay on the east shore of San Miguel Island.

Bayles [Shasta]. The post office was established August 10, 1875, at Delta with A. M. Bayles, son of Judge Bayles, a settler of 1855, as postmaster (Steger). December 4, 1884, it was changed to Bayles, and May 1, 1948, again to Delta.

Bealville [Kern]. When the Southern Pacific built this section in the 1870's, it named the station for General Edward F. Beale, a veteran of the Mexican and Civil wars, who was superintendent of Indian affairs in California in the 1850's. Beale owned about 200,000 acres in the county. **Beale, Camp** [Yuba]. Established in August, 1942, and named by the War Department in honor of the same officer.

Beal Well [Imperial]. Probably named for Willis F. Beal, who came to the county in

1903, and later became county supervisor, assemblyman, and a director of the irrigation district.

Bean Hollow Lake [San Mateo]. The reservoir was named after the Arroyo de los Frijoles, 'kidney bean creek,' from which it is impounded. There are several Bean Creeks and Bean Canyons in the State. Asa Bean Ridge [Mendocino] and the Santa Fe station Bean [Kings] were apparently named for settlers.

Bear. Approximately five hundred geographic features in California bear the name of the largest and most notable of our native animals. With the exception of the desert regions the name is found in all parts of the State. It is more frequent in the Coast Ranges than in the Sierra Nevada, where prospectors, who were given to overstatements, were likely to call a bear a 'grizzly.' There are seven Bear Rivers, twenty-five Bear Mountains, more than thirty Bear Canyons and as many Bear Valleys, a hundred or more Bear Creeks, and an assortment of Bear Lakes, Meadows, Flats, Basins, Buttes, Gulches, and Sloughs. Added to these are a Bear Dome [Fresno], Bear Haven Creek [Mendocino], three Bear Wallow Creeks [Kern, Mendocino, Los Angeles], and a number of Beartrap Creeks and Beartrap Canyons. **Bear Pen Creek** and **Bearpen Creek** [Sonoma] recall the frontiersmen's method of catching bears alive in an enclosure. **Bear Valley** [Mariposa], named by Frémont in 1848, is Historic Landmark 331. **Bearpaw: Cave, Butte** [Modoc]. When Tom Durham, an early-day bear hunter, had his camp here, he nailed a bear paw to a juniper tree whenever he killed a bear (Howard). **Bearpaw Meadow** [Sequoia National Park] was assertedly so named because a bear's paw was found nailed to a tree; **Bearskin Meadow,** east of General Grant Grove, because the last snow patch to melt under the summer sun resembled in shape a bearskin (Farquhar). Many features were named Bear because some encounter with the animal took place in the vicinity: **Bear River** [Humboldt] was so named because Lewis K. Wood of the Gregg party was badly mangled by a wounded grizzly in January, 1850; **Bear Creek Gulch** [San Mateo], because of "Grizzly" Ryder's encounter with a bear which left him nearly dead (Wyatt). **Bear Lake** [San Bernardino] was named as early as 1845 by "Don Benito" Wilson, whose men killed a number of bears there while on an Indian campaign. The present Big Bear Lake is not Wilson's lake but an artificial lake created by the Bear

Valley Irrigation Company in 1884. The original Bear Lake is probably the half-dry lake called Baldwin. **Bear Creek** [Contra Costa]. The name has been on the maps since the 1860's. In 1965 it was damned for the Briones Reservoir. **Bear Paw** [Del Norte, Siskiyou]. The spur of the Siskiyou Mountains was so named because it is linked to Bear Mountain like a paw to a bear (Geographic Board, 1965). Some of the Bear names may be translations from the Spanish *Oso*.

Beard Creek [Alameda]. The name for the tidal channel commemorates E. L. Beard, who settled near Mission San Jose about 1846 and acquired part of the mission lands. His residence north of the mission, and Beard Embarcadero, are shown on Hoffmann's map of the Bay region (1873).

Bear Flag Monument [Sonoma]. Dedicated in 1914 to commemorate the raising of the Bear Flag and the proclamation at Sonoma of the short-lived California Republic on June 14, 1846. Historic Landmark 7.

Bearup, bẹr'-ŭp: **Lake** [Yosemite National Park]. Named by Lieutenant N. F. McClure, in 1894, for a soldier in his detachment (Farquhar).

Beasore, bā'-sô: **Meadow, Creek** [Madera]. Named for a stockman of the 1860's, who is said to have spelled his name Beausore (Farquhar).

Beatrice [Humboldt]. The original name, Salmon Creek, was changed to the present name to honor Mrs. Beatrice White, the first postmaster, when the post office was established in the 1880's (M. H. Cloney).

Beatys Icebox [Borrego State Park]. When the trail to Highway 99 was built through the desert in 1929 there was a base camp here, and a cool cave served as a natural icebox. A.A. "Doc" Beaty was an early homesteader and promoter of the road. The cave was washed away but the name remains for the canyon. (Parker, p. 33.)

Beaumont, bō'-mŏnt [Riverside]. In 1887 a group of capitalists bought the townsite and gave it the French name, meaning 'beautiful mountain.' Originally the name had been Edgar Station, for a physician who accompanied a survey party there in the early 1850's. In 1875 it was changed to Summit, and in 1884 to San Gorgonio, after the mountain of that name.

Beaver. The beaver was once found in great abundance on woodland streams of the continent. It was gradually killed off as the settlement of the country progressed, but it left its name in hundreds of places. Before the American occupation of California the beaver had been almost exterminated by Hudson's Bay Company and other trappers; hence the name is found in only a few places, mainly in the northern counties. Beaver River was the trappers' name for Scott River.

Beck Lakes [Madera]. Named about 1882 for John Beck, a prospector of the Minaret district (Farquhar).

Beckwith: Pass, Butte; Beckwourth: post office [Lassen, Plumas]. The names commemorate one of the most colorful of frontiersmen, James Beckwourth, a native of Virginia, who came to California in 1844, participated in the campaign against Micheltorena, and returned after the discovery of gold. Since "Old Jim" could not spell, his name varies between Beckwourth and Beckwith. In 1851 he discovered the pass, which soon became an important immigrant route and later the route of the Sierra Valley and Mohawk Railroad and finally that of the Western Pacific. The Marysville *Herald* reports, June 3, 1851: "Mr. Jas. P. Beckwith, the discoverer and projector of this new and important route, . . . states that he has now several men at work cutting a wagon road" (Boggs, p. 84). In 1852 Beckwourth built the first house in Sierra Valley and set up a trading post. The von Leicht–Craven map (1874) shows the spelling Beckworth for the pass, the peak, and a part of Sierra Valley. The Land Office map of 1879 shows the town with the spelling Beckwith; the post-office name was so spelled until 1932, and the Geological Survey retained this spelling for town, butte, and pass on the 1942 edition of the Sierraville atlas sheet. Gannett erroneously assumed that these places were named for Lieutenant E. G. Beckwith of the Pacific Railroad Survey, who explored the Honey Lake route in 1854. In June, 1950, the Geographic Board ended the confusion by adopting for the pass and the peak the spelling used by the post office, which had been Beckwourth since July 1, 1932.

Bee. A Bee Tree Ridge [Sonoma], several Bee Tree Creeks, a Bee Wash [Imperial], and an assortment of some twenty-five Bee Creeks, Canyons, and Valleys record the presence of the honey-gathering insect. **Beehive** [Santa Cruz] was so named because its outline resembles that of a beehive. **Beegum: Peak, Creek,** settlement [Tehama]. The name was probably given to the peak by a Southerner because of its shape. The word "beegum" was applied in the South originally to a bee colony in a hollow gum tree, but since about 1850 it refers also to a common beehive made of boards. As a geographical term it seems to be used in California only. The name appears on the von Leicht–Craven map as Bee Gum Creek and on the Mining Bureau map of 1891 as Bee Gum Butte. The peak is of limestone and is honeycombed with holes many of which are actually inhabited by bees.

Beer Creek. Several surface waters are named for the effervescent drink, probably because of their bubbling waters. On the Seiad and Sawyers Bar atlas sheets Beer Gulch appears with other mouth-watering names: Spirit Lake, Whiskey Creek, Tea Creek, Applesauce Creek, Sauerkraut Gulch.

Begg Rock [Ventura]. Named by the Coast Survey for the ship *John Begg*, which grounded on a near-by rock on September 20, 1824.

Belden [Plumas]. The Western Pacific station and the post office were named in 1909 for Robert Belden, a miner and property owner.

Bell [Los Angeles]. The name was applied in 1898 by J. G. and Alphonso Bell, founders of the town. The post office was called Obed until the name was changed to Bell, May 3, 1898.

Bella Vista [Shasta]. The town was founded by the Shasta Lumber Company; the post office was established in 1893 and given the Spanish name, meaning 'beautiful view.' It was moved to the present location in 1920. (Steger.)

Bell Canyon [Orange]. So named because a large granite rock, when pounded, gave forth a peal that filled the canyon. It had been known in Mexican times as *Cañada de la Campana,* 'canyon of the bell.' (Stephenson.)

Bellflower [Los Angeles]. Established by F. E. Woodruff in 1906 and named Somerset in 1909 when the post office was established. The Post Office Department rejected the name because there was a town named Somerset in Colorado. An orchard of bellflower apples in the northern section of the ranch on which the town was laid out suggested the new name.

Bell Gardens [Los Angeles]. When the vegetable tracts developed by Japanese gardeners were subdivided in 1930, the area was named after nearby Bell, and in 1961 the town was incorporated (Co. Hist., 1965, IV, 65)

Bellota [San Joaquin]. The place is shown as Donnel on Hoffmann's map of 1873 and as Belota on the von Leicht–Craven map of

1874. The present spelling, which is that of the Spanish word for 'acorn,' was adopted when the post office was established in 1879.

Bell Spring Mountain [Mendocino]. In 1860 when the settlers pursued the Wylackies who had killed the Sprowell brothers, the Indians were betrayed by two cowbells they carried. Jim Graham found the bells near the spring from which the mountain later received its name. (Asbill.)

Bell Valley [Yuba]. Named for the notorious highwayman, Tom Bell, who used the valley as a hide-out.

Bellyache Canyon [Mariposa]. According to a decision of the Geographic Board, Sept.-Dec., 1963, the name was reportedly applied to the canyon because of an early resident named Billy Aike, or Ache.

Belmont. The name, a variant of the French *Beaumont*, meaning 'beautiful mountain,' is found in various European and American countries. The oldest and most important Belmont of the State, in San Mateo County, developed around the hotel built in 1850–1851; it was named by Steinburger & Beard because of the "symmetrically rounded eminence" near by (Co. Hist., 1878, p. 29). The town is mentioned in the *Statutes* of 1855; it was the county seat in 1856.

Belvedere. An international place name of Italian origin, meaning 'beautiful view.' It is usually spelled Belvidere in the United States. The town in Marin County was founded about 1890 by the Belvedere Club of San Francisco on what was formerly known as Peninsular (or De Silva's) Island.

Benali [Sacramento]. A contraction of the two middle names of James Ben Ali Haggin, a San Francisco lawyer, who was part owner of Rancho del Paso in the 1860's.

Benbow, bĕn'-bō [Humboldt]. Named in 1926 for the Benbow family, who established the summer resort there.

Bend [Tehama]. In early days the place was known as Horsethief Bend because the bend in the Sacramento River afforded an ideal hide-out for outlaws. This was later named Sander's Bend for an early settler, and finally simplified to Bend. (Dorothy Dorland.)

Bendire Canyon [Inyo]. The canyon in the Argus Mountains was name for Lieutenant Charles Bendire, native of Germany and veteran of the Civil War, who led a military expedition through Death Valley in 1867. On Wheeler atlas sheet 65-D the name appears as Bendere's Cañon.

Benedict Canyon [Los Angeles]. Named for Edson A. Benedict, a Los Angeles storekeeper, who filed a claim to the land in 1868 (W. W. Robinson, p. 166).

Benedict Meadows [Madera]. The meadow northwest of Shaver Lake was named in memory of Maurice A. Benedict, from 1909 to 1944 supervisor of Sierra National Forest, who had died in 1959 (Geographic Board, Jan.-April, 1960) .

Ben Hur [Mariposa]. Named by the community about 1890, for the hero of Lew Wallace's novel *Ben-Hur,* then at the height of its popularity (Grace Quick).

Benicia, bĕ-nē'-shá [Solano]. On December 23, 1846, Mariano G. Vallejo and Robert Semple signed an agreement for the founding of a city on the northern shore of Carquinez Strait, a logical place for a metropolis of the West. It was to be named Francisca, in honor of Vallejo's wife, and the agreement was recorded and translated in Yerba Buena on January 19, 1847, by the *alcalde,* Washington A Bartlett. This agreement and the town's name prompted Bartlett to bring about the change of the name of Yerba Buena to San Francisco, a name well known because of the mission and the bay. Nothing was done to found Francisca, and on May 19 Vallejo transferred his interest in the venture to Thomas O. Larkin and Semple. Before the end of May, Jasper O'Farrell began laying out the townsite. Until June 5, lots in Francisca were advertised, but one week later, on June 12, Semple referred to the town as Benicia (another of Señora Vallejo's Christian names); on June 19 he made official and public announcement in the newspapers that the change was made. (Bowman.) Benicia, too, was the name originally chosen for the county that was named Solano in 1850. **Benicia Arsenal Reservation.** The arsenal was established in 1851, and the army post was designated as Benicia Barracks by General Orders, No. 6, Division of the Pacific, in 1852. The present name was bestowed in 1924 by General Orders, No. 14, War Department. **Benicia Shoal.** The name was applied by the U.S. Bureau of Lighthouses.

Ben Lomond: town, **Mountain** [Santa Cruz]. The post office existed as early as 1872 and was named presumably after the mountain in Scotland. The name may also have been used locally for the mountain. The form Ben Lomond Mountain was used by the Geological Survey when it mapped the region about 1900; its literal meaning is 'Mountain Lomond Mountain,' as *ben* is a term used in

Scotland for 'mountain.' Several towns and mountains in the United States derive their name directly or indirectly from the stately landmark above Loch Lomond. A Ben Lomond in Butte County is shown on the von Leicht–Craven map.

Ben Mar Hills [Los Angeles]. Established in 1920 and named by Ben Mark, promoter of the subdivision (R. F. Flickwir). The "k" in the family name was obviously omitted to make it sound "Spanish."

Benmoore: Canyon, Valley, Creek, Glades [Lake]. The canyon was named for Ben Moore, a stock rustler, about 1851 (Mauldin). In 1960 the Geographic Board decided for the spelling Benmore, which was apparently the original spelling of the name.

Bennett, Point [San Miguel Island]. Named by the Coast Survey before 1900, possibly for W. H. Bennett, who had been engaged with George Davidson in the defense of Philadelphia in 1863.

Bennett Creek [Tulare]. Named for William F. Bennett, a stockman of the 1870's (Farquhar).

Bennetts Well [Death Valley National Monument]. The name commemorates Asahel Bennett, a member of a party which crossed Death Valley in 1849–1850. Although it is not certain that the Bennett-Manly party camped here, the name Bennetts Spring was affixed to this spot by the von Schmidt-Gibbs map of 1869. On the Wheeler atlas sheet 65-D of 1877 it appears as Bennett's Wells. According to Wheelock, it may not refer to Asahel Bennett but to a teamster, "Texas" Bennett.

Benson: Lake, Pass [Yosemite National Park]. Named in 1895 for Harry C. Benson (1857–1924), acting superintendent of the park from 1905 to 1908 (Farquhar).

Benton: town, Range, Crossing [Mono]. The town came into existence during the mining boom of 1865; the post office is listed in 1867. Since it was chiefly a silver-mining district it may have been named for Senator Thomas H. Benton of Missouri, Frémont's father-in-law, who was an advocate of metallic currency.

Berdoo Canyon, bĕr-dōō′ [Joshua Tree National Monument]. The popular name for San Bernardino, used by many persons but frowned upon by the Chamber of Commerce, was applied to the canyon through the Little San Bernardino Mountains and was placed on the Pinyon Well atlas sheet by the Corps of Engineers in 1944. The names of the trian-

gulation hills of the district are playful abbreviations of San Bernardino, with or without the descriptive adjectives: Bern, Bernard, Dino, North Dino, Berdoo, Round Berdoo, Little Berdoo.

Berenda. *See* Antelope.

Berg [Sutter]. The name was applied by the Central (now Southern) Pacific in the 1870's for the owner of the property (possibly John Berg, pioneer of 1850) on which the station was built.

Berkeley: city, Hills [Alameda]. The name for the new college town was adopted on May 24, 1866, after many months of discussion, by the trustees of the College of California (now the University of California). The verses which George Berkeley, Bishop of Cloyne, wrote when he sailed for Rhode Island in 1728 with the ultimate aim of forming a college in the Bermudas and extending its benefits to the Americans:

> Westward the course of empire takes its way;
> The four first acts already past,
> A fifth shall close the drama with the day;
> Time's noblest offspring is the last,

inspired Frederick Billings to propose the name.

Bernardino Mountains. *See* San Gabriel Mountains.

Bernardo Mountain [San Diego]. The mountain and a small settlement (now usually called Lake Hodges) preserve the name of the San Bernardo land grant, dated February 16, 1842. *El Paraje o Cañada de San Bernardo* is mentioned in mission archives before 1822 (Arch. MSB, III, 261) and repeatedly in later years. The San Dieguito River is shown as *Arroyo de S. Bernardo* on a diseño of 1841, and on the Land Office map of 1859.

Bernasconi: Hot Springs, Pass, Hills [Riverside]. Named for Bernardo Bernasconi, who developed the springs in the 1880's.

Bernice Lake [Yosemite National Park]. Named for the wife of W. B. Lewis, superintendent of the park from 1916 to 1927.

Berrendo. *See* Antelope.

Berros; Los Berros: Creek, Canyon [San Luis Obispo]. *Berros* (watercress) in the district was mentioned by Crespi on September 4, 1769. Los Berros Creek is shown as *Arroyo de los Berros* on Hutton's map of Rancho Nipomo, 1850. The town was founded and named in 1891.

Berry Creek [Butte]. The creek was named after a rich mining bar of the 1850's. The post office was established May 10, 1875, at Virginia Mills, but was named after the creek. Gold mining was carried on until the

1920's. The place is shown on the Bidwell Bar atlas sheet. The creek may have been named for Henry Berry, of Pennsylvania.

Berryessa, bĕr-ĭ-ĕs′-à: post office, **Creek** [Santa Clara]. Named for an old family which came directly from Spain and settled in the Santa Clara Valley. Nicolás Berreyessa was grantee, May 6, 1834, of the land grant Milpitas, through which the creek flows. José Reyes Berreyesa was grantee of the San Vicente grant, August 1, 1842. The family name is variously spelled.

Berryessa, bĕr-ĭ-ĕs′-à: **Valley** [Napa]. The valley preserves the names of José Jesús and Sisto Berryessa, soldiers in the San Francisco company and in 1843 grantees of Rancho Las Putas. By decision of the Geographic Board in 1957, the former Monticello Reservoir is now known as Berryessa Lake.

Bestville [Siskiyou]. The one-time metropolis of Salmon River was named for Captain Best, who in 1850 led the first party of prospectors into the wilderness (Luddy).

Bethany: town, **Ferry** [San Joaquin]. First called Mohr Station, for John Mohr, who deeded the site to the Southern Pacific. In order to avoid confusion with another station called Moore's Station, the name was changed to Bethany, probably after the place in Palestine.

Betteravia [Santa Barbara]. From the French word *betterave,* meaning 'beet.' The sugar-beet industry was introduced here in 1897 by the Union Sugar Refining Company. (AGS: *Santa Barbara,* p. 182.)

Beverly Hills [Los Angeles]. A newspaper account in 1907 which reported that President Taft was spending a few days at Beverly Farms suggested the name to Burton E. Green, president of the Rodeo Land and Water Company. The post office was established in 1907 as Beverly and the name was changed to Beverly Hills in 1911.

Bicycle Lake [San Bernardino]. The intermittent lake has become well known because of the army antiaircraft range here, which is named after the lake. The story that an unfortunate traveler left a bicycle here while attempting to cross the desert was confirmed by Washington W. Cahill, a long-time official of the borax company, who told L. Burr Belden that the teamsters of the company found a rusty bicycle here around 1890. However, according to an old resident of Barstow, the young men of Daggett in its flourishing days used the lake for bicycle races when it was dry (Arda Haenszel). In

1957 an aerial photograph, taken by Pilot Don Krogh and widely published, shows a corpse lying beside a bicycle in the Mojave Desert not far from the lake.

Biderman, Mount [Mono]. Named for J. W. Biderman, prospector and promoter in the Bodie Mining District in the early 1860's. The name was incorrectly transcribed on the Bridgeport atlas sheet as Biedeman. (Maule.)

Bidwell: Bar, Creek, Butte, State Park [Butte], **Lake** [Lassen], **Peak** [Modoc]; **Fort Bidwell:** town, **Indian Reservation** [Modoc]. The bar in Feather River, now Historic Landmark 330, was called Bidwell's Bar after John Bidwell (*see* Glossary) discovered gold here in July, 1848. The fort in Modoc County was named in 1865 for Bidwell, who was at that time a congressman and a general of California militia. The post office was established in the 1870's. The state park was presented as a memorial by his widow. Bidwell Point in Mendocino National Forest was named by the Forest Service in 1934 because the pioneer had spent an anxious night there in 1844 in fear of an attack by Indians.

Bieber [Lassen]. The post office was established in 1879 and named for Nathan Bieber, who in 1877 built the first store and house at the crossing of Pit River known as Chalk Ford.

Bielawski, Mount [Santa Clara]. Named by J. D. Whitney in 1861 for the chief draughtsman of the Surveyor General's office. Captain Casimir Bielawski came to California in 1853 and for forty-five years was connected with the U.S. Land Office in San Francisco.

Big. The adjective is used in geographical nomenclature for various reasons. First, a physical feature is actually "big": Big Basin [Santa Cruz]; Big Lagoon [Humboldt]; Big Creek [Fresno]; and the numerous Big Bars of goldmining days, of which those in Amador (Historic Landmark 41) and Trinity counties are best known. Second, a feature is called "big" in comparison with a smaller feature named previously or at the same time. The most notable example of this is the Big Bear cluster in San Bernardino County, which originated with Bear Lake, so named by "Don Benito" Wilson in 1845. The result of this unimaginative method of naming is confusing because it is often not clear whether the specific or the generic term is modified by "big": Big Coyote Knoll [San Mateo], Big Salmon Creek [Mendocino]. Sometimes composite names with a humorous effect are evolved: Butte County has a Big Chico Creek and a Little Chico Creek, i.e., a big and a little "little" creek; on the Caliente Road in Sequoia National Forest two water sources are designated as Big Last Chance Can and Little Last Chance Can. Third, the adjective is applied because it clearly modifies the specific term: Big Oak Flat [Tuolumne], named for a big oak; Big Bird Lake [Tulare], because the tracks of a large bird were found on its shore; Big Rock Creek [Los Angeles], because of a huge boulder in the creek; Big Brother Slough [San Joaquin]. Some names are translations of the Spanish *grande*. Big Sur River [Monterey] was *Rio Grande del Sur* (big river of the south); Big River [Mendocino] is shown as *Rio Grande* on a *diseño* of the Albion grant, dated October 30, 1844. The adjective also occurs in the names of a number of post offices and communities: Big Bear: Lake, City, Park [San Bernardino], Big Chief [Placer], Big Flat [Siskiyou], Big Gum [Shasta], Bigpine [Inyo], Big Trees [Calaveras, Santa Cruz], Big Bend [Shasta], and others. **Big Oak Flat** [Tuolumne]. The place was named for a giant oak near which a rich mining town started to develop in 1849. The post office was established January 21, 1852, and the place is shown on the maps of that year. It is now Historic Landmark 406, and the name is preserved in the Big Oak Flat Road. **Big Basin Redwoods** [Santa Cruz]. The state park was established in 1961 with the assistance of the Save-the-Redwoods League and the Sierra Club. **Big Bear Lake** [San Bernardino]. The artificial lake was created in 1884 by building the Old Bear Valley Dam, now Historic Landmark 725.

Bigelow Peak [Yosemite National Park]. Named for Major John Bigelow, Jr., acting superintendent of Yosemite National Park in 1904 (Farquhar).

Biggs [Butte]. The station was named in 1870 by the California and Oregon Railroad for Major Marion Biggs, who was the first rancher to ship grain from there (Co. Hist., 1882, p. 246).

Bighorn Lake [Fresno]. Named shortly before 1900 by Lincoln Hutchinson's party: "An exclamation of surprise burst from one of the party, and we found directly before us a band of 'big-horn' sheep. We had supposed the animal long since extinct in the Sierra, and at first we could scarcely believe our eyes. . . . Deep down in the amphitheater below us lay an azure lake." (*SCB*, IV, 202 f.) In a footnote he adds, "This we named Big Horn Lake." **Bighorn: Spring, Gorge** [Death Valley Na-

tional Monument]. E. W. Nelson of the Merriam expedition camped by the spring in 1891 while hunting sheep. The name was applied to the gorge by the Park Service in 1939. The bighorn is now a permanent resident of the National Monument area; the last census showed about six hundred head (Death Valley Survey).

Bigler, Lake. *See* Tahoe.

Bihler: Landing, Point [Sonoma]. Named for William ("Dutch Bill") Bihler, a German butcher who came round the Horn to California in 1848 and became a large landowner and stockbreeder in Sonoma County. The landing was called Black Point Harbor on the county map of 1879, but the Coast Survey used the name Beeler in 1876, and in 1915 the present name was placed on the Plantation atlas sheet of the tactical map by the Corps of Engineers.

Bijou, bē'-zhōō [El Dorado]. The French word for 'gem' or 'jewel' was applied to the resort in the 1880's, probably because it was a good publicity name. The name is found elsewhere in the United States. In 1843 Frémont camped on Bijou Creek in Colorado, but since none of the detailed maps show the place in California before 1890 it is not likely that it was an early transfer name.

Biola [Fresno]. The name was coined by William Kerchoff of Los Angeles from the initial letters of *Bi*ble *I*nstitute *o*f *L*os *A*ngeles when he established the town in 1912.

Birch. The birch is rare among native California trees; hence only a few places are named for it. The water birch, *Betula occidentalis*, is found in eastern and northern regions of the State. There is a Birch Creek in Deep Springs Valley [Inyo] and there are two in Owens Valley, after one of which the stately **Birch Mountain** was named, a name approved in 1938 by the Geographic Board. Old-timers are of the opinion that **Birch Creek** in the San Bernardino Mountains was named for a tree mistaken for a birch, as there are no birch trees there (O. J. Fisk). Birchville, a ghost town in Nevada County, was named in 1853 "by common consent . . . in honor of L. Burch [!] Adsit, a prominent citizen" (Co. Hist., 1880, p. 61).

Bird. About twenty-five geographic features, mainly islands and rocks, were given this name because of the presence of birds. Alcatraz Island [San Francisco Bay] was once known as Bird Island. **Big Bird Lake** [Tulare] was named in 1902 by James Clay because tracks of a large bird were seen on the shore (Farquhar). Santa Clara County has a Blackbird Valley, and Orange County a Blue Bird Canyon. **Bird Rock** [San Diego], a subdivision started by M. Hall, took its name from a rocky formation which resembled a bird (Hunzicker). *See* Pajaro.

Birds Crossing [Butte]. Probably named for Ralph Bird, one of the founders of Ophir City (Oroville) in 1855.

Birds Landing [Solano]. Formerly the shipping point of John Bird, who had a storage and commission business. Bird, a native of New York, settled here in 1865 (Hoover).

Bishop: Creek, town [Inyo]; **Pass** [Kings Canyon National Park]. Named for Samuel A. Bishop, a well-known cattleman, who came from Virginia to California in 1849, served as an officer in the Mariposa Battalion in 1851, lived in Owens Valley from 1860 to 1863, and became a supervisor of Kern County in 1866.

Bishop Rocks [San Diego]. These rocks, part of the Cortes Bank, were discovered in 1855 when the Philadelphia clipper *Bishop* struck one of them. The name was applied by the Coast Survey in 1856.

Bismarck Knob [Napa, Sonoma]. The peak is probably the same as Carnero Mountain, mentioned in the *Statutes* of 1850. In later years it became known as Mount Nebo (D. T. Davis). When the Napa quadrangle was surveyed by the Geological Survey in 1899, the present name was applied, probably in memory of the great German statesman, who had died in the preceding year.

Bitter, Bitterwater. The palatability of water, especially in the arid sections of the State, is of great importance to herdsmen, prospectors, and surveyors, and a creek or lake with bitter-tasting water is almost invariably so designated. There are more than fifty Bitter Creeks and Lakes and Bitterwater Canyons in California. *See* Amargosa.

Bixby: Landing, Creek [Monterey]. Named for Charles H. Bixby, who came to Monterey County in 1868.

Bixby Slough [Los Angeles]. In Spanish days this was known as *Cañada de Palos Verdes.* In 1884 it appeared on maps as *Lagunita,* and by 1900 it had come to be known as Bixby Slough, for Jotham Bixby, pioneer and landowner (HSSC: *Q,* XIX, 9, 19).

Black. Of the adjectives of color used in descriptive geographic names, black is by far the most common, followed by red and white. It is chiefly applied to orographic features which appear black because of the geological

formation, or the dark green chaparral, or the atmospheric condition. California has almost one hundred Black Mountains, some thirty Buttes, about ten each of Peaks, Cones, and Rocks, but only a few Hills. The twenty-five or more Black Canyons were doubtless so named because of their dark and forbidding appearance; most of the Black Lakes, Springs, and Creeks are not black, but were named after a Black Mountain near by. Often the generic term is preceded by a specific term modified by black: Black Crater Mountain, Black Lake Canyon, Black Butte River, Blackcap Mountain, Blackoak Mountain, Blackhawk Creek, Black Rabbit Canyon Creek. Merced County has a Black Rascal Creek, but the sinister story behind its naming is not known. Black Rascal Hills are mentioned in a railroad survey of 1873. **Black Lassic Creek** [Trinity] was named after a black peak: neither Lassic (an Indian chief) nor the creek is black. *See* Lassic. **Black Butte** [Siskiyou]. The peak was so known in the early 1850's because it was "black as the darkest iron ore" (Pac. R.R. *Reports,* Vol. II, Pt. 2, p. 50). The Geographic Board changed the name first to Wintoon Butte, then to Cone Mountain, and finally (June 6, 1934) back to the original name. **Black Star Canyon** [Orange]. The *Cañada de los Indios,* so named because of the large Indian village there (Historic Landmark 217), became known by the present name after Joseph Yoch opened the Black Star Coal Mine in the canyon in the late 1870's (Stephenson, I, 49). **Black Rock Pass** [Sequoia National Park]. This name for the pass was recorded in 1896 by Lieutenant M. F. Davis because a band of black rock is in noticeable contrast to the red and white formations near by (Farquhar). **Black Giant** [Kings Canyon National Park]. Named in 1904 by J. N. LeConte. When the U.S. Geological Survey made the map of the Mount Goddard quadrangle, 1907–1909, it placed the name Mount Goode on this peak, apparently unaware of the name given by LeConte. The earlier name was restored in 1926 by decision of the U.S. Geographic Board, and the name Goode was transferred to another peak. (Farquhar.) **Black Divide** [Kings Canyon National Park]. The ridge south of Black Giant was named by George R. Davis, topographer, when the Mount Goddard quadrangle was surveyed, 1907–1909. **Blackeye Grade, Canyon** [Lake]. Named at the turn of the century for "Blackeye" Herndon, who lived at the top of the grade and was so nicknamed because he had big black eyes, or because one of his eyes was blacked in a fight (Mauldin). **Black Butte Dam** [Glenn]. The 140-foot high earth-filled dam on Stony Creek, which was built to create the Stony Gorge Reservoir, was dedicated in June, 1963.

Black Mountain [Marin]. The name commemorates James Black, a Scottish sailor, who came to California in 1832. He was grantee of Cañada de Jonive, February 5, 1846; owner of part of Rancho Nicasio and part of Olompali, 1852; judge in 1850; assessor in 1852. The mountain is shown as Black's Mountain on a county map of 1873. **Black Point** [Marin] was probably named for the same pioneer. A surveyor's plot (1859) of Rancho Novato shows Black's Store in Novato Valley. Hoffmann's map of the Bay region (1874) has a settlement Black John two miles north, and J. Black four miles north, of the point. The three names are on Rancho San Jose, whose owner, the widow of Ignacio Pacheco, James Black married in 1865. The post office, named after the point, was established January 11, 1865. In 1905, real-estate promoters succeeded in having the name changed to Grandview Terrace; April 1, 1944, the old pioneer name was restored (H. W. Hobbs).

Blairsden [Plumas]. Named about 1903 after the country home of James A. Blair, prominent in the early financing of the Western Pacific Railway (*Headlight*, July, 1942).

Blakes: Sea, Ravines [Riverside, San Diego]. Parker uses these names in his guide book (*see* Glossary). They commemorate William P. Blake, the geologist with the Pacific Railroad Survey, 1853–1854. Blakes Sea is the ancient lake bed (the middle of which is now covered by Salton Sea) which was explored by Blake and named Lake Cahuilla. The Ravines are strange, washed-out canyons, west of Highway 99. (Parker, pp. 39 f., 46 f.) *See* Cahuilla, Coachella, Salton Sea.

Blanco, Blanca. The Spanish word for 'white' is found in the names of about fifteen orographic features: Penon Blanco [Tuolumne, Mariposa], from *peñón*, 'rocky mountain'; Muro Blanco [Fresno]; Pico Blanco [Monterey]; Blanco Mountain [Mono]; Piedra Blanca Creek [Ventura]; and others.

Blanco [Monterey]. Tom White, who deserted ship at Monterey in 1840, and who was known as Tomás Blanco (white) to his Spanish-speaking neighbors, received on August 27, 1844, a small grant on Salinas River. His place became known as Blanco Crossing, and in the fall of 1872 the name was given to the

Southern Pacific station. It is a coincidence that the Portolá expedition had given the name *Real Blanco* (white camp) to a site about 25 miles southeast of the present settlement, on September 28, 1769, because of the white appearance of the earth in the vicinity (Crespi, p. 199).

Blaney Meadows [Fresno]. The original name, Lost Valley, was changed to the present name for a sheepman who camped there every year (Farquhar).

Blind Spring: Hill, Valley [Mono]. An underground spring which was hard to find gave the name to the hill and the valley. In early days a barrel casing made the water available to miners on the hill. (Robinson.) There are several Blind Canyons in the State, which probably, like "blind" roads, lead nowhere.

Bliss Rubicon Point State Park [El Dorado]. Named in memory of Duane L. Bliss and after Rubicon Point at Lake Tahoe. The park was given to the State in 1929 by William, Walter, and Hope Bliss.

Blocksburg [Humboldt]. Named for Benjamin Blockburger, an immigrant of 1853 and participant in Indian fights, who established a store at this place in 1872. When the post office was first established, January 30, 1877, the name was spelled Blocksburgh; since April 29, 1893, the spelling has been Blocksburg.

Bloody. The names of about twenty features in the State include the word "bloody" or "blood." Usually the name was applied because blood flowed there for some reason, though sometimes it may have been used in jest, or because of a cursing Englishman, or because the rocks looked bloody red. **Bloody Island** [Tehama] was named in 1844 by Samuel J. Hensley, of Sutter's Fort, because Indians had attacked his party there. It is shown as *Isla de la Sangre* on a *diseño* of Rancho Buenaventura. **Bloody Island** [Lake] was the scene of the "Bloody Island Massacre" in December, 1849. *See* Battle Island. **Bloody Point** [Modoc]. On the promontory jutting out into Tule Lake, Modoc Indians ambushed parties coming over the Oregon Trail. In September, 1852, a party of sixty-four was massacred here, only one man escaping. Historic Landmark 8. (W. S. Brown.) **Bloody Rock** [Mendocino]. According to Powers (pp. 136 ff.), the last of the *Chumaia* (a part of the Yuki) perished here by leaping from the boulder upon which they had been driven by white settlers. **Bloody Canyon** [Mono]. "The horses were so cut by sharp rocks that they [the early prospectors] named it 'Bloody Canyon,' and it has held the name—and it is appropriate" (Brewer, p. 416). **Bloody Mountain** [Mono]. The slope of this peak was said to have been the scene of a bloody fight between escaped convicts and a posse in September, 1871. *See* Convict Lake. But according to Wheelock, the name probably originated from the "bloody" red rocks of the peak. **Blood Gulch** [Amador]. The old mining town was so named because miners noted blood mingled with water and found a dead man when they went upstream. **Bloody Run** [Nevada] "took its name by virtue of the greater than ordinary number of murders once committed along its course" (Ritchie, pp. 363 f.).

Bloomfield [Sonoma]. The place was first settled in 1855. When the post office was established, July 12, 1856, it was named for Dr. Frederick G. Blume, a German surgeon who had been a prominent pioneer in the county since 1847. Blumefield, which was probably the intended form, was easily changed to the popular American place name.

Bloomington [San Bernardino]. This popular American name for a town was applied to the development by the Semi-Tropic Land and Water Company, organized in 1887 (Co. Hist., 1904, p. 619).

Blossom Lakes [Sequoia National Park]. Named in 1909 by R. B. Marshall of the U.S. Geological Survey, for Charles W. Blossom, park ranger (Farquhar).

Blossom Rock [San Francisco Bay]. A rock slightly below the surface of the water halfway between Alcatraz and Yerba Buena islands. Discovered and named by F. W. Beechey for his ship *Blossom,* which anchored near by in November and December, 1826. The danger to shipping was removed when A. W. von Schmidt blew off the peak with twenty-three tons of powder, April 23, 1870.

Blucher [Sonoma and Marin]. The name of a Mexican land grant dated June 5, 1842, and October 14, 1844, and granted to Juan J. Vioget, a native of Switzerland and pioneer surveyor of San Francisco. Vioget was generally known as "Blucher" because he strongly resembled the Prussian field marshal Gebhard von Blücher, Wellington's comrade-in-arms at Waterloo. (Bowman.)

Blue. There are some twenty-five Blue Mountains, Ridges, and Hills throughout the State, apparently so named because of their appearance under certain atmospheric conditions, or because of the presence of bluish rock formations; or because the slopes were covered by wild lilac or other blue blossoms. The ten-odd Blue Canyons were probably named for the same reason. Since the adjective was used in Spanish times (*Sierra azul* on several *diseños*), some names may be translations. The many Blue Creeks and Blue Lakes were apparently all named because of the color of the water. The name of the feature was sometimes transferred to settlements: **Blue Lake** [Humboldt], **Blue Rock** [Mendocino], **Blue Canon** [Placer]. The last received its name from the blue smoke of the camps when extensive lumbering was done in the 1850's. According to Loye Miller, however, the canyon was originally named for Old Jim Blue, who mined there in the 1850's. **Blue Nose** [Siskiyou]. Derived its name from the Blue Nose gold mine, an enterprise started by a group of Nova Scotians, sometimes called Blue Noses. A post office was established June 1, 1917 (R. W. Bower). Imperial County has a railroad station called Blue Goose, and San Bernardino County a post office named Blue Jay. Often, not the generic but the preceding specific name is modified: Blue Canyon Peak [Fresno], Bluejay Mountain [Shasta], Blue Tent Creek [Tehama]. The Blue Nose and Blue Rock Mountains [Plumas, Trinity, Shasta, Mendocino, Monterey] were probably all named because of the presence of glaucophane or other bluish rock formations.

Bluff. The name is found as a generic term, especially along the coast, for a steeply rising bank or cliff with a broad front. The city of Red Bluff and a number of Bluff Creeks, Coves, and Canyons were named after bluffs near by. **Bluff Creek** [Humboldt, Del Norte]. "We camped [October 9, 1851] opposite the high point which forms a land-mark from the Bald Hills, and which gives the name of Bluff creek to a stream . . . called by the Indians Otche-poh" (Gibbs, in Schoolcraft, III, 147). *See* Gold Bluffs; Red Bluff.

Blunts Reef [Humboldt]. The reef off Cape Mendocino was discovered by Vancouver but left nameless. In 1841 Wilkes named it for Simon F. Blunt, a midshipman on the U. S. S. *Porpoise.* The name was placed on the map by the Coast Survey in 1850.

Blythe [Riverside]. Established in 1908 by the Palo Verde Land and Water Company, and named for Thomas H. Blythe, a San Francisco capitalist who in 1875 had bought the land in Palo Verde Valley on which the irrigation project was later developed.

Boardman: Canyon, Ridge [Lake]. Named in the 1880's for Oscar Boardman and his brother, who homesteaded in the rugged country north of Lake Pillsbury and ran stock on the ridge there (Mauldin).

Boardman, Mount. This mountain, on the peak of which the boundaries of Alameda, Santa Clara, San Joaquin, and Stanislaus counties intersect, was named in memory of W. F. Boardman, surveyor of Alameda County, city engineer of Oakland (1864–1868), and builder of the dams that created Lake Chabot and Lake Temescal (E. T. Planer).

Boca. In Spanish times the term for 'mouth' was often found not only for the mouth of a river but also for the entrance to, or the outlet of, an estuary, a valley, or a port. The term was contained in the names of three land grants: Boca de Santa Monica [Los Angeles], June 19, 1839; Boca de la Cañada del Pinole [Contra Costa], June 21, 1842; Boca de la Playa [Orange], April 18, 1845, and May 7, 1846. **Boca** [Nevada] is a modern application. The name was given to the station of the Central Pacific when the Truckee-Verdi section was built in 1867 because it is situated not far from the mouth of Little Truckee River.

Bodega, bȯ-dā′-gȧ: **Bay, Head, Port, Rock,** town [Sonoma]. The bay was entered by Juan Francisco de la Bodega, captain of the *Sonora*, on October 3, 1775, and named for him. Bodega's map of 1775 (Wagner, Pl. XXXIV) shows *Pto y Rio del Capitan Vodega*. On later maps the bay is usually designated as *Puerto de la Bodega*. Kotzebue, in the report (1821) of his first expedition, gives the abbreviated form, *Port Bodega* (*Rurik*, p. 62). Between 1812 and 1841 the bay was used by the Russians as a harbor and often called *Romanzov* (variously spelled), in honor of the chancellor of the empire (1809–1814) and patron of the *Rurik* expedition. Kotzebue, in 1830, records *Hafen Bodega oder Port Romanzov*. The modern version, Bodega Bay, was established by the Coast Survey in 1850. The cape was called *Pte. Bodega* by La Pérouse (1797). Duflot de Mofras (1844) follows Kotzebue: *Pte. de la Bodega ou C. Romanzoff*. Tyson, 1850, has Bodega Point; and the Coast Survey, 1851, Bodega Head. A settlement called Bodega on the north shore of the bay is shown on Tyson's map of 1850. The present village was settled by George Robinson in 1853 and is recorded as Bodega Corners on Hoffmann's map of 1873. Two land grants dated July 15, 1841, and September 12, 1844, were called Bodega. *Presidio de Bodega* was a name sometimes used for Fort Ross. *See*

Presidio. For the current local name of Bodega Head, *see* Campbells Point.

Bodfish Creek [Santa Clara]; **Bodfish:** town, **Peak** [Kern]. The name is shown on a map of the land grant Las Animas [Santa Clara] in 1855. One Orlando Bodfish of Massachusetts was a registered voter in Santa Clara County, January 10, 1867; the death of an Orlando Bodfish, in Havilah, Kern County, was reported in the San Francisco *Alta California,* June 27, 1868. Boyd, p. 44, also mentions a Bodfish Creek, tributary to Kern River, and a George H. Bodfish as the owner of mines in Keyesville.

Bodie: post office, **Creek, Mountain** [Mono]. Waterman S. Body discovered the ore deposits here in 1859. He lost his life in a snowstorm in May, 1860, but the settlement preserved his name. The change in spelling was perhaps caused by the desire to keep the proper pronunciation, bȯ′-di. The name is sometimes spelled Bodey. Historic Landmark 341.

Boga [Butte and Sutter]. The name of two land grants, dated February 21, 1844. Although *boga* means 'rower, oarsman,' the name may be the Spanish rendering of an Indian word. An Indian village named *Boga* is shown on the *diseños* of the Boga and Fernandez grants. The rancho was also known as Rio de las Plumas because of its location on Feather River, and as Flugge (i.e., Rancho de Flugge) for the grantee, Charles W. Flügge, native of Germany and pioneer of 1841.

Boggs Lake [Lake]. Named for H. C. Boggs, owner of the sawmill which stood on the shore of the lake in the 1870's.

Bogue [Sutter]. Named for Virgil G. Bogue, chief engineer of the Western Pacific (Drury). *See* Virgilia.

Bogus. Like humbug, a common term for fake or sham, used by disappointed prospectors, mainly for creeks. In Placer County there is also a Bogus Thunder Bar, so named because a near-by waterfall produces a sound like thunder. Bogess Creek in San Mateo County may originally have been Bogus Creek because it dries up in summer (Wyatt). **Bogus: Country, Creek** [Siskiyou]. The district drained by Big Bogus Creek and Little Bogus Creek came by its name from the operations of counterfeiters who had a furnace in a thicket near a spring (*WF*, VI, 376 f.). Bogus post office was listed in the 1880's and 1890's.

Bohemian Grove [Sonoma]. The name came into existence when the Bohemian Club of San Francisco in 1880 held a Midsummer

High Jinks in the redwood forests of Russian River. It was applied to the present grove in 1891.

Bohemotash, bô-hē′-mŏ-tăsh: **Mountain** [Shasta]. Named after a big Indian campground northwest of Shasta Dam (Steger). *Bohem* is the Wintu word for 'large' (Kroeber).

Bolam: Creek, Glacier [Siskiyou]. The name of the creek on the north slope of Mount Shasta is apparently of Wintu origin and may contain the word for 'peak.' *See* Bally.

Bolinas, bô-lē′-năs: **Bay, Lagoon, Point, Ridge, town** [Marin]. *La Cañada que llaman los Baulenes* (the valley that they call the *Baulenes*) is mentioned by Ignacio Martínez in 1834 as one of the boundaries of the *pueblo* of San Rafael and was probably the valley through which Olema Creek flows (SP Mis., X, 11). A map of about the same date has the word "Baulenes" on the peninsula which now includes Bolinas Point, Duxbury Point, and the town of Bolinas. The name *Baulenes,* possibly from a Coast Miwok word of undeterminable meaning, no doubt referred to the Indians who inhabited the region. The *Cañada de Baulines* is shown on a *diseño* of Punta de los Reyes, 1835, running into the *Estero de Tamales* (Tomales Bay) on the north. From 1852 to 1910 the name is spelled Ballenas on the charts of the Coast Survey, obviously through mistaken analogy to the Spanish word for 'whale.' In the 1869 edition of his *Coast Pilot* (Directory) George Davidson erroneously assumed that the bay was named for Francisco de Bolaños of Vizcaíno's expedition. This gave rise to the spellings Bolanos and Boliñas. In 1873, Baulinas on Hoffmann's maps approximated the original spelling, but the Geological Survey and the Geographic Board adopted the spelling Bolinas which had been used when the post office was established in 1863. *See* Baulenes.

For the name of the bay and the lagoon on Ringgold's chart, *see* Rialto.

Bolivar Lookout [Siskiyou]. The ranger station preserves the old name of what is now called Craggy Peak on the Etna atlas sheet. The name of the South American revolutionary leader, Simon Bolivar, was often used for place names in the United States.

Bollibokka: Mountain, Creek [Shasta]. A combination of the two Wintu words *bolla,* 'black,' and *boka,* 'bush,' referring to the black-berried manzanita as distinguished from the red-berried (Towendolly).

Bollinger Canyon [Contra Costa]. In 1855 Joshua Bollinger settled in the canyon east of the present site of Saint Marys College (County History, 1882).

Bolling Memorial Grove [Humboldt]. Dedicated in 1921 and named in honor of Colonel Raynal Bolling, an American army officer killed in action in World War I (Drury).

Bolo [San Bernardino]. The original name, Bristol, was changed by the Santa Fe in 1898 to Bombay then to Bengal, and in 1915 to Bolo for operating convenience (Santa Fe).

Bolsa. The Spanish word means 'pocket' and is used in a geographical sense for a semi-enclosed or shut-in place, usually for a neck of land surrounded by water or a swamp and accessible from one side only. The term, extremely popular in Spanish times, was the chief or secondary name of no fewer than twenty-four land grants and claims. It has been preserved as a place name in Orange, San Luis Obispo, San Benito, and San Mateo counties.

Bolton Brown, Mount [Kings Canyon National Park]. Chester Versteeg and Rudolph Berls made the first ascent on August 14, 1922, and named the peak "in honor of Bolton C. Brown, of the Sierra Club, who was the first to explore, map and write of the Upper Basin of the So. Fork of the Kings River" (*SCB*, XI, 426). Bolton C. Brown was professor of drawing and painting at Stanford University from 1891 to 1902 (Farquhar).

Bonanza. The word, derived from the Spanish word for 'prosperity,' is used in the West for anything highly profitable, especially a richly yielding mine. Although commonly used in California, it appears as a place name apparently for only four minor features—in Kern, San Bernardino, Merced, and Lake counties.

Bond Pass [Yosemite National Park]. Named for Frank Bond, member of the Yosemite National Park Boundary Commission in 1904, later chairman of the U.S. Geographic Board (Farquhar).

Bonita [San Diego]. In 1884 Henry E. Cooper named his estate Bonita Ranch, and the name was later applied to the post office. The Spanish word *bonita,* a diminutive of *buena,* means 'pretty.'

Bonita, Point; Bonita: Channel, Cove [Marin]. The point was named *Punta de Santiago* by Ayala in 1775 and was so designated as late as 1825. On other maps the point is shown as *Punta Bonete* (Wagner, p. 377), probably because there were originally three heads, each of which resembled the bonnet of a clergyman (Davidson). The term *Punta de Bonetas* used in 1809 (PSP, XIX, 226 f.) was probably intended for a plural and was not a folk-etymological rendering (*bonetas*, 'pieces of extra canvas'). Beechey in 1826 spelled the name *Punta Boneta* (II, 424) and this version was used by Duflot de Mofras (1844), the Coast Survey (1851), and Gibbes (1852). Williamson-Abbot (1855) have Pt. Bonita, and the Bancroft maps of the 1860's fixed this now accepted version, meaning literally 'pretty point.' Until about 1900 the Coast Survey charts spelled the name Bonito, probably because it was assumed that the point was named for the bonito, a fish which lives in channels where there are currents.

Bonner Grade [Modoc]. For John H. Bonner, who planned and managed the construction of the road over the summit of the Warner Range, in northeastern California, in the 1860's. Historic Landmark 15.

Bonsall [San Diego]. For James Bonsall, a native of Pennsylvania, who set up a nursery here in the 1870's. When a post office was established in 1889, his name was selected from those submitted by the residents (Susie K. Worris).

Boomer. According to local tradition, the Boomer Mine in Trinity County was so called because it was a big producer. The word is also a mining term denoting the contrivance by which the accumulation of water (in placer mining) is suddenly discharged. The name is found in other mining regions of the State: Boomer Creek [Butte].

Boonville [Mendocino]. The town was founded as Kendall's City in 1864. Soon afterward, W. W. Boone bought the store of Levi and Straus and changed the name of the town to Booneville. The "e" was dropped when the post office was established in the 1880's.

Boot Lake [Modoc]. Named by early residents on account of its shape (W. S. Brown).

Borax. About twenty features are so named because of the presence of borax deposits. The oldest is probably Borax Lake in Lake County, discovered and named by Dr. John A. Veatch in September, 1856.

Borden [Madera]. When the Southern Pacific reached the place in the spring of 1872, the station was named for Dr. Joseph Borden, a member of the near-by community popularly called the Alabama settlement.

Boreal Ridge [Nevada]. The elevation between the old and the new route of Highway 40 was so named because it lies north of Donner Pass and the Southern Pacific crossing of the Sierra Nevada. The name is derived from the Latin *borealis*, 'northern.'

Borego. *See* Borrego.

Boron [Kern]. From 1912 until 1938 the Santa Fe station was called Amargo (bitter), probably from the taste of the borax deposits, and the settlement is still so known. After the Pacific Coast Borax Company moved from Death Valley to Amargo, the railway station and the near-by post office took the name Boron, for the nonmetallic element in borax. (Santa Fe.)

Boronda Creek [Monterey]. Named for the Boronda family, early settlers of the district. José M. Boronda was, in 1839, a co-grantee of Rancho Los Laureles, eight miles northwest of the creek.

Borosolvay, bō-rō-sŏl'-vā [San Bernardino]. The name is a combination of the names of the two firms which established the community in 1916, the Pacific Coast Borax Company and the Solvay Process Company.

Borrego, Borrega. The word for 'lamb' (or 'sheep') was repeatedly used for place names in Spanish times, usually in the feminine form. It appears in the names of land grants in Contra Costa, Santa Clara, and Santa Barbara counties and is also preserved in Borego, bô-rā'-gō: Mountain, Valley, Spring [San Diego], Sanjon [ditch] de Borregas [Santa Cruz]. In San Diego County it has become an important cluster name, which probably originated because of the presence of the Nelson bighorn sheep—**Borrego: State Park, Badlands, Desert, Mountain, Palm Canyon, Sink, Spring, Springs, Wells.** Borrego Springs post office was established May 16, 1949. Borego post office, established March 1, 1928, has been discontinued.

Bosquejo [Tehama, Butte]. The name of two land grants, granted to Peter Lassen on July 26, 1844, and in December, 1844. On the *diseño* of the former is the following inscription: *Bosquejo del terreno solicitado por Pedro Lawson,* 'sketch of the land solicited by Peter Lassen.' Apparently someone took the Spanish word for 'sketch' as the name of the rancho. Or perhaps *bosquejo* means 'small tract of wooded land.' The ending *-ejo* denotes something poor, bad, hence small (Morley).

Bostonia [San Diego]. Named in 1895 by the promoters of the town after the Boston Ranch, on which part of the town is situated. The former name was Meridian District.

Bothe-Napa Valley State Park [Napa]. The park was established in 1960 and bears the name of the former owner of the property, who operated a commercial enterprise under the name of Bothe's Paradise.

Bottlerock Mountain [Lake]. The names of mountains and other orographic features consisting chiefly of obsidian often include the descriptive term "Glass." In Lake County, according to Mauldin, obsidian is "bottle-rock" in common speech.

Boulder. This is an extremely popular place name in the West. California probably leads the other states with almost a hundred Boulder Creeks, Lakes, etc. **Boulder Creek** [Santa Cruz]. In the 1880's the lumber town Lorenzo took the name of the Boulder Creek post office, which had been established in the 1870's. In Siskiyou County the spelling variant Bowlder is used for two creeks and a lake.

Boulevard [San Diego]. Town and post office were so named because they are situated on the "boulevard" (U.S. Highway 80) to the Imperial Valley.

Boundary. Surveyors sometimes used the word to name a feature at a boundary. **Boundary Hill** [Yosemite National Park] was named by Lieutenant Montgomery M. Macomb of the Wheeler Survey because it was on the line of Yosemite State Park. The hill is now near the center of Yosemite National Park. Boundary Peak in the White Mountains suffered a similar misfortune. When A. W. von Schmidt established the California-Nevada boundary in 1872, the line ran through the peak. The corrected boundary placed the mountain well into the state of Nevada. Madera County has a Boundary Creek and Inyo County a Boundary Canyon.

Bouquet Canyon [Los Angeles]. When a French sailor named Chari settled in the canyon, it became known by his Spanish nickname *El Buque* (the ship). In the 1850's, surveyors, believing the name to be French, recorded it as *Bouquet,* and their version is still used. (HSSC:*P,* XIV, 197.) Now, the name is generally pronounced bō-kĕt'.

Bourns: Gulch, Landing, Rock [Mendocino]. The features were named for the Bourn family, early settlers, whose family cemetery is located near the mouth of the gulch (Geographic Board, May-Aug., 1962).

Bower Cascade [Mono]. "One of the smallest of the cascades [of Bloody Canyon Creek], which I name the Bower Cascade, is in the lower region of the pass, where the vegetation is showy and luxuriant" (Muir, p. 301). Bower is found elsewhere as a descriptive specific term: Bower Cave [Mariposa].

Bowles Prairie [Humboldt]. Named for one of the partners of Bowles, Bowles, and Coding-ton, large property owners and, according to the assessment roll of 1853–1854, "heavy merchants of Uniontown."

Bowman [Placer]. Named for Harry H. Bowman, a merchant and agriculturist, and the first commissioner of horticulture of Placer County (H. P. Davis).

Bowman Lake [Nevada]. Named for James F. Bowman, a native of Scotland, who settled at what became known as Little Bowman Lake in the early 1860's. In 1873, Big and Little Bowman Lakes were consolidated, providing a source of water supply for hydraulic mining. The lake is now the principal reservoir of the county irrigation district. (H. P. Davis.)

Box Springs: Canyon, Mountains, town [Riverside]. The two springs which were once "boxed in" to supply water for domestic use doubtless suggested the name. *See* Cajon.

Box S Spring [San Bernardino]. Named after the near-by Box S Ranch, which derived its name from the owner's cattle brand, a square enclosing the letter "S."

Boyden Cave [Sequoia National Park]. The cave in the canyon of the South Fork of the Kings River was named for its discoverer, Pete Boyden.

Boyes Hot Springs [Sonoma]. Named for Captain H. E. Boyes, owner and developer of the springs. The Indians had previously used the waters for medicinal purposes. The post office is listed in 1912.

Bradbury [Los Angeles]. Incorporated in 1957 and named for L. L. Bradbury, owner of property at the turn of the century (Co. Hist., 1965, III, 126).

Bradley [Monterey]. The Southern Pacific reached the place in October, 1886, and named the station for the owner of the land, Bradley V. Sargent, State senator, 1887–1889.

Bradley, Mount [Kings Canyon National Park]. Named by Robert M. Price, Mrs. Price, and Joseph C. Shinn—who made the first ascent on July 5, 1898—for Cornelius B. Bradley (1843–1936), professor of rhetoric at the University of California, 1894–1911 (Farquhar). Mount Bradley in the Shasta-Trinity National Forest was also named for Professor Bradley. He spent many summers at the Castle Crags Resort and always dragged his friends to the top of the mountain, which commands a splendid view (Schrader).

Branch. The geographical term for a fork of a river is rarely used in California nomenclature: Spring Branch of Willow Creek [Tehama], South Branch of Pleasant Grove

Creek [Placer], West Branch of San Pablo Creek [Contra Costa]. Sometimes the term is used to avoid repetition of "Fork": South Branch of Middle Fork of Feather River; Dusy Branch of Middle Fork of Kings River; East Branch of East Fork of North Fork of Trinity River. *See* Fork.

Branciforte Creek [Santa Cruz]. The creek takes its name from the *Pueblo* or *Villa de Branciforte*, established in 1797 at the site of the present town of Santa Cruz and named in honor of the viceroy of New Spain, the Marqués de Branciforte. From February 18 to April 5, 1850, Branciforte was the provisional name of Santa Cruz County.

Brand Park [Los Angeles]. Landmark 150 was registered January 11, 1935, and named for L. C. Brand, who gave to the park the great Star Fountain, which had been built by Indians under the direction of the padres.

Brandy. *See* Whiskey.

Branigan Lake [Yosemite National Park]. Named by Lieutenant N. F. McClure in 1894 for a soldier of his detachment, who was later killed in action in the Philippines (Farquhar).

Brannan Island [Sacramento]. The island opposite Rio Vista is the only place in California to commemorate Samuel Brannan, who came to California in 1846 in charge of the Mormon colonization and, after the discovery of gold, which he publicized far and wide, became the most spectacular financier and speculator in central California.

Branscomb [Mendocino]. The settlement and post office (1895) were named for the first postmaster, probably Benjamin Branscomb, a native of Ohio. The Branscomb who "shot three bear in one tree December, 1900" (Co. Hist., 1914, p. 101) may have been the same gentleman.

Brawley [Imperial]. Laid out and named by the Imperial Land Company in 1902, on property that had belonged to J. H. Braly of Los Angeles. Although the locality had begun to be called after him, he feared a failure of the project and refused permission to use Braly as a name for the proposed town. A. H. Heber, general manager of the land company, suggested as a compromise that Brawley, the name of one of his Chicago friends, be substituted. (Tout.)

Brawley Peaks [Mono]. Named for James M. Brawley, a prospector of the 1860's (Maule). Recorded as Braly Mountain on the Whitney maps.

Bray [Siskiyou]. When the post office was estab-

lished, June 7, 1907, it was named after the Bray Ranch, situated about half a mile from the present settlement (D. Steffenson).

Brea, brā′-à. The beds of asphaltum (Spanish, *brea*) in Los Angeles County were mentioned by the Portolá expedition and repeatedly in later years. In these beds thousands of skeletons of extinct animals have been discovered. As a geographical term, the word *brea* appears in the names of five land grants in Santa Clara, Monterey, Los Angeles, and Orange counties. It is still preserved in Labrea Creek [Santa Barbara] and some minor features. **Brea:** town, **Canyon** [Orange]. Named after the grant Rincon de la Brea [Los Angeles, Orange], dated February 23, 1841. *See* Asphalt, Pismo.

Breakfast Canyon [Death Valley National Monument]. "Dude wranglers" of Furnace Creek Inn are in the habit of eating breakfast in this colorful gorge after a morning ride; hence the name (Death Valley Survey).

Breakneck Canyon [Inyo]. Named in 1871 by Lieutenant D. A. Lyle of the Wheeler Survey because of the difficulties encountered in crossing it. Shown on Wheeler atlas sheet 65. Another very steep canyon by that name is in Butte County, and there is a Breakneck Creek in San Bernardino County.

Breckenridge Mountain [Kern]. Named after the Breckenridge sawmill on Lucas Creek, which in earlier days provided much of the lumber for Bakersfield. The Pacific Railroad Survey had named the elevation Cañon Mountain. At the time of the Civil War the new name arose, probably having been given by Southern sympathizers for John C. Breckinridge, prominent soldier, statesman, and in 1860 candidate for the Presidency (W. H. Boyd). The mountain was also known as Cross Mountain, named after the Cross Brothers lumber mill.

Breeze: Creek, Lake [Madera]. Named in 1896 by Lieutenant H. C. Benson for his brother-in-law, William F. Breeze of San Francisco.

Breisgau [Tehama and Shasta]. A Mexican land grant dated July 26, 1844, and named by the grantee, William Benitz, after his home district in southwestern Germany.

Brentwood [Contra Costa]. Named after Brentwood in Essex, England, the ancestral home of John Marsh, who had owned Rancho Los Meganos (on which the present town is situated). The town was laid out in 1878 on land donated by the owners of the property.

Brewer, Mount [Kings Canyon National Park]. Named by the Whitney Survey for William

H. Brewer after he and Charles F. Hoffmann had made the first ascent on July 2, 1864. Brewer, professor of natural sciences at the University of California, 1863–1864, professor of agriculture at Yale, 1864–1903, was the principal assistant of Whitney in the California State Geological Survey, 1860–1864. **Brewer Creek** [Siskiyou] was apparently also named for Professor Brewer, who identified the weeping spruce, *Picea breweriana,* in the Mount Shasta region.

Brewery Gulch [Mendocino]. The name survives from a brewery that flourished here in the "early days" (George R. Stewart) .

Breyfogle: Canyon, Buttes [Death Valley National Monument]. The names commemorate Charles C. Breyfogle, one of the fabulous prospectors of Death Valley. The Breyfogles, father and several sons, had mined for gold on the North Yuba River near Downieville in 1850. The father, Joshua, wrote an interesting diary, and their camp was named for them. One of the sons, Charles, resided in Oakland later and was assessor and treasurer of Alameda County from 1854 to 1859. In 1864 he claimed to have discovered a rich gold deposit in or near the canyon. He was captured by Indians and after his release he could not find the place of his discovery. In the jargon of Death Valley's gold seekers, "breyfogling" became the synonym for "searching for lost mines." Numerous articles and monographs about the confusing subject have been published. In some of these his first name is given as Jacob, in others as Anton, identified as a German from Austin, Nevada.

Briceland [Humboldt]. Named for John C. Briceland, a native of Virginia, who, about 1889, bought the ranch on which the present town has been developed (Co. Hist., 1915, p. 1190). The post office is listed in 1892.

Bridalveil: Fall, Creek [Yosemite National Park]. Apparently named by Warren Baer, editor of the Mariposa *Democrat,* on August 5, 1856. James M. Hutchings asserts that he suggested the name on his first visit to Yosemite in 1855. (Farquhar.) The Indians called it *Pohono* and, according to Kroeber, connected the word with *Pohonichi,* the Yokuts name for the Miwok group in the vicinity. There is no evidence that *pohono* means 'evil wind.' However, in 1920 C. Hart Merriam informed Loye Miller that an Indian had told him that *pohono* means 'coming down in chunks.' This is quite descriptive of the fall, but it might be just an Indian inven-

tion. At the time of the Whitney Survey the Indian name was apparently still in common use (Brewer, Notes, June 16, 1863).

Bridge. One of the most popular designations for a place ever since people have built bridges and settled near them. **Bridgeport:** town, **Valley, Canyon, Creek** [Mono]. The town was settled in the late 1850's and became the seat of Mono County in 1864. The valley was first called Big Meadows because of the large area of grass around the settlement. Another Bridgeport, mentioned in the 1850's, was situated on Yuba River at a covered bridge, which is still standing today. **Bridgeville** [Humboldt] was so named because of its location at the bridge over the Van Duzen River. The word occurs in the names of seven other districts or settlements in the State, including Bridge Creek [Lassen] and Bridgeport Landing [Mendocino].

Brier [Inyo]. Named for the Rev. J. W. Brier and his family, who crossed Death Valley in 1849 and settled in Los Angeles (*Desert Mag.,* Sept., 1938).

Brighton [Sacramento]. Laid out in 1849 about a mile north of the present site, near Sutter's gristmill (built in 1847), by a party of Sacramento speculators and named after Brighton, England. The name appears in the *Statutes* of 1851, and on Gibbes' map of 1852. *See* Perkins.

Briones: Hills, Valley [Contra Costa]. Named for Felipe Briones' family, who were allowed to settle on Martínez' rancho in 1831. Briones himself was killed by Indians in 1840.

Brisbane [San Mateo]. The town was established in 1908 under the name of Visitacion City. To avoid confusion with the near-by Visitacion Valley, the name was changed to Brisbane for the well-known journalist, Arthur Brisbane, when the post office was established in 1931. According to Stanger (pp. 47 ff.), the name was applied by the promoter Arthur Annis, a native of Brisbane, Australia.

Briscoe Creek [Glenn]. Named for Watt Briscoe, a stockman of the district in the early 1850's. Sometimes spelled Brisco.

Brites Valley [Kern]. Named for John M. Brite, who came to the Tehachapi region in 1854 (Co. Hist., 1914, p. 185). According to Crites (p. 266), it was named for W. F. Brite, one of the first supervisors of the county.

Brittans Knoll [San Mateo]. The elevation near San Carlos was named after the Nat Brittan Ranch, established in 1856 (A. K. Brown) .

Britton, Lake [Shasta]. The reservoir was

formed in 1925 and named in memory of John A. Britton, general manager of the Pacific Gas and Electric Company (Steger).

Brockway [Placer]. Before 1900, Frank Brockway Alverson was associated with "Lucky" Baldwin and built a hot spring resort on the north side of Fallen Leaf Lake. It was named for "Uncle Nathaniel" Brockway. The post office was established March 16, 1901.

Broderick [Yolo]. The town was laid out in February, 1850, by the widow of James McDowell and named Washington. In 1854 the Postal Guide lists two Washingtons, one in Yolo County and one in Nevada County. Both post offices were discontinued before 1858, but the one in Nevada County was reëstablished before 1867. About 1890, when the town in Yolo County again petitioned for a post office, a new name had to be found. It is not known why the name Broderick was chosen; perhaps it was given in memory of Senator Broderick. *See below.*

Broderick, Mount [Yosemite National Park]. David C. Broderick, U.S. senator from California, 1857–1859, was killed (near San Francisco) by Judge David S. Terry in 1859 in the last formal duel fought on California soil. The Whitney Survey had placed his name originally on what is now known as Liberty Cap. The latter name was given in 1865, and the name Mount Broderick was later transferred to its present location. (Farquhar.)

Broken Rib Mountain [Del Norte] and also **Wounded Knee Mountain** (two miles west) indicate that a party of the Geological Survey had tough going when they surveyed the Preston Peak quadrangle in 1915.

Brooklyn Basin [Alameda]. The name in Oakland's Inner Harbor preserves the memory of the town of Brooklyn, now part of Oakland. The section of Oakland around Mills College had a post office named Brooklyn from 1855 to 1878. A town was created March 10, 1856, when the Supervisors of Alameda County amalgamated the settlements Clinton and San Antonio. According to Annaleone Patten, the place was named after the ship *Brooklyn,* which brought Sam Brannan and 238 Mormons to San Francisco in 1846.

Brooks [Yolo]. The name was selected at a public meeting on March 3, 1884, as an appropriate name for the post office because a brook flows past the site (Earl Smith).

Brooks Canyon [Riverside]. The canyon in the Cleveland National Forest was named in 1960 in memory of Andrew C. Brooks, a Forest Service employee who lost his life in the Decker fire of August, 1959.

Brooks Island [San Francisco Bay]. The Spanish name of the island was *Isla del Carmen* (Cañizares, 1776). When the Coast Survey charted the bay in 1850, it was used as a triangulation point and called Rocky Island. On Eddy's map (1854) it is labeled Brooks Island, probably for the owner of the island. It is also popularly known as Sheep Island.

Brother Jonathan Rock [Del Norte]. This is the name of a submerged rock about four miles off the shore near Crescent City, upon which the steamer *Brother Jonathan* was wrecked on July 30, 1865. The name was applied by the Coast Survey; it is mentioned as Jonathan Rock in a letter to Davidson, October 10, 1869.

Brothers. It is an old international custom to designate a group of two or more orographic features of similar appearance as brothers or sisters. Two rocks at San Pablo Point [Contra Costa] are called The Brothers, and the two rocks on the opposite shore [Marin], The Sisters. Another group of bare rocks called The Brothers is south of Cape Mendocino. In Fresno, as well as in Riverside County, there are mountain groups called Three Sisters, and four peaks in Del Norte County are named Four Brothers. *See* Three Brothers.

Brown. The brown slopes of the California landscape are so common a sight during the long dry season that this color adjective has seldom been used in place naming. Fewer than ten orographic features, including Brown Cone [Fresno], are so named; most of these derive their names from the color of rock formations.

Brown Mountain [Los Angeles]. The mountain was named for the sons of the fiery abolitionist of Harpers Ferry fame, Jason and Owen Brown, whose ranch was at the foot of the mountain. It should, perhaps, properly honor John Brown himself, whose body lay a-mouldering in the grave, but whose soul went marching on throughout the Civil War. John Brown's family had moved to California after the Civil War (Shasta *Courier,* April 22, 1865).

Browns Flat [Mariposa]. "Here the adventurous pioneer David Brown made his headquarters for many years, dividing his time between gold-hunting and bear-hunting" (Muir, p. 35).

Browns Valley [Napa]. Apparently named for John E. Brown, who had purchased a slice of Salvador Vallejo's enormous Napa grant "for a horse and buggy" (Doyle) and was the successful claimant for the section in 1853.

Browns Valley: settlement, **Ridge** [Yuba]. Named for a prospector who is reported to have taken within a few weeks' time, in 1850, $12,000 in gold-bearing quartz from near the base of a huge boulder. The name is mentioned in Trask's *Report, 1854* (p. 90).

Brownsville [Yuba]. Named for I. E. Brown, who erected the first sawmill there in 1851 (Co. Hist., 1879, p. 91).

Bryn Mawr [San Bernardino]. The post office was established about 1895 and was probably named after the town in Pennsylvania, which had been named after the town in Wales.

Bryte [Yolo]. Because of its location on the Sacramento River the place was at first called Riverbank. When the post office was established in 1914, the present name—for George Bryte, a local dairyman—was chosen in order to avoid confusion with Riverbank in Stanislaus County. (F. V. Wike.)

Bubbs Creek [Kings Canyon National Park]. The name was applied by the Whitney Survey for John Bubbs, a prospector, who crossed Kearsarge Pass from Owens Valley in 1864 (Farquhar).

Buchon, bŭ-shŏn′, **Point** [San Luis Obispo]. The Portolá expedition, on September 4, 1769, found in Price Canyon north of Pismo a settlement of Indians whose chief had a goiter or tumor which hung from his neck. "On account of this the soldiers named him El Buchón, which name he and the village retained. I named the place San Ladislao." (Crespi, p. 183.) The San Luis Range is shown as the *Sierra de Buchon* on Costansó's map of 1770, and San Luis Obispo Bay is called *Bahia de Buchon* by Padre Palou in a letter of 1772 (Palou, IV, 317). On 19th-century maps the range appears as Mount Buchon or Monte del Buchon. The Coast Survey mapped the district during the Civil War and called the nameless cape Point Buchon. For several years it also retained the designation Monte del Buchon; the highest elevation on it was later named Saddle Peak.

Buck. More than one hundred geographic features in California are named Buck—almost as many as are named Deer. The word appears mainly with Creek, Mountain, and Peak. Since the name is often used as a nickname, or to designate an Indian man (in contrast to squaw), not all such names refer to a male deer or antelope. There are a number of Buckhorn Creeks and Flats, and in Lake County there is a Bucksnort Creek.

Buckeye. The striking California buckeye, native to the Coast Ranges and the Sierra foothills, has given its name to at least fifty geographic features. Since the tree is found chiefly near water, it is not surprising that about half of these features are creeks. It was in Buckeye Ravine [Nevada] that a new method of gold mining, "hydraulicking," originated in 1852 (H. P. Davis). The tree is not found east of the Sierra Nevada. The cluster name in Mono County, **Buckeye: Creek, Ridge, Pass, Hot Springs,** was taken from the Buckeye Mill which was owned and operated in the 1860's by E. Roberts (Maule). **Buckeye:** town, **Creek** [Shasta]. The town was founded in 1856 and named by settlers from Ohio after their home, the "Buckeye State."

Buckingham: Peak, Bluffs, Peninsula, Point, Park, Island [Lake]. Named for the family connected with the well-known western shoe firm Buckingham & Hecht. The family resided here in the 1880's and 1890's. (Mauldin.)

Buckman Springs [San Diego]. Named for Amos Buckman, who settled in the valley in 1868 or 1869 and owned the property which includes the springs.

Bucks Flat [Tehama]. In the 1850's the Indians stole from a rancher an old ox named "Buck," killed it at this place, and hung the meat up to jerk. This act precipitated one of the last Indian fights of the region. The name commemorates the sad end of old "Buck." (Carl Turner.)

Bucksport [Humboldt]. Named for David A. Buck, formerly of New York, a member of the Josiah Gregg party of 1849, who laid out the town in 1851.

Bucks: Valley, town, **Creek, Mountain, Lake, Reservoir** [Plumas]. Named for Horace (or Francis) Bucklin, popularly known as "Buck," who settled here in 1850. Historic Landmark 197.

Budd: Creek, Lake [Yosemite National Park]. The name was applied by the Geological Survey before 1910, for James H. Budd, governor of California from 1895 to 1899.

Buellton [Santa Barbara]. The post office was named in 1916 by William Budd, the first postmaster, for Rufus T. Buell, a native of Vermont who had settled there in 1874.

Buena, bwä′-nà: **Park** [Orange]. Founded in 1887 and given its hybrid name (*buena*, 'good'). As the town grew, it reached the railroad station Northam, which the Santa Fe renamed Buena Park in 1929.

Buenaventura. After the Lewis and Clark expedition had definitely dispelled the legend of a great "River of the West" traversing the western part of the continent and entering the ocean somewhere in Oregon Territory, the mythical river was shifted south. In the early part of the 19th century a *Buenaventura* (good fortune) River was supposed to flow from the Rocky Mountains via Great Salt Lake and through a gap in the Sierra Nevada into the ocean somewhere in central California. The name *Bonaventura* was used for the Sacramento by the Hudson's Bay Company trappers, who usually entered central California along its course, and map makers found it convenient to use this name for the new "River of the West." Jedediah Smith's journeys exploded the myth of a river flowing from Salt Lake to the sea, and Burr's map of 1839 (based largely on Smith's discoveries) places the name Buenaventura River on what is now the Sacramento River, and the name Valley of the Buenaventura on the Sacramento and San Joaquin valleys. Hood's map of 1838 has Buenaventura R. apparently for what is now the Humboldt River in Nevada; a dotted line from Humboldt Sink to the Sacramento Valley indicates a possible connection with the California river system. Coulter's map of 1835 and Hood's map also label the Salinas, *R. Buenaventura.* Wilkes' party in 1841 left the name *Buenaventura* for the Salinas on the map, preceding it with an *S* [i.e., *San*] for good measure. The report of the expedition calls the San Joaquin Valley, Buena Ventura Valley. After that the name was used only sporadically and in the 1850's it disappeared altogether. The Salinas is called *San Buenaventura* as late as 1857 (Pac. R.R. *Reports,* Vol. V, Pt. 2, p. 139). It is interesting to note that the official *Mapa de los Estados Unidos Mejicanos* (Paris, 1837) has a complete *Rio S. Buenaventura* reaching the ocean north of San Luis Obispo, and that Frémont, too, was convinced of the existence of the river almost until he reached Sutter's Fort in March, 1844 (*Expl. Exp.,* 1853, pp. 286, 300, 309). **Buenaventura** [Shasta and Tehama]. The former name of the Sacramento River was given to the Mexican land grant, dated December 4, 1844, granted to Pierson B. Reading.

Buena Vista, bwä'-nȧ vĭs'-tȧ. The term, meaning 'beautiful view,' is probably the most common place name of Spanish origin in the United States. Many places bear this name in commemoration of Taylor's decisive victory over Santa Anna on February 23, 1847.

However, no evidence has been found to indicate that any of the Buena Vistas in California were named for this battle. The peaks in Amador, Mariposa, Madera, and Tulare counties were probably so named because they command a *buena vista.* Other place names go back to Spanish times, when the term was very popular and was used repeatedly for land grants and geographic features. **Buena Vista: Lake, Valley, Creek, Hills** [Kern]. The oldest Spanish place name in the San Joaquin Valley. An Indian village, *Buena Vista,* is mentioned by Fages in 1772 (*CHSQ,* X, 218 f.) and again by Zalvidea in 1806 (Arch. MSB, IV, 51). The lake is recorded as *Laguna de Buenavista* on Estudillo's sketch map of 1819, and elsewhere in Spanish times. It is repeatedly mentioned in the Pacific Railroad *Reports.* On April 30, 1855, a Buena Vista County was created (*Statutes,* 1855, p. 203), but it did not materialize. The names were officially applied to creek, valley, and hills by the Geographic Board, April 7, 1909. **Buena Vista** [Monterey]. A place called *Buenavista* is mentioned by Font on April 14, 1776. It appears on Narváez' Plano and Duflot de Mofras's map. The name was applied to a land grant before 1795 and to another grant in 1822. It is repeatedly found on maps and in records. **Buena Vista: Creeks, Hills; Buena** [San Diego]. The name was applied to a land grant dated June 17, 1845, doubtless after a rancheria called Buena Vista. The rancheria is mentioned by Emory in 1847 (*Mil. Rec.,* p. 116). In 1890 the San Diego Central extended its line across the rancho and named a station Buena Vista. When in 1908 a name was needed for another station, the old one was simply called Buena and the new one, Vista. Another creek and a canada in the county (Ramona atlas sheet) take their name from a spring mentioned as Buena Vista in 1821 (Arch. MSB, IV, 217).

Bueyes, Rincon de los [Los Angeles]. The name was applied to the land grant, dated December 7, 1821. *Bueyes* is the Spanish word for 'oxen.' *See* Rincon.

Buhne, bōō'-nȧ, **Point** [Humboldt]. Named for Captain H. H. Bühne, who entered Humboldt Bay on April 9, 1850, as second officer of the *Laura Virginia,* and who later became a prominent lumberman.

Bull. The old English custom of using the stem "Ox" in place names has never taken root in America. "Bull" and to a lesser degree "Cow" and "Cattle" are used instead. In California more than fifty names contain the word Bull, including Bull Barn Gulch [Sonoma] and Bull Tail Valley [Marin]. The word Bullpen, used for a number of features, is western slang for sleeping quarters in camps, or for "pens" in general. Bullhead Creek [Siskiyou] was probably named for the fish. **Bulls Head Point** [Suisun Bay] took its name from "Large House (Bull's Head)" shown on surveyor's plats of Rancho Las Juntas (April, 1864), and **Bullwheel Ridge** [Kings] from a bull wheel used in drilling. Since the Spaniards also frequently used the name *Toro* (bull), some of the Bull Creeks in the southern counties were doubtless originally *Arroyos del Toro*. **Bull: Creek, Flat** [Humboldt] were so named because in the early 1850's Indians stole a bull from a white settler near Briceland, slaughtered it at the creek, and were killed by the settlers in retaliation (Humboldt *Times*, Sept. 15, 1931). Thanks to the Save-The-Redwoods League a large part of the beautiful redwood growth of Bull Creek Watershed is now protected by a state park and the Rockefeller Forest.

Bullards: Bar, Dam, Power Reservoir [Yuba]. Perpetuates the name of a forty-niner, Dr. Bullard of Brooklyn, N.Y., for whom the settlement Bullards Bar, now covered by the reservoir, had been named.

Bullfrog Lake [Kings Canyon National Park]. John Muir called it Bryanthus Lake, but local custom prevailed. Since trout have been planted, it is no longer distinguished for its bullfrogs; yet the name remains.

Bullion. The term for gold or silver in bars or bulk was used for several place names in California and has survived in Mount Bullion [Alpine], listed as a mining town in 1864. *See* Mount Bullion. **Bullion Bend** [El Dorado]. The bend in the South Fork of American River, west of Riverton, became known by this name because in the 1850's a gang of stage robbers hid the stolen gold in a deep hole in the river, from which it was later retrieved ("The Knave," Sept. 22, 1946).

Bull Run. *See* Run.

Bullskin Ridge [Shasta]. The ridge was named for "Bullskin Jack," a saloonkeeper, who was so nicknamed by Jim Smith, a stage driver, when the latter saw a bull's skin drying on the fence in front of the saloon (Steger).

Bully, Bully Choop. *See* Bally.

Bumpass: Mountain, Hell [Lassen National Park]. Named for Kendall V. Bumpass, hunter, guide, and prospector, who was last seen at Morgan Springs in 1870 (Doyle). The editor of the Red Bluff *Independent* wrote in 1865: ". . . We took up the line of march with Mr. K. V. Bumpass as guide. . . . On turning the ridge all the wonders of Hell were suddenly before us . . . This basin was discovered by our guide last year while hunting . . ." (D. J. Tobin.) The generic Hot Springs is a map name used only by the Geological Survey.

Bunker Hill. The place where American patriotism received its baptism of fire has always been a favorite place name in the United States. There seems to have been no settlement so named in California, but the name is preserved in three "hills" in Amador, Nevada, and Plumas counties, the one in Plumas County being 7,290 feet higher than Bunker Hill near Boston. However, there is also a Bunker Hill between Colton and San Bernardino, and one within the city limits of Los Angeles, which are about the size of the original hill.

Bunnell: Point, Cascade, Cliff [Yosemite National Park]. The point was named for Dr. Lafayette H. Bunnell (1824–1903), a member of the Mariposa Battalion, which was the first party of white men to enter Yosemite Valley, March 25, 1851. It was Bunnell who proposed the name Yosemite for the valley. He was an army surgeon in the Civil War. (Farquhar.)

Burbank [Los Angeles]. The city was laid out in 1887 on the Providencia rancho, and was named for one of the subdividers, Dr. David Burbank, a Los Angeles dentist.

Burbank Memorial Park [Sonoma]. Named in honor of Luther Burbank (1849–1926), the horticulturist. The park was his home and experimental garden. He is buried there under a cedar of Lebanon of his own planting. The **Luther Burbank Grove** in the Prairie Creek Redwoods State Park was established through the efforts of the Save-the-Redwoods League in 1949.

Burcham Flat [Mono]. For James Burcham, reported to have been a Confederate deserter, who grazed cattle here in the 1860's (Maule).

Burdell: Mountain, Island, station [Marin]. Named for Dr. Galen Burdell, who came to California on the *Duxbury* in 1849, married the daughter of James Black, a pioneer of Marin County, and settled on Rancho Olompali in 1863.

Buriburi Ridge [San Mateo]. The Register of Mission Dolores lists *Urebure* as one of the rancherias under its jurisdiction soon after its founding. In a letter of July 24, 1798, the new *Rancho de Real Hacienda* in *el parage nombrado* [the place named] *Buriburi* is mentioned (SP Mis. & C., I, 74). Beechey, in November, 1826, mentions a farm called Burri Burri, with a small cottage, about twelve miles from San Francisco. On his map (1827–1828) a place called *Bourri* is shown near what is now San Bruno. Duflot de Mofras has *Buri (Plan* 16) in the same location. The name Buri Buri was applied to a provisional land grant, dated December 11, 1827. Later the entire region between San Bruno Mountain and San Mateo became known as Buri Buri. The meaning of the name is unknown. The name of Burra Burra Peak [Santa Clara] may come from the same stem. Both are in Costanoan territory.

Burkhalter [Nevada]. Probably named for M. E. Burkhalter, president of the Pacific Wood & Lumber Company (Myrick). A post office named Burkhalter was established June 5, 1891.

Burlingame [San Mateo]. Named in 1868 by William C. Ralston for his friend Anson Burlingame (1822–1870), well-known orator and diplomat, who was U.S. Minister to China, 1861–1867, and head of the Burlingame mission of the Chinese government, 1867–1870.

Burney: Creek, town, **Falls** [Shasta]. When the post office was established in 1872, R. M. Johnson named it Burney Valley in memory of Samuel Burney, a trapper and immigrant guide of Scottish origin, who was killed by Indians in the late 1850's. The Post Office Department changed the name to Burney in 1894. *See* McArthur–Burney Falls State Park.

Burnham, Mount [Los Angeles]. Named by the Geographic Board in 1951 in honor of Major Frederick R. Burnham, explorer and scout leader.

Burns Valley [Lake]. Named for an early settler of the Lower Lake region (Co. Hist., 1881, p. 140).

Burnt. Although there are several Burnt Mountains, Hills, and Valleys in the State, the number is small in view of the fact that grass and forest fires are of frequent occurrence. The Coso District was once called Burnt District and may have been called that by the Indians in their own tongue. (*See* Coso.) There is a unique Burn*ed* Mountain in Monterey County. Often a geographic feature is named Burnt because a man-made structure has burned there: Burnt Mill Creek [San Bernardino], Burnt Camp Creek [Sequoia National Park], Burnt Bridge Creek [Yuba], Burnt Corral Creek [Fresno], Burnt Ranch [Tehama]. **Burnt Ranch** [Trinity]. The former important mining center, which had a post

office as early as 1858, was so named because in 1849 Canadian miners burned down an Indian rancheria (De Massey, *A Frenchman in the Gold Rush,* p. 100; Schoolcraft III, 135). The often-told story of the Indians burning down a settler's ranch is purely imaginative. *See* Quemado.

Burrel [Fresno]. The railroad station was named in 1889, for Cuthbert Burrell (or Burrel), an immigrant of 1846 and one of the pioneers in stock raising in Fresno County, where he lived from 1860 to 1869. Before the coming of the railroad the place had been known as Elkhorn Station, after Burrel's Elkhorn Ranch. The post office was named in 1912.

Burrill Mountain [Humboldt]. It was named "in the early days" for Robert Burrill, who had a cattle ranch at the foot of the mountain (Irene Quinn).

Burro. The Spanish name for 'jackass' is repeatedly found in place names, though not nearly so often as the English term. The cluster of names in Monterey County is derived from the name of the Los Burros Mining District of the 1870's. It is possible that some places were named for the *buro,* 'mule deer,' a large herd of which was observed by Font on April 3, 1776, near Antioch (*Compl. Diary,* p. 382). West of Santa Barbara there is a state park called Arroyo Burro.

Burson: Valley, Springs, post office [Calaveras]. The places were named for a railroad man, David S. Burson, when the post office was established, December 2, 1884 (Frances Bishop). The name of the railroad station, however, was Helisma.

Burt Canyon [Mono]. Named for C. H. Burt, who herded sheep in this canyon before the establishment of the Mono National Forest (Maule).

Burton Mound [Santa Barbara]. This Indian burial mound was named for Lewis T. Burton, who came to California with the Wolfskill party in 1831, lived in an adobe on the site, and later was a claimant for the Bolsa del Chamizal and Jesus Maria grants. *See* Mesa.

Butano, bū′-tá-nō: **Creek, Ridge, Falls, Forest** [San Mateo]. Probably an Indian word made to sound Spanish. *El Butano* was mentioned by Padre Jaime Escudet, July 7, 1816 (Arch. Arz. SF, III, 101). *Arrollo del Butano* is shown on a *diseño* of the San Antonio or El Pescadero grant (1833). A land grant called El Butano was granted in 1838 and in 1844; one of its *diseños* shows *Bolsa del Butano.* According to Frances M. Molera, *butano* is what early Californians called a drinking cup made out of the horn of a bull or other animal. It is not certain whether such a drinking horn was found at the place or a waterfall or a spring in the rocks suggested the name.

Butcher Ranch [Placer]. Mentioned as a farming settlement in the Sacramento *Union*, June 16, 1858; it was probably named for the original owner of the land. The name Butchers appears on the Placerville atlas sheet.

Butte, būt. The origin of the word was probably a Teutonic stem designating a blunt extension or elevation, found in the English *butt*. In the French language it became a geographical term and stood for a small isolated elevation, a knoll, mound, or hillock. It was introduced into the northwestern states by the French-Canadian trappers of the Hudson's Bay Company. The first Americans to use it as a generic term were probably the members of the Lewis and Clark expedition. It was Frémont, however, who gave the term a sort of official blessing. "The French word *butte,* which so often occurs in this narrative, is retained from the familiar language of the country, and identifies the objects to which it refers. It is naturalized in the region of the Rocky mountains, and, even if desirable to render it in English, I know of no word which would be its precise equivalent. It is applied to the detached hills and ridges which rise rapidly, and reach too high to be called hills or ridges, and not high enough to be called mountains." (*Expl. Exp.,* 1853, pp. 214 f.) This distinction soon disappeared in California. High peaks like Shasta and Lassen were called buttes (often spelled bute), and for some time it seemed that the term might replace "mount" and "peak." There are in the State today some five hundred Buttes, many of them more than 5,000, and some more than 10,000 feet high. Most of them are in the north, but some are found in almost every county. A great number of creeks, lakes, meadows, etc., and five settlements are named after near-by buttes. **Butte: County, Creek, Basin, Slough, Meadows, Sink.** The cluster name had its origin in the three buttes which now are called the Sutter Buttes or Marysville Buttes, the impressive landmark in the Sacramento Valley. When Butte County was created and named, February 18, 1850, the buttes were within its borders; they are now in Sutter County. **Butte City** [Glenn]. "This is the name given to a new town which we learn has been surveyed on the east bank of the Sacramento river" (S.F. *Alta California,*

March 23, 1850). The city is situated on the Llano Seco grant and was likewise named after the Sutter Buttes. The place is shown as Butte on Eddy's map (1854) but apparently did not develop until the Butte Ferry was established by the Marysville-Shasta stage line about 1875.

Butterbread: Canyon, Peak, Well [Kern]. In the 1860's Frederick Butterbredt, a native of Germany, settled here as a "ranchero," married an Indian girl, and had a large family. When the Geological Survey mapped the Mojave quadrangle in 1912–1913 the surveyors misspelled the name. One of the pioneer's grandsons has adopted the spelling Butterbread for his family name (H. C. Topp). It is quite possible that the original name of the settler was really *Butterbrot,* 'buttered bread, sandwich.'

Butterfield Stage Station [Riverside]. Historical Landmark 188 seems to be the only place named for the famous stage line, which inaugurated in 1858 the first overland service to California. The route itself is Historical Landmark 471.

Buttermilk: Hill, Country [Inyo]. The name arose in the early 1870's when "Old Joe" Inman, father of State Senator Joseph Inman, had a dairy there and the teamsters from Tim Lewis' sawmill on Birch Creek stopped at his place for a drink of buttermilk (Robinson).

Buttonwillow: town, Ridge [Kern]. The name was applied to the station and post office when the branch line from Bakersfield reached the place in 1895. It goes back to the early days of Miller and Lux, when the cowboys used the lone buttonwillow tree by the slough bank as a landmark. (W. D. Tracy.) There is also a Buttonwillow Peak in Tulare County. The name is a California localism for the buttonbush (*Cephalanthus occidentalis*) and arose because buttonbush leaves somewhat resemble those of the willow. Under favorable circumstances the bush will grow into a tree.

Butt: Valley, Creek, Mountain, Reservoir [Plumas]. Named for Horace Butts, a successful miner at Dutch Hill, who settled in the lower part of the valley now known as Butt Valley. Butt Valley Reservoir was named in 1921 by the Great Western Power Company. (Co. Library.)

Buzzard. The heavy, slow-flying bird of prey is a common sight in many sections of the State and appears in some twenty-five place names, including two mountains called Buzzard

Roost [Tulare, San Joaquin].

Byrnes Ferry [Calaveras]. Named for Patrick O. Byrne, who operated a ferry at the place where the road between Copperopolis and Mountain Pass crosses the Stanislaus River. The river was first bridged in 1853, and the settlement that sprang up retained the original name. The site is also known as O'Byrne Ferry, and Historic Landmark 281 is so called.

Byron: town, **Hot Springs** [Contra Costa]. The name was applied to the station of the Southern Pacific in 1878, probably after one of the numerous Byrons "back East." The springs (without the name) are indicated on Hoffmann's map of the Bay region (1873) as Sulphur, Salt, and Hot Springs.

Cabazon, kăb′-à-zŏn: town, **Peak** [Riverside]. The station was named by the Southern Pacific in the 1870's, after a near-by Indian rancheria which appears as Cabezone on the Land Office map of 1859. The town was laid out and named after the station in 1884. The peak was named by the Geological Survey in 1901. "These settlements in Coahuilla Valley comprise about 800 . . . Coahuilla Indians, or . . . 'diggers.' They . . . recognize Cabezon as their head chief and supreme authority. . . . His name 'Cabezon' was given him by the Californian-Mexican population, on account of the unusually large size of his head." (S.F. *Alta California*, July 17, 1862.)

Cabeza de Santa Rosa [Sonoma]. The name of a land grant dated September 30, 1841. *Cabeza* was used in a geographical sense like the corresponding English term 'head' (of a canyon, etc.).

Cabrillo, Point [Mendocino]. Named in 1870 by the Coast Survey in honor of Juan Rodríguez Cabrillo (*see* Glossary) at the suggestion of George Davidson. **Cabrillo National Monument** [San Diego]. This area, which in all probability includes Cabrillo's first landing place in what is now the State of California, was created and named by proclamation of President Wilson in 1913. **Cabrillo Point** [Monterey]. Named in 1935 by the Geographic Board because Cabrillo anchored near it on November 16, 1542. The pronunciation varies: kà-brē′-ŏ, kà-brē′-yŏ, kà-brĭl′-ŏ. The Geographic Board Decisions, 1964, (Sept.-Dec.) list a **Cerro Cabrillo**, "mountain peak with an elevation of about 912 feet," southeast of Morro Bay in San Luis Obispo County.

Cachagua Creek [Monterey]. On a *diseño* of the Los Tularcitos grant the stream, a tributary to the upper Carmel River, is unnamed, but near it appear the words *Cañada* and *ojo de agua*. It is not impossible that a later map maker garbled these words into Cachagua. There is a Mexican word *cachagua*, meaning 'sewer,' 'gutter,' which might be the source of the name.

Cache, kăsh: **Creek** [Yolo]. The name *Rivière la Cache* was applied to the stream by Hudson's Bay Company trappers, sometime before 1832, because they had a cache or hiding place for their traps on its banks. In Mexican documents of the 1840's the creek is called *Rio* (or *Arroyo*) *de Jesus Maria*, a name which had been bestowed upon the Sacramento River north of its junction with the Feather by Gabriel Moraga in 1808 (*CFQ*, VI, 73 f.). In the *New Helvetia Diary*, under date of January 25, 1846, the stream is called Cash Creek, and this phonetic spelling is often found in the early American period. Derby's map of 1849 has the present spelling. Cacheville was the name of Yolo in the 1850's, and an Indian village of Kachitule (!) appears on the map of Kroeber's *Handbook* facing page 354. In pioneer times the name was quite common in the American West. The spelling was usually "cash." Kern County has a Cache Peak and a Cash Creek.

Cachuma, kà-chōō′-mà: **Creek, Mountain** [Santa Barbara]. Apparently the American version of an Indian name which on the maps of the Tequepis grant looks like *Juichama* and *Juichuneas*. Cachuma Lake was created by impounding the Santa Ynez River in 1960.

Cactus. The four species of cactus native to California have given the name to a number of places in the southern counties, including settlements in Imperial and Riverside counties. *See* Chollas.

Cadenasso [Yolo]. Named for Nicolo Cadenasso, who bought the Adobe Ranch, west of Capay, in 1880. In 1885 he gave part of his land for a school, and the near vicinity became known as Cadenasso, now quite generally spelled Cadanassa.

Cadiz, kā′-dĭz: station, **Lake, Valley** [San Bernardino]. The station was named in 1883 by the Atlantic and Pacific Railroad, probably after one of the towns of the same name in the eastern United States. *See* Amboy.

Cady Mountain [San Bernardino]. The name preserves the memory of Camp Cady, a military post active in 1864 to protect travelers along the San Bernardino–Fort Mojave road (Myrick). The camp had been named for Albemarle Cady, a major in the Mexican War and a brigadier general in 1865.

Cahill Ridge [San Mateo]. Named for Anthony Cahill, a native of Ireland and a farmer in the district in 1867. Spelled Cahil on the Santa Cruz atlas sheet.

Cahoon: Meadow, Mountain, Creek [Tulare]. The mountain and meadow were named for George Cahoon, who lived near by (Farquhar). The name was placed on the map by the Geological Survey in 1902–1903.

Cahto [Mendocino], **Cahto Creek** [Humboldt]. The name is from a Pomo word meaning 'lake,' according to Goddard (*AAE*, V, 67). Since *cah* means 'water' and *to* means 'mush,' in the Pomo dialect (Kroeber), the interpretation 'mush lake' or 'mush water' for the swampy lake that once covered the valley is not impossible. John P. Simpson and Robert White came here in 1856 and started the settlement known later as Cahto. A post office was established July 22, 1863. Cahto Mountain is mentioned by John Rockwell in 1878.

Cahuenga, ká-hŭng′-gà, ká-wĕng′-gà: **Pass, Peak, Park** [Los Angeles]. The name probably comes from that of an Indian rancheria, "undoubtedly named from some Gabrielino Shoshonean word" (Kroeber). A *sitio de Caguenga* is mentioned on June 27, 1802 (Docs. Hist. Cal., IV, 117). The name was used for three Mexican land grants, dated May 5, 1843, February 7, 1845, and July·29, 1846, and is found repeatedly, with many spelling variants, in documents and *expedientes* of the following decades. It gained historical significance when Andrés Pico surrendered to Frémont at *Campo de Cahuenga*, January 13, 1847. The site, now within the limits of Universal City, is Historical Landmark 151.

Cahuilla, kä-wē′-à: **Indian Reservation, Valley, Mountain,** post office [Riverside]. The Cahuilla Indians are a wide-spread division of Shoshoneans, who occupied the territory on both sides of the San Jacinto Mountains and are still found in a number of reservations. According to Rupert Costo, a member of the tribe, the name means 'leader,' and the Indians would prefer to spell it Ka-we′-a, as it is indeed pronounced. The Geological Survey spells the name Coahuila on the San Jacinto atlas sheet, and various forms may be found in the literature. In 1963 the present form, Cahuilla, was made official. A *gentil* [heathen] *Cuchuil* is mentioned as early as July 30, 1782 (Arch. Mont., VII, 15) . In the records of the 1820's and 1830's the name is usually spelled Cagüilla; June 21, 1845, the modern spelling variant Cahuillas is recorded for the first time (DSP,

VI, 43) . On Warren's map (1859) the habitat of the tribe is indicated along the mountain ranges between longitude 116° and 118° and the name is spelled Coahuillas. As a geographical term the name was used for the valley northeast of the San Jacinto Mountains on the Land Office map of 1859 with the spelling Cohuilla, by the Whitney Survey (1873) with the spelling Coahuila, and with similar spellings on all maps published before 1891. This valley is now called Coachella Valley. Salton Sea was called Lake Cahuilla by the Pacific Railroad Survey and is still so called by some geologists. The modern names do not refer to features in Coachella Valley but to those in the valley *southwest* of the San Jacinto range and south of the San Bernardino National Forest, where another band of the Cahuilla lives. The post office Cahuilla in this valley, established April 12, 1888, west of Anza, was apparently the first geographical name from which the cluster name in this region developed; the name of the post office was changed to Anza, Sept. 16, 1926. It is not known whether the name Cahuilla has any linguistic connection with the name Kaweah applied to the Kaweah Peaks in the Sequoia National Park.

Cajalco Canyon [Riverside]. This is near the Cajalco Tin Mine, the name of which was probably coined from the name of the company operating the mine.

Cajon. The Spanish word for 'box' was used as a geographical term to describe boxlike canyons. It is included in the names of five Mexican land grants or claims—all in southern counties. **Cajon**, ká-hōn′: **Pass, Canyon, Creek,** town [San Bernardino]. The original *Cajon* was el cajon que llaman *Muscupiavit* (the canyon that they call Muscupiavit), as it was referred to before 1806, Muscupiavit being an Indian rancheria, the name of which has been spelled in various ways (SP Mis. & C., I, 241). On November 24, 1819, Padre Nuez named it solemnly el Caxon de San Gabriel de Amuscopiabit (Arch. MSB, IV, 140). The name appears in the following decades with various spellings. The abbreviated form, Cajon Pass, is used on Gibbes' map of 1852. The town was laid out when the California Southern Railroad (Santa Fe) began operations through the pass in 1885, but a settlement called Cajon had already appeared on Williamson's map of 1853. *See* El Cajon.

Cal-, Cali-. The first three or four letters of the name of the State have been used in the coining of a number of place names. Most of them are border names: Calada, Calneva, Calvada are found along the Nevada line; Calor connects with Oregon, Calzona with Arizona, Calexico with Mexico. Some have been coined from the names of business firms: Calwa [Fresno] from California Wine Association; Calpack [Merced] from California Packing Corporation; Calgro [Tulare] from California Growers Wineries, Caldor [El Dorado] from California Door Company. In others, the letters prefix another name: Calipatria [Imperial] from Latin *patria*, 'fatherland'; Calimesa [Riverside] from Spanish *mesa*, 'flat-topped hill.' Califa [Madera] and Calime [Butte] may also belong here. *See* Calistoga.

Calabazas. The Spanish name meaning 'pumpkins,' 'squash,' or 'gourds' was quite important in the cultural history of the Southwest because the gourd was an essential fruit for the Indians, who used it for food as well as for making drinking vessels and other utensils. The word appears sometimes on *diseños* to indicate a patch of pumpkins or squash, and it has survived in several place names in California. **Calabasas,** kăl-*á*-băs'-*ăs*: town, **Peak, Canyon** [Los Angeles]. The name was applied to the site, or to a rancheria at the site, prior to August 18, 1795, when it is recorded that Padre Santa María slept there (Arch. MSB, II, 11). **Calabazas Creek** [Santa Clara]. The name seems to have been especially popular south of San Francisco Bay. Besides the creek, there is a Calabasas School in the southern part of Santa Clara County. A *laguna de las calabasas* is shown on *diseños* of the Corte de Madera and Las Pulgas grants. **Calabazas Creek** [Sonoma]. The word Calabazas is shown on a *diseño* of part of the Agua Caliente grant (1840), a little west of *Arroyo de los Guilicos.* This stream may be the present Calabazas Creek. The name of the Laguna de las Calabazas grant [Santa Cruz], dated December 17, 1833, is not preserved as a current name; but there is a Calabazal Creek in Santa Barbara County.

Calaboose Creek [Monterey]. The colloquial western American term for 'jail' (from Spanish *calabozo*) was put on the map by the Geological Survey when the Jamesburg quadrangle was surveyed in 1917. The reason for the naming is not known. There is a Jail Canyon in Inyo County.

Calada. *See* Cal-.

Calaveras. The name, meaning 'skulls,' was repeatedly used in Spanish times for places where human skeletons testified to a fight or a famine. **Calaveras,** kăl-*á*-vĕr'-*ăs*: **River, Creek, County, Reservoir, Big Tree State Park.** According to John Currey ("Incidents in California," 1878, MS, Bancroft Library), John Marsh and his party in 1836 or 1837 came upon a place near the present Calaveras River where they found a great many skulls and skeletons, and afterward always referred to the place as Calaveras. Beechey in his *Narrative* (II, 28), writing in 1826, mentions "the river of *Yachicumé*," doubtless referring to the Yatchicomnes Indians, whose rancheria is shown on the Plano ... de San Jose. One of the Spanish names for the river was apparently *Rio San Juan;* this appears on Wilkes' maps of 1841 and 1849. Eld's sketch has a *San Juan* as well as a Calaveras. Frémont and Preuss fixed the latter name on the stream, *Rio de las Calaveras* (map of 1845). The county, one of the original twenty-seven, was created and named by act of the legislature, February 18, 1850. The state park was named because of its location in the county. **Calaveras: Creek, Valley, Dam** [Alameda, Santa Clara]. A *parage de las Calaveras* is mentioned as early as 1809 (Arch. SJ, III, 75), and Monument Peak at one time was known as *Cerro de las Calaveras.* José Romero, who was born in San Jose in 1800, testified in 1860 that it was so called "because when it was first discovered by the first inhabitants it was recognized ... as a place where the Indians ... kept their idols. Some remains of idols [probably skulls and bones] were found there." (*WF*, VI, 374.) Beechey (II, 426) and Duflot de Mofras (*Plan* 16) applied the name (*Calavaros*) to Coyote Creek, seven miles to the west. On the Parke-Custer map of 1855 Coyote Hills are called Calaveras Point; Hoffmann (1873) designated the upper part of Arroyo Hondo as Calaveras Creek. A *Cerro de la Calavera* is shown on the San Luis Rey, and a *Cañada de las Calaveras* on the Lompoc, atlas sheet. A land grant called Calaveras in San Joaquin County, dated July 11, 1846, was later rejected by the U.S. Supreme Court.

Calaveritas, kăl-*á*-vĕ-rē'-*tăs*: **Creek,** ghost town [Calaveras]. The name of the creek, a tributary to the South Fork of Calaveras River, is a diminutive in the sense of 'Little Calaveras River.' Hoffmann (1873) has Calaveritas River. The site of the town is Historic Landmark 255.

Caldor. *See* Cal-.

Caldwell Butte, Ice Cave [Lava Beds National

Monument]. Named for a "professor from Boston," who settled in the vicinity with his wife and two daughters and started a horse ranch (Howard).

Calera. The word for 'limekiln' was repeatedly used in Spanish times for place names. **Arroyo Calero, Calero Reservoir** [Santa Clara]. A *paraje de la Calera* is mentioned on August 16, 1803 (Prov. Recs., XI, 183). The misspelling is now found on all maps. **Calera Creek** [Santa Clara]. This tributary to Coyote River was named for a *calera* mentioned on October 24, 1807 (Arch. SJ, IV, 17). As a geographical name, *el paraje de la Calera*, it is used in 1828 (Registro, p. 19). **Calera Valley** [San Mateo]. *Cañada de la Calera* is shown on a *diseño* of the San Pedro land grant, 1838. The limekiln was on a point south of Laguna Salada. **La Calera y las Positas** [Santa Barbara]. The name, meaning 'limekiln and water holes,' was applied to a land grant dated May 8, 1843, and July 1, 1846.

Calexico. *See* Cal-.

Calgro. *See* Cal-.

Calico Hills [San Bernardino], **Calico Peaks** [Death Valley National Monument]. "The colors . . . are a kaleidoscopic mixture of light and dark—the light shades are yellowish-white to buff, and the dark shades dull pinkish to red. Such assemblages of particolored Tertiary volcanic rocks are called calico by the prospectors throughout the desert region, and the hills formed from them are called calico hills, the Calico Peaks being themselves an example of this usage." (Geol. Soc. *Bulletin*, LII, 969.) According to Weight (*Desert Magazine*, July, 1953), Walter Knott bought the ghost town in 1951 to restore "the greatest southern California silver camp as it was in the heyday of its 1880's boom."

Caliente, kăl-ĭ-ĕn'-tĭ: **Mountain, Range** [San Luis Obispo]. The name, meaning 'hot,' does not refer to the temperature of the mountains. It has its origin in the Ojo Caliente, recorded on the Parke-Custer map of 1855 in the Cuyama Valley, south of the mountain, and refers obviously to the hot spring. **Caliente: town, Creek, Canyon** [Kern]. A trading post for Indians and cowboys was established here in the 1870's and named Caliente because of the hot springs in the canyon. The name was retained by the Southern Pacific when the company established a grading camp in 1874. The settlement had originally been called Allens Camp, because a sheep owner named Allen had his camp here. *See* Agua Caliente.

Califa. *See* Cal-, Cali-.

California. The discovery of the New World by Columbus gave a strong momentum to the age-old search for an earthly paradise with unbounded productiveness without labor, with beautiful women, gold, and pearls. Among a number of such utopias, created by the fertile imaginations of fiction writers and ambitious explorers, was the rich island of *California*, inhabited by handsome black women like Amazons. The story of this extraordinary realm and its queen Calafia was recounted and published about 1500 in *Las sergas de Esplandián*, by the Spanish writer, Montalvo, as a continuation of the famous romance, *Amadís de Gaula*. It was the distinguished American writer, Edward Everett Hale, who in 1862 pointed out the probable connection between the name of the utopia and the name of the State. The location attributed to this island, "at the right hand of the Indies, . . . very close to that part of the Terrestrial Paradise, which was inhabited by black women . . . ," places it definitely in the same group as El Dorado, the Seven Cities of Cibola, Quivira, and other realms eagerly sought by the Spanish conquerors. The name was probably coined and has no definite meaning. It is, of course, possible that the author may have thought of the Arabic *caliph* (supreme ruler) and *caliphat* (sovereignty) when he formed the word. In spite of the Christians' hatred for the Moslem, the Mohammedan Orient had exercised, since the days of the Crusades, a strong influence upon Western European culture. Indeed, a similar name for the Arabic domain, *Califerne*, is found in the French epic, the *Chanson de Roland*. (For a detailed discussion of the various theories about the origin and etymology of the name, *see* Ruth Putnam, "California: The Name," *UCPH*, IV, 356–362; Chapman, chap. vi; Stewart, pp. 14 ff.) The precise date and circumstances of the application of the name to some part of what is now called Lower California is not known. The historian Antonio de Herrera in 1601 stated definitely that it was Cortés himself "who placed this name upon it" (*que le puso este nombre*). However, it seems more probable that the mutinous pilot of the Becerra expedition, Fortún Jiménez, discovered the peninsula in the winter of 1533, and it is not impossible that he called the newly discovered land

California. Upon hearing of the discovery of the territory and the finding of pearls, Cortés himself set out for the new land in

April, 1535; but he called the harbor in which he anchored Santa Cruz (Chapman, p. 65) and on his map shows the peninsula as Santa Cruz (Wagner, p. 16). By 1542, however, navigators were using the name California (report of the Cabrillo-Ferrer voyage in Bolton, *Span. Expl.,* pp. 3–39). It is a matter of conjecture whether Jiménez applied the name and sailors kept it alive by word of mouth, or another navigator after 1535, believing that he had come upon the land of the Amazons, applied the name. It took several decades for it to get on the maps and thus become definitely established. If its appearance on Castillo's map of 1541, which is considered to be a later interpolation (Wagner, p. 32), be disregarded, the name perhaps first appears on two maps of 1562: *Golfo de la California* on the map of South America in the Olives atlas in the Vatican (Wagner, No. 60), and *C[abo] California* on Diego Gutiérrez' map (reproduced by Putnam, *op. cit.*). The great Mercator himself applied the name to the peninsula now called Lower California, in 1569; his map of the North Polar regions (reproduced in Nordenskiöld, p. 95) shows the peninsula with the legend: *Califormia* [!] *regio sola fama Hispanis nota* (California region known to the Spanish by hearsay only). The name remained restricted to the peninsula. Map makers frequently placed the mythical kingdom of Quivira in the general vicinity of what is now the State of California. After Drake (1579) had applied the name New Albion to the region north of San Francisco, this name, as well as Quivira, was often used. When, throughout most of the 17th century, cartographers believed that the peninsula was really an island, there was no longer any space left for Quivira and New Albion on the maps, but California remained as the name of the island. However, even before Kino reëstablished the peninsular character of California in 1705, the French cartographer Guillaume Delisle had extended the name into the area included in the present State of California (Wagner, No. 459). The Spaniards, for the sake of priority of claim, applied the name to the entire coast, while the British, for the same reason, again called the region which is now within our State, New Albion. When the Spaniards in 1769 renewed their interest in colonizing the coast, the terms *Baja California* and *Alta* (or *Nueva*) *California* were applied. In common American usage, however, the term Califor-

nia referred to the region now within the State's borders, even before the American occupation. (For further information on the name, see *Names,* II, 121 ff., 196, 249 ff., 275.)

Calime. *See* Cal-, Cali-.

Calimesa. *See* Cal-.

Calipatria. *See* Cal-.

Calistoga [Napa]. In 1859 Sam Brannan bought the place called Agua Caliente and developed it as a resort. His recent biographer, Reva Scott, lets Sam tell the story of its naming: "As I was saying, I named Calistoga in the first place . . . 'Someday I'll make this place the Saratoga of California,' I started to say, but my tongue slipped and what I said was, 'I'll make this place the Calistoga of Sarafornia' " (*Samuel Brannan*, p. 384).

Callahan [Siskiyou]. Named for M. B. Callahan, who built a cabin at the foot of Mount Bolivar in 1851 and opened a hotel there in 1852 (Co. Hist., 1881, p. 215).

Callan, Camp [San Diego]. Established by the War Department in 1940 as a training center for antiaircraft artillery and named in honor of General Robert E. Callan (1874–1936), a veteran of the Spanish-American War and World War I.

Calleguas, käl'-ê-gäs: **Creek** [Ventura]. Padre Vicente de Santa María visited in August, 1795, an Indian rancheria the name of which he spelled *Cayegues* (Arch. MSB, II, 9–17). The name appears with the present spelling as the name of a land grant dated May 10, 1837, and again in the Land Office reports. The Parke-Custer map of 1855 has Cayegua. According to Kroeber, the name is derived from a Chumash word meaning 'my head.'

Calneva. *See* Cal-.

Calor. *See* Cal-, Cali-.

Calpack. *See* Cal-.

Calpella, käl-pĕl'-á [Mendocino]. Kalpela, the name of the chief of a northern Pomo village (Barrett, *Pomo*, p. 143), was applied to his people, and later to all the Indians of Redwood Valley, by the white settlers (Kroeber). Redick McKee mentions the chief under date of August 21, 1851, and uses the present spelling (Indian Report). The possible meaning is 'mussel bearer,' from *khal, hal,* 'mussel,' and *pela, pelo,* 'carry,' 'pack' (Kroeber). The town was founded in 1858 by C. H. Veeder.

Calpine [Sierra]. The place developed in 1919 around the mill and yards of the Davies-Johnson Lumber Company and was known as McAlpine. After the Post Office Department rejected the name for the post office in 1922, the abbreviated form was used. (L. C.

Hjelte.)

Caltech Peak [Tulare]. The high peak bears the general popular abbreviation for California Institute of Technology.

Calvada. *See* Cal-

Calwa. *See* Cal-.

Calzona. *See* Cal-.

Camajal y Palomar [San Diego]. A land grant dated August 1, 1846. *Mesa de Camajal* and *Cañada de Palomar* (valley of the pigeon roost) are shown on a *diseño*. *Camajal* was the name of two Indian villages in 1852, according to B. D. Wilson. *See* Palomar.

Camanche, kȧ-măn′-chĕ [Calaveras]; **Comanche: Creek, Point** [Kern]. A transfer name from the Middle West. The Comanche were the only Shoshonean tribe that moved to the plains and "lived on the buffalo." This is perhaps the reason that they were called *Kumantsi,* meaning 'different,' 'distinctive.' (Leland, *CFQ,* V, 391.) The town in Calaveras County was named in 1849 after the town in Iowa. It is now covered by the Camanche Reservoir, completed in 1963.

Camarillo, kăm-ȧ-rē′-ō [Ventura]. When the Ventura section of the Southern Pacific was built in the 1880's, the name was applied to the station in memory of Juan Camarillo, owner of Rancho Calleguas from 1859 until his death in 1880.

Cambria [San Luis Obispo]. The place was settled in the 1860's and called Slabtown. When the town became more self-conscious, the names Santa Rosa and Rosaville were suggested because it was built on Rancho Santa Rosa. A Welshman named Llewellyn wanted the place to be known by the Roman name of his homeland. He hung the sign "Cambria Carpenter Shop" over the door of his place of business and won the day. The new name is mentioned in a letter of November 18, 1870 (Pico Docs., III, 394), but the von Leicht–Craven map of 1874 still shows both names: Cambria and Santa Rosa.

Camel. Most of the Camel Hills, Humps, and Mounds of the State were so named because of their shape. Some of the creek names may refer to the camels imported in 1857 when an expensive and abortive attempt was made to introduce the "ship of the desert" as a transportation animal into California; others were so called because the fossils of a prehistoric camel were found there.

Cameron Creek [Tulare]. The name is shown on Williamson's map of 1855, and was probably applied for a settler. The notion that the name is derived from the Spanish *camarón,*

'shrimp,' is hardly admissible. There were no Spanish settlements in this region.

Cameron Valley [San Diego]. Named for the first settlers here. A Cameron Station on the Yuma stage route is mentioned on October 27, 1870, in the San Diego *Union.*

Camino. The Spanish word meaning 'road,' 'trail,' or 'route' has been applied to communities in El Dorado and Los Angeles counties, probably just for its sound. **El Camino Real,** kȧ-mē′-nō rä-äl′. In Spanish days *camino real, camino nacional,* or *camino principal* designated the public roads and trails between presidios, missions, and settlements (Bowman). The name is now applied to the modern highways connecting the missions and is often erroneously interpreted to mean the 'king's highway.'

Camp. Military reservations are listed under their specific names.

Camp. Besides military reservations, the names of many summer resorts are preceded or followed by this generic term. Many creeks and canyons and some settlements were named after some camp now disappeared. Camp Two [Siskiyou], Camp Seven [Mendocino], Camp Nine [Humboldt] survived from numbered railroad or lumber camps. *See* Camphora. **Camp Meeker** [Sonoma]. In 1876 the place was known as Meeker's, later as Camp Meeker, for Melvin C. Meeker, an early settler and lumberman. **Camp Steffani** [Monterey]. Joseph Steffani, a native of Switzerland, settled here about 1888 and later subdivided part of his two-thousand-acre ranch for summer homes. The original name, Camp Carmel, was changed to the present name in 1910. It is misspelled Stephani on the Jamesburg atlas sheet. (F. Feliz.) **Camp Curry** [Yosemite National Park]. Established June 1, 1899, by David A. Curry (1860–1917) and Jennie Curry (1861–1948). **Camp Independence** [Inyo]. Historic Landmark 349. *See* Independence. **Camp Inis,** ē′-nĕz [Lake]. The name, applied in the 1890's, was coined from the name Campini's Campgrounds (Mauldin). **Camp Creek** [El Dorado]. The important affluent to Cosumnes River was named by the Mormons on their march from Sutters Fort to Salt Lake City. They camped here on July 16, 1848 (Bigler, p. 114).

Campbell: Creek, town [Santa Clara]. The creek was named for William Campbell, an immigrant of 1846, who established a sawmill here in 1848 and a stage station in 1852. The stream was also known as Arroyo Quito, Big

Moody Creek, and Saratoga Creek. The town was founded by his son, Benjamin Campbell, in 1885. By decision of the Geographic Board (May, 1954) the stream now officially bears the name Saratoga Creek. *See* Saratoga.

Campbell Creek [Shasta]. Jeremiah B. Campbell was a settler of 1855 and a prominent ichthyologist (Steger).

Campbell, Mount [Fresno]. The mountain was named for William Campbell, who operated a store at Poole's Ferry on the Kings River (Co. Hist., 1956).

Campbells: Point, Cove [Sonoma]. The point, officially known as Bodega Head, near the spot where Bodega brought his sloop to anchor in 1775, is known locally as Campbells Point, for Captain John Campbell, a pioneer ranch owner.

Camphora, kăm-fôr′-à [Monterey]. Mexican railroad workers referred to Camp Four, a construction camp set up here in 1873, as Camphora. The railroad officials adopted the name for the station. (Paul Parker, *CFQ*, I, 295.)

Campito: Peak, Meadow [Mono]. The coined name, suggesting 'little field' or 'little camp,' was probably applied by a surveyor who tried to bring a touch of Spanish into the White Mountains. Blanco Peak and Tres Plumas Flat are close by.

Campo. The Spanish word for 'field' is preserved in the names of a number of physical features and of two communities in San Diego and Calaveras counties. In Mexican Spanish the word also means 'mining camp' and in California was often simply used in the sense of 'camp.' Hence the old mining town Campo Seco [Calaveras] was probably not a 'dry field,' but a 'dry camp,' and the land grant **Campo de los Franceses** [San Joaquin], dated January 13, 1844, was simply 'Camp of the Frenchmen,' so named because the French-Canadian trappers made their camp there in the 1830's.

Camptonville [Yuba]. In 1850 or 1851, J. M. and J. Campbell built a hotel, the Nevada House, at this place. In 1854 the town was named for the blacksmith, Robert Campton. (Co. Hist., 1879, p. 98.)

Camuesa, kă-mōō′-sà: **Canyon, Peak** [Santa Barbara]. The name is probably derived from Spanish *camuza* (or *gamuza*), 'chamois,' and was applied because the squaws tanned buckskin when the Indians camped here while on a hunt (Wm. S. Brown). Buckhorn Creek and Indian Creek, near by, seem to bear out this statement. Camuesa is the Mexican name of

Opuntia robusta, but this particular species of cactus is not native to California.

Camulos, kăm′-ŭ-lŏs [Ventura]. The name was originally that of a Chumash village or was the Chumash name of a Shoshonean village. According to Kroeber, it contains the root *mulus*, the name of an edible fruit. A *paraje de Camulo (Camulus le llaman los Naturales* [Camulus the natives call it]) is mentioned in a letter of April 27, 1804 (Arch. Arz. SF, II, 36). This apparently was just on the line between Chumash and Shoshonean territory. In a report of May 19, 1821, a rancho called *Camulus* is mentioned (Arch. Arz. SF, Vol. IV, Pt. 1, p. 61), and the name Camulos appears repeatedly in documents. A *diseño* of the land grant Camulos or Alamos y Agua Caliente, dated October 2, 1843, shows a *Rio*, a *Lomeria*, and a *Cañada de Camulos*. The name does not seem to be recorded on early American maps and was preserved probably when the Southern Pacific reached the place in the 1880's and gave the old Indian name to the station.

Cañada. The Spanish word for 'valley' was perhaps the most common generic term used before the American occupation. Unlike the related terms, *cañon* and *arroyo*, it did not survive as a generic term. In Ventura and Santa Barbara counties, to be sure, American surveyors not only kept the existing Canadas, but applied the generic term to many gulches. Neither spelling nor pronunciation of the word is uniform. The Corps of Engineers has restored the Spanish spelling, Cañada, on most of its atlas sheets. The following pronunciations are current in different parts of the State: kăn′-à-dà, kà-nä′-dà, kăn-yăd′-à, kàn-yä′-dà, the last approximating the proper Spanish pronunciation. **Canada Verruga**, 'wart valley' [San Diego]. "It was named by the public from the fact that in 1864 an old Indian squatter settled here. He was more intelligent than the rest, but was known particularly by all the settlers of these parts as Verruga because of a very large and prominent wart on the side of his neck. His ranch was always spoken of as Verruga Ranch and so this canyon came to be known as Canada Verruga." (J. Jasper.) **La Canada**, kăn-yăd′-à [Los Angeles]. The post office was established about 1890 and named after the land grant La Cañada, dated May 12, 1843. **Cañada Verde** [San Mateo]. The name, 'green valley,' was given to a land grant dated March 25, 1838. **Cañada Larga o Verde** [Ventura]. The name of a land grant dated January 30, 1841.

Other names of land grants beginning with Cañada are listed under their specific names.

Canadian Creek [Trinity]. This and several other features were obviously named for settlers from Canada. The Canadian element in California was much stronger than these few names seem to indicate, but the French Canadians were ordinarily called "French" and the British were not sufficiently distinguished from other English-speaking people.

Canby; Fort Canby [Modoc]. The post office was named for General Edward R. S. Canby, murdered in 1873 during the Modoc War.

Candlestick: Point, Cove, Park Stadium [San Francisco]. In 1894 the Coast Survey established a triangulation station here and named it after Candlestick Rock, an eight-foot sharp pinnacle shown on the map of the Board of Tide Land Commissioners, 1869. The extreme eastern part of the stadium structure marks the approximate location of the pinnacle. (F. B. Rogers)

Canebrake Creek [Kern]. The Pacific R. R. Survey applied the Indian name Chay-o-pooya-päh, 'creek of the bullrushes,' in 1853 (*Reports*, Vol. V, Pt. 1, p. 15). The modern name ('place overgrown with cane') was used by the Geological Survey in 1908. *See* Kane Spring.

Canfield [Kern]. The name commemorates C. A. Canfield, who, with other former gold miners, started prospecting for oil with pick and shovel about 1895, and discovered the rich deposits near Fellows.

Canoas. The Spanish word for 'canoes,' used in Mexico also for 'troughs,' is preserved in the names of two creeks [Fresno, Santa Clara] and in Cinco [five] Canoas Canyon [Monterey].

Canoe River. *See* Cow Creek.

Canoga Park [Los Angeles]. The name Canoga was applied to the station when the Southern Pacific branch from Burbank was built in the 1890's. Park was added when the community developed. It was probably named after Canoga, New York, which had taken its name from the Indian village *Ganogeh*, 'place of floating oil' (Hodge). The original name of this section of Los Angeles was Owensmouth, which is still used for the name of a street (Gregory Stein). The name of the post office was also Owensmouth from 1912 to 1931.

Canon. The names of the creeks in Humboldt and Trinity counties are probably American renderings of the Spanish term *cañon*. *See* Canyon.

Canthook: Creek, Mountain, Prairie [Del Norte]. The name of the important tool used to turn logs seems very appropriate as a place name in the midst of a lumber district.

Cantil [Kern]. The name was given to the station when the Nevada and California Railroad was extended from Owens Lake to Mojave in 1908–1909. The Spanish word means 'steep rock,' but it may have been applied only because the location engineer was fond of names beginning with "C." Cambio, Cinco, Ceneda are other station names in this sector.

Cantu [Imperial]. The name of the Mexican colonel, Esteban Cantú, was applied to the station when the branch of the Inter-California Railroad (Southern Pacific) was built from Calexico to Yuma, 1904–1909. The post office name is Andrade.

Cantua Creek [Fresno]. Cantua Creek, mentioned in the 1850's, is said to have been one of the retreats of Joaquin Murieta, the bandit. It is shown on Goddard's map of 1857 and was named for a member of the Cantua family, in Mexican times prominent in the Monterey district. Waltham Creek at Coalinga was formerly also known as Cantua Creek (Geographic Board, May 6, 1908).

Canyon. "The Spaniards . . . had a word meaning pipe or cannon, and in Mexico they had come to use it also for a narrow watercourse among mountains. The trappers needed such a word; they took over *cañon*, and spread it across all the West as *canyon*." (Stewart, p. 221.) In California, as in other western states, the word has become a true generic term and is used more frequently than older English terms. However, it has assumed the meaning of 'narrow valley,' 'ravine,' 'gulch'; hence the numerous tautological Canyon (sometimes Canon) Creeks. **Canyon** [Contra Costa]. Abbreviated from New Redwood Canyon, where the post office was established in the 1910's. In the early 1920's the name was temporarily changed to the more melodious name Sequoya. The word is found in the names of other inhabited places: Canyondam [Plumas], Canyon Park [Humboldt], Canyon Tank [Tuolumne].

Capay, kä-pä': town, **Valley, Canal** [Yolo]. The origin of the name is found in the Southern Wintun word for 'stream' (Kroeber). A rancheria named *Capa* in what is now Colusa County is mentioned October 27, 1821 (Arch. MSB, IV, 169–190). The name appears with the present spelling in the land grant Cañada de Capay, dated January 26, 1846. Gibbs, in 1851, applied the name with the spelling

Copéh to the Indians living on Putah Creek. The town in Yolo County was first called Munchville, then Langville, both for early settlers. The name Capay appears also in two other land grants in Tehama, Glenn, and Butte counties, but here it did not survive as a place name.

Cape Horn. Many of our pioneers on their journey to California experienced the "rounding of the Horn," and Cape Horn became a favorite name for places where the going was tough. The name is preserved in San Diego, Los Angeles, Fresno, Mendocino, Shasta, Siskiyou, and Placer counties. The Southern Pacific station near Colfax [Placer] was named by the construction engineers in 1866 because of the difficult curve and grade. Lassens Horn, the old name of Fandango Pass [Modoc], was doubtless named in analogy to Cape Horn. Dana jokingly called Point Conception "the Cape Horn of California, where ... it begins to blow the first of January, and blows until the last of December."

Capell Creek [Humboldt]. The name is derived from that of an Indian village, mentioned by Heintzelman in 1858. Waterman (p. 248) spells the name *Ke'pel* and translates it as 'house-pit.' Goddard's map of 1857 shows the name Capell west of the confluence of Klamath and Trinity rivers.

Capell: Valley, Creek [Napa]. Named for the first settler in the valley. The Indian name of the creek had been *To-bi-pa,* 'running water.' (D. T. Davis.)

Capistrano Beach [Orange]. The post office was established October 1, 1925. On March 1, 1931, the name was changed to Doheny Park, for E. L. Doheny, a California oil promoter, who had laid out the townsite in the 1920's. On January 1, 1948, the name was changed back to Capistrano Beach. Capistrano is a short form for San Juan Capistrano. *See* San Juan Capistrano.

Capitan; Canada del Capitan; El Capitan Beach [Santa Barbara]. *Arroyo de Capitan* is mentioned in 1804 (Prov. Recs., XI, 104), and *paraje del Capitan* in 1817 (PSP, XX, 177). The *cañada* is shown on a *diseño* (1840) of Rancho Cañada del Corral. The name may commemorate *el Capitán* José Francisco Ortega, though the valley is several miles east of the boundaries established for the Ortega grant. *See* El Capitan.

Capitancillos, Cañada de los [Santa Clara]. The name was applied to a land grant dated June 16, 1842. *Capitancillo* is a diminutive of *capitán,* 'captain' or 'chief.'

Capitan Grande Indian Reservation [San Diego]. The land was set aside and named by executive order of President U. S. Grant, December 27, 1875. The canyon of the upper San Diego River in which the reservation lies was formerly known as the Capitan Grande Canyon. *See* El Capitan.

Capitola [Santa Cruz]. The place was developed as a resort by F. A. Hihn in 1876 and called Camp Capitola, apparently a publicity name coined from "capitol." Mr. Hihn is mentioned as a German living in Santa Cruz in the 1880's. According to the *Mining Bureau,* XVII, 235, he is said to have founded his fortune on a large amount of gold taken from a huge boulder in a creek issuing from Ben Lomond Mountain.

Captain Jacks: Stronghold, Ice Cave [Lava Beds National Monument]. The two names honor "Captain Jack," the heroic Indian leader in the Modoc War of 1872–1873.

Carbondale [Amador]. This name, and that of near-by Lignite, keep alive the memory of one of the greatest coal booms in California history. The deposits in Ione Valley were discovered before 1870, and in 1877 the Central Pacific built a branch line from Galt with Carbondale as the principal station for shipping "black diamonds." Although the coal proved useless for locomotives, these mines were profitably worked for a number of years. Carbon [Mendocino], Carbona [San Joaquin], Carbondale [Orange], Historical Landmark 228, and various other combinations with 'carbon' or 'coal' are reminders of other booms.

Carbonera, La [Santa Cruz]. A land grant dated February 3, 1838. A *carbonera* is a place where charcoal is made.

Cardiff-by-the-Sea [San Diego]. The town was laid out in 1911 by J. Frank Cullen and named after the seaport in Wales. The place was formerly called San Elijo after the near-by lagoon.

Cardinal: Mountain, Lake [Kings Canyon National Park]. The mountain was thus named by George R. Davis, of the Geological Survey, because the brilliant coloring of the mountain's summit looked like the red hat of a cardinal (Farquhar).

Careaga: Canyon, station [Santa Barbara]. Named for Juan B. Careaga of the firm Careaga and Harris, which cultivated a tract near Los Alamos in the early 1880's (Co. Hist., 1883, p. 295).

Caribou. The name of the finest representative of Canada's fauna is included in a number of place names in Trinity, Siskiyou, Shasta, Lassen, and Plumas counties. There is even a Caribou Creek in the Mojave Desert [San Gorgonio quadrangle]. These names arose when California prospectors returned from British Columbia, where the famous Cariboo mines were opened in 1858. Some were probably taken directly from the mines, and others may have been given for persons nicknamed Caribou. (Stewart, *CFQ*, V, 393 ff.)

Carillon, Mount [Sequoia National Park]. The bell-tower shape of the mountain suggested this name to Chester Versteeg, and it was adopted by the Geographic Board in 1938.

Carlotta [Humboldt]. When the Northwestern Pacific was built in 1903, John M. Vance, a pioneer of 1865, laid out the town and named it for his youngest daughter, Carlotta, later Mrs. Lester W. Hink of Berkeley.

Carlsbad [San Diego]. Known in 1884 as Frazier's Station, for John A. Frazier, who discovered the spring. In 1886 Gerhard Schutte and his associates tested the waters, found them like those of Karlsbad, Bohemia, and transferred the name to the town. Carlsbad Beach State Park was named after the town in 1933.

Carmel, kär-mĕl': **River, Valley, Bay, Mission, Point; Mount Carmel; Carmel-by-the-Sea** [Monterey]. The river was discovered by Vizcaíno, January 3, 1603, and called *Rio del Carmelo,* probably because three friars of the Carmelite order were members of the expedition (Wagner, p. 379). In 1771, Serra and Crespi removed Mission San Carlos from Monterey to the site by the *Rio del Carmelo* (Engelhardt, II, 87), and it soon became known as Mission Carmelo although officially the old name was retained. Except for the town which developed in modern times, and Mount Carmel, which received its name from the Coast Survey in 1856, all the features were named in Spanish times. Malaspina's map of Monterey Bay, 1791, records *Rio del Carmelo, Punta del Carmelo,* and *Ensenada de Carmelo.* Although the form Carmel appears as early as 1798 for the river (English translation of La Pérouse, *Voyage,* II, 204) and for the triangulation point of the Coast Survey (Mount Carmel, 1856), the Americanization of the name was slow. Bancroft established the modern version in his popular maps of the 1860's. Wood's *Gazetteer* (1912) still has Carmelo River. A creek emptying into Glicko Creek, a tributary to the Carmel River, is named Carmelocitos River on the Land Office map of 1907. Modern Carmel-

by-the-Sea was so named to distinguish it from another Carmel which was some ten miles inland. A land grant called *Carmel,* in Yolo County, dated May 4, 1846, was rejected by the U. S. Supreme Court. For the application of the name Point Carmel to Point Lobos, *see* Lobos Rocks [Monterey].

Carmenita [Los Angeles]. Laid out in the boom year of 1887 on the land grant Los Coyotes. In the region of Granada, Spain, *carmen* means country home, and this form might have been considered a diminutive. It might also have been a girl's name.

Carmen Lake. *See* Kirman.

Carmichael [Sacramento]. Named in 1910 by the owner of the land, for himself (G. H. Artz).

Carnadero Creek [Santa Clara]. The word *carnadero* (or *carneadero*), probably meaning 'butchering place,' is recorded for a place in the vicinity as early as January 23, 1784 (PSP, V, 70). In the following decades the name appears repeatedly in documents and on maps, and was used as an alternate name for the Las Animas grant. Carnadero River is mentioned by Trask in 1854 and is shown on Hoffmann's map of 1873.

Carne Humana [Napa]. A land grant dated March 14, 1841, appears in the records with various spellings: *Huilic Noma, Caligolman, Colijolmanoc. See* Bale.

Carnelian Bay [Placer]. The bay which indents the northwest shore of Lake Tahoe was named by the Whitney Survey because of the presence of the variety of chalcedony known as carnelian and as Cambay stone. The name is shown on the von Leicht–Hoffmann Tahoe map of 1874. The post office is listed in 1910.

Carneros Creek [Napa]. The name (*carneros,* sheep) is derived from that of the land grant Los Carneros (part of the Entre Napa grant), dated May 9, 1836. *Arroyo de los Carneros* is shown on *diseños* of the Huichica grant of 1844 and others of the period. Carnero Creek and Carnero Mountain (probably Bismarck Knob) are mentioned in the *Statutes* of 1850; Carnero Ridge, in *Hutchings' Illustrated California Magazine* (III, 355). Land grants in Monterey County, dated May 13, 1834, August 16, 1839, and October 5, 1842, were, named Los Carneros, a name from which apparently no present-day name has sprung. Kern County has a Carneros Spring and a Carneros Canyon (Geographic Board, April 7, 1909). **Carneros Valley** [Santa Barbara]. A place *Los Carneros* is shown on a *diseño* of the land grant Dos Pueblos (1842), and an arroyo is labeled Carnero on a *diseño* of La Goleta (1846). The name is misspelled Cameros on the Goleta atlas sheet.

Carpenter Valley [Nevada]. The small settlement at the north fork of Prosser Creek was probably named for John S. Carpenter, who in the 1860's was engaged in hauling logs to "Old Hobart Mills" (H. P. Davis).

Carpinteria, kär-pĭn-tĕ-rē'-à: **Creek, Lagoon, town, State Park** [Santa Barbara]. The Portolá expedition reached the Indian village at this place on August 17, 1769. "The Indians have many canoes, and at the time were building one, for which reason the soldiers named this town *La Carpintería* [the carpenter shop], while I christened it with the name of San Roque." (Crespi, p. 164.) The name La Carpinteria is repeatedly mentioned in early manuscripts. The post office was named Carpinteria in 1868. The park was created and named in 1932. A land grant Cañada de la Carpinteria, in Monterey County, was dated October 12, 1831, and September 25, 1835.

Carquinez, kär-kē'-nĕs: **Strait, Point, Bridge** [Solano, Contra Costa]. The strait and Suisun Bay were discovered by the Fages expedition in 1772. Font (*Compl. Diary*, p. 336) in 1776 called it *Boca del Puerto Dulce* (mouth of the fresh-water port). The present name is derived from the Karquin Indians, many of whom were mentioned in the baptismal records of Mission Dolores between 1795 and 1821. In a geographical sense the name is used by Abella in 1807: *Rancheria de los Karquines* and *Estrecho de los Karquines* (Arch. Arz. SF, II, 55). Belcher (I, 118) used the same spelling in 1837. In 1837, at Santa Ynez, Padre Arroyo wrote down a number of words spoken by the natives of the *Rancheria de Karkin* which he had heard at Mission Dolores in January, 1821. In the manuscript "Lecciones de Indios" (p. 20) he makes the statement: *el Karkin, que significa trocar* (... which means 'exchange' or 'barter'). Hence *Rancheria de los Karquines* could have meant 'village of the traders.' The present spelling, although official (*Statutes*, 1850), was not generally adopted until the 20th century. The Coast Survey used the spelling Karquines until 1905.

Carriger Creek [Sonoma]. Named for Nicholas Carriger, pioneer of 1846, mail carrier from Sonoma to San Rafael during the Mexican War, farmer in the district after 1850.

Carrillo Beach State Park [Los Angeles]. The name was applied in 1953 for the prominent southern California family. Leo Carrillo, the actor, later became a member of the State Park Commission.

Carrisalito: Spring, Creek [Merced]. The name is derived from the name of the land grant Panoche de San Juan y Los Carrisalitos (reed sugar of St. John and the little patches of reed grass), dated February 10, 1844.

Carrizo. The word means 'reed grass, bunch grass, cane'; it appeared frequently as a place name in Spanish times because the plant was of great importance to California Indians, who made their sweetening substance, *panoche,* from it. **Carrizo: Creek, Gorge, Station** [San Diego, Imperial]. The *carrizo* was mentioned by Font when the Anza party camped at the junction of Carrizo and San Felipe creeks, December 13, 1775 (*Compl. Diary*, p. 130). The name is recorded on Wilkes' map (1841) as Carisal, and by Emory as Cariso Creek in 1848, and appears with various spellings in the Pacific Railroad *Reports*. An attempt to Americanize it to Cane Creek was unsuccessful. **Carrizo Creek** [San Diego]. *Carizal* is shown on a *diseño* of Agua Caliente (1840 or 1844). The name has also survived in San Luis Obispo and Riverside counties.

Carroll Creek [Inyo]. Named for A. W. de la Cour Carroll, of Lone Pine, a charter member of the Sierra Club (Robinson).

Carrville [Trinity]. Named for the James E. Carr family, on whose land the town was built. The Carr ranch had been established in 1852 and was first called Ruch ranch.

Carson: Creek, Flat, Hill [Calaveras]. The town Carson Hill, the Slumgullion of Bret Harte's story, was named for James H. Carson, a native of Virginia who came to California as a soldier in 1847. In 1848 he discovered gold here, and his diggings became known as Carson's Creek. He was a member-elect of the legislature when he died in 1853. Hill and Creek are shown on Gibbes' map of 1852. *See* Melones. Carson Hill is Historic Landmark 274.

Carson: River, Valley, Pass, Hill, Range [Alpine]. The river, which appeared for the first time on the Preuss map of 1848, was named by Frémont for his guide, Christopher (Kit) Carson (1809–1868), with whom he had crossed the Sierra Nevada in 1844. Kit Carson Marker (Kit Carson Pass) is Historic Landmark 315. The stream had been named Pilot River on August 5, 1848, by Bigler and the Mormons on their march to Salt Lake City.

Carsons [Humboldt]. Probably named for William Carson, who came to California in 1850 from New Brunswick and was prominent as a banker and lumberman in Humboldt County.

Cartago [Inyo]. The Spanish name for the ancient city in North Africa was applied to the station by the Southern Pacific when the Mojave-Owenyo branch reached the place in 1909, and was given to the post office in 1919. A settlement and a creek near by bear the Engish version, Carthage.

Cartridge Creek [Kings Canyon National Park]. Named in the 1870's by Frank Lewis: "While hunting there with a young friend, Harrison Hill, I wounded a bear and told him to finish it. He became excited and threw all the shells out of his Winchester without firing a shot." (Lewis to Farquhar.)

Caruthers [Fresno]. Named in the 1890's for W. A. Caruthers, a local farmer.

Cary Peak [Alpine]. Named for the Carey (or Cary) brothers, settlers in the vicinity in the early 1850's. William Carey owned a small ranch; John Carey established a sawmill at the place which later became known as Woodfords.

Casa. The Spanish word for 'house' is found in a number of place names, apparently all applied in American times. **Casa Diablo: Mountain, Lake, Hot Springs** [Mono]. The mountain was named after the Casa Diablo Mine on the west slope. The name was also transported to the springs (and lake) about fifteen miles west. **Casa Blanca** [Riverside]. When the railroad station was built in 1887, a white house visible from the right of way prompted the Santa Fe to bestow the Spanish name. In both Riverside and Orange counties there is an ungrammatical combination: Casa Loma instead of Casa de la Loma.

Casaba [Imperial]. The name was applied to the Southern Pacific station when the branch from Niland was built in 1916–1917. The casaba is a melon which was grown originally in Kasaba, Asia Minor.

Cascade Range. The name applies now to the entire range from British Columbia to the gap south of Lassen Peak (Geographic Board, *Fifth Report*, 1920). The name is derived from that of the Cascades of the Columbia River. Cascade Mountains and Cascade Range of Mountains are mentioned in the journal (1823–1827) of the botanist David Douglas. Because of the orographic vagueness of the section extending into California, the name did not appear on the maps of the State until recently. For a full discussion, see Lewis A. McArthur, *Oregon Geographic Names*. In addition to the Cascade Range, which is really an Oregon name, about fifteen features in California, mostly creeks, are named Cascade. The best known are the Cascades and Cascade Cliffs in Yosemite National Park.

Case Mountain [Tulare]. Named for Bill Case, who used to run a team of four different animals: a horse, a mule, a burro, and a steer (Farquhar).

Casitas: Creek, Springs, Pass, Valley [Ventura]. The *Arroyo de las Casitas* (creek of the little houses) is recorded on a plat of the lands of Ex-Mission San Buenaventura in 1864. Lake Casitas was created in the late 1950's by impounding Coyote Creek.

Caslamayomi [Sonoma]. A land grant of this name, also called Laguna de los Gentiles (lake of the heathen), was granted March 21, 1844. On maps of the grant a *Rio de Caslamayom* (or possibly *Caslamayoni*) is shown. The ending *-yomi* means 'place' in Southern Pomo and Coast Miwok (Kroeber). *See* Collayomi

Casmalia, kăz-măl′-yȧ: town, **Hills** [Santa Barbara]. The name, probably the Spanish rendering of an Indian word of unknown origin, appears under date of April 6, 1837, in the *expediente* of a land grant; on *diseños* of various dates it is sometimes spelled Casmali and Casmaria. Maps made soon after the American occupation do not show the name. The name of the town is shown as Casmale on Goddard's map (1860), and, with the modern spelling, on the von Leicht–Craven map (1874).

Caspar: town, Point, Creek, Anchorage [Mendocino]. Named for Siegfrid Caspar, who settled there before 1860. In 1861 Kelley and Randall built a sawmill on Caspar Creek. When Jacob Green purchased the property in 1864, he named the community Caspar (Borden). The name for the point appears on the Coast Survey chart of 1872. In 1878 the hill southeast of the point was used as a triangulation point and was given the proud name Great Caspar, which it still bears on the topographical map.

Cassel [Shasta]. The former name, Hat Creek, was changed to the present name by the Post Office Department in 1888 at the instigation of a real-estate promoter named Myers, whose birthplace was Cassel, Germany.

Castac: Lake, Valley [Kern]; **Castaic**, kăs′-tāk: **Creek, town** [Los Angeles]. An Indian rancheria *Castec* is mentioned in 1791 (AGN, p. 46). It is spelled *Casteque* in 1806 (Arch. MSB, IV, 49-68). Still another spelling is recorded on June 27, 1824 (DSP, I, 48): *paraje llamado Casitec, y por nosotros S. Pablo,* 'place called Casitec, and by us San Pablo.' It appears as Castec for a land grant of November 22, 1843. Early American maps do not show the name, but the *Statutes* of 1851 mention a Rancho Casteque, and Blake refers to Casteca Lake in 1853 (Pac. R. R. *Reports,* Vol. V. Pt. 2, p. 47). The official spelling (Geographic Board, *Fifth Report*) was established by the von Leicht-Craven map as Castac Ranch and Lake, but post office and local usage prefer Castaic. In 1960 the Geographic Board decided for Castac Lake and Valley in Kern County and for Castaic Creek, Valley and town in Los Angeles County. The post office is not at the site of the original rancho. According to Kroeber, the name was originally applied to the Shoshonean village by the neighboring Chumash and means 'my eyes' or 'our eye.'

Castella [Shasta]. The castle-like formation of the near-by granite pinnacles known as the Crags doubtless inspired the fanciful name (Latin, 'castles') which has appeared continuously on railway maps since 1900. Between 1900 and 1911 the name of an adjacent station to the north, similarly inspired, fluctuated from Castle Crag (1900–1904) to Castle Rock (1905–1909) and back to Castle Crag (1910–1911), and in 1913 disappeared entirely.

Castilleja, kăs-tĭ-lā'-yá [Sequoia National Park] Named in 1896 by Bolton C. Brown. "This we named Castilleja Lake, the castilleja blossoms [Indian paintbrush] being especially perfect and brilliant upon its shores." (*SCB,* II, 21.)

Castillo, Point [Santa Barbara]. The Spanish name for 'castle' or 'fort' is applied to the southern limits of the Santa Barbara harbor.

Castle. A popular descriptive term for orographic features resembling, or assumed to resemble, a castle. In California about fifteen rocks, peaks, cliffs, etc., are so named. **Castle Crags State Park** [Shasta]. The park was established in 1934 and named after the granite formation known as Castle Crags. Castle Rock, the most outstanding peak, was known as Devil's Castle until 1852, when the name was changed by the boundary survey (*Statutes* of 1852, p. 233). There is a Vulcans Castle

in Lassen National Park, and a Kings Castle in Siskiyou County. *See* Dunderberg Peak.

Castro. Several place names bear this Spanish family name, which is common in California. **Castroville** [Monterey]. The town was laid out and named in 1864 by Juan B. Castro on the Rancho Bolsa Nueva del Cojo, the first parcel of which had been granted to his father, Simeón Castro, February 14, 1825. **Castro: Creek, Point, Rocks** [San Francisco Bay] preserve the name of Joaquín I. Castro, owner of Rancho San Pablo, first granted provisionally to his father, Francisco, April 15, 1823. **Castro Valley** [Alameda]. The name commemorates Guillermo Castro, who became grantee of parts of the San Lorenzo and San Leandro lands on February 23, 1841. His rancho is shown on Duflot de Mofras's map of 1844. The name for the valley appears on Hoffmann's map of the Bay region. **Castro Flats** [Santa Clara]. Mostly on Las Animas Rancho, granted August 17, 1802, to José Mariano Castro, son of Joaquín Castro who had come with the Anza expedition in 1776. The name also appears in other counties: for a peak [Los Angeles], a canyon [Santa Barbara], and a settlement [Santa Clara] founded in 1867.

Caswell Memorial State Park [San Joaquin]. Established in 1952, and named for the Caswell family, several members of whom were donors of the park.

Catacombs Cave [Lava Beds National Monument]. The peculiarly formed niches in the walls make the cave look like a subterranean cemetery of the early Christians.

Catacula [Napa]. A land grant dated November 9, 1844. The valley now called Chiles Valley is shown as *Valle de Catuculu* on an early map of the grant. The word is of Wintun origin, but its meaning is not known. *See* Chiles.

Catalina Island. *See* Santa Catalina Island.

Cataract Creek [Fresno]. "Down ... tumbled the foaming stream, a long line of silver, lost here and there amongst the talus-piles. Cataract Creek, we called it." (J. N. LeConte, *SCB,* V, 10.)

Cathay [Mariposa]. The post office was established April 6, 1882, and apparently named for James or Nathaniel Cathay, both residents of the township.

Cathedral. A number of peaks are so named because of their resemblance to a cathedral. **Cathedral: Canyon, City** [Riverside]. When Colonel Henry Washington made the first survey of the canyon in 1858, he applied the name because he thought the canyon resembled the interior of a cathedral. The city was mapped in 1925 and named because of its location at the desert fan of the canyon. (W. R. Hillery.) **Cathedral: Peak, Pass, Range** [Yosemite National Park]. The peak was named in 1862 by Henry G. Hanks, James Hutchings, and Captain Corcoran, representatives of the San Carlos Mining and Exploration Company, while on a trip to the mines near Independence (Chalfant, *Inyo*, pp. 125 f.). The peak had first been designated as Cathedral Spires, but the Whitney Survey changed the name to Cathedral Peak. Cathedral Spires and Rocks are now the names of the rock formations opposite El Capitan in Yosemite Valley.

Cathey: Valley, Mountain [Mariposa]. The places were named for Andrew Cathey, a native of North Carolina, who settled in the valley about 1850. The post office, 1879 to 1881, was called Catheys Valley.

Cat Mountain [San Bernardino]. The mountain between Baker and Yermo is called Cat Mountain because the elements have cut the figure of a sitting cat on its front (Doyle).

Cattle. In comparison with the many places named Bull and Cow, there are only a few Cattle Creeks and Hills in the State, including a Wild Cattle Creek in Sonoma County.

Caution [Trinity]. The little town in the Trinity Alps near the Mendocino County line was founded in, or before, 1901. It was probably so named because it is situated in a rugged district which could be reached only on foot or on horseback.

Cavallo Point [Marin]. A *Punta de los Caballos* (point of the horses) is shown on a *diseñó* of the Tamalpais grant of 1845, and a *Plaza de los Caballos* appears on Duflot de Mofras's *Plan* 16. The present version was used by the Coast Survey on the charts of San Francisco Bay in the early 1850's. The Spanish letters "b" and "v" were formerly often interchanged. It may be assumed from a note of Padre Payeras in 1819 (Docs. Hist. Cal., IV, 270) that the name arose because horses were kept here for travel in what is now Marin County. The bay partly formed by the point is called Horseshoe Bay because of its shape. Besides Cavallo Point and two obsolete place names, *Ojo de Caballo* [Contra Costa] and *Arroyo de la Caballada* [San Diego], no names containing the Spanish word for 'horse' could be found. In Spanish and Mexican times the horse played an important role, but was so common a sight and was held in so little

esteem that few places were named for him until the American occupation. *See* Horse.

Cave City [Calaveras]. Named after the near-by limestone caves (Doyle). The place is shown on Hoffmann's map (1873).

Cayetano Creek [Alameda, Contra Costa]. A *Cañada de San Cayetan* appears on a *diseño*, 1834, of the land grant Las Positas. It is shown as Arroyo Cayetano on the Mount Diablo atlas sheet. There is also a Cayetano Creek in Napa County. *See* San Cayetano.

Caymus [Napa]. This land grant, dated February 23, 1836, was named after an Indian village at the site of modern Yountville. The Caymos Indians are mentioned on March 29, 1824 (Arch. Ariz. SF, Vol. IV, Pt. 2, p. 126).

Cayton: Valley, Creek, town [Shasta]. The valley was settled by William Cayton about 1855 (Steger).

Cayucos, kī-yōō′-kăs: town, **Creek, Point, Landing** [San Luis Obispo]. The word was used to designate small fishing boats in California, and occurs elsewhere in American Spanish. It is a Spanish rendering of the Eskimo *kayak*. A minute description of a *cayuco* is given in Font's *Complete Diary* on March 27, 1776. A document, dated July 16, 1806, mentions *canoas ó cayucos de las qꞌ usan en Noka*—"canoes or kayaks, the kind they use in Nootka" (PSP, XIX, 134 f.), and the word appears frequently thereafter in Spanish documents to designate the *bidarkas* of the Aleuts who were employed in hunting sea otter along the California coast. The word is found also in the name of the land grant Moro y Cayucos, dated December 28, 1837, and April 27, 1842. The town was laid out and named in 1875, and is shown on the Land Office map of 1879.

Cazadero, kăz-ȧ-dâr′-ō [Sonoma]. The station was named when it became the terminus of the North Pacific Coast Railroad in the late 1880's. The name is California Spanish for 'hunting place.' Cazadores [Sacramento]. The name of an unconfirmed land grant dated July 26, 1844, means literally 'hunters.'

Cebada Canyon [Santa Barbara]. *Cebada* is the Spanish word for 'barley,' once one of the chief crops in the Lompoc district.

Cecilville [Siskiyou]. The place was named for John Baker Sissel, who came to Shasta Valley sometime before 1849 (Mary Bridwell). The name was misspelled on Goddard's map of 1857 and again when the post office was established June 25, 1879. *See* Sissel Gulch.

Cedar. The name has been applied to more than one hundred places throughout the State, as Cedar Hill, Flat, Gulch, Glen, etc.

The popularity of the name, which rivals Pine, is due to the application of the term to a variety of native coniferous trees, many of which are not cedar but cypress. The name is also used for a number of towns and settlements, some of which may have been named for plantings of cedars or similar trees: Cedar Glen, Cedarpines Park [San Bernardino], The Cedars, Cedar Kress [Nevada], Cedar Crest [Fresno]. **Cedarville** [Modoc] is a transfer name. The town was named by J. H. Bonner in 1867 after his home town in Ohio.

Cedric Wright, Mount [Fresno]. The mountain was named in 1961 in memory of George Cedric Wright, who died in 1959. The internationally known photographer had made significant contributions to the appreciation of the natural scene. (Geographic Board, Sept.-Dec., 1961) .

Center Peak [Tulare]. The peak was named by Cornelius B. Bradley and his party in July, 1898. "A third [mountain], standing more detached, and in the very center of the mighty cirque at the head of the valley, we named Center Peak." (*SCB*, II, 272.)

Centerville. The name has always found favor in the United States. As early as 1854 *Lippincott's Gazetteer* lists sixty-three occurrences of it, all spelled Centreville. **Centerville** [Alameda], one of the earliest and now the largest of the several in California, was settled before 1850. **Centerville** [Fresno]. Named about 1870 by residents because of its central location in the Kings River Valley. For many years the post office name was Kings River. There are other Centervilles in Butte and Shasta counties. *See* Grass Valley.

Centinela Creek [Los Angeles]. The creek emptying into Ballona Lagoon derives its name from the Aguaje del Centinela (spring of the sentinel) grant, dated September 14, 1844, on the territory on which it rises. The post office was established July 24, 1889, but was discontinued in 1895. Centinela Springs is Historical Landmark 363.

Central Valley [Shasta]. When construction was begun in 1938 on Shasta Dam, the main unit of the Central Valley Project, two boom towns sprang up and were named after the project, one Central Valley and the other Project City.

Ceres, sḗ'-rēz [Stanislaus]. The railway station of the Southern Pacific was named in 1874 for the goddess of growing vegetation by Elma Carter, daughter of one of the first settlers.

Cerrito, sĕ-rē'-tō. The word, meaning 'hillock,'

was a favorite geographical term in Spanish California. **Cerritos** [Los Angeles]. Los Cerritos was the name of a land grant dated May 22, 1834. For many years this was also the name of the eminence now known as Signal Hill and of a station of the Pacific Electric Railroad. **El Cerrito** [Contra Costa]. The little hill is mentioned in the records since 1820 as *Cerrito de San Antonio,* a name possibly applied by the padres of Mission Dolores for Anthony of Padua, a patron saint of the Franciscans. (Bowman.) Cerrito Creek is shown on Hoffmann's map of the Bay region (1873). The popular name Cerrito Hill is a tautology, 'little hill hill'; the elevation is also known as Albany Hill. The community north of the hill was first known as County Line. In 1909 the post office was established and named Rust, for William R. Rust, a pioneer of 1888 and first postmaster. When the city was incorporated in 1917, the name was changed to El Cerrito. **Potrero de los Cerritos** [Alameda]. The name, meaning 'pasture of the hills,' was given to the land grant dated March 21, 1844.

Cerro, sĕr'-ō. The term for 'mountain' or 'high hill' was commonly used in Spanish times and has survived as the generic term in the names of several mountains, particularly in San Diego and San Luis Obispo counties. According to tradition, the well-known **Cerro Gordo** (big hill) in Inyo County was named in the 1860's when Pablo Flores and two other Mexicans discovered the rich ore deposits there. The various Cerros followed by Alto, Ultimo, Lodoso, etc., on the atlas sheets of the Kettleman oil district, are affectations of American surveyors and are not used locally. **Cerro Romualdo** [San Luis Obispo]. The name commemorates an Indian, Romualdo, grantee of the Huerta de Romualdo or Chorro land grant dated 1842 and July 10, 1846.

Chabot, shă-bō', **Lake** [Alameda]. An artificial lake, created in 1868-1869 and named for Anthony Chabot, a Canadian, who played an important role in the gold rush. Later he was associated with A. W. von Schmidt in establishing the first water supply system for San Francisco. He is the donor of the Chabot Observatory in Oakland.

Chagoopah: Plateau, Falls, Creek [Sequoia National Park]. The falls were named in 1881 by W. B. Wallace and his party, for an old Paiute chief (Farquhar). Chagoopah is almost certainly a Mono word, according to Kroeber, though its meaning is unknown. *Pah* is the common Shoshonean term for 'water.' The name is spelled Chagoopa on the maps of the Geological Survey.

Chalfant [Mono]. A post office was established in 1913 and named for W. A. Chalfant. (*See* Glossary.)

Chalk. The presence of chalk or chalklike deposits is indicated in the names of about twenty peaks, buttes, and mountains in California. Chalk Mountain [Shasta] is mentioned by Reading as early as 1843 (Steger).

Chalk Bluff Ridge [Nevada]. The ridge was named after the mining camp Chalk Bluff, which was later called Red Dog.

Challenge [Yuba]. Named about 1856, after the Challenge Lumber Mill, around which the settlement developed (Co. Hist., 1924, p. 204).

Chalone, shă-lōn′, chă-lōn′: **Mountain, Creek** [San Benito, Monterey]. According to Henry Henshaw (in Hodge), Chalone was the name of a division of the Costanoan family which lived east of Soledad Mission. *La lengua Chalona* (the Chalone language) is mentioned in a letter of January 13, 1816 (Arch. Arz. SF, Vol. III, Pt. 1, p. 6). On a *diseño* of the San Lorenzo grant the mountain is shown as *Cierro Chalon.* The Parke-Custer map (1855) places a Mount Chelone farther south, approximately in latitude 36° 20′. Goddard (1860) likewise misspells the name, but he has it in the right position. Hoffmann established the modern spelling for the name of mountain and creek. There is probably no connection with the rancheria *Cholam* or *Cholan,* which was in Salinan territory. *See* Cholame. Chalone Peaks are now called The Pinnacles. *See* Pinnacles and Metz.

Chambers Lodge [Placer]. The post office was established in 1928 and named after the resort, Chambers Lodge (Florence Slade).

Chamise, shă-mēs′, **Chamisal,** shăm-ĭ-săl′. Botanists now associate this name with our native white-flowering greasewood, *Adenostoma fasciculatum:* chamise (Rowntree). The Indians of the San Fernando Mission used the word *chamiso* for islay, *Prunus ilicifolia:* "islai, called chamiso by them" (*AAE,* VIII, 12 f.), while the Luiseño Indians farther south called the same shrub *chamish* (*AAE,* VIII, 232). The name became extremely popular in Spanish times and appears in various spellings: *chamish, chamisso, chemise,* etc., but to all indications it identified neither the islay nor the greasewood. On *diseños,* chamisal, chemisal, or chamiso seems to designate brushwood or chaparral. The name appears in three land grants: Chamisal, November

15, 1835 [Monterey]; Bolsa del Chamisal, May 11, 1837 [San Luis Obispo]; Punta de Lobos or Chamisal de los Lobos, June 25, 1846 [San Francisco]. In American times the word was used as a generic name in early documents and plats. At the time of the Whitney Survey the shrub was in some degree identified with greasewood: "dense chaparral, composed more exclusively of the *Adenostoma fasiculata* [!], or 'chamiso' . . . Where the *chamiso* predominates, the thick undergrowth is usually designated as 'chamisal' " (Whitney, *Geology,* Vol. I, p. 65). Hoffmann's map of the Bay region designates several large areas as *Chamisal.* The name is preserved in Chemisal Ridge [Monterey], Chemissal and Chemisal Creeks [Colusa], Chemise Ridge [San Benito], Chemise Creek [Mendocino], Chamisa Gap [Lake], and some minor places. In the old Spanish domain some of the names may not refer to the shrub. *Chamiso* was also the term used in Mexico for a person of mixed white, black, and Indian blood (Leon).

Chanchelulla: Mountain, Gulch [Trinity]. The name occurs in Wintu territory, but the meaning is not known. It does not appear on early maps, but, like many others in this district, was preserved orally. The Mining Bureau map of 1891 records it, and the Land Office map of the same year has Chanche Lulla Mountain.

Chandler Grove [Humboldt]. The grove in the Avenue of the Giants was established in 1966 and named in memory of the late Harry Chandler, publisher of the Los Angeles *Times* until 1941.

Chandon [Butte]. Named in 1906 by the Northern Electric Railroad for the owner of the land on which the station was built (Florence Campbell).

Channel Islands. The collective name for the islands which are separated from the mainland by the Santa Barbara Channel. The group was discovered by Cabrillo in October, 1542, and named for Saint Luke, whose feast day is October 18 (Wagner, p. 503). In the 18th century the individual islands were named and renamed for various saints. In 1841 the Wilkes expedition affixed to the three largest islands the respective names which they still bear: San Miguel, Santa Rosa, Santa Cruz, an alignment which had appeared probably for the first time on a map of about 1794 (cf. Wagner, p. 360). *See* San Miguel; Anacapa. **Channel Islands National Monument,** created by presidential proclamation in 1938, includes the two westernmost islands of the Anacapa group and Santa Barbara Island, south of this group.

Chanslor [Kern]. The name commemorates J. A. Chanslor, one of Charlie Canfield's partners in the discovery and development of the rich oil fields. *See* Canfield.

Chaparral, shăp-*á*-răl′. The Spanish word designated a place where the evergreen oak (*chaparro*) grows. In California the word is used to describe the dense brush covering of our hillsides, and since these hills are a common sight only a few bear the name. The name of Chaparrosa Spring, southeast of Bear Valley [San Bernardino], is probably from the same root. *See* Chamisal, the corresponding term usually used on *diseños* of land grants.

Chariot: Canyon, Mountain [San Diego]. The canyon, leading off from Banner Canyon, was named after the Golden Chariot Mine, the ore deposits of which were discovered by George N. King on February 13, 1871 (Hunzicker).

Charity Valley. *See* Hope Valley.

Charles Creek [Shasta]. Named for Charles Keluche, son of an Indian doctor.

Charleys Butte [Inyo]. The lava butte near the highway, about eighteen miles north of Independence, preserves the memory of Charley Tyler, a Negro and former slave. On March 7, 1863, Indians attacked the party with which he was traveling. Charley gave up his horse to help the women escape, and, failing to catch another, was captured and killed by the Indians. (Brierly.)

Charlotte: Lake, Creek [Fresno]. A Lake Charlotte is recorded on Hoffmann's map of 1873. It was probably named by a member of the Whitney Survey for some young lady.

Charlton Flat [Los Angeles]. Applied to an open space near Pine Mountain, for the late R. H. Charlton, supervisor of Angeles National Forest from 1905 to 1925.

Charter Oak [Los Angeles]. The community developed in the late 1890's and was probably so named because a large oak tree reminded someone of the famous Charter Oak in Hartford, Connecticut. The post office is listed in 1904. There is no evidence to support the local tradition that the place was named when a party of Americans achieved a victory near the oak at some time in the War with Mexico.

Charybdis. *See* Scylla.

Chatsworth: town, Peak, Reservoir [Los Angeles]. The place was named in the boom year of 1887, after Chatsworth in England.

Chatterdowen Creek [Shasta]. The tributary to the McCloud River bears obviously a Wintu name. According to Steger, the word means 'digger pine' and should be spelled Chattidown.

Chemawa [Riverside]. The name of the Pacific Electric station may be a spelling variant of the name of the Chemehuevi Indians on the Colorado, mentioned by Heintzelman in 1853 as Chemawawas. The name Chemawa also occurs in Marion County, Oregon.

Chemehuevi, shĕm-*ê*-hwā′-vĭ: **Valley, Mountains, Indian Reservation** [San Bernardino]. "A Shoshonean tribe, apparently an offshoot of the Paiute" (Hodge), is repeatedly mentioned by this name in Spanish and early American times under a great variety of spellings. The modern version was established by Whipple in 1853 (Pac. R.R. *Reports,* Vol. III, Pt. 3, p. 16): Chemehuevis (from a Paiute informant) or Chemehuevitz (from a Yuma). In 1904 the Geological Survey dropped the *-s,* probably believing that the ending *-i* indicates a plural.

Chemise, Chemisal. *See* Chamise.

Cherokee, chĕr′-ô-kē. The name of the tribe of the southern Appalachian region is one of our romantic and truly American names and is used as a place name in many states. At the time of the gold rush several parties of Cherokees came to California; of the five mining towns named for them, only one, in Butte County, survives. The one in Calaveras County is remembered in the name of a creek and the one in Sierra County in the name of a creek and a bridge. There is a Cherokee Station on the Central California Traction Railroad in San Joaquin County. Cherokee Flat of the 1850's is now Altaville [Calaveras], and Cherokee [Nevada] is the site of Paterson on the Smartsville atlas sheet. **Cherokee** [Tuolumne]. Historic Landmark 445, two miles north of Tuolumne City, indicates the site of the mining camp where gold was discovered in 1853 by the Scott brothers, descendants of Cherokee Indians.

Cherry. No true cherry is indigenous to California, but a number of the native shrubs have cherry-like berries, especially the western chokecherry, *Padus demissa,* and the holly-leaved cherry, *Prunus ilicifolia.* (*See* Islay.) Most of the twenty-odd places originally named Cherry were so called because of the presence of these shrubs. Some, however, may be named for orchards or for places "back East," where the name is popular. There are also a few Chokecherry Creeks and Canyons in the southern part of the State.

Chester [Plumas]. Named after Chester, Vermont, by Oscar Martin in the 1900's (G. Stover).

Chianti, kĕ-ăn'-tĭ [Sonoma]. The station on the Northwestern Pacific was named, like near-by Asti, after a wine-producing district in Italy.

Chicago. The metropolis of the Middle West has been used repeatedly for place names in various sections of the State. **Chicago Park** [Nevada]. The name was given by Paul Ullrich and a group of German settlers from Chicago, Illinois, in the 1880's (Elizabeth Beukers). **Port Chicago** [Contra Costa]. The place was founded in 1906 by the C. A. Smith Lumber Company and called Bay Point. The present name was chosen for the post office in 1931, after the name Chicago had been rejected by the Post Office Department.

Chickahominy Slough [Yolo]. According to the County History of 1940 (p. 240), the slough was named because two ranchers, Joseph Griffin and J. McMahon, had a fight here at or about the time of the Civil War battle in Virginia, June 27, 1862.

Chickering Grove [Humboldt]. The grove in the Prairie Creek Redwoods State Park was established in 1958 in honor of Allen and Alma S. Chickering. Allen Chickering (1877-1958) had been a member of the Sierra Club since 1896, the Save - the - Redwoods League since 1919 and one of its Councillors for 28 years, the California Historical Society since 1923 and a Director for 27 years.

Chico, chĕ'-kō [Butte]. The origin of the name is found in the creek which suggested the name for the land grant Arroyo Chico (little stream), granted November 7, 1844, to William Dickey and sold in 1849 to Bidwell, both formerly connected with Sutter's Fort. City and Creek are recorded in the *Statutes* of 1850, but the modern city was not laid out until February, 1860. The original *Arroyo Chico* is now called Big Chico Creek (literally, 'big little creek,' and the stream to the south, Little Chico Creek 'little little creek'). Chico is found in the names of twenty or more features in California, including Bolsa Chico Lake [San Luis Obispo].

Chico Martinez Creek [San Luis Obispo], near the Kern County line, was named for Chico Martínez, "king of the mustang runners," mentioned by Rensch and Hoover (p. 139). *See* Chiquito.

Chihuahua, chĕ-wä'-wä: **Valley, Creek** [San Diego]. José Melandras, a goatherd who loved solitude, settled first near Warner Hot Springs. When too many people came to the valley, he moved farther inland to a place near Dead Mans Hole, and finally to the valley which became known by the name of his native state in Mexico, Chihuahua. (Mary Connors.)

Chilao [Los Angeles]. Formerly Chileo, or Chilleo. Named for José Gonzales, a herder and a member of Tiburcio Vasquez' bandit gang, who killed a grizzly bear in that area, with only a hunting knife. He was nicknamed Chileo ('hot stuff') by his companions for that exploit. (Angeles National Forest.)

Chilcoot [Plumas]. Named, about 1900, after Chilcoot Pass, Alaska, the gateway to the Klondike, at the time of the gold rush to the Yukon (R. F. Ramelli).

Chile, Chili, Chilean. Of all South American countries, Chile sent the largest contingent of miners to California during the gold rush. Some of the many camps and physical features named for them are still found on the maps. **Chili Bar** [El Dorado]. The place on the South Fork of the American River was a gold mining camp in 1851 and was first called Chillian Bar. **Chili Camp** [Calaveras]. The rich mining camp east of Lancha Plana was first mentioned in 1850. It is no longer on the map although gold mining was carried on until the twentieth century. **Chili Gulch** [Calaveras]. The place south of Mokelumne Hill was mentioned as Chile or Chilean Gulch as early as 1850. The place was so named when a Dr. Concha imported Chilean peons to the gulch, and their presence led to the so-called "Chilean War" in 1850. The gold deposits proved to be very rich, and in 1857 a post office was established with the name Chili. Historic Landmark 265.

Chileno. The Spanish designation for a native of Chile is preserved in Chileno Valley [Marin], Chileno Creek [Merced], and Chileno Canyon [Los Angeles]. *See* Chili Gulch.

Chiles: town, Valley [Napa]. Named for Joseph B. Chiles, of Kentucky, who came across the plains in 1841 and was grantee of the Catacula grant in Napa County, November 9, 1844.

Chilnualna: Creek, Falls, Falls Trail, Ranger Station [Yosemite National Park]. An Indian name of unknown meaning, shown as Chilnoialny Creek on the Hoffmann-Gardiner Yosemite map of 1867.

Chimiles [Napa]. The name, probably of Indian origin, was given to the land grant dated

May 2, 1846.

Chimney. Some of the thirty-odd Chimney Rocks, Canyons, Gulches, etc., were named because of chimney-like rock formations; others from the presence of "pay chimneys," i.e., lodes of gold-bearing quartz; still others possibly from the vertical cleft in rocks called a "chimney" by mountain climbers. **Chimney Peak** [Imperial]. The famous landmark for early explorers and travelers in the Colorado Desert was so named because of its shape. *See* Picacho. **Chimney Rock** in Modoc County was so named because Thomas L. Denson, who had settled here in the early 1850's, had cut a fireplace and flue out of the rock. In the Lava Beds National Monument the term is repeatedly used with reference to "chimneys" created by the cooling of lava.

China, Chinese. China and Chinese are among the most popular of California place names derived from nationalities. They bear witness to the important part that Chinese labor played in the building of the State. Some of the places in the mountains, like **Chinese Camp** (locally: Chinee Camp) in Tuolumne County, date from the gold-rush days; others were named in the 1860's and 1870's when large numbers of Chinese were employed in mining and railroad building. Some of the names along the coast point to the trade with China, and others to the presence of Chinese fishermen in the district. **China Slide** in Trinity County, however, was named not only because of extensive tunneling by Chinese miners, but also because the disastrous slide occurred on Chinese New Year's Day, 1890 (W. E. Hotelling). **China Lake** [Kern]. The post office was established in 1948 and named after the large dry lake near by.

Chino: town, Creek, Valley [San Bernardino]; **Canyon** [Riverside]. The name is derived from that of the Santa Ana del Chino land grant, dated March 26, 1841. The term *chino* is used in most Spanish American countries for persons of mixed blood. For the Mexican *chino* see Nicolas Leon. The word was used in a geographical sense before 1830 (Bancroft, II, 352, map), probably as the name of an Indian rancheria whose chief was a *chino*. Early American maps and reports have the spelling *China*, but in the *Statutes* of 1853 the original spelling was restored. The settlement is shown on the Land Office map of 1862. The name appears in several other features in the southern part of the State and in Chino Creek [Butte]. An unclaimed grant, Rancheria del Chino, in Santa Clara County, might have

something to do with Chino Rodríguez, patentee of the San Gregorio grant [San Mateo].

Chinquapin [Yosemite National Park]. The ranger station was named for the chinquapin, *Castanopsis sempervirens*, native to California and Oregon. According to Rowntree, there is a good stand of this shrub at the station. The name seems not to have been recorded until the Geological Survey mapped the valley in 1893–1894.

Chiquito, chĭ-kē′-tō, **Chiquita.** The word is a diminutive of *chico*, 'small,' 'little,' and is found in the name of Chiquita station north of Healdsburg [Sonoma] on the Northwestern Pacific, and of Chiquito Creek in Shasta County. **Chiquito: Creek, Ridge, Pass, Lake** [Madera]. The name goes back to the Chiquito Joaquin (little Joaquin), probably applied to this tributary of San Joaquin River by Mexican prospectors in the mining days. Hoffmann (1873) also calls the highest peak of the Ridge, Chiquito, and has Chiquito Meadows for Beasore Meadows.

Chittenden: Peak, Pass [Yosemite National Park]. Named for Captain Hiram M. Chittenden (1858–1917), later a brigadier general in the Corps of Engineers and in 1904 a boundary commissioner for Yosemite National Park.

Chocolate. The word is repeatedly used to indicate chocolate coloring. The best-known features so named are the Chocolate Mountains [Imperial], Chocolate Peak [Inyo], Chocolate Creek [San Diego].

Chokecherry Creek. *See* Cherry.

Cholame, shŏ-lăm′, chŏ-lăm′ [San Luis Obispo]; **Cholame: Creek, Hills** [Monterey, San Luis Obispo]. *Cholam* was a Salinan rancheria, fourteen leagues from Mission San Miguel. It is mentioned under date of January 29, 1804, as *Cholan* (PSP Ben. Mil., XXXIV, 7). The name appears as Cholame on a *diseño* of the San Miguel grant in 1840, and on a *diseño* of the Cholam land grant of February 5, 1844. The Parke-Custer map (1855) has a Chelame Pass for the valley between Shandon and Cholame. The Land Office map of 1859 has Choloma Creek. The current spelling of the name was used by Hoffmann in a letter to Whitney, April 7, 1866, and is so recorded on the von Leicht-Craven map of 1873. *See* Chalone.

Chollas, chŏl′-ăs, choi′-ăs: station, **Reservoir; Las Choyas,** choi′-ăs: **Valley** [San Diego]. Originally the name of a large Indian village near the present Indian Point, mentioned November 30, 1775 (PSP Ben. Mil., I, 1), and shown on Pantoja's map of 1782 as *Rancheria de las Choyas*. A. B. Gray's map of 1849 has Las Choyas; that of the Coast Survey, 1857, Choyas Valley; and Coast Survey, 1858, Choya Point. On the *Official Map of ... San Diego*, 1870, is the spelling variant Chollas Valley. The etymology of the word is uncertain. In Spanish, *choya* is 'crow' or 'jackdaw,' *cholla* is 'skull' or 'head,' but in Mexican and California Spanish "y" and "ll" represent the same "y" sound. Both place names are probably folk-etymological renderings of the Indian name for the succulent plant, now called cholla cactus, which grows here luxuriantly. There is a Cholla Creek in San Benito County.

Chorro Creek [San Luis Obispo]. *Chorro* in a geographical sense corresponds to the American term 'rapids.' The creek is shown on the *diseño* of the Huerta de Romualdo (o del Chorro) grant (1842 and 1846) as *Arroyo del Chorro* and *Aguage [aguaje,* 'spring'] *del Chorro*. An adjoining grant, Cañada del Chorro, dated October 10, 1845, was doubtless named after the same arroyo.

Chowchilla, chou-chĭl'*á*: **River, Mountains,** town, **Canal** [Madera, Mariposa]. According to Hodge and to Kroeber (*Handbook*, p. 443), there was a Yokuts tribe on the lower, and a Miwok tribe probably on the upper, course of the river. A *rancheria de los Chauciles* is mentioned December 8, 1834 (Pico Docs., p. 128), and *indios Chauciles y Joyimas* are mentioned by the *alcalde* of San Jose, February 5, 1835 (Arch. SJ, I, 40). Both references (which relate to horse stealing) doubtless are to the Yokuts tribe or village. The Chauciles were aggressive, and the name may mean 'killers.' Kroeber (*Place Names*) thinks it likely "that the Miwok Chauchilas were so named by Americans, or by English-speaking Indians, after the name of the stream." At any rate, in the various Indian reports of the early 1850's the two tribes are obviously confused and the name is recorded in various spellings. The stream is shown on most maps of the 1850's. The present version is found on the maps of the Pacific Railroad Survey. The first ascertainable recording is *rancheria de Chausila*, by Sebastian Rodriguez in April, 1828.

Choyas. *See* Chollas.

Christine [Mendocino]. A number of Swiss families settled here before 1856, and the place became known as Guntley's, for one of the pioneers. When a post office was established in the 1870's it was named Christine, for a

daughter of John Geschwend, another pioneer, who had built the first sawmill in the valley. (Co. Hist., 1914, p. 35.)

Chual, chōō'-ăl, **Mount** [Santa Clara]. The name originated in Mexican times and is recorded on C. S. Lyman's manuscript Mapa ... de Nuevo Almaden (1848) as *Picacho de Chual*. Hoffmann's map of the Bay region calls it Choual Mountain. It contains obviously the Costanoan word *chual*, for *Chenopodium album,* the common pigweed (or lamb's quarters), used by the Indians as food. **Chualar,** chōō'-á-lär [Monterey]. This Spanish word means 'place where the *chual* grows.' In 1830 the place was one of the landmarks delineating the jurisdiction of Monterey (Legis. Recs., I, 147). The name was preserved through two land grants, dated September 23, 1831, and January 5, 1835. The present town is recorded on the von Leicht–Craven map.

Chubbuck [San Bernardino]. When the Santa Fe line from Cadiz to Blythe was built in 1910, the station was named Kilbeck for an employee of the railroad. When the post office was established in 1937, the name was changed to Chubbuck for the owner and developer of the local lime deposits. (Santa Fe.)

Chuchupate, chōō-chōō-păt'-ĭ [Kern]. The name for the district between Mount Pinos and Frazier Mountain in Los Padres National Forest, and for the old Tejon ranger station, is derived from the local Indian name of a yellow-flowered plant, probably the arrowleaf balsamroot, the roots of which were valued by the natives as a food (Forest Service).

Chuckawalla: Mountains, Valley [Riverside]; **Chuckwalla: Canyon** [Death Valley National Monument], **Mountain** [Kern]. These places were named for the chuckwalla, a species of lizard, native to the southeastern part of the State. Chuckwalla Wells is mentioned in the 1870's as a stopping place of the Butterfield stages.

Chuckchansi Indian Reservation [Fresno]. The name of a Mariposan (Yokuts) tribe mentioned with various spellings in the Indian reports after 1851.

Chuck Pass [Fresno]. Apparently named by the Geological Survey in 1907–1909 after Woodchuck Creek, a tributary to the North Fork of Kings River.

Chula Vista, chōō'-lá vĭs'-tá [San Diego]. *Chula* is a Mexican word, meaning 'pretty,' 'graceful,' 'attractive.' The town was laid out and named by the San Diego Land and Town Company in 1888. Through the efforts of

Eldredge and Davidson the post-office name was changed from Chulavista to the present form in 1906.

Chumash Peak [San Luis Obispo]. The 1,250-foot elevation northwest of San Luis Obispo is the only cartographical record of the name of the Indian tribe, which left a great number of place names in their language on the maps. *See* Chumash in Glossary.

Chupadero. The word is Spanish American for a 'brackish pool where animals come to drink.' It was used as the name of a land grant in Monterey County before 1795 (DSP, XIII, 267), and the word is shown on *diseños* of several other grants. A mountain, Chupedero, is mentioned by Trask (*Report*, 1854, p. 91) and is shown on Goddard's map in latitude 36° 35'.

Chupines, chŭ-pē'-nĕs: **Creek** [Monterey]. The name probably includes the Spanish word *chopo*, meaning 'black cottonwood'—a tree native to the region. A place called *Chupines* is mentioned in 1828 (Registro, p. 11), and an *Arroyo de los Chupines* (or *Chopines*) is recorded on a *diseño* of the land grant Los Tularcitos.

Church Creek [Monterey]. The Church family, members of which still reside in the vicinity of Monterey and Carmel, was the first to settle on the creek.

Churn Creek [Shasta]. A hole in the rock bottom of the creek, made by a waterfall and resembling an old-fashioned churn, suggested the name. The creek is mentioned in the Sacramento *Union* of July 9, 1851. Churntown, now vanished, was named after the creek.

Chute Landing [Santa Barbara]. Because of the high rates charged at the wharf of Point Sal, a company of farmers commissioned a French Canadian named St. Ores to build a chute, or slide, down the cliff to a wharf (Co. Hist., 1883, pp. 300 f.).

Cienaga, sĭ-ĕn'-à-gà. The Spanish generic term *ciénaga* was widely used before the American occupation. It means 'marsh' or 'miry place,' but in the southwestern states was applied also to a marshy meadow. Although the word appears in the names of about ten land grants or claims, it seems to have survived in only a few place names. **Cienega: Creek, Valley** [San Benito]. Here the name was preserved through the land grant Cienega de los Paicines, dated October 5, 1842. The *ciénaga* is shown on a *diseño* of 1834. The term is still used at times in a generic sense: Cienaga Seca [San Bernardino], Cooper Cienaga [San Diego]. There is also Cienaga Canyon in the Angeles National Forest, southwest of Liebre Mountain. **Cieneguitas.** The name, meaning 'little swamps,' was given to a land grant [Santa Barbara], dated October 10, 1845, which was also known as Paraje [place] de la Cieneguita, or Suerte [lot] en las Cieneguitas.

Ciervo, sĭ-ĕr'-vō: **Hills, Mountain; Arroyo Ciervo** [Fresno]. The word for 'elk' was repeatedly used in Spanish times and ¬has survived in this cluster name as well as in Canada del Cierbo [Contra Costa].

Cima, sē'-mà [San Bernardino]. The Spanish word for 'summit' was given to the station in 1907 when the San Pedro–Los Angeles–Salt Lake Railroad reached the place. It is at the top of the pass between Kelso and Ivanpah. (R. B. Gill.) **Cima Mesa** [Los Angeles]. So named because of its location above Antelope Valley.

Cinco Canoas Canyon. *See* Canoas.

Cinder Cone. *See* Cone.

Cinnabar. The vermilion-colored mercury ore is found in various parts of the State and has given its name to several places, of which Cinnabar Camp and Springs [Siskiyou] are the best known.

Cirque. The geographical term for a steep-walled, semicircular depression in a mountain, caused by glacial action, is repeatedly found as a specific name in High Sierra features: Cirque: Mountain [Mono], Crest [Fresno], Peak [Inyo]. Glacier Divide, now part of the boundary of Kings Canyon National Park, was named Cirque Ridge on LeConte's map of 1905. "We stood [July, 1904] upon the brink of an immense cirque, or amphitheater, filled with snow and ice.... This cirque was one of a chain of cirques which formed the northern face of the ridge." (*SCB*, V, 158.) The same party named Cirque Lake, a name likewise disregarded by the Geological Survey: "This little lake is located in the bottom of the cirque into which we had descended, and for that reason we named it 'Cirque Lake' " (*ibid.*, p. 160).

Cisco [Placer]. Named in 1865 by the Central Pacific Railroad, for John J. Cisco, treasurer of the company (1863–1869), at the suggestion of Charles Crocker, one of the organizers of the railroad. It was formerly known as Heaton Station.

Citrus. The citrus-fruit industry in the State has given rise to a number of place names: Citro [Tulare], Citrona [Yolo], Citrus [Sacramento]. *See* Lemon; Orange.

City of Industry [Los Angeles]. Created in 1957 on undeveloped land in La Puente

Valley and incorporated for the sole purpose of industrial development. Later additional nonresidential corridors in other areas were annexed. (Co. Hist., 1965, II, 108 ff.).

City of Six Ridge [Sierra]. The ridge preserves the name of the mining town, City of Six. near Downieville, which was often mentioned in the 1850's as yielding large gold nuggets. See Jackassville.

Claiborne Creek [Shasta]. Named by Sim Southern (see Sims), owner of the Eagle Hotel in old Shasta, for G. B. Claiborne, a banker from Stockton.

Clair Engle Lake [Trinity]. The artificial lake created by Trinity Dam in 1965 was named in honor of the late Clair Engle, 1911-1964, U.S. Senator from California.

Clairville [Plumas]. The transfer point from rail to teams was named for Claire Bowen, Mrs. W. E. Clarke (Myrick). The name was applied to the post office from July 20, 1896, to October 15, 1910.

Claremont [Los Angeles]. The Pacific Land and Improvement Company, a subsidiary of the Santa Fe, offered to name the town, which it platted in 1887, for H. A. Palmer, owner of the land. Mr. Palmer declined the honor and suggested a number of Spanish names descriptive of the grand view of the mountains. The directors, from Boston, called for equivalents in their own language and, influenced by one among them who formerly lived in Claremont, New Hampshire, chose the present name. (Willis Kerr.)

Clarence King, Mount [Kings Canyon National Park]. The peak was named Mount King in 1864 by the Brewer party of the Whitney Survey, for Clarence King, a member of the party. King (1842–1901) was connected with the State Geological Survey from 1863 to 1866 and later became the first chief of the United States Geological Survey, 1879–1881. The full name is recorded on the 1939 edition of the Mount Whitney atlas sheet, but King Spur, named after the mountain, retains the shorter form.

Clark, Mount [Yosemite National Park]. Named for Galen Clark, mountaineer and first guardian of Yosemite State Park. The Whitney Survey had named the peak The Obelisk because of its odd shape. Clark's Station, stage stop and home of Clark in the 'sixties and 'seventies, is now Wawona.

Clark Lake [San Diego]. Named in the 1890's for the Clark brothers, who developed the lake for watering their stock (J. Jasper).

Clark Mountain [San Bernardino]. The name was placed on the map by the Death Valley Expedition of 1891. Like Clark County in Nevada, it honors Senator William A. Clark of Montana, famous for his copper mines and builder of the Las Vegas and Tonopah Railroad (E. C. Jaeger, Desert Magazine, July, 1954, p. 14).

Clarksburg [Yolo]. Named for Judge Clark, who settled there in 1849 (Co. Hist., 1940, p. 216).

Clarks: Lake, Peak, Spring [Lake]. Named for Peter Clark, who took up a homestead in Big Valley soon after the arrival of the earlier settlers of 1854 (Mauldin).

Clarks Point [San Francisco]. The point was named when William S. Clark, an emigrant of 1846, acquired the property at Montgomery and Sacramento streets and built a wharf and a warehouse here.

Claus [Stanislaus]. Established in the 1890's by the San Francisco and San Joaquin Valley Railroad (now the Santa Fe) and named for Claus Spreckels, who was instrumental in having the railroad built.

Clawhammer Bar [Siskiyou]. "In '54 there came to Hardscrabble on the 4th of July a stranger attired in clawhammer coat and plug hat to attend the celebration. He had plenty of dust and of congenial spirit, but alas, coat and hat were destroyed by the wild happy crowd, but the incident added the name Clawhammer Bar to one of the richest spots on Salmon." (Luddy.)

Clay [Sacramento]. The post office was established July 26, 1878, and was possibly so named because of the composition of the soil in the district.

Clayton [Contra Costa]. Named for Joel Clayton, who settled here in 1857. Hoffmann in his notes of September 23, 1861, refers to the place as Clayton's, and two days later as Claytonville. The town was for many years the trade and social center for the Mount Diablo coal mines.

Clear Creek. There are about forty Clear Creeks, mostly in the mountainous sections of the State. Clear Creek in Shasta County is Historic Landmark 78, commemorating the discovery of gold at Readings Bar on Clear Creek by Pierson B. Reading in 1848.

Clearinghouse [Mariposa]. This was the name of a gold mine on the Merced River named by Frank X. Egenhoft. During the panic of 1907, when clearinghouse certificates were in circulation, the mine was a clearinghouse for gold bullion. It subsequently failed and closed, but the name continues in the railroad station and the post office across the river. (J. W. Warford.)

Clear Lake [Lake]. The lake was called *Laguna* and *Laguna Grande* (large lake) in Spanish times and so appears on a number of early American maps. The present name is recorded in Gibbs' Journal (1851). The Indian name was doubtless *Kah Shoh,* the word for 'lake' used by the Clear Lake Valley Indians and recorded in 1850 by Dr. J. S. Griffin (Schoolcraft, III, 421, 430). The names of three post offices include the name of the lake: Clearlake Highlands, Clearlake Oaks, and Clearlake Park. **Clear Lake: Reservoir, Hills** [Modoc]. The large body of clear fresh water in Tule Lake Valley gave the name to the reservoir, which was surveyed in 1870 and repeatedly enlarged. The outline of the reservoir resembles Rhett Lake on the Frémont-Preuss map of 1848, though the latter was probably what is now Tule Lake.

Clearwater [Los Angeles]. Founded in 1887 by the California Cooperative Land Colony, and named by Colonel F. A. Atwater after a near-by lake, dry since 1914. **Clearwater Creek** in Mono County had been named McLean's River by Lieutenant Tredwell Moore, in 1852, for a member of his party. The name is used for several other creeks and lakes in the State.

Cleary Reserve [Napa]. The 400-acre reserve in Pope Valley was established in 1962 by the Biological Field Studies Association and the Nature Conservatory as an area for the study of wild life. It was named in honor of the generous owners of the land, Ernest W. and Mary Edna Cleary.

Cleghorn, Mount; Cleghorn: Canyon, Pass [San Bernardino]. Named for Mathew Cleghorn and his son John, who leased land near by in the 1870's for a lumber business (Co. Library).

Clements [San Joaquin]. Named for Thomas Clements, on whose land a settlement and trading center developed in the 1870's.

Cleone, klē-ōn' [Mendocino]. According to Hodge, the name is derived from the name of the *Keliopoma,* the northernmost branch of the Pomo Indians. However, it may be just a girl's name.

Cleveland National Forest. Created by executive order of President Theodore Roosevelt, July 1, 1908, and named in memory of President Grover Cleveland, who had died on June 24 of that year. Trabuco Canyon and San Jacinto national forests were combined to form the new area.

Clews Ridge [San Bernardino]. Apparently named for Joe Clews, a prospector in the 1860's (Geographic Board, Jan.-Apr., 1961).

Clikapudi Creek [Shasta]. According to Steger, the name may have been derived from *klukapuda,* meaning in Yana dialect 'to kill,' because a band of Indians was once poisoned here by some traders. The name appears on the Redding atlas sheet (1901), but it seems not to be recorded on older maps.

Clio, klī'-ō [Plumas]. In the 1870's the post office was established and named Wash, for a pioneer. In 1905 the name was changed to Clio. According to local tradition, the new name was suggested to the postmaster, Fred King, by the trade name of a heating stove. (*Headlight,* Oct., 1942.) Thus the name of the muse of epic poetry and history entered California by way of a lowly stove. However, Clio was then already a popular place name: a Clio mine in Tuolumne County is listed by Browne in 1869, and the Postal Guide of 1892 lists nine Clios in different states.

Clipper. The name was applied in the 1830's to sailing vessels designed primarily for speed. Before the era of the steamship, American clipper ships had a short but brilliant career, and from this the word was transferred in the sense of speed to the terms clipper mill, plow, sled, etc. In California the geographical terms probably owe their origin to near-by clipper mills. Besides the two communities, **Clipper Gap** [Placer], applied to the Central Pacific station in the summer of 1865, and **Clipper Mills** [Butte], established as a post office August 13, 1861. There is a Clipper Mountain northwest of Danby [San Bernardino], a Clipper Creek east of Applegate [Placer], and Clipper Creek and Clipper Ravine in Nevada County.

Cloud: Creek, Canyon [Kings Canyon National Park]. "I named it 'the Cloud Mine' because the clouds hung so low overhead. At the same time I named the creek Cloud Creek and put the name in my notebook." (W. B. Wallace, *SCB,* XII, 47 f.) On many maps the canyon is erroneously labeled Deadman Cañon, the name of the canyon immediately to the west (Farquhar).

Clouds Rest [Yosemite National Park]. So named "because upon our first visit [1851] the party exploring the 'Little Yosemite' turned back and hastened to camp upon seeing the clouds rapidly settling down to rest upon that mountain, thereby indicating the snow storm that soon followed" (Bunnell,

1880, p. 201).

Clough Cave [Tulare]. "So named in honor of William O. Clough (1851–1917), who discovered this cave in 1885" (Geographic Board, *Sixth Report*).

Clough: Creek, Gulch [Shasta]. Named for Noah Clough, who settled at the creek in the 1850's (Steger).

Clover. A favorite name in regions where this fodder grows. There are about ten places in the State so named, including a Red Clover Valley [Plumas] and a settlement, Clover Flat [San Diego]. **Cloverdale** [Sonoma]. The post office was established August 15, 1857. Previously, the settlement had been known as Markleville, for R. B. Markle, former owner of the land.

Clovis [Fresno]. The Southern Pacific named its station for Clovis Cole, owner of the large wheat ranch through which it built a branch line in 1889.

Clyde [Contra Costa]. The name originated during World War I, when the Clyde Shipyard was located here (J. Silvas).

Coachella, kṑ-chĕl'-ȧ: **Valley, town** [Riverside]. The name of the valley between the San Bernardino County line and Salton Sea was known until about 1900 as Cahuilla Valley because it was within the habitat of the Kawea or Cahuilla Indians. In 1901 the section north of Palm Springs appears on the atlas sheet of the San Jacinto quadrangle as Coachella Valley. The post office was established November 30, 1901. No evidence of the early use of the name could be found, but a number of etymologies have been advanced. Since shells could be found in the valley, obviously remnants of the time when the region of Riverside and Imperial counties was under water, Dr. Stephen Bowers in a lecture before the Ventura Society of Natural History in 1888 called it Conchilla Valley, after the Spanish *conchilla*, 'shell.' According to Elmo Proctor in *Desert Magazine*, November, 1945, the valley was generally called Salton Sea Sink and when the region was surveyed by the Geological Survey before 1900, A. G. Tingman, a storekeeper in Indio, proposed the change of the name to Conchilla Valley. This name was accepted by the prospectors and homesteaders, and apparently also by W. C. Mendenhall of the Geological Survey. At any rate, he used the name Conchilla as late as 1909 (WSP, No. 225). But the cartographers apparently misread the name and it appeared as Coachella Valley on the San Jacinto atlas

sheet—a "bastard name without meaning in any language," as Mr. Tingman is reported to have remarked. But other inhabitants of the valley considered the name "unique, distinctive and euphonious," and in 1909 the the Geographic Board made the name official.

Coal. The Coal Creeks and Coalmine Canyons in various counties are reminiscent of the many "coal booms," which were widely publicized and heavily financed but always failed to produce valuable coal. The hope of discovering coal in California was foremost in the minds of industrial and mining circles from the American occupation until the large-scale exploitation of oil deposits. A land grant in Santa Cruz County, dated February 3, 1838, was called La Carbonera, but this name probably referred to a place where charcoal was made, not to a coal mine. There is a Charcoal Ravine in Sierra County.

Coalinga, kṑ-lĭng'-gȧ [Fresno]. The place was known as Coaling Station after the Southern Pacific had built a branch line to the district in 1888, when deposits of lignite were widely publicized as great coal seams. According to local tradition, the sonorous name was created by an official of the Southern Pacific who added an "a" to "coaling" (Laura Lauritzen). Coalmine Canyon northeast of the town also recalls the "Coalinga coal boom," which petered out like the other California coal booms and in later years was replaced in this district by a more substantial oil boom.

Coarsegold [Madera]. The name was given in 1849 by Texan miners, probably because they found coarse gold nuggets in the placer.

Coast Range. The name was used spontaneously by early American explorers and cartographers as a collective term for the various *sierras* along the coast, some of which had previously borne the names of saints. Coast Ranges is now loosely though officially applied to the entire group of mountains from Mexico to Canada. In the singular it is commonly restricted to the coastal mountains of central California.

Cobb: Valley, Creek, Mountain, town [Lake]. Named for John Cobb, a native of Kentucky, who built a combined sawmill and gristmill in the valley in 1859. Cobb Mountain is on the von Leicht–Craven map of 1874.

Coches. The Mexican provincial word for 'hogs' was repeatedly used for geographical terms and was applied to a number of land grants and claims. **Coches,** kṑ'-chĕs: **Creek, Canyon** [San Diego]. Cañada de los Coches (valley of the hogs) was the name of a land grant dated May 16, 1843. In mission days there was a hog farm in the vicinity, and wild hogs were found there for many years afterward. Other grants were Ojo de Agua de la Coche (hog spring) [Santa Clara], August 4, 1835; Los Coches [Santa Clara], October 10, 1840, at San Jose; Los Coches [Monterey], June 14, 1841. Las Pulgas, a land grant in San Mateo County, was also known as Cochenitos, 'little hogs,' probably only a folk-etymological rendering of the name of a rancheria, *Chachanegtac*. Arroyo de los Coches, the creek by Milpitas (shown as *Arroyo del monte de los coches* on a *diseño* of Los Tularcitos), has no connection with the two grants in Santa Clara County. There is a Coche Canyon in Ventura; Los Coches Mountain and Canada de los Coches in Santa Barbara County; and Coche Point and Coches Prietos (blackish hogs) Anchorage on Santa Cruz Island.

Cockatoo Grove [San Diego]. The name was applied by a former Austrian sailor named Seiss, who had a vineyard and winepress here (Emily Richie). It was probably applied in jest; a cockatoo is a popular bird among sailors, and the German *Kakadu* has a decidedly funny connotation. *Katuktu* was the Indian name for Moro Hill in San Diego County (*AAE*, VIII, 157, 191), but this is in Luiseño territory and probably has no connection with this name.

Cockscomb Crest [Yosemite National Park]. So named in 1919 by François E. Matthes, of the Geological Survey, because of its appearance (Farquhar). **Coxcomb Mountains** [Riverside, San Bernardino]. A proper descriptive term, since from certain angles the granite crags look like cocks' combs. On some maps they were called the Granite Mountains. The present name, locally long current, is shown on the Metropolitan Water District maps and the Cadiz Valley atlas sheet of the Corps of Engineers.

Cocopah, kō'-kô-pä: **Mountains, Indian Reservation** [Imperial]. The name of a still existing Indian tribe of the Yuman family, mentioned as *Cucapa* by Garcés in 1775 and described by Heintzelman in 1853. The present spelling was used in 1852 (Schoolcraft, II, 116).

Codornices, kō-dôr-nē'-sĕs: **Creek, Village** [Alameda]. The creek was named by José Domingo Peralta in 1818, when he and his brother found on its bank a nest of quail's eggs (*codorniz*, 'quail'). "We ate the eggs and

called the creek Codornices Creek" (*WF*, VI, 371).

Coe State Park [Santa Clara]. The park was named for Henry W. Coe, who gave the land to the county, which in turn transferred ownership to the state. In 1959 it was made a state park.

Coffee. There are a number of Coffee Creeks in the State, the best known of which is in Trinity County. The color of the water probably gave rise to these names, although an incident like the loss of a bag of coffee in the stream (*see* Sardine; Sugar) may have provided the reason. According to Jessie Gummer ("The Knave," Sept. 9, 1951), the creek in Trinity County was so named because a pack mule loaded with coffee was swept away by the high water.

Coffin: Canyon, Peak [Death Valley National Monument]. The canyon has been thus known since the Greenwater boom of 1906 and was probably so named in analogy to the other morbid names in Death Valley.

Cohasset [Butte]. When the Post Office Department in 1887 rejected the name North Point, Miss Welch, the teacher, and Marie Wilson chose the name of the town in Massachusetts for the new post office (*WF*, VI, 266 ff.). Since the name is derived from the Algonkian *koowas-et*, 'place of pine trees,' it fits nicely into the pine-covered region.

Cojo. The word, meaning 'lame' or 'lame man,' was a favorite sobriquet in Spanish times and was several times transferred to a place. The two land grants in Monterey County which include the word seem to have left no trace in California geography, but there is a Coja Creek (lame woman's creek) in Santa Cruz County, the *Arroyo de San Lucas* or *Las Puentes* of the Portolá expedition (Crespi, p. 216). **Canada del Cojo**, kō'-hō [Santa Barbara]. The Portolá expedition reached this place August 26, 1769, and camped by an Indian village. "Their chief is lame in one leg, for which reason the soldiers called it Ranchería del Cojo, but I christened it Santa Teresa" (Crespi, p. 174). The anchorage at this point, which is the *Puerto de Todos Santos* of Cabrillo, became known as *Ensenada* (or *Puerto*, or *Rada*) *del Cojo*. When A. M. Harrison of the Coast Survey made the topographical survey of Point Conception in August and September, 1850, he called the canyon Valley of the Coxo, and on Goddard's map a place called Caxa appears; but when the Coast Survey established a triangulation point at this place in 1873, the spelling was changed to Cojo (Letter to Davidson, Sept. 25, 1873).

Colby Mountain [Yosemite National Park]. Named in 1909 by R. B. Marshall in honor of William E. Colby, a well-known San Francisco attorney and mountaineer. **Colby Meadow** [Fresno]. Named in 1915 by members of the Forest Service engaged in building the John Muir Trail. **Colby: Pass, Lake** [Kings Canyon National Park]. The pass was discovered by a Sierra Club party led by William E. Colby on July 13, 1912, and was named by the party for its leader. (Farquhar.) The name was applied to the near-by lake by another Sierra Club party in 1928.

Cold, Coldwater. The adjective appears in the names of almost a hundred creeks, lakes, springs, and canyons. Some are doubtless translations of the common Spanish designation *Agua Fria*. **Cold Mountain** [Yosemite National Park] is not colder than the other peaks, but was so named simply because of its location west of Cold Canyon. **Cold Creek** [Amador], however, was originally Cole Creek, named for a settler (Co. Surveyor).

Cole Creek [Lake]. The Indian name for the stream was apparently *chibidame*, but the Indians accepted the American name Cold Creek, which in their pronunciation became Cole Creek (Mauldin).

Colegrove Point [Sutter]. The projection into Sutter Basin was named for G. S. Colegrove, a settler of 1851 (Co. Hist., 1879, p. 98).

Coleman [Death Valley]. The place was named for William T. Coleman, of San Francisco Vigilance Committee fame, who had extensive borax interests there until 1888. *See* Furnace Creek Ranch.

Coleman Valley [Sonoma]. The original name was Kolmer Valley, for Michael Kolmer, a German immigrant, who came to California in 1846 and in 1848 became the first permanent settler in this vicinity. Tyson, placing the name on the map in 1849, apparently misunderstood the name and therefore misspelled it.

Cole Slough [Tulare]. Named for William T. Cole, who in 1868 dug the irrigation ditch which formed a new channel for the Kings River during a flood (Wallace Smith, p. 192).

Coleville [Mono]. Named for Cornelius Cole, congressman 1863–1867, U.S. senator 1867–1873 (Maule).

Colfax [Placer]. The naming of the station by the Central Pacific was one of the many honors bestowed upon Schuyler Colfax when he visited California in the summer of 1865.

At that time Colfax was Speaker of the House. In 1868 he was elected Vice-President, and served during Grant's first term.

Collayomi, kăl-ĭ-ō′-mĭ: **Valley** [Lake]. The *Coyayomi* or *Joyayomi* were probably the division of the Miwok Indians, designated as Lake Indians on the map in Kroeber's *Handbook,* dwelling on both sides of the St. Helena Range. Luis Argüello, November 6, 1821 (MS, Bancroft), mentions a rancheria named *Cuaguillomic,* and the records of Mission San Francisco Solano include the name Collayomi with various spellings. The land grants Caslamayomi, March 21, 1844, Colloyomi, June 17, 1844, Colijolmanoc (Carne Humana), March 14, 1841, and possibly Locoallomi (also spelled Coallomi), 1845, may or may not preserve the same tribal name. The name of the valley was preserved through the Colloyomi grant.

College. A favorite name for real-estate subdivisions in the vicinity of colleges and often applied to physical features near them. **Collegeville** [San Joaquin]. Named in 1867 by the founders of Morris College, a Presbyterian institution, which was destroyed by fire in 1874. **College City** [Colusa]. The town grew up around the former Pierce Christian College, founded in the 1870's and endowed by the legacy of Andrew Pierce. **College Terrace** [Santa Clara]. The town was laid out in 1888 on the land purchased from Peter Spacher and F. W. Weisshaar and named Palo Alto. Stanford, who called his ranch Palo Alto, objected and suggested College Place. The property owners, however, adopted the present name, ·proposed by Edgar C. Humphrey in 1891 (Guy Miller, *WF,* VI, 78 f.). **College Heights** [San Bernardino]. Named in 1909 or 1910 by L. W. Campbell because of its proximity to Pomona College.

Collins Valley [San Diego]. The place in Coyote Valley was named for John Collins, who took up a homestead there in the 1890's but had to leave because of a conflict with the cattlemen (Parker).

Collinsville [Solano]. Named for C. J. Collins, who settled here in 1859. The name was changed to Newport in 1867, but the old name was restored in 1872.

Colma, kōl′-má [San Mateo]. On older maps the place was simply designated as Station (of the San Francisco–San Jose Railroad). Because of its location near the schoolhouse it became known as School House Station and this was the name given to the post office in

1869. The name Colma is given in Wells, Fargo & Co.'s Express Directory of 1872 and is shown on the county map of 1877. The post office is listed in 1891. The origin of the name is not known. William T. Coleman, the "Lion of the Vigilantes," owned part of the Buri Buri Rancho two miles south, and a Thomas Coleman was a registered voter in the district in the 1870's; it is not impossible that Colma was coined from this name. Since most of the settlers of those years were apparently German or Irish, it may be a transfer name from the "old country." Switzerland has a Colma, and Alsace a Colmar. Another possible origin is suggested by Beeler (*WF*, XIII, 276): in the San Francisco dialect of Costanoan, *colma* means 'moon.' However, no Indian rancheria called *Colma* is shown on any *diseño* or early map of the vicinity. Finally, there is the possibility of a literary origin. Colma occurs as a personal name in MacPherson's *Songs of Selma,* one of the Ossianic fragments (Arthur Hutson).

Coloma, kȯ-lō'-mȧ [El Dorado]. The settlement developed around Sutter's mill after the discovery of gold by James Marshall on January 24, 1848. It was named after a near-by Southern Maidu village and appears in the *New Helvetia Diary* under date of March 17, 1848, as *Culloma.* It is spelled *Colluma* on Derby's map of 1849. The post office, established November 8, 1849, was Culloma until January 13, 1851. The present spelling was first used on Tyson's map of 1849. The statement by Bancroft (IV, 27) and repeated by others, that the original name means 'beautiful vale' is a figment of American romanticists. Studebaker's shop, where the later automobile builder made wheelbarrows for the miners, is Historic Landmark 142 and the Gold Discovery site is Historic Landmark 530.

Colony: Meadow, Peak, Mill [Tulare]. The name goes back to the establishment in 1886 of the Kaweah Co-operative Colony, headed by Burnette G. Haskell, whose purpose was the cutting and marketing of lumber on a socialistic basis. Internal dissension, the countermeasures of the lumber barons, and the creation of Sequoia National Park brought about the collapse of the colony in 1891. (Cf. *Pac. Hist. Rev.,* XVII, 429 ff.)

Colorado River. The name Colorado was first applied by the Oñate expedition in October, 1604, to what is now the Little Colorado in Arizona, "because the water is nearly red" (Bolton, *Span. Expl.,* p. 269). The transfer to the larger river (called *Rio Grande de Buena Esperanza* by Oñate in January, 1605) seems to have been made by Kino in 1699 (Bolton, *Kino,* I, 193). In October, 1700, Kino mentions the "very large volumed, populous, and fertile Colorado River, which ... is that which the ancient cosmographers ... called Rio del Norte" (*ibid.,* p. 252). On his map of 1701 it appears as *Rio Colorado del Norte.* Other early names had been *Rio de Buena Guia* (river of good guidance) given by Alarcón in August, 1540 (*CHSQ,* III, 385 f.), and *Rio del Tizon* (firebrand river, because the Indians carried firebrands) given by Melchior Díaz in 1541 (Wagner, p. 519). The hybridization, Colorado River, is found, apparently for the first time, on Cary's map of 1806. Attempts were made by American cartographers of the 1840's and 1850's to call it Red River of the West or Red River of California. According to Whipple's sketches, based on information from natives in 1853, the Southern Paiute called the river *Uncah Pah,* and the Yuma, *Hah Weal Asientic* (Pac. R.R. *Reports,* Vol. III, Pt. 3, p. 16). The latter echoes clearly the name *Javill,* the Yuma name for the river as recorded by Garcés in 1775 (Coues, *Trail,* p. 144). In 1853, William P. Blake of the Pacific Railroad Survey applied the name Colorado Desert, after the river, to the region now known as the Imperial and Coachella valleys. Mesa de Colorado [Riverside] and the station Colorado [Imperial] were likewise named after the river. Elsewhere the Spanish adjective is found in place names in Contra Costa, Mariposa, Tehama, Alpine, San Benito, and Monterey counties. *See* Palo Colorado.

Colton [San Bernardino]. The place was settled by the Slover Mountain Colony in 1873. When the Southern Pacific reached the settlement two years later, it named the station for David D. Colton, financial director of the Central Pacific and Broderick's second in his duel with Terry.

Columbia. One of the most popular of our geographical names and in the early years of the republic a serious contender for the name of the United States. California has its share of Columbias, including the tall peak, Columbia Finger, in Mariposa County. **Columbia** [Tuolumne]. The discovery of gold at "Hildreth's Diggings" in March, 1850, precipitated a rush to the place. "The honor of bestowing upon the new camp its present name, Columbia, is due to Majors Farnsworth and Sullivan and Mr. D. G. Alexander, who formally named the place on the 29th of April" (Co. Hist., 1882, p. 26). The name is prominently displayed on Gibbes' map of the Southern Mines (1852). The town is now Historic Landmark 123, and since 1945 has been part of the State Park system. **Columbia Hill** [Nevada]. Named in 1853 by N. L. Tisdale and other miners for the Columbia Consolidated Mining Company.

Columbine Lake [Tulare]. The name was given by Joseph Palmer, a pioneer of the Kaweah region, because of the great quantities of columbines growing on the shores of the lake.

Colusa, kȯ-lōō′-sȧ: **County**, town, **Basin**. The rancheria named *Coru* is mentioned by Padre Blas Ordaz on October 28, 1821 (Arch. MSB, IV, 169 ff.), obviously in Patwin territory. The name was applied to two land grants: Coluses or Colussas (July 26, 1844) and Colus (October 2, 1845). Although simpler than other Indian names, it seems to set the record for spelling variants, ranging from *Corusies* to *Colouse*. The town was founded in 1850 by Charles D. Semple, claimant of the Colus rancho and brother of lanky Robert, and was called first Salmon Bend, then Colusi. The post office is listed in 1851 as Colusi's, but newspaper accounts of the same year have the modern spelling. The county, one of the original twenty-seven, was organized February 18, 1850, and likewise called Colusi until 1854.

Comanche. *See* Camanche.

Combie Lake [Placer, Nevada]. The reservoir was named after Combie (or Coombe) crossing and ranch, now submerged by the lake. Combie was a Frenchman who reached Bear River in the mining days. He is said to have introduced alfalfa into California. (Doyle.)

Complexion: Canyon, Spring [Lake]. Because the mineral water is reputedly good for the complexion, an attempt was made to commercialize the spring when a toll road was built between Bear Valley and Bartlett Springs in the 1870's (Mauldin).

Comptche, kŏmpt′-chĭ [Mendocino]. Probably an Indian name, possibly from the *Pomo* village *Komacho* (Barrett, *Pomo*, p. 178).

Compton [Los Angeles]. The name was given to the station of the Los Angeles and San Pedro Railroad in 1869, for Griffith D. Compton, founder of a Methodist temperance colony on the Domínguez rancho and in 1880 one of the founders of the University of Southern California.

Conard Meadows, Mount Conard [Lassen National Park]. Black Butte and Black Butte

Meadows were renamed in 1948 at the instigation of the Park headquarters, in memory of Arthur L. Conard, of Red Bluff, who had been instrumental in the establishment of the national park (P. E. Schulz).

Conception, Point; Concepcion, kŏn-sĕp′-shŭn [Santa Barbara]. The cape was named *Cabo de Galera* by Cabrillo, October 18, 1542, because it looked to him like a seagoing galley. The new name was apparently applied by Vizcaíno in 1602, for he reached the point about December 8, the day of the *Purísima Concepción* (Immaculate Conception). It appears on Palacios' plan as *Punta de la Limpia Concepcion* (Wagner, p. 381). On August 27, 1769, the Portolá expedition reached an Indian village north of the cape, where a native stole the sword of a soldier. "For this reason [the men] called it Rancheria de la Espada, so that with this reminder the soldier would be more careful. I gave it the sweet name of Concepcion de Maria Santisima, in view of the neighborhood of the point which has had this name for so many years" (Crespi, pp. 175 f.). On May 10, 1837, the name was applied to a land grant, Punta de la Concepcion, on which the town of Concepcion now stands. The Anglicized name, Point Conception, appears in Vancouver's *Voyage* and again on Gibbes' map (1852). The Coast Survey adopted this form in 1855, although the *Coast Pilot* and many maps continued for many years to use the Spanish spelling. The name of the post office is still spelled Concepcion but is pronounced in the American way.

Concha, Conchilla. The Spanish word for 'shell' and its diminutive are often found in geographical nomenclature, especially along the coast. *See* Abalone, Aulon, Coachella.

Concord [Contra Costa]. In 1862 Salvio Pacheco, owner of the Monte del Diablo rancho, selected the site for a town. He called the new settlement Todos Santos and offered a free lot to anyone who would build. The project succeeded, but the strong New England influence soon changed the name (Doyle). In 1868, Lewis Castro still made a survey of Todos Santos, but Juan Galindo's ledger shows that the name had been changed to Concord before June, 1869 (Robert Becker). The new name appears on Hoffmann's map of the Bay Region, 1873.

Concow, kŏn′-kow: **Valley, Creek** [Butte]. The Concow Indians, a branch of the Maidu, lived in the valley until they were transferred to the Round Valley reservation. They kept the name in their new abode (Kroeber). According to Powers (p. 283), the name was derived from the Maidu word *ko'-yoang-kau* (*ko'-yo*, 'plain'; *kau*, 'earth' or 'place').

Condor Peak [Los Angeles]; **Condor Point** [Santa Barbara]. These two features and Vulture Rock [San Luis Obispo] record the presence of the California condor or vulture, which once ranged as far north as British Columbia but is now found only occasionally in the southern part of the Coast Ranges. *See* Sisquoc.

Cone. The Cones and Cone Peaks in the State are apparently all named for their conical shape. "There are a great number of volcanic cones, more or less regular in outline, scattered over the plain to the northwest of Mount Shasta. . . . One of these conical mountains, which was much higher than any of the others, and which lay close at the western base of Mount Shasta, was so beautifully regular in its outline that we gave it the name of Cone Mountain." (Whitney, *Geology*, I, 345.) There are three Cinder Cones on the slopes of Mount Shasta, and others in Lassen National Park and in Modoc Lava Bed National Monument; also Ventana, South Ventana, and Ventana Double Cone [Monterey]; Brown Cone and Volcanic Cone [Fresno]; Dardanelles Cone [Alpine]; Red Cinder Cone [Shasta].

Conejo. The word for 'rabbit' was often used in Spanish times and is preserved in San Diego, Ventura, Fresno, Stanislaus, and Monterey counties. **Conejo,** kŏ-nā'-ō: **Mountain, Valley, Creek, Grade** [Ventura]. A watering place, *Los Conejos*, is mentioned by Font (*Compl. Diary*) on February 23, 1776, and appears repeatedly in the provincial records as the name of an Indian village and as the name of a rancho. It is again recorded in the *expediente* of the land grant El Conejo (or Nuestra Señora de Altagracia, 'Our Lady of High Grace'), dated October 10, 1822. The place is recorded on the Narváez Plano of 1830, and again on the Parke-Custer map (1855); Conejo Pass is shown on the von Leicht-Craven map of 1874. *See* Newbury Park.

Confidence: Springs, Hills, Peak, Wash [Death Valley National Monument]. Named after the Confidence Mill operated by Mormons in the 1870's. It was hoped the name might inspire confidence in the valley, so full of disappointments. A settlement called Confidence in Tuolumne County, mentioned as early as 1880, was likewise named after a mine.

Conglomerate Mesa [Inyo]. The prominent mesa, listed in the decisions of the Geographic Board, Sept.-Dec., 1963, was apparently so named on account of the conglomerate soil.

Congress Springs [Santa Clara]. The springs, discovered in the 1850's by Jud Caldwell, were originally named Pacific Congress Springs because the water is similar to that of Congress Springs, Saratoga, New York.

Conness, kŏ-něs', **Mount; Conness: Creek, Glacier** [Yosemite National Park]. "Named by the Whitney Survey in 1864 for John Conness (1821–1909), a native of Ireland; member of the State legislature, 1853–1854 and 1860–1861, U.S. senator, 1863–1869, who sponsored, in 1860, the bill that established the Geological Survey of California, and, in 1864, the bill by which Yosemite Valley and the Mariposa Grove were granted to the State" (Farquhar).

Conn Valley [Napa]. Commemorates John Conn, who came to California in 1843, possibly with the Chiles-Walker party, and who in 1853 was claimant of the Locoallomi grant. *See* Locoallomi.

Connick Grove [Humboldt]. The grove in the Prairie Creek Redwoods State Park was established in 1965 and named in honor of Arthur E. and Florence R. Connick. Connick was president of the Save-the-Redwoods League from 1951 to 1960.

Consultation Lake [Inyo]. Named in 1904 when the men who laid out the first trail to the summit of Mount Whitney from the east had a consultation here on which direction the trail should take.

Contra Costa, kŏn'-trá kŏs'-tá: **County.** One of the original twenty-seven counties, organized and named February 18, 1850. It took its name from the term used by the Mexicans to designate the 'coast opposite' San Francisco. The term Contra Costa (or Contracosta) is found in Spanish documents as early as 1797. It referred sometimes to the northern shore of the Bay: in *Hutchings' Illustrated California Magazine* Marin County is called "Contracosta" as late as August, 1860. In a letter of January 22, 1835, however, the East Bay district is clearly so designated (DSP Mont., IV, 91). The name lost its appropriateness when Alameda County was formed in 1853 and the larger part of the 'contra costa' was included in the new county.

Converse: Basin, Mountain [Fresno]. Named for Charles Converse, who came to California in 1849 and took up timber lands in the valley in the 1870's. He built the first jail in Fresno County and was the first person confined in it. (Farquhar.)

Convict: Creek, Lake [Mono]. On the morning of September 24, 1871, an engagement was fought here between convicts escaped from Carson City, Nevada, and a posse led by Robert Morrison. Morrison was killed, but the convicts were rounded up a few days later. The name of the creek had formerly been Monte Diablo Creek. (Chalfant, *Inyo*, pp. 214 ff.) *See* Morrison; Bloody.

Conway Lake [Trinity]. Named for Frederick E. Conway (1857–1951), early trapper, hunter, miner, and finally settler in the region (Geographic Board, May, 1954).

Cony Crags [Yosemite National Park]. The ridge was so named because of the abundance of "conies" (*Ochotona princeps muiri*) which inhibit the talus around the crags (Geographic Board, May-Aug., 1963).

Cooke, Camp [Santa Barbara]. Named by the War Department in honor of Philip St. George Cooke, who led the Mormon Battalion to San Diego in 1847 and became a general in the Union army in the Civil War.

Cool [El Dorado]. An old placer mining camp of the 1850's. Mining was carried on until the end of the nineteenth century. A post office was established October 20, 1885.

Coolbrith. *See* Ina Coolbrith.

Coon. About fifty physical features in the State, mainly creeks, are thus named, mostly because of the occurrence of the raccoon, although some may have been named for settlers named Coon. There is a Coon Hunters Gulch near Gilroy Hot Springs.

Cooper Canyon [Los Angeles]. Named for the brothers Ike and Tom Cooper, hunters and trappers in this area between 1870 and 1890 (Forest Service).

Coopertown [Stanislaus]. The town developed on the Rock River Ranch of William F. Cooper, who served as an officer in the Mexican War under General Scott (Paden-Schlichtmann). A post office with this name was established July 27, 1901.

Copco [Siskiyou]. Coined from *Ca*lifornia *Ore*gon *Power Co*mpany and applied to the post office in 1915 when the company's hydroelectric project was under construction.

Copernicus Peak [Santa Clara]. Named in 1895 by the staff of the Lick Observatory for the great Polish-German astronomer, Nicolaus Copernicus (1473–1543).

Copper. Only a few features in the State bear this name, given because of the presence of the ore or for the copper color of a mountain. In San Bernardino County there is a Copper Mountain Valley but apparently no Copper Mountain. **Copperopolis** [Calaveras]. The Greek word *polis*, meaning 'city,' was combined with the word "copper" to form the name of the town which grew up around the mines. "The Reed Lode was discovered by Mr. W. K. Reed, July 4th, 1861, and the first house built at what is now the thriving town of Copperopolis, September 5th" (Whitney, *Geology*, I, 255). Copper City [Shasta] and Copper Vale [Lassen] were prosperous mining towns and had post offices.

Coquette Creek [Plumas]. Like many Lady and Squaw Creeks it is probably a euphemistic term for a less respectable local name. The falls of Bolam Creek on the north slope of Mount Shasta are called Coquette Falls.

Cora Lakes [Madera]. Named by R. B. Marshall for Mrs. Cora Cressey Crow, probably when the Mount Lyell quadrangle was mapped in 1898–1899.

Coralillos Canyon. *See* Corralitos.

Coral Reef [Riverside]. "The rocky wall a few miles south of Indio is an isolated hill, close to the main rise of the mountain, noticeable for the strongly marked beach line, which is seen in a broad band of dark brown that reached 10 to 12 feet above the soil. The so called 'Coral' is really travertine or calcium carbonate." (Doyle.) *See* Travertine Rock.

Corcoran [Kings]. The establishment of the settlement was promoted by H. J. Whitley of Los Angeles in 1905, and the town was named for a civil engineer of the Santa Fe.

Cordelia [Solano]. The place was settled in 1853 by Robert H. Waterman, the clipper-ship captain, and was named Bridgeport after the town in Connecticut. When the post office was established about 1869, the Post Office Department insisted upon a less common name and Cordelia was chosen in honor of Waterman's wife. The name Cordelia for a section of the town had been mentioned since 1858. Hoffmann's map of the San Francisco Bay Region, 1873, still records the town as Bridgeport, but the post office and the slough as Cordelia. The place received the name definitely when the Wells Fargo agency was established in 1880.

Cordell Bank [Marin]. The shoal west of Point Reyes was explored in June, 1869, by Captain Edward Cordell and named for his fellow countryman J. A. Sutter (both were natives of Baden, Germany). After Cordell's sudden death on January 26, 1870, the Coast Survey renamed the bank in his memory.

Cordero, kôr-dĕr'-ō. This place name, found for several minor geographic features, is derived either from the family name or from the Spanish word *cordero,* 'lamb.'

Cordilleras. A geographical term designating the mountain ranges bordering a continent, applied in particular to South America. Emory in 1846 or 1847 (*Notes,* p. 102) called apparently both the Sierra Nevada and the Coast Range, Cordilleras of California. In the 1850's the Pacific Railroad Survey tried to make this official: "I am informed that it is now proposed to term the entire chain of mountains, extending through to the northern part of Oregon, and running south into lower California, 'Cordilleras of Western America'. . ." (Trask, *Report,* 1854, p. 13). In 1870, Whitney proposed the name for the entire orographic system of western North America, and it was actually applied until geographers realized that there is no need for such a collective name. There is a Cordilleras Creek in San Mateo County.

Cordova Village [Sacramento]. So named because the Cordova Vineyards were situated in the center of the Rancho de los Americanos grant. The post office was established May 16, 1955, and given the name Rancho Cordova.

Corkscrew Peak [Death Valley National Monument]. The name was suggested in 1936 by Don Curry, naturalist of the monument, because, in a certain light, peculiar folds in the rocks give it the appearance of a corkscrew. **Corkscrew Canyon** has been so called since 1910 because of its meandering course (Death Valley Survey).

Cornaz Lake [Shasta]. Named for Julius Cornaz, pioneer settler of Burney Valley, who built the Cornaz Trading Post in 1863 (Steger). *See* Freaner Peak.

Corning [Tehama]. The town was laid out in 1882 by the Pacific Improvement Company, a subsidiary of the Central Pacific Railroad, and named in memory of John Corning, general manager of the railroad, who died in 1878. The post office, established April 5, 1881, was first named Riceville, for a settler of 1872.

Corona. The Latin name for 'wreath' or 'circle' (which is also the Spanish word for 'crown') has always been a favorite place name in the United States. In California there are, or were, at least six communities so named.

Corona, kŏ-rō'-nȧ [Riverside]. The city was laid out by the South Riverside Land and Water Company in 1886 and named South Riverside. When the city was incorporated in 1896 the present name was suggested by Baron Harden-Hickey, owner of the El Cerrito orchards (Janet Gould). It was accepted by popular referendum on June 26. Because of the circular drive around the city it was sometimes called Circle City, a name popularized when Barney Oldfield and Eddie Rickenbacker gained their laurels in the spectacular auto races, 1913–1916. **Corona del Mar** [Orange]. The place was developed and named by George E. Hart in 1904. In 1915 the major interests were acquired by the F. D. Cornell Company, and for advertising purposes the name was changed to Balboa Palisades. Public sentiment brought about the restoration of the old name, which means 'crown by the sea.' (Sherman, pp. 154 f.)

Coronado [San Diego]. The townsite was surveyed and named in October, 1887, by the Coronado Beach Company. The name was doubtless suggested by the islands, called Los Coronados, off the coast of Lower California. These had been named by the friars of the Vizcaíno expedition in November, 1602, because November 8 was the day of the *Cuatro Coronados,* four brothers allegedly put to death for their Christian faith in the time of Diocletian.

Corral, kŏ-räl'. The Spanish word for 'enclosed space' or 'poultry yard' is used in the western United States to designate a pen for livestock or almost any outdoor enclosure. The word appears in the names of a number of Mexican land grants and often has survived as a place name. In California the word was first used in a geographical sense when the soldiers of the Portolá expedition, on August 8, 1769, called a village near Castaic [Los Angeles] *Rancheria del Corral* because "the inhabitants lived without other protection than a light shelter of branches in the form of an enclosure" (Costansó). **Corral de Piedra Creek** [San Luis Obispo]. The name is derived from the land grant Corral de Piedra, dated February 11, 1841. A *Corral de Piedra,* possibly a natural stone corral, is shown on the *diseño.* Parke, in the Pacific Railroad *Report,* 1854, calls the stream Corral de Piedras Creek. **Corral Hollow: Canyon, Creek, Pass** [Alameda, San Joaquin]. The canyon appears as *Portezuela* [pass] *de Buenos Ayres* on the *diseño* of Las Positas in 1834, and as *Arroyo Buenos Ayres* on Gibbes' map of the

Southern Mines (1852). In the 1850's the name was spelled Corall by Trask and Goddard. The canyon was perhaps so named because at its mouth there was a large corral for catching wild horses. In fact, this may have been the "caral" mentioned in the *California Star* on March 18, 1848: "We are credibly informed . . . that a number of our countrymen with several Californians are actively engaged in building an extensive caral, or enclosure, in the valley of the river San Joaquin, for the purpose of capturing wild horses. The caral . . . will enclose twenty-five acres of land . . ." According to local tradition the place was named for Edward B. Carroll, a settler of the 1850's. However, James Capen Adams, who was there in 1855, spells the name of the man Carroll and (as did Brewer in 1861) the name of the place Corral Hollow. California Kerlinger, who was born there in 1873, believes that the name referred to an old sheep corral which she remembers seeing there when she was a child. **Canada de Corral** [Santa Barbara]. The name of the gulch near El Capitan Beach preserves the name of a land grant dated November 5, 1841.

Corralitos: Lagoon, Creek, town [Santa Cruz]. A lake was called *Laguna del Corral* by Portolá's men in October, 1769, because "a piece of fence . . . was constructed between the lake and a low hill in order to keep the animals penned by night with few watchmen" (Costansó, p. 91). The present name, meaning 'little corrals,' is mentioned in 1807 (Arch. Arz. SF, II, 60) and was given to a land grant dated April 18, 1823. The name apparently did not appear on American maps until 1873 (Hoffmann), but Cronise (p. 129) mentions a town of Corallitos of "nearly one thousand five hundred inhabitants" in 1868. **Coralillos Canyon** [Santa Barbara]. A *Corral de Guadalupe* is shown on the south side of the *Arroyo de Guadalupe* (probably Corralillos Canyon) on a *diseño*, 1837, of Rancho Guadalupe. The word is another diminutive of *corral*.

Corte Madera. The term *Corte de Madera*, meaning 'a place where wood (or lumber) is cut,' was often found in Spanish times near pueblos or other settlements. It was applied to several land grants and has survived in a number of place names. **Corte Madera,** kôr'-tĕ mȧ-dâr'-ȧ: town, **Creek** [Marin]. The *Corte de Madera del Presidio* was so named because it supplied the San Francisco presidio with lumber. October 2, 1834, this name was applied to the grant of John Reed (or

Read, or Reid). The sawmill which he built was the most important source of lumber for the Bay district. The present abbreviated form of the name was used by Theodor Cordua, who leased part of the rancho in 1846. A Corte de Madera Creek in San Mateo County runs through the two grants, Cañada del Corte de Madera (May 18, 1833) and El Corte de Madera (May 1, 1844). There is a Corte Madera Mountain, and Valley, in San Diego County, and El Corte de Madera Creek is shown on the Santa Cruz atlas sheet.

Cortes Bank [San Diego]. The bank was charted by the Coast Survey in 1856 and named for the steamer *Cortes*, from the bridge of which Captain Cropper had first seen the shoal in March, 1853. The name of the bank was at first spelled Cortez, but this spelling was later corrected by Davidson. *See* Lost Islands.

Cortina: Creek, Valley, station [Colusa]. Probably named for an Indian chief. According to Barrett (*Pomo*, p. 324), Kotina was the name of a captain or head man of a Southern Wintun village. The name of the station is spelled Cortena.

Cosmit Indian Reservation [San Diego]. The Diegueño name is Kosmit, too, but its meaning is not known (Kroeber).

Coso, kō'-sō: **Range, Peak, Hot Springs,** settlement [Inyo]. The etymology of the word is not certain. Bailey says it means 'broken coal' and Kroeber adds that words beginning with *ku-* mean 'charcoal' in several Shoshonean dialects of the vicinity. This seems to connect with two older interpretations. An undated clipping from the Visalia *Delta* (about 1862) says: "Coso means fire in the dialect of the Indians inhabiting that region, and is not the name of a tribe. . . . The Coso District is, in fact, the fire, or burnt district" (Bancroft Scrapbooks, XVI, 16). Another clipping, dated April 10, 1863, says: "The Coso, or Fire District, as it is called by the Indians" (Bancroft Scraps, Mining, I, 348). The name began to appear on maps when prospectors invaded the region. On Goddard's map (1860) the vast territory between Owens Lake and the Nevada line is designated as Coso Diggings. On the von Leicht–Craven map the mountains are named, and on Wheeler atlas sheet 65-D Coso Peak appears, and Coso Valley is shown between Coso Mountains and Argus Range. The Geological Survey in 1913 retained the name but changed Coso Mountains to Coso Range. In 1864 the legislature approved a proposal for a new county, south of Mono County, to be called Coso, but it did not come into existence, and two years later Inyo County was established. Coso post office is listed in 1925.

Costa Mesa, kōs'-tá mā'-sá [Orange]. The place was originally known as Harper. When a subdivision was opened here about 1915, it was necessary to select a new name because there was a station called Harper on the Pacific Electric Railroad. As the result of a contest the present name was chosen. (Stephenson.) The two words (meaning 'coast' and 'tableland') are Spanish, but the combination is not. The post office was established and named in 1921.

Cosumnes, kŏ-sŭm'-nĕs: **River** [El Dorado, Sacramento]. The village of the Indians called *Cossomenes* is indicated on the Plano . . . de San Jose (about 1824), and the name appears in the following years with various spellings. The name may consist of the Miwok word *kosum,* 'salmon' (Bailey), plus the suffix *-umne,* 'tribe' or 'people.' The present spelling was established by Sutter, who mentions the *tribas Cosumnes y Cosolumnes* in 1841 in a letter to Alvarado (DSP, XVII, 90). It was also probably Sutter who suggested the name for the river. This is shown on Wilkes' map of 1841 as Cosmenes R., and is mentioned by Eld as Rio Cosomes. Although Frémont and Preuss used Sutter's spelling on their official maps of 1845 and 1848, the spelling was not uniform until the Geographic Board decided on May 5, 1909: "Cosumnes . . . not Consumne, Cosumne, Cosumni, Mokesumne, nor Mokosumne." The Board was less successful in trying to force upon the settlement on State Highway 16 another decision of the same day: "Cosumne . . . not Bridge House, Cosumnes, Howells, nor McCosumne." The name of the place is still spelled like that of the river. Two land grants in Sacramento County, dated December 22, 1844, and November 3, 1844, included Cosumnes in their names.

Cotati: town, **Valley** [Sonoma]. The land grant, also spelled Cotate, is dated July 6, 1844. On the *diseño* a range north of the grant is designated as *Lomas de Cotate.* Meaning and origin of the name are unknown. Barrett (*Pomo,* p. 311) lists a former Coast Miwok village, *Kotati,* north of the present town.

Cottaneva: Creek, Cove, Needle, Ridge, Rock, Valley [Mendocino]. The name of the creek emptying into Rockport Bay is shown on older maps as Cottonwood Creek. John Rockwell of the Coast Survey gives the name as Cottaneva Creek in 1878, and the county history of 1880 (pp. 470 f.) gives Cotineva as an alternate name for Rockport. The origin of the name is probably an Athabascan Indian word of unknown meaning.

Cotter, Mount [Kings Canyon National Park]. Named for Richard D. Cotter, a packer of the Whitney Survey, who accompanied Clarence King on his memorable ascent of Mount Tyndall in 1864. The name was applied by David R. Brower in 1934 and was approved by the Geographic Board in 1938. The mountain was called "Precipice Peak" by Bolton C. Brown on his sketch map (*SCB,* III, 136).

Cottonwood. Among deciduous trees the willow and the cottonwood are the favorites for place names in California. About a hundred creeks and as many other geographic features are named Cottonwood. There is hardly a county that has not at least one creek so named. The one between Shasta and Tehama counties is shown on the Frémont-Preuss map of 1848. Two settlements [Shasta and Inyo] retain the name. The reason for its popularity is the widespread occurrence of both the black and the common (or Fremont) cottonwood, the former throughout the State, the latter mainly in its southern part. The decision for Cottonwood Creek (not Tia Juana River) in Cleveland National Forest was one of the very few contributions to California nomenclature made by the Geographic Board between January, 1945, and July, 1947. *See* Alamo.

Coulterville [Mariposa]. Named for George W. Coulter from Pennsylvania, who opened a store there in 1849 and later became one of the first commissioners of the Yosemite Valley grant. The post office was established in 1852 and was called Maxwells Creek until 1872. The place is shown on Trask's map, 1853, and on all other early maps because it became one of the important trading centers of the southern Mother Lode. Historic Landmark 332. *See* Maxwell Creek.

Courtland [Sacramento]. Named for Courtland Sims, son of the owner of the land on which a steamboat landing was built in the 1860's (*Grizzly Bear,* April, 1922).

Courtright Reservoir [Fresno]. The dam and lake on Helms Creek were completed in 1958 and named in memory of H. H. "Kelly" Courtright (1887-1956), general manager of the Pacific Gas and Electric Company.

Coutolenc, kō'-tŏ-lĭnks [Butte]. Originally Coutolanezes, for Eugene Coutolanezes, but abbreviated to the present form when a post office was established in the 1880's (S. A. Vandegrift).

Covelo, kŏ'-vĕ-lō [Mendocino]. According to Bailey, the name was given in 1870 by Charles H. Eberle, after a fortress in Switzerland. Since no such place is mentioned in the gazetteers of Switzerland, the name may be a misspelling of Covolo, the name of an old Venetian fort in Tirol, not very far from the Swiss border. Covelo exists as a place name in Spain. The town in Mendocino County is recorded on the Land Office map of 1879.

Covina, kŏ-vē'-nȧ [Los Angeles]. This pleasant-sounding name was applied to a subdivision of La Puente Rancho in the late 1880's. It is shown on the Land Office map of 1891. Locally the name is said to mean 'place of vines.'

Cow. Although not as popular as the bull in geographical nomenclature, the cow is represented in some twenty-five features in California. Of these, the oldest is doubtless **Cow Creek** [Shasta], of which Frémont speaks in his *Memoirs:* "So named as being the range of a small band of cattle, which ran off here from a party on their way to Oregon. They are entirely wild, and are hunted like other game" (p. 477). Bidwell, too, says that the animals of this herd were the wildest he ever saw. Besides simple Cow Creek, a Little, an Old, a North, and a South Cow Creek flow through the same valley. **Cow Mountain** [Mendocino] was so named because it was the range of a herd of cattle, probably the stock of Andrew Kelsey which ran wild after he was killed by the Indians in 1849. **Cowhead Potrero** [Ventura] and **Cowhead Lake** and **Spring** [Modoc] were probably so named because the skull of a cow was found nailed to a post. Kern County has a Cow Heaven Canyon, and Mendocino County a Curly Cow Creek. **Cow Creek** [Death Valley National Monument]. When Phi and Cub Lee moved a herd of cattle through the valley they lost many animals here. The cows had had no water for twenty-four hours and "riled" the water of the small creek in a stampede. (Death Valley Survey.) **Cowskin Island** [Tuolumne]. The island on Woods Creek became so known because the Mexicans covered their huts here with hides from the slaughterhouse on the island (Doyle).

Cowell [Contra Costa]. Named for Henry Cowell, of the Cowell Lime & Cement Company, which built the cement works there in 1908. **Cowell Redwood State Park** [Santa Cruz]. The park was named in honor of Henry Cowell in 1954 after his son had donated the large area of redwood groves to the old Welch County Park.

Coxo. *See* Cojo.

Coyote. The name is a western American adaptation of the Aztec name for the prairie wolf, *coyotl,* and is an extremely popular place name. Many geographic features in California were named directly or indirectly after the animal, including a pass, a ridge, an Indian reservation, a land grant, and several settlements. The pronunciation of the name varies, even in the same locality, between kī-ō'-tĕ and kī'-ōt. The oldest name is probably **Coyote River,** in Santa Clara County, mentioned by Anza as *Arroyo del Coyote,* March 31, 1776, and appearing as *Arollo de Collote* on Joseph Moraga's map of San Jose, 1781. Historically interesting is **Los Coyotes** [San Diego], where Heintzelman defeated the Indians in 1851. It is Coyote on the von Leicht–Craven map and now Los Coyotes Indian Reservation. **Coyote Wells** [Imperial]. The wells were discovered in 1857 by James E. Mason of the "Jackass Mail Line," who saw a coyote scratching in the sand for water (*Desert Magazine,* May, 1939). Vanished Coyoteville in El Dorado County and several geographic features were named not for the animals but for the type of mining known as coyoteing. This method of burrowing into the ground and throwing dirt and gravel about the mouths of the shafts was apparently first used in what is now Nevada County. "The resemblance of these holes with their burrows of dirt ... to those made by the coyote [was so strong that] the system of mining was at once called 'coyoteing' and the hill was named Coyote Hill. This was the first working of the great coyote range that was so famous in early days." (Wells, *Hist. of Nevada Co.,* 1880, p. 197). In Mexico the term *coyote* is used for a certain kind of half-breed. It is not impossible that some place names applied in Spanish or Mexican times had this origin.

Crabtree: Creek, Meadow [Sequoia National Park]. Named for W. N. Crabtree, an early stockman of the region (Farquhar).

Crafton, Craf [San Bernardino]. The post office is listed in 1887 as Crafton Retreat, the name of the resort developed by Myron H. Crafts in the 1870's. The present town was laid out and named by the Crafton Land and Water Company about 1885. In 1908 the Santa Fe named its station for the same pioneer, but abbreviated it to Craf to avoid confusion with the Southern Pacific station, Crafton.

Crag. This topographical term, like many other

generic names, is of Celtic origin. It is often found for a broken cliff or projecting rock: Chaos Crags [Lassen National Park], Eagle Crags [San Bernardino], Temple Crag [Inyo], Devils Crags [Kings Canyon National Park]. There is also a Crag Peak in Tulare County.

Craig Peak [Yosemite National Park]. Named in 1898 by R. B. Marshall for John White Craig, at that time a second lieutenant in the Fifth Cavalry.

Craigy Peak [Siskiyou]. The peak was given this name, a Scottish spelling variant of craggy, because of its rugged appearance.

Crane. Crane Flat in Yosemite National Park and the places called Crane in Alameda, Lake, Madera, Napa, Sonoma, and Tuolumne counties, were named because of the presence of the bird. Flocks of the Mexican or sandhill crane are often observed on their journey between the arctic and the tropics. The soldiers of the Portolá expedition, on October 7, 1769, named a lake near Del Monte Junction *Laguna de las Grullas* because they saw many cranes (*grullas*) there (Crespi, p. 209).

Crannell [Humboldt]. The post office was named in 1924 for Levi Crannell, president of the Little River Redwood Company. From 1901 to 1924 the place was known as Bullwinkel (or Bulwinkle) for Conrad Bullwinkel, owner of the site.

Crater. The volcanic nature of the Sierra Nevada and the Cascades has given rise to a large number of Crater Peaks, Mountains, Buttes, or simply Craters. Some are really not extinct craters, but only have that appearance. The highest is Crater Mountain [Fresno]. The name is sometimes used as a generic term: Black Crater [Siskiyou], Crescent Crater [Lassen National Park]. We have a miniature Crater Lake in Lassen County and a Crater Creek in Madera County.

Crazy. *See* Mad.

Creek. In England the word designates a tidal channel, but in America it has taken the meaning of a stream smaller than a river (Stewart, pp. 60 f.). The word "estuary" is now used instead of "creek" to designate an arm of a larger sheet of water or the tidal channel of a stream, but has not become common in geographical nomenclature. The tidal channels of central California are still called, as in England, "creek," or else "slough," the latter word having meant originally a muddy place. The wide channel between Oakland and Alameda, commonly known as the "Estuary," is officially San Antonio Creek; the

wide channel between Pittsburg and Browns Island [Contra Costa] is called New York Slough; the long channel north of Suisun Bay is designated as Montezuma Slough on the Antioch atlas sheet, but as Montezuma Creek on the Napa sheet. A good example of the use of the term "creek" in the American language can be found in the watercourse along the boundary of Marin and Sonoma counties. The tidal channel has been known since Spanish times as Estero Americano (American estuary). In Wood's *Gazetteer* and on Punnett's map of Sonoma County both the estuary and the stream entering it are called Estero Americano Creek. On the Sebastopol atlas sheet the ambiguity is avoided by calling the estuary Estero Americano and the stream Americano Creek.

Crescent. This word of Latin derivation has found more favor in place naming in the United States than its Anglo-Saxon equivalent, 'half-moon.' In California the name is found in about twenty places and features, including Crescent Bay [Orange], Crescent Hill [Plumas], Crescent Lake [Yosemite National Park]. Crescent Crater and Cliff [Lassen National Park] are both shaped like a crescent. Of the five towns on the maps of the 1850's, two have survived: **Crescent Mills** [Plumas], a post office since 1870, and **Crescent City** [Del Norte]. The latter was founded by J. F. Wendell in 1853 and was so named because of the crescent-shaped bay, formerly known as Paragon Bay. The name appears in the *Statutes* of 1853 and is recorded on the Coast Survey charts of the same year. There are two fanciful creations in Los Angeles County: La Crescenta and Crescentia. The latter may have been suggested by the botanical name of the calabash tree, now grown in southern California.

Cressey [Merced]. Named by the Santa Fe for Calvin J. Cressey, a native of New Hampshire, owner of the land. The name appears as Cressy on the Santa Fe map of 1902; this spelling was adopted by the Post Office Department in 1910 but was later corrected. *See* Livingston.

Crest. The word is not only a common generic term, but is a favorite for naming places at or near a crest: Crest [Lassen], Crestmore [Riverside], Creston [Napa], Crestview [Mono]. **Creston** [San Luis Obispo]. Founded and named in 1887 by J. V. Webster of Alameda County, owner of a part of the Huerhuero grant. **Crestline** [San Bernardino]. The name was suggested by Dr. Thompson when the post office was established in 1920 (F. M. Spencer). **Crest Park** [San Bernardino]. When the post office was established, September 16, 1949, it was named after the Crest Park Camp grounds, on which it is situated (Doris Olson). The Spanish equivalent is found in Cresta [Butte] and Cresta Blanca [Alameda].

Crissy Field [San Francisco]. In 1919 Major H. H. Arnold, an Air Service officer in San Francisco (later chief of Air Staff) chose the site of the race track of the Panama-Pacific International Exposition of 1915 for an airfield. He named it in memory of Major Dana H. Crissy, who had been killed in a transcontinental air race in the same year.

Cristianitos Canyon [San Diego]. The Portolá expedition camped here on July 22, 1769, and Crespi named it for Saint Apollinaris, whose feast day is July 23. However, the soldiers, impressed by the fact that the padres of the expedition baptized two little Indian girls here, called the place *Los Cristianos* (the Christians), also *Cañada de los Bautismos* (valley of the baptisms). (Crespi, p. 135.) Later the diminutive form came to be used.

Crocker, Mount [Fresno, Mono]. When the Geological Survey mapped the region, 1907–1909, its chief geographer, R. B. Marshall, named the four peaks of the divide, surrounding the Pioneer Basin, in memory of the "Big Four" of the Central Pacific Railroad: Charles Crocker, Mark Hopkins, Collis P. Huntington, Leland Stanford (Farquhar). The four peaks are almost equal in height.

Crocker Ridge [Tuolumne]. Named after Crockers Sierra Resort at the foot of the ridge, established in 1880 by Henry R. Crocker.

Crockett [Contra Costa]. The town was laid out by Thomas Edwards in 1881 on the property of Judge J. B. Crockett, who had received 1800 acres as fee for settling a land case.

Cromberg [Plumas]. Until 1880 this was known as Twenty-Mile House because it was twenty miles from Quincy on the road to Reno. When the post office was established, Gerhard A. Langhorst, owner of the post, chose the Americanized form of his mother's family name, Krumberg (German for 'curved mountain'), as appropriate for the place on the winding road. (Minnie Church.)

Cronise: Valley, Mountains, Lake [San Bernardino]. Sometimes spelled Cronese. Probably named for Titus F. Cronise, a California pioneer and author of *The Natural Wealth of California*.

Cronkhite, Fort [Marin]. Established by the War Department in June, 1937, as a training center for Coast Artillery troops, and named in memory of Adelbert Cronkhite (1861–1937), a major general in World War I.

Crooked Spring Gulch [Calaveras]. A near-by gulch is called Straight Spring Gulch.

Cross Roads [San Bernardino]. The name was applied because a road to the river crossed the highway at this spot. The road was washed out by floods, but the name remained and was given to the post office in 1939. (E. U. Oettle.)

Crow. Some twenty features in the State bear this name. Most of them, including Crows Nest in San Luis Obispo County, were doubtless named for the bird. Others were named for men named Crow, or may be abbreviations of "Jim Crow," the once widely current nickname for a Negro.

Crow Creek [Shasta]. Named for Isaac Crow, a miner, who had his home at this tributary of Cottonwood Creek in the late 1860's.

Crowles Mountain [San Diego]. Named for George A. Crowles, who owned a ranch on the north slope in 1878. On the La Jolla atlas sheet it is designated as Black Mountain. (B. B. Moore.)

Crowley Lake [Mono]. The reservoir of the Los Angeles water system was named in 1941 for Father John J. Crowley in recognition of his services to the people of Inyo and Mono counties.

Crown: Mountain, Ridge, Creek [Kings Canyon National Park]. The mountain was named about 1870 by Frank Dusy because of a crownlike cap of rocks (Farquhar). The descriptive name is found elsewhere: Crown Point [Mono].

Crows Landing [Stanislaus]. The original Crows Landing perpetuates the name of Walter Crow and his sons, who settled along Oristimba Creek after 1849. According to the Co. Hist., 1881 (p. 218), the place was named for John Bradford Crow, a native of Kentucky, who acquired 4,000 acres of land along the San Joaquin River in 1867. The post office was established June 27, 1870.

Crucero, krŏō-sâr'-ō [San Bernardino]. In 1906 the Tonopah and Tidewater Railroad connected with the Los Angeles–Salt Lake Railroad at Epsom. In 1910 the name of the station was changed to the more melodious Crucero, the Spanish word for 'crossing.'

Crumbaugh Lake [Lassen National Park]. Named in memory of Peter C. Crumbaugh, an early sheepman and pioneer of Red Bluff

(Steger). Also spelled Crumbo.

Crystal. California has more than thirty geographic features the names of which include the descriptive term. Most of them are lakes and creeks so named because of their crystal-clear water. Crystal Creek [Shasta], Crystal Cave [Sequoia National Park], and Crystal Mine [El Dorado] were named because of the presence of crystal formations. Monterey County has a Crystal Knob, and Nevada County a settlement called Crystal Lake. **Crystal Springs Lake** [San Mateo]. The reservoir of the San Francisco water system was created in the 1870's and named after Crystal Springs, a community which was mentioned as early as 1856 and was situated a little to the northwest of present Crystal Springs Dam. **Crystal Lake** [Placer]. The lake near Cisco was named by the owner of Crystal Lake Hotel on the old Dutch Flat Road (clipping from Sacramento *Union*). **Crystal Cave** [Lava Beds National Monument]. The deepest cave in the monument was so named by J. D. Howard because the right side of the wall of the lower level was covered with ice crystals.

Cuaslui Creek [Santa Barbara]. The name *Guaslay* is shown on the southwest part of the *diseño* of the land grant La Zaca (1838). It is a Chumash name of unknown meaning.

Cuate. The Mexican word for 'twin,' from the Aztec *coatl*, was used in the names of three Mexican land grants: Huerta [garden] de Cuati, October 12, 1838, and Prospero o Cuati, May 16, 1843, both in Los Angeles County, and Corral del Cuate (also spelled Cuati, Quate, and Quati), November 14, 1845, in Santa Barbara County. A place called *Cuate* is mentioned, July 21, 1822, by a padre of Santa Ynez (Guerra Docs., V, 266). *See* Quatal.

Cuba. This became a very popular name at the time of the Spanish-American War. In 1898 California had a post office [Lassen] and several communities of that name. Only Cuba in Merced County is still found on maps and in gazetteers.

Cuca [San Diego]. A land grant dated May 7, 1845. *Los gentiles de Cucam* (the heathen Indians of Cucam) are mentioned February 27, 1842 (DSP Ang., VI, 97). *Cuca* is said to be the Indian name of a root or fruit.

Cucamonga, kŭ-kȧ-mŏng′-gȧ: **Canyon, town, Peak, Park** [San Bernardino]. A Shoshonean Indian place name meaning 'sandy place' (O. J. Fisk). *Un parage llamado* [a place called] *Cucamonga* is mentioned by Padre.

Nuez under date of November 23, 1819, when he was on an expedition commanded by Gabriel Moraga. He named it *Nuestra Señora del Pilar de Cucamunga*. (Arch. MSB, IV, 140.) January 25, 1839, the name was given to a land grant; an *Arroyo de Cucamonga* is shown on the *diseño*. The settlement developed around the old winery; it is mentioned in 1854 in the Pacific Railroad *Reports* (Vol. III, Pt. 1, p. 134) and is shown on the von Leicht–Craven map of 1873. The post office, the oldest in the county, listed in 1867, is still on the grant, but the railroad station established in 1879 is several miles southeast.

Cuddeback Lake [San Bernardino]. The dry lake took its name from John Cuddeback, who during the latter part of the 19th century hauled ore from Randsburg to Kramer and who had a quicksilver mine at the edge of the lake. The valley is known as Golden, Cuddeback, or Willard Valley. (Carma Zimmerman.)

Cuesta, kwĕs′-tȧ: **Pass** [San Luis Obispo]. The word has the general meaning of 'grade' and was applied in Spanish times here and elsewhere. It is shown as *Cañada de la cuesta* on a *diseño* of the Potrero de San Luis Obispo (1842). The name Cuesta was applied to a camp and a station north of the pass when the construction engineers of the Southern Pacific achieved, between 1887 and 1894, the difficult task of crossing the Santa Lucia Mountains. The Pacific Railroad Survey had called the pass San Luis Pass when it proposed the same route in the 1850's.

Cuffey: Cove, Inlet [Mendocino]. The name appears on the charts of the Coast Survey in 1870 as Cuffee's Cove, but it is not known whether Cuffee (or Cuffey) was actually a person's name or the nickname of a Negro settler.

Culbert L. Olson Grove [Humboldt]. The grove was dedicated by Matthew Gleason, chairman of the California State Park Commission, on June 28, 1940, and named in honor of Culbert L. Olson, governor of California, 1938–1942.

Culbertson Lake [Nevada]. The reservoir was named for J. H. Culbertson, who built the dam in the early 1850's.

Culver City [Los Angeles]. Named for Harry H. Culver, who came from Nebraska in 1914 and acquired and subdivided part of the Ballona land grant.

Cumbre. The Spanish word for 'top' or 'summit' is used in the name of La Cumbre Peak [Santa Barbara].

Cummings [Mendocino]. Named for Jonathan Cummings, a native of Maine who came to California in 1856 and in the early 1870's preëmpted a homestead on the Eel River (Co. Hist., 1914, p. 1025).

Cummings: Valley, Creek, Mountain [Kern]. Named for George Cummings—an Austrian despite his English name, according to the County History (1914, p. 1531). He came to California in 1849, took up a homestead in the valley in the 1870's, and became a successful stock raiser.

Cunningham [Sonoma]. The railroad station was named in 1904 for the Cunningham family, who had large holdings in the vicinity.

Cupertino, kū-pêr-tē′-nō [Santa Clara]. An *Arroyo de San Jose Cupertino*, named in honor of an Italian saint of the 17th century, was mentioned by Anza and Font when the expedition camped at the creek, March 25, 1776. When in the late 1840's Elisha Stephens (or Stevens) settled there, it became known as Stevens Creek. Hoffmann's map of the Bay region (1873) has "Stephen's or Cupertino Creek." The Geological Survey in 1899 decided for Stevens Creek, but the old name was preserved in the name of the post office, established in 1882. After this post office was discontinued, the name was transferred to the one at West Side in 1895 as a result of a petition.

Curry, Lake [Napa]. The reservoir of the Valley Water Supply was named about 1925 for Congressman Charles F. Curry (D. T. Davis).

Curry–Bidwell Bar State Park [Butte]. In 1947 T. E. Curry gave the land for the park, which includes the place where John Bidwell discovered gold on July 4, 1848.

Cushenbury: Canyon, Springs, Grade [San Bernardino]. The names go back to a short-lived Cushenbury or Cushionberry City at the east end of Holcomb Valley, named for a miner who operated there during the gold rush of 1860 (*Mining and Scientific Press*, April 27, 1861).

Cutler: town, Park [Tulare]. Named by the Santa Fe in 1903 for John Cutler, a pioneer of the district and for many years a county judge. In 1898 Cutler had given the right of way through his land, with the proviso that the station be named for him. The park was given by John Cutler, Jr., in 1919, to be known as Cutler Park in memory of his parents.

Cutten [Humboldt]. The post office was established in 1930 and named for the Cutten family, prominent since the early 1850's in the industrial and political history of Humboldt County.

Cut-throat Gulch [Trinity]. So named because, about 1860, "Blind Lee," a Chinese prospector who was thought to have struck it rich, was found there with his throat cut (J. D. Beebe).

Cuyamaca, kwē-á-măk′-á: **Peak, Valley, Reservoir, State Park** [San Diego]. An Indian rancheria, *Cullamac*, is recorded on August 10, 1776 (PSP, I, 229), and is mentioned as *Cuyamac* in the early records of Mission San Diego. The present spelling is used in the title of a land grant dated August 11, 1845; the *Sierra de Cuyamaca* is shown on the *diseño;* and an Indian village named Cuyamaca is mentioned as late as 1852. The common designation of the mountains as "Queermack" seems to bear out Kroeber's contention that the origin of the name is Diegueño *ekwi-amak*, 'rain above.'

Cuyama: River, Peak, settlement [Santa Barbara, San Luis Obispo]. An *arroyo llamado de Cuyam* is mentioned in 1824 (DSP, I, 48). The name Cuyama was given to two land grants, dated March 16, 1843, and June 9, 1846. Cuyama Plain and Mountains are mentioned by Parke in 1854–1855 (Pac. R.R. *Reports*, Vol. VII, Pt. 1, p. 6). The name was doubtless that of an Indian rancheria, shown as *Cullama* and *Cuyama* on *diseños* of the land grants. The word is Chumash and means 'clams,' according to Harrington. The pronunciation varies according to locality: kōō-yä′-má, kwē-ä′-má, kwē-yăm′-á, kwē-ăm′-á.

Cuyapaipe. *See* Guyapipe.

Cuyler Harbor [San Miguel Island]. Named in February, 1852, by James Alden of the Coast Survey schooner *Ewing* for Lieutenant R. M. Cuyler: "a very good anchorage, which I have named '*Cuyler's Harbor*,' in honor of one of the officers attached to the party" (*Report*, 1852, p. 105).

Cypress. In spite of the existence of five different native species of the tree and the striking shape of the Monterey cypress, the name is connected with only a few geographic features. This is because most members of the cypress family are commonly called cedars. **Point Cypress** [Monterey] is the only feature which is named after the Monterey cypress. Tomás de la Peña (June 15, 1774) calls it, in his diary, *La Punta de cipreses* (HSSC:*P*, Vol. II, Pt. 1, p. 85), and it is so named on several maps. It was used for the name of a land grant, February 29, 1836. The trees which suggested the name are mentioned by Palou

(II, 285 f.): "They [Portolá, Crespi, and Fages] also found a grove of cypresses on a point which is on the little bay [Carmel Bay] to the south of the Point of Pines." In 1852 the Coast Survey translated the name as Point Cypress. There is a **Cypress Mountain** in San Luis Obispo County, doubtless named after the Sargent cypress, which is found in the Santa Lucia Mountains. **Cypress** [Orange], **Cypress Grove** [Los Angeles and Marin], and **Cypress Lawn** [San Mateo] were named either for plantings of the tree or after other places so named.

Daggett [San Bernardino]. Named in 1882 by the Southern Pacific Railroad (the name was retained in 1884 by the Santa Fe) for John Daggett, lieutenant governor of California (1883–1887), who built one of the first houses here and laid out the townsite. Daggett Pass in Alpine County was apparently likewise named for John Daggett.

Dairy Valley [Los Angeles]. A "rural city" surrounded by a populated area was incorporated in 1956 to protect its dairy and agricultural industry (Co. Hist., 1965, IV, 106).

Dalton [Los Angeles]. The Big and the Little Dalton Wash, and the Big and Little Dalton Canyons, commemorate Henry Dalton, an English trader from Lima, grantee of the San Francisquito and claimant of the Azusa and Santa Anita ranchos.

Dalton Mountain [Fresno]. So named because Grattan Dalton of the Midwestern Dalton gang hid out in the area after his escape from the Visalia jail in 1891 (Co. Hist., 1956).

Daly City [San Mateo]. The city came into existence when many people found a refuge there after the San Francisco earthquake and fire of 1906. It was incorporated in 1911 and named for John Daly, owner of a dairy ranch. (Wyatt.)

Damnation Peak [Shasta]. So named because of the desperate struggle between entrapped Indians and a detachment of the Fourth Infantry under Lieutenant George Crook in July, 1859. Damnation Creek [Del Norte] was doubtless named for some similar reason.

Dana [Shasta]. The town was laid out in 1888 and named for Loren Dana, who had settled at the Big Springs in the late 1860's (Steger). The post office is listed in 1892.

Dana, Mount; Dana Creek [Yosemite National Park]. In 1889, J. N. LeConte copied from a record found on the summit: "State Geological Survey, June 28, 1863. J. D. Whitney, W. H. Brewer, Charles F. Hoffmann, ascended this mountain June 28th and again

the 29th. We give the name of Mount Dana to it in honor of J. D. Dana, the most eminent American geologist." James Dwight Dana (1813–1895) was professor of geology at Yale at that time (*SCB*, XI, 247.) "Messrs. Dana and Lyell expressed themselves as highly gratified over the honor done them; as well they might, for a thirteen-thousand-foot peak is no mean memorial for any man, while of all human monuments few endure like place names" (Whitney, July 10, 1863). *See* Lyell.

Dana: Point, Cove; Dana Point (town) [Orange]. Neither point nor bay was prominent enough to have found a place on early maps. The bay was called *Bahia* [on Humboldt's map: *Ensenada*] *de San Juan Capistrano* when this mission used it as an anchorage in the early part of the 19th century. Early American maps failed to show a name for the bay, but in 1884 the Coast Survey called a triangulation point on the promontory, Dana, doubtless in memory of Richard H. Dana, who once "had swung down [the cliff] by a pair of halyards to save a few hides." On the Capistrano atlas sheet, edition of 1902, the Geological Survey applied the name to the point and the cove. The Coast Survey accepted the name, but the Hassan map of the Geological Survey (1929) and the Corps of Engineers atlas sheet use the name San Juan Capistrano Point. The post office, Dana Point, was established in 1929 and named after the point.

Danby. *See* Amboy.

Dan Hunt: Mountain, Meadows [Shasta]. Named for Dan Hunt, who settled in the county in 1852 and became one of the early cattle kings (Steger).

Dantes View [Death Valley National Monument]. The name, doubtless inspired by Dante's description of the Inferno, had already been used locally when it was chosen in the early 1930's by the National Park Service for the best-known view point of Death Valley. W. C. Mendenhall (WSP, No. 224) in 1909 mentioned Dante Springs near Soda Lake, about eighty miles southeast.

Danville [Contra Costa]. In an issue of the Danville *Sentinel* of 1898, Daniel Inman, who had settled here in 1858, told the story of the naming of the post office in 1867. "Then the people wanted a post office. Of course it had to have a name, and quite a number were suggested. At first they thought of calling it 'Inmanville,' but my brother Andrew and I objected to that. Finally, 'Grandma' Young, my brother's mother-in-law, said: 'Call it

Danville' and as much or more out of respect to her, as she was born and raised near Danville, Kentucky, it took that name." (R. R. Veale.) However, a post office Danville was already established August 31, 1860, and it is shown on a plat of Rancho San Ramon.

Dardanelles, The; Dardanelles: Cone, Creek; Dardanelle post office [Alpine, Tuolumne]. The peaks were apparently named by the men of the Whitney Survey in the 1860's because they saw a resemblance between the volcanic rock formations and the mountain castles which guarded the entrance to the Sea of Marmora in Turkey. By a strange coincidence, the contour lines on the topographical atlas sheet resemble the outline of Gallipoli Peninsula and the opposite coast of Asia Minor. The watercourse, however, does not bear the classical name Hellespont, but is called McCormick Creek. Near by is another group of peaks called Whittakers Dardanelles, shown on the Stanislaus National Forest map. (*WF*, VI, 79, 178.) The name of the straits in Turkey was repeatedly used for mines and mining companies, doubtless because the Crimean War (1854) made the name Dardanelles known all over the world. In a letter of March 10, 1861, Whitney mentions "Dardanelles Diggings, way up in Placer County," and Brewer mentions the name on November 7, 1863 (Notes).

Darrah Creek [Shasta]. The branch of Battle Creek was named for Simon Darrah, a pioneer of 1857, who guided lumber rafts down the Sacramento (Steger).

Darwin, Mount; Darwin: Glacier, Canyon, Creek [Kings Canyon National Park]. The highest peak in the Evolution Group was named in 1895 by T. S. Solomons, in honor of Charles Darwin. *See* Evolution.

Darwin: Wash, Canyon, town [Inyo]. The wash was named in 1860 by Dr. Darwin French when he led a party into Death Valley to search for the mythical "Gunsight Lode." Darwins Canon is mentioned by the Nevada Boundary Survey on July 31, 1861. Darwin Cañon and the mining town appear on Wheeler atlas sheet 65-D. According to Weight (p. 9), Dr. E. Darwin French had a ranch at Fort Tejon and was with a party of prospectors in this canyon in the fall of 1850.

Daulton [Madera]. Named for Henry C. Daulton, who came to Fresno County in 1857 and was made chairman of the commission to organize Madera County. The name was applied by the Southern Pacific in the late 1860's because Daulton gave to the railroad

eight miles of right of way through his property.

Davenport [Santa Cruz]. Named about 1868 after the near-by whaling station, Davenport Landing, established by Captain John P. Davenport in the 1850's.

Davidson, Mount [San Francisco]. The highest elevation in San Francisco County had been known as Blue Mountain since Beechey placed it on a map in 1827. In 1912, after the death of George Davidson, the mountain was named in memory of that great scientist. The change was made at the instigation of the Sierra Club, and the ceremony of christening was performed by Davidson's friend and associate, Alexander McAdie. On some maps the elevation is still labelled San Miguel Hills. **Davidson Seamount** [75 miles west of Point Piedras Blancas]. Discovered in 1932 by the Coast Survey ship *Guide* and named in 1938 in honor of Davidson. "The generic term 'seamount' is here used for the first time, and is applied to submarine elevations of mountain form whose character and depth are such that the existing terms bank, shoal, pinnacle, etc., are not appropriate." (Geographic Board, *Decisions*, 1938.)

Davidson City [Los Angeles]. *See* Dominguez.

Davis [Yolo]. Originally called Davisville for Jerome C. Davis, who settled here in the early 1850's. With the coming of the railroad in the 1860's the town grew and became known by its present name.

Davis, Lake [Plumas]. The artificial lake was formed by the Grizzly Valley Dam in the 1950's and named for Lester T. Davis, conservationist and leader in behalf of the project, who had died in 1952 (Geographic Board, Jan.-Mar., 1965).

Davis Creek [Inyo]. Named for David Davis, who came to the region about 1866, married Lizzie Wiles, an Indian woman, and raised cattle and potatoes for the mining camps (Robinson).

Davis Lake [Kings Canyon National Park]. Named in 1925 in memory of George R. Davis (1877–1922), topographic engineer with the U.S. Geological Survey. Davis mapped and assisted in mapping about thirty topographical quadrangles. (Farquhar.) There is another Davis Lake on the same quadrangle (Mount Goddard) in Mono County.

Davis Mountain [Mono]. Named in 1894 by Lieutenant N. F. McClure, for Lieutenant Milton F. Davis, who had made the first ascent on August 28, 1891. Davis was chief of staff of the Army Air Service during World War I. (Farquhar.)

Davy Brown Creek [Santa Barbara]. The name has been current since the 1860's, when it was the favorite back-country haunt of an early settler, Davy Brown, who had served under Jackson at New Orleans (Wm. S. Brown).

Dawson, Mount [Los Angeles]. Named for R. W. Dawson, a miner in San Gabriel Canyon about 1876, and in 1890 operator of the first resort in what is now Angeles National Forest.

Day [Modoc]. The post office is listed in 1892 and was named possibly for Nathaniel H. Day, a pioneer, whose name is recorded in the Great Register of 1879.

Day, Mount [Santa Clara]. The peak, near the Alameda County line, recorded on maps since the 1860's, was named probably for Sherman Day, State senator representing Alameda and Santa Clara counties, 1855–1856, U.S. surveyor general for California, 1868–1871. Sherman Island [Sacramento] was also named for Senator Day.

Daylight: Spring, Pass [Death Valley National Monument]. The name of the spring was first Delightful, then Delight, and finally Daylight Spring (AGS: *Death Valley*).

Days Needle [Sequoia National Park]. The pinnacle was named for William C. Day (1857–1895), of Johns Hopkins University, later professor of chemistry at Swarthmore College. He was engaged in solar observations on Mount Whitney in 1881 with the party led by the astronomer Samuel P. Langley. (Farquhar.)

Dead. The adjective is applied to a number of features, mainly mountains, because of their forbidding appearance. Best known are the Dead Mountains extending from San Bernardino County into Nevada. More than twenty-five geographic features, including Dead Horse Glen [Del Norte] and Dead Horse Reservoir [Modesto], were named because a dead horse was found at each of them. There is also an assortment of Dead Indian, Dead Cow, Dead Pine Creeks, Gulches, Mountains, etc. *See* Deadman; Death Valley; Muerto.

Deadman. A convenient and often-used term for places where a corpse was found. More than ten Deadman Creeks and as many Deadman Canyons appear on maps of California, as well as various Deadman Gulches, Sloughs, Forks, Flats, Lakes, Points, and Islands. **Dead Mans Island** [Los Angeles]. Thus named because, before 1836, an English sea captain was buried on its highest point. In later years it served as a convenient burial ground for persons who died aboard ships. The name was mentioned by Richard H. Dana in 1835, and again in Robert C. Duvall's Log of the *Savannah:* On November 11, 1846, William H. Berry "departed this Life from the effects of a wound received in Battle. Sent his body on 'Dead Mans Island,' so named by us" (*CHSQ*, III, 118 f.). The island, now only a shoal in San Pedro harbor, was also known as *Isla del Muerto*. **Deadman's Hole** [San Diego]. The springs became thus known after a driver for the Butterfield stages found a corpse there in 1858. **Deadman Canyon** [Kings Canyon National Park]. At the lower end of the west branch of Roaring River is the grave of a sheepherder, concerning which there are many legends. The name is incorrectly given to the east branch on some maps. (Farquhar.) **Deadman: Creek, Pass, Summit** [Mono]. The creek became known by this name because the headless body of a man was found there in the 1860's. It was probably the body of Robert Hume, of Carson, who had been killed by a fellow miner.

Deadwood. The word was a typical gold miner's term meaning "sure thing." During the gold rush it was applied to numerous camps, the name of one of which, in Trinity County, has survived .Some of the twenty orographic and hydrographic features in the State may actually have been applied for dead or burned forests.

Dearborn Park [San Mateo]. Named for Henry Dearborn, a lumberman of the early logging days (Wyatt).

Death Valley; Death Valley: Buttes, Canyon, post office, **National Monument.** The name was probably used for the valley by gold seekers of the 1850's because of its forbidding appearance and because of the skeletons of unfortunate wanderers found there. Most maps of the period leave the region blank, but Lapham and Taylor (1856) designate the valley as Armuyosa (!) Desert. The present name was probably applied if not bestowed by the Nevada Boundary Survey. Its earliest known mention is an entry written by a member of the Boundary Commission, dated February 24, 1861: "... Death Valley, which forms the grand retort for all its [Amargosa's] damned ingredients, and which is ... a vast and deep pit of many gloomy wonders ..." (Sacramento *Union,* July 9, 1861). Soon afterward everyone called the region Death Valley as if it were an old name (Wheat, *SCB*, XXIV, 108). The first map recording of the name seems to be that of Farley (1861). William L.

Manly, a member of the ill-fated Manly-Bennett party of 1849, wrote, forty-five years later: "Just as we were ready to leave and return to camp we took off our hats, and then overlooking the scene of so much trial, suffering and death spoke the thought uppermost saying, '*Goodbye, Death Valley!*'" (*Death Valley in '49*, Santa Barbara: Hebberd [1929], p. 221). No contemporary evidence, however, has been discovered to indicate that the name was used before 1861. The names Lost Valley and Amargosa Desert were also used for the valley or parts of it until the Geographic Board by decision of February 7, 1906, made the present name official. The national monument was created and named in 1933 by proclamation of President Hoover. *See* Amargosa.

Declezville, dĕ-klĕz'-vĭl [San Bernardino]. When the Southern Pacific built a spur to the large granite quarries, it named the junction Declez and the terminal Declezville, for William Declez, owner of the granite works. Declez is now South Fontana.

Decoto [Alameda]. Named by the Southern Pacific for Ezra Decoto, who had come from Canada in 1854, bought a large farm with his brothers in 1860, and sold the right of way to the railroad in 1867.

Dedrick [Trinity]. The settlement was formerly an important trading center and the post office for the mines between Trinity Alps and Trinity River. The identity of Mr. Dedrick could not be determined.

Deer. There are at least 150 Deer Creeks, Canyons, Flats, Parks, etc., in the State. In place names derived from the animal kingdom only Bear outranks Deer as a favorite. There are a number of Deerhorn Meadows and Creeks, probably so named because horns were found there. In Tulare County there is an Old Deer Creek Channel, and in Trinity County a settlement, Deer Lick Springs. Some of the names are translations from the Spanish: Deer Creek [Tehama] is shown on *diseños* as *Arroyo de los Venados* and *Rio de los Venados*. **Deer Creek** [Nevada]. The stream was named by Isaac Wistar and a companion named Hunt in August, 1849, when they abandoned a freshly killed deer because they feared hostile Indians. "Next day we reached camp before dark, and described to eager listeners our creek—then and there christened Deer Creek—with the promising appearance of its vicinity . . ." (Wistar, I, 125). Hunt returned to the creek, struck one of the richest and most famous gold deposits, and named

the place Deer Creek Dry Diggings. This was the nucleus of Nevada City.

Deer Flat [Shasta]. So named because "Deer Flat," a chief of the Hat Creek Indians, lived there (Steger).

Deerhorn Mountain [Kings Canyon National Park]. Named by Joseph N. LeConte in 1895 because of the resemblance of its double summit to two deerhorns (Farquhar).

De Haven [Mendocino]. Named for John J. De Haven, a native of Missouri, who came to California in 1849 and was district attorney 1867–1869, assemblyman 1869–1871, and finally state senator (Co. Hist., 1882, p. 177).

Dehesa, dĕ-hē'-sȧ [San Diego]. The Spanish word for 'pasture ground' was applied to a post office, June 18, 1888. Shown on the Land Office map of 1891. **Dehesa, Mount** [Lake]. According to Mauldin, the name was applied by Salvador Vallejo. It is commonly pronounced desh'-a.

Dekkas Creek [Shasta]. According to Steger, the name of the tributary to McCloud River is derived from Wintu *da-kas*, which is said to mean 'climb up.'

Delamar [Shasta]. The mining town was named in 1900 by M. E. Dittmar, for Captain J. H. Delamar of New York, owner of the Bully Hill mines (Steger).

Delaney Creek [Yosemite National Park]. Named, apparently by John Muir, for Pat Delaney, the sheepman who accompanied him on his first trip to the Sierra in 1869 (Farquhar).

Delano, dĕ-lā'-nō [Kern]. The Southern Pacific reached the place on July 14, 1873, and named the station for Columbus Delano, at that time (1870–1875) Secretary of the Interior.

Delavan [Colusa]. The Southern Pacific station was named, probably after one of the four Delavans then existing in the Middle West, when the line from Woodland to Willows was built in the 1870's. The name of the post office is spelled Delevan.

Delgada, dĕl-gä'-dȧ, **Point; Delgada Canyon** [Humboldt]. The descriptive name, meaning 'narrow point,' was applied to Point Arena apparently by Bodega in 1775. In 1792 Vancouver changed this name to Barro de Arena, and cartographers were obliged to find a new point for Delgada. La Pérouse (1797) placed it just south of Cape Mendocino, and, with the exception of Humboldt's, apparently all subsequent maps have a Point Delgada somewhere near latitude 40°. The cautious Duflot de Mofras placed two such names on his map, one south of Cape Mendocino, one north of

Point Arena. Wilkes in 1841 finally applied it to the point above Shelter Cove, although this particular point is not at all narrow. The name for the submarine canyon, seven miles off the coast, was applied by the Coast Survey and approved by the Geographic Board in 1938.

Delhi. The name of the historic city in India, famed for its gardens, is a favored place name in the United States. In California it has been used at least three times. **Delhi,** dĕl′-hī [Merced]. The place is shown on the Mining Bureau map of 1891. The modern town was laid out in 1911. **Delhi** [Solano] was listed as a railroad station by McKenney in 1884 and still appears in the gazetteers. **Delhi** [Orange] is mentioned in the county history of 1921.

Delleker, dĕl′-ĕ-kĕr [Plumas]. The name of W. H. Delleker, a lumberman, was applied to the station of the Western Pacific in 1908 (*Headlight,* Dec., 1942).

Del Loma [Trinity]. The name, meaning 'of the hill' or 'by the hill,' was given to the post office in 1927.

Del Mar [San Diego]. The seaside town was founded in 1884 by Colonel Jacob S. Taylor of Oklahoma. The wife of T. M. Loop, one of the promoters, is said to have suggested the name because the site was not far from the setting of Bayard Taylor's poem, "The Fight of Paso del Mar." (Santa Fe.)

Del Monte, dĕl mŏn′-tĭ [Monterey]. The name, meaning 'of (or by) the grove,' was given to the hotel by Charles Crocker in 1886. It was probably suggestèd by the beautiful oak groves near by, rather than by the land grant Rincon de la Punta del Monte, twenty-five miles to the southeast.

Del Norte, dĕl nôrt: **County.** The bill proposing the creation of the new county in 1857 proposed the name Buchanan, for the newly elected President of the United States. The legislature, in spite of its Democratic majority, rejected the name of the President and insisted upon a Spanish name. Del Norte, meaning 'of the north,' was chosen in preference to Alta, Altissima, Rincon, and Del Merritt (!) , the other suggested names. The area comprising Del Norte Coast Redwoods is now a state park.

Del Paso, dĕl păs′-ō [Sacramento]. The post office is listed in 1904 and was named after the Mexican grant, Rancho del Paso, dated December 18, 1844, which in turn had been named after *El paso de los Americanos,* the ford in American River, northeast of Brighton. The town was platted in 1911. The post-

office name is now Del Paso Heights. *See* American River; Paso.

Delpiedra, dĕl-pĭ-ā′-drá [Fresno]. When the Santa Fe spur from Reedley was built in 1910, the terminal was called Piedra (stone). In 1923 the post office was established, and was given the name Del Piedra, a pseudo-Spanish combination. The railroad station retained the original name.

Del Rey, dĕl rā [Fresno]. The town was settled by the Wilkinson brothers in 1884, and the post office was established the following year with the name of Clifton. When the railroad reached the place in 1898, the present name was adopted because the station was on the Rio del Rey (river of the king) ranch. (Santa Fe.)

Del Rosa [San Bernardino]. The post office and the town bore the name Delrosa (possibly a family name) until 1905, when Zoeth S. Eldredge, a Spanish language enthusiast, petitioned the Post Office Department for the change. The result is an incorrect combination of a feminine noun with a masculine article.

Delta. In geographical terminology the fourth letter of the Greek alphabet is applied to any formation having its shape (Δ). Because of the fame and fertility of the Nile Delta, the word is frequently applied to any alluvial deposits at the mouth of a river, even if no triangular shape is evident; as, for example, the Sacramento and San Joaquin Delta. There is a Delta Lake in Modoc County; a Santa Fe siding, La Delta, in San Bernardino County; a Delta Canyon and a Pacific Electric station named Delta in Los Angeles County. **Delta** [Shasta]. The place was so named because the level land on top of the hill and the intersection of the Sacramento with Dog Creek form the Greek letter *delta* (Steger). A post office named Delta was established August 10, 1875, and again May 1, 1948. The name is shown on the Land Office map in 1879. Between 1884 and 1948 the post office name was Bayles, for A. M. Bayles, the postmaster, whose father had been a settler of 1855 (Steger) .

De Luz, dĕ lōōz: **Creek,** station, town [San Diego]. According to local tradition, a pioneer Englishman named Luce built a large enclosure for his horses, and his Spanish-speaking neighbors called it *Corral de Luz.* When the post office was established in the 1880's, this name was abbreviated to the present form.

Democrat Mountain [Shasta]; **Democrat Hot**

Springs [Kern]. Former generations not only were fond of bestowing the names of political leaders upon places but sometimes commemorated their parties in geographical names. *See* Knownothing.

Denair, dê-nâr' [Stanislaus]. Named by John Denair, a former superintendent of the Santa Fe division point at Needles, when he purchased the townsite in 1906. The original settlement was known as Elmdale, then as Elmwood Colony. (Santa Fe.)

Denlin [Tulare]. Originally named Linden, for John and Emma Linden, who sold the right of way to the Santa Fe in 1917. To end confusion with another Linden, the syllables were reversed in 1927 to form the present name. (Santa Fe.)

Denniston Creek [San Mateo]. Probably named for James G. Denniston, an assemblyman from San Mateo County who had come to California with Stevenson's New York Volunteers in 1847 (Wyatt).

Denny [Trinity]. The place was settled in 1882 and called New River City. When the Post Office Department rejected the name a few years later, the miners chose the present name, for Denny Bar, owner of the store. In 1920 the town was abandoned and the post office moved to Quimby, which soon afterward was renamed Denny. (W. Ladd.)

Denverton [Solano]. Named in 1858 for James W. Denver, California's secretary of state, 1853–1855, and congressman from the district, 1855–1857, in recognition of his stand against a bill to confirm all existing grants less than ten leagues in area. Denver later became governor of Kansas Territory, and his name is commemorated in Denver, Colorado. Denverton was formerly known as Nurse's Landing, for Dr. Stephen K. Nurse. *See* Nurse Slough.

Derby Dike [San Diego]. Named for Lieutenant George H. Derby, of the U.S. Corps of Topographical Engineers, who in 1853 supervised the construction of a dam across the course of the San Diego River, diverting the water into False Bay (now Mission Bay). The original structure was washed out in 1855 and replaced in 1876. Derby was the early California humorist who wrote under the name John Phoenix. *See* Honey Lake.

Dersch Meadows [Lassen National Park]. The name commemorates Fred and George Dersch, prominent pioneers in Shasta County in the 1860's and 1870's. Dersch Homestead, east of Anderson, is Historic Landmark 120.

De Sabla, dê săb′-lá: Reservoir, town [Butte].

Named for Eugene De Sabla, who initiated the construction of the power plant for the Pacific Gas and Electric Company in 1903.

Descanso dĕs-kăn′-sō: town, Valley, Creek [San Diego]. The Spanish word for 'rest' or 'repose' was applied to the post office February 16, 1877. The place is mentioned in a diary of 1849 with the drawing of a mission-style building (SCP: *Q*, VI, 96), but this may refer to a place on the Descanso land grant, just south of the international boundary in Lower California. There is also a Descanso Bay on Catalina Island.

Desert. The desert has a strong fascination for those who know it, and the name is used not only for a number of buttes, creeks, and springs, but also for several communities: Desert Center, Desert Hot Springs [Riverside]; Desert [San Bernardino].

Desolation. The name is repeatedly used in California nomenclature to designate isolated or uninviting spots. The name Desolation Lake was applied to the largest of the lakes of Humphreys Basin [Fresno] by J. N. LeConte in 1898 (Farquhar).

Detachment Meadow. *See* Soldier Meadow.

Devil. There are in California between 150 and 200 topographic features which are named for the Prince of Darkness. Probably no other state can equal this number. We have not only many forbidding places in mountains and forests where he might abide, but also an assortment of weird formations of basalt, sandstone, and lava, as well as numerous evil-smelling pools and wells, which people like to connect with the devil. Besides the common generic terms, the following are most popular in combination with this name: Gate (10 in number), Punchbowl (5), Den (5), Kitchen (3), Gap (3), Backbone (3). There are a number of unusual combinations: Devils Speedway [Death Valley National Monument], Devils Rock Garden [Shasta], Devils Playground [San Bernardino], Devils Half Acre [Shasta], Devilwater Creek [Kern], Devils Parade Ground [Tehama], Devils Heart Peak [Ventura], Devils Nose [Calaveras], Devils Potrero [Ventura], Devils Pulpit [Mount Diablo State Park], Devils Head Peak [Napa]. The name is also applied to a town: Devils Den [Kern]. The bend in the Sacramento, north of Colusa, was once known as Devil's Hackle. The "devilish" names in Geyser Canyon [Sonoma] were already current in 1867—Devils: Gristmill, Inkstand, Laboratory, Pulpit, Quartzmill, etc. Well-known features are Devils Postpile National

Monument [Madera], a strange pile of basalt columns established as a national monument, July 6, 1911; **Devils Crags** [Kings Canyon National Park], named by J. N. LeConte in 1906; **Devils Golf Course** [Death Valley National Monument], a wide expanse of jagged salt hummocks on which only the devil could play golf; **Devils Garden** [Riverside], an immense thicket of cactus. **Devils Bathtub** [Fresno] is shown in perfect outline on the Mount Goddard atlas sheet. **Devils Homestead** [Lava Beds National Monument]. So named because of the weird appearance of the formation along the west boundary of the Monument caused by a recent (i.e., only a few centuries old) lava flow. **Devils Mush Pot Cave** [Lava Beds National Monument]. J. D. Howard originally applied the name Devils Mush Pot to the small crater near Indian Well, and the name Pots to the cave south of Hercules Leg because there were "two stone whirlpools" on the floor of the lower chamber. *See* Diablo.

Devines Gulch [El Dorado]. The gulch near Georgetown was named for Caleb Devine, who discovered gold here in 1850. According to an unidentified newspaper clipping the discoverer was later hanged by a mob.

Devore, dĕ-vôr′ [San Bernardino]. The station was named for John Devore, a landowner of the district, when the California Southern (now the Santa Fe) completed the railroad through Cajon Pass in 1885. It was formerly called Kenwood for a Chicago clothier who owned a large tract of land here. (Santa Fe.)

Dexter Peak [San Diego]. Named in memory of John Porter Dexter, an early resident of the area and public-spirited citizen, who died in 1960 (Geographic Board, Sept.-Dec., 1960).

Diablo, dĭ-äb′-lō, dĭ-äb′-lō, **Mount; Diablo: Valley, Creek, Range,** post office. The earliest name of the mountain was apparently *San Juan Bautista* (Dalrymple, 1790). In October, 1811, Ramón Abella, in his diary, mentions the peak as *Cerro Alto de los Bolbones* (high hill of the Bolbones, i.e., the Indians who live at its foot). The ridge was later designated as *Sierra de los Bolbones* (or *Golgones*, and other variants). The name *Monte del Diablo* (devil's woods) appears on the Plano topografico de la Mision de San Jose about 1824, where there was an Indian rancheria perhaps near a thicket at the approximate site of the present town of Concord. On August 24, 1828, the name was applied to the Monte del Diablo land grant for which Salvio Pacheco

had petitioned in 1827. The story, for some time accepted by the State Park administration, that the peak had a Costanoan Indian name, *Koo Wah Koom,* meaning 'laughing mountain,' was a hoax ("The Knave," Feb. 26, 1961). Vallejo in his *Report* of 1850 tells the story of a fight between a detachment of soldiers from the San Francisco presidio and the Indians at the foot of the mountain in 1806. The appearance of "an unknown personage, decorated with the most extraordinary plumage," made the soldiers take to their heels, believing the devil had allied himself with the Indians; hence they applied then and there the present name to the mountain. This is quite certainly fanciful. Marsh in 1850 stated that Vallejo was incorrect in placing the engagement near the mountain, and that it had occurred in the vicinity of a thicket of willows near the house of Salvio Pacheco (i.e., near present Concord), at a later date. The name was transferred to the peak by non-Spanish explorers who associated 'monte' with a mountain and applied the Italian form *Monte Diavolo* or *Diabolo.* Belcher (I, 119, writing in 1837) calls the range *Sierras Bolbones* and speaks of "the high range of the Montes Diavolo" on his left (!) as he entered the Sacramento River. The Wilkes expedition of 1841 definitely fixed the name on the lofty mountain peak. Duflot de Mofras in 1844 cautiously gives both names, *Monte del Diablo* and *Sierra de los Bolbones* (*Plan* 16). Finally, Frémont and Preuss, on their map of 1848, give the proper latitude and call it Mount Diabolo. Trask's and other maps of the early 1850's established the modern spelling, although Monte Diablo is found as late as 1873 (Hoffmann). The orographic identity of the range headed by Mount Diablo was recognized by cartographers in Mexican and early American times. The Geographic Board, by decision of May 15, 1908, designated the entire range from Carquinez Strait to Antelope Valley in Kern County as Diablo Range to distinguish it from the other chains of the Coast Ranges. Diablo post office is listed in 1917.—This Spanish word for Satan was used repeatedly for other place names in Spanish times, although not as often as the word "devil" in American times. It occurs in two other land grants: Rincon del Diablo [San Diego], May 18, 1843, Cañada del Diablo (or San Miguel) [Ventura], May 30, 1845. Point Diablo [Marin] and Diablo Point [Santa Cruz Island] can also be traced to Spanish times. Other

Diablos in various counties were applied in American times.—*See* Devil.

Diamond. The occasional discovery of small genuine diamonds and of quartz crystals which look like diamonds has given rise to some twenty place names in California. The oldest is probably **Diamond Spring** [El Dorado], where the finding of pretty specimens of quartz crystals in 1849 brought about the first large-scale rumor of the discovery of diamond fields. Sometimes the name is used because of the diamond shape of the feature. Diamond Peak [Inyo] and Diamond Mesa [Sequoia National Park] received their names because the contour lines on the topographic map form a more or less perfect diamond.

Diaz: Creek, station [Inyo]. Named for the brothers Rafael and Eleuterio Diaz, who owned a cattle ranch on the creek in the 1860's (Farquhar).

Dickinson. *See* Legrand.

Didallas, dĭ-dăl′-ăs: **Creek** [Shasta]. The name of this tributary of Squaw Creek is probably of Wintu origin and has been interpreted to mean 'daybreak.'

Digger. "Root-Diggers. . . . This name seems to embrace Indian tribes inhabiting a large extent of country west of the Rocky Mountains. . . . With these tribes, roots are, for the great portion of the year, their main subsistence" (Schoolcraft, IV, 221). The diggers also valued as food the green cones and the seeds of the *Pinus sabiniana,* whence the common designation, Digger Pine. In California the name seems to have been used in a geographical sense mainly in Wintu territory. With the exception of a Digger Creek which empties into the ocean near Beaver Point [Mendocino], the existing Digger names are in Shasta, Tehama, and Trinity counties. The natives on Kings River were called Root Digger Indians in the Indian Report (pp. 236 f.).

Diggings. Since the beginning of the 19th century this word has been used in the American language to designate pits made by searchers for minerals. With the discovery of gold in California the term gained new significance and was raised to the dignity of a generic term. A number of places on the map of the State are still called Diggings; in this book they are listed under their specific names.

Di Giorgio [Kern]. The station was named by the Southern Pacific in 1923 for Joseph Di Giorgio, president of the Earl Fruit Company. The post office was established May 26, 1944.

Dike. *See* Dyke.

Diller, Mount [Shasta]. Named for Joseph S. Diller, a geologist for the Geological Survey in the 1880's and the author of *Geology of the Lassen Peak District,* 1889.

Dillon Beach [Marin]. The post office was established in 1923 and named for the Dillon family. George Dillon, a native of Ireland, had settled here before 1867.

Dinkey: Creek, Lake, Meadow, Mountain; Dinkey Creek, town [Fresno]. The creek was named by four hunters, whose dog Dinkey was injured there in a fight with a grizzly bear in August, 1863. John Muir mentions in 1878 a grove of sequoias called Dinkey Grove, on Dinkey Creek. (Farquhar.) The other features were named after the creek when the Geological Survey mapped the Kaiser quadrangle in 1901–1902.

Dinuba, dĭ-nōō′-bȧ [Tulare]. A number of theories concerning the origin of the name have been advanced, but none has been substantiated. It is probably a fanciful name applied by the construction engineer when the branch line was built in 1887–1888. Stations between Sanger and Exeter bear these typical railroad names: Fortuna, Smyrna, Dinuba, Taurusa. The original name was Sibleyville, for James Sibley, who had deeded 240 acres to the Pacific Improvement Company [Southern Pacific].

Dirty Sock Hot Springs [Inyo]. Sulphur odor in the water might have given rise to the name. However, since this odor is hardly noticeable, the story that the miners washed and hung their socks in the natural washroom probably accounts for the name having been given to the place. (Wheelock.)

Disappearing Creek [Kings Canyon National Park]. Applied by T. S. Solomons in 1895 to the creek in the Enchanted Gorge between Scylla and Charybdis (Farquhar). A number of other watercourses are so named because the surface stream disappears.

Disappointment, Mount [Angeles National Forest]. In the early 1890's a party of the Geological Survey climbed the mountain to use it as a triangulation point; to their "disappointment" they found that near-by San Gabriel Peak was 100 feet higher (Harry Grace).

Disaster: Peak, Creek [Alpine]. Named by Lieutenant Montgomery M. Macomb of the Wheeler Survey because on September 6, 1877, his topographer, W. A. Cowles, accidentally dislodged a huge boulder and was severely injured. The mountain was formerly known as King's Peak (*WF*, VI, 270).

Disneyland [Orange]. The deceased producer, Walt Disney, created the unique and extensive amusement park in 1955.

Ditch. Although the building of ditches in mining and in irrigation was of great importance in the development of California, the word has survived in only a few place names as a generic term, the most notable of which are Big Ditch near Yreka and Milpitas Ditch near Mission San Antonio in Monterey County. *See* Zanja.

Divide, The [Placer]. The mining country between the North and Middle forks of the American River, adjoining and just east of the Auburn district, formerly known as Yankee Jim's Divide, is now called the Forest Hill Divide, abbreviated locally to "the Divide" (State Library). The name is found elsewhere in the State: Divide Peak [Santa Barbara], Divide Ridge [Alameda, Contra Costa], and is given to two railroad stations in Sonoma and Santa Barbara counties. *See* Great Western Divide; LeConte Divide.

Dixie. There are a number of Dixies in the State, including two cluster names in Lassen and Plumas counties; most of these were probably applied by Southerners at the time of the Civil War when Union was a place name favored by Northerners. The name Dixieland [Imperial] was chosen by promoters in 1909 in the hope that irrigation would make the district suitable for cotton growing.

Dixon [Solano]. Named in 1870 for Thomas Dickson, who gave ten acres for the townsite. The present spelling was adopted by the Post Office Department through an error.

Doane: Valley, Creek [San Diego]. Named for the Doane brothers, who took up homesteads in the valley in the late 1860's (Co. Library).

Dobbins: Creek, town [Yuba]. For William M. and Mark D. Dobbins, brothers who settled at the creek in 1849.

Docas [Monterey]. The name of the Southern Pacific station was coined from San Ar*do* and San Lu*cas*, between which it is situated ("The Knave," March 17, 1935).

Dockweiler Beach State Park [Los Angeles]. The Venice-Hyperion beach area was made a park in 1947 and named for Isidore B. Dockweiler, a State Park Commissioner, 1939–1947.

Doctor Rock [Del Norte]. An American interpretation of the Indian name for the rock. The Indians prayed here to bring good to themselves and evil to their enemies (J. Endert).

Dodge Gulch [Shasta]. Named for Wilbur S. Dodge, a prospector of 1850, who later owned the American Ranch in Trinity County (Steger).

Doe. The word for female deer appears in the names of a number of physical features, including Little Doe Ridge in Mendocino County.

Dog. More than twenty-five features, mainly creeks, are named for the faithful canine. The usual reason for naming was doubtless the finding of a stray dog, or some incident concerning a dog. **Dog Lake** [Yosemite National Park] was named by R. B. Marshall in 1898 because he found there a sheep dog with a litter of puppies (Farquhar). In Kern County there is a Five Dog Creek, and elsewhere features are named for red, black, and yellow dogs. Doghead Peak [Yosemite National Park] and Dogtooth Peak [Fresno] are obviously descriptive. *See* Red Dog.

Dogtown. A popular miners' term for camps with huts or hovels "good enough for dogs to live in." The sites of some of them are still shown on the topographical map [Jackson, Clements. Mother Lode atlas sheets]. A well-known **Dog Town** [Mono] was so named because of the makeshift huts of numerous Chinese placer miners in the late 1850's. The creek there should be called Dog Town Creek instead of Dog Creek. **Dog Town** [Butte]. In 1850 the place was a gold camp named Mountain View. According to the County History, 1882, p. 252, the name Dogtown was applied because Mrs. Bassett, the wife of the first permanent settler bred and sold dogs to the miners. In 1861 the name was changed to Magalia, which was the name of the post office.

Dogwood. Except for the Peak and Creek in Plumas and the Canyon in Fresno County, no geographic features seem to have been named for the dogwood, the best-known native species of which are *Cornus nuttallii*, distinguished by its handsome white flowers, and *C. californica*, a red-stemmed shrub or tree.

Doheny Park. *See* Capistrano Beach.

Dollar Lake [San Bernardino]. The lake is like a silver dollar in shape and color. Big Bird Lake [Kings Canyon National Park] was formerly called Dollar Lake although it is not perfectly round.

Dolly Varden Creek [Humboldt]. The stream was named for the well-known Dolly Varden trout (*Salvelinus malma spectabilis*), common in the waters of northern California. Dolly Varden was a frivolous character in Dickens' novel *Barnaby Rudge* who wore a bright flower-sprinkled dress. About 1870 her name was applied to many gay and colorful things, including the beautifully marked trout.

Dolomite [Inyo]. The name was given to the station of the Carson and Colorado Railroad after 1900 because of the occurrence there of dolomite, a carbonate of lime and magnesia, found in the mountainous sections of the State, especially in Inyo and Mono counties. White Mountain Peak [Mono] received its name because its summit, composed of this rock, looks as if it were covered with snow.

Dolores, Mission [San Francisco]. The common designation of the San Francisco mission. The name *Los Dolores* or *Nuestra Señora de los Dolores* (Our Lady of Sorrows) was given to a spring and a small stream by Anza on March 29, 1776, and *Mision San Francisco de Asis*, founded near it later that same year, afterward came to be popularly known as *la mision de los Dolores*.

Dome. In California the word is used, almost exclusively, as a generic term for dome-shaped mountains in the Sierra Nevada between 36° and 38° latitude, where it occurs about forty times. In other parts of the State the word is sometimes used as a specific term: Dome Mountain [Siskiyou and San Bernardino].

Dominguez, dṓ-mĭn'-gĕz: town, **Hills** [Los Angeles]. The place preserves the family name of the grantees of the vast San Pedro or Dominguez Rancho, granted first to Juan José Dominguez before November 20, 1784. From 1923 to 1937 the station was known as Davidson City, for the Davidson Investment Company; prior to that time as Elftman, for the owner of the land (Co. Surveyor). **Laguna Dominguez** is the new name adopted by the Los Angeles Board of Supervisors on March 30, 1938, for the swampy lake formerly known as Nigger Slough.

Donahue [Sonoma]. The place, for many years the terminus of the Northwestern Pacific branch from Petaluma, was named in 1870 for Peter Donahue. Donahue, a native of Scotland of Irish parentage, was a well-known San Francisco financier, who in 1869–1870 built the railroad, first called the San Francisco and North Pacific.

Doney Creek [Shasta]. The tributary to the Sacramento was named for William K. Doney, who settled there in 1860 (Steger).

Donnells Reservoir [Stanislaus]. The name of one of the dams and reservoirs of the Tri-Dam project commemorates one of the partners of Donnell and Parsons, of Columbia, who in 1855 constructed the first water system between Donnells Flat and Columbia.

Donner: Lake, station, **Peak, Pass, Monument** [Nevada, Placer]. The names commemorate one of the worst disasters in the history of the American West. Eighty-one immigrants, led by George and Jacob Donner, were obliged to winter in the vicinity of the lake in 1846–1847. Thirty-six died from cold and starvation. The lake had been discovered by the Stephens-Murphy-Townsend party in 1844 and called Truckee Lake. The present names for the lake and peak appear on the von Leicht–Hoffmann map of Lake Tahoe (1874) and were doubtless applied by the Whitney Survey.

Donohue: Pass, Peak [Yosemite National Park]. Named by Lieutenant N. F. McClure in 1895, for a soldier in his detachment (Farquhar).

Don Pedro Reservoir [Tuolumne]. A place on Tuolumne River called Don Pedro's Bar is mentioned by Audubon in 1849 and appears on Gibbes' map of 1852. It is sometimes incorrectly spelled Dom Pedro. It was named for Pierre ("Don Pedro") Sainsevain, a French pioneer of 1839, who mined here in August, 1848. He was a member of the first California Constitutional Convention. The town is now covered by the reservoir, but the San Francisco Light and Power Company has preserved the old name.

Doré: Cliffs, Pass [Mono]. Named about 1882 by Israel C. Russell of the Geological Survey in honor of Paul Gustave Doré (1832–1883), the celebrated French illustrator.

Dorn Valley [Lake]. The valley was named for Max Dorn, who with his family settled in it in 1871 (Mauldin).

Dorothy Lake [Yosemite National Park]. Named by R. B. Marshall for Dorothy Forsyth, daughter of the acting superintendent of the park, 1909–1912 (Farquhar).

Dorris [Siskiyou]; **Dorris Reservoir** [Modoc]. The station was named by the Southern Pacific about 1907. The name commemorates Presley A. Dorris and his brother, Carlos J. Dorris, stock raisers in Little Shasta in the 1860's. In 1870 they left their home to take up claims near Pit River in what is now Modoc County. The settlement which developed around the bridge built by Presley Dorris was called Dorris' Bridge until 1876, when the name was changed to Alturas.

Dorst Creek [Sequoia National Park]. Named for Joseph H. Dorst (1852–1916), a captain in the Fourth Cavalry and first acting superintendent of Sequoia and General Grant national parks, 1891–1892 (Farquhar).

Dos Palmas [Riverside]. The watering place close to Mecca was known by this name when the Arizona pioneer, Hermann Ehrenberg was killed there by Indians in 1868. At that time there were two palms at the oasis, as indicated by the Spanish name, but now the place has more than thirty Washingtonia palms.

Dos Palmas [Riverside]. The oasis near the highway between Pine and Palms is described in *Desert Magazine,* November, 1945. In 1945 the place had three palms. *See* Palm.

Dos Palos, dôs păl′-ŏs: **Slough,** town [Merced]. The name, meaning 'two trees,' was applied to the station when the Southern Pacific reached the place in 1889. The two trees and the words *Dos Palos* are shown on the *diseño* of the Sanjon de Santa Rita grant of 1841, a few miles northeast. A Dos Palos Colony was established in 1892. The name of the post office was spelled Dospalos for many years, but in 1905 Eldredge succeeded in having the Spanish version restored. The modern town was founded and named by the Pacific Improvement Company in 1907. *See* Palo.

Dos Piedras. *See* Two Rock.

Dos Pueblos, dôs pwĕb′-lōs: **Canyon, Creek** [Santa Barbara]. The name is derived from two Indian villages (at the mouth of the canyon), the inhabitants of which differed greatly in appearance and speech; these villages were noted by Cabrillo in 1542. The canyon apparently formed the boundary between two dialectal divisions of the Chumash Indians. (Wagner, p. 384.) It is doubtless the same place as that recorded by Anza on April 28, 1774: "I came to camp for the night at the place which they call Dos Rancherias." The *dos pueblos* are mentioned in 1795 (PSP, XIII, 29) and thereafter appear frequently in the records. On April 18, 1842, the name Dos Pueblos was given to the land grant, which includes the creek and canyon.

Dos Rios, dôs rē′-ōs [Mendocino]. The situation of the town at the junction of two branches of the Eel River suggested the name, which is Spanish for 'two rivers.'

Double. This adjective is used much less frequently than "twin" for pairs of geographic features. Only some twenty them include the word in their names, among them Double Cone Rock [Mendocino], Doublehead and Doublehead Lake [Modoc], Double Point [Marin], Double Butte [Riverside]. **Double Gate**

Ridge [Trinity] was so named because of a drift fence, separating a sheep range from a cattle range, near which a sheepherder named Newtervin was killed in a feud between cattle owners and sheep owners in 1885. **Double Springs,** Historic Landmark 264, was once a prosperous mining town and in 1850 was the county seat of Calaveras County. Promoters claimed that there were not only double springs near the town but "six or eight never failing springs of the best water in California" (J. A. Smith, Calaveras).

Dougherty: Creek, Meadow [Kings Canyon National Park]. Named for Bill and Bob Dougherty, pioneer sheepmen (Farquhar).

Douglas City [Trinity]. Settled in the early 1860's and named in memory of Stephen A. Douglas, the "Little Giant," who died in 1861. Although unsuccessful as a presidential candidate, defeated by Lincoln, Douglas was admired as an upright and uncompromising political leader. The post office is listed in 1867.

Douglasflat [Calaveras]. The post office was established in the 1870's and named after an old mining camp. A place, Douglass and Raney, is shown twenty-five miles east of Stockton on Gibbes' map of 1852. Douglass Flat is shown on Goddard's map of 1860 at the location of the present settlement.

Downey [Los Angeles]. In 1865 John G. Downey, governor of California from 1860 to 1862, subdivided Rancho Santa Gertrudis and later gave his name to the new town. The highest peak of the Santa Ana Range had been named for him by the Whitney Survey in 1861.

Downieville [Sierra]. Named for "Major" William Downie, a native of Scotland, who mined at the forks of the Yuba River in November, 1849. The place, at first called merely "the Forks," was named Downieville the next spring by a group of miners, at the suggestion of James Galloway.

Doyle [Lassen]. The name appears on the railroad map of 1900 as a station of the Nevada-California-Oregon Railway. John W. and Stephen A. Doyle had been settlers in Long Valley since the 1860's.

Doyles: Camp, Springs [Tulare]. The name commemorates John J. Doyle, one of the farmers who served a jail sentence for taking part in the Mussel Slough affair in 1880 (Wallace Smith, pp. 287 f.). *See* Mussel Slough.

Dragon Channel [Del Norte]. On April 23, 1792, Vancouver christened the cape north of Crescent City in honor of Saint George and at the same time called the rocks (probably in jesting analogy) Dragon Rocks. This name was used for many years by the Coast Survey, but at present the individual rocks have local names. Vancouver's name, however, is preserved in the name of the channel between Mansfield Break and The Great Break. *See* Saint George.

Dragon: Peak, Lake [Kings Canyon National Park]. The peak was so named because its outline as seen from Rae Lake suggests a dragon (Farquhar). **Dragon Head** [Lava Beds National Monument]. Named by J. D. Howard because of the appearance of the rock formation at the "skylight" of a cave.

Drakesbad [Plumas]. Formerly known as Hot Spring Valley, or Drake's Place, or Drake's Hot Springs, for E. R. Drake, who settled there in the 1860's. When the Sifford family bought the place in 1900, it also became known as Sifford's. To avoid confusion, the Sifford family added the common German generic *-bad* (watering place), for the hot mineral springs, to the name of the former owner, who had always wished that his name be retained. (R. D. Sifford.) Near-by Drake Lake was named by the Geological Survey in 1925.

Drakes: Bay, Estero, Head [Marin]. The bay was discovered by Rodríguez Cermeño and was named *Puerto y Bahia de San Francisco,* November 7, 1595. Vizcaíno, on January 8, 1603, renamed the bay *Bahia de Don Gaspar* in honor of Gaspar de Zuñiga y Açevedo, Conde de Monterey. On his map of 1625, Henry Briggs ignored both names and applied the name *Puerto Sr Francisco Draco* to a port north of Point Reyes—apparently an attempt to support the English claim to the coast of California. In 1790, Arrowsmith's map applies the name Sir Francis Drake to what is now San Francisco Bay (Wagner, No. 744). The Spanish explorer and cartographer Martínez y Zayas in 1793 placed Drake's name at the present location: *P[uer]to de Fran[cis]co Drak.* Vancouver likewise called it Bay of Sir F. Drake. The Coast Survey uses the name Sir F. Drake's Bay in 1850, and the modern abbreviated form in 1854. The actual anchorage of Drake in June and July, 1579, has never been established. *See* Estero de Limantour.

Dripping Blood Mountain [Inyo]. The peak received the name because of its sanguine coloring.

Drum Barracks [Los Angeles]. Historic Landmark 169. Established 1862, abandoned 1866.

Named by the War Department for Richard Drum, who in the Civil War was a lieutenant colonel and assistant adjutant general of the Department of California.

Drum Bridge [Plumas]. Pipes about the diameter of a snare drum were filled with concrete to serve as piers and looked from the ends like drums; hence the name. There are other such bridges in the State. (Stewart.)

Drum Reservoir [Placer]. Named for Frank G. Drum, president of the Pacific Gas and Electric Company, 1907-1920. The Drum Powerhouse on Bear River was the first generating plant constructed after the earthquake of 1906. The dam and reservoir were built in 1924.

Drury Grove [Calaveras]. The grove in Calaveras Big Trees State Park was established in 1965 in memory of Aubrey Drury (1891-1959), who had been associated with the Save-the-Redwoods League from 1918-1959. Aubrey was a well-known California author, the son of the pioneer western journalist, Wells Drury, and the brother of Newton Drury, former director of the U.S. National Park Service.

Dry. There are more than one hundred Dry Creeks and about twenty-five Dry Lakes in the State, together with an assortment of Dry Sloughs, Gulches, Valleys, Arroyos, and Lagoons. Most of these were named in the dry seasons; there are very few which are dry all the year round. **Dry Lake** [Modoc]. The name of Sorass Lake was changed to Dry Lake in 1873 when, in the Modoc War, soldiers expecting to get water there found it dry. At daylight on May 10, 1873, the lake bed was the scene of a crushing defeat inflicted upon Captain Jack and his Indians (Wm. S. Brown). **Drytown** [Amador]. So named by the miners in 1849 or 1850 because the camp's rivulet could not supply enough water for washing gold. Historic Landmark 31. **Drylyn** [Imperial]. The name contains the Gaelic generic term *lin* or *lyn,* 'spring,' 'pool.' **Dry Lagoon Beach State Park** [Humboldt], created and named in 1931, is an example of unimaginative official place naming.

Duarte, dwär'-tĭ [Los Angeles]. The settlement developed when the Rancho Azusa, which had been granted to Andrés Duarte, was subdivided in 1864-1865. It became the nucleus of the town promoted in the boom years 1886-1887. The land had been granted to Duarte on May 10, 1841.

Dublin: town, Canyon [Alameda]. James W. Dougherty of Tennessee acquired a parcel of

Amador's Rancho San Ramon and settled on it after 1852. When the post office was established in the 1860's, it was named Dougherty's Station. The story that Dougherty called the part south of the road Dublin because so many Irishmen lived there (Doyle) has its merits: on Hoffmann's map of the Bay region the settlement north of the road is labeled Dougherty and the one south of it Dublin. The name of the post office was not changed to Dublin until the 1890's.

Ducor, dōō′-kôr [Tulare]. In 1899 the Southern Pacific reached the place known as Dutch Corners because four Germans had adjoining homesteads here. For euphony and convenience the name was shortened to Ducor.

Dulzura, dŭl-zōōr′-á: town, **Creek** [San Diego]. The Spanish name, meaning 'sweetness,' was applied to the place because the honey industry was introduced into this region in 1869 by John S. Harbison. There is a Honey Spring Ranch to the north and a Bee Canyon to the south. According to local tradition, the name was suggested by Mrs. Hagenbeck, a lover of wild flowers, when the post office was established in 1887 (Hazel Sheckler).

Dumbarton: station, **Point, Bridge** [Alameda, San Mateo]. The name of the county in Scotland was given to the station when the Oakland–Santa Cruz line was built in 1876. The highway bridge, the first to cross San Francisco Bay, was constructed and named in 1927.

Dumbbell Lake [Kings Canyon National Park]. Named in 1903: "... a lonely lake. This, from its shape, we called Dumb-bell Lake ..." (J. N. LeConte, *SCB*, V, 7).

Dume, dōōm: **Point, Cove, Canyon** [Los Angeles]. The name was given to the point by Vancouver in honor of his host, Padre Francisco Dumetz of Mission San Buenaventura. Vancouver, who often erred in the spelling of names, gave the form Dume. The maps of the Pacific Railroad Survey recorded it as Duma and this spelling was generally accepted until 1869, when the Coast Survey changed it to Dume, doubtless after consulting Vancouver's map.

Dumont Meadows [Alpine]. Named for one of the French-Canadian woodcutters who in the 1870's were engaged in the slaughter of Alpine's forests for timbering in the Comstock mines (Maule). There are Dumont Sand Dunes and Little Dumont Dunes in Death Valley National Monument, but probably not named for the same man.

Duncan: Creek, Canyon, Peak [Placer]. The tributary of "the Middle Fork of the Middle Fork of the American" was named for Thomas Duncan, who came overland from Missouri in 1848, according to James Marshall, discoverer of gold at Coloma (Co. Hist., 1882, p. 381).

Duncan Creek [Shasta]. The tributary of Cottonwood Creek was named for the Duncan brothers, early settlers (Steger).

Duncan Reservoir [Modoc National Forest]. The reservoir was constructed by Charles Duncan, a pioneer settler and horse raiser in Modoc County (R. B. Sherman).

Duncans Mills [Sonoma]. Named for S. M. and A. Duncan, who built a mill there in 1860. The post office was established December 20, 1862.

Dunderberg Peak [Mono]. The peak appears as Castle Peak on Goddard's and Hoffmann's maps. On September 19, 1878, a party of the Wheeler Survey headed by Lieutenant M. M. Macomb renamed it Dunderberg, after the famous mine on Dog Creek on the north slope of the mountain. (Farquhar.) This mine was probably named after the Union man-of-war *Dunderberg,* launched in New York in July, 1865. The vessel in turn probably derived its name from the mountain in New York, Dunderberg (Dutch, thunder mountain). Thus it may well have been that a mountain in California was named after a mountain in New York via a warship and a mine. (*See* Kearsarge.) In June, 1947, Birge M. and Malcolm Clark of Palo Alto found the following record of the Macomb party in a metal can on the peak: "This peak is called 'Dunderberg' instead of 'Castle Peak' in view of the fact that there is a peak north of Summit Station, Cal., on the C.P. [Central Pacific] R.R. to which the name is more appropriate. Also because the name 'Castle Rocks' has been given to some peaks north of the Relief Trail at the head of the Stanislaus." The present name appears on the Bridgeport atlas sheet (1911).

Dunlap [Fresno]. The post office was first established November 13, 1882, and the place is shown on the Land Office map of 1891. It was named for George Dunlap Moss, the first postmaster and a schoolteacher in the early 1880's (Co. Hist., 1956).

Dunnigan: Creek, town [Yolo]. When the Northern Railway reached this point in 1876, the station was named for the owner of the land, A. W. Dunnigan, who had settled here in 1853.

Dunsmuir [Siskiyou]. The Southern Pacific

reached this section in August, 1886. When Alexander Dunsmuir, a "coal baron" of British Columbia and San Francisco, passed through Cedar Flat, a station consisting of a boxcar, he promised the settlers a fountain if they would name the future town for him. The proposal was accepted, and at the beginning of January, 1887, the name and the boxcar were moved to the present site, which previously had been called Pusher. The fountain was erected at the railroad station, where it still stands. (Marcelle Masson.)

Durham [Butte]. When the railroad reached the place in the 1870's, the station was named for W. W. Durham, a millowner and assemblyman from Butte County (1880).

Dusy: Branch, Meadow [Kings Canyon National Park]. In 1879, L. A. Winchell named this branch of the Middle Fork of Kings River for Frank Dusy (1836–1898), a native of Canada and well-known stockman and mountaineer (Farquhar).

Dutch, Dutchman. With the exception of the Yankees, the Germans seem to be the only settlers whose presence is recorded by their nickname. "Dutch" is the English way of pronouncing *Deutsch*, 'German,' and until the 18th century it was common in England to call the Germans "High Dutch" and the Netherlanders "Low Dutch." The American habit of calling Germans "Dutch" and "Dutchmen" became general in the first half of the 19th century, when the "Dutch" began to play an important part in the settlement of the West. In California, as well as in many other states, Dutch has practically replaced the adjective German in geographical nomenclature: there are only two German Creeks, against almost a hundred Dutch Creeks, Flats, Canyons, Valleys, etc., and even these two creeks may not have been named for German settlers but for members of Spanish families by the name of German. Very often the adjective is combined with a given name: Dutch Bill, Ed, Henry, John, etc. Some of the names were doubtless given for Hollanders, or even Scandinavians: "Europeans ... save French, English, and 'Eyetalians,' are in California classed under the general denomination of Dutchmen" (Borthwick, *Three Years in California* [1857], p. 329). **Dutch Flat** [Placer]. Two Germans, the brothers Charles and Joseph Dornbach, settled there in 1851. The place became known as Dutch Charlie's Flat, and the name was later abbreviated to Dutch Flat. In the 1870's an attempt was made to change the name to

German Level. The town is Historical Landmark 397. *See* Ducor.

Dutch Creek [Shasta]. Named by Sim Southern in the 1860's for Dr. William Dutch, a San Francisco dentist and frequent visitor in the region (Steger).

Dutschke Hill [Amador]. The elevation near Ione was named for the pioneer family of Charles Dutschke. Formerly also known as Jones Butte (Geographic Board, Sept.-Dec., 1963).

Duxbury: Reef, Point [Marin]. The ship *Duxbury* was grounded on the reef on August 21, 1849. The name is shown on the Coast Survey charts of 1851. In Mexican times the cape was known as *Punta de Baulenas*.

Dyer, Mount [Plumas]. The mountain was named in honor of Assistant U.S. Surveyor General Ephraim Dyer, who came to California in 1850 and between 1861 and 1870 surveyed the land along the California-Nevada line from Lake Tahoe to Oregon.

Dyerville [Humboldt]. The town, on Highway 101, is said to have been named for a "tin peddler" by that name. It had a post office from 1890 to 1933.

Dyke. The word, as designating an igneous rock wall which has resisted erosion, is occasionally used as a generic term (*see* Jackass Dyke). **Grand Dike** [Kings Canyon National Park]. "Just at the junction of the forks [main forks of Kings River], the end of the divide is crossed by a broad red stripe, bearing about northwest . . . This, which seemed to be a great dyke of volcanic rock, but which was afterwards found to be a vein of granite, led to giving this divide the name of 'Dyke Ridge'" (Whitney, *Geology*, I, 370). The divide itself is now called Monarch Divide, and Dyke Mountain [Hoffmann's map], ten miles northwest, is Crown Mountain. Dike Creek on the Mount Lyell atlas sheet was doubtless so named because its source is on the dyke formation of the Minarets.

Eagle. The favorite bird for place names in the State. There are about ten Eagle Peaks and as many Eagle Rocks, as well as a large number of Eagle Meadows, Canyons, Lakes, Nests, etc. The name is sometimes used for communities: Eagleville [Modoc], listed in the Great Register of 1879; Eagle Tree [San Joaquin]. Not all features are named for the presence of the bird. **Eagle Rock** [Los Angeles] was so named because its shadow resembles the outline of an eagle, and **Eagle Prairie** [Humboldt] was named for an old settler nicknamed "Old Eagle Beak." *See* Graeagle. Some names were translations of the Spanish *águila*, 'eagle': **Eagle Canyon** [Santa Barbara] is shown as *Agalia* on copies of the *diseños* of the Dos Pueblos grant (about 1842) and as *Arroyo de Agalia* on the plat of the same grant (1862).

Eagle Scout: Peak, Creek [Sequoia National Park]. Named by Francis P. Farquhar and a group of Boy Scouts from the San Joaquin Valley at the time of the first ascent, July 15, 1926.

Earl [Los Angeles]. Established in 1937 and named after the Earl Estate, formerly owned by E. T. Earl of the Earl Wholesale Fruit Company, Los Angeles.

Earl, Lake [Del Norte]. The name is mentioned by A. W. Chase of the Coast Survey in 1869, but the identity of Mr. Earl is not known.

Earlimart [Tulare]. When the Southern Pacific reached the place in 1873, the station was called Alila, probably just a "railroad name," which could be spelled forward or backward. In 1909, real-estate promoters changed the name to Earlimart to indicate that crops mature early here.

Earp, ûrp [San Bernardino]. At the request of residents, and of the Santa Fe, the Post Office Department gave the name in 1929, for Wyatt Earp, Arizona pioneer, peace officer, and miner, who came to California in the 1860's. The railroad station had been Drennan since 1910.

Eastberne [San Bernardino]. The name, coined from East San Bernardino, was applied to the subdivision about 1880 (Santa Fe).

Easter Bowl [Death Valley National Monument]. So named because the natural amphitheater is used for the annual Easter services, inaugurated in 1927 by H. W. Eichbaum.

East Highlands. *See* Highland.

East Lake [Kings Canyon National Park]. Named by a State Hydrographic Survey party in 1881 or 1882, for Thomas B. East, a hunter, trapper, and cattleman of Eshom Valley (Farquhar).

Easton [Fresno]. The town was first named Covell for A. T. Covell, resident manager of the Washington Irrigated Colony, founded in the 1870's. When the post office was established in 1882, the place was renamed for O. W. Easton, land agent of the colony.

East Pasadena [Los Angeles]. Originally named Lamanda Park for Amanda, wife of Leonard J. Rose, on whose property the town was founded. The post-office name was changed to East Pasadena in 1930; the railroad station retained the old name. *See* Lamanda Park.

East Riverside. *See* Highgrove.

Eastwood Grove [Humboldt]. The grove in the Prairie Creek Redwoods State Park was established in 1953 in memory of Alice Eastwood, (1859-1953), noted California botanist, who was Curator of Botany at the California Academy of Sciences for 57 years.

Eaton Canyon [Los Angeles]. Named for Judge Benjamin S. Eaton, who settled at Fair Oaks in 1865 and utilized the water of the canyon for his vineyards. Eaton, a native of Connecticut, had come to Los Angeles in 1852, and was district attorney in 1855–1856 (Reid, p. 378).

Ebabias Creek [Sonoma]. The name *Ebabais* is shown on a *diseño* of the Cañada de Pogolimi grant (1844). It is probably a word of Pomo origin, but its meaning is not known.

Ebbetts Pass [Alpine]. "The pass we called Ebbets' pass, in memory of Major Ebbets, who went over it in the spring of 1851, with a large train of mules, and who found no snow there in April" (Surveyor General, *Report*, 1854, p. 90). John Ebbetts came to California in 1849 as captain of the Knickerbocker Exploring Company, and died April 15, 1854, in the wreck of the *Secretary* in San Pablo Strait. The Whitney Survey left the pass nameless: "In 1863 this was a simple trail, and it crossed by the route designated on Britton and Rey's map as 'Ebbett's Pass'; this name is, however, one no longer known in that region, as we could find no one who had ever heard of it" (Whitney, *Geology*, I, 446). The old name was restored when the Geological Survey surveyed the Markleeville quadrangle in 1893.

Echo. A favorite term for places where an echo is heard. The best-known features bearing the name in California are Echo Lake [El Dorado], Echo Rock [Los Angeles], and Echo Peak [Yosemite National Park]; the last was named by the Wheeler Survey in 1879.

Eckhard [Yolo]. Probably named for Conrad Eckhardt, a native of Germany and a farmer, who was registered as a voter at West Cottonwood in 1878.

Eckley [Contra Costa]. Commodore John L. Eckley, who had come to California as a land agent for D. O. Mills, Thomas O. Larkin, and W. D. M. Howard, bought the cove for a yacht harbor in the 1870's (Purcell, Co. Hist., 1940, p. 732). The name was applied to the station after 1878 when the Central Pacific built the line from Berkeley to Tracy.

Eddy, Mount [Siskiyou]. Named for Nelson Harvey Eddy, a native of New York State, who arrived in 1854 with one yoke of oxen and one cow, lived on the slope of the mountain until 1867, and then became a successful rancher in Shasta Valley (Schrader). According to Towendolly, the Wintu name of the peak was *Num-mel-be-le-sas-pom,* 'west blaze mountain.'

Eden. Of all names alluding to an earthly paradise, Eden is the most popular. The map of the United States is dotted with hundreds of Edens, Edendales, Eden Valleys, etc. California has about fifteen places or topographic features so named. Some may have been derived from the well-known English surname. **Mount Eden:** town, **Creek** [Alameda]. Eden Landing was established by the Mount Eden Company, an association of farmers, in 1850, and Eden township was formed in 1853. On Hoffmann's map of the Bay region both Eden Landing and Mount Eden are shown. Since there is no "Mount" to justify the name, it is either a transfer name, or members of the large Eden family may have settled in the district as early as 1850 and provided the name. **Eden** [Riverside]. The Eden Hot Springs were named by the owner, John Ryan, in 1890. The post office Eden was established March 7, 1924. Hoopa Valley [Humboldt] was formerly Eden Valley.

Edgar Peak [Yolo]. Probably named for James Edgar, a native of Canada, who had a 1,500-acre farm in the region in 1870.

Edgewood [Siskiyou]. The place was first known as Butteville. In 1875 Joseph Cavanaugh changed the name to Edgewood, which he considered more appropriate for its situation at the edge of the forest bordering the Shasta Valley.

Edison [Kern]. Named by the Southern California Edison Company when it built a substation there in 1905. **Lake Thomas A. Edison** [Fresno] near the Inyo County line, was named in the 1950's directly for the great inventor (1874-1931).

Edna Lake [Yosemite National Park]. Named (about 1900) by R. B. Marshall for Edna Bowman, later Mrs. Charles J. Kuhn of San Francisco (Farquhar).

Edom. *See* Palm.

Edwards: Air Force Base, post office [Kern]. The name of old Muroc Air Field was changed to Edwards Air Force Base January 27, 1950, in memory of Captain Glenn W. Edwards, who was fatally injured in the crash of an experimental YB-49 "Flying Wing." The name of the post office was changed to Edwards, November 1, 1951.

Edwards Canyon [Riverside]. The canyon in the Cleveland National Forest was named in 1960 in memory of Boyd M. Edwards, a U.S. Forest Service employee who lost his life in the Decker fire in August, 1959.

Edyth Lake [Yosemite National Park]. Named in 1910 by Major William W. Forsyth, acting superintendent of the Park, for the daughter of Colonel John T. Nance (Farquhar).

Eel: River, Canyon, Rock [Mendocino, Humboldt]. The river was named in January, 1850, by the Gregg party because L. K. Wood obtained a large number of eels from the Indians in return for small pieces of a broken frying pan. The name was placed on the map by C. D. Gibbes in 1852. According to George Gibbs, the Indians called the middle fork of Eel River *Ba-ka-wha* (Schoolcraft, III, 115), and Eel River itself *Wee-yot* (*ibid.*, p. 127). Eel Rock was the name applied to the station of the Northwestern Pacific when the section was built in 1910. A few other features, including Eel Point [San Clemente Island], were probably so named because eel fishing was profitable there.

Egg Lake [Modoc]. The lake, in the Modoc National Forest, was so named because it is a favorite nesting place for various species of waterfowl (Forest Service).

Ehrnbeck Peak [Yosemite National Park]. Named for Lieutenant Arthur R. Ehrnbeck, a native of Wisconsin, who made a report in 1909 on a comprehensive road-and-trail project for Yosemite National Park (Farquhar).

Eiler Lake [Shasta]. Named for Lu Eiler, who discovered Thousand Lake Valley (Steger).

Eiler Mountain [Alameda]. Named for the Eiler brothers who settled here in 1853 (Still).

Eisen, Mount [Sequoia National Park]. Named in 1941 in memory of Dr. Gustavus A. Eisen (1847–1940), a native of Sweden and a well-known scientist. He accompanied the German geographer Friedrich Ratzel on his trip to California in 1874, and later was instrumental in the establishment of the Sequoia and General Grant national parks.

Eisenecke: Valley, Creek [San Diego]. The name was applied by Mr. and Mrs. Billie Bloch to their ranch and to the creek which flows through it. The name, German for 'iron corner,' appears on the Cuyamaca atlas sheet (1903) and was probably applied because the huge granite cliffs form a natural gateway.

El. Spanish names preceded by the masculine article *el* which are included in cluster, group, or folk names will be found in the alphabetical order of the name proper. Example: El Cerrito will be found under Cerrito.

El Cajon, ká-hōn': **Valley, Mountains,** town [San Diego]. The name is mentioned on September 10, 1821, as another name for the *sitio rancho Santa Monica* (Arch. MSB, IV, 210). *Cajón,* the Spanish word for 'box,' was applied because the place is boxed in by the hills. (*See* Cajon.) The name appears in the *expediente* of a provisional grant of August 22, 1844, and is mentioned by B. D. Wilson as the name of a Diegueño village in 1852. The valley is called Cajon Valley on the von Leicht–Craven map of 1873, and the ranch was known in 1875 as Cajon Ranch. When the modern town developed, the original name El Cajon was restored. The name of the post office was written Elcajon until 1905, when the Post Office Department separated the two words at the insistence of Zoeth S. Eldredge.

El Camino Real. *See* Camino.

El Capinero [Tulare]. The name shown on the Tobias Peak atlas sheet has been the subject of considerable controversy (*WF,* VIII, 370; IX, 155 f.). Morley's suggestion that it is a misspelling of *sapinero,* 'plain of pines or junipers,' is plausible, especially since the place is near Pine Flat. However, a Spanish adaptation of an Indian word or a fanciful creation by a surveyor is not impossible.

El Capitan, kä-pǐ-tän' [Yosemite National Park]. The name was applied by the Mariposa Battalion in 1851: "To-tor-kon, is the name for a sand-hill crane, and ni-yul-u-ka, is the Pai-ute for head . . . [but] it appears to me most probable that Tote-ack-ah-noo-la is derived from 'ack' a rock, and To-whon-e-o, meaning chief . . . In adopting the Spanish interpretation, 'El Capitan,' for Tote-ack-ah-noo-la, we pleased our mission interpreters and conferred upon the majestic cliff a name corresponding to its dignity." (Bunnell, p. 211). Brewer gathered the information that the Indians saw in the rock the face of the highest deity and that their name meant really the 'great captain' (Notes, June 16, 1863). The name El Capitan is used also for a towering rock in Siskiyou County near the Del Norte line, and for a new state park in San Diego County.

El Casco [Riverside]. The name was applied to the Southern Pacific station before 1891. *Casco* in a geographical sense refers to a mountain which looks like the upper part of a skull; it corresponds to the American term

'round top.'

El Centro [Imperial]. When the town was platted in 1905, the real-estate company chose the Spanish term to indicate that the town was in the center of the Imperial Valley. The railroad station had previously been called Cabarker for C. A. Barker, a friend of W. F. Holt, owner of the land on which the town developed.

El Cerrito. *See* Cerrito.

Elder. Although several species of the common shrub or tree are native to various sections of the State, the name is applied to not more than ten creeks and canyons and two inhabited places, Elderwood [Tulare] and Elder Creek [Sacramento]. The Elder Creek which gave the name to the latter settlement appears on Bidwell's map of 1844 as *Arroyo de los Saucos* (arroyo of the elders).

El Dorado. The name, meaning 'the gilded one,' appears at the beginning of the 16th century as that of a mythical Indian chief in the tableland of Bogotá, who was said to have been covered with gold during the performance of religious rites. This chief was eagerly sought by the German and Spanish conquerors of northern South America until his abode was assertedly found in 1537. After that, the name designated one of the golden utopias which played such an important role in the conquest of America. With the discovery of gold in California the name assumed a new significance. Charles Preuss, on his map of 1848, which he was finishing when news of the discovery of gold reached Washington, placed the legend "El Dorado or Gold Region" along Plumas River and the South Fork of American River. **El Dorado County.** One of the original twenty-seven counties, created and named by the legislature on February 18, 1850. **El Dorado** [El Dorado]. At its inception in 1849 the town was known as Mud Springs, but at its incorporation, April 16, 1855, the name was changed to El Dorado, after the county. **Eldorado National Forest.** Created and named by presidential proclamation in 1910.—The name was applied to a number of communities in the 1850's and its popularity soon spread to other states. There is another El Dorado in Calaveras County, and there are Eldorado Creeks in Mariposa, Placer, and Santa Barbara counties. **El Dorado Hills** [Sacramento]. The settlement on either side of Highway 50 is a modern real estate development, established 1962.

Eldridge [Sonoma]. The post office, established

about 1895, was named for James Eldridge, to whom part of Rancho Cabeza de Santa Rosa had been patented, January 5, 1880.

Eleanor, Lake; Eleanor Creek; Lake Eleanor Reservoir [Yosemite National Park]. The Whitney Survey named the lake in the 1860's for Josiah D. Whitney's daughter Eleanor. The lake was converted into a reservoir for the water system of San Francisco in 1913. (Farquhar.)

Electra Peak [Yosemite National Park]. The name appears on the Mount Lyell atlas sheet, published in 1901, and was perhaps given because the anticlerical drama, *Electra*, by the Spanish author, Benito Pérez Galdós, attracted world-wide attention in the same year. **Electra** [Amador]. The post office and the P.G. and E. station, built in 1902, may have been named for the same reason. The plant was established by André Poniatowski, president of the Standard Electric Company and son-in-law of the founder of the Sperry Milling Company.

Elena [Shasta]. Named in memory of Elena Haggen, one of the first women to settle in Big Bend (Steger).

Elephant. Several mountains in the State bear the name because of their resemblance to the animal: Elephant Back [Alpine, Tulare], Elephants Head [Santa Clara], Elephant Rock [Yosemite National Park]. **Elephant Hill** [Fresno]. "The name refers to the fact that fossil remains of an elephantine, Plio-mastodon, were found on the top of this hill" (Geographic Board, *Decisions*, 1932). **Elephants Playground** [Plumas] was suggested by the elephantine scale of the boulders in the meadow (Stewart). "To see the elephant" was a common expression for having mined gold during the gold rush, and a number of mines were named Elephant.

El Granada, grá-nä'-dá [San Mateo]. The post office was named in 1910. If it was named after the last Moorish stronghold in Spain, it does not need the article; if the name chosen was the Spanish word for 'pomegranate,' the feminine article, *la,* should have been used.

Elizabeth. The most popular of all given names in the State's toponymy. There are about ten Elizabeth Lakes, several Creeks, and at least one Mountain. The oldest is apparently Elizabeth Lake [Los Angeles], mentioned in 1853 in the Pacific Railroad *Reports* as Lake Elizabeth. The lake in Tuolumne County was named in 1909 by R. B. Marshall of the Geological Survey, for the daughter of Dr. Samuel

E. Simmons of Sacramento. The pass in Kings Canyon National Park was named by Stewart Edward White for his wife when they crossed the divide in 1905. **Elizabethtown** [Plumas], named in 1852 for Elizabeth Stark Blakesley and popularly known as Betsyburg, is Historic Landmark 231.

El Jaro Creek. *See* Jarro.

Elk, Elkhorn. Although not so popular as the deer, the elk is represented in more than fifty geographic features in the State. In 1837, Belcher calls the mountains of Solano and Napa counties Elk Range, and even speaks of an Elk station (I, 119 ff.). The names Elkhorn Peak and Elkhorn Slough [Solano] are apparently not derived from the name given by Belcher, but offer additional evidence that the now vanished animal once abounded in this region. **Elk River** [Humboldt] was named by the Gregg party on Christmas Day, 1849, after they had celebrated the day with a dinner of elk meat. An Indian name of the river was *Ka-sha-reh* (Schoolcraft, III, 131 f.). **Elk Grove** [Sacramento] also dates from pioneer days. In 1850 James Hall opened his Elk Grove House, with an elk's head painted over the door. The name is found in a number of other post offices and communities: Elk [Mendocino and Fresno], Elk Creek [Glenn], Elkhorn [Monterey], Elk Horn [Yolo], Elks Retreat [Butte], Elk Valley [Del Norte].

Ellery Lake [Mono]. Named for State Engineer Nathaniel Ellery, who built the road between Tioga Pass and Mono Lake in 1909 (Farquhar).

Ellis Landing [Contra Costa]. Named for Captain George Ellis, who operated a schooner on San Francisco Bay in the 1850's. It was best known for its shell mound.

Ellis Meadow [Tulare]. Named for Sam L. N. Ellis, for many years head ranger of the U.S. Forest Service in the region and one-time supervisor of Tulare County (Farquhar).

Ellwood [Santa Barbara]. The name commemorates Ellwood Cooper, one of California's notable pioneers in horticulture, who was instrumental in introducing the eucalyptus tree and in developing olive culture in southern California. He served as president of the State Board of Horticulture from 1883 to 1903.

Elmira [Solano]. When the California Pacific Railroad from Vallejo to Sacramento was built in 1868, the name Vaca, after Vacaville three miles west, was applied to the station. When the extension to Rumsey was built, about 1875, Vacaville itself became a railroad station and the station Vaca was renamed

Elmira, after the city in New York.

El Mirage: Dry Lake, Valley, post office [San Bernardino]. The lake west of Victorville was named for the optical illusion frequently occurring in the desert, plus the Spanish indefinite article, for good measure. The settlement El Mirage, south of the lake, had a post office from 1917 to 1934.

El Modena, mŏ-dĕ′-nȧ [Orange]. The settlement was named Modena after the Italian city, or more likely after one of the several American towns by that name. When the post office was established, about 1890, the Spanish article El was added to the name to avoid confusion with Madera. In 1910 the Post Office Department realized that in Spanish a masculine article cannot be followed by a feminine noun, and changed the name to El Modeno. In 1965 (Apr.-June) the Geographic Board confirmed the form El Modeno.

El Monte, mŏn′-tĭ [Los Angeles]. The town was settled in 1852 by squatters who believed that there was a flaw in the title to the land. The place was called El Monte (the thicket) because of a dense stand of willows. It is mentioned as Monte in the Statutes of 1854 (p. 223) and in the Pacific Railroad Reports (Vol. III, Prel., p. 27). The original post-office name was also Monte; this was changed to El Monte before 1880. About 1895 the Post Office Department contracted the two words into one, but in 1905 it changed back to El Monte at Zoeth S. Eldredge's insistence.

Elms Canyon [Los Angeles]. Named in 1882 or 1883 for Dr. Henry Elms, owner of the land at the mouth of the canyon.

El Piojo Creek [Monterey]. The tributary of Nacimiento River was named after the land grant El Piojo, dated August 20, 1842. Piojo is the Spanish word for 'louse,' but it is not known whether the disagreeable name was deliberately chosen or whether its application is due to a misunderstanding.

El Portal, pôr-tăl′ [Mariposa]. In 1907 the Yosemite Valley Railroad gave the Spanish name to its terminus at the 'gateway' to the park.

El Rio, rē′-ō [Ventura]. The town was founded in 1875 by Simon Cohn and called New Jerusalem. About 1895 the Post Office Department changed the name to Elrio, and in 1905, upon Eldredge's insistence, to El Rio. See Rio.

El Segundo, sĕ-gōōn′-dō [Los Angeles]. The name, meaning 'the second,' was applied in 1911 by Colonel Rheem, of the Standard Oil Company, to the company's second refinery in California.

Elsinore: town, Lake, Mountain, Valley [Riverside]. In 1883 Donald M. Graham, William Collier, and F. H. Heald purchased and subdivided Rancho La Laguna, which doubtless had been so named because of the lake formerly called La Laguna Grande or Lake Laguna. The township of one section was called Laguna to preserve the old name. When a post office was established in 1884, the Post Office Department insisted upon a new name because there was already a Laguna post office in the State. Hence Donald Graham chose the name of the Danish castle made famous by Shakespeare's Hamlet. In the 1860's the stage station at the place was called Machado in memory of the first owner of the rancho, Agustín Machado. The Luiseño Indian name for the place is said to have been Etengvo Wumoma.

El Sobrante. See Sobrante.

Elterpom Creek [Trinity]. The name of the tributary of the South Fork of the Trinity, spelled Eltapom on the national forest map, is obviously Wintu. Pom means 'ground' or 'land,' but the meaning of the specific part is not known.

El Toro. See Toro.

El Verano, vĕ-rä′-nō [Sonoma]. About 1890, George H. Maxwell, a lawyer and later a well-known irrigationist, whose parental home adjoined El Verano, chose the Spanish name, meaning 'the summer,' because "the climate here was considered about perfect" (Ruth Denny).

Elverta [Sacramento]. The town was named in 1908 for Elverta Dike, whose husband had given a building lot for a community church (Lizzie Silver). The post office is listed in 1915.

Elysian Valley [Lassen]. The beauty of the valley inspired Daney H. Keatley and L. N. Breed to bestow upon it the name Elysian when they settled there in the summer of 1856.

Embarcadero, ĕm-bär-kȧ-dâr′-ō. The Spanish term for 'landing place' was commonly used in Spanish times and has survived in a number of places. A land grant in Santa Clara County, dated June 18, 1845, was named Embarcadero de Santa Clara.

Emerald. The name of the bright green precious stone is repeatedly used for place names, mostly for bodies of water [Los Angeles, El Dorado, Santa Catalina Island], but also for mountains [Kern, Fresno] and for settlements [San Mateo, Los Angeles]. Emerald

Peak [Kings Canyon National Park]. Named by T. S. Solomons in 1895 on account of its color (Farquhar).

Emeric: Creek, Lake [Mariposa]. Named by Lieutenant N. F. McClure, in 1895, for Henry F. Emeric, president of the State Board of Fish Commissioners and a charter member of the Sierra Club (Farquhar).

Emerson, Mount [Inyo]. John Muir wrote, in 1873: "I have named a grand *wide-winged* mountain on the head of the Joaquin Mount Emerson. Its head is high above its fellows and wings are white with ice and snow." Muir had become acquainted with Ralph Waldo Emerson when the latter visited Yosemite in May, 1871. Muir's Mount Emerson was probably the present Mount Humphreys. (Farquhar.) The present Mount Emerson is about two and one-half miles southeast of Mount Humphreys.

Emeryville [Alameda]. Named in 1897 for Joseph S. Emery, a native of New Hampshire, who came to California in 1850 and bought in 1859 the land on which Emeryville now stands. Emery School District was organized and named in 1884. ("The Knave," Oct. 6, 1946.) Emeryville Shell Mound is Historic Landmark 335.

Emigrant. There are about twenty Emigrant Passes, Lakes, Meadows, etc., along the routes by which trains of immigrants (usually called emigrants) reached the State in the early days. Among the oldest and best known of these are Emigrant Gap in Placer County, Emigrant Pass in Tuolumne County, and Emigrant Canyon in Death Valley National Monument.

Emma Lake; Mount Emma [Mono]. Two small lakes were presumably named for Anna and Emma Mack, sisters of Senator Maurice Mack, whose parental home was near by in the 1870's (Maule).

Emory, Fort [San Diego]. Named on December 14, 1942, by the War Department, General Order No. 67, in honor of William H. Emory, topographical engineer of Kearny's detachment in 1846–1847, member of the commission to establish the boundary between the United States and Mexico, major general in the Civil War. The name was suggested by Colonel P. H. Ottosen of Fort Rosecrans.

Empire [Stanislaus]. Founded as Empire City (probably named after New York, the "Empire City") in 1850, but shown on Gibbes' map (1852) as Empire. Although twice almost destroyed and deserted (1852 and 1855), the place has survived with the name. **Empire**

Creek [Sierra]. The stream was officially known as Little North Fork of Middle Fork of North Fork of Yuba River. In 1950 the Geographic Board abolished this monstrosity by naming the stream after the Empire Ranch, through which it flows.

Encanto [San Diego]. The Spanish word for 'charm,' 'fascination,' was selected for the town by Miss Alice Klauber because of the charming climate and the fascinating view (Sanchez). The post office is listed in 1910.

Enchanted Gorge [Kings Canyon National Park]. Named by T. S. Solomons in 1895 for the gorge between Scylla and Charybdis (Farquhar).

Encina, Encinitas, ĕn-sē'-nà, ĕn-sĭ-nē'-tăs. Americans use the word 'oak' indiscriminately for any type of that tree, but the Spanish distinguish between *encina* (or *encino*), 'live oak,' and *roble*, 'deciduous oak.' The words *encina, encinitas,* 'little oaks,' and *encinal,* 'oak grove,' were included in the titles of seven land grants and have survived in the names of a number of communities and geographic features. The site of part of the present city of Oakland was once called *Encinal de Temescal.* **Encinitas: Creek,** town [San Diego]. The Portolá expedition gave the name *Cañada de los Encinos* to the valley through which the creek runs, July 16, 1769. The name Los Encinitos was applied to the land grant, July 13, 1842. The modern community dates from 1881, when Nathan Eaton, "hermit, keeper of bees, and brother of General Eaton of Civil War fame" (Santa Fe), built the first house. The Santa Fe station was named Encenitos in 1881; the Postal Directory of 1892 and the Official Railway Map of 1900 have the modern spelling. **Encino: post office, Park, Reservoir** [Los Angeles]. The Portolá expedition found many live oaks in the vicinity and called San Fernando Valley *Santa Catalina de Bononia de los Encinos,* August 5, 1769. A provisional grant, Encino, was made about 1840 and was regranted to three Indians on July 18, 1845. The name was applied to the station when the Southern Pacific extension from Burbank was built in the 1890's. The post office is listed in 1939.

Enderts Beach [Del Norte]. Named for Fred W. Endert of Crescent City.

Engels, Engelmine [Plumas]. The place was named for the Engel brothers, who developed the big copper mining company around 1900. When a post office was established July 22, 1916, it was called Engelmine.

Englebright: Dam, Reservoir [Nevada]. The dam was named by the California Hydraulic Miners Association in 1945 in memory of Harry L. Englebright of Nevada City, congressman, 1926–1943.

English. About ten geographic features in California bear the name English, sometimes perhaps from the family name. Not only were English miners and settlers less numerous than either the Scots or the "Dutch," but their presence was less conspicuous.

Enterprise [Butte]. Probably named for the Union Enterprise Company, which built flumes there in 1852 (*Grizzly Bear*, June, 1921).

Epidote, ĕp′-ĭ-dōt: **Peak** [Mono]. The name was apparently applied by the Geological Survey when the Bridgeport quadrangle was surveyed, in the years 1904–1909, because of the presence of the mineral, a composition of calcium, aluminum, and iron.

Ericsson, Mount [Sequoia National Park]. When Professor Bolton C. Brown and his wife made the first ascent in 1896, they named the peak Crag Ericsson in honor of John Ericsson, designer of the *Monitor*, the ironclad which fought the *Merrimac* in the Civil War (Farquhar). The generic term was changed to 'Mount' probably when the Geological Survey mapped the Mount Whitney quadrangle in 1906.

Escalon, ĕs′-kȧ-lŏn [San Joaquin]. James W. Jones, so the story goes, came upon the Spanish word meaning 'step of a stair' in a book in the Stockton Public Library. Pleased with the sound of the word, he reserved it for the town which he laid out on his land with the coming of the railroad in 1895–1896.

Escarpines. The word appears in the name of the Bolsa de los Escarpines grant [Monterey], dated October 7, 1837. *Escarpin* means 'sock' or 'light shoe,' but the word may have something to do with *escarpe,* 'bluff,' 'declivity,' 'sloped bank,' or *escorpina,* 'a small saltwater fish.' On Land Office maps and on the Salinas atlas sheet the name is spelled Bolsa de las Escorpinas. *See* Espinosa Lake.

Escondido, Escondida. The Spanish word for 'hidden' was used in a geographical sense mainly with watering places. The Anza expedition camped "at the place called Agua Escondida" on February 22, 1776 (Anza, Font). There are Escondido Creeks in San Diego, Los Angeles, and Santa Barbara counties. **Escondido,** ĕs-kŏn-dē′-dō [San Diego]. In 1885 a syndicate of Los Angeles and San Diego businessmen bought the Rancho El Rincon del Diablo, laid out the town at the crossroads called Apex, and named it Escondido after the creek. Lake Wohlford was formerly known as Lake Escondido.

Escorpion [Los Angeles]. The Spanish word for 'scorpion' is mentioned by Fages as a place name as early as September, 1783 (Prov. Recs., III, 130). In July, 1834, it is recorded as the name of a sheep and horse ranch (DSP Ben. Mil., LXXIX, 89). August 7, 1845, it was applied to a grant of half a league, conveyed to three Indians, Urbano, Odon, and Manuel. "The Sierra Santa Susanna ... ; this range is also familiarly known as the 'Scorpion Hills'" (Whitney, *Geology*, I, 120).

Eshom: Creek, Valley, Point [Tulare]. Named for John Perry Eshom, a native of Illinois, who settled in the Tule River precinct before 1866.

Esmerelda [Calaveras]. The name, probably derived from the near-by Esmeralda (emerald) Mine, is shown on the Land Office map of 1891 as Esmeralda. In the Postal Guide of 1892 it was misspelled Esmerelda; this has not been corrected. The name was very popular in the 19th century, partly because of Esmeralda, the heroine of Victor Hugo's novel *Notre-Dame de Paris.*

Espada Creek [Santa Barbara]. "At this place a soldier lost his sword; he allowed it to be stolen from his belt, but he afterwards recovered it as the Indians who had seen the act ran after the thief ... For this reason the name of Rancheria de la Espada stuck to the village" (Costansó, August 27, 1769).

Esparto, ĕs-pär′-tō [Yolo]. The Vaca Valley Railroad (now the Southern Pacific) reached the place in 1875 and called the station Esperanza. When the post office was established in the 1880's, the name had to be changed because there was another Esperanza, in Tulare County. Esparto is the Spanish word for 'feather grass.'

Esperanza. The Spanish word meaning 'hope' is found as an optimistic name for settlements in various parts of the world. California has two railroad stations so named [Orange, Siskiyou] and an **Esperanza Creek** [Calaveras]. The latter is mentioned in *Hutchings' Illustrated California Magazine* (III, 490) and was probably named after the mine between Mountain Ranch and Railroad Flat. A land grant in Monterey County, dated November 29, 1834, was named Encinal y Buena Esperanza (oak grove and good hope).

Espinosa Lake [Monterey]. Perpetuates the

names of José and Salvador Espinosa, who owned adjoining ranchos, the boundary between them running through the lake. *El rancho de los Espinosas llamado* [called] *San Miguel* is mentioned as early as 1828 (Registro, p. 14).

Espiritu Santo. The Spanish words, meaning 'Holy Ghost,' are found in the names of two land grants. Lomerias Muertas (dead or bare ridge) or Lomerias del Espiritu Santo [San Benito] was granted August 16, 1842. *Loma del Espiritu Santo* [San Benito], a grant dated April 15, 1839, but not confirmed by the United States, may have been named for the grantee, María del Espíritu Santo Carrillo, and not directly for the Holy Ghost.

Esquon [Butte]. The name of the land grant, dated December 22, 1844, was apparently derived from that of an Indian rancheria, shown as *Rª Esque* on a *diseño* (about 1844) of the Aguas Frias grant. According to Kroeber (*AAE*, XXIX, 267), *Esken* was the name of a tract of land held by northwestern Maidu Indians. The grant was also known as Neal's Rancho for the co-grantee, Samuel Neal, a Pennsylvania German who came with Frémont in 1844. The station Esquon of the old Sacramento Northern was so named because it was on land included in the grant.

Essex [San Bernardino]. The station had been called Edson by the Atlantic and Pacific Railroad in 1883. In 1906 the Santa Fe changed the name for operating convenience. According to local tradition, Essex was the name of a pioneer miner. (Santa Fe.) There is another Essex in Humboldt County.

Estanislao. *See* Stanislaus.

Estero, ĕs-târ'-ō. The word corresponds to the English 'estuary,' but was also used for an inlet or lagoon near the sea. It was frequently applied as a geographical term in Spanish times and has survived in the names of several coastal features. **Estero: Bay, Point** [San Luis Obispo]. The *estero* was mentioned by Costansó under date of September 9, 1769, and *Punta del Estero* is shown on his map. The bay appears on later Spanish maps as *Los Esteros*. Vancouver (II, 446) has *Ponto* [!] *del Esteros;* and Wilkes' map, Esteros Point. Point Esteros and Esteros Bay are shown on the Coast Survey chart of 1852, and Estero Bay is mentioned in the *Report* of 1858 (p. 322). Parke in 1854 called Carrizo Plains [west of Antelope Valley] the Estero, "another remarkable feature ... a broad, smooth plain" (Pac. R.R. *Reports*, Vol. VII, Pt. 1, p. 8), and the Parke-Custer map shows

Llano Estero. Here the name refers not to a coastal feature, but to the salt marsh, which is sometimes called *estero* in Spanish. **Estero Americano** [Sonoma]. The name arose in Spanish times, probably because American ships engaged in the fur trade sometimes anchored at the mouth of the *estero*. In 1810 Gabriel Moraga came across three Americans from such a ship, who were hunting deer a few miles from the inlet (PSP, XIX, 279). The name was applied to a land grant dated September 4, 1839, and in the *Statutes* of 1855 the stream is mentioned as forming the boundary between Marin and Sonoma counties. Duflot de Mofras (1844) and Ringgold (General Chart, 1850) have Estero Americano for Tomales Bay. *See* Creek. **Estero de Limantour** [Marin]. The name was first applied to what is now Drakes Estero for José Yves Limantour, supercargo of the *Ayacucho*, which was wrecked at the entrance to the *estero* in 1841. Limantour was a French trader, naturalized in Mexico, who gained wide notoriety in the 1850's by presenting to the authorities no fewer than seven claims for grants, totaling more than 124 leagues—all rejected as fraudulent. On the chart of Drake's Bay (1860) the Coast Survey renamed the estuary Drake's Estero. Two years later the Survey officials tried to restore the original name in spite of their belief that the wreck of Limantour's vessel had been a fake too: "[Limantour] asserted that in trading upon this coast in 1841 he lost the Mexican vessel Ayachuco [!] at the entrance to this estero" (*Report*, 1862, p. 326). Davidson, however, in his 1869 edition of the *Coast Pilot* kept Drake's name for the large estuary, and Limantour's name was transferred to the smaller inlet farther east.

Estrella, ĕs-trä'-yȧ: **Creek,** town, **Army Air Field** [San Luis Obispo]. The name Estrella (star) is shown north of the creek, a tributary to the Salinas, on the *diseño* of San Miguel, 1840. On July 16, 1844, the name was given to part of the land grant conveyed to the Christian Indians of San Miguel; the grant was not confirmed by the United States. The town is shown on G. H. Derby's map of 1850, (misspelled Estrelta, although it is spelled correctly in his report).

Estuary. *See* Creek.

Ethanac, ĕ'-thăn-ăk [Riverside]. The post office was established June 25, 1900; the name was coined from that of Ethan A. Chase, a landowner and political leader. When the Santa Fe reached the place in 1905, the name was applied to the station.

Eticuera, ĕt-ĭ-kwâr′-à: **Creek** [Napa]. Probably the Spanish rendering of a Patwin name. *Etécuero* is shown on a *diseño* of Las Putas grant (175 ND) about 1843.

Etiwanda [San Bernardino]. George and William Chaffey started the settlement in 1882 and named it for the chief of a tribe near Lake Michigan. The Santa Fe station is Etiwanda, and the near-by Southern Pacific station is Etiwa.

Etna [Siskiyou]. The original name, Rough and Ready, was changed by statute in 1874 to the more conventional name of the near-by flour mill (spelled Aetna).

Ettawa [Lake]. The Indian-sounding name was coined before 1900 by the owner of the springs, from the name of his mother, Etta Waughtel (F. M. Andres).

Ettersburg [Humboldt]. In 1894 Albert F. Etter took up a homestead here, and two years later he started the Ettersburg Experimental Place, where he has since created a large number of fruit varieties by his unique methods. The post office is listed in 1916. The name commemorates Ettersburg, the castle on the Rhine which the Etter family left 200 years before.

Eureka. The Greek expression for 'I have found it,' associated with the great geometrician, Archimedes, has common currency in Western civilization. As a geographical term it apparently originated in California: the gazetteers of the 1840's mention no such place in the United States—in 1880 there were forty of them. The motto became popular after the California constitutional convention, on October 2, 1849, approved the great seal of the State, with the inscription "Eureka." The expression became popular also as a trade and mining term, and is still retained in the names of about fifteen features in the State. **Eureka** [Humboldt]. The settlement was established by the Union and Mendocino companies, headed by C. S. Ricks and J. T. Ryan of San Francisco, and named on May 13, 1850 (Doyle). **Eureka Valley** [Death Valley National Monument]. The name has been used since 1888 and was either applied in derision or because something, perhaps water, was actually found. Lieutenant D. A. Lyle of the Wheeler Survey called it Termination Valley, since he could find no source of water in it.

Evans: Glade, Peak [Mendocino National Forest]. Named for the Evans family who lived in a cabin in the glade. The name for the peak is no longer used locally.

Evelyn. Next to Elizabeth and Helen, this is the most popular girl's name used in California geography. **Evelyn Lake** [Sequoia National Park]. Named for Evelyn Clough, sister of William O. Clough, who discovered Cloughs Cave (Farquhar). **Evelyn** [Inyo]. When F. M. ("Borax") Smith built the Tonopah and Tidewater Railroad in 1907, he named this station for his wife. **Evelyn Lake** [Yosemite National Park]. Named for a daughter of Major William W. Forsyth, acting superintendent of the park from 1909 to 1912 (Farquhar).

Evergreen [Santa Clara]. The popular American place name was applied about 1875 to the post office, now discontinued.

Everitt Hill [Siskiyou]. The elevation on the slope of Mount Shasta was named for John Samuel Everitt, supervisor of the Shasta National Forest, who lost his life in a forest fire on this spot, August 25, 1934 (Schrader).

Evolution: Group, Creek, Valley, Lake, Meadow, Basin [Kings Canyon National Park]. Six peaks in this group were named in July, 1895, by T. S. Solomons, in honor of Charles Darwin, Thomas Huxley, Herbert Spencer, and Alfred Wallace, the British exponents of the theory of evolution, and for Ernst Haeckel, the German scientist, and John Fiske, the American historian and philosopher (Farquhar). The creek was named by J. N. LeConte in January, 1905. "The locality . . . is drained by what is known as the Middle Branch of the South Fork of the San Joaquin River, a name clumsy and objectionable to the last degree. I therefore propose to reject it, the sheepmen to the contrary notwithstanding, and refer to it as Evolution Creek . . ." (*SCB*, V, 229). The other features were named when the Geological Survey mapped the district, 1907–1909. Two other peaks of the group have since been named in honor of distinguished scientists: one in 1912 for Jean Lamarck, the French pre-Darwinian evolutionist, and the other in 1942, by David R. Brower, for Gregor Mendel, the German-Austrian author of the Mendelian law of heredity.

Exeter [Tulare]. The town was founded in 1880 by D. W. Parkhurst for the Pacific Improvement Company and was named after his home city in England (I. G. Simmons). The post office was established June 17, 1889.

Explorers Pass [Imperial]. Named on January 12, 1858, by Lieutenant Joseph C. Ives while he was exploring the Colorado River: "... below the pass, which we call after our little steamboat, the Explorer's Pass ..." (Ives, *Report*, p. 47).

Eyese, ī'-ēz: **Creek** [Siskiyou]. The name of the affluent of the Klamath is derived from that of the Karok village *Ayiis* at the mouth of the creek (Kroeber, *AAE*, XXXV, 38).

Fagan [Butte]. Named by the Southern Pacific for Edward Fagan, on whose land a siding was constructed about 1903.

Fairbank Point [San Luis Obispo]. The point south of the town of Morrow Bay was named in memory of Dr. and Mrs. Charles Oliver Fairbank, who had lived near-by (Geographic Board, Sept.-Dec., 1962).

Fairfax [Marin]. Named for Charles Snowden Fairfax, of Fairfax County, Virginia, popularly known as Lord Fairfax, who settled in 1856 on what was once a part of Rancho Cañada de Herrera (or Providencia).

Fairfield [Solano]. In 1859, Robert H. Waterman (1808–1884), a famous captain of famous clipper ships, lived here in a house which he modeled after the prow of a ship. He gave the land for a new city, which he named after Fairfield, Connecticut, his former home.

Fairfield Peak [Lassen National Park]. Named for Asa M. Fairfield, a pioneer educator and historian of Lassen County. The name appears on the atlas sheet of the Geological Survey, made in 1925–1926, and in the *Sixth Report* of the Geographic Board.

Fair Oaks [Sacramento]. The name was applied to the post office about 1895. Other combinations with the adjective "fair," a favorite in American place names, include: Fairmead [Madera], Fairmont [Los Angeles], Fairport [Modoc], Fairview [Fresno], Fairville [Sonoma].

Fair Play [El Dorado]. N. Sisson and Charles Staples settled here in 1853; the post office is listed in 1862. According to local tradition, the name arose from an incident in which an appeal for fair play forestalled a fight between two miners. However, Fair Play was a popular place name in the days before the Civil War. *Lippincott's Gazetteer* of 1854 lists eight towns of that name in various states.

Faith Valley. See Hope Valley.

Falda [San Diego]. The name was applied to the station of the San Diego Central after 1890. It was probably chosen because the place is near the steep slope of Loma Alta, since in Spanish geographical terminology *falda*, meaning 'skirt,' is used for the lower part of a slope.

Fales Hot Springs [Mono]. Samuel Fales, a native of Michigan, settled in Antelope Valley before 1868 and developed the springs in 1877 (Maule).

Falk [Humboldt]. Named for the brothers Noah H. and Elijah H. Falk, of Pennsylvania German stock, who came to California in 1852 and 1878, respectively. Both were prominent lumbermen, and Elijah H. was mayor of Eureka in 1915.

Fallbrook [San Diego]. Named after Fallbrook, Pennsylvania, the former home of Charles V. Reche, who settled in the district in 1859 and became its first postmaster in 1878. After the town was washed out in the early 1880's, a new settlement developed around the railroad station, which had been named North Fallbrook by the California Southern Railroad in 1882.

Fallen Leaf Lake [El Dorado]. Apparently named by the Whitney Survey because from the surrounding heights the outline of the lake resembles a fallen leaf. The name appears on the von Leicht–Hoffmann map of Lake Tahoe (1874).

Fallen Moon, Lake of the [El Dorado]. Named by Frank Ernest Hill, who made the lake the subject of a poem, "The Lake of the Fallen Moon," published in 1923 in the *Sierra Club Bulletin* (Farquhar).

Fallon [Marin]. The station on the North Pacific Coast Railroad was named in the 1890's, probably for a member of the pioneer Fallon family. Luke Fallon settled in the Tomales township in 1854; James L. Fallon settled there five years later (Co. Hist., 1880, pp. 405 f.).

Fall River, Fall River Mills [Shasta]. The river was so named by Frémont in 1846 because of its cascades. The name appears on the Frémont-Preuss map of 1848 and is repeatedly mentioned in the reports of the government surveys in the 1850's. Eddy's map shows also a Fall Lake. The town took the name Fall River Mills from the mills built in 1872 by W. H. Winters, although on the county map of 1884 it is shown as Fall City (Steger). **Fall River** [Butte]. The stream was so named because of the waterfalls which are near the junction of the river with the Middle Fork of Feather River. **Fallsvale** [San Bernardino]. When the post office was established November 25, 1929, it was given an abbreviated version of the name Valley of the Falls.

False. The adjective is often used, especially by navigators, to describe an unnamed geographic feature which resembles and may be mistaken for another feature already named.

False Cape [Humboldt]. It was probably this cape upon which Hezeta in 1775 bestowed the name *Punta Gorda*. In 1851 it is mentioned as False Cape Mendocino, a term used by American sailors. Davidson in 1854 applied the old Spanish name to the present Punta Gorda south of Cape Mendocino and renamed the False Cape, Cape Fortunas, a name originally bestowed upon Point Arena by Ferrer in 1543. "We have ventured to call this headland Cape Fortunas, to avoid the repetition of Mendocino, and to commemorate Ferrelo's [Ferrer's] discoveries." (Coast Pilot, 1858, p. 68.) The present version, long used by navigators, was officially established by decision of the Geographic Board in 1940. *See* Punta Gorda. **False Klamath: Cove, Rock** [Del Norte]. The cove was so named because from aboard a ship it resembles the cove at the mouth of Klamath River. The rock was named by the Coast Survey after the cove, although there is no "true" Klamath Rock. **False Bay** [San Diego]. *See* Mission Bay.

Famoso [Kern]. When the Southern Pacific reached the place in the 1870's, it called the station Poso after Poso Creek. When the post office was established about 1890, the Post Office Department applied the name Spottiswood because the old name was too much like Pozo in San Luis Obispo County. The residents did not like the Anglo-Saxon name and requested the Post Office Department to change the name to Famoso, which is the Spanish word for 'famous,' 'noteworthy.'

Fandango: Valley, Creek, Mountain, Pass [Modoc]. The valley was named by members of the "Wolverine Rangers," an immigrant party of 1849. "After camping one night the weather grew so terribly cold that the men had to dance to keep warm, and named their wild camping place 'Fandango Valley'" (Oliver Goldsmith, a forty-niner, quoted in Bruff, I, 580 f.). The often-repeated story that a band of Indians in the early 1850's surprised and massacred an immigrant party while they were dancing and making merry in celebration of their successful crossing of Lassen's Pass is more romantic but less authentic. The name is recorded in early reports and on county maps and was given currency by the Wheeler atlas, in which sheet 38-B shows Valley, Creek, and Peak.

Farallon, fâr'-á-lŏn: **Islands; Gulf of the Farallones** [San Francisco]. The Spanish name for 'small rocky islands in the sea' is repeatedly shown on maps of the 16th and 17th centuries in different latitudes. The rocky islands off the Golden Gate were called Islands of Saint James by Drake (1579), and appear with that name on English maps of the 18th century. The Vizcaíno expedition (1602–1603) referred to them as "farallones" and named them *Los Frayles* (the friars). Gonzáles referred to them as *los Farallones* in 1734, and Bodega in 1775 called them *Farallones de los Frayles*. Most of the Spanish and Mexican maps used *Farallones de San Francisco*, or simply *Farallones*, but Davidson and the Coast Survey used Bodega's *Farallones de los Frayles* until the 1870's. On modern maps the islands are usually designated individually as North, Middle, and South Farallon (or Farallone and Farallones).

Farley [Mendocino]. When the Northwestern Pacific was extended north from Ukiah in 1911, the station was named for Jackson Farley, a native of Virginia who settled in the district about 1857.

Farmersville [Tulare]. The convenient descriptive name came into being when the post office was established in the 1870's.

Farmington [San Joaquin]. A common American place name applied about 1859 by W. B. Stamper. The settlement is in the center of a rich farming area.

Farnsworth Bank [Santa Catalina Island]. Named for Samuel S. Farnsworth, who built a road on the island, 1893–1902 (Geographic Board, 1936).

Farwell [Butte, Glenn]. Rancho Arroyo Chico, granted to Edward A. Farwell of Boston, Massachusetts, on March 29, 1844, was also known as Rancho de Farwell.

Faucherie: Lake, Creek [Nevada]. The lake was named for B. Faucherie, a pioneer hydraulic engineer of the 1850's and 1860's who also created French Lake and the Magenta flume.

Fauntleroy Rock [Humboldt]. The rock south of Cape Mendocino was named for the Coast Survey brig *R. H. Fauntleroy*, Davidson's survey vessel between 1854 and 1858. The brig, in turn, was named in memory of Robert H. Fauntleroy of the Coast Survey, son-in-law of the Scottish reformer Robert Owen and father-in-law of George Davidson. There is another Fauntleroy Rock in Crescent City harbor.

Fawnskin Meadows [San Bernardino]. Skins were stretched on trees by a party of hunters in 1891 and allowed to remain there for many years; hence the name (V. W. Bruner). The settlement Fawnskin which developed on

Highway 18, north of Big Bear Lake, received a post office in May 18, 1918.

Feather Falls [Butte]. The post office was established in 1921. The name was apparently suggested by Feather River and the well-known waterfalls of Fall River, several miles north.

Feather River [Butte, Plumas]. The river was known by the present name to the trappers of the Hudson's Bay Company in the 1830's. There is no conclusive evidence that it was named *Rio de las Plumas* by the Spaniards. The Spanish and the English versions probably became current as Sutter used both: "I named Feather River, 'Rio de las Plumas,' from the fact that the Indians went profusely decorated with feathers, and there were piles of feathers lying around everywhere, out of which the natives made blankets" (p. 62). Wilkes' map of 1841 shows Feather River; a *diseño* of the Arroyo Chico grant (1843) and the Frémont-Preuss map of 1845 have *Rio de las Plumas*. Gibbes' map of 1852 still has the Spanish version, but Eddy's official map and most of the other American maps have Feather River. Jedediah Smith's name for the stream in 1828 had been *Ya-loo* (*Travels*, pp. 70, 176). *See* Plumas.

Felis. *See* Los Felis.

Feliz [San Mateo]. This land grant, also called Cañada de las Auras, dated April 30, 1844, was known by the name of the grantee, Domingo Feliz.

Feliz, fā'lĭz: **Creek** [Mendocino]. Named for Fernando Feliz, grantee of the Sanel rancho, November 9, 1844.

Fellows [Kern]. Named in 1908 for Charley A. Fellows, a building contractor, by the Sunset Western Railroad Company, which built the line now jointly owned and operated by the Santa Fe and the Southern Pacific.

Felton [Santa Cruz]. The town was founded in 1878 and named by George Treat, the owner of the land, for his friend Charles N. Felton, State assemblyman (1880–1881), later congressman (1885–1889), U.S. senator (1891–1893), and member of the State Board of Prison Directors (1903–1907). Charles N. Felton Memorial Grove [Humboldt] was named in his memory.

Fender Mountain [Shasta]. Named for W. H. Fender, who had a furniture factory near Kenyon Sulphur Springs in the 1880's (Steger).

Fenner. *See* Amboy.

Fermin, fĕr'-mĭn, **Point** [Los Angeles]. Vancouver, in 1793, gave this name to the western point at the entrance of San Pedro Bay, to honor his friend Padre Fermín Francisco de Lasuén. The name is spelled Firmin on some maps.

Fernandez [Butte]. The name of a rancho granted to the brothers Dionisio and Máximo Fernández on June 12, 1846.

Fernandez Pass [Yosemite National Park]. Named for Joseph Fernandez, a first sergeant of the Fourth Cavalry, who, with Lieutenant Harry C. Benson, explored the headwaters of the Merced, 1895–1897 (Farquhar).

Ferndale [Humboldt]. The town was founded about 1870 and appropriately named because of the luxuriant growth of ferns in the valley. Other communities bear similar names: Fern [Shasta], Fernbridge [Humboldt], Fern Cove [Sonoma], Fern Canyon [Marin]. Some fifteen Fern Creeks, Canyons, Hills, and Mountains are shown on topographical atlas sheets, and many more such names are used locally.

Ferris Canyon [Mono]. Named for Andrew Ferris, who obtained a patent to land near Sweetwater (Maule).

Ferrum [Riverside]. The Latin word for 'iron' was applied to the railroad station in 1948 when Henry J. Kaiser built a branch line to haul iron ore from Eagle Mountains to the steel mill at Fontana (John Hilton, *Desert Magazine*, March, 1949, p. 7).

Fetters Hot Springs [Sonoma]. George Fetters, a native of Pittsburgh, Pennsylvania, struck flowing hot water when prospecting for mineral water here, on land which he had bought in 1907 (Co. Hist., 1911, pp. 618 f.).

Fiddletown [Amador]. "In the days of the gold rush the mining settlement got its name Fiddletown because a large number of miners were from Missouri and had brought their fiddles with them. It was said to be a common sight to see one miner working on the claim while his partner played the fiddle for their enjoyment." (Doyle). According to another version an old lady claimed that her family were the first settlers at the place and called it Violin City because four members of the family played the violin (*CHSQ*, XXIV, 167). May 24, 1878, the name of the post office was changed to Oleta, but on July 1, 1932, the old name was restored. There is a Fiddle Creek in Sierra County and a Fiddler Gulch in Kern County. A Violin Canyon runs parallel to Highway 99 in Los Angeles County.

Fidler Creek [Shasta]. Named for Captain Hercules Fidler, who had his house here from the late 1860's to 1876 (Steger).

Fieldbrook [Humboldt]. The place was originally known as Bokman's Prairie. When the town was laid out in 1900, the name was changed to Fieldbrook because there were brooks east and west of it. (Regina Schneitter.)

Fields Landing [Humboldt]. The name is mentioned in the Business Directory of the county in 1890 and appears on the Mining Bureau map of 1891 as a station of the Eel River and Eureka Railroad. The station was named for Waterman Field, who had been a resident of the county since the 1860's.

Figarden [Fresno]. Named for the large fig orchards there. The name appeared originally on the Santa Fe Railroad map of 1921 as Fig Garden. On succeeding maps it has its present form.

Fig Tree John Springs [Riverside]. The springs were so named because Juan Razón, a Coahuila Indian popularly known as "Figtree John," lived near them. The place was submerged by the Salton Sea in 1907. The springs reappeared when the water subsided, but John had moved to a safer place, Agua Dulce.

Figueroa Mountain [Santa Barbara]. The mountain was named for a member of the well-known southern California family, the most eminent of whom was José Figueroa, governor of California 1833–1835.

Fillmore [Ventura]. Named by the Southern Pacific in 1887 for J. A. Fillmore, general superintendent of the company's Pacific system.

Fin Dome [Kings Canyon National Park]. Named in 1899 by Bolton C. Brown. He compared the ridge above Rae Lake to a sea serpent and on his sketch map marked "The Head," "The Fin," "The Tail." (SCB, III, 136.)

Finger. About ten mountains and rocks, including the high peaks in Kings Canyon and Yosemite national parks, are so named because of their shape. The name also occurs as a generic term: Columbia Finger [Yosemite National Park].

Finley [Lake]. The town was started by John Syler, April 20, 1889. From a list of names he submitted, the Post Office Department selected the name Finley for the Post office established October 25, 1907. It was the middle name of his father, Samuel Finley Syler (Mauldin).

Finney Creek [San Mateo, Santa Cruz]. Named for Seldon J. Finney, State assemblyman 1869–1870, State senator 1871–1874, whose home was on the creek.

Firebaugh [Fresno]. In 1854, A. D. Fierbaugh established a trading post and a ferry across the San Joaquin River. The name was misspelled Firebaugh's Ferry as early as 1856, and this version was used when the place became a station on the Gilroy-Sageland stage line in the 1860's.

Fir Top Mountain [Sierra]. An excellent example of a descriptive name. The mountain has a bare appearance except at its rather flat top, which is covered with trees, presumably firs. (Stewart.) The fir, in spite of its frequent occurrence in the mountain areas, is seldom found in place names. The sound of the name, unlike "cedar" or "pine," does not seem apt for euphonious combinations.

Fish. There are not more than about twenty-five Fish Creeks, Valleys, and Canyons in California, a small number for a state in which fish are abundant. The word appears occasionally in the names of mountains: Fish Valley Peak [Mono], Fish Spring Hill [Inyo], Fish Creek Mountain [Madera], and in several settlements, Fish Rock [Mendocino], Fish Camp [Mariposa], Fish Spring [Imperial]. Fish Creek Mountain [San Bernardino]. *See* Grinnell Peak.

Fishermen. About twenty geographic features, mainly bays and coves along the coast, or canyons and creeks in the mountains, were so named because they were favorite fishing places. Mount Whitney was once, for some reason, known as Fisherman's Peak.

Fiske, Mount. *See* Evolution.

Fitch Mountain [Sonoma]. The mountain was known to Indians and earlier settlers as *Sotoyome*, and later was named for Henry Delano Fitch (1799–1849) of San Diego, who in 1841 was granted the Rancho Sotoyome, on which the mountain is situated. Fitch's romantic elopement with Josefa Carrillo in 1829 is famous in California literature.

Fitzhugh Creek [Modoc]. Named for the Fitzhugh family, pioneer settlers of the 1870's (Irma Laird).

Five-and-Ten Divide [Siskiyou]. The ridge west of Happy Camp forms the divide between Fivemile Creek and Tenmile Creek (Geographic Board, July-Sept., 1965).

Five Points [Fresno]. The post office was established July 28, 1944, and so named because five roads converge at this point.

Flatiron. About ten hills, buttes, and ridges are so named because of their shape. The best-known features are the ridges in Mono County and in Lassen National Park.

Flea Valley; Flea Valley Creek [Butte]. Apparently the only place in the State with the American name of this obnoxious little insect; at any rate, it is the only survivor from earlier days. Flea Valley House is shown on the Mining Bureau map of 1891. The near-by Western Pacific station and post office, established about 1907, bear the Spanish word for 'flea,' *pulga. See* Pulgas.

Fleener Chimneys [Lava Beds National Monument]. Named for Sam Fleener, a homesteader in the vicinity (Geographic Board, December, 1948). A post office named Fleener is listed between 1889 and 1893.

Fleischmann Lake [Plumas]. Named for Major Max C. Fleischmann in appreciation of his support of the Boy Scout movement in America (Geographic Board, May, 1954).

Fleming Point [Alameda]. The site of the race track, Golden Gate Fields, was named for J. J. Fleming, who settled in the vicinity in 1853 (Ferrier, p. 116). His name is shown on Hoffmann's map of the Bay region.

Fletcher: Lake, Creek [Yosemite National Park]. Named in 1895 by Lieutenant N. F. McClure, for A. G. Fletcher, a State fish commissioner, who was instrumental in stocking the streams of Yosemite.

Flinn Springs [San Diego]. Possibly named for W. E. Flinn, a native of North Carolina, who was a farmer at Ranchita in 1866.

Flint. The name has been given to several geographic features where obsidian deposits provided the Indians with arrowheads. The origin of the name of the most prominent feature, **Flint Rock Head** [Del Norte], however, is shrouded in mystery. The name was applied by the Coast Survey and is apparently an interpretation of the Yurok *o-kne'-get,* 'where they get arrow points.' When Waterman pointed out to his informants that they could not possibly get arrowheads there, the Indians told him that some spirit had "tried" to change the granite into obsidian for their benefit, and that he "almost did it" (Waterman, pp. 232 f., 272). *See* Pedernales.

Flintridge [Los Angeles]. When part of Rancho la Cañada was subdivided in 1920, the tract was named by Frank P. Flint, U.S. senator from California, 1905–1911.

Florence Lake [Fresno]. Named in 1896 for Florence Evelyn Starr by her brother, Walter A. Starr, who, with Allen L. Chickering, camped here when on a trip through the High Sierra from Yosemite to Kings River Canyon. The lake, enlarged by a dam, is now a reservoir of the Southern California Edison Company's system. (W. A. Starr.) **Florence,**

Mount; Florence Creek [Yosemite National Park]. The mountain was named at the suggestion of B. F. Taylor in 1886, in memory of Florence, a daughter of James M. Hutchings. She was born in Yosemite Valley on August 23, 1864, and died there September 26, 1881 (Farquhar). There is a Florence Peak of almost the same height in Sequoia National Park.

Flores, flôr'-ĕs. The word for 'flowers' was used repeatedly for place names in Spanish times and appears in the titles of a number of land grants and claims. **Las Flores** [San Diego]. Font (*Compl. Diary,* p. 189) mentions, on January 9, 1776, a lake called *Las Flores.* This was probably in the valley which the Portolá expedition had called *Santa Praxedis de los Rosales* because of "innumerable Castilian rosebushes and other flowers" (Crespi, p. 133). *Las Flores,* apparently the name of a rancheria, is recorded in 1778 (PSP, II, 1). Later, an *asistencia* of Mission San Luis Rey and an experimental Indian pueblo were established at Las Flores. On October 8, 1844, the land was purchased by the Pico family and became part of their Rancho Santa Margarita y San Onofre. Emory (*Mil. Rec.,* p. 117) in 1846–1847 mentions Las Flores as "a deserted mission." About 1888 the name was given to the station of the Santa Fe. **Las Flores** [Tehama]. The town was laid out in 1916 and named after the Las Flores land grant (of December 24, 1844), on which it is situated. The name is also preserved in Los Angeles and Santa Barbara counties. In Orange County there is a fancifully named Miraflores.

Flores, flôr'-ĕs: **Peak** [Orange]. The name of the peak in Santiago Canyon commemorates the Mexican outlaw Juan Flores, part of whose band was captured here in 1857. *See* Barton Mound; Sheriffs Springs.

Florin [Sacramento]. The name was given to the station by E. B. Crocker of the Central Pacific Railroad when the line was constructed, between 1863 and 1869. The florin is a silver coin long used in Europe and still minted in England (a two-shilling piece); but the coin may not be the source of the name. According to the County History of 1880, p. 235, the name was applied because of the large number of flowers in the region.

Floriston [Nevada]. The railroad station established in the 1870's bore the name Bronco, after the creek a mile to the south. When the post office was established in 1891 the new name was chosen. It is probably a coined word with the stem *flor*, 'flower.' There are other fanciful names on the Truckee-Verdi section: Polaris, Boca, Iceland, Mystic, Calvada.

Flournoy; flûr'-noi [Tehama]. The post office, listed in 1910, was named for the Flournoy family, who had been farmers in the Henleyville district since the 1870's.

Flying Dutchman Creek [Kern]. The name appears on the Breckenridge Mountain atlas sheet of the Corps of Engineers for a tributary to Havilah Canyon Creek. Whether it was named for the fabled Dutch mariner, or for Wagner's opera, or for some fleet-footed German, is not known.

Foerster: Peak, Creek [Yosemite National Park]. Named in 1895 by Lieutenant N. F. McClure, for Lewis Foerster (1868–1936), soldier and mountaineer, a native of Germany. "His service was outstanding, and it was in recognition of his achievements and because of his close association with the particular region that I gave his name to a prominent peak." (*SCB*, XXII, 102.)

Folger Peak [Alpine]. Named either for Robert M. Folger, proprietor of the Alpine *Chronicle*, founded in 1864, the first newspaper on the eastern slope of the Sierra, or for his brother, Alexander M. Folger, first postmaster at Markleeville (Maule).

Folsom [Sacramento]. The town was laid out in 1855 by Theodore D. Judah as the temporary terminus of the Sacramento Valley Railroad, the first in California. It was named for Captain Joseph L. Folsom, who had come to California as assistant quartermaster of Stevenson's New York Volunteers and had bought Rancho Rio de los Americanos, part of the vast Leidesdorff estate, on which the railroad station was built. The settlement of 1849 had been called Negro Bar because the first placer miners there were Negroes, according to the County History, 1880, p. 222. This, however, was another camp near Folsom.

Fontana, fŏn-tăn'-á [San Bernardino]. A town was laid out here by the Semi-Tropic Land and Water Company in the "boom year" 1887, but it failed to develop. Before 1905 the Fontana Development Company bought the interests, and a new town was started by A. B. Miller, under the name of Rosena. It is uncertain whether the company took its name from a family or from the Spanish poetical word for 'fountain.' In 1913 the name Rosena was changed to Fontana in a solemn ceremony, Judge B. F. Bledsoe presiding and Mrs. E. B. Miller, mother of the "father of Fontana,"

officiating (Santa Fe).

Forbestown [Butte]. Named for Ben F. Forbes, a native of Wisconsin, who established a general merchandise store at this place in 1850. Mentioned in the *Statutes* of 1853 (p. 313).

Fordyce Lake [Nevada]. The reservoir was built in 1873–1875 by the South Yuba Canal Company and was named for the hydraulic engineer who began building flumes and canals in that region in 1853. Jerome Fordyce of Fordyce Valley is listed in a directory of 1867.

Forest. This word, usually combined with City, Grove, Hill, Home, Knoll, etc., is an extremely popular place name in the United States. California has ten places so named, the oldest of which is probably **Forest Hill** [Placer], settled in the early 1850's and so named because of the dense pine forest surrounding the place. **Forest** [Sierra]. In 1862, William Hughes of Forest City, answering Bancroft's questionnaire, stated that the town was settled in 1852 and that it was given the name Forest City by a woman (he crossed out 'lady') named Mrs. Moody (Bancroft Scrapbooks, XIII, 73). Another source states that the name came into use when a Mrs. Forest Mooney "dated" her newspaper articles "Forest City" (Hittell, III, 100). The name of the post office was abbreviated to Forest, January 17, 1895. The names of several other post offices include the word: Forest Ranch [Butte], June 7, 1878; Forest Home [San Bernardino], May 1, 1906; Forest Knolls [Marin], March 22, 1916; Forest Glen [Trinity], March 9, 1920. **Forest Falls** [San Bernardino] post office was established July 1, 1960. The name is a combination of two discontinued post offices: Fallsvale and Forest Home. **Forest Hill Divide** [Placer] *See* Divide, The.

Forester Pass [Sequoia National Park]. The pass was discovered on August 18, 1929, by a party which included S. B. Show, Jesse W. Nelson, and Frank Cunningham, all of the Forest Service. At the suggestion of Cunningham, then supervisor of Sequoia National Forest, the new route to the headwaters of Kern River was named Forester Pass for the men who had discovered it. The name was approved by the Geographic Board on January 24, 1938. (W. I. Hutchinson.)

Forestville [Sonoma]. This place at the edge of the timber country was originally named Forrestville for its founder, A. J. Forrester. By the end of the 1880's the present spelling was generally used. Andrew Jackson Forrester, a native of Illinois, saloonkeeper at Russian River, was a registered voter in 1866.

Fork. The practice of designating as "forks" the branches or important tributaries of a river system seems to have prevailed in California more frequently than in other parts of the United States and is especially noticeable on the west slope of the Sierra Nevada. Stewart has explained this predilection for "forking" rivers to the rapidity of settlement after the discovery of gold and to the circumstance that the gold seekers (and later the surveyors) proceeded upstream (*American Speech*, XIV, No. 3). Most of the specific names which modify the term "fork" indicate the relative location: north, east, middle, etc.; but some are descriptive, or are the names of other features: Triple Peak Fork of the Merced, Wheatfield Fork of the Gualala, Fish Fork of the San Gabriel, etc. Others are names of men: Stewart Fork of the Trinity, Dana Fork of the Tuolumne, Lewis Fork of the Fresno, etc. In many places the practice is carried to the second degree: North Fork of North Fork of Navarro River, Silver Fork of South Fork of American River, East Fork of West Fork of Mojave River, etc. The Yuba has actually an East, a Middle, a North, and a South Fork of the North Fork. In a few places the "forking" was carried to a third degree and has led to amusing monstrosities such as East Branch of East Fork of North Fork of Trinity River, or West Fork of South Fork of North Fork of San Joaquin River. Although such combinations are never used locally, the streams are so designated by the Geological Survey. A more sensible naming is found in a few places where the term "fork" is avoided: East and West Walker River, Natchez and Rocky Honcut Creek.

Forks of Salmon [Siskiyou]. So named when the post office was established in 1859, because of its situation at the confluence of the North and South forks of Salmon River. A place called Salmon is shown on Eddy's map (1854), not here, but at the junction of the East Fork and the main stream.

Forsythe Creek [Mendocino]. Named for Benjamin Franklin Forsythe, a native of Pennsylvania, who settled in Calpella township in 1857.

Forsyth Peak [Yosemite National Park]. Named for Colonel William W. Forsyth (1856–1933), U.S. Army, who was acting superintendent of Yosemite National Park, 1909–1912.

Fort. Military reservations are listed under their specific names.

Fort. The word is found not only as a generic term in the names of military reservations and as part of the names of communities which developed around old forts, but also as a descriptive term in orographic features. **Fort Mountain** [Calaveras]. Whitney referred to the mountain near Railroad Flat as Fort Hill and said that it was so called because of its "fancied resemblance to a fortress" (*Geology*, I, 266). It was Phil Schumacher of the Whitney Survey who named the mountain. In a letter datelined Railroad Flat, June 29, 1872, he states that the top is "so even and horizontal that it will give room to measure a base-line" (Davidson papers). **Fort Mountain** [Shasta] was no named because it seems to stand guard over the site of old Fort Crook (Steger).

Fort Benson [San Bernardino]. Jerome Benson, a former Mormon, joined by other settlers, fortified his house when the court decided that he had settled (1856) within the boundaries of the San Bernardino Rancho, which belonged to the Mormons. Registered as Historical Landmark 617, September 11, 1957.

Fort Bidwell. *See* Bidwell.

Fort Bragg [Mendocino]. When the town was founded in 1885, it was named after the military post which had been established in 1857 by Lieutenant H. G. Gibson and named in honor of Lieutenant Colonel Braxton Bragg of Mexican War fame. In the Civil War battles of Murfreesboro and Chickamauga, Bragg was the Confederate opponent of Rosecrans, whose name is commemorated in Fort Rosecrans [San Diego].

Fort Crook [Shasta]. Historic Landmark 355 commemorates old Fort Crook, named in 1857 for Lieutenant George Crook. Crook later served with distinction as a general in the Civil War.

Fort Dick [Del Norte]. Fort Dick Landing is first mentioned in the Civil War records. The "fort" was a log house, built by the citizens for defense against the Indians and was probably named for a settler. In 1888 the four brothers Bertsch moved their shake-and-shingle mill to the place and called it Newburg. With the establishment of the post office in 1896 the old name was revived.

Fort Jones [Siskiyou]. The fort was established on October 16, 1852, by companies A and E, First Dragoons, and named for Colonel Roger Jones, Adjutant General of the Army (F. B. Rogers). The garrison evacuated the post on June 23, 1858, but in 1860 the settlers of Wheelock renamed their settlement Fort

Jones in gratitude for the military protection they had received. On November 19, 1860, the name was also adopted for the post office, until then called Ottitiewa for the Scott Valley branch of the Shasta Indians. On Goddard's map, 1857, Fort Jones is shown, but not Ottitiewa.

Fort Point [San Francisco]. The name was applied to the point by the Coast Survey in 1851 because there were still to be seen on it the ruins of an old Spanish fort, the *Castillo de San Joaquin.* Ayala had called it *Punta de San Jose* in August, 1775. On Cañizares' Plano of 1776 it is shown as *Punta de San Josef o Cantil Blanco* (white cliff). It is the site of modern Fort Winfield Scott.

Fort Reading. *See* Reading Peak.

Fort Ross [Sonoma]. The fort was the nucleus of Russian activities in California from 1812 to 1841. The name Ross, selected from lots placed at the base of an image of Christ, was bestowed upon the settlement when it was dedicated on September 11, 1812 (*CHSQ,* XII, 192). It is an obsolete, poetical name for "Russians." The fort was sometimes called by the Spanish *Presidio Ruso* or *Presidio de Bodega. See* Presidio. A post office was established and named Fort Ross on May 23, 1877.

Fort Seward [Humboldt]. The town takes its name from the military post which was established September 26, 1861, and named for Lincoln's secretary of state. The post office is listed in 1913.

Fort Sutter. *See* Sutter.

Fort Tejon. *See* Tejon.

Fortuna [Humboldt]. The place was opened for settlement in the late 1870's by a minister named Gardner, who owned the land. He named it Fortune because he believed it was an ideal place in which to live. Later, for the sake of euphony, he changed its appellation to Fortuna, at that time a unique name in the United States. Names which did not survive were Springville, for the many springs near by, and Slide, for the landslide northwest of the town. (Marie Linser.)

Fortunas, Cape. *See* False Cape.

Fort Yuma. *See* Yuma.

Foss Lake [San Diego]. Probably named for David R. Foss of New Hampshire, who was a merchant in San Luis Rey in 1871.

Foster City [San Mateo]. Established in 1965 and named for T. Jack Foster, who deeded a large parcel of real estate to the county.

Foster Lake [Trinity]. Named for William Foster (1869–1950), because he had assisted in

maintaining sport fishing in the area (Geographic Board, May, 1954).

Four Gables [Fresno, Inyo]. Probably named by the Geological Survey when the Mount Goddard quadrangle was surveyed, 1907–1909, because of the four gable-like formations, two extending northward and one each eastward and westward. The Seven Gables are four miles west.

Fourth Crossing [Calaveras]. This was the place where travelers forded the fourth fork of Calaveras River on the road between Stockton and Murphy's Diggings. A post office of this name was established June 2, 1855, and again February 15, 1892. The present settlement is not on the Calaveras River but east of it, on San Antonio Creek. There was also a Second and a Third Crossing along the same route.

Fouts Springs [Colusa]. Named for John F. Fouts, who discovered the springs in 1873.

Fowler [Fresno]. Named for Thomas Fowler, State senator from Fresno, 1869–1872 and 1877–1878. The name Fowler's Switch was applied to the railroad switch which was built on the Fowler ranch in 1872 and around which the present town developed.

Foxen Canyon [Santa Barbara]. The canyon which cuts through the Tinaquaic rancho preserves the name of the grantee, Benjamin ("Don Julian") Foxen, an English sailor who came to California in 1828.

Fox Meadow [Kings Canyon National Park]. Named for John Fox, for many years a hunter, packer, and guide in the Kings River region (Farquhar).

Frances. *See* Irvine.

Franklin [Sacramento]. Named after the Franklin House, built by Andrew George in 1856. Until 1887 the place was also known as Georgetown, although the post-office name has been Franklin since 1862.

Franklin Canyon [Contra Costa]. Named for Edward Franklin, who bought Vicente Martínez' share of the Ignacio Martínez estate, October 6, 1853, and lived in the canyon until 1875.

Franklin K. Lane Grove [Humboldt]. Dedicated in 1924, and named in honor of the Secretary of the Interior in Woodrow Wilson's cabinet and the first president of the Save-the-Redwoods League.

Franklin: Lakes, Pass [Sequoia National Park]. The name for the two lakes was "derived from the 'Lady Franklin' mine located in this vicinity in the seventies" (Geographic Board, *Sixth Report*).

Franklin Point [San Mateo]. The cape appears as Middle Point on the early charts of the Coast Survey. It was changed after the ship *Sir John Franklin* was wrecked there on January 17, 1865. For a probable early name, *see* Ano Nuevo, Point.

Frazier: Mountain [Ventura]; **Game Refuge, Park** [Kern]. The mountain was named after the Frazier Mine on the south slope. According to the story, a man named Frazier, while tracking down a wounded deer, found a rock rich in gold ore and began his mining operations at that spot (Elizabeth Topping). The mine is mentioned as Frazer Mine in October, 1875 (Co. Hist., 1883, p. 426). The town was named after the mountain by Harry McBain in 1926.

Freaner Peak [Shasta]. The name of Stoney Peak was officially changed to Freaner Peak by the Geographic Board in 1947, at the instigation of the Shasta Historical Society. Colonel James L. Freaner in 1852 undertook to build a road between the Upper Sacramento and Oregon. In July of the same year, he was killed by Indians while on his way from Yreka to the Democratic state convention at Benicia. Beckwith in 1854 mentions a "lake [now Cornaz Lake] called Freaner, the name of an unfortunate gentleman who is supposed to have been killed by the Indians in its vicinity" (Pac. R.R. *Reports*, Vol. II, Pt. 2, p. 57).

Fredericksburg [Alpine]. The town was started in 1864 and may have been named for Frederick Frevert, who operated a sawmill near by (Maule). In view of the strong Confederate sentiment in this region, the scene of Burnside's defeat at Fredericksburg, Virginia, in December, 1862, may have had something to do with the naming.

Fredonyer, frā-dŏn'-yēr: **Pass, Peak** [Lassen]. Named for Dr. Atlas Fredonyer, who discovered the pass in 1852 and built the first house in Mountain Meadows.

Freedom [Santa Cruz]. Originally known as Whiskey Hill, doubtless because of the quenchless thirst of the residents, served by eleven saloons in 1852. In 1892 or 1893 an enterprising purveyor of alcoholic beverages had a huge sign put across the front of his place of business, sporting two American flags and the legend "The Flag of Freedom." The place became known as Freedom, a name which was finally applied to the entire town. (J. E. Gardner, *WF*, V, 199.)

Freel Peak [Alpine, El Dorado]. When William Eimbeck of the Coast Survey used the highest point of Jobs Peaks for triangulation in 1874, he called it Freel's Peak, for James Freel, a settler at the foot of the mountain. *See* Jobs Peak.

Freeport [Sacramento]. The place was established in 1862 by the Freeport Railroad Company as a shipping center. It was really a "free port" as compared with Sacramento, which at that time levied a tax on all transit across the levee.

Freestone [Sonoma]. The town developed around Ferdinand Harbordt's store and was so named because of a quarry of easily worked, free sandstone. The post office is listed in 1870.

Freezeout: Creek, Gulch, Flat [Sonoma]. These places near Duncans Mills are the only survivors of a number of early-day Freezeouts. They were probably all named after the card game, in which a player drops out as soon as his capital is exhausted. *See* Ione.

Fremont. One of the most spectacular and most controversial characters in American history, John C. Frémont, is honored in more than a hundred place names throughout the West. In California the name Fremont was especially popular soon after the Mexican War, but its popularity did not last: Fremont County became Yolo County; Fremont Canyon is now Sierra Canyon; the peak in San Benito County where Frémont raised the Stars and Stripes on March 6, 1846, is officially Gabilan Peak; the town Fremont in Yolo County, founded by Jonas Spect, March 21, 1849, vanished soon after the post office was discontinued in 1864; Fremont Pass, north of Los Angeles, is replaced by San Fernando Pass. At the end of the nineteenth century the name was remembered in California geography only by a moderately high peak and a railroad siding in San Bernardino County. Now the maps show the state parks [San Benito and Monterey], Fremont Ford [Merced], and the promising city in Alameda County. **Fremont Peak State Park** [San Benito]. The park was created in 1934, and the former Gabilan Peak, named Fremont Peak by the Geographic Board in 1960, was made Historic Landmark 181. Frémont did not raise the flag on the peak in 1846, but on Hill 2146 at the head of Steinbach Canyon, two miles distant, and not within the park area (Fred B. Rogers). **Fremont** [Alameda]. The towns of Centerville, Niles, Irvington, Mission San Jose, and Warm Springs—all listed separately in this book—united to form this city, incorporated

January 24, 1956. The name was selected by the Incorporation Committee.

Fremont Canyon [Orange]. Named for Fremont Smith, a stock herder of the 1870's.

French, Frenchman. About seventy-five places in the State have names which include the word French. Most of these were so named because of the presence of French prospectors or settlers; some, because French-Canadian trappers of the Hudson's Bay Company were active in those parts; others doubtless for other foreigners who were thought to be French; and still others, probably for persons named French. **French Camp** [San Joaquin]. This was the southernmost regular camp site of the trappers after La Framboise had established his headquarters here in 1832. By the Spanish Californians it was called Campo de los Franceses, a name preserved in the land grant of January 13, 1844. When Charles M. Weber had the townsite plotted in 1850 he called it Castoria (from French *castor*, 'beaver'), but popular usage retained the old name, French Camp, and it was applied to the post office in 1859. **French Corral** [Nevada]. A stock pen built by a French settler provided the name for the town which developed after a rich gold placer was discovered in the vicinity in 1849. **French Gulch** [Shasta]. The post office was established in 1856 and named after the gulch where French miners had prospected in 1849 or 1850. Historic Landmark 166. **Frenchmans Lake** [Santa Clara]. Named for Peter Coutts (Paulin Caperon), a colorful Frenchman who settled near it in the 1870's (Hoover, pp. 539 ff.).

Freshwater Lagoon [Humboldt]. The Yurok name for the lagoon south of Orick was *Pe'-gwi*, which means, according to Waterman (p. 264), 'freshwater lagoon.' Men came from the Indian village at the site of Orick to bathe here after a sweat bath. **Freshwater: Slough, Creek, Corners,** town [Humboldt]. The name is derived from the "fresh water" in the slough as compared with the salt water in Eureka Slough. The name occurs elsewhere in the State. Suisun Bay was sometimes called Freshwater Bay on early maps, after the Spanish *Boca del Puerto Dulce* (Font, *Compl. Diary*, p. 369).

Fresno, frĕz'-nō: **River, Flats, Dome, Grove of Big Trees** [Madera]; **Fresno: County, city.** Fresno is the Spanish name for 'ash' and was doubtless applied because the Oregon ash, *Fraxinus oregona*, was native there. Goddard's map shows Ash Slough north of the river. Rio Fresno is mentioned in the San Francisco *Alta California* of April 2, 1851, and the name appears as Fresno River on Tassin's map of the same year. The stream is shown as Fresno Creek on Gibbes' map of 1852 and is mentioned as Frezno River in the Indian Report. This phonetic spelling was also used when the county was created and named, April 19, 1856 (*Statutes*, p. 183). Before 1860 an attempt was made to establish a Fresno City at the site of the present station of Tranquility (Goddard's and Hoffmann's maps). When the Central Pacific reached the site of the present city, May 28, 1872, the name was applied to the station. In 1874, Millerton, county seat and all, moved to the new station. In Mexican times the name was used in other regions: Bear Creek [Shasta] is shown as *Arroyo de los Fresnos* on a *diseño* of the Breisgau grant (1844). It is not impossible that *el monte redondo*, mentioned by Sebastian Rodriguez on April 23, 1828, when he was in the vicinity of the present city of Fresno, was a round grove of *fresnos* and may have been the origin of the name. *See* Roeding Park.

Friant: town, **Dam** [Fresno]. The town is situated at the landing of the old Converse (later Jones) Ferry, established in 1852 by Charles Converse. When the place became the terminus of the Southern Pacific branch from Fresno in 1891, the station was named Pollasky for Marcus Pollasky, an agent of the railroad and its promoters. In the early 1920's the town was renamed for Thomas Friant of the White-Friant Lumber Company.

Fruitland [Humboldt]. The name of a Dutch colony sponsored by David P. Cutten. The post office is listed in 1891.

Fruto [Glenn]. The Spanish word for 'fruit' or 'produce' was given to the post office about 1890.

Frys Point [Sequoia National Park]. Named by R. B. Marshall in 1909 for Walter Fry, a native of Illinois. Fry worked for a lumber company in the 1890's, revolted at cutting down more of the big trees, entered the government service, and was superintendent of Sequoia and General Grant national parks from 1914 to 1920 (Farquhar).

Fuller: Canyon, settlement [Lake]. Named when the family connected with the well-known W. P. Fuller paint company settled in the vicinity about 1905 (Mauldin).

Fuller Lake [Nevada]. The reservoir was created before 1871 by the Meager Mining Company and, like other lakes of the company, was probably named for one of its officials.

Fullerton [Orange]. The town was founded in 1887 by Edward and George Amerigue, the Wilshire brothers, and the Pacific Land and Improvement Company. George H. Fullerton, president of the land company and "right-of-way man" of the California Central (Santa Fe), routed the new railroad through the property of the Amerigues, and received in return an interest in the townsite and the honor of having the new city named for him.

Fulton [Sonoma]. Founded and named in 1871 by Thomas and James Fulton, natives of Indiana, who were residents of Santa Rosa in 1867.

Funeral: Mountains, Peak [Death Valley National Monument]. The identity of the range has never been definitely established. The Black Mountains and the Amargosa Range have been so designated, and on the Furnace Creek atlas sheet (1910) the name is applied to part of the latter. Chalfant (*Death Valley*, 1936, p. 49) quotes a passage from R. H. Stretch's diary, published in the Virginia *Enterprise* (1866): "The name of the mountains is probably due to their peculiar appearance. They are principally light-colored rocks, but are frequently capped with heavy masses of black limestone or basalt, the débris of which, running down the slopes, gives them the appearance of being fringed with crape, a species of natural mourning." There is no evidence that the mountains were named by J. B. Colton of the "Jayhawkers" because four members of the party died there.

Funks Creek [Colusa]. The slough was named for John Funk, who owned a large parcel of land there in the 1850's.

Funston, Fort [San Francisco]. Named by the War Department in 1917, in honor of Major General Frederick Funston (1865–1917), a hero of the Spanish-American War, who had been in command of the Department of California at the time of the San Francisco earthquake of 1906. It had previously been known as Laguna Merced Military Reservation.

Funston: Meadow, Creek, Camp [Sequoia National Park]. Named for James Funston, who grazed sheep in the vicinity about 1870 (Farquhar).

Furnace Creek: Wash, Ranch, Pass [Death Valley National Monument]. Probably so named because of the extreme heat. According to Hanks (p. 31), Dr. Darwin French and his party named the creek in 1860. The tradition that Mormons had built a furnace there in the 1850's to extract lead from galena is

apparently without foundation. Furnace Creek Ranch, established in 1870, was called Greenland in the 1880's and sometimes Coleman, for the owner, William T. Coleman, "Lion of the Vigilantes"; it was given its present name by the Pacific Coast Borax Company after 1889. The summit southwest of Pyramid Peak is locally known as Furnace Creek Pass. According to a statement by W. L. Manly, made in 1893 (*The Jayhawkers' Oath*, Los Angeles, 1949), Asahel Bennett and his party built a furnace there in 1860. **Furnace Canyon** [San Bernardino], shown on the San Gorgonio atlas sheet, although within the territory of the Mormon settlements, was so named because of the extreme heat (O. J. Fisk).

Gabb, Mount [Fresno]. The Whitney Survey named a peak for William M. Gabb (1839–1878), paleontologist of the party. It is uncertain whether this peak is the Mount Gabb shown on LeConte's map of 1907 and on the present Mount Goddard atlas sheet.

Gabbro Peak [Mono]. Named because of the rock of granitic texture which occurs here. The name was probably applied when the Bridgeport quadrangle was surveyed, 1905–1909.

Gabilan. The Spanish word for 'sparrow hawk' (*gavilán*) was repeatedly used for names of mountains in Spanish times. **Gabilan**, găb'-ĭ-lăn: **Peak, Creek, Range** [Monterey, San Benito]. *Un gran cerro llamado del "Gavilan"* (a high hill called [hill] of the hawk) is mentioned in 1828 (Registro, p. 14). The creek is shown as *Arroyo del Gavilan* on a *diseño* of San Miguelito (1841). A land grant, Cienega del Gabilan, was granted October 26, 1843. The range was called *Sierra de Gavilan* in the 1840's (Castro Docs., II, 44), is mentioned as San Juan or Gavilan or Salinas Range by Blake in 1857 (Pac. R.R. *Reports*, Vol. V, Pt. 2, p. 139), and is shown as Sierra Gabilan on Goddard's map. The three geographic features now called Gabilan and a town of that name appear on the maps of the Whitney Survey. *See* Fremont. Riverside County has both a Gavilan Peak and Mountain. The letters "b" and "v" are often interchanged in Spanish.

Galena, gȧ-lē'-nȧ: **Canyon** [Death Valley National Monument]. This canyon and several other geographic features were named because of the occurrence of galena, a common ore of lead found in California.

Gale Peak [Yosemite National Park]. Named in 1894 by Lieutenant N. F. McClure for

Captain (later Colonel) George H. Gale (1858–1920), a native of Maine and acting superintendent of Yosemite National Park in 1894 (Farquhar).

Gallagher: Beach, Canyon [Santa Catalina Island]. The places were named for Tom Gallagher, who for many years lived on the beach as a squatter. When the squatters were asked to leave the island, Tom moved to San Clemente Island, where another beach was named for him. (Windle, p. 118.)

Gallinas, gà-lē′-năs: **Valley, Creek; Las Gallinas** [Marin]. A *sitio de las Gallinas* (place of the hens) is mentioned by Padre Payeras in 1819 (Docs. Hist. Cal., IV, 341). On February 12, 1844, the name was incorporated into the San Pedro, Santa Margarita y las Gallinas land grant. The Creek is recorded on Hoffmann's map of the Bay region.

Galt [Sacramento]. Named in 1869 by John McFarland, an early settler, after his former home in Ontario, Canada, which had been named for John Galt, the Scotch novelist.

Garapito, gàr-à-pē′-tō: **Creek** [Los Angeles]. The name was probably applied by a surveyor who noticed water bugs and who knew their Spanish name, *garapito*.

Garberville [Humboldt]. Named for Jacob C. Garber, a native of Virginia, who was a resident of Rohnerville in 1871 and soon afterward settled at the place which bears his name. Garberville is shown on the Land Office map of 1879 and is listed as a post office in 1880.

Garcia, gär-sē′-à: **River** [Mendocino]. Probably named for Rafael García, who was granted nine leagues on the coast north of *Presidio Ruso* (Fort Ross), November 15, 1844. García was also grantee of Tamales y Baulenes [Marin]; the place Garcia, listed in Rand McNally, is on this grant.

Garden. Place names containing the generic term garden are popular in all sections of the United States. California has (or had) a dozen such communities, the most important of which are **Gardena** [Los Angeles] and **Garden Grove** [Orange]. **Garden Valley** [El Dorado], according to local tradition, received its name because people realized that it was more profitable to raise vegetables than to mine for gold. However, the post office was established December 16, 1852, as Garden Valley while it was still a rich gold camp (as late as 1857 a nugget worth $525 was found there). There is a Garden Canyon Creek in Stanislaus and a Garden Valley in Yuba County.

Gardiner, Mount; Gardiner Creek [Kings Canyon National Park]. Named in 1865 for James T. Gardiner (1842–1912) by the Whitney Survey, of which he was a member from 1864 to 1867. The Whitney Survey had spelled the name Gardner in accordance with Gardiner's own spelling of the name at that time. At the instigation of the Sierra Club, and with the approval of the Geographic Board, the spelling was changed to conform to the original form of the family name as later adopted by Gardiner himself.

Garey [Santa Barbara]. Established in 1889 and named for Thomas A. Garey, who came to California in 1852 and settled first in Pomona Valley. Garey was a well-known nurseryman and horticulturist, specializing in the culture of citrus fruit.

Garfield: Grove Big Trees, Creek [Sequoia National Park]. Named by the Geological Survey in 1902 in memory of James A. Garfield, the twentieth President of the United States.

Garlic. *See* Onion.

Garlock [Kern]. The old railroad station west of Randsburg was named for Eugene Garlock, who set up the first stamp mill of the Randsburg Mining District in 1895 at the place known as Cow Wells.

Garnet. The common red glasslike mineral occurs in various parts of the State and has given its name to orographic features in Calaveras, Madera, Mariposa, and Riverside counties. **Garnet** [Riverside]. The name was applied to the Southern Pacific station in 1923 after the hill west of it. On the Palm Springs atlas sheet of the Corps of Engineers only the triangulation point, not the hill itself, bears the name.

Garrapata, gàr-à-pä′-tà: **Creek** [Monterey]. The creek is shown in 1835 on a *diseño* (Docs. Hist. Cal., I, 484) as *Arroyo de las Garrapatas,* and was probably named because of the presence of wood ticks, which thrive especially where wild lilac grows. Misspelled Garrapatos on some maps.

Garrote. *See* Groveland; Second Garrote.

Garus [Santa Barbara]. The name was coined by transposing the letters of the word sugar. The place is in a sugar-beet region ("The Knave," March 17, 1935).

Garzas Creek [Stanislaus, Merced]. A *parage llamado ... las Garzas* (a place called the herons) is mentioned July 4, 1840 (DSP Mont., III, 86), and the creek is shown as *Arroyo de las Garzas* on a *diseño* of the Orestimba grant (1843).

Gaskill Peak [San Diego]. Named for the Gaskill brothers, who operated a hotel, a store, and a blacksmith shop there in the 1870's (Hazel Sheckler).

Gas Point [Shasta]. The name was given to the place because the old prospectors gathered here to "gas and spin yarns" (Steger). From 1875 to 1933 it was the name of the post office.

Gasquet [Del Norte]. Named for a member of the Gasquet family. Horace Gasquet, a native of France, came to Del Norte County before 1860 and had a ranch in Mountain township. Howard Gasquet is listed in McKenney's Directory of 1883 as the postmaster and hotelkeeper at Gasquet.

Gate of the Antipodes [Sierra]. The name "China," shown west of this narrow pass, may have suggested the fanciful term to the surveyor. China was often considered to be just opposite America on the globe. (Stewart.)

Gatos. The Spanish word for 'cats' (in this case, wildcats) was often found in geographical names, including two land grants, Los Gatos or Santa Rita in Monterey County, dated 1824 and regranted September 30, 1837, and Rinconada [corner] de los Gatos in Santa Clara County, dated May 21, 1840. Names of creeks in Santa Clara, San Benito, and Fresno counties, and Cañada del Gato in Santa Barbara County, still include the word. **Los Gatos,** gắt′-ŏs: **Creek,** town [Santa Clara] preserve the name of the land grant Rinconada de los Gatos. The Santa Cruz Mountains are called *Cuesta de los Gatos* by Frémont (*Geog. Memoir,* 1848, p. 33) and are so designated on the German edition of Eddy's map (1856), whereas Eddy's original map has the modern name Santa Cruz Mountains. The Creek is shown on the maps of the Whitney Survey. The town was laid out in 1850 by J. A. Forbes (Co. Hist., 1876, p. 16). The post office is listed in 1867, and the station was named when the railroad from San Jose reached the place, June 1, 1878. **Los Gatos Creek** [Fresno]. The creek which flows past Coalinga and which also bore the names Arroyo Pasajero and Arroyo Poso de Chane was officially named Los Gatos by decision of the Geographic Board in 1964 (May-Aug.) .

Gavilan. *See* Gabilan.

Gaviota, gắv-ĭ-ō′-tȧ: **Canyon, Pass, Creek, Peak,** town [Santa Barbara]. The Portolá expedition camped in the valley on August 24, 1769. Crespi says that he "called this place San Luis, King of France, and the soldiers know it as La Gaviota, because they killed a sea-gull [*gaviota*] there" (Crespi, p. 172). This name appears frequently in documents of the succeeding years. The *Cajon de la Gaviota* is mentioned in 1795 (PSP, XIV, 76), and Gabiota (for the canyon) is shown on the *diseño* of the Rancho Nuestra Señora del Refugio, 1838. Parke in his report and on his map misspells it Gaviote Pass. The correct spelling appears again on Goddard's map (1860).

Gaylor Lakes [Yosemite National Park]. Named for Jack Gaylor, a ranger in the park until his death in 1921 (Farquhar).

Gazelle, gȧ-zĕl′ [Siskiyou]. The name of the small African antelope was given to the post office in 1870; many places had been named for the native antelope. In the 1850's a steamer *Gazelle* plied between San Francisco and the upper Sacramento River.

Gazos Creek [San Mateo]. The name may be a misspelling either of *garzas* (herons) or of *casas* (houses). On the creek the Portolá expedition found an Indian village (Crespi, p. 219).

Gem: Lake, Pass [Mono]. The lake was named Gem-o'-the-Mountains by Theodore C. Agnew before 1896 (Farquhar). When the Geological Survey mapped the region in 1898–1899 it shortened the name, and gave this also to the pass north of the lake.

Gemini [Kings Canyon National Park]. The name for the twin-peaked mountain north of the Pinnacles was proposed by Chester Versteeg of the Sierra Club and approved by the Board on Geographical Names (March, 1957). Gemini is the name of the constellation including the twin stars Castor and Pollux.

General Creek [El Dorado]. Named for General William Phipps, for whom Phipps Lake and Peak were also named. The general, a native of Kentucky and veteran of Indian wars, came to Georgetown in 1854. (W. T. Russell in "The Knave," July 23, 1944.)

General Grant Grove [Kings Canyon National Park]. When General Grant National Park was incorporated into Kings Canyon National Park in 1940, its identity and name were preserved in the name of the grove. The largest *Sequoia gigantea* in the park had been christened General Grant by Mrs. L. P. Baker of Visalia in August, 1867, in honor of Ulysses S. Grant, and the name of the tree was given to the national park when it was established in 1890 at the suggestion of David K. Zumwalt, the important attorney of the Southern Pacific Railroad.

Genesee: Valley, settlement [Plumas]. The

Postal Guide of 1867 spells the name Geneseo, but that of 1880 has Genesee; Genesee Valley is mentioned in January, 1863 (Bancroft Scrapbooks, VIII, 114). The older gazetteers of New York State likewise have Geneseo for the town, but Genesee for the valley. The name may have been brought from New York by the Ingalls family, who settled in (and perhaps named) Genesee Valley in the 1860's. *See* Ingalls.

Genevra [Colusa]. The name was given by the Southern Pacific Railroad to replace the name Berlin, originally given by the Northern Railroad. The post office, established August 18, 1876, retained the name Berlin until its discontinuance, June 30, 1934.

Genevra, Mount [Sequoia National Park]. Named for Mrs. Genevra Magee in 1899 by J. N. LeConte and his party, who were with Mrs. Magee on the summit of Mount Brewer (Farquhar).

George J. Hatfield State Park [Merced]. The park was created in 1953 and named for the former District Attorney and Lieutenant Governor.

Georges Creek [Inyo]. The leader of the band of Paiute Indians who fought the white intruders in the mid-southern part of Owens Valley in 1863 was named George. His rancheria was on the creek which now bears his name.

Georges Gap [Plumas]. The gap was named for George Geisendorfer, who lived just south of it. Geisendorfer's settlement is shown on Bowman's map (1873), but the pass is labeled Georgia Gap. There is another Georges Gap [Los Angeles] on the Angeles Great Highway, on the saddle between Arroyo Seco and Tujunga watersheds (Wheelock).

George Stewart, Mount. *See* Stewart.

Georgetown [El Dorado]. The settlement was started in 1849 by George Ehrenhaft (Bancroft, VI, 482), but it is uncertain whether it was named for him or for George Phipps, a sailor who led a party of prospectors to the place in 1849 (Rensch-Hoover, pp. 104 f.). It was repeatedly mentioned in 1850 as one of the most important mining centers. An earlier name, or nickname, was Growlersburg. Historic Landmark 484.

Gerber [Tehama]. Named in 1916 by the Southern Pacific Railroad for H. E. Gerber, of Sacramento, who sold the land to the railroad. The post office is listed in 1917.

Gerle Creek [El Dorado]. The tributary of Rubicon River was named for Christopher C. Gerle, a native of Sweden, who settled in

El Dorado County before 1860. On Wheeler atlas sheet 56-B the name is spelled as pronounced, Gurley.

German. There are two German Creeks in the State [Los Angeles and Mendocino], and there was a mining town, German Bar [Nevada], in the 1850's. Artois [Glenn] was formerly called Germantown. Elsewhere the nickname Dutch is used in place of German in California toponymy. Even the two creeks may not have been named for German settlers; German was quite a common family name in Spanish California.

German [Sonoma]. A land grant dated April 8, 1846. The name is probably a Spanish phonetic rendering of the German name *Hermann*, which Ernest Rufus, the grantee, had apparently intended to apply to his rancho. "H" is a silent letter in Spanish, and the aspirate sound is, before *e* and *i*, expressed by "g." The name *Rancho de Hermann* appears on the *diseño*, but the *expediente* has German. The name of Hermann, victor over the Romans in the Teutoburg Forest, 9 A.D., was favored in place naming by German immigrants to the United States in the middle of the 19th century. *See* Gualala.

Geyser. The name is found in Sonoma County and elsewhere where hot springs appear in the form of small geysers. **Geyserville** [Sonoma] was founded in 1851 by Elisha Ely and so named to advertise the near-by "geysers." Originally the place was known as Clairville (!) for John Clar, for many years engaged in translating and transcribing Spanish archives (Bowman).

Giant [Contra Costa]. The name was applied when the Giant Powder Company of Wilmington, Delaware, built its west coast plant in 1880. "Giant powder" was the early common name of dynamite.

Giant Forest [Sequoia National Park]. Discovered in 1858 by Hale Tharp and named in 1875 by John Muir. "This part of the Sequoia belt seemed to me the finest, and I then named it 'the Giant Forest'" (Muir, *Our National Parks*, p. 300).

Gibbs, Mount [Yosemite National Park]. Named by F. L. Olmsted on the first ascent, August 31, 1864, for Oliver Wolcott Gibbs (1822–1908), professor of science at Harvard and a lifelong friend of J. D. Whitney.

Gibson [Shasta]. The name was applied to the station of the Southern Pacific when the extension from Redding was built in 1886. The name honors Reuben Gibson, who led the whites and the Wintus against the Modocs at Battle Rock in June, 1855 (Steger).

Gibsonville [Sierra]. An old mining town on Little Shasta Creek which was first called Gibsons New Diggings and was probably named for the same man who discovered one of the Secret Canyons in Placer County.

Gigling [Monterey]. The Southern Pacific station was named about 1920 for the Gigling (or Geigling) family. Valentine Geigling, a native of Germany, settled in the county as a farmer before 1857.

Gilbert, Mount [Kings Canyon National Park]. Named for Grove K. Gilbert (1843–1918), geologist of the Geological Survey and author of numerous monographs. The name was confirmed by the Geographic Board, July 19, 1911.

Gillette [Tulare]. The station was named for King C. Gillette, of safety-razor fame, who owned a citrus orchard of five hundred acres there (Santa Fe).

Gillett Mountain [Tuolumne]. Named in 1909 by R. B. Marshall for J. N. Gillett, congressman, 1903–1906, governor of California, 1907–1911 (Farquhar).

Gilman Hot Springs [Riverside]. The springs, already known to the Indians, were developed by the Branch family in the 1880's under the name San Jacinto Hot Springs. The present name originated when William E. and Josephine Gilman bought the place in 1913. The post office was established June 1, 1938.

Gilman Lake [Mono]. Named in 1905 for Robert Gilman Brown, vice-president and general manager of the Standard Consolidated Mining Company, by one of the company's engineers, who was engaged in mapping the district (Farquhar).

Gilroy: town, **Hot Springs** [Santa Clara]. John Gilroy, a Scotch sailor and the first permanent non-Spanish settler in California, was left ashore in Monterey in 1814 by the Hudson's Bay vessel *Isaac Todd* because he was sick with scurvy. His real name was Cameron, but he changed it to his mother's family name because he had left home as a minor and was in danger of being sent back. He settled in the Santa Clara Valley, where he married María Clara Ortega, the grantee (June 3, 1833) of part of the San Isidro land grant. The settlement which developed on the rancho became known as San Isidro, and later as Gilroy. Bowen's *Post-Office Guide* of 1851 lists Gilroy's. After the coming of the railroad in 1869, the name Gilroy appears on the map for the station, and Old Gilroy (San

Isidro post office) for the older settlement (von Leicht–Craven). The springs were discovered in 1865 by a Mexican sheepherder while he was hunting for some of his flock, and were named after the town years later. The Spanish name for Gilroy Valley was Llano de las Llagas. *See* Llagas.

Girard: Creek, Ridge [Shasta]. Named for Louis Girard, a French Canadian, who discovered gold on the creek (Steger).

Giraud, jǐ-rō′: Peak [Kings Canyon National Park]. Probably named for Pierre Giraud, sheepman of Inyo County, known as "Little Pete." The name is spelled Giroud on the Mount Goddard atlas sheet and on other maps. *See* Little Pete Meadow.

Glacier. Of the numerous geographic features so called, **Glacier Divide** and **Glacier Lake** and **Creek** [Kings Canyon National Park] were named because of the actual presence of glaciers. On the crest of the divide are eight small glaciers; the lake and creek are just south of Palisade Glacier. **Glacier: Ridge, Monument, Creek** in the same park, as well as **Glacier Point** in Yosemite, were so named because of the evidence of glacial action in former periods. Glacier Point was named by the Mariposa Battalion in 1851. Its Indian name was said to be *Pa-til-le-ma* (Bunnell, 1880, p. 213). **Glacier Canyon Creek** [Mono] has its origin in a glacier on the north slope of Mount Dana.

Glade. The old Germanic term for an open space in the forest has become a common generic name in North America. Most of the "glades" in California are in northern counties. According to Mauldin, there are about sixty open spaces or clearings so called in Lake County alone.

Glamis, glăm′-ĭs [Imperial]. The post office is listed in 1887 and the station is shown on the Official Railway Map of 1900. Glamis (or Glammis) is a castle in Scotland, made famous by Shakespeare's *Macbeth*.

Glass Mountain [Modoc and Siskiyou]. The mountain is chiefly of obsidian which varies in shades from crystal-clear through milky white to jet black. Glass Mountain and Creek [Mono] were probably named also for the presence of obsidian.

Glaucophane Ridge [San Benito]. Named because of the occurrence of glaucophane, probably by the Geological Survey when the Panoche quadrangle was mapped, 1908–1911. In the United States the mineral, a silicate of aluminum, sodium, iron, and magnesium, occurs chiefly in the Coast Ranges of California.

Gleason Mountain [Los Angeles]. Probably named for George Gleason, a resident in the county in 1872.

Glen. The Celtic generic term, meaning 'narrow valley,' became the most popular of the obsolete or almost obsolete geographical names which were revived by the Romantic movement in the 19th century. It is seldom used as a true generic term replacing "canyon," but it has provided the first element of numerous composite place names. California has not only its share of Glenbrooks, Glenburns, Glendales, and Glenwoods, but also a number of unique combinations: Glen Alder [Placer], Glen Alpine [El Dorado], Glen Arbor [Santa Cruz], Glen Frazer [Contra Costa], Glen Una [Santa Clara]. **Glen Ellen** [Sonoma]. The name was given to the settlement in 1869 by Charles V. Stuart, a native of Pennsylvania and a pioneer of 1849, for his wife, Ellen Mary. The post office was established and named July 19, 1871. **Glencoe** [Calaveras]. The place is shown on Hoffmann's map (1873) as Mosquito. When the post office was established about 1878, a new name was chosen because there was a Mosquito post office in El Dorado County. At that time there were eighteen other Glencoes in the United States, directly or indirectly named after the valley in Scotland. Historic Landmark 280. **Glendale** [Los Angeles]. The town developed soon after the railroad was built from Los Angeles to San Fernando in 1873–1874 and was named Riverdale (Co. Map, 1881). Since the name was refused by the Post Office Department in 1886 because of the Riverdale already existing in Fresno County, the post office was called Mason. Soon afterward it was changed to Glendale; this name is shown on the Land Office map of 1891. There were twenty-five other Glendales in the United States at that time. **Glendora** [Los Angeles]. The name was created in 1887 by George Whitcomb from the word *glen* and his wife's name, Le*dora*. **Glen Blair** [Mendocino]. The place was named after the Glen Blair Mill Company, founded by Captain Blair "soon after Fort Bragg was in operation" (Co. Hist., 1914, p. 67). **Glenavon** [Riverside]. The name, a combination of *glen* and another Celtic term, *avon* (meaning 'river'), was chosen by L. V. W. Brown in 1909 (A. C. Fulmor). **Glen Aulin** [Yosemite National Park]. Here the name is used as a true generic. "It was probably in the winter of 1913–1914 . . . I . . . suggested

[to R. B. Marshall] Glen Aulin, 'beautiful valley or glen,' and wrote it for him in this way, that it might be correctly pronounced—the '*au*' as in *author*. The correct Gaelic (Irish) orthography is *Gleann Alainn*." (James McCormick to F. P. Farquhar.) **Glenwood** [Santa Cruz]. The town was founded by Charles C. Martin, who had come round the Horn in 1850. It was known as Martinville until the post office was established, August 23, 1880. Colusa County has Glen Valley Slough, and Santa Barbara a Glen Anne Creek.

Glendale. *See* Glen.

Glenn: County, station. The county was formed by act of the legislature, March 11, 1891, from the northern part of Colusa County, and named for Dr. Hugh J. Glenn, whose estate gave financial backing to a proposal for creating and naming the new county. Dr. Glenn came to California from Missouri in 1849, bought Rancho Jacinto in 1867, and became the most important wheatgrower of the State. The station was named after the county when the Southern Pacific branch from Colusa was built in 1917.

Glenn Ranch [San Bernardino]. The resort was established on the old Glenn Ranch, on which Jerry Glenn, an immigrant from Texas, had settled in the 1860's.

Glennville [Kern]. The post office was established in the 1870's and was named for James Madison Glenn, a native of Tennessee, who had settled in Linn's Valley in 1857.

Glen Pass [Kings Canyon National Park]. Named for Glen H. Crow, a ranger in the Forest Service and an assistant in the Geological Survey, when the Mount Whitney quadrangle was surveyed in 1907 (Farquhar).

Glorietta. So named are communities in Contra Costa and Fresno counties, and a bay in San Diego harbor. A subdivision in Orange County is spelled Gloryetta. The name was probably chosen for its sound. In Spain and Mexico the word *glorieta* is used for a small plaza from which several streets radiate.

Goat. Since no goats are native to California, the various Goat Mountains, Buttes, and Rocks were probably so named because antelope or mountain sheep were mistaken for goats. Yerba Buena Island in San Francisco Bay was called **Goat Island** for many years because at the time of the gold rush it was populated by several hundred goats, descendants of half a dozen which had been placed on the island in 1842 or 1843 by Nathan Spear and John Fuller, merchants in Yerba

Buena (Davis, p. 266).

Gobernadora, gō-bĕr-nä-dôr'-à: **Canyon** [Orange]. The name appears as *Cañada de la Gobernadera* on a *diseño* of the Trabuco grant. The canyon probably received its name because of the presence of the gobernadora (*Zygophyllum tridentatum*), a plant native in the dry sections of northern Mexico. The name is shown on the Corona atlas sheet as Canada Gubernadora. Gobernador Creek in Santa Barbara County, Governador on a map of El Rincon grant, perhaps also was named for the shrub; there seems to be no reason for connecting it with the Spanish word for 'governor.'

Goddard, Mount; Goddard: Divide, Canyon, Creek [Kings Canyon National Park]. The peak was named in 1865 by the Whitney Survey for George H. Goddard (*see* Glossary). "Thirty-two miles north-northwest is a very high mountain, called Mount Goddard, in honor of a Civil Engineer who has done much to advance our knowledge of the geography of California, and who is the author of 'Britton & Rey's Map'" (Whitney, *Geology,* I, 382). The names of the other features appear on the atlas sheet of 1912 of the Geological Survey.

Goethe, Mount; Goethe: Cirque, Glacier, Lake [Fresno]. The highest peak of Glacier Divide was named by the U. S. Forest Service and the Sierra Club in 1949, the bicentennial of the birth of Johann Wolfgang Goethe, poet, philosopher, scientist. The name was suggested by David R. Brower and Erwin G. Gudde and was confirmed by the Geographic Board in August, 1949.

Goethe Grove [Humboldt]. The Mary Glide Goethe Grove in the Prairie Creek Redwoods State Park, established through the efforts of the Save-the-Redwoods League in 1948, memorializes Mary Glide Goethe, wife of the late Charles M. Goethe, of Sacramento. The area below the Grove is called Goethe Addition. Mr. and Mrs. Goethe were well-known philanthropists and outstanding leaders in nature conservation.

Goffs. *See* Amboy.

Gold. The name of the precious metal so intimately connected with the history of the "Golden State" is found in the names of more than a hundred geographic features. Kern County has a Goldpan Canyon, Madera County a Coarse Gold Creek, a Fine Gold Creek, and a Little Fine Gold Creek. In Death Valley National Monument are Goldbelt Springs and Goldbar. **Gold Run** [Ne-

vada]. The stream is mentioned on August 26, 1849: ". . . on the banks of Deer Creek and Gold Run—as they have ever since been called—they struck some of the richest and most famous diggings ever known in California" (Wistar, I, 126). **Gold Lake** [Plumas]. The name commemorates what seems to have been the first large-scale hoax perpetrated after the discovery of gold. Early prospectors, noting that the gold became coarser as they proceeded upstream, believed there must be a lake or other source of gold high in the mountains. The first rumor of a lake rich with golden pebbles seems to have started in 1849. In the summer of 1850 some traders utilized these rumors by deliberately spreading the news of the actual discovery of such a gold lake, which, they said, could unfortunately not be exploited by small parties because of hostile Indians. All doubts vanished when, in July, Peter Lassen, who knew the region between Honey Lake and Sacramento Valley better than any other man, fell for the hoax. From Lassen's Ranch alone four expeditions set out about August 1, and by the end of the year the floating population of the mines swarmed through the northern Sierra Nevada in search of the lake. The traders reaped rich profits, but the gold hunters "didn't diskiver nare a Gold Lake" (Bruff, II, 825). The name apparently became attached to the lake in Plumas County because it fits the general description of the mythical lake: deep-seated, near several buttes, two days' travel from Honey Lake. The range northeast of it was known as Gold Lake Mountains in the 1850's. The name of Gold Lake in Sierra County may also have some connection with the "great Gold Lake hunt." Some writers think that this is the lake. In fact neither this nor the Gold lakes in Sierra and Butte counties have anything to do with the "Gold Lake hunt" or the "Goose Lake hunt," as Schaeffer sarcastically calls it in his account. The Gold Lake of 1849 remains a phantom in spite of the numerous modern accounts, including the fascinating story in J. C. Tucker, *To the Golden Goal,* and the tales about Thomas R. Stoddart, which were started by the ghost writer of William Downie's *Hunting for Gold.* The best direct contemporary account is given by Schaeffer, pp. 81 ff. He and his party left Washington City, a mining camp on the South fork of the Yuba River, on June 7, 1850, but gave up in disgust after four days. This did not prevent other parties from joining the "Goose Lake hunt." Bruff in *Gold Rush* gives many interesting but somewhat confusing data. *See* Last Chance. **Gold Bluffs** [Humboldt]. Almost contemporary with the Gold Lake hunt was the rush for the sandhills. This time it was no hoax. The Gold Bluffs were discovered in April, 1850, by Hermann Ehrenberg, in later years a famous pioneer of Arizona. They were so called because gold had been washed from them, but the yield from washing the sand proved to be unprofitable. **Gold Run** [Placer]. The name refers to a run of auriferous gravel worked there by early miners. The present town developed around O. W. Hollenbeck's trading center in 1862, and the post office was established and named on July 15, 1863. **Gold Discovery Site** [El Dorado]. The site of Sutter's sawmill, in the tailrace of which James W. Marshall discovered gold on January 24, 1848, became a state historical monument in 1942; excavation in 1947 showed that the actual site of the discovery is not on state property (*CHSQ*, XXVI, 129 f.). *See* Oro; Placer.

Golden. A number of geographic features, including Golden Valley [San Bernardino], were named because of the golden glow at sunset or the presence of fields of golden poppies. **Golden Canyon** [Death Valley] was named because of the yellowish clay there.

Golden Gate. The name was given to the entrance of San Francisco Bay by Frémont in the spring of 1846. He chose this name because he foresaw the day when the riches of the greater Orient would flow through the Golden Gate just as the riches of the lesser Orient had once flowed into the Golden Horn. In a footnote to page 32 of his *Geographical Memoir* (1848) Frémont justifies his choice: "Called *Chrysopylae* (golden gate) on the map, on the same principle that the harbor of *Byzantium* (Constantinople afterwards) was called *Chrysoceras* (golden horn). ... The form of the entrance into the bay of San Francisco, and its advantages for commerce, (Asiatic inclusive,) suggests the name which is given to this entrance." Frémont was apparently determined to fix the Greek name on the entrance, but Preuss cautiously put "Chrysopylae or Golden Gate" on his map of 1848, and the latter was naturally the name accepted. **Golden Gate Park** [San Francisco]. Created and named by act of the legislature, April 4, 1870: "The land ... is hereby designated and shall be known as the 'Golden

Gate Park.' " **Golden Gate Bridge.** The name was spontaneously used when the project was first discussed in 1917 by M. H. O'Shaughnessy, city engineer of San Francisco, and Joseph B. Strauss, who later constructed the bridge. It became official with the incorporation of the Golden Gate Bridge and Highway District by act of the legislature, May 25, 1923. **Golden Gate National Cemetery** [San Mateo]. Named by General Orders No. 4, War Department, 1939. The name Golden Gate is found for a creek in Amador, a hill in Calaveras, and a "gate" in Colusa County.

Golden Trout Creek [Tulare]. This tributary of the Kern River was once called Whitney Creek, then Volcano Creek. The present name was applied by the Geological Survey (probably when the Olancha quadrangle was surveyed in 1905) because Dr. B. W. Evermann identified here in 1903 a new species of trout, *Salmo roosevelti*. (Farquhar.)

Goldstein Peak [Tulare]. Named for Ike Goldstein of Visalia, who ran hogs on the mountain at one time (A. L. Dickey).

Goldtree [San Luis Obispo]. An Americanization of the surname of Morris Goldbaum, who settled here in the 1890's ('tree' is *Baum* in German).

Goler: Wash, Canyon, Heights [Death Valley National Monument]. The names are reminiscent of one of the strangest incidents in the history of Death Valley. Among the Argonauts who crossed Death Valley in 1849 were two Germans, John Galler (or Goler or Goller) and possibly Wolfgang Tauber. Tauber apparently discovered gold in either the Canyon or the Wash (which are 50 miles apart). In 1912 Carl Menge discovered a rich pocket of gold at his Oro Fino Claim in Goler Wash (*Death Valley Guide*, p. 62). If at all, it was probably here where Tauber found the gold. Both W. Tauber and John Galler or Goller are listed as members of sections of the Jayhawkers Party (HSSC:*Q*, XXII, 102 ff; John Ellenbecker, *The Jayhawkers of Death Valley*). Tauber died at sea in 1850, and in later years Galler or Goller tried to find the mysterious gold deposits .Hence, the find became known as Goler's mine or nuggets. (Weight, pp. 31 ff.) The well-known pioneer carriage maker of Los Angeles, John Goller, is apparently identical with the gold seeker; although Harris Newmark, who knew Goller very well, does not mention the Death Valley episode in his *Sixty Years in Southern California*. The story of Goller's nugget was still alive enough in 1893 to give the name to Goler Gulch, miles away from Death Valley, in Kern County, where the discovery of gold led to the development of the Johannesburg-Randsburg district.

Goleta, gō-lē'-tá [Santa Barbara]. The community developed on the land grant La Goleta, dated June 10, 1846. In 1875 the town was laid out and named after the grant. According to Michael C. White (MS, 1877, Bancroft Library), the place was originally so named because a schooner (*goleta*) was built there in 1829. According to other and probably more authentic sources, the name originated because an American schooner, stranded in the estuary, lay there for many years (AGS: *Santa Barbara*, p. 168). A *diseño* of La Goleta grant shows a wreck at the mouth of the estuary.

Gomez, gō'-mĕz [Sutter]. Named in 1906 by the Northern Electric Railroad for Nathaniel Gomez, a native of Portugal, because the right of way cut through his property (H. H. Harter).

Gonzales, gŏn-zä'-lĕs [Monterey]. Teodoro Gonzales, then *regidor* and acting *alcalde* at Monterey, was granted Rincon de la Punta del Monte de la Soledad, September 20, 1836, on which the place is situated. Duflot de Mofras on his map of 1844 shows a Gonsales south of the present location, perhaps indicating the rancho of José Rafael Gonzales, San Miguelito. The present Gonzales may have been named for Teodoro's sons, Alfredo and Mariano, who were prominently associated with the Monterey and Salinas Railroad (Bancroft, III, 761).

Goodale: Creek, Mountain [Inyo]; **Pass** [Fresno]. The creek and mountain were named for Ezra and Thomas Goodale, who settled here in the 1870's. The pass may be named for Gus G. Goodale, son of the latter, at one time a ranger in the Forest Service.

Goode, Mount [Kings Canyon National Park]. In mapping the Mount Goddard quadrangle, 1907–1909, the Geological Survey inadvertently placed a second name upon a peak already known as Black Giant. This name, which honors Richard U. Goode (1858–1903), geographer in charge of the Geological Survey in the western United States, was transferred to the present peak by decision of the Geographic Board in 1926.

Goodwin Dam [Stanislaus]. The two diversion dams on the Stanislaus River were named for A. D. Goodwin, Manteca rancher and manufacturer of farm equipment, who was one of the principal boosters of the Tri-Dam project, completed in 1957.

Goodyears: Bar, Creek, Hill [Sierra]. The name was first used for the river bar opposite the present settlement, where Miles and Andrew Goodyear discovered gold in 1849. In 1851 the name was applied to the settlement, which previously had been known as Slaughter's Bar.

Goose. More than fifty geographic features in the State, including a Goose Nest Mountain [Siskiyou], were named because of the presence of this bird, so important as a food for travelers in the early days. **Goose Lake** [Modoc]. The sheet of water, now only a lake bed, was probably the one called Pit Lake (after Pit River) by John Work in 1832 (*CHSQ*, XXII, 205). Pit Lake on Hood's map (1838), however, has no connection with what was later called Goose Lake. Pitts Lake on Wilkes' map of 1841 was apparently intended for Goose Lake but is placed more than one degree of longitude too far 'east. The name Goose Lake probably arose spontaneously in the 1840's, because the honkers were as numerous in the region then as they are now. The name appears on Williamson's map (1849) and in his report (Tyson, Pt. 2, p. 22). According to McArthur, the Klamath Indian name was *Newapkshi*. Miguel Costansó of the Portolá expedition mentions a *Llano de los Ansares* (plain of the geese) in what is now San Mateo County on October 28, 1769 (p. 102).

Goose Creek [Modoc]. This creek, emptying into Upper Alkali Lake near Lake City, was named for a German homesteader of the late 1860's whose name was Goos (W. S. Brown)

Gordo, Gorda. The Spanish word for 'big' or 'fat' is used in a geographical sense for massive promontories along the coast, usually with Punta. **Punta Gorda; Gorda: Rock, Seavalley** [Humboldt]. The name was given by Hezeta in 1775 to a bold headland north of Cape Mendocino. It was shown on the maps in the latitude of present False Cape as late as 1846 (Tanner). In the first edition of his Coast Pilot (1858) Davidson applied the name to the point south of Mendocino: "Punta Gorda is 17 miles . . . from Shelter Cove, and, as its name implies, is a large, bold rounding point" (p. 67). **Gorda** [Monterey]. Settlement, mine, and school preserve the old name of the near-by cape, Punta Gorda, which the Coast Survey changed to Cape San Martin in 1862. **Cerro Gordo: Mine, Spring, Mountain** [Inyo]. The names

Cerro Gordo Peak (tautological: 'peak big peak') and Cerro Gordo Mountains (for Inyo Mountains northeast of Owens Lake) are shown in 1871 on Wheeler atlas sheet 65. *See* Cerro.

Gordon: Creek, Hill [Mendocino]. The names were applied by the Coast Survey for Alexander Gordon, a native of Canada, who came to California in 1863, settled first at Caspar, and in 1875 purchased the ranch north of Westport on which are Gordon Creek and Hill.

Gordons Ferry [Kern]. Historic Landmark 137 marks the place where roads and trails met at the Kern River in the 1850's and 1860's and where there was a station of the Butterfield stages, 1858–1860. Major Gordon operated the ferry.

Gordon Valley [Yolo, Napa]. Named for William ("Julian") Gordon, the first white settler in what is now Yolo County, grantee of the Quesesosi or Jesus Maria grant, January 27, 1843. *See* Quesesosi.

Gorge of Despair [Kings Canyon National Park]. Named in 1879 by Lilbourne A. Winchell, who spent five months of that year exploring the High Sierra (Farquhar).

Gorman [Los Angeles]. The post office, Gorman's Station, was established December 18, 1877, and reëstablished as Gorman on September 29, 1915. It was obviously named for H. Gorman, the first postmaster.

Goshen, gō'-shĕn [Tulare]. Named by an employee of the Southern Pacific when the railroad reached this point in 1872. The name of the "best of the land" in Egypt given by Pharaoh to Jacob has been a favorite for places throughout the United States.

Gossage Creek [Sonoma]. The stream was probably named for Jerome Bonaparte Gossage, from Ohio, who is listed in the Great Register of 1867.

Gottville [Siskiyou]. A mining town named for William N. Gott, whose family owned one of the large mines in the 1880's. The post office name has been Klamath River since 1934.

Gould, Mount [Kings Canyon National Park]. The name University Peak had been given to this mountain in honor of the University of California by J. N. LeConte and a party at the first ascent in 1890. July 12, 1896, LeConte transferred this name to the present University Peak, when, with Helen Gompertz and Belle and Estelle Miller, he made the first ascent. The following day he climbed the old University Peak and named it for his companion, Wilson S. Gould of Oakland.

Goumaz, gōō'-măz [Lassen]. Probably named for Philip J. Goumaz, a native of Switzerland, who came to California in 1863 and settled in Lassen County in 1866.

Government. A number of places are so designated because they were at some time occupied by a federal agency. **Government: Well, Lake** [Shasta]. In the late 1850's a detachment of soldiers from Fort Crook established a camp here to protect the freighters from the Indians and dug a well to provide water for the camp. The near-by lake was named after the well. (Steger.)

Grabners [Fresno]. The post office was established in 1915 and named for F. Grabner, on whose land the office was originally situated (Marie Goodrich).

Grace Lake [Shasta]. The two artificial lakes near Noble's "castle" were named for Grace and Nora, daughters of H. H. Noble (Steger).

Grace Meadow [Yosemite National Park]. The meadow in the upper Jack Main Canyon was named for Grace Sovulewski, daughter of Gabriel Sovulewski, for many years an official of the park (Farquhar).

Graciosa, gräs-ĭ-ō'-sà: **Ridge, Canyon** [Santa Barbara]. The Portolá expedition camped in a valley southwest of the canyon on August 31, 1769. Since it was the first time the soldiers saw native women dance, they called the lagoon *Baile de las Indias*, 'dance of the Indian women.' Other members of the party called it *La Graciosa* because a soldier through a slip of the tongue said that he had seen *una laguna graciosa*, 'a graceful lagoon.' As this adjective is ordinarily used only for persons, the soldier may have been thinking of one of the Indian dancers. However, on February 29, 1776, Font mentions the *Laguna Graciosa* and says it was so called because "it is small and of very fine water" (*Compl. Diary*, p. 266). The ridge, *la cuesta de la graciosa*, is mentioned on March 19, 1824 (DSP, I, 166), and *Cañada de la Graciosa* is shown on a *diseño* of 1841. A station was named La Graciosa when the Pacific Coast Railroad was built in the early 1880's.

Graeagle, grä-ē'-g'l [Plumas]. The post office was established in 1919 and named Davies Mill. In 1921 the name was changed to the present one, a contraction from near-by Gray Eagle Creek. This name may have some connection with Edward D. Baker, the "Gray Eagle of Republicanism," who was in the mining region in 1856 while stumping the State for Frémont.

Grafton. *See* Knights Landing.

Grand. The word is frequently used in geographical nomenclature as a synonym for 'great,' 'high,' or for 'majestic,' 'imposing.' Usually the adjective describes an orographic feature: Grand Mountain [Yosemite National Park], Grand Sentinel [Kings Canyon National Park], Grand Bluff [Fresno], Grand Dike [Kings Canyon National Park]. In view of the popularity of the word for names of communities in other parts of the United States, it seems strange that it is not contained in a single California post office name. There is a subdivision Grand Terrace near Colton [San Bernardino], and Black Point [Marin] was for some time called Grandview Terrace.

Grande. The Spanish word for 'great' or 'large' is found in a number of geographical names as a descriptive adjective, the best known of which are Arroyo Grande [San Luis Obispo] and Mesa Grande [San Diego]. *See* Arroyo.

Grandview Terrace. *See* Black Point.

Grangeville [Kings]. The popular American place name, derived from French *grange,* 'barn,' was applied to the post office (now discontinued) in the 1870's when the town was the center of the Lucerne district.

Granite. More than fifty geographic features in mountainous areas of the State have been named for this rock formation. The cluster name between the Middle and South forks of Kings River, where large masses of granite are found, originated with the Whitney Survey. Placer County has a Granite Chief, Inyo County a Granite Park, and Madera County a Granite Stairway. Sometimes the name has been applied to settlements: Granite Gate [Los Angeles], Granite Creek [Madera], Granite Hill [El Dorado]. In some cases the places may have been named for the "Granite State," New Hampshire. **Graniteville** [Nevada]. The rich old gold-mining town was known as Eureka as early as 1850. When the post office was established August 27, 1867, the new name was chosen to avoid confusion with other post offices named Eureka.

Grape, Grapevine. Among wild plants bearing edible fruit, the grapevine, next to the strawberry, is the most popular for place names. The most important geographic feature named for it is the long range of Grapevine Mountains, extending from Inyo County into the State of Nevada; Grape Vine Canon is mentioned by the Nevada Boundary Survey in the Sacramento *Daily Union* of August 10, 1861. The names of Grapevine Canyon and Creek in Kern County can be traced back to Spanish times: Fages had noticed the wealth of wild grapes in 1772, and an expedition gave the name *Cajon de las Uvas* (canyon of the grapes) on July 29, 1806 (Arch. MSB, IV, 49 ff.). The railroad stations Grape [Imperial], Grapegrowers [Fresno], Grapeland [San Bernardino] were named because of grape culture there. *See* Uvas.

Grapit, grăp'-ĭt [Glenn]. The name of the Southern Pacific station is a coined name suggested by a near-by gravel pit ("The Knave," March 17, 1935).

Grass Valley [Nevada]. "A little valley among the hills, whose verdure, surrounded by the red, dry mountain earth of that region, suggested for a name to the first discoverer, that of Grass Valley" (Delano, p. 66). The settlement was started in the fall of 1849, when a sawmill was erected. The first log cabin was built by a man named Scott, and the first quartz gold was discovered accidentally on Gold Hill in 1850 by a German (Vischer, pp. 244 ff.). This started the town on its phenomenal development as a gold mining center. In the early days the names Grass Valley and Centerville were used alternately. On July 10, 1851, the post office was established with the name Centerville, but on August 20, 1852, it was changed to Grass Valley. The name Grass Valley became very popular in California. Amador, Plumas, Trinity, and other counties have places so named. In Kings County there is a Pepper Grass Valley.

Graton, grā'-tŏn [Sonoma]. The community was founded in 1904 by James H. Gray and J. H. Brush of Santa Rosa and was named for the former by abbreviating Graytown to Graton (F. L. Perkins).

Grave Creek [Trinity]. The tributary of Trinity River was so named because near by is the grave of a young Englishman whose tombstone bears this inscription: "In memory of Joseph Martin. Drowned in Trinity River, June 15, 1862. Age 33 years. Native of Darbyshire, England." (R. H. Cross in "The Knave," Dec. 15, 1946.)

Gravelly Valley [Lake]. So called because the valley is strewn with gravel and debris brought by winter floods (Doyle). The names of more than twenty other geographic features contain the adjective "gravelly" or the noun "gravel."

Graves Grove [Del Norte]. This fine stand of redwood was presented to the State by

George F. Schwarz, of New York, and named in honor of Henry S. Graves, of the Yale University School of Forestry and former chief forester, U.S. Forest Service (Doyle).

Graveyard: Meadows, Peak [Fresno]. Sheepmen named this meadow, where two of their number were murdered and buried (Farquhar). Graveyard Canyon [Los Angeles] and several other places were so named because of the presence of Indian burial grounds.

Gray. The adjective is found in the names of about twenty-five geographic features, mainly rocks, peaks, and buttes, but also several creeks and valleys. Most of them were doubtless named because of the color; some were named for persons. Placer County has a Gray Horse Valley and Canyon, and Plumas County a Gray Eagle Valley and Creek.

Grayback. A common folk name used for orographic features which look grey. The popular name of San Gorgonio Peak in San Bernardino County is still Grayback.

Gray Eagle Creek. *See* Graeagle.

Grayson [Stanislaus]. Andrew J. Grayson, a native of Louisiana, came to California in 1846, was active in the Mexican War, and in later years became a well-known authority on Pacific Coast birds. The town which he founded in 1850 is shown on Gibbes' map of 1852 and is often mentioned in the Pacific Railroad *Reports*.

Grays Well [Imperial]. A camp for men constructing the plank road to Yuma was established in 1915 and named for Newt Gray, a Holtville pioneer and road builder.

Great. This adjective is used with the names of a few physical features to describe their magnitude and importance. **Great Basin.** The wide desert-like plains covering most of Nevada, parts of Utah, and the southeastern corner of California were given this name by Frémont in 1843. "As most of the streams known to exist in it are known to lose themselves, it has been called, very properly, the 'Great Basin' " (Williamson in Pac. R.R. *Reports*, Vol. V, Pt. 1, p. 9). **Great Central Valley** is the commonly accepted designation of the inland basin formed by the Sacramento and San Joaquin valleys. The first to use the word "great" as a common name for both valleys was probably Lansford W. Hastings, who referred to the Great California Valley in his *Emigrants' Guide* (1845, p. 75). Other designations were Valley of California and Great Interior Valley. **Great Western Divide.** "The Great Western Divide lies parallel with the Main Crest west of Mt. Whitney. The southern end of it is between the Kern River watershed and the headwaters of the Kaweah River. Further north it is between the Kern and Roaring River, a tributary of the Kings, and still further north between two tributaries of the Kings, ending in Mt. Brewer. I named it [1896] because it was nearly as high as the Main Crest, parallel with, and about 15 to 20 miles west of it." (J. N. LeConte.)

Great Cliffs [Kings Canyon National Park]. The Geological Survey probably applied the name to the mighty monolith on the Middle Fork of Kings River when the Mount Goddard quadrangle was mapped in 1907–1909.

Green. More than fifty geographic features are called Green. Most of them are valleys so named because of the luxuriant vegetation; some are springs and sloughs which look greenish; others were named for persons named Green. The name is occasionally a translation from the Spanish: **Green Valley** [Contra Costa] is shown in 1833 as *Cañada Verde* on the *diseño* of the San Ramon grant (322 ND). **Green Valley** [Santa Cruz] is *Cañada Verde* on the *diseño*, 1844, of the Los Corralitos grant. In combination with -field, -ville, -wood, -spot, -view, -dale, etc., this adjective of color is the most popular for communities in the United States, and California has about twenty such combinations. **Greenwater: Springs, Valley** [Death Valley National Monument]. The springs were so named because their waters have a greenish tinge. The place has been known by this name since 1884, but it did not become famous until 1905, when the discovery of copper deposits caused a short-lived boom. **Greenspot** [San Bernardino]. Named in the early 1900's by the Cram family, early settlers, because it was the only green spot at the upper end of the San Bernardino Valley (Clara Patridge). **Greenfield** [Monterey]. The town was laid out on the Arroyo Seco Rancho by the California Home Extension Association between 1902 and 1905 and was called Clarke City for John S. Clarke, one of its principal officers. In 1905 the Post Office Department declined to use the name and selected the present name from a large number submitted by residents. (R. W. Dunham.)

Green Creek [Shasta]. This tributary of the Sacramento was named for Myron Green, who was in charge of the U.S. trout hatchery at Baird Station from 1879 to 1883 (Steger).

Greenhorn. The common designation for a newcomer was a favorite for place names in

California in mining days and has survived for some fifteen geographic features and for a railroad station in Plumas County. **Greenhorn River** [Nevada]. This is probably the oldest feature so named. "There we found a small camp of overlanders [new arrivals from the East] washing successfully for gold. They called the creek 'Greenhorn,' and showed us quite a lot of bright, shining, yellow scales . . ." (Wistar, I, 117; Aug. 25, 1849.) The following story about **Greenhorn Creek** in Siskiyou County is still current: "A greenhorn came to Yreka in the mining days, and being a greenhorn asked around and about as to where was the best place to mine. The old-timers of course sent him off to a place where no one had found gold and where there seemed to be no likelihood. He struck it rich, and had the laugh on them—and so it was known as Greenhorn." (Stewart.) Similar stories have been told about the prominent range, the Greenhorn Mountains, in Kern and Tulare counties, and about other places so named which are still on maps or on the atlas sheets of the Geological Survey and the U.S. Forest Service. Most of these names can be traced back to the gold-rush period.

Greenlead Creek [San Bernardino]. Probably so named because of the occurrence of pyromorphite, or green lead ore.

Green Valley Creek [Sonoma]. This may be the stream mentioned by Padre Mariano Payeras as Arroyo Verde, on October 21, 1822. He accompanied a *comisionado* to Fort Ross. The official became sick and vomited 'green,' at this place. (Arch. MSB, XII, 416.)

Greenville [Alameda]. Named for John Green, a native of Ireland, who came to California in 1857 and for many years had a store and a farm at Dublin.

Greenville [Plumas]. A man by the name of Green built a house here in the mid-1850's. Because his wife served meals to the miners, the house became known as Green's Hotel, and the settlement as Greenville.

Greenwater Spring [Death Valley National Monument]. The only name on the maps reminiscent of the once bustling town of Greenwater. The town was established in 1906 by Arthur Kunze and for some years was the center of extensive copper mining in the area.

Greenwood [El Dorado]. The name commemorates John Greenwood, son of the famous trapper and guide Caleb Greenwood. John had guided a party overland to California in 1845, had served in the Mexican War, and had established a trading post here before 1850. Greenwood Valley is mentioned in 1850. The place became an important mining center, and October 9, 1852, the post office was transferred from Louisville.

Greenwood: Creek, Ridge [Mendocino]. Named after the settlement Greenwood, founded about 1862 at the mouth of the creek by Britton Greenwood, member of the second Donner relief party and brother of John (of El Dorado County).

Grenada, grĕ-nā′-dá [Siskiyou]. The region was originally known as Starve-Out because of its poor land (Ella Soulé). After the formation of the irrigation district it was renamed, possibly after Grenada County in Mississippi, a region known for its fertile soil.

Grider Creek [Siskiyou]. W. T. Grider settled in Seiad Valley in 1870. The Creek is recorded on the county map of 1883.

Gridley [Butte]. Named in 1870 by the Southern Pacific for George W. Gridley, owner of the land on which the town was built.

Griffith: Park, Observatory [Los Angeles]. The park was named on December 16, 1896, by the Los Angeles city council, for its donor, Griffith J. Griffith. The observatory was named February 25, 1932, by the park commissioners. (Public Library.)

Grigsby Creek [Plumas, Lassen]. Named for Challan Grigsby of the Forest Service (Stewart).

Grigsby Soda Springs [Napa]. The place became known by this name in 1946 when T. B. Grigsby purchased the Samuel Soda Springs.

Grimes [Colusa]. Named about 1865 for Cleaton Grimes, who settled there in 1851.

Grindstone Creek [Glenn]. Named for the first commercial industry of the county: the making of grindstones as early as 1845 by Lassen, Ezekiel Merritt, and other pioneers. The creek is shown on Bidwell's 1844 map and on *diseños* as *Rio de Capay. See* Stone.

Grinnell, Lake Joseph [Fresno]. The lake, south of Red and White Mountain, was named in December, 1946, by Leon A. Talbot of the Division of Fish and Game, in memory of Joseph Grinnell, professor of zoölogy and director of the Museum of Vertebrate Zoölogy at the University of California from 1908 to 1939. **Grinnell Peak** [San Bernardino]. The mountain northeast of San Gorgonio Peak had been labelled Fish Creek Mountain by the Geological Survey. Upon petition of the Sierra Club it was renamed for the zoologist who had made studies here at the beginning of the twentieth century. (Wheelock.)

Griswold: Hills, Canyon, Creek [San Benito]. Brewer (p. 137) mentions "Griswold, a hard looking customer, [who] expatiated on the qualities of his 'ranch'—squatter claim of course" in this location. There is also a Griswold Creek in Tuolumne County.

Grizzly. The grizzly bear, *Ursus horribilis,* now disappeared from the mountains of California, has played an important role in the lore of the State, and about two hundred place names preserve its memory. The majority of these names are found in the Sierra Nevada and the foothills. This does not necessarily prove that the grizzly was less common in the coast ranges: the prospectors often used the term for any bear, whereas the farmers were able to distinguish between the different types. Three settlements bear the name: Grizzly [Plumas], Grizzly Bluff [Humboldt], and Grizzly Flats [El Dorado]. A number of geographic features were named Grizzly because of an incident. **Grizzly Mountain** [Trinity]. "Jim Willburn, my wife's grandfather, wounded a bear on this mountain. The bear charged him before the gun could be reloaded and caught Willburn in a hug. Willburn stabbed the bear with a homemade hunting knife and finally killed it after being badly mauled. Local people then came to use the name Grizzly Mountain." (L. P. Duncan.) **Grizzly Camp** [Humboldt]. "Back in 1880, Bob Pratt camped at this site with his mules and cargo destined for the New River Miners. Feed being plentiful the mules were turned out to graze on the near-by slope. Sometime during the night the Packer was awakened by distress bawling of a mule. Rushing to the rescue of the animal with rifle in hand, expecting to find a Grizzly Bear tearing the mule to bits, the Packer found instead the mule down and under a large Sugar Pine log where it had slipped from the rolling ground. The animal was extricated and being somewhat disgusted the Old Packer decided to name the place 'Grizzly Camp.'" (D. Dartt.) **Grizzly Creek Redwoods State Park** [Humboldt]. The park was established in 1943 and named after the tributary of the Van Dusen River.

Grossmont [San Diego]. Promoted about 1900 as an artists' colony by Colonel Ed Fletcher and William B. Gross, realtors, and named for the latter. The post office is listed in 1912.

Grouse. About thirty geographic features, including two high mountains in Inyo and Mono counties, a meadow in Kings Canyon National Park, and a ridge in Nevada County, are named for the bird whose drumming is a familiar sound in the woods.

Groveland [Tuolumne]. A peaceful name, perhaps reminiscent of a town "back home," was chosen by residents to replace the earlier name, Garrote, which had been applied in 1850 when miners hanged a thief here. Garrote post office is listed from 1854 to about 1875. When a place near by was called Second Garrote for a similar reason, the original Garrote became First Garrote. Hoffmann's map of 1873 still has 1st and 2nd Garrota, but on the Land Office map of 1879 the former appears as Groveland.

Grover City [San Luis Obispo]. The town was named Grover, for Henry Grover, in 1892. In 1937, H. V. Bagwell renamed it Grover City.

Grover Hot Springs [Alpine]. Named for Alvin M. Grover, on whose homestead the springs were situated, and who was county assessor for many years ("The Knave," Aug. 19, 1956). Grover Hot Springs is now a state park.

Groves Prairie [Humboldt]. Named for Dave Groves, who squatted on the area in the late 1860's with the intention of raising horses and cattle (Forest Service).

Grub Gulch [Madera], **Grub Flat** [Plumas]. These are apparently the only survivors from gold-rush days of several place names which contained the miners' term "grub," meaning food earned the hard way.

Grunigen Creek [Tulare]. So named because it runs by the home of the Grunigen family, who formerly spelled their name von Grueningen (Farquhar).

Guachama Rancheria [San Bernardino]. Historical Landmark 95 preserves the name of the Guachama Indians, a division of the Serrano Shoshonean tribe.

Guadalasca [Ventura]. A land grant dated May 6, 1836, and April 6, 1837. The meaning of the name is uncertain. The stem *guad-,* from the Arabic word for 'river,' is found in numerous place names in Spain and Mexico, but apparently the name of the land grant, like the name Guadalupe, is just a transfer name. A transcript of the *expediente* (Legis. Recs., III, 13) has the version Guadalaesa, probably a misspelling.

Guadalupe. The name is derived from the patron saint of Catholic Mexico, the Virgin of Guadalupe, and was an extremely popular place name in early California. The modern pronunciation varies: gwä-dá-lōōp', gwä-dá-lōō'-pĭ, gwä-dá-lōō'-pä. **Guadalupe: River, Creek, Slough** [Santa Clara]. The river was named by the Anza expedition on March 30, 1776, *Rio de Nuestra Señora de Guadalupe,* in honor of the Mexican saint, who was also the principal patron saint of the Anza expedition of 1775. The name is frequently mentioned in documents. It appears on Font's map of the Bay region (1777), and again on Eld's sketch of 1841, and on Duflot de Mofras's map of 1844. **Guadalupe: Lake,** town [Santa Barbara]. The name Guadalupe appears on Narváez' Plano of 1830, and a rancho of that name is mentioned in 1834 (PSP, LXXIX, 106). On April 8, 1837, the name was applied to a land grant. Wilkes' map of 1841 shows the Santa Maria River as *Rio Guadalupe.* The name was adopted for the post office in 1872. The lake, which appears by its present name on the maps of the Land Office in the 1850's, had been named *Laguna Grande de San Daniel* and *Laguna Larga* by the Portolá expedition, September 1, 1769. This name was apparently preserved locally, for on the Parke-Custer map of 1855 it is shown as Guadalupe Largo. **Guadalupe Valley** [San Mateo]. A place called *Cañada de Guadalupe y Visitacion* is mentioned on February 8, 1835, by Manuel Sanchez in a petition for a grant (Docs. Hist. Cal., I, 482). This name was included in the name of the land grant to Jacob P. Leese, July 31, 1841. **Guadalupe: Valley, Mountains** [Mariposa]. The name goes back to the vanished mining town, Guadalupe, shown on Gibbes' map of 1852, and again on Hoffmann's map of 1873. The name has no connection with the river named, in 1806, *Nuestra Señora de Guadalupe;* this was probably the Stanislaus. **Guadalupe y Llanitos de los Correos,** a land grant in Monterey County, dated September 23, 1831, May 18, 1833, and February 10, 1835, has left no trace in the nomenclature of the district. A now vanished town in Nevada County was called Walloupa by the miners in 1852, for an Indian chief, Guadalupe (Co. Hist., 1880, p. 71).

Guajome, wä-hō'-mĕ [San Diego]. According to Kroeber, the name of the land grant, dated July 19, 1845, is derived from Luiseño *Wakhaumai.* Engelhardt (*San Juan Capistrano,* p. 244) lists *Guajaumere* and *Guajaimeie* among the rancherias mentioned in the baptismal register of Mission San Juan Capistrano. According to local tradition, the meaning of the Indian word is 'home of the frog,' i.e., 'swamp with plenty of frogs.'

Gualala, wä-lä'lä: **River,** post office, **Point** [Sonoma, Mendocino]. The origin of the name may never be satisfactorily explained. Anthropologists who have studied the problem—Powers, Barrett, Kroeber, Leland—insist that it is the Spanish rendering of Pomo *Walali,* 'where the waters meet.' County histories and local tradition are just as insistent that it is the Spanish version of Walhalla, in Teutonic mythology the abode of heroes fallen in battle. The name was apparently applied to the river by Ernest Rufus, captain of Sutter's Indian Company in the Micheltorena campaign and grantee of Rancho German. Since Rufus intended to name his grant *Hermann,* in honor of the Teutonic hero, it is quite possible that he might also have given the romantic name Walhalla to the beautiful valley. (*See* German.) The name *Arroyo Valale* is on the *diseño* of the grant (1846). Padre Payeras in 1822 mentions an Indian chief of the region whose name he spells *Valli:ela* (Arch. MSB, XII, 429). If this personal name is the source of the place name (Spaniards often called villages by the names of their chiefs), it would be a strong argument in favor of the theory of the Indian origin of the name. In a recently published monograph by Robert L. Oswalt ("Kashaya Texts," *UCPL,* XXXVI, 1964, p. 8) it is stated that there was an Indian settlement at the site of modern Gualala: *q^hawálali,* 'water coming down place, rivermouth.' If this name was known in 1846, Ernest Rufus might deliberately have used it, changing the spelling to Walhalla. Most American maps show the German version with various spellings; the Coast Survey used the spelling Walalla until recent years. The Spanish spelling, Gualala, was used for the name of the post office, September 9, 1862. The name giver wrongly assumed that the name was Spanish and hence used this spelling because the English "w" appears in Spanish as "gu." The spelling Gualala was accepted by the Land Office maps in the 1870's and is now generally used. A proposal of the Coast Survey in April, 1879, to restore the spelling for the post office was rejected by the Post Office Department because "the name 'Gualala' has been used for nearly 17 years" (letter to Davidson, April 10, 1879). According to Emanuel Fritz, the name is often pronounced Wal Hollow, and is so spelled on at least one map.

Guasti, gwä'-stĭ [San Bernardino]. The railroad

station was called South Cucamonga when the Southern Pacific line was built in the 1890's. When the Italian Vineyard Company began its operations here, soon after 1900, the new name was given for Secondo Guasti, founder of the company and for many years one of the leading viticulturists of the State.

Guatay, gwä'-tī: **Creek, Valley,** town, **Indian Reservation** [San Diego]. A *Valle de Guatay* is shown on a *diseño* (about 1845) of the Cuyamaca grant. According to Kroeber, a Diegueño Indian stated that *kwaitai* means 'large.'

Gubserville [Santa Clara]. A post office was established on the stage route from San Jose to Saratoga, July 5, 1882, and named for Frank Gubser, the first postmaster. Registered as Historical Landmark 447, November 2, 1949.

Guejito y Cañada de Palomea [San Diego]. The land grant is dated September 20, 1845; *Sierra de Guejito,* shown on the *diseño,* seems to be Roderick Mountain and surrounding hills. Guejito is probably a diminutive of *guijo,* 'pebble.' Palomea is obviously a misspelling: *Cañada Paloma,* 'pigeon valley,' is mentioned in 1845 (DSP Ben. P & J, II, 73).

Guenoc [Lake]. The name was given to a land grant dated December 8, 1844, and August 8, 1845. It appears on the *diseños* as the name for a small stream and for a *laguna*. Anthropologists seem to agree that it is a Spanish rendering of a Lake Miwok place name, *Wenok* (*AAE,* XXIX, 367). However, since no such place has been identified, Bancroft's statement (III, 766) may have some merit: "Greenock, 1846, ment. by Revere as the frontier settler on a journey from Napa Val. to Clear Lake. I think there may be some connection between this name and 'Guenoc,' that of a Lake Co. rancho granted in '45 to Geo. 'Rock.' Guenoc is still the name in use." Finally there is a possibility that an Indian, baptized for Saint Gwynoc, a Welsh saint of the 6th century, may have given his name to a village, after which the land grant was named. *See* Novato; San Anselmo; San Quentin.

Guerneville, gûrn'-vĭl [Sonoma]. The place was settled in 1860. When the post office was established in the 1870's it was named for George E. Guerne, a native of Ohio, who had built a saw- and planing-mill there in 1864.

Guernsey [Kings]. Named for James Guernsey, landowner. The name first appeared on the Santa Fe railroad map of 1902.

Guesesosi. *See* Quesesosi.

Guijarral, gē-hȧ-räl' [Fresno]. The Spanish word designates a 'place where cobblestones are found.' *See* Ballast Point.

Guilicos, wĭl'-ĭ-kŏs [Sonoma]. The name of the land grant dated November 13, 1837, is derived from an Indian tribe, mentioned on April 10, 1823, by Padre Amorós as *la nacion Guiluc* (Arch. Arz. SF, Vol. IV, Pt. 2, p. 84). The name appears repeatedly in mission records with various spellings. The name of the grant was spelled Guilucos until 1859, when the spelling Los Guilicos is shown on a surveyor's plat of the rancho. There was an inhabited village, *Wi'lok-yomi,* south of Middletown. The name is Miwok, but the site was perhaps originally Wappo. (*AAE,* XXIX, 367.) The name Los Guilicos for the station of the Northwestern Pacific is shown on the maps after 1890.

Guinda, gwĭn'-dȧ [Yolo]. The Spanish word for 'cherry' was given to the station by the Southern Pacific in the early 1890's because an old cherry tree was then standing at the southeast corner of the townsite.

Gulch. The word gulch (or gulsh), of uncertain origin, evolved as a term for chasm or ravine in America early in the 19th century. It was rarely used as a true generic term until the discovery of gold in California, when nearly every ravine, particularly those that yielded gold, became a "gulch." Now it is in general use throughout the State for a small, short canyon.

Gull. An island south of Santa Cruz Island and a number of rocks and coves along the coast, as well as Gull Lake in Mono County, are named for the most common aquatic bird. Not a single feature seems to be called "sea gull." *See* Gaviota.

Gulling [Plumas]. The place was named for Charles Gulling, an early lumberman and organizer of the Grizzly Creek Ice Company (Myrick).

Gulnac Peak [Santa Clara]. The mountain was named either for William Gulnac or for one of his sons. Gulnac came to California in 1833 and later was the grantee of Campo de los Franceses.

Gustine [Merced]. The town was laid out by Henry Miller and named in memory of his daughter Augustine, who had been thrown from a horse and killed. The station is shown on the Official Railway Map of 1900.

Guthrie Canyon [Riverside]. The canyon in the Cleveland National Forest was named in memory of John D. Guthrie, a California Division of Forestry employee who lost his life in the Decker fire of August, 1959.

Guthrie: Creek, Gulch [Humboldt]. Probably named for Alexander P. Guthrie, who settled in the Eel River district in the 1860's.

Guyapipe, gwē'-á-pīp: **Indian Reservation** [San Diego]. The name of the reservation in Die-gueño territory is not mentioned in the Indian Reports until 1902. Hodge spells the name Cuiapaipa but does not explain its origin or meaning. Kroeber derives it from Diegueño *ewi-apaiɬ* or *awi-apaiɬ,* 'rock lie on.' The Corps of Engineers spells the name of the reservation and the quadrangle Cuya-paipe (1944).

Guyot, gē'-ō, **Mount; Guyot: Pass, Creek, Flat** [Sequoia National Park]. The name for the mountain was suggested by F. H. Wales, and was applied by Captain J. W. A. Wright and his party, on September 3, 1881, in honor of Arnold H. Guyot (1807–1884), a native of Switzerland, explorer of the Appalachian Mountains, and for many years professor of geography and geology at the College of New Jersey (later Princeton). The other features were named after the mountain by the Geological Survey in 1907.

Gypsum. The frequent occurrence of the mineral in California accounts for a number of place names derived from the word, including two railroad stations, Gypsum [Orange], Gypsite [Kern], and Gyp Hill in Death Valley, named in 1937 by Don Curry, park naturalist.

Ha Amar Creek [Humboldt]. The name is recorded on the Tectah Creek atlas sheet of the Corps of Engineers for the stream which enters Klamath River at lat. 41° 19', long. 123° 51'. Waterman, map 11, shows a *Ho'-ome'ᴿ Wroi* about half a mile upstream, but gives no meaning of the name.

Habra. *See* La Habra.

Hacienda, hä-sĭ-ĕn'-dá. The Spanish word for 'estate' or 'farm' is found as a place name in Alameda, Kings, Los Angeles, and Sonoma counties.

Hackamore: station, Reservoir [Modoc]. This is a western American word for a halter used mainly in breaking horses. Its origin is the Spanish *jáquima* (headstall of a bridle), and in this form (often spelled Jaquina) it was applied to the station of the Nevada-California-Oregon Railroad in 1910. It was possibly a folk-etymological rendering of an Indian word. In 1928 the Southern Pacific changed the spelling to the American form, which had always prevailed in speech.

Haeckel, hĕk'-ĕl, **Mount** [Kings Canyon Na-

tional Park]. Named in 1895 by T. S. Solomons, in honor of Ernst Haeckel (1834–1919), the best known of the German Darwinists and author of the law of recapitulation. *See* Evolution.

Hagerman Peak [Santa Clara]. The name for the peak north of Pacheco Pass was probably given for one of the descendants of George "H. F." Hageman, a native of Germany and hotelkeeper in Gilroy township in 1875, although none can be identified with it at this time.

Hahn, Mount [Death Valley National Monument]. The mountain was named for C. F. R. Hahn, who had guided the Lyle detachment of the Wheeler Survey into Death Valley and disappeared in August, 1871, near Last Chance Spring.

Haiwee, hã'-wä: **Creek,** post office, **Reservoir** [Inyo]. According to Chalfant, the name was applied to the land now covered by the reservoir. Its former spelling was Haiwai (as it is still pronounced), and it is the Indian word for 'dove.' (*Inyo,* p. 180.) This interpretation is possible because the district still abounds with wild pigeons. Haiwee Meadows are mentioned by the Nevada Boundary Survey (Sacramento *Union,* August 10, 1861), and Haiwee Meadows as a settlement is recorded on the von Leicht–Craven map (1874) several miles east of the road. The spelling Haway is also found, but the Geological Survey, when it surveyed the Olancha quadrangle in 1905, accepted the spelling used by the Whitney Survey map.

Halagow Creek [Humboldt]. The name of the tributary of Klamath River is the American version of Yurok *Helegä'ä Wroi.* The name probably has something to do with a feature of the deerskin dance, performed in two boats on Klamath River, floating down as far as this creek (Waterman, p. 240).

Halcyon, hăl'-sĭ-ŭn [San Luis Obispo]. The place was established in 1903 by a group of Theosophists (Robert Hine, p. 54). Halcyon means 'calm, peaceful,' and is another name for the kingfisher, which is believed to calm the waves. The name is found repeatedly as a place name in the southeastern United States.

Half Dome [Yosemite National Park]. The descriptive name was applied by the Mariposa Battalion in 1851 to the split mountain which is also known as South Dome. The Indian name, *Tissaack,* is said to have been the name of a woman who was transformed into the mountain.

Halfmoon Bay; Half Moon Bay: town [San Mateo]. The Coast Survey gave this name to the bay because of its shape. It appears first on the sketch of 1854 as the name for a triangulation station on the hill east of the town. The settlement was first known as Spanish Town and appears thus on the maps of the Whitney Survey. The post office is listed as Halfmoon Bay in 1867, and this name for the town appears on the Land Office map of 1879. Since about 1905 the Post Office Department has spelled the name Half Moon Bay. By a decision of the Geographic Board, May-Aug., 1960, this spelling in three words for both the town and the bay is now official.

Half Moon Lake [El Dorado]. The name was given to the lake because of its shape, probably by the Geological Survey when the Pyramid Peak quadrangle was mapped in 1889.

Halleck Creek [Marin]. The name of the stream commemorates Henry W. Halleck, in 1852 co-claimant of the part of the Nicasio grant through which the creek flows. Halleck was California's secretary of state and custodian of the Spanish archives after the Mexican War, and was General-in-Chief of the Union armies, 1862–1864.

Halloran Springs [San Bernardino]. The origin of the name for the springs and the mining district has not been established, but the name was in existence in 1875, when Eric Bergland was leading a detachment of the Wheeler Survey through the region (Belden).

Halls Flat [Lassen]. Named by the Forest Service for W. G. Hall and sons, who had a summer cattle camp here about 1880.

Hambre. *See* Alhambra.

Hambright Creek [Glenn]. Named for Robert Hambright, a Mexican War veteran, who had settled on the bank of the stream. It is shown as Hambright Slough on the Mining Bureau map of 1891.

Hamburg: town, **Gulch** [Siskiyou]. Established as a mining camp in the fall of 1851 and named by Sigmund Simon, probably after the seaport in Germany. It was also known as Hamburg Bar. (Co. Hist., 1881, p. 218.)

Hamilton, Mount [Santa Clara]. Named by William Brewer and Charles Hoffmann of the Whitney Survey, for the Rev. Laurentine Hamilton. Hamilton accompanied the two surveyors to the top of the mountain on August 26, 1861. Brewer, in a letter dated January 31, 1888, states: "Hoffmann and I were encumbered with our instruments, and, as we neared the summit, Mr. Hamilton pushed on ahead of us, and reaching it, swung his hat in the air and shouted back to us: 'First on top—for this is the highest point.' ... When we worked up our notes in the office, and failing to find any old name in use, Hoffmann and I, after discussing two names, agreed to call it Mt. Hamilton." The date of naming is confirmed in Hoffmann's field notes: on August 26 he calls the mountain the highest peak of the Mount Diablo range; on August 27 he calls it Mount Hamilton. Hamilton was at that time preaching in San Jose. In 1864 he moved to Oakland, where he died in the pulpit of his Independent Church on Easter Sunday, 1882. (F. J. Neubauer.) By a strange irony of fate it was later discovered that the peak climbed by Brewer and Hoffmann not only had had an old name, Isabel, but also that the peak two miles southeast of the site of the Lick Observatory was fourteen feet higher. The Geological Survey promptly (1895) placed the old name upon this peak; but the entire mountain remains known as Mount Hamilton. *See* Isabel.

Hamilton City [Glenn]. The settlement was started by a sugar company in 1906, and named for J. G. Hamilton, promoter of the town. The railroad name is Hamilton. The Hamilton mentioned in the *Statutes* of 1851 as the county seat of Butte County was thirty miles southeast on the Feather River.

Hamilton Field [Marin]. Named in 1932 by the War Department in honor of Lieutenant Lloyd A. Hamilton, of the 17th Aero Squadron, U.S. Army, who won the Distinguished Service Cross for heroism in Belgium and was killed in action in France in 1918. Before the site was given to the government by the county it was known as Marin Meadows.

Hamilton: Lakes, Creek [Sequoia National Park]. The lakes were named for James Hamilton, former owner of Redwood Meadow and Wet Meadow (Farquhar).

Hammarskjold Grove [Humboldt]. The grove on Pepperwood Flat was selected by the Save-The-Redwoods League in 1962 and named Dag Hammarskjold Memorial Redwood Grove in honor of the late Secretary-General of the United Nations.

Hammer Field [Fresno]. The Hammer Field Army Air Base was activated August 1, 1941, and named in memory of Lieutenant Earl M. Hammer, the first aviator from California to achieve an air victory in World War I and the first to be killed in action while on a mission over Germany.

Hammerhorn Mountain [Mendocino]. In the late 1860's the name was given by a man named Fleming to the mountain on which he had shot a deer that had round knobs at the tips of the horns (Forest Service).

Hammonton [Yuba]. Named in 1905 for W. P. Hammon, an official of a gold-dredging company.

Hampshire Rocks [Placer]. The rocks were named after New Hampshire, the "Granite State" because they were of "real hard granite." (Sacramento *Union*, July 11, 1864)

Hanaupah: Canyon, Spring [Death Valley National Monument]. According to Kroeber, the word is almost certainly Shoshonean. The last syllable, *pah*, means 'water' in Shoshonean. F. V. Coville (Death Valley Survey) states that the Indian name was *Wishi Honopi*, *wishi* being the name of the Indian hemp, *Apocynum cannabinum*, and *honopi*, a Panamint word for 'canyon.' This theory has its merits, for the tough fibers from the stalks of this plant were used as twine by the Indians.

Hanford [Kings]. Named in 1877 by the Central Pacific (now the Southern Pacific) for its treasurer, James Hanford.

Hangtown Creek [El Dorado]. The creek preserves the nickname of Placerville, which was called Hangtown in the 1850's because its citizens had hanged several robbers in 1849.

Hanna Mountain [Mono]. The peak was named for Thomas R. Hanna, son-in-law of John Muir. Hanna made the preliminary survey of the Hetch Hetchy project in 1905, and was owner of the May Lundy Mine from 1920 to 1940.

Hansen Dam [Los Angeles]. The U.S. District Engineer's Office named the dam and the flood-control basin after Hansen Hill, which was at the site of the spillway. The name had been used locally because Dr. Homer A. Hansen had his home on the hill for many years. (N. B. Hodgkinson.)

Happy. A typical folk name, as popular with the prospectors in the gold-rush days as with modern real-estate developers. **Happy Camp** [Siskiyou]. A number of stories are told about the naming of the old mining town in 1851. H. C. Chester, who interviewed Jack Titus in 1882 or 1883, states that Titus named the camp because his partner James Camp, upon arriving there, exclaimed: "This is the happiest day of my life." Redick McKee mentions the camp on November 8, 1851, as "Mr.

Roache's 'Happy Camp,' at the place known as Murderer's Bar" (Indian Report, 1853, p. 178). **Happy Isles** [Yosemite National Park]. Named in 1885 by W. E. Dennison, guardian of Yosemite Valley: "... I have named them the *Happy Isles,* for no one can visit them without for the while forgetting the grinding strife of *his* world and being happy." (Farquhar.) **Happy Gap** [Kings Canyon National Park]. The pass between Kings River Canyon and Tehipite Valley was named before 1896. According to J. N. LeConte, anyone who succeeds in getting a pack train to this point at once perceives the appropriateness of the name. (Farquhar.)

Harbin: Hot Springs, Creek, Mountain [Lake]. Named for James M. Harbin, who came overland in 1846 and was claimant of part of Salvador Vallejo's Napa grant in 1853. About 1857 he settled at the springs which became known as Harbin Hot Springs.

Harbison Canyon [San Diego]. John S. Harbison, apiarist, came to San Diego County in 1869 and settled in the canyon which bears his name (Co. Library).

Harbor City [Los Angeles]. The city, in the "shoestring strip," was named Harbor Industrial City when it was laid out by W. I. Hollingsworth in 1912. When the expected connection with Los Angeles harbor (then being developed by dredging the slough) did not materialize, the less pretentious form of the name was adopted.

Harden Lake [Yosemite National Park]. Apparently named by the Whitney Survey for the owner of Harden's Ranch on the South Fork of the Tuolumne. Both ranch and lake are spelled Hardin on the Hoffmann-Gardner map of 1867.

Hardin Butte [Lava Beds National Monument]. Named in memory of Major Charles B. Hardin, who died June 7, 1939; the name was approved by the Geographic Board in June, 1940.

Harding: Canyon, Creek [Orange]. Named for Ike Harding, who had a goat farm in the canyon (Stephenson).

Hardin Mountain [Del Norte]. The mountain was named for Silas T. Hardin, one of the pioneer settlers of Summit Valley (Co. Hist., 1953).

Hardins: Flat, Hill [Tuolumne]. Named for an eccentric Englishman, "Little Johnny 'Ardin," who had a sawmill on the flat in the 1850's (Paden-Schlichtmann).

Hardscrabble. The old American place name became a typical frontier name used wherever the scrabble for daily grub was hard. It was repeatedly used for mining camps in the gold-rush days. Today only two Hardscrabble Creeks are left—in Mendocino and Del Norte counties. The once famous mining town in Siskiyou County was named in the 1850's by two former residents of Hardscrabble, Wisconsin (Luddy).

Hardwick [Kings]. When the branch road was built in the 1890's, the station and townsite were named for a traffic official of the Southern Pacific. The post office is listed in 1910.

Harkless Flat [Inyo]. Named for a pioneer rancher near Big Pine, who cut and sold wood in this area (Brierly).

Harkness, Mount [Lassen National Park]. The peak originally bore the name Mount Juniper because of a single fine specimen of the Sierra juniper on its slope, and the lake north of it is still called Juniper Lake. The present name, shown on the Mining Bureau map of 1891, was given in honor of Dr. Harvey W. Harkness, president of the California Academy of Sciences in the 1890's.

Harlan Canyon [Riverside]. The canyon in the Cleveland National Forest was named in 1960 in memory of Nelson D. Harlan, a U.S. Forest Service employee who lost his life in the Decker fire in August, 1959.

Harlem Springs [San Bernardino]. The promoters of the resort in 1887 accepted the proposal of Mrs. Crawford, a property owner near by, to name their "town" and hotel in remembrance of her alma mater, the Harlem School for Young Ladies, New York.

Harmony. The name, always a favorite for pioneer settlements, was especially popular in Civil War days. *Lippincott's Gazetteer* of 1868 lists twenty-four towns with this name. **Harmony: Valley,** town [San Luis Obispo]. The name was applied to the valley by settlers in the 1860's. When the post office was established in 1915, the name was adopted at the suggestion of Marius G. Salmina, of the Harmony Valley Creamery Association. **Harmony Ridge** [Nevada] was named after the two Harmony mines on the south slope.

Harper Lake [San Bernardino]. Named for J. D. Harper, who lived at the edge of the lake, on what is now known as Black's Ranch.

Harris [Humboldt]. Probably named for William C. Harris, a native of Wisconsin, who is listed as the postmaster and hotelkeeper at Harris in McKenney's Directory of 1883–1884.

Harrisburg Flat [Death Valley National Monument]. The place name, long in use locally, commemorates "Shorty" (Frank) Harris, who from the 1890's until his death in 1934 was one of the most colorful and best-known "single-blanket jackass prospectors" of the Death Valley region. This particular place became associated with Shorty's name because he found a rich deposit of gold here in 1906.

Harrison, Mount [San Bernardino]. In the 1880's Myron H. Crafts named three peaks in the region in honor of three Presidents: Garfield, Lincoln, and Harrison. Only the last is still shown on maps. *See* Crafton.

Harrison Gulch [Shasta]. Named for W. H. Harrison, the first judge of Shasta County, who settled on the North Fork of Cottonwood Creek in 1852 (Steger).

Harrison Pass [Sequoia National Park]. The pass, probably used by sheepmen as early as 1875, gradually became known by its present name, which is for Ben Harrison, part Cherokee Indian, who herded sheep in the upper Kern region in the 1880's (Farquhar).

Harter [Sutter]. Named in 1908 by Clyde B. Harter, owner of the land, for his father, George Harter, a pioneer. The name replaced the name Las Uvas (the grapes), which the Northern Electric had given to the station in 1906 because the right of way crossed a vineyard.

Hartoum [San Bernardino]. The former name, Khartoum, after the city in the Anglo-Egyptian Sudan, fitted into the scheme of fanciful railroad names in the desert—Bengal, Siam, Java, Nome, Klondike, etc. The Santa Fe has used the present form since 1903.

Harvard, Mount [Los Angeles]. The peak, formerly called South Gable Promontory, was named in honor of Harvard University when, on April 7, 1892, the university's president, Charles W. Eliot, visited the point, near by, where the Harvard photographing telescope had stood in 1889–1890 (Reid, pp. 364 ff.).

Harwood, Mount [San Bernardino]. The mountain in the San Gabriel Mountains is named in memory of Aurelia Squire Harwood, educator and conservationist, who died in 1928 (Geographic Board, July-Sept., 1965).

Haskell: Peak, Creek [Sierra]. Named for Edward W. Haskell, father of Burnette G. Haskell, founder of the Kaweah Cooperative Colony in Tulare County. *See* Colony. Edward Haskell had a ranch for many years at the foot of the peak. (Oscar Berland.)

Hastings: Creek, Cut, Slough, Tract [Contra Costa]. The creek was probably named for

Lyman H. Hastings, a native of Ohio and a farmer at Marsh Creek, who discovered quicksilver on the east side of Mount Diablo in 1860.

Hatchet: Creek, Mountain, Mountain Pass [Shasta]. According to Steger, the creek was so named because Indians "slyly appropriated" a hatchet from a party of immigrants.

Hat: Creek, Mountain, Lake, post office [Lassen National Park]. The mountain may well have been named because of its shape, and the creek after the mountain. However, since Hat Creek but not Hat Mountain is mentioned in early reports (Beckwith, 1854; Brewer, 1863), the creek may have been named first. According to Steger, it was named when a member of the party blazing the trail for the Noble route in 1852 lost his hat in the stream. The Indian name for the creek was *Hat'-te we'-we* (Merriam, *Pit River*, p. 29). This may point to an Indian origin of the name, or may be an Indian adaptation of the American name. Hat Creek post office was established in 1884 but the name was changed to Cassel in 1888; the present Hat Creek post office was established in 1909. For mountains the name is used elsewhere: a Hat Peak is shown on the Alturas atlas sheet and a Hat Mountain on the Modoc National Forest map.

Haupt Creek [Sonoma]. The name commemorates Charles Haupt, a German immigrant, who settled here in the 1860's, married a Pomo girl, and was held in high esteem by the Indians of the district (Leland). It is shown as Charley Haupt Creek on the county map of 1879.

Havasu, hăv'-à-soo: **Lake** [San Bernardino]. An artificial lake on the Colorado River named by John C. Page; the name was approved by the Geographic Board in 1939. *Havasu* is a word from the Mojave language, meaning 'blue.' It is said that it was the name given to the lake by an old Mojave Indian, Harani, and his wife, when they first saw the new lake with its clear blue water.

Havens: Anchorage, Neck [Mendocino]. The name was given to the anchorage by the Coast Survey before 1855. According to the County History (1880, pp. 380 f.), it was named for a "commander of a Government coast surveying vessel by the name of Haven." In 1855 Lieutenant Edwin J. De Haven was assistant in the Coast Survey and in charge of the *Arago*, then off the coast of Texas. Since his name cannot be connected with the California place, it is more likely that the anchorage was named for H. W. Havens, a member of

a detachment of the Laura Virginia party (*see* Humboldt Bay) which explored along the coast north of the Golden Gate in 1850 (cf. Co. Hist., 1882, pp. 96 ff.).

Havilah: town, **Canyon** [Kern]. Named in 1864 by the founder, Asbury Harpending, a native of Kentucky, after the Biblical gold land, Havilah, mentioned in Gen. 2:11. Historic Landmark 100.

Hawkins, Mount [Los Angeles]. Named by the Forest Service for Nellie Hawkins, about 1890 a popular waitress at near-by Squirrel Inn.

Hawkins Peak [Alpine]. Named for John Hawkins, who squatted on a ranch east of the peak in 1858 (Maule).

Hawthorne [Los Angeles]. Named about 1906 for Nathaniel Hawthorne, the American novelist, by Mrs. Laurine H. Woolwine, daughter of H. D. Harding, who was one of the founders of the town.

Hay. The numerous place names containing this word testify to the importance of hay to immigrants and settlers. **Hayfork: River, Mountain, Bally,** town [Trinity]. When the Ruch family settled there in 1852, the region was known as Hayfields because it was the largest farming section of the county. Later the name Hayfork was applied to a branch of the Trinity River, and this in turn gave the name to the town. Hayfork Bally is shown on the map of Trinity National Forest, but on the Big Bar atlas sheet the generic appears as Baldy. *See* Bally. **Hayfield Reservoir** [Riverside]. The site of the reservoir and the pump lift of the Metropolitan Water District had been humorously named the Hayfields because a thin growth of grass there was used by cattlemen for pasturage. **Haypress: Creek, Valley** [Sierra]. The remains of the handmade hay press of "early days" can still be seen about half a mile from the forest-guard station (Stewart). The name occurs elsewhere in the State: Haypress Flat [Alpine], Haypress Meadow [Siskiyou]. **Haystack.** About twenty orographic features resembling the outline of a haystack are so named, usually in combination with Hill, Peak, or Mountain; two elevations in Siskiyou and Del Norte counties, however, are named simply Haystack.

Hayden Hill [Lassen]. The hill was named for J. W. Hayden, who located several mines here in 1869. A post office named Hayden was established April 13, 1871; after 1878 it was called Haydenhill.

Hayward [Alameda]. In 1852 William Hayward opened a hotel here after he had settled inadvertently on another part of Guillermo Castro's Rancho San Lorenzo. When Castro laid out the present town in 1854 he retained the name. The post office was established January 6, 1860, with the name Haywood, although William Hayward is listed as postmaster. March 22, 1880, the name was changed to Haywards, and January 15, 1911, to the present spelling.

Hazard: post office [Los Angeles]. Opened October 2, 1950, and named for Henry G. Hazard, who had come to California in 1853 and was mayor of Los Angeles in 1889.

Hazel. Only a few physical features bear the name of the native hazel or hazelnut bush, the oldest of which is probably Hazel Green Creek just west of Yosemite National Park, named by the Mariposa Battalion in 1851 (Bunnell, 1880, p. 316). Hazel Creek post office [Shasta] was named in 1877, after having been called Portuguee since 1870. A site in Santa Cruz County was called *Los Avellanos* (the hazelnuts) *de Nuestra Señora del Pilar* by the Portolá expedition on November 23, 1769 (Crespi, p. 239). On Hazel Creek in El Dorado County a rich gold deposit was discovered in 1948 and was being exploited with modern equipment. According to the *Mining Bureau*, LII, 416, the assay was expected to be as high as $500 per ton.

Hazelbusch [Butte]. The name was applied to the station by the Northern Electric about 1903, for one of the Hazelbusch families from Germany who had settled there in the 1870's. On some maps it is spelled, probably correctly, Haselbusch.

Healdsburg [Sonoma]. The name was applied by the Post Office Department in 1857 for Harmon G. Heald, who had had a trading post there since 1846 and had built the first store in the town in 1852. From 1854 to 1857 the post office name was Russian River.

Hearst [Butte]. The station was named by the Southern Pacific in the 1890's, for George Hearst, U.S. senator from 1887 to 1891. **Hearst** [Mendocino]. The post office was established in 1892 and was probably likewise named in memory of George Hearst, who had died the preceding year.

Heber, hē'-bēr [Imperial]. Founded in 1903 by the California Development Company and named for its president, A. H. Heber, one of the leaders in the development of the Imperial Valley.

Hecker Pass [Santa Clara]. When the highway was opened in 1928, the pass was named for Henry Hecker, a county supervisor. The monument erected on the pass bears this legend: "This testimonial dedicated to Henry Hecker, whose foresight made possible the completion of the Yosemite-to-the-Sea Highway, May 27, 1928." Henry Hecker was the nephew of Friedrich Hecker, leader of the Baden insurrection of 1848, "Latin farmer" at Belleville, Missouri, colonel of a Union regiment in the Civil War. *See* Hilgard.

Hector [San Bernardino]. The station was named by the Santa Fe in 1902. This name, like others on this sector, was chosen from classical literature. Hector was the bravest of the Trojans.

Hedionda, hĕd-ĭ-ŏn'-dä: **Creek** [Santa Clara]. The Spanish adjective, meaning 'fetid,' was repeatedly applied to creeks or ponds with unpleasant odors. In the Las Animas land grant case, in 1861, Manuel Larios testified that the creek which empties into Pescadero Creek was so named "from the fact of being stinking water." Two days later, John Gilroy made the more refined statement that "the Hedionda Creek derives its name from a sulphur spring." But two days later still, in the Juristac case, he too labeled it "stinking spring." (*WF*, VI, 372.) *See* Agua.

Heenan Lake [Alpine]. Probably named for a Mr. Heenan who worked in the Leviathan Mine near by and was killed in the 1860's by a blast (Maule, p. 5).

Heffernan Honor Grove [Humboldt]. The grove in the Prairie Creek State Park was established in 1966 in honor of Helen Heffernan, former chief of the California Bureau of Elementary Education.

Heins Lake [Monterey]. Named for a farmer who had settled at the lake before 1868. The lake itself was recently drained and the land is being farmed.

Helen. Next to Elizabeth this is probably the most popular feminine name for lakes. R. B. Marshall of the Geological Survey was so infatuated with the name that he bestowed it upon three lakes in the Sierra: one east of Kuna Crest, for the daughter of George Otis Smith, director of the Geological Survey; another at the East Fork of Cherry Creek, for Mrs. Helen Keyes, the daughter of Colonel William W. Forsyth; and a third northeast of Muir Pass, for Muir's daughter, Mrs. Helen Funk. This is all the more astonishing because there was already a Helen Lake (now Starr King Lake) in Yosemite National Park. **Helen Lake** [Lassen National Park]. Named in 1864 for Helen Tanner Brodt, the first white woman to ascend Lassen Peak. **Helendale** [San Bernardino]. The Santa Fe station originally called Point of Rocks was named Helen on December 15, 1897, for the daughter of A. G. Wells, vice-president of the company. On September 22, 1918, the name was changed to Helendale. (Santa Fe).

Helix, Mount [San Diego]. The trail which winds around to the summit of the cone-shaped mountain suggested the appropriate name (Latin, 'spiral'), which was given by Captain Rufus K. Porter in the early 1870's. Gardeners are familiar with the term as used in *Hedera helix,* the English ivy. The boom town conceived and named Helix in 1887 did not flourish.

Hell. The realm of the fallen angels was never as popular for place names as the name of His Satanic Majesty. A few mining camps which included the word in their names dropped it when the country became respectable; the only survivor is Helltown, shown on the Chico atlas sheet five miles northeast of Paradise, in Butte County. The canyon between Montezuma and Borrego valleys [San Diego] is still known as **Hellhole,** named so by W. Helm, an early cattleman. The name **Hell-for-Sure Pass** [Fresno] was applied to the Baird trail by J. N. LeConte in 1904. LeConte may have thought of the old Hell-for-Sartain Pass in Southern Highlands (Drury). **Hell's Hollow,** near the town of Bear Valley [Mariposa], was so called because of the many accidents to men and animals traversing the rough trail in early days (Doyle). **Hell Gate** [Death Valley National Monument]. The name is appropriate because travelers are struck by the marked change in temperature when crossing the pass on a hot day (Death Valley Survey). **Hell Hole** [Placer], a deep gorge on the Rubicon River, is a favorite of deer hunters (Morley). Devils Half Acre in Shasta County is matched by Hells Half Acre in Lake County. *See* Bumpass Hell.

Helm; Helms: Meadow, Creek [Fresno]. Named for William Helm, a native of Canada, who came to California in 1859, settled at Big Dry Creek in 1865, and for many years raised more sheep than anyone else in central California.

Hemet, hĕm'-ĕt: **Valley, Dam, Lake, Butte,** town [Riverside]. The dam was built between 1886 and 1890, the post office is listed in 1898, the station is shown on the Official Railway Map of 1900. No evidence has been found that the name dates from Spanish times. However, according to Kroeber, it sounds as if it might be Luiseño Shoshonean. It may have been the Indian name of the valley, supplied to the promoters by the inhabitants of the Pochea village south of Hemet. A derivation from Swedish *hemmet* (in the home) is also possible.

Hemlock. A number of places in the Sierra Nevada and the Coast Ranges were so named because of the occurrence of the mountain hemlock or of the Douglas fir, often called hemlock. Hemlock Creek [San Bernardino] and some other places were probably named for the growth of water hemlock (*Cicuta*), a deadly poisonous plant of the carrot family, highly dangerous to cattle that feed on the tubers.

Hendy Redwood Grove [Mendocino]. The grove was named for Joshua Hendy, its former owner.

Henley [Siskiyou]. The original mining settlement of the 1850's was named Cottonwood, after the creek on which it was situated. The post office is listed as Henley as early as 1858. It was named for a prominent citizen named Henly [!] (Co. Hist., 1881, p. 210).

Henleyville [Tehama]. Probably named for William N. Henley, a native of Indiana, who registered as a voter at Henleys, August 3, 1866.

Hennerville Peak. *See* Hunewill.

Henness Pass [Nevada]. The pass was discovered by Patrick Henness (or Hanness) and his partner Jackson. The former returned to the Atlantic seaboard, but Jackson remained on his ranch and in 1852 built a wagon road across the pass which continued to bear his partner's name. The name is mentioned in the *Report* of the state surveyor general of 1856 (p. 191): "... the route known as the Henness, or Downieville, Route."

Henness Trail [Yosemite National Park]. The trail was named for James A. Hennessy, a native of Ireland, whose residence is shown on the Hoffmann-Gardner map of 1867 at the confluence of Indian Creek with Merced River. The name was misspelled Henness by the Wheeler Survey, and this spelling is now generally accepted. The Yosemite National Park map of the Geological Survey (1932) still shows a place called Henness west of El Portal.

Hennigers Flat [Los Angeles]. The place on the west slope of Mount Harvard was so named because William K. Henniger had a squatter's claim here in the 1880's (Reid,

p. 365).

Henry, Mount [Kings Canyon National Park]. Named by J. N. LeConte in honor of Joseph Henry (1797–1878), an eminent physicist, who was professor of natural history at the College of New Jersey (now Princeton University), 1832–1878, and president of the National Academy of Sciences, 1868–1878 (Farquhar).

Henshaw, Lake [San Diego]. The reservoir was created in 1924 and named for William G. Henshaw, who owned that part of the old Warner's Ranch which is now flooded.

Hercules [Contra Costa]. Named in the 1890's when the Hercules Powder Company was established there. The post office is listed in 1915.

Herlong [Lassen]. When the Sierra Ordnance Department was established there, the War Department named the place in honor of Captain Henry W. Herlong (1911–1941), the first American ordnance officer to lose his life in World War II.

Hermit. The name is repeatedly found in the State for isolated peaks or rocks. The best known are The Hermit [Kings Canyon National Park], named by T. S. Solomons in 1895, and Hermit Butte [Modoc], named by the Forest Service.

Hermosa, hûr-mō'-sà: **Beach** [Los Angeles]. The advertising name, a Spanish word meaning 'beautiful,' was used by the Hermosa Beach Land and Water Company when the original subdivision was laid out in 1901. The name has been used elsewhere in southern California; in San Bernardino County it was once combined with the name Iowa to form the unique name Ioamosa for adjoining tracts of land formerly called Hermosa and Iowa Tract and now called Alta Loma.

Hernandez: town, **Valley** [San Benito]. Two farmers, Rafael and Jesus Hernandez, are listed in the Great Register of 1879 as residents of the county, but they cannot now be identified with this place.

Herndon [Fresno]. The Central Pacific (Southern Pacific) crossed the San Joaquin River at the point called Sycamore in 1872 but abandoned its plan to lay out a townsite here and chose instead the present site of Fresno. Sycamore station was renamed Herndon about 1895, for a relative of the promoter of a local irrigation project. (B. R. Walker.)

Herpoco [Contra Costa]. Coined from *Her*cules *Po*wder *Co*mpany and applied to the station in 1919 by the Santa Fe to distinguish it from the Southern Pacific station Hercules.

Herrera, Cañada de [Marin]. A land grant dated August 10, 1839. One Francisco Herrera, a *soldado de cuero* (leather-jacket soldier) was sponsor of four Indians baptized December 14, 1817, at San Rafael, but it is not certain whether the valley was named for him.

Herscheys Hollow [Plumas]. In the early 'seventies a murderer named Herschey, who was said to have buried $20,000, was killed and buried in the hollow, which is two miles south of Vinton (R. F. Ramelli).

Hesperia, hĕs-pē'-rĭ-à [San Bernardino]. The station was named in 1885 by the California Southern (Santa Fe), possibly after Hesperia, Michigan. Greek and Roman poets used the name in the sense of "The Western Land."

Hester Lake [Kings Canyon National Park]. The lake was named in 1960 in memory of Robert M. Hester and his father, Clinton Hester. Robert Hester was the co-pilot of a B-24 bomber which crashed here in 1943. His body was not discovered until 1960. (Geographic Board, Sept.-Dec., 1960.)

Hetch Hetchy: Valley, Falls, Dome, Reservoir, Junction [Yosemite National Park]. According to Kroeber, the name is from a Central Miwok word denoting a kind of grass or plant with edible seeds. Powers maintains that the original form was *Hatchatchie* (p. 357). Hoffmann, however, who explored the valley in 1866, stated: "Tuolumne Valley, or Hetch-Hetchy, as it is called by the Indians (the meaning of this word I was unable to ascertain) . . . The latter [northern Paiutes] still visit the valley every fall to gather acorns, which abound in this locality" (California Academy of Natural Sciences, *Proceedings . . . 1867*, 1868, pp. 368 ff.). It may be that the name means 'acorn valley,' instead of 'grass-seed valley.' The reservoir was constructed by the city of San Francisco from 1914 to 1923.

Hetten, Ketten. The Wintu word for 'camass' or 'camas' (wild hyacinth), valued as food by the Indians of the Northwest, is found in the names of a number of geographic features in Trinity and Humboldt counties. **Hettenshaw: Valley, Peak** [Trinity]. *Hetten Chow* means 'camass valley,' according to Powers (p. 117), who reports that the Indians "used to gather immense quantities of cammas (*Cammasia* [!] *esculenta*)." **Kettenpom Valley** [Trinity]. *Hetten Pum* means 'camass earth,' according to Powers. The Indian name was apparently preserved by the Whitney Survey: von Leicht–Craven record Ketten Pom and Ketten Chow valleys. A Ketin-shaw Trail is mentioned in 1861. Hetten in the southwest corner of Trinity County was once a mining town and had a post office between 1890 and 1900.

Hewes Park [Orange]. Named about 1890 for David Hewes of San Francisco, on whose ranch the park is situated (Stephenson). Hewes was Leland Stanford's brother-in-law and supplied the golden spike for the cere-monies of the meeting of the Union Pacific and the Central Pacific in May, 1869.

Hexie Mountain [Riverside]. The mine at its base was originally called Hexahedron, sometimes shortened to Hexie (Wheelock).

Hickey Grove State Park [Mendocino]. Cre-ated in 1921 and named in memory of Edward R. Hickey.

Hickman [Stanislaus]. Named in 1891 by the Southern Pacific for Louis Hickman, an early settler and one-time mayor of Stockton, who owned the ranch adjacent to the station.

Hicks. *See* Hodge.

Hi-corum [San Bernardino]. The mining dis-trict at the west end of the Providence Moun-tains was named for Hi-corum, a Chemehuevi Indian, discoverer of the ore deposits of the Orange Blossom Mine near Bagdad and probably discoverer of Mitchells Caverns (O. J. Fisk).

Higgins Mountain [Del Norte]. Named for Lew Higgins, who discovered the first copper deposits in the district.

High. The adjective is often used with a generic term to form a place name. In addition to the seven communities listed in the gazetteers a number of physical features include the word in their names: High Dome and High Plateau Mountain [Del Norte], Highland Peak [Alpine], High Valley [Colusa]. The phonetic spelling which is sometimes used produces a comical effect: Hydril Hill [Kings] (from "high drill"), Hipass [San Diego], Hytree [Del Norte], Hi Vista [Los Angeles]. **Highgrove** [Riverside]. The townsite was mapped and recorded in 1887 by A. J. Two-good and S. H. Herrick and named because there were orange groves on the hillside there. The name of the California Southern railroad station here had been East River-side since 1882 (Santa Fe). **Highland: Lake, Creek, Peak, Reservoir** [Alpine]. The cluster name commemorates the short-lived High-land City which was on the high land of the divide between the Carson and the Stanis-laus. City, Lake, and Creek are shown on the maps of the Whitney Survey. **Highland, East**

Highlands [San Bernardino]. Both names were applied to stations when the Santa Fe was built through the valley in 1894–1895. The two places are actually in the lowlands; they were named after the narrow fertile tableland several hundred feet above the valley, which had been called Highland when the school district was organized in 1883. The name of the post office was Messina until 1898. East Highland was formerly Cramville, named for Louis Cram, the first settler. **Hipass** [San Diego]. The post office was established November 12, 1917, and named because of its situation. In 1956 the name was changed to Tierra del Sol. **Hi Vista** [Los Angeles]. Named in 1930 by Mrs. M. R. Card, wife of the man who developed the place, because it commands a beautiful view of the Sierra Madre and the San Ber-nardino Mountains (Mrs. M. R. Card). **High Sierra.** A commonly accepted name for the part of the Sierra Nevada which in-cludes the high peaks. It was used by the Whitney Survey to designate the highest regions as distinguished from the mining and stock-running regions.

Highway Highlands [Los Angeles]. The origi-nal subdivision was so named in 1923 by one of the promoters, Mark S. Collins, because of its situation on the state highway (Foothill Boulevard). The gazetteers also list a High-way in Monterey County and a station of the old Sacramento Northern, Highway Cross-ing, in Solano County.

Hildreth Mountain [Madera]. Named for either Jonathan or Emphrey Hildreth, farmers from Missouri, who settled in the region about 1870. There is another Hildreth Mountain in Los Padres National Forest.

Hilgard, Mount [Fresno]. Named before 1896 by T. S. Solomons, at the suggestion of Ernest C. Bonner, an admiring former student of Professor Hilgard (Farquhar). Eugene W. Hilgard (1833–1916), the father of scientific agriculture in California, was a scion of a family of "Latin farmers" (i.e., professors, doctors, lawyers, etc., who tilled the soil) who had left Germany for political reasons and settled at Belleville, Missouri.

Hillsborough [San Mateo]. The town was in-corporated in 1910 and named after Hills-boro (or Hillsborough) New Hampshire, the ancestral home of W. D. M. Howard, the former owner of the site. California has an-other Hillsborough and several names with the word Hill as the first element.

Hillyer, Mount [Los Angeles]. Named by the

Forest Service, for Margaret Hillyer, an employee at the Angeles National Forest.

Hilmar [Merced]. The town, established in 1917, was named after the Hilmar Colony, founded as a colony of Swedes by Nels O. Hultberg and probably named for his son Hilmar, or for Hilmar A. Carlson, a pioneer citizen.

Hilton [Sonoma]. The name was chosen by the Post Office Department in 1894 from a list submitted by the residents. Hilton Ridenhour was the son of the oldest pioneer, around whose ranch the settlement grew up.

Hilton, Mount [Trinity]. The mountain in the Trinity Alps is named for James Hilton, author of *Lost Horizon* (Geographic Board, July-Sept., 1966).

Hilton: Creek, Lakes [Mono]. Named for Richard Hilton, a blacksmith from Michigan, who settled in Round Valley about 1870 and later operated a "milk ranch" in Long Valley.

Hilts [Siskiyou]. John Hilt came to Siskiyou County in 1855 and built a sawmill on Cottonwood Creek. In 1903 a group of lumbermen bought the estate and named their company and the town for its original owner. The name of the station is Hilt; the post office, transferred from Coles, July 6, 1903, is Hilts.

Hinkley [San Bernardino]. Named upon the arrival of the railroad in 1882, by D. C. Henderson, of Barstow, for his son Hinckley. Formerly spelled Hinckley.

Hiouchi, hī-ōō'-chī: **Redwoods, Bridge** [Del Norte]. *Hiouchi* is an Indian word meaning 'blue waters,' according to Drury (p. 356).

Hipass. *See* High; Tierra del Sol.

Hirz Creek [Shasta]. This tributary of McCloud River was named for Christian Hirz, who mined here in the late 1860's (Steger).

Hitchcock, Mount [Sequoia National Park]. Named by the Rev. F. H. Wales, of Tulare, on September 7, 1881, when he ascended near-by Mount Young. Charles H. Hitchcock (1836–1919) was a professor of geology at Dartmouth and the first scientist in the United States to conduct a high mountain observatory.

Hites Cove [Mariposa]. The place was named for John R. Hite, a lucky miner whose yields from his claims in the Sweetwater district are said to have run into millions. The mine at the Cove was opened in 1864. The name appears on the Hoffmann-Gardner map (1867) and is listed as a post office until about 1890. The Yosemite map of the Geological Survey shows Hite Cove.

Hi Vista. *See* High.

Hoaglin [Trinity]. Named for a member of the Hoaglin (or Hoaglen) family, who settled in the district before 1900.

Hobart Mills [Nevada]. A post office was established about 1900 and was named after the Hobart Mills, which had been operating there since 1897. Walter Scott Hobart was one of the leading lumbermen of the Lake Tahoe district from the 1860's until his death in 1892.

Hobergs [Lake]. Gustave Hoberg settled here in 1885 and his summer resort became known by his name. In 1929 the Post Office Department accepted the name for the post office.

Hobo Hot Springs [Kern]. The place was first known as Clear Creek Hot Springs. When in the early 1900's the crew of a compressor camped there and helped themselves to cattle and sheep on the fields, the farmers complained to Sheriff Fred McCracken.

> After hearing these men with their tales and woes
> Said sheriff dubbed the campers a lot of Hoboes.
> Thereafter when conversation hit on such things
> There was always some reference to 'Hobo Hot
> Springs.'
> (Earl E. Lambert.)

This name was applied to the post office when it was established, February 4, 1934, and was changed to Miracle Hot Springs on November 1, 1947.

Hockett: Meadows, Lakes, Trail [Sequoia National Park]. Named for J. B. Hockett, a pioneer of the region as early as 1849, who built the trail in the years 1862–1864 (Farquhar).

Hock Farm [Sutter]. Established by Sutter in 1841 and named after an Indian village. It was Sutter's residence from 1849 to 1865. Historic Landmark 346.

Hodge [San Bernardino]. At the suggestion of Arthur Brisbane, a well-known journalist in the early part of the 20th century and owner of a ranch in the Mojave Desert, the Santa Fe changed the name of its station in 1926 from Hicks to the present name, for Gilbert and Robert Hodge, of Buffalo, New York, owners of a ranch in the desert since 1912. The name Hicks appears with Hodge on some present-day maps.

Hodges, Lake [San Diego]. In 1922 the Santa Fe dammed the San Dieguito River at the Carroll reservoir site in order to create a lake to supply water for its park development. The lake was named for W. E. Hodges, vice-president of the company.

Hodges Peak [Los Angeles]. The peak was named for Dr. J. S. Hodge, who purchased a tract in 1888 and built a wagon road to the summit.

Hoffmann, Mount [Lassen National Park]. The mountain was named for George J. Hoffmann, who camped and hunted near it for many years. He was the son of Charles F. Hoffmann, Whitney's topographer. The name of the mountain is misspelled Hoffman on the topographical maps.

Hoffmann, Mount [Modoc]. Named for John D. Hoffmann, a brother of Whitney's topographer. John D. Hoffmann was one of the group of German civil engineers who played an important part in the scientific delineation and recording of the geography of California. He is co-author of the first topographical map of the Tahoe region.

Hoffmann, Mount [Yosemite National Park]. "June 24 [1863] we climbed a peak over eleven thousand feet high, about five miles from camp, which we named Mount Hoffmann, after our topographer [Charles F. Hoffmann]. It commanded a sublime view." (Brewer, p. 407.) *See* Glossary.

Hoffmeister Creek [Shasta]. Named for Charles Hoffmeister, who had a cattle range here (Steger).

Hog. The maps show about twenty Hog Creeks, Canyons, Mountains, and Islands in California, and doubtless many more such names are used locally. The State had no native hogs, but in the early days of American occupation herds of wild hogs—descendants of domestic animals which had escaped from missions and ranchos—were still encountered. *See* Coches. **Hog Flat Reservoir** [Lassen]. The meadow now covered by the reservoir was called Hog Flat when the farmers of the irrigation district fattened huge herds of hogs on the luxurious vegetation which grew there after the first dam built to create the artificial lake had broken. The name is perpetuated in the name of the reservoir. (A. G. Brenneis.)

Hogback. The term has been used repeatedly as a descriptive name for orographic features. A Hogback Ridge is found in Death Valley National Monument, a Hogback Peak in Kings Canyon National Park, and a plain Hogback in Sonoma County. There is a Hogback Creek west of Haiwee Reservoir [Inyo], but the peak after which it was apparently named is now Round Mountain.

Holbrook Grove [Humboldt]. The grove became a part of the state park system in 1933, and was dedicated by Mrs. Silas H. Palmer to the memory of her father, Charles Holbrook (1830–1925), a pioneer dealer in stoves

and iron and a leading businessman and philanthropist of Sacramento and San Francisco.

Holcomb Valley [San Bernardino]. Named for William F. Holcomb, a native of Indiana, who came to California in 1850. In May, 1860, while employed as a bear hunter for prospectors in Bear Valley, he discovered gold in the valley which bears his name. According to L. Burr Belden (August 4, 1963), he "scooped up a handful of gravel" which he found "literally loaded with grains of gold."

Hole. Although this word is not a generally accepted generic term, it is sometimes used for depressions in the ground, for water holes, and instead of the term 'hollow' or 'cove.' In the 1870's a landmark along the road from Yreka to the Lava Beds was called Hole in the Ground, and on the Burney atlas sheet the same name is shown just west of Lassen Volcanic National Park. A depression in the land on the boundary between Fresno and Kings counties is called The Dark Hole, and in Death Valley there is a Hole in the Rock Spring. *See* Hollow; Jolla.

Hollenbeck: Flat, Butte [Modoc]. Named for Asa Hollenbeck, a cowman who used the near-by range from the 1880's to the 1920's (W. S. Brown).

Hollenbeck Park [Los Angeles]. Given to the city of Los Angeles by William H. Workman and Mrs. J. E. Hollenbeck, when Workman was mayor (1887–1888), and named at his request in memory of Mr. Hollenbeck, his "old and cherished friend" (Workman, pp. 221 ff.).

Hollister [San Benito]. Named in 1868 by the San Justo Homestead Association of farmers, for Colonel W. W. Hollister, who had driven the first flock of sheep across the continent and had acquired the San Justo grant on which the new community was established. When someone suggested at the first town meeting that the name of the land grant be retained, one citizen protested so violently against the adding of another to the long list of saints' names in the State that San Justo was rejected.

Hollister Peak [San Luis Obispo]. The name was applied by the Coast Survey in 1884 for the Hollister family, who had established a ranch at the base of the mountain in 1866. It appears as Cerro Alto (high hill) on older maps, and was also known as Morro Twin.

Hollow. The descriptive generic term is repeatedly used in geographical nomenclature, especially for depressions for which the terms valley, canyon, and glen are not suited. In Butte County north of Chico four canyons, through which tributaries to Mud Creek flow, are called Grizzly, Sheep, Cabin, and Sycamore hollows. *See* Corral Hollow; Herscheys Hollow.

Hollywood [Los Angeles]. The town which was destined to become the film center of the world was laid out and named by Horace H. Wilcox in 1886. The name is a transfer name. There is a Hollywood in the County of Dourn in Ireland, and the word occurs as a place name in the states of Arkansas, Georgia, Maryland, and North Carolina, where the American holly *(Ilex opaca)* is native, and in Minnesota, where it is apparently a transfer name, like our Hollywood. According to Tom Patterson, Mrs. Wilcox heard the name from a fellow passenger on a trip east. Mr. Wilcox imported two holly trees to justify the name but they did not survive in the temperature of southern California. The name and derivations of it became very popular after Hollywood attained its fame.

Holmby Hills [Los Angeles]. Named after Holmby, England, birthplace of Arthur Letts, Sr., founder of the Broadway Department Store, Los Angeles. In 1919 he bought Rancho San Jose de Buenos Ayres, on which the place is situated.

Holmes [Humboldt]. The place was named, in 1908, Holmes Camp, for the head man of the logging company operating there. The generic term was dropped when the post office was established in 1912. (Ruth Nalander.)

Holt [San Joaquin]. When the Santa Fe took over the San Francisco and San Joaquin Railroad in 1900, the station and town were established and named for Charles Parker Holt, who had extensive farming interests on Roberts Island and was the original builder of caterpillar tractors (Santa Fe).

Holtville [Imperial]. Established and named Holton in 1903 by W. F. Holt, president of the Holton Power Company and one of the organizers of the irrigation project for the Imperial Valley in 1899. At the request of the Post Office Department the name was soon changed to the present form.

Holy City [Santa Clara]. The town was founded in 1920 by W. E. Riker as a religious community for people of the "white race" and named so "because of the principles revealed for an indisputable solution for the Economic, Racial and Spiritual problems of this world" (E. Allington). The post office is listed in 1927.

Holy Jim Canyon [Orange]. James ("Cussin' Jim") Smith had an apiary here and the name was applied in irony (Stephenson).

Homer. *See* Amboy.

Homers Nose [Sequoia National Park]. Named in 1872 for Joseph Homer, a veteran of the Mexican War. "As my father and the two government surveyors were looking at the mountain Mr. Powell laughingly remarked, 'Homer, that south projection looks like your nose.' 'All right,' said Mr. Orth, 'I am marking it on my map as Homers Nose' and so it was named." (E. B. Homer to F. P. Farquhar.)

Homestead Valley [Marin]. Named in 1903 by the Tamalpais Land and Water Company, after the country home of S. M. Throckmorton.

Honcut: Creek, town [Butte, Yuba]. The name comes from *Hoan'kut*, the Maidu village on the Yuba just below the mouth of the creek (Powers, p. 283). Theodor Cordua, grantee of the land grant dated December 22, 1844, mentions the name in his *Memoirs* (p. 6): "This name I had given my ten-league grant, because the Honcut River formed the northern boundary of my . . . holdings . . . The names of the rancherias or Indian villages I found rather pretty, for instance . . . Honcut." The creek was apparently the one which Jedediah Smith had called Red Bank Creek (*Travels*, p. 71). It appears on a *diseño* of Rancho Honcut as *Arroyo Honcut*, and in the present form in the *Statutes* of 1850 (p. 62) and on Gibbes' map of 1852. The post office is listed in 1867.

Hondo, Honda. The Spanish adjective for 'deep' is combined with Creek or Arroyo in about ten California place names and is also found as the name for a number of communities. **La Honda,** hŏn'-dà: **Creek,** town [San Mateo]. The creek is shown as *Arroyo ondo* on several *diseños* of land grants, and as *Arroyo Hondo* on a map of Rancho Cañada de Raymundo (1856). On Hoffmann's map of the Bay region (1874) the valley of San Gregorio Creek west of La Honda Creek is designated as Honda. The post office La Honda is listed in 1880. After 1895 the name was spelled Lahonda, but the original form was restored in 1905, owing to Eldredge's efforts. **Hondo** [Los Angeles]. The post office was established in 1919 and was named after Rio Hondo, the creek on which it is situated. On *diseños* of several land grants the stream is called *Rio de San Gabriel, Rio hondo* [?] *de* *asuza,* and *Zanja Onda* (deep ditch). The San Gabriel River took a new course in 1867; the old channel became known as Rio Hondo after July, 1888 (Bowman). **Honda** [Santa Barbara]. The station was named after the Cañada Honda Creek when the last link of the Southern Pacific coast line between Surf and Ellwood was completed in 1900.

Honey Lake [Lassen]. Bruff records on October 5, 1850 (II, 871): "As this country has never been explored,—I shall take the liberty of naming this beautiful Lake, after my highly esteemed friend, Derby, of the U.S. Topographical Engineers. Capt. [George H.] Derby is now engaged in surveying in the southern part of California." And on November 7 (II, 925): "The older Hough [Lassen's former bookkeeper] related to me their first visit to Honey Lake, as they called it, from the sweet substance which they found exuding from the heads of wild oats in the basin. (I have named it L. Derby.)" The older name stuck to the lake and was placed on the map by Blake in 1853. The "honey" was not exuding from the oats, however: "This substance is deposited by the honeydew aphis, a species of bee sometimes found in dry and barren countries. It is a sweetish ... liquid, resembling honey, and ... is gathered by the Indians, who ... make a sort of molasses, of which they are fond." (Cronise, p. 222.) Most of the other physical features named Honey (including a Honey Run in Butte County) probably received their names because wild honey was found there. In Humboldt County there is a post office called Honeydew.

Hood [Sacramento]. Named in 1910 by Madison P. Barnes, for William Hood, at that time chief engineer of the Southern Pacific.

Hood: Creek, Mountain [Sonoma]. Named for William Hood, a Scotch carpenter, who came to California in 1846 and in the 1850's bought the Guilicos rancho. The mountain and creek are on this rancho.

Hoodoo. A typical miner's term, used either in the abstract sense or for an unusual rock formation. The name is preserved in Hoodoo Creek [Lake] and probably in some other topographic features.

Hooker: Canyon, Creek [Sonoma]. Named for Joseph ("Fighting Joe") Hooker (1814–1879), who had come to California in 1849, after serving as an officer in the Mexican War. Hooker purchased part of Rancho Agua Caliente in 1851 and lived there for several years. In the Civil War he commanded the Army of the Potomac, January–June, 1863.

(*CHSQ,* XVI, 304–320.)

Hooker: Creek, station [Tehama]. The creek was named for J. M. Hooker, who settled near its mouth in 1852; the railroad station took the name of the creek (McNamar). A post office was established November 20, 1885, reëstablished May 31, 1889, and discontinued October 31, 1928.

Hookton: Channel, Slough [Humboldt]. These names commemorate Hookton, an important shipping center of the lower Eel River region in the 1860's and 1870's.

Hoopa: Valley, Valley Indian Reservation [Humboldt]. "This [Hoopah], which is the name given by the Weits-pek, and other Klamath Indians, to the lower part of the Trinity and its inhabitants, I have retained for their language" (Gibbs, 1851, in Schoolcraft, III, 422). The story that the Indians used the name after they heard the drivers shout "whoop-ah, whoop-ah" in rounding up the mules of a pack train (W. N. Speegle) sounds like folk etymology; so-called "Indian names,". however, sometimes originate in this manner. The present spelling is used by Heintzelman in 1858. The name Hupa Mountain, east of Trinidad Head, is a spelling variant. Hupa is the spelling now usually used by ethnologists to designate this group of the Athabascan family. Hoopa Valley was formerly called Eden Valley.

Hooper [Siskiyou]. The place was known as Hoopersville for Frank Hooper, a miner (Co. Hist., 1881, p. 217). The shorter form was apparently used when the name was applied to a station of the McCloud River Railroad in the 1890's.

Hooper, Mount; Hooper Creek [Fresno]. R. B. Marshall of the Geological Survey named the mountain (probably at the time the Mount Goddard quadrangle was surveyed, 1907–1909) in memory of Major William B. Hooper, a native of Virginia and at one time owner of the Occidental Hotel in San Francisco, who died in 1903. The Geographic Board by decision of June 7, 1911, called the mountain Hooper Peak, but since there is already a Hooper Peak, in Yosemite National Park [Mount Lyell atlas sheet], the Geological Survey and common usage prefer Mount Hooper.

Hoover Lake [Mono]. Named in 1905 by an engineer of the Standard Consolidated Mining Company, for Theodore J. Hoover, who was at that time manager of the company at Bodie. Hoover, a brother of the former President of the United States, was professor of mining and metallurgy at Stanford University, 1919–1941.

Hoover Wilderness Area [Mono]. The name was applied in 1928 by the Forest Service, in honor of Herbert Hoover, thirty-first President of the United States, in the year of his election (G. B. Doll).

Hope Ranch [Santa Barbara]. On June 10, 1870, a patent was issued to Thomas W. Hope for 3,281.7 acres of the land grant La Calera y las Positas or Cañada de Calera. The name was changed to Hope Ranch and was transferred to the modern subdivision by the heirs.

Hopeton [Merced]. The place is an old mining camp and was named Forlorn Hope, apparently after the name of a mine, when it was still in Mariposa County. A post office was first established as Forlorn Hope, August 17, 1854. The name was then changed to Hopetown and when the post office was reëstablished, October 2, 1866, the present name was used.

Hope Valley [Alpine]. The Mormons on their trek from Sutters Fort to Salt Lake City crossed the summit here and Bigler recorded under date of July 29, 1848, "campt at the head of which we called Hope Valley as we began to have hope." In analogy, O. B. Powers and a party of surveyors in November, 1855, called the two beautiful grassy valleys to the south Faith Valley and Charity Valley.

Hopkins, Mount. *See* Crocker.

Hopland [Mendocino]. The town was started in 1859 when Knox, Willard, and Conner opened a saloon and R. (or Thomas) Harrison established a store. The place was called Sanel after the land grant on which it was situated, and is so shown on the von Leicht–Craven map. When in 1874 a toll road was built on the east side of Russian River, the town (with the exception of a brick store) was moved across the river. The name was changed to Hopland because Stephen Knowles' experiment of growing hops there had proved successful. This name appears on the Land Office map of 1879. When in 1890 the California Northwestern was extended to Ukiah, the tracks were laid on the west side of the river. Business flowed back to Sanel, and the old Indian name was given to the railroad station and the post office. In 1891 or 1892 the Post Office Department discontinued the old Hopland office but gave the name Hopland to the one at Sanel. *See* Feliz; Sanel. Attempts to grow hops on a large scale were made in other parts of the State, but the only

name reminiscent of them is Hopyard Road in the Livermore Valley, where in 1903 the Pleasanton Hop Company had four hundred acres in cultivation (E. T. Planer).

Hoppow Creek [Del Norte]. Named after the Yurok village *Ho'opeu* or *Ho'päu* (Kroeber).

Horicon [Sonoma]. The name of the school district was probably chosen by an admirer of James Fenimore Cooper. The latter, in *The Last of the Mohicans,* had called Lake George in New York "The Horicon." (Leland.)

Hornblende Mountains [El Dorado]. When the Geological Survey mapped the Placerville quadrangle in 1887, the name for a variety of amphibole was applied apparently because of the occurrence of the mineral.

Hornbrook [Siskiyou]. Named in 1886 by the Southern Pacific, after the brook which ran through the property of David Horn.

Hornitos, hôr-nē′-tŏs [Mariposa]. The town was first settled in 1852 by Mexican miners who had been driven out of Quartzburg (Kernville). The post office was established as Hornitas, June 18, 1856, and changed to present spelling August 20, 1877. In 1858 the place gained wide recognition when the Mount Gaines Quartz Mill built two arrastras (*see* Arrastre) driven by an engine of 30 h.p. The word is a diminutive of *horno,* 'bake oven,' 'kiln.' In the volcanic districts of Latin America *hornito* describes a low oven-shaped mound. But the name is doubtless a transfer name, probably from *Los Hornitos* in the Mexican state of Durango. The often repeated stories that the shallow graves of the Mexican miners looked like *hornitos,* or that German miners built little bake ovens of stones and mud belong obviously in the field of folk etymology. The little *hornitos* of brick on and near the cemetery give the impression of having been built in later years to justify the name.

Horse. In Spanish times the horse was so common a sight and was held in such little esteem that the word *caballo* rarely appears in place names. *See* Cavallo. When the first Americans and Europeans filtered into the Mexican province they found not only a wealth of domestic horses, but large herds that had gone wild. The name Horse was given to numerous creeks, canyons, flats, and lakes from the very beginning of American occupation. Today there are probably some five hundred Horse names in the State, including numerous places named for dead and blind horses, gray and black horses, wild and stud horses. Sometimes the name was transferred to post offices and communities: Horse Creek [Siskiyou], Horse Lake [Lassen], White Horse [Modoc]. About twenty Horsethief Creeks, Canyons, Points, etc., commemorate the hideouts of horsethieves or places where they were caught and punished. **Horsetown** [Shasta]. The historic landmark preserves the name of one of the richest diggings in the northern mining district in the 1850's. The original name, One-Horse Town, was probably given to the camp in derision. According to an item in the Bancroft Scrapbooks (XIII, 30), "it was named in honor of a favorite horse, the only one at the time about the camp." The abbreviated name is shown on Lapham and Taylor's map of 1856. **Horsehead Mountain** [Trinity]. The mountain was given this name because the skull of a horse which had fallen there and died could for many years be seen from the trail (K. Smith). **Horse Grotto** [Lava Beds National Monument]. When J. D. Howard explored the cave, about 1918, he found six horses belonging to a settler, Frank Adams, seeking shelter from the wind.

Horse Linto Creek [Humboldt]. A popular rendering of the name of the Hupa village at the mouth of the creek, given by Gibbs (Schoolcraft, III, 139) as Has-lintah; by McKee (Indian Report, Oct. 7, 1851) as Kas-lin-ta; by Goddard (*AAE*, I, 12) as Xaslindiñ; and by Kroeber as Haslinding. Local residents pronounce the name hôs-lĭn'-tĕn, but map makers have recorded it as Horse Linto.

Horseshoe. A popular descriptive term applied to about fifteen lakes resembling a horseshoe and to as many U-shaped river bends. The name is also found combined with Bar, Bay, Cove, Creek, Point, and Slough. The finding of a horseshoe may sometimes have been the reason for the naming.

Horton: Creek, Lakes [Inyo]. Named for William Horton, who settled in Round Valley in 1864 (Robinson).

Hospital. The names of about ten geographic features in the State include this word. **Hospital Creek** [San Joaquin, Stanislaus]. The origin of the name can be traced to the Indian sweathouses (*temescales*) near the springs in the canyon (Still). The creek is shown on Hoffmann's map of 1873. The name, however, may have resulted from a misunderstanding. On a *diseño* of El Pescadero (1843) *Ospital* seems to be a stream flowing from the hills; Goddard's map of 1860 shows the stream as *Arroyo del Osnito*. **Hospital Rock** [Sequoia National Park]. The name was given to the

huge boulder in 1873 by Hale D. Tharp when Alfred Everton, accidentally shot in a bear trap, found a temporary hospital in the shelter formed by the overhanging rock. Others had found shelter here under similar circumstances, and the Potwisha Indians had used it for their sick. (Farquhar.) **Hospital Rock** [Modoc]. The shelter formed by the rock at the south end of Tule Lake was used as a hospital by the soldiers in the Modoc War, 1872–1873 (Doyle). **Hospital Cove** [Angel Island State Park]. In 1870 the army constructed two hospital buildings in what was known as Morgan's Cove and renamed the site.

Hosselkus: Creek, Valley [Plumas]. Named for a large family of Palatinate Germans from Mohawk Valley, New York, who settled here in the early 1850's. Edwin D. Hosselkus had a general store with the Blood brothers in Indian Valley in 1855.

Hot Rock [Lassen National Park]. The rock erupted from Mount Lassen in 1915, and was thrown a distance of three miles. It retained its heat for more than a week, but the name still stuck to the rock after it cooled. (Doyle.)

Houghs Creek [Plumas]. The stream was probably named for Lassen's bookkeeper and associate in the Gold Lake hunt (1850), a man by the name of Hough (or Huff).

Howards Bluff [Humboldt]. Named for Major E. H. Howard, who owned the land on which the bluff is situated (Co. Hist., 1882, p. 128).

Howard Springs [Lake]. Named for C. W. Howard, who opened the springs to the public in 1877 (Co. Hist., 1881, p. 153).

Howlands Landing [Santa Catalina Island]. Named for William Howland, of Los Angeles. His sons Frank and Charlie acquired a sheep concession on San Clemente, where another Howlands Landing was named for them. (Windle, p. 124.)

Hoya. *See* Jolla.

Huasna, wäz'-nà: **River, Creek, Valley** [San Luis Obispo]. The Chumash name (probably of an Indian village) was transmitted through the Huasna land grant, dated December 8, 1843. *Lomeria colindante con Guasna* (hills adjacent to Guasna) is shown on a *diseño* of the Arroyo Grande grant (1842), and *Arroyo del Huasna* on a *diseño* of the Huasna grant. The name appears as *Rio Wasna* on the Parke-Custer map (1855), and on the von Leicht–Craven map Huasna Creek is shown for what is now Huasna River.

Huckleberry. Although the native evergreen huckleberry is widespread in northern and central California, only a few geographic features are named for it, including the lakes in Tuolumne and Shasta counties. The name is doubtless used locally for other features.

Huddart Park [San Mateo]. The mountain tract north and west of Woodside was named for J. M. Huddart, who bequeathed the area to the city of San Francisco in 1935 (Wyatt).

Huecos [Santa Clara]. The name of a land grant, dated May 6, 1846. The Spanish word *hueco* means 'hole,' 'gap,' 'hollow.' The name is found in other parts of the State. On March 28, 1822, the Los Nietos grant [Los Angeles] is described as consisting of the *parages llamados Los Coyotes, Las Bolsas, y Huecos y Naciós* (DSP, Ben., P & J, VI, 25).

Hueneme, wĭ-nē'-mê: **Point, Canyon,** town [Ventura]. The name was applied to the point in 1856 by James Alden, in charge of the Coast Survey steamer *Active*. The settlement was founded and named after the point by W. E. Barnard and his partners in 1870. The name is derived from the Chumash village *Wene'me* or *Wene'mu* (Kroeber). The name of the post office in 1870 was Wynema; in 1874 it was changed to Hueneme, and in 1940 to Port Hueneme.

Huerhuero, wâr-wâr'-ō: **Creek, Soda Springs** [San Luis Obispo]. The name was taken from the name of the land grant Huerhuero, dated May 9, 1842, and March 28, 1846, which in turn was derived from a *parage nombrado* [site called] *"Huergüero,"* recorded May 26, 1843 (Legis. Recs., IV, 58 f.). Rancho Huerhuero is recorded by Parke-Custer (1855), Huer Huero Creek by von Leicht–Craven (1874). The origin of the name may be the Mexican Spanish *huero*, 'putrid,' 'rotten,' especially referring to eggs, and here perhaps referring to the odor of sulphur water. There is a tendency among local people to anticipate the final *o* by pronouncing the name wâr-ô-wâr'-ō.

Huerta. The Spanish word for 'garden' or 'orchard,' once a popular generic term, which appeared in the principal or secondary name of about ten land grants or claims, does not seem to have survived as a place name. Three of the grants so named were confirmed by the United States. *See* Cerro Romualdo; Cuate; Noche Buena.

Hughes Lake [Los Angeles]. The lake is recorded as Hughe's Lake in 1898, and was doubtless named for G. O. Hughes, who owned the adjoining land (R. Flickwir).

Hughes: Valley, Mountain [Fresno]. Named for John R. Hughes, the first settler in the valley.

Hughson [Stanislaus]. Named for Hiram Hughson, owner of the land on which the firm of Flack and Jacobson laid out the town in 1907.

Huichica, wĭ-chē'-kà: **Creek** [Napa]. *Arroyo de Huichica* is shown on a *diseño* of El Rancho de Huichica, granted to Jacob Leese, July 6, 1844. According to Barrett (*Pomo*, p. 312), the name was apparently derived from that of an Indian village, *Hū'-tci*, near the plaza of the town of Sonoma. However, on a *diseño* of the Entre Napa grant (1835) a locality Huichica is shown quite a bit southeast of Sonoma.

Huling Creek [Shasta]. The tributary of Eagle Creek was named for William Huling, who settled here in 1851 (Steger).

Hull Mountain [Mendocino]. In 1856 James Hull, a settler in the Sacramento Valley, built a hunting cabin near the top of the mountain. In a fight with a grizzly he killed the animal but was so badly mauled that he died of his wounds. (Forest Service.)

Humboldt: Bay, Point, County, Creek, Hill, State Park. The bay was discovered in the summer of 1806 by Jonathan Winship, an American in the employ of the Russian American Company. It was described in Russian documents as a "bay of Indians" (Davidson, *Humboldt Bay*, pp. 10 ff.), and its entrance was named for Nicolai Resanof, the hero of the most celebrated romance of Spanish California, who was in San Francisco in the spring of 1806. The Indian name for the bay, as ascertained by Davidson in the 1850's, was *Qual-a-wa-loo*. When the Gregg party reached the bay on December 20, 1849, they believed that they had found Trinidad Bay and gave it the English version of the name, Trinity. On April 8, 1850, Captain Hans Bühne of the Laura Virginia Company entered it in a boat and a few days later piloted the company's schooner through the channel. He and Douglas Ottinger, commander of the expedition, are responsible for the present name, which honors Alexander von Humboldt (*see* Glossary), who was then at the height of his fame. A short-lived Humboldt City existed in the early 1850's. Fort Humboldt, now Historic Landmark 154, was established in 1853. The county was created and named by act of the legislature, May 12, 1853.

Humbug. A favorite prospector's term to express disappointment when a claim did not yield as much as expected, or when a creek was found to be dry. Two cluster names in Placer and Siskiyou counties originated at the time of the gold rush; the camp in Siskiyou County disproved its name by yielding richly. About ten other places still bear this name, including Big Humbug Creek [Tuolumne] and Little Humbug Creek [Sierra]. North Bloomfield [Nevada] flourished in the 1850's as Humbug or Humbug City.

Hume Lake [Fresno]. The lake was impounded from the flow of Tenmile Creek by the Hume and Bennett lumber firm, which operated a mill there at the turn of the century (Co. Hist., 1933, p. 85). A recreation area has been developed at Hume Lake by the Forest Service.

Humphreys [Fresno]. The station was named for John W. Humphreys, a pioneer lumberman and stock raiser of the Tollhouse and Pine Ridge area (Co. Hist., 1956).

Humphreys, Mount; Humphreys Basin [Fresno]. The name was applied by the Whitney Survey in honor of Andrew A. Humphreys, who played an important role in the topographical survey of the western United States and distinguished himself as a general in the Civil War.

Hunewill, hŭn'-ĭ-wĭl: **Peak, Hills** [Mono]. Named for N. B. Hunewill, who operated a sawmill in Buckeye Canyon in the 1860's to supply lumber for the mining towns. The name is misspelled Hennerville on the Bridgeport atlas sheet.

Hungry. More than ten valleys, creeks, and hollows include this word in their names, among them Hungrymans Gulch [Santa Cruz Island]. All were probably named because of failure to find food at a certain place. Some may go back to Spanish times when the adjective *hambre* was used for place names for the same reason. **Hungry Creek** [Siskiyou]. "... The place referred to delights in the significant cognomen of 'Hungry Creek,' so called doubtless from the fact of its discoverers having been hemmed in by the snows without any provisions" (Shasta *Courier,* March 19, 1853; Boggs, p. 157). *See* Raggedy-ass Gulch. **Hungry Bills Ranch** [Death Valley National Monument]. Hungry Bill was a Panamint Indian, who had served as a scout in the Modoc War and had received the ranch for his services (Death Valley Survey). There is a Hungry Packer Lake one mile northeast of Mount Wallace.

Hunters Point [San Francisco]. The place was named for Robert E. Hunter, who in 1849 participated in a project to found on the point a city called South San Francisco. On Hoffmann's map of the Bay region of 1874 the promontory is called Hunter's Point,

while the point itself bears the old name. Avisadero. Geological Survey and Coast Survey make the same distinction but spell the name Hunter Point. Hunters Point is the generally accepted designation for the entire promontory. *See* Avisadero.

Hunters Valley [Mariposa]. Hunter's Valley is mentioned by Browne (*Resources,* pp. 30 f.) in 1869 as a site of mines. It was probably named for William W. Hunter, an engineer from Pennsylvania, a resident of Mariposa in 1867 and of Hornitos in 1879.

Huntington. Henry E. Huntington, a nephew of Collis P. Huntington and promoter of most of the electric railroads in the southern part of the State, has been honored in more place names than any other of our later industrial pioneers. He will best be remembered as the donor of the Huntington Library and Art Gallery in San Marino. **Huntington Park** [Los Angeles]. Laid out in 1903 and named by the subdivider, E. V. Baker, for his friend Huntington. **Huntington Beach** [Orange]. Originally called Pacific Beach, its name was changed by the townsite company in 1903 (Stephenson). **Huntington Lake** [Fresno]. The reservoir was named in 1912 by the Pacific Light and Power Corporation, for its president, Henry E. Huntington.

Huntington, Mount. *See* Crocker.

Huntoon Valley [Mono]. Named for R. S. Huntoon, who settled here in the 1870's, or for some one of his relatives (Maule).

Hupa. *See* Hoopa.

Hurd Peak [Inyo]. The peak bears the name of the engineer, H. C. Hurd, who in 1906 made the first known ascent.

Hurdygurdy. This was a typical miner's term, applied to hand organs and to the "hurdygurdy girls." It was also the trade name of a widely used water wheel. The name is preserved in Hurdygurdy Butte and Creek in Del Norte County and in some local geographical names.

Hurleton [Butte]. The name was given in 1880 to the post office, the first postmaster of which was Smith H. Hurles, a native of Ireland. He had named his place Boston Ranch after Boston, Massachusetts, where he formerly lived.

Huron [Fresno]. The name was applied by the Southern Pacific in 1877 to a station on the proposed route from Goshen to Tres Pinos. This was the name given by the French to a group of four Iroquoian tribes in Ontario, and it became a popular place name in the United States.

Hurricane Deck [Santa Barbara]. Since early

days the name has been used for this remote and rugged section of Los Padres National Forest because of the heavy winds which frequently blow there (W. S. Brown).

Hutchings, Mount [Kings Canyon National Park]; **Hutchings Creek** [Yosemite National Park]. Named for James M. Hutchings, a native of Northamptonshire, England, who came to California in 1849. He is best known for his *Illustrated California Magazine* (1856–1861) and for his enthusiastic books on Yosemite.

Hutchinson Meadow [Fresno]. Named for James S. Hutchinson, a native of San Francisco and explorer and mountain climber in the Sierra for many years (Farquhar).

Huxley, Mount [Kings Canyon National Park]. Named in honor of the English biologist, Thomas H. Huxley (1825–1895), by T. S. Solomons in 1895. *See* Evolution.

Hyampom, hī′-ăm-pŏm [Trinity]. *Pom* is 'land' or 'place' in the Wintu tongue, but the meaning of the specific part is unknown (Kroeber). The name is sometimes spelled Hiampum. According to the County History, 1858, p. 28, the place was settled January 12, 1855, by Hank Young. The post office was established October 22, 1890.

Hyatt Lake [Tuolumne]. Named in 1909 by R. B. Marshall for Edward Hyatt, at that time topographic engineer of the Geological Survey, since 1927 the state engineer.

Hyde Park [Los Angeles]. The post office preserves the name of one of the "ghost towns" of the "boom year" of 1887, laid out by Moses L. Wicks and named for the owner of a lumber yard at the site.

Hydesville [Humboldt]. Named in 1858 for John Hyde, owner of the land on which the town was built (Ruth Stover). The post office is listed in 1867.

Hynes [Los Angeles]. The original name of the station and town was South Clearwater. When the post office was established, July 15, 1898, the name was changed to Hynes, for C. B. Hynes, superintendent of the Salt Lake Railroad. The town is now a part of Paramount.

Iaqua, ī′-ă-kwā: **Buttes** [Humboldt]. The name is probably derived from the native salutation still heard in Humboldt County. Bruff writes, on February 12, 1851 (II, 951): "He [the leader of a band of Indians] came up, and saluted me, as usual with them, saying '*Ay-a-qui-ya?*' (How do you do?) which I reciprocated and shook hands." The present spelling was used in November, 1864, when

a detachment from Fort Humboldt went to Camp Iaqua (Pico Docs., III, 171). The town "at old Fort Iaqua" is mentioned in the County Business Directory of 1895–1896, and the post office is listed in 1910.

Ibex: Spring, Hills, Pass, Wash [Death Valley National Monument]. Named for the desert bighorn, a sheep which the desert dwellers often called ibex, the name of the European mountain goat (Death Valley Survey).

Ibis: Mountain, station [San Bernardino]. In 1896 the Santa Fe named the siding Ibex (the wild goat of the Old World) to fit into the alphabetic order of stations of this section. In 1904 the name was changed to Ibis, after Ibis Mountain (left nameless on the Bannock atlas sheet), which in turn had been named for the Ibis Mine on the east slope. The ibis was a sacred bird of the Egyptians.

Icaria, ī-kâr′-ī-á [Sonoma]. The name was given by Armand J. DeHay to a French socialistic community, established here in 1881 (S. G. Morley). The Greek place name had been used by Etienne Cabet in 1840 and was adopted by the Fourierists for their utopian settlements.

Iceberg, The; Iceberg: Meadow, Peak [Alpine]. The prominent grayish rock has the appearance of an iceberg when viewed from the meadow (J. Ellis). Meadow and Peak were named after this rock when the Geological Survey mapped the Dardanelles quadrangle in the 1890's. **Iceberg Lake** [Madera]. So named because the Clyde Minaret glacier at one time discharged bergs into it. Ice still remains on the lake well into summer, owing to its elevation. (D. R. Brower.) **Iceberg Cave** [Lava Beds National Monument]. So named by J. D. Howard, in January, 1917, because there was a 20-foot-high ice pinnacle in it formed by water dropping through the ceiling.

Iceland [Nevada]. The name was given to the Southern Pacific station about 1902. Like Polaris, Floriston, Mystic, on the same sector, it is apparently just a railroad name, although appropriate enough for the place in wintertime. For Iceland Lake [Tuolumne] *see* Lewis Lakes.

Ickes, Mount [Fresno]. The mountain in Kings Canyon National Park was named in honor of Harold L. Ickes, Secretary of the Interior from 1933 to 1946 (Geographic Board, Jan.-Apr., 1964).

Idria, ĭd′-rĭ-á [San Benito]. Named after the New Idria quicksilver mine (Historic Landmark 324), which in turn had been named in the early 1850's after Idria, a production center of quicksilver on the Adriatic Sea. Brewer (Notes, July 19, 1861) calls the place New Idria, and this was the name of the first post office, established March 22, 1869. When the new post office was established, December 22, 1894, the abbreviated name was used.

Idyllwild [Riverside]. The name, suggested by Mrs. Laura Rutledge as descriptive of the timbered resort area, was accepted by the Post Office Department in 1899. Places called Idlewild are in Del Norte and Placer counties.

Ignacio, ĭg-nä'-shō [Marin]. Named for Ignacio Pacheco, a soldier of the San Francisco company after 1827 and in 1840 grantee of the San Jose grant on which the settlement is situated. The place is shown as Pacheco on Hoffmann's map of the Bay region, but with the establishment of the post office about 1895 the name was changed because there was a Pacheco in Contra Costa County.

Igo [Shasta]. According to Steger, the name was suggested in 1868 by Charles Hoffmann because he heard the little son of George Mc-Pherson say: "Daddy, I go, I go," whenever the latter left for the mine. However, the von Leicht–Craven map of 1874, revised by Hoffmann himself, has the old name, Piety Hill. The post office was established and named Igo in 1873, and the place is shown on the Land Office map of 1879. In folk etymology the name is associated with near-by Ono: Igo was named when a Chinaman driven from his claim there said, "I go," and Ono was named when the same Chinaman said, "Oh, no!" when American prospectors tried to drive him from this site too. It could not be ascertained whether this story accounts for the names of two places, Igo and Ono, in San Bernardino County which are within twenty miles of each other.

Ikes: Creek, Falls [Humboldt]. Named for a Karok Indian, "Little Ike," who lived by the falls (Kroeber). Ike's Karok Indian name was 'é:hkan (Bright, *WF*. XI, 122) .

Illilouette: Canyon, Creek, Fall [Yosemite National Park]. This outlandish name was given to the canyon because of a misunderstanding. "Tululowehäck. The cañon of the South Fork of the Merced, called the Illilouette in the California Geological Report, that being the spelling given by Messrs. King and Gardner,—a good illustration of how difficult it is to catch the exact pronunciation of these names. Mr. Hutchings spells it Toolulu-wack." (Whitney, *Yosemite Book,* 1870, p. 17.)

Bunnell (*Discovery,* 1880, p. 202) gives the original Indian name as *Too-lool-lo-we-ack,* a name which "would not bear a translation."

Immanuel Peak [Monterey]. Named for Immanuel Innocente, a neighbor of Michael Pfeiffer, for whom Pfeiffer Redwoods State Park was named (AGS: *Monterey Peninsula,* 1941, p. 184).

Imola, ī-mō'-là [Napa]. The name of the ancient city in Italy was applied in the 1920's to the post office and to the station for the state hospital. The name Imola was apparently chosen because there is a large hospital for the insane in the Italian city.

Imperial: Valley, city, County, Dam. The name came into existence when the California Development Company organized a subsidiary to colonize the newly reclaimed south part of Colorado Desert. The leading men of the project, George Chaffey, Anthony H. Heber, and L. M. Holt, considered Colorado Desert a name unlikely to attract settlers and called the promoting organization Imperial Land Company and the region Imperial Valley. The "mother town," Imperial, was platted early in 1901; the county was organized August 15, 1907. **Imperial Beach** [San Diego]. The name was applied to the seaside town apparently because of its advertising value. The post office is listed in 1910.

Ina Coolbrith, Mount [Sierra]. Named by the U.S. Geographic Board, February, 1932, at the request of the State Geographic Board, acting on behalf of the Ina Coolbrith Circle and other organizations. The mountain was formerly called Summit Peak. Ina Donna Coolbrith (1842–1928) came to California in 1849 with a party led by Jim Beckwourth (for whom a near-by pass is named). In 1915 she was named poet laureate of California by the legislature.

Inaja Indian Reservation [San Diego]. According to Kroeber, the name is derived from Diegueño Indian *Any-aha,* 'my water.' The prefix *any-* is unaccented, hence the syncopation.

Incline [Mariposa]. Named in 1923 by the Yosemite Valley Railroad for the Incline Logging Railroad, an engineering feat of lumber transportation over a 68 per cent grade (J. Law). The post office is listed in 1924.

Independence. The word has had a fascinating ring to American ears since the days of the Revolution and is used in a great number of place names. In California there are about twelve features and places so named. Some may be transfer names from the East: Independence, Missouri, was the starting point of many immigrant trains. **Independence** [Inyo]. In 1861 Charles Putnam built a stone house at the site and the place was first known as Putnam's, later as Little Pine. The present townsite was laid out by Thomas Edwards in 1866 and named after near-by Camp Independence, which had been established by Lieutenant Colonel George S. Evans, of the Second Cavalry, on Independence Day (July 4), 1862. **Independence Lake** [Nevada]. Named on Independence Day of 1852 or 1853 by Lola Montez, the actress, who was living in near-by Grass Valley at that time. *See* Lola, Mount. However, according to his manuscript in the Bancroft Library, Augustus Moore claims to have named the lake on the Fourth of July, 1862.

Indian. It stands to reason that the general racial designation of America's original inhabitants is more frequently used in place names than any other adjective of race or nationality. More than three hundred names in the State contain the term, including some ten settlements and one fanciful Indianola [Humboldt]. Some names go back to early mining and exploration days: Indian Valley [Plumas], Indian Diggins [El Dorado], Indian Creek [Siskiyou], Indiangulch [Mariposa], Indian Springs [San Diego]. Several mountains and rocks are so called because of their assumed or real resemblance to an Indian: Indian Head [Tulare], Indian Rock [Yosemite National Park], The Indians [Monterey]. There are also combinations like Dead Indian Creek [Riverside], Lake of the Lone Indian [Fresno], Indian Joe Spring [Inyo]. Trinity River was once Indian Scalp River and the site of Concord [Contra Costa] was known as Drunken Indian. **Indian Canyon** [Yosemite National Park]. "A locality in the Yosemite Valley once famous for its supply of . . . arrow-wood, was the ravine called by the Yosemites 'Le-Hamite' [the arrow-wood] . . . but which is now designated as 'Indian Cañon' " (Bunnell, 1880, p. 131).

Indio: town, **Hills, Mountain** [Riverside]. When the Sunset Route of the Southern Pacific reached the place in May, 1876, the station was named after the near-by (still existing) Indian Wells. Before 1879 the name was changed to the Spanish name for 'Indian.'

Infant Buttes [Fresno]. Named by T. S. Solomons (Farquhar). The name was perhaps applied because the buttes, although more than 10,000 feet high, look like infants when compared with the giants east of them.

Infernal Caverns [Modoc]. Historic Landmark 16 marks the site of a battle, fought on September 26 and 27, 1867, between United States soldiers, commanded by General George Crook, and a band of Indians.

Ingalls, Mount [Plumas]. The mountain was named for the Ingalls family, from New York State, who settled in the Genesee Valley before 1870.

Ingalls: Bluffs, Creek [Sonoma]. Probably named for Timothy A. Ingalls from New York, who had a farm in Knights Valley in the 1870's.

Inglewood [Los Angeles]. The town was founded in 1887 on the part of Rancho de la Centinela owned by Daniel Freeman. It was probably named by a visitor from Inglewood, Canada, who was the sister-in-law of N. R. Vail, one of the promoters (Bertha H. Fuller).

Ingomar [Merced]. A railroad name applied to the station in 1889 and to the post office January 28, 1890. The name of the successful play *Ingomar, the Barbarian,* a translation of *Der Sohn der Wildnis* by Friedrich Halm (E. F. J. Münch-Bellinghausen), probably suggested the name. (R. F. Wood.) The play was revived on the American stage in 1885.

Ingot [Shasta]. The mining town has been known as Ingot since about 1900 because of the foundry there in which metals are cast into convenient forms (ingots) for shipping. Ingot post office was established in 1919 and discontinued in 1940. (Steger.)

In-ko-pah: Gorge, Mountain [Imperial]. The name on Highway 80 was applied by the Division of Highways on the basis of an existing older name, apparently of Indian origin. According to a manuscript in the San Diego Public Library on San Dieguneo names, *in-ke-pah* is the Indian word for 'mountain tribes' (Zelma Locker).

Inskip: settlement, Creek [Butte]. Established in 1857 and named for a "Dutchman" (probably a Pennsylvania German) named Enskeep, who had discovered gold near by. **Inskip Hill, Little Inskip Hill** [Tehama] may have been named for the same man. The Marysville *Weekly Express,* July 2, 1859, reported that a Dr. Inskip had been on a trapping expedition in the Mount Lassen country that year.

Inverness: town [Marin]. Alexander H. Baily, with a Scot named Thompson, camped there in 1888 or 1889. The resort was laid out on land owned by James M. Shafter and was named, either by Shafter or by Baily, after Inverness, Scotland (Thompson's birthplace), which is said to be similar in appearance and climate. By a coincidence, James Black, who lived on the opposite side of Tomales Bay from about 1848 to 1870, and his friend Edward M. McIntosh, were also natives of Inverness-shire.

Inwood [Shasta]. The combination of words, suggesting 'hidden in the woods,' was applied to the post office on January 6, 1887 (Steger).

Inyo: Mountains, County, National Forest. The mountain range east of Owens Lake is clearly shown on the maps of the 1850's, but no name is attached to it. In April, 1860, a group of twenty or more men led by Colonel H. P. Russ and Dr. S. G. George organized the Russ Mining District in this region. When they inquired of the Indians about names, "Chief George," later a leader in the Indian war fought in that district, informed them that the name of the mountains was "Inyo" and that its meaning was apparently "dwelling place of a great spirit" (Chalfant, *Inyo*, p. 83). *See* Bally. The county was created on March 22, 1866. The national forest was established and named by executive order of President Theodore Roosevelt, May 25, 1907.

Inyokern [Kern]. The earlier name, Magnolia, was changed at the request of the Post Office Department because there was another town of the same name. The present name was adopted in 1913 by a meeting of the residents because the place is near the boundary of Inyo and Kern counties.

Ione: Valley, town [Amador]. According to an often-repeated story, the name was applied in 1848 by Thomas Brown for one of Bulwer-Lytton's heroines. It may also have been named after Ione, Illinois. On Baker's map of 1856 the valley is called Lone Valley, and one would be inclined to seek here the origin of the name. But Ione City is already mentioned in the San Francisco *Alta California* of March 3, 1852, and Ione Valley in the *Statutes* of 1854. The Placerville *Herald* of September 24, 1853, has this amusing story concerning the town: "First named 'Ione City'; then to please some, it was changed to Rickeyville, but as that name was not funny enough for the gamblers . . . they named it 'Freeze Out,' then 'Hardscrabble,' and lately it was called "Woosterville.'" Another far-fetched story is told in the publication of the Book Club of California (1945), entitled *Heraldry of New Helvetia* (p. 75). William Hicks of Tennessee came to California with the Chiles-Walker party

of 1843 and settled on the Cosumnes River, where the town Hicksville was named for him. The town of Ione was also situated on his land and was reportedly so named because he often used the phrase "I own," indicating his great wealth. The town was originally in Calaveras County. The post office was established September 3, 1852 with the name Jone Valley. On February 16, 1857 it was called Jone City; then Ione City; in 1861 Ione Valley; and in 1880 finally Ione. The actual origin and meaning of the name has never been established.

Iowa Hill [Placer]. The only survivor of several places named by miners from Iowa after their home state. Gold was discovered here in 1853, and the settlement is mentioned in the *Statutes* of 1854 (p. 222).

Ireland: Lake, Creek [Yosemite National Park]. Named by Lieutenant Harry C. Benson for Dr. M. W. Ireland, of Indiana, who was on duty in the park in 1897 and during World War I was surgeon general of the Army (Farquhar).

Irish. Maps of today show about fifteen geographic features so named—comparatively few in view of the strong Irish element among miners and settlers and the number of place names which they transferred from Ireland to California. The old mining town Irishtown [Amador] is Historical Landmark 38.

Irmulco [Mendocino]. The name of this station of the California Western Railroad was coined in 1908 from "Irvine and Muir Lumber Company" (Borden).

Iron. The word occurs in the names of about thirty mountains, probably all applied because of the presence or supposed presence of iron deposits. The fifteen-odd Iron Creeks and Springs probably owe their names to the iron content of the water. **Iron Mountain** [Shasta]. The settlement developed around the iron mines located by William Magee, deputy to the U.S. surveyor general for California, and by Charles Camden. The claim for 320 acres of unsurveyed land, including the iron deposits, was published in the Shasta *Courier*, October 21, 1871 (Boggs, p. 564).

Ironwood Mountains [Imperial]. The range was so named because of the growth of *Olneya tesota*, known as desert ironwood, the *arbol de hierro* of the Spanish Californians.

Irvine, Mount [Sequoia National Park]. Named by Norman Clyde on the first ascent in June, 1925, in honor of Andrew Irvine, who was lost on the British Mount Everest expedition in June, 1924 (Farquhar).

Irvine: town, **Park, Dam, Lake** [Orange]. About 1870, James Irvine, of San Francisco, purchased Rancho San Joaquin and established his famous orchards. When the Santa Fe built the line to Fallbrook Junction in 1888, it named the station for him. In 1913 it named a siding on the spur to Venta, Myford, for Irvine's son, and in 1923 it named another siding in memory of Irvine's wife, Frances. *See* Kathryn. The post office, established May 20, 1899, was named Myford, because there was another post office in Calaveras County at that time named Irvine, and not until March 17, 1914, was the name Myford changed to Irvine. When the University of California at Irvine was established in 1965, the Irvine post office became East Irvine, and the same year the railroad name was changed to Valencia.

Irvington [Alameda]. The place was known in the 1870's as Washington Corner (and Corners), after the township in which it is situated. March 24, 1884, the Post Office Department changed the name to Irving in order to avoid confusion with Washington in Nevada County. In spite of the protests of citizens, the Central Pacific changed the name of the station to Irvington; on March 15, 1887, this name was applied also to the post office. The name of one of our greatest writers, then at the height of his fame, had doubtless something to do with the change.

Irwin [Merced]. The town was laid out and named by W. A. Irwin in 1907 (Co. Hist., 1925, pp. 372 f.).

Irwindale [Los Angeles]. Named for a citrus grower in the area (Co. Hist., 1965, III, 256). The post office was established May 20, 1899, and the place was incorporated in 1957.

Isabel, Mount; Isabel: Creek, Valley [Santa Clara]. The peaks of what is now called Mount Hamilton were known in Spanish times as *Sierra de Santa Isabel*, as is shown on the *diseños* of several land grants. Mount Isabel is mentioned by Edward S. Townsend, April 23, 1850: "On your right rises the middle range, Mount Diablo and Mount Isabel the crowning point of the ridge..." (*CHSQ*, XI, 360). William Brewer and Charles Hoffmann of the Whitney Survey, when they climbed the mountain on August 26, 1861, named what they believed to be the highest peak Mount Hamilton, unaware that it already had a name. The valley east of the peak, however, is called Isabel Valley on the maps of the Whitney Survey. When the Geo-

logical Survey in 1895 discovered that the peak two miles southeast of the site of the Lick Observatory is really fourteen feet higher, this point was properly labeled Mount Isabel, although the mountain group itself retained the name Hamilton. *See* Hamilton.

Isabella [Kern]. Named in 1893, the year of the Columbian Exposition, by Stephen Barton, the founder of the town, "because no town on the continent of North America has been named after the good queen who financed the expedition of Columbus" (A. O. Suhre). There were at that time at least nine Isabellas in the United States, but Mr. Barton was apparently certain that none had been named for the Spanish queen. The town is now inundated by the waters impounded by the Isabella Dam.

Isabel Valley [Humboldt]. The valley was named in 1850 for Captain R. V. Warner's brig, *Isabel* (Co. Hist., 1882, p. 101).

Ishberg: Pass, Peak [Yosemite National Park]. The pass was named by Lieutenant N. F. McClure for a soldier in his detachment, a native of Norway, who in 1895 discovered the route while prospecting for sheepherders' trails (Farquhar).

Island Mountain [Trinity]. The mountain was named in the 1850's by the first settlers because it is nearly encircled by a river and two creeks. John Rockwell of the Coast Survey mentions Island Peak in 1878. The post office, established in 1905, was called Island until 1907, and then Irma until August 16, 1915, when it was given its present name.

Islay. *Slay* was the name used by the Salinan Indians for the so-called hollyleaf cherry, the *Prunus ilicifolia* (Harrington). It is mentioned as *yslay* by Fages in 1775 and soon it became the Californians' name for the shrub and its fruit, a favorite Indian food. **Islais Creek** [San Francisco]. The name *Los Islais* is recorded on the *diseño* of the petition for the grant Salinas y Visitacion in 1834. *El arroyo de los Yslais* is mentioned in a petition of Manuel Sánchez, dated February 8, 1835. In American times it is recorded as Islar in 1851 and as Islais in 1853. The early Coast Survey charts call the creek Du Vrees, for a settler, but in 1859 V. Wackenreuder restores the old name on his map. It is still used for the estuary and the bridge (*CFQ*, IV, 281 ff.; V, 298 ff.). **Islay: Creek, Hill** [San Luis Obispo]. The name was preserved through the grant Cañada de los Osos y Pecho y Islai, (valley of the bears, the breast, and the islay), dated September 24, 1845.

Isleton [Sacramento]. This unique name was given by Josiah Pool and John Brocas to the town which they built on Andrus Island in 1874.

Islip, Mount; Islip Canyon [Los Angeles]. The peak was named for George Islip, who settled about 1880 on land now included in the Angeles National Forest (Forest Service). He was probably the same George Islip, a Canadian, who had a place north of Stanislaus River in the 1850's.

Isthmus: Cove, Landing [Santa Catalina Island]. The name was applied by the Coast Survey because of the isthmus formed by the cove and by Catalina harbor.

Italian. This adjective of nationality is found in the names of about twenty physical features, most of them applied in modern times when Italian settlers played an important role in Californa agriculture, especially in viticulture.

Italy, Lake [Fresno]. Named by the Geological Survey about 1907. With a little imagination one can see on the topographical map the resemblance of the lake to the outline of Italy.

Ivanhoe [Tulare]. The name of Walter Scott's novel was first applied to the school district in 1885 at the suggestion of Mrs. Ellen Boas. The original name for the settlement was Klink for George T. Klink, auditor of the Southern Pacific. The name Venice Hill, proposed by the Venice Hill Land Company, was refused by the residents. The present name was bestowed in 1924 through the efforts of the Ivanhoe Farm Bureau. (Edith Williams.)

Ivanpah, ī'-văn-pô: **Valley, Mountain,** station [San Bernardino]. Ivanpah Valley and a settlement, Ivanpah, just east of Clark Mountain, are shown on von Schmidt's boundary map (1872). This settlement, obviously a trading camp for the mines that developed around 1870, is now vanished. When the Santa Fe built a spur into the valley it appropriated the name for the terminal. The spur was discontinued in 1920, but the name was not lost: the Union Pacific used it for its station which was formerly called Leastalk (coined from "salt lake" by shaking up the letters and putting them together again). According to O. J. Fisk and R. B. Gill, Ivanpah is Southern Paiute and means 'good (or clear, white) water.' This explanation appears logical, since the original Ivanpah was situated at one of the clear springs at the foot of Clark Mountain.

Izaak Walton, Mount [Fresno]. The name for the peak at the head of Fish Creek Canyon was proposed in 1919 by Francis P. Farquhar. It honors the author of *The Compleat Angler,* which was first published in 1653. The **Isaac Walton League of America Grove** in the Prairie Creek Redwoods State Park was dedicated October 3, 1954. The League is one of the oldest conservation organizations in the United States.

Jacalitos, jăk-á-lē'-tŏs: **Creek, Hills** [Fresno]. *Jacalito,* a diminutive of Mexican Spanish *jacal,* means 'little Indian hut.' The name probably does not go back to Spanish times, but, like many others in the region, may have been applied by American surveyors.

Jacinto, jă-sĭn'-tō [Glenn]. The place preserves the first name of Jacinto Rodríguez, who on September 2, 1844, was granted land that was sometimes called Rancho de Rodriguez (Bidwell map, 1844) and sometimes Rancho Jacinto.

Jackass. More than twenty-five place names in the State testify to the wide use of jackasses as pack animals in the mining days. Most of them originated from an incident in which a jackass played a role; some were probably applied in derision. Jackass Creeks are the most numerous, but there are also Jackass Buttes, Peaks, Rocks, Meadows, etc.; the best-known is probably the cluster name west of the junction of the Middle and South forks of San Joaquin River [Madera]. **Jackassville** [Siskiyou]. A mining camp called City of Six by its first six inhabitants was known in the neighboring camps as the "camp of half a dozen jackasses," later as Jackassville (C. L. Canfield, *The City of Six,* Chicago, 1910). **Jackass Hill** [Tuolumne] was the home of James W. Gillis, who is immortalized in Mark Twain's writings as "The Sage of Jackass Hill." **Jackass Dyke** [Fresno] is one of the few places in California where 'dyke' (i.e., an igneous rock wall which has resisted erosion) is used as a generic term. It was not named after the animal, but after Jackass Meadow. **Jackass Flat** [Shasta]. The sad story of a jackass that kicked against progress is told in the Redding *Republican Free Press* of March 7, 1885 (Boggs, p. 709): "The locomotive started ahead, when the animal threw up his tail, kicked up his heels, and blazed away. But alas for the jack, he landed partially on the track, and the remorseless wheels of the locomotive cut off poor jack's fore and hind leg. The poor fellow rolled down the bank, and his kind master came along and put an end to his misery. The railroad boys have named the terrible scene of disaster, 'Jackass Flat.' "

Jack London Historic State Park [Sonoma]. The park, honoring one of California's famous literary men, was created in 1960 on Jack London's ranch near Glen Ellen.

Jack Main Canyon [Yosemite National Park]. Named for Jack Main (or Means), who ran sheep in this canyon for many years, beginning in the early 1870's (Farquhar).

Jacks Backbone. *See* Backbone.

Jackson: town, **Gate, Valley, Creek, Butte** [Amador]. The mining camp was first known as Bottileas because of the many bottles (*botillas*) which had accumulated near the spring where travelers stopped on their way to the southern mines. When "Colonel" Alden M. Jackson, a lawyer from New England, opened an office in the camp and became generally liked for settling quarrels out of court, the grateful miners named the place for him. The post office was established July 10, 1851, while the town was still in Calaveras County. It is said that the original name of the butte was Polo Peak, named for an Indian chief. The "Gate," a fissure in the reef of rocks which crosses the creek, was discovered by a boy from Sacramento in 1849 and is now Historic Landmark 118. **Jacksonville** [Tuolumne] was named for the same Jackson; both towns appear on Gibbes' map of 1852.

Jacks Valley [Lassen]. Named for John Wright, known as "Coyote Jack," who settled here in 1864 (Doyle).

Jacoby Creek [Humboldt]. Named for A. Jacoby, an early settler. In the 1850's and 1860's Jacoby's brick store in Union (now Arcata) was used as a refuge during Indian attacks (Coy, *Humboldt*, p. 199). The name was placed on the map by von Leicht and Craven as Jacoby River.

Jacumba, hȧ-kŭm'-bȧ: **Mountains, Valley, Hot Springs,** town [San Diego]. *La Rancheria llamada en su idioma Jacom* (the village called Jacom in their language) is mentioned May 13, 1795 (PSP, XIII, 222). The name is repeatedly found in documents, with various spellings. It is recorded for the mountains as *la sierra de Jacum,* June 8, 1841 (DSP Ben. P & J, IV, 14), and Jacum Pass is mentioned in the Pacific Railroad *Reports* (Vol. V, Pt. 1, p. 41). The name was preserved in the old Jacumba House around which the town developed when the San Diego and Arizona

Eastern was built in 1917. The word may be Diegueño with the stem *aha,* 'water.'

Jail Canyon [Inyo]. The name appears on Wheeler atlas sheet 65-D (Topography) and may have been given because the canyon might easily be converted into a jail by guarding the entrance. The "Land Classification" of the same atlas designates it as Tail Canyon. *See* Calaboose Creek.

Jalama, hȧ-lăm'-ȧ: **Creek,** station [Santa Barbara]. A Chumash rancheria, *Jalama,* of Mission La Purisima is mentioned as early as 1791 (Arch. MPC, p. 10), and *una cañada* ... *Jalama* is recorded July 25, 1834 (DSP Ben. Mil., LXXIX, 105). The name also appears on several *diseños* with the same spelling. According to Kroeber, the Indian name was *Halam,* but its meaning is unknown.

Jamacha, hăm'-ȧ-shô [San Diego]. According to Kroeber, the name is derived from Diegueño *hamacha,* 'a small wild squash plant.' A rancheria *Xamacha* is mentioned November 30, 1775 (PSP Ben. Mil., I, 5); this is called *Rancheria de Jamacha* the next year (SP Sac., VIII, 72), and in a later record *Jamocha* or *San Jacome de la Marca.* The Indians of the village participated in the attack upon San Diego Mission, November 4, 1775. The land grant Jamacha or Jamacho is first recorded December 1, 1831. The spelling of the Geographic Board is Jamacao (*Sixth Report*).

Jamesburg [Monterey]. Named for John James, who founded the town in 1867.

Jamestown [Tuolumne]. The name was given to the town which was started in 1848 by Colonel George F. James, a San Francisco lawyer. It appears on Gibbes' map of 1852. After a series of disputes with Mexican settlers, which ended in James' ruin and departure, the name of the town was changed to American Camp, but later the old name was restored. Locally the place is known as "Jimtown."

Jamul, hä-mōōl': **Creek, Butte, Mountains,** town [San Diego]. According to Kroeber, the name is derived from Diegueño *ha-mul* (from *aha,* water) and means 'foam' or 'lather.' A *capitanejo de Jamol* is mentioned by *Comandante* Rivera, San Diego, August 10, 1776 (PSP, I, 227), the *Jamol* apparently being an Indian rancheria. The *sitio de Jamul* is repeatedly mentioned in records of the 1820's, and on April 20, 1831, Pío Pico was given permission to occupy provisionally *el parage llamado* [the place called] *Jamul* (Dep. Recs., IX, 98). In 1837 the rancho was attacked by Indians and the caretakers were slain. It was regranted to Pío Pico, December 23, 1845.

Janes Creek [Humboldt]. Named for H. F. Janes, formerly of Janesville, Wisconsin, who came to California in 1849.

Janesville [Lassen]. The post office was named in 1864 by L. N. Breed, the first postmaster, either for Jane Bankhead, wife of the village blacksmith, or for Jane Hill, who was born here on May 17, 1862; possibly for both.

Japatul, hä′-pȧ-tool: **Valley** [San Diego]. The name probably preserves the name of the Indian village, *Japatai*, which was still in existence in the early 1880's. The first syllable may be from Diegueño *aha*, 'water.' According to J. C. Hayes, the name is derived from an Indian word *japa*, designating the fruit of the prickly pear, and was first applied to a placer-mining area across the border in Lower California (San Diego *Union*, Dec. 7, 1873).

Jaquima. *See* Hackamore.

Jarro. The Spanish word for 'jug' or 'pitcher' was used repeatedly in Spanish place names and is preserved in two names. **El Jarro Creek** [Santa Barbara]. A *cañada* called *el Yarro* is mentioned July 25, 1834 (PSP Ben. Mil., LXXIX, 105), and an *Arroyo del Jarro* is shown on the *diseño*, 1837, of the San Julian grant. **El Jarro Point** [Santa Cruz]. The Agua Puerca y las Trancas grant was first made on October 12, 1839, as El Jarro (also spelled Tarro). The *diseño* of 1843 shows *Arroyo de Jarro* (probably Scott Creek). Lorenzo, an old Indian of Mission Santa Cruz, stated that there was an Indian tribe called *Jaraum* who lived "up the coast" (Co. Hist., 1892, p. 46). The Coast Survey did not apply the name to the point until after 1910.

Javon: Canyon, Creek [Ventura]. The name of the canyon one mile southeast of Seacliff is derived from the Spanish *jabón* (soap) and is reminiscent of one of the strangest of the numerous California mineral booms. It was started in 1875 when H. L. Bickford began to work the so-called "rock soap" mine in the canyon. Within a short time a number of companies, including the Pacific Soap Company, were organized to take soap right out of the earth (Co. Hist., 1883, pp. 423 ff.). Extravagant claims were made for the miracle product, which was made into scrubbing soap, toilet soap, salt-water soap, and even tooth powder. The same year, samples of this mineral were shown at the Paris Exposition and attracted considerable attention (Hanks, *Report*, 1884, p. 345). It turned out, however, that the mineral was infusorial earth suitable

only for polishing jewelry and silverware, and California's soap bubble burst.

Jawbone Canyon [Kern]. The name was applied by prospectors because the outline of the canyon suggests a jawbone. Other physical features bear this name; most of them were probably so named because the jawbone of some animal was found at the place.

Jayhawker: Spring, Well [Death Valley National Monument]. The spring, by which the Jayhawkers (*see* Glossary) camped in 1849, was so named in 1936 by the Park Service; it was formerly known as Hitchens' Spring for James Hitchens, who camped there in 1860. The well, by which they also camped, was long known as McLean's Spring.

Jedediah Smith: Redwoods State Park; Memorial Grove [Del Norte]. The prominent features of the Smith River–Mill Creek State Park honors one of the greatest pathfinders of the West. The grove was established at the suggestion, and with the support, of Charles M. Goethe of Sacramento. *See* Smith River.

The Jedediah Smith Mountain, 15 miles northeast of Gasquet, was for some reason changed to Jedediah Mountain by a decision of the Geographic Board, July-Dec., 1965) .

Jeff Davis: Peak, Creek [Alpine]. The peak appears on Wheeler atlas sheet 56-B as Sentinel Rock. The present name was apparently not recorded on maps until the district was mapped by the Geological Survey in 1889; it may, however, have long been used locally, as many of the inhabitants of near-by Summit City (now abandoned) were Confederate sympathizers during the Civil War.

Jellico [Lassen National Forest]. The name was applied to the section-crew camp of the Western Pacific about 1930. The near-by Jelly Camp may have suggested the name.

Jelly Camp [Lassen National Forest]. The name was given to a sheepherder's camp in the early 1890's, probably by Victor Ayle, a homesteader. It is shown on the maps of the Forest Service, but the reason for its application is not known.

Jenkinson Lake [Mono]. Named for Walter E. Jenkinson, who was chiefly responsible for creating the reservoir by damming up Sly Park Creek (Geographic Board, March, 1957).

Jenner: Creek, town [Sonoma]. Probably named for Elijah K. Jenner, a native of Vermont, or for his son Charles, a native of Wisconsin; both were living in the county in the 1860's.

Jennie Lake [Kings Canyon National Park].

Named by S. L. N. Ellis for his wife, Jennie, in 1897 (Farquhar).

Jenny Lind [Calaveras]. Established as a mining camp in the early 1850's and named in honor of the Swedish singer, whose tour of eastern cities in 1850–1852, managed by the great Barnum himself, created a furor of excitement throughout America. Despite the persistent legend, Jenny Lind never visited California. The place is now Historical Landmark 266. In the columns of *Las Calaveras* there are various stories concerning the origin of the name: Jenny Lind *had* come to California during her tour through the United States; a man by the name of Dr. J. Y. Lind founded the place; the braying of mules prompted the miners to use the name of the great singer in sarcasm. The name was popular and was often used because the "Swedish nightingale" was so widely known. Big Arroyo in Tulare County was formerly called Jenny Lind Creek, after a mine near its banks.

Jerusalem Creek [Shasta]. The branch of Cottonwood Creek was named by Jewish settlers (Steger). **Jerusalem Valley** [Lake]. Named by Saphonia, daughter of Charles Copsey, who came from Missouri in 1856 with an emigrant train ("The Knave," June 30, 1957). El Rio [Ventura] was once called New Jerusalem, and Brewer (Notes, June 7, 1862) mentions an "Old Jerusalem," apparently in Alameda County.

Jesmond Dene [San Diego]. Named in the 1920's by a Scotchman, after the public park in Newcastle-upon-Tyne, northern England.

Jess Valley [Modoc]. Named for Jonathan Jess and his brother, pioneers of the 1860's.

Jesus Maria. *Rio Jesus Maria*, as the name for a stream, was used in 1808 by Gabriel Moraga for that part of the Sacramento which is north of the junction with the Feather River. Within the next forty years the name was applied to various rivers, real or imaginary: the upper Sacramento, a branch of the San Joaquin, an eastern branch of the lower Sacramento, a river between the Sacramento and the San Joaquin, a river rising near Cape Mendocino and emptying into the northwestern part of San Francisco Bay, and finally to Cache Creek in Yolo County. (Bowman.) On October 21, 1843, the name Rio de Jesus Maria was applied to a land grant in what is now Yolo County. *See* Quesesosi. **Jesus Maria** [Santa Barbara]. The name of a land grant, dated April 8, 1837.

Jesus Maria Creek [Calaveras]. The creek and

a settlement (Historic Landmark 284) were named for a Mexican by that name who raised vegetables there in the mining days. The place is shown on Lapham and Taylor's map of 1856. The local pronunciation is sōōs má-rē'-á.

Jim Crow: Creek, Ravine [Sierra]. "While we were camped at Slate Range [in the fall of 1849], one of our men went back for a Kanaka and an Indian. The Kanaka he returned with, was Jim Crow, whose name still lives in those regions" (Wm. Downie, *Hunting for Gold*, p. 35). "Our next meeting [with Jim Crow] was in the following spring, at Crow City, at the head of Jim Crow Canyon, as these places are now called " (*ibid.*, p. 52).

Jim Dollar Mountain [Lake]. Probably named for James Henry Dollar, a native of Indiana, who settled in the county in 1867 or earlier.

Jimeno, hǐ-mē'-nō [Yolo]. Named after the Jimeno land grant, dated November 2, 1844, which was so called for its grantee, Manuel Jimeno Casarin, a well-known political figure in the last decade of Mexican rule.

Jimgrey [San Bernardino]. A contraction of the name of Jim Grey, a road foreman of engineers, given to a railroad siding established by the Santa Fe in 1900.

Jim Jam Ridge [Trinity]. Jim jams was a term used by the miners of the district for the result of overindulgence in alcohol, now commonly called the "jitters." In the 1890's three miners on a "sobering-up" hike had so many "sobering-up" drinks that one of them rolled into the campfire, with his pocket full of 30-30 shells. His companions were so affected by "jim jams" that they named the spot for it. (Bill Noble to W. E. Hotelling.) The name was put on the map of the Trinity National Forest in 1935.

Joaquin Rocks. *See* Murieta.

Jobs: Peak, Sister [Alpine]. In the early 1850's Moses Job opened a store in Sheridan at the foot of the mountain which soon became known by his name. The State Surveyor General's *Report* of 1856 speaks of Job's Group of Mountains (p. 141), and Hoffmann's map of 1873 calls the peaks of the range collectively Job's Peaks. In 1893 the Geological Survey applied the name Jobs Sister to the middle peak and Freel Peak to the western peak.

Jobs Peak [San Bernardino]. The peak northwest of Lake Arrowhead was so named because a cow (or a mule) called Job wandered up the slope and got lost (Wheelock).

Johannesburg [Kern]. Named about 1897 by

the founders, Chauncey M. Depew and associates, after the famous mining center in the Transvaal, South Africa. It is popularly known as Joburg.

John Little State Park [Monterey]. In 1953, Elizabeth Livermore Schmidt presented the park to the State and named it for a friend, John Little, a pioneer of the area.

John Muir Trail. *See* Muir.

Johnson, Mount [Kings Canyon National Park]. The name was originally bestowed by R. B. Marshall upon the present Mount Lewis, for Willard D. Johnson (1861–1917), a member of the U. S. Geological Survey. To avoid confusion with the near-by Johnson Peak, the name was transferred to its present location.

Johnson Canyon [Riverside]. The canyon in the Cleveland National Forest was named in 1960 in memory of Steven W. Johnson, a U.S. Forest Service employee who lost his life in the Decker fire in August, 1959.

Johnsondale [Tulare]. The mill town was named in 1938 by the Mount Whitney Lumber Company for Walter Johnson, one of its officials (Mitchell).

Johnson Peak [Yosemite National Park]. Named by R. B. Marshall, for a teamster and guide with his survey party in the 1890's (Farquhar).

Johnsons Ranch [Yuba]. The land grant, dated December 22, 1844, was first known as Rancho de Pablo, for Pablo Gutiérrez, the grantee. Gutiérrez, Sutter's old Mexican employee, was killed in the Micheltorena campaign, and the title to part of the grant was subsequently acquired by William Johnson, a native of Boston who came to California in 1840. For several years after 1845 Johnson's Ranch was well known as the first settlement reached by the overland immigrants after crossing the Sierra.

Johnstone Peak [Los Angeles]. Named by the Forest Service for the late W. A. Johnstone, for many years a leader in forest conservation. Approved by the Geographic Board in 1940.

Johnstonville [Lassen]. The settlement was originally known as Toadtown because, according to tradition, little toads covered the ground after a rainstorm. In December, 1864, the Board of Supervisors changed the name to Johnstonville, for Robert Johnston, pioneer farmer in the valley.

Johnsville [Plumas]. Founded in 1876 and known as Johnstown, for William Johns, manager of the Plumas Eureka Mine. The present name was adopted when the post office was established in 1882.

Jolla, hoi'-à. *Jolla* (or *joya*, or *hoya*) is a common Mexican geographical term referring to a hollow in the mountains, a hollow worn in a river bed, or a hollow on the coast worn by waves. Peñafiel calls it a *corrupción de la palabra castellana Hoya que significa concavidad ó excavación de la tierra* (corruption of the Castilian word *hoya*, which means hollow or excavation in the ground). The name occurs in three different sections of San Diego County but is also found in other parts of the State. **La Jolla Creek** [Fresno] is shown on the Dark Hole atlas sheet; an intermittent creek rising in the Lompoc Hills [Santa Barbara] is called La Hoya; and a third spelling variant is found in **La Joya Peak** [Ventura]. The Portolá expedition called the "hollow" at their camping place, in what is now Monterey County, on September 17, 1769, *La Hoya de la Sierra de Santa Lucia* (Crespi, p. 192), a name which did not survive. The sodomites among the Indians were called *joyas* (Fages, p. 33), but this application of the word cannot be connected with any of the place names. Bunnell mentions the use of the word by the Yosemite Indians in the 1850's: "Ho-yas . . . referred to certain holes in detached rocks west of the Sentinel, which afforded 'milling privileges' for a number of squaws, and hence, the locality was a favorite camp ground. The 'Sentinel' or 'Loya' . . . marked the near locality of the Ho-yas or mortars." (Bunnell, 1880, pp. 212 ff.) **La Jolla Valley** [San Diego]. An Indian rancheria called *La Joya* is mentioned in 1828 (Registro, p. 37). The name for the valley, three miles southwest of Lake Hodges, is shown as *La Hoya* on a *diseño* of the San Bernardo grant (1841); and two *diseños* of the Encinitas grant (1845) show *Joya* about where Olivenhain now is. **La Jolla Indian Reservation** [San Diego]. Here the name was preserved through an unconfirmed land grant to two Indians, dated November 7, 1845. The *diseño* of the grant shows an *Arroyo de la Hoya* as a tributary of what is now San Luis Rey River. The name is spelled La Joya on some maps. **La Jolla:** town, **Point, Bay, Caves, Mesa, Canyon** [San Diego]. It is not known whether the name at the coast has any connection with La Jolla Valley on the San Bernardo grant or whether it was applied independently. The present town was laid out in 1869. The Pascoe map of 1870 shows clearly lot numbers 1286 and 1288 in a hollow, called La Joya, just back of the Beach and Tennis Club (H. F. Randolph). On the maps of the Coast Survey and the Land Office the name is shown variously spelled, in one or in two words. The first post office, established February 29, 1888, was called La Jolla Park; the second, established August 17, 1894, Lajolla. This was changed, on Eldredge's insistence, to La Jolla, June 19, 1905. The popular tradition that the name is derived from the Spanish word *joya*, 'jewel,' sounds plausible since "y" and "ll" were interchangeable, but it is supported by no evidence.

Jolon, hŏ-lōn': **Creek**, post office [Monterey]. Jolon is an aboriginal site of Salinan Indians (Kroeber); the meaning of the name is 'valley of dead trees,' according to Paul Parker. Bancroft shows the name of the locality near San Antonio Mission on his map (1885) of the Monterey district as it existed in 1801–1810 (II, 145). *Cañada de Jolon* is recorded on a *diseño* of the Los Ojitos grant (1842). The name does not seem to appear on early American maps, but Jolon ranch and post office are mentioned by Brewer, May 8, 1861 (p. 93).

Jones Valley [Shasta]. The valley near Bear Mountain was named for a Mrs. Jones who was killed there by Modoc Indians in 1864 (Steger).

Jonive, hŏ-nē'-vĕ: **Hill** [Sonoma]. The hill west of Sebastopol preserves the name of the grant Cañada de Jonive, one of James Black's grants, dated February 5, 1846. A *Cañada de Jonive* is shown on the *diseño*. The name is probably the result of a misspelling or misunderstanding; it is not in any Spanish dictionary and it sounds neither Pomo nor Wappo Indian.

J. O. Pass [Sequoia National Park]. The name was given in 1889 by S. L. N. Ellis and stands for the first two letters of *J*ohn W. Warren's name, which had been carved in a tree by Warren a few years before.

Jordan, Mount [Sequoia National Park]. Named in 1925 by the Sierra Club in honor of the educator and scientist, David Starr Jordan (1851–1931), president and chancellor of Stanford University. Jordan himself had proposed the name Crag Reflection for a part of the peak.

Joseph Grinnell, Lake. *See* Grinnell.

Josephine, Mount [Los Angeles]. Named for the daughter of Phil Begue, a ranch owner in the vicinity.

Josephine Lake [Kings Canyon National Park]. Named by S. L. N. Ellis for Miss Josephine Perkins (Farquhar).

Josephine Peak [Los Angeles]. The peak was named for Josephine Lippencott, whose husband used the elevation for a triangulation station (W. C. Mendenhall).

Joshua Tree National Monument [Riverside, San Bernardino]. Created in 1936 by proclamation of President Franklin D. Roosevelt. A post office, Joshua Tree, was established July 16, 1946. The desert tree (*Yucca brevifolia*) was named Joshua tree by the Mormons, to whom it seemed to be a symbol of Joshua leading them to the promised land. However, the names Twenty-nine Palms Oasis, Fortynine Palms Canyon, Lone Palm Oasis, Lost Palm Canyon, although they are within the monument, derive their names not from the Joshua tree, sometimes called yucca palm, but from the *Washingtonia filifera* (E. N. Fladmark). *See* Palm.

Jota [Napa]. The land grant La Jota, conveyed to George C. Yount, October 21, 1843, may have been named for the Spanish dance *la jota*. *See* Polka.

Jovista [Tulare]. When a spur of the Southern Pacific was built in 1923, railroad officials coined the name for the station from the two initial letters of Joseph Di Giorgio's given name and the Spanish word vista, 'view.' *See* Di Giorgio.

Jubilee Pass [Death Valley National Monument]. This name, placed on the Avawatz atlas sheet by the Geological Survey in 1933, was suggested by that of the Jubilee Mine.

Jughandle Gulch [Mendocino]. So named because the old road across it made a turn in the shape of a jughandle (Stewart).

Judah, Mount [Placer]. The name, approved by the Geographic Board in 1941, was given, at a rather late date, in memory of the great railroad construction engineer Theodore D. Judah, who built the first California railroad and was the guiding spirit in building the Central Pacific across the Sierra Nevada.

Judson Reservoir [San Diego]. Named in the 1880's, probably for Lemon Judson, who owned a ranch in the district.

Julian [San Diego]. Laid out in 1870 by Drew Bailey and named for his cousin, Mike S. Julian, a mining recorder on whose government claim gold quartz had been discovered.

Jumbo Knob [Los Angeles]. The terminal knob of the Linda Vista crescent of hills was named in 1884 because of a fancied resemblance to Barnum's elephant, Jumbo (Reid, p. 374).

Jump-Off Creek [Mendocino]. Named after a former road, which was so steep at this point that wagons descending it were braked with drags of hewn trees (F. Price).

Junction. This geographical term is commonly applied to places where railroads, highways, mountain ranges, rivers, and county borders meet. **Junction City** [Trinity]. The post office was transferred from Messerville, August 19, 1861 and was named Junction because of the old mining center which had developed at the junction of Canyon creek with Trinity River about 1850. **Junction: Meadow Peak** [Sequoia National Park]. The meadow at the junction of the Kern and Kern-Kaweah rivers was named by W. B. Wallace in 1881, and the peak by J. N. LeConte in 1896, because it is at the junction of the Kings-Kern Divide with the main Sierra crest (Farquhar). **Junction: Butte, Bluffs** [Madera]. The names were applied because butte and bluffs are situated at the junction of the North and Middle forks of San Joaquin River, probably by the Geological Survey when the Mount Lyell quadrangle was surveyed in 1898–1899. **Junction Ridge** [Kings Canyon National Park]. The continuation of Monarch Divide west of Wren Peak was first called Junction Dike when the Geological Survey mapped the Tehipite quadrangle in 1903. At the western end of the ridge is the junction of Middle Fork and South Fork of Kings River.

Juniper. The occurrence of at least one of the four native species of juniper in almost all parts of the State has given the name to more than twenty-five physical features and settlements. **Juniper Lake** [Lassen National Park]. The lake was named after the peak south of it, which was once called Juniper Peak because a beautiful specimen of *Juniperus occidentalis* was on its slope. The peak was renamed Mount Harkness in the 1890's.

Junipero Serra, hŭ-nĭp'-ĕ-rō sĕr'-à: **Peak** [Monterey]. The name honors Padre Junípero Serra (1713–1784), founder of nine missions in Alta California during his presidency of the missions from 1769 until his death. The Native Daughters of the Golden West had first (June, 1905) bestowed the name upon a peak in the High Sierra, but the name was transferred to the former Santa Lucia Peak upon the recommendation of the Sierra Club, and the transfer was affirmed by the Geographic Board in 1907. "He was familiar with the Mountain [range] of Santa Lucia . . . and it is believed that he never saw the Sierra Nevada . . . The name of Junípero Serra in the Sierra Nevada will be simply a geographical record; his name upon one of these coast peaks that barred the expedition of 1769 and 1770, will be a living designation to some

marked and well known landfall, appealed to every day by the mariner and traveller." (Letter of George Davidson, Oct. 5, 1905.)

Juntas [Contra Costa]. A land grant dated October 20, 1832, and February 12, 1844. Since the grant is just south of Suisun Bay, it is probable that the name was derived from *Junta de los quatro Evangelistas* (junction of the four evangelists), a name, probably referring to the "meeting" of the waters, shown on the Ayala-Cañizares map of 1775 and on later maps. For many years the name was preserved in Las Juntas station of the old San Ramon branch of the Southern Pacific.

Juristac [Santa Clara]. The name of the land grant, dated October 22, 1835, includes a Costanoan place name. The locative ending *-tak* is frequently found in Costanoan village names (Kroeber). The grant was also known as La Brea and as Los Germanos (Antonio and Faustino German were the grantees).

Jurupa, hŭ-rōōp'-à: **Mountains,** station [Riverside, San Bernardino]. The name was applied because the range and the railroad station are situated on the territory of the Jurupa land grant, dated September 28, 1838. Jurupa, even earlier, had been a rancho of Mission San Gabriel. According to Kroeber, the name is Serrano or Gabrielino Shoshonean, *Hurupa* or *Hurumpa*, but its meaning is unknown. Jurupa is mentioned as a place by Ord in 1849 (p. 119) and is shown on his sketch of the Los Angeles plains. Riverside was apparently first called Jurupa (*see* Riverside); however, the von Leicht–Craven map of 1874 shows the two names in different locations.

Kagel Canyon [Los Angeles]. Named for Henry Kagel, who took up a claim on government lands at the mouth of the canyon (T. R. Wilson).

Kaiser [San Bernardino]. The station was named by the Southern Pacific for Henry Kaiser, "miracle man" of World War II, one of whose war plants was in near-by Fontana. **Kaiser: Creek, Creek Diggings, Pass, Peak, Peak Meadows, Ridge** [Fresno]; **Creek Ford** [Madera]. According to L. A. Winchell, Kaiser or Keyser Gulch was mentioned as early as 1862 (Farquhar). It appears as Kaiser Gulch on Hoffmann's map of 1873 and as Kaiser Creek on Bancroft's map of 1882. The other features were named by the Geological Survey and are shown on the Kaiser atlas sheet of 1904. It is possible that the gulch was named for Elijah Keyser, a native of Pennsylvania and argonaut of 1849. (*CFQ*, IV, 92 f.) He struck it rich somewhere in the mines, but neither he nor any other person named Keyser has been identified with this particular location. It is also not impossible that the gulch was originally named for Richard Keyes, a successful miner of 1853, and that the present version is the result of a misunderstanding. At the time of World War I, many places in the United States named Kaiser were changed, but the three other Kaiser Creeks in California, all probably named for local residents, likewise weathered the storm.

Kanaka, kȧ-năk′-ȧ. The common designation for a native of the Hawaiian Islands is contained in the names of about twelve geographic features, apparently all in northern counties, including Kanaka Glade [Mendocino]. (Glade is a generic term rarely used in California.) Kanakas were widely employed as sailors, and some accompanied early trapping parties even before Sutter brought his islanders in 1839. All Kanaka place names probably originated in the mining days, but the term was loosely used and some names may have been applied for reasons other than the presence of Pacific Islanders. There is no evidence to show that the names Kanaka Creek [Sierra] and Kanaka Bar [Trinity] have anything to do with sons or cousins of King Kamehameha, as has often been asserted. *See* Jim Crow.

Kanawyers, kȧ-nô′-yẽrz [Kings Canyon National Park]. Napoleon ("Poly") Kanawyer for many years maintained a camp at Copper Creek near its confluence with the South Fork of Kings River (Farquhar).

Kane Spring [Imperial]. According to an article in the *Overland Monthly* (Nov., 1904), the spring was named for the first owner. Since the name is also spelled Cane the origin may perhaps be found in the growth of canes at the place. *See* Canebrake. **Kane: Springs, Lake** [Kern]. The springs northeast of Cantil were apparently named for Grover Kane, repeatedly mentioned in Marcia Wynn's book. Near-by Koehn Lake was also known as Kane Lake.

Kangaroo. Several place names in northern counties, including Kangaroo Mountain [Siskiyou], were probably given because of the presence of the kangaroo rat. "Nice, harmless animals . . . on my ranch where they danced around in large numbers on beautiful summer evenings" (Cordua, p. 26).

Kaseberg Creek [Placer]. Named for James W.

Kaseberg, a native of Germany, who had a large ranch adjoining Roseville.

Kashia Indian Reserve [Sonoma]. The name, of unknown origin, was applied by the Indian Office, about 1920, to the reserve upon which it settled a band of Pomo Indians (Leland).

Kathryn [Orange]. Named in 1923 by the Santa Fe, for Kathryn Irvine, daughter of James Irvine, owner of the San Joaquin rancho (Gertrude Hellis). *See* Irvine.

Kavanaugh Ridge [Mono]. The ridge was named for Stephen ("Steve") Kavanaugh, who was employed about 1900 by M. P. Hayes to drive a tunnel along a gold vein high on the ridge from the East Fork of Green Creek. Steve never became rich, although the Chemung Mine, which he located and named after his home town in Illinois, has produced more than a million dollars' worth of ore. (Maule.)

Kaweah, kä-wē′-ȧ: **River, Peaks,** post office, **Basin, Gap** [Sequoia National Park]. The name is derived from the name of the Yokuts tribe *Kawia* or *Gȧ′-wia* (Kroeber), who lived on the edge of the plains on the north side of the river. The tribal name appears as *Cah-was* in the Johnston Report (Aug. 31, 1851), as *Cahwia* in the Indian Report (p. 254), and with many spelling variants in other documents of the 1850's and 1860's. The name seems to have no relation to that of the Cahuilla Indians in Riverside County, although it is similarly pronounced. The river itself had been discovered and named *San Gabriel* by a Spanish expedition in 1806 (Arch. MSB, IV, 40). It is mentioned by Padre Juan Cabot in 1814 and is shown on the Estudillo (1819) map as *Rio de San Gabriel*. Derby's map (1850) records "River Frances or San Gabriel." In the Indian Report the first of the four creeks forming the delta is called Cowier on April 28, 1851, and in the Johnston Report the Cahuia River is mentioned on September 26, 1851. It is shown as Cahwia on Tassin's map (1851). In the Pacific Railroad *Reports* the stream is mentioned as the "Pi-pi-yu-na, or Kah-wée-ya, . . . very commonly known as the Four Creeks" (Vol. V, Pt. 1, p. 13). Most maps of the 1850's label the river system Four Creeks. The modern version, Kaweah, appears on Goddard's map (1860). Mount Kaweah was named in September, 1881, when J. W. A. Wright, F. H. Wales, and W. B. Wallace made the first ascent. They named the other three peaks of the group Mount Abert, Mount Henry,

Mount LeConte, but these are now known as Black, Red, and Gray Kaweah (Farquhar). The post office was named Kaweah in 1889 because it was at the headquarters of the Kaweah Co-operative Colony, founded by Burnette G. Haskell. *See* Colony. Kaweah was once commonly called Ragtown. *See* Rag.

Keane Wonder; Keane Spring Canyon [Death Valley National Monument]. The names are reminiscent of the Keane Wonder Mine, near Chloride Cliff, discovered by Jack Keane and associates in 1903.

Kearney [Fresno]. Named for M. Theo. Kearney, a wealthy landholder, who came to the county about 1873 and died in 1906 (Co. Hist., 1919, pp. 218 ff.).

Kearny, Camp [San Diego]. The reservation was named by the War Department at the time of World War I, in memory of General Stephen W. Kearny, whose name has been associated with this area since he led the "Army of the West" from New Mexico to San Diego in 1846. A town on Bear River [Yuba], doubtless named in his honor, is mentioned in the *Statutes* of 1850 (p. 101).

Kearsarge, kẹr'-särj: **Peak,** station [Inyo]; **Pass, Lakes, Pinnacles** [Kings Canyon National Park]. After the Confederate raider *Alabama* had sunk the Union warship *Hatteras* off the coast of Texas, January 11, 1863, the range north of Owens Lake was named Alabama Hills by Southern sympathizers. When the Union man-of-war *Kearsarge* in turn destroyed the *Alabama* off the coast of France, June 19, 1864, Thomas May and his partners called their claims the Kearsarge Mining District (organized September 19, 1864). Kearsarge is mentioned as a stage station on June 23, 1866 (S.F. *Alta California*), and Kearsarge Mountain is shown on Hoffmann's map. Since the Union warship was named after Mount Kearsarge, New Hampshire, we have (as with Dunderberg) a California peak named after an eastern peak via a warship and a mine. The names were applied to the other features by the Geological Survey when the Mount Whitney quadrangle was mapped in 1905.

Keddie: Ridge, Peak [Plumas, Lassen]; post office [Plumas]. Named for Arthur W. Keddie, a native of Scotland who came to California in 1863, was surveyor of Plumas County 1870–1871 and 1874–1877, and made the original survey for the Western Pacific route. The post office is listed in 1910.

Keeler [Inyo]. The station was named in 1882 for J. M. Keeler, manager of the Inyo County Marble Quarry. Keeler was a fortyniner, who went back east to fight in the Civil War, in which he earned a captaincy.

Keeler's Needle [Sequoia National Park]. Named in 1881 by S. P. Langley, for his assistant in the Mount Whitney expedition, James E. Keeler (1857–1900), later a well-known astronomer and director of Lick Observatory (Farquhar).

Keen Camp [Riverside]. Named in 1880 for the Keen family, the first white settlers of the district (H. D. King). The post office is listed in 1910.

Keene [Kern]. The post office was first established February 13, 1879, and was doubtless named for a member of the Keene family, prominent in the district.

Keith, Mount [Kings Canyon National Park]. Named by Helen M. Gompertz in July, 1896, in honor of the well-known California landscape painter, William Keith (1838–1911), a native of Scotland and frequent companion of John Muir in his High Sierra travels (Farquhar).

Kekawaka, kĭk'-à-wä-kê, **Creek** [Trinity]. According to its sound, the name might be from the local Lassik dialect of Athabascan (Kroeber). Local tradition gives *keka* for 'creek,' and *waka* for 'frog' (Church Willburn). The creek is shown on the Mining Bureau map of 1892; the station was named when the last link of the Northwestern Pacific was built in 1910.

Keller: Peak, Creek [San Bernardino]. Apparently named for Francis D. Keller, a native of Illinois and pioneer farmer in the district after 1854.

Kellogg, Mount. *See* Rodgers Peak.

Kelly Mountain [Plumas]. Named for the head of the Kelly family, the first settlers in the vicinity.

Kelsey [El Dorado]. Named for Benjamin and Samuel Kelsey (brothers of Andrew of Kelseyville), who opened the diggings here in 1848. The place is shown on Trask's Mining District map of 1853.

Kelseyville, Kelsey Creek [Lake]. The town was established in the 1860's and called Kelsey Town in memory of Andrew Kelsey, the first settler in the county and a troublesome character, who was killed in 1849 by the Indians in revenge for his mistreatment of them. The post office name at first was Uncle Sam, after the mountain of the same name. About 1885 the names of the town and the post office were changed to Kelseyville. *See* Konocti.

Kelso [San Bernardino]. Named for a railroad official in 1906 when a railroad siding was established there by the San Pedro, Los Angeles and Salt Lake Railroad (now the Union Pacific).

Kelso Creek [Kern]. Named for John W. Kelso, who brought goods by ox team from Los Angeles during the Kern River gold rush in the 1860's.

Keluche Creek [Shasta]. The tributary of McCloud River was named for Dr. Keluche, Sr., who supervised an Indian orphanage on his rancheria (Steger).

Kendrick: Peak, Creek [Yosemite National Park]. The peak was named in 1912 by Colonel W. W. Forsyth in honor of Henry L. Kendrick (1811–1891), veteran of the Mexican War and professor of chemistry at the U.S. Military Academy from 1857 to 1880.

Kennedy: Lake, Peak [Tuolumne]. The name was applied because the lake was included in the strip of land patented to Andrew L. Kennedy, August 27, 1886, for grazing purposes (Forest Service).

Kennedy Peak [Inyo]. The mountain near the Nine Mile Canyon Road was named for a local rancher (Wheelock).

Kennedy Table [Madera]. The plateau northwest of Kerckhoff Powerhouse was probably named for Alexander Kennedy, a native of Maryland and a stock raiser at Millerton in the 1860's.

Kennett [Shasta]. The town, the site of which is now covered by the waters of the Shasta reservoir behind Shasta Dam, was named in 1884 by the Central Pacific Railroad for Squire Kennett, a stockholder. During World War I it was a thriving copper-smelting and shipping center. The name is now preserved only in the Kennett Division of the U.S. Bureau of Reclamation.

Kenshaw Spring [Shasta]. Apparently a Wintu Indian name of unknown origin and meaning. According to Powers, *shaw* or *chow* means 'valley.' *See* Hetten.

Kensington Park [Contra Costa]. Named after Kensington, England, by Robert Bousefield, when the tract was opened in 1911 (L. Ver Mehr).

Kentfield [Marin]. Albert Emmett Kent established his home here in 1872 and called it Tamalpais. The adjacent station of the North Pacific Coast Railroad was also called Tamalpais until the 1890's, when it was changed to Kent to avoid confusion with the name of the newly built Tamalpais Scenic Railway. When the post office was established about 1905, the name was changed to Kentfield. (Elizabeth Kent.)

Kent Grove [Humboldt]. Named in memory of William Kent (1864–1928), who had donated the grove for public use. He had previously given Muir Woods to the federal government but had declined President Theodore Roosevelt's suggestion to name it Kent Woods. Kent (a congressman from 1911 to 1917) was the son of Albert Emmett Kent, of Kentfield.

Kenwood [Sonoma]. Named before 1887 by a Mrs. Yost, after the town in Illinois.

Kerckhoff: Dam, Lake, Dome [Fresno]. The lake and dam derive their names from the Kerckhoff plant, which was put into operation by the San Joaquin Power Company on August 5, 1920. William G. Kerckhoff, of Los Angeles, was a well-known promoter and philanthropist and one of the organizers of the company. Kerkhoff Canyon [Los Angeles] was probably named for the same man.

Kerman [Fresno]. The Southern Pacific station was named Collis (for Collis P. Huntington) when the connecting line from Fresno was built in 1895. In 1906, when W. G. Kerckhoff and Jacob Mansar of Los Angeles established a colony of Germans and Scandinavians from the Middle West, the settlement and the station were called Kerman, a name coined from the first three letters of each promoter's last name.

Kern: River, County; Kernville [Kern]. **Kern: Canyon, Flat, Hot Springs, Lake, Peak, Point, Ridge; Little Kern River, Little Kern Lake, Kern-Kaweah River** [Tulare]. The name of the river was given by Frémont in 1845 for his topographer and artist, Edward M. Kern, of Philadelphia, who narrowly escaped drowning while attempting to cross the stream. *See* Rio Bravo. Francesco Garcés had named the river *Rio de San Felipe* on May 1, 1776 (Coues, *Trail*, I, 280 ff.). In August, 1806, Padre Zalvidea renamed it *La Porciuncula* for the day of the Porciuncula Indulgence, August 2 (S.F. *Bulletin*, June 6, 1865). The name continued to be used locally and elicited this statement from Williamson in 1853: "This stream was, and is now, known to the native Californians as the Po-sun-co-la, a name doubtless derived from the Indians" (Pac. R.R. *Reports*, Vol. V, Pt. 1, p. 17). As late as 1860 "Kern or Porsiuncula R." is found on Goddard's map. A Kerns Pass is given on Gibbes' map, apparently for the now nameless pass at Kern Flat. The same map shows a Kern Lake (now disappeared) in Kern County. The lake in Tulare County was formed by a landslide in 1867–1868 and was named after the river. Kernville was known as Whiskey Flat in the early 1860's. The county was created from parts of Tulare and Los Angeles counties and named by act of the legislature, April 2, 1866. The name Kern-Kaweah River was bestowed by a Stanford University party in July, 1897, upon the west branch of the river which had been known since 1881 as Cone Creek.

Kerrick Canyon [Yosemite National Park]. Named for James D. Kerrick, who took sheep into the mountains about 1880 (Farquhar).

Kessler: Spring, Peak, Range [San Bernardino]. The names perpetuate the memory of a settler named Kessler, who was killed supposedly by Indians about 1890. One of the suspected Indians was tried and was hanged from an oak tree at Kessler Spring, but it is not certain that he was guilty. (Gill.)

Keswick [Shasta]. Named by the Mountain Copper Company, Ltd., for its president, Lord Keswick, of London, when operations were begun in 1896 (M. E. Dittmar).

Kettenpom Valley. See Hetten.

Kettle. A favorite descriptive term for kettle-like depressions as well as for kettle- or dome-shaped mountains. **The Kettle** [Kings Canyon National Park] was the name applied by the Whitney Survey to the natural amphitheater at the upper course of Sugarloaf Creek: "From this camp, and the next . . . two miles farther up the divide, an examination was made of an interesting and characteristic feature in the topography of this granitic region, and to which the name of 'The Kettle' was given" (*Geology*, I, 374). This name has apparently never appeared on maps (not even on those of the Survey), but the mountain southwest of this amphitheater is Kettle Peak. There are also a Kettle Dome and a Kettle Ridge in the park, north of the Middle Fork of Kings River. Another Kettle Peak is found in Mono County, a Kettle Mountain in Shasta County, and a Kettle Rock in Plumas County.

Kettleman: Plain, Hills, City [Kings]. Named for David Kettleman, who came to California in 1849, went back to the Missouri River, and returned with a herd of cattle, which he pastured in the hills west of Tulare Lake (J. W. Beebe). Kettleman Plains and Kettleman School House are shown in the county atlas of 1892. The Geographic Board approved the name Kettleman, "not Kittleman," for the plain and hills on May 6, 1908. Kettleman City was laid out in 1929 as the first "oil

town" in the county by A. Mansford Brown.

Keyes, kēz [Stanislaus]. The name was given to the Southern Pacific station about 1897, probably in memory of Thomas J. Keyes, who died in 1895. Keyes had represented the county in the State senate from 1871 to 1874.

Keyes Peak [Yosemite National Park]. Colonel W. W. Forsyth named the peak in 1912, for his son-in-law, Lieutenant Edward A. Keyes (Farquhar).

Keyesville [Kern]. The ghost town, which is Historic Landmark 98, was named for Richard Keyes, whose discovery of gold in Key's (or Keyes) Gulch about 1853 caused the Kern River gold rush. *See* Kaiser Creek.

Keys Creek [Marin]. Named for John Keys, a native of Ireland, who came to California in 1849, used this once-important waterway in 1850, and took up land along the creek (Co. Hist., 1880, pp. 402 ff.).

Keystone: Mountain, Ravine; Ravine Creek [Sierra]. The names go back to the rich Keystone Mine, which was developed before 1857 and in 1866 had a twelve-stamp mill.

Kiavah Mountain [Kern]. The name of the mountain west of Walker Pass was apparently not placed on the map until the Geological Survey mapped the Kernville quadrangle in 1906. According to Crites (pp. 225, 267), the peak was known as Scodie Mountain but was renamed for the chief of a tribe that came from Panamint Canyon and took up residence in Sage Canyon.

Kibbie: Creek, Lake, Ridge [Yosemite National Park]. Named for H. M. Kibbie, who owned land in the vicinity (Farquhar).

Kibesillah, kĭb-ĕ-sĭl'-à [Mendocino]. The name of the region and of the bare rock north of Fort Bragg may contain the Southwestern Pomo words, *kabe*, 'rock,' and *sila*, 'flat' (Kroeber). Another interpretation is that it means 'head of the valley' and refers to the point where the mountain spurs project into the ocean and the valley ends (Co. Hist., 1880, p. 168). Kibesillah Mountain is mentioned by John Rockwell of the Coast Survey in 1878 and this name appears on the maps of the Survey.

Kimball Island [Sacramento]. The island opposite Antioch was named for George W. Kimball, who came from Maine to California in 1850 as captain of a sailing vessel. He settled at the site of Antioch and was the first postmaster, first notary public, and first justice of the peace in New York township. When his land was declared part of Los Medanos grant, he bought the island which now bears his name.

Kimball Plains [Shasta]. The plains were named for "Kimball Bill," who was in charge of the sheep range of Cone & Kimball of Red Bluff (Steger).

Kimshew Creek [Butte]. According to Powers (p. 283), the name is from the Maidu Indian *ki-wim se'-u,* 'little water.' The Indians may not have applied the term to this particular stream. Kimshew is mentioned by Browne in 1868 (p. 160) as a place where a tunnel had been run to strike the old channel under Table Mountain. *See* Nimshew. On this as well as on Little Kimshew Creek there were prosperous gold-mining camps in the 1850's and 1860's.

King, Mount. *See* Clarence King, Mount; Starr King, Mount.

King City [Monterey]. Named for C. H. King, who laid out the town on his Rancho San Lorenzo when the Southern Pacific was extended to that place in 1886.

Kingdon [San Joaquin]. The place was called West Lodi when the Western Pacific reached it in 1909. In 1915 the railroad renamed the place for Kingdon Gould, a grandson of Jay Gould. (Amy Boynton.)

Kings Beach [Placer]. Named by the residents for Joe King, in recognition of his gifts to the community. The post office was established March 25, 1937.

Kingsburg. *See* Kings River.

Kings: Meadows, Creek, Falls [Lassen National Park]. The meadows were named for James W. King, who ran horses and mules in the mountains near Lassen Peak and owned a race track at Pine Grove in the 1860's (Steger).

Kings Mountain [San Mateo]. The highest elevation of the Sierra Moreno is quite commonly called Kings Mountain, from the Kings Mountain House, which was operated for many years by Mrs. Honora King (Wyatt). Honora was probably the widow of Frank King, who had come from Indiana to California in 1852 and in the 1860's acquired the Mountain Brow House and eighty acres of land (Co. Hist., 1878, p. 39).

King Spur. *See* Clarence King.

Kings Ridge [Sonoma]. Doubtless named for William King, a native of Canada, who settled at West Austin Creek after 1876 and later was for many years a supervisor and assessor of the county (Co. Hist., 1911, pp. 941 ff.).

Kings: River, River Canyon, County, Canyon National Park; Kings-Kern Divide. The river was discovered and named *Rio de los Santos Reyes* [river of the Holy Kings] by a party of Spanish explorers in 1805, according to Padre Muñoz' diary of the Moraga expedition of 1806 (Arch. MSB, IV, 1–47). The first party probably reached the river on January 6, the festival of the three Magi; hence the name. Padre Cabot used the name *Rio de Reyes* in 1814 (Arch. MSB, VI, 67–72), a form which appears on Estudillo's map of 1819 and on later maps. Jedediah Smith in 1827, ignorant of the Spanish name, called it the *Wim-mel-che,* for the Indians living on the river (Merriam in *SCB,* XI, 376). Frémont reached the river on April 8, 1844, at a time of the year when most of the flood flow passes southward to Tulare Lake. Hence he called it "River of the Lake" (*Expl. Exp.,* p. 363). After he had learned of the Spanish name, he spoke of "*Rio Reyes* of Tulárè Lake" (*Geog. Memoir,* 1848, p. 30). Preuss labeled the stream on both of his maps "Lake Fork," a name also used by Frémont (*op. cit.,* p. 18). Derby's map (1849) and Williamson's report (Pac. R.R. *Reps.,* Vol. V, Pt. 1, p. 13) have the translation King's [!] River, but the *Statutes* of 1852 (p. 240) as well as Gibbes', Blake's, and Eddy's maps have the modern version. Kings River Canyon was explored and named by the Whitney Survey in 1864. Kings County was created from a part of Tulare County and named on March 22, 1893; the national park, in 1940. **Kingston** [Kings]. Historic Landmark 270 preserves the name of the old ferry station opposite Laton, first known in 1856 as Whitmore's Ferry, then as Kings River Station, finally as Kingston. **Kingsburg** [Fresno]. The name was adopted in 1875 for the settlement which was originally known as Kings River Switch, then as Drapersville, and later as Wheatville.

Kingston: Springs, Peak, Range, Wash, settlement [San Bernardino]. Kingston Spring is mentioned by the Nevada Boundary Survey on February 20, 1861 (Sacramento *Union,* June 29, 1861). It is said that the name was applied by a member of Frémont's second expedition, after Kingston, New York (O. J. Fisk). Frémont's party traversed the region in the spring of 1844, but Preuss fails to record the name on his maps. However, on June 2, 1854, Peg-leg Smith told S. N. Carvalho (*Travels and Adventures . . . ,* New York, 1859, p. 234) that the name Kingstone Springs had long been in use. The peak is shown on the von Schmidt boundary map of 1872, and the name was affixed to the mountains, including Nopah Range, by the Whitney and Wheeler surveys. *See* Nopah.

Kinney Lakes [Alpine]. The lakes near Ebbetts Pass, known in the 1860's as Silver Lakes, were named for David Kinney, a native of Iowa, who was a farmer at Silver Mountain in 1873.

Kinyon [Siskiyou]. The old post office White Horse, across the line in Modoc County, was given the name of the boss of the logging camp on August 1, 1952.

Kirker Creek, Pass [Contra Costa]. The stream through the old coal-mining district was known as Quercus Creek. When the Mt. Diablo quadrangle was surveyed in 1898 the name Kirker Creek was applied. The name of the pass originated about 1852 when James "Don Santiago" Kirker, a native of Belfast, Ireland, and a well known Indian fighter in New Mexico and Chihuahua, lived here in his cabin in Oak Springs near the pass.

Kirkville, Kirk Lake [Sutter]. Named for T. D. Kirk, who in 1874 laid out a town which he called Kirksville at the place known as Colegrove Point (Co. Hist., 1879, p. 98). *See* Colegrove.

Kirkwood [Tehama]. When the section of the Central Pacific from Willows to Tehama was built in 1882, the station was named for Samuel J. Kirkwood, Secretary of the Interior in 1881 (Ruth L. Zimmerman).

Kirkwood Lake. *See* Lake Kirkwood.

Kirman Lake [Mono]. The lake was named for Richard Kirman, Sr., an early cattleman (Maule). The name is misspelled Carmen on the Bridgeport atlas sheet.

Kit Carson: Pass [Alpine]; post office [Amador]. The pass was named by Frémont for his guide in crossing the Sierra Nevada in February, 1844. *See* Carson. The post office was established June 16, 1951.

Kittinelbe [Humboldt]. The place derives its name from an old Indian village given as *Ketinelbe* by C. Hart Merriam (Drury). Although this name still appears on Thomas' map and in its Index, the place is now known by the name of the post office, Phillipsville.

Klamath: River, Lake, National Forest. The name is derived from *Tlamatl*, the Chinook name for a sister tribe of the Modocs who called themselves *Maklaks*, 'people' (Kroeber). The first person to use the derivative in a geographical sense was apparently Peter Ogden, who refers to "Claminitt Country" in a letter of July 1, 1826 (McArthur), and to the "waters of the Clammitte" in his diary of

November 27, 1826 (*OHQ*, XI, 209 ff.). An English-speaking person easily substitutes initial "kl" for "tl" because the latter does not occur in English at the beginning of a word. On the maps the name of the river appears variously with "tl" and "kl" (or "cl") as initial letters and with many spelling variants. Duflot de Mofras's map of 1844 shows the position of the river fairly accurately. The Yurok Indians at the junction of the Klamath and Trinity rivers called the river below, *Poh-lik*, signifying 'down,' and the one above, *Peh-tsik*, meaning 'up' (Schoolcraft, III, 138). The lower Klamath was apparently the stream upon which Jedediah Smith's name had been bestowed in 1828 (Wilkes' map, 1841). *See* Smith River. The present spelling of the name became current when the short-lived Klamath County was established, April 25, 1851. Klamath National Forest was established and named by presidential proclamation in 1905. The bay four miles north of the mouth of the Klamath is named False Klamath Cove, probably because its outline when seen from the ocean resembles that of the bay at the river mouth; False Klamath Rock was obviously named (or misnamed) after the cove, for there is no "true" Klamath Rock. The name was repeatedly applied to settlements and post offices. A now-vanished town, Klamath, near the site of Requa, existed in 1851. Two communities in Del Norte County are called Klamath and Klamath Glen. The settlement called Klamath River [Siskiyou] was first called Honolulu, then (until 1934) Gottville for William N. Gott. **Klamathon** [Siskiyou]. In 1890 James McLaughlin built a mill here and named it Pokagama, an Indian name which he had brought from Wisconsin. When John R. Cook ran the mill in 1892 he renamed it Klamathton, the name of the river plus the suffix -*ton* (town). The name Pokagama was then applied to the logging camp near Shovel Creek Springs. (Schrader.) Klamathton appears as Klamathon on modern maps.

Klinefelter. *See* Amboy.

Klondike [San Bernardino]. The choice of this name by the Santa Fe in 1897 for one of the hottest spots in the Mojave Desert was doubtless influenced by the discovery of rich gold deposits on the river in Canada. Klondike Lake [Inyo] and Klondike Canyon [Monterey] probably owe their origin likewise to the Klondike gold rush in 1897.

Kneeland [Humboldt]. The post office was established before 1880 and named after Knee-land's Prairie, a place which had been named for a settler of the early 1850's, John A. Kneeland (Co. Hist., 1882, p. 148).

Knightsen [Contra Costa]. Founded in 1898 when the San Francisco–San Joaquin Valley Railroad (now the Santa Fe) was built, and named for G. M. Knight, a prosperous farmer who had donated the right of way to the railroad. The name was suggested by Mr. Knight and includes the suffix of his wife's maiden name, Christen*sen*.

Knights Landing [Yolo]. The name commem-orates William Knight, of Indiana, who settled here in 1843. The town was laid out in 1850 and is shown on Gibbes' map. The post office name was for many years Grafton, for the man who established the mail route from Benicia to Yolo in 1855 (Co. Hist., 1940, p. 235). **Knights Ferry** [Stanislaus]. After the discovery of gold, William Knight moved to this place, where he operated a ferry. When he died in 1849, John C. and Lewis Dent (General Grant's brothers-in-law) and James Vantine took over the busi-ness. No evidence has been found to support Bancroft's statement that it was called Dent-ville (VI, 514). The *Statutes* of 1850, the In-dian Report (1851), and Gibbes' map (1852) all have the present name.

Knights Valley [Sonoma]. Named for Thomas Knight, the first permanent settler in the val-ley in the 1850's. Knight's Creek and Knight's Valley are mentioned by Brewer in 1861.

Knob. The American generic term for a round hill or small mountain is found in California in the names of about fifty orographic fea-tures. Most of these are in the southern half of the State; in the north the term butte is generally used for this type of elevation. Since the word ordinarily refers to an isolated hill, or at least one jutting out above others, it is often combined with the word Pilot to desig-nate a landmark [Fresno, Imperial, Kern, San Bernardino]. Kern and Mariposa counties each have a tautological Knob Hill. The post office Knob [Shasta] is named after a near-by knob, and the Southern Pacific station Knob [Imperial], formerly Pilot Knob, after the old landmark near the corner where Califor-nia, Arizona, and Mexico join.

Knotts Berry Farm [Orange]. The famous ber-ry farm was developed by Walter Knott in the 1920's. In 1940 he added a "ghost town" to his farm. It consisted of relics from real ghost towns in Southern California and Ari-zona. *See* Caliente.

Knowland State Park [Alameda]. The park and arboretum, opened September 9, 1951, were named for the late Joseph R. Know-land (1873-1966), for many years publisher of the Oakland *Tribune*.

Knowles [Madera]. Named by the Southern Pacific in 1890 for F. E. Knowles, the founder of the town.

Knownothing Creek [Butte, Siskiyou]. The names of the two creeks are reminiscent of the American party, usually called the Know-Nothing party because its members, when questioned, replied that they "knew noth-ing" about the party. Its short but spectacular career shook the country in the 1850's. In the seventh session of the State assembly (1856) the American party had the majority, though only a few members were rabid "Know-Nothings"; most of them were Whigs, whose party was disintegrating. Knownoth-ing was a favorite name for mines, and the creek in Siskiyou County (a tributary to Salmon River) was named after the Know-nothing Mine at Gilta.

Knox Mountain [Modoc]. The mountain in the Modoc National Forest was named for Robert Knox, who built a sawmill here in 1874 (Forest Service).

Knoxville [Napa]. Named for one of the pro-prietors of the Manhattan Quicksilver Mine. A post office was established November 30, 1863. The place is mentioned in a letter from Hoffmann to Whitney, November 29, 1870, and in the reports of the Mining Bur-eau until modern times. It was in Lake County until 1872.

Knulthkarn Creek [Humboldt]. The name of the tributary of Klamath River (south of Pekwan Creek) is an American rendering of Yurok *Knū'Lkenọk Wroi* (Waterman, map 11).

Koehn Lake [Kern]. The now dry lake south of the road from Mojave to Randsburg was named for Charley Koehn, a German home-steader at Kane Springs. His place was a stopping point before the discovery of the gold deposits in 1893, and it had a post of-fice from 1893 to 1898. (Wynn, p. 60.) The lake is also known as Kane Lake, or Desert Lake.

Kohler, Camp [Sacramento]. Named in 1942 by the War Department for Lieutenant Frederick Kohler, the first Signal Corps offi-cer killed in World War II, a graduate of the University of California.

Koip: Peak, Crest [Yosemite National Park]. The name for the mountain was fixed by

Willard D. Johnson of the Geological Survey about 1883. It is probably a Mono Indian word; according to Kroeber, *koipa* means 'mountain sheep' in the closely related Northern Paiute dialect.

Kokoweep, kō-kō-wēp′: **Peak** [San Bernardino]. According to James Fletcher Morris, a prospector at Mineral Springs, the name Kokoweep means 'canyon of winds' in the local Paiute dialect and refers to the canyon from Mineral Springs through Ivanpah Mountain to the valley in which the peak is situated. The name is misspelled Kokoweef on the Ivanpah atlas sheet. (Gill.)

Kolmer: Creek, Gulch [Sonoma]. Named for Michael Kolmer, who settled here in 1848. *See* Coleman Valley.

Konocti, kŏ-nŏk′-tī, **Mount** [Lake]. George Gibbs had named the isolated peak Mount M'Kee for Colonel Redick McKee, who explored the Clear Lake region in 1851 (Schoolcraft, III, 109 f.). In 1854 Martin Hammack and Woods Crawford named it Uncle Sam Mountain and it appears with that name on the von Leicht–Craven map. The Geographic Board (*Sixth Report*) decided for the local Indian name of the peak, which, according to Barrett (*Pomo,* p. 183), was *Kno'ktai,* derived from *kno,* 'mountain,' and *xatai,* 'woman.' The locally accepted interpretation of *konocti* is 'thrown horse'; it is said that the name arose because of the peculiar shape of an open space on the mountainside—now covered but not obscured by a walnut orchard—which looks like a fallen horse with its head held down (Ruth Lewis). This interpretation, as well as the story that the horse was shot down while carrying two lovers, doubtless belongs in the realm of white men's lore.

Korbel [Humboldt]. The place was known as North Fork when the Korbel brothers built their mill there in 1882. June 24, 1891, the post office was established under the name Korbel (Borden). Korbel Rock is mentioned in Davidson's correspondence as early as 1872. Near-by Korblex is obviously derived from Korbel.

Kosh Creek [Shasta]. The tributary of Pit River was named for John Kosh, a native of Russia who was superintendent of the Silver City Mine in the 1860's and later operated a ferry across the Pit River (Steger).

Kramer: station, Hills [San Bernardino]. The Southern Pacific in 1882 gave the name to the junction from which a branch led to the Johannesburg and Randsburg mines. The

Santa Fe retained the name for the present station. One Moritz Kramer, a native of Germany, is listed in the Great Register of 1879.

Kreyenhagen Hills [Fresno, Kings]. The range was named for the Kreyenhagen brothers, large-scale cattle breeders, whose headquarters were on Zapato Creek at the foot of the hills. Their father, Gustave Kreyenhagen, a native of Germany, had come to Merced County in 1867 and had settled at the place which became known as Kreyenhagen's. *See* Los Banos. Kreyenhagen Shale of the oil-producing geological formation around Coalinga was named after the original Kreyenhagen Ranch.

Kruse Rhododendron Reserve State Park [Sonoma]. This part of the old Rancho German was given to the State by Edward, Emil, and Mollie Kruse, and was made a state park January 8, 1934.

Kuna: Peak, Crest, Ridge, Creek [Yosemite National Park]. The name of the peak was fixed, about 1883, by Willard D. Johnson of the Geological Survey. *Kuna* means 'firewood' in the Mono dialect, and 'fire' in Shoshonean, according to Kroeber.

Kunkle Reservoir [Butte]. The reservoir was named after the mining place Kunkles, shown on the county map of 1862 and named for a settler of the region.

Kyburz, kī′-bûrz [El Dorado]. The post office was established in 1911 and named for the first postmaster, Albert Kyburz, the son of Samuel Kyburz, a native of Switzerland and an important figure at Sutter's Fort before and during the gold rush.

La. Names preceded by the Spanish feminine article *la* which are included in cluster, group, and folk names will be found under the first letter of the name proper. Example: La Canada is listed under Canada.

Labrea Creek. *See* Brea.

Lac [Sonoma]. A place called *Lac* by the Indians is mentioned in the petition of May 21, 1844, for the land grant of this name, dated July 25, 1844 (Bowman).

Lacjac [Fresno]. Coined by Daniel J. Ellis in 1899 from the names of the firm *Lac*hman & *Jac*obi, for whom he built at this place a winery and distillery, at that time the largest in the world.

Lack Creek [Shasta]. Named for De Marcus Franklin Lack, who settled at the creek, a tributary of Bear Creek, about 1860 (Steger).

La Crescenta [Los Angeles]. The place was settled in the early 1880's and named by Dr. Benjamin B. Briggs. From his home he could see three crescent-shaped formations, which suggested to him the artificial name with the Romanic touch. The name was accepted for the post office in 1888. (H. A. Scheuner.)

Ladder Butte [Lassen National Forest]. The Forest Service gave the name about 1929, when it built a lookout station there.

Ladybug. A number of canyons, as well as a peak in Sierra County, bear this name because they are hibernation refuges of the brightly colored beetle (properly a ladybird, the Vedalia), so valuable in the control of California citrus pests.

Lady Franklin Rock [Yosemite National Park]. Named for Lady Jane Franklin, widow of John Franklin, the British naval officer whose attempt to discover the Northwest Passage in 1847 led to one of the worst Arctic disasters. Lady Franklin visited Yosemite in 1863 and admired the view of Vernal Fall from this rock (Farquhar).

Lafayette: town, Creek, Ridge, Reservoir [Contra Costa]. The town stands among the fifty or more other places in the United States named in honor of the great Frenchman who fought in our War of Independence, the Marquis de Lafayette. The first settler was Elam Brown, who bought the Acalanes rancho and settled near the site of Lafayette, February 7, 1848 ("The Knave," Feb. 8, 1948). The settlement was named in 1853 by Benjamin Shreve, the owner of the store; the post office was established March 2, 1857, with the name spelled La Fayette originally.

Lagoon. Both the English 'lagoon' and the Spanish *laguna* are derived from Latin *lacuna*, 'pool,' 'pond,' but in English-speaking countries the term is now almost entirely restricted to a sheet of water near or communicating with the ocean. The most prominent feature for which the generic term is used in this sense is the Big Lagoon [Humboldt]. Since *laguna* was used in Spanish and Mexican times for any kind of lake, inland lakes in California are sometimes designated as lagoons. The swampy lake north of Irvington [Alameda] is called The Lagoon; it was originally called La Laguna, and its overflow passes through Arroyo de la Laguna.

La Grange [Stanislaus]. The place was known in the early 1850's as French Bar, but it appears on Baker's map of 1856 as Owen's Ferry. In the same year the settlement was made the county seat, and the present name, probably for one of the French settlers, was applied. La Grange was the name of Lafayette's country home and was then already

very popular as a place name in our country.

Laguna, là-gōō'-nà. The Spanish geographical term designates generally a small lake, but Clear Lake, a large body of water, was formerly known as the *Laguna* (Bryant, p. 278), and the shallow, marshy Tulare Lake was once called *Laguna de Tache*. The word *laguna* appears in the names of more than thirty land grants and claims. It has survived as a semigeneric term and has also become a specific term in the names of mountains, canyons, creeks, and subdivisions. It occurs tautologically as Laguna Lake in Imperial, San Benito, and San Luis Obispo counties. **Punta de la Laguna** [Santa Barbara, San Luis Obispo]. The land grant, dated December 26, 1844, took its name from the lake named by the Portolá expedition, *Laguna Grande de San Daniel*, on September 1, 1769 (Crespi, p. 181). Costansó records on the same day that the valley was named *el valle de la Laguna Larga* (p. 54). **Laguna Seca** [Santa Clara]. *La Laguna Zeca* (the dry lake) is mentioned on October 31, 1797 (PSP, XV, 158), at a time of the year when many California lakes are dry. In 1823 the name was used for the Laguna Seca (or Refugio de la Laguna Seca) provisional grant, which was definitely granted July 22, 1834. **Laguna Seca** [Monterey]. *La laguna seca* is mentioned on July 24, 1830 (Legis. Recs., I, 147), and a name *Laguna* is shown on a *diseño* of the Laguna Seca (or Cañadita) grant, dated May 18, 1833, and January 9, 1834. **The Lagoon; Arroyo de la Laguna** [Alameda]. The lake north of Irvington is shown as *Laguna Permanente que es nacimiento de este Arroyo* (the permanent lake which is the source of this arroyo) on a *diseño* of the San Ramon grant (1834). **Laguna Peak** [Ventura]. The mountain was obviously named after the *Laguna* (now called Mugu Laguna), shown on a *diseño* of the Guadalasca grant (1836). **Laguna Creek** [Santa Cruz]. The stream is shown as *Arroyo de la laguna* on a *diseño* (1836) of the land grant bearing the same name. **Laguna Salada** [San Mateo]. The name, 'salt lake,' here actually a lagoon, is shown on a *diseño* (1838) of the San Pedro grant. **Arroyo de la Laguna** [Alameda]. The tributary of Alameda Creek was named after the *Laguna* shown on a *diseño* of the Valle de San Jose grant (1839). **Laguna Honda** [San Francisco]. At the site of the reservoir at the edge of Sutro Forest there was formerly a 'deep lake,' which is shown on several *diseños*. Laguna Honda Home was named after it.

Laguna: Canyon, Beach [Orange]. The canyon is shown as *Cañada de Las Lagunas* on a *diseño* (1841) of the Niguel grant. The town of Laguna Beach was named after the canyon. **Laguna Mountains** [San Diego] have been known since the 1870's by this name because two lakes called Laguna Lakes are on the summit of the mountain range.

Lagunita, là-gōō-nē′-tà. This diminutive, meaning 'little lake,' was used in Spanish times much less often than the term *laguna*. **Lagunitas: Creek, Lake,** town [Marin]. The origin of the name is found in the little lakes north of Mount Tamalpais, now converted into reservoirs. The one now called Lagunitas Lake (little lakes lake) is shown as *Laguna* on a *diseño* of the Cañada de Herrera grant (1839). The canyon through which Little Carson Creek flows is labeled Puerto Zuelo Lagunitas (*portezuela*, 'little mountain pass') on Hoffmann's map of the Bay region (1873). On the county map of the same year the stream on the north slope of Mount Tamalpais emptying into Lagunitas Lake is called Lagunitas Creek. On modern maps the name Lagunitas Creek is applied to the entire stream to Tomales Bay. This watercourse appears on a *diseño* of Rancho Nicasio (1844) as *Arroyo de San Geronimo,* and is designated on American maps as San Geronimo Creek. It is also known as Paper Mill Creek because in 1856 Samuel P. Taylor built a paper mill at the site of Taylorville. When the Geological Survey mapped the Tamalpais quadrangle in 1895 the name San Geronimo was restricted to the tributary of Lagunitas Creek. The post office is listed in 1908. **Lagunita Lake** [Monterey]. The 'little lake lake' at the Salinas–San Juan Bautista highway is shown as *Laguna* on a *diseño* of the Vergeles grant (1834).

La Habra, hä′-brà: **Valley,** town [Orange]. *Habra* (which in modern Spanish is spelled without the initial "h") means 'gorge' or 'pass through the mountains' and refers here to the pass through the Puente Hills, traversed by the Portolá expedition on July 30, 1769. The term was used in the name of a land grant, La Cañada del Habra (Legis. Recs., III, 62), dated October 22, 1839. In American land-grant papers the name was given as La Habra, and this form was applied to the valley and in 1912 to the post office.

La Honda. *See* Hondo.

La Jolla. *See* Jolla.

Lake. The shores of a lake have been since primitive times most conducive to settlement, and the word "lake" is probably found in the names of more American communities than any other geographical generic term with the exception of "mount" and "mountain." In California it is used in combination with "shore," "side," "view," "wood," etc., for about fifteen communities, and at least seven additional lake names were copied in naming a town or a post office. Some of the name-giving lakes have long since disappeared. Several mountains and creeks are likewise named after near-by lakes. **Lake City** [Nevada] was founded in 1857 and named after the numerous small lakes in the vicinity (Co. Hist., 1880, pp. 59, 172). **Lake County** was created on May 20, 1861, from part of Napa County and so named because Clear Lake is the principal feature of the county. **Lakeport** [Lake]. The place was settled in 1859 and first called Forbestown, for William Forbes, the owner of the land. When the community became the seat of the newly created Lake County, the name was changed to Lakeport because it is on the edge of Clear Lake. **Lakeville** [Sonoma]. The place is shown on Hoffmann's map of the Bay region (1873). Its situation on the shore of the lakelike expansion of Petaluma Creek doubtless suggested the name. **Lake City** [Modoc]. The post office was established in the 1870's and was so named because it is situated between Upper and Middle Alkali Lakes (locally known as Surprise Valley Lakes). **Lakeside** [San Diego]. The town was laid out on the shore of Lake Lindo in 1886 by El Cajon Valley Company and was named after the lake (Hunzicker). **Lakeview: post office, Mountains** [Riverside]. The post office was established about 1895 and was given this name because of the view of Lake Moreno. The lake, long since drained, was formerly called Brown's Lake (*moreno,* 'brown'). *See* Moreno. **Lake Hughes** [Los Angeles]. The post office was named in 1925 after the lake. *See* Hughes Lake. **Lakewood Village** [Los Angeles]. The subdivision was laid out in 1934 on the land of Rancho Los Cerritos by Clark J. Bonner of the Montana Land Company and Charles B. Hopper, promoter of the development, and was named Lakewood Village because it is near Bouton Lake (C. B. Hopper). **Lake Kirkwood** [El Dorado]. The post office was established October 11, 1941, and named after Kirkwood Lake, which in turn had been named for Zachariah S. Kirkwood, owner of the adjoining land in the early 1860's. The log cabin erected as a hostelry and stage depot in 1864 at the juncture of Alpine, Amador, and El Dorado counties is Historical Landmark 40.

Lake Mountain [Trinity]. The post office, established April 18, 1878, and later discontinued, was reëstablished March 25, 1936 (Leona Miller). **Lakehead** [Shasta]. The name was applied to the station at the northern "head" of Shasta Lake by the Southern Pacific after completion of Shasta Dam. The post office was established November 1, 1950, and named after the station (Edith Ramey).

Lake Arrowhead [San Bernardino]. When the post office was established, April 29, 1922, at Arrowhead Lake, the generic name was placed first to avoid confusion with other Arrowhead names in the vicinity. *See* Arrowhead.

Lamanda Park [Los Angeles]. In 1886 Leonard J. Rose laid out the subdivision on his famous Sunnyslope Farm and named it by prefixing the initial letter of his given name to his wife's name, Amanda. In 1905, zealous Zoeth S. Eldredge, scenting a Spanish name, persuaded the Post Office Department to "restore" it to La Manda. Fortunately, the Santa Fe station kept the name Lamanda, and in 1920 the post office restored the old form.

Lamarck, Mount. *See* Evolution.

Lambert Dome. *See* Lembert.

La Mesa. *See* Mesa.

La Mirada, mĭ-rä′-dȧ [Los Angeles]. The name was applied to the station of the Santa Fe when the line to San Diego was built in 1888. It is a Spanish word meaning 'glance,' 'gaze.' In 1953 an olive grove in the area was subdivided and the settlement was named after the station (Co. Hist., 1965, II, 132 f.) .

Lamoine [Shasta]. Named in 1898 by the Coggins brothers, owners of the Lamoine Lumber & Trading Company, after their native home in Maine (Steger). The name is spelled La Moine by the Post Office Department.

Lamont [Kern]. Named by the MacFadden family, landholders, after their former home in Scotland (Santa Fe).

Lanare [Fresno]. Coined from the name of L. A. Nares, chief promoter of the colonization project, and applied in 1911 when the Laton and Western Railway was built.

Lancaster [Los Angeles]. Named in 1877 by settlers, after their former home in Pennsylvania.

Lancaster Mountain [San Diego]. Named for A. W. Lancaster, who purchased a farm near the mountain in 1872 (Hunzicker).

Lancha Plana [Amador]. Historic Landmark 30 commemorates the mining town settled probably in 1848. In 1850 two prospectors, Kaiser and Winter, built a raft of casks lashed together for a ferry across the Tuolumne River; hence the name "flat boat."

Lane Memorial Grove. *See* Franklin K. Lane Grove.

Lanfair [San Bernardino]. The station was named for E. L. Lanfair, an early settler, when the Southern Pacific branch from Needles to Mohave was built in 1884. A post office was established in 1912.

Lang [Los Angeles]. Named for John Lang, a native of New York who was a farmer at Soledad in the 1870's. In the State Gazetteer of 1888 he is listed as postmaster, hotelkeeper, and real-estate agent at Lang.

Langille, lăn′-jĭl: **Peak** [Kings Canyon National Park]. Named by the Geological Survey, at the suggestion of Charles H. Shinn, then head ranger, for Harold D. Langille, a forest inspector for the U.S. General Land Office, after his tour of inspection in 1904 (Farquhar).

Langley, Mount [Sequoia National Park]. Named in 1905 in honor of Samuel P. Langley (1834–1906), astronomer and physicist, who organized an expedition to Mount Whitney in 1881 for research in solar heat, and who was well known for his experiments in the problem of mechanical flight. In 1864 Clarence King had named the peak Sheep Mountain. In 1871 Albert Bierstadt made a painting of the peak and named it for William W. Corcoran, donor of the Corcoran Art Gallery, Washington, D.C., where the painting later hung. The same year, Clarence King mistook his Sheep Mountain for Mount Whitney, which he and his companions had named seven years before. The mistake was corrected by W. A. Goodyear, July 27, 1873, and Whitney's name was restored to the peak for which it was intended. The Geographic Board approved the name Mount Corcoran until 1943, when, upon the instigation of the Sierra Club, because "Langley" had become established through usage, it reversed its decision and made the present name official.

Langley Hill [San Mateo]. Named for Frank and Laban Langley, who owned five sections of land here in 1877.

La Paleta: Valley, Creek [San Diego]. The Spanish word *paleta* has several meanings: 'shovel,' 'shoulder blade,' 'artist's palette.' It may have been applied to the valley to indicate its shape or coloring, or, like many other place names in southern California, for the pleasant sound of the name.

La Panza: settlement, **Range** [San Luis Obispo]. The place is shown as La Pansa on the von Leicht–Craven map, and as La Panza on the Land Office map of 1879, at the site of present La Panza Ranch. The discovery of gold in the canyon in 1878 precipitated a small-scale gold rush, and was followed by the establishment of a post office. For some years the residents suffered the name to be spelled in one word until Eldredge in 1905 prevailed upon the Post Office Department to restore its rightful form. According to Sanchez, the name arose because hunters used the paunch (*la panza*) of a beef to catch bear. It appears to be the same place recorded as *paraje la Panza* by Sebastian Rodriguez on April 27, 1828.

La Patera, pä-tĕr'-*à* [Santa Barbara]. The name was applied to the Southern Pacific station when the line westward from Santa Barbara was built in the 1880's. *Patera* means 'place where ducks congregate,' and is shown on a *diseño* of the Dos Pueblos grant (1842) as the name for a stream which flows into the *estero*. The hinterland of Goleta Point, commonly designated La Patera, was a good duck hunting area until the building of the airport.

La Porte [Plumas]. Named in 1857 after La Porte, Indiana, the birthplace of Frank Everts, a local banker. *See* Rabbit.

La Puente [Los Angeles]. The post office was established as Puente, September 15, 1884. The place was so known until the Geographic Board decided for La Puente in 1955. *See* Puente.

La Quinta, kēn'-tà [Riverside]. The post office was established in 1931 and named after the La Quinta Hotel, which had been opened by a Mr. Kiener. *Quinta* means 'country estate.' (Mary Brooks.)

Larabee: Creek, station, **Buttes** [Humboldt]. Named for a stock raiser, Larabee, whose ranch was burned by Indians in the spring of 1861. The stream is shown on the von Leicht–Craven map as Lariby Creek, and Laribee Buttes are mentioned by Rockwell in 1878. A post office, Laribee, was established April 6, 1888. The present spelling was used for the station in 1908 and for a new post office September 30, 1921.

Largo [Mendocino]. The name was applied to the station of the Northwestern Pacific in 1908. It is a Spanish word meaning 'long,' and may have been chosen because the station was on the land of Lemuel F. Long, resident in the county since 1858, assemblyman 1877–1878.

Larkin's Children [Colusa, Glenn]. The grant, dated December 14, 1844, was made to the three minor children of Thomas O. Larkin, a native of Massachusetts, who came to California in 1832 and was U.S. consul at Monterey after 1843. The land could not be granted to Larkin himself, because he never became a Mexican citizen.

Larkspur [Marin]. The town was founded in 1887 and named because blue larkspur grew profusely in the vicinity.

Las. Names preceded by the Spanish feminine plural article *las* which are not listed here will be found under the first letter of the name proper. Example: Las Flores is listed under Flores.

Las Aguilas, ä'-gĭ-lăs: **Creek, Canyon, Mountains, Valley** [San Benito]. In 1854 Manuel Larios testified in the Real de las Aguilas land case that "the name . . . was given to said place in 1826 in consequence of two persons by the name of Aguila having encamped there while lassoing cattle" (*WF*, VI, 371). The two Aguilas, however, were not the grantees of the land grant called Real de las Aguilas and dated January 16, 1844.

Las Choyas. *See* Chollas.

Las Cruces, krōō'-sĕs [Santa Barbara]. The name, 'the crosses,' is derived from a land grant, dated July 12, 1836, and May 11, 1837. A *Rancho de las Cruces*, probably belonging to Mission Santa Ynez, is mentioned on July 21, 1822 (Guerra Docs., V, 266), and *Lomas de las Cruces* is shown on a *diseño* of Rancho Santa Rosa (about 1835). The canyon labeled Canada de las Cruces on the Lompoc atlas sheet is shown as *Arroyo de las Cruces* on a *diseño* of the Las Cruces grant. A post office Las Cruces is listed in 1880.

Las Plumas [Butte]. This community, named from the Feather River on which it is situated, was inhabited mainly by the employees of the large P. G. and E. Big Bend powerhouse. The first post office was established November 24, 1908. Since 1966 it has been under the waters of the Oroville Dam project.

Las Posadas Forest [Napa]. In 1938, Mrs. Anson S. Blake of Berkeley donated the Moores Creek Ranch to the State Board of Forestry to preserve and study the unique flora of the forest. The ranch had been a portion of the La Jota land grant and the name owes its origin to the fact that *las posadas,* the guest houses, were apparently located at this beautiful spot (*CHSQ*, XXXV, 1 ff.) . *See* Moores Creek.

Lassen: Peak, County, National Forest, Volcanic National Park; Lassen: Meadow, View [Plumas]; **Lassen Creek** [Modoc]. In a geographical sense the name of the noted Danish pioneer (*see* Glossary) was probably applied first to the mountain. In 1827 Jedediah Smith, who often called a range a "mountain," applied the name Mount Joseph to the entire chain between latitude 39° and 41° (Burr's map). Wilkes' map of 1841 limited the term to what is now Lassen Peak, but, influenced by the holy names farther south, placed "St." before it. This name, Mount St. Joseph, is shown on most maps until the middle 1850's. Bruff in 1850 calls it Snow-Butte or Mount St. Jose (II, 810). The people, however, attached to the peak the name of the generally respected pioneer, as is shown by the reference to "Mount Saint Joseph, (sometimes called Lassen's Peak,)" in the Pacific Railroad *Reports* (Vol. II, Pt. 2, p. 51). H. L. Abbot, of the same survey, speaks of "Lassen's butte" in 1851 (*ibid.*, Vol. VI, Pt. 1, p. 128), and Blake, the geologist of the survey, used the form Lassens Butte on his map, an early example of the omission of the apostrophe, a simplification which is now required by the Geographic Board. The now generally accepted name is Mount Lassen, although officially it is Lassen Peak (Geographic Board, June 2, 1915). The county was created, from parts of Plumas and Shasta counties, and named on April 1, 1864, by the legislature; the national forest in 1908, by presidential proclamation; the national park in 1916, by act of Congress. Fandango Pass [Modoc] was formerly Lassen Pass or Lassen Horn or Lassen Cut-off, and the meadows in Nevada where the Humboldt changes its course from west to south were Lassen Meadows. Former misspellings: Lawson, Lasson, and Lassin.

Lassic, Mount; Black Lassic: Peak, Creek; Red Lassic: Peak, Creek [Trinity]. According to P. E. Goddard, the mountain preserves the name of a people of the Athapascan family, named after their last chief, Lassik (Hodge). The spelling is that of the Forest Service. Black Lassic Creek is a typical absurdity caused by thoughtless naming after other features. Neither Lassic nor the creek could be called black, but only the peak after which the creek was named.

Last Chance. A name favored by prospectors and explorers, especially for places where they had found water when about to give up from thirst. The name may sometimes have been applied because the place was the last at which one could obtain supplies of water or liquor before entering a desert or a mountain fastness. E. J. McKenney tells the story of three men working a mine near Coloma [El Dorado] who were ready to give up when a Sacramento firm staked them with a few months' supplies. They took up work, struck it rich, and called their claim the Last Chance. ("The Knave," Dec. 29, 1946.) There are more than twenty "last chance" names in the State, including a Last Chance Ditch [Kings]. On the Caliente Road in Sequoia National Forest two water-supply places are designated as Big and Little Last Chance Can. **Last Chance: Spring, Range** [Inyo]. In August, 1871, the Lyle detachment of the Wheeler Survey, completely exhausted after their guide, C. F. R. Hahn, had disappeared, fortunately reached the spring. The name appears on the von Schmidt boundary map (1872) and on Wheeler atlas sheet 65. **Last Chance Creek** [Plumas]. A prospector led the first party to discover Gold Lake from Nevada City about June 5, 1850. After a long fruitless search, the leader was given a "last chance" to find the lake within forty-eight hours, or else . . . Schaeffer (p. 87) relates that the threat was not carried out because some believed that his "reason was dethroned." **Last Chance** [Placer]. According to local tradition, the miners applied the name to their claim when they shot a deer with their last bullet after all their provisions were gone.

Las Trampas: Ridge, Peak, Creek [Contra Costa]. On the *diseños* of several ranchos of the district the ridge is labeled *Sierras pequeñas del . . . arroyo San Ramon alias las trampas* (little ridge of the . . . arroyo San Ramon alias *las trampas*). The abbreviated versions Las Trampas and Arroyo de las Trampas appear on the *diseño* of Laguna de los Palos Colorados. *Trampa* means 'trap' or 'snare,' and according to the testimony of José Martinez, in land grant case 276 N.D. (1862), traps were set in the chaparral of these hills to catch elk (Cutter).

Lasuen, Point [Los Angeles]. In November, 1792, Vancouver named the southeast point of San Pedro Bay for his friend, Padre Fermín Francisco de Lasuén. *See* Fermin.

Las Virgenes Creek [Ventura, Los Angeles]. *El paraje de las Virgenes* (the place of the virgins) was the name of a land grant in 1802 (Docs. Hist. Cal., IV, 121). This grant was later abandoned, but the name was preserved through a new grant, dated April 6, 1837.

Las Yeguas Canyon [Santa Barbara]. Shown on the *diseño* of the Cañada del Corral grant as *Cañada de las Yeguas*, 'valley of the mares.' On the *diseño* of the Dos Pueblos grant the same valley is labeled *Arroyo de las Llagas*, 'arroyo of the stigmata.' Since *y* and *ll* were often interchanged in Mexican spelling, we have here an obvious confusion. *See* Llagas, Yegua.

Lathrop [San Joaquin]. Laid out in 1887 and named by Leland Stanford, for his brother-in-law, Charles Lathrop.

Laton [Fresno]. Named for Charles A. Laton of San Francisco, who with L. A. Nares acquired a part of the Laguna de Tache ranch in the 1890's.

Latour Butte [Shasta]. The elevation was named for James La Tour, whose homestead is now included in La Tour State Park (Steger).

Latrobe [El Dorado]. When the Placerville and Sacramento Valley Railroad reached the place in August, 1864, F. A. Bishop, the chief engineer, named the station for Benjamin H. Latrobe, who had constructed the famous Thomas Viaduct over the Patapsco River for the Baltimore and Ohio Railroad in the 1830's.

Laurel. The occurrence of the California laurel, *Umbellularia californica,* in almost all sections of the State, either as a tree or a shrub, has given rise to some twenty-five Laurel Creeks, Lakes, Mountains, and Hills. Most of the places named for the laurel tree are in the central and southern parts of the State. In the northern counties the laurel is usually called pepperwood, bay tree, or spice tree.

Laureles. The Spanish word for 'laurel trees' appears in the names of two land grants in Monterey County, dated September 19, 1839, and March 4, 1844. It has also survived in Los Laureles Canyon [Santa Barbara]. However, *Laureles Arroyo,* shown on a *diseño* of Las Pulgas (1835), was translated into Laurel Creek [San Mateo].

Lauterwasser Creek [Contra Costa]. The tributary to San Pablo Creek was formerly a large clear stream for which the name, meaning 'pure water,' was highly descriptive, but it was named for F. P. Lauterwasser, a German butcher from San Francisco, one of the earliest settlers in the Orinda district.

Lava. The presence of lava flow is indicated in the names of about ten orographic features, including Lava Top on the boundary line of Plumas and Butte counties. **Lava Beds**

National Monument [Modoc, Siskiyou]. Created and named by presidential proclamation in 1925. The name Lava Beds for the volcanic formations had long been in use, and it gained prominence after the Modoc War of 1872–1873, in which the Indians used them as strongholds.

La Verne [Los Angeles]. Named in 1916 after La Verne Heights, a subdivision west of the town which had been given the first name of the promoter. The former name was Lordsburg, for I. W. Lord, who laid out the town in 1886. (Santa Fe.)

Lavezzola Creek [Sierra]. This name of an early settler was applied by the Geographical Board in 1950 to the stream formerly known as North Fork of the North Fork of Yuba River.

Lavic: Lake, Mountain, settlement. [San Bernardino]. The places west of Ludlow were apparently named for a prospector. The lake is dry; the mountain is known for its manganese deposits. The settlement had a post office from 1902 to 1909.

Lavigia, lä-vĭg′-ĭ-á: **Hill** [Santa Barbara]. The hill is mentioned as *el cerro de la Vigia* (lookout hill) in a description of Rancho Nuestra Señora del Refugio in 1828 (Registro, p. 31). When W. E. Greenwell of the Coast Survey charted the Santa Barbara Channel, between 1856 and 1861, he used the hill for a triangulation point and kept the Spanish name.

Lawlor, Mount [Los Angeles]. The mountain was named by the Forest Service for Oscar Lawlor, a prominent Los Angeles attorney, about 1890.

Lawndale. This popular American place name, which preserves the old English generic term *dale* (valley), is represented in California by **Lawndale** [Los Angeles], established and named by Charles Hopper in 1905; **Lawndale** [San Mateo], named in 1924 by the Associated Cemeteries at the suggestion of M. Jensen, later mayor of the town; and **Lawndale** [Sonoma], a station of the Northwestern Pacific.

Lawrence Creek [Humboldt]. The stream was probably named for either Asa or William H. Lawrence, farmers at Rohnerville, whose names appear in the Great Register of 1879.

Laws [Inyo]. The Carson and Colorado Railroad built the narrow-gauge road in 1883 and named the station, which was near the site of old Owensville, for R. J. Laws, assistant superintendent.

Laytonville [Mendocino]. Named for Frank B. Layton, who came to California from Nova Scotia, Canada, in 1867 and settled here in

1875 (Co. Hist., 1880, pp. 583 f.).

League. Some Mexican land grants were described as a number of *sitios*, each *sitio* being a parcel of land 5,000 *varas* square. In American land-grant papers the *sitio* was translated as "league." There were three grants called Four Leagues [Napa, Sacramento, San Francisco], two Five Leagues [Yolo], six Eleven Leagues [Butte, Fresno, Glenn, Madera, Stanislaus]. Since the *vara* (yard) was not uniform in practice, the size of a *sitio* or league differs. The provincial league was 4,438.19 acres; the league around 1850 was 4,340.28 acres; and the present league, used since June, 1857, in the patent surveys for land grants, 4,438.68. (Bowman.)

Leavitt: Meadow, Peak, Creek [Mono]. In 1863 Hiram L. Leavitt built a hotel at the east end of Sonora Pass to accommodate the traffic between Aurora and Sonora (Maule). Leavitt's is recorded on Hoffmann's map, and Levitt Peak on the Mining Bureau map of 1891.

Lebec, 'lĕ-bĕk' [Kern]. The place was named for a man who was killed here by a grizzly bear, probably a member of a trapping party. His comrades buried him and cut this inscription on an oak tree, "Peter Lebeck, killed by a X bear, Oct. 17, 1837." The inscription is now in Kern County Museum. It was first seen and recorded by Bigler, July 31, 1847. September 29, 1853, William Blake of the Pacific Railroad Survey recorded it again but misspelled the name, Le Beck. This gave rise to the stories that Lebeck was a veteran of Napoleon's armies, a settler in the region, that his name was Pierre Lebeque—all unproven fantasies. When the post office was established September 6, 1895, the Post Office Department further corrupted the name to Lebec.

Lechler Canyon [Los Angeles]. The canyon with the intermittent stream was named by the Geological Survey after the Lechler Ranch in Oak Canyon, when the Camulos quadrangle was surveyed, 1900–1901. The name was also spelled Leckler. Geo. W. Lechler died in Piru City, December 10, 1906 (HSSC:P, VII, 85).

Lechusa Canyon [Los Angeles]. *Lechuza* is the Spanish word for the 'barn owl' and is also applied to "owlish persons." The canyon is on the Malibu grant; the name probably goes back to Spanish times.

LeConte: Canyon [Kings Canyon National Park], **Point** [Yosemite National Park]. The point was named for J. N. LeConte (*see*

Glossary) by R. B. Marshall in 1909. The name for the canyon was applied before 1908, and was approved with the spelling Leconte by the Geographic Board, June 7, 1911.

LeConte Falls [Yosemite National Park]. The falls were named by R. M. Price and his party in the summer of 1894: ". . . in many respects the most majestic cascade in the whole [Tuolumne] cañon, the LeConte Cascade, so named by us in honor of our esteemed Professor, Joseph LeConte" (SCB, I, 204). **Mount LeConte** [Sequoia National Park]. "Forms one of the most striking points of the whole range . . . Some time ago those residents of the Lone Pine district who are interested in the mountains decided upon naming this peak LeConte, in honor of Professor Joseph LeConte. . . . It was then determined to make the ascent of the mountain and erect a monument. . . . in a small can we put a photograph of the Professor, with the following memorandum: 'To-day, the 14th of August, 1895, we, undersigned, hereby named this mountain LeConte, in honor of the eminent geologist Professor Joseph LeConte. . . . A. W. de la Cour Carroll, Stafford W. Austin.' " (SCB, I, 325 f.) **LeConte Divide** [Kings Canyon National Park] between San Joaquin and Kings rivers was approved (with the spelling Leconte) by decision of the Geographic Board, June 7, 1911. The location of Mount LeConte in Death Valley, named in 1883 by James J. McGillivray, of New York, has not been definitely established (Death Valley Survey). *See* Glossary.

Leek. *See* Onion.

Leesville [Colusa]. Named about 1876 for "Lee" Harl, the owner of the land, who acquired his nickname (according to local tradition) because he was an ardent admirer of the great Southern commander, Robert E. Lee.

Leevining: Creek, Peak, settlement [Mono]. A contraction of the name of Lee (Leroy) Vining, of Laporte, Indiana, who came to California in 1852 in search of gold. Vining settled on the creek named for him and operated a sawmill. (Maule.) The creek is shown on maps as early as 1863; the post office was established March 1, 1928. In 1957 the Geographic Board decided that the name should be spelled in two words: Lee Vining.

Leggett [Mendocino]. The place was long known as Leggett Valley, for an early pioneer. When the post office was established, October 16, 1949, the name was abbreviated by the Post Office Department.

Legrand [Merced]. Established in 1896 by the

San Francisco and San Joaquin Valley Railroad (now the Santa Fe) and named for William Legrand Dickinson, a Stockton resident, who owned large tracts of land there. The name Dickinson itself was given to the railroad siding three miles south of Legrand.

Leidig Meadow [Yosemite National Park]. The name commemorates the Leidig family, Pennsylvania Germans, who came to Yosemite Valley in 1866. George F. Leidig owned the Leidig and Davaney Hotel at the foot of Sentinel Rock in the 1860's and 1870's and had a winter house in the meadow which now bears his name. His son, Charles, the first white boy born in the valley (1869), was later a ranger in the Park Service.

Leidy Creek [Mono]. Named for George Leidy, of Fort Madison, Iowa, who settled in Fish Lake Valley in 1882 (Robinson).

Lembert Dome [Yosemite National Park]. In 1885 John B. Lembert took up a homestead at the foot of the dome to which his name was applied in the 1890's. The name was placed on the map by the Geological Survey in 1901. The Wheeler Survey had named the prominent landmark Soda Spring Dome (atlas sheet 56-D).

Lemon. Next to the orange the lemon is California's most important citrus fruit, and its name has been used for a number of places in southern counties: Lemon Grove [San Diego], Lemoncove [Tulare], Lemon Heights [Orange], a fancy Lemona [Riverside], and two plain Lemons, one in Ventura, the other in Los Angeles County—a post office established December 11, 1895, and renamed Walnut on December 22, 1908.

Lemoore [Kings]. The place was settled by John Kurtz in 1859. In 1871 Dr. Lovern Lee Moore arrived, called the settlement Latache, and founded the Lower Kings River Ditch Company. When the post office was established, September 21, 1875, its name was coined from Moore's name.

Lempom [Tulare]. The name, given to the railroad station in 1917, was coined from *lem*on and *pom*egranate (Santa Fe).

Lennox [Los Angeles]. Named after Lenox, Massachusetts, the former home of a resident of the settlement, who met with a group of other citizens to choose a name for their community. It had been known in the early days as Inglewood Rancho and later for a short time as Jefferson. In 1921 the Los Angeles County Board of Supervisors officially recognized the name by changing the name of Olivian Avenue to Lennox Avenue, now

Lennox Boulevard. (Co. Library.)

Lenwood [San Bernardino]. Coined from the name of Ellen Woods, whose husband, Frank Woods, subdivided land and planned a town here in the early 1920's (Santa Fe).

Leonard Lake [Mendocino]. Named for John Leonard, who, according to local tradition, obtained title to the lake from Jim Patrick, a bear hunter, in exchange for a pinto horse.

Leonis Valley [Los Angeles]. Named for Miguel Leonis, a Basque sheepherder, who settled in the San Fernando Valley before 1868 and later became the owner of Rancho El Escorpion.

Le Parron Peak [Six Rivers National Forest]. Named for an early prospector and hunter who built a log cabin on what later became known as Le Parron Flat (W. E. Hotelling).

Lerdo [Kern]. The name was applied to the station by the Southern Pacific when the railroad reached the place in the fall of 1872. It looks like a typical railroad name; according to Sanchez, it is a surname. Sometimes spelled Ledro (Land Office map, 1891).

Leucadia [San Diego]. Established in 1885 by a group of English colonists with a predilection for Greek. Leucadia (or Santa Maura) is one of the Ionian Islands. From one of its cliffs Sappho is said to have leaped into the sea. All street names in the California town are Greek: Hygeia Street, Athena Street, etc. (G. E. Thrailkill). The post office was established March 27, 1888.

Leviathan: Creek, Peak [Alpine]. Probably named after the mine which was worked in the 1860's and, like many mines, was given a name suggestive of tremendous riches.

Lewis, Mount [Yosemite National Park]. Named in memory of Washington B. Lewis, a native of Michigan, who for many years was connected with the Geological Survey and was superintendent of Yosemite National Park, 1916–1927. The former name was Mount Johnson. **Lewis Creek** [Yosemite National Park], also known as Maclure Fork, was named for the same man.

Lewis: Creek, Canyon [Kings Canyon National Park]. Named for the brothers Frank M. and Jeff Lewis, pioneer stockmen, prospectors, and hunters (Farquhar).

Lewis Lakes [Tuolumne]. A group of three lakes was named in memory of Bert Lewis, of the Forest Service, who was killed in World War I, May 27, 1918. Another near-by lake, also called Lewis Lake, was named Iceland Lake by decision of the Geographic Board, Jan.-Mar., 1965.

Lewiston: town, **Lake** [Trinity]. The town was settled by B. F. Lewis in 1853 and has had a post office since May 24, 1854. The lake was created by impounding the Trinity River in the late 1950's.

Lexington. The scene of the first bloody conflict between colonists and British troops, on April 19, 1775, is one of the most popular place names in the United States. For Southern sympathizers the name gained new significance when the siege of Lexington [Missouri] in August, 1861, ended in one of the early Confederate victories. Of a number of Lexingtons applied to communities, mines, and physical features in California, only Lexington Hill [Plumas] seems to have survived.

Liberty Cap [Yosemite National Park]. "Owing to the exalted and striking individuality of this boldly singular mountain . . . , it had many godfathers in early days; who christened it Mt. Frances, Gwin's Peak, Bellows' Butte, Mt. Broderick, and others; but, when Governor Stanford (now U.S. Senator) was in front of it with his party in 1865, and inquired its name, the above list of appellatives was enumerated, and the Governor invited to take his choice of candidates. A puzzled smile lighted up his face and played about his eyes, as he responded, 'Mr. H., I cannot say that I like either of those names very much *for that magnificent mountain;* don't you think a more appropriate one could be given?' Producing an old-fashioned half-dollar with the ideal Cap of Liberty well defined upon it, the writer suggested the close resemblance in form of the mountain before us with the embossed cap on the coin; when the Governor exclaimed, 'Why! Mr. H., that would make a most excellent and appropriate name for that mountain. Let us so call it.' *Thenceforward it was so called;* and as everyone preferentially respects this name, all others have been quietly renunciated." (Hutchings, *Sierras,* 1886, p. 445.)

Lick. Several Lick Creeks and a Licking Fork (of the South Fork of the Mokelumne) were probably so named after salt licks for cattle or game.

Lick Observatory [Santa Clara]. The name commemorates the donor of the observatory to the University of California, James Lick (1796–1876), a Pennsylvania German, real-estate speculator and public benefactor. The name was suggested by George Davidson in 1873 after Lick had accepted his plan to establish the observatory on what is still called Observatory Point at Lake Tahoe (von Leicht–Craven map, 1874). In 1874 the choice of site was changed to Mount Hamilton. The road to the peak was built in 1876 by Santa Clara County and named Lick Avenue. Lick came to California shortly before the discovery of gold with a small fortune acquired in South America, which he augmented by clever real-estate speculation. In addition to giving the observatory to his adopted state, he endowed the California Academy of Sciences and made numerous other bequests. Lick Mills in San Jose is the site of his mahogany-finished flour mill, built in 1855.

Liebel, lē'-bĕl: **Peak** [Kern]. The mountain was named in the 1930's for Michael Otto Liebel, a prospector of German descent who came into the Paiute Mountain country in 1876. He married an Indian girl, settled at the foot of the mountain, and brought up a large family. All eleven children and their parents were still living in 1947.

Liebre, lē-ā'-brĕ: **Mountain, Gulch** [Los Angeles]; **Liebre Twins** [Kern]. The land grant, La Liebre, dated April 21, 1846, was evidently named after *el paraje que llaman la Cueba de la liebre* (the place that is called the burrow of the hare), mentioned in October, 1825 (Docs. Hist. Cal., IV, 767). Sierra de la Liebre is shown on Wheeler atlas sheet 73-c. The modern names (all of which are outside the boundaries of the land grant) were used when the Geological Survey mapped the Tejon quadrangle. By mistake the name Liebre Twins was transferred on the atlas sheet to a single-top higher peak to the west (Wheelock).

Lieutenants, The [Siskiyou]. The two peaks in the Siskiyou Mountains were thus named as Lieutenants for the towering El Capitan, close to the southwest of them (Geographic Board, July–Sept., 1965).

Lights Creek [Plumas]. Named for Ephraim Light, a pioneer rancher north of Indian Valley. He later was one of the first men to commercialize hot springs in Santa Rosa (R. Batha).

Lignite. *See* Carbondale.

Likely [Modoc]. In 1878 the settlers had to find a new name for their place because the old name, South Fork, had been rejected by the Post Office Department. They suggested three other names and each was rejected because the name existed elsewhere. The settlers met again and one remarked dejectedly that it was not likely that they would ever get a name. Another spoke up and said,

"What's the matter with 'Likely?' It is not likely that there will be another post office in the state called 'Likely.'" The suggestion was adopted and the Post Office Department approved the name. The mountain southwest of the town is now called Likely Mountain instead of South Fork Mountain (Geographic Board, July-Sept., 1965).

Lillis [Fresno]. Named for Simon C. Lillis, a superintendent of the Laguna de Tache cattle ranch before 1917.

Limantour. *See* Estero.

Lime, Limestone. There are some fifteen geographic features so named because of the occurrence of limestone. None seem to have been named for the citrus fruit. There is a Lime Saddle in Butte County and a Lime Point in San Francisco. There are also several Limekiln Creeks and Canyons, and three settlements: Lime [Tuolumne], Limestairs [Trinity], Limestone [El Dorado]. *See* Calera.

Lincoln [Placer]. "The TOWN of LINCOLN, at Auburn Ravine, Placer county, was laid out about two years ago, under the auspices of C. L. Wilson, projector of the California Central Railroad, and soon afterward a sale of town lots at auction took place at the St. George Hotel in this city. The town does not take its name from the President of the United States, but from its founder, whose middle name is Lincoln." (Sacramento *Union*, Nov. 4, 1861.) Lincoln Acres [San Diego] and Lincoln Park [Los Angeles], like scores of other communities in the United States, may have been named for Abraham Lincoln.

Linda [Yuba]. Laid out by John Rose in January, 1850, as a rival of Marysville. Named after the miniature steamer *Linda*, launched on the Sacramento River in December, 1849. The steamer had been named after the seagoing *Linda*, which had brought round Cape Horn the engine, scow, and wheel for the little *Linda*. (Ramey.)

Lindemann Lake [Modoc]. The lake was named for J. B. Lindemann, a native of Germany and a resident of Eagleville in the 1870's.

Linden, Linden Road [San Joaquin]. In 1860 the place was known as Linden Mills. The name was shortened to the present form when the post office was established in 1867. Since no species of the linden tree is native in the State, it is probably a transfer name from the East, where the name is popular.

Lindero, lĭn-dĕr'-ō: **Canyon** [Los Angeles]. *Cañada del Lindero* [boundary valley] is

shown on a *diseño* of El Conejo grant on the boundary of Las Virgenes grant.

Lindo, Linda. This Spanish adjective, meaning 'pretty,' or 'handsome,' has been repeatedly used in place naming. There is a **Lindo Lake** in San Diego County and a **Linda Creek** in both Placer and Sacramento counties. **Linda Vista** (pretty view) in San Diego County was mentioned as a new settlement in the San Diego *Union*, April 22, 1886. During World War II the name was applied to a large housing project on Kearny Mesa, five miles east of the old place (San Diego Public Library). There is another Linda Vista in Santa Clara County.

Lindsay [Tulare]. Captain A. J. Hutchinson chose the maiden name of his wife for the town which he founded in 1888.

Linn, Mount [Tehama]. The name was given by Frémont, probably to the highest peak of the Yolla Bolly group, in honor of Lewis F. Linn, a senator from Missouri, 1833–1843, who took an active part in the struggle for the acquisition of the Oregon Territory. Mt. Linn and Mt. Tsashtl (Shasta) are the only California mountains named on Preuss's map of 1848. Von Leicht–Craven (1874) show "South Yallo Balley or Mt. Linn." The Mining Bureau map of 1891 transferred the name to a peak farther east, and Douglas' gazetteer places it at latitude 40° 03', longitude 122° 46'.

Linns Valley [Kern]. Named for William Lynn, who settled in the district in 1854 (Co. Hist., 1914, p. 188).

Linora [Merced]. Applied to the station by the Southern Pacific when the line was built about 1890. A typical railroad name, probably coined like other fanciful names on this section.

Lion. The presence of cougars or mountain lions in various parts of the State is indicated in the names of more than fifty geographic features, mainly canyons. **Lion: Rock, Lake** [Sequoia National Park]. The rock was so named because Mansell Brooks, a sheepman, killed a mountain lion near there in 1883 (Farquhar). **Lion Rock** [San Luis Obispo]. This rock was named because of the presence of sea lions; it was already known in Spanish times as *El Lobo* (the [sea] wolf), as shown on a plat of part of the land grant Cañada de los Osos y Pecho y Islai.

Lippincott Mountain [Sequoia National Park]. Named by the Geological Survey in 1903, for Joseph B. Lippincott, at that time hydrographer for the Survey.

Litchfield [Lassen]. Named for the Litch family, pioneer settlers, by Mrs. B. F. Gibson (Clara Litch), when the townsite was laid out in 1912. The post office is listed in 1915.

Little. The adjective is used frequently for geographic features which resemble another more prominent feature near by, e.g., Little Yosemite Valley. This unimaginative method of naming often produces a comic effect: Little Shuteye Peak [Madera] is not named for a little shut-eye but is a peak that is smaller than the real Shuteye Peak; likewise, Little Bear Creek [Los Angeles] is not named for a little bear, nor Little Rattlesnake Mountain [Del Norte] for a little rattlesnake. A tributary of San Gabriel River is called Little Santa Anita Canyon Creek. Sometimes, however, the specific name is actually modified: **Little Lake Valley** [Mendocino] is named after a diminutive lake near its southern border; **Little Lakes Valley** [Inyo] because there are some forty little lakes in it; **Little Pete Meadow** [Kings Canyon National Park] for Pierre ("Little Pete") Giraud (Farquhar); and **Little Claire Lake** [Sequoia National Park] for the seven-year-old daughter of Ralph Hopping (Farquhar). Often, similar features in the same locality receive the adjectives "big" and "little" at the same time: Big and Little Maria Mountains [Riverside], Big and Little Five Lakes [Sequoia National Park]. Sometimes a feature is modified by "little" because it is thought to resemble a well-known feature elsewhere, e.g., Little Gibraltar [Santa Catalina Island]. A number of mining towns and settlements were named after states or cities: Little Texas [San Diego], Little York [Nevada]. "Little" geographic features often have namesakes in near-by post offices and communities: Little Lake [Inyo], Littleriver [Mendocino], Little River [Humboldt], Littlerock [Los Angeles], Little Shasta [Siskiyou], Little Valley [Lassen]. **Little Norway** [El Dorado] was so named in 1961, replacing the former name Vade.

Live Oak. The common designation of several species of California's evergreen native oak is contained in some twenty geographical names, including a number of communities and post offices: Live Oak [Sutter], named in 1874 by H. L. Gregory; Live Oak Acres [Ventura], named about 1925 by W. C. Hickey; Live Oak [Sacramento]; Live Oaks [Sonoma]; Live Oak Springs [San Diego]. See Encina; Oak.

Livermore: city, **Valley, Pass** [Alameda]. Robert Livermore (1799–1858), an English sailor,

came to California in the 1820's and became co-grantee of Rancho Las Positas, April 10, 1839. After the American occupation his residence became known as Livermore's and is so designated on maps of the 1850's. The town did not come into existence until 1864. It was first named Laddville, for Alphonso S. Ladd, who erected the first building. In 1869 the post office was established and named Nottingham after Livermore's home town. However, in the same year William H. Mendenhall, a member of the Bear Flag party, platted the townsite and named it Livermore in memory of the pioneer. The name was accepted for the post office and the railroad station.

Livingston [Merced]. When the valley route of the Southern Pacific reached the place in 1871 the station was named Cressey for the owner of the land. In 1872 the postmaster, O. J. Little, also a landholder, objected to the name (according to Outcalt's Co. Hist., 1925, p. 366), and the name of the explorer of central Africa, David Livingstone (minus the final "e"), was chosen instead. The old name was not lost but was applied to a Santa Fe station, three miles east, about 1900. See Cressey.

Llagas, lyä′-gȧs: **Creek** [Santa Clara]. Padre Palou, on November 25, 1774, named a place near the creek *Las Llagas de Nuestro Padre San Francisco* (the wounds [stigmata] of Our Father Saint Francis). Anza refers to it as Las Llagas in 1776, and Josef Moraga calls the creek *Arroyo de las Llagas de Nuestro Padre San Francisco* (Anza, III, 411). *Llano de las Llagas* was the Spanish name for Gilroy Valley (Beechey, II, 48). A land grant, San Francisco de las Llagas, is dated February 3, 1834. Trask's *Report* of 1854 (p. 8) mentions Llagos River. The present version is recorded in Hoffmann's notes on August 20, 1861.

Llanada [San Benito]. A post office, now discontinued, was established here about 1900 and given the Spanish name, meaning 'plain,' 'level ground,' because it is situated on the wide expanse of Panoche Valley.

Llano. The Spanish word means 'level field' or 'even ground,' and was commonly used as a generic geographical term. Six land grants include the word in their titles; another has the diminutive, Llanitos. **Llano,** yä′-nō [Los Angeles]. A post office with this name was established in 1890. It was discontinued in 1900, but when the well-known socialist leader Job Harriman of Los Angeles founded the colony Llano del Rio, the post office was reëstablished, January 23, 1915. The socialistic colony was moved to Louisiana in 1917, but the post office remained.

Lobdell Lake [Mono]. Named for J. B. Lobdell, who is said to have hidden out here in the 1860's to escape military service (Maule).

Lobitos: Creek, settlement [San Mateo]. The name, 'little wolves,' may refer to coyote or seal pups. The stream is shown as *Arroyo de los Lovitos* on a *diseño* of the Cañada Verde grant (about 1838), and as *Arroyo de los Lobitos* on a *diseño* of the San Gregorio grant (about 1839).

Lobo, lō'-bō. The geographical names, current or obsolete, with the Spanish word for 'wolf' seem to occur only along the coast and refer to the 'sea wolf,' *lobo marino* (seal or sea lion). **Point Lobos; Lobos Creek** [San Francisco]. The name of the westernmost point of San Francisco is as appropriate now as it was when it originated. *Punta de los Lobos* is mentioned by Chamisso in 1816 (*Rurik*, p. 73), and June 25, 1846, the name *Punta de Lobos* was given to a land grant (later rejected by the U.S. courts), which included this point as well as the presidio. The English version, Point Lobos, is used by Beechey in 1826 (II, 424) and by the Coast Survey in 1851. **Point Lobos; Lobos Rocks** [Monterey]. "Innumerable sea wolves" were observed in the vicinity by Crespi and Fages in May, 1770 (Palou, II, 284). *Punta de Lobos* is shown on a *diseño* of the San Jose y Sur Chiquito grant (1839). On American maps the entire cape was generally designated as Point Carmel; the map of the Coast Survey of 1855 has Point Lobos, but the Survey's special map of Monterey Bay of 1878 has Pyramid Point, because the projecting rock, now called Pinnacle Point, is pyramid-shaped. The name Point Lobos for the entire cape has been used since 1890; it was made permanent in 1933 by the creation of the Point Lobos Reserve, a state park.

Lockeford [San Joaquin]. The name was first applied to the ford which crossed the Mokelumne River on land of Dr. D. J. Locke, a graduate of Harvard, who settled there in 1851. In 1860 John A. Clapp used the name for his hotel, and shortly thereafter the town was laid out and named. The post office is listed in 1867. Locke's Ford is Historic Landmark 365.

Locoallomi [Napa]. The land grant, dated September 30, 1841, may preserve the tribal name of a division of Wappo Indians. The name of these Indians is spelled *Aloquiomi*, *Loaquiomi, Liaquiomi, Loaquiomis,* etc., in the records of Mission San Francisco Solano (Arch. Mis., I). Barrett (*Pomo*, p. 273) connects the name with Wappo "*lō'knōma,* from lok, 'goose,' and nōma, 'village,' or *laka'-hyōme* (Northern Moquelumnan [Miwok] dialect name)." Both variations, the Wappo and Miwok, obviously existed, because the name of the land grant is also written Loconoma. The confusion concerning this name may never be cleared up. *See* Collayomi Valley.

Loconoma Valley [Lake]. The name preserves one of the most puzzling Indian tribal names. *See* Collayomi, Locoallomi.

Loco Siding [Inyo]. When the California-Nevada Railroad was built in 1910, the name Loco, probably a local Indian name, was applied to the station. Other stations of this sector bear Indian names—Coso, Haiwee, Olancha. Loko Indians are mentioned by Hodge (I, 932) as a division of the Mono-Paviotso group.

Lodi, lō'-dī [San Joaquin]. The station was called Mokelumne when the Central Pacific reached the place in 1869. To avoid confusion with similar names the present name was chosen in 1874. Lodi in Italy was the scene of Napoleon's first spectacular victory, May 10, 1796, and in the 1870's more than twenty communities in the United States were already so named. A famous race horse called "Lodi" may have had some connection with selection of the name in California.

Lodoga [Colusa]. The place is shown on a map of 1902 as Ladoga. It may have been named after the large lake between Finland and Russia, or after Ladoga in Indiana or Wisconsin, or just for its pleasant sound. The post office was established February 1, 1898, with the name spelled Lodoga.

Loftus [Shasta]. A post office was established in 1922 at Steinaker's service station and named after Pollock Bridge, which had been built across the Sacramento in 1916 by George Pollock. In 1939, when the bridge and settlement became victims of the Shasta Dam project, the post office, together with the old name, was moved five miles north, and in 1940 another two miles north. (Stella Woolman.) As the post office was often confused with Pollock Pines in El Dorado County, it was renamed in 1944 for Charles T. Loftus, a resident of the canyon and son of Tom Loftus, creator of the famous Banner strawberry (Steger).

Logan Lake [Shasta]. Named for P. B. Logan,

who had his summer range here (Steger).

Log Cabin [Yuba]. The settlement was named in 1927 when a post office (now discontinued) was established in a log cabin (Maudelene Cleveland).

Log Meadow [Sequoia National Park]. A huge, hollow, fallen Sequoia at the edge of a meadow was first seen by Hale D. Tharp in 1858 and later used by him as a summer cabin.

Lokoya, lō-koi'-yȧ [Napa]. This Indian name, which had been preserved locally, was applied in 1925 to the post office formerly called Solid Comfort. *La tribu de Locaya* is mentioned on August 6, 1845 (DSP Ben., V, 384). A connection with Locoallomi is indicated.

Lola, Mount [Nevada]. The mountain preserves the memory of the great courtesan and lesser actress, Lola Montez, who precipitated a revolution in Munich in 1848 and in the 1850's found a fruitful field for her endeavors in Grass Valley and other mining towns of California. *See* Independence Lake.

Loleta, lō-lē'-tȧ [Humboldt]. When the local railroad was built in 1883 the station was named Swauger for Samuel A. Swauger, the owner of the property. In 1893 the residents, wishing a change, accepted Mrs. Rufus F. Herrick's choice of the present name, which according to local tradition is an Indian word. (W. F. Dickson.)

Loma. The Spanish geographical term, *loma*, designates a low, long elevation or hill, but apparently even in Spanish times it was occasionally applied to higher hills or mountains. It has survived as a semigeneric term in the counties which were in the Spanish domain: with Alta, 'high' [Marin, Monterey, Santa Barbara, San Diego], Pelona, 'bald' [San Luis Obispo, Santa Barbara], Atravesada, 'oblique' [Fresno], Chiquita, 'little' [Santa Clara], Verde, 'green' [Los Angeles]. Las Lomas [Kings], unlike other fancy map names in the Kettleman Hills, is really descriptive of the feature. *Las Lomas Muertas* [San Diego] is a name which was repeatedly used in Spanish times for bare hills. Loma has also become a favorite specific term, often used for a "Spanish" effect without regard to meaning or idiomatic usage: Del Loma [Trinity], Loma Rica [Yuba], Loma Mar [San Mateo], Oro Loma [Fresno], Casa Loma [Orange], Loma Portal, Loma Alta Mountain [San Diego]. **Point Loma** [San Diego]. The name *Punta de la Loma* was applied to the tip of the peninsula because of its promontory. It appears first on Juan Pantoja's *plano* of 1782 (Wagner, p. 395). Wilkes (1841) has Loma

Point, and the Coast Survey chart of 1851, Point Loma. The post office was established about 1895. **Loma Prieta** [Santa Clara]. In 1854 the peak was used as a primary triangulation station by the Coast Survey and named in honor of their chief, Alexander D. Bache, a grandson of Benjamin Franklin and superintendent of the Survey from 1843 to 1867. The Whitney Survey and the State Mining Bureau accepted the Coast Survey name, but the Land Office maps continued to use the old Spanish name, and this was accepted by the Geological Survey when the New Almaden quadrangle was surveyed in 1916. "The name 'Loma Prieta' is very commonly given by the Spanish-Mexican population to any high chaparral-covered point which looks black in the distance. Mount Bache is one of these 'Black Mountains'" (Whitney, *Geology*, I, 65). A short-lived post office, Loma Prieta, is listed in 1892. **Loma Linda** [San Bernardino]. When the Colton-Indio sector of the Sunset Route was built in 1875–1876, the name Mound Station was applied to the stop, doubtless because of the slight elevation south of it; it is so named on the Land Office map of 1879, but later Southern Pacific maps have Mound City. When the Seventh Day Adventists built a sanatorium in the 1890's and a post office was established January 14, 1901, the name Loma Linda, 'pretty hill,' first spelled Lomalinda, was chosen.

Lomerias Muertas, lō-mĕ-rē'-ȧs mōō-ĕr'-tȧs [San Benito]. The elevations north of San Juan Bautista were given this name, meaning 'dead hills,' because they are almost entirely without trees. August 16, 1842, the name was applied to a land grant. Lomerias Muertas are often mentioned in Hoffmann's notes in the summer of 1861.

Lomita, lō-mē'-tȧ. The Mexican-Spanish diminutive of *loma*, which means 'low, long hill,' was rarely used before 1846. One of the names which can be traced to Spanish times is **Lomita de las Linares**, a hill one mile slightly west of south of Rucker in Santa Clara County. From about 1780 to the middle of the 19th century it was a well-known landmark. In 1875 the origin of the name was revealed in the testimony of Justo Larios in Circuit Court case 1397, San Francisco: "... the Lomita de las Linares was named after my grandmother. They were on the road from Monterey to San Jose and passing this spot they saw wild animals, elks, and they went to chase the deer and left my grandmother upon this spot and in that way it came to be named the Lomita de las Linares. . . . They left her upon the lomita so she could not be frightened while they went to chase the deer. Her name was Linares." (*WF*, VI, 374.) Lomita Mountain, eight miles west of this hill, means literally "little hill mountain." **Lomita** [Los Angeles] also had its origin in Spanish times. On the surveyor's plat of the San Pedro Rancho is shown a *Lomita del Toro*, a few miles east of the modern city. Lomita Park [San Mateo] and the many other Lomitas are modern realtors' applications.

Lompoc, lŏm'-pŏk: town, **Hills** [Santa Barbara]. A Chumash place name of uncertain meaning. A rancheria *Lompoc o Lompocop* under the jurisdiction of Mission La Purisima is recorded in 1791 (Arch. MPC, p. 10). A rancho, Lompoc, is mentioned in 1835 (DSP, IV, 48–51); the land was granted to Joaquín and José Carrillo on April 15, 1837. In 1874 the California Immigrant Union purchased a portion of the rancho, laid out the town, and sold lots with the condition that the sale and consumption of alcohol be prohibited.

Lone. There are about twelve Lone Rocks, Mountains, Lakes, etc., on the maps of the State, and as many Lone Tree, Pine, Rock, etc., combinations. There is also a Lonely Gulch near Lake Tahoe. **Lake of the Lone Indian** [Fresno]. In 1902 a party which included Lincoln Hutchinson gave the name to the lake because the mountain above it shows distinctly the profile of the face of a reclining Indian (*SCB*, IV, 197). **Lone Pine** [Inyo]. The Hill party camped here in 1860 while prospecting the Iowa silver mine, and named the place for the tall pine which was a landmark for many years until it was undermined by the creek. The name and a picture of the pine are shown on Farley's map of 1861. Other inhabited places having names which include the adjective are: Lone Star [Fresno], possibly for Texas, the "Lone Star State"; Lone Hill [Los Angeles]. The names of the post office Lonoak in San Benito County and the Southern Pacific siding Lonoke in Santa Clara County seem to have been coined from "lone oak." **Lone Point** [Santa Catalina Island]. The Coast Survey named the cape Long Point, but most maps label it Lone Point. The atlas sheet of the Corps of Engineers (1943) has Long Point, but Lone Point Light.

Long. The descriptive adjective "long" is included in the names of more than a hundred features, mainly valleys, but also bars, beaches, gulches, canyons, and lakes. There are a great number of Long Valley Creeks, even a Long Grade Canyon Creek [Ventura] and a Long Pine Canyon Creek [San Bernardino], but the number of simple Long Creeks is very limited, because length is a general characteristic of creeks, not a distinguishing one. Long Creek in Sierra National Forest is so named because it rises on Long Mountain, properly so named. There is a Long Dave Canyon and Valley in Los Padres National Forest. Long Barn [Tuolumne] and Longvale (from Long Valley) [Mendocino] are settlements. Long Lake [Plumas] was probably named for a man, because it is not at all long. **Long Beach** [Los Angeles]. The town was founded in 1882 by William E. Willmore and named Willmore City. In the "boom year," 1887, the Long Beach Land and Water Company acquired the interests and applied the new, truly descriptive name.

Longley Pass [Kings Canyon National Park]. Discovered and named in August, 1894. "As the writer [Howard Longley] had been first to reach its summit, the party concluded to call it Longley's Pass, as a means of identification in the future" (*SCB*, I, 190).

Lookout. The term is often given to elevations which command a wide view. The State has more than twenty Lookout Mountains, about ten Peaks and ten Points, and a few Ridges, Hills, and Rocks. **Lookout** [Modoc]. The settlement was named about 1860 after the hill above the town on which, as the story goes, the Pit River Indians had a lookout when the Modocs were on wife-stealing expeditions (Doyle). *See* Lavigia.

Loomis [Placer]. Named in 1884 by the Southern Pacific for Jim Loomis, the local railroad agent, express agent, postmaster, and saloonkeeper. Twenty years before, the station had been named Pino to distinguish it from the near-by settlement of Pine Grove, but the railroad and the Post Office Department found that the name was confused with Reno, and therefore changed it.

Loomis Peak [Shasta]. Named for B. F. Loomis, an early settler, according to the *Sixth Report* of the Geographic Board. Benjamin Franklin Loomis was the author of *Pictorial Lassen* (Steger).

Loon Lake [El Dorado]. Recorded on Hoffmann's map of 1873 and doubtless so named because the loon, an aquatic bird, was found there.

Los. Names preceded by the Spanish masculine

plural article *los* which are not listed here will be found under the first letter of the name proper. Example: Los Coyotes is listed under Coyote.

Los Altos [Santa Clara]. The post office was established in 1908 and took the Spanish name, meaning 'the heights,' which the subdivider had chosen for the site in 1907.

Los Angeles, lôs ăn'-jĕ-lĕs, lôs ăng'-glĕs: **River, city, County**. According to Kroeber (*AAE*, VIII, 39), the place where Los Angeles now stands was known to the Indians as *Wenot* "because of a large river there." The word for stream is *wanic* in Cahuilla and *wanut* in Serrano dialect. Hugo Reid (Dakin, *Paisano*, p. 220) says that the name of the rancheria on the site of the city was *Yang-na*. The mission padres, however, called it *Yabit* (*CHSQ*, XIII, 195). The Portolá expedition camped on the bank of the river on August 2, 1769, and named it in honor of *Nuestra Señora de los Angeles de Porciuncula*, whose feast day they had celebrated the preceding day. The Portiuncula chapel, the cradle of the Franciscan order, is in the basilica of 'Our Lady of the Angels' near Assisi, Italy. Crespi and Costansó simply called the stream *Porciuncula*. This abbreviated form was commonly used; Palou, however, in December, 1773, gives the full name: *Nuestra Señora de los Angeles de Porciuncula* (*Hist. Mem.*, III, 220). The name was not preserved through the river, but through the name of the *pueblo*, the projected establishment of which is mentioned on December 27, 1779 (PSP, I, 59): *la ereccion de un pueblo con el titulo de Reina de los Angeles sobre el rio de la Porciuncula*, 'the founding of a town with the name Queen of the Angels on the river of the Porciuncula.' On August 26, 1781, Governor Neve issued the final instruction for the founding of the town, which took place on September 4, 1781. Although the place was not named for the Angels, but for the Virgin, the most common designation of the future metropolis seems to have been *Pueblo de Los Angeles*. After the American occupation there was some confusion about the proper use of the name. Stockton date-lined his general order of January 11, 1847, after the occupation of the place by the U.S. forces, *Ciudad de los Angelos*, and Emory gives the English equivalent of this version, City of the Angels (*Mil. Rec.*, p. 121). Ord shows City of Los Angeles on his sketch of August, 1849, and the present abbreviated version was definitely established when the county was

organized, February 18, 1850, and the city incorporated, April 4, 1850. The controversy over the "correct" pronunciation of the name of the great city which has been carried on in years past with a fierceness worthy of a better cause seems to have been settled by the younger generation. There are still some enthusiasts who insist upon a "Spanish" pronunciation, not realizing, however, that the Spanish *g*, correctly pronounced, is an entirely foreign sound to Americans. The city will doubtless continue to flourish with its name pronounced euphoniously and rhythmically: lôs ăn'-jĕ-lĕs. In fact, September 12, 1952, a jury appointed by the mayor decided that this is the official pronunciation of the metropolis (*Names*, I, 35 ff.) .

Los Banos, băn'-ŏs: **Creek, town, Game Refuge** [Merced]. The creek took its name from the pools near its source, called *Los Baños* [the baths] *del Padre Arroyo*, for Padre Felipe Arroyo de la Cuesta, who was at San Juan Bautista Mission from 1808 to 1833. According to tradition, he used to refresh himself in the pools when on missionary trips to the San Joaquin Valley. The pools are called *Baños del Padre Arroyo* on *diseños* of the San Luis Gonzaga (1841) and Panocha de San Juan (1844) grants. It is possible that these were the "baths" mentioned on October 20, 1798, as *los Baños de S. Juan* (Prov. Recs., V, 282). About 1870, Gustave Kreyenhagen, a German immigrant, built a store at the old wagon road about three miles west of the creek on land leased from Henry Miller (of Miller & Lux). The place became known as Kreyenhagen's and is shown on the maps of the Whitney Survey. A post office was established at the store in 1874 and named Los Banos after the creek. After the railroad was built in 1889, Miller & Lux laid out the present town, which has since been the headquarters of that famous cattle firm.

Los Buellis Hills [Santa Clara]. A misspelling of Los Buelles (i.e., *bueyes*, 'oxen') shown on the *diseño* of the Pueblo Lands of San Jose, 1838.

Los Felis [Los Angeles]. The name of the land grant, which included the site of modern Griffith Park, preserves the name of José Feliz (or Felix), mentioned as having cultivated a garden here in 1813 (Bancroft, II, 349). After his death the widow married Juan Diego Berdugo, but when the land was granted to her on March 22, 1843, the grant was named Los Felis, i.e., Señora Feliz and her children of the first marriage.

Los Gatos. *See* Gatos.

Los Nietos, nĭ-ĕt'-ŏs: town, **Valley** [Los Angeles]. Manuel Nieto was the grantee of one of the first California land grants, dated November 20, 1784. It is called *rancho de Nieto* (PSP, XVI, 250) and *rancho de los Nietos* (Prov. Recs., V, 262) in 1797. On May 22, 1834, the large rancho (33 leagues) was regranted to his five heirs (*los Nietos*) in five parcels: Los Alamitos, Los Cerritos, Santa Gertrudis, Los Coyotes, Las Bolsas. The name is shown as *Nieto* on Narváez' Plano (1830) and on Duflot de Mofras's map (1844), and as Los Nietos on the von Leicht–Craven map. The first post office bearing the name was established June 14, 1867; it was reëstablished May 29, 1891, after the Santa Fe had given the name to the station.

Los Olivos, lōs ō-lē'-vōs [Santa Barbara]. When the Pacific Coast Railroad built the extension from Los Alamos about 1890, the terminal was called Los Olivos because of the extensive plantings of olive cuttings made there by the Hayne brothers. The immense olive orchard disappeared, but the name remained.

Los Padres National Forest. Named in 1936 by order of President Franklin D. Roosevelt, to commemorate the Franciscan padres who founded the California missions, eight of which are in or near the forest area. The present name replaces the name Santa Barbara National Forest, which had been given by order of President Theodore Roosevelt in 1903 to a combination of forest reserves and which was extended in 1910 to include San Luis Obispo National Forest, and in 1919, Monterey National Forest.

Lospe Mountain [Santa Barbara]. According to Lawson (March 28, 1883), the name is Chumash, *ospe,* meaning 'flower field,' and the present version arose because the word was believed to be Spanish.

Los Penasquitos, pĕn-ăs-kē'-tŏs: **Canyon, Creek** [San Diego]. The name (*peñasquitos,* 'small rocks') appears in the *expediente* of the land grant of Santa Maria de los Peñasquitos, June 15, 1823, and is mentioned as Panasquitas by Emory in 1849. Von Leicht–Craven (1873) have Penasquito Creek, but Coast Survey and Geological Survey used the plural form.

Lost. The adjective "lost" in a place name generally indicates an incident or story behind the name. There are almost one hundred such names in the State, mostly for creeks and rivers which suddenly go underground, or for meadows, hills, mines, canyons, etc.,

which were discovered, "lost" for a time, and later found again. Sometimes a feature because of its isolation or seclusion may seem to be lost. There are also a number of names referring to something that was actually lost: Lost Horse (Cow, Man, etc.) Creeks. In Humboldt County there is a Little Lost Man Creek as well as a Lost Man Creek. El Dorado County has a Lost Corner Mountain; Riverside County, where the groups of Washington palms have provided many place names, a Lost Palm Canyon. **Lost Cannon: Creek, Canyon, Peak** [Mono] were so named on the erroneous assumption that Frémont abandoned his howitzer here in 1844 (Maule). **Lost Wagons** [Death Valley National Monument]. In the summer of 1889, C. B. Zabriskie was obliged to abandon here one or two wagons of the Pacific Coast Borax Company. The place and name have been associated with the burning of the wagons of the Jayhawker party of 1849, which actually occurred much farther south. **The Lost Arrow** [Yosemite National Park]. The authorities seem to agree that this is the translation of the Miwok Indian *Ummo, Hammo,* or *Ummoso.* **Lost Hills** [Kern]. In 1910 the town took its name from the so-called Lost Hills, slight elevations which seem to belong to the Kettleman Hills but look as if they were "lost." **Lost River** [Modoc]. The river is literally lost between Clear Lake and Tule Lake. Reclamation engineers have tried in vain to find an underground flow. **Lost Islands** [San Diego]. This is the common name for the two submarine mountains west of the Coronados, called Cortez Bank and Tanner Bank by the Coast Survey. *See* Cortes Bank.

Los Trancos Creek. *See* Tranca.

Los Viejos [Kings]. The name, meaning 'the old ones,' was applied by American surveyors "because the hills are older physiographically than those directly north" (Geographic Board, No. 20).

Lotus [El Dorado]. The place was first named Marshall for James W. Marshall, the discoverer of gold at Sutter's mill. After the admission of the State into the Union, in 1850, the name was changed to Uniontown. When the post office was established, January 6, 1881, the new name was chosen, probably to avoid confusion with Union House [Sacramento]. There was no other Uniontown in the State at that time; Uniontown in Humboldt County had been Arcata since 1860. According to W. T. Russell ("The Knave," July 23, 1944), the first postmaster, George E.

Gallaner, suggested the new name because in his opinion the inhabitants were as easygoing as the lotus eaters in the Odyssey.

Love. A number of geographic features in various parts of the State bear names like Love, Lovejoy, Loveland, but usually they were named for persons (as Lovelady and Lovelock were) and have nothing to do with tender emotions. El Dorado, Santa Clara, and Placer counties, however, each have a Lovers Leap. This is a favorite American name for a cliff, not because a lover ever jumped from one so named, but because it would be "a good place to take off, if anyone wanted to" (Stewart, p. 129). By decision of the Geographic Board, May-Aug., 1961, the name of Point Aulon (*see* Abalone) was changed to Lovers Point.

Love Creek [Santa Cruz]. Named for Henry (Harry) Love, captain of the California Rangers who in 1853 killed one of the bandits called Joaquin Murieta.

Lovelady Ridge [Mendocino National Forest]. Named for Joshua Lovelady, who settled at the foot of the ridge in the 1860's.

Lovelock [Butte]. The place was originally named Lovelocks, for George Lovelock, who founded the mining town in 1855 by opening a hotel and store (Co. Hist., 1882, p. 260).

Lowe, Mount [Los Angeles]. The peak was named in honor of Thaddeus S. C. Lowe by his companions on the first horseback ascent, September 24, 1892. Lowe (1832–1913), a versatile scientist and inventor, was chief of the Aeronautic Corps of the U.S. Army in the Civil War. "It was discovered that until this time this giant peak, the monarch of the Sierra Madres, was unnamed. One of the party suggested, that whereas Prof. T. S. C. Lowe, the great scientist, had first ridden to the top, had made the first trail to its lofty summit, was the first man to have *planted the stars and stripes on its highest point*, and was the first man to conceive the project of reaching its dizzy height with a railroad and with courage and means to put such a project into execution, as was now being done, no more fit and appropriate name could be given this mountain than the name of 'Mount Lowe.'" (Auglaize, Ohio, *Republican,* Dec. 1, 1892, quoted by Reid, p. 445.)

Lower Lake [Lake]. The town was established in 1860 and named from its proximity to the southeasterly tip of Clear Lake, at that time generally known as Lower Lake. The post office is listed in 1859. The adjective "lower" is used elsewhere in the State: Lower Coon

Mountain [Del Norte], Lower Alkali Lake [Modoc], Lower Salmon Lake [Sierra], Lower Sardine Lake [Sierra], Lower Soda Springs [Shasta].

Loyalton [Sierra]. Named by the Post Office Department in 1863, at the suggestion of the Rev. Adam G. Doom, the first postmaster, who considered the name expressive of the strong Union sentiment of the place. The settlement was previously known as Smith's Neck, perhaps because the Smith Mining Company was operating there at that time.

Loyd Meadows [Tulare]. Named for John W. Loyd, who ran sheep there in the 1870's (Farquhar).

Lubeck Pass [San Bernardino]. Named for Bill Lubeck, who settled on the Colorado River in pre-railroad days (*Desert Mag.,* April 1941).

Lucas Valley [Marin]. Probably named for John Lucas, who inherited from his uncle, Timothy Murphy, the rancho of which the valley is a part.

Lucerne. The name of the medieval town and the beautiful lake in Switzerland, the locale of Wilhelm Tell's exploits, is a popular place name in the United States. There are fourteen post offices (often spelled Luzerne) and a great number of lakes and other features so called. California has its share with at least four Lucernes, one of which, however, was named for the European name of our alfalfa and not for the Swiss city. **Lake Lucerne** [San Mateo]. The name of the lake in Switzerland replaces the former name Bean Hollow Lagoon, an American version of the Spanish name, *Laguna del Arroyo de los Frijoles* (Wyatt). Bean Hollow Lake is now the name of the reservoir farther upstream. **Lucerne Valley** [Kings]. The reclaimed district was known by the name of the stream which traverses it, Mussel Slough. Frank L. Dodge, editor of the Hanford *Weekly Sentinel,* and other boosters disliked the name "slough" because to Easterners the name still suggests a muddy backwater. In an article of April 21, 1887, the district was rechristened Lucerne Valley because the distant mountains, the glittering Tulare Lake, the richness of the soil made the reclaimed tule land "eminently worthy to be a namesake of that old, rich and venerable Lucerne of Europe." *See* Mussel Slough. **Lucerne Valley** [San Bernardino]. James E. Goulding settled in the valley in 1897. When questioned about a name for it, Goulding said, "Well, if we get water, I know from past experience that we can raise plenty of alfalfa in this country, or lucerne, as the Mormons called it in southwest Colorado . . . Why not called it Lucerne Valley?" (quoted in *CHSQ*, XXVII, 120) . In 1912, Dr. F. J. Gobar and his family homesteaded at the site of the present town and found that lucerne or alfalfa actually could be grown successfully in the valley (Belden, July 26, 1963) . A post office was established September 9, 1912. **Lucerne** [Lake]. The situation on the shore of Clear Lake, which presumably resembled the Swiss lake, suggested the name for the hotel and post office established July 2, 1926.

Lucia, loo-sē'-*a* [Monterey]. The post office, now discontinued, was established about 1900, and was obviously named because the settlement is at the foot of the Santa Lucia Mountains.

Ludlow [San Bernardino]. Named in the 1870's by the Central Pacific (now Southern Pacific), for William B. Ludlow, master car-repairer of the Western Division. The name of the post office was Stagg from 1902 to 1926.

Luffenholtz: Creek, settlement [Humboldt]. Named for the millowner, who settled here in the spring of 1851. His name was originally spelled Luffelholz. On the county map of 1886 the stream is labeled Lutfenholts Creek.

Lugo [Los Angeles]. The station of the Pacific Electric commemorates Antonio María Lugo, on whose Rancho San Antonio the place is situated.

Lugo [San Bernardino]. It is not certain for which of the numerous Lugos the Santa Fe station was named. Three members of the Lugo family were grantees of San Bernardino Rancho, some eighteen miles south of the station. The district formerly called Lugonia was on part of the San Bernardino grant; the name was coined from the family name in 1877.

Lukens Lake [Yosemite National Park]. Named in 1894 by R. B. Marshall, for Theodore P. Lukens, mayor of Pasadena at that time; he was a noted advocate of reforestation. Mount Lukens [Los Angeles], named for the same man, is the common designation for Sister Elsie Peak, *see* Sister Elsie Peak.

Lunada Bay [Los Angeles]. The Spanish word, meaning 'formed like a half-moon,' was applied in modern times to the crescent-shaped bight.

Lundy: Lake, Canyon, settlement [Mono]. William O. Lundy obtained a timber patent here in 1880. The settlement near the May Lundy Mine was first known as Mill Creek.

Luther Pass [El Dorado, Alpine]. Named for Ira M. Luther, who crossed the pass in a wagon in 1854 and later was active in an attempt to route the Central Pacific over it.

Luzon [Contra Costa]. The station of the San Francisco and San Joaquin Valley Railroad was named at the time of the Spanish-American War, when Philippine place names were exceedingly popular (Santa Fe).

Lyell, Mount; Lyell: Canyon, Fork (of the Merced), **Fork** (of the Tuolumne), **Glacier** [Yosemite National Park]. The peak was named in 1863 for the English geologist Charles Lyell (1797–1875) by Brewer and Hoffmann of the Whitney Survey: "As we had named the other mountain Mount Dana, after the most eminent of *American* geologists, we named this Mount Lyell, after the most eminent of *English* geologists" (Brewer, p. 411).

Lynwood [Los Angeles]. The name was first applied to a dairy, for Lynn Wood Sessions, the wife of the owner. The station and subdivision were named after the dairy. (W. E. Wellinger.) The place was incorporated July 16, 1921.

Lyons Peak [Siskiyou]. Named by the Forest Service for George Washington Lyons, supervisor of the Modoc National Forest, who died of injuries incurred while he was on duty (W. S. Brown).

Lyons Springs [Ventura]. Named for Gertrude A. Lyons, owner of the property (*WSP*, No. 338, p. 63).

Lyons: Valley, Peak [San Diego]. The names of these features preserve the name of General Nathaniel Lyon, who was instrumental in keeping Missouri in the Union at the beginning of the Civil War and was killed in the battle of Wilson's Creek, August 7, 1861. In the early 1850's he was stationed in San Diego and acquired a section of land in the valley. *See* Battle Island.

Lytle Creek [San Bernardino]. Named for Captain Andrew Lytle, a former officer of the Mormon Battalion, who in 1851 led a division of the Latter-day Saints into San Bernardino Valley.

Lytton [Sonoma]. Named for Captain Litton, who developed the place as a resort in 1875. The name was misspelled when the Northwestern Pacific applied it to a station on the railroad built in the 1880's.

Maacama. *See* Mayacmas.

Maahcooatche [Shasta]. The name of the Indian settlement near the Lincoln schoolhouse may be translated as 'where the deer come down to drink' (Steger).

McAdams Creek [Siskiyou]. Named for a Scot who mined at the creek in 1854 (Co. Hist., 1881, p. 216).

McAdie, mȧ-kā'-dĭ: **Mount** [Sequoia National Park]. Named in 1905 in honor of Alexander G. McAdie, who was forecast official (1895–1902) and in charge (1903–1913) of the U.S. Weather Bureau, San Francisco. He was professor of meteorology, Harvard University, and director of the Blue Hill Observatory from 1913 to 1931. "Our party had the honor of naming the peak directly south of Lone Pine Pass Mt. McAdie, to commemorate your services in advancing the science of climatology" (J. E. Church, *SCB*, V, 317).

McAfee, măk'-ȧ-fē: **Creek, Meadow** [Mono]. Named for A. G. McAfee, a rancher who settled in Fish Lake Valley in 1864 (Robinson).

McArthur [Shasta]. Named about 1896 by the John McArthur Company for John McArthur, who had settled in the Pit River Valley in 1869 and who owned most of the land in the district.

MacArthur, Fort [Los Angeles]. On January 10, 1914, the War Department named the fort in honor of Lieutenant General Arthur MacArthur (1845–1912), U.S. Army, a veteran of the Civil and Spanish-American wars and father of General Douglas MacArthur.

McArthur–Burney Falls State Park [Shasta]. The original 160 acres were given to the State in 1920 by Frank McArthur, in memory of his mother, Catherine Clark McArthur (Steger). *See* Burney.

McCabe: Lakes, Creek [Yosemite National Park]. Named in 1900, for Lieutenant Edward R. W. McCabe, 17th Infantry.

McCall Creek [Shasta]. The tributary of Dog Creek was named for John McCall, who owned sixty acres of mining claims on this creek (Steger).

McCann [Humboldt]. The name was applied in 1881 to a station on the stage route, for an old settler who had a mill here (L. M. Armstrong). The settler was probably Willard O. McCann, who came to the county in 1869.

McClelland Field [Sacramento]. Named in 1939 by the War Department in memory of Major Hez McClelland of the Army Air Corps.

McCloud: River, town [Siskiyou, Shasta]. The river took its name from Alexander R. McLeod, leader of a Hudson's Bay Company brigade that trapped in California in 1828–1829. The name is spelled McLoud on Reading's map and in Trask's *Report* (1854, p. 45), and McCloud by Beckwith in 1854 in the Pacific Railroad *Reports* (Vol. II, Pt. 2, p. 54),

doubtless because the name McLeod is ordinarily so pronounced. Butler's (1851) and Eddy's (1854) maps have the correct spelling: McLeod's Fork. After Ross McCloud settled here in 1855 and became prominent in the development of the region, the river was usually associated with his name. Various spellings were used until the Whitney Survey decided for McCloud (von Leicht–Craven, 1874).

McClure Lake [Madera]. Named for Nathaniel F. McClure, lieutenant, Fifth Cavalry, stationed 1894–1895 in Yosemite National Park (Farquhar). Probably named by R. B. Marshall in 1899.

McClure Meadow [Kings Canyon National Park]. Named for Wilbur F. McClure, State engineer from 1912 to 1926, in recognition of his assistance in building the John Muir Trail (*SCB*, X, 86). **McClure, Lake** [Mariposa]. Named in 1927 by the Merced Irrigation District, in memory of the same McClure, who had died in the preceding year.

McColl [Shasta]. The station was named in memory of John McColl, State senator from Shasta and Trinity counties from 1932 to 1938 (Steger).

McComber Lake [Shasta]. In the late 1850's George W. McComber settled on the meadow along Battle Creek that became known as McComber Flat. A dam was built in 1906; the lake formed by the inundated meadow kept the name McComber (McNamar).

McConnell [Sacramento]. The station was named by the Central Pacific in the 1870's for Thomas McConnell, a native of Vermont who had settled in the county in 1855 and engaged in raising sheep.

McConnell State Park [Merced]. In 1949 the land for the park was given to the State by Mr. and Mrs. Warren F. McConnell.

McCoy: Mountains, Spring [Riverside]. Probably named for James McCoy, a native of Ireland who had come to San Diego in 1850 as a soldier, was sheriff of San Diego County, 1861–1871, and State senator, 1871–1874.

MacCullough: Lake, Valley [Lake]. Named for H. V. S. MacCullough, who settled in the county and had a homesite in the valley before 1900 (Mauldin).

Macdoel [Siskiyou]. When the Southern Pacific extension from Weed to Klamath Falls was built in 1906, the station was named for the owner of the land, William MacDoel.

McDonald Creek [Sonoma]. Named for William McDonald, who came to Napa Valley in 1847 and in 1850 built a house on the banks of this creek (*WF*, VI, 372).

McDonald Lake [Trinity]. Named for Warren P. McDonald because of his aid in conservation of wildlife (Geographic Board, May, 1954).

McDowell, Fort [Angel Island]. Named by the War Department in 1900, in honor of Irvin McDowell, commander of the Union army at the first battle of Bull Run and, later, of the Department of the Pacific.

McDuffie, Mount [Kings Canyon National Park]. Named by the Sierra Club in memory of Duncan McDuffie, an outstanding mountaineer and conservationist, who died April 21, 1951. The **Duncan and Jean McDuffie Grove** in Prairie Creek Redwoods State Park was established in 1951 through the efforts of the Save-the-Redwoods League; the Sierra Grove bearing their names was established in the Calaveras Big Trees State Park in 1959.

McFarland [Kern]. Named in 1908 for J. B. McFarland, one of the founders of the town.

McGee, Mount; McGee Lakes [Kings Canyon National Park]. Named in memory of W. J. McGee (1853–1912), well-known American geologist and anthropologist.

McGee: Creek, Canyon, Mountain, Meadow [Mono, Inyo]. The names commemorate the four McGee brothers, early cattlemen in Mono and Inyo counties, of whom Alney ("Allie"), John, and Bart played important roles in pioneer days. The tributary of Owens River in Long Valley [Mono] became known as McGee Creek because the brothers had their headquarters there. McGee Creek west of Bishop received its name because John McGee, at one time sheriff of Inyo County, owned a ranch where the creek debouches upon the valley. (Brierly.)

McGinty: Point, Reservoir [Modoc]. The point was named about 1917 for J. B. McGinty, a near-by homesteader (W. S. Brown).

McGonigle Canyon [San Diego]. Named in the early 1870's for Felix McGonigle, an early settler and landholder in this district, which was formerly known as Cordero Valley and Canyon for the Cordero brothers, Spanish soldiers in the Portolá expedition (San Diego Public Library).

McIntyre Creek [Tulare]. Named for Thomas McIntyre, a pioneer of Tulare County, who ran sheep here in the 1880's (Farquhar).

MacKerricher Beach State Park [Mendocino]. The land for the park was a gift from the MacKerricher family, whose forebears Duncan and Jessie had come from Canada and settled on it in 1864.

McKinley Grove [Fresno]. When the Geological Survey mapped the Kaiser quadrangle in 1901–1902, R. B. Marshall named the grove of big trees in memory of William McKinley, twenty-fifth President of the United States, who had died, the victim of an assassin, on September 14, 1901. **McKinleyville** [Humboldt]. Named by Isaac Minor, in memory of the President. A post office is listed in 1904.

McKinleyville [Humboldt]. The settlement on Highway 101 was named in honor of President McKinley after his assassination September 14, 1901. It had a post office from 1903 until 1921.

McKinney: Creek, Bay [Placer, El Dorado]. Named for John McKinney, a miner, hunter, and trapper, who came to El Dorado County in the early 1850's and later opened one of the first Lake Tahoe resorts, on the southern shore of McKinney Bay (W. T. Russell in "The Knave," July 23, 1944).

McKinstry: Peak, Lake, Meadow [Placer]. The mountain is labeled McKinstry's Mountain on Bowman's map (1873), and M'Kinstry Peak on sheet 47-D of Wheeler's atlas. It has been suggested that the name may commemorate George McKinstry, Jr., who was one of the best known of Sutter's men and the first sheriff of the northern district (1846–1847); it seems more likely, however, that the places were named for Elliott McKinstry, a miner at Oregon Bar in 1866, or for Lee McKinstry, a miner in Georgetown township [El Dorado] in 1867.

McKittrick: town, Valley, Field, Summit [Kern]. When the Southern Pacific built the extension from Bakersfield to the asphaltum beds in the early 1890's, the terminal was named Asphalto. When the oil fields were developed, the railroad extended the tracks in 1900 and named the new station for Captain William H. McKittrick, son-in-law of General William Shafter and owner of the land.

McLaren Park [San Francisco]. Named April 14, 1927, by action of the Board of Park Commissioners, in honor of John McLaren, superintendent of San Francisco parks from 1890 to 1943. **McLaren Meadows** [Contra Costa]. Named in 1943 for John McLaren by resolution of the East Bay Regional Park Board in recognition of his assistance in creating the local regional parks.

Maclure, Mount; Maclure: Fork, Creek, Glacier, Lake [Yosemite National Park]. The Whitney Survey named the mountain in 1868, in honor of the Scotch-American geologist, William Maclure (1763–1840). "To the pioneer of American geology . . . one of the dominating peaks of the Sierra Nevada is very properly dedicated" (Whitney, *Yosemite Book*, 1869, p. 101). In 1901 the Geological Survey applied the name to this branch of the Lyell Fork of Tuolumne River. The other features were named in 1932 by the Geographic Board. On some maps the name is erroneously spelled McClure.

McNears: Landing, Point [Marin]. This point had been known as Point San Pedro since 1811. In the 1870's an important fishing industry was developed here by Chinese (Co. Hist., 1880, pp. 346 f.), and the landing, and later the point, became known as McNears, for the firm, McNear & Brothers, the owners of the land.

Macomb Ridge [Yosemite National Park]. Named for Lieutenant Montgomery M. Macomb of the Wheeler Survey, who mapped the region in 1879.

McPherson [Orange]. The post office, now discontinued, was established about 1885, and named for Robert McPherson, station agent and first postmaster.

McQuaide, Camp [Santa Cruz]. Established September 17, 1940, by the War Department as a special training center and named in honor of Joseph P. McQuaide, a chaplain in the Spanish-American War and in World War I (Shirley Potter).

Mad. Among miners and settlers this adjective was a favorite descriptive term in place naming, used in the sense of 'crazy,' 'enraged,' 'angry,' and was applied usually because of an incident. Several of these names have survived. Names including the adjective "crazy" were less common, and only one such name appears on California maps: Crazy Mule Gulch [Yosemite National Park]. **Mad River**; **Mad River: Ridge, Rock** [Humboldt, Trinity]. The stream was named in December, 1849, by members of an exploring party led by Dr. Josiah Gregg. The leader became very angry with his companions for not waiting for him when he wished to determine the latitude of the mouth of the river. "As the canoes were about pushing off, the Doctor . . . hastily caught up his instruments and ran for the canoe, to reach which, however, he was compelled to wade several steps in the water. His cup of wrath was now filled to the brim; but he remained silent until the opposite shore was gained, when he opened upon us a perfect battery of the most withering and violent abuse. Several times during the ebul-

lition of the old man's passion, he indulged in such insulting language and comparisons, that some of the party . . . came very near inflicting upon him summary punishment by consigning him, instruments and all, to this beautiful river. Fortunately for the old gentleman, pacific councils prevailed . . . This stream, in commemoration of the difficulty I have just related, we called Mad River." (Wood, *Discovery*, p. 12.) Mad River is mentioned in the *Statutes* of 1851 (p. 179) and was apparently put on the map by Gibbes in 1852. **Mad Canyon Creek** [Placer]. The tributary of the Middle Fork of American River was named after the Mad Cañon Diggings, a mining camp mentioned in the Sacramento *Daily Transcript* of March 15, 1851. **Mad Mule Canyon, Mad Ox Canyon** [Shasta]. The incidents which led to the naming of the two canyons on Whiskey Creek are not known. The former was known as a gold-mining site in 1851 and was a voting precinct in 1853 (Steger); the latter is mentioned in the Shasta *Courier* of May 29, 1852.

Maddox, Mount [Kings Canyon National Park]. Named in memory of Ben M. Maddox of Visalia, who died in 1933 (Farquhar).

Madeline: Plains, post office [Lassen]. The name commemorates a little girl by that name, killed when a party of immigrants were attacked by Indians in the early 1850's (H. E. Risdon). It was first applied to the pass west of Mud Lake [Nevada] and appears in the Pacific Railroad *Reports* as Madelin Pass. The plains are shown by von Leicht–Craven with the present spelling. The post office was named in the 1870's.

Madera, má-dâr'-à: city, **County, Peak.** When the California Lumber Company built a flume from the forest area to the railroad in 1876, the pleasant-sounding Spanish word for 'lumber' was chosen as an appropriate name for the new lumber town. On March 11, 1893, the part of Fresno County north and west of San Joaquin River was organized as a new county and named after the town. The name of Black Peak was changed to Madera Peak by the Geographic Board (*Sixth Report*) at the request of various organizations of the county. **Madera Creek** [Santa Clara]. The stream is shown as *Arroyo del Matadero* (slaughtering place) on *diseños* of the 1830's and 1840's and on American maps until the 1870's. The name may have been changed accidentally because of the similarity in sound. *See* Corte Madera.

Madison [Yolo]. In 1877, when the Vaca Valley

and Clear Lake Railroad extended its line from Winters to a point one mile beyond the old trading center Cottonwood, a new townsite was laid out at the terminus and named Madison (Co. Hist., 1879, p. 71). The name was not given in honor of our fourth President; it was applied in 1870 by Daniel Bradley Hulbert, a native of Madison, Wisconsin, according to William E. Ashton.

Madonna, Mount [Santa Clara]. The Italian designation for the Virgin Mary was applied to the peak west of Gilroy by Hiram Wentworth, a pioneer of the region (Doyle).

Madrone, má-drōn'. The common designation for one of our most beautiful native trees (*Arbutus menziesii*) is derived from its Spanish name, *madroño*, and is found in numerous place names, chiefly in the mountains, foothills, and gravelly valleys of the Coast Ranges, the principal habitat of the tree. Madrona is a common variant of the name.

Magalia, má-gāl'-yá: post office, **Reservoir** [Butte]. The settlement was started in 1850 by E. B. Vinson and Charles Chamberlain and became known as Dogtown. In 1862, so the story goes, A. C. Buffum, a citizen, suggested the Latin word for 'cottages' as a more fitting name for the town which, he declared, was, after all, a town of cottages and not dog houses (Doyle). The new name was probably applied when the post office was transfered from Butte Mills, November 14, 1861.

Magee Peak [Shasta]. Named for William Magee, a deputy to the U.S. surveyor general, who surveyed this district in the 1860's.

Maggie, Mount [Tulare]. Named in the 1870's by Frank Knowles, for Maggie Kincaid, a schoolteacher in Tulare County (Farquhar).

Magnesia Spring Canyon [Riverside]. The canyon was named after the magnesia spring in the canyon which opens into Coachella Valley. The spring was known to the Indians, who called it, according to Chase (*Desert Trails*, p. 27), *Pah-wah'-te*. *Pah* is the Shoshonean generic term for 'water.'

Mahnke Peak [Lake]. The mountain on which Bear Creek rises was named for the pioneer family Mahnke, who killed three bears there, one as recently as 1946 (Mauldin).

Mahogany Flat [Death Valley National Monument]. Named by Colonel J. R. White, for the desert mahogany, a shrub or scraggy tree native in our desert regions.

Maidens Grave [Amador]. Historic Landmark 28 marks what is believed to be the grave of Rachel Melton, a girl from Iowa, who came to California in a covered wagon in 1850. The name of the girl and the location of the grave have never been definitely established. (State Library.)

Mailliard Redwoods State Park [Mendocino]. The park was named in 1954 for John Ward Mailliard, Jr., a distinguished philanthropist and conservationist, who died July 11, 1954.

Main Canal [Stanislaus, Merced, Fresno]. By decision of the Geographic Board, May-Aug., 1963, this is the official name for the important irrigation canal hitherto known as Old, San Joaquin, or Kings River Canal.

Malaga [Fresno]. The post office was established about 1885 and named for the malaga grape, which is grown commercially in the district.

Malakoff Diggings State Park [Nevada]. The state park, created in 1966, commemorates one of the richest gold diggings in the state. The original mine was opened during the Crimean War, 1855, and was named after the Malakoff Tower near Sebastopol, Russia.

Malapai Hill [Joshua Tree National Monument]. The name is an Americanism derived from *malpais*, American Spanish for 'rough terrain,' 'badlands,' especially in lava-bed country. But the miners used the word also for basaltic formations, and this hill was apparently named for its basaltic rocks.

Malibu, măl'-ĭ-bōō: **Creek, Point, Lake, Beach** [Los Angeles]. The origin of the name is in the name of a rancheria (probably Chumash) *Umalibo*, which was under the jurisdiction of Mission San Buenaventura (Engelhardt, *Mission San Buenaventura*, p. 166). The present spelling appears in the name of the Topanga Malibu Sequit grant, dated July 12, 1805. A spelling variant is recorded on December 31, 1827, *la cierra de Maligo* (DSP, II, 49), and the rancho is called Malago in the *Statutes* of 1851 (p. 172). Similar variants persist until about 1880 (Goddard, 1860: Malico; Wheeler atlas sheet 73-C, 1881: Malaga). On the county map of 1881 the spelling Malibu is restored.

Mallacomes. *See* Mayacmas.

Mallory, Mount [Sequoia National Park]. Named in memory of George H. L. Mallory, a member of the British Mount Everest expeditions of 1921, 1922, and 1924, who was lost in June, 1924, after reaching a height above 28,000 feet. The name was proposed by Norman Clyde, who made the first ascent of Mount Mallory in July, 1925.

Malpaso, măl-păs'-ō: **Creek, Canyon** [Monterey]. Applied by the Coast Survey from

Arroyo de mal paso (creek of tough going or difficult to cross), shown on a *diseño* of the Sur Chiquito grant, dated April 2, 1835. **Mal Paso, Mallo Pass Creek** [Mendocino], **Mal Pass** [Humboldt]. This queer assortment is shown on the Saddle Point and Point Delgada atlas sheets of the War Department. When the Coast Survey charted the sector in 1869–1870, the name Mal Passo was applied to the steep gulch, probably because the surveyors knew the creek in Monterey County and because this one was really "mal paso." In the *Coast Pilot* it became Mal Pass, but neither name appears in the Coast Survey Gazetteer of 1940.

Mama Pottinger Canyon. *See* Pottinger.

Mammoth. The descriptive name occurs for about fifteen geographic features and places in the State, including mighty Mammoth Peak in Tuolumne County. A number are survivals of mining-boom days, when the name was a favorite. **Mammoth Peak** [Yosemite National Park]. "A very high and massive peak was seen to the east of Mount Lyell, which it nearly equalled in altitude; it was called Mammoth Mountain" (Whitney, *Geology*, I, 401). This is probably the peak later named Mount Ritter. It is possible that the Geological Survey, when the Mount Lyell quadrangle was mapped, transferred the name to the present Mammoth Peak, which is due north of Mount Lyell. **Mammoth: Mountain, Lakes, Creek, Pass, Crest** [Mono, Madera, Fresno]. The cluster recalls the big boom town, Mammoth City, which flourished briefly after the organization of the Mammoth Mining Company, June 3, 1878.

Manchester [Mendocino]. The post office was established in the 1870's and was probably named after one of the thirty-five Manchesters which already existed in the United States. Two farmers named John Manchester were residents of the county in 1879–1880, but their residence was in the Sherwood district, forty-five miles distant.

Mandeville Island [San Joaquin]. Named probably for James W. Mandeville, former assemblyman, State senator, U.S. surveyor general, and State controller.

Manhattan Beach [Los Angeles]. Named in 1902, after New York's Manhattan Island, at the suggestion of Stewart Merrill, founder of the town. The place was formerly known as Shore Acres, a name given to the station established by the Santa Fe (Edna Alterton.)

Manikin: Creek, Flat [Tulare]. The places were named for an early settler by that name (Jesse

Pattee). The Great Register of 1872 lists James Henry Mankins, a native of Arkansas, farmer at Venice.

Manly: Peak, Pass, Fall [Inyo]; **Peak, Beacon** [Death Valley National Monument]. The features in Inyo County (recorded on the Searles Lake atlas sheet) commemorate William Lewis Manly, who played a prominent role in one of the Death Valley expeditions of 1849. In 1936 the National Park Service, dissatisfied with having Manly's name on only a minor peak, changed the name of the double peak marked Baldy on the Ballarat atlas sheet, designating the north peak as Manly Peak, for Manly, and the south peak as Rogers Peak, for John Rogers, as a fitting tribute to the two men who led their starving party out of Death Valley.

Mann: Ridge, Gulch [Alameda]. Named for George Mann, who settled in the district in 1855. The name is misspelled Man on the Tesla atlas sheet (Still).

Manteca, măn-tĕ'-kȧ [San Joaquin]. In 1904 or 1905 the Southern Pacific named the station, according to an often-told story, after a local creamery, which had taken its name from the Spanish word for 'butter' or 'lard.' The former name of the station was Cowell, for Joshua Cowell, who had given the railroad the right of way in 1870.

Manton [Tehama]. Named in 1892 by J. M. Meeder, probably after the town in Rhode Island (G. L. Childs).

Mantor Meadow [Kern]. This High Sierra meadow was named for a pioneer sheepherder named Mantor (Crites, p. 269).

Manvel [San Bernardino]. When the railroad spur was built north from Goffs, Isaac Blake named the station for A. A. Manvell, president of the Santa Fe (Myrick). A post office was established March 30, 1893 and changed to Barnwell February 21, 1907.

Manzana Creek [Santa Barbara]. The Spanish word for 'apple' was bestowed upon the creek in the 1870's because a large apple orchard was adjacent to it at that time (W. S. Brown).

Manzanar [Inyo]. Before its acquisition by Los Angeles for the Owens Valley water project, the site was the center of an important fruit-growing industry, whence it received its Spanish name, meaning 'apple orchard.' A post office is listed in 1912.

Manzanita, măn-zȧ-nē'-tȧ. The common name for the genus *Arctostaphylos* is the Spanish word *manzanita*, which means 'little apple.' The name is appropriate because the berries of the shrub, valued as a food by the Indians, actually look like tiny apples. This beautiful shrub, with its twenty-eight species ranging from the tall Common Manzanita to the creeping *A. Uva-ursi*, grows abundantly in all parts of the State. (Rowntree.) More than a hundred geographic features are named for it, including Manzanita Chute [Shasta], a smooth slope covered with manzanitas.

Maple. About twenty-five creeks are so named because of the occurrence of one of the three native species, the big-leaf, the vine, and the Sierra maple. Whereas most of the names are found in the northern Coast Range, where the tree thrives best, a number occur in other sections less favorable to its growth and where its presence is more notable when it is found.

Marble. The frequent occurrence of marble or similar limestone formations has given rise to more than twenty-five geographical names, including the impressive range Marble Mountains [Siskiyou], topped by a summit of limestone which looks like snow from a distance.

March Field [Riverside]. The air base was named in March, 1918, in memory of Lieutenant Peyton C. March, Jr., who had lost his life in an airplane accident in San Antonio, Texas, on February 13, 1918.

Marconi, mär-kō'-nǐ [Marin]. In 1914 the Radio Corporation of America installed a station 'here and named it in honor of the famous Italian pioneer in wireless communication, Guglielmo Marconi (D. J. Steele).

Marcuse [Sutter]. The name for the station is recorded on the Official Railway Map of 1900 and was probably given for Abraham and Jonas Marcuse, who came from Germany before 1870 and acquired large land holdings in the county.

Mareep Creek [Humboldt]. The Yurok name of the stream was *Me'rip Wroi; Merip* was an Indian village near the confluence of the creek with Klamath River (Waterman, map 17).

Mare Island [Solano]. The island (or rather part of a peninsula) was called *Isla Plana* (flat island) by Ayala in 1775. According to a generally accepted story, the island was named *Isla de la Yegua* (isle of the mare) by M. G. Vallejo when his favorite white mare saved herself from a capsized boat by swimming to the island, from which she was later retrieved (Co. Hist., 1879, p. 247). A different story is told by Joseph W. Revere: "This island is famous for being the resort of a large herd of these animals [elk], which are invariably accompanied by a *wild mare*, who has found

her way thither. But although we saw this beautiful band, feeding in company with their equine friend, we could not get near enough for a shot . . ." (*Tour of Duty*, 1849, p. 67.) This report is confirmed by another reliable witness, Bayard Taylor (*El Dorado*, 1855, p. 215). Vallejo's mare and the mare that joined the elks were perhaps one and the same, not a favorite horse but an ordinary animal not worth the trouble of retrieving. Isla de la Yegua was the name of the grant of the southern tip of the peninsula, dated October 31, 1840, and May 2, 1841; litigation over this grant continued until May 25, 1942, when the U.S. Supreme Court rejected the claim of the U.S. Navy for the entire peninsula. In the *Statutes* of 1850 (p. 60) and on Gibbes' map of 1852 the hybrid Yegua Island occurs, but the Coast Survey established the English version. Mare Island Strait is shown on the Coast Survey sketch of San Francisco Bay in 1850. Mare Island Navy Yard was established and named by act of Congress, August 31, 1852.

Maricopa [Kern]. The name was applied to the new terminal when the spur of the Southern Pacific was extended from Sunset (now Hazelton) in 1903–1904. Sunset Valley had apparently once been called Maricopa Valley (Geographic Board, *Sixth Report*). It is doubtless a transfer name from Arizona, where the name of the Maricopa Indians on the Gila River is included in the names of a county and eight other places and features.

Marie Lake [Fresno]. The lake was named when the Mount Goddard quadrangle was mapped, 1907–1909, by R. B. Marshall, for Mary Hooper, later Mrs. Frederick L. Perry, eldest daughter of Major William B. Hooper (Farquhar).

Marin, mȧ-rǐn': **Islands, County, Peninsula.** The bay between San Pedro and San Quentin points, in which the two islands lie, was named *Bahia de Nuestra Señora del Rosario la Marinera* by Ayala in 1775, doubtless for the patron saint of his vessel, the *San Carlos*. This name is shown on the maps of Ayala and Cañizares (1775, 1776, and 1781) and Dalrymple (1790). Although another map shows the abbreviated version *Bahia del Rosario* (Wagner, p. 492), it is possible that a different abbreviation *Bahia de la Marinera* survived locally, and that the name *Marinera* was also applied to the islands. *Ya* [*Ysla*] *de Marin* is shown near the two islands on a *diseño* of the Corte Madera del Presidio grant (about 1834), and in 1850 the islands are designated as Marin Islands on Ringgold's charts and in the *Statutes* (p. 60). The larger island may be the one called *del Oro* by Payeras, May 28, 1819 (Docs. Hist. Cal., IV, 341). Vallejo, in 1850, in his Report told the story of a great Indian chief and military leader named Marin, for whom he said the islands had been named. That the Indian was a chief is questionable, and the stories of his prowess are doubtless fictional, but apparently there actually was an Indian, a boatman, by the name of Marin at Mission San Rafael (*CFQ*, IV, 166 f.), who quite possibly lived for a time on one of the islands. Whether the islands were named for this Indian or whether Ayala's *Bahia de . . . la Marinera* was the origin of the modern name is still an unanswered question.

Marina, má-rē´-na. The name, meaning 'shore' or 'seacoast,' is used for a post office in Monterey County and for a district in San Francisco; it does not seem to have been used in California as a place name in Spanish times.

Marion: Lake, Peak [Kings Canyon National Park]. The lake was named in 1902 by J. N. LeConte, for his wife, Helen Marion, who was with him on a pioneering trip up Cartridge Creek (Farquhar).

Mariposa, mâr-ĭ-pō´-zà: **Creek, town, County, Grove** [Mariposa]; **Mariposa Peak** [Merced]. Padre Muñoz, who accompanied Gabriel Moraga on his expedition through the San Joaquin Valley in 1806, records in his diary (Arch. MSB, IV, 1–47), September 27, 1806: "This place is called [place] of the *Mariposas* [butterflies] because of their great multitude, especially at night and morning . . . One of the corporals of the expedition got one in his ear, causing him considerable annoyance and no little discomfort in its extraction." It is, of course, not certain that the arroyo at which the expedition camped is identical with present Mariposa Creek. The name Las Mariposas was given to two land grants, dated September 19, 1843, and February 22, 1844. Frémont in his *Memoirs* (p. 444) speaks of Mariposas River in connection with his third expedition (1845–1846). In 1847 Frémont acquired the claim for the rancho which had been granted to Juan B. Alvarado in 1844. In his *Memoirs* (p. 447) the great trail blazer expresses his own ideas of the origin of the name: "On some of the higher ridges were fields of a poppy which, fluttering and tremulous on its long thin stalk, suggests the idea of a butterfly settling on a flower, and gives to this flower its name of *Mariposas*—butter-

flies—and the flower extends its name to the stream." Frémont's version of the origin of the name of the stream is hardly acceptable even without Muñoz' direct evidence. Ina Coolbrith, to be sure, calls the lovely *Calochortus*, commonly known as Mariposa lily or tulip, "Thou winged bloom! thou blossom butterfly!" But such poetic thoughts were foreign to the men of Moraga's expedition even though the flower may have grown at their camping place, for its blossom is especially attractive to butterflies and other insects. When the county (one of the original twenty-seven and at first including most of southern California) was created on February 18, 1850, the singular form, Mariposa, was chosen. The town sprang up when gold was discovered on Mariposa Creek in 1849; it was moved to the present site early in 1850. Mariposa Grove in Yosemite National Park was discovered by Galen Clark and Milton Mann in May, 1857, and was so named because it was in Mariposa County. It is mentioned as Mammoth Grove of Mariposa in *Hutchings' Illustrated California Magazine* of December, 1858. The name for the peak at the junction of Merced, San Benito, and Santa Clara counties was apparently applied by the Geological Survey when the Quien Sabe quadrangle was mapped in 1917–1918.

Marjorie, Lake [Kings Canyon National Park]. Named for Marjorie Mott, later Mrs. David C. Berger, daughter of Ernest J. Mott of San Francisco (Farquhar).

Markham [Sonoma]. The place near the mouth of the Russian River was named for Andrew Markham, who built a sawmill there in the late 1880's (Borden).

Markham, Mount [Los Angeles]. Named by the Forest Service, for Henry H. Markham, governor of California from 1891 to 1895.

Markleeville: town, Creek, Peak [Alpine]. The post office was established October 21, 1863, and was named for Jacob J. Marklee, a settler of 1861 who was later killed in a quarrel over the land on which the town was built. The town was incorporated by act of the legislature in 1864, and kept the name of the post office. The site of Marklee's cabin is Historical Landmark 240.

Mark West: Springs, Creek, station [Sonoma]. The places preserve the name of Mark (or William Marcus) West, an Englishman who came to California from Mexico in 1832, was naturalized in 1834, and received the San Miguel grant, November 2, 1840. The Indian name of the stream had been *Potiquimi*. The post office at the station and the old mill existed from 1865 until 1917. In 1894-1895 the short-lived utopian colony Altruria existed here.

Markwood Meadow [Fresno]. The meadow southeast of Shaver Lake was named for William Markwood, a sheepman of the 1870's (Farquhar).

Marshall [Marin]. Originally called Marshalls, for Alexander S. Marshall and his brothers James, Hugh, and Samuel, who settled in the county in the 1850's and built a hotel here in 1870 (Co. Hist., 1880, pp. 413 f., 503).

Marshall Historical Monument [El Dorado]. The monument at Coloma was erected by the State in 1890 in honor of James W. Marshall, the discoverer of gold at Sutter's mill January 24, 1848. Historic Landmark 143 and state park.

Marsh Creek [Contra Costa]. The only feature which preserves the name of John Marsh, one of the foremost pioneers of central California. (*See* Glossary.) The creek, on which Marsh built his home, was formerly called *Arroyo de los Poblanos*. His shipping point, four miles west of Antioch, was for many years known as Marsh's Landing.

Martell [Amador]. The post office was established about 1906 and was probably named for a descendant of Louis Martell, who came from Canada before 1866 and settled in nearby Jackson.

Martha Lake [Kings Canyon National Park]. The lake at the foot of Mount Goddard was named in 1907 by George R. Davis, topographer of the Geological Survey, for his mother (Farquhar).

Martin Creek [Sonoma]. Probably named for Martin E. Cook, co-patentee of part of the Mallacomes grant, through which it flows.

Martinez, mär-tě′-něs [Contra Costa]. Named in 1849, for Ignacio Martínez, born in Mexico City in 1774, *comandante* at the Presidio of San Francisco, 1822–1827. The town was laid out in 1849 by Colonel William M. Smith on Rancho El Pinole, which had been granted to Martínez in 1823 in recognition of military service. *See* Pinole.

Martins Beach [San Mateo]. Named for Nicholas Martin, a prosperous rancher, who came to California in 1850 and at one time owned this beach (Wyatt).

Marvin Pass [Kings Canyon National Park]. The pass between Mount Maddox and Mitchell Peak was named by Sam L. N. Ellis, of the Forest Service in this region, for his son Marvin (Farquhar).

Mar Vista [Los Angeles]. The original name, Ocean Park Heights, was changed by the community in 1904 to avoid confusion with Ocean Park (E. A. Johnson). Mar Vista is pseudo-Spanish, suggesting 'view of the sea.' The post office is listed in 1925.

Mary Austin, Mount [Inyo]. The mountain west of Independence was named for the author of *Land of Little Rain* and many other books and articles on the Southwest, and a long-time resident of the area (Geographic Board, Jan.-March, 1966) .

Mary Blaine Mountain [Trinity]. The mountain was named before 1870 after the mine named for Mary Blaine, who operated a roadhouse at the junction of the old Trinity and and Klamath trails (J. D. Beebe).

Marysville [Yuba]. Theodor Cordua, a native of the duchy of Mecklenburg, Germany, established a ranch at the site of modern Marysville in the fall of 1842, on land which he had leased from Sutter. He was the first settler in the Sacramento Valley north of New Helvetia. "I called my whole settlement New Mecklenburg, hoping that I would be able to share it with many of my own countrymen" (*Memoirs*, p. 7). Cordua called the grant which he received on December 22, 1844, Honcut, but on most maps it is labeled Mecklenburg, or New Mecklenburg, or Cordua's Rancho. The present city was laid out in the winter of 1849–1850 by Auguste Le Plongeon, a French ·surveyor, for Covillaud and Company, who had acquired Cordua's land grant. Sutter, in conveying his equity in the townsite to Covillaud and his partners, had used the name Jubaville (Yubaville), and many would have favored this name had it not been for Yuba City across the river. Sicardoro (for Theodore Sicard), Circumdoro, and Norwich were proposed. Finally, at a public meeting in January, 1850, the town was named Marysville, in honor of Mary Murphy Covillaud, a survivor of the Donner party and the wife of Charles Covillaud, the principal owner. The name Marysville had already been used in advertisements prior to the meeting. The prominent peaks west of the city are called Marysville or Sutter Buttes.

Mason, Fort [San Francisco]. The name was given to the fort at Point San Jose by the War Department in 1882 in memory of General Richard B. Mason, who had been military governor of California, 1847–1849.

Masonic: Gulch, Mountain, settlement [Mono]. Named after the mines, which were first worked in 1862 by a group of Masons from

Aurora (Maule).

Massacre Canyon [Riverside]. The name was applied to the canyon a few miles north of San Jacinto because it had once been the scene of a battle between the Ivahs and the Temeculas over a supply of wild grain (Drury, p. 127).

Matagual Valley [San Diego]. *Matagua* is mentioned as the name of a rancheria in the *Valle de San Jose* in 1795 (SP Mis., II, 55 ff.). On a map of the valley of 1844 the name *Matajuai* is shown near the southeastern end of what is now Matagual Valley (J. J. Hill, *Warner's Ranch*, pp. 29, 207). According to Kroeber, the name *Matajuai* is derived from Diegueño *Amat-ahwai*, 'earth-white,' and was given to the place because white scum, used by the Indians as paint, was found there.

Matanzas Creek [Sonoma]. The stream is labeled Matanza Creek on a map of Part of Cabeza de Santa Rosa Rancho (1859) and Matanzas Creek on a map of Los Guilicos Rancho. "At the killing season, cattle were driven from the rodeo ground to a particular spot on the rancho, near a brook or forest. It was usual to slaughter from fifty to one hundred at a time ... The occasion was called *the matanza*." (W. H. Davis, pp. 45 f.)

Mather, măth'-ēr: **Field** [Sacramento]. Named by the War Department in 1936, in memory of Lieutenant Carl Mather, Aviation Section, Signal Officers' Reserve Corps.

Mather, măth'-ēr: **Pass** [Kings Canyon National Park], station [Yosemite National Park], **Grove** [Humboldt]. These names commemorate Stephen T. Mather, a native of San Francisco and first director of the National Park Service (1917 to 1929). The pass was named on August 25, 1921, by a party which included Mr. and Mrs. Chauncey J. Hamlin, of Buffalo, New York, probably the first group to cross with a pack train. The name was applied to the station on the Hetch Hetchy Road by M. M. O'Shaughnessy, city engineer of San Francisco. The post office at the station is listed in 1921.

Matheson [Shasta]. Named in 1920 by the Mountain Copper Company, a subsidiary of Matheson and Company of London, in memory of the founder of the famous firm, James Matheson (W. F. Kett). The post office is listed in 1924.

Mathews, Lake [Riverside]. The major reservoir of the Colorado River Aqueduct was named about 1940 for W. B. Mathews (1865–1931), the first general counsel of the Metropolitan Water District of Southern Califor-

nia, Los Angeles, and a leader of the building project (Riverside Public Library).

Matilija, má-tĭl'-ĭ-hä: **Canyon, Hot Springs,** station [Ventura]. *Matilja* was one of the Chumash rancherias under the jurisdiction of Mission San Buenaventura and is mentioned in its archives (I, 27). *Arroyo de Matilija* is recorded in 1827 (Dep. Recs., V, 74), and *Rancheria de Matilija* is shown on a *diseño* of El Rincon. The name is mentioned by Taylor with the phonetic spelling Matiliha on October 18, 1861, and with the Spanish spelling Matilija on July 24, 1863. The name was applied to the Southern Pacific station when the extension from Ventura to Nordhoff (Ojai) was built in 1898. The meaning of the word is unknown. Since the matilija poppy grows in abundance in the canyon, and since the Indians valued the plant highly for its medicinal properties, it is not impossible that the name may actually have been the Chumash name for the plant with the spectacular blossom.

Matterhorn: Peak, Canyon [Yosemite National Park]. The name of one of the grandest Alpine peaks was applied in 1877 by Muir, perhaps to Banner Peak near Mount Ritter (Farquhar), and in 1878 was applied by the Wheeler Survey to the peak and the canyon which still bear the name (atlas sheet 56-D). "That the name is a poor one there can be no doubt, for ... there is only the barest suggestion of resemblance to the wonderful Swiss mountain after which it is called" (L. Hutchinson, *SCB*, III, 162 f.). The name Matterhorn Peak on LeConte's map and the Geological Survey map is tautological: *horn* is a German generic term for 'peak.'

Matthes, măth'-ĕs: **Crest** [Yosemite National Park]. The name was proposed in 1946 by Reid Moran, then a Yosemite ranger-naturalist, in honor of Dr. François Emile Matthes, Senior Geologist, U.S. Geological Survey, who made outstanding contributions to the knowledge of the physiography of the Sierra Nevada between 1913 and 1948, the year of his death. The crest is the cotype of a geological form first generically described by Matthes as a cockscomb. (David Brower.) *See* Cockscomb Crest.

Mattole, má-tōl': **River, Canyon** [Humboldt]. The name commemorates an Athabascan tribe who were practically exterminated because of their fierce resistance to the white intruders. According to Powers in 1877 (p. 107), the original name was *Mattóal;* the present spelling, however, appears as early as

1862 on the Land Office map. According to Kroeber, the Wiyot Indians of Humboldt Bay called the Athabascans of this vicinity *Medol,* a name which may have the same root. Local tradition interprets the name as meaning 'clear water' (Co. Hist., 1882, p. 126). The canyon is submarine, one mile off shore at latitude 40° 17', and was named by the Geographic Board in 1937.

Maturango Peak [Inyo]. The Whitney Survey left the highest peak of the Argus Range nameless, but the name appears in 1877 on sheet 65-D of the Wheeler atlas. On later maps the name is usually misspelled. The Geological Survey restored Wheeler's version when the Ballarat quadrangle was mapped in 1905–1906 and 1910–1911. The origin of the name is unexplained.

Mawah Creek [Humboldt]. The name is derived from the Yurok name *Mä'wä Wroi; wroi* is the Indian word for 'creek' (Waterman, map 17); the meaning of the specific name is not known.

Maxon: Resort, Dome, Meadow [Fresno]. Named for Charles N. Maxon, an early setler who operated a hotel at the site of the modern resort (Co. Hist., 1956).

Maxwell [Colusa]. Established in 1878 and named for George Maxwell, an early resident.

Maxwell Creek [Mariposa]. The tributary to Merced River was named for George Maxwell, a gold miner of 1849. The post office at Coulterville was called Maxwell Creek from 1852 to 1872. *See* Coulterville.

Mayacmas, mā-yăk'-măs, mȧ-ăk'-ȧ-măs: **Mountains, Maacama Creek** [Sonoma, Lake]. The mountain chain, forming the divide of the headwaters of Russian River and Clear Lake, was named for the Indians on the west slope, probably a division of the Yuki. According to Barrett (*Pomo,* p. 269), there was a Yukian Wappo village, *Maiya'kma,* one mile south of Calistoga. *Serro de los Mallacomes* [Mount Saint Helena] is shown on a *diseño* of the Caymus grant (1836). Later the name appears in the title and on the *diseños* of a land grant Mallacomes y Plano de Agua Caliente or Moristul, dated September 3, 1841, and October 11 and 14, 1843. The present spelling is used in the *Statutes* of 1850 (pp. 60 f.). Although this version was also used by the Whitney Survey, confusion persists to the present day. The Geographic Board (*Fifth Report*) decided for Miyakma, but in 1941 it reversed this decision in favor of Mayacmas ("not Miyakma, Cobb Mountain Range, Malacomas, Mayacamas, nor St. Helena

Range"). The stream is still called Maacama Creek.

Mayfield [Santa Clara]. In 1853 Elisha O. Crosby, who had been a member of the California Constitutional Convention of 1849, bought a tract of land which he called "Mayfield Farm." The name Mayfield was given to the post office in 1855, to the railroad station in 1863, and to the town which was laid out by William Paul in 1867. In 1925 the town was annexed to Palo Alto. Mayfield is a very popular American place name.

Mayfield Canyon Battleground [Inyo]. The place was registered as Historical Landmark 211 on June 20, 1935, in commemoration of the battle fought by California cavalry and settlers against the Indians in April, 1862. One leader of the settlers, named Mayfield, was killed.

Mayhew [Sacramento]. The name is shown on the Land Office map of 1879. According to the county history of 1890, Mayhew Station was one of the first stations on the Sacramento Valley Railroad built by Theodore D. Judah in 1856, and was named for the station agent. In McKenney's Directory of 1880 it is listed as Mahews, with L. Mahew as agent.

May Lake [Yosemite National Park]. Named by Charles F. Hoffmann, for Lucy Mayotta ("May") Browne, who became his wife in 1870 (Farquhar).

Maywood [Los Angeles]. This popular American place name was chosen for the town by a vote of the citizens, probably at the time of the incorporation in 1924 (Myrtle Reed).

Mc. *See* Mac. The Postal Guides and most modern gazetteers list all names with this prefix under Mac.

Meachim Hill [Sonoma]. Probably named for Alonzo Meacham, who in 1853 established a general store and trading post in Santa Rosa.

Meadow. The common generic term has also been repeatedly used as a specific term, especially in connection with Creek and Lake. A number of Meadow names have been transferred to towns and stations. Meadow Valley [Plumas], once a rich gold-mining center, has a post office, established October 3, 1855, and Meadow Lake [Nevada] is a reminder of the even richer mining town of the 1860's, Meadow Lake City.

Meads [Shasta]. The station was named for Dr. Elwood Mead (1858–1936), late commissioner of the U.S. Bureau of Reclamation (Steger).

Mears Creek [Shasta]. The tributary of the Sacramento was named for Henry Mears, a trapper, who built a rock fort on this creek in the winter of 1862 as a protection against the Indians (Steger).

Mecca: town, **Hills** [Riverside]. When this part of the desert was reclaimed through irrigation for date culture, the name of the Arabian city was considered more appropriate than Walters, the name by which the settlement had been known since 1896. The name was changed to Mecca, September 26, 1903, at the suggestion of R. H. Myers, founder of the Mecca Land Company (*Westways*, February, 1951).

Medanos, mĕ-dä'-nōs, **Point** [San Diego]. The name, meaning 'sand banks' or 'dunes,' was applied to the cape by the Coast Survey in modern times. On a *diseño* of the Pueblo Lands of San Diego some *meganos* (another spelling) are shown near *Punta Falza* (False Point). **Los Medanos,** mĕ-dä'-nōs [Contra Costa]. The name was applied to the Southern Pacific station in 1878 because it was situated on the land grant Los Medanos, dated November 26, 1839. The spelling variant Meganos had been used earlier for another grant in the district, dated October 13, 1835, which was finally patented to John Marsh's daughter. A *paraje que llaman los Meganos* (place called the sand dunes) is mentioned in Durán's diary on May 24, 1817.—In both sections of the State the accent of this Spanish name has shifted from the first to the second syllable.

Meder Creek [Santa Cruz]. Named for Moses A. Meder, a Mormon who had come to San Francisco in 1846 with Samuel Brannan and who later acquired the property through which the creek runs.

Medicine Lake [Siskiyou]. According to local Indian tradition, the Indians held here "big medicine" rites and, apparently, puberty rites. Shastan youths, in acquiring adult status, were compelled to run from Strawberry Valley to Medicine Lake carrying stones in thongs passed through slits in their flesh. (Schrader.) The name does not seem to appear on older maps. The Land Office map of 1890 has the present name, but the Mining Bureau map of 1891 has Crystal Lake. There are about twenty-five other Medicine Lakes, Creeks, and Gulches in the State. Some names may go back to Indian times, others doubtless were applied because the water or nearby herbs proved to be of healing value to exhausted travelers.

Meeks: Bay, Creek [El Dorado]. The name appears on the maps of the 1870's: Micks Bay and Meadow (von Leicht–Hoffmann, Wheeler), Meeks Bay (Bowman). Several Meeks were registered in the county, but none can be definitely connected with the place.

Meganos. *See* Medanos.

Meiners, mī'-nĕrs: **Oaks** [Ventura]. Named in 1925 for Carl Meiners, a landowner in the district (H. M. Rider).

Meloland [Imperial]. The place was named about 1910 by the well-known author Harold Bell Wright, because of the mellow nature of the loamy soil (L. G. Goar).

Melones: post office, **Reservoir** [Calaveras]. The present name of the place on the Stanislaus River between Angels Camp and Sonora did not appear on the maps until the name of the post office was changed from Robinsons to Melones, February 15, 1902. The name itself, however, goes back to 1850. The San Francisco *Alta California,* June 16, 1851, refers to a Meloneys Diggings, and other newspapers to a Melones claim. A rich mine on the slope of Carson Hill, called Melones, is frequently mentioned. This mine once had a mill with 120 stamps and is claimed to have produced 4.5 million dollars by 1934. In 1896 it was consolidated with five other quartz mines to form Melones Consolidated Mines. This group of mines was called the largest mining town of the state by Browne (p. 59). Edward Vischer describes the origin but not the meaning of the name: "Only a few miles from the southern end of the town [Angels Camp] . . . is the famous Carson Hill, called 'el Cerro de Melones' [hill of melons] by the Mexicans . . . That was in the summer of 1851 when the wealth of Carson Hill seemed inexhaustible. . . . There were several productive dry diggings . . . called 'Meloncitos' by the Mexicans to differentiate them from the mountain." (*CHSQ,* XI, 324.) That Carson Hill was called *Cerro de Melones* cannot be proved, although this statement has often been repeated. Likewise unproved is the generally accepted story that the Mexicans found gold flakes in the shape of melon seeds there. Flakes that looked like melon or cucumber seeds were in fact actually found in various places (Browne, p. 51; Hittell *Mining,* p. 46). This does not prove however, that Mexicans called a camp, not to mention a hill, *Melones,* the Spanish word for melons, not melon seeds. *Melones* as a place name is found in other Spanish-speaking countries and it may be just a transfer name. It is also possible that Melones is a misreading of the name McLeans or McLanes, applied to a camp or mine and repeatedly mentioned in old diaries and recorded on Gibbes', Goddard's, and other early maps close to Robinsons Ferry. The rare compound of tellurium and nickel is called Mellonite, after the Melones mine where it was found. The idea that Melones was once called Slumgullion existed only in the vivid imagination of Bret Harte.

Melville, Mount [San Mateo]. Named in memory of Melville B. Anderson, professor of English literature at Stanford University.

Mendel, Mount. *See* Evolution.

Mendenhall Peak [Los Angeles]. Named by the Forest Service for Frank Mendenhall, a hunter.

Mendenhall Valley [San Diego]. Named for Enos Mendenhall, who settled here in 1870.

Mendocino, měn-dō-sē'-nō, **Cape** [Humboldt]; **Mendocino: County,** town, **National Forest, Canyon.** The origin of the name cannot be satisfactorily explained. A *Cabo Mendocino* in the general region appears on the maps of Ortelius in 1587 (Wagner, pp. 396 f.). Padre Antonio de la Ascensión wrote the following account a few years after his return from the Vizcaíno expedition (1602–1603): "There may be some curious person who may wish to know why this cape or point of land came to be named 'Mendocino.' The reason was that when Don Antonio de Mendoza was viceroy of New Spain in 1542, he sent two ships to the Philippines . . . the first land seen [by them] returning by that latitude was this Cabo Mendocino, to which they gave the name in honor and remembrance of the viceroy . . ." (Wagner's translation, *CHSQ*, VII, 366). This story remained current and was repeated, somewhat garbled, more than two centuries later by Duflot de Mofras (p. 97). It has never been substantiated, but neither can it be refuted. Since the name apparently does not appear on maps until 1587, it is, of course, possible (and more plausible) that the cape was named for Lorenzo Suárez de Mendoza, viceroy of New Spain from 1580 to 1583. If one of the two viceroys was thus honored, the place name originated by the relatively rare method of using the adjective form of the personal name, comparable to Smithsonian, Wagnerian, etc. (In Argentina, a *Mendocino* is a man from the city of Mendoza.) It is also not impossible that some European cartographer simply placed the name on the map. It is the oldest name of a cape that has survived the various phases of real and imaginary California geography with the same spelling and in the same general location, although it was not definitely identified with the cape at latitude 40° 27' until Malaspina (1791) placed it at 40° 29' (Wagner, *ibid.*). The county, one of the original twenty-seven, was created on February 18, 1850, and named Mendocino after the cape although the latter was, and is, not within the county. The town was settled and probably named by William Kasten in 1852; the post office is listed in 1853. The national forest was created as Stony Creek Forest Reserve in 1907, was named California National Forest in 1908, and received its present name in 1932. The submarine canyon, two miles off the coast, was named by the Coast Survey, and in 1938 the name was approved by the Geographic Board.

Mendota [Fresno]. The name was given to the station in 1895 when the Southern Pacific built the extension from Fresno. Like many railroad stations, it was probably named after a town "back home." There were a number of Mendotas in the Middle West at that time.

Menlo Park [San Mateo]. In August, 1854, D. J. Oliver and D. C. McGlynn, brothers-in-law, from Menlough, county Galway, Ireland, erected an arched gate at the joint entrance to their ranches with the inscription "Menlo Park" and the date. When the San Francisco and San Jose Railroad reached the place in 1863, it adopted the name for the station. The gate stood until July 7, 1922, when an automobile struck and destroyed the landmark. (Stanger, p. 152.)

Mentone [San Bernardino]. The land was purchased by the Mentone Company in 1886, and the town was laid out in 1887 (Santa Fe). The name was probably chosen for advertising purposes; the asserted resemblance to the Riviera resort is imaginary.

Merced, měr-sěd', **Lake** [San Francisco]. When Palou and other members of the Anza expedition camped here on September 22, 1775, they named the *laguna* for *Nuestra Señora de la Merced*, 'Our Lady of Mercy' (Palou, IV, 40). It is shown as *Laguna de la Merced* on Cañizares' 1776 map. In 1798 some of the cattle of the San Francisco presidio were kept in *el parage de la Laguna de Merced* (SP Mis. & C., I, 74). September 25, 1835, the name was applied to a land grant. The hybrid name, Lake Merced, came into use in the early 1850's, although Eddy's and other maps retained the all-Spanish name. The name La Merced was also applied to a land grant in

Los Angeles County, dated October 4, 1844. **Merced: River, County, Falls** (post office), city [Merced]; **Grove, Peak, Pass, Lake** [Yosemite National Park]. The name *Nuestra Señora de la Merced* was given to the river by an expedition headed by Gabriel Moraga on September 29, 1806 (Muñoz), five days after the feast day of Our Lady of Mercy. Frémont speaks of *Rio de la Merced* in his *Exploring Expedition* (1853, p. 360), and Tuolumne River is labeled *Rio de la Merced* on Preuss' map of 1845. In his *Geographical Memoir* (pp. 14, 21) Frémont mentions an Indian name for the stream, *Aux-um-ne,* and this name appears in the plural on Preuss' map of 1848 and Wilkes' map of 1849, obviously referring to the natives on the banks of the stream. According to Powers, the Indians called the river *Wa-kal'-la* (p. 362). The modern name seems to have come into general use with the gold rush. A short-lived settlement, Merced City, on the San Joaquin north of the mouth of Merced River, is mentioned in the San Francisco *Alta California* on February 7, 1850. The mining town Merced Falls was founded soon afterward; the post office is listed in 1858. The county, carved out of Mariposa County, was named on April 19, 1855. The modern city came into existence after the Southern Pacific reached the place, January 15, 1872. The grove of Big Trees was discovered (or rediscovered) in 1871 or 1872 by surveyors for the Coulterville Road and named by John T. McLean, president of the Turnpike Company (Farquhar). Merced Peak is shown on Wheeler atlas sheet 56-D. Merced Pass was discovered by Corporal Ottoway in 1895 and was named by Lieutenant H. C. Benson (Farquhar). The lake above Little Yosemite Valley was discovered by John Muir in 1872 and named Shadow Lake, but it has been designated as Merced Lake by the Geographic Board (No. 30).

Mercur Peak [Yosemite National Park]. Named in 1912 by Colonel W. W. Forsyth, for James Mercur (1842–1896), professor of civil and military engineering at West Point from 1884 until his death.

Mercy Hot Springs [Fresno]. Probably named for John N. Mercy, a native of France, a stock raiser in the county in the 1860's and 1870's.

Meridian [Sutter]. The name was given to the post office in 1860 because the place is only one-fourth mile west of the Mount Diablo meridian.

Merriam, Mount [Fresno]. The peak was named by the Sierra Club in 1932 in honor of C.

Hart Merriam. *See* Glossary.

Merriam Mountains [San Diego]. The range near Escondido was named for Major G. F. Merriam, one of the earliest settlers in the area (San Diego Public Library).

Merrill Ice Cave [Lava Beds National Monument]. This cave with permanent ice was named for Charles H. Merrill, who homesteaded the land on which it is situated (Geographic Board, December, 1948).

Merrillville [Lassen]. A post office (now discontinued) was established before 1880 and probably named for C. A. Merrill, a native of Maine, who came to Lassen County in 1874 (Co. Hist., 1882, p. 504). "Merrill & Marker, tunneling Eagle Lake," are mentioned in McKenney's Directory, 1883–1884.

Merrimac [Butte]. The now discontinued post office was established about 1885 and given the popular American place name which originated in New England.

Merritt [Yolo]. The Southern Pacific station was named for Hiram P. Merritt, who came to California from Vermont in 1852 and settled in the county before 1866.

Merritt, Lake [Alameda]. The slough of San Antonio Creek became a "lake" through the efforts of Dr. Samuel J. Merritt, mayor of Oakland in 1869. It was named Lake Peralta, but was renamed Lake Merritt when it and the surrounding land became a city park in 1891.

Merritt Island [Yolo]. Probably named for Ezekiel Merritt, who is said to have had a hunting or trapping camp here. Merritt was a tough character connected with Sutter's Fort and participated in every fight in the last troublesome years of Mexican rule.

Mesa, mā'-sȧ. The Spanish word for a flat-topped hill with steep sloping sides is generally used in the American Southwest as a generic term, but it has not wholly replaced the corresponding English term "table." Five of the twenty-odd Mesa names in the State are land-grant names; others may also have originated in Spanish times, but most of them are probably modern applications. Monterey County has a Mesa Grande, Las Mesas Potrero, and a Mesa Coyote; Riverside County has mesas de Burro, de Colorado, and de la Punta. Some Mesa names are hybrids: The Mesa [San Diego], Burton Mesa· [Santa Barbara], Mount Mesa [Los Angeles]. Mesa Peak [Los Angeles] is actually a peak and was perhaps so named because of the real but unnamed mesa on Malibu Creek to the southeast. Some settlements derive their names from near-by mesas: Mesa Grande [San Diego], Mesaville [Riverside]. **La Mesa Battlefield** [Los Angeles], the site of one of the last engagements in the Mexican War, January 9, 1847, is Historic Landmark 167. **La Mesa** [San Diego]. The name was first used as La Mesa Heights in 1886. In 1894 a new town was started at Allison Springs (for Robert Allison, sheep rancher in the 1860's) and called La Mesa Springs. When the town was incorporated in 1912 the abbreviated form was used. The post office name had always been La Mesa; it was spelled in one word for a number of years until Eldredge came to the rescue in 1905.

Mescal. The name is of Aztec origin (Robelo, p. 598: *Me-xcalli*) and designates the fleshy edible parts of several species of Agave. This plant was of great value to the Indian tribes on both sides of the present Mexican boundary from the Rio Grande to the Pacific Coast. They used it chiefly for food but also for the making of rope, baskets, and the like. In Mexico *mescal* (usually spelled *mezcal*) is also an intoxicating drink, made from the juice of the same plant. As a place name, Mescal occurs in Los Angeles, Monterey, Santa Barbara, and San Bernardino counties. **Mescal Island** [Santa Barbara]. The Portolá expedition camped in the vicinity on August 20, 1769, near several fairly rich Indian villages: "The soldiers named these towns Mescaltitlan, but others call them the towns of La Isla; I christened them with the name of Santa Margarita de Cortona" (Crespi, p. 168). The Aztec-Mexican suffix *-titlan* means 'among'; hence the meaning of the place name, 'among the mescal.' The *mescal* may have referred to the ordinary red tuna or prickly pear. This plant grew luxuriantly on the island before the soil was used as fill for the Santa Barbara airport (O. H. O'Neill). The abbreviated form of the name appears on the 1903 edition of the Goleta atlas sheet; locally the island is also known as Mescalitan Island. **Mescal: Range, Springs** [San Bernardino]. The *Yucca mojavensis* grows plentifully in the Ivanpah Mountains. The Indians prepared the plant by roasting it in pit ovens, the common native method of preparing the food (Gill).

Mesquite, mĕs-kēt′. Mesquite is the common name for several species of the genus *Prosopis* in the acacia tribe of the pea family. The word is of Aztec origin (*mizquitl*) but is no longer used by Mexicans, who call the tree *algarroba*. The two species native to Califor-

nia are the only trees which grow, without traceable water supply, in the arid regions of the Great Basin. They are valued by Indians and desert dwellers for their seed pods and their wood. A number of places testify to their presence or former presence: Mesquite Valley (northwest arm of Death Valley); Mesquite Flat and Well [Death Valley]; Mesquite Dry Lake [San Bernardino]; a Southern Pacific station [Imperial]; and minor features.

Messelbeck Reservoir [Shasta]. The reservoir was built in 1875 and named for Frank Messelbeck, the former owner of the property (Steger).

Messick [Sutter]. Apparently named for Charles C. Messick, a native of Woodland, who came to the Meridian district in the 1870's (Co. Library).

Metropolitan [Humboldt]. Originally known as McDairmids Prairie, the place was renamed in 1904 when the Metropolitan Redwood Lumber Company built their mill there (Borden).

Mettah Creek [Humboldt]. A translation of Yurok *meta′ wroi* (Waterman, map 11). The creek (*wroi*) was named after the Indian village *Meta,* situated below the confluence of the creek with Klamath River.

Metz [Monterey]. When the Southern Pacific reached the place in 1886 the station was named Chalone, after Chalone Peaks (now The Pinnacles). In 1891 a post office was established and named for the first postmaster, W. H. H. Metz, a native of Ohio, who had settled here as a stock raiser in 1871.

Meyers [El Dorado]. The post office was established October 6, 1904, and named for the homesteader who had settled on the land before 1860. Brewer mentions the settlement in his Notes, November 7, 1863.

Meyers Canyon [Imperial, San Diego]. Named for a Doctor Meyers, cattleman and rancher near Descanso (*Desert Mag.,* June, 1939).

Miami Mountain [Mariposa]. The name is perhaps the local Indian (Yokuts) name *Mē-ah-nee* (W. M. Sell); association with the well-known eastern place name, Miami, may account for the spelling. **Miami Creek** [Madera, Mariposa]. By decision of the Geographic Board, Jan.-Apr., 1964, this is the new name for the North Fork of Fresno River.

Mica Butte [Riverside]. Probably named because a deposit of mica, a mineral very common in the State, was found there. There is a Mica Gulch near Igo in Shasta County.

Michie Peak [Yosemite National Park]. Named

in 1912 by Colonel W. W. Forsyth, in memory of Peter S. Michie (1839–1901), a native of Scotland, a general in the Civil War, and professor of natural and experimental philosophy at West Point from 1871 until his death.

Michigan: Bar [Sacramento], **Bluff** [Placer]. Miners from Michigan gave both names in the early 1850's. Michigan Bar was originally applied to the river bar and was soon transferred to the settlement known as Live Oaks. Michigan Bluff started as Michigan City one-half mile away and assumed its new name and new location when mining operations threatened the foundations of the houses (Doyle). There is also a Michigan Flat in Lassen County.

Mid, Middle. The map of the United States is dotted with hundreds of names containing these adjectives. The name is applied for a place either halfway between two other places, or in the center of a valley, etc., or amid trees, etc. For physical features it is often purely descriptive: Middle Fork, Middle Palisade, Middle Alkali Lake. **Midway: Valley, Peak; Midoil; Midland** [Kern]. The valley probably received its name because it is situated midway between San Joaquin Valley and Carrizo Plains. The name became widely known when C. A. Canfield and his associates developed the Midway oil fields in the 1890's. There are **Mid Hills** in San Bernardino County, connecting the New York Mountains with the Providence Mountains, and a creek on Henness Pass Road [Sierra] bears the unique generic: **Middle Waters.** The old Middletown [Shasta], which vanished in the 1860's, was named because it was about midway between Shasta and Horsetown, and the new **Middletown** [Lake] was named in the 1860's when it was the stage stop halfway between Lower Lake and Calistoga. Midway City [Orange] derived its name from its location exactly midway on Bolsa Avenue between Santa Ana and the beach; the post office is listed in 1930. **Midpines** [Mariposa] was named by N. D. Chamberlain in 1926 because it is "amidst the pines and midway between Merced and Yosemite." There are many other settlements and towns named for similar reasons: Middle Creek [Shasta]; Middle River [San Joaquin]; Midlake [Lake]; Midvale [Madera]; Midway Well [Imperial]; Midway [Alameda]. **Midland** [Riverside], however, is a transfer name from Michigan, given in 1928 by O. M. Knode of the U. S. Gypsum Company.

Miguel, mĕ-gĕl': **Meadow, Creek** [Yosemite National Park]. "Next day we proceeded . . . to McGill's, where I again camped . . . The ranch belongs to Mr. Miguel D. Errera, but his American friends have corrupted *Miguel* into *McGill* and by that name is his house known." (N. F. McClure, *SCB*, I, 184 f.) The original spelling has been restored by the Geographic Board.

Milagro Valley [San Mateo]. *Milagro* is the Spanish word for 'miracle,' but the name was applied apparently in modern times; it is shown neither on the *diseños* of Rancho San Pedro nor on early maps of the county. The name is spelled Milagra on the San Mateo atlas sheet.

Mile. In early California geography the word "mile," modified by a number, was a convenient and widely used specific term, and it has survived in some thirty place names. It was combined mainly with House or Creek, sometimes with Canyon, Hill, Point, River, Ridge, Rock, and Slough. With creeks the number of miles seems usually to have designated the distance along a trail from the crossing of one stream to that of another; in only a few names the length of the stream itself is indicated. In slow foot travel the distance covered was naturally small: the longest distance indicated in this manner seems to be Twelvemile Creek [Modoc]. Fortymile Creek, a little stream southwest of Placerville [El Dorado], was probably applied in jest or through a misunderstanding. Running off from Klamath River in Township 6 N, Range 6, 7 W is a trail having Four Mile, Five Mile, and Ten Mile Creeks. The first two distances are approximately correct, but the distance between the last two is something over two miles, not five miles. Such discrepancies are found elsewhere and may indicate that sometimes the miles get longer after one has walked a while in the mountains. (Stewart.) Larger numbers are found when places are designated by distance of miles along a road: Fifteen Mile Point, a projection north of Bear Lake Road [San Bernardino], is exactly fifteen miles east of Victorville. On Hoffmann's map of the Bay region (1873), Seven, Eight, Thirteen, Fourteen, Fifteen, Eighteen, and Twenty-one Mile Houses are indicated along the road from San Jose to Gilroy. On the old country road to Gasquet [Del Norte], Ten Mile, Eleven Mile, Twelve Mile, Eighteen Mile Creeks are shown, counting from the Oregon line or a point just above it. **Mile Rocks** [San Francisco]. These were called

One-mile Rocks by Beechey in November, 1826, because they were one mile south of the channel (half a mile south of Point Bonita) by which ships entered the Golden Gate. The Coast Survey applied the present name (*Coast Pilot*, 1869, p. 59.) **Ten Mile River** [Mendocino]. The stream was so named in the 1850's because it is ten miles north of Noyo. People now usually assume that the name refers to the distance from Fort Bragg, which is only about eight miles. (F. F. Spalding.) **Five Mile Gulch** [Shasta]. The Irish Placer Mining Company dug a ditch five miles long from this gulch to bring water to French Gulch for placer mining. The ditch itself is called Five Mile Ditch. (Steger.) **Three Mile Valley** in Plumas National Forest is exactly three miles long.

Milestone: Mountain, Plateau, Bowl, Creek [Sequoia National Forest]. Prospectors used this name because the abrupt mountain summit resembles a milestone. It is recorded on Hoffmann's map of 1873. The bowl and plateau were named after the mountain in 1902 by Professor W. R. Dudley, of Stanford.

Miley, Fort [San Francisco]. Named in 1900 by the War Department, in memory of Lieutenant Colonel John D. Miley, who died in Manila, September 19, 1899.

Milford. *See* Mill.

Mill. There are in the State more than one hundred Mill Creeks, all named, so far as could be ascertained, because there was or had been a mill on the creek. In addition to several Mill Gulches the maps show also Mill Spur [Yolo]; Mill Potrero [Kern]; Chino Mill Creek [Riverside]; Burnt Mill Creek [San Bernardino]. The name-giving mill was usually a gristmill or a sawmill, but some places may have been named after a stamp mill, and at least two were named after a windmill: Windmill Creek [San Luis Obispo], Windmill Canyon [Monterey]. Some of the Mill Creeks were translations of the Spanish *molino*. **Mill Valley** [Marin]. The valley was locally so known because John Reed (Reid, or Read), grantee of Rancho Corte de Madera del Presidio, had built a sawmill there in 1834 and operated it for many years. The place itself is shown as Read on Hoffmann's map of the Bay region (1873). In 1889 the Tamalpais Land and Water Company acquired the land, built a branch of the North Pacific Coast Railroad to it, and laid out the town of Mill Valley. **Mill Creek** [Tehama]. The stream is shown on *diseños* as *Arroyo* and *Rio de los Molinos;* the latter name was applied to the land grant dated December 20, 1844, and granted to Albert G. Toomes, the pioneer of Tehama. It was, however, called Mill Creek by Bidwell and others as early as 1843 and is so designated on Reading's map of 1849. The resort was first called Mill Creek Homesite, after the creek. When the post office was established in 1937, the present name was adopted at the suggestion of E. J. and W. H. Foster. **Millville** [Shasta]. One of the first gristmills of Shasta County was built here by D. D. Harrill, of Shasta. The place was known as Harrill's Mill in 1855, as Buscombe (after Harrill's birthplace in North Carolina) in 1856, and under the present name in 1857 (Steger). **Milford** [Lassen]. When J. C. Wemple built a gristmill here in 1861, he thought the name appropriate for the settlement (Co. Hist., 1916, p. 239). **Mills** [Sacramento]. The place, formerly known as Hangtown Crossing, was named after a gristmill (Co. Hist., 1913, p. 321). The station is shown on the Official Railway Map of 1900. **Millseat Creek** [Shasta]. The branch of the North Fork of Battle Creek, formerly also called Millsite, was so named because several early mills were built on this stream (Steger). **Mill Creek Redwood State Park** [Del Norte]. The nucleus of the park was the Franklin D. Stout Memorial Grove, given to the State in 1929. Since then, several magnificent groves of redwoods have been added, including the National Tribute Grove and the Hiouchi Redwoods. (Drury.)

Millard Canyon [Los Angeles]. Named for Henry W. Millard, a native of Missouri, who settled at the mouth of the canyon in 1862, raised bees, and hauled wood to Los Angeles.

Millbrae [San Mateo]. In the 1860's Darius O. Mills, one of San Francisco's leading bankers and promoters, acquired part of the Buri Buri rancho and built his residence south of the townsite. The name Millbrae (*brae* is Scottish for 'hill slope') was applied first to the railroad station, and in 1867 to the post office. The San Francisco Municipal Airport was originally called Mills Field, because it was acquired from the estate. **Mount Mills, Mills Creek** [Fresno]. At the suggestion of the Sierra Club the name was applied by the Geographic Board after Mills' death in 1910. Mills was a charter member of the club.

Mill Creek. *See* Mill.

Miller [Marin]. The name preserves the memory of James Miller, a native of Ireland, who came to California with the Stevens-Murphy-Townsend party in 1844 and settled in the county in 1845.

Miller [Santa Cruz]. The Southern Pacific station was named before 1900 for Henry Miller (of Miller & Lux), whose Bloomfield Farm was here (Hoover, p. 494).

Miller, Fort. See Millerton.

Miller Lake [Yosemite National Park]. Named by Lieutenant N. F. McClure in 1894, for a soldier in his detachment (Farquhar).

Miller Peak [Riverside]. Named by the California State Park Commission, November 9, 1935, in memory of Frank A. Miller (1858–1935), proprietor of the Mission Inn, Riverside, and civic leader.

Millerton Lake [Fresno, Madera]. In 1851 Lieutenant Tredwell Moore established a fort at the river and named it in honor of Major Albert S. Miller, a Mexican War veteran and at that time commanding officer at Benicia. In 1854 the mining town of Rootville, about one mile below, was renamed after the fort; It appears as Millerstown in the *Statutes* of 1854 (p. 222) but as Millerton on the maps. It was the county seat of Fresno County from 1856 to 1874. The reservoir, formed by Friant Dam, has now obliterated the site of the historic town, but it preserves the name.

Millikin Corners [Santa Clara]. Named for John Millikin, a native of Pennsylvania, who settled in Santa Clara County in 1852 and lived on his farm until his death in 1877. The name is often misspelled Millican.

Mills. See Mill.

Mills, Mount. See Millbrae.

Millsaps [Glenn]. Named for George W. Millsaps, of Kentucky, who came to California in 1854.

Mills College [Alameda]. In 1871 Dr. Cyrus Mills moved the Young Ladies Seminary from Benicia to Oakland. It became generally known and was incorporated under the present name in 1886. The post office was named Mills Seminary before 1880 and was changed to Mills College in 1888. Dr. Mills had intended to give the name Alderwood Seminary and had erased his name from all blueprints except the one which was in the hands of the architect and which was shown by the latter to a reporter (Wolfe).

Mills Creek. See Millbrae.

Millseat Creek. See Mill.

Millsholm [Glenn]. The station was named for Edgar Mills when the Southern Pacific spur to Fruto was built through his land in the 1880's. *Holm* is a Teutonic generic term meaning 'island' in English and Scandinavian but 'hill' in German. The latter meaning

is indicated by the surrounding hills.

Millux [Kern]. The name was applied to the station when the Sunset spur of the Southern Pacific was built in 1901. It is coined from that of the stock-raising firm Miller & Lux, which had large holdings near by (Santa Fe).

Mill Valley. See Mill.

Millville. See Mill.

Milo [Tulare]. The post office of Mountain View Valley was established in 1882 and named Cramer, for Eleanor Cramer, one of the first settlers. When the Post Office Department requested a change of name in 1888, Henry Murphy sent in a list of names, from which the Department selected Milo. (Mitchell.) There were at that time eleven other Milos in the United States.

Milpitas, mǐl-pē'-tăs [Santa Clara]. The word is a diminutive of *milpas*, 'cornfields,' apparently used to designate vegetable gardens. *Milpa* is of Aztec origin, from the noun *milli*, 'land sown with seed,' and the preposition *pa*, 'in' (Robelo, pp. 229, 269). The name was preserved through the Milpitas grant, dated September 28, and October 2, 1835. Máximo Martínez testified in the U.S. District Court on October 13, 1861, that the place was so called because his father "sowed, cultivated, and lived there, and after raising the crop, left for the pueblo [San Jose]. Some Indians were living with us." (Bowman.) The town was founded in the 1850's. Milpitas Village is shown on a plat of the Rincon de los Esteros grant in 1858, and the post office was established May 31, 1856. **Milpitas Ditch, Las Milpitas** [Monterey]. The names near San Antonio Mission are reminiscent of the Milpitas grant, dated May 5, 1838.

Milton [Calaveras]. The name was applied to the terminus of the Stockton and Copperopolis Railroad in 1871. It is not known whether the station name was given for Milton Latham, governor of California for five days in 1860, U.S. senator, successful banker, and unsuccessful railroad builder, or whether it had been intended for W. J. L. Molton, a director of the railroad, and was misspelled on maps.

Minarets, The; Minaret Creek [Madera]. "To the south of [Mount Ritter] are some grand pinnacles of granite . . . to which we gave the name of 'the minarets' " (Whitney, *Yosemite Book*, 1868, p. 98).

Mindego: Hill, Creek [San Mateo]. Named for Juan Mendico, who owned two sections of land here in 1877. The misspelling occurred on early maps and has not been corrected.

Mineral [Tehama]. When the post office was

established, June 4, 1894, it was so named because it was near the Morgan Mineral Springs. When the post office was moved to the new location, the old name was retained.

Mineral King [Tulare]. The settlement, which grew up around the mine opened here in 1872, was first called Beulah but was changed to Mineral King when a mining district was organized and proclaimed "the king of mineral districts" (Farquhar). The post office was established March 15, 1877.

Minkler [Fresno]. When the Santa Fe spur from Reedley to Delpiedra was built in 1910, the station was named probably for Charles O. Minkler, a farmer at Sanger, or for a member of his family.

Minneola [San Bernardino]. In 1902 the Santa Fe named the siding after the now vanished boom town which had been built at the site as the terminus of an irrigation canal about 1895. The name was given for Mihnie Dieterle, the wife of an official of the Southern California Improvement Company, which had built the canal. (Santa Fe.)

Minor Creek [Humboldt]. The name may have been given for Isaac Minor, who settled in Humboldt County in 1853.

Mira. One of the most popular Spanish words used in coining pleasant-sounding place names. The word does not mean 'view,' as is generally assumed, but is an imperative: 'Look!' 'Behold!' The favorite combinations are: Miramar, Mira Monte, and Mira Loma. Although these names are not Spanish for 'sea view,' 'mountain view,' 'hill view,' their application is perfectly legitimate. *Miramar* and *Miraflores* are sometimes found even in Spanish-speaking countries. **Miramar,** mĭr′-à-mär [San Diego]. The name was given by E. W. Scripps to his Linda Vista Ranch. It appears in the San Diego *Union*, August 5, 1891, and was applied to the post office in April, 1892. (Co. Library.) **Mira Loma,** mĭr-à lō′-mà [Riverside]. The original name, Stalder, for an old settler, was changed to Wineville when the Charles Stern Winery was built there. The present name replaced the alcoholic name when the post office was established, November 1, 1930. (C. E. Faulhaber.) **Miraleste,** mĭr-à-lĕs′-tĭ [Los Angeles]. The name was applied in 1924 by the Palos Verdes Project, a land-development company, after consultation with several Spanish scholars (Co. Library). *Leste* means 'east' and 'east wind.' **Miramonte,** mĭr-à-mŏn′-tĭ [Fresno] and **Mira Monte** [Ventura] were so named because of the mountain view. "Monte" may

mean mountain, but usually means 'woods' or 'bush.'

Miracle Hot Springs. *See* Hobo Hot Springs.

Mirador [Tulare]. The name, meaning 'balcony' or 'gallery,' was applied to the Santa Fe station in 1923.

Miramontes, mĭr-à-mŏn′-tĕs: **Point,** ridge [San Mateo]. The name can be traced to the Miramontes family of San Francisco, who settled south of Pilarcitos Creek in 1840 and became grantees of Arroyo de los Pilarcitos, January 2, 1841. The name was first applied to the northern headland of Halfmoon Bay by the Coast Survey in 1854. When Halfmoon Bay was charted in 1862, the name Pillar Point was chosen for this cape, and the name Miramontes was transferred to the nameless point five miles south, which was actually on the property of the rancho. The name was later given to the chain of hills north of Pillar Point without a generic name, the cartographer probably assuming that "montes" stands for mountains.

Miranda [Humboldt]. The name was applied to the post office about 1906; it is not known whether the name giver had in mind a girl or the well-known Spanish place name and family name.

Mirror Lake [Yosemite National Park]. According to Barrett (*Myths,* p. 27) and other sources, the Indian name of the lake was *Awa'ya*. The modern commonplace name was applied by C. H. Spencer, of the Mariposa Battalion.

Mission, mĭsh′-ŭn. The importance of the Franciscan missions in the early culture of the State is reflected in some fifty place names, not all of them in the proximity of an old mission. The names of the twenty-one California missions will be found under the specific names. **Mission: Bay, Bay State Park, Beach, Valley** [San Diego]. Crespi referred to the bay as the second but closed harbor of San Diego (p. 122), and Font called it *Puerto Anegado,* 'overflowed port' (p. 237). On Pantoja's map of 1782 it is shown as *Puerto Falso* (Wagner, p. 453), and this name it retained— later translated to False Bay by the Coast Survey—until the Geographic Board changed the name to Mission Bay by decision of June 2, 1915. The state park was named in 1929. **Mission: Creek, Rock** [San Francisco]. The tidal channel originally extended to Mission Dolores, making possible communication by water with downtown San Francisco. It is shown on a *diseño* of Limantour's land claim (1842) as *Estero de la Mision.* The bay between Steamboat and Potrero points, long since filled in, had been named *Ensenada de los Llorones* by Ayala in 1775, but became known to Americans as Mission Bay. Twin Peaks were sometimes known as Mission Peaks. **Mission San Jose,** săn ô-zā' [Alameda]. The mission was founded June 11, 1797, as the *Mision del Gloriosissimo Patriarco San Joseph*. In Spanish times it was commonly known as the Misión de San José. This became Mission San Jose when the post office was established, April 9, 1850. The Indian name of the site was *Oroysom*.

Mitchell: Canyon, Creek [Contra Costa]. In 1853 Captain Mitchell located a claim in the canyon south of the present town of Clayton (Co. Hist., 1882).

Mitchell: Meadow, Peak [Tulare]. The meadow was named for Hyman Mitchell, of White River, and the peak for Susman Mitchell, his son (Farquhar).

Mitchells Caverns [San Bernardino]. The caves were discovered before 1895, probably by Hi-corum, a Chemehuevi Indian, and were named for J. E. Mitchell, who later developed them.

Miter, The [Sequoia National Park]. The peak was named by Chester H. Versteeg, about 1935, because its shape resembles that of the ornamental headdress worn by bishops.

Mi-Wuk Village, mī-wŏŏk [Tuolumne]. When Harry Hoefler developed the community in 1955, he selected the name after consultation with Chief Fuller of a near-by Miwok village (Mary E. Storch).

Moaning Cave [Calaveras]. The large domelike vault was so named because of a curious sound heard at the entrance. The "moaning" disappeared after the circular stairway was built in the main chamber (Doyle). The original name was Solomons Hole. It was believed among gold seekers that it had been worked for gold in Mexican, or even Spanish times, until Trask disproved this in 1851.

Moccasin, mŏk'-à-sĭn. This word from the Algonkian Indian language, designating the footgear of American Indians, is found in the names of several California communities and physical features. **Moccasin: Creek, Peak,** post office [Tuolumne]. The creek is shown as Mocosin on Gibbes' map of 1852. The stream was so named because miners mistook the numerous water snakes for moccasin snakes, found in swampy regions in the South.

Mocho, mō'-chō, **Arroyo; Mocho Mountain** [Alameda, Santa Clara]. "It was on account

of this creek having no outlet, but sinking into the ground (except in wettest weather) after spreading out into many smaller streams between Livermore and Pleasanton, that it was given the name Arroyo Mocho, meaning 'cut-off creek' " (Still). On August 8, 1838, it is recorded in the Archives of San Jose (V, 32) that the body of Juan Carrasco had been found in the *Arroyo mocho ... haber muerto de hambre* (he having died of hunger). The arroyo is also shown on several *diseños* of the 1830's. Although the hybridization Mocho Creek is recorded as early as 1852 (*Statutes*, p. 178), the all-Spanish version is still used. When in 1875 William Eimbeck of the Coast Survey established a triangulation station on the near-by mountain, he was not sure of the meaning of the name and changed the spelling to Macho, 'mule.' In 1887 Davidson restored the original spelling of the name of the creek and the mountain (*Names,* December, 1957). The name was used elsewhere in California, but apparently it has not survived, except possibly in Los Machos Hills [Monterey], where it may refer to 'mules,' or may be the result of a similar misunderstanding.

Mococo [Contra Costa]. The name was coined in 1912 from *Mountain Copper Company,* the name of the company that owned the copper smelter at Bulls Head Point. From 1910 to 1912 the Southern Pacific station was called Lewis, for the general manager of the company.

Modesto, mô-děs'-tō [Stanislaus]. The Central Pacific reached the place on November 8, 1870, and it was intended to name the station for William C. Ralston, one of the railroad's directors and the most colorful of San Francisco's financiers. According to the often-repeated story, Ralston, upon hearing of the honor, modestly declined, whereupon the name was changed to the Spanish adjective meaning 'modest.'

Modin Creek [Shasta]. The branch of Squaw Creek was named for Jim Modin, whose home is on the stream (Steger).

Modjeska: Canyon, Island, Peak [Orange]. In the 1870's the actress Helena Modjeska and her husband, Count Bozenta, financed a farming project for Poles in the canyon. The island (also called Bay Island) was named Modjeska in 1907 when the actress bought a house there. After her death in 1909, J. B. Stephenson, forest ranger, named the mountain in her memory.

Modoc, mō'-dŏk: **County, National Forest.** The

county was created from a part of Siskiyou County by act of the legislature of February 17, 1874, and named for the Indian tribe which had been subdued after severe fighting in the Modoc War of the preceding year. Modoc National Forest was created and named in 1908. According to Livingston Farrand, the name is derived from the Klamath *Móatokni*, meaning 'southerners,' i.e., the people living south of the Klamath tribe (Hodge). The modern spelling was used in the Indian Report of 1854 (p. 471). In a geographical sense the name was apparently not applied until the creation of the county, although immigrants, traveling over the bloody trail from Lassens Pass, used the term Modoc country.

Moffett Creek [Siskiyou]. The tributary of Scott River preserves the name of a prospector who had settled at the creek for a short time in 1850 (Schrader).

Moffett Field [Santa Clara]. The air field was transferred from the Navy to the Army in 1935. The following year, the War Department named it in honor of Rear Admiral William A. Moffett.

Mohave. *See* Mojave.

Mohawk: Valley, Creek, settlement [Plumas]. The region was settled by descendants of the Palatinate Germans of New York. *See* Hosselkus. The settlement had a post office from 1881 to 1926. Mohawk is one of the most popular place names of Indian origin in the United States, hallowed by the blood of Herkimer and the settlers of Mohawk Valley at Oriskany in the War of Independence.

Mojave, mō-hä′-vĕh: **River, Valley, Sink** [San Bernardino], **Desert** [San Bernardino, Kern, Los Angeles]; town [Kern]. **Mohave: Mountains, Canyon, Rock, Wash, Indian Reservation** [San Bernardino]. The name is derived from the populous and warlike Yuman tribe on the Colorado where California, Arizona, and Nevada now meet. These Indians are mentioned in 1775–1776 as *Jamajabs* in the diaries of Font and Garcés. Kroeber refutes the explanation that the name is derived from *hamok* (three) and *avi* (mountain), i.e., the three "needles." It is fairly certain, however, that *avi* or *habi* is the Mohave word for mountain (*WF*, VII, 169). In literature the name appears with more spelling variants than any other Indian name in California. In Whipple's report the Yuman version is given as *Mac-há-vès* and the Paiute version as *A-mac-há-vès* (Pac. R.R. *Reports*, Vol. III, Pt.

3, p. 16). A spelling approximating the modern version, *Mohawa*, is used as early as 1833 (James O. Pattie, *Personal Narrative* . . . p. 93). In a geographical sense the name was first applied by Frémont for the river on April 23, 1844: "The two different portions in which water is found had received from the priests two different names [*Arroyo de los Martires* by Garcés, March 9, 1776]; and subsequently I heard it called by the Spaniards the *Rio de las Animas,* but on the map we have called it the *Mohahve* river" (*Expl. Exp.*, 1853, p. 377). Frémont's reason for applying this name to the river in the Great Basin, separated by several mountain ranges from the territory of the Mohave Indians, has been a puzzle to scholars. Kroeber believes that it arose from the "erroneous impression that this [river] drained into the Colorado in the habitat of the Mohave." The explorer, however, applied the name although he knew the river was not in Mohave territory. He had met on the day he named the stream a party of six roving Mohaves, one of whom told him that "a short distance below, this river finally disappeared" (*ibid.*), and also gave him interesting information about his tribe. This meeting induced Frémont to name the stream Mohahve. Mojave River had been called Inconstant River by Jedediah Smith in 1826 (*Travels*, p. 15), and it is thus designated on Burr's (1839) and Wilkes' (1841) maps. Mojave Valley is repeatedly mentioned in the Pacific Railroad *Reports*. Sink of Mohave is recorded on Goddard's map (1860); it is now also known as Soda Sink. The term Mohave Desert seems to have been applied by the Wheeler Survey in 1875 (atlas sheet 73-c), although it was doubtless used before that date. The town in Kern County came into existence when the Southern Pacific reached the place on August 8, 1876, and called the station Mojave because it was at the western end of Mojave Desert. The names of the places straddling the Colorado in San Bernardino County and in Mohave County [Arizona] arose because they were all in or near the habitat of the Mohave Indians. The mountains east of the Colorado are called *Hamook Häbi* on the Whipple-Ives map (1854). The Geographic Board (*Sixth Report*) decided for the spelling Mojave for the California names in the Great Basin but left the spelling Mohave for the names on the Colorado, thus accentuating the difference in the origin and application of the two name clusters, despite their common source. Lorraine M. Sherer published in the *Southern California Quarterly*, March, 1967, a long article on the history of the origin and meaning of the name. According to her, it consists of the two Indian words *aha*, 'water' and *makhave, macave*, 'along or beside,' and Mohave or Mojave, meaning 'people who live along the water.'

Mokelumne, mô-kĕl′-ŭ-mĭ, mô-kŏl′-ŭ-mĭ: **River** [San Joaquin]; **Hill** [Calaveras]; **Peak** [Amador]. According to Barrett (*Miwok*, p. 340), the name is derived from a Plains Miwok village near Lockeford. The ending *-umne* means 'people' (*see* Cosumnes, Tuolumne), but the meaning of the specific term is unknown. The Indians are called *Muquelemnes* by Durán on May 23, 1817, and their name appears with similar spellings elsewhere (Arch. Arz. SF, Vol. III, Pt. 2, pp. 83 f., 104, etc.). On the Plano topographico de la Mision de San Jose (about 1824) a village of heathen Indians, *Muguelemnes*, is indicated near the site of the present city of Lodi. The name was applied to the river by the Wilkes party, probably at the suggestion of Sutter: *Rio Mokellemos* (Eld), *Mogneles River* (Wilkes map, 1841). The name Sanjon [ditch] de los Moquelemes was used for a land grant, January 24, 1844, and the name of the river appears in the titles of several other grants. The present spelling, Mokelumne River, was used by Frémont (*Geog. Memoir*, 1848, p. 16). Mokelumne Hill, first called Big Bar, then known as Mok Hill or The Hill, developed as a mining camp in 1848 and became one of the important centers of the southern mines. The post office was established July 10, 1851. In the early days the French element among the miners predominated. They published a newspaper in the French language and had their own name for the place, *Les Fourcades*. Mokelumne City [San Joaquin], now Historic Landmark 162, was deserted when the Central Pacific built a station about ten miles southeast, which it called Mokelumne until 1874, when the name was changed to Lodi.

Molaine Corrals [Trinity]. The place has been known by this name since 1887 when Jim Molaine had a holding pasture here for his cattle (W. E. Hotelling).

Molate, mô-lä′-tė: **Point, Reef** [Contra Costa]. The name *Moleta* was applied in Mexican times to the island now known as Red Rock, probably because its shape resembles the conical stone (called *moleta* in Spanish) used by painters to grind colors. Beechey in 1826 mis-

spelled the word Molate, and this version was adopted in 1851 by the Coast Survey when it used the island as a secondary triangulation station. Molate Point was named by the Survey in 1854 and Molate Reef in 1864. *See* Red Rock.

Molino, mô-lē′-nō. The Spanish word for 'mill' was repeatedly used as a geographical term and has not only survived in a number of places but has been used for place naming by Americans. **Molino** [Sonoma]. The place was so named because it is on the Molino land grant, dated February 24, 1836. **Los Molinos** [Tehama]. The town was named after the land grant El Rio de los Molinos, dated December 20, 1844. The post office is listed in 1908. *See* Mill. **Molino Creek** [Santa Cruz]. The stream is shown as *Arroyo del Molino* on a *diseño* of the San Vicente grant (1846). On another *diseño* of the same grant it is misspelled *Aroyo del Moly-llo*. **Molino** [San Bernardino]. The Santa Fe station was named in 1909 because the Brookings Lumber Company had built a mill here in 1896 (Santa Fe).

Molybdenite: Creek, Canyon [Mono]. Named on account of an outcropping of ore of molybdenum, a metallic element of the chromium group.

Monache, Mono. A division or dialectic group of the Shoshonean Indians. Kroeber (*Handbook*, map) indicates their main habitat along the eastern slope of the Sierra Nevada from about forty miles north of Mono Lake to slightly north of Owens Lake. Their western neighbors, the Yokuts, called them *monachi*, i.e., 'fly people,' because their chief food staple and trading article was the pupae of a fly, *Ephyda hyans*, found in great quantities on the shores of the Great Basin lakes (*CFQ*, IV, 90 f.). It is certainly not accidental that their name is preserved mainly in two clusters, one at Mono and the other at Owens Lake. **Monache**, mō-nǎch′-ē: **Meadow, Creek, Mountain** [Tulare]; **Monachee** [Inyo]. The name was recorded in a geographical sense when the people of Owens Valley petitioned the legislature in February, 1864, to create a new county south of Mono County and name it Monache (Chalfant, *Inyo*, p. 175). The von Leicht–Craven map (1874) shows the phonetic spelling Monatchay Meadows; the Mining Bureau map of 1891 has the now accepted spelling. The name Monache was applied to the mountain and the creek when the Geological Survey mapped the region in 1905. With an additional "e" to indicate the pronunciation, the name was applied to the station when the California-Nevada Railway was built in 1908. **Mono**, mō'-nō: **Lake, Pass, County, Valley, Dome, Craters** [Mono]; **Divide, Rock** [Fresno]. As a geographical term the shorter and more common form of the name is the older. It was applied to the lake by Lieutenant Tredwell Moore in the summer of 1852 and appears on Trask's maps of 1853. The county was created and named by act of the legislature, April 24, 1861. There was a short-lived mining town, Monoville, after Cord Norst found gold in the hills around Owens Valley in July, 1859. Powers (p. 576) records *mo'-nekh* as the word for 'fly' among the Yokuts of the Tule River Reservation.

Monarch Divide [Kings Canyon National Park]. The divide between the Middle and South forks of Kings River was named Dyke Ridge by the Whitney Survey (*see* Dyke). The new name was apparently applied by the Geological Survey when the Tehipite quadrangle was mapped in 1903 and may have been used in somewhat jesting analogy to Kings River.

Monmouth [Fresno]. The station was named in the 1890's by the Santa Fe after Monmouth, Illinois, former home of a settler.

Mono. *See* Monache.

Monocline Ridge [Fresno]. The ridge, near the San Benito County line, was so named, probably by the Geological Survey when the Panoche quadrangle was mapped, 1908–1911, because it appears to have only one inclination or slope, extending into San Joaquin Valley.

Mono Creek [Santa Barbara]. This name may contain the Spanish adjective for 'pretty,' 'cute,' 'funny,' or the noun for 'monkey,' both of which dictionary etymologists have tried to connect with the name of the Indian tribe.

Monolith [Kern]. The place was named in 1908 by William Mulholland, builder of the Los Angeles Aqueduct after the Monolith Portland Cement Company, which is still in operation there.

Monroe Meadow [Yosemite National Park]. Named for George F. Monroe, who from 1868 to 1888 drove stages on the Wawona Road to Yosemite Valley.

Monroeville [Glenn]. The place was named for U. P. Monroe, who settled here before 1851. When Colusa County was organized in 1851, Monroe's Rancho became the first county seat. The post office is listed as Monroeville the same year.

Monrovia: city, **Hill** [Los Angeles]. Named for

William N. Monroe, a railroad construction engineer, who with his associates laid out the town in 1886 on sixty acres of Ranchos Santa Anita and Azusa de Duarte. The form of the place name reflects Monrovia in Liberia, named for President Monroe in a Latinizing period.

Monserrate Mountain [San Diego]. The name is derived from the Monserrate land grant, dated May 4, 1846. According to tradition, the peak was named in Spanish times because it resembled Monserrat, a mountain in Spain (Hist. San Bernardino Co., 1883, p. 180).

Monson [Tulare]. A railroad name applied to the station in 1887. There was at that time a Monson in Massachusetts and another in Maine.

Montague [Siskiyou]. When the Southern Pacific extension was built from Dunsmuir to the state line in 1886–1887, the station was named for S. S. Montague, chief engineer of the Central Pacific (Southern Pacific).

Montalvo, mŏn-tăl'-vō [Ventura]. The name was applied to the station when the Southern Pacific reached the point in the summer of 1887. Montalvo is thought to be the author of *Las sergas de Esplandián* (about 1510), in which the name California appears probably for the first time. Montalvo is also the name of James Phelan's estate in Santa Clara County, now semipublic (Drury).

Montana de Oro State Park [San Luis Obispo]. The name does not stand for a 'mountain of gold' but is symbolic of the blaze of spring flowers on its slope. It was the name of a rancho and the site was purchased by the state in 1965.

Montara, Point; Montara: Mountain, post office [San Mateo]. The name, spelled Montoro, was used for the mountain and the point by the Whitney Survey in 1867, and in 1869 the present form was used by the Coast Survey (*Coast Pilot*, 1869, p. 54). Both are probably misspellings of one of several similar Spanish words referring to forest and mountain: *montuoso, montaraz, montaña.* A *Cañada Montosa* (valley full of woods and thickets) was shown, about 1838, on a *diseño* of near-by Rancho San Pedro.

Montclair. The name is often used in the United States. Among the many districts and subdivisions so named the most important is the rapidly growing, rich citrus-producing Montclair in San Bernardino County, named in 1960.

Monte. The Spanish word for 'woods,' 'grove,' 'thicket,' was often used as a generic geographical term in Spanish times. Although Spanish dictionaries list *monte* also with the meaning 'mountain,' no evidence has been found that it was so used in Spanish-speaking countries except where a hill or mountain was densely covered with trees. A *diseño* of the San Antonio or El Pescadero grant (1833) bears out the use of the word in Spanish California: Butano Ridge is called *Lomas* and *Sierra con monte*, 'hills' and 'ridge with woods.' Americans believed (and still do) that *monte* means 'mountain,' as it does in Italian. Mount Diablo appears as Monte Diablo as late as 1874 (Hoffmann's maps), and the word is still used for elevations: Monte de Oro [Butte], Monte Arido [Santa Barbara]. The term has also been used for communities: Monte Rio [Sonoma], Monte Vista [Santa Clara, San Bernardino, Placer], Monte Nido [Los Angeles]. Where *monte* is used with an Italian specific term, the combination is grammatically correct: Monte Bello (beautiful mountain) Ridge [Santa Clara]. The name Monte Cristo, which occurs in Los Angeles, Mono, and Sierra counties, was doubtless chosen because of Dumas's popular novel, *The Count of Monte Cristo. See* Del Monte: El Monte; Diablo.

Montebello [Los Angeles]. In 1887 Harris Newmark, one of the grand old men of the southern metropolis, purchased part of the Repetto ranch. The entire settlement was called Montebello, an international name of Italian origin (beautiful mountain), but the town itself was named Newmark. This name was dropped on October 16, 1920, in favor of Montebello: "another of the many instances in recent years of the lack, among Californians, of proper historic respect for pioneer names," as Newmark's son remarks in the 1926 edition of his father's book, *Sixty Years in Southern California* (pp. 555, 668).

Montecito: town, **Creek, Peak** [Santa Barbara]. A place called Montecito (little woods) is mentioned by Fages as early as December 5, 1783, as a site suitable for a mission (Prov. Recs., III, 55), and there Mission Santa Barbara was founded in 1844. The name appears repeatedly in mission and land-grant papers. The present town of Montecito is farther east, on Santa Barbara pueblo lands; a *Terreno de Montecito* was given to José Rosas, probably a former soldier, on May 15, 1834. The town is mentioned as Monticito in the *Statutes* of 1850 (p. 172).

Monte Cristo Channel [Sierra, Nevada]. The name of the old river bed, stretching from

north of Downieville to North Bloomfield, goes back to the early 1850's, when rich gold deposits were discovered along its course. Alexandre Dumas's novel *The Count of Monte Cristo* was then at the height of its popularity.

Monterey, mŏn-tĕ-rā´: **Bay, Harbor, Presidio,** city, **County, Canyon.** The bay was discovered by Cabrillo on November 16, 1542, and named *Bahia de los Pinos;* Cermeño crossed it on December 10, 1595, and named it *San Pedro,* in honor of Saint Peter Martyr, whose feast day is December 9 (Wagner, p. 398). Seven years later, on December 16, 1602, Vizcaíno anchored in what is now Monterey Harbor and named it *Puerto de Monterey,* in honor of the Conde de Monterey, then viceroy of New Spain. When Portolá was sent north in 1769, he was commissioned to find this harbor, which had been described as an excellent port by Vizcaíno. On June 3, 1770, a presidio and a mission were established, both named San Carlos Borromeo. The presidio, however, was known by the name Monterey even in Spanish times, and in 1904 the U.S. War Department renewed this name in perpetuation of the first Spanish military post in California. The county, one of the original twenty-seven, was named on February 18, 1850. The submarine canyon, probably the same in which Cabrillo had anchored, was named by the Coast Survey and the name was confirmed by the Geographic Board in 1938. The Salinas River was called *Rio de Monterey* by Font on March 4, 1776, and was called Monterey River as late as 1850 (*Statutes,* p. 59).

Monterey Park [Los Angeles]. A subdivision on the Repetto ranch was developed in 1906 and named Ramona Acres. At the time of its incorporation the city was renamed after Monterey Pass to the west (Gertrude Shearer). The pass is now often called Coyote Pass.

Montezuma. The name of the Aztec chief at the time of Cortés' invasion of Mexico was suggested as a new name for Alta California by José María Echeandía, governor of the province, 1825–1831. The *Diputación* (provincial legislature) adopted the suggestion in 1827, but the Mexican government refused to concur. (Chapman, p. 460.) The name Montezuma was frequently used as a place name in the United States and after the Mexican War became very popular in California, where it still survives in a few places. **Montezuma,** mŏn-tĕ-zōō´-má: **Landing, Hills, Creek, Island, Slough,** station [Solano]. The names recall one of the many attempts of the Mormons to settle in California. Lansford W. Hastings, their agent, laid out Montezuma City at the head of Suisun Bay in 1847. Although often mentioned in contemporary newspapers and books, the "city" never seems to have developed beyond Hastings' own adobe. Montezuma Hills appear on Ringgold's general chart (1850); they are mentioned in *Hutchings' Illustrated California Magazine,* March, 1858. **Montezuma** [Tuolumne]. Historic Landmark 122 preserves the memory of Montezuma House, a prosperous trading post, established by Sol Miller and P. K. Aurond in 1850 and named after Montezuma Flats.

Montgomery Creek [Shasta]. The post office was named Montgomery Ferry in 1877, but the name was changed to the present form in 1878. The creek from which the town derives the name was probably so called because Zack Montgomery once made a big haul when fishing there in the early 1850's. (Steger.)

Montgomery: Creek, Peak [Mono]. The creek is shown on Wheeler atlas sheet 57 but the peak is labeled White Mountain Peak. The man for whom the creek was named was perhaps the owner of the mill which is shown on Hoffmann's map (1873) halfway down the course of the stream near the edge of the talus. In 1917 the Geological Survey renamed the peak and transferred the old name to a peak sixteen miles farther south.

Montgomery Memorial State Park [San Diego]. Created in 1952 in memory of John J. Montgomery, the first American to experiment with nonpowered aircraft of the heavier-than-air type; Montgomery was killed in a glider fall in 1911. **Montgomery Hill** [Santa Clara]. The hill east of San Jose was also named for the pioneer in aviation (Geographic Board, Jan.-Apr., 1964).

Monticello [Napa]. An extremely popular place name in the United States since the time of Jefferson, who gave to his Virginia estate the name of the town in northern Italy. The post office was established July 8, 1867. The town is now inundated by Berryessa Lake, but Monticello Dam keeps alive the old name.

Montpelier [Stanislaus]. The station was named in 1891 upon completion of the Southern Pacific from Oakdale to Merced, probably after the capital of Vermont. The name of the post office (now discontinued) was spelled Montpellier, but the present spelling is shown on the Official Railway Map of 1900.

Montrose [Los Angeles]. The name, which has long been a popular place name in the United States, was chosen, as the result of a contest, for the subdivision established in 1913 on part of the La Crescenta development.

Monument. About fifteen orographic features bear this name, and in addition a number of Monument Creeks are named after them. Most of the peaks so named are at the boundaries of the State where surveying parties had erected a "monument." The name **Monument Peak** at the intersection of El Dorado, Alpine, and Douglas [in Nevada] counties was apparently placed on the map—atlas sheet 56-B—by the Wheeler Survey because of the proximity of the peak to one of the granite monuments erected by the boundary survey of 1872. Some Monument Mountains were named because of their appearance.

Moody Creek [Shasta]. The branch of Stillwater Creek was named for M. G. and Elizabeth Moody, who filed a land claim on this creek in 1852 (Steger).

Moon. The word is often found in the United States as the name of a lake, but only one Moon Lake [San Bernardino] could be found in California. Moonshine Creek [Yuba] was probably named because "moonshiners" were active here; Moonlight Peak [Plumas, Lassen] must have been named by a romantic settler or surveyor.

Moon Creek [Shasta]. The tributary of Rainbow Lake was named for Arch Moon, who filed a homestead claim here in 1883 (Steger).

Mooney, Mount [Los Angeles]. Named in memory of John L. Mooney, of the Forest Service, who died in France in World War I.

Mooney Flat [Yuba]. Named for Thomas Mooney, who in 1851, in partnership with Michael Riley, established a hotel and a trading post on the near-by Empire Ranch, which was on the route of the California Stage Company.

Moonstone Beach. Three beaches [Humboldt, San Luis Obispo, Santa Catalina Island] are so named because of the moonstones washed in by the breakers.

Moorehouse Creek [Tulare]. Named for Gus Moorehouse, an early prospector (Farquhar).

Moorek [Humboldt]. The name is derived from *Mureku,* a Yurok village on the north side of the lower Klamath (Kroeber).

Moores Creek [Napa]. The creek and the ranch were named for "Old Lady Moore," the wife of a settler in the 1850's who had died under suspicious circumstances *(CHSQ,* XXXV, 9). *See* Las Posadas.

Moores Flat [Nevada]. Named for H. M. Moore,

who built the first house and store here in 1851, after having driven a herd of cattle across the continent (*Brown and Dallison's Nevada, Grass Valley Directory,* 1856).

Moorman Meadow [Mono]. Named after the pioneer Moorman Ranch, but spelled Mormon on the Bridgeport atlas sheet (Maule).

Moorpark [Ventura]. The town was founded about 1900 and named for the well-known English variety of apricot, which has always been one of the favorite varieties in southern California. The post office is listed in 1904.

Moosa: settlement, **Canyon** [San Diego]. According to the file of the San Diego Public Library, the name is an abbreviation of *Pamoosa,* which in turn is derived from *Pamusi,* a rancheria mentioned July 23, 1805. A post office, Moosa, now discontinued, is listed in 1887.

Moose, Moosehead. These names, found mainly in northern counties, were applied because large specimens of elk were mistaken for moose, which have never been observed in California. **Moose Lake** [Sequoia National Park]. The lake northeast of Giant Forest was so named because its outline on the map resembles the head of a moose.

Mopeco [Kern]. The name of the railroad siding was coined from *Mo*hawk *Pe*troleum *Co*rporation (Santa Fe).

Moraga: Valley, settlement [Contra Costa]. Preserves the name of Joaquín Moraga, a soldier in the San Francisco Company in 1819 and in 1835 co-grantee of the Laguna de los Palos Colorados grant. He was the son of the better-known Gabriel Moraga. The post office was established May 5, 1886, and reëstablished December 16, 1915, when the town was developed.

Moraine. Although the deposits of ancient glaciers are frequently found in California, the term is included in the names of only about ten features. The best known are **Moraine Lake** [Sequoia National Park], named by a party of the Sierra Club in 1897, and Mount Moraine, Moraine Ridge, and Moraine Creek [Tulare]. There is another Moraine Ridge in Tuolumne, a Moraine Dome in Mariposa, and a Moraine Mountain in Madera County.

Moran [Lassen]. The siding of the Southern Pacific was established February 28, 1953, and upon the suggestion of David F. Myrick was named for Charles Moran, builder of the Nevada-California-Oregon Railway.

Morena, mȯ-rē′-nà: station, **Butte, Valley, Dam** [San Diego]. The name is shown for the Santa Fe station on the Official Railway Map of

1900. It is not known whether its origin is a family name or the Spanish descriptive adjective meaning 'brown.'

Moreno, mȯ-rē′-nō [Riverside]. When F. E. Brown declined to have his name used for the town which he and E. C. Judson laid out in 1881–1882, the Spanish word for 'brown' was substituted (Co. Hist., 1912, p. 170).

Morgan, Mount [Inyo]. Named on August 28, 1878, by the Wheeler Survey, for one of its members, J. H. Morgan, of Alabama.

Morgan Hill [Santa Clara]. The settlement which developed on the Morgan Hill Ranch was named about 1892, for Morgan Hill, who had acquired the ranch when he married Diana Murphy, daughter of Daniel Murphy, a wealthy landholder and stock raiser.

Morgan Territory [Contra Costa]. The district was named for Jeremiah ("Jerry") Morgan, a Cherokee Indian, who came to California in 1849, and in 1856 claimed 10,000 acres of unsurveyed land east of Mount Diablo.

Morgan Valley [Lake]. Named for Charles Morgan, who settled in the valley in 1854 (Co. Hist., 1881, p. 141).

Moristul [Sonoma]. The alternate name of the three Mallacomes grants is derived from that of the former Wappo village *Mutistul* (*muti,* 'north'; *tul,* 'large valley'), four and a half miles west of Calistoga (Barrett, *Pomo,* pp. 270 f.). However, the name is already shown with the spellings Maristul and Muristul on *diseños* of the grants.

Mormon. The participation of the Latter-day Saints in the Mexican War, their connection with the discovery of gold, and their various attempts to settle in California have left distinct traces in our toponymy. More than twenty-five places with the name are still current, including three inhabited places. Mormon Creek [Tuolumne], Mormon Island [Sacramento], Mormon Bar [Mariposa], Historic Landmark 323, Mormon Point [Inyo] are names with historical implications. **Mormon Meadow** in Mono County, however, is one of the misspellings on the Bridgeport atlas sheet and should be Moorman, for a pioneer settler (Maule).

Morongo: Valley, Creek, Pass, Indian Reservation [San Bernardino, Riverside]. The names are derived from a Serrano Shoshonean village in the valley, *Maronga,* 'the largest village' (Kroeber, *AAE,* VIII, 35). Marengo (!) Pass is shown on the Land Office map of 1859 and on the von Leicht–Craven map. The name was preserved locally by settlers in the valley, and when the post office was established, July 1, 1947, it was named Morongo.

Moro Rock [Sequoia National Park]. "Mr. Swanson of Three Rivers in the sixties of the last century had a blue roan mustang—the color that the Mexicans call *moro* . . . This moro pony of Swanson's often ranged up under the rock and they called it 'Moro's Rock.' " (John R. White to Francis P. Farquhar.) Adams gives *moro*, 'a horse of bluish color,' as a Western word. There is a Moro Cojo [lame blue roan] Slough near Capitola [Santa Cruz]. *See* Morro.

Morrison, Mount [Mono]. Named for Robert Morrison, of Benton, who with a posse pursued a number of convicts escaped from the Nevada State Penitentiary and was killed by one of them on September 24, 1871. *See* Convict; Bloody.

Morro. The Spanish geographical term for a crown-shaped rock or hill, the best known of which is El Morro in the harbor of Havana, Cuba, was repeatedly used in Spanish times and has survived in San Luis Obispo, Ventura, and San Diego counties. **Morro: Rock, Bay, Creek, Beach** [San Luis Obispo]. The Portolá expedition camped in the valley of what is now Morro Creek on September 8, 1769, and Crespi mentions the rock at the entrance of the bay: "a great rock in the form of a round *morro*" (p. 186). In the expediente of the land grant, provisionally granted December 28, 1837, the word is spelled with one "r" (*Moro y Cojo* or *Moro y Cayucos*), probably because a relation to *moro* ('Moor' or 'blue roan horse') was assumed. *See* Moro. This remained the common spelling until the Coast Survey changed it back to Morro in the 1890's. A town, Moro, is shown on the von Leicht–Craven map of 1874. Morro Bay State Park was named in 1932 and Morro Strand in 1934. **Morro Hill** [San Diego]. This prominent isolated hill (also spelled Moro and Mora) was called *Katukto* by the Luiseño Indians. According to them, this hill was used as a refuge during a flood. (Constance DuBois, *AAE*, VIII, 157.) It is shown as Morro on a *diseño* of the Santa Margarita y Las Flores grant. Point Sur [Monterey] had been named by Costansó in 1769, *Morro de la Trompa*, because it looked like a rock in the shape of a trumpet (APCH:P, II, 125).

Mortmar [Riverside]. The Southern Pacific station was named Mortmere in the 1890's because of the proximity of Salton Sea (*mort*, 'dead'; *mere*, 'lake'). It is shown on the Official Railway Map of 1900, but on modern maps the Anglo-Saxon *mere* is replaced by the

Spanish *mar*.

Mosaic Canyon [Death Valley National Monument] is so called from the appearance of the rock (a breccia), which is exposed on many smooth surfaces and resembles many-colored mosaic work (Stewart).

Moscow [Sonoma]. The place on the Russian River is mentioned in the County Historical Atlas of 1877 (p. 24). It is uncertain whether the name was chosen because the settlement is on the Russian River or whether the name is an American rendering of an Indian name, *Meskua* (*Overland Monthly*, Oct., 1904), which in turn might have preserved an original "Moscow" applied by the Russians.

Moses, Mount [Tulare]. Moses, the nickname of an elderly member of a fishing party, was applied to the mountain by Frank Knowles in the 1870's (Farquhar).

Mosquito. Some fifty creeks, gulches, and lakes bear the name of the annoying little insect. Although the word came into the English language from the Spanish ('little fly'), and although the Spaniards doubtless were bothered as much by mosquitoes as were Americans, apparently none of the names date from Spanish times. The name was very popular in gold-rush days. There was once a post office Mosquito in El Dorado County, and Glencoe [Calaveras] was formerly Mosquito Gulch. The creek from which the first water was conveyed for the dry diggings in Nevada City was called Musketo Creek (Ritchie, p. 93).

Moss Beach [San Mateo]. The beach was so named because of the presence of the remarkable marine plant life, commonly called moss. There is another Moss Beach in Santa Cruz and a Moss Creek in Mariposa County.

Moss Landing [Monterey]. According to an often-repeated story, Charles Moss built a wharf here about 1865, and the place became an important whaling station. It was abandoned in 1888. The anchorage is not recorded on the detailed Coast Survey charts until about 1900. Hoffmann's map of 1873 shows Morse's Landing.

Mother Grundy Peak [San Diego]. The name was given to the peak by Mrs. Hagenbeck because it shows the distinct upward-facing profile of a large nose and a protruding chin (Hazel Sheckler).

Mother Lode. In early mining days it was believed that a huge vein of gold extended from the Middle Fork of American River to a point near Mariposa and that the known veins were offsprings of this "mother lode."

Although this idea has long since been discarded by geologists, the name continues to be used and cherished.

Mott [Siskiyou]. "The new town of Mott, south of Sisson, . . . was named after M. H. Mott, the energetic and popular road master of the railroad company" (Yreka *Journal*, July 16, 1887).

Mott Lake [Fresno]. "Named in honor of Ernest Julian Mott, mountain explorer" (Geographic Board, *Sixth Report*).

Mount. California has ten post offices and communities named after a near-by mountain; several others are transfer names. **Mount Bullion** [Mariposa]. Named in 1850 after the eminence on Frémont's Mariposas estate, which Frémont had named for his father-in-law, Thomas Hart Benton (1782–1858). The senator from Missouri had been nicknamed "Old Bullion" because he advocated the adoption of metallic currency. The post office is listed in 1862. Mount Bullion was formerly known as Princeton, named after the Princeton Mine, which in turn had been named, tradition says, for Mr. Prince Steptoe, one of the discoverers of the ore deposit. **Mount Hebron:** peak, town [Siskiyou]. The name is that of an ancient town in Palestine. It appears as Mount Hebron for a settlement on the Land Office map of 1891. The peak, six miles south, may have been named first. This would explain the generic in the name of the town. **Mount Hermon** [Santa Cruz]. In 1905 a group of Christian people purchased "The Tuxedo," a pleasure resort. Five women of the group were entrusted with the selection of a new name, and they chose that of the lofty mountain peak in Palestine. (Inga Hamlin.) **Mount Owen** [Kern]. When a railroad reached the community in 1909 the station was named Front. The name was later changed to Brown, for George Brown, owner of the hotel, and in 1949, to Mount Owen, after the peak which overlooks the valley (L. A. *Times*, June 24, 1951). **Mount Baldy** [San Bernardino]. The community was originally known as Camp Baldy, but on July 1, 1951, the name of the post office was changed to Mount Baldy upon petition óf the residents. For names with "Mount" as a generic term see entry under specific name.

Mountain. Of the generic geographical terms used as the specific part of a place name, "mountain" is the most popular in the United States. In California there are about twenty-five Mountain Lakes, Passes, Springs, etc., as well as a Mountain Top [Calaveras] and a Mountain View Peak [Madera]. Lake Tahoe was once called Mountain Lake, so named by Frémont; Mountain Lake near the U.S. Marine Hospital [San Francisco] was in Spanish times *Laguna de Loma Alta,* 'lake of the high hill,' referring to the 400-foot elevation of the Presidio. The term is also found in names of communities: Mountain View [Kern, Nevada, Santa Clara]; Mountain Ranch [Calaveras]; Mountain King [Mariposa]; Mountain House [Alameda]; Mountain Spring [San Diego]. **Mountain View** [Santa Clara]. The settlement which developed in the early 1850's around the stage station was named Mountain View because the Santa Cruz Mountains, Mount Diablo, and Mount Hamilton could be seen from the place (D. M. Burke). In 1864 the name was also given to the railroad station about one mile north and to the new town which grew up there and eventually merged with the old town.

Mountain Charlie Gulch [Santa Cruz]. Named for Charles McKiernan, better known as Mountain Charlie, an early pioneer and "noted character." He built the first road in these mountains, still called Mountain Charlie Road, and collected toll for many years. Near Glenwood on Bear Creek is Mountain Charlie Tree, a redwood 260 feet high. (Doyle.) *See* Schultheis.

Mount Bullion. *See* Mount.

Mountclef Village [Ventura]. The community northwest of Thousand Oaks and Mountclef Ridge is listed in the Geographic Board Decisions of 1964 (Jan.-Apr.) . The name is apparently a combination of Mount and the French *clef*, 'key.'

Mount Hebron. *See* Mount.

Mount Hermon. *See* Mount.

Muah Mountain [Inyo]. The location of the peak and the sound of the word indicate a Shoshonean origin, probably Mono (Kroeber). The name is not shown on older general maps and was probably applied by the Geological Survey from local information when the Olancha quadrangle was mapped in 1905.

Mud. The term is contained in the names of more than thirty features on the map, mostly springs, but also creeks, sloughs, and lakes. There is a tautological Mud Run Creek in Fresno County. Riverside County has the strange Mud Hills, so named because they seem to be wrought of mud. Mud Town was the name of Watts before it was incorporated in Los Angeles.

Muerto, moo-ĕr'-tō. The Spanish word for

'dead' or 'dead man' was frequently used in place naming in Spanish times; it has survived in the names of a number of places in the original form and sometimes in translation. When the adjective is used with a generic orographic term, it usually designates 'barren': Las Lomas Muertas [San Diego], Lomerias Muertas [San Benito]. The noun *muerto* in a name refers to a place where a corpse was found, or to a burial ground. *See* Dead; Deadman; Punta de los Muertos.

Mugu: Point, Lagoon, Canyon [Ventura]. According to Kroeber, the name is from the Chumash Indian word *muwu*, meaning 'beach,' and was used as a specific village or place name. The Indian village was mentioned by Cabrillo in 1542, and may thus have the distinction of being the oldest recorded California name still in existence (*CFQ*, V, 197 f.). It is mentioned again in early mission records (Arch. Mis. S. Buen., I, 27). Vizcaíno in 1603 called the cape *Punta de la Conversion*, and it appears thus on the maps until the 19th century. For some unknown reason the Coast Survey did not accept the name but applied it only to a triangulation point, and called the cape Point Laguna. The name Point Mugu for the cape appears in the report of Subassistant W. M. Johnson, who surveyed the sector in 1856 (Coast Survey *Report*, p. 100). He doubtless chose the name because the Indian village still existed at that time. It is shown on the Land Office map of 1859, and in 1863 it replaced the former name on the charts of the Coast Survey. The canyon is submarine. Its name was approved by the Geographic Board in 1938.

Muir. The great naturalist and mountaineer, John Muir (*see* Glossary), has been commemorated in the nomenclature of the State more than any other person. **Muir Gorge** [Yosemite National Park]. "We named [1894] this gorge Muir Gorge, after John Muir, the first man to go through the cañon" (R. M. Price, *SCB*, I, 206). **Muir Grove** [Sequoia National Park] and **Pass** [Kings Canyon National Park] were named by R. B. Marshall in 1909. **Muir, Mount** and **Lake** [Tulare]. The name was given to the peak by Alexander G. McAdie, of the U.S. Weather Bureau. **Muir** [Contra Costa]. The station was named by the Santa Fe in 1904 because Muir's residence was near by. **Muir Woods National Monument** [Marin]. The area was given to the United States by William and Elizabeth Kent (of Kentfield) to preserve the virgin stand of coast redwood. The name was bestowed at

their request when the national monument was created in 1908. The near-by beach was named after the monument. **John Muir Trail.** At the instigation of the Sierra Club the legislature appropriated in 1915 the first installment for the construction of the High Sierra trail. It was named in memory of Muir, who had died the preceding year. (Farquhar.) **Muirs Peak** [Los Angeles]. The summit of the ridge forming the east wall of Rubio Canyon was so named because John Muir made the first ascent in August, 1875 (Reid, p. 369). **Muir Crest** [Sequoia National Park]. The culminating crest of the Sierra Nevada between Shepherd and Cottonwood passes was named for Muir in 1937 by François E. Matthes of the Geological Survey. "The small peak that bears Muir's name at present seems hardly commensurate in importance among the features of the Sierra Nevada with the greatness of the man whose love for the 'Range of Light' inspired the movement for the conservation of its scenic treasures" (*SCB*, XXII, 6).

Mulberry. The station of the Sacramento Northern in Butte County, the town in San Benito County, and several physical features named Mulberry, for plantings of the tree, are reminiscent of a widely heralded California industry which failed to develop. Louis Prevost, a native of France and expert in silk culture, planted the first mulberry trees, in San Jose, and in 1856 imported the first silkworm eggs from France. In 1866 the promoters of the industry prevailed upon the legislature to offer handsome premiums for plantings of mulberry trees and for production of cocoons. With true California enthusiasm the people covered the land with mulberry groves. The trees flourished but the silkworms failed to thrive. In August, 1869, Prevost, the pioneer of the movement, died; a few months later the legislature repealed the law; and in 1871 a heat wave killed most of the surviving silkworms. Today a few geographical names are the only remnants of an industry that once looked so promising.

Mule. Since the mule played a less important part than the jackass as a pack animal in early mining and mountaineering days, only a limited number of features were named for the animal, including a Mule Mountain and a Mad Mule Gulch [Shasta], a Crazy Mule Gulch Creek [Yosemite National Park], the famous Mule Springs, originally Dead Mule Springs [Nevada], and several mining camps. Shasta County once had a One Mule Town as well as a One Horse Town (Steger).

Mulholland Hill [Contra Costa]. The name was apparently applied to the elevation south of Orinda when the Concord quadrangle was mapped in 1892–1894. It may preserve the name of one of the three Mulhollands, farmers from Ireland, who settled in the San Pablo district in 1867.

Mulligan Hill [Monterey]. The elevation, shown as *Cabeza de Milligan* (Milligan's Head) on a *diseño* of the Bolsa del Potrero grant, was long known as Mulligan Head. It was named for John Milligan, an Irish sailor and one of the earliest foreign residents of the country. He arrived before 1819, taught the art of weaving to Indians at several missions, and became part owner of Rancho Bolsa del Potrero; he died in 1834. (Bancroft, IV, 747 f.)

Muniz [Sonoma]. The name of a land grant, dated December 4, 1845. It is called *Rancho de Maniz* on a *diseño*, but the origin of the word is unknown.

Murderer. The many acts of violence committed in the gold-rush days and during Indian fights have left their mark upon California's toponymy, though numerous names containing the word have disappeared. **Murderers Bar** [El Dorado]. The place received its name because five Oregonians were killed here (probably in 1849) in retaliation for the murder of three Indians who had been slain in an attempt to protect their women (Hittell, III, 77). **Murderers Gulch** [Siskiyou]. The gulch northeast of Forks of Salmon was named after Murderers Bar. "The bar itself takes its name from the killing of three men, by the people [Indians] living on the creek opposite" (Gibbs, in Schoolcraft, III, 155 f.), i.e., the creek in Murderers Gulch called *Yoteh* by the natives.

Murdock Lake [Tuolumne]. Named by N. F. McClure in 1895, for William C. Murdock, of the State Board of Fish Commissioners (Farquhar).

Murieta. Joaquin Murieta was the "John Doe" of five or more Mexican bandits of the early 1850's. The name has left its mark in several geographical names, two of which are still in use: Joaquin Murieta Caves [Alameda], east of Brushy Peak, and Joaquin: Rocks, Ridge [Fresno]; both localities were favorite hideouts, according to tradition. Joaquin Peak near San Andreas in Calaveras County was so named because Murieta is said to have fought the Chaparral skirmish here in January, 1853.

Muro Blanco [Kings Canyon National Park]. The west slope of Arrow Ridge, which looks like a solid whitish wall, apparently suggested the Spanish name, which was applied by the Geological Survey in 1904.

Muroc: station, **Dry Lake, Army Air Field** [Kern]. The Santa Fe named the station on December 25, 1910, by spelling backwards the surname of Clifford and Ralph Corum, homesteaders. The station was built in 1882 and had borne several other names. Since January 27, 1950, the airfield has been called Edwards Air Force Base in honor of Captain Glenn W. Edwards, who was killed in a test flight in 1948. Muroc post office, established December 17, 1910, was renamed Edwards, November 1, 1951.

Murphy Creek [Yosemite National Park]. Named for John L. Murphy, an early settler on the shore of Tenaya Lake (Farquhar).

Murphys [Calaveras]. Established as a mining camp in 1848 or 1849 and named for John M. Murphy, a member of Weber's Stockton Mining Company. With his father, Martin Murphy, and other members of the family, he came from Missouri to California in the Stevens party in 1844. In 1849 the family settled in Santa Clara County, where John later held several county offices and was mayor of San Jose. (Bancroft, IV, 749.) Murphys Peak near Morgan Hill [Santa Clara] is also named for the family.

Murphy Spring [Mono]. The spring at the site of the old stage station on the Big Meadows and Bodie Toll Road was owned by J. C. Murphy in the 1880's.

Murray [Kings]. The post office was established in 1919 and named for David Murray, who was a leader in introducing olive culture into the region (J. E. Meadows).

Murray Canyon [Riverside]. Named for Dr. Welwood Murray, who built a health resort and hotel at Palm Springs about 1885.

Murrieta: town, **Valley, Creek, Hot Springs** [Riverside]. The post office was established about 1885, and named for John Murrieta, ranch owner and for many years bookkeeper in the sheriff's office.

Muscupiabe [San Bernardino]. The name of the land grant, dated April 29, 1843, is derived from *el cajon de Muscupiavit*, mentioned about 1785 (SP Mis. & C., I, 241) and repeatedly in later years. According to Kroeber, the name consists of Serrano Shoshonean *muskupia*, of unknown meaning, and the locative suffix *-vit*.

Musick Peak [Fresno]. Named for either

Charles or Henry Musick, both of whom were connected with the mill company at Shaver (Farquhar). The name is misspelled Music on the Kaiser atlas sheet.

Muslatt: Mountain, Lake [Del Norte]. The mountain is so called by the Big Flat Indians, but its meaning is unknown (J. Endert).

Mussel. About twenty features, chiefly rocks, are named because of the presence of mussels. Most of these names occur along the coast, where large colonies of marine mussels are a common sight. On October 30, 1769, the men of the Portolá expedition gave the name *Punta de las Almejas* (point of the mussels) to what is now Pedro Point [San Mateo], "on account of the large number of mussels which they found on the beach, very good and large" (Crespi, p. 226). The point five miles north of it is now called Mussel Rock.

Mussel Slough [Kings]. The branch of Kings River was named Muscle Creek because freshwater mollusks were found there. This spelling variant persisted on maps until the 1890's, though the stream as well as the district was popularly known as Mussel Slough. The name gained historical significance through the bitter struggle between settlers and the Southern Pacific from 1876 until the bloody encounter in May, 1880—an episode immortalized in Frank Norris' novel *The Octopus*. *See* Lucerne Valley.

Mustang. The word formerly designated the small half-wild horse of the Western plains, but is now practically synonymous with horse throughout the American Southwest. It is apparently derived from a combination of *mesteno*, pertaining to *mesta*, 'cattle industry,' and *mostrenco*, 'belonging to no one' (Bentley). Some of the California place names were probably given because in the vicinity wild horses, descendants of horses that had escaped from the missions or ranchos, were seen or captured.

Mustard. No feature seems to have been named for our wild mustard, in spite of the striking appearance of wide mustard fields in the California landscape and in spite of the fact that Santa Barbara County supplies much of the mustard for the United States. **Mustard: Canyon, Hills** [Death Valley National Monument] were so named because of the mustard-yellow rocks in which the canyon is cut.

Musulacon [Sonoma]. Rincon de Musulacon was the name of a land grant, dated May 2, 1846. "This branch [the Mi-sal'-la Ma-gun'] of the nation [Pomo] was named after a famous chief they once had. A Gallinomero

told me the name was a corruption of *mi-sal'-la-a'-ko,* which denotes 'long snake.' Another form for the name is Mu-sal-la-kūn'." (Powers, p. 183.)

Myers Flat [Humboldt]. The settlement was known as Myers, after the Grant Myers ranch. When the post office was established, January 1, 1949, the present name was chosen to avoid confusion with Myers in El Dorado County. (Mary Mosby.)

Myford [Orange]. Named in 1923 by the Santa Fe for Myford Irvine, son of James Irvine, owner of the San Joaquin Rancho (Gertrude Hellis). *See* Irvine.

Nacimiento, nä-sĭm-ĭ-ĕn'-tō: **River, station** [San Luis Obispo, Monterey]. The name for the river apparently arose through a misunderstanding. The Portolá expedition camped on the river on September 21, 1769, and Crespi (p. 194) called it "a very large arroyo, whose source [*nacimiento*], so they said, was not far off." When the Anza expedition came to the same river, Anza apparently assumed that the previous expedition had named this river *Nacimiento,* perhaps associating the word with 'the Nativity,' another meaning of the word, and not with 'source of the river.' Anza mentions the name of the stream on April 16 and 24, 1774. On August 27, 1795, a padre speaks of *el nacimiento* between San Antonio and San Luis [Obispo]; the small "n" seems to indicate that here again the meaning 'source' was intended (SP Mis., II, 56 f.). However, later documents mention the *rio del Nacimiento.* Parcels of land called Gallinas, Nacimiento, and Estrella were granted to the Christian Indians of San Miguel July 16, 1844, but the claims were later rejected by the United States. In the *Statutes* of 1850, Nacimiento River is mentioned as forming part of the northern boundary of San Luis Obispo County as originally defined (pp. 59 f.). The Southern Pacific station was named after the river in 1905.

Nacional. The livestock ranchos of the presidios, unless they had a specific name, were generally called *rancho del rey* in Spanish times. After Mexico became independent this designation was changed to *rancho nacional.* (Bowman.) Two of the ranchos which later became land grants kept the name: that of Monterey presidio, dated April 4, 1839, and that of San Diego presidio, dated July 26, 1843; the latter was also known as Rancho de la Nacion. *See* National City.

Nadeau [Los Angeles]. The Santa Fe station was named after the Gernert & Nadeau Beet

Sugarie (!) established at this place in 1881. Remi Nadeau, a French Canadian, had come to Los Angeles in the 1860's and organized the first freight transportation service by mule teams from the silver mines of Cerro Gordo, Calico, and Lookout across the Mojave Desert.

Najalayegua [Santa Barbara]. An Indian rancheria so named is mentioned as early as June 28, 1785 (PSP, V, 157), and repeatedly in later years. September 23, 1845, the name appears in the title of the Prietos y Najalayegua land grant. The word is obviously Chumash but its meaning is unknown.

Najoqui. *See* Nojogui.

Nance Peak [Yosemite National Park]. Named for Colonel John Torrence Nance, professor of military science in the University of California (1904–1927).

Napa, năp'-à: **Valley,** city, **County, River, Creek, Slough, Junction, Soda Springs.** The name is mentioned in the baptismal records of Mission Dolores after 1795 and again in the diaries of Padre José Altimira and José Sánchez in June, 1823, when they were looking for a suitable site for Mission San Francisco Solano. They came upon a large arroyo in the beautiful plain of Napa, *asi llamado de los Indios que antes lo habitaban* (SP Sac. XI, 30 ff.), 'so called for the Indians who formerly inhabited it.' The name appears in the titles of two land grants: Entre Napa, May 9, 1836, and Napa or Trancas y Jalapa, September 21, 1838. The Caymus land grant was sometimes called Paraje en Napa. The city was laid out in 1848 by Nathan Coombs, a native of Massachusetts, who had come to California in 1843 and had bought a portion of Salvador Vallejo's Napa grant. The county, one of the original twenty-seven, was named February 18, 1850. River and creek are mentioned in the *Statutes* of 1850 (pp. 60 f.). In 1858, Vaca Mountains are called Napa Range and Clear Lake is called Laguna Grande de Napa (*Hutch. Cal. Mag.*, II, 397; III, 146). The meaning of the name Napa has never been satisfactorily explained, although there are probably more theories about it than about any other Indian name in California. According to Kroeber, *napa* is the southern Patwin designation for 'grizzly bear.' This is doubtless correct, but it does not necessarily follow that the word is the source of the place names. It is quite certain that the geographical term originated in northern Patwin territory. In 1851 George Gibbs stated that the word *napo* meant 'house' and was used by the

Indians south of Clear Lake in their appellation for themselves as well as in their designation of neighboring tribes: *Habe-napo,* 'stone house'; *Ná-po-batin,* 'many houses' (referring to the first six tribes collectively); *Boh-Napo-batin,* 'western many houses,' designating the Russian River tribes (Schoolcraft, III, 110). Two tribes, *Ca-ba-na-po* and *Ha-bi-na-pa,* were represented at the great council at Camp Lupiyuma on August 18, 1851 (Indian Report). A third plausible interpretation was advanced by Mariano Vallejo's son, Plutón, who had learned the language of the Suisun Indians. According to him, the meaning is 'near mother,' 'near home,' or 'motherland' (San Francisco *Bulletin*, February 7, 1914) . This is, of course, not in contradiction to the meaning 'house,' 'houses,' or 'habitat.' For an application of the term *Wye* in Napa Wye, *see* Wyeth.

Naphus Peak [Mendocino]. Jim Naphus, a Missourian who came with the Asbills in 1854, was an Indian fighter and later a bandit. Once when he returned from a hunt he had so much red soil of the mountain on him that he claimed the peak as his own. (Asbill.)

Naples [Santa Barbara]. The Southern Pacific station was named in 1887, after the city in Italy. **Naples** [Los Angeles]. The community was founded in 1905 by A. C. and A. M. Parson, and was named likewise after the Italian city.

Naranjo, ná-răn'-hō [Tulare]. When citrus-fruit growing developed in this region in the early 1900's, the Spanish word for 'orange tree' was given to the community and to the station of the Visalia Railroad. The post office, now discontinued, is listed in 1904.

Narod [San Bernardino]. When the old railroad to Salt Lake City was built in 1904, the station was given the name Narod, the section foreman's name spelled in reverse (Belden) .

Nashmead [Mendocino]. The station and post office were named Nash, for the first postmaster, when the Northwestern Pacific reached the place in 1907; the name was changed to the present form in 1916 (D. O. Strock). Mead is an old English term for 'meadow' still used in place naming and in poetry.

Nashville [El Dorado]. The name was applied at the time of the gold rush by miners from Nashville, Tennessee (Co. Hist., 1883, p. 198). The name is not found on older maps but is mentioned in the *Statutes* of 1854 (p. 222).

Natchka Creek [Humboldt]. An American rendering of *No'xtska-hipū'r Wroi* (Waterman, map 11). *Wroi* is the Yurok term for 'creek.' A village *No'htskum* or *Nohxtska* is shown about three-fourths of a mile southeast.

National City [San Diego]. The town, which was laid out on the part of Rancho de la Nacion owned by Frank, Warren, and Levi Kimball, was named National Ranch in 1868 and National City in 1871. The Spanish name lingered for many years: the Santa Fe station was called Nacion as late as 1886. *See* Nacional.

National Tribute Grove [Del Norte]. The grove in Jedediah Smith Redwoods State Park was created in 1945 representing every state in the Union, including Hawaii and Alaska, which were still territories at that time.

Natividad: Valley, Creek [Monterey]. The place called *La Natividad* (The Nativity) is mentioned by Font on March 23, 1776, two days before the day of the Annunciation, i.e., the day on which the Archangel Gabriel announced to the Virgin Mary the coming nativity of Christ. Anza's diary on the same day calls the camping place *La Assumpcion*. The text leaves no doubt that both names refer to the same place, "at the beginning of a canyon." La Natividad as a place is mentioned again on September 15, 1795 (Arch. MSB, IV, 192 ff.), and repeatedly in later years. The name was given to a land grant, dated May 30, 1823, and November 16, 1837. The place gained historical significance when the "Battle of Natividad" was fought on the rancho, November 16, 1846, between a party of Americans under Captain Charles Burroughs and the Californians. The post office, now discontinued, is listed in 1858.

Natoma, ná-tō'-má [Sacramento]. The name of an Indian village *Natomo* on the American River was repeatedly mentioned in the *New Helvetia Diary* of 1847 and 1848 in connection with the building of Sutter's gristmill. This is not the site of Natoma or Notoma founded by Brannan on Mormon Island in 1848, shown on maps of 1849 (Jackson) and 1851 (Butler), and mentioned by F. P. Wierzbicki (*California*, 1849, p. 41). A third site, the present town, southwest of Folsom, is shown on Gibbes' map of 1852; the post office was established December 2, 1884. The name includes the Maidu Indian word *noto,* which according to Powers (p. 315) means 'easterners,' and according to Kroeber probably means 'up-stream'—i.e., 'east.'

Navalencia [Fresno]. The name was coined by combining the names of two varieties of oranges: Navel and Valencia. It was applied to the station by the Santa Fe in 1913 because it is situated in one of the best citrus regions of the valley. The post office is listed in 1919.

Navarro, ná-vâr'-ō: **River, Head, Point,** post office [Mendocino]. The name Novarra (or Novarro) is shown on a *diseño* of the Albion grant (1844). It was probably an Indian name, and it was perhaps by accident that it was transcribed to resemble the name of the Spanish province Navarra, or the family name Navarro. The name for the river is on the Land Office map of 1862; the Coast Survey did not use the name until about 1870. The name of the lumber town and the post office was Wendling until about 1914, when it was changed to Navarro.

Nawtawaket: Creek, Mountains [Shasta]. The name of this tributary of McCloud River is a combination of the Wintu words *naw,* 'south,' and *waket,* 'creek.' According to Towendolly, the word for 'south' in Wintu is really *nor.* (Steger.)

Neall Lake [Yosemite National Park]. Named for John M. Neall, Fourth Cavalry, who was stationed in the park, 1892–1897 (Geographic Board, No. 30).

Neal's Rancho. *See* Esquon.

Needham Mountain [Sequoia National Park]. Named by W. F. Dean of Three Rivers, for James C. Needham of Modesto, a congressman from 1899 to 1913 (Farquhar).

Needle. The word is sometimes used to describe orographic features. It occurs as a generic: Agassiz Needle, the former name of Mount Agassiz [Fresno], The Needles [Tulare]; and also as a specific term: Needle Peak [Placer], Needle Rock Point [Santa Cruz].

Needles [San Bernardino]. The post office and the station of the Atlantic and Pacific Railroad (now the Santa Fe) were established on February 18, 1883, on the Arizona side of the Colorado River and named after the near-by pinnacles. On October 11 of the same year the railroad transferred the name to a new town on the California side, a location which it considered better suited for a projected division point. (Barnes.) The name was originally applied to the peaks by the Pacific Railroad Survey, in whose reports they are frequently mentioned. The Whipple-Ives map of 1854 labels with both Indian and English names the peaks on both sides of the river: Asientic Häbî or The Needles.

Neeley Hill [Sonoma]. Probably named for Robert Neely, a native of Pennsylvania, who came to the county in 1866 or earlier.

[218]

Neenach [Los Angeles]. The place is shown on the Land Office maps after 1890; it is probably of Shoshonean origin but its meaning is not known.

Negit Island [Mono Lake]. "The island second in size we call [1882] Negit Island, the name being the Pa-vi-o-osi [Mono Indian] word for blue-winged goose" (I. C. Russell, U.S. Geol. Survey *Report*, VIII, 279).

Negro, Nigger. The names have occurred frequently in times past, particularly in mining days, not because there were large numbers of Negroes but because the presence of a single one was sufficiently conspicuous to suggest calling a place Negro Bar or Nigger Slide. The name is also found in Spanish times: Lytle Creek was known as *Arroyo de los Negros,* and the pass northwest of San Bernardino as *El Puerto de los Negros.* The grant El Cajon de los Negros is dated June 15, 1846. Although the form Nigger was occasionally changed to Negro when California nomenclature tried to become respectable, the nickname still far outnumbers the name Negro. Among the thirty-odd features so called are some interesting names, such as Nigger Bill Bend in the San Joaquin, south of Stockton; Nigger Head [Mendocino] and Niggerhead Mountain [Los Angeles], because of their outline; Nigger Rube Creek [Tulare]; Nigger Jack Slough [Yuba]; Niggerville Gulch Creek [Siskiyou]. The name of one of the old mining towns is preserved in Nigger Bar [Sacramento]. Among the names which include Negro are Negro Butte and Negro Butte Dry Lake [San Bernardino], and a creek with a rare generic, Negro Run [Plumas]. **Negro Canyon** [Los Angeles]. Named for Robert ("Uncle Bob") Owen, who came from Texas in 1853, secured a contract to supply firewood to the soldiers, invested his money wisely, and became the richest colored man in the county (Reid, p. 386). **Nigger Jack Peak** [Tuolumne]. Named for "Nigger Jack" Wade, a former slave, who owned 460 acres at the base of Table Mountain. (Paden-Schlichtmann.)

Neighbours [Riverside]. Named for J. E. Neighbors, the first postmaster (Co. Hist., 1935, p. 213). The post office (now discontinued) is listed in 1908 as Neighbours.

Nelson [Butte]. Established in the early 1870's as a station on the California and Oregon Railroad (now the Southern Pacific) and named for A. D. Nelson and his sons, farmers in the district.

Nelson [Tulare]. Named for John H. Nelson, a pioneer of the Tule River region (Far-

quhar).

Nelson: Creek, Point [Plumas]. The creek appears on Gibbes' map of California (1852). It was named for the "tall, sandy haired, thin faced, good natured *hombre*" (Delano, p. 19) who had a store at the confluence of the creek and the Middle Fork of Feather River. The bar and the diggings on the creek proved to be the richest gold-producing placers of the region. They were discovered in 1850 and were shown on the maps as early as 1851. The first post office was established March 30, 1855.

Nemshas. *See* Nimshew.

Neponset [Monterey]. An Indian transfer name from Massachusetts, meaning 'little summer place' according to Leland (*CFQ*, IV, 406). The former name, Martin Station, was changed by the Southern Pacific about 1900.

Nestor [San Diego]. The post office was named about 1890 for Nestor A. Young, State assemblyman, 1887–1893.

Nevada. The name of the mighty range, Sierra Nevada, has given to California nomenclature two sonorous names, often applied without regard to their meaning: Sierra (range) and Nevada (snow-covered). **Nevada City** [Nevada]. The place at the site of the city was called Deer Creek Dry Diggings in the fall of 1849 by a prospector named Hunt, who struck rich gold deposits here. *See* Deer Creek. It became known also as Caldwell's Upper Store, for Dr. A. B. Caldwell, who set up his trading post here in October, 1849, a short time after he had opened a "lower store" seven miles down Deer Creek. In May, 1850, the settlers at a public meeting adopted the name Nevada, probably suggested by O. P. Blackman, and in March, 1851, the town was incorporated as City of Nevada (H. P. Davis). The name Nevada City is shown on Bancroft's map of 1858 but it was used earlier to distinguish the city from the county. The post office is listed as Nevada City as early as 1851. **Nevada County.** The county was established and named after the city by act of the legislature on April 25, 1851. City and county were not named after the State of Nevada as has been sometimes assumed; indeed, according to H. P. Davis, the Territory, later the State of Nevada, was in all probability named after the California places. The gold rush to the Washoe country in Nevada, which led to the creation of a new political unit carved from Utah Territory, was started in Nevada City. The "blue-black stuff" was brought across the Sierra and assayed by citizens of

Nevada City, and after the Nevada *Journal* on July 1, 1859, had published the facts about the amazing gold and silver content of the ore the people of the city were in the vanguard of the argonauts to the Washoe mines. Stewart, however, states that the name which Congress gave to the territory was a shortening of the name of the mountain range (pp. 303 f.). **Nevada Fall** [Yosemite National Park]. The name was suggested by Bunnell when the Mariposa Battalion entered the valley in 1851. "The white, foaming water, as it dashed down Yo-wy-we [the Indian name for the fall] from the snowy mountains, represented to my mind a vast avalanche of snow" (Bunnell, *Discovery*, 1880, p. 205).

New. The principal use of the adjective "new" is in connection with transfer names which immigrants brought from the home country. California has had comparatively few such names: New Chicago, New Helvetia, New Mecklenburg, New Philadelphia, New Texas, New Vernon—all have vanished. Occasionally the adjective was used in emulation of another place: New Almaden, New Jerusalem, New Albion. Sometimes the word was used to distinguish a newly founded settlement from an older one: New Rio Dell, Nubieber. In several names "new" was combined with an abstract noun: New Hope was to have been the name of a Mormon colony which Sam Brannan tried to found on the Stanislaus in 1846; the gazetteers list Newhope Landing [San Joaquin], New Hope Rock [San Diego], Newlove [Contra Costa]. Most of the names of California communities with the prefix "New" are direct transfer names, in which the "New" is no longer descriptive: New England Mills, Newport, etc. The Pacific Electric station Greenville [Orange] was formerly actually known as Old Newport. Because of the peculiar hydrographic conditions in several sections of the State, there are, finally, a number of New Creeks, Lakes, and Rivers, the best known of which is New River [Imperial], named as early as 1849, when the dry river bed was suddenly filled by overflow from the Colorado. *See* Nuevo. The more important names with the adjective "New" are listed separately.

New Albion. From June 17 to July 23, 1579 (June 27 to August 8, New Style), Francis Drake anchored his *Golden Hinde* in a bay which was probably the one still called Drakes Bay. During his stay he took possession of the country for the English crown and named the country Nova [New] Albion:

"Our Generall called this countrey Noua Albion, and that for two causes: the one in respect of the white bankes and cliffes, which lie toward the sea; and the other, because it might haue more affinitie with our Countrey in name, which sometime was so called." (Quoted in H. R. Wagner, *Sir Francis Drake's Voyage Around the World*, pp. 276 f.). It was the first challenge to Spain's claims, and "New England" was to be the nucleus of a British empire in North America. The British claim to the coast of northern California was not given up until the Oregon treaty of 1846. On most British and on many other non-Spanish maps the English name appears for the rather undefined territory otherwise often labeled with the mythical name *Quivira*. The The name New Albion gained new significance after the Spaniards started the colonization of Upper California. The renewed British claim for California is reflected on the maps: Arrowsmith (1790) and Cary (1806) place the name New Albion neatly within the present boundaries of the State. It remains unexplained why the Russians, who had planted themselves squarely in the British claim, should retain the English name. A Spanish padre in July, 1818, complains that the Russians use the name as dictated to them by Great Britain: *es uno de los dictados de la Gran Bretaña* (Guerra Docs., V, 66), and Kotzebue writes in 1824: "The whole of the northern part of the [San Francisco] bay, which does not properly belong to California, but is assigned by geographers to New Albion ..." (*New Voyage,* 1830, II, 112). *See* Albion.

New Almaden. *See* Almaden.

Newark [Alameda]. The South Pacific Coast Railroad Company named its station in 1876 after the former home (in New Jersey) of A. E. Davis and his brother.

Newberry [San Bernardino]. The Southern Pacific named the station in 1883. In 1919 the Santa Fe changed the name to Water because for a long period the springs there supplied the Santa Fe with all the water it needed. In 1922 the name Newberry was restored. (Santa Fe.)

Newbury Park [Ventura]. "The Conejo Postoffice, styled 'Newbury Park' in the postal guide, was established in 1875 with E. S. Newbury as Postmaster" (Co. Hist., 1883, p. 392).

Newcastle [Placer]. The station of the Central Pacific was named in 1864 after the old mining town near by, which in turn had doubtless been named after one of the "old" Newcastles in the eastern United States. The post office is listed in 1867.

Newcomb Pass [Los Angeles]. Named by the Forest Service for Louis T. Newcomb, a ranger in the timberland reserve which is now the Angeles National Forest (Forest Service).

Newell [Modoc]. The place, at the time of World War II a Japanese relocation center, was named for Frederick H. Newell, the first chief engineer of the U.S. Reclamation Service (State Library).

New England Mills [Placer]. The name was applied to a station of the Central Pacific about 1877 after the near-by mill, which was operated by Captain Starbuck and his partners from New England, and which supplied timber for the railroad (Virginia Major). The post office name is Weimar.

Newhall: town, **Creek, Pass** [Los Angeles]. A station of the Southern Pacific was established October 28, 1876, at the present site of Saugus and named for Henry M. Newhall (1825–1882), the owner of the land, a prominent California pioneer, railroad promoter, and resident of San Francisco. February 15, 1878, the depot and the name were transferred to the new site. (Co. Surveyor.)

New Helvetia [Sacramento]. The settlement was founded by Sutter on August 13, 1839, and given the Roman name of Switzerland, the home country of his ancestors. June 18, 1841, and February 25, 1845, the Spanish version, Nueva Helvetia, was applied to Sutter's vast land grant. *See* Sacramento; Sutters Fort.

New Hope [Stanislaus]. Historic Landmark 436 near Ripon is the only reminder of the New Hope Colony of Mormons, which was established by Sam Brannan in 1847. *See* Stanislaus City.

Newhope Landing [San Joaquin]. The name is reminiscent of the New Hope Ranch established by Arthur Thornton, about 1855, at the site of present Thornton. From 1880 to 1907 New Hope is listed as a post office. *See* Thornton.

Newman [Stanislaus]. The town was established in 1887 when the Southern Pacific reached the place, and was named for Simon Newman, who donated the land for the right-of-way of the railroad. The residents of nearby Hills Ferry and of Dutch Corners, a German settlement, moved to the new town.

Newport: Bay, Beach, Heights [Orange]. In 1873 the McFadden brothers, of Delaware, bought the dock and warehouse which had been built the previous year and established a lumber business. In 1876 they named their

steamer *Newport,* and in 1892 they had the townsite Newport platted as a beach resort, in which lots were not sold but leased. Later the property was sold to W. S. Collins and associates, who on February 16, 1904, filed the map for the subdivision Newport Beach. (Sherman, pp. 9 ff.)

New York. Of all names transferred from the East in pioneer days, New York was the most common in California. It has been retained in about fifteen place names, including the mountain range separating Ivanpah and Lanfair valleys in San Bernardino County. New York Point and Slough and York Island [Contra Costa] are reminiscent of a proud New York of the Pacific, founded in 1849. *See* Pittsburg.

Nicasio, nĭ-kăsh'-ō: **Creek, Hill,** town [Marin]. The name was applied to two land grants, dated March 13, 1835, and February 2, 1844. *Arroyo de Nicasio, Casa de los Indios de Nicasio,* and *Roblar de Nicasio* are shown on a *diseño* of the 1844 grant. Nicasio was probably an Indian who had received the name of one of several saints (Saint Nicasius) at his baptism. The place was settled by Noah Corey in 1852; the post office was established April 13, 1870 (Co. Hist., 1880, pp. 284 ff.).

Nice, nēs [Lake]. The old name, Clear Lake Villas, was changed to the present name by the citizens in 1927 or 1928 because the general topography of the district was thought to resemble the Riviera landscape near Nice in France (Helen Bayne).

Nichols [Contra Costa]. Established as a siding by the Santa Fe in 1909 and named for the William H. Nichols Syndicate (now the General Chemical Company of California), the principal landholder in the district (Santa Fe).

Nicolaus, nĭk'-ô-lǎs [Sutter]. Nicholaus Allgeier, a native of Germany, came to California in 1840 as a trapper for the Hudson's Bay Company and in 1842 received from Sutter a tract of land on the Feather River, where he built a hut and operated a ferry. "The public spirited proprietor of the tract of land heretofore known as Nicolaus' Ranche has responded to the repeated requests of the people, and has caused one mile square of it to be laid off into a town, to which he has given the name of the ranche. The name is not so euphonious as some 'we wot of,' but our friend Shakspeare has told us, and with some truth, that 'a rose by any other name would smell as sweet'; we argue from this that 'Nicolaus' will lose none of the great advantages it possesses in consequence of its name." (Sacramento *Placer Times*, Feb. 16, 1850; Boggs, p. 42.) The maps of 1849 record the place as Nicholas Ferry and Nicholas Alleger. The Postal Guide of 1851 and Schaeffer's sketches have the German spelling Nicholaus.

Nicoll, nĭk'-ĕl: **Peak** [Kern]. The mountain south of Weldon was named for John Nicoll, who came to Southfork Valley in 1852 and took up a homestead. The name is misspelled Nichols on most maps.

Nido, nē'-dō. The Spanish word for 'nest,' often used in the applied sense of 'abode' or 'home,' is found in three places: El Nido [Los Angeles and Merced] and Rionido [Sonoma]. The latter is pseudo-Spanish suggesting 'river nest.'

Nietos. *See* Los Nietos.

Nigger. *See* Negro.

Night Cap [Sacramento]. The name was applied to the mountain near Sonora Pass by the Geological Survey in the 1890's, probably because the outline resembles an old-fashioned nightcap. *See* Liberty Cap.

Niguel Hill [Orange]. A place called *Niguili* by the Indians is mentioned in Boscana's *Chinigchinich* before 1831 (1933, pp. 83, 215), and appears in later records with various spellings. The name is used for the Niguel land grant, dated June 21, 1842. On a *diseño* the hill is shown, spelled *Lomaria de Neuil*. The Coast Survey used the hill as a triangulation station in the 1870's but spelled the name Nihail, a spelling that continued on the maps of the survey for many years.

Niland [Imperial]. A contraction of "Nile land," selected in 1916 by the Imperial Farm Lands Association because of the fertility of the irrigated region. When the Southern Pacific built its branch line into the Imperial Valley, the name of the station was Old Beach, and from 1905 to 1916 it was Imperial Junction.

Nilegarden [San Joaquin]. The Western Pacific applied the name about 1915 to the shipping station near the Nile Garden Irrigation Farms, which the promoter, C. B. Hubbard, had named in analogy to the Nile delta in Egypt.

Niles [Alameda]. The name was given in 1869 by the Central Pacific, for Judge Addison C. Niles, who was elected to the State supreme court in 1871. The place had been known as Vallejo Mills in the 1850's for José de Jesús Vallejo, who had built a flour mill on Alameda Creek. Niles Flour Mill is Historic Landmark 46.

Nimshew [Butte]. A division of the Maidu Indians, Nemshaw, near the headwaters of Butte Creek, is noted by Horatio Hale (Wilkes, VI, 631) and appears in various spellings in the *New Helvetia Diary* and in the records of the 1850's. According to Powers (p. 283), there was a creek, Nim'-shu, from *nem se'-u*, 'big water' (either Big Butte Creek or West Branch of Feather River). The name of the Nemshas grant, dated July 26, 1844, probably comes from the same source although the grant was much farther south. Nimshew mining tunnel under Table Mountain is mentioned by Browne in 1868 (p. 160). *See* Kimshew.

Nipinnawasee [Madera]. Edgar B. Landon brought the name from Michigan, where, according to the Indians of his native district, it means 'plenty of deer.' He applied it to his settlement in 1908, and in 1915 it was accepted by the Post Office Department.

Nipomo, nĭ-pō'-mō: **Valley, Creek, Hill,** town [San Luis Obispo]. The name of a Chumash rancheria, *Nipomo*, is mentioned in the records of La Purisima Mission between 1799 and 1822 (Merriam). April 6, 1837, the name was applied to the land grant. The place is mentioned by Brewer on April 9, 1861; the modern town was laid out in 1889 by the heirs of William G. Dana, the original grantee of the rancho, a cousin of Richard H. Dana, the writer.

Nipple, The [Alpine]. The Geological Survey adopted the local name for the mountain when the Markleeville quadrangle was mapped in 1889. A number of hills are so named in various parts of the State, including Nellies Nipple [Kern], shown on the Emerald Mountain atlas sheet.

Nipton [San Bernardino]. According to local tradition, the station was named for one of the engineers of the survey party when the San Pedro, Los Angeles, and Salt Lake (now Union Pacific) Railroad was built in 1904. However, the Southern Pacific map of 1905 shows the name Nippen for the station; the present name does not appear until 1910.

Nisene Marks State Park [Santa Cruz]. The park was established in 1963 and named for Nisene Marks, the mother of the donors of the property. The land was donated through the Nature Conservancy, and the full name is The Forest of Nisene Marks State Park.

Noble Pass [Lassen]. The pass was named for William H. Noble, who in the summer of 1852 began to build a wagon road over the cut-off which had been discovered in 1851.

Noble Pass Route (Viola entrance to Lassen National Park) is Historic Landmark 11. By decision of the Geographic Board, 1966 (July-Sept.), the name was changed to Nobles Pass, because the pioneer's name was apparently spelled that way.

Noche Buena [Monterey]. The land grant, dated November 15, 1835. was also known as Huerta de la Nacion. *Nochebuena* means 'Christmas Eve.'

Nogales. The California walnut was noticed by the very first overland expedition on August 5, 1769 (Crespi, p. 151). Later the word *nogales* (walnuts) was used in the names of two land grants in Los Angeles County: Nogales, October 11, 1838, and March 13, 1840; Cañada de los Nogales, August 30, 1844. Neither the Pacific Electric station Los Nogales, near Universal City, nor the Union Pacific station Walnut, southwest of Spadra, derives its name from these grants.

Nojogui, nō'-hō-wē: **Creek, Falls** [Santa Barbara]. *Najague* or *Najajué* was one of the rancherias under the jurisdiction of Mission La Purisima (Arch. MPC, p. 10), and is repeatedly found in land-grant papers with various spellings. The canyon through which the creek flows is shown as *Cañada de Najao-ui* on a *diseño* of Las Cruces grant; *Cuchilla de Nojogue* and *Planecita Nojoque* appear on the *diseño* of the Najoqui grant (1842). According to Kroeber, the name seems to come from the Chumash Indian *Onohwi,* which still finds its echo in the local pronunciation; its meaning, however, is unknown.

Nomi-Lackee [Tehama]. The former Indian Reservation is now Historic Landmark 357. Long ago the Indians to the east had engaged in a lengthy war. By the terms of the treaty one of the tribes was to move west—in their dialect *Noom-Hy.* Hence the name, Nome Lackee ('west talk'). (*Alta California,* April 28, 1858.) Powers confirms that *noam* is 'west' and *lak-ki* is 'tongue' or 'branch' in Wintu (p. 230).

Nomwaket Creek [Shasta]. *Waket* is the Wintu word for 'creek'; hence the name means "west creek creek."

No Name Canyon [Kern]. The canyon north of Inyokern received the unusual name because the surveyors for the Los Angeles Aqueduct could find no local name in use and apparently did not have the necessary imagination to give it a name of their own (Wheelock). *See* Unnamed Wash.

Noonday Rock [San Francisco]. The rock off the Farallon Islands was named by the Coast Survey for the clipper *Noonday,* which struck it on January 2, 1863, and sank within one hour.

Nopah Range [Inyo]. The mountains were considered part of the Kingston Range by the Whitney and the Wheeler surveys. When the Geological Survey mapped the region (1909–1912) the name Kingston was applied only to the southern part, and the northern part was designated as Nopah, a name doubtless supplied by local sources. *Pah* is the generic term for 'water' in Shoshonean and is often found in the region of the Great Basin: Ivanpah, Pahrump, etc. Nopah, in fact, may be a hybrid created by surveyors: "No Water Range." *See* Kingston.

Nora, Lake. *See* Helen.

Norco [Riverside]. The name was coined from *Nor*th *Co*rona Land Company by Rex B. Clark in 1922. **Lake Norconian** was so named in 1925 because it is part of the Norco development.

Nord [Butte]. Laid out in 1871 by G. W. Colby and named Nord (German, 'north') by his wife (Co. Hist., 1882, p. 246).

Norden; Lake Van Norden [Nevada]. The dam was built in 1900 and the lake was later named for Dr. Charles Van Norden, of the South Yuba Water Company. The post office was established in 1927 and named after the lake.

Nordheimer Creek [Siskiyou]. The stream was named for a prospector who lived in the vicinity until the 1930's (Ella Soulé). George A. Nordheim, a native of Prussia, is listed in the Great Registers of the early 1870's. Nordheimer Creek and Ditch are mentioned by Browne in 1868 (p. 202). Another possibility is that the name commemorates B. Nordheimer, who was one of the first to try to wash gold at Gold Bluffs in 1850 (Alex Rosborough in "The Knave," Aug. 26, 1956).

Nordhoff Peak [Ventura]. The peak was named by the Geological Survey in 1903 after the town of Nordhoff, which had been named for Charles Nordhoff (1830–1901), a native of Germany, well-known author, and grandfather of Charles B. Nordhoff, co-author of *Mutiny on the Bounty. See* Ojai.

Norris Butte [Trinity]. The mountain was named for a settler who lived at the foot of it. The name is misspelled Norse on some maps. (K. Smith.)

North Bloomfield [Nevada]. The town which developed after the discovery of gold here in 1851–1852 was first called Humbug, or Humbug City. When the post office was about to be established, the popular American town name Bloomfield was chosen at a public meeting. As there was already a Bloomfield post office, in Sonoma County, "North" was added to distinguish the two places.

North Columbia [Nevada]. The post office was established in the 1860's and named after Columbia Hill, a well-known mining camp. The "North" was added to distinguish it from Columbia post office in Tuolumne County.

North Dome [Yosemite National Park]. Named in 1851 by Major Savage's party of the Mariposa Battalion. The Indians called it *To-ko-ya,* according to Bunnell (1880, p. 212); the interpretation, 'the basket,' which he suggests, is very questionable.

North Fork [Madera]. The town came into existence after several mining companies opened up the district in 1878 and was named because of its location on the North Fork of San Joaquin River. The post office was established December 18, 1888, as Northfork, and many maps still spell the name as one word.

North Guard [Kings Canyon National Park]. The names North Guard and South Guard for the two peaks which flank the somewhat higher Mount Brewer appear on Lieutenant Milton F. Davis' map of 1896 (Farquhar).

Northridge [Los Angeles]. When the Southern Pacific Railroad built the San Fernando branch line about 1908 the place was known by the Biblical name Zelzah because it was actually a 'watering place in the desert.' In 1933 the name was changed to North Los Angeles, and in 1935 to Northridge, a name proposed by Carl S. Dentzel because the home of the Northridge Stampede lies at the base of San Fernando Valley's northern ridge.

North Sacramento [Sacramento]. The North Sacramento Land Company purchased a part of the Rancho Del Paso in 1910, laid out a subdivision, and named it for its location north of the city of Sacramento (H. S. Wanzer).

North San Juan; San Juan: Hill, Ridge [Nevada]. When the rich gold deposits were found in 1853, one of the discoverers, Christian Kientz, a veteran of the Mexican War, named the hill because its shape reminded him of San Juan de Ulloa in Mexico. When the post office was established May 21, 1857, the adjective North was added to distinguish it from San Juan in San Benito County.

Nortonville [Contra Costa]. Named for Noah Norton, a native of New York, who located

the Black Diamond coal mine and in 1861 built the first house in the town. The mine was one of the centers of the Mount Diablo coal boom, the decline of which began with the explosion in this mine on July 24, 1876. *See* Coal, Coalinga, Pittsburg, Somersville.

Norwalk [Los Angeles]. The place was settled by Atwood and Gilbert Sproul in 1877 and called Corvallis, after their former home town in Oregon. In 1879, when the post office was established, it was renamed after Norwalk, Connecticut, the former home of some of the settlers (Co. Hist., 1965, IV, 180).

Nose Rock [Mendocino]. The name was applied to the rock opposite Cuffey Cove by the Coast Survey, probably because of its outline. *See* Homers Nose.

Nosoni Creek [Shasta]. The name of the tributary of McCloud River, according to Steger, is from the Wintu *nous-sono,* 'pointing south.'

Nova Albion. *See* New Albion.

Novato, nô-vä'-tō: **Valley, Creek,** town [Marin]. A *Cañada de Novato,* where cattle from Mission San Rafael grazed, was mentioned in 1828 (Registro, p. 4). The name is from that of a chief of the Hookooeko Indians, according to Merriam (*Mewan Stock,* p. 355); this chief had probably been baptized for Saint Novatus. On November 18, 1836, the name was applied to a land grant, and on February 2, 1856, to a post office.

Noyo: River, Canyon, town, **Anchorage, Seavalley** [Mendocino]. According to Barrett (*Pomo,* p. 134), *Noyo* was the name of a former Northern Pomo village near the mouth of Pudding Creek. This creek was called *Nō'-yō-bida* by the Indians but the name was later transferred to the river south of Fort Bragg, doubtless by the Coast Survey: *Report,* 1855, Noyou River; *Coast Pilot,* 1858, Noyon River. *See* Pudding Creek.

Nubble, The [Sonoma]. This rare topographical term was applied to a little knob projecting at the end of a sloping hill, probably when the Geological Survey mapped the Tombs Creek quadrangle.

Nubieber [Lassen]. In 1931 the extensions of the Great Northern Railroad and the Western Pacific Railroad met at this place, which was called New Town at that time. When the newly selected name, Big Valley City, was rejected by the Post Office Department, L. H. Martin of the Chamber of Commerce of Bieber christened the settlement after the pioneer town. *See* Bieber; New.

Nueces y Bolbones [Contra Costa]. The name

Arroyo de las Nueces y Bolbones (creek of the nuts and the Bolbones) was the name of the land granted to Juana Sánchez de Pacheco, July 11, 1834. The Bolbones [Indians] are often mentioned in Spanish records. *See* Diablo; Walnut Creek.

Nuestra Señora. In place naming, the Franciscan missionaries used this title, referring to 'Our Lady,' i.e., the Virgin Mary, in preference to Santa María. It was usually combined with one of her special titles: de Altagracia, de los Dolores, de los Angeles, de la Merced, del Rosario, etc. The Nuestra Señora part of these names was naturally soon dropped for practical purposes, even in Spanish times; but the special title has survived as a place name in numerous instances.

Nuevo, Nueva. The Spanish adjective meaning 'new' was frequently used in Spanish times and has survived in a few places: Nuevo Canyon [Ventura], Nuevo Creek [Santa Barbara]. Nueva Flandria, Nueva Helvetia, Nueva Mecklenburg, and Nueva Salem were land grants. Nuevo post office in Riverside County was named in 1916. *See* New.

Nurse Slough [Solano]. The tidal channel .was named after Nurse's Landing (now Denverton), which in turn had been named for Dr. Stephen K. Nurse. *See* Denverton.

Nutter Lake [Mono]. Named in 1905 by an engineer of the Standard Consolidated Mining Company, of Bodie, for the assistant superintendent, Edward H. Nutter (Farquhar).

Oak. The seventeen species of native live and deciduous oaks have left their mark upon the nomenclature of the State. Oak is included in almost 150 names on the maps and, next to Willow and Pine, is the most popular name derived from a tree. While the Spanish distinguished between *encina* (live oak) and *roble* (deciduous oak), we have only a few place names modified by "live" or "white" or "black." Because especially beautiful specimens grow on level ground, the number of Oak Flats is rather large. In Shasta County there is a tautological Oak Run Creek. There is an Oak Hall Bend in the river south of Sacramento and a Seven Oaks Creek in Sonoma County. Rand McNally's Gazetteer lists at least thirty towns and settlements bearing the name in one form or another, some of which are only conventional applications.

Oakland [Alameda]. In Spanish times part of the site of the city was called *Encinal del Temescal* (oak grove by the sweathouse) because of the luxuriant growth of oaks. The city was laid out for Horace W. Carpentier, Edson Adams, and Andrew J. Moon by a surveyor, Julius Kellersberger, in 1850. When it was incorporated as a town the present name was spontaneously chosen. **Oakdale** [Stanislaus]. Established and named when the Copperopolis and Visalia Railroad reached the place in 1871 (Santa Fe). **Oakville** [Napa]. The name was applied to the station when the Napa-Calistoga sector of the railroad was built in the early 1870's. Shown on the von Leicht–Craven map of 1874. **Oakley** [Contra Costa]. Settled in 1896 and 1897 and named for the abundance of native oak trees by R. C. Marsh, who became the first postmaster in 1898. The Old English suffix *-ley* for 'field' or 'meadow' was commonly used for places in the United States, although many such names were doubtless transfers from England. **Oak View Gardens** [Ventura]. Named in 1925 at a public meeting because of the garden-like appearance of the oak groves. **Oak Creek Pass** [Kern]. The pass by which Frémont's second expedition crossed the Tehachapis on April 14, 1844, is Historical Landmark 97. According to *California Historical Landmarks* [1963], this was the pass used already by Padre Garcés when he returned from the exploration of San Joaquin Valley in 1776. **Oak Glen** [San Bernardino]. The original name was Potato Canyon and is still shown on the San Gorgonio atlas sheet, 1954. When apple growing replaced potato growing in the fertile valley, Isaac Ford, substituted the present more euphonious name (Buie, Sept. 22, 1964) . *See* Encina, Roble.

Oasis [Mono]. Named after the fertile and productive Oasis Ranch, on which N. T. Piper and his brother Samuel settled in 1864 (Robinson). **Oasis de Mara** [Riverside]. On September 22, 1950, the Twenty-Nine Palms Corporation presented the 60-acre oasis to Joshua Tree National Monument (O'Neal).

Oat. There are about twenty Oat Hills and Mountains on California maps, together with a number of Oat Creeks and Canyons and an Oat Knob [Tulare]. Sonoma County has Big and Little Oat Mountain and Red Oat Ridge. Oat Creek [San Luis Obispo] on the Land Office maps should be Old Creek. *See* Avena.

Oban [Los Angeles]. The station is shown on Southern Pacific maps after 1904 and was probably named after the seaport in Scotland or the town in Kansas.

Obelisk [Fresno]. The name was applied to the peak by the Geological Survey in 1903 because of its shape. The Whitney Survey had named the Clark Range "Obelisk Group." The word is occasionally used as a generic.

O'Brien: Creek, Mountain [Shasta]. Named for Con O'Brien, who bought the old Conner Hotel on the Sacramento-Yreka road in 1873 (Steger).

Observatory, Observation. Several peaks, hills, and points are so called because they were used for geodetic or astronomic observation. **Observatory Point** [Lake Tahoe]. In 1873 this was the prospective site of the observatory later established on Mount Hamilton. The von Leicht–Craven map and the von Leicht–Hoffmann Tahoe map of 1874 show Lick's Observatory here. After the site was changed to Mount Hamilton the abbreviated name clung to the point. **Observation Peak** [Kings Canyon National Park]. The name was applied by J. N. LeConte in 1902 because he used the peak for a triangulation point (Farquhar).

O'Byrne Ferry [Calaveras]. Historical Landmark 281, registered January 1, 1938, commemorates Patrick O. Byrne, who established a ferry and later (1852) built a bridge across the Stanislaus River to Mountain Pass. *See* Byrnes Ferry.

Occidental [Sonoma]. The name was first given to a Methodist church erected here in April, 1876, on land given by M. C. Meeker, who then laid out the town. The post office was established December 7, 1876. As a place name, Occidental was unique at that time and seems to have remained so in the United States. The railroad station was called Howards until 1891, for William Howard, a settler of 1849.

Ocean. The best known and one of the oldest of the many names along the coast with the stem Ocean is **Oceanside** [San Diego], founded in 1883 and named by J. C. Hayes. **Ocean Beach** [San Diego]. The town was laid out and named by William H. Carlson and Albert E. Higgins in May, 1888 (C. A. McGrew, *San Diego*, I, 133 f.). **Ocean Park** [Los Angeles]. The community was founded and named in 1892 by Abbot Kinney and F. G. Ryan (Newmark, 1916, p. 603). A post office in San Luis Obispo County bears the Spanish name Oceano, and Marin County has an Ocean Roar.

Ockenden [Fresno]. Named for Tom Ockenden, who had a trading post here (Farquhar).

Ocotillo [San Diego]. The post office on Highway 79, established November 16, 1957, and several physical features are named because of the presence of the shrub ocotillo, *Fou-*

quieria splendens. The name is of Aztec origin, probably containing a root meaning 'prickly.' The name occurs frequently in the Borrego State Park. *Ocote* is a common name for a Mexican pine.

Odessa [Kings]. The name appears on Santa Fe maps after 1905. As the place was in a wheat-growing district, it was doubtless considered appropriate to name it after the greatest wheat-exporting port in Europe.

Offield Mountains [Siskiyou]. Probably named for a local Indian family by that name.

Ohm [San Joaquin]. The Southern Pacific siding was named about 1900 after the Ohm Ranch, which was established by Thomas Ohm, a native of Germany, who settled there in 1868 and raised grain on a large scale (Co. Hist., 1923, pp. 972, 975).

Oil. The exploitation of California's oil resources has played in our century as important, albeit less romantic, a role as the discovery of gold in the middle of last century, and has likewise made its mark upon our nomenclature. In Kern County there is a whole cluster: Oil: City, Center, Junction; Oildale. A town in Fresno County is called Oilfields, a mountain ridge in Ventura County is named Oil Ridge, and several minor features bear the name.

Ojai, ō'-hī: **Valley, town** [Ventura]. The word is a Chumash place name, *A'hwai,* and means 'moon' (Kroeber). *Aujai o Aujay* is on the list of rancherias of Mission San Buenaventura (Arch. Mis. S. Buen., I, 28), and a rancheria *de Ojai* is shown on a *diseño* of El Rincon, about 1834. April 6, 1837, it was applied to a land grant, spelled Ojay and Ojai. In 1874 R. G. Surdam laid out the town and named it for Charles Nordhoff, the writer, who had given enthusiastic accounts of the valley in his articles. In 1916 the town was renamed after the valley. *See* Nordhoff.

Ojitos [Monterey]. The name Los Ojitos, meaning 'the little springs,' was applied to the land grant, April 5, 1842. A *diseño* of the grant shows *Ojo de agua de los Ojitos.* The geographical term was used in other parts of California in Spanish times, but does not seem to have survived. *See* Ojo.

Ojo. The Spanish-American word for 'spring,' often given as *ojo de agua,* 'water spring,' was widely used as a geographical term in Spanish times and appears as the principal name of several land grants: Ojo de Agua de Figueroa [San Francisco], September 16, 1833; Ojo de Agua de la Coche (sow spring) [Santa Clara], August 4, 1835; Tres Ojos de

Agua [Santa Cruz], March 18, 1844; Ojo de Agua [Sonoma], December 20, 1844; it is also included in the alternate names of other land grants. The peak on the old land grant west of Morgan Hill [Santa Clara], labeled El Toro on the Morgan Hill atlas sheet, was probably one of the "remarkable hills . . . named *El ójo del cóche*" mentioned by Beechey in 1826 (1831, II, 48), and recorded as Peak of "Ojo del Agua de la Coche" in Hoffmann's notes on August 21, 1861. Ojo Grande [Riverside] was the name of a spring at the head of Carrizo Creek mentioned by Emory in 1846–1847 (p. 103). None of the names seem to have survived.

Olancha: Peak, town, **Creek** [Inyo]. The Olanches, obviously a Shoshonean village or band south of Owens Lake, were mentioned by Taylor in 1860. The name appears for a settlement, south of Owens Lake, shown as Olanche on Farley's map of 1861, and for the peak shown as Olancha on Wheeler atlas sheet 65. The name of the town is recorded on the Land Office maps of the 1870's. Kroeber leaves open the possibility that the word was taken from the name of a Yokuts tribe on the other side of the Sierra Nevada who called themselves Yaudanchi and were called by their western neighbors Yaulanchi.

Old. This descriptive adjective was applied to a number of communities and physical features, usually after another place had been given the original name. There is an Old Inspiration Point in Yosemite and an Old Mountain View in Santa Clara County. Orange County had for some time an Old Newport as well as a Newport. In some names the adjective is not used in contrast to a "new" name: Old Barn [Sacramento], Old Man Mountain [Nevada, Santa Barbara], Oldwomans Creek [San Mateo]. **Old Diggings** [Shasta]. A mining district was so named because abandoned mines of the 1850's were reopened in later years (Steger). **Old Station** [Shasta]. The site of the Hat Creek stage station and military post, called Old Station after it was abandoned in 1858 (Steger). **Old Woman: Mountains, Springs** [San Bernardino]. According to *WSP*, No. 224, p. 70, the range was so named because the granite pinnacle at its crest resembles an old woman, and the *Desert Magazine* (Dec., 1940) indicates that the Indian name for the mountains was *Nomopeoits*, which likewise meant 'old woman.' L. Burr Belden, however, states that the place was so named because Colonel Henry Washington found

two old Indian women at the springs when he surveyed the base line in 1855. **Old Dad Mountains** [San Bernardino]. According to O. J. Fisk, the mountains were actually named because of their appearance. **Old Harmony Borax Works** [Death Valley National Monument]. Historic Landmark 773 commemorates the famous works from which the first twenty-mule teams transported borax. The borax works were built in 1882 by William T. Coleman. Old Baldy and Old Grayback [San Bernardino] are the local names for San Antonio and San Bernardino or San Gorgonio peaks.

Olema, ō-lē'-mȧ: post office, **Creek** [Marin]. The approximate site of modern Olema was probably occupied by an Indian village mentioned repeatedly as *Olemos* and *Olemus* in the baptismal records of Mission Dolores after 1802 (Arch. Mis., I, 87 ff., 108). According to Merriam, the Hookooeko Indian name of the place was *O-lā'-mah* (*Mewan Stock*, p. 355). The Coast Miwok village of *Olemaloke*, 'coyote valley,' mentioned by Barrett (*Pomo*, p. 307), was obviously not at the site of the present-day Olema but was some ten miles north, in what is now called Chileno Valley. What seems to be a tribal name, *Olemoloque*, is mentioned on October 14, 1805 (Arch. Mis., I, 89), and the same root is found in '*Olemochoe*' in the territory of the Laguna de San Antonio grant at the Sonoma County line. The occurrence of the stem of the name in different regions confirms Kroeber's assumption that it had become a "tribal" name (*Olamentke*) for the Indians in northern Marin County. According to Barrett, the word ō' le is Coast Miwok for 'coyote' (*Pomo*, p. 307). Olema post office was established February 28, 1859. The Olema station of the Wells Fargo Company was named Point Reyes Station, April 1, 1883. *See* Reyes, Point.

Oleta. *See* Fiddletown.

Oleum [Contra Costa]. The name of the town at the Union Oil Company refinery was created by lopping off the first four letters of petro*leum*. The post office is listed in 1912.

Olinda [Shasta]. Originally a Portuguese name, preserved in the Brazilian city near Pernambuco, but now international. Samuel T. Alexander, a settler, transferred the name from the Hawaiian Islands in the early 1880's. **Olinda** [Orange]. The former name Petrolia was changed about 1900 by Mr. Bailey, president of the Olinda Oil Company.

Olive. The olive tree was introduced into California by the Franciscan padres who planted seed, brought from Mexico, in the mission gardens. Today olive orchards are cultivated commercially in a large area of the State.

Olive [Orange]. The olive trees on near-by Burruell Point suggested the name Olive Heights when the town was laid out in 1880. The generic was dropped when the post office was established about 1890. **Olivenhain**, ō-lĕ'-vĕn-hīn [San Diego]. The place was a German coöperative colony, which was in existence in July, 1885, according to the journal of J. E. Hauswirth, a member of the colony. He spells the name Olivenheim, meaning 'home of the olives,' whereas the present name is Olivenhain, 'olive grove.' The chief crop is now beans. Other places are called: Olive View [Los Angeles]; Olivehurst [Yuba]; Olive Oak Springs [San Diego]; Oliveto [Sonoma]. *See* Los Olivos.

Olive Lake [Tuolumne]. The lake near Huckleberry Lake was named in memory of Olive Hall, a local resident and conservationist, who died in 1964 (Geographic Board, July-Sept., 1965) .

Olmsted Grove [Humboldt]. The grove in the Prairie Creek Redwoods State Park was established in 1953 in honor of Frederick Law Olmstead (1870-1957), noted landscape architect, who for many years was consultant to the California state parks system and active in the redwoods conservation program.

Olney: Creek, Gulch [Shasta]. Named for Nathan Olney, of Oregon, who mined here with his Walla Walla Indians before the gold rush of 1849 (Steger).

Olompali [Marin]. The school preserves the name of a former large Coast Miwok village. The Olumpali or Olompalis Indians are mentioned by members of the Kotzebue expedition in 1816, and Padre Payeras records a *cañada de los Olompalis* in 1819 (Docs. Hist. Cal., IV, 341 ff.), and *el punto de Sta Lucia Onompali* on October 20, 1822 (Arch. MSB, XII, 411). *La rancheria de Olimpali o Santisimo Rosario* is mentioned in 1828 in the *Registro*, p. 4, and the baptismal records of Mission Dolores show the variant *Olompalico.* The present spelling was used for the name of a land grant, October 22, 1843. According to Barrett (*Pomo,* p. 325), *o'lōm* means 'south.' An arroyo *Olom* or *Holom,* fifteen miles south, mentioned in the papers of the Corte Madera del Presidio grant near San Rafael, seems to indicate a connection with the "tribal" name *Olamentke. See* Olema.

Olympia [Santa Cruz]. The post office was established and named in 1915. Olympus, the mountain throne of the Greek gods, and Olympia, the site of the Olympic games, have repeatedly been used for American place names.

Olympic Valley [Placer]. The name of the post office was changed from Squaw Village to Olympic Valley, August 1, 1960, in anticipation of the Winter Olympic Games at Squaw Valley.

Omagaar Creek [Humboldt, Del Norte]. The name of the tributary of the Klamath is derived from *Omega''a Wroi* (Waterman, map 9); *wroi* is Yurok for 'creek,' the meaning of the specific name is not known. The spelling is that of the Forest Service on the Tectah Creek atlas sheet.

Omega [Nevada]. Two mining towns, named after the first and the last letter of the Greek alphabet, are listed as post offices in 1858. Omega, founded in 1851 by E. Paxton, John Douglass, and others, is still on the maps, but only a road sign indicates the diggings at old Alpha.

Omenoku [Humboldt]. The name of the small promontory north of Trinidad Head is a genuine Yurok geographical term. According to Waterman (p. 269), *O-meno'qᵂ* means 'where it projects.' *Omen* is apparently a Yurok generic term, probably meaning 'ground' or 'land.' A location *Omen* is recommended by Heintzelman in 1858 (p. 639) as the northern boundary of Klamath Indian Reservation.

Omjumi Mountain [Plumas]. The name of this mountain, which is in Maidu territory, probably contains the Maidu generic term *om,* 'rock' (Kroeber).

Omochumnes [Sacramento]. The land grant, dated January 8, 1844, was named after the *Rancheria de los Omochumnes,* shown on a *diseño* of the grant. According to Merriam (*Mewan Stock,* p. 349), who spells the name *Oo-moo'-chah,* the village was situated at the site of modern Elk Grove. The suffix *-umne* means 'people' and the first syllable is probably the Maidu word for 'rock.'

Omo Ranch [El Dorado]. The place is shown on the Land Office map of 1891, and is listed as a post office in 1892. According to Merriam (*Mewan Stock,* p. 344), it was named after an Indian village, *Omo.*

O'Neals [Madera]. The post office, established October 4, 1887, took its name from Charles O'Neal's Hotel.

O'Neill Forebay [Merced]. The reservoir was

named for J. E. O'Neill, rancher and business leader in the San Joaquin Valley (Geographic Board, Oct.-Dec., 1966) .

O'Neill Lake [San Diego]. Named for Richard O'Neill, who owned a part of the Santa Margarita Ranch (J. Davidson).

Oneonta Park [Los Angeles]. The Pacific Electric station was named after Oneonta, New York, birthplace of Henry E. Huntington, the promoter of the railroad.

Onion. About twenty-seven native species of the genus *Allium* are found in California, especially in hilly and mountainous sections; their occurrence has given rise to almost a hundred Onion, Leek, and Garlic place names, including two settlements called Onion Valley, in Plumas and Calaveras counties, respectively.

Onlauf Canyon [Ventura]. Named for the Anlauf family of Santa Paula, who owned property in this section (J. H. Morrison). The spelling "on" approximates the pronunciation of the German "an."

Ono [Shasta]. When the post office was established in 1883 at Eagle Creek the settlers chose the name of the Biblical town (I Chron., 8:12), at the suggestion of the Rev. William S. Kidder (Steger). There are (or were at that time) several Onos in the Middle West, and there is now another Ono in California [San Bernardino]. *See* Igo.

Onofre. *See* San Onofre.

Ontario: town, **Peak** [San Bernardino]. The town was laid out in 1882 by George B. Chaffey on the old Cucamonga Rancho and named for his former home province, Ontario, Canada.

Onyx: post office, **Peak** [Kern]. The place had been known as Scodie's Store since the 1860's. When the post office was established in 1890, the name Scodie was rejected because of its similarity to Scotia in Humboldt County. William Scodie chose, therefore, the present name because it is short and unique. (A. J. Alexander.)

Opahwah, ō-pä'-wä: **Butte** [Modoc]. The mountain, also known as Centerville or Rattlesnake Butte, was given this name by the Geographic Board (*Sixth Report*) in the 1920's. Opahwah is the name by which the butte is known to the Indians.

Ophir [Placer]. This is the only survivor of five mining towns named after Ophir, the land of gold mentioned repeatedly in the Bible. The town was known as Spanish Corral in 1849 but took the Biblical name in 1850 after a rich lode was discovered in the vicinity.

It is Historical Landmark 463. Ophir City was the original name of Oroville. Mount Ophir [Mariposa] was the site of one of the first mints to coin California gold pieces.

Orange. The importance of the orange in California fruit culture is shown in the number of places—including at least seven communities or settlements—which have been named for it. **Orange:** city, **County.** The town, laid out by Glasell and Chapman in the 1870's, was first called Richland; then its name was changed to Orange because there was another Richland in Sacramento County (Santa Fe). The Land Office Map of 1879 shows neither name, but Orange post office was established September 1, 1873. It is assumed that the name was chosen to accent the developing orange culture in the district. However, it is also possible that it is a transfer name from the East. Andrew Glassell, one of the founders of the town, was a native of Virginia, where in the early 1700's a county had been named Orange in honor of the son-in-law of King George II. By 1880 there were Orange counties in six other states, as well as numerous towns and post offices so named. The California county, carved from Los Angeles County, March 11, 1889, to be sure, was named because the orange industry flourished there: "This county was given its name by the Legislature because of the orange groves for which it is justly famous" (*Blue Book*, 1907, p. 278). **Orange Cove** [Fresno]. The community, situated in a "cove" in the Sierra foothills where citrus fruit thrives, was named in 1913 after the Orosi Orange Lands Company, managed by E. M. Sheridan and M. S. Robertson (Santa Fe).

Orchard Spring [Lassen]. The spring in the lower end of Little Tuledad Canyon had various names until the Geographic Board decided in 1964 (Jan.-Apr.) for the present name because it is near an abandoned apple orchard.

Orcutt [Santa Barbara]. The town was laid out by the Union Oil Company in 1903 and named for the company's geologist, W. W. Orcutt (AGS: *Santa Barbara*), p. 180.

Ord, Fort [Monterey]. In 1933 the War Department named the military reservation Camp Ord, in memory of General Edward O. C. Ord, who had first come to California as a lieutenant of the Third Artillery in 1847. In 1849 he was commissioned to make the first official survey of the city of Los Angeles. He was a distinguished general in the Civil War, and in 1868 became commander of the Department of the Pacific. August 15, 1940, the name was changed to Fort Ord by General Order No. 7. The name is also preserved in the Southern Pacific station Ordbend [Glenn] on the extensive Ord Ranch, owned in the 1850's by E. O. C. Ord and two of his brothers. **Ord Mountains** [San Bernardino]. According to local information, the mountains were named after the "Ord Group," a number of claims located here by Sandie Lochery about 1876. The mines were named for General Ord, under whom the prospector may have served. (O. J. Fisk.)

Oregon: Hills, Peak, Gulch [Butte]; **Oregon Bar** [El Dorado]; **Oregon House** [Yuba]; **Oregon Creek** [Sierra]; **Oregon Gulch** [Shasta]— all these names are survivors of the many camps and features named in mining days by gold seekers who came from or via Oregon.

Orestimba Creek [Stanislaus]. An *arroyo de orestimac* is mentioned in Father Viader's diary of October, 1810 (Arch. MSB, IV, 92). On a *diseño* of the Rancho del Puerto, 1843, there is an *Arroyo de Horestimba,* and a *diseño* of the Orestimba land grant (February 21, 1844) shows an *Arroyito de Orestiñoc.* The name contains Costanoan words, the first, *ores,* denoting 'bear' (Kroeber). A tributary is called Oso (Bear) Creek and a near-by mountain, Mount Oso. Locally the stream is usually referred to as Orris Timbers Creek.

Orick [Humboldt]. "The Indians of Redwood creek, called by the whites Bald Hill Indians . . . are termed Oruk by the Coast Indians, and Tcho-lo-lah by the Weits-peks". (Gibbs, in Schoolcraft, III, 139). A Yurok Indian village *Ore'q*ᵂ was near the site of the present town (Waterman, p. 262).

Oriflamme: Canyon, Mountains [San Diego]. Named after a quartz mine operating there about 1900; sometimes spelled Oroflamme, doubtless because of association with Spanish *oro,* 'gold.' Oriflamme is used in English for anything suggestive of the red flag carried into battle by early French kings. According to Wheelock, the first miners during the Julian gold rush boom of 1870 arrived aboard the sidewheeler *Oriflamme,* and this may be the origin of the name.

Orinda, ō-rĭn′-dȧ [Contra Costa]. About 1880, Theodore Wagner, then U. S. Surveyor General for California, called his estate between Bear and Lauterwasser creeks, Orinda Park. March 13, 1888, it was favored with a post office and in 1890 Orinda Park Station became the provisional terminal of the California-Nevada Railroad. From the Wagner estate it was transferred in 1895 to what is now Orinda Village, and in 1945, as Orinda, to the "cross roads," formerly known as Bryant. Like similar names with a Latin flavor it was probably coined for its pleasing sound although "General" Wagner might have read the name Orinda by which the poetess Katherine Fowler Philips was known.

Orland [Glenn]. The name was given to the station when the Central Pacific built the connecting line between Willows and Tehama. According to the county history (1918), the place was named after Orland, England, the birthplace of an early settler. The name was drawn from a hat in which three proposed names had been placed, including Leland and Comstock.

Orleans: town, Mountain [Humboldt]. The place was settled in 1850 and called New Orleans Bar, probably after the city in Louisiana. The name was shortened to Orleans Bar in 1855 when the settlement became the county seat of short-lived Klamath County. The present form was used by the post office in 1859.

Ornbaum: Valley, Hot Springs [Mendocino]. The places were named for John S. Ornbaum, a native of Indiana, who came to the county in 1854 and operated a large stock ranch in the valley (Co. Hist., 1914, p. 880).

Oro. The Spanish word for 'gold' was naturally a favorite word in naming places in California. Oro was the name intended for what became Tuolumne County, and it was the name given to the first county seat of Sutter County, a short-lived town founded in 1850 three miles above the mouth of Bear River (now in Placer County). Often the name was first given to a gold mine, and frequently it was applied without regard to idiomatic usage: Oro Loma [Fresno]; Oro Chino [Mariposa]; Oroleeve, Monte de Oro [Butte]; Orocopia Mountains [Riverside]. The combination Oro Fino was especially popular and this name is preserved in Monterey, San Luis Obispo, and Siskiyou counties. **Oroville** [Butte]. The place was settled in 1849 by Colonel John Tatam and other miners and became known as Ophir City, in analogy to the ancient gold land mentioned in the Old Testament. When the post office was established in 1855 the name had to be changed because there was an Ophir in Mariposa County and an Ophirville in Placer County. Judge J. M. Burt preserved the golden glimmer by coining the new name from the Spanish *oro.* **Oro Grande** [San Bernardino]. The name goes back to a gold-mining camp of 1878. The post office was established January 3, 1881, and was named Halleck, for the chemist of the stamp mill. May 1, 1925, the name of the post office and of the town was changed to Oro Grande, after the nearby Oro Grande mine, which was operating at that time.

Orosi, ō-rō′-sá [Tulare]. The town was founded in 1888 by Daniel R. Shafer and associates. The name was coined from *oro,* 'gold,' by Neal McCallan because the fields around were covered with golden poppies. The post office is listed in 1892.

Oroville. *See* Oro.

Orrs Springs [Mendocino]. The hot sulphur springs are on the Orr ranch, established in 1858 by Samuel Orr, a native of Kentucky who had come to California in 1850 (Co. Hist., 1880, p. 658). The place is shown on the Official Railway Map of 1900.

Ortega: Hill, station [Santa Barbara]. The name for the station appears on maps after 1890 and was given for a member of the Ortega family, well known in the annals of the county. The intermittent creek west of Summerland is labeled Arroyo de las Ortegas on the Santa Barbara atlas sheet. This is doubtless on the property mentioned as *otro parajito nombrado* [other little place called] *las Ortegas* in July, 1834 (DSP Ben. Mil., LXXIX, 96). There is another Ortega Hill (4,970 feet!) in Ventura County and a station of the Western Pacific called Ortega in San Joaquin County.

Ortigalita: Creek, Peak [Merced]. *Ortigalita* is a diminutive of Spanish *ortiga,* 'nettle.' The name may have been chosen for its pleasing sound without regard for its meaning. A post office Ortigalito is listed in 1880.

Osdick [San Bernardino]. In 1905 the Santa Fe named the station on the recently acquired Kramer-Johannesburg branch for P. J. ("Pete") Osdick, a pioneer in the Rand mining district. After a dispute with the mining interests in 1931 the name was officially changed to Red Mountain, but school and voting district as well as the Osdick Group of Mines preserve the old pioneer's name.

Oso. The Spanish word for 'bear,' the most notable of our native animals, was frequently used for place names in Spanish times and has survived in the names of more than ten geographic features. **Oso Flaco: Valley, Creek, Lake** [San Luis Obispo]. The Portolá expedition camped here on September 2, 1769, and some of the soldiers killed a bear. Crespi gave

the place a holy name, some of the soldiers called it *Las Vivoras* (on account of the many vipers), and others *El Oso Flaco* (the lean bear), although the bear must have weighed 375 pounds (Crespi, p. 182). Since then, Oso Flaco is repeatedly mentioned in Spanish manuscripts as the name for the lake and for a *sitio*. A *diseño* of the Guadalupe grant records *Meganos de Oso Flaco,* and of the Bolsa de Chamisal (1837), *Terrenos del Oso Flaco.* **Los Osos: Valley, Creek** [San Luis Obispo]. "In this valley we saw troops of bears, which kept the ground plowed up and full of holes which they make searching for roots . . . The soldiers went out to hunt and succeeded in killing one . . . This valley they named Los Osos, and I called it La Natividad de Nuestra Señora" (Crespi, pp. 184 f.). The name was preserved by the land grant Cañada de los Osos, dated December 1, 1842, which on September 24, 1845, was combined in a grant with the extraordinary name Cañada de los Osos y Pecho y Islai (valley of the bears and breast [after a rock] and islay). **Cañada de los Osos** [Santa Clara]. A *Rancheria de los Osos* is mentioned on June 7, 1799 (PSP, XVII, 327), and probably did not refer to bears but to bad Indians called *Osos* by the Spaniards (Prov. Rec., VI, 120). *Cañada de los Osos* is shown on a *diseño* of Rancho Ausaymas, 1833; this name was used for a land grant, dated October 20, 1844. The diminutive, *Osito,* was occasionally used. Crespi records under date of September 10, 1769: "They brought a little bear which they had reared and offered it to us, but we did not accept it. From this circumstance the soldiers took occasion to name the spot El Osito, but I called it San Benvenuto." *See* Bear; Poza.

Ossagon Creek [Humboldt]. An Americanization of Yurok *O'segen Wroi.* The *wroi* (creek) was named after the settlement *O-segen* situated at the mouth of the stream (Waterman, map 9). The spelling given here is that of the Forest Service on the Orick atlas sheet.

Ostrander: Rocks, Lake, Trail [Yosemite National Park]. Named by the Whitney Survey for Harvey J. Ostrander, descendant of one of the early Dutch settlers of New Amsterdam, who came to California at the time of the gold rush and in the 1860's took up a homestead at the junction of Glacier Point and Old Mono trails. The rocks and the homestead are shown on the Hoffmann-Gardner Yosemite map of 1867. Bret Harte's mother was a member of the Ostrander family.

Oswald [Sutter]. The place was probably named for August Oswald (or Ostwald), a native of Germany, who had come to California in 1847 as a member of Company B of Stevenson's Volunteers and was later one of Allgeier's men at Nicolaus.

Otay, ō′-tī: **River, Valley, Mesa, Mountain,** town, **Reservoirs** [San Diego]. The name is from the Diegueño Indian word *otai* and means 'brushy,' according to Kroeber. An Indian rancheria *Otai* is mentioned in 1775 (PSP Ben. Mil., I, 5), and a *gentil de Otay* is recorded in the following year (PSP, I, 230). The form Otay was used for two land grants, March 24; 1829, and May 4, 1846, and the river is shown as *Arroyo de Otay* on a *diseño* of 1833. Boundary Survey, 1849, has Rio Otay; Coast Survey, 1857: Valley of Ohjia (!); von Leicht–Craven, 1874: Otay Creek. Otay post office is listed in 1870.

Otterbein [Los Angeles]. In 1910 Bishop William M. Bell established a settlement for retired ministers of the Church of the United Brethren in Christ, and named it in honor of the founder of the church, Philip W. Otterbein (C. H. Bell).

Otter Creek [El Dorado]. The name of the tributary of the Middle Fork of American River is the only reminder of the land otter which once inhabited our riverbanks. Wilkes' map of 1841 shows an Otter River, apparently the Merced.

Ottoway: Peak, Creek, Lakes [Yosemite National Park]. The peak was named in 1895 by Lieutenant N. F. McClure, for a corporal in his detachment.

Outside Creek [Tulare]. The creek was so named because it was on the "outside" edge of the swamp area created by the delta of Saint Johns and Kaweah rivers.

Ouzel: Basin, Creek [Kings Canyon National Park]. Named in 1899 by David Starr Jordan because "here John Muir studied the waterouzel [or American Dipper] in its home, and wrote of it the best biography yet given of any bird" (Jordan, *The Alps of the King[s]-Kern Divide*, pp. 18 f.).

Ovis Bridge [Lava Beds National Monument]. The generic name for 'sheep' was suggested to J. D. Howard by a naturalist when they examined the skulls of bighorns lying under the bridge.

Owens Creek [Merced, Mariposa]. The stream is labeled Owen's Creek on Hoffmann's map of 1873, and may have been named for Richard H. Owen, a native of Connecticut and a miner in Mariposa County in the 1870's.

Owens: Lake, Valley, Point [Inyo]; **River** [Mono, Inyo]; **Mountain** [Fresno]; **Peak** [Kern]. John C. Frémont named the lake in 1845 for Richard Owens, of Ohio, a member of his third expedition (1845–1846), captain of Company A of the California Battalion, and his "Secretary of State." "To one of the lakes . . . on the east side of the range I gave Owens' name" (Frémont, *Memoirs,* 1887, p. 455). The river was also named by Frémont; at least it appears on Preuss' map of 1848. The Indians called the lake *Pacheta,* and the river, *Wakopee.*

Owens Mountain [Fresno]. The mountain was probably named for George W. Owens, a native of Ohio, who came to California in 1862 and had a stock ranch in the foothills in the 1870's.

Owenyo [Inyo]. A railroad name, coined from the name of the lake and the second syllable of the county, and applied to the station of the Carson and Colorado Railroad in 1905. When the extension to Mojave was built in 1910, the station was shifted to the present location and called New Owenyo, but the prefixed adjective was dropped the following year.

Owlshead Mountains [San Bernardino]. The highest peak of the mountains was named Owlshead Peak by the Wheeler Survey (atlas sheet 65), doubtless because of its appearance from a certain angle. By a strange coincidence the contour lines of the mountains on the Avawatz Mountains atlas sheet present the picture of an owl's face, with Lost Lake and Owl Lake for eyes and the center ridge for the beak.

Oxalis [Fresno]. When the line from Los Banos to Fresno was built in the 1890's, the Southern Pacific applied to the station the botanical name for wood sorrel. When another siding was established a few miles to the south, it received the same name spelled backwards: Silaxo.

Oxnard [Ventura]. When the Southern Pacific branch from Ventura to Burbank was built in 1898–1900, the station was named for Henry T. Oxnard, who had established a beet-sugar refinery here in 1897.

Pachalka Spring [San Bernardino]. The spring was named before 1895 for a Paiute Indian who had his camp there. Pachalka was a sort of headman (not a recognized chief) of a small group of Las Vegas Indians. (O. J. Fisk.) The name was spelled in various ways until the Geographic Board on December 6, 1911, decided for the present version: "Not Pachaca,

Pachanca, Pachapa, Pachauca, Pechaca, nor Pechapa."

Pachappa [Riverside]. The name was applied to the station when the Santa Fe line was built from Riverside to Santa Ana in 1890. It is apparently a Gabrielino name of unknown meaning. Since Pachalka [San Bernardino] was also known as Pachapa and Pechapa, a relationship between the two names is indicated.

Pacheco, pȧ-chä′-kō: **Hill** [Marin]. Named for Ignacio Pacheco (1808–1864), a native of San Jose and in 1840 grantee of the San Jose land grant, on which the hill is situated.

Pacheco, pȧ-chä′-kō: **Pass** [Merced]; **Peak, Creek, Canyon** [Santa Clara]. The names are in the territories of the San Luis Gonzaga and Ausaymas y San Felipe grants, the former granted in 1843 to Juan P. Pacheco, and the latter in 1833 and 1836 to Francisco Pacheco, who had come to California in 1819. The pass is shown as Pacheco's Pass on the Frémont-Preuss map of 1848. Pacheco Peak is mentioned in 1854 in Trask's *Report* (p. 39). Hoffmann mentions a Pachecoville (which has since vanished) in his notes of September, 1861. Sierra de Pacheco is shown on a *diseño* of the Soberanes land grant, which later became the nucleus of the vast landholdings of Miller and Lux.

Pacheco, pȧ-chä′-kō: **Valley, Creek,** town [Contra Costa]. Salvio Pacheco, a native of Monterey and a former soldier, settled in 1844 on Rancho Monte del Diablo, which had been granted to him in 1834. The present town was laid out by Dr. J. H. Carothers in 1857 and named Pacheco in 1858.

Pacific. California's location on the shore of the Pacific Ocean is reflected in a number of place names, including the half-Spanish Pacifico Mountains [Los Angeles]. The oldest of the names still in existence is probably that of the post office in El Dorado County, which goes back to the early 1870's. **Pacific Grove** [Monterey] was established as a tent city by Methodists in 1875, and the present town was laid out by the Pacific Improvement Company in 1883. **Pacific Beach** [San Diego]. The name was apparently chosen by the founders of San Diego College of Letters, a short-lived institution established in 1887 (San Diego *Tribune,* Dec. 7, 1934). **Pacific Palisades** [Los Angeles]. The town was founded and named in 1921 by a Methodist church organization. The post office was established October 6, 1924. **Pacific Valley** [San Luis Obispo]. "The only stretch of level land along Santa Lucia

coast" is "dignified with the name of Pacific Valley though there is nothing at all valley-like about it" (Chase, *Coast Trails*). **Pacific Ridge** [Lake]. Bears the name of the now-vanished Pacific City, which was built mainly of tents during the copper boom of the 1860's (Mauldin).

Pacifica [San Mateo]. On October 29, 1957, the inhabitants of Linda Mar, Sharp Park, Edgemar, Westview, Pacific Manor, Rockaway Beach, Fairway Park, Vallemar, and Pedro Point voted to incorporate as the city of Pacifica, a name indicative of its situation by the shore of the Pacific Ocean.

Pacoima, pȧ-koi′-mȧ: **Canyon, Creek, Dam, Wash,** city [Los Angeles]. The name is derived from a Gabrielino Shoshonean word, and may mean 'running water' (Keffer, p. 63). The town was established about 1887 by Senator Charles Maclay, Judge Robert M. Widney, and others; the post office is listed in 1915.

Padre Barona: Valley, Creek [San Diego]. The name was apparently first applied to one of the mesas in the region: a land grant, dated January 25, 1846, is called Cañada de San Vicente y Mesa del Padre Barona. José Barona was a friar at San Diego (1798–1811) and at San Juan Capistrano (1811–1831).

Pahrump, pä′rŭmp: **Valley** [Inyo]. The valley extending from Nevada into California is shown as Pahrimp in Wheeler's atlas (sheet 66). The name can be referred to Southern Paiute *pa·* (water) and *timpi* (stone), which after the root *pa* would be modified phonetically to *rimpi,* or *rumpi.* 'Water-stone' probably refers to a spring in a rock. (Stewart.)

Pahute Mountain. *See* Piute.

Paicines, pī-sē′-nĕs [San Benito]. The post office was established before 1880 and named after the Rancho Cienega de los Paicines, granted October 5, 1842. The specific term refers to a Costanoan village, *Paisi-n,* on San Benito River (Kroeber, *Handbook,* p. 465). This spelling approximates that of *Cienega de los pasines,* shown on a *diseño* of the rancho. *Ciénega* is the common Spanish generic term for 'marsh.' *See* Tres Pinos.

Paige [Tulare]. The Santa Fe station was named for Timothy Paige, a San Francisco banker and owner of the Paige & Morton Ranch, when the branch from Tulare to Corcoran was built in the middle 1890's.

Painted. The participle is used to describe physical features which because of their surface composition appear "painted" in a certain light, or which are actually marked with pictographs made by former dwellers. Painted Canyon [Riverside], with fantastic color combinations in sunset light; Painted Gorge [Imperial], with highly colored coralline formations; Painted Rock [Placer]; Painted Hill [Riverside] belong in the former class. Painted Cave [Santa Barbara], in which picture writings were discovered by Dr. W. J. Hoffman in 1884, and Painted Rock [San Luis Obispo], known to the Spaniards as *La Piedra Pintada*, belong in the latter class.

Paintersville [Sacramento]. Named for Levi Painter, who came to California in 1853 and laid out the town in 1879 (Doyle).

Paiute. *See* Piute.

Pajaro, pä′-hȧ-rō: **River, Creek, Gap,** town; **Mount Pajaro** [Santa Cruz, Monterey]. The river was named by the soldiers of the Portolá expedition on October 8, 1769. "We saw in this place a bird which the heathen had killed and stuffed with straw; to some of our party it looked like a royal eagle.... For this reason the soldiers called the stream Rio del Pajaro, and I added the name of La Señora Santa Ana" (Crespi, pp. 210 f.). *Llano* [plain] *del Pajaro* is mentioned on September 17, 1795 (Arch. MSB, IV, 193). The name of the river is repeatedly recorded in mission and state papers and appears later in the titles of several land grants. Beechey (followed by Gannett) was apparently unaware of the circumstance of the naming, as he states that the river was "appropriately named Rio de los Paxaros, from the number of wild ducks which occasionally resort thither" (II, 48 f.). Pajaro Valley is mentioned by Tyson in 1850 (p. 51), and Pajaro River in the *Statutes* of 1850 (p. 59). Pajaro is called a "considerable" town by Cronise in 1868 (p. 123). The name was used elsewhere in Spanish times: *Islas de Pajaro* (perhaps The Brothers) are shown on a *diseño* of Rancho de San Pablo [Contra Costa]. Pajaro River was apparently once called Sanjon (ditch) de Tequesquito. *See* Tequesquito.

Pala [Santa Clara]. The name of the land grants, Pala, dated November 5, 1835, and Cañada de Pala, dated August 10, 1839, are derived from an Indian *capitanejo*, named Pala, who was mentioned as early as July 29, 1795 (DSP San Jose, I, 50).

Pala, pä′-lȧ: **Mountain, Indian Reservation,** town [San Diego]. A rancheria called *Pala* appears in mission records as early as September 28, 1781 (Arch. Mont., VII, 3). In 1816 the Mission San Luis Rey built a chapel there and called the *asistencia, San Antonio de*

Pala. There were three Mexican land claims called Pala, the first dated November 5, 1835. The name is recorded by Williamson in 1855. The Indian Reservation was established and named by executive order of President Grant, December 27, 1875. A Luiseño version of the naming is given by DuBois (*AAE*, VIII, 152): "In the cañon he [Nahachish, the Temecula chief] drank water and called it Pala, 'water,' and Pame, 'little water.' "

Palermo, pȧ-lĕr′-mō [Butte]. Named in 1887 after Palermo, the capital of Sicily. The name was chosen because the land and climate are suited for olive growing, as in Sicily. (H. Huse.)

Palisade: peaks, **Creek, Lakes** [Kings Canyon National Park]; **Glacier** [Inyo]. The collective name Palisades was applied to the peaks by the Whitney Survey in 1864. The two highest peaks are now called North and Middle Palisade. In 1879 North Palisade, the highest, was named by L. A. Winchell, for Frank Dusy, and in 1895 by Bolton C. Brown, for David Starr Jordan. Neither name prevailed. Split Mountain was at one time called South Palisade, but it does not really belong to the group and the name has been discontinued. (Farquhar.) A steep elevation along Nacimiento River [Monterey] is called The Palisades. The name is also found as a generic term on the ocean shore, where the sea-facing bluffs are usually so designated. *See* Pacific Palisades.

Palm. The isolated groups of the California fan palm, *Washingtonia filifera*, in Riverside and San Diego counties have suggested a number of place names. Indeed, so conspicuous and so important is the tree that it comes quite natural to call a place where it grows Palm Spring, or Palm Canyon, or Palm Valley. "In the talk of desert men the palm figures constantly . . . the names mean to the traveller not only water, but shade, with the chance of grass for his animals, and the relief of verdure for his sorely harassed eyes." (Chase, *Desert Trails*, p. 16.) The number of trees found in a place often becomes a part of the name: Lone Palm, Dos Palmas, Two Bunch Palms, Seven Palms Valley, Seventeen Palms, Twentynine Palms, Thousand Palms; these names survive even when they lose their appropriateness. In Spanish documents places named for the *palmas* are repeatedly mentioned. None of these seem to have survived although some were doubtless for the same places now bearing the American form. Dos Palmas [Riverside] was named in American times. The land grant Valle de las Palmas is situated in Lower California. Las Palmas [Fresno] and several other places were not named for the native palm. These were named either for cultivated palms or for other trees which were called palms. **Palm Springs** [Riverside]. The name was originally Palmetto Spring: "The fine large trees which mark the course of the run have furnished the name by which it is known—'Palmetto Spring'" (Whipple, 1849, pp. 7 f.). The place is shown as Big Palm Spring on the von Leicht–Craven map of 1874. Later it was known as Agua Caliente because of the hot springs. When the post office was established about 1890 the name Palm Springs was chosen because there was already a post office named Agua Caliente, in Sonoma County. The Southern Pacific station, now called Garnet, was named Palms when the sector from Colton to Indio was built in 1875–1876. On the Southern Pacific map of 1889 it appears as Seven Palms, and in 1900 as Palm Springs. In 1923, when Palm Springs station became Garnet, the name was transferred to the old White Water station. **Thousand Palms: Canyon,** post office [Riverside]. The largest colony of fan palms has been called Thousand [i.e., many] Palms since the "early days," although on the von Leicht–Craven map of 1874 the place is modestly called 100 Palm Spring, and on the Land Office map of 1891 it is likewise labeled 100 Palms. In 1946 there were actually about a thousand palms in the canyon, approximately seven hundred old trees, and three hundred from ten to twenty feet tall. Paul Wilhelm's recent plantings of 60,000 seedlings will give new significance to the name. The post office was established in 1915 and called Edom after the ancient country in Asia. In 1939 the name was changed to Thousand Palms upon petition of the residents. The railroad name is still Edom. There is another Thousand Palms Canyon in Anza Desert State Park, some fifteen miles northeast of Warners Springs. **Two Bunch Palms** [Riverside]. The name is derived from two groups of fan palms, one upper bunch and one lower bunch. Both have small springs and were Indian camps and later resting places for desert prospectors (*Desert Magazine*, May 1939, p. 40). **Twenty-nine Palms** [San Diego]. Named in 1852 by Colonel Henry Washington, the surveyor of the San Bernardino base line, who found 29 "cabbage trees" here. This was the common name for the Washingtonia palm before the

German botanist Wendland named it in 1879 for the father of our country, or for Henry Washington. There are numerous other Palm names in Riverside and San Diego counties: Biskra, Curtiss, Macomber, and Willis, Palms, Pushawalla Canyon Palms, One Palm, Lost Palms, Hidden Palms, Palm Desert.

Palmas. *See* Palm.

Palm City [San Diego]. When the post office was established, January 13, 1914, it was so named because it was situated on a road lined by palm trees.

Palmdale [Los Angeles]. The tree for which this town and several other places were named was not a true palm but the Joshua tree, sometimes called yucca palm. The place was settled by German Lutherans in 1886 and called Palmenthal. The post office was established June 7, 1888, and the name was changed to Palmdale on August 13, 1890.

Palmer, Mount [Death Valley National Monument]. This peak in the Grapevine Mountains was named by the Geographic Board for Dr. T. S. Palmer after his death in 1955. Palmer was a member of the biological expedition to Death Valley in 1891 and the author of *Place Names of the Death Valley Region*, 1948.

Palmer: Mountain [Kings Canyon National Park]; **Cave** [Sequoia National Park]. Named for Joe Palmer, a pioneer miner and mountaineer of the region and discoverer of the cave.

Palo. The word *palo* means 'stick,' 'log,' 'timber,' 'mast,' but was used in Spanish California for 'tree,' in combination with purely descriptive adjectives, as in *palo seco*, 'dry tree,' *palo prieto*, 'dark tree,' as well as for definite species of trees: *palo colorado*, 'redwood,' *palo verde*, a tree with green bark in the desert regions, still called palo verde. It has survived from Spanish times in a number of geographical names and has also been used for place naming in American times. **Palo Alto,** păl'-ō ăl'-tō [Santa Clara]. Tradition connects the origin of the name with the tall tree still standing near the railroad station. However, since this redwood had a twin, which fell in 1885 or 1886, it can hardly be the *palo alto* described by the Anza expedition, as is generally assumed by historians. Under date of November 28, 1774, Palou (III, 264) records in his diary: "Near the crossing there is a grove of very tall redwood trees, and a hundred steps farther down another very large one of the same redwood, which is visible more than a league before reaching the arroyo, and appears from a distance like a tower." Palou, from a distance, might have taken "twin redwoods" for one large tree, but Anza and Font in their diary entries of March 30, 1776, leave no doubt that the *palo alto* was a single tree. Font's map of the Bay region (*Compl. Diary*, opposite p. 302) shows likewise only a single tree. Whether this tree was the redwood a mile downstream, carried away by high water in March, 1911, or whether it was another tree, which has left no trace, will probably remain an unanswered question. In a geographical sense the name was used when the San Francisquito rancho was sold in 1857: "a certain tract of land known as the Rancho of Palo Alto." This name was doubtless used to avoid confusion with the two adjoining ranchos which included the name San Francisquito in their full names. Various surveyor's plats of these ranchos after 1858 show clearly that the name "Palo Alto" was at that time associated with "Twin Redwoods." Stanford established his country estate in 1876 on the rancho. Gradually he acquired a total of 8,000 acres, which he called Palo Alto Farm. After the founding of Stanford University, Timothy Hopkins laid out the present town in 1888, naming it University Park. At the same time a real-estate company developed a new subdivision adjoining Mayfield and named it Palo Alto. Stanford brought an injunction against the company for using "his" name; through an amicable settlement Palo Alto became College Terrace, and University Park was rechristened Palo Alto on January 30, 1892. (Cf. Guy Miller, *WF*, VI, 78 f.; VII, 284 ff.) **Laguna de los Palos Colorados** [Alameda, Contra Costa]. The name was applied to the land grant, dated October 10, 1835, because a lake and some of the *palos colorados* of Redwood Canyon were on the territory of the grant. These (as well as other stands of redwood in the San Francisco Bay region) are shown as *Bosques de Palo Colorado* on Ayala's *Plano* (1775). In a geographical sense the name is used as early as September 2, 1797, when the baptismal records of Mission San Jose show that an Indian woman, Gilpae, *de los Palos Colorados*, was christened Josepha. **Palo Colorado Canyon** [Monterey]. The canyon is shown as *Arroyo del palo Colorado* on a *diseño* of Rancho Sur Chiquito, 1835. **Palo Escrito,** păl'-ō ĕs-krē'-tō: **Peak** [Monterey]. A *terreno* called *palo escrito* is mentioned February 21, 1833 (Arch.

Mont., VI, 56), and *Cañada de Palo Escrito* is recorded in a petition for a grant in 1840 (Bowman Index). Palo Scrito Hills are mentioned by Whitney (*Geology*, I, 111) and Palo Escrito Mountain is shown on Hoffmann's map. The name probably originated because there was a tree, mentioned as *palo escrito* in 1828 (Registro, p. 11), with carved symbols. *See* Alamo Pintado. **Palos Verdes,** păl'-ōs vûr'-dēz: **Estates** [Los Angeles]. The name is derived from *Cañada de los Palos Verdes* (valley of green trees or timber), now known as Bixby Slough. The land had been occupied by José and Juan Sepúlveda since 1827, was mentioned as a rancho named Palos Verdes in 1844 (DSP Ang., VIII, 2), and was formally granted on June 3, 1846. The subdivision was laid out on part of the rancho in 1922. **Palo Cedro,** păl'-ō sē'-drō [Shasta]. A townsite laid out in 1891 and given the Spanish name because of a cedar tree on the place. The original tree is no longer there. (Steger.) The post office, listed in 1893, was for a number of years spelled Palocedro. **Palo Verde,** păl'-ō vûr'-dē: **town, Lagoon, Mountains** [Imperial]. The name was probably derived from the Spanish name for a small tree with bright green (*verde*) bark, *Cercidium torreyanum*. The post office was established January 13, 1903, as Paloverde, and on July 1, 1905, the name was changed to Palo Verde. The Portolá expedition, September 26, 1769, called an Indian village in what is now Monterey County, *Rancheria del Palo Caydo,* because the Indians "lived in the open near a fallen oak tree" (Costansó, p. 234). This, the first place name in California containing the word *palo,* as well as many *palo* names shown on *diseños,* has not survived.

Paloma, Palomar. The Spanish word for 'pigeon' and, with the locative ending -*r,* for 'place of the pigeons' was often used for place names in Spanish times. Paloma is mentioned as a place name in San Diego County (DSP Ben. P. & J., II, 73) and in Los Angeles County (Bowman Index). Today the name is found in Calaveras, Monterey, Riverside, and San Luis Obispo counties, in some instances probably applied by Americans because of its pleasant sound: pȧ-lō'-mȧ. **Palomar,** păl'-ō-mär: **Mountain, State Park** [San Diego]. A *Cañada de Palomar* is shown on a *diseño* of the Camajal y Palomar grant (1846). (*See* Camajal.) From 1859 to 1868 Joseph Smith lived on his Palomar ranch at the side of the mountain, and after he met a violent death the peak became known as Smith Mountain.

In December, 1901, the Geographic Board, upon a petition of Julia Wagenet and other local residents, restored the old name officially. The post office Palomar Mountain was established December 19, 1920, and the state park in 1933. The Indian name of the mountain was *Paauw*, and the names of its peaks were *Wikyo* and *Ta'i* (Sparkman, p. 191).

Palomar [Los Angeles]. The station of the Pacific Electric, on Rancho San Jose, was doubtless named for Ignacio Palomares, one of the patentees of the grant.

Palomares Creek [Alameda]. Probably named for Francisco Palomares (or a member of his family), who was a resident of San Jose after 1833, an Indian fighter, and a judge.

Palomas Canyon [Los Angeles]. The name probably originated by folk etymology through association of *paloma*, 'pigeon,' with *pelonas*, 'bald.' *Lomas pelonas* (bald hills) are shown on a *diseño* of the Temascal grant, through which the canyon runs.

Palowalla [Riverside]. The name of the place on highway 60-70 may be of Chemehuevi Indian origin, or it may be just a combination of Spanish *palo*, 'tree,' and the second part of the name "Chuckwalla." The Little Chuckwalla Mountains are a few miles to the southwest.

Pamo Valley [San Diego]. An Indian rancheria called *Pamo* is mentioned in Spanish records as early as 1778 (PSP Ben. Mil., I, 41). The Valle de Pamo, or Santa Maria, land grant is dated November 21, 1843. *Pamo* is a Diegueño word of unknown meaning.

Pampa Peak [Kern]. The peak was named after the former Southern Pacific station, shown on the Official Railway Map of 1900. Pampa, like Bena and Ilmon on the same sector, is probably a railroad name, without meaning.

Panama: town, **Slough** [Kern]. The place was settled before 1866 and was probably so named because the settlers considered the land on which they were living an isthmus, formed by two river channels (H. S. Allen). On November 27, 1874, the name was given to the Panama Ranch, established by Miller and Lux. Panama Slough is mentioned in court records of August 6, 1900. (V. J. McGovern.)

Panamint, păn'-*å*-mĭnt: **Valley, Range, Springs, Dry Lake** [Inyo]. The name is derived from a division of Shoshonean Indians formerly occupying this region, perhaps the "nation" called Beñemé by Garcés in 1776 (Coues, *Trail*, p. 238). It appears as Panamint in the report of the Nevada Boundary Commission

in 1861 (Sacramento *Union*, July 13, 1861), and was probably applied by the Darwin French party in the preceding year. (*See* Darwin Wash.) The orographic identity of the mountains on the maps remained vague. The map of the State Mining Bureau (1891) and again the Ballarat and Avawatz Mountains atlas sheets designate the various chains from Tin Mountain to Wingate Gap collectively as Panamint Range. On the Searles Lake atlas sheet the Quail Mountains are added for good measure.

Pancho Rico Creek [Monterey]. The tributary of Salinas River commemorates Francisco ("Pancho") Rico, grantee of the San Lorenzo grant, November 16, 1842. The name was misspelled Poncho Rico until the Geographic Board restored the proper form in 1961 (May-Aug.).

Panoche: Creek, Hills, Valley, town [Fresno, Merced, San Benito]. *Panoche* (or *panocha*) was a kind of sweet substance which the Indians extracted from reeds and wild fruit. The etymology of the word is not entirely clear, but it is quite certain that it is of Aztec origin and referred to the making of sugar or syrup from plants. *Nochtli* is the Aztec word for 'prickly pear' (*Cactus opuntia*), used by the Mexicans in making sweets and wine; Robelo lists also *pancololote*, another "plant from whose fruit a sweet syrup is made" (pp. 616, 630). *El punto* [place] *de la Panocha*, twenty leagues east of San Juan Bautista, is mentioned June 7, 1830 (DSP Ben. Mil., LXXII, 10), and *parage llamado la Panocha* (place called the Panocha) mentioned on July 4, 1840 (DSP Mont., III, 86). It is improbable that the name has any connection with Narciso Panocha, who was given permission to go after neophytes from Monterey in 1827 (Dep. Recs., IV, 79). The name appears in the titles of two land grants: Panocha de San Juan y Carrisalitos in Merced County, dated February 10, 1844, and Panoche Grande in San Benito County, dated March 14, 1844, but the latter was not confirmed by the United States. Paneche Pass is shown on Derby's map (1850), and Penoche Valley is mentioned in Hoffmann's notes in July, 1861.—The name was used elsewhere: *Panocha* is shown on a *diseño* of the Cuyama grant [Santa Barbara], and the diminutive Panochita, a name shown as *La Panochita* on several *diseños*, is used for a hill southwest of Mount Hamilton. The place was mentioned by Sebastian Rodriguez on April 22, 1828: *el paraje llamado la Panochita.*—The production of California *panoche* is described by Fages, pp. 79 ff.: "Native sugar is made from the olive-like fruit produced by a very leafy, tufted shrub, six feet high with a stem of reddish color and leaves like those of the mangrove. The preparation ... consists in gathering the ripe fruit, separating the pulp from the seed, and pressing it in baskets to make cakes of sugar ..." The *Indian Report* of 1853 (p. 57) mentions an Indian dish, *penocha* or *penona,* made of acorns with sugar.

Panther. This name is sometimes used for the mountain lion and is found in the names of about twenty geographic features, including Panther Den and Panther Beds Ridge [Sonoma]. Most of these names are in northern counties, where this name for the mountain lion is apparently more commonly used than elsewhere. **Panther: Creek, Gap, Peak** [Sequoia National Park]. The creek was so named because a panther was killed here by Hale Tharp (Farquhar).

Paoha Island [Mono Lake]. The name was given to the island by I. C. Russell in 1882: "We may therefore name the larger island Paoha Island, in remembrance, perhaps, of the children of the mist that held their revels there on moonlit nights in times long past" (Geological Survey, *Report,* VIII, 279). *Pauha* is a Mono word for 'water babies,' naked female spirits with long, flowing tresses (Gifford). The Land Office map of 1879 shows the island as Anna Herman Island.

Paper Mill Creek [Marin]. The first paper mill on the Pacific Coast was built and operated about three miles southeast of Olema by Samuel P. Taylor, in 1856. The mill is recorded on Hoffmann's map, on which the creek is still called Arroyo San Geronimo. On the maps of the Coast and Geological surveys the entire creek is called Lagunitas Creek.

Paradise. In California some fifty features are so named because of their assumed resemblance to the abode of the blessed; to some the name was no doubt applied in irony. In Siskiyou County there is a Paradise Craggy and in San Joaquin County a Paradise Dam. **Paradise** [Butte] is one of several settlements so named which has survived. It is shown on the Land Office map of 1879. On the Official Railway Map of 1900 it is recorded as Paradice. It could not be ascertained whether this spelling confirms the old story that the town was named after the "Pair o' Dice" saloon, or whether it was a misspelling which gave rise to the story. Helltown is a short distance

away.

Paraiso Springs [Monterey]. The Spanish word for 'paradise' was occasionally used for place names in California in Spanish times—far less often than Paradise in American times. The name in Monterey County seems to be the only survivor. A *Cañada del Paraiso,* now the upper San Jacinto Valley [Riverside], is mentioned by Font on December 16, 1775.

Paraje. The common Spanish generic term, sometimes spelled *parage,* for 'place' or 'site.' It is often found in land-grant and mission records and seems to have been used interchangeably with *sitio. See* Sitio.

Paramount [Los Angeles]. When the cities of Hynes and Clearwater were merged in 1948, Frank Zamboni, president of the Kiwanis Club, proposed the new name because the main street was Paramount Boulevard, named for the motion picture company (Betty Doheney).

Pardee Reservoir [Amador]. Named by the East Bay Municipal Utility District, October 19, 1929, for George C. Pardee, mayor of Oakland, 1893–1895, governor of California, 1903–1907, president of the board of directors of the utility district, 1924–1941.

Parker Dam [San Bernardino]. When the new branch of the Santa Fe was built in 1905–1907 the station in Arizona was named Parker, both for Earl H. Parker, location engineer of the railroad, and after Parker, an Indian settlement in the vicinity (Barnes). The general area became known as Parker, and the name was transferred to the proposed dam for water diversion into Arizona and then to the dam for Havasu Lake. The post office is listed in 1936.

Parker Mountain [Los Angeles]. The name is shown on the Tujunga atlas sheet of 1900 and probably commemorates James L. Parker, a ranger in the San Gabriel Forest Reserve in 1898 (County Surveyor). Older maps designate the peak as Mount Parkinson.

Parker: Pass [Yosemite National Park]; **Creek, Lake, Peak** [Mono]. The tributary to Mono Lake is labeled Cranes Creek on Eddy's map (1854) but is left nameless on other older maps. The present name, for an old settler on the banks of the creek, was apparently not applied until the Mount Lyell quadrangle was mapped in 1898.

Parkfield [Monterey]. After the Post Office Department had rejected the original name, Russelsville, Postmaster Sittenfelt, in 1883, selected the present name because of the surrounding natural oak park (Myrtle Flentge).

Parks Bar [Yuba]. Named for David Parks, who settled there in 1848 (Co. Hist., 1879, p. 88).

Parlier [Fresno]. The post office, established in 1898, was named for its first postmaster, I. N. Parlier, who had settled in the district in 1876.

Parsons: Peak, Memorial Lodge [Yosemite National Park]. Named in 1901 by R. B. Marshall for Edward T. Parsons (1861–1914), for many years a director of the Sierra Club. The lodge was erected and named by the Sierra Club in 1915.

Par Value Lake [Mono]. The lake was named after the adjacent mining claim called Par Value (Maule).

Pasadena, păs-á-dē′-ná [Los Angeles]. The community was founded in 1874 and called Indiana Colony because the original promoters came from Indiana. When the post office was established in 1875 another name had to be chosen, and rarely have pioneer settlers gone to more trouble to select a name for their town than the good people of Indiana Colony. Hiram Reid's account of the naming (pp. 338 ff.) sounds more convincing than various other stories: Judge B. S. Eaton, in discussing with another stockholder, Calvin Fletcher, the possibility of finding a suitable Spanish name for the proposed post office, recalled a conversation he had had with Manuel Garfías, the patentee of Rancho San Pascual, on part of which the town was situated. When asked why he had chosen so impractical a place for his house, Garfías replied, "Porque es la llave del Rancho." Fletcher was disappointed, because "yavvey," the only word he caught, would never do for a place name. Judge Eaton then translated Garfias' reply as 'key of the rancho.' This was at least a cue to a suitable name. Dr. T. B. Elliott, the president of the Indiana Colony, then took up the idea. He wrote to a friend who was a missionary among the Chippewa Indians in the Mississippi Valley for an Indian version of 'Key of the Ranch,' or 'Entrance to the Upper Part of the Valley,' and received in due course these suggestions: *Weoquán Pá sá de ná*, 'Crown of the Valley'; *Gish ká de ná Pá sá de ná*, 'Peak of the Valley'; *Tape Dáegun Pá sá de ná*, 'Key of the Valley'; *Pe quá de na Pá sá de ná*, 'Hill of the Valley.' Since Dr. Elliott could not very well propose the name Tapedaegunpasadena or Weoquanpasadena, he quietly dropped the specific part and submitted to the townspeople the pleasing and euphonious name, Pasadena. The interpretation that *pasadena* alone means 'crown of the valley' has persisted until the present day. The etymology of the original Chippewa word has received various interpretations. Casimir Vogt, another missionary among these Indians, derives the word from *passa-an*, 'I split something,' and interprets *passadena* as a "space formed by intersecting a range of hills or mountains" (Reid, *ibid.*), a somewhat roundabout way of saying 'valley.' According to Leland, the word is derived from *passajeck*, 'valley,' and *odena*, 'town'; the second element is preserved in Wadena, Minnesota, and Odanah, Wisconsin.

Paskenta [Tehama]. The name is derived from Central Wintun *paskenti*, 'under the bank' (Kroeber). The post office was established September 3, 1872.

Paso. The Spanish word is a common geographical term for 'pass,' 'passage,' 'crossing,' 'ford,' 'narrows,' 'channel.' It was often used in Spanish times and appears as a generic term in the names of six land grants, and as a specific term in one. **Paso Robles,** păs′-ŏ rŏ′-b'ls: city, **Creek** [San Luis Obispo]. The deciduous oaks which later provided the name for the place are mentioned by Font under date of March 4, 1776. *Paso de Robles* (passage through the oaks) is recorded as a rancho where the padres of San Miguel sowed wheat in 1828 (Registro, p. 17). May 12, 1844, the name was used for a land grant. The city was founded on the rancho in 1886 and incorporated in 1889 with the name Paso de Robles. In common usage the name is abbreviated to Paso Robles. *See* Bartolo Viejo; Del Paso. **El Paso Creek** [Kern]. The stream was named Pass Creek on April 14, 1844, when Frémont and Preuss crossed the Tehachapi Mountains. Later surveyors Hispanicized the name. **El Paso: Peak, Mountains** [Kern]. The pass north of Mojave, which gave the name to the orographic features, was discovered and named by Jacob Kuhrts in 1857. The well-known German pioneer of Los Angeles passed through Bedrock Canyon together with John Searles (of Searles Lake) on his way to Los Angeles (HSSC:Q, XXIX, 141).

Pastoria de las Borregas [Santa Clara]. The name, meaning 'sheep pasture,' was applied to the land grant on January 15, 1842. **Pastoria Creek** [Kern] was so named because the plateau through which it runs was used as the government pasture lands in the days of the Indian reservation at Rancho El Tejon in the 1850's (Rensch-Hoover, p. 132).

Patch [Kern]. The place was known as Weedpatch from the many weeds which grew there because of subirrigation. The Santa Fe abbreviated the name for the railroad siding, to distinguish it from the settlement Weed Patch farther south. *See* Algoso.

Patchin [Santa Clara]. The post office was established March 28, 1872, and named for a famous race horse. It was registered as Historical Landmark 448, November 2, 1949.

Pate Valley [Yosemite National Park]. Part of the Grand Canyon of Tuolumne River. The place is not shown on the maps of the Whitney and Wheeler surveys. It may have been named for Francis M. Pate of Alabama, a resident of Indian Gulch in 1867. However, the name appears as Pait in the early 1890's, which suggests a sheepman (Farquhar).

Patrick: Creek, Point, State Park [Humboldt]. The name Patrick Point is shown on the county map of 1886. It was doubtless given for Patrick Beegan, whose preëmption claim is recorded in the Trinidad Record Book on January 13, 1851, and whose tract six miles north of Trinidad was known as Patrick's Ranch (Joseph P. Tracy).

Patterson [Stanislaus]. Thomas W. Patterson, a Fresno banker, laid out the town about 1910 and named it for his uncle, John D. Patterson, who had purchased the land in 1864.

Patterson, Mount [Mono]. The highest peak in the Sweetwater Mountains was named possibly for James H. Patterson, a native of Ohio, who settled at Big Meadows before 1867.

Patterson Mountain [Fresno]. Probably named for John A. Patterson, a native of Georgia, who brought the first cattle into the upper Kings River region in 1853, was county supervisor in 1856, and assemblyman, 1875–1876.

Patterson: Pass, Run [Alameda]. Andrew Jackson Patterson was one of three brothers who settled in the district in the 1850's. Once when he and his wife were driving through the pass, a heavy windstorm came up. The wagon turned over and Mrs. Patterson's leg was broken. It is said that the pass received its name from this incident. (Lila McKinne.)

Patton [San Bernardino]. The Santa Fe station was called Asylum in 1891 because it was the station for the Southern California State Hospital. When the post office was established in 1895 it was named for Henry Patton of Santa Barbara. (Santa Fe.) In 1909 the station appears on the Santa Fe map as Patton.

Pattymocus [Siskiyou]. The name of the mountain means 'basket upside down' in Wintu Indian, a plausible interpretation (C. W. Lewis).

Pauba [Riverside]. The name of a land grant,

dated October 18, 1844, and February 4, 1846. It is probably a Luiseño word but its meaning is not known. A place *Pauba* is shown on one *diseño*, and *Las Páubas* on another.

Pauley Creek [Sierra]. The Geographic Board gave this name to the East Fork of the North Fork of Yuba River in 1950. An early settler named Pauley had built the first sawmill on the stream.

Paulsell [Stanislaus]. Named in 1897 by the Sierra Railroad for A. C. Paulsell, a native of Tennessee, the owner of the property. Paulsell came to Dent Township in 1854, was president of the Farmers' Co-operative Union, assemblyman 1873–1874, member of the State Harbor Commission 1884–1890.

Pauma: Valley, Creek, Indian Reservation [San Diego]. The name goes back to a rancheria of Luiseño Indians, mentioned in the records of the 1790's (PSP, XV, 182). *Potreros de Paoma* are mentioned on November 27, 1841 (Arch. LA, II, 120), and on November 8, 1844, the name was applied to the land grant, Pauma or Potrero de Pauma. The meaning of the word is not known, but since the place is near Pala, a connection with Luiseño *pame,* 'little water,' is possible. *See* Pala.

Paxton [Plumas]. The post office was established September 3, 1917, and was named for Elmer E. Paxton, general manager of the Indian Valley Railroad and the Engel Mining Company (Helen Strong).

Paynes Creek [Tehama]. A settlement, Payne's Creek, is listed in the Directory of the Marysville *Appeal* of 1878, apparently named after Paines Creek, shown on the Land Office map of 1879. The post office Paynes Creek is listed in 1892. A Mr. Payne had a sawmill farther south, on Sacramento River, perhaps as early as 1851, and John Paine (or Payne) was a resident of Red Bluff in the 1860's.

Payson Canyon [Inyo]. The canyon was named for "Old Lew" Payson, who lived for many years at Antelope Springs (Robinson).

Peach. Several physical features bear the name of the fruit: Peaches Creek [Sonoma], Peachtree Canyon [San Bernardino], Peachtree Creek [Stanislaus], Peachtree Valley [Monterey]. San Bernardino County has a Peachy Canyon. The community **Peachton** [Butte] was named in 1907 by the Sacramento Northern because a large peach orchard flourished there (Florence Campbell).

Peanut [Trinity]. In 1898 the settlers around Cuff's store decided to apply for a post office and name it for Cuff's wife. When the matter was submitted to A. L. Paulsen, postmaster at Weaverville, he suggested instead the name Peanut, because it would be a unique name and because he was very fond of peanuts and was eating them at the time. The petitioners agreed to enter it on the application as a second choice. The Post Office Department apparently agreed with Mr. Paulsen and chose the name Peanut, January 20, 1900.

Pearblossom [Los Angeles]. Named in 1924 by Guy C. Chase because it was then a center of pear orchards. The name remained after the pears were killed by blight and replaced by peaches. (R. M. Yost.) **Pearland** [Los Angeles]. An advertising name applied to the subdivision in 1919.

Pear Lake [Sequoia National Park]. The name was given to the lake because, as on the Tehipite atlas sheet, it presents a perfect outline of a pear.

Pease [Sutter]. The station of the Sacramento Northern was named for George Pease, through whose property the railroad was built in 1907.

Pebble Beach [Monterey]. The name developed locally because there is a beach with pebbles at this point, and it was accepted by the Pacific Improvement Company when it acquired the property in 1880. The post office is listed in 1910.—There are several other Pebble Beaches and Creeks in the State.

Pechanga Indian Reservation [Riverside]. Luiseño Indians told Constance DuBois (*AAE*, VIII, 151 f.) the story of a Temecula chief who named this and other places. "He went to Picha Awanga, Pichanga, between Temecula and Warner's Ranch, and named that place. There were a lot of people there having a fiesta, and there was plenty of food. They passed everything to him, and there was a sort of mush of a light gray color. So he said, 'My stomach is picha.' So they called the place by that name." This story has the earmarks of folklore.

Pecho: Rock, Creek [San Luis Obispo]. *Pecho,* 'breast,' was used in a geographical sense for rocks and hills shaped like a woman's breast. *Arroyo del Pecho* is shown on a *diseño* of the San Miguelito grant (1839). *El Pecho* (for the rock) and *Cañada* and *Arroyo del Pecho* are shown on several *diseños* of the grants which were combined in 1845 in the Cañada de los Osos y Pecho y Islai grant.

Pecks Canyon [Tulare]. Named for a man who ran sheep here about 1870 (Farquhar). One James Peck, a native of Kentucky, is registered in Visalia in 1879.

Pecwan. *See* Pekwan.

Pedernales, pĕd-ēr-nä′-lĕs, **Point** [Santa Barbara]. On August 28, 1769, the Portolá expedition camped somewhere near Point Arguello and found an Indian rancheria. "In this village the soldiers gathered good flints for their weapons; for this reason they named it Los Pedernales" (Crespi, pp. 176 f.). On Spanish maps the headland, of which Arguello is the principal point, was called *Punta Pedernales,* while on American and European maps Arguello was used, in various spellings. In the 1850's the name had become attached to Purisima Point: "This is known on the coast as Point Pedernales, signifying Point of Flints, but generally and erroneously printed Pedro Nales" (Coast Pilot, 1858, p. 24). When the Coast Survey recharted this section in 1873–1874, it called a triangulation point Pedernales but designated the present point as Promontory. The name was not attached to the point at latitude 34° 36′ until after 1900 (*Coast Pilot,* 1904). *See* Arguello.

Pedley [Riverside]. When the railroad from Ontario to Riverside (now the Union Pacific) was built in 1905, the station was named, probably for Francis X. Pedley, who was at that time engaged in real-estate promotion at Arlington. Pedley was a native of England, who had come to California in 1882 and to Riverside County in 1894. (Co. Hist., 1912, pp. 598 f.)

Pedro, pē′-drō: **Point, Creek, Valley, Hill** [San Mateo]. *San Pedro* as a rancho of Mission Dolores is mentioned as early as 1791. January 26, 1839, the name was used for a land grant. The anchorage San Pedro is shown on Duflot de Mofras's map. The point, situated on the grant and originally named *Punta del Angel Custodio* (guardian angel) by Crespi and *Punta de las Almejas* (mussels) by Portolá's soldiers, October 30, 1769, appears as Point San Pedro on sketch J2 (1850) of the Coast Survey. The "San" has been dropped by common usage and by the Post Office Department, but is still used on most maps. The post office is listed in 1939. *See* San Pedro.

Peeler Lake [Mono]. Named for Barney Peeler, an early settler (Maule).

Pegleg Mountain [Lassen]. J. J. ("Pegleg") Johnson, a trapper and Indian fighter, had taken a homestead near the mountain in the 1850's, and by local usage the mountain was given his nickname (A. G. Brenneis).

Pekwan Creek [Humboldt]. The name is derived from that of the Indian village at the confluence of the creek with Klamath River. The Pak-wan "band" is mentioned in the Indian Report under date of October 6, 1851. The name is spelled Pecwan on most maps.

Pelican. Three points, two bays, and one rock on the coast are named for the largest of our aquatic birds. The oldest is probably Pelican Bay [Del Norte], shown on Gibbs' map of 1851. *See* Alcatraz.

Pelona. The Spanish word for 'bald' was used as a descriptive name for orographic features devoid of trees. It is preserved in Sierra Pelona and Sierra Pelona Valley [Los Angeles] and in Loma Pelona [Monterey; Santa Barbara]. *See* Bald; Palomas.

Peñasquitos [San Diego]. The word is a diminutive of *peña*, 'rock,' and was applied to a land grant dated August 11, 1832, and May 5, 1834. *Santa Margarita de los Peñasquitos* was one of the ranchos and localities under the jurisdiction of Santiago Argüello, December 31, 1830 (Engelhardt, *San Diego*, p. 229).

Pendleton, Camp [San Diego]. Named in 1941 in memory of Marine Major General Joseph H. Pendleton, a veteran of the "banana" wars in Central America during the 1920's, who was instrumental in getting Marine Corps units based on the West Coast (Frances Kracha).

Penitencia, pĕn-ĭ-tĕns′-ĭ-ä: **Creek, Canyon** [Santa Clara]. The tributary of Coyote Creek was named after the Penitencia adobe house which stood at the highway and which probably had been used as a house of confession and penitence in mission times (Bowman). *La Penitencia*, apparently still the adobe house, is shown on Eld's sketch of 1841, and *Arroyo de la Penitencia* is shown on a *diseño* of the Pueblo Lands of San Jose (1840).

Penngrove [Sonoma]. Penn's Grove is mentioned as a station of the San Francisco and North Pacific Railroad in 1880 and was possibly named after Penn's Grove, New Jersey. The contraction was used by the Post Office Department in 1908.

Penon Blanco: Point, Ridge [Mariposa]. Named after the Peñon Blanco mine, which "takes in nearly the whole of the prominent Peñon Blanco hill" (Browne, p. 35). *Peñón blanco* is Spanish for 'large white rock.'

Penryn [Placer]. Established in 1864 by Griffith Griffith, owner of local granite quarries, and named after his home, Penrhyn, Wales. When the Central Pacific Railroad built a station there, the officials struck the "h" from the original spelling.

Pentz [Butte]. The post office (now discontinued) was established between 1864 and 1867, and was named for Manoah Pence, the first postmaster. The name was misspelled apparently by the Post Office Department (Co. Hist., 1882, p. 251). The county map of 1861 shows the name Pences north of Oroville.

Peoria: Pass, Basin, Creek, Mountain [Tuolumne]. The pass is shown on Hoffmann's map (1873) and was probably named after the town in Illinois or another of the ten Peorias then existing in the United States.

Pepperwood. About ten geographic features are so named, apparently all in the northern Coast Ranges, where the California laurel is called 'pepperwood.' **Pepperwood** [Humboldt]. The post office was established about 1900 and so named because of the presence of one of the finest groves of this pepperwood in the State.

Peral, pĕ-rāl′ [Tulare]. The Spanish word for 'pear tree' was applied to the Santa Fe station when the line from Visalia to Fresno was built, about 1895.

Peralta, pĕ-rāl′-tä [Orange]. The settlement was founded before 1900 and named in memory of Juan Pablo Peralta, in 1810 co-grantee of the Santiago de Santa Ana grant, on which the place is situated. The group of hills near the place in the Santa Ana Mountains is now called Peralta Hills (Geographic Board, July-Sept., 1965).

Peregoy Meadows [Yosemite National Park]. In 1869 Charles E. Peregoy, a native of Maryland, built a hotel, known as the Mountain View House, on the old horse trail from Clark's to Yosemite Valley. The remains of the old building are still visible on the meadow. His place is shown as Peregoy's on the Hoffmann-Gardner map, and the name is mentioned repeatedly in Brewer's Notes of the summer of 1864.

Perkins [Sacramento]. The post office was established about 1866 and named Brighton. About 1885 the name was changed to Perkins for Thomas C. Perkins, a native of Massachusetts, who had settled here in 1861 and had been the first postmaster. *See* Brighton.

Perkins, Mount [Kings Canyon National Park]. Named by Robert D. Pike in 1906, for George C. Perkins (1839–1923), governor of California 1880–1883, U.S. senator from California 1893–1915 (Farquhar).

Permanente Creek [Santa Clara]. The creek is shown as *Arroyo Permanente* on a *diseño* of Rancho San Antonio (1839). Permanente post office, established in 1938, and Henry Kaiser's Permanente Cement Company were named after the stream (J. H. Rogers). *Per-*

manente is often found on Spanish maps to designate a surface water which does not dry up in summer.

Perris: town, **Valley** [Riverside]. The town was laid out in 1886 and named for Fred T. Perris, chief engineer for the California Southern Railroad and one of the founders of the town. The valley was formerly called San Jacinto Plains, after the land grant San Jacinto. Before 1885 the town was two miles south of Perris and was called Pinecate after a near-by gold mine. Because of some litigation, both the site of the town and the name were changed (Co. Hist., 1935, p. 228). *See* Pinecate.

Perrott Grove [Humboldt]. This unit of Humboldt State Park was named for the donor, Mrs. Sarah T. Perrott.

Perry [Los Angeles]. The station was named in 1905 for the president of the Pacific Electric Railroad, at the suggestion of John Kirsch, owner of the local store.

Perry, Mount [Inyo]. The mountain in Death Valley was named for John W. S. Perry, 1848-1898, who designed the twenty-mule team wagons used to haul borax from Death Valley (Geographic Board, Jan.-Apr., 1961).

Perry Aiken Creek [Mono]. Named for Perry Aiken, a settler there in 1870 (Robinson).

Persian: Creek, Canyon [Tulare]. The name of the tributary to Cottonwood Creek is not reminiscent of any Persian settlers on its banks, but of the old John Persian ranch (A. L. Dickey). James Persian, a native of Pennsylvania, and John, Silas, and Henry Persian, natives of Missouri, were residents of the county in 1867.

Persido Bar [Siskiyou]. The name is an Anglicization of *Patsiluvra,* a former Karok Indian hamlet about 250 yards upstream (Gifford).

Persinger Canyon [Los Angeles]. Named by the Forest Service for the Persinger family, homesteaders of 1888 (Forest Service).

Pescadero, pĕs-kȧ-dâr'-ō. In maritime Spanish the word is used for 'fishing place.' On the older maps there are various places *de los Pescadores* (of the fishermen), but the five land grants and the surviving names have only Pescadero. **Pescadero Creek** [Santa Clara]. In 1861 Manuel Larios testified in the Las Animas land-grant case that the Castros "had an Indian boy who went to this creek to fish" and so it was called the Pescadero. Two days later John Gilroy testified in the same case that "the Pescadero draws its name from the fact of our catching salmon there." And two days later still, in the Juristac

land-grant case, Gilroy stated that "the Castros, I and an Indian gave it that name in 1814, being a place where we used to catch salmon" (*WF*, VI, 371 f.). *Arroyo del Pescadero* is shown on *diseños* of the 1830's. The stream is mentioned as Pescadero River in Trask's *Report* (1854, p. 8). **Pescadero: Creek,** town, **Point** [San Mateo]. The name is mentioned in the *expediente* of the land grant El Pescadero or San Antonio, December 17, 1833. On the charts of the 1860's the Coast Survey called the creek Pescador River. The town was settled by Spanish-speaking people in the early 1850's and was called Pescadero from the beginning. **Pescadero: Point, Rocks** [Monterey]. *La punta del pescadero* is mentioned in a letter of April 2, 1835 (Legis. Recs., III, 61). The name El Pescadero was applied to a land grant, February 29, 1836, and Pescadero appears on the early charts of the Coast Survey. **Pescadero Colony** [San Joaquin]. The name of the tract was preserved from the land grant, El Pescadero, dated November 28, 1843. The name may go back to the *Rio del Pescadero* (probably the old channel of the San Joaquin) named by Fernando de Rivera in December, 1776 (PSP, XIV, 13 f.). **Pescadero Creek** [San Benito] is recorded as *Sanjon del Pescadero* on a *diseño* of the Paicines grant.

Petaluma, pĕt-ȧ-lōō'-mȧ: city, **Creek** [Sonoma]. According to Barrett (*Pomo*, p. 310), the name contains the Coast Miwok words *pe'ta,* 'flat,' and *lū'ma,* 'back,' and was applied to a village site on a low hill east of the creek as well as to the hill itself. Since an elevation of this kind would be called *loma* in Spanish, an Indian adaptation of the Spanish word might be indicated. The Coast Survey chart of 1850 actually spells the name Petaloma. However, in the Spanish manuscripts examined this spelling has not been found, nor has the name been found applied to a hill. *El llano de los Petalumas* (the plain of the Petaluma Indians) is mentioned by Padre Payeras, May 31, 1819 (Docs. Hist. Cal., IV, 341 ff.), and the name of the Indians is found in even earlier records. Moreover, the second element suggests the Miwok word *yome* or *lume,* 'place.' *See* Tocaloma. On June 21, 1834, the name Petaluma was applied to a land grant, of which Mariano G. Vallejo was grantee. Part of the rancho was preempted in 1850 by G. W. Keller, who laid out the city in 1851 and kept the Indian name. The post office was established and named on February 9, 1852.

Peter, Lake [Tulare]. According to Judge W. B. Wallace, the name was bestowed upon the little lake in 1877 by his companion, Joe Palmer, because the dim trail they had followed "petered out" at that place (Farquhar).

Peter Peak [Kings Canyon National Park]. Named by the Sierra Club in 1938, in memory of Peter Grubb, who had made the first recorded ascent in July, 1936 (Farquhar).

Peters [San Joaquin]. The station of the Stockton and Copperopolis Railroad was named in the 1870's for J. D. Peters, owner of the land. Peters, an associate of Frank Stewart in land speculation, had come to California at the time of the gold rush and later gained a fortune in the grain and shipping business, with headquarters at Stockton.

Petrified Forest. There are several petrified forests in the State, so named because of the presence of petrified trees. The two best known are in Sonoma and Kern counties.

Petroglyph Point [Modoc]. So named because the rock wall near the Oregon line is covered with petroglyphs carved by aborigines.

Petrolia [Humboldt]. The first California oil deposits to be exploited commercially were found northeast of the town by a U.S. Army officer. Reports of the discovery were published, with reservations, in the Sonoma *Journal* and the *Mining Press*, February 1, 1861, and in the summer of 1865 the San Francisco newspapers reported the first shipment of oil. The name of the post office, established September 13, 1865, was originally spelled Petrolea. The site of the first drilled oil wells is Historic Landmark 543.

Petticoat Mountain [Lake]. So named because it is shaped like an old-fashioned petticoat (Mauldin). The once well-known mining camp Petticoat Slide was, according to tradition, so named because a lady slid in the mud, fell, and exposed her petticoats.

Pettit Peak [Yosemite National Park]. The peak was named by Colonel W. W. Forsyth, acting superintendent of the park, 1909–1912, for James S. Pettit, colonel of the Fourth U.S. Volunteer Infantry in the Spanish-American War.

Pfeiffer, fíf′-ĕr: **Point, Rock, Redwoods State Park** [Monterey]. The name was given to the point for Michael Pfeiffer, a pioneer settler, when the Coast Survey resurveyed this sector, 1885–1887. The state park was created and named in 1933. Pfeiffer preëmpted a claim in Sycamore Canyon in the Big Sur valley in November, 1869 (AGS: *Monterey*, p. 183). The Julia Pfeiffer State Park, made possible

by a land gift of 1,700 acres, was created in 1961.

Phelan [San Bernardino]. The post office was named Nov. 25, 1916, for Senator James D. Phelan, who had used his influence in establishing it (Ruth Mannigel).

Phillipsville [Humboldt]. George Stump Phillips settled here about 1865 and the place became known as Phillips Flat. When the post office was established, March 12, 1883, the name was changed to Philippsville. C. Hart Merriam changed the name to Kittinelbe after the Indian village at the site, but when the post office was reëstablished, August 1, 1948, the old name was again chosen.

Philo [Mendocino]. Named after 1868 by Cornelius Prather, landowner and first postmaster, for his favorite girl cousin, whose given name was probably Philomena.

Phipps Peak [El Dorado]. Named for General William Phipps, a native of Kentucky and veteran of Indian wars, who came to Georgetown in 1854 and was famous for his marksmanship (W. T. Russell in "The Knave," July 23, 1944).

Picacho, pĭ-kä′-chō: **Peak, Mines, Wash,** settlement; **Little Picacho** [Imperial]. The peak, which has the appearance of an obelisk, is a well-known landmark. Font mentions it as *La Campana* (the bell) on December 4, 1775 (*Compl. Diary*), and Garcés calls it *Peñon de la Campana*, 'rock of the bell' (Coues, *Trail*, pp. 162, 215). In early American times it became known as Chimney Rock, a name still used locally. *See* Chimney. The present name is tautological: *picacho* itself means 'peak.' Picacho Mines are Historic Landmark 193.— The Sutter Buttes were called *Picachos* in Spanish times, and the hill southeast of Arroyo Grande [San Luis Obispo] is still called Picacho.

Picayune, pĭk-á-yōōn′: **Valley** [Placer]. The mining district formed in 1864 apparently failed to yield a golden harvest; hence the name. A picayune was the smallest coin (five cents) of the mid-19th century and the term came to mean 'paltry' or 'insignificant.' *See* Poverty Hills.

Pickel Meadow [Mono]. The meadow was named for Frank Pickel, stockman and prospector of the 1860's. It had formerly been known as Duffields Valley (Maule, p. 10). The name is misspelled Pickle Meadow by the Geological Survey.

Picket Guard Peak [Tulare]. Named before 1898. "There is a fine pyramidal peak at the eastern end of the third range, which was always in the background of the view as we entered and ascended the narrow cleft of the Kern-Kaweah. This was named the Picket Guard." (William R. Dudley, *SCB*, II, 189.)

Pickett Peak [Alpine]. The name recalls an early stage station, Pickett Place, which was near the peak and was named for Edward M. Pickett (Maule).

Pico, pě'-kō [Los Angeles]. The name was applied to the station of the San Pedro, Los Angeles, and Salt Lake Railroad in 1904 because it was situated on that part of the Paso de Bartolo Viejo grant which was owned by Pío Pico, the last governor of Mexican California. **Pico: Canyon, Oil Field** [Los Angeles]. Named for Andrés Pico, brother of Pío Pico, and the last commanding Mexican officer to surrender in 1847. "Andreas Pico knew the locality now called Pico Cañon ... and had made oil for San Fernando Mission in a small way. ... He was probably the pioneer coal oil manufacturer of the State" (Hanks, *Report*, 1884, p. 294).—Pico Heights [Los Angeles], listed as a post office in 1904, and a few physical features were named for some members of the large Pico family.

Pico Blanco [Monterey]. "A striking white mountain called Pico Blanco [white peak], the second highest point of the range. It looked strangely white, almost as though it were snow-covered." (Chase, *Coast Trails*, p. 208.) The geographical term *pico* was used here in the original sense: 'peak of the mountain.' It has survived (or was applied by Americans) in the names of several other orographic features: *see* the specific names.

Pico: Creek, Rock [San Luis Obispo]. The creek was named for José de Jesús Pico, patentee (1876) of the Piedra Blanca grant (1840), through which the creek flows. The Coast Survey applied the name to the bare rock south of San Simeon.

Pico Rivera [Los Angeles]. In January, 1958, the towns of Pico and Rivera incorporated under the new name, which is confusing because the two post offices were not amalgamated.

Piedmont [Alameda]. This name, of Italian or French origin, is one of the popular American place names with an aristocratic ring. It is here actually descriptive because the city is situated at the 'foot of the mountain.' About 1876 an organization which called itself the Piedmont Springs Company purchased a tract of land on which there was a sulphur spring and soon afterward erected the Piedmont Springs Hotel (Co. Hist., 1928, I, 532). The residential district was developed about 1900; the post office is listed in 1904.

Piedra. The Spanish word really means 'stone' but was used in California nomenclature for 'rock,' just as "stone" in American terminology was formerly used for "rock." Some Piedra names have survived from Spanish times: Piedras Altas [Monterey], Piedra Azul Canyon [Merced], Piedra Gorda [Los Angeles], Piedra de Lumbre (flint stone) Canyon [San Diego], Corral de Piedra Creek [San Luis Obispo]. **Piedras Blancas:** rocks, **Point** [San Luis Obispo]. The two large, white, pointed rocks were noticed by early navigators, although no name for them is found on the maps. *La Piedra blanca* is mentioned on April 27, 1836 (Docs. Hist. Cal., I, 255), and on January 18, 1840, the name, also in the singular, was applied to a land grant. The Coast Survey has used the name Piedras Blancas since the early 1850's. **Piedra** [Fresno]. In 1911 the Santa Fe constructed a branch line to handle rock from a quarry and gave the siding its Spanish name. The name of the post office is Delpiedra, a nice-sounding but ungrammatical combination.

Pierce Mountain [Humboldt]. Named for President Pierce by Henry Washington when he established on the peak the initial point of the Humboldt base line: "It has been named Mount Pierce, as a compliment to the President, and the monument ... was erected ... on the 6th. of October, 1853" (*CHSQ*, XXXIV, 14).

Piercy [Mendocino]. The name was given to the post office in 1920 for Sam Piercy, the oldest white settler of the district (C. C. Kirk).

Pierpont Bay [Ventura]. The bay was named for Ernest Pierpont, a native of Virginia, who was a resident of Ojai Valley in the 1890's.

Piety Hill [Shasta]. The old mining town was named after Piety Hill, Michigan, the former home of "Grandma" McKenny, a beloved and respected resident (Steger). The place is now called Igo.

Pigeon Point [San Mateo]. The name was applied by the Coast Survey because the clipper ship *Carrier Pigeon* was wrecked here on May 6, 1853. The Spanish name for the point as shown on several *diseños* was *Punta de las Ballenas* (point of whales). *Punta Falsa de Año Nuevo* on Camancho's map of 1785 was probably modern Pigeon and Franklin points. See Ano Nuevo, Point.

Pike. The expression "Pike" or "Pike Countyan" was used in California in the 1860's, or earlier, for a person who had supposedly come from Pike County, Missouri, but actually it was applied to anyone of migratory habits. The name, used in one sense or another, found its way into geographical names, some of which have survived. **Pike County Peak** [Yuba]. The peak was named after the Pike County House, a hotel built and named by a Mr. Thompson in 1860 (Co. Hist., 1879, p. 92). **Pike** [Sierra]. The post office was established as Pike City in the 1870's and may have been named for a family named Pike. The "City" was dropped when the Post Office Department in the 1890's systematically simplified many of its names.

Pilarcitos, pĭl-ĕr-sē'-tōs: **Creek, Lake** [San Mateo]. The Portolá expedition camped at the creek on October 28, 1769, and Crespi named it Arroyo de San Simon y San Judas in honor of the Apostles Simon and Jude because it was their feast day. The name Arroyo de los Pilarcitos, i.e., creek of the little pillar-like rocks, was given to a land grant January 2, 1841, but the name is recorded in land-grant papers as early as 1836. The grant was also known as Rancho de Miramontes and as San Benito. In 1862 the Coast Survey placed the name Pilarcitos Creek on its chart of Half-moon Bay. **Pilarcitos: Canyon, Ridge** [Monterey]. A place, Pilarcitos, about midway between missions San Juan Bautista and Soledad, is shown by Bancroft on his map of the Monterey district, 1801–1824 (II, 145). A *sitio de los Pilarcitos* is mentioned on July 24, 1830 (Legis. Recs., I, 147), and in later records. On June 23, 1834, the place was made a temporary grant, which, however, was called Chamisal when granted in 1835 (Bowman Index).

Pillar: Point, Rock, Reef [San Mateo]. A *parage llamado el 'Pilar'* (the place called the 'pillar') is mentioned on October 18, 1796 (PSP, XIV, 19), and in later records. It was probably so named because a rocky formation at the near-by point resembled a pillar, and was not the place (in Santa Cruz County) named in honor of *Nuestra Señora del Pilar* by Crespi, October 12 and November 23, 1769. Narváez' Plano of 1830 and some of the later maps show a settlement Pilares at the approximate site of the present town of Half Moon Bay. The cape is called Miramontes on the Coast Survey chart of 1854, but when Halfmoon Bay was charted in 1862 this name was replaced by Pillar Point.

Pillsbury Lake [Lake]. The reservoir, filled for the first time in February, 1922, was named

for E. S. Pillsbury, who with Senator C. N. Felton had organized the Snow Mountain Water and Power Company in 1906 (*Pacific Service Magazine*, XVII, 344 ff.).

Pilot. The word, usually combined with Peak, Hill, or Knob, was a favored name with overland immigrants, prospectors, and surveyors, for a landmark which would "pilot" them in the right direction. In California there are at least twenty orographic features called "Pilot," including Pilot Knob west of Humphreys Basin [Fresno] and the unique Pilot Pinnacle [Lassen National Park]. **Pilot Knob** [Imperial]. This black rock was called *San Pablo* in Anza's diary entry of February 10, 1774. The present name was used as early as 1846 by soldiers, surveyors, and immigrants, and seldom has a name been applied more appropriately. The Indian name for the knob was *Ha-bee-co-la-la* (Whipple, 1849), or *Avie Quah-la-Altwa* (Emory, *Report*, p. 104). *Avi* or *habi* is the Yuman word for 'mountain.' **Pilot Knob** [Siskiyou]. The high peak of the Siskiyou Mountains has been thus known since the 1840's when it "piloted" the caravans using the old California-Oregon trail. **Pilot Hill** [El Dorado]. The name of the elevation between the Middle and South forks of the American River goes back to the early mining days. As early as 1849 it was the center of a rich placer-mining region. On April 18, 1854 a post office was established.

Pinchot, pĭn'-shō, **Mount; Pass** [Kings Canyon National Park]. ". . . there stood a great rounded mass of red slate on the Main Crest, and I allowed myself to change the name Red Mountain given it by Professor Brown, and already applied to scores of the slate peaks of the Sierra, to Mt. Pinchot" (J. N. LeConte, *SCB*, IV, 262). Gifford Pinchot was at that time chief of the U.S. Division of Forestry, later professor of forestry at Yale and governor of Pennsylvania.

Pincushion Peak [Fresno]. The peak near the Madera County line was so named because its regular outline resembles a pincushion. The name, which probably had already been in use locally, was applied by the Geological Survey when the Kaiser quadrangle was mapped in 1901–1902.

Pine. The existence of almost twenty varieties of true pines in the State and the great commercial value of a number of them have made this tree one of the most popular for naming places. About two hundred physical features bear some form of the name Pine on the maps, and many more are so called locally.

Some Pine names are translations from the Spanish: Pine Canyon [Monterey] was *Arroyo del Pino;* Pine Creek [Tehama, Butte] was *Arroyo de los Pinos;* Pine Ridge [Santa Clara] was *Pinalitos. See* Pinos. Occasionally the name of the species is added: Digger Pine Flat, Sugar Pine Hill, Torrey Pines Park. Some names are modified by Lone, Big, or Little, or by a number. "Piney" in Piney Ridge and Creek [Mariposa] is a common term for 'pine-covered.' No fewer than sixteen towns and settlements are named after the tree; among these are several post offices: Pinecrest [Tuolumne], Pinedale [Fresno], Pine Grove [Amador], Pineridge [Fresno], Pine Valley [San Diego], Bigpine [Inyo], Lone Pine [Inyo], Pine Knot and Pine Lake [San Bernardino].

Pinecate, pē'-nĕ-kä'-tĭ: **Peak** [San Benito]. *Los Pinacates* are mentioned on April 6, 1817 (Arch. Arz. SF, Vol. III, Pt. 2, p. 11). *Cañada de los Pinacates* is shown on several *diseños* in different locations but was probably the valley through which the road winds. An unconfirmed land grant called *Cañada de los Pinacates* is dated April 20, 1835. *Pinecate,* derived from Aztec *pinacatl,* is a Mexican word for a black beetle which lives in damp places.

Pinnacles. The name is applied to pillar-like formations created by erosion. The most notable are the Pinnacle Rocks [San Benito], mentioned by Vancouver in 1794 and included, since 1908, in Pinnacles National Monument, and the Pinnacles in Yosemite National Park. With the exception of Pilot Pinnacle [Lassen National Park] the word does not seem to have been used as a generic term. Pinnacle Point is the modern name of the rocky promontory of Point Lobos near Monterey. In 1878 the Coast Survey recorded the name Pyramid Point for the projecting rock. The Pinnacles in the National Monument in San Benito County were formerly called Chalone Peaks. *See* Chalone.

Pinole, pē-nōl': **Point, Creek, Ridge,** town, **Shoal** [Contra Costa]. The word is derived from the Aztec *pinolli,* designating ground and parched or toasted grain or seeds. Fages (p. 79) reports that the California Indians made a chocolate-colored *pinole* from the seeds of the cattail reed, and from the flower in season they made a yellow and sweet *pinole.* It may have been a *pinole* of this kind which the Indians gave to José de Cañizares in 1775 (Eldredge, *Portolá,* pp. 66 f.), and because of this incident the name may have

become attached to the region. According to a legend, however, the name was given in Mexican times: A detachment of soldiers, prevented from crossing Carquinez Strait because of high winds, ran out of provisions. "On their march they found a village of Indians, who had corn from which they manufactured meal (Pinole). That camp they named El Pinole." (Co. Hist., 1878, p. 12.) In 1823, possessory rights to Pinole y Cañada de la Hambre were granted to Ignacio Martínez in recognition of his military services. The formal land grant is dated June 1, 1842. Another grant, Boca de la Cañada del Pinole, is dated June 21, 1842. The point was called Penoli on Ringgold's maps, and Penole on the Coast Survey chart in 1850. The Parke-Custer map, in 1855, gives the correct spelling, but the Coast Survey did not correct the mistake until fifty years later. The post office was established and named in the 1870's.

Pinon Hills [San Bernardino]. The community, about 40 miles northwest of San Bernardino, first bore the name Smithson Springs for the owner of a cattle ranch, later Desert Springs, and in 1962 Pinon Hills (Belden). The name is derived from the Spanish word *piñon,* 'pine nut kernel.'

Pinos. The wealth of native pines in California made this tree the most popular for place naming, even in Spanish times. The name was repeatedly used by explorers who were struck by the pine-covered mountains and promontories after their passage along the treeless shores of Lower California. Monterey Bay was the *Bahia de los Pinos* and Point Reyes was probably the *Cabo de Pinos* which Cabrillo named in 1542. From Monterey Bay southward there are still about fifteen geographic features called Pinos. **Point Pinos,** pē'-nōs [Monterey]. The name *Punta de Pinos* was given to the cape by Vizcaíno in December, 1602 (Wagner, p. 402). It was applied to a land grant, dated May 24, 1833, and October 4, 1844. The generic part was Americanized by the Coast Survey in 1855. **Potrero Los Pinos; Los Pinos Mountain** [San Diego]. The names originated with the Potrero Los Pinos, a part of the Potreros de San Juan Capistrano land grant, dated April 5, 1845. In Santa Barbara County, there was a land grant Cañada de los Pinos, dated March 16, 1844, and the Santa Cruz Mountains are called *Sierra Verde de Pinos* on Crespi's map of 1772. *See* Tres Pinos; Pine.

Pinoso, Arroyo [Fresno]. The valley south of Coalinga had several other names before the

Geographic Board decided in 1964 (May-Aug.) for the present name, which is the Spanish word for 'piny.'

Pintado. In Spanish and even in early American times the Spanish adjective for 'painted' was often used for colored canyons and mountains as well as for trees or rocks with Indian symbols and figures.

Pinto. The word means 'mottled' in the Southwest and is now usually applied to a piebald horse. It was used as a name for a mountain chain near the Mojave Sink as early as 1776: ". . . the sierra that I named Pinta for the veins that run in it of various colors" (Garcés, March 9, 1776; Coues, *Trail*, p. 238). **Pinto Peak** [Death Valley National Monument]. The name was applied to the range north of Towne's Pass and to its highest peak by the Wheeler Survey in 1871 and appears on its atlas sheet 65-D. The name was later extended to the ridge south of the pass (Carson and Colorado Railroad map of the 1880's). On the Ballarat atlas sheet it is transferred, without reference to its meaning, to a drab and colorless peak. The range, left nameless on the atlas sheet, is locally called Moigne Mountain, for an old prospector. Pinto Lake in Santa Cruz County was probably named for a person.

Pinyon. The Spanish word *piñón* designates the edible pine-nut seed. In California the name is applied to the two species of pines, *Pinus parryana* and *monophylla,* both of which bear these nuts. They were of great value to the Indians. Except for the two Pinyon peaks in Monterey County, places bearing the name are all found in the arid sections of the State, where the trees are native.

Piojo. *See* El Piojo.

Pioneer Basin [Fresno]. When the Mount Goddard quadrangle was surveyed, between 1907 and 1909, R. B. Marshall named four peaks of the Silver Divide for the pioneer railroad builders (*see* Crocker, Mount) and called the depression surrounded by the peaks Pioneer Basin (Farquhar).

Pioneertown [San Bernardino]. The town was originally built as a set for Western movies. The late actor Dick Curtis applied the name on Labor Day, 1946 (Hester Downing). The word is used in other parts of the State; in Amador County a post office named Pioneer was established June 1, 1947.

Pipe Creek [Mendocino]. So named by the settlers in-the early 1860's because they found near the stream two corncob pipes belonging to the Sprowell brothers (Asbill). *See* Spro-

well Creek; Bell Spring Mountain.

Pipe Line Canyon [Lake]. In the 1890's an iron pipe line four miles long was laid from Chicken Springs to the Highland Springs Resort (Mauldin).

Piru, pī-rōō: **River, Creek, Canyon,** town [Ventura]. According to Kroeber, the name is derived from Shoshonean *pi'idhu-ku,* the name of a plant. A place called *Piru* is mentioned on May 31, 1817 (Arch. Arz. SF, Vol. III, Pt. 1, p. 132), and with various spellings in the following years; the *Arroyo de Piruc* is shown on a *diseño* of the San Francisco grant, 1838. In American times, the name appears as Piro in the *Statutes* of 1850 (p. 59) and as Rio Peru on the Parke-Custer map of 1854–1855. The town was laid out in 1888 and called Piru City after the Piru ranch developed by the Chicago publisher, David C. Cook.

Pisgah, pĭz'-gȧ: **Mountain,** station [San Bernardino]. The extinct volcanic crater was named after Mount Pisgah in Palestine, from which Moses saw the promised land. The station was named after the mountain in 1905 (Santa Fe).

Pismo, pĭz'-mō: **Beach, Creek, Lake, State Park** [San Luis Obispo]. The town was laid out in 1891 when the last link of the Southern Pacific coast route was built from San Luis Obispo to Ellwood. It was named Pismo because of its situation on the Pismo land grant (dated November 18, 1840); the generic term Beach was added to the name after 1904. The state park was established and named in 1935. *Pismu* was the Indian word for 'tar' (Fages, p. 82). *See* Asphalt; Brea.

Pitas, pē'-tȧs: **Point** [Ventura]. The point received its name from an Indian village called by the Portolá expedition *Los Pitos* (the whistles): "Two leagues beyond is the village of Los Pitos, so called because of the whistle which the men of the first expedition of Commander Portolá heard blown there all night" (Font, *Compl. Diary,* pp. 248 f.). Crespi had recorded the same incident under date of August 15, 1769: "During the night they [the Indians] disturbed us and kept us awake playing all night on some doleful pipes or whistles." He adds that he called the village *Santa Conefundis,* but does not say that the soldiers named it *Los Pitos. El citio llamado* [the place called] *de los Pitos* is mentioned July 25, 1822 (Docs. Hist. Cal., IV, 583). The Coast Survey left the point nameless until 1868, when it was labeled Las Petes. In 1889 Davidson changed the name to Point Las

Pitas, probably assuming that it was named for the American agave or century plant, *pita* in Spanish. The Coast Survey chart still keeps Davidson's name although the point is commonly called Pitas Point.

Pitman Creek [Fresno]. Named for Elias Pitman, who had a hunting cabin on the banks of the creek "in the early days" (Farquhar).

Pit River. Like the Missouri and the Mississippi, the Pit and the Sacramento present a geographical anomaly. Above the confluence with the Little or Upper Sacramento the Pit is the main stream; consequently, the entire course from Goose Lake to Suisun Bay should be called either Pit *or* Sacramento. The Pit River had been known to the trappers of the Hudson's Bay Company since the 1820's and was so called because the Indians dug pits on its banks as traps. A graphic account of these pits is given by Joaquin Miller in his *Life amongst the Modocs* (p. 373): "We crossed the McCloud, and our course lay through a saddle in the mountains to Pit river; so called from the blind pits dug out like a jug by the Indians in places where their enemies or game are likely to pass. These pits are dangerous traps; they are ten or fifteen [!] feet deep, small at the mouth, but made to diverge in descent, so that it is impossible for anything to escape that once falls into their capacious maws. To add to their horror, at the bottom, elk and deer antlers that have been ground sharp at the points are set up so as to pierce any unfortunate man or beast they may chance to swallow up. They are dug by the squaws, and the earth taken from them is carried in baskets and thrown into the river." Hood's map of 1838 has the correct spelling, but Wilkes' map of 1841 has Pitts River and Pitts Lake. The observant Eld, to be sure, crossed out one "t" in his manuscript when he learned the reason for its naming, but his journal was not published. In 1850 Williamson tried to rectify the mistaken idea that the river was named for the great English statesman: "We passed many pits about six feet deep and lightly covered with twigs and grass. The river derives its name from these pits, which are dug by the Indians to entrap game. On this account, Lieut. Williamson always spelled the name with a single t, although on most maps it is written with two." (Pac. R.R. *Reports,* Vol. VI, Pt. 1, p. 64.) His efforts were in vain: although the newspapers of the northern counties usually spelled the name correctly, most maps of the 1850's and 1860's have Pitt River. Scholfield in 1851 applied the name Sacramento to both the Pit and the Sacramento. The Whitney Survey tried again to call the entire waterway Sacramento River and at the same time restored the proper spelling. The von Leicht–Craven map has Upper Sacramento *or* Pit River. However, Brewer in his field notes uses consistently the spelling Pitt, and most maps continued the wrong spelling until the Geological Survey issued the Redding atlas sheet in 1901.

Pittsburg: Landing, city, **Station** [Contra Costa]. Colonel J. D. Stevenson, of the New York Volunteers, and Dr. W. C. Parker bought Rancho Los Medanos in 1849 and laid out the "City of New York of the Pacific" at the site of modern Pittsburg. When the coal deposits, discovered in the hills north of Mount Diablo in 1852, were commercially exploited after 1858, two railroads were built, one terminating in this New York, the other at the wharf of the Pittsburg Coal Company at the present site of Pittsburg Landing (plat of Rancho Los Medanos, 1865). The coal company was doubtless named after the industrial city in Pennsylvania. On Hoffmann's map of the Bay region (1873) both terminals of the railroad—the one at the river as well as the one in the hills—are labeled Pittsburgh. The struggle to make the exploitation of the deposits of inferior coal pay dividends was finally given up, and both cities declined. After 1900 the steel industry instilled new life into the sleeping communities: old New York was named Pittsburg (or Pittsburgh) and old Pittsburg became Pittsburg Landing. With the exception of the large city in Pennsylvania, which insists upon the retention of the final "h," the spelling Pittsburg is now generally used in the United States.

Pittville [Lassen]. The post office was established in 1878 and named after the river, its name then still incorrectly spelled Pitt. Another town, Pittsburg, obviously named after the river, is mentioned by Beckwith in the Pacific Railroad *Reports* (Vol. II, Pt. 2, p. 55).

Piute, pī-ūt'. In California this spelling is now generally accepted for most of the places named for the tribe. The Paiute—as anthropologists prefer to spell the name—are a branch of the Ute, a division of the Shoshonean Indians, whose name is preserved in the name of the state, Utah. There is no reasonable doubt that the original name was *Pah-Ute,* 'water ute'; the generic *pah,* 'water,' is preserved in numerous place names in California and in Arizona. The earliest ascertainable recording of the name of the tribe is found in Garcés' diary of 1776: *Payuches* (Coues, *Trail,* p. 351) and *Payuchas* (p. 405). The spelling in later years naturally varies; the version Paiute, later simplified to Piute, was generally used by the men of the Pacific Railroad Survey in the 1850's. In early American times the name seems to have been loosely applied to most of the Indians east of the Sierra Nevada. **Piute Creek** [Lassen], a tributary of Susan River, appears to be the only feature named for what anthropologists now designate as Northern Paiute (or Paviotso). **Piute: Mountain, Creek** [Yosemite National Park]; **Piute Mountain** [Mono]; **Piute: Pass, Creek, Canyon** [Fresno]; **Paiute Monument** [Inyo]. These places are in the territory of the Eastern Mono, commonly called Paiute. According to Kroeber, these Mono-speaking Indians are not related to the Paiute farther south, but "affiliate with the 'false' or Northern Paiute." The Sierra pass on the Fresno-Inyo county line was named by L. A. Winchell because it was used by Owens Valley Indians. The name was applied to the creek by J. N. LeConte in 1904 to avoid the name North Branch of the South Fork of the San Joaquin River (Farquhar). *See* Winnedumah. **Piute: Range,** station [San Bernardino]. These places are really in Paiute territory— Southern Paiute or Chemehuevi, according to anthropologists, who try to avoid the use of the designation Paiute because of its vagueness. The station was named by the Santa Fe in 1903 or 1904. A near-by Pah-Ute Springs, shown on the Santa Fe map of 1880, doubtless suggested the name. **Piute Butte** [Los Angeles]; **Piute: Mountains, Peak,** town; **Pahute Peak** [Kern]. These places are decidedly outside of Paiute territory but close enough to justify their naming. When rangers of Sequoia National Forest climbed a peak near Piute Peak about 1945, they found a tube containing a record left by earlier climbers indicating that this was the original Piute Peak. Since, however, the name givers had spelled the name Pahute, the rangers left this name on the new peak and we now have both names. (Stewart.)

Pixley [Tulare]. The name of Frank Pixley, founder and editor of the San Francisco *Argonaut,* was given to the settlement in the 1880's (Co. Hist., 1913, p. 51).

Pizzlewig Creek [Siskiyou]. The fork of Crawford Creek (tributary to Salmon River) formerly known as Sweet Pizzlewig Creek has retained the shortened form. The story behind the name was told by "Hardscrabble"

in August, 1900: "A poor forlorn woman deficient in virtuous ways settled on top of the mountains to be free from the temptations of the world, but her charm seemed to be so catching that the babbling brook that flowed by her door paused for a moment and secreted away that poetical name and shall now forever be known as Sweet Pizzlewig for its momentary folly" (Luddy).

Placentia [Orange]. Founded in 1910 and named after the school district, which had been named by Mrs. Sarah J. McFadden in 1884, probably after the town and bay in Newfoundland.

Placer, plăs'-ĕr. This western American term of Spanish origin designates alluvial or glacial deposits containing gold particles, which can be obtained by washing. In the "golden days" the word was frequently used for place names. **Placerita Creek** [Los Angeles]. The name of the intermittent tributary of Santa Clara River near Saugus is reminiscent of the discovery of gold by Francisco López six years before Marshall's find. For a few years after 1842 a placer on Rancho San Francisco was worked with moderate success. **Placerville** [El Dorado]. The site was first settled in 1848 by William Daylor of Sutter's Fort and became known as Dry Diggings. In 1850 the camp was named Placerville because the streets of the camp were almost impassable on account of the numerous placering holes. The town never bore the name Hangtown, as is often asserted by contemporary as well as modern writers. It was simply a nickname given to the place because of an incident which occurred on January 22, 1849, a Sunday, when two Frenchmen and one Chileno were hanged, as witnessed by E. Gould Buffum (p. 65). "The name of 'Hangtown' was originally given to the town, in consequence of the carrying into effect in a summary manner, some of Judge Lynch's sentences, and the citizens find it somewhat difficult to get rid of the objectionable soubriquet" (Sacramento *Union,* April 2, 1853). **Placer County.** The county was created April 25, 1851, from parts of Sutter and Yuba counties, and was so named because of many placers in its territory.

Plainsburg [Merced]. In 1869, after Farley's hotel was opened near the settlement known as Welch's Store, the place was named Plainsburg (Co. Hist., 1925, p. 363). It is actually a "burg in the plains." *See* Athlone.

Planada. plá-nä'-dá [Merced]. From a number of names submitted in a contest held in 1911 the Spanish word for 'plain' was chosen as a suitable name for the town, which is situated in a rich fertile plain (Frances Osterhaut). The former post-office name was Geneva; the former railroad name, Whitton.

Plano, plä'-nō [Tulare]. *Plano* is the Spanish word for 'level ground,' 'plain,' 'flat,' but is obsolete as a generic term. It was selected when the post office was established in 1871, probably by A. J. Adams, the first postmaster.

Plantation [Sonoma]. The post office was established about 1900 and was named after the old Plantation House, a roadhouse shown on the county map of 1879.

Plaskett: Creek, Rock [Monterey]. Probably named for William L. Plaskett, a native of Indiana, or one of his sons, who were farmers in near-by San Antonio in the 1870's.

Plaster City [Imperial]. The post office was established in August, 1936, and was so named because the Portland Cement Company (now United States Gypsum Company) had its main office there.

Platina, plăt'-ĭ-nà [Shasta]. The post office was established April 23, 1921, and was so named because it is in a platinum ore area (Steger). The term *platina* is a derivative of *plata* (silver), a metal which platinum resembles, and, according to Hanks, was originally applied to platinum in South America, where it was first found (*Report,* 1884, p. 309)

Playa. The generic name means beach, but has a number of meanings in different sections of Spanish America. In the name of the land grant Boca de la Playa [Orange], dated May 7, 1846, and in La Playa [San Diego] the term is obviously used for beach. Playa del Rey [Los Angeles], named in 1902 for the unsuccessful venture of Port Ballona, was advertised as meaning 'playground of the king' with a certain justification, for in parts of Argentine and Chile it means 'playground.' In the case of Rancho de la Playa, which belonged to the Mission Santa Barbara before the secularization, and the many other playas found on *diseños* in various places of the state the meaning is as in Tabasco, Mexico, dry lake or river bed.

Pleasant. A favorite American specific term used to describe places of beauty and tranquillity. California has about fifty features so named, including four communities [Contra Costa, El Dorado, Mariposa, Sutter]. More than half of the names refer to valleys. **Pleasant Valley** [El Dorado]. The valley was discovered and named by Henry W. Bigler, June 18, 1848. On July 3rd the Mormons from

Coloma and Mormon Island started their trek here to Salt Lake. It had a post office from March 23, 1864, till December 31, 1917. **Pleasant Grove** [Sutter]. The post office was established in the late 1860's, and the pleasant name was probably applied to offset the old ugly name Gouge Eye (Co. Hist., 1879, p. 98).

Pleasanton [Alameda]. The origin of the name is not in "pleasant town" as the present spelling would suggest. The town was named in 1867 for General Alfred Pleasonton by John W. Kottinger, a native of Austria and pioneer of 1851, who may have served with Pleasonton in the Mexican War. The name was misspelled probably through a clerical error when the post office was established on June 4, 1867. An attempt was made in later years to correct the error (Postal Guide, 1898), apparently without success, for within a few years the name appeared again as Pleasanton.

Pleasants Peak [Orange]. Adopted in 1933 by the Geographic Board at the suggestion of the Orange County Historical Society, for J. E. Pleasants, a forty-niner, whose name had been associated with the peak since 1860. J. E. Pleasants was a son of James M. Pleasants, for whom Pleasants Valley in Solano County was named. The original name of the peak was Sugarloaf.

Pleasants Valley [Solano]. The valley, between Vacaville and Winters, was named for James Marshall Pleasants, a native of Kentucky, and his son William James, who arrived here December 6, 1850, and settled as farmers. William James Pleasants later described his experiences in *Twice across the Plains* (San Francisco, 1906).

Pleasant Valley [Inyo]. Named for James ("Cage") Pleasant, a dairyman from Visalia, who was killed by the Indians here in 1862 (Chalfant, *Inyo,* p. 116).

Pleito: Hills, Creek [Monterey]. The place called *el Pleito* is mentioned as early as September, 1796 (Prov. Recs., VI, 172), and a rancho San Bartolome or Pleito is repeatedly mentioned in later years. It was made a land grant on July 18, 1845. Modern maps show a locality Pleyto on the territory of the grant. *Pleito* is a Spanish legal term, meaning 'litigation,' 'dispute,' and may have been applied because there was some dispute between the missions of San Miguel and San Antonio. concerning the property rights of Rancho de San Bartolomé. The name is found also in Kern County. Pleito: Hills, Creek, and a playful diminutive, Pleitito

Creek, are shown on the Mount Pinos atlas sheet.

Plumas. Feather River was known as *Rio de las Plumas* in Mexican times and appears with this name on American maps as late as 1852 (Gibbes). When **Plumas County** was formed from a portion of Butte County on March 18, 1854, the old name was revived. A flourishing town on the east bank of the Feather River, founded in 1850 and named Plumas City, has vanished. Two Western Pacific stations are called Plumas [Lassen] and Las Plumas [Butte]. A lake in Yuba County, exceedingly irregular in shape, is called Plumas Lake; the near-by Sacramento Northern station is named after the lake. **Plumas National Forest** was created and named by presidential proclamation in 1905. *See* Feather River.

Plum Valley [Sierra]. The valley is first mentioned in 1858 and was so named because of the great quantities of wild plums found there.

Pluton Creek [Sonoma]. The name, derived from the name of the god of the lower world in classical mythology, Pluto, may have been applied to the stream by Forrest Shepherd in February, 1851, when he saw the hot geysers rising from lower strata. Pluton Geysers, Pluton Valley, and Pluto's Cauldron are mentioned in an article by Shepherd in the *American Journal of Science and Arts,* November, 1851 (pp. 153 ff.). Only the north fork now bears the name; the main stream is called Sulphur Creek. There is a Mount Pluto in Placer County, and Pluto's Cave near Mount Shasta is mentioned by Brewer on November 11, 1863. The presence of plutonic rock may have some connection with these names.

Plymouth [Amador]. The site of an old gold-mining camp called Puckerville, or Pokerville. A post office was established there September 8, 1871, and was named after the Plymouth Mines, which had been in operation since the early 1850's. Historic Landmark 470.

Poblanos [Contra Costa]. *Arroyo de los Poblanos* is shown for Marsh Creek on the Plano topographico de la Mision de San Jose (about 1824) and part of it is still shown as Canada de los Poblanos on the Mount Diablo atlas sheet. The name is probably another version of the name of the Bolbones Indians at the foot of Mount Diablo.

Poe: Canyon, Reservoir [Plumas]. The canyon was named for Edgar Allen Poe by Mrs. Virgil Bogue in 1908. The lake and the powerhouse were built by the Pacific Gas and Electric Company in 1958, in anticipation of the construction of the Oroville Dam.

Pogolimi [Sonoma]. The name of the land grant Cañada (valley) de Pogolimi (or Pogolomi or Pogolome), dated February 12, 1844, is apparently derived from an Indian word of unknown origin and meaning.

Pohono. *See* Bridalveil Fall.

Point. Names of coastal features preceded by the generic Point will be found listed under the specific name.

Point Arena, *à-rē′-nà*: town, **Creek** [Mendocino]. The town developed around the store built in 1859 and was named after the near-by cape. The post office name was Punta Arenas in 1867, but the von Leicht–Craven map, 1874, has Point Arena. *See* Arena.

Point Loma. *See* Loma.

Point Reyes. *See* Reyes, Point.

Poison. The word is frequently found attached to names of physical features. Poison Rock in Mendocino County [Eden Valley atlas sheet] probably preserves the name of a meadow or creek no longer so known. Poison Meadows and Canyons are often properly so named because poisonous plants grow there which are known to have killed livestock, especially sheep. In relation to surface waters the term is loosely applied: the arsenic and other "poisons" are only Glauber's and Epsom salts, which, of course, may be fatal if drunk in excess by thirsty desert travelers. **Poison Lake** [Lassen]. "It was [so] called, from the innumerable quantity of animalculae and frogiponiana in its waters, which could only be rendered drinkable by filtration" (Delano, p. 36). **Poison Valley** [Alpine]. The meadows and streamside of Poison Valley were shunned, or herding there was watchfully done, by early cattlemen after some of their stock had died from eating water hemlock (*Cicuta*) and larkspur (*Delphinium*) (Maule).

Poker Flat [Sierra]. The site in the rich gold-producing Slate Creek region, still shown on the Downieville atlas sheet of 1907, is the only remnant of several Poker flats, bars, and "villes" named during the gold rush. The scene of Bret Harte's "The Outcasts of Poker Flat" is purely fictional and has nothing to do with the place.

Pokywaket Creek [Shasta]. The name of the tributary of McCloud River is derived from Wintu *po-kee,* 'raw,' and *waket,* 'creek.' Black acorns were brought here to be cured.

(Steger.)

Polaris [Nevada]. The Latin name of the North Star is one of the fanciful railroad names applied to stations of the Truckee-Verdi section in 1867.

Polita: Canyon, station [Inyo]. The Southern Pacific station was named after the canyon, which had been named after the Poleta Mine. A Mexican or Spaniard named Poleta located the mine in the early 1880's. (Robinson.)

Polka [Santa Clara]. The land grant was part of the original San Isidro grant (1808); it is dated June 19, 1833. In 1849 Daniel Murphy bought the rancho, and in his claim, filed February 17, 1852, he calls it La Polka, a name probably suggested by the new dance which was at the peak of its popularity in those years.

Pollard Gulch [Shasta]. Named for John Pollard, a miner who lived here for a short time in the early 1880's (Steger).

Pollock Bridge. *See* Loftus.

Pollock Pines [El Dorado]. The post office was established in 1935 and named for the grove of pines belonging to the Pollock family, the first settlers.

Polly Dome [Yosemite National Park]. Named by R. B. Marshall, for Mrs. Polly McCabe, daughter of Colonel W. W. Forsyth (Farquhar).

Polvadero: Gap, Creek [Fresno]. *Polvadera* means 'cloud of dust.' The name (with the wrong gender) was applied to the gap between Kettleman and Guijarral Hills, probably because of the frequent occurrence of dust storms.

Pomins [El Dorado]. The post office, now discontinued, was named after Pomins Lodge, owned by Frank and Marion Pomin (F. Slade). William Pomin, a pioneer, had built the Tahoe House in 1864.

Pomo [Mendocino]. A post office (now discontinued) was named in the 1870's, probably after the Indian village, *Pomo,* which stood at the site of the Potter Valley flour mill (Barrett, *Pomo,* p. 140). This is the only place which bears the name of the Pomo, a linguistic family in Mendocino, Lake, and Sonoma counties. *Pomo* simply means 'people' and was often used as a suffix of village names.

Pomona, pŏ-mŏ´-nà [Los Angeles]. The name was applied to a new settlement by the Los Angeles Immigration and Land Co-operative Association on August 20, 1875, as a result of a contest for a name, won by Solomon Gates, a nurseryman. The Roman goddess of orchards and gardens had already given her name to at least six other communities in the United States. Pomona College was originally in Pomona and was named after the city in 1887.

Pomponio Creek [San Mateo]; **Canada Pomponio** [Marin]. Both features were named for a renegade Christian Indian, notorious for his depredations between San Rafael and Santa Cruz, who was captured and executed in 1824. *Cuchilla de Pomponio* is shown on a *diseño* of the San Gregorio grant (1839).

Ponderosa Way [Sierra Nevada foothills]. A firebreak of some two hundred miles, most of which was completed in the 1930's. It was so named because it separates the higher country, where the ponderosa pines grow, from the highly inflammable and not very valuable lower country. (Stewart.)

Pondosa [Siskiyou]. The post office was established in 1926 and named Pondosa, the trade name of ponderosa pine, *Pinus ponderosa* (E. Fritz).

Ponto [San Diego]. The name, poetical Spanish for 'sea,' was applied to the Santa Fe station in 1919. The place had previously been known as La Costa.

Pony. Ponies, small but hardy horses, were greatly valued in pioneer days. The name became very popular as a place name when the famous (though short-lived) pony express was inaugurated in 1860. About fifteen geographic features bear the name.

Poonkiny Creek [Mendocino]. According to Kroeber's *Handbook* the name of the stream was the Yuki Indian word *punkini,* meaning 'wormwood.'

Poopout Hill [San Bernardino]. The name appears in the Decisions of the Geographic Board, Oct.-Dec., 1966. The name of this hill near San Gorgonio Mountain probably contains the American slang word for exhausted because the elevation is also known as Trail Head Hill.

Poorman Creek [Nevada, Butte]. According to the journal of John Steele written during his California mining adventure in 1850, "... both streams, we were told, [derive] their names from the same pioneer miner, Mr. Poorman" (Bidwell, *Echoes,* p. 163). San Luis Obispo County has a Poorman Canyon, Plumas County a Poorman Creek, and Mendocino County a Poor Mans Valley. The name was often used in gold-mining days, sometimes because the diggings were really poor, at other times to scare away new prospectors by pretending unprofitable results.

Pope: Valley, Creek [Napa]. Valley and creek

preserve the name of William (Julian) Pope, a member of Pattie's party in 1828 and grantee of the Locoallomi grant, September 30, 1841. The Indian name for Pope Creek was *Nombadjara* (D. T. Davis). The latter name is shown on a *diseño* of the Las Putas grant.

Poplar. Besides the town in Tulare County and the cluster name on the Middle Fork of Feather River [Plumas] only a few places in the State bear the name of the tree. There are three species native to the State, *Populus: Fremontii, trichocarpa,* and *tremuloides,* but the first two are commonly called cottonwood, and the last, aspen; hence the lack of Poplar place names. In the eastern states the Poplar names outnumber the Cottonwood names. *See* Alamo.

Porcupine. The name of the prickly animal was used repeatedly for geographical names. The best-known feature is Porcupine Flat in Yosemite Valley, mentioned in a letter of Hoffman to Whitney, September 8, 1867.

Portal. A name sometimes used in place of "gate." The best-known instances of its use are El Portal [Mariposa] and Portal Ridge [Los Angeles].

Port Animal Depot. [Los Angeles]. Established by the War Department on September 7, 1944, and so named because the post was a "staging area" for animals (mules, war dogs, carrier pigeons, etc.) to be shipped overseas during World War II. It is commonly called Puente Animal Depot because of its proximity to the town of Puente. (Marian Guntrup.)

Port Chicago. *See* Chicago.

Port Costa [Contra Costa]. The name was applied to the station of the Southern Pacific in 1878, obviously because it was in Contra Costa County and situated at the coast.

Porterville [Tulare]. In 1859, Royal Porter Putnam, who was known by his middle name, operated a stage depot known as Porter's Station, and later he had a store called Porter's Trading Post or Store. In 1864 he laid out the town and named it Portersville. The Official Railway Map of 1900 shows the present form.

Port Kenyon [Humboldt]. The name was applied by the Coast Survey to the shipping point on the land of J. G. Kenyon (Co. Hist., 1882, p. 158).

Portola. Gaspar de Portolá, leader of the expedition of 1769, is honored in the name of a post office in Plumas County (listed in 1910), a settlement and valley in San Mateo County, and in **Portola Redwoods State Park.** This last name was suggested by Aubrey Drury at a Park Commission meeting and was adopted on motion of Commissioner Leo Carrillo, a descendant of members of the Portolá expeditions. The current pronunciation of the name is pôr-tō'-lå. The name of the state park is often pronounced the Spanish way, the accent on the last syllable (Drury). *See* Glossary.

Portuguese Bend [Los Angeles]. The name was applied for Joseph Clark (Machado), a native of the Azores, who owned a fleet of whalers around 1860 (*CHSQ,* XXXV, 238). **Portuguese Flat** [Shasta], locally pronounced pôr'-tŭ-gē, was named for Portuguese settlers in the mining days. Hazel Creek post office in Shasta County was called Portuguee from 1870 to 1877.

Posa. *See* Poza.

Posey. *See* Poza.

Posita. The name is a Mexican localism for 'pond' or 'water hole,' a diminutive of *pozo* (well). **Las Positas,** pō-sē'-tăs: **Creek** [Alameda]. Padre Viader mentions *una posa de buena agua,* 'a pool of good water,' in the *Valle de San Jose* (Livermore Valley) in August, 1810 (Docs. Hist. Cal., IV, 74), and Joaquín Piña mentions a *Paraje nombrado de las Positas del Valle,* 'called a place of the little pools of the valley,' on May 26, 1829 (Piña, Expedicion). The name appears in the title of the land grant Las Positas or Las Pocitas del Valle de San Jose, granted April 10, 1839, to Livermore and Noriega. It is shown as *Los Positos* on Eld's sketch of 1841 and as *las Pocitas* on several *diseños.* The Land Office maps of the 1850's have Posita Creek; Hoffmann's map of 1873 has Las Positas Creek. On the Pleasanton atlas sheet of 1906 it appears as Arroyo las Positas. **Positas** [Santa Barbara]. The name appears in the *expediente* of the land grant La Calera y las Positas, dated May 8, 1843.

Poso. *See* Poza.

Posolmi y Posita de las Animas [Santa Clara]. The name of a land grant, dated February 15, 1844, which is also known as Rancho de Ynigo, from the name of the grantee, Lupe (or Lopez) Ynigo, an Indian. The name seems to be somewhat garbled: *posita de las ánimas* would mean 'little pool of the souls'; the word *posolmi* may include the root *poso,* pool.' *See* Animas.

Post Office: Cave, Bridge [Lava Beds National Monument]. The presence of many pigeonholes in the walls suggested the name to J. D. Howard. Ballarat [Death Valley] was formerly Post Office Springs.

Post Peak [Yosemite National Park]. Named

for William S. Post, of the Geological Survey, when the Mount Lyell quadrangle was surveyed in 1898–1899.

Potato. More than twenty-five geographic features, mainly hills, bear the name of this staple food. **Potato Canyon** [San Bernardino], now called Oak Glen, was so named because potatoes were once grown there, and **Potato Hill** [Tehama] because it has the shape of a potato. Some hills may resemble the shape of a "potato hill" rather than the potato itself; others may have been named because potatoes were planted on the slope. Santa Cruz Island has a Potato Harbor. Mineral Peak [Tulare] was known as Half Potato Hill in the 1880's; the Twin Peaks in San Francisco were once called *Las Papas,* 'the potatoes,' and appeared with this name on many early maps.

Potem Creek [Shasta]. This tributary of Pit River was named by the Indians for the first white settler, who befriended them (Steger).

Potholes. The term is used by geologists to describe regularly shaped holes in rocks, like those found in the canyon of the North Fork of Mokelumne River. It was once believed that they had been made by Indians, but most of them were formed by glacial action or by running water in stream beds: The Pothole and Pothole Creek [Tulare]; Pothole Valley and Pothole Spring [Modoc]. Sometimes the name is used for a natural or excavated but regular depression in the ground: Pothole Lake [Inyo] seems to be literally in a pothole. **Potholes** [Imperial]. The name was applied to the terminus of the spur built by the Southern Pacific from Yuma in 1907. According to Doyle, it is the site of an old mining town and was probably so named because the gold was found in "pots or pockets." There is no documentary evidence that gold was mined here in the eighteenth century, as often asserted, but small-scale gold washing was carried on here until the 1930's, mainly by Mexicans.

Potrero. The Spanish name for 'pasture' was one of the most common generic terms in California and appears in the names of more than twenty land grants or claims. It has survived in the name of one community in San Diego County, a district in San Francisco, and in the names of numerous physical features. It is commonly pronounced pō-trār'-ō. Although *potrero* has not entered the American language like corral and canyon it is still used, especially in southern California, as a true generic term: The Potrero, Big Potrero,

Round Potrero [San Diego]; Potrero Chico, Potrero Grande, Potrero de Felipe Lugo [Los Angeles]; Potrero Seco [Ventura]; Mill Potrero [Kern]; La Carpa Potreros, Montgomery Potrero, Pine Corral Potrero, Salisbury Potrero, etc. [Santa Barbara]. It is also found as a specific term combined with Creek, Hill, Peak, Point, and sometimes tautologically with Meadow.

Potter Point [Yosemite National Park]. The name was given in 1909 by R. B. Marshall for Dr. Charles Potter of Boston (Farquhar).

Potter Valley [Mendocino]. William Potter and his brother were the first white settlers in the Chico region. In 1853 they moved to the valley which bears their name. According to the County History of 1880 (p. 167), the Indian name was *Be-loh-kai,* 'leafy valley.'

Pottinger Canyon [Kern]. The canyon in Santa Maria Valley was probably named for Thomas B. Pottinger, a native of Maryland and a resident of Bakersfield in 1879. Near-by Mama Pottinger Canyon may have been named for his wife or for his mother.

Potwisha, pŏt-wĭsh'-à [Tulare]. The locality at the junction of the Marble and Middle forks of Kaweah River was named by the Geographic Board (*Sixth Report*) at the suggestion of George W. Stewart, for a branch of the Yokuts Indians who once camped there.

Poverty Hills [Inyo]. Since gold was mined in rather large quantities in the near-by Fish Springs Hills in the 1870's and none was found in these hills, it is quite likely that for this reason the latter then received their present name (Brierly). **Poverty Bar** [Trinity] was probably named for a similar reason, although it is said that Chinese reopened the diggings and made good wages. **Poverty Hill** [Sierra] near Scales has a rich gold mine; the name is ironic (S. G. Morley).

Poway, pou'-wā, pou'-wī: **Valley,** town [San Diego]. The name is derived from a rancho of Mission San Diego, mentioned in 1828 as *Paguay* (Registro, p. 37). *Cañada y Arroyo de Paguay* is shown on a *diseño* of Rancho San Bernardo (1841). The post office is listed in 1880. The Diegueño as well as the Luiseño call the place *Pawai* (Kroeber); the meaning of the name is, according to E. D. French (San Bernardino Co. Hist., 1883, p. 178), 'it is finished' or 'the end of the valley.'

Powder Mill Flat [Santa Cruz]. The name is derived from the California Powder Works, which were operated here between 1865 and 1916 (Hoover, p. 575).

Powell, Mount [Kings Canyon National Park].

Named in 1912 by R. B. Marshall in memory of John W. Powell (1834–1902), who was in charge of the expedition which navigated the Colorado through the Grand Canyon in 1869. Powell was director of the Geological Survey, 1881–1894, and director of the Bureau of Ethnology, Smithsonian Institution, 1879–1902. (Farquhar.)

Powellton [Butte]. The post office was established in the 1870's and named for R. P. Powell, who had acquired a ranch here before 1853. It exemplifies the use of the old English suffix '-ton' (town) in the formation of a California place name.

Poza, Pozo. In Spanish geographical nomenclature a distinction is made between *poza,* 'puddle,' and *pozo,* 'well.' In Spanish California, however, either word (also spelled *posa* and *poso*) was apparently used indiscriminately for 'water hole' in the widest sense. The various spellings were found in the names of several land grants and on many *diseños;* some of these names have survived. The word has even been actively used in place naming in American times. **Arroyo las Pozas** [Ventura]. A place called *las pozas o simi,* between San Buenaventura and San Fernando, is mentioned on January 28, 1819 (Arch. Arz. SF, Vol. III, Pt. 2, p. 52). The land grant Las Pozas, named after the place, is dated May 15, 1834. *Arroyo de las pozas* and *Cuchilla de las pozas* are shown on a *diseño* of Calleguas grant (1837). **Posa** [Santa Clara], the name of a land grant also designated as Posa de San Juan Bautista and Posa de Chaboya, dated March 10, 1839, and **Posa de los Ositos** [Monterey], the name of another grant, meaning 'water hole of the little bears,' and dated April 16, 1839, do not seem to have survived as place names. *See* Oso. **Pozo** [San Luis Obispo]. "G. W. Lingo, Esq., a well known citizen, had the honor of proposing the name of the post-office in the valley. *Pozo,* in Spanish, means a well or hole, whence the likeness of the valley itself to a place of this sort, and the Spanish word *Pozo* was adopted as the name of the post-office." (Co. Hist., 1883, p. 366.) In the same county is Poso Ortega, a little lake in the Temblor Range. A tributary of Nacimiento River [Monterey] is called Pozo Hondo Creek. In Spanish times the site of San Miguel mission was known as *Las Pozas* (SP Mis., II, 56 f.). **Poso: Creek, Camp, Flat; Mount Poso** [Kern, Tulare]; **Posey:** post office [Tulare]. This is apparently the stream called *Rio de Santiago* by Garcés on May 1, 1776 (Coues, *Trail,* p. 283). Wil-

liamson, in 1853, calls it O-co-ya or Pose Creek (Pac. R.R. *Reports,* Vol. V, Pt. 1, p. 14). The maps of the 1850's have both names or either name. In the Indian Report of 1854 and on Goddard's map (1860) it is spelled Posa. Brewer mentions Posé Flat and Little Posé Flat on June 7, 1863 (p. 394). The older Land Office maps have Poso Creek for the lower course and Posey Creek for the upper course. The post office is listed in 1915. This name, as well as Poso Slough [Merced] and others, may be derived from *poso,* 'sediment.' *See* Famoso.

Prado, prä′-dō: station, **Dam, Reservoir** [Riverside]. The Spanish name for 'meadow' was given to a station of the Santa Fe in 1907 and later was applied to the dam built by the Corps of Engineers. **El Prado** [Fresno]. The name was given to the station when the San Joaquin and Eastern Railroad was built from here to Huntington Lake.

Prairie. The word, so familiar throughout the American West, is rarely used in California names. In the northwestern section of the State, especially in Humboldt County, the term is used as a true generic for glade or clearing: Groves, Hancorn, Pitt Place, Bukers, Stevens, Boyes, and Elk prairies. Sometimes Prairie is found as the specific term of a name: Prairie Creek [Humboldt], Prairie Creek [Yuba], Prairie Fork of the San Gabriel River [Los Angeles]. Prairie Buttes [Sutter] was a former name of Sutter Buttes. Prairie City in Sacramento County is Historic Landmark 464. **Prairie Creek Redwoods State Park** [Humboldt, Del Norte]. The park was created in 1923 and its area was increased in the following years to cover 12,000 acres.

Prater, Mount [Inyo, Fresno]. Named in memory of Alfred Prater, who, with his wife, made probably the first ascent in 1928.

Prather [Fresno]. The post office, listed in 1915, was so named because it is on the Prather Brothers Lodge Ranch, which was established about 1912 by Joseph E. and Fred Prather.

Prattville [Plumas]. The settlement, known as Big Meadows, was named for the first postmaster, Dr. Willard Pratt, when the post office was established in the 1870's. The name of the post office is now Almanor.

Prenda [Riverside]. The optimistic name, a Spanish word meaning 'pledge,' 'security,' was given to the terminus when the Santa Fe spur was built into the newly developed citrus district in 1907 (Santa Fe).

Presidio. The Spanish word means 'garrison'

or 'fortified barracks.' In Spanish California there were four *presidios,* the names of which are still in use: Monterey Presidio was established in 1770; the San Diego mission guard was made a royal presidio on January 1, 1774; the one in San Francisco was founded in 1776; the one in Santa Barbara in 1782. The Sonoma garrison (1836) was really a *presidio,* but it was rarely so called. The Russian establishment, now Fort Ross, was sometimes called by the Spanish *Presidio Ruso* or *Presidio de Bodega.* (Bowman.) The current pronunciation is generally prĕ-sē'-dĭ-ō.

Price Creek [Humboldt]. Preserves the name of Isaac Price, a settler of 1852 (Co. Hist., 1915, p. 828).

Price Creek [Yosemite National Park]. Named for Lieutenant George Ehler Price, a veteran of the Spanish-American War (Farquhar).

Priest Grade [Tuolumne]. Named about 1870 for W. C. Priest, owner of Priest's Hotel near Big Oak Flat. The name is repeatedly mentioned in the Davidson correspondence.

Prieto, Prieta. The descriptive adjective, meaning 'dark,' 'blackish,' was repeatedly used in Spanish times and is preserved in the names of several mountains. The word is used in the name of the Prietos y Najalayegua grant [Santa Barbara], September 23, 1845. *Rancho de los Prietos* is mentioned in the Guerra Documents (VII, 147), and *Corral de los Prietos* is shown on a *diseño* of San Marcos.

Primer Cañon [Tehama]. The name, meaning 'first canyon,' was applied to the land grant on May 22, 1844. This grant is also known as Rio (or Arroyo) de los Berrendos.

Primero [Tulare]. The Spanish word for 'first' was applied to the station because it is the first station north of Orosi on the Santa Fe branch to Porterville, built in 1913–1914 (Santa Fe).

Prince Island [Del Norte]. The island was named by the Coast Survey about 1900, probably for Francis Prince, a native of New York who settled at Smith River before 1879.

Princeton [Colusa]. The post office, listed in 1858, was named at the suggestion of Dr. Almon Lull, a graduate of Princeton University (E. L. Hemstreet). There is another Princeton in San Mateo County.

Princeton [Mariposa]. *See* Mount Bullion.

Prisoners Harbor [Santa Cruz Island]. The name was put on the map by the Coast Survey, which published a hydrographic sketch of the harbor in 1852. The name may preserve the memory of an interesting historical incident. At one time the Mexican govern-

ment intended to make California a penal colony; eighty criminals, sent on the *Maria Ester,* arrived in Santa Barbara in March, 1830. When the Californians refused to receive them, many of the prisoners were provided with tools, cattle, fishhooks, and a little grain and were shipped to Santa Cruz Island. It is most likely that they were landed at this bay because plenty of wood and water could be obtained in its vicinity. When a fire destroyed their possessions the convicts built a raft and returned to the mainland, landing at Carpinteria. (Bancroft, III, 48.)

Proberta [Tehama]. The name was applied to the Southern Pacific station in 1889 for Edward Probert.

Project City [Shasta]. The town started and grew with the Central Valley Project; the name was adopted at a public meeting in the spring of 1939 (W. K. Gaslin).

Prospect Peak [Shasta]. Prospectors for gold have searched hereabouts without success (Steger).

Prospero [Los Angeles]. The land grant is dated May 16, 1843, and was so called because the grantee was Prospero Valenzuela, an Indian.

Prosser Creek [Nevada]. The name is shown on the von Leicht–Hoffmann Tahoe map of 1874. According to Williams' *The Pacific Tourist* (1876, p. 224), a man by that name operated a hotel there "in the early days." One Wm. Jones Prosser, a native of England and resident of Truckee, is listed in the Great Register of 1872, but he could not be identified with the place.

Providence Mountains [San Bernardino]. The name is shown on the maps after 1857 for the entire range of New York Mountains, Mid Hills, and Providence Mountains. It was probably applied by early travelers and immigrants because they found numerous springs on the range, which is situated between desert valleys. When the Geological Survey mapped the Ivanpah quadrangle in 1909–1910, it limited the name to the southern end of the range.

Providencia [Los Angeles]. The land grant is dated March 1, 1843; the name is an example of the rare use of an abstract noun (providence, i.e., divine providence) for a land grant. Providencia was an alternate name of another grant, Cañada de Herrera [Marin].

Pudding Creek [Mendocino]. The Coast Survey charts show Padding River in 1870 and Pudding River in 1871. According to a local story, sailors called Noyo River "Put In Creek" because its mouth provided the only safe anchorage (E. C. Cretser). This name may later have been transferred to the stream north of Fort Bragg and changed to the present form by folk etymology. *See* Noyo River. It is, of course, possible that the name simply arose because of the presence of conglomerate, or pudding stone. There is a Pudding Stone Reservoir in Los Angeles County.

Pueblo. In Spanish California *pueblo* was a common generic name corresponding to the American "town." The oldest civic community is *Pueblo de San Jose de Guadalupe*, founded in 1777, now the city of San Jose. The term *ciudad* (city) was occasionally used for Los Angeles, and *villa* (town) was used only once: *Villa de Branciforte,* modern Santa Cruz. (Bowman.) It is strange that the convenient and euphonious word Pueblo is found in California today only in the name of a siding of the San Diego and Arizona Eastern Railroad. *See* Dos Pueblos.

Puente, poo-ĕn'-tĭ: town, **Hills** [Los Angeles]. The name, meaning 'bridge,' obviously goes back to the Portolá expedition, which camped at San Jose Creek on July 30, 1769. "In order to cross the arroyo it was necessary to make a bridge of poles, because it was so miry" (Crespi). On the return journey the expedition camped in the same place, on January 17, 1770, and Portolá mentions the plain as *Llano de la Puente.* On November 22, 1819, a *rancho llamado La Puente,* 'ranch called The Bridge,' is mentioned, and on July 22, 1845, the name was used for the rancho granted to two well-known pioneers of the Los Angeles district, John Rowland and William Workman. (*WF,* VI, 269 f.) When the Los Angeles–Colton section of the Southern Pacific was built in 1875, the name was applied to the station. The post office was established September 15, 1884 as Puente. In 1955 the Geographic Board decided for La Puente. The name of the land grant Rincon de la Puente del Monte, in Monterey County, dated September 20, 1836, is a misspelling of Rincon de la Punta del Monte.

Puerto; Puerta. The generic term *puerto,* 'port,' was frequently used along the coast in Spanish times, but apparently it has not survived in this sense. It also means a 'mountain pass,' and Whipple, in 1849, mentions such a Puerto in San Diego County. **Puerto,** poo-ĕr'-tō: **Canyon, Creek** [Stanislaus]. Apparently the feminine form *puerta,* 'door,' 'gate,' was used also, since the creek appears as *Arroyo de la Puerta* on a *diseño* of Rancho del Puerto, granted January 10, 1844, as well as on a

diseño of the Pescadero grant (1843). Brewer mentions Cañada del Puerto and Puerto Canyon on June 10, 1862: "the canyon comes through by a very narrow 'door,' which gives the name to the valley behind."

Pulgas. Although Americans were as much molested by fleas (*pulgas*) as the Spaniards were, they seldom used the word for place names (*see* Flea Valley). In Spanish times, however, quite a number of places were named for the little insect, some of which have survived. **Pulgas,** pŏŏl'-găs: **Ridge, Creek** [San Mateo] were so named because they are on the Pulgas (or San Luis or Cochenitos) land grant, dated 1795 and again November 27, 1835. Beechey (1831, II, 44) mentions "a farm-house ... called Las Pulgas" in November, 1826: "a name which afforded much mirth to our travellers, in which they were heartily joined by the inmates of the dwelling, who were very well aware that the name had not been bestowed without cause." The soldiers of the Portolá expedition had given the name *Rancheria de las Pulgas* to a deserted village on Purisima Creek, about ten miles southwest of the Pulgas rancho, on October 27, 1769 (Crespi, Costansó). **Las Pulgas Canyon** [San Diego]. *Las Pulgas* was a *sitio* of Mission San Luis Rey in 1828 (PSP, Presidios, I, 98). **Pulga** [Butte]. The station, near Flea Valley, was named when the Western Pacific built the line in 1907. It is a renewal of the name of the old mining camp Pulga Bar, which later was apparently called Big Bar.

Punta. In Spanish times the word *punta* was found frequently in names of less prominent headlands on the coast. The word corresponds exactly to the English word 'point'; hence the Spanish term has survived in only a few places. There is a Punta del Castillo in Santa Barbara County, a Mesa de la Punta in Riverside County, a station, Punta, in Ventura County, and a Punta Arena on Santa Cruz Island. The generic term also appears in the names of eight land grants. **Punta Gorda,** pŏŏn'-tá gôr'-dá [Humboldt]. Bruno de Hezeta, when he was in Trinidad Bay, June, 1775, gave this Spanish name, meaning 'massive point,' to a broad point to the south. It is not certain whether the name was applied to Table Bluff or to False Cape. On his large map Hezeta places it in the latitude of the former, on his small map in the latitude of the latter (Wagner, p. 458). Later cartographers identify the name with the promontory which is now called False Cape. In 1854 the Coast Survey, trying to save the name Cape Fortunas for False Cape, moved the name Point Gorda southward to the cape which some maps show as Cabo Vizcaino (Wagner, p. 523). In 1870 the Coast Survey restored the Spanish name, Punta Gorda. **Punta de los Muertos** [San Diego Harbor]. The name was applied in Spanish times to the point just south of the present Municipal Pier and appears on maps since 1782. It was named 'point of the dead' because a squadron had anchored at that place and buried a number of sailors carried off by an epidemic. After the American occupation the morbid name disappeared because "New Town" developed at exactly this place and its promoters expected it to be very much alive. The old Spanish name was recalled when an explosion on the U.S.S. *Bennington,* anchoring off this point, caused the death of sixty-five sailors on July 21, 1905. Historic Landmark 57. **Rincon de la Punta del Monte** [Monterey] is the name of a land grant, dated September 20, 1836. The word Punta (point) is given as Puente (bridge) on the Land Office maps.

Purificacion. The word, referring to the Purification of the Virgin Mary, is found in the name of a land grant, Lomas [hills] de la Purificacion [Santa Barbara], dated December 27, 1844. The word is shown on a *diseño* of the grant, apparently designating a valley.

Purisima, pŭ-rĭs′-ĭ-má: **Point, Hills, Canyon** [Santa Barbara]. These geographic features were named after Mission La Purisima Concepcion (Immaculate Conception of the Virgin Mary), founded by Lasuén on December 8, 1787. The mission is Historic Landmark 350. *See* Conception. **Purisima: Creek,** town [San Mateo] are so named because they are on the Cañada Verde y Arroyo de la Purisima (green valley and Purisima creek) land grant, dated March 25, 1838, and June 10, 1839. A post office, spelled Purissama, is listed from 1880 to 1898. The name of the land grant *La Purisima Concepcion* [Santa Clara], dated June 30, 1840, does not seem to have survived in a geographical name.

Pushawalla Canyon [Imperial]. The canyon with the beautiful stand of Washington palms in the Indio Hills is described in the *Desert Magazine* of December, 1945. The name, like Chuckawalla, is obviously of Indian or Aztec origin, but its meaning is not known.

Putah Creek [Lake, Napa, Solano]. The stream preserves the name of a branch of the Patwin Indians who once dwelt on its banks. Its similarity to Spanish *puta,* 'harlot,' is purely accidental. In the records of Mission San Francisco Solano (Sonoma Mission) of 1824, the natives are mentioned with various spellings from *Putto* to *Puttato.* In the baptismal records of Mission Dolores an *adulto de Putü* is mentioned in 1817, and the wife of Pedro Putay, in 1821 (Arch. Mis., I, 94, 81). In 1842 the stream was well known by its name: "I know that the Rio was called 'Putos' . . . it is well known by the name which has been given it" (J. J. Warner, Land Grant Case 232 ND). The name was probably fixed by William Wolfskill, who named his grant, dated May 24, 1842, Rio de los Putos. In 1843 the name was used in the titles of three other land grants, in one of which the spelling Putas occurs. In the *Statutes* of the early 1850's, in the Indian reports, and in the Pacific Railroad *Reports* the spelling of the name is in complete confusion. The present version was applied to a town in 1853, was used in the *Statutes* of 1854, was made popular by the Bancroft maps, and finally was adopted by the Geological Survey. The Whitney Survey and some other maps have the spelling Puta. It was probably this version which gave rise to the persistent tale that in central California there is a stream called 'whore creek.' Even the fact that *Putto* and *Putos* were older than *Puta* has not dismayed some "scholars." (See Preface.) In certain parts of Spanish America, they argue, the word *puto* is used for a masculine prostitute, and there are place names of that origin. But until some evidence of this sort is produced for Putah Creek, we shall have to assume that its name is derived from the name of the Indian village of *Puta-to,* mentioned by Kroeber (*Handbook,* p. 356) and that the name contains the Patwin root *pu,* 'east.'

Putnam Peak [Solano]. The peak was probably named for Ansel W. Putnam, who had settled as a farmer at Vacaville before 1867.

Pyramid. Some twenty-five features in California—mostly peaks, rocks, and hills—are called Pyramid because of their shape. Among these are two high peaks in Sequoia National Park and in Inyo County, and Pyramid Head on San Clemente Island. For the application of the name Pyramid Point to Point Lobos, *see* Point Lobos [Monterey] in the entry Lobo.

Pywiack Cascade [Yosemite National Park]. The name was recorded by John Muir in 1873 and was made official by decision of the

Geographic Board (No. 30). *Py-we-ah* or *Py-we-ack* was the Indian name for Tenaya Creek and Lake.

Quail. Coveys of this distinctive bird are a familiar sight in many sections of California, and it is not surprising that some twenty-five geographic features are named for it. One of the three species, the valley quail, is our state bird. *See* Codornices.

Quarry. A quarry on a hill or mountain slope often leads to naming the whole feature after it. Most features named after quarries are hills, but there is a high mountain, Quarry Peak, in Yosemite National Park.

Quartz. The mineral has always been of great importance in California because gold is often imbedded in it. The maps show a number of Quartz Mountains, Hills, and Rocks; also several Canyons and Creeks; and a Quartzite Peak [Inyo]. Two settlements called Quartz are in Butte and Tuolumne counties, and there is a ghost town, Quartzburg, in Mariposa County.

Quatal Canyon [Ventura, Santa Barbara]. The name possibly was derived from the presence of the Mexican plant *cuate, Eysenhardtia polystachya. Quate* and *cuate* were interchangeable, and the suffix *-al* is a common locative. The Mexican *cuate,* 'twin,' is another possible derivation. *See* Cuate.

Quati. *See* Cuate.

Quemado. The word for 'burnt' was used for several place names in Spanish times. The only survivor seems to be **Arroyo Quemado** [Santa Barbara], mentioned as early as December, 1794, and shown on the *diseño* of Rancho Refugio, 1838.

Quentin. *See* San Quentin.

Quesesosi [Yolo]. The land grant, sometimes written Guesesosi, and also known as Jesus Maria, is dated January 27, 1843. A *diseño* bears the legend: TERRENO QUE SE SOLI [on the left side], CITA EN [across the top], and CANTIDAD DE OCHO SITIOS [at the bottom], which, put together, means "Land which he asks for of the amount of eight *sitios.*" It has been suggested that the three words *que se soli* may have been mistaken for the name of the *terreno* and that the name Quesesosi was finally evolved through this mistake (*WF,* VI, 82). The *diseño* on which this legend was noted, to be sure, was made two years after the name Quesesosi had been used on another *diseño* (*WF,* VII, 171 ff.). Earlier maps, no longer available, may, however, have had this same notation. It is therefore not impossible that the name Quesesosi, or Guesesosi,

may have originated in this way.

Quicksilver. The places in Los Angeles and Sonoma counties are the only survivors of a number of names which arose when the discovery of small amounts of quicksilver raised hopes of finding large deposits of the valuable metal. *See* Almaden.

Quien Sabe Creek [San Benito]. The Spanish phrase 'Who knows?' is found in the name of a land grant, Santa Ana y Quien Sabe, dated April 8, 1839. It had been used previously (April 15, 1836) for a grant which was not confirmed. The maps of the Santa Ana y Quien Sabe grant show *Cañada de Quien Sabe* and *Sierra de Quien Sabe* for a part of Diablo Range. The name is recorded as *arroyo llamado Quien sabe* by Sebastian Rodriguez on April 21, 1828. The name was applied either in jest or because of some incident.

Quijarral. *See* Guijarral.

Quinado Canyon [Monterey]. The name is a Spanish rendering of a Costanoan word, meaning 'evil-smelling,' and refers to the sulphur springs (Paul Parker, *CFQ,* I, 295). On a *diseño* of the San Bernabe grant the designation *Quenas* appears where the road goes through the mountains; on another map of the grant *Guinado* is shown in the same place. Most maps designated the canyon as Kent Canyon until the Geographic Board restored the Indian name in 1935.

Quincy [Plumas]. The place grew around the hotel which H. J. Bradley built on his American Ranch in the early 1850's. When it became the seat of the newly formed Plumas County in 1854, it was called Quincy, after Bradley's native town in Illinois.

Quinliven Gulch [Mendocino]. The gulch near Anchor Bay was named for the Quinliven family, who settled early in the area (Geographic Board, May-Aug., 1962).

Quinn: Horse Camp, Peak [Sequoia National Park]. Named for Harry Quinn, a native of Ireland, who came to California in 1868 and became a sheep raiser in Tulare County (Farquhar).

Quintin. *See* San Quentin.

Quinto Creek [Stanislaus]. *Quinto,* the Spanish word for 'fifth,' may have referred to a share of land, or it may have been applied here to indicate that this creek was the fifth one from some point on the road. It is spelled Kinto on the Land Office map of 1879.

Quito [Santa Clara]. When the Southern Pacific was built from San Jose to Los Gatos in 1878, the siding was named Quito because it was on the land grant of this name, dated March 12, 1841. *Quito* is the Spanish word for 'quits.' The name, however, may have been the result of an error; the grant was also called Tito, for an Indian who occupied a part of the former Mission Santa Clara.

Rabbit. The various species of rabbits, easily hunted and trapped, were an important source of meat for miners and settlers. Probably more than fifty creeks and canyons, as well as a number of flats, islands, and at least one peak [San Diego], are named for the little animal. The mining camp at the site of modern La Porte [Plumas] had been named Rabbit Creek for the presence of the "snowshoe" rabbits, but the settlers became indignant when the Post Office Department tried to bestow the name Rabbit Town upon them. Rabbit Creek Hotel Monument is Historic Landmark 213. *See* Conejo.

Raccoon: Strait, Shoal [San Francisco Bay]. The channel between Angel Island and Marin County was named for the British warship *Raccoon,* which anchored in San Francisco Bay in 1814 to make repairs (PSP, XIX, 368). Raccoon Strait is shown on Tyson's map of 1850 and on the charts of the Coast Survey after 1858.

Racetrack [Death Valley National Monument]. "The Racetrack in Death Valley is a circular dry lake in the northwest corner of the Monument immediately adjacent to Ubehebe Peak. It is so named because it is almost a true circle in shape and has two rock formations protruding, which by stretch of imagination could appear to be a judges' stand and a grand stand." (T. R. Goodwin.)

Rackerby [Yuba]. The place was known as Hansonville for James H. Hanson, who had settled here in 1851. In 1884, William M. Rackerby, a pioneer of 1849, came to Hansonville as a merchant and rancher; when the Hansonville post office was discontinued in 1892, a new post office was established with Rackerby as postmaster, and it was named for him.

Radec [Riverside]. The post office (now discontinued) was established about 1885 and given the name Cedar spelled backward. *See* Sniktaw.

Rademacher, rä'-dĕ-mä-kĕr: station, **Mountains** [Kern]. The Southern Pacific station, on the branch line built in 1909 from Mojave to Owens Lake, was probably named for Alexander Rademacher, a native of Germany and resident at Greenwich in 1879.

Radio Hill [Plumas]. This sharp hill just outside of Quincy used to have no name, except that it was occasionally called Cemetery Hill because of the cemetery there. After the Forest Service established its key radio station for the region on top of this hill about 1945, it became generally known as Radio Hill. (Stewart.)

Rae Lake [Kings Canyon National Park]. The lake was named by R. B. Marshall in 1906 for Rachel ("Rae") Colby, wife of William E. Colby, the well-known conservationist and mountaineer (Farquhar).

Rafferty: Creek, Peak [Yosemite National Park]. Named in 1895 by Lieutenant Nathaniel F. McClure, for his companion, Captain Ogden Rafferty (1860–1922), an army surgeon (Farquhar).

Rag, Ragged. These have been used as specific terms in place names, either to describe physical features, mainly peaks, points, canyons, or to indicate the dilapidated condition of a camp or its settlers. Kaweah was once commonly called Ragtown because most of the inhabitants lived in makeshift tent-houses. **Raggedyass Gulch** [Siskiyou]. The tributary of Beaver Creek became so known because the miners in this gulch looked more dilapidated than the ordinary miners of the period. It is shown as Raggedass Creek on the map of Klamath National Forest. (Schrader.) Hungry Creek, another tributary of Beaver Creek, seems to confirm the story of hardship.

Railroad Flat [Calaveras]. The camp was settled in 1849, and later so named because a short track conveyed the lorries with gold ore and waste to and from the diggings. The place had a post office in 1857 and 1858, which was reëstablished March 17, 1869 and continues to the present time. Historic Landmark 286. **Railroad Canyon** [Riverside]. So named because the Santa Fe Railroad passed through it. After the railroad bed was washed out one winter, the line was re-routed via Corona, but the name remained and is now applied to the reservoir (Wheelock).

Raimundo, Cañada de [San Mateo]. The name of a land grant dated August 4, 1840, also spelled Raymundo. One Raimundo, a native of Baja California, is mentioned on June 20, 1797, as having been sent out after Indians who had run away from Mission San Jose (PSP, XV, 16). On a plat of Pulgas rancho (1856) Laguna Grande or Lake Raymundo seems to be the one now called Crystal Springs Lake.

Rainbow Lake [Shasta]. The artificial lake formed from Moon Creek was so named because it is stocked with rainbow trout (Steger).

Rainbow Mountain [San Bernardino]. The mountain west of Ivanpah Range was so named because the stratified volcanic rock resembles the rainbow (Gill).

Raines Valley [Fresno]. The valley east of Centerville was named for James Raines, a settler of 1863, who, according to Doyle, later served a term in a penitentiary and was finally lynched.

Raisin [Fresno]. The post office was established about 1906 and named for the chief product of the district.

Raker Peak [Lassen National Park]. Named for John E. Raker, a congressman from 1910 to 1926, who introduced the bill to create Lassen Volcanic National Park.

Ralston Peak [El Dorado]. The name for the peak above Echo Lake appears on atlas sheet 56-D of the Wheeler Survey, which mapped the region in 1876. It was probably given (not necessarily by the Wheeler Survey) in memory of William C. Ralston, whose spectacular career had ended with his tragic death on August 27, 1875. *See* Modesto.

Rambaud Peak [Kings Canyon National Park]. Named for Pete Rambaud, a Basque sheepman, who brought the first sheep into the region of the Middle Fork of Kings River from the Inyo side, through Bishop Pass, in 1877 (Farquhar).

Ramona [San Diego]. The name was given to this community, as well as to several others, soon after 1884, when Helen Hunt Jackson's sentimental romance *Ramona* was at the height of its popularity. The post office is listed in 1892. Two railroad stations are called Ramona [Sacramento] and Ramona Park [Los Angeles]. Riverside County has Ramona Hot Springs. *See* Alessandro; Romoland.

Ramshaw Meadows [Tulare]. Named for Peter Ramshaw, a stockman in this region from 1861 to 1880 (Farquhar).

Rana. The Spanish word for 'frog' was sometimes used in place naming. Cienega [marsh] de las Ranas was the original name of the San Joaquin grant [Orange], dated April 8, 1837; a tributary of Tularcitos Creek [Monterey] is still called Rana Creek; and there is a Santa Fe station Rana in San Bernardino County.

Rancheria, răn-chĕ-rē'-à. The Spanish word, originally designating 'a collection of ranchos or rude dwellings' (Bentley), has taken the meaning of 'hamlet' or 'village' in Amer-

ican Spanish. It was invariably used in Spanish California for Indian villages. Although the word has not entered our language as a generic term, it was frequently used in early American times outside of the old Spanish domain; it gradually disappeared from common speech as the old villages themselves gradually vanished. As a specific term it is preserved in more than thirty geographic features, mainly creeks on the banks of which there was once a rancheria. The best known is the cluster Rancheria: Creek, Falls, Mountain, Trail, in Yosemite National Park.

Ranch House [San Diego]. The Santa Fe station was originally called Margarita because it was on the Rancho Santa Margarita y las Flores. Before 1900 the name was changed to Ranch House because it was near the adobe house of the Picos, onetime owners of the rancho (Santa Fe).

Rancho. In American Spanish the word *rancho* was applied originally to a hut or a number of huts in which herdsmen or farm laborers lived. In Spanish times the word was often used in this sense in reference to the farms of the missions, pueblos, and presidios. A presidio rancho was called *rancho del rey*, and later, in Mexican times, *rancho nacional*. In Mexico the word acquired the meaning of 'a small farm'; at the fringe of the Spanish empire, in the present southwestern states of the United States, the term evolved as the designation for a grazing range. When the private land grants were separated from the public domain the word rancho became synonymous with 'landed estate'—called *hacienda* in other Spanish American countries. It was really used as a generic geographical term. The western American term 'ranch' is an abbreviation of 'rancho.' **Rancho Mirage** [Riverside] received an official name when the post office was established February 1, 1961. The name of a post office in San Diego County, Ranchita, is a diminutive of *rancho*. The name Ranchial Creek, given to a tributary of Estrella Creek [San Luis Obispo], is probably used in the sense of 'pertaining to a ranch.'

Rancho Santa Fe [San Diego]. In 1906 the Santa Fe purchased the San Dieguito Ranch for experimental planting of eucalyptus trees and gave it the present name. In 1927 the railroad sold the ranch to promoters, who subdivided it but kept the old name.

Randsburg; Rand Mountains [Kern]. The name was applied as a good omen to the town and the district in 1895, after Witwatersrand in the Transvaal, commonly called "The Rand," which is a rocky ridge that has been known since 1886 as one of the richest gold-mining districts in the world.

Rankin Peak [Los Angeles]. Named for the late Edward P. Rankin, a resident of Monrovia, who was actively interested in the mountains of the area (Geographic Board, September, 1949).

Ransom Point [Contra Costa]. Named for Leander Ransom, who, as a deputy U.S. surveyor, established the Mount Diablo base and meridian lines in 1851.

Rattlesnake. Nearly two hundred features on the maps of the State are named for the venomous serpent, and many more are so named locally. The name is usually connected with a creek or a canyon, but there are also Rattlesnake Ridges, Mountains, Buttes, Meadows, Gulches, Valleys, and Points; a Rattlesnake Bridge joins El Dorado and Placer counties. In early mining days the name was also used for communities: Rattlesnake Flat is shown on Gibbes' map of 1852, south of the South Fork of Tuolumne River, and Rattlesnake Bar, on the North Fork of American River, is mentioned in the *Statutes* of 1854 (p. 222). **Rattlesnake Creek** [Humboldt] is said to have been named because a winding road near the creek was first called Snake Road, then Rattlesnake Road.

Ravendale [Lassen]. The post office is listed in 1910. Unlike other combinations with the word "raven" (*see* Ravenswood), the California Ravendale seems to be the only one in the United States.

Ravenna [Los Angeles]. This typical railroad name was applied to the station when the last section of the valley route was built in 1876. There were at that time a number of Ravennas in the East, all probably named after the Italian city.

Ravenswood: Point, Slough [San Mateo]. The names preserve the name of the town of Ravenswood, which had been laid out in the 1850's when the Central Pacific was expected to cross lower San Francisco Bay, and which was probably named after one of the several Ravenswoods in the East. When the railroad bridge was finally built in 1920, the town had disappeared, but it left its name in a railroad siding, still listed by Rand McNally.

Rawhide [Tuolumne]. The place west of Jamestown seems to be the only survivor of the once popular name for California gold mines. The rich mining town of the nineteenth century, formerly called Rawhide

Ranch, is still shown on the Sonora 1939 atlas sheet.

Raymond [Madera]. The name was applied to the terminal of the Southern Pacific spur from Berenda, about 1885, for Walter Raymond of the Raymond-Whitcomb Yosemite Tours, which started at this point (F. E. Knowles).

Raymond, Mount [Yosemite National Park]. Named by the Whitney Survey in 1863, for Israel W. Raymond (1811–1887), one of the chief proponents in the campaign to set aside Yosemite Valley for public enjoyment and for many years a member of the state commission which managed Yosemite Valley before it became a national park (Farquhar).

Raymond Peak [Alpine]. Named in 1865 by the Whitney Survey for Rossiter W. Raymond, a graduate of the famous mining school of Freiberg, Germany, for many years U.S. Commissioner of mining statistics in the Treasury Department. Reed's map of the county, 1865, shows a Raymond City north of the peak.

Reading Peak [Lassen National Park]. The peak, formerly known as White Mountain, was named in memory of Pierson B. Reading by the Geographic Board, October 19, 1943. Next to Bidwell and Marshall, Reading was the best known of Sutter's men, and the real pioneer of Shasta County. He was grantee of Rancho Buenaventura in 1844, participated in the Bear Flag Revolt, and discovered gold in the Trinity region in July, 1848. Reading Peak, Reading Adobe (Historic Landmark 10), Readings Bar (Historic Landmark 32), and Fort Reading (Historic Landmark 379) commemorate the great pioneer; Readings Springs and Diggings have vanished. *See* Redding; Shasta.

Real de las Aguilas. *See* Las Aguilas.

Recess Peak [Fresno]. Named because of its proximity to the First Recess of Mono Creek, which had been discovered with the other three Recesses by Theodore S. Solomons in 1894 (Farquhar).

Reche: Canyon, Mountain, Wells [San Bernardino]. The places were named for Charles L. Reche, an early homesteader who dug the first well in the area (Geographic Board, 1960). It is said that Reche killed himself when his daughter ran away with one of his sheepherders.

Reconnaissance Peak [Plumas]. The peak was so named because of the timber reconnaissance work done there in 1914–1915 (D. N. Rogers).

Rector Canyon [Napa]. Named for a man who settled here before 1847 (Doyle), possibly John Potter Rector, whose name is recorded in the Great Register of Napa County, 1867–1868.

Red. Next to black, red is the most common adjective of color used in place names. The maps of the State have more than 150 names which include this adjective, and many more are used locally. Usually the word is found to describe hills, peaks, cliffs, and points. Most of the Red Lakes and Creeks (unless they contain the nickname of a person) are doubtless named after red orographic features or because the soil looks red, but there are some notable exceptions: Red River of California, as the Colorado River was sometimes called, was so named because its water appears "reddish." Often the adjective does not describe the feature but another preceding specific or generic term: Redrock Mountain, etc. [Los Angeles and elsewhere]; Red Bridge Slough [San Joaquin]; Red Fox Canyon [Los Angeles]; Red Rover Canyon [Los Angeles]; Red Reef Canyon [Ventura]; Red Pass Lake [San Bernardino]; Red Clover Creek [Plumas]; Redbird Creek [El Dorado], and many others. **Red Rock** [San Francisco Bay]. The conspicuous landmark was known in Spanish times as *Moleta* (misspelled Molate by Beechey in 1826) for its conical shape. It was also known as Golden Rock because pirates were supposed to have buried vast treasures there. It was possibly the island mentioned by Padre Payeras in 1819 (Docs. Hist. Cal., IV, 341 ff.): *otra mucho mas chica* [isla] *cerca Sn. Rafael llamada del oro* (another much smaller island near San Rafael called golden). The name Golden Rock is the official name (*Statutes*, 1850, p. 60), but as early as 1848 the present name was in use (Ord's map). The Coast Survey kept the name Molate Rock until 1897. **Red Bank Creek** [Tehama] is shown as *Baranca Colorada* on Bidwell's map of 1844, a name also applied to the land grant Barranca Colorada (red ravine), dated December 24, 1844. In the 1850's the creek was sometimes called Red Bluff Creek (*Statutes*, 1851; Gibbes' map, 1852). **Red Cap: Bar, Creek** [Humboldt]. ". . . we came to Red-Cap's bar; . . . so called from a sub-chief living there . . . 'Red-Cap' was so called from a greasy-looking woollen headpiece, with which some miner had presented him, and which ordinarily constituted his sole dress" (Gibbs, 1851: Schoolcraft, Vol. III, pp. 148 f.). **Red Lassic: Peak, Creek**

[Trinity]. The color refers to the peak, not to Lassik, last chief of an Athabascan tribe, and is used here to distinguish it from Lassik and Black Lassik peaks. (*See* Lassic.) **Red Lake Peak** [Alpine]. The peak was formerly called Red Mountain, and the small, marshy, half-dry lake at its foot was named Red Lake, after the mountain (Surveyor General, *Report*, 1856, p. 105). The name of the mountain was apparently lost, but it stuck to the lake, which was made into a reservoir. When it became necessary to have a name for the mountain, it was named after the lake: Red Lake Peak! According to George Stewart, however, the lake was originally Reed Lake. *See* Reed. There is another Red Lake and a Red Lake Mountain in Shasta County. **Red Slate Mountain** [Mono]. Named by the Whitney Survey and recorded on Hoffmann's map of 1873. **Red and White Mountain** [Fresno]. Named by Theodore S. Solomons in 1894. When Lincoln Hutchinson and his party made the first ascent, July 18, 1902, they kept the name because "it is peculiarly descriptive of the great peak of red slate fantastically streaked with seams of white granite" (*SCB*, IV, 201). **Red Hill** [Orange]. The old landmark, so called because of its cinnabar coloring, is Historic Landmark 203. **Red Box Divide** [Los Angeles] marks the boundary between the watersheds of Arroyo Seco and San Gabriel River and was given this name because a large red box used by forest rangers for storing fire-fighting equipment was visible from the road (AGS: *Los Angeles*, p. 298). Many communities have been named after near-by physical features. **Red Bluff** [Tehama]. Early in May, 1850, Bruff (pp. 789, 794) refers to the plans of Sashel Woods and Charles L. Wilson to lay out the town at Red Bluffs or "the Bluffs"; in the same year, the town Red Bluffs is mentioned in the *Statutes* (p. 62). According to Bancroft (VI, 496), the name is said to have been Leodocia at first. In 1853 it was known as Covertsburg (S.F. *Alta California*, Jan. 15, 1853). Eddy's map of 1854 shows the town as Red Bluffs. **Redlands** [San Bernardino]. The district formerly known as Lugonia was developed after the California Southern built a line to connect with the Santa Fe in 1885. *See* Lugo. The present name, descriptive of the soil, was given to the town, which was platted in 1887 by E. G. Judson and Frank E. Brown. **Redbanks** [Tulare]. The Santa Fe named the station in 1914 after the Redbanks Orchard Company, which had been so named because the soil in the district was red. **Red Mountain** [San Bernardino]. The post office was named in 1929 after the near-by reddish-colored mountain. *See* Osdick.

Red Bluff. *See* Red.

Redding [Shasta]. A town was laid out south of the present city and was first called Latona, and later Reading, in honor of Pierson B. Reading (*see* Reading Peak). "While upon this matter we have to record an objection to the name 'Latona.' It is not a proper name for a town or anything else that we know of. As well as we can remember, Latona was the name of one of the high old goddesses of Grecian mythology, who conducted herself in a very improper manner. We would take the liberty of suggesting the name of 'Reading' as by far the more appropriate." (Shasta *Courier*, Nov. 2, 1861; Boggs, p. 397.) After the Central Pacific had acquired the right of way, the present town was laid out in 1872 by B. B. Redding, land agent of the company, former secretary of state of California and future State fish commissioner, and was named for him. The local people, however, wished to keep the pioneer name, and in January, 1874, the legislature enacted solemnly: "That the name of the Town of Redding, Shasta County, shall hereafter be known and spelled Reading, in honor of the late Major Pearson [!] B. Reading, the pioneer of Shasta County" (Boggs, p. 595). This did not end the confusion, for the railroad refused to recognize the change. In the end the friends of the living railroad official were more influential than those of the dead pioneer, and in April, 1880, the legislature changed the name back to Redding (*ibid.*, p. 666). Mr. Redding showed his appreciation by donating a fine 245-pound bell to the Presbyterian church of Redding (Sacramento *Record Union*, March 9, 1881).

Redding Canyon [Inyo]. Named for John Redding, an old miner who lived in the canyon in 1879 (Robinson).

Redding Rock [Humboldt]. The name was given to the rock by the Coast Survey in 1849 or 1850 (*Report*, 1862, p. 341). Since the name of the pioneer, Pierson B. Reading, was pronounced rĕd'-ing and often so spelled, it is not impossible that it may have been named for him.

Red Dog [Nevada]. The once famous mining town was named in the early 1850's by Charlie Wilson after his former home, Red Dog Hill, Illinois (H. P. Davis), which in turn may have been named for the popular card game, or in allusion to "Red Dog" banks and bank notes, a well-known term current about 1850, synonymous with "wildcat." Red Dog is mentioned in Brewer's Notes of November, 1861. It had a post office from 1855 to 1869. The former name was Chalk Bluff.

Redinger Lake [Fresno]. Named in 1955 for Daniel H. Redinger, for many years resident engineer of the Big Creek hydroelectric project of the Southern California Edison Company.

Redlands. *See* Red.

Redondo, rĕ-dŏn'-dō: **Beach** [Los Angeles]. The city was founded in 1881 and incorporated in 1892 (Santa Fe). Although the city is on the territory of Rancho San Pedro, the name was doubtless derived from adjacent Rancho Sausal Redondo (round willow grove). The post office was established July 15, 1889. The adjective *redondo* was often used in the names of bays, lakes, and valleys. The part of San Francisco Bay now called San Pablo Bay was originally known as *Bahia Redonda* (Crespi, 1772; Cañizares, 1776, 1781).

Red Rock. *See* Red.

Reds Meadow. *See* Satcher Lake.

Redwood. The popular name for the *Sequoia sempervirens* is included in the names of more than fifty places in the regions of its habitat along the coast. In some places the name-giving redwoods have long since disappeared. As early as 1769 the distinctiveness of the tree and its abundance were noticed by Crespi, who already used the term *palo colorado* (pp. 211, 232 f.). Redwood Creek and Canyon [Contra Costa] are among the places which were known in Spanish times as *los palos colorados*. The name redwood, or Sierra redwood, is frequently applied to the *Sequoia gigantea:* on the Tehipite atlas sheet [Tulare, Fresno], Redwood: Meadow, Creek, Canyon, Mountain are shown. **Redwood City** [San Mateo]. The place received its name not so much because of the beautiful stands of redwoods once surrounding the site as because of their commercial exploitation on a large scale. In the early 1850's it was known as Mezesville, for S. M. Mezes, but it is shown as Redwood City on Goddard's map of 1860. **Redwood Empire.** The popular name for the area traversed by the Redwood Highway from Marin to Del Norte counties was first used by Aubrey Drury, in 1915. *See* Palo; Sequoia. **Redwood Creek** [Humboldt]. The stream became well known in 1963 when Paul A. Zahl of the National Geographic Society discovered here the tallest redwoods ever measured.

Redwood Memorial Groves. Through the efforts of the Save-the-Redwoods League many groves have been established in state parks and in other redwood reserves. Some of these memorialize organizations, such as the California Federation of Women's Clubs (1931), Garden Clubs of America (1931), and Native Daughters of the Golden West (1930) in the Humboldt Redwoods State Park; California Garden Clubs (1949), California Real Estate Association (1953), National Council of State Garden Clubs (1949), and Rotary Clubs (1952) in the Prairie Creek Redwoods State Park; Daughters of the American Revolution (1949) in the Jedediah Smith Redwoods State Park. Many other groves memorialize individuals, some of which are listed separately in this book.

Reed. Names of hydrographic features distinguished by the growth of reeds are rarely found in California, the Mexican Spanish word *tule,* from Aztec *tullin,* being used almost exclusively. The former Reed Lake near Carson Pass in Alpine County, apparently the only sheet of water named originally because of the broad margin of reeds, has become Red Lake (Stewart). *See* Red Lake Peak.

Reed [Marin]. When the Northwestern Pacific was built in the 1870's, the station was named for John Reed (or Read, or Reid), owner of the Corte Madera Rancho, on which the station is situated.

Reedley [Fresno]. Named for Thomas L. Reed, a veteran of Sherman's march to the sea, who in 1888 gave half of his holdings to the city. Since Reed objected to the use of his name for the city, the directors of the Pacific Improvement Company added the suffix.

Reflection Lake. There are several lakes so named, the best known of which is the one in Lassen National Park, reflecting Lassen Peak. Reflection Lake [Kings Canyon National Park], one of the most beautiful lakes in the High Sierra, was named by Howard Longley and his party in 1894 (Farquhar).

Refugio. The Spanish word for 'refuge' was repeatedly used as a place name and appears in the names of land grants in Santa Barbara, Santa Clara, and Santa Cruz counties. Refugio Creek and Refugio Valley [Contra Costa], east of Pinole, are shown on the chart of the Coast Survey. **Canada del Refugio** [Santa Barbara]. The name preserves the name of the land grant Nuestra Señora del

Refugio, granted provisionally in November, 1794, and definitively in July, 1834. The name is also preserved in Refugio Pass.

Regulation Peak [Yosemite National Park]. In 1895, when Lieutenant Harry C. Benson, accompanied by a trumpeter named McBride, was placing copies of the park regulations on trees in the park, McBride suggested the name Regulation Peak for a peak between Smedberg Lake and Rodgers Lake, and Benson put it on his map of 1897. On the 1901 edition of the Mount Lyell atlas sheet the name was put on the wrong peak; to the true Regulation Peak, thus left vacant, the name of Volunteer Peak was assigned, and it still goes by that name. (Farquhar.)

Reiff [Lake]. Named for John Reiff, on whose ranch a post office was established May 18, 1881.

Reinhardt Redwoods [Contra Costa]. Named in 1941 by the East Bay Regional Park Board, in honor of Aurelia Henry Reinhardt, for many years president of Mills College (R. E. Walpole).

Reinstein, Mount [Kings Canyon National Park]. Named by R. B. Marshall for Jacob B. Reinstein, a charter member of the Sierra Club and from 1897 until his death in 1911 a regent of the University of California (Farquhar).

Reister: Knoll, Canyon, Rock [Mendocino National Forest]. The knoll was named for George Reister, an old settler. The other names are not used locally.

Relief: Valley, Creek, Peak, Reservoir, Camp [Tuolumne]. The valley was named in the early 1850's when an immigrant train, having abandoned its wagons, found shelter here, sent a party ahead, and got help (Rensch-Hoover, p. 502). The broad valley marked Relief Valley on the Dardanelles atlas sheet is not the original Relief Valley. This was the narrow valley five miles north, mentioned in *Hutchings' Illustrated California Magazine* in May, 1858 (II, 494). On Hoffmann's map of 1873 the present Relief Valley is called Green Flat. The Wheeler Survey is responsible for the naming of the creek and the peak, and for the transfer of the name from the former to the present Relief Valley (atlas sheet 56-B).—The name has been applied to several other geographic features. There is a small settlement, Relief, in Nevada County, east of North Bloomfield, doubtless named after Relief Hill. According to an item in *CHSQ,* X, 351, this hill was so named because James F. Reed here came to the relief of nineteen members of the Donner Party in 1847.

Reliz. The Spanish-Mexican term *reliz*, 'landslide,' was repeatedly used in place naming and has survived in at least two places. **Reliez,** rĕ-lēs': **Valley** [Contra Costa]. This is the locally accepted spelling for the valley west of Walnut Creek; the name is spelled Raliez on the Concord atlas sheet of the Corps of Engineers and Reesley on that of the Geological Survey. **Reliz Creek** [Monterey] has become Release Creek by popular etymology, but the original spelling has been restored on the Junipero Serra atlas sheet.

Represa, rĕ-prĕs'-ȧ [Sacramento]. The post office for Folsom prison was established about 1895. It is not certain whether the Spanish name, which means 'dam' and also 'restriction,' was chosen because of its sound, or because there was a dam near by in the American River, or because someone thought it was appropriate for a prison post office.

Requa [Del Norte]. "Each village has its chief; the clan and village are of the same name ... *Rech-wa* is the name of the village and clan on the N. side of the mouth of the Tlamath river" (Bruff [writing in 1851], p. 955). According to Waterman (*Yurok*, p. 231), the name was *Re'kwoi* and means 'creek mouth.'

Rescue [El Dorado]. Among the names submitted by townspeople about 1895, the Post Office Department chose the one suggested by Andrew Hare, who owned a mine called Rescue (State Library).

Reseda, rĕ-sē'-dȧ [Los Angeles]. The name Reseda (the botanical name for mignonette) was originally applied to a station on the Southern Pacific branch line which was built from Burbank to Chatsworth about 1895. After 1920 the name was transferred to the station of the Pacific Electric previously known as Marion.

Reservation Point [Los Angeles]. So named in 1915 when the Treasury Department acquired the site east of the entrance to the inner harbor of San Pedro and established a quarantine station there.

Resting Spring [Inyo]. On April 29, 1844, Frémont had named the place Hernandez' Spring in commemoration of a Mexican traveler murdered here by Indians. In the 'fifties the spring was given the present name because Mormon immigrants bound for San Bernardino stopped there to rest and recuperate.

Return Creek [Yosemite National Park]. The name appears on Wheeler atlas sheet 56-D.

Its application was doubtless prompted by some incident, as were a number of other names given by the Wheeler Survey.

Reversed: Creek, Peak [Mono]. "The ancient drainage has been reversed by the deposition of morainal debris; we have therefore called the stream draining June and Gull lakes, Reversed Creek" (Geological Survey, *Report*, 1887, p. 343). The peak is not at all reversed, but takes its name from the creek.

Rey. The term *del Rey*, found in geographical nomenclature in Spanish times, designated a place belonging to the king, i.e., national or public property. After Mexico became independent the term was officially changed to *de la Nacion* or *nacional*; the old term survived, however, and is even today often used by realtors in naming new subdivisions.

Reyes, rāz, **Point** [Marin]. The cape is probably the one discovered by Cabrillo, November 14, 1542, and named *Cabo de Pinos*. The Vizcaíno expedition passed the point on January 6, 1603, the day of the "three holy kings." They named the present Drakes Bay, where they found shelter, *Puerto de los Reyes*, a name which did not stick. The point was probably named at the same time and appears quite regularly as *Punta de los Reyes* on the maps of the following centuries. On March 17, 1836, and again on January 4, 1842, the name was given to land grants. Hood's map (1838) misspells the name a Point Keys [!]. The present hybrid form is shown on Wilkes' map of 1841. The Spanish version is shown as late as 1860 (Goddard), but the Coast Survey and most maps have used the modern form since 1855. **Point Reyes.** The name Point Reyes Station was applied to the former Olema station of the Wells Fargo Company, April 1, 1883. The post office, Point Reyes, is listed in 1887; when a new post office was established on the headland and named Point Reyes, the old station south of Tomales Bay was renamed Point Reyes Station. Both post offices have been listed since 1892.

Reyes Peak [Ventura]. The peak may have been named for Jacinto D. Reyes, a resident at Cuyama in 1892.

Reynolds Peak [Alpine]. Named in memory of G. Elmer Reynolds, for many years editor of the Stockton *Record* and long active in forest conservation. (Geographic Board, October, 1929.)

Rheem [Contra Costa]. Donald L. Rheem, owner of the property on the east slope of Mulholland Hill, started the development in the fall of 1944 and called it Rheem Center.

Rialto [San Bernardino]. The colony was founded and named in 1887 by a group of Methodists from Halstead, Kansas. Rialto was originally a contraction of Rivus Altus, the deep or grand canal of Venice; it gradually became synonymous with place of business, and this accounts for its popularity as a place name in various parts of the world. Bolinas Bay and Bolinas Lagoon are shown as Rialto Cove on Ringgold's General Chart of 1850.

Ribbon: Fall, Fall Creek [Yosemite National Park]. The Indian name was something like *Lungyotuckoya,* interpreted correctly by Whitney as 'Pigeon Creek' (*Yosemite Book,* 1869, p. 16); *lunguti* is the name of the band-tailed pigeon in Central Miwok dialect (Gifford). The Whitney Survey maps record the high but trickling fall as Virgin Tears Creek and Virgin Tears Fall. According to Clarence King, p. 136, James M. Hutchings is responsible for this sentimental name: "We [camped] at the head-waters of a small brook, named by emotional Mr. Hutchings, I believe, the Virgin's Tears, because from time to time from under the brow of a cliff just south of El Capitan there may be seen a feeble waterfall. I suspect this sentimental pleasantry is intended to bear some relation to the Bridal Veil Fall opposite." However, it was apparently not Mr. Hutchings who was responsible for the Virgin Tears but some sentimental woman; Hutchings gave the falls the more commonplace name, Ribbon Fall, which is first recorded on Wheeler's Yosemite atlas sheet, 1870.

Ricardo [Kern]. So named for the innkeeper, an Indian, when this was a stop on the old stage route from Bishop to Los Angeles.

Rice: station, Air Base [San Bernardino]. The station of the Parker branch of the Santa Fe was named before 1919, for Guy R. Rice, chief engineer of the California Southern Railroad (Santa Fe).

Rich. Combinations with this adjective were very popular in mining days and have retained their popularity, although they are applied no longer to gold deposits but to fertile soil. **Rich Bar** [Plumas]. This place on the North Fork of Feather River is the only survivor of several mining camps so named. The gold deposits which three Germans found in August, 1850, at the time of the Gold Lake excitement, turned out to be one of the most spectacular discoveries of the gold rush. Bruff records the news under date of August 18: "Brittle, from Myer's diggings,

gives us a rich account of the mining there . . . He says that the spot where Lassen and comrades prospected, and found only a *trace* of gold, was yielding not less than 50 dolls. worth pr day to each miner, and some had taken out 60 lbs. of gold in a day. That 3 men there had made in three days an average of $2,000 each, and then sold out for several thousand dollars more, each, and left for home. They have named this place 'Rich Bar.' " (II, p. 1066.) **Richvale** [Butte]. The subdivision was developed and named in 1909 by Samuel J. Nunn. When the post office was established in 1912 the original name, Richland, had to be changed because there already was a post office by that name in the State. **Richgrove** [Tulare]. Developed and named in 1909 by S. R. Shoup and W. H. Wise of the Richgrove Development Company. The post office is listed in 1912.

Richardson Bay [San Francisco Bay]. The name commemorates one of the foremost pioneers of San Francisco. William A. Richardson, a native of England, arrived in San Francisco in 1822, put up the first house, a tentlike structure, in San Francisco in 1835, and in the same year was made captain of the port of San Francisco. In 1838 he was grantee of Rancho Sausalito, adjoining the bay which bears his name. Ringgold's maps of 1850 show Richardson's Bay, and the Coast Survey had a station called Richardson in the early 1850's. The Spanish name of the bay had been *Ensenada de la Carmelita,* named by Cañizares on August 6, 1775, "because in it was a rock resembling a friar of that order" (Eldredge, *Portolá,* p. 56). It is shown as *Ensenada del Carmelita* on Ayala's 1775 map. Another name was Puerto de los Balleneros, which was translated later into Whaler's Harbor. *See* Ballena.

Richardson Grove [Humboldt]. Created in 1922 and named for Friend W. Richardson, publisher of the Berkeley *Gazette* for many years, governor of California 1923–1927.

Richardson Peak [Yosemite National Park]. Named in 1879 by Lieutenant M. M. Macomb of the Wheeler Survey, for his companion, Thomas Richardson, an early sheepman (Farquhar).

Richardson Springs [Butte]. The springs became known by this name because they were on the property of the four Richardson brothers, cattle and sheep raisers. The first hotel was built by J. V. Richardson in 1889. (Co. Hist., 1918, pp. 1098 f.)

Richgrove. *See* Rich.

Richmond, Point; Richmond [Contra Costa]. The point was named Point Stevens by the U.S. Coast Survey in 1851. In 1852 the name was changed to Richmond Point, probably after one of the many Richmonds in various sections of the United States. The geological map of the Williamson *Reports* of 1853 places the name on the point now called Shoal Point. In 1897 the Santa Fe secured the site just north of the point for its terminal and called it Point Richmond; the settlement which developed there was called Santa Fe. The town that was laid out on the Barrett ranch by A. S. Macdonald and his associates was named Richmond. The post office, established at "old town" in August, 1900, had also been called Richmond. The city was incorporated August 7, 1905.

Richter Creek [Inyo]. The name should probably be Rittgers Creek, for Israel P. and John A. Rittgers, who settled in the district in the 1860's.

Richvale. *See* Rich.

Riggs [San Bernardino]. The station on the Tonopah & Tidewater Railroad was named for the owner of a silver mine (Myrick).

Rincon, Rinconada, rĭng'-kŏn, ring-kŏ-nä'-dȧ. In modern Spanish geographical nomenclature *rincón* simply designates a small portion of land, while *rinconada* is an inside corner formed by hills, woods, roads, or slopes. In California both terms were apparently used interchangeably, frequently for the "inside corner" of a projection extending into the sea, into the plains, into the neighboring property, and sometimes for just a corner or piece of land. Rincon is found in the names of more than twenty land grants and has survived in the names of a number of hills, points, and valleys. Rinconada appears in three land-grant names. The word "rincon" is still current in the southwestern United States for 'nook,' 'secluded place,' and 'a bend in the river' (Bentley), but it does not seem to have been used actively in place naming in California after the American conquest. In 1857 it was proposed for a newly formed county in the northwest "corner" of the State, but was rejected in favor of Del Norte. In the Kettleman Hills, where many names are Spanish (on the map), we find without surprise El Rincon, south of Avenal Gap. **Rincon: Point, Creek, Mountain** [Ventura, Santa Barbara]. Crespi called the Indian village near this point *Santa Clara de Monte Falco,* but Portolá's soldiers called it *El Bailarin* because one of the chiefs was "a great dancer"

(Crespi, p. 162). The Anza expedition on February 24, 1776, disregarded these names: Anza mentions *Rancherias del Rincon,* and Font (*Compl. Diary*), *La Rinconada*. The land grant El Rincon (or Matilija) is dated January 8, 1834, and June 22, 1835. Rincon Point is recorded on the Land Office map of 1862. **Rincon Point** [San Francisco]. The elevation at the San Francisco terminus of the Bay Bridge was a true "rincon" until a part of the water front was filled in. The hill was a prominent landmark often mentioned in early reports; it was used by the Coast Survey as a secondary triangulation point as early as 1850.

Ringgold Creek [El Dorado]. The tributary to Weber Creek is a remembrance of the once prosperous town of Ringgold, the first settlement on the road from Carson Pass in the early gold-rush days. It might have been named for Cadwalader Ringgold of the Wilkes Expedition, who explored the region in 1841. The name of the creek is spelled Ringold on the Placerville atlas sheet. *See* Ringgold in Glossary.

Rio, rē'-ō. The Spanish word for 'river' (*río*) was naturally a common generic term and is found in the names of at least seven land grants, which are listed under their specific names. It is still found in a few names as a true generic term: Rio Hondo [Los Angeles], Rio Bravo [Kern]. More frequently it is found in names of post offices and communities, sometimes without regard to meaning or Spanish usage. **Rio Vista** [Solano]. The town was founded in 1857 by Colonel N. H. Davis and called Brazos del Rio because it was near the three arms of the Sacramento. In 1860 the name was changed to Rio Vista. When the town was wiped out by a flood on January 9, 1862, it was rebuilt at the present site, and at first called New Rio Vista. **Rio Dell** [Humboldt]. The place was first called Eagle Prairie. When the post office was established about 1890, the name River Dell was proposed as an appropriate name, but was rejected because of its similarity to Riverdale, in Fresno County. The Spanish word for 'river' was then substituted, and the name was accepted. **Rio Bravo** [Kern]. The name was given to the station when the Southern Pacific built the line from Bakersfield to the asphaltum beds in the early 1890's. It preserves the old name of Kern River, which was called Rio Bravo because it was difficult to cross. This is confirmed by the fact that Edward Kern, for whom the river was then named by Frémont, almost drowned in 1845, while swimming it. Rio Bravo had a post office from 1912 to 1919. **Rio Oso** [Sutter]. The station of the Sacramento Northern was named about 1907 because of its location on Bear River. *See* Oso. **Rio Linda** [Sacramento]. The town was founded and named in 1913 by a member of the firm of Sears Roebuck & Company. Rio Lindo means 'pretty river.' **Rionido** [Sonoma]. The resort was developed about 1910 and was apparently so named because this combination of Spanish words has a pleasing sound. The post office is listed in 1912. *See* El Rio; Nido; Dos Rios; River.

Ripgut Creek [Shasta]. This tributary of Pit River was so named by William Bowersok, a cattleman, because his clothes were torn to shreds on the haw shrub which abounds here (Steger).

Ripley [Riverside]. The terminus of the Ripley branch of the Santa Fe was named in 1921 for E. P. Ripley, former president of the railroad.

Ripon, rĭp'-ŏn [San Joaquin]. In 1876, the first postmaster of the town, Applias Crooks, chose the name of his former home in Wisconsin to replace the earlier name, Stanislaus City.

Rising River [Shasta]. The tributary of Hat Creek was so named because it has no distinct source but apparently rises out of a marshy meadow (Steger). Hat Creek is perhaps the only creek which has the distinction of having a "river" as a tributary.

Ritter, Mount; Ritter Range [Madera]. Named by the Whitney Survey in 1864, in memory of Karl Ritter (1779–1859), progenitor of scientific geography. Ritter was one of the luminaries of the University of Berlin when Whitney was a student there in the 1840's.

River. The term is often used in the names of settlements at or near a river. California has sixteen or more communities with names in which River is combined with -bank, -bend, -dale, -glen, -side, -view, etc. A town in El Dorado is simply called River. **Riverside: city, County, Mountains.** A settlement was started on the Rancho Jurupa in 1869 by Louis Prevost, who had learned silk culture in France and intended to develop a silk-producing colony. After Prevost's death, John W. North of the Southern California Colony Association acquired the property and retained the name Jurupa. In September, 1870, the company started building the upper canal of the Santa Ana River, and when the canal reached the settlement in June, 1871, the name was changed to Riverside (Co. Hist., 1883, p. 131). Riverside post office is listed June 12, 1871. It is, however, possible that both Jurupa and Riverside existed side by side: the von Leicht–Craven (1874) map shows both places on two different channels of the Santa Ana about three miles apart. The county was created by act of the legislature of March 11, 1893, and named after the city. **Riverdale** [Fresno]. The place was originally known as Liberty Settlement. When the post office was established in 1875 the new name was chosen because of its proximity to Kings River. **Riverton** [El Dorado]. The place was long known as Moore's Station because it was on the toll road between Sacramento and Virginia City, built and operated by John M. Moore, a former member of the San Francisco Vigilance Committee (J. W. Winkley in "The Knave," Sept. 22, 1946). When a post office was established, about 1895, another name had to be chosen in order to avoid confusion with Moore's Station [Butte]. The location at the bank of the South Fork of American River suggested the new name. **Riverbank** [Stanislaus]. In 1911 the Santa Fe Railroad established a new terminal and division point south of Burneyville and named it Riverbank for its location on the Stanislaus River. The older settlement, now on the edge of Riverbank, had been named for Major James Burney, an early settler and the first sheriff of Mariposa County.

Rivera, rĭ-vĕr'-à [Los Angeles]. The district was named Maizeland in 1866 because the chief crop was corn. In 1886, when the Santa Fe reached the town, the name was changed to Rivera, a name considered appropriate because the place is between two rivers: Rio Hondo and San Gabriel River. (Ada Moss.)

Rixford, Mount [Kings Canyon National Park]. Named in 1899 by Vernon L. Kellogg and a party from Stanford University, for Emmet Rixford, professor of surgery at Stanford University, who had previously climbed the peak (Farquhar).

Roach Creek [Humboldt]. The stream may have been named for M. Roach, a dairyman at Alliance in the 1890's.

Roads End [Tulare]. The post office was named Roads End because it was at the end of the road from Kernville. Now the road goes on but the old name remains.

Roaring River. Of the several "roaring rivers" in the State, the best known are in Shasta

County and in Kings Canyon National Park. Why the lazy tidal channel in Suisun Bay should ever have been called Roaring River (Hoffmann, 1873) and in modern times Roaring River Slough is no longer determinable.

Robbers. The word is found in about ten place names, probably all applied to places where robbers had their hideout or where a robbery had been committed. **Robbers Roost** [Los Angeles]. The rocks on the high ridge between Soledad and Mint canyons were once the hiding place of Tiburcio Vasquez, a famous bandit of the early 1870's (Doyle). *See* Vasquez. **Robbers Roost** [Monterey] was likewise named because Vasquez and his band robbed a stage here (Co. Hist., 1881, p. 152). **Robbers Ravine** [Sacramento]. So named because notorious highwaymen of stagecoach days had their meeting place here. **Robbers Creek** [Lassen, Plumas]. The stream was named after James Doyle had been robbed here by armed men in 1865 or 1866 (Lassen Co. Hist., 1916, p. 406).

Robbins [Sutter]. Named in 1925 by the Sutter Basin Company for its president, George B. Robbins. The former name had been Maddox, for a manager of the same company. (W. J. Duffy.)

Robbs Peak [El Dorado]. Named for Hamilton D. Robb, an early-day stockman (W. T. Russell in "The Knave," July 23, 1944); Forest Service records, however, say that it was for a Lieutenant Robb, who, while leading a detachment of cavalry on an exploration trip, climbed the mountain and left a tin cylinder on it (E. F. Smith).

Robert [Alameda]. The Southern Pacific station was doubtless named after Robert's Landing when the line from Alameda Point to Newark was built in 1876–1878. Captain William Robert (or Roberts), a native of England, was one of the earliest settlers of Eden township and had hay and grain warehouses at the landing in the 1870's and 1880's.

Roberts Canyon [Los Angeles]. Named for H. C. Roberts, settler of 1856 (Forest Service).

Robertson Creek [Mendocino]. The stream was named for William E. Robertson, who was in charge of the Indian agency in Ukiah in the 1870's (Asbill).

Robertsville [Santa Clara]. Named for J. G. Roberts, owner of a ranch in the district (Wyatt and Arbuckle).

Robinson: Creek, Peak [Mono]. In the 1860's Moses Robinson operated a sawmill on the creek which bears his name.

Robinson: Point, Reef [Mendocino]. The names were applied by the Coast Survey, doubtless for Cyrus D. Robinson, a native of Pennsylvania who came to California in 1849 and settled at Gualala in 1858, where he engaged in hotelkeeping, shipping, and farming.

Robinson's Ferry [Calaveras]. Historical Landmark 276, registered October 7, 1937, commemorates the ferry and trading post established by John W. Robinson and Stephen Mead on the Stanislaus River in 1848.

Roble, Roblar. The Spanish words for 'deciduous oak' and for the 'place where deciduous oaks grow' were used for place naming less often than *encina,* the word for 'live oak.' They are found in the names of two land grants, Paso de Robles [San Luis Obispo], May 12, 1844, and Roblar de la Miseria [Sonoma], November 25, 1845. The Rincon de San Francisco grant [Santa Clara] was known as the Robles Rancho, not because *robles* were present but because the grantees were Teodoro and Secundino Robles. In modern times the name is found in Los Angeles, Monterey, San Luis Obispo, Santa Barbara, Sonoma, and Tehama counties. The two railroad stations called Robla [Sacramento, Tulare] are probably derived from the same word. *See* Paso Robles; Encina; Oak.

Rock, Rocky. Besides the wide use of Rock as a generic term there are in California more than two hundred names for natural features in which the noun or the adjective is used as a specific term. The oldest is doubtless Rocky Point, for the point at the north entrance of Trinidad Bay, given by Vancouver in 1792. There is a Rockpile in Sonoma County and a Rockpile Peak and Creek in Mendocino County (Ornbaum atlas sheet). Rock, or Rocky, in some form or combination, appears in the names of about ten inhabited places; a few of these may be for a person. **Rocklin** [Placer]. The name was applied to the station when the Central Pacific built the line from Sacramento to Newcastle in 1863–1864. The extensive quarries doubtless suggested the name; *lin* is the common Celtic generic term for 'spring' or 'pool' as well as for 'ravine' or 'precipice.' **Rockport: post office, Bay, Creek** [Mendocino]. A chute and a wharf were erected on the rocky coast in 1876; in 1880 Rockport is given as an alternate for Cotineva (Co. Hist., 1880, p. 471). Rockport post office is listed in 1892. **Rock Creek** [Shasta]. The tributary of Pit River was named for the

"Rock Indians," who buried their dead in an upright position among the rocks (Steger). **Rock Island: Lake, Pass; Rock Canyon** [Yosemite National Park]. "I named the stream Rock Creek, and the lake Rock Island Lake, from a large granite island that was visible near the northern end" (N. F. McClure, *SCB*, I, 178).

Rockaway Beach [San Mateo]. Doubtless named after Rockaway, Long Island, a name which was derived from the Delaware *regawihaki*, 'sandy land' (Leland, *CFQ*, IV, 405). The post office is listed in 1910. Folk etymology derives the name from the large quarry where they take "rock away."

Rockefeller Forest [Humboldt]. The large area of redwood trees in the Humboldt Redwoods State Park was donated by John D. Rockefeller, Jr. (1874-1960), philanthropist, who gave $478,000,000 to charities during his lifetime.

Rockwood [Imperial]. Named for Charles R. Rockwood, engineer of the California Development Company and the Imperial Irrigation District, who had been actively engaged in promoting the irrigation of the Colorado Desert since 1892.

Rodeo, rō-dā'-ō, rō'-dĕ-ō. The word was used originally for an enclosure at a fair or market where cattle were exhibited for sale. In Mexico, it developed as a designation for the periodical rounding up of cattle for counting and marketing. It appears in the names of three land grants in Los Angeles, San Francisco and San Mateo, and Santa Cruz counties. Since "rodeo" has become the common American term for a cowboy contest, some of the Rodeo Canyons, Creeks, Lagoons, etc., may have been applied in American times. **Rodeo: Creek, town** [Contra Costa]. A place, Rodeo, is shown on a *diseño* of the Pinole grant near the center of the rancho. Rodeo Valley appears on a plat of the rancho in 1860, and Rodeo Creek on another in 1865. The post office is listed in 1898.

Rodgers: Peak, Lake [Yosemite National Park]. The peak was named in 1895 by Lieutenant N. F. McClure, for Captain Alexander Rodgers, acting superintendent of Yosemite National Park at that time. Independently, Lieutenant H. C. Benson in the same year christened Rodgers Lake and gave the same name to the peak south of it. To avoid the duplication, the Geological Survey substituted for the latter the name Regulation Peak, which had previously been intended for another peak. On LeConte's map of 1896

Rodgers Peak is called Mount Kellogg, a name probably given by John Muir for the botanist, Albert Kellogg. (Farquhar.)

Roeding Park [Fresno]. The name commemorates Frederick Roeding, a native of Hamburg, Germany, who came to California in 1849 and settled in Fresno County in 1868. He was one of the leaders of the "German Syndicate," which in 1868 subdivided an area of 80,000 acres, on which the modern city of Fresno was developed. The first of his famous nurseries was established in 1883.

Rogers Peak. *See* Manly.

Rohnert Park [Sonoma]. The town was developed by Paul Golis and incorporated August, 1962. It was named after the Waldo Rohnert Seed Farm.

Rohnerville [Humboldt]. Named for Henry Rohner, a native of Switzerland who, with a man named Feigenbaum, opened a store here in 1859. The post office is listed in the 1870's.

Rolph [Humboldt]. Named for James ("Sunny Jim") Rolph, mayor of San Francisco 1911–1930, governor of California 1931–1934 (Laura Prescott). The **Governor James Rolph Grove** in the Humboldt Redwoods State Park was dedicated in his memory in 1934.

Romero Creek [Merced]. Named for José Romero, who led an exploring party to the creek and, according to F. F. Latta (p. 18), was killed by the Indians on this trip.

Romoland [Riverside]. About 1925 the promoters chose the name Ramola for the new development in the Ramona country. When the Post Office Department requested another name, to avoid confusion with Ramona, the present name was substituted. *See* Ethanac.

Romualdo. *See* Cerro.

Roops Fort [Lassen]. Historic Landmark 76, in Susanville, also known as Old Fort. The blockhouse was built in 1854 by Isaac N. Roop, and there the settlers of Honey Lake Valley met in 1856 to form the "Territory of Nataqua." It earned the title "fort" when it served as fortified headquarters during the "Sagebrush War" in 1863. The settlers of Honey Lake Valley with Roop as provisional governor were for some time in authority.

Root Creek [Shasta]. Named for Orin T. Root, who diverted the waters of a spring near Castle Dome to form the stream. Root settled at Castle Rock Spring in 1864 and kept an inn there for fifteen years. (Steger.)

Rosamond: town, Dry Lake [Kern]. The station was named about 1888 for the daughter of an official of the Southern Pacific.

Rose. The common wild rose, *Rosa californica,* especially noteworthy in the hot summer when few flowers bloom, has given rise to some fifty Rose, Rosebush, and Wildrose Canyons and Valleys. Las Pulgas [the fleas] Canyon [San Diego] was named *Cañada de Santa Praxedis de los Rosales* by the Portolá expedition on July 21, 1769, because of the many rosebushes. Ten or more California communities and railroad stations include the word "rose" in their names, but none of these need have any connection with the flower; the word is very commonly used throughout the United States to form pleasant-sounding place names.

Rose Canyon [San Diego]. The canyon and the former settlement, Roseville, were named for Louis Rose, who built a wharf there in 1870.

Rosecrans, rō'-zĕ-krănz, **Fort** [San Diego]. The site of the old Spanish Fort Guijarros was reserved by the War Department in 1852, and the building of the fortifications was begun in 1897. In 1899 the fort was named in memory of General William S. Rosecrans, who had died in 1898. Rosecrans was one of the ablest strategists among the Union generals and was commander of the Army of the Cumberland, 1862–1863. After the war he settled in the Los Angeles district (where Rosecrans Avenue is named for him) and was a congressman from 1880 to 1884. His Confederate opponent in the Tennessee campaign is honored in the name of Fort Bragg.

Rose Lake [Fresno]. Named by R. B. Marshall for the painter of miniatures, Rosa Hooper, sister of Selden S. Hooper, an assistant of the Geological Survey (Farquhar).

Rosemead [Los Angeles]. The name was originally (in the 1870's) applied to the famous horse farm on Leonard J. Rose's Sunny Slope estate. The post office was established September 1, 1927.

Roseville [Placer]. The name was applied to the station when the Central Pacific reached the place in the spring of 1864. It was chosen by the residents, at a picnic, for the most popular girl present (Sacramento *Bee,* Oct. 20, 1931). Other similar stories are told about the origin of the name, but it is just as possible that it was chosen because of its pleasant sound, like the many other Rosevilles then in existence.

Ross, Fort. See Fort Ross.

Ross: town, Valley [Marin]. Named for James Ross, who acquired the Rancho Punta de Quintin in 1859. Ross Landing is shown on Hoffmann's map of the Bay region.

Rossmoor. The first of the Rossmoor adult communities in California was established in 1961 and named for Ross W. Cortese, the originator of the idea. In 1967 there were three Rossmoor Leisure World communities in the state, situated in, or near Laguna Hills [San Diego], Seal Beach [Orange], and Walnut Creek [Contra Costa].

Rough and Ready. The phrase was popular as a place name after the Mexican War because it was General (later President) Zachary Taylor's nickname. California had three towns so named, of which the one in Nevada County survives. It was founded in 1849 by the Rough and Ready Company, led by Captain A. A. Townsend, who had served under Taylor. The post office was reëstablished in 1948. The name of the town in Siskiyou County was changed to Etna by statute in 1874. The name in San Joaquin County is preserved in Rough and Ready Island, now a naval supply depot. **Rough and Ready Creek** [Tuolumne], a tributary of the North Fork of Tuolumne River, was named for the Rough and Ready Company, which started working their rich claim in 1854 (Browne, pp. 41 f.).

Roughs, The [Sonoma]. A topographical name applied to the steep slope of Red Oat Ridge (Cazadero atlas sheet).

Round. The descriptive adjective, applied to about one hundred features, is used mainly for mountains and valleys. Half of all the elevations designated as "tops" are Round Tops. The best-known feature named Round is Round Valley in Mendocino County, where the old Indian reservation is situated. Big Valley [Modoc] was named Round Valley by Frémont in 1846: ". . . the next day [April 30] again encamped . . . at the upper end of a valley, to which, from ·its marked form, I gave the name *Round Valley*" (*Memoirs,* 1887, I, 480). There is a Round Corral Meadow in Fresno County, a Round Potrero in San Diego County, a Round Corral Canyon in Santa Barbara County, and a Roundtop Hill in Riverside County. The post office at Round Mountain [Shasta] was named after the mountain northwest of the town.

Routier [Sacramento]. A railroad station was established here in 1866 and named for Joseph Routier, a native of France who had settled here in June, 1853, as agent of Captain Folsom (*see* Folsom), and who later became assemblyman, State senator, and fish commissioner.

Rowdy Creek [Del Norte]. The name was probably applied to distinguish this creek from the commonplace Rough, Roaring, and Wild Creeks.

Rowell Meadow [Tulare]. The name became attached to the meadow because Chester and George Rowell, uncles of the late well-known newspaperman Chester Rowell, used to run sheep there and had a sort of "shotgun" title to the meadow (Farquhar).

Royal Arches, The; Royal Arch: Cascade, Creek [Yosemite National Park]. The name The Royal Arch, for the seventh degree of the Masonic fraternity, was applied to the rock formation by a member of the Mariposa Battalion in 1851 (Bunnell, 1880, p. 212). The plural form is shown on the King-Gardner map of 1865. Bunnell gives the Indian name as *Scho-ko-ni*, with the fanciful interpretation: a movable shade to a cradle forming an arched shade over the infant's head. Powers (p. 364) gives one name *cho-ko-nip'-o-deh*, 'baby basket,' and another form, *cho-ko'-ni*; "either one means literally 'dog-place' or 'dog-house'"!

Royce, Mount [Fresno]. The name was proposed in 1929 by the State Geographic Board and was accepted by the U.S. Geographic Board in memory of Josiah Royce (1855–1916), philosopher and educator, a native of Grass Valley, and the author of *California: from the Conquest in 1846 to the Second Vigilance Committee in San Francisco*.

Rubicon: River, Point, Peak, Lodge [El Dorado]. The upper course of the Rubicon River is called "The Rubicon" on the von Leicht–Hoffmann Lake Tahoe map (copyrighted 1873), probably in jesting analogy to Caesar's crossing of the Rubicon. The name for the point on Lake Tahoe appears on the same map. The less romantic Amos Bowman has Rubicon River on his map of the same year and Wheeler's atlas sheets 47-B, -D have Rubicon Creek. In 1889 the Geological Survey applied the name to the entire river and also named the peak. Wells Drury related that a resort owner thereabouts, a German, called his place Rubicund (Drury).

Rubidoux, Mount [Riverside]. Named for Louis Robidoux (as he spelled his name), a French pioneer who acquired large land holdings, including a part of Rancho Jurupa, on which the hill is situated. His house and his gristmill are Historic Landmarks 102 and 303.

Rubio Canyon [Los Angeles]. Named for Jesus Rubio, a native Californian who became an American citizen by the treaty of peace of 1847 and settled as a squatter at the mouth of the canyon in 1867 (Reid, p. 379).

Rucker Lake [Nevada]. The reservoir was created by the Meager Mining Company, before 1871, and was probably named for one of its officers.

Rudolph Hagen Canyon [Kern]. Named for Rudolph Hagen, a gold hunter who settled in the Mojave Desert (Doyle).

Ruffy Lake [Siskiyou]. Named for an Indian called Ruffy, who seined some trout out of Etna Creek and planted them in the lake (R. Baker).

Rumsey [Yolo]. The town was laid out in 1892 and named for Captain D. C. Rumsey, the owner of the land (Co. Hist., 1940, pp. 228 f.). The post office is listed in 1892.

Run. The use of the word as a generic term for a small creek originated in Virginia (Stewart, p. 60). It has never achieved general currency, but the two battles of Bull Run in the Civil War made this particular combination known everywhere. **Bull Run Peak** [Alpine]. The presence of a strong Southern element in the district during the Civil War probably explains the application of the name, which commemorates the two Confederate victories. **Bull Run Pass** [Tulare], a name used for a stock driveway from Lynns Valley to Bull Run Basin by Joel Carver in the early 1880's (Mitchell), and the tautological Bull Run Creek [Plumas, Tulare], Mud Run Creek [Fresno], Oak Run Creek [Shasta], indicate that "run" may sometimes mean trail and not creek. There are, however, a number of "runs" where the term actually designated a small stream: Bloody Run [Nevada], Honey Run, Sucker Run [Butte], Negro Run [Plumas], Whiskey Run [Placer].

Runyon [Sacramento]. The Western Pacific station was named for the sports writer, Damon Runyon. The place was formerly called Sims, for an old settler. (*Headlight*, July, 1942.)

Ruppert Point [Mendocino National Forest]. Named for a member of a pioneer family who settled here in the 1880's (Annie Lovelady).

Ruskin, Mount [Kings Canyon National Park]. Named in 1895 by Bolton C. Brown in honor of John Ruskin (1819–1900), the great English critic and author (Farquhar).

Russell, Mount [Sequoia National Park].

Named in memory of Israel C. Russell (1852–1906), assistant geologist with the Wheeler Survey in 1878; professor of geology at the University of Michigan, 1892–1906 (Farquhar).

Russ Grove [Humboldt]. Named in memory of Joseph Russ, a native of Maine, who settled in Humboldt County in 1852 and became a large landowner and prominent politician (Co. Hist., 1882, p. 168).

Russian. Besides the names in Sonoma County which commemorate the Russian establishment there are about fifteen other names which include the word. Most of them are in northern counties (including a Yellow Russian Gulch on the Sawyers Bar atlas sheet) and were probably all given for settlers from Russia or other Slavic countries. **Russian: River, Gulch** [Sonoma]. An early Spanish name for the river was *San Ygnacio*, mentioned November 8, 1821, in the diary of Padre Blas Ordaz (Arch. MSB, IV, 169 ff.). The Russian colonists themselves called it *Slavianka*, 'Slav woman' (Kotzebue, *New Voyage*, 1830, II, 119). "The river Slavianka, called in the language of the natives *Shabaikai*" (Russian America, V, No. 2, MS, Bancroft Library). In Mexican records and in land-grant papers the river (or part of it) appears with various names. The Spanish version of the modern name is mentioned, perhaps for the first time, in the petition for the Bodega grant, dated July 19, 1843: *la boca del Rio Ruso*, 'the mouth of the Russian River.' On the *diseños* of the Bodega and Muniz grants the name is recorded as *Rio Ruso o San Ignacio*. The American form, Russian River, is shown on Gibbes' map of 1852, but was doubtless current before the publication of this map. **Russian Spring** [San Diego]. This spring or well, rediscovered in 1952, owes its name to a rather fantastic story, according to Dallas Wood in the Palo Alto *Times*. About 1830 a Russian whaler was wrecked on the strand south of the present Hotel Coronado, and the sailors dug the well with their bare hands. Later a girl led sailors from a Mexican boat to the spring, where the bodies of seven Russians were found. **Russian Gulch** [Mendocino]. According to local tradition, it was so named because a deserter from Fort Ross had settled there (Stewart).

Ruth [Trinity]. The post office was established in 1904 and named for Ruth McKnight, the daughter of a pioneer family (Albert Burgess).

Rutherford [Napa]. Railroad station and post office were named in the 1880's for Thomas L. Rutherford, who had married a granddaughter of the pioneer George C. Yount of near-by Yountville (Doyle).

Rutherford Lake [Madera]. Named for Lieutenant Samuel M. Rutherford of the Fourth Cavalry, who was stationed in Yosemite National Park in 1896 (Farquhar).

Ryan: town, Wash [Death Valley National Monument]. The old town at the site of the Lila C. mine, as well as the present town on the site formerly called Devair, were named for John Ryan, for many years manager of the Pacific Coast Borax Company. In 1936 the Park Service gave this name to the southern fork of Furnace Creek Wash. (Death Valley Survey.)

Ryde [Sacramento]. William A. Kesner bought the land from Judge Williams in 1892 and laid out the town. When the post office was established in 1893, Kesner became first postmaster but refused to have it named for himself. Judge Williams then suggested the name Ryde, after the town on the Isle of Wight, the situation of which is similar to that of the California town on Grand Island. (Patricia Kesner.)

Ryer Island [Solano]. The name commemorates the former owner of the island, Dr. W. M. Ryer, a pioneer physician of Stockton, who vaccinated some two thousand Indians in the San Joaquin Valley in the summer of 1852. The name appears on Ringgold's chart of 1850.

Sablon [San Bernardino]. When the Santa Fe line from Cadiz was built in 1909 the station was named Randolph. In 1912 the present name (from Spanish *sablón*, 'gravel') was applied.

Sabrina, Lake [Inyo]. Named about 1908 for Sabrina Hobbs, wife of C. M. Hobbs, general manager of the Nevada-California Power Company.

Sacate [Santa Barbara]. The name is shown for the station on the Southern Pacific map of 1905. *Sacate* is Mexican Spanish for 'grass,' 'hay.'

Saco [Kern]. The Spanish word for 'sack' was applied to the Southern Pacific siding after 1900. Since the word is used as a place name in Maine and other states, it may be a transfer name.

Sacramento, săk-rȧ-měn'-tō: **River, city, County**. The Spanish name for 'Holy Sacrament' is found often as a place name in Spanish-speaking countries. Gabriel Moraga on October 8, 1808, gave the name Sacramento to the Feather River (Diario de la tercera expedicion). The lower Sacramento was still being called *Rio de San Francisco* by Abella in October, 1811 (Bancroft, II, 322), but the name given by Moraga soon came to refer to the lower Sacramento as well as to the Feather. Durán in May, 1817, records going up the *Rio del Sacramento* with Luis Argüello; they probably got almost as far as the mouth of Feather River (APCH:*P*, II, 332 ff.). On the Plano topografico de la Mision de San Jose (about 1824) the lower course of the river is shown as R. del Sacram[en]to. The trappers of the Hudson's Bay Company called the stream "the big river" or Bonaventura, and as Buenaventura River it appears on Burr's map of 1839. Hood's map of 1838 shows Sacramento River, and the Wilkes expedition in 1841 definitely established the name Sacramento for the river south of the confluence of Pit and Little or Upper Sacramento rivers. The latter is labeled Destruction River on Wilkes' map. In the fall of 1848, John A. Sutter, Jr., and Sam Brannan, against the wishes of the elder Sutter, laid out a town at the embarcadero of Sutter's Fort, and named it Sacramento, after tne river. This name had been mentioned previously for Sutter's settlement at the Fort (S.F. *Californian*, July 31, 1847: Fort Sacramento). The county, one of the original twenty-seven, was established and named on February 18, 1850. *See* Pit River; Buenaventura. The name Sacramento is also found for the mountain range west of Needles [San Bernardino]. Sacramento Buttes [Sutter] was a former name of Sutter Buttes.

Saddle, Saddleback. These descriptive terms are found in the names of more than twenty-five buttes, peaks, and mountains. Sometimes they are even used in a generic sense, as in Salt Tree Saddle, north of Cazadero [Sonoma], and in Saddleback on the Calistoga atlas sheet. A number of creeks and lakes have been named after the orographic features. **Old Saddleback** [Orange]. The Indian name for this mountain was *Kalawpa*. Its two peaks are now Santiago and Modjeska. (Stephenson, II, 117.)

Sadler: Peak, Lake [Madera]. The name was applied in 1895 by Lieutenant N. F. McClure for a corporal in his detachment (Farquhar).

Sage. The presence of sagebrush, of the genus *Artemisia,* characteristic of our western plains, has been the reason for giving a number of names in the arid regions of the State.

Until 1942 there was a post office named Sage in Riverside County. A mining camp in 1860 in Kern County was called Sageland. A railroad station in Lassen County and several physical features were named for the sage hen, the popular name of the western grouse, *Centrocercus urophasianus.*

Sailor. The characteristics peculiar to seafaring men made sailors readily recognizable among miners, and a number of bars, flats, and ravines were named for them. Some of these names have survived in Humboldt, Nevada, Placer, 'and Sierra counties. One may commemorate "Sailor Jack," the Finn who turned the joke on the miners of Pinchemtight by finding a $50,000 pocket in the "worthless" claims which they had induced him to stake out (C. M. Goethe, *Sierran Cabin . . . ,* pp. 143 ff.).

Saint George, Point; Saint George: Reef, Channel [Del Norte]. The name was given to the point by Vancouver on April 23, 1792, the day of the patron saint of England, Saint George. It is shown on most American maps and on the first sketch of the western coast by the Coast Survey in 1850. Vancouver named the rocks below the point Dragon Rocks, in analogy to Saint George and the dragon; this name is preserved in Dragon Channel, south of the Reef. Vizcaíno had named the point *Cabo Blanco de San Sebastian,* on January 19, 1603, "the eve of that glorious martyr" (*CHSQ,* VII, 367).

Saint Helena, Mount [Sonoma]; **Saint Helena Creek** [Lake, Napa]. The first mentioning of the name Mount Saint Helena, as far as could be ascertained, is in a report on the geysers in the *American Journal of Science and Arts,* November, 1851, p. 154. No evidence has been found to show when and why the peak was so named. On *diseños* of the Caymus (1836) and the Mallacomes (1841) land grants the mountain is apparently designated as *Serro* [Cerro] *de los Mallacomes,* for the Indians living on the west slope. Mayacmas Mountains is still the official name of what is commonly known as Saint Helena Range. In 1853 a plate was discovered on the peak which showed that the Russian scientist and traveler J. G. Woznesenski had climbed the mountain in June, 1841; thereafter, it was generally assumed that the Russians had named the peak. This belief received the sanction of Whitney: "named in honor of the Empress of Russia" (*Geology,* I, 86). The name of the empress in 1841, however, was Alexandra, not Helena. The story became more romantic as the years passed: no less than Princess Helena de Gagarin, "a niece of the Czar," braved the chaparral and the rattlesnakes and christened the mountain in honor of her patron saint, Saint Helena, the mother of Constantine the Great (of Constantinople), while the Russian flag fluttered above in the breeze. Erman's map of 1849, based on Russian information, shows the mountain range but leaves it nameless. It is nevertheless possible that the Russians did give the name, though no record of it has been found. One of the Russian vessels bore the name *Saint Helena*, and since the peak is the highest point in this latitude and visible as far as seventy-five miles off shore, the naming from aboard ship would be more likely than the christening by a princess. After the American conquest the mountain was known as Devil's Mount. On January 29, 1848, the *California Star* prints this item: "It is related of a Russian botanist, who eight or ten years ago, climbed the 'Devil's Mount,' and on its summit affixed a plate of brass commemorative of the feat. . . ." Bartlett (*Personal Narrative*, 1854, II, 28) writes in March, 1852, of "Mount Helena or Moyacino of the Russians." Until the time of the Whitney Survey the name is often given as Helen or Hellen, with and without the Saint. **Saint Helena** [Napa]. Henry Still, who had settled here in 1853, founded the town in 1855 and named it "from the name given to the Division of the Sons of Temperance established there about that time . . . On account of the fine view obtained of St. Helena mountain, the Division was named St. Helena, and the Division gave the name to the town." (Co. Hist., 1873, pp. 186, 119.) The post office is listed in 1858.

Saint John, Mount [Glenn]. According to the county history of 1880, peak and settlement were named for A. C. St. John, a settler in the early 1850's. Mt. St. John is shown on Baker's map of 1856 and is mentioned in *Hutchings' Illustrated California Magazine*, 1857, p. 484.

Saint John Mountain [Napa]. The peak was named Mount Henry by Brewer in 1861, for Professor Joseph Henry of Princeton University. This name, however, did not appear on maps, and when the region was surveyed between 1896 and 1899, the Geological Survey applied the present, probably local name.

Saint Johns River [Tulare]. Named for Loomis St. John, who had a cabin near Kaweah River in 1850. St. John was a member of the Court of Sessions in 1852 and county supervisor in 1853 (Mitchell).

Saint Louis Mountain [Sonoma]. The mountain was named after the vanished town of Saint Louis, mentioned in the *California Star* of December 25, 1847. In 1859 a Saint Louis post office [Sierra] is listed. Both settlements were probably named by settlers who came from the city in Missouri.

Saint Marys College [Contra Costa]. The Catholic institution was established in Oakland in 1863 and was moved to the present site in 1927. The post office is listed in 1928. The name of the saint occurs elsewhere in California: Saint Marys Creek [Lake], Saint Marys Peak [Merced].

Saint Orres Gulch [Mendocino]. According to a report received by the Geographic Board, May-Aug., 1962, the gulch was named for the St. Orres family, early settlers of the region.

Sal, Point [Santa Barbara]. Named by Vancouver in 1792 for Hermenegildo Sal, at that time *comandante* at San Francisco, in recognition of favors received from him. It appears on the Lahainaluna *Carta* of 1839 (Wheat, No. 12), and was used by the Coast Survey in 1852.

Salada. The Spanish word for 'salty' was used for surface waters with a strong saline content and has survived in a number of place names. The feminine form seems to be used exclusively, although with Arroyo [Orange, San Diego, Imperial] the masculine Salado would be correct. **Salada,** så-lä′-då: **Beach; Laguna Salada** [San Mateo]. Laguna Salada is shown on a *diseño* of the San Pedro grant, 1838. *See* Salinas; Salt; Sharp Park.

Salida, så-lī′-då [Stanislaus]. When the Southern Pacific reached the place in 1870, it named the station Salida, the Spanish word for 'departure,' because it seemed to be an appropriate name for a railway station.

Salinas, så-lē′-nǎs: **River, Valley,** city [Monterey]. The origin of the name is found in the *salinas* (salt marshes) near the river mouth, which were commercially important in Spanish times. The word is included in the names of several land grants in Monterey County, the oldest of which was granted before 1795 (PSP, XIII, 269). The river itself had various names in Spanish times: *Santa Delfina, San Antonio, Rio de Monterey*. When the legend arose in the 1820's that a mythical river, the Buenaventura, coming from the Rocky Mountains, entered the ocean somewhere south of San Francisco, the Salinas was at times confused with this river and bore its name (often with a San in front of it) long after the myth of the great river was exploded. (*See* Buenaventura.) Salines River is mentioned in a letter by Larkin on March 6, 1846 (Castro Docs., II, 31), and *Rio San Buenaventura* or *Rio Salinas* is recorded by Frémont-Preuss in 1848. Both names were used until about 1860, except by those cartographers who could not decide one way or the other and left the important waterway without a name (Wilkes, 1849; Derby, 1850). The post office is listed in 1858; the town, named after the river, is shown on Goddard's map of 1860. **Rincon de las Salinas y Potrero Viejo** [San Francisco, San Mateo] was the name of a land grant dated October 10, 1839, and May 30, 1840. *See* Salt.

Saline Valley [Inyo]. So named because of its salt deposits. This seems to be the only important geographic feature in the State which bears this name. In other states the word is commonly used as a place name. *See* Salt.

Salmon. The name of the common and valuable fish is found in the names of almost fifty features, mainly creeks. Since the fish occurs seldom south of 38° latitude, the names are confined to the northern counties, except Salmon Creek and Falls [Tulare], Salmon Cove and Creek [Monterey]. Salmon Mountains, Salmon Alps, and Forks of Salmon are named after Salmon River in Siskiyou County; the river is mentioned in the *Statutes* of 1852 (p. 233), but the name had probably been in use since 1849. Truckee River was called Salmon Trout River by Frémont in 1844 (*Expl. Exp.*, 1853, p. 323). A post office was established at Salmon Creek [Humboldt], Feb. 19, 1884, and named Beatrice. *See* Beatrice.

Salsberry: Spring, Pass [Inyo]. Named for John Salsberry (or Salisbury), a prospector in the early 1900's.

Salsipuedes. The Spanish phrase, meaning 'get-out-if-you-can,' was repeatedly used in geographical nomenclature, usually for narrow enclosures or for canyons where the terrain is very rough. **Salsipuedes** [Santa Cruz, Santa Clara]. A *sitio* in *el plan de los corralitos llamados* [the plain of the little corrals called] *Sal si puedes* is mentioned on May 25, 1806 (Estudillo Docs., I, 160). The padres of Santa Cruz mission were granted land called *Bolsa de Salsipuedes* (or *sitio de Salsipuedes*) on which to put their cattle, in 1817 (Arch. Arz. SF, Vol. III, Pt. 1, pp. 134 f.; Vol. III, Pt. 2, p. 79), and in June, 1823, the name was

applied to a private land grant. The stream shown on a *diseño* (1836) of the grant as *Arroyo de Salsipuedes* seems to be Corralitos Creek on modern maps. **Salsipuedes,** säl-sĭ-pōō-ĕd'-ĕs: **Creek** [Santa Barbara]. A *sitio de Sal si puedes,* belonging to the *Mision de la Purisima,* is mentioned in 1817 in Documentos . . . Historia de California (IV, 321 f.), and on May 18, 1844, the name was given to a grant, Cañada de Salsipuedes. The stream is shown on a *diseño* of the grant as *Arrollo [arroyo] de Salsipuedes.*—The term has also survived as a name for creeks in Monterey and San Luis Obispo counties.

Salt. Since earliest times this name has been used for places in all parts of the world. California has more than a hundred Salt names, mostly for creeks, sloughs, wells, springs, and lakes. There is a Salt Marsh in Ventura County and a Salt Pool in Death Valley National Monument. Only a few indicate the occurrence of salt in sizable quantities; most of them, especially on the coast and in the Great Basin, simply describe the peculiar taste of the water, which may come from the presence of common salt or medicinal salts. Two settlements are named Saltdale [Kern] and Salt Works [San Diego]. A number of names are doubtless translations from the Spanish. *See* Salada; Salinas; Saline.

Saltmarsh [San Bernardino]. Named in 1921 by the Santa Fe, not for salt beds but for S.M. Saltmarsh, car accountant for the Santa Fe.

Salton: station, **Sea, Creek** [Riverside]. The ancient lake bed was discovered and explored by William Blake of the Pacific Railroad Survey in 1853–1854; it was called Lake Cahuilla for the Indians of the region. *See* Coachella. This name, although still used by geologists, has never become current. The present name, first given to the Southern Pacific station, was transferred by Frank Stevens to the lake bed in 1892, and was retained for the sheet of water (much smaller than the old bed) which formed in 1907 after the overflow of the Colorado. The name was apparently coined from "salt."

Saltus [San Bernardino]. The name, probably coined from "salt," like Salton, was given to the Santa Fe station in 1915.

Salyer [Trinity]. The post office was established April 16, 1918, and named for Charles Marshall Salyer, a prominent mining man (Bess Moore).

Samagatuma Valley [San Diego]. The name is derived from that of an Indian rancheria *Jamatayune* shown on a *diseño* (about 1845) of the Sierra de Cuyamaca grant.

Samoa [Humboldt]. The place was originally known as Brownsville for James D. H. Brown, who established a dairy ranch in 1859. In 1889 a group of Eureka businessmen formed the Samoa Land and Improvement Company, so named because the crisis in the Samoan Islands was emphasized in the newspapers and because Humboldt Bay was assumed to be similar to the harbor of Pago Pago. The lumber town, which developed in the 1890's, was called Samoa; it is now the center of operations of the Hammond Lumber Company.

Sampsons Flats [Inyo]. Named for a Digger Indian chief called Sampson, who in 1858 piloted a party across Kearsarge Pass (Chalfant, *Inyo*, 1922, p. 76).

Samuel P. Taylor State Park [Marin]. The park was created in 1955 and named for Samuel P. Taylor, who had come to San Francisco in 1850 and established the first paper mill here in 1856. *See* Taylorville.

San Agustin Creek [Santa Cruz]. The name of Saint Augustine, Bishop of Hippo, was given to a land grant, dated November 23, 1833, and April 21, 1841. The stream, which may have been named before the grant, is on the rancho and was mentioned as *Rio San Augustine* in 1854 (Trask, *Report*, 1854, p. 24). The Southern Pacific station San Augustine in Santa Barbara County is probably another survivor from Spanish times. The Coast Survey still spells the name of the settlement the Spanish way, San Agustin.

San Alejo. *See* San Elijo.

San Andreas. Saint Andrew, one of the apostles and patron saint of Scotland, called ¯San *Andrés* in Spanish, is honored in several living place names and in several obsolete names. San Clemente Island, San Pedro Bay, and Pinole Point once bore the name *San Andres*. **San Andreas,** ăn-drā'-ăs: **Valley, Lake** [San Mateo]. The valley was named *Cañada de San Andres* by Palou on November 30, 1774, the feast day of the saint (Anza, II, 418 f.). Hoffmann's map of the Bay region (1873) has Cañada San Andres; the name of the reservoir which was created in 1875 was spelled San Andreas from the beginning (Co. map, 1877). **San Andres** [Santa Cruz]. The name of a land grant, dated May 21, 1823, and November 21, 1833. **San Andreas,** ăn'-drăs [Calaveras]. The place on San Andreas Gulch was settled by Mexicans in 1848 or 1849. The town is mentioned in the *Statutes* of 1854 (p. 222), and the post office is listed in 1858.

San Anselmo, ăn-sĕl'-mō [Marin]. *Cañada de Anselmo* appears in the papers of the Punta de Quintin grant of 1840 and was applied in the present form to the North Pacific Coast Railroad station in the 1890's. It is very likely that the *cañada* (valley) was named for a baptized Indian and that the *San* was added to the name later.

San Antonio. The name was extremely popular as a place name, in mission days especially, because Saint Anthony of Padua was a patron saint of the Franciscan Order. The name appears in the titles of many land grants and claims; it has survived in a number of places. **San Antonio: River, Mission, Creek, Valley** [Monterey]. The mission was founded by Serra on July 14, 1771; the river had been named by him previously (Engelhardt, II, 87 ff.). A post office San Antonio is listed from 1867 to 1887. **San Antonio: Creek, Canyon, Mountains, Peak, Heights** [San Bernardino]. The name of the arroyo called San Antonio is mentioned by Garcés on March 21, 1774 (Anza, II, 346). A place named *San Antonio* is recorded on March 24, 1821 (PSP, XX, 287), and *Arroyo de San Antonio* is shown on a *diseño* of the Cucamonga grant (1839). Von Leicht–Craven (1874) have San Antonio Mountain for the highest peak of San Gabriel Mountains. San Antonio Heights district was known by this name before 1888 (Minnie Goodrich); San Antonio post office is listed after 1892. Locally San Antonio Peak is now called Old Baldy because winds have denuded its top of vegetation (Doyle). It is labeled Old Baldy Peak on the Cucamonga atlas sheet of the Corps of Engineers. **San Antonio Creek** [Alameda]. The name was applied to the channel between Alameda and Oakland, popularly known as "The Estuary," because it is on the territory of the San Antonio grant, first granted to Luis María Peralta on August 3, 1820. Rio San Antonio and San Antonio (the rancho) are shown on Narváez' Plano of 1830. The Coast Survey charts show the name in 1850. San Antonio Creek, a tributary of Alameda Creek (south of Sunol), is not on the territory of the grant. **San Antonio Creek** [Ventura]. A place called *San Antonio* is shown on a *diseño* of the Ojai grant (1837), and is mentioned on April 4, 1841 (DSP Ang., VI, 2). **San Antonio Creek** [Sonoma, Marin]. The stream is on the Laguna de San Antonio grant, dated May 6, 1839, and November 25, 1845. A station of the Northwestern Pacific was also called San Antonio after the grant. Estero de San Antonio, flowing into Bodega Bay, is outside the territory of the grant. **San Antonio Creek** [Santa Barbara]. The stream traverses Rancho Todos Santos y San Antonio, dated August 28, 1841. A rancho San Antonio is mentioned on March 11, 1813 (Arch. MSB, VI, 173), and the place is shown on Narváez' Plano of 1830. The grants called San Antonio in Los Angeles, Santa Clara, and Sonoma counties seem to have left no traces in present-day place names; there is, however, another San Antonio Creek northeast of Mount Hamilton [Santa Clara].

San Ardo [Monterey]. The town was laid out in 1886 when the Southern Pacific reached the place and was named San Bernardo by M. J. Brandenstein, who had bought the San Bernardo Rancho, originally granted June 16, 1841. When the Post Office Department objected to the name because of possible confusion with San Bernardino, Brandenstein created a new saint name by lopping off "Bern."

San Augustine. *See* San Agustin.

San Benancio Gulch [Monterey]. A *diseño* (1834) of Rancho El Toro shows the *Cañada de San Benancio* running north and south parallel to *Arroyo del Toro;* another shows it in approximately its present location. The name probably honors one of the four Saint Venantiuses; *b* and *v* are often interchanged in Spanish.

San Benito: River, Valley, Mountain, County, town. The Spanish name for Saint Benedict, the founder of the Benedictine Order, was applied to what is now San Juan Creek by Crespi on March 21, 1772, Saint Benedict's feast day. Palou, on November 24, 1774, remarked that the valley had been named *Cañada de San Benito* by the expedition of 1772. The name became well known and is often mentioned in mission and provincial records. What is now San Benito River was formerly San Juan River, and it is still so labeled on the Land Office map of 1861. However, Goddard's map of 1860 calls the stream San Benito ·down to its confluence with Pacheco Creek, where it becomes Pajaro River, an alignment still in use. The legislature created the county from a portion of Monterey County and named it on February 12, 1874. The name was also used for a land grant in Monterey County, dated March 11, 1842.

San Bernabe [Monterey]. The land grant, dated March 10, 1841, and April 6, 1842, derived its name from *Cañada de San Bernabe,* named for Saint Barnabas the Apostle, and mentioned by Font on April 15, 1776.

San Bernardino, bĕr-nȧ-dē′-nō:**Valley, Mountains, Peak,** city, **County, National Forest.** Saint Bernardino of Siena, Italy, the great Franciscan preacher of the 15th century, was honored during mission days in a number of place names. An *asistencia* of Mission San Gabriel was established southeast of the site of the modern city, in 1819, at a place called *Guachama* (or *Guachinga*) by the Indians, and named San Bernardino by the padres (Arch. MSB, III, 268). It is mentioned as a rancho of the mission in the early 1820's (Arch. Arz. SF, Vol. IV, Pt. 2, p. 129). According to an often-repeated story, the name was first applied to a temporary chapel by Padre Dumetz and a party from Mission San Gabriel on May 20, 1810, the feast day of the saint. June 21, 1842, the name was applied to a land grant. In 1851 a group of Mormons bought the rancho and founded the ·colony which developed into the modern city. The county, created from part of Los Angeles County, was named April 26, 1853. The peak is shown as Mt. Bernardino on Wilkes' map of 1841. The Luiseño Indian name of the mountain is *Pewipwi* (Sparkman, p. 191); locally this peak and San Gorgonio Peak, which rise from a common base, are known as Old Grayback (Doyle). For the mountain range W. P. Blake had suggested the name Bernardino Sierra because he considered it a prolongation of the Sierra Nevada (Pac. R.R. *Reports,* Vol. V, Pt. 1, p. 8), but the name San Bernardino Mountains has been generally used since the 1850's. The name is now restricted to the chain between Cajon and San Gorgonio passes. The National Forest was established and named in 1893 by order of President Harrison; from 1908 to 1925 it was part of Angeles National Forest. *See* Berdoo Canyon.

San Bernardo Creek [San Luis Obispo]. The name is derived from that of the land grant San Bernardo, dated February 11, 1840. Wagner (Saints' Names) identifies the saint with the 12th-century French saint, Bernard of Clairvaux, who organized the Second Crusade. *See* San Ardo; Bernardo.

San Bruno: Mountain, Point, Canal, town, **Creek** [San Mateo]. The name, apparently applied by Palou in November or December, 1774 (Font, *Compl. Diary,* p. 348), was given to the creek which rose on the north slope of San Bruno Mountain, paralleled the highway between Colma Schoolhouse and Baden Station, and emptied into the sloughs south of San Bruno Point. This creek is mentioned by Beechey in 1826 and is shown on *diseños* in the 1830's. What is left of it no longer bears the name, but an intermittent stream flowing east from the Buriburi Ridge is now called San Bruno Creek. San Bruno was a German saint of the 11th century, founder of the Carthusian Order. A place *San Bruno,* apparently a cattle range of the San Francisco presidio, is repeatedly mentioned in early provincial and mission records. The mountain and its foothills are mentioned as *Sierra de San Bruno* by Beechey in 1826 (II, 42), and as *Montes San Bruno* by Eld, October 29, 1841; they are shown on Greenhow's map of 1844 as San Bruno Mountains. *Pta. San Bruno* appears on Duflot de Mofras's *Plan* 16, and Point San Bruno on the Coast Survey chart of 1851. The town developed around Richard Cunningham's San Bruno House (1862) on the San Bruno toll road; the name of the station of the San Francisco and San Jose Railroad was announced in the itinerary, dated October 16, 1863. There is a San Bruno Canyon in Santa Clara County; it is shown as *Cañada de San Bruno* on a map of the Rancho de la Laguna Seca (1847).

San Buenaventura, bwā'-nȧ-vĕn-tōōr'-ȧ [Ventura]. The establishment of a mission at Santa Barbara Channel named San Buenaventura, for a Franciscan saint of the 13th century, was one of the projects with which José de Gálvez, the *visitador general* of New Spain, had charged the Portolá expedition. When the expedition reached the site on August 14, 1769, Crespi considered it well suited for a mission and named the populous Indian village there *La Asuncion de Nuestra Señora* (The Assumption of Our Lady). The mission, however, was not established and named until Easter Sunday, March 31, 1782. The mission is Historic Landmark 310. *See* Buenaventura; Ventura.

San Carlos. The mission, San Carlos Borromeo [Monterey], was established on June 3, 1770, near the presidio of Monterey, but was transferred to the present site in 1771; it was named for Saint Charles Borromeo, Archbishop of Milan in the 16th century. The mission is Historic Landmark 135, and is now generally known as Mission Carmel. **San Carlos Pass** [Riverside]. On March 16, 1774, the Anza expedition crossed the mountains by this pass into the coastal region of Cali-

fornia. The *Puerto Real de San Carlos* was named by Anza on March 15, 1774 (Anza, II, 199), and is mentioned repeatedly in Anza's and Font's diaries. The old but apparently forgotten name was revived when the Native Sons of the Golden West erected a monument at the pass in 1924. **Potrero de San Carlos** [Monterey]. The name, 'pasture of San Carlos,' was given to a land grant October 9, 1837. **San Carlos de Jonata** [Santa Barbara]. The name of a land grant dated September 24, 1845. *Jonata* was the name of a Chumash rancheria, mentioned in the mission records in 1791 and later. **San Carlos** [San Mateo]. The name does not go back to Spanish times but was applied to the town in 1887 when "Captain" N. T. Smith and his associates founded it. The name San Carlos was chosen because it was believed that the Portolá expedition first saw San Francisco Bay on November 4, 1769, St. Charles' feast day, from the hills behind the present town (Stanger, pp. 128 f.). *Punta de San Carlos* on the Marin shore of the Golden Gate (probably Lime Point) appears on Ayala's map of 1775 and on some later maps; it was apparently named for the first ship to enter the Golden Gate, as well as for the saint. There is a San Carlos Peak in San Benito County and a San Carlos Canyon in Monterey County.

San Carpoforo Creek [Monterey, San Luis Obispo]. In September, 1769, the Portolá expedition entered the Santa Lucia Range through the canyon of this creek, called *Santa Humiliana* by Crespi (p. 190). The present name, for one of several saints called Carpophorus, was the name of a rancho of Mission San Antonio in 1836 (SP Mis., V, 51). *Camino de S. Carpoforo* is shown on a *diseño* (1841) of the San Miguelito grant. In Wood's *Gazetteer* the name is spelled San Carvoforo. "This name suffers many variations. I have read it 'San Carpoco,' 'San Carpojo,' 'Zanjapoco,' and 'Zanjapojo,' while in speech the changes are rung on 'Sankypoco,' and 'Sankypoky'" (Chase, *Coast Trails,* p. 167). These pronunciations doubtless came about through association with the more familiar sănk'-ē, the California folk pronunciation of Spanish *zanja* and *zanjón,* 'ditch.'

San Cayetano Mountain [Ventura]. The mountain was so named because it is on the territory of the Sespe or San Cayetano land grant, dated November 22, 1833. The name of the 16th-century Saint Cajetan (or Gaetano) of Lombardy was also given to a grant in Monterey County, Bolsa de San Cayetano, dated

October 12, 1822; to a rejected grant, Huerta de San Cayetano [Alameda]; and as an alternate name of the Moro y Cojo grant [San Luis Obispo]. The Moraga expedition of 1806 named a stream along its route *Arroyo que llamanos S. Cayetano* ('creek which we call St. Cajetan'—Muñoz, p. 35), but the name has not survived.

Sanchez, Paraje de [Monterey]. *El parage de Sanchez* (Sánchez' place) is mentioned on October 16, 1806 (Arch. Arz. SF, II, 11), and was made a private land grant June 8, 1839. Of the many Sanchezes, José Antonio, a well-known Indian fighter and enemy of the clergy, seems to be the one most likely connected with the *paraje*.

San Clemente, klĕ-mĕn'-tĭ: **Island** [Los Angeles]. The island was named by Vizcaíno about November 25, 1602, for Saint Clement (Wagner, p. 408), the third Pope and Bishop of Rome, whose feast day is November 23. Among the many saints' names applied on or near feast days, this one seems to be fitting for the place: Saint Clement discovered, through a miracle, a clear spring of water on a barren island. The name was definitely affixed to the island when Costansó used it on his map of 1770. The Luiseño Indian name was *Kimki harasa* (Sparkman, p. 191). **San Clemente:** town, **Beach State Park** [Orange]. The seaside resort was developed in 1925 by Ole Hanson, former mayor of Seattle, and was probably named after the island sixty miles off shore. It is known as "The Spanish Village" because of its architecture. (Santa Fe.) The state park was created and named in 1931.—The name San Clemente was used in other parts of the State and is still found in San Clemente Canyon [San Diego] and San Clemente Creek and Ridge [Monterey].

Sand, Sandy. About fifty Sand or Sandy Hills, Creeks, Canyons, Flats, Points, etc., are shown on the maps, and many more similar names are used locally. There is a Sand Spit Park in Santa Barbara, a Sandy Mush Country in Merced, and a Sand Rock Peak in Los Angeles County. Several orographic features are named for Sandstone. *See* Arena.

Sandberg [Los Angeles]. The post office was established April 22, 1918, and was named for the first postmaster, Harold Sandberg, who operated an inn on the old Ridge Route (G. Hamilton).

Sanders [Fresno]. Probably named for C. E. Sanders, who was the first postmaster when the post office was established, October 15, 1879.

Sandia, săn-dē'-á [Imperial]. The Spanish name for 'watermelon' was applied to the station when the Southern Pacific line from Calipatria was built in 1924. Like Casaba, the name advertises one of the principal products of Imperial Valley.

San Diego, dē-ā'-gō: **Bay, Mission,** city, **River, County.** The bay was discovered by Cabrillo on September 28, 1542, and named San Miguel for Saint Michael, whose feast was the following day. From November 10 to 14, 1602, Vizcaíno anchored in the port and renamed it in honor of San Diego de Alcalá de Henares (Saint Didacus), a Franciscan saint of the 15th century, whose feast fell on November 12, and whose name had also been given to Vizcaíno's flagship. The first published map to show the modern name San Diego is that of Abraham Goos (Wagner, No. 292), in the *West-Indische Spieghel* (Amsterdam, 1624). When Serra founded the first mission in Alta California on July 16, 1769, he dedicated it to the same saint and called it *La Mision de San Diego de Alcala*. The original Mexican pueblo at Presidio Hill is now Old Town. New San Diego was laid out in 1850 but did not flourish until the coming of A. E. Horton in 1867. The county, one of the original twenty-seven, was created and named by act of the legislature on February 18, 1850.

San Dieguito, dē-ā-gē'-tō: **Valley, River** [San Diego]. The stream and a place spelled *San Dieguillo* are mentioned by Font on January 10, 1776. The diminutive was doubtless used to distinguish the place from San Diego. An Indian rancheria, *San Dieguito,* under the jurisdiction of San Diego Mission, is mentioned in 1778 (Arch. MSB, I, 158; PSP Ben. Mil., I, 41), and an Indian pueblo, San Dieguito, was established before 1834 (Engelhardt, III, 531). In 1840 or 1841 the name was applied to a rancho, which was finally granted August 11, 1845.

San Dimas, dē'-măs: town, **Canyon, Wash, Junction** [Los Angeles]. In 1886–1887 the San Jose Land Company laid out and named the town at the site formerly known as Mud Springs (Santa Fe). Saint Dismas was the penitent robber crucified at the side of Christ. The name may go back to Spanish times, but the often-repeated story that Ygnacio Palomares, grantee of Rancho San Jose, chose the name in allusion to the unrepenting Indian robbers who stole his cattle has not been substantiated by documentary evidence.

San Domingo. The name of Saint Dominic, a Spanish saint of the 13th century and founder of the Dominican Order, was occasionally used in place naming in Spanish times. Creeks in Calaveras and Sacramento counties still bear the name of this saint. The correct Spanish form would be Santo Domingo.

San Elijo, ĕ-lē'-hō: **Valley, Lagoon** [San Diego]. The Portolá expedition camped not far from Batequitos Lagoon on July 16, 1769, and called the place where they camped *San Alejo* (Crespi, pp. 127 f.), in honor of Saint Alexius, whose feast day is July 17; Costansó mentions the *cañada de San Alexos* on July 16, 1769. The name of the valley was preserved in the alternate name of the Encinitos grant, Cañada de San Alejo, July 13, 1842. The present San Elijo Lagoon is the southern boundary of this grant. It is not known who is responsible for the change in spelling. The name does not appear on the older charts of the Coast Survey, but San Elejo Creek is shown on the Land Office map of 1891. Cardiff-by-the-Sea was formerly called San Elijo. *See* Cardiff-by-the-Sea.

Sanel Mountain [Mendocino]. A populous Pomo Indian village called *Se-nel* or *Shanel* (Kroeber: from *shane*, 'sweathouse, ceremonial house') was situated southeast of East Hopland; its site is still shown on the Hopland atlas sheet as Rancho Del Sanel. On November 9, 1844, the name was used for the land grant Sanel; on the *diseños, Rancheria de Sanel* and *Rio permanente de Sanel* are shown. Gibbs (in Schoolcraft, III, 109 ff.) mentions these Indians on August 20 and 21, 1851, and seems to distinguish between a village, *Shanel-kaya*, and a "band," *Sah-nel,* which he mentions in connection with other "bands" like the Pomo and Yukai. In 1859 it was applied to the settlement west of the river, now Hopland. The name for town and mountain are shown on the von Leicht-Craven map of 1874.

San Emigdio, ĕ-mĭd'-ĭ-ō: **Canyon, Creek, Mountain** [Kern]. The names are derived from the name of a rancho of Mission Santa Barbara, mentioned in 1823 and 1824 (Arch. Arz. SF, Vol. IV, Pt. 2, p. 91; DSP, I, 42). On July 13, 1842, the property became a private land grant, usually spelled San Emidio. The saint for whom the name was given was apparently Emygdius (or Emidius), a German who was converted to Christianity and became a martyr in 303 or 304 A.D. The name is mentioned repeatedly as San Amidio and Emidio in Brewer's Notes in the spring of 1863.

San Felipe. The name has survived as a place name in San Diego, San Benito, and Santa Clara counties. There were at least four well-known holy Philips; Wagner (Saints' Names) ascribes the names to the first-century saint who was crucified in Asia Minor and whose feast day is May 1 (or August 1). **San Felipe,** fĕ-lē'-pē: **Valley, Creek** [San Diego]. On April 18, 1782, Pedro Fages and his party gave the name San Phelipe to a place where they camped (*Diary,* p. 94). The name soon spread to the valley and to an Indian village in it: the *gentiles de San Felipe* are mentioned on April 27, 1785 (PSP, V, 210). The name of the creek, which is also in Imperial County, probably comes from this source. The rancheria, the valley, and the *Sierra de San Felipe* are repeatedly mentioned in early records. On February 21, 1846, the name Valle de San Felipe was applied to a land grant. The place, San Felipe, is recorded on Coulter's and Wilkes' maps, and is mentioned as San Felippe by Emory in 1846–1847 (*Mil. Rec.,* p. 104). **San Felipe,** fĕ-lĭp'-ĕ: **Creek, Hills, Lake,** town, **Valley** [San Benito, Santa Clara]. The names were preserved through three land grants: San Felipe, April 1, 1836; Bolsa de San Felipe, November 13, 1837; Cañada de San Felipe y las Animas, August 17, 1839, and August 1, 1844. The stream is recorded as San Felipe River on Wilkes' map of 1841. Creek and lake are mentioned in the *Statutes* of 1850 (p. 59). Padre Garcés had given the name to Kern River on May 1, 1776, and it is shown as *Rio de San Philipe* on Font's map of 1777 (Coues, *Trail,* pp. 282 f.).

San Fernando: Mission, Valley, Pass, city, **Reservoir** [Los Angeles]. The valley was mentioned under various names by the Portolá and Anza expeditions. The present name comes from the *Mision San Fernando Rey de España,* founded September 8, 1797, and named in honor of Ferdinand III, King of Castile and Leon (1200–1252). Many other features named after the mission (peak, range, hills, pass) by the Pacific Railroad Survey received different names when the Geological Survey mapped the region in the 1890's. The city was laid out in 1874 on part of the lands in San Fernando Valley formerly owned by Eulogio de Celis.

San Francisco. The number of saints named Francis and especially the fame of Saint Francis of Assisi have made this name one of the most popular in Roman Catholic countries. Franciscan friars accompanied Portolá to

California, and in 1776 the Franciscans were entrusted with the spiritual work in both Californias. The name was used for the land grants San Francisco de las Llagas [Santa Clara], February 3, 1834, and San Francisco [Los Angeles and Ventura], January 22, 1839, and as an alternate name for several other grants. **San Francisco,** frăn-sĭs′-kō: **Bay,** city, **County.** The name San Francisco appears on Plancius' map of 1590, and is shown on his map of 1592 (Wagner, Pl. XX) for a cape in a location which, according to the distances to Cape Mendocino and to Cabo San Lucas, on the peninsula of Lower California, appears almost exactly in the latitude of present-day San Francisco. Although Wagner (p. 500) is doubtless right in assigning Plancius' *Cabo de San Francisco,* which is shown on some later maps, to the realm of imaginary geography, it is a remarkable coincidence that a Dutch cartographer in 1592 should attach this name to a spot on the map where centuries later it would actually occur as one of the greatest place names. On November 6, 1595, Rodríguez Cermeño entered the harbor now known as Drakes Bay, and the following day he named it *Bahia* or *Puerto de San Francisco* (Wagner, p. 499). The date is not close to any of the feast days of the several saints named Francis, but since the christening was performed by a member of the Franciscan Order it may be assumed that it was in honor of the saint of Assisi. Bolaños' *derrotero* (1603) records this *Puerto de San Francisco* (Wagner, p. 118) about one degree north of the actual latitude of present San Francisco Bay. Until 1769 the name remained a vague geographical conception, although, by another coincidence, Anson's map of 1748 shows the outline of the bay, the Farallones, the strait now known as the Golden Gate, the peninsula, and Point Reyes—all in fairly proper position (Wagner, Pl. XXX). British and other non-Spanish maps after 1625 usually label the uncertain bay with the name of Francis Drake in accordance with the English claim to this part of the coast. *See* New Albion. On October 31, 1769, a detachment of the Portolá expedition beheld from the hills near Pedro Point [San Mateo] the large body of water between them and Point Reyes (now known as the Gulf of the Farallones) and believed they had rediscovered the original *Bahia de San Francisco.* A few days later, when they saw the bay now called San Francisco, they called it merely an estuary (*estero*) of the port. Costansó's map of 1770

records both the *Puerto* (Drakes Bay) and the *Estero de San Francisco.* On Ayala's map of 1775 the name *Puerto de San Francisco* indicates San Francisco Bay. The presidio was dedicated and formally named•on the day of the Wounds of Saint Francis, September 17, 1776; *La Mision de Nuestro Serafico Padre San Francisco de Asis a la Laguna de los Dolores* (mission of our seraphic father Saint Francis of Assisi at the Lake of [Our Lady of] the Sorrows) was founded June 29, and dedicated on October 8 or 9, 1776. The pueblo at the presidio was established November 3, 1834, and the pueblo on Yerba Buena cove was founded by order of Governor Figueroa in 1835. William A. Richardson and Jacob P. Leese were the first settlers. This village became the most important of the three settlements, eventually absorbing the villages at the presidio and the mission. It was known as Yerba Buena; but when Bartlett, its chief magistrate, recorded the agreement to found the town of Francisca (*see* Benicia), he feared that the name of the new port at Carquinez Strait would be confusing and also detrimental to the interests of Yerba Buena and hence decided to establish the name as San Francisco. He published the following proclamation in the issues of January 23 and 30, 1847, of the *California Star:* "Whereas the local name of Yerba Buena as applied to the settlement or town of *San Francisco,* is unknown beyond the immediate district; and has been applied from the local name of the Cove on which the town is built—therefore to prevent confusion and mistakes in public documents, and that the town may have the advantage of the name given on the published maps, It is hereby ordered that the name of *San Francisco* shall hereafter be used in all official communications, or records appertaining to the town." Bartlett, however, had no authority to confirm the name, and it was not made official until March 10, 1847, when General Stephen W. Kearny, the military governor, decided for San Francisco. (Bowman.) The county, one of the original twenty-seven, was named February 18, 1850.

San Francisco Solano Mission. *See* Solano.

San Francisquito. The diminutive suffix *-ito,* or *-ita,* was frequently used in Spanish times to designate a geographic feature smaller than another one previously named. When applied to saints' names this way of naming one feature after another often results in ambiguous combinations and sometimes produces a comic effect. *Arroyo de San Francis-*

quito might properly be translated as 'Little San Francisco Creek'—but it is not the Holy Francis who is little, but the creek. The name San Francisquito is found as the principal or alternate name of eight land grants, and at least three such names have survived. **San Francisquito,** frăn-sĭs-kē'-tō: **Creek** [San Mateo, Santa Clara]. Palou camped on the bank of the creek near the site of Palo Alto on November 28, 1774, and selected the spot as a suitable place for a mission to be dedicated to Saint Francis of Assisi (*Diary,* pp. 411 f.). Anza's diary of March 26, 1776, mentions the *Arroyo de San Francisco* and adds that the spot had been found unsuitable for a mission because of lack of water there in the dry season. After the San Francisco mission (popularly called Mission Dolores) was established, the stream came to be known as *Arroyo de San Francisquito.* This name was given to three land grants: San Francisquito, May 1, 1839, on which Stanford University is now situated; Rinconada del Arroyo de San Francisquito, February 16, 1841; and Rincon de San Francisquito, March 29, 1841. The modern hybrid name for the stream is mentioned in the *Statutes* of 1850 (pp. 59 f.). **San Francisquito Flat, Sierra de San Francisquito** [Monterey]. Both places are on the San Francisquito land grant, dated November 7, 1835. The flat is probably *el llanito de San Francisquito,* mentioned as early as 1822 (Arch. MSB, III, 297). **San Francisquito Canyon** [Los Angeles]. The canyon is on the San Francisco land grant. It is more or less the collective name for the various gold discoveries in San Fernando Valley, six years before the discovery at Sutters Mill. Francisco Lopez discovered the gold deposits in March, 1842, and was for some time in partnership with a Frenchman, Charles Baric. Duflot de Mofras's map of 1844 records the *Mine d'or de Mr. Baric.* Rancho San Francisquito and San Francisquito Pass are shown on the Parke-Custer map of 1855 and are repeatedly mentioned in the Pacific Railroad *Reports.* The often-repeated story that the Franciscan mission padres mined gold here and in other canyons of the San Fernando Valley has never been verified.

San Gabriel, gā'-brĭ-ĕl: **Valley, Mission, River, Mountains, Peak,** city, **Dams; Gabriel Canyon** [Los Angeles]. The valley was discovered by the Portolá expedition and named *San Miguel Arcangel* on July 30, 1769 (Crespi, pp. 144 f.). The *Mision del Santo Arcangel San Gabriel de los Temblores* (Mission of the

Holy Archangel Saint Gabriel of the Earthquakes) was established and named September 8, 1771, and was moved to the present location in 1776. The word *temblores* was added to the name because earthquakes had been felt at this place by the Portolá expedition (Arch. MSB, I, 101; PSP, I, 118), or because the intended site for the mission had been on the *Rio de los Temblores,* now Santa Ana River (Palou, II, 323). The *Arroyo de San Gabriel* is mentioned by Font on January 4, 1776, but this was probably not the present San Gabriel River. However, on Pantoja's map of 1782 the name is already identified with that river. The stream is shown but not labeled on the Frémont-Preuss map of 1848. Williamson called the upper part Johnson's River "after the soldier who found it for us" (Pac. R.R. *Reports,* Vol. V, Pt. 1, p. 30). The mountain chain of which San Gabriel Mountains are an important part was vaguely called Sierra Madre by the missionaries, but a *Cierra* [*Sierra*] *de San Gabriel* is mentioned in August, 1806 (Arch. MSB, IV, 67), and later. Blake, 1853, mentions as local names *Qui-Quai-mungo* Range and San Gabriel Range (Pac. R.R. *Reports,* Vol. V, Pt. 2, p. 137). The Whitney Survey adopted the name San Gabriel Range, but the Geographic Board in 1927 decided for San Gabriel Mountains. San Gabriel post office was established July 26, 1854.

Sanger [Fresno]. The station was named for Joseph Sanger, Jr., an official of the Pacific Improvement Company, an affiliate of the Southern Pacific, when the branch from Fresno to Porterville was built in 1888.

Sanger Meadow [Inyo]. Named for the Sanger family, pioneers of Inyo and Kern counties, who ran horses here (Brierly).

San Geronimo, jĕ-rŏn'-ĭ-mō: **Creek,** town [Marin]. The name Cañada de San Geronimo was applied to a land grant, dated February 12, 1844. *Cañada* or *Arroyo de San Geronimo* is shown on the *diseños* and maps of the grant. It is not known whether the place was named for one of several Saint Jeromes or whether it was named for an Indian who had received the name Geronimo at his baptism. On Hoffmann's map of the Bay region, present Lagunitas Creek is called Arroyo San Geronimo, and present San Geronimo Creek is labeled Arroyo Nicasio. The name was applied to the station of the North Pacific Coast Railroad in 1875. The post office is listed in 1898. San Geronimo land grant [San Luis Obispo], dated July 24, 1842, does not seem to have left any traces in present-day place names.

San Gorgonio: Pass, River, Creek, Mountain [San Bernardino, Riverside]. *San Gorgonio* was a cattle ranch of Mission San Gabriel in 1824 (DSP, I, 27), named for Gorgonius, a third-century martyr, whose feast day is September 9 (Wagner, Saints' Names). The name appears in the land grant San Jacinto y San Gorgonio, dated March 22, 1843. *Arroyo* and *Valle de San Gorgonio* are shown on the *diseño*. The pass, now traversed by the Southern Pacific, is shown as Pass St. Gorgonie on Gibbes' map of 1852. The Pacific Railroad Survey gave this name to a peak and mountain, but these appear on modern maps as San Jacinto Peak and Mountains. The present-day San Gorgonio Mountain was formerly called Grayback. The town Beaumont [Riverside] was once named San Gorgonio, after the mountain. *See* Beaumont.

San Gregorio: Creek, Valley, post office, **Mountain** [San Mateo]. *Arroyo de San Gregorio* is shown on a *diseño* of the San Gregorio grant, dated April 16, 1839. The name honors the Benedictine saint, Gregory the Great, Prefect of Rome and Pope, whose feast day is March 12 (Wagner, Saints' Names). The post office was established in the 1870's. A place in Los Angeles County was called San Gregorio by Crespi on August 4, 1769, and Anza named a place in Borrego Valley [San Diego] San Gregorio on March 12, 1774, for Gregory the Great. These names did not survive.

Sanhedrin, Mount; Sanhedrin Creek [Mendocino]. The peak is given as Sanhidrim on the von Leicht–Craven map of 1874. A few years later the Coast Survey established a triangulation station there and used the present spelling. The region was first settled by Missourians; it is possible that they named the mountain after Mount Sanhedrin in their home state, which in turn may have been named after the supreme council of the Jews.

San Isidro [San Benito, Santa Clara]. The name of one of several Saint Isidores was given to a land grant conveyed to Ignacio Ortega in 1808 or 1809, and in 1833 regranted in three parts to his heirs. The name is shown on Narváez' Plano of 1830, and is often mentioned in mission and land-grant records, usually spelled San Ysidro.

Sanitarium [Napa]. In 1878 the Seventh-Day Adventists established the Saint Helena Sanitarium and called the place Crystal Springs. The community developed around the institution, and the name was soon changed by popular usage to Sanitarium. (E. L. Place.)

San Jacinto, já-sĭn'-tō, há-sĭn'-tō: **River, Valley, Peak, Mountains,** town, **Lake, Indian Reservation** [Riverside]. *San Jacinto* [*Viejo*] was a cattle ranch of Mission San Luis Rey as early as 1821, and was called by the natives *Jaguara* (Arch. MSB, IV, 223). Between 1842 and 1846 the name of the saint appears in the names of four different land grants. The name honors the Silesian-born Dominican, Hyacinth, whose feast day is August 16. The mountain is mentioned in *Hutchings' Illustrated California Magazine* of February, 1859. The modern town developed around the store built in 1872 by a Russian exile, Procco Akimo (Santa Fe); the post office, however, had already been in existence since July 27, 1870.

San Joaquin, wä-kēn'. Saint Joachim, honored by Roman Catholics as the father of the Virgin Mary, was often commemorated in place names, and his name has survived in one of the most important geographical names of the State and in the names of several lesser features. **San Joaquin: River, County, Valley, Bridge;** post office [Fresno]. Crespi saw the river on March 30, 1772, when with Fages he was attempting to reach Point Reyes, and he named it *San Francisco* for Saint Francis of Assisi. Gabriel Moraga gave the name San Joaquin to the river when he reached its southern part in 1805 or 1806, according to Padre Muñoz' diary (Arch. MSB, IV, 1 ff.). Saint Joachim's feast day is March 20. Before and after Moraga's visit, various sections of the river had different names. However, in the records after 1810 San Joaquin is mentioned as if it was a well-known name. The name appears for the upper course of the river on Estudillo's map of 1819, and three main channels of the lower course are shown with this name on the Plano topografico de la Mision de San Jose (about 1824). The accounts of Kotzebue, Beechey, and Wilkes allow no doubt about the river's identity. On Narváez' Plano of 1830, to be sure, the San Joaquin Valley is shown covered by an enormous swamp, *Cienegas ó Tulares*. The maps of Wilkes (1841) and Frémont-Preuss (1845) definitely identify the name with the major part of the river. The former has San Joachim, but Frémont uses the Spanish version. The county is one of the original twenty-seven, created and named February 18, 1850. A San Joaquin City existed in 1850 (S.F. *Alta California*, Feb. 7, 1850) but soon vanished. The name San Joaquin Valley seems to have come into general use at the time of the Pacific Railroad Survey, 1853–1854. The bridge across the river was built by the Central Pacific in 1869, and the station was named San Joaquin Bridge (Mary Seamonds). A post office in San Joaquin County is listed as San Joaquin in the 1880's; the post office in Fresno County was established in 1915. **San Joaquin Peak** [San Benito]. The peak was so named because it is on the San Joaquin or Rosa Morada grant, dated April 1, 1836. **San Joaquin Hills** [Orange]. The hills were so named because they are on the Bolsa de San Joaquin grant, dated May 13, 1842. **Castillo de San Joaquin** [San Francisco]. Historic Landmark 82 preserves the name of the old Spanish fort which stood at the site of Fort Winfield Scott. **San Joaquin** [Contra Costa]. The name was given by W. H. Davis to his mother-in-law's ranch (part of Rancho Pinole). To the middle name of his father-in-law, José Joaquín Estudillo, Davis "added San . . . then it became the name of a Saint." (W. H. Davis, p. 531.)

Sanjon. *See* Zanja.

San Jose. Of all saints' names, that of San José, Saint Joseph, husband of the Virgin Mary, is probably the most popular for place names in Spanish-speaking countries. In California, from the beginnings of colonization, the name has been intimately connected with geographical nomenclature. José de Gálvez, *visitador* of all New Spain, in a solemn proclamation of November 21, 1768, named Saint Joseph the patron saint of the first expedition to settle Alta California, and the new ship built at San Blas which was to bring part of the Portolá expedition to Monterey was named in his honor. The vessel was disabled and after being repaired was lost at sea—an ill omen, which did not deter the Spaniards from their venture. The name appears as the principal or alternate name for about fifteen land grants and claims and has survived for more than ten geographic features. **San Jose,** săn ô-zā' [Santa Clara]. A village was founded by José Joaquín Moraga on November 29, 1777, under instructions from Governor Felipe de Neve, who named it *Pueblo de San Jose de Guadalupe*, for Saint Joseph and for the river on which the town was situated. It was the first Spanish pueblo in what is now the State of California; thus the modern city has the distinction of being the oldest civic municipality of the State. In 1849 it became the State of California's first capital when the legislature convened there on December 15. On older maps *Rio de San Jose* is found

for Guadalupe River, *Port San Jose* for Alviso, *Estrecho de San Jose* for the southern arm of the Bay. The mission named San Jose [Alameda] was established on June 11, 1797, at a place known as *San Francisco Solano,* at some distance from the pueblo in accordance with Spanish methods of colonization. *See* Mission San Jose. **San Jose Valley** [San Diego]. The valley, now partly covered by the Henshaw Reservoir, was named San Josef (or San Jose) by the priests of San Diego Mission in 1795 or before (Arch. MSB, IV, 200 ff.); in 1821 it appears as *el Valle de San Jose o Guadalupe (ibid.,* 209 ff.). The name is recorded for two land grants called Valle de San Jose, dated April 16, 1836, and November 27, 1844. The grantee of the latter was Juan J. Warner, who developed his famous ranch on this grant. **San Jose: Creek, Hills, Peak, Wash** [Los Angeles]. These features were so named because they are partly on the territory of the San Jose grant, dated April 15, 1837, and March 14, 1840. **Arroyo San Jose** [Marin]. The name of the creek, mentioned in 1828 (Registro, p. 147), was preserved through the San Jose grant, dated March 24, 1838, and October 3, 1840. **San Jose Creek** [Monterey]. The name of the stream east of Point Carmel is on the territory of the San Jose y Sur Chiquito grant, dated April 16, 1839.

San Juan. Besides the important place names derived from the missions San Juan Bautista and San Juan Capistrano, the name was used in several land grants and has survived in a number of geographical names. Wagner (Saints' Names) lists six Saint Johns honored in California nomenclature.

San Juan Bautista, wän bô-tēs'-tá: **Mission,** post office; **San Juan: Creek,** town [San Benito]. The mission was founded and named in honor of Saint John the Baptist, by Padre Lasuén, on June 24, 1797, the feast day of the saint. The present San Benito Valley was called *Llano de San Juan* by Beechey in 1826 (II, 49); it appears as San Juan Valley on Wilkes' map of 1849 and is so called by Trask in his *Report,* 1854 (p. 67). In the 1850's the Gabilan Range was called San Juan Range. The post office was established under the name San Juan in 1852; this name was changed to the present form about 1905. The name *Rio de San Juan Baptista* is given to the San Joaquin on Ayala's map of 1775. On March 30, 1844, the name San Juan Bautista was applied to a land grant in Santa Clara County.

San Juan Capistrano, wän käp-ĭ-strä′-nō: **Mission,** post office; **San Juan: Creek, Canyon, Rock, Hot Springs, Seamount** [Orange]. The name San Juan Capistrano was first given by Crespi, on July 18, 1769, to the valley in San Diego County now known as San Luis Rey Valley. In 1775 Viceroy Bucareli gave instructions to name the next mission in honor of the fighting priest, Saint John Capistrano (1385–1456), who took a heroic part in the first defense of Vienna against the Turks. The site of the mission was first dedicated October 30, 1775, but because of the Indian revolt at San Diego in November, 1775, the mission was not formally founded until November 1, 1776. Serra bestowed upon the new mission the name *San Juan Capistrano de Quanis-savit,* the last name doubtless referring to the Indian rancheria at the site. (Palou, *Vida . . . Serra,* pp. 174 f.; Engelhardt.) On early American maps the name is usually shortened to San Juan, and on a military map of 1847 it is San Campistrano (!). Bancroft (1858) and Goddard (1860) record the name San Juan Capistrano. The short form Capistrano was used for the post office from the time it was established, June 5, 1867, until October 23, 1905, when Zoeth Eldredge prevailed upon the Post Office Department to restore the original name. *See* Capistrano. Point San Juan appears on Duflot de Mofras's map of 1844. Von Leicht–Craven, 1874, give Point Capistrano, and the Coast Survey, Dana Point. Although the name Dana Point should be considered official, the Geological Survey and the Corps of Engineers call the cape San Juan Capistrano Point. Dana Cove was known in Spanish times as *Bahia de San Juan Capistrano.* The creek is shown as San Juan River on the Coast Survey charts of the 1880's. The name San Juan Capistrano was apparently applied to the San Joaquin River at some time, and Wilkes' map of 1841 still has a *R. St. Juan* for a tributary to the San Joaquin. A land grant, San Juan Capistrano del Camote [San Luis Obispo], is dated July 11, 1846.

San Juan Hill [Nevada]. *See* North San Juan.

San Julian [Santa Barbara]. The name of one of a number of Saint Julians was applied to a rancho in the jurisdiction of the presidio of Santa Barbara before 1827 (Docs. Hist. Cal., IV, 811 ff.). It is shown on Narváez' Plano of 1830, and was made a land grant April 7, 1837.

San Justo [San Benito]. It is uncertain which

Saint Justin or Justus was honored in the names of two land grants, dated February 18, 1836 (not confirmed), and April 15, 1839. In modern times the name is preserved only in the name of a school. *See* Hollister.

Sankey [Sutter]. The station of the Sacramento Northern was probably named for Calvin Sankey, a native of Missouri, who was a farmer in the Vernon district in 1866.

San Leandro, lē-ăn′-drō: **Creek, city, Bay, Hills, Reservoir** [Alameda]. *Arroyo de San Leandro* is mentioned in 1828 (Registro, p. 6) and *Rio San Leandro* is shown on Narváez' Plano of 1830. The saint honored was probably Saint Leander, Archbishop of Seville, "Apostle of the Goths" in the sixth century. A land grant, San Leandro, is dated August 16, 1839, and October 16, 1842; the name also appears in the titles of several other grants. The settlement of the grantee, José J. Estudillo, is shown north of the creek on Duflot de Mofras's map of 1844. The town south of the creek was laid out in 1855; the post office, however, had already been established, May 3, 1853.

San Lorenzo River [Santa Cruz]. The river was named by the Portolá expedition on October 17, 1769 (Crespi, p. 215). The saint honored was probably Saint Laurence, whose feast day is August 10. The name appears in the title of a grant, Cañada del Rincon [canyon of the corner] en el Rio San Lorenzo (July 10, 1843), and the Americanized version is mentioned by Trask (1854, p. 8). **San Lorenzo: Creek, town, Village** [Alameda]. The creek was named *Arroyo de San Salvador de Horta* by Crespi on March 25, 1772 (p. 287). "It is known also as the Arroyo de la Harina, for so the soldiers called it during the journey of Señor Fages, because in it a load of flour [*harina*] got wet . . ." (Font, *Compl. Diary,* p. 355). The name San Lorenzo was applied to two land grants dated February 23, 1841, and October 10, 1842. The name, however, had been used much earlier. Joaquín Castro testified on February 18, 1854, in the San Lorenzo (1842) land-grant case (300 ND): "In 1812, it was then called by the same name." *Rancho de San Lorenzo* is also shown on the Plano topografico de la Mision de San Jose (about 1824). The creek forms part of the boundary of the two grants, but it is not known whether the creek or one of the ranchos was named first. The town was laid out in 1854 by Guillermo Castro, grantee of the 1841 rancho. *See* Castro Valley. The town is mentioned in the *Statutes* of 1854 (p. 223).

San Lorenzo Creek [Monterey]. A *sitio de San Lorenzo* is mentioned on July 20, 1823 (SP Sac., X, 13), and *Arroyo de San Lorenzo* is shown on a *diseño* of San Bernabe (1841). The name was applied to three grants, dated August 9, 1841, November 16, 1842, February 18, 1846.

San Lucas [Monterey]. The Spanish name of Saint Luke the Evangelist was applied to the land grant, dated May 9, 1842. When the Southern Pacific built the section from King City to Paso Robles in the fall of 1886 the station was named after the grant, although it is outside of its boundaries. The post office is listed in 1892. Saint Luke's name was used for other place names in Spanish times. Crespi's *Arroyo de San Lucas* for Coja Creek in Santa Cruz County (p. 216) did not survive, but there is a San Lucas Creek, a tributary of Santa Ynez River, in Santa Barbara County.

San Luis, lŏŏ'ĭs: **Creek, Hill** [Merced]. A place, discovered by an expedition sent out from the presidio of San Francisco probably in 1805, was named *San Luis Gonzaga,* because it was discovered on June 21, the day of Saint Aloysius Gonzaga, an Italian Jesuit of the 16th century. Padre Muñoz mentions the place on September 22, 1806, and Padre Viader on August 24, 1810. On October 3, 1843, the name San Luis Gonzaga was applied to a land grant.

San Luisito, lŏŏ-ĭ-sē'-tō: **Creek** [San Luis Obispo]. The creek was named after the San Luisito grant, dated August 6, 1841. There is no "little Saint Louis"; the name is simply a diminutive of near-by San Luis Obispo. *See* San Francisquito.

San Luis Obispo, lŏŏ'-ĭs ō-bĭs'-pō: **Mission, Bay,** city, **County, Creek, Peak; San Luis: Canyon, Hills, Range; Port San Luis.** The mission was founded by Serra on September 1, 1772, and named in honor of Saint Louis, Bishop of Toulouse, son of the King of Naples and Sicily (13th century). The Indian name of the site was *Tixlini,* and in early records the names *de Tixlimi* and *de los Tichos* are found attached to the name of the mission (Arch. MSB, I, 125; Docs. Hist. Cal., IV, 12). The bay (*ensenada*) is recorded as San Luis on Narváez' Plano of 1830. Potrero de San Luis Obispo is the name of a grant, dated November 8, 1842. The county, one of the original twenty-seven, was established and named on February 18, 1850. The town was laid out and named by William R. Hutton in August, 1850; the post office is listed in 1851. Port San Luis, the city's harbor, was formerly called Port Harford for John Harford, who had built a wharf in 1872–1873.

San Luis Rey, lŏŏ'-ĭs rā': **Mission, River,** post office [San Diego]. The valley through which the river flows was named *San Juan Capistrano* by the Portolá expedition on July 18, 1769, and was intended as the site of a mission (Crespi, p. 131). In October, 1797, the site was again recommended and chosen but was referred to as *San Juan Capistrano el Viejo* (Old Capistrano) because in the meantime the name had been used for a mission elsewhere (Engelhardt, II, 496). Padre Lasuén founded the new mission on June 13, 1798 (Prov. Recs., V, 277), and, upon the request of the viceroy, named it in honor of Saint Louis, King of France. The site had been called *Jacayme* by the natives (Prov. Recs., VI, 98). *Boca del rio* [mouth of the river] *San Luis* is shown on a *diseño* (1845) of Santa Margarita y Las Flores grant. The post office was established before 1867.

San Marcos. Saint Mark the Evangelist was often honored in place names in Spanish times. Tehachapi Range and the south. end of the Sierra Nevada had been named *Sierra de San Marcos* by Garcés in 1776 (Coues, *Trail,* pp. 270 f.). The name is shown on Font's map of 1777 (Davidson copy), and on Humboldt's map (1811) it designates the central part of the Sierra Nevada. **San Marcos: Valley, Creek, Mountains,** town [San Diego]. *El Valle San Marcos* is mentioned in a letter in 1797. In 1835 San Marcos was the name of one of the ranchos of Mission San Luis Rey (SP Mis., VI, 10 f.). The name appears in the land grant Los Vallecitos [little valleys] de San Marcos, dated April 22, 1840; the *vallecitos* are shown on a *diseño.* The patent of the grant was not issued until 1883; the town developed after the "boom year," 1887, around the Santa Fe station (Santa Fe). **San Marcos Pass** [Santa Barbara]. *San Marcos* is mentioned as a rancho of Mission Santa Barbara in 1817 (PSP, XX, 178). The place is shown on Narváez' Plano of 1830. On June 8, 1846, the name was given to the land grant. San Marcus Pass across Santa Ynez Mountains is mentioned by John G. Parke in 1855 (Pac. R.R. *Reports,* Vol. VII, Pt. 1, p. 2). **San Marcos Creek** [San Luis Obispo] is mentioned as *El arroyo de San Marcos* as early as 1795 (Arch. MSB, II, 18 ff.).

San Marino, mȧ-rē'-nō [Los Angeles]. In 1878, James de Barth Shorb built a home on the land which he and his wife had received from his father-in-law, "Don Benito" Wilson.

He named the estate San Marino, after his birthplace in Emmitsburg, Maryland, which in turn had probably been named after the tiny European republic. In 1903 Henry E. Huntington bought the property and retained the name for his estate, the site of the Huntington Library and Art Gallery. (Edith Shorb Steele.)

San Martin, mär-tēn′ [Santa Clara]. Martin Murphy, a native of Ireland, and his large family came to California in 1844 and settled on the San Francisco de las Llagas grant, which was later patented to James Murphy, one of the sons. As a devout Roman Catholic, Martin Murphy followed the Spanish custom and named his settlement in honor of his patron saint.

San Martin, Cape [Monterey]. "This point [Punta Gorda] is the *Cape San Martin* of Cabrillo. He placed it in latitude 37° 30′ N.; but applying the correction obtained from his erroneous determination of San Diego, we obtain 35° 50′ N. as the position of San Martin, which is very nearly its proper latitude. As there is one point under Cape Mendocino, more generally known as Punta Gorda, it is recommended that this point retain the name given to it by Cabrillo, especially as all his names have been cast aside." (Davidson, in Coast Survey *Report*, 1862, p. 294.)

San Mateo. The name of the evangelist and apostle, Saint Matthew, was repeatedly used in Spanish times and has survived in two large cluster names. **San Mateo,** må-tä′-ō: **Creek, Point,** city, **County, Slough, Bridge.** *Arroyo de San Matheo* is mentioned in the diaries of Anza and Font on March 26, 1776, and in the vicinity of the creek, in the 1790's, Mission Dolores had a sheep ranch called *San Mateo,* which developed into an unofficial "Mission" San Mateo (*CHSQ,* XXIII, 247 ff.). *Esteros de San Mateo* and *Punta de San Mateo* are mentioned by Argüello in 1810 (PSP, XIX, 280). The name appears in a petition for a land grant, December 22, 1836, and on May 5 or 6, 1846, it was applied to another grant. Arroyo, point, and settlement are shown on most maps, and until 1850 their names are usually spelled San Matheo. The county, carved out of San Francisco County, was created and named on April 19, 1856. The modern city was laid out by C. B. Polhemus in 1863 when the San Francisco–San Jose Railroad was built; the first train reached the station on October 18, 1863. **San Mateo: Canyon, Creek, Point, Rocks** [San

Diego]. *Arroyo de San Mateo* and a place, probably a rancheria, are mentioned in March, 1778 (PSP, II, 1). A petition for a land grant, San Mateo, was filed in 1839, but no grant is recorded. A Rancho San Mateo existed in 1828 (Registro, p. 41); it is shown on Duflot de Mofras's map of 1844. The creek is shown as *Rio San Mateo* on a *diseño* of 1845, and San Mateo Creek is mentioned in the *Statutes* of 1850 (pp. 58 f.).

San Miguel. The Spanish form of the name Saint Michael was a favorite in Spanish California nomenclature. Among places which once bore the name are San Diego Bay, San Gabriel Valley, San Joaquin River, and a stream of the Kaweah River system. All the San Miguel names still in existence were probably bestowed, according to Wagner (Saints' Names), in honor of the archangel. **San Miguel: Island, Passage** [Santa Barbara]. Juan Rodríguez Cabrillo discovered this island and Santa Rosa Island probably on October 18, 1542, and named them *Islas de San Lucas.* He renamed one island *Posesion* after having taken possession of it, and this was afterward named by Ferrer, in his memory, *Juan Rodriguez.* The island appears on the maps of the following centuries with various names until about 1790, when the name San Miguel became attached to it, a name which Miguel Costansó had in 1770 applied to what is now Santa Rosa Island. (Wagner, p. 411.) This new alignment of the Channel Islands became fixed when Vancouver used it for his maps, although until Wilkes in 1841 adopted Vancouver's alignment, older names persisted: Juan Rodriguez (Bonnycastle, Tanner); San Bernardo (Humboldt, Narváez). **San Miguel: Mission, Canyon,** town [San Luis Obispo]. The mission was founded and named San Miguel Arcangel on July 25, 1797. When the Southern Pacific reached the place in the fall of 1886 the name of the mission was applied to the station. The post office is listed in 1887. **San Miguel Canyon** [Monterey]. San Miguel was an alternate name of the Bolsa de los Escarpines grant, dated October 7, 1837; *Cañada de San Miguel* is shown on a *diseño* of the grant. **San Miguel Hills** [San Francisco]. The elevation, now generally known as Mount Davidson, is still labeled San Miguel Hills on maps because it is on the San Miguel land grant, dated December 23, 1845. The San Miguel grants in Sonoma (November 2, 1840) and Ventura (July 6, 1841) counties have apparently left no trace in modern nomenclature, but in San Diego County there is a San Miguel Mountain, which is shown as *Sierra de San Miguel* on a *diseño* of Rancho de la Nacion, 1843.

San Miguelito. The name was applied to three land grants dated April 8, 1839 [San Luis Obispo], September 25, 1839 [Monterey], and May 30, 1845 [Ventura]. There is no "little Saint Michael"; San Miguelito is a diminutive of the place name San Miguel. A place *San Miguelito* in San Luis Obispo County is shown on Narváez' 1830 Plano. (*See* San Francisquito; Santa Anita.) The name is preserved in modern geography in San Miguelito Creek, an intermittent stream in Santa Barbara County.

San Nicolas Island [Ventura]. The island was evidently given this name by the crew of Vizcaíno's launch *Tres Reyes* on December 6, 1602, the feast day of Saint Nicholas of Myra, the patron of sailors, travelers, and merchants (Wagner, p. 412). It is also known as Passing Island because the sand is gradually being blown away and the island will eventually be reclaimed by the sea (Doyle).

San Onofre, ô-nō'-frè: **Creek, Canyon, Mountain, Hill, Bluff,** post office [San Diego]. The name of the remarkable Egyptian saint, Saint Onuphrius, is mentioned as the name of a rancho of San Juan Capistrano Mission in 1828 (Registro, p. 41). It appears in the name of the Santa Margarita y San Onofre grant, dated February 23, 1836, and May 10, 1841, but does not appear on early American maps or on the charts of the Coast Survey. It was given to the station when the Santa Fe built the coast line from Los Angeles to Oceanside in the late 1880's. *See* Flores; Santa Margarita. **Canada San Onofre** [Santa Barbara]. The valley, shown as Cañada de San Onofre on the Lompoc atlas sheet, is probably the San Onofre mentioned in 1795 (PSP, XIV, 62) and was doubtless named for the same saint.

San Pablo, păb'-lō: **Point, Strait, Bay, Creek,** town, **Reservoir** [Contra Costa]. The names San Pedro and San Pablo (Peter and Paul) for the points on opposite shores of San Pablo Strait originated probably at the same time. They are mentioned in Abella's diary in October, 1811, and *Punta de San Pablo* is recorded by Durán on May 13, 1817. The name San Pablo was used for a land grant, dated April 15, and April 23, 1823. On the Plano topografico de la Mision de San Jose (about 1824) the narrows are called *Estrecho de San Pablo,* and Rancho San Pablo is

shown. The name of the bay itself had been called *Bahia Redonda* by Crespi in 1772, and by Cañizares in 1776; on the Plano topographico it is called *Bahia de Sonoma.* The two points are mentioned by Beechey (1831, II, 425) ; on Duflot de Mofras's *Plan* 16 the name San Pablo appears also for the bay. The town San Pablo is shown on Butler's map of 1851; the post office was established November 15, 1854.

San Pascual [Los Angeles]. Rancho San Pascual is mentioned December 27, 1833 (Arch. LA, IV, 74). The land, which had belonged to Mission San Gabriel, became public property with secularization of the mission; one part was made into a land grant dated July 27, 1838, and another, September 24, 1840, and July 10, 1843. This grant and the places called San Pasqual in San Diego County were probably both named for Saint Paschal, a Franciscan of the 16th century. After the American occupation the spelling San Pasqual was ordinarily used in official reports and in land-grant records. **San Pasqual,** păs-kwôl': town, **Valley** [San Diego]. The name was evidently applied to an Indian village under the jurisdiction of San Diego Mission. It appears as S. Pascual on Bancroft's map of the San Diego district 1800–1830 (II, 105), and was applied in 1835 to the pueblo composed of former neophytes of Mission San Luis Rey (San Diego Public Library). The present spelling was used in army reports after the "battle of San Pasqual" had been fought between Kearny's and Andrés Pico's forces on December 6, 1846.

San Pedro. The Spanish form of the name Saint Peter was very popular for place names in Spanish times. It was given to five land grants, and about twelve geographic features still bear it. Not all the names honor the apostle; some honor other saints named Peter. **San Pedro,** pĕ'-drō: **Bay, Channel, Hill, Hills,** post office [Los Angeles]. The bay had been named *Bahia de los rumos* or *Fuegos* by Cabrillo on October 8, 1542, because smokes from numerous fires were visible. According to Wagner (p. 412), the name San Pedro was applied to the bay by one of Vizcaíno's men, probably because it was sighted on November 26, 1602, the feast day of the Saint Peter who was martyred in Constantinople. It appears in the Bolaños-Ascensión *derrotero* and on the maps based upon Vizcaíno's discoveries. *Bahia de San Pedro* is mentioned in Vila's diary on April 26, 1769 (APCH:*P,* II, 86), and repeatedly in the reports of the Anza expedition. Later, the name San Pedro was applied to one of the land grants bordering the bay on the north, granted before November 20, 1784, to Juan José Domínguez, and regranted at various times to other members of the Domínguez family. Narváez' Plano of 1830 shows an *Ensenada* and a *Punta* San Pedro. On Duflot de Mofras's map (1844) San Pedro is shown with an anchorage; Los Angeles River and Long Point are also labeled *San Pedro*. The town of San Pedro is mentioned in the *Statutes* of 1854 (p. 223); the post office is listed in 1858. **San Pedro Point** [Marin]. Abella mentions an Indian rancheria *San Pedro* in the region on February 28, 1807 (Arch. Arz. SF, II, 54 f.), and *Punta de San Pedro* in 1811 (Arch. MSB, IV, 321). San Pedro is shown near the point on the Plano topografico de la Mision de San Jose, about 1824. The name is also found in the name of the land grant San Pedro, Santa Margarita y las Gallinas, dated November 18, 1840, and February 12, 1844. Beechey mentions *Puntas* San Pablo and San Pedro (1831, II, 425), and these are shown on Duflot de Mofras's *Plan* 16, and on sketch J (1850) of the Coast Survey. Point San Pedro is now generally called McNears Point. *See* McNears Point; San Pablo. **San Pedro** [San Mateo]. *See* Pedro.

San Quentin, Point; San Quentin [Marin]. The name was not given in honor of the Roman officer who resigned his commission to become a Christian missionary but for his namesake, an Indian named Quintin, a notorious thief, according to Bancroft; a subchief and daring warrior, according to Vallejo. The point was called *Punta de Quintin* because the chief or (and) thief was captured there (1824). September 24, 1840, the name was applied to a land grant. *Punta Quintin* is shown on the *diseños* of the Corte de Madera del Presidio grant (1834) and of the Punta de Quintin grant (1840). In the meantime a point on the bay shore of San Francisco, just north of Potrero Point, had been named for the saint (Forbes' map of 1839). When the Coast Survey charted the bay in 1850 it Americanized both points to Quentin and added a "San" to the point in Marin County. For many years both names were on the maps until the old Mission Bay was filled in and the confusion ended.

San Rafael. The archangel Saint Raphael, the guardian angel of humanity, was frequently honored in place names, and a number of these have survived in Los Angeles, Marin,

Santa Barbara, and Ventura counties. **San Rafael,** rȧ-fĕl': **Hills** [Los Angeles]. The hills are on the territory of the Rancho San Rafael, one of the oldest land grants in California, dated October 20, 1784, and January 12, 1798. The grant, conveyed to José María Verdugo, was known as Hahaonuput, or Arroyo Hondo, or Zanja, and later as San Rafael. It is one of two known grants made to soldiers marrying Indian girls, in accordance with a decree of August 12, 1768. (Bowman Index.) **San Rafael,** rȧ-fĕl': **Mission, Bay,** city, **Creek, Rock** [Marin]. The mission was founded as an *asistencia* of Mission Dolores on December 14, 1817, at a site called by the Indians *Nanaguanui* (Engelhardt, *Franciscans,* p. 440), and was named San Rafael Arcangel. The city had its beginnings when Timoteo Murphy was granted a lot near the mission and built a house on it sometime before 1841. Both the mission and Murphy's residence are shown on Duflot de Mofras's *Plan* 16. The post office was established on November 6, 1851. **San Rafael,** rȧ-fĕl': **Mountains** [Santa Barbara]. The range is shown as *Sierra de San Rafael* on a *diseño* of the San Marcos grant, 1846. The American version is mentioned in the Pacific Railroad *Reports* (Vol. VII, Pt. 1, p. 6).

San Ramon, rȧ-mōn': **Valley, Creek,** town [Contra Costa]. The name is used for several land grants, the oldest dated June 5, 1833. This name did not originally honor a saint. The "San" was simply added to make the whole name conform to the usual name of this type. José María Amador testified in 1855 in the San Ramon land grant case that "The name was given it [the creek] by a *mayor domo* [of Mission San Jose] by the name of Ramon who had the care of some sheep there a long time ago. It was also called Arroyo del Injerto from the fact that there is a singular tree growing there, which is an oak with a willow ingrafted on it." (*WF,* VI, 373.) The town came into existence in the 1850's and is shown on Goddard's maps. The post office is listed in 1859. The early Bancroft maps designate Pacheco Creek as San Ramon Creek. On Hoffmann's map of the Bay region the name is applied to the present creek. Crespi, on August 31, 1769, had honored Saint Raymond Nonnatus by calling a lake or lagoon *San Ramon Nonato,* but the soldiers' name, La Graciosa, prevailed. *See* Graciosa.

San Roque, rō'-kĕ: **Canyon, Creek** [Santa Barbara]. The names are derived from a *paraje*

llamado [place called] *San Roque,* one and a half leagues from Mission Santa Barbara, mentioned June 22, 1824 (DSP, I, 49). The name of Saint Roque, a French Carmelite of the 14th century, was repeatedly used for place names. The rancheria at the site of Carpinteria was called *San Roque* by Crespi, August 17, 1769; the lower course of the Sacramento is called *Rio de San Roque* on Cañizares' map of 1776.

San Sevaine Flats [San Bernardino]. The place in the wilderness area above Etiwanda was named for the well-known French pioneer of 1839, Pierre ("Don Pedro") Sainsevain, obviously spelled the way his Spanish neighbors pronounced the name. In the 1870's Sainsevain had a well dug here to irrigate his vineyard in Cucamonga (Buie) . *See* Don Pedro Reservoir.

San Simeon, sĭm'-ê-ŏn: **Bay, Creek, Point,** town [San Luis Obispo]. A *rancho de San Simeon,* belonging to Mission San Miguel, is mentioned on January 31, 1819; on November 26, 1827, it is recorded that the mission kept cattle and horses there (Engelhardt, *San Miguel,* p. 28). The name honors Saint Simeon, whose feast day is February 18 (Wagner, Saints' Names). *Arroyo de San Simeon* is shown on a *diseño* of the Santa Rosa grant, 1841. The rancho was made a private land grant, dated October 1, 1842; the settlement and anchorage appear on Duflot de Mofras's map of 1844. The name of the bay is shown on the Coast Survey charts since 1852. The post office was established three times, 1864, 1867, 1873, and each time it was soon discontinued. In 1874 or 1875 Leopold Frankl, an Austrian emigrant of 1849, opened the first store here and became the postmaster of the definitive post office, established August 9, 1878. When Senator George Hearst began to develop his vast estate here, Frankl sold most of his land to him. The Hearst Castle became a state park after the heirs of William Randolph Hearst donated it to the state.

Santa Ana. The name of Saint Anne was repeatedly used in Spanish times for place names; probably all honor the mother of the Virgin Mary. These names have survived in various sections of the State. **Santa Ana,** ăn'-à: **River** [San Bernardino, Riverside, Orange], **Mountains, city** [Orange]. The Portolá expedition camped on the stream on July 28, 1769, and the padres bestowed on it *el dulcisimo nombre de Jesús de los Temblores* (the most sweet name of Jesus of the Earthquakes) "on ac-

count of the earthquakes that we felt when on it" (Crespi, pp. 32, 142). To the soldiers the stream was known as Santa Ana (*ibid.,* p. 142), and thereafter *Rio de Santa Ana* is mentioned repeatedly in the early records. Saint Anne's feast day is July 26. This seems to be the only time that the soldiers of the expedition applied a holy name to a place. *Rio de Santa Ana* is shown on Narváez' Plano (1830). Five land grants in Orange, Riverside, and San Bernardino counties were named after the river. The mountain chain along the Orange-Riverside line, southwest of Corona, is recorded as *Sierra de Santa Ana* on the Parke-Custer (1855) and von Leicht–Craven (1874) maps, and as Santa Ana Mountains on the Land Office map of 1879. A settlement Santa Anna is mentioned by Emory in 1846–1847 (p. 118) and is shown on Butler's (1851) and Bancroft's (1858) maps, but the modern city at the present site on the Rancho Santiago de Santa Ana was not founded and named until 1869 (Stephenson). **Santa Ana: Creek, Valley, Peak** [San Benito]. The name may go back to the Portolá expedition when Crespi, on October 8, 1769, added the name of *La Señora Santa Ana* to the name of *Rio del Pajaro* (Crespi, p. 211). Santa Ana Creek is connected with Pajaro River through Tequesquite Slough. April 16, 1836, the name was used in the Santa Ana y Santa Anita grant, unconfirmed by the United States, and April 8, 1839, in the Santa Ana y Quien Sabe grant. The creek, valley, and peak are on this grant. Two mountains are called *Picacho de Santa Ana* on a *diseño* of the grant. The present Santa Ana Peak is mentioned in Hoffmann's notes of July 10, 1861, and it is still commonly so known, although it is labeled Santa Ana Mountain on the Hollister atlas sheet. A pass north of Pacheco Pass is called Pass of Santa Aña on Derby's map (1850). **Santa Ana: Creek, Valley** [Ventura]. The names were preserved through the Santa Ana land grant, dated April 14, 1837.

Santa Anita, ă-nē'-tà: **Canyon, Creek, station, Park** [Los Angeles]. The places are on the Santa Anita land grant, dated April 16, 1841, and March 31, 1845, which was developed in the 1880's by "Lucky" Baldwin into one of the spectacular ranchos of southern California. The name is found in the titles of five other land grants or claims. There is no "Saint Annie"; the name Santa Anita is simply a diminutive of the place name Santa Ana. According to the Forest Service, the canyon was not named after the land grant but for Baldwin's daughter Anita. Place names formed by the addition of "San" or "Santa" to a personal name are not unusual. *See* San Quentin, San Ramon.

Santa Barbara: Channel, Island, Mission, Harbor, County, city, Point, Canyon. The name *Canal de Santa Barbara* was applied to the passage between the mainland and what are now the Channel Islands by Vizcaíno on December 4, 1602, the feast day of the Roman maiden who was beheaded by her father because she had become a Christian. Vizcaíno also named an island for Saint Barbara, probably the easternmost of the Anacapa Islands, although Palacios' chart (Wagner, No. 236) shows it almost in the same relative position as the present Santa Barbara Island, which belongs to Los Angeles County. The name *Canal de St. Barbaria* is shown on a Briggs type map of 1625 (Wagner, Pl. XXIII). The Presidio de Santa Barbara, Virgen y Martir, was established April 21, 1782, on the land called *Yamnonalit* by the Indians (Engelhardt, II, 369) and *San Joaquin de la Laguna* by the Spaniards (Prov. Recs., II, 61). On December 4, 1786, Saint Barbara's day, a great cross was raised at a spot called *Pedregoso* (stony), which had been selected as the site for the mission (Arch. MSB, V, 3), and the mission was formally declared founded on the sixteenth (*ibid.*, II, 434). The county, one of the original twenty-seven, was named February 18, 1850; the city was incorporated April 9, 1850. What are now the Channel Islands were named Santa Barbara Islands by the Coast Survey; the mountains opposite the town are called Santa Barbara Mountains in the Pacific Railroad *Reports* (Vol. VII, Pt. 1, p. 7). *See* Los Padres National Forest.

Santa Catalina, kăt-*ȧ*-lē'-nȧ: Island; Gulf of Santa Catalina; Catalina: Harbor, Head. Cabrillo named the island *San Salvador* in October, 1542, after one of his ships. Vizcaíno renamed it Santa Catalina on November 25, 1602, the feast day of Saint Catherine, the royal virgin and martyr of Alexandria. All older maps consulted show this name except Homem's of 1559 (Wagner, No. 42). Yet the name given by Cabrillo lasted until modern times. Bonnycastle (1818) has *San Salvador* for Santa Catalina Island, Duflot de Mofras (1844) has it as an alternate name for San Clemente, and Tanner (1846) has a San Salvador Island at the latitude of San Diego. Ysla de Santa Catalina was one of the last private land grants made under Mexican rule

(July 4, 1846). Catalina Harbor has been recorded on the Coast Survey charts since 1852; the name is used for the gulf between San Pedro and San Diego by Davidson in the 1889 edition of his Coast Pilot. The Luiseño Indian name of the island was *Ponga'* (Sparkman, p. 191).

Santa Catarina Springs [Borrego State Park]. Anza's expedition camped here March 14, 1774. "We arrived at a spring or fountain of the finest water . . . and to the place I gave the name Santa Catarina" (Anza, II, 86 f.). The springs are known as Willow or Reeds Springs, but in recent years the Spanish name has come into use again.

Santa Clara River [Los Angeles, Ventura]. The Portolá expedition rested at the river on August 9, 1769, and Crespi named the valley Santa Clara in honor of Saint Clare of Assisi, co-founder of the Franciscan Order of Poor Clares. Her feast day is August 12. The river soon came to be known as *Rio de Santa Clara;* this name appears on Pantoja y Arriaga's map of 1782 and on many others. The name was used in the titles of two land grants on the river: Santa Clara, May 18, 1837, and Rio de Santa Clara, May 22, 1837. Gibbes' map of 1852 shows Santa Clara Creek, but the Pacific Railroad Survey used the name Santa Clara River. **Santa Clara: Mission, city, County, Valley.** The mission was founded by Padre Tomás de la Peña on January 12, 1777, and named according to instructions from Mexico, *Mision de Santa Clara de Asis.* On the Plano topografico de la Mision de San Jose (about 1824) the lower part of San Francisco Bay is called *Estero de Santa Clara.* The highest peak of Montara Mountain is designated as *Mont Santa Clara* on Duflot de Mofras's *Plan* 16. February 29, 1844, the name is used for a land grant, Potrero de Santa Clara. The county, one of the original twenty-seven, was named on February 18, 1850. The name Santa Clara Valley seems to have come into general use in the 1850's and is repeatedly found in the Pacific Railroad *Reports.*

Santa Cruz. The words for 'holy cross' are frequently found as a place name in Spanish-speaking countries. Santa Cruz might easily have become the name of the State, for when Cortés came to the peninsula of what was later called California he named his landing place *Santa Cruz.* One of the first names bestowed by the Portolá expedition in what is now our State was *Triunfo de la Santa Cruz,* a place near San Elijo Lagoon [San Diego]

(Crespi, p. 126). **Santa Cruz,** krōōz: **Island, Channel.** The name, given to one of the islands in Santa Barbara Channel early in April, 1769, had no immediate religious significance but arose from an incident. A party from the *San Antonio,* a ship commanded by Juan Pérez, landed on the island. A friar in the party lost a staff with a cross on it; this was found by an Indian and returned to him the next day (Wagner, p. 414). From the maps and reports of the expedition it is not clear which of the Channel Islands was so named. The name was not definitely fixed upon the present Santa Cruz Island until the voyage of Vancouver (ed. 1798: II, 448 and atlas). The Indian name of this island was *Limu* or *Limun;* Ferrer in 1543 had named it *San Sebastian;* Vizcaíno in 1602 called it *Isla de Gente Barbuda* because one of his men said that he had seen bearded natives there. **Santa Cruz: Mission,** city, **County, Mountains, Harbor, Point.** An arroyo of running water (probably Majors Mill Creek) was named *Santa Cruz* by the Portolá expedition on October 18, 1769 (Crespi, p. 216). The mission was founded and named August 28, 1791. On January 27, 1797, the viceroy, the Marqués de Branciforte, ordered the establishment of a pueblo near the mission, although this was contrary to the royal decrees which forbade white settlements within a league of an Indian mission. The pueblo was founded by Governor Borica on July 24, 1797, and named *Villa de Branciforte* in honor of the viceroy. (Engelhardt, II, 454, 519.) The county, one of the original twenty-seven, was created February 18, 1850, and was named Branciforte, but the name was changed to Santa Cruz by act of the legislature, April 5, 1850. The town was established in 1849 and from the beginning bore the name Santa Cruz (S.F. *Alta California,* Sept. 27, 1849). The post office is listed as Santa Cruz in 1850. Santa Cruz Mountains are mentioned in the *Statutes* of 1850 (p. 59). The mountains are shown as *Cierra [Sierra] Madre de Santa Cruz* on a *diseño* of the San Antonio grant (1838). Frémont called the mountains *Cuesta de los Gatos. See* Gatos. **Santa Cruz: Creek, Peak** [Santa Barbara]. *Cañada de Santa Cruz* is shown on *diseños* of the Tequepis (1845) and San Marcos (1846) grants. There is also a Santa Cruz Mountain in Mariposa County.

Santa Fe. The Spanish term for 'Holy Faith,' which has given to the Southwest one of the best-known place names of Spanish origin,

seems to have been little used in California. The alternate name of a land grant in San Luis Obispo County, usually designated in documents as "1,000 Varas," was Ranchito de Santa Fe (September 18, 1842); Gabilan Range [Monterey, San Benito] is labeled *Sierra de Santa Fe* on several *diseños.* The Coast Survey Gazetteer gives the channel between Potrero Point and Brooks Island [San Francisco Bay] as Santa Fe Channel, a name derived from that of the railroad settlement near by, or from the name of the railroad itself.

Santa Fe Springs [Los Angeles]. In 1886 the Santa Fe purchased and renamed the mineral springs where J. E. Fulton had established a sanitarium in 1873 under the name of Fulton Sulphur Springs and Health Resort. *See* Rancho Santa Fe.

Santa Gertrudis Creek [Riverside]. An *ojo de agua* (spring) called *Santa Gertrudis* is mentioned on September 24, 1821 (Arch. MSB, IV, 223), and is shown on a *diseño* of the Temecula grant. According to Wagner (Saints' Names), the name honors the holy Gertrude whose feast day is August 17. **Santa Gertrudis** [Los Angeles, Orange]. One of the five parts into which the large Nieto grant (dated November 20, 1784) was divided after the death of Manuel Nieto in 1804 was called Santa Gertrudis; this was regranted July 27, 1833. Another Santa Gertrudis grant, dated November 22, 1845, was apparently in Lower California.

Santa Inez. *See* Santa Ynez.

Santa Isabel. *See* Santa Ysabel.

Santa Lucia, lōō-sē'-à: **Range** [San Luis Obispo, Monterey]. In November, 1542, Cabrillo named this important link in the Coast Ranges *Sierras de San Martin* and called its northern part *Sierras Nevadas* because there was snow on it. About December 14, 1602, Vizcaíno named it *Sierra de Santa Lucia* in honor of Saint Lucy of Syracuse, a saint of the early days of Christianity, whose feast day is December 13. The *Sierra de Santa Lucia* is repeatedly mentioned in the diaries of the Portolá expedition, apparently for the entire range. Font in his *Complete Diary,* March 1, 1776, states: "It is the very high, rough and long Sierra de Santa Lucìa, which begins here [near San Luis Obispo] and ends at the mission of Carmelo near Monterey." The Parke-Custer map (1855) extends the name south to Santa Clara River, but the Coast Survey established as the southern limit the divide southeast of San Luis Obispo.

Santa Lucia Canyon [Santa Barbara]. The canyon is shown as *Cañada de Santa Lucia* on a *diseño* of the Jesus Maria grant (1837).

Santa Manuela [San Luis Obispo]. The name was applied to the land grant on April 6, 1837. It honors the Santa Manuela whose feast day is June 24 (Wagner, Saints' Names).

Santa Margarita: River, Canyon, Mountains [San Diego, Riverside]. The Portolá expedition camped near the river on July 20, 1769. "Because we arrived at this place on the day of Santa Margarita [Saint Margaret of Antioch] we christened it with the name of this holy virgin and martyr" (Crespi, p. 133). A rancheria Santa Margarita is mentioned in August, 1795 (Arch. MSB, IV, 200 ff.). The name was given to the land grant Santa Margarita y San Onofre, dated February 23, 1836, and May 10, 1841. **Santa Margarita: Creek,** town [San Luis Obispo]. The site and river of Santa Margarita are mentioned in Anza's diary on March 4, 1776. The name had doubtless been applied by the padres of San Luis Obispo Mission in honor of Margaret of Cortona, a saint who in 1769 had been honored in a place name near Santa Barbara (Crespi, p. 168). Before 1790 the mission used the place near San Luis Obispo for a hog farm (Engelhardt, III, 643 f.); it is mentioned on July 15, 1790 (DSP, San Jose, I, 37). Later Santa Margarita became an *asistencia*. *El rancho de Santa Margarita de Cortona* is mentioned on December 16, 1833 (Guerra Docs., I, 246), and the name Santa Margarita was given to a land grant, September 27, 1841. The present town developed in the 1870's. It is shown on the Land Office map of 1879; the post office is listed in 1880. **Santa Margarita Valley** [Marin]. The name goes back to the San Pedro, Santa Margarita y las Gallinas grant, dated February 12, 1844.

Santa Maria, má-rē′-à. The name was a favorite place name and has survived in San Diego, Santa Barbara, and Kern counties. These names were probably given in honor of a saint other than the Virgin, who was usually referred to as *Nuestra Señora*. **Santa Maria: Valley, Creek** [San Diego]. The name was preserved through a land grant, Valle de Pamo or Santa Maria, dated November 21, 1843. The rancho is mentioned by Emory in 1846 (*Mil. Rec.*, p. 107), and the valley by Audubon in October, 1849 (p. 170). **Santa Maria: River** [San Luis Obispo, Santa Barbara]; city, **Valley** [Santa Barbara]. The name was applied in Spanish times and was preserved through a land grant, Tepusquet or

Santa Maria, dated April 6, 1837. Rancho and river (the latter called Creek) are recorded in the *Statutes* of 1850 (p. 59). At least three different versions of the founding of the modern city have been published. Y. A. Storke's account that it was laid out in 1874 by R. D. Cook, the owner of the land (Co. Hist., 1891, p. 515), seems to be the most plausible. The place is shown on the Land Office map of 1879. The post office is listed in 1880. The river is called Cuyama River above its junction with the Sisquoc, its principal tributary.

Santa Monica, mŏn′-ĭ-kà: **Mountains, Bay, Canyon,** city [Los Angeles]. Wagner (p. 415) thinks that the mountains were named by Portolá's party on May 4, 1770, the feast day of Saint Monica, mother of Saint Augustine, while on their way to found the mission and presidio at Monterey. In June, 1822, *parage de Santa Monica* and *sierra de Santa Monica* are recorded in the Guerra Documentos (VII, 107). The name was used for two grants: Boca de Santa Monica, June 19, 1839, and San Vicente y Santa Monica, December 20, 1839, and June 8, 1846. The all-Spanish name for the mountain range was retained for several decades: *Sierra de la Monica* (Parke-Custer), *Sierra Monica* (Goddard's), *Sierra de Santa Monica* (Land Office, 1879). The popular designation Santa Monica Mountains appears on the county map of 1881. The town was founded in 1875 on Rancho San Vicente y Santa Monica by Senator John P. Jones of Nevada and Colonel Robert S. Baker. The post office is listed in 1880. **Santa Monica** [San Diego] was the alternate name of the Cajon de San Diego grant, dated September 23, 1845. A mission rancho *Santa Monica* at this place is mentioned in 1821 (Arch. MSB, IV, 210). There is a Santa Monica Creek west of Carpinteria in Santa Barbara County.

Santa Paula: city, **Canyon, Creek, Peak, Ridge** [Ventura]. A stock ranch called *Santa Paula*, belonging to Mission San Buenaventura, in the heathen district *Atugu′*, is mentioned in July, 1834 (DSP Ben. Mil., LXXIX, 93). The place was probably named for Saint Paula, a noble Roman matron who became a disciple of Saint Jerome. The name was applied to a land grant, Santa Paula y Saticoy, dated July 31, 1834, and April 28, 1840. The modern town was founded on the grant by Nathan W. Blanchard and E. L. Bradley in 1872.

Santa Rita. The name appears in the names of four land grants and has survived in a number of places. According to Wagner (Saints' Names), the saint honored is Santa Rita de Cassis, an Augustinian, whose feast day is May 22. **Santa Rita, rē'-tà: Slough, Park** [Merced]. Muñoz in his diary mentions the place *Santa Rita* on September 22, 1806, and says that it had been discovered by Gabriel Moraga and named previously (Arch. MSB, IV, 4 f.). *Arroyo de Santa Rita* is repeatedly mentioned in provincial and mission records and is shown on Estudillo's map of 1819 for Fresno Slough. September 7, 1841, the name Sanjon [ditch] de Santa Rita was applied to a land grant. The post office Santa Rita Park is listed in 1941. **Santa Rita** [Monterey]. The town was laid out in 1867 and was so named because it is on the Los Gatos or Santa Rita grant, dated September 30, 1837. **Santa Rita: Hills,** settlement [Santa Barbara]. The places were so named because they are on the Santa Rita land grant, dated April 10, 1839. **Santa Rita** [Alameda]. The name of the community preserves the name of the Santa Rita grant, dated April 10, 1839. There is a Santa Rita Peak southeast of New Idria [San Benito], named or confirmed by the Geographic Board on March 6, 1912, and another Santa Rita Peak in San Bernardino County.

Santa Rosa. The name was extremely popular for naming places and appears as part of the name of at least ten land grants. Most places were doubtless named for the Dominican saint, Rosa de Lima, until recent times the only female saint of the Americas; some may have been named for Saint Rosa de Viterbo, a Franciscan of the 13th century. **Santa Rosa: Creek, Hills** [Santa Barbara]. "We named this river, . . . the largest that we have encountered, for San Bernardo and his companion, but, because we arrived on this day [August 30, 1769, the feast day of the saint of Lima], it is also called Santa Rosa" (Crespi, p. 178). Although the name of the river was changed to Santa Ynez sometime after 1801, the name Santa Rosa remained for a rancheria and a *cañada*. These and the *cuchilla de Santa Rosa* are repeatedly mentioned in the records, and *Cañada* as well as *Lomas de Santa Rosa* are shown on various *diseños*. July 30, 1839, the name was given to a land grant. **Santa Rosa Island.** The Indian name of the island was *Nicalque;* Cabrillo in 1542 named it *San Lucas;* Vizcaíno in 1602 named it *San Ambrosio.* The name *Santa Rosa* was used, apparently for what is now San Miguel Island, in the journal of Juan Pérez of his expedition of 1774 (Wagner, p. 415). On a

map of about 1794 (Wagner, No. 825) Santa Rosa is the middle one of the three chief channel islands, and this name became fixed when it was adopted by Vancouver. The island was made a private land grant on October 4, 1843. **Santa Rosa: Creek,** city [Sonoma]. According to a clipping dated June 5, 1876, in Bancroft's Scraps (V, 263), "the stream was named by a missionary priest who, before the settlement of the country, captured and baptized in its waters an Indian girl, and gave her the name of Santa Rosa, in honor of the saint on whose day in the calendar this interesting ceremony was performed." Although this story has never been substantiated it has found its way into literature complete with the name of the priest and the exact date. The name was doubtless applied by the padres of Sonoma Mission, who claimed the site as property of the mission. The name appears in the *expediente* of a land grant under date of January 8, 1831 (PSP Ben. Mil., LXXI, 7), a grant which was not consummated because of the opposition of the Mission. *Arroyo de Santa Rosa* is mentioned by Vallejo in May, 1833 (SP Mis. & C., II, 102). In 1841 there was a grant Cabeza de Santa Rosa, and in 1844 another grant called Llano de Santa Rosa, southwest of the present city. Camp Santa Rosa is mentioned by John McKee in the Indian Report on August 11, 1851; the post office was established and named April 23, 1852. **Santa Rosa: Mountain, Mountains** [Riverside, San Diego]. There was a Santa Rosa land grant, dated April 28, 1845, and January 30, 1846, in the western part of what is now Riverside County; peak and range are not near this grant.

Santa Susana: Mountains, Pass, Tunnel, station [Los Angeles, Ventura]. *El camino* [the road] *de Santa Susana y Simi* is mentioned as early as April 27, 1804 (Arch. Arz. SF, II, 36). *Una gran cuesta conocida por Santa Susana,* 'a large ridge known as Santa Susana,' probably Chatsworth Peak between Simi and San Fernando valleys, is recorded in July, 1834 (DSP Ben. Mil., LXXIX, 89). *Sierra de Santa Susana* is shown on a *diseño* of Las Virgenes (1837). Santa Susana Mountains are mentioned in the *Statutes* of 1850 (p. 59). Station and tunnel were named when the Somis branch of the Southern Pacific was built in 1902. The original name apparently honored Saint Susanna, the Roman virgin and martyr of the third century; her name is included in the missal of the College of

San Fernando, Mexico, from which Junípero Serra was sent to California.

Santa Teresa Hills [Santa Clara]. The hills were so named because they are on the Santa Teresa or Laguna de Santa Teresa land grant, dated July 11, 1834. The name probably has no connection with the *Laguna de Santa Teresa* named by Crespi on October 15, 1769, the feast day of the Carmelite Saint Theresa of Avila; this lagoon was several miles south of the land grant.

Santa Ynez, ĕ-nĕz′: **Mission, River, Valley, Mountains, Peak,** town [Santa Barbara]. The mission was founded on September 17, 1804, and named in honor of Santa Inés (Saint Agnes), one of the four great virgin martyrs of the early Roman church (about 300 A.D.). The river had been called *Santa Rosa* and *San Bernardo* by the Portolá expedition on August 30, 1769. In 1817, the site of the mission had the Indian name *Calahuasa* and the stream is mentioned as *Rio de Calaguasa* (PSP, XX, 176). After the founding of Mission La Purisima it was sometimes called *Rio de la Purisima*. On a *diseño* (1835) of the Santa Rosa grant, the name *Rio de Santa Ynes o la Purisima* appears, and on an 1865 map of the Lompoc grant the stream is labeled Santa Ynez or La Purisima River. The mountain range is mentioned as Santa Inez range by W. P. Blake of the Pacific Railroad Survey (*Reports,* Vol. V, Pt. 2, p. 137), but the all-Spanish name *Sierra de Santa Ines* persisted on many maps until the Whitney Survey fixed the commonly used name, Santa Inez Mountains. The spelling varied until the Geographic Board decided for Santa Ynez (*Sixth Report*). The town was founded in 1882 as a trading center for the large College Ranch.

Santa Ysabel, ĭz′-à-bĕl: **Creek, Indian Reservation,** town [San Diego]. The Spanish name for Saint Elisabeth appears in the records in 1818 for a place where the missionaries planned to build a chapel (Prov. Recs., XII, 165), and there was some kind of mission establishment there in 1822 (Arch. MSB, III, 261). The saint honored in the name is probably Elisabeth of Portugal, daughter of the King of Aragon, whose feast day is July 8. The site of the chapel is now Historic Landmark 369. The name (sometimes spelled Isabel) was applied to a land grant, dated November 8, 1844. The Indian Reservation was set aside by executive order of President Grant, December 27, 1875. The town is shown on the Land Office map of 1879; the post office is listed in 1892. **Santa Ysabel** [San Luis Obispo]. *Santa Ysabel* and *Arroyo de Santa Ysabel* are mentioned on August 27, 1795 (SP Mis., II, 56 f.), and the name of a rancho, *Santa Ysabel,* belonging to Mission San Antonio, is recorded under date of May 2, 1801 (Estudillo Docs., I, 58), and later. May 12, 1844, the rancho was made a private land grant. It is not known for which of several holy Isabels the place was named. *See* Isabel. In Spanish times the name was much more popular than the surviving names indicate. One of the first names applied by the Portolá expedition (July 15, 1769) was *Valle de Santa Isabel,* for Soledad Canyon in San Diego County. Font, on February 22, 1776, gave the name *Santa Ysabel* to what is now San Fernando Valley.

Santee [San Diego]. The post office, named for the first postmaster, is listed in 1892. The community was first known as Fanita, for Mrs. Fanita McCoon, then also as Cowles, until by popular vote the people accepted the name of the post office in 1902. (Dorothea Hoffmann.)

Santiago. The name of the apostle and patron of the Spains, Santiago (Saint James), was frequently used in Spanish times for place names, but except for the names in Orange County it seems to have survived only in Santiago Creek [Kern]. Point Bonita appears as *Punta de Santiago* on Ayala's map (1775) and on later maps; Poso Creek [Kern] was named *Rio de Santiago* by Garcés in 1776. **Santiago,** săn-tĭ-ä′-gō: **Creek, Hills, Peak, Reservoir** [Orange]. The creek was named by the Portolá expedition on July 27, 1769, two days after Santiago's feast day (Crespi, p. 140). *Arroyo de Santiago* is mentioned in a petition for a grant, December 8, 1801 (Bowman). Santiago de Santa Ana was the name of a land grant, dated July 1, 1810. The Spanish name of Santiago Hills was given to another grant, Lomas de Santiago or Lomerias de Santiago, dated May 26, 1846. The mountain known locally as Old Saddleback was labeled Santiago Peak when the Geological Survey mapped the Corona quadrangle in 1894.

San Timoteo, tĭm-ō-tā′-ō: **Canyon, Creek** [Riverside, San Bernardino]. A place called San Timoteo is mentioned on December 31, 1830 (SP Mis., IV, 37 f.). The name was used as an alternate name of the Yucaipa grant, dated March 22, 1843. The saint honored may be Timothy, a disciple of Paul, who died Bishop of Ephesus, according to ancient Roman martyrology.

San Tomas Aquinas Creek [Santa Clara]. In the 1850's the stream is shown on the plats of several land grants as *Arroyo de San Tomas Aquinas*. It seems somewhat grotesque that the great philosopher of scholasticism in the 13th century should be honored by the name of an intermittent creek.

San Vicente. The name was very popular as a place name; it is found in the names of eight land grants and claims and has survived in at least five localities. There were a number of holy Vincents, three of whom Wagner (Saints' Names) has identified in California place names. **San Vicente Mountain** [Los Angeles]. A *parage* [place] *de San Vicente* is mentioned as early as August 31, 1802 (Docs. Hist. Cal., IV, 121). A provisional land grant was so named in 1828, and later the name was incorporated in the San Vicente y Santa Monica land grant, dated December 20, 1839, and June 8, 1846. The mountain was named San Vicente because it is on the grant. **San Vicente Creek** [Santa Cruz]. The creek is on the land grant San Vicente, dated April 16, 1839. *Arroyo de S. Vicente* is shown on a *diseño* (about 1836) of the Arroyo de la Laguna grant. **San Vicente: Valley, Creek** [San Diego]. The places are on the Cañada de San Vicente y Mesa del Padre Barona land grant, dated January 25, 1846. The valley is shown as *Cañada de S. Vicente* on a *diseño* of the grant. The San Vicente grants in Monterey (September 20, 1836) and Santa Clara (August 1, 1842) counties have apparently left no traces in geographical nomenclature, but there is another San Vicente Creek in San Mateo County.

San Ysidro, ĭ-sē′-drō: **Mountains,** town [San Diego]. A rancho *San Ysidro*, probably a San Diego Mission rancho, is mentioned in 1836 (Hayes Docs., p. 110). The name probably honors the Spanish saint, Isidore the Plowman, whose feast day is May 10. In the 1870's and for many years thereafter town and post office were called Tia Juana, like the town across the border, but when the Little Landers Colony was established in 1909, William E. Smythe, the founder, considered the name too "sporty" and applied the present name.

Saranap [Contra Costa]. The name was coined in 1913 from *Sara Naph*thaly, the name of the mother of Samuel Naphthaly, vice-president of the Oakland and Antioch Railway, and was applied to the station previously known as Dewing Park (Jessie Lea).

Saratoga [Santa Clara]. The town was founded in 1851 and called McCarthysville, for the miller, Martin McCarthy. When the post office was established in 1867 it received the present name, chosen because the waters of near-by Pacific Congress Spring resemble those of Congress Spring at Saratoga, New York. The town was known by both names until the 1870's. **Saratoga Springs** [Death Valley National Monument]. The well-known bathing pool was probably named by the Wheeler Survey. A now vanished Saratoga in El Dorado County is mentioned in the *Statutes* of 1854 (p. 222). **Saratoga Springs** in Lake County was settled in 1874 by J. W. Pearson; it was formerly known as Pearson Springs (Mauldin). **Saratoga Springs** [Death Valley National Monument]. The name was apparently applied to the pool of water at the southern boundary of the monument by the Geological Survey in 1900. It is the only supply of fairly fresh water in the swampy region.

Sarco Creek [Napa] is shown as *Arroyo Sarco* on a *diseño* of Tulucay (about 1836–1841), and as Sarco Creek on a plat (1858) of Rancho Yajome. The name is probably the Spanish rendering of an Indian word.

Sardella Lake [Tuolumne]. The little lake in the Sierra Nevada was named in memory of Giovanni Domenico Sardella, a noted local resident, who died in 1955 (Geographic Board, July-Sept., 1965).

Sardine Lake [Mono]. According to a local story (Chase, *Yosemite Trails*, p. 299), a mule, carrying a load of sardines, rolled off the trail and was drowned in the lake. There is a Sardine Lake and Creek in Sierra County.

Sargent [Santa Clara]. When the Southern Pacific reached the place in 1869, the station was named for James P. Sargent, a farmer and stock breeder.

Sarvorum Mountain [Six Rivers National Forest]. The name commemorates the rancheria of Karok Indians south of the confluence of Boyce Creek and Klamath River (W. E. Hotelling).

Satcher Lake [Madera]. The lake as well as Reds Meadow and Creek were named for "Red" Satcher, who lived at the meadow and is said to have raised vegetables there for sale at Mammoth during the Mammoth mining boom in the years after 1878 (Robinson). The name is spelled Sotcher on the Mount Lyell atlas sheet.

Saticoy, săt′-ĭ-koi [Ventura]. The name is derived from the name of a Chumash rancheria; its meaning is not known. A *sitio de Saticoy* is mentioned on May 20, 1826 (Dep. Recs., IV, 47), and the name appears repeatedly in land-grant papers. The Santa Paula y Saticoy grant is dated July 31, 1834, and April 28, 1840. The modern town started when J. L. Crane settled there in 1861; the post office is listed in the 1870's. The Indian village, Saticoy, existed as late as 1863 (Taylor, July 24, 1863).

Sattley [Sierra]. Named in 1884 for Mrs. Harriet Sattley Church, the oldest lady in the town at that time.

Sauce. The Spanish word for 'willow' and its derivatives *sausito*, 'little willow,' *sausal*, 'grove of willows,' and *sausalito*, 'little grove of willows' were frequently used in place naming, and some of the names have survived. **Sausal Redondo** [Los Angeles]. The name of the land grant, dated March 15, 1822, and May 20, 1837, means 'round willow grove'; its specific part has survived in the name of the city, Redondo. **Sausalito,** sôs-á-lē'-tō: town, **Point, Cove** [Marin]. The cove was a convenient place to get water and wood and served generally as anchorage for foreign whalers. On the charts of the Coast Survey it is called Horseshoe Bay. Beechey mentions the name Sausalito in November, 1826, and on a *diseño* of the Corte Madera del Presidio grant (1834) a sort of building, probably John Reed's shanty, is labeled Sausalito. February 11, 1838, a land grant called Sausalito was conveyed to William A. Richardson, captain of the port of San Francisco. After the American occupation the spelling grew confused: Saucilito, Sausolita, Sausolito, Sousoleto, Sausaulito, Sauselito, etc., until the form Saucelito, used by the Pacific Railroad Survey, came to be generally accepted. The present town was started when the Saucelito Land and Ferry Company subdivided the land in 1868 and established ferry service to San Francisco. The post office was established and named Saucelito, December 12, 1870. The original and correct spelling, Sausalito, was restored by the Post Office Department November 12, 1887. Nevertheless, the other spelling persisted until after 1900. Saucito, mentioned as a rancho on June 12, 1822 (PSP, LIII, 32 f.), is the name of a grant dated May 22, 1833, and Sausal that of another, dated August 2, 1834, and August 10, 1845, both of which are in Monterey County. **Los Sauces Creek** [Ventura]. The stream is shown as *Arroyo de los Sauces* on a surveyor's map of the El Rincon grant.

Saucos [Tehama]. The Rancho Los Saucos was granted December 20, 1844, to Robert H. Thomes. This seems to be the only recorded place name using the Spanish word *saúcos* for 'elders.' It is possible that some of the names supposed to be from *sauce*, 'willow,' may be derived from *saúco. See* Elder; Tehama.

Sauerkraut Gulch. *See* Beer Creek.

Saugus [Los Angeles]. The name of the railroad station was originally Newhall, for Henry M. Newhall. When this name was transferred on February 15, 1878, to the station two miles south, the old station was renamed Saugus after Newhall's birthplace in Massachusetts. The name means 'outlet' in Algonkian dialects and by chance fits the locality near the outlets of San Francisquito, Bouquet, Mint, and Soledad canyons (*CFQ*, IV, 404 f.). *See* Newhall.

Saurian Crest [Tuolumne]. Named in 1911 by William E. Colby because the crest resembles the sawtoothed back of the ancient monster. (Farquhar.)

Sausal. *See* Sauce.

Sausalito. *See* Sauce.

Savage Dam [San Diego]. The building of the dam, first called Lower Otay, was begun in 1917; in 1934 the name was changed, in honor of H. N. Savage, the engineer who had planned and directed the construction.

Sawmill. About twenty features in California bear this name; the best known are Sawmill Creek, Pass, and Point in Inyo County, and Sawmill Flat on Woods Creek in Tuolumne County, now Historical Landmark 424.

Sawpit Flat [Plumas]. A pit was built on the flat in 1850 for the use of a whipsaw; hence the name (Co. Hist., 1882, p. 290).

Sawtooth. About fifteen orographic features in the State are so named because of their appearance. Among these are the well-known peak in Sequoia National Park and the imposing ridge on the northern boundary of Yosemite National Park. Since 1960, Glacier Pass on the Kings and Tulare counties boundary has been called Sawtooth Pass (Geographic Board, Jan.-April, 1960).

Sawyer Ridge [San Mateo]. Named after Sawyer's Camp, the headquarters of a trainer of circus horses in San Andreas Canyon (Wyatt).

Sawyers Bar [Siskiyou]. The bar was named in the 1850's for Dan Sawyer, who lived and mined near the site of the present town. Later, the name was applied to the settlement recorded on the von Leicht–Craven map of 1874.

Scaffold Meadow [Kings Canyon National Park]. The meadow became known by this name because sheepmen had a scaffold there to protect their supplies from bears and other animals (Farquhar).

Scarface [Modoc]. The name of the Great Northern station preserves the name of Scarface Charlie, who fought with Captain Jack in the Modoc War of 1873 (Beth Bowden).

Scarper Peak [San Mateo]. The name should have been spelled Scarpa because the peak was named for a family by that name residing in the district (Wyatt).

Schallenberger Ridge [Placer]. The name for the mountains south of Donner Lake was applied by the Geological Survey in honor of young Moses Schallenberger, who wintered at the lake, 1844-1845. Schallenberger was a member of the Stevens-Murphy-Townsend party.

Schellville [Sonoma]. The Northern Pacific Railroad named the station before 1888 for Theodore L. Schell, who owned 160 acres of land there in the 1850's and was active as a merchant in Sonoma and San Francisco. He died in San Francicso in 1878. (San Jose *Pioneer and Register,* January 12, 1878) . On some maps the name is spelled Shellville. There is a prominent Schell Mountain in Shasta County and a Schell Creek in Sierra County, but they could not be identified with any of the Schells, the first of whom came to California during the gold rush.

Schilling [Shasta]. The place was settled in 1849 and was first known as Franklin City, then as Whiskey Creek, and finally as Whiskeytown. The post office was established in 1881 and bore successively the names Blair, Stella, and in 1917 Schilling, the last for John Frederick Schilling, a resident and storekeeper in the early 1900's. (Steger) . The post office was named Whiskeytown again on July 1, 1952, following the modern trend of reverting to bawdy but "historical" names. *See* Whiskeytown.

Schofield Peak [Yosemite National Park]. Named by Major William W. Forsyth in honor of General John M. Schofield, Secretary of War, 1868–1869; Commander-in-Chief of the Army, 1888–1895 (Farquhar).

Schonchin, scŏn′-shĭn: **Butte** [Lava Beds National Monument]. The name commemorates the old chief of the Modocs who signed a treaty with representatives of the government in 1864. Looking for something to give emphasis to his pledge, so the story goes, he pointed to the dominant lone butte and declared that that mountain would fall before Schonchin ever would raise his hand against

his white brothers (W. S. Brown). He kept his pledge and lived peaceably with his people in the Klamath reservation, but his younger brother, Schonchin John, became a leader in the Modoc War eight years later.

Schramsberg [Napa]. Historical Landmark 561 was registered December 31, 1956, in memory of Jacob Schram, a pioneer vineyardist.

Schultheis: Lagoon, Pass [Santa Clara]. Named for John Martin Schultheis (or Schultheiss), a native of Germany, who homesteaded here in 1852 (Hoover, p. 533). This is doubtless the same Schultheis who, according to Doyle, found Charlie McKiernan seriously wounded by a bear and took him to a doctor. *See* Mountain Charlie Gulch.

Schwaub [Death Valley National Monument]. According to the Death Valley Survey the mining camp was promoted in 1906 by Charles Schwab of the Bethlehem Steel Works. Charles M. Schwab had a large interest in the Greenwater copper mining district. But the Desert Valley literature often mentions a Charles Schwab as an active prospector and promoter of mineral projects after 1900, when the great industrialist was already the president of the Carnegie Steel Corporation. The name of the place is spelled as the surname is commonly pronounced.

Scodie: Canyon, Spring [Kern]. Named for William Scodie, who established a store at the mouth of the canyon in the 1860's. *See* Onyx.

Scotia, skō-shà [Humboldt]. When the Pacific Lumber Company built their mill in 1885 the town was first called Forestville. When the post office was established, July 9, 1888, the present name was chosen because many of the men working in the mill were natives of Nova Scotia (Borden).

Scott. About forty geographic features in California are named Scott and several more are called Scotty and Scotchman. Most of the Scott names are from the family name; some were meant to be Scot but were spelled like the surname. In Tehama County the name is combined with a rare generic term: Scotts Glade. **Scotts Valley** [Santa Cruz]. Named for Hiram Daniel Scott, a sailor who came to Monterey Bay in 1846 and in 1852 purchased Rancho San Agustin (Hoover, p. 574). **Scott: Bar, Valley, River, Mountain** [Siskiyou]. John W. Scott discovered gold in 1850, and his name has been perpetuated in a number of geographic features. The bar and the valley are mentioned in 1851 (Indian Report, pp. 170 f.). The stream is shown as Scotts Fork on Gibbes' map of 1852 and is mentioned as Scott's River in the *Statutes* of 1852 (p. 233). The river had been called Beaver River by the Hudson's Bay Company trappers. **Scottys: Castle, Canyon** [Death Valley National Monument]. In 1923 Walter ("Death Valley") Scott, a former champion roughrider in Buffalo Bill's show, and A. M. Johnson of Chicago bought the old Staininger Ranch and began building the fabulous "castle" for which the millionaire Johnson, who had come to Death Valley for his health, apparently provided the money.

Screwdriver Creek [Shasta]. The tributary of Pit River was so named because of its "screwy movement through the canyon and flat" (Steger).

Scylla [Kings Canyon National Park]. In 1895, when T. S. Solomons and E. C. Bonner came down from Mount Goddard to Simpson Meadow by way of Disappearing Creek and the Enchanted Gorge, they passed between two peaks which they named Scylla and Charybdis, from Homer's *Odyssey* (Farquhar). "Sheer, ice-smoothed walls arose on either side, up and up, seemingly into the very sky, their crowns two sharp black peaks of most majestic form. A Scylla and a Charybdis they seemed to us, as we stood at the margin of the lake and wondered how we might pass the dangerous portal." (*Appalachia*, 1896, p. 55.)

Seal. The species of seal, sometimes called the sea lion, common along our coast has given the name to a number of places, including the well-known Seal Rocks below the Cliff House in San Francisco. The charts of the Coast Survey show six other Seal Rock or Rocks, two Coves, one Island, and one Creek. *See* Lobo. **Seal Beach** [Orange]. The place, first called Bay City, was given the present name by Philip A. Stanton and other interested persons (Stephenson). The post office is listed in 1915.

Seal Creek [San Mateo] may have been named for Henry W. Seale, who at one time owned part of Rancho Rinconada del Arroyo de San Francisquito.

Sea Lion. The name is much less frequently used than the popular form "seal," hence there are only three barren Sea Lion Rocks and one Sea Lion Gulch in California. *See* Lobo.

Seamans Gulch [Shasta]. Named for George Seaman, who located a claim here in the 1860's (Steger).

Searles Lake [San Bernardino]; **Searles** [Kern]. The dry lake was named for John and Dennis Searles, brothers, who discovered borax there in 1863, and in 1873 began to exploit the rich deposits of minerals. A post office, established August 20, 1898, at the shipping point across the line in Kern County was named Searles. The Searles Lake Borax Discovery is now Historic Landmark 774 at Trona.

Sears Point [Sonoma]. The name was applied to the station of the old Northwestern Pacific before 1888, probably for Franklin Sears, who came to California in 1845, took part in the Mexican War, and settled in Sonoma Valley in 1851.

Searsville Lake [San Mateo]. The name recalls the old town of Searsville, named for John H. Sears, who came from New York in 1849 and built the Sears Hotel in 1854. In 1890, the lake was created as a reservoir of the Spring Valley Water Company, and was named after the town, now vanished.

Seaside [Monterey]. The town was laid out in 1888 by Dr. J. L. D. Roberts and named East Monterey. When the Post Office Department declined this name in 1890, Roberts chose the present name.

Seavey Pass [Yosemite National Park]. Named by R. B. Marshall for Clyde L. Seavey, president of the State Railroad Commission in 1923, who later was a member of the Federal Power Commission (Farquhar).

Sebastopol, sĕ-băs'-tṓ-pŏl [Sonoma]. The sole survivor of five Sebastopols, all named in or soon after 1854 when the siege of the Russian seaport by the British and French excited the whole world. The town in Napa County is now Yountville; those in Tulare, Sacramento, and Nevada counties no longer exist. The town in Sonoma County was founded by H. P. Morris in 1853 as Pine Grove, and according to tradition the name was changed to Sebastopol at the time of the Crimean War because of a local fight in which one party found its Sebastopol in the general store. The post office is listed in 1859.

Seco, Seca. Since many watercourses in California dry out in summer and many others have become permanently dry, the Spanish word corresponding to the English term 'dry' was a common specific name in Spanish and Mexican times, especially with *Arroyo* and *Laguna*. It was also used with *Campo* (field) and *Llano* (plain) to indicate the absence of water. The adjective is still found in more than ten place names, including the settlements Arroyo Seco [Monterey] and Campo Seco [Calaveras], and is commonly pronounced sā'-kō.

Second Garrote, gä-rō'-tê [Tuolumne]. Modern Groveland was formerly called Garrote because a Mexican was hanged from a tree there in July, 1850, for having stolen two hundred dollars from two miners (Bancroft Scrapbooks, XVI, 127). A similar incident in a camp two miles southeast led to naming it Second Garrote, thereby distinguishing it from the original Garrote. *Garrote* is the Spanish designation for capital punishment by strangulation, or for the scaffold on which the punishment is inflicted. The name of the post office was spelled Garrote from 1854 until it became Groveland in the 1870's, but the maps never got the name straight. Trask's Map of the Mineral Regions has two Garots. Lapham & Taylor (1856) show a 2nd Garota but no first; Goddard (1860) has a Garota and a 2nd Garota. Hoffmann and Gardner (1867) use the Spanish spelling, Garrote, but the other maps of the Whitney Survey have Garrota. On the Sonora atlas sheet of the Geological Survey the name is spelled Second Garrotte. *See* Groveland.

Secret. The word was frequently used for camps, gulches, springs, ravines, and the like during the gold rush. The places were named "secret" either because they were hard to find, or because some successful miners did not want to make their finds known. In modern times only two small localities are still recorded on maps: **Secret Ravine** [Placer] near Newcastle, and **Secret** [Lassen], an old railroad station. Both formerly had post offices.

Sedco [Riverside]. The place was established about 1915 and given this name, coined from *South Elsinore Development Company* (L. E. Burnham).

Seeley [Imperial]. After the destruction of Blue Lake and the surrounding district by the overflow of New River, 1905–1907, a new town was started several miles to the north and was named for Henry Seeley, one of the pioneers in the development of Imperial Valley.

Segunda [Monterey]. *La Cañada llamada de la Segunda* is mentioned in 1822 (Arch. MSB, III, 296), but it is not known why the canyon should be called 'of the second.' April 4, 1839, the name Cañada de la Segunda was applied to a land grant. On the Monterey atlas sheet the *cañada* is called Canyon Secundo.

Seiad, sī-ăd': **Creek, Valley** [Siskiyou]. The place is in the former territory of the Shasta Indians, and the name, spelled Sciad originally, may be derived from their language. Brewer of the Whitney Survey mentions, on November 15, 1863, Sciad Creek and Sciad Ranch, a thriving place settled in 1854 by a farmer from New York named Reeves (p. 480). The post office is listed in 1867 with the spelling Seiad. This spelling is now generally accepted by the residents although Wood's *Gazetteer* lists the stream as Sciad Creek. The word may be Yurok Indian, meaning 'far-away land,' i.e., far away from the Yurok habitat on the coast (Ellen Wilson).

Seigler, sēg'-lēr: **Springs, Valley, Creek, Mountain** [Lake, Napa]. The springs were named for the discoverer and original owner, Thomas Sigler, a native of New York. They are listed as Hot Sigler Springs (!) in the Pacific Coast Business Directory, 1876–1878. The name is spelled Siegler in the County History of 1881, but the spelling Seigler, used by the Whitney Survey, finally won out.

Selby [Contra Costa]. The post office was established about 1887 and named for Prentiss Selby, superintendent of the Selby Smelting and Lead Works and first postmaster.

Selden Pass [Fresno]. Named by R. B. Marshall of the Geological Survey, for Selden S. Hooper, who was a member of the Survey from 1891 to 1898 (Farquhar). In a decision of February 3, 1915, the Geographic Board misspelled the name Seldon, and this version is found on some maps.

Selma [Fresno]. Established by the Southern Pacific in 1880 and named for the daughter of Max Gruenberg, assertedly at the request of Leland Stanford, to whom Gruenberg had shown a picture of his baby daughter. Another version was published in the *Centennial Almanac* of 1956 (p. 170). According to Ernest J. Neilsen of Selma, the station was named for Selma Michelson Kingsbury, the wife of an official of the Central Pacific Railroad.

Seneca [Plumas]. Named by R. K. Dunn, a pioneer settler, after the township, which had been named about 1854 doubtless after one of the many places of this name in the East and Middle West. The name is from Algonkian *assini*, 'stone,' and *ka*, 'people,' which by folk etymology came to be pronounced and spelled like the name of the Roman philosopher (Leland, *CFQ*, V, 392).

Senger, Mount; Senger Creek [Fresno]. Named in 1894 by T. S. Solomons, for Joachim H. Senger (1848–1926), professor of German at the University of California and one of the four founders of the Sierra Club (Farquhar).

Sentenac Canyon [San Diego]. Named for Paul Sentenac, a French settler, who raised goats here in the early 1890's (J. Kelly).

Sentinel. About twenty orographic features are so named because of their real or fancied resemblance to a watchtower, including the imposing Grand Sentinel in Kings Canyon National Park. **Sentinel: Dome, Rock** [Yosemite National Park]. In 1851 the Mariposa Battalion applied the name South Dome to the mountain. At the time of the Whitney Survey the present name was current: "A prominent point, which . . . from its fancied likeness to a gigantic watch-tower, is called 'Sentinel Rock' " (Whitney, *Geology*, I, 412). The Indian name was *Loya* and may be derived from the Spanish word *hoya,* 'hole.' (*See* Jolla.) Bunnell believes the Indian name is from the Spanish *olla,* 'earthen pot,' and means 'basket.' The rock is supposed to resemble a long, pointed basket. (*Discovery*, 1880, pp. 212 f.) **Sentinel Cave** [Siskiyou]. The grotto in the Lava Beds National Monument was so named because nine pillar-like formations stand like sentinels before the entrance.

Sepulveda, sĕ-pŭl′-vĕ-dà [Los Angeles]. The name was applied to the station east of the present town, when the railroad from Los Angeles to San Fernando was built in 1873, probably for Fernando Sepúlveda, whose adobe was near the base of the Verdugo Mountains.

Sepulveda Canyon [Los Angeles]. The name commemorates Francisco Sepúlveda, grantee of the San Vicente y Santa Monica grant in 1839.

Sequan: Peak, Indian Reservation [San Diego]. An application for a grant called *Secuan* is recorded in 1835 (San Diego Arch., Hayes, C & R, p. 58), and an Indian rancheria (or rancho) called *Socouan* is mentioned on February 1, 1836 (Hayes, Mis., I, 292). On May 2, 1839, the grant was made, but no claim was ever filed. According to Kroeber, the name is derived from the Diegueño Indian word *sekwan,* denoting a kind of bush.

Sequoia, sĕ-kwoi′-à. In 1847 the Austrian scholar, Stephan L. Endlicher, published his monumental *Synopsis Coniferarum,* in which he established the California giant trees as a separate genus with two species: *Sequoia sempervirens* and *Sequoia gigantea*. Both, however, proved to be one and the same, the coast redwood. In 1854, the French botanist, J. Decaisne, transferred the latter name to

the big tree of the Sierra Nevada. In applying the name, Endlicher, who was also a great linguist, doubtless wished to honor Sequoya (George Gist), the creator of the Cherokee alphabet. The meaning of the name is less beautiful than its sound: 'opossum' or 'member of the opossum clan,' the latter probably a clan of half-breeds, so called because the Cherokee evidently considered the opossum an animal of mixed breed (Leland, *WF*, VI, 269). Among the few places bearing the name are Sequoia Ridge [Fresno, Tulare]; two railroad stations, Sequoia [Humboldt] and Sequoya [Contra Costa]; and several minor features. **Sequoia National Park** was established by act of Congress of September 25, 1890, and christened by John W. Noble, Secretary of the Interior, at the suggestion of George W. Stewart. **Sequoia National Forest** was established and named by executive order of President Theodore Roosevelt, July 2, 1908 (Farquhar). *See* Redwood; Palo.

Serra [Orange]. In 1910 the Santa Fe named the station after the newly formed school district, which had been named presumably in honor of Padre Junípero Serra. The former name of the station was San Juan by the Sea.

Serrano [San Luis Obispo]. The station was named in 1893 by the Southern Pacific for the Serrano family, from whom the right of way was obtained. Miguel Serrano, a native of Mexico, had settled in the county in 1828.

Serrano Boulder [Riverside]. Named for Leandro Serrano, major-domo of Mission San Juan Capistrano and, after 1818, ranchero in Temescal Valley. Registered as Historical Landmark 185, June 20, 1935.

Serret Peak [Kern]. The high mountain north of Kernville was named for a Basque sheep owner of the region in "the early days."

Sespe, sĕs′-pê: town, **Creek, Gorge, Hot Springs, Oilfields** [Ventura]. The name can be traced to a Chumash rancheria, called Cepsey in 1791 (AGN, California, p. 46). It was often recorded, with various spellings, in the archives of Mission San Buenaventura. The meaning of the word is probably "kneepan," according to Harrington. It is doubtful that the word has anything to do with the place name. Henshaw lists the word for 'kneepan' as *pi·ke·le′-li* in the Santa Barbara Indian dialect. The present spelling is used in a letter of May 5, 1824 (Arch. Arz. SF, Vol. IV, Pt 2, p. 102), and for the land grant Sespe or San Cayetano, dated November 22, 1833. The Parke-Custer map of 1854 has Cespai

River; Goddard's map of 1860, Sespe River. The name was applied to the Southern Pacific station in 1887 and to the post office in 1894. Henshaw, however, about the same time gives the spelling Cespe Ranch and calls the Indian village *sek-pe*.

Seven Gables [Fresno]. Named by T. S. Solomons and Leigh Bierce on September 20, 1894: "The south wall of the gap we found to be the side of a peak, the eccentric shape of which is suggested in the name Seven Gables, which we hastened to fasten upon it" (*SCB*, I, 230).

Seville [Tulare]. In 1913, when the Santa Fe built the line from Minkler to Exeter through the newly developed citrus-fruit region, the location engineers chose Spanish-sounding names as appropriate station names: Primero, Orosi, Seville, Rayo, Sur, Fruta, etc.

Seward Creek [Mendocino]. The tributary of Forsythe Creek was named, about 1880, for Anson J. Seward (H. McCowen).

Shackleford Creek [Siskiyou]. The stream was named for John M. Shackleford, who built an eight-stamp quartz mill on the creek in 1852 (Co. Hist., 1881, p. 215).

Shadow: Mountains, Mountain [San Bernardino]. The range was so named because a dark-colored peak appears to be the shadow of a neighboring lighter-colored peak. Shadow Mountain is not a part of the range but stands seven miles east. The word is used elsewhere in place naming: **Shadow Lake** [Madera] on the headwaters of the North Fork of the San Joaquin is known as one of the most beautiful lakes in the High Sierra; the same name had once been applied to Merced Lake in Yosemite by John Muir.

Shafter [Kern]. Named in memory of General William ("Pecos Bill") Shafter, 1835–1906, commander of the U.S. forces in Cuba during the Spanish-American War. General Shafter lived on his ranch of 10,520 acres near Bakersfield from the time of his retirement in 1901 until his death in 1906. In 1914 the land was subdivided and the town of Shafter was established.

Shagoopah. *See* Chagoopah.

Shake City. *See* Shingle.

Shamrock Lake [Yosemite National Park]. The outline of the little lake north of Benson Pass suggested the name, which was probably applied when the Bridgeport quadrangle was mapped, 1905–1907.

Shandon [San Luis Obispo]. In 1891 the Post Office Department accepted the name, which was unique at that time among post offices in the United States. It was suggested by Dr. John Hughes, supposedly from a story published in *Harper's*.

Shanty Creek [Trinity]. So named because of the bark-covered Indian huts called shanties by the white people (L. P. Duncan).

Sharktooth Peak [Fresno]. The peak was so named by T. S. Solomons in 1892 because of its shape (Farquhar).

Sharp Park [San Mateo]. When the district was developed in 1905, the Ocean Shore Land Company named the place Salada Beach after the near-by Laguna Salada. When the Post Office Department in 1936 requested another name to avoid confusion with a similar one, the name was changed to Sharp Park, after the park and recreation area given to the city of San Francisco by Honora Sharp. The county map of 1877 shows that two sections of Rancho San Pedro were owned by G. F. Sharp.

Shasta, Mount; Shasta: River, Valley, Springs, Retreat; Mount Shasta (town) [Siskiyou]; **Shasta: County,** town, **Bally Mountain, Dam, Lake** [Shasta]; **Shasta National Forest.** The origin of the place name is found in the name of the Indians who in the early part of the 19th century inhabited the region of the upper Rogue, middle Klamath, Scott, and Shasta rivers. The name of the Indian tribe is mentioned in an entry under date of January 31, 1814, in the journals of Alexander Henry and David Thompson: "They [the Indians] said they were of the Wallawalla, Shatasla, and Halthwypum nations" (Coues, *New Light*, p. 827). Under the date of February 10, 1827, Peter Ogden records: "Here we are among the Sastise," and four days later he gave the name of the tribe to a river and a mountain: "I have named this river Sastise River. There is a mountain equal in height to Mount Hood or Vancouver, I have named Mt. Sastise. I have given these names from the tribes of Indians." In later entries, March 9 and 13, he spells the name Sasty. (*OHQ*, XI, 213 ff.) Ogden's sketchy diary does not make clear which peak and river he named. It is, however, fairly certain that it was Mount Shasta and equally certain that it was not Shasta River. Merriam (*Journal,* Washington [D.C.] Academy of Science, XIV, 522 ff.) believes that Ogden referred to Mount McLoughlin and Rogue River in Oregon, and the maps of the 1830's support this belief. Abert's map of 1838, a U.S. government publication, shows Shasty River (and a tributary, Nasty River!) flowing into Klamath River from the north, as well as Mount Shasty, all in Oregon. In the summer of 1841 Wilkes expressly mentioned the mountain in his instructions to Emmons and Ringgold, who were to explore the interior: "particularly the Shaste Peak, the most southern one in the territory of Oregon" (Wilkes, V, 521). However, the Emmons detachment definitely applied the name to the present Mount Shasta, and Eld's sketches have Sasty Peak and River in California, and Sasty Country and Sasty or Cascade Mountains straddling the line. On Duflot de Mofras's map of 1844 the names for both mountain and river (Mont Sasté and R. des Sastés) are in their new location. There are numerous spelling variants on early maps (Frémont-Preuss, 1848: Mt. Tsashtl), and as late as 1852 Horn's *Overland Guide* uses the name Shaste for the Rogue River. Brewer, under date of October 5, 1862, states that an Indian pronounced the name "tschasta." Since the spelling Chasty or Chasta occurs on some early maps it may be assumed that this was the approximate native pronunciation and that there was a relation to the Chastas in Oregon. Other early American maps called the peak Mount Jackson, and Gibbs says the Indian name was *Wy-e-kah* (Schoolcraft, III, 165). *See* Yreka. According to Towendolly, the Wintu name is *Bo-lem-poi'-yok,* 'high peak.' The sponsor of the modern version was apparently Madison Walthall, assemblyman from the Sacramento district, who proposed the name Shasta County for the county in the northeast corner of the State instead of the name Reading County, which was proposed by others. With the creation of the twenty-seven original counties, on February 18, 1850, the name became official. The spelling Shasta is used on Scholfield's map of 1851. Some of the other maps of the 1850's have Mt. Shasté and Shasta Butte. The town known as Reading's Springs or Diggings was changed to Shasta City in 1850. The name was abbreviated to Shasta with the establishment of the post office in 1851. The town in Siskiyou County, first known as Strawberry Valley, and from 1886 to 1922 as Sisson (for H. J. Sisson, an early settler), was changed to Mount Shasta in 1922. The national forest was created and named by presidential proclamation in 1905, and Shasta Dam was officially named by John C. Page, Commissioner, Bureau of Reclamation, September 12, 1937.

Shastina [Siskiyou]. The playful feminine form of the name Shasta has been applied to the west peak of Mount Shasta.

Shauls Lake [Lake]. This sheet of water, now only a lake bed, was named for Ben F. Shaul, a settler of 1865, on whose ranch the lake was situated (Mauldin).

Shaver Lake, reservoir, post office; **Shaver Crossing** [Fresno]. According to L. A. Winchell, the place was named for C. B. Shaver, of the Fresno Flume and Irrigation Company, which built a reservoir and sawmill here in the 1890's. The Southern California Edison Company retained the name for the enlarged reservoir (Farquhar). However, a settlement, Saver, and Saver's Peak are shown in this locality on the maps of the Whitney Survey as early as 1873. It is quite possible that this original name was changed when Mr. Shaver became associated with the region. *See* McCloud River for a similar shifting of names.

Shaws Flat [Tuolumne]. Named by Mandeville Shaw, who planted an orchard here in 1849 (Kazmarek).

Sheep. Among the fifty or more features so named on the maps of the State are four peaks that rise more than ten thousand feet, several Sheep Hollows and Sheep Corrals, a Sheephead Mountain and Pass [Death Valley National Monument], a Sheep Thief Creek [Stanislaus], a Sheep Crossing [Madera], and a Sheep Repose Ridge [Sonoma]. The majority of the names doubtless refer to herds of domestic sheep, but some were applied because of the presence of the mountain or desert bighorn sheep. **Sheep Rock** [Siskiyou], the oldest Sheep name in California, was given by Hudson's Bay Company trappers probably in the 1820's. "It is said to be one of only three places, where the bighorn, or mountain sheep, is at present found, west of the Sierra Nevada" (Gibbs, 1851, in Schoolcraft, III, 168). **Sheepranch** [Calaveras]. The town was named after a gold mine, which in turn had been named after a sheep corral. *See* Carneros.

Sheetiron: Springs, Mountain [Lake]. Sometime between 1860 and 1880 a man camped by the springs for his health. His shelter was a sheet-iron hut. After he abandoned it, the hut fell apart, and for years hunters and campers used the pieces for fire plates and camp stoves (Mauldin).

Sheldon [Sacramento]. The settlement which developed on the Omochumnes (or Cosumnes) land grant was named for Jared Sheldon, grantee in 1844.

Shell. About twenty places in California, chiefly along the ocean shore, are named for the occurrence of sea shells; included are one post office, Shell Beach [San Luis Obispo], and several communities. Along the coast are numerous places designated as Shell-mounds, some of which are now protected in state parks; these were refuse heaps and burial mounds which had developed near Indian villages, and were so named because they consist mainly of fragments of shells.

Shelter Cove [Humboldt]. The name was applied to the small natural harbor by the Coast Survey when making a hydrographic survey of it in 1854. It afforded "an anchorage from northwest winds, and may, perhaps, be regarded as a harbor of refuge for small coasters which have experienced heavy weather off Cape Mendocino, and are short of wood and water, both of which may be obtained here from one or two gulches opening upon the sea" (Coast Pilot, 1858, p. 66).

Shenandoah Valley [Amador]. Blood Gulch running through the valley seems to indicate that some miniature battle took place here which reminded the name giver of the many bloody engagements in the valley in Virginia during the Civil War. According to Doyle, however, John Jameson, who settled in the valley in the early 1850's, named it after his birthplace.

Shepherd. More than ten geographic features are so named because some shepherd had his cabin there. The spelling Shepard occurs in Alameda, Glenn, and Inyo counties. The creek and pass in Inyo County, however, owe their name to a pioneer family named Shepherd (Farquhar).

Sheridan [Placer]. As the Roseville-Marysville branch of the Central Pacific was built during and immediately following the Civil War, the station was doubtless named in honor of General Philip Sheridan, the distinguished cavalry leader.

Sheridan Creek [Shasta]. The tributary of Bear Creek was named for George Sheridan, who settled here in the 1850's (Steger).

Sheriffs Springs [Orange]. So named because Sheriff James Barton and his posse were murdered here by Juan Flores and his band in 1857. See Flores Peak.

Sherlock Gulch [Mariposa]. The gulch northeast of Bullion Mountain was named after Sherlock's Diggings, discovered in the summer of 1849 "by a man named Sherlock, who with a company of seventy Mexicans worked these deposits on shares ... Sherlock has gone

into the mountains ... and we have elected a new Alcalde, who ... issued an order for all Mexicans to decamp" (S.F. *Alta California,* Oct. 25, 1849).

Sherman Island [Sacramento]. Named for Sherman Day, State senator, 1855–1856, U.S. surveyor general for California, 1868–1871. The island, on which Day owned a ranch, is shown on Ringgold's General Chart of 1850. *See* Mount Day.

Sherwin: Creek, Lakes, Hill [Mono]. Named for James L. C. Sherwin, a native of Kentucky, who came to California in 1850 and settled in Round Valley in the early 1860's. Sherwin took an active interest in Indian affairs and was a member of the California state assembly in 1858.

Sherwood Valley [Mendocino]. Named for Alfred Sherwood, who settled in the valley in 1853 and lived there until his death in 1900.

Shiloah [Shasta]. The mineral spring was named by Charles Dougherty after the ancient spring near Jerusalem, Palestine, noted for its healing qualities (Steger).

Shingle [El Dorado]. The first house in the settlement known as Shingle Springs was built in 1850 by a man named Bartlett. The name came "from a shingle machine used for the manufacture of shingles at a cluster of springs, situated on the western extremity of the village." (Co. Hist., 1883, pp. 199 f.) Shingle Spring post office was established February 3, 1853. It was changed to Shingle, May 11, 1895, and back to Shingle Spring, January 13, 1955. In Shasta County there is a post office called Shingletown, and Mendocino County has a settlement named Shake City.

Shinn, Mount [Fresno]. Named in 1925 by members of the Forest Service in memory of Charles H. Shinn (1852–1924), who was for many years connected with the Forest Service and was a charter member of the Sierra Club (Farquhar).

Ship. The several Ship Mountains and Rocks in the State apparently were given this name because of their shape. The mountain in Siskiyou County was originally known as Four Brothers and was given the present name in 1909 by A. W. Lewis (Forest Service).

Shirttail. This favorite name in the bawdy and colorful nomenclature of mining days has survived in several places. **Shirttail: Gulch, Peak** [Shasta]. In the late 1850's a group of miners working on the East Fork of Clear Creek were swept down the stream by a slide. All were killed except Wilbur Dodge, whose wife was able to rescue him because his shirttail had caught on a snag at the mouth of the creek. (Steger.) **Shirttail Canyon** [Placer]. The explanation that it was so named in 1849 because a prospector was found working there clad only in a shirt is the most plausible of the half dozen theories about the origin of the name.

Shivelly Gulch [Amador]. Named for Charles Shivelly, who came to California in 1849 and apparently found a fortune in the gulch in 1852 ("The Knave," Sept. 22, 1946).

Shively [Humboldt]. Probably named for William R. Shiveley, a pioneer of Humboldt County, who came to California from Ohio in 1852.

Shoemaker Bally. *See* Bally.

Shorb Junction [Los Angeles]. A station of the Southern Pacific was named before 1900 for James de Barth Shorb. *See* San Marino.

Shoshone, shō-shō′-nĕ [Inyo]. The name was applied to the station when the Tonopah and Tidewater Railroad was built shortly after 1900. The post office is listed in 1915. It is apparently the only place in California named for the widespread family of Shoshonean Indians. The name of the tribe, Shoshoni, is derived from *tso,* 'head,' and *so′ni,* 'tangled, curly,' referring to the hairdress of the Indians (W. L. Marsden, *American Anthropologist,* N.S., XIII, 725).

Shot Gun. A number of places are so named because of some incident in which a shotgun played a role. **Shotgun Pass** [Sequoia National Park] and **Shot Gun Creek** [Shasta], a tributary of Sacramento River, seem to be the only survivors. According to old-timers, a miner named Brand, instead of paying his helper, ran him out with a shotgun, and so the creek in Shasta County got its name. (Steger). A bend in the road to Angels Camp was once called Shot Gun Bend because highwaymen could easily hold up a stage at this point.

Showalter Hill [Calaveras] Named for John Showalter, who had a cabin near the top of the hill on which extensive coyote mining was carried on (*Las Calaveras,* October, 1957).

Showers Pass [Humboldt]. Probably named for Jacob O. Showers, a farmer at Rohnerville, who summered his cattle here in the 1860's. According to local tradition the pass was so called because Showers once rode across it at breakneck speed to escape a band of Indians (Arthur Renfroe).

Shuman Canyon [Santa Barbara]. The canyon north of Casmalia was long known by the name of an early settler, who spelled it Schumann. The Geographic Board decided for the present spelling, June, 1949.

Shuteye: Peak, Pass [Madera]. Named for Old Shuteye, an Indian who was blind in one eye. One of the main trails across the Sierra passed through his rancheria. The peak has a namesake called Little Shuteye Peak. *See* Little.

Siberia [San Bernardino]. Named by the Southern Pacific Railroad when the original line (now Santa Fe) was built in 1883. The choice of the name was probably inspired by the striking contrast in the temperature of the desert and of Siberia. *See* Klondike.

Siberian: Outpost, Pass, Pass Creek [Sequoia National Park]. The region was named Siberian Outpost by Harvey Corbett in 1895 because of its bleak appearance. The pass had been called Rampart Pass by Wallace, Wales, and Wright in 1881. (Farquhar.) In 1907 the Geological Survey used the present name for the pass and the creek.

Sicard: Bar, Flat [Yuba]. Named for Theodore Sicard, a French sailor who came to Sutter's Fort in 1842, and in 1848 mined and traded at the places which became known by his name and which now exist in name only. In 1849 he was associated with Covillaud in the establishment of Marysville, and some people favored the name Sicardoro for the new place.

Sidewinder: Mountain, Road [San Bernardino]. The peak was named after the Sidewinder Mine northwest of it, which in turn was probably named because of the occurrence of the rattlesnake called sidewinder.

Sierra, sĭ-ĕr′-à. The descriptive name for 'mountain range' was frequently used in Spanish times: any two or more peaks in a row were usually called "sierra." The word appears also in the chief or secondary names of six land grants. Although it has not become a generic term in California, it is occasionally so used, as in Sierra Azul [Santa Cruz], Sierra Morena [San Mateo], Sierra de Salinas [Monterey], Sierra Pelona [Los Angeles]. **Sierra: Peak, Canyon; La Sierra** [Riverside, Orange]. These names are derived from the two land grants, Sierra or Sierra de Santa Ana, both dated June 15, 1846, and granted to Bernardo Yorba and Vicente Sepúlveda respectively. **Sierra: City, County, Valley, Buttes; Sierraville.** All these places were named directly or indirectly for their location in the northern part of the Sierra Nevada. The county, formed from a portion of Yuba County, was established and named on April 16, 1852. Sierraville post office is listed in 1867. **Sierra**

Point [Yosemite National Park]. This vantage point of Yosemite Valley was discovered by Charles A. Bailey, Warren Cheney, W. E. Dennison, and Walter E. Magee and named on June 14, 1897, as a compliment to the Sierra Club (Farquhar). **Sierra National Forest** is one of five national forests created in 1908 by division of the area that included the original Sierra Forest Reserve, established and named by executive order of President Harrison in 1893.

Sierra Madre, sĭ-ĕr'-à mădʹ-rė [Los Angeles]. The name means 'mother range' and was applied in Spanish times to a number of ranges in different sections of California. The various ranges in Kern, Los Angeles, San Bernardino and Riverside counties were called *Sierra Madre de California* by Font in 1775 (*Compl. Diary*, p. 122). "The whole chain ... was formerly called *Sierra Madre* by the Padres—probably from the fact that the Sierra Nevada, the Coast Mountains, and other ranges seem to spring from it" (Blake, 1853, Pac. R.R. *Reports*, Vol. V, Pt. 2, p. 137). There is today no collective name for these ranges. The name was given to the town in Los Angeles County when Nathaniel C. Carter subdivided part of Rancho Santa Anita in 1881. The Sierra Madre Villa is recorded in 1881. By decision of the Geographic Board, Jan.-Mar., 1965, the range between Cuyama and Sisquoc rivers in Santa Barbara County is now tautologically called Sierra Madre Mountains.

Sierra Nevada, sĭ-ĕr'-à nĕ-văd'-à. The name existed in California more than two centuries before it was identified with the lofty mountain range. It is a common descriptive Spanish name for a range covered with snow. As *Sierras Nevadas* the name was first applied by Cabrillo in November, 1542, to the Santa Lucia Mountains south of Carmel. On the Bologna-Ayer map of 1556 (Wagner, No. 37) a large section of the present State is covered by a glacial mass, called *Sierra Neuados*, and on Zaltieri's map (*Geographical Report*, opposite p. 504) of 1566, a well-defined *Sierra Nevada* runs east-west in the latitude of Alaska. For more than a century the cartographers used the name for mountains or points along the coast, variously spelled and in various latitudes, until California had become an island on the maps and names were dropped for lack of space. The present-day Sierra Nevada was first seen (but not named) by Crespi in 1772. It was seen again by Font on April 3, 1776, from a hill near the junc-ture of the Sacramento and San Joaquin rivers: "If we looked to the east we saw on the other side of the plain at a distance of some thirty leagues a great *sierra nevada*, white from the summit to the skirts, and running about from south-southeast to north-northwest." On Font's map of 1776 the name appears for the northern part of the Sierra Nevada and also for the Coast Ranges in the southern counties. The latter were then already known by this name, as Padre Garcés records under date of April 25, 1776, "I ... came upon another large sierra which makes off from the Sierra Nevada and extends north-eastward; to which I gave the name of San Marcos" (Coues, *Trail*, pp. 270 f.). On Font's map of 1777 (Davidson's copy), which incorporated both his and Garcés' discoveries, the entire range first appears. The San Gabriel Mountains are called *Sierra Nevada;* the Tehachapi and Piute mountains and the south end of the modern Sierra Nevada are left nameless; between latitude 36° and 38° it is *Sierra de San Marcos;* and between about 38° and 39° again Sierra Nevada. This extraordinary map presents, on the whole, the same orographic picture of the southern half of the State which we see on modern maps. Unfortunately, Font's map of 1777 was unknown to later cartographers, and Humboldt's map of 1811 has only a vague *Sierra de San Marcos* between latitude 36° and 39°. Langsdorff in 1806 repeatedly mentions the name Sierra Nevada, but he did not publish a map. American and European cartography remained vague about the location of the range, and it was sometimes confused with the Rocky Mountains. Narváez' Plano of 1830, finally, gave again a fairly accurate location but left the range nameless. Wilkes' map of 1841 calls it California Range, and the Frémont-Preuss map of 1845 records Sierra Nevada of California. Several American cartographers attempted in vain to substitute Snowy Mountains or California Range. Muir suggested the sentimental name Range of Light. The present northern limitation of the range is indicated at 40° 20' on Erman's map of 1849 where it is labeled Sierra Nevada or *Blaue Berge* (Blue Mountains). By decision of the Geographic Board (*Sixth Report*) the range is limited on the north by the gap south of Lassen Peak, on the south by Tehachapi Pass. The range is often spoken of colloquially as "the Sierra Nevadas," "the Sierras," or the tautological "Sierra Nevada Mountains."

Sifford Lakes [Lassen Volcanic National Park]
The lakes were named for the Sifford family,
who acquired Drakesbad in 1900; the name
was approved by the Geographic Board in
1937.

Signal. It is common usage in place naming to
attach this word to an eminence which serves
as a signal station in warfare and in explorations and surveys. California has more than
thirty such names, mainly Buttes and Hills,
but also a number of Creeks. **Signal Lake;
Mount Signal** [Imperial]. The lake and the
settlement were named after Signal Mountain, which is just across the border in Mexico. This mountain was named during the
Boundary Survey: "The prominent mountain lying about four miles S. 10° E. from
camp, and apparently 2,000 feet in height,
must serve as a beacon to travelers crossing
from the Colorado, and may probably be
found a convenient point from which to flash
gunpowder for the determination of the difference of longitude between San Diego and
the mouth of the Rio Gila. Hence it may be
called 'Signal mountain,' and this lake so
near its foot 'Signal lake.' (Whipple, *Extract,*
1849, p. 9.) **Signal Hill** [Los Angeles]. The
eminence had been known since Spanish
times as *Los Cerritos.* When the Coast Survey
established the Los Angeles Base Line in
1889–1890, John Rockwell erected a signal
on the hill and it became known as Signal
Hill. The Coast Survey charts and other maps
retained the old Spanish name for some time,
but the popular name became official after
the discovery of oil in 1921. "I recognize a hill
near the town on which I erected a signal and
which bears the name of Signal Hill to this
day" (Rockwell to Davidson, Feb. 5, 1905).

Silaxo. *See* Oxalis.

Sill, Mount [Kings Canyon National Park].
Joseph N. LeConte named the peak in 1896,
in memory of Edward R. Sill (1841–1887),
poet, and professor of English at the University of California from 1874 to 1882.

**Silliman, Mount; Silliman: Creek, Crest, Lake,
Pass** [Sequoia National Park]. Named by the
Whitney Survey in June, 1864, in honor of
Benjamin Silliman, Jr. (1816–1885), profes-
sor of chemistry at Yale (Farquhar).

Silsbee [Imperial]. The town was laid out in
1902 and named for Thomas Silsbee, a cattleman of San Diego, who had pastured his
stock here.

Silurian: Valley, Lake [San Bernardino]. The
valley southwest of Death Valley was named
because of the Silurian (Paleozoic) rocks.

Silva: Flat, Reservoir [Modoc National Forest]
The flat became known as Silva's because a
man named Silva drove his sheep from the
Sacramento Valley to pasture here in summer. The reservoir was constructed in the
1920's and named after the flat (R. B. Sherman).

Silver. This word is found in the names of more
than seventy-five physical features in California. A number of these, including the
peak, creek, valley, and the old mining
towns Silver Mountain and Silverking in
Alpine County, were named for the occurrence of silver ore. Most of them, however,
especially the many creeks and lakes, were
given the name because of their silvery appearance. **Silver Lake** [San Bernardino]. The
station of the old Tonopah and Tidewater
Railroad was named in 1906 because it is at
the edge of a large dry lake known as Silver
Lake (W. W. Cahill). **Silver: Creek, Peak,
Pass, Divide** [Fresno]. The cluster name had
its origin in Silver Creek, which was given the
name in 1892 by T. S. Solomons because of
its silvery appearance (Farquhar). The peak
was named after the creek, by Solomons also,
but the name for the pass and divide were
applied by the Geological Survey when the
Mount Goddard quadrangle was surveyed in
1907-1909. **Silver: Creek, Mountain** [Alpine].
Rich silver deposits were discovered here
about 1860 and a mining town, now disappeared, is said to have been established by
Scandinavian miners and called Kongsberg
after the mining town in Norway. The post
office established on May 12, 1863, was
named Konigsberg; in 1865 it was changed
to Silver Mountain, and in 1879 to Silver
Creek. The "Silver" in some names refers to
the occurrence of quicksilver, often called
"silver."

Silverado: Canyon, town [Orange]. The name
was coined in analogy to Eldorado, connot-
ing silver instead of gold. It was given to the
canyon when silver was discovered there in
the 1870's (Stephenson). The post office is
listed in 1932. **Silverado** [Napa]. The now
vanished mining community flourished in
the early 'seventies. In the summer of 1880
Robert Louis Stevenson lived here with his
bride and wrote *The Silverado Squatters.*
There is also a Silverado Canyon in Mono
County.

Silveyville [Solano.] Named for Elijah S. Silvey,
who built a tavern there in 1852. A post office
was established July 25, 1864.

Simi, sē-mē′: Hills, Peak, town [Ventura]. The

name is recorded in its present form in 1795 as the name of a land grant, regranted March 8, 1821, and April 25, 1842. *Un Balle [Valle] que se llama Simi,* 'a valley called Simi,' is mentioned on February 3, 1796 (Arch. MSB, II, 10), and the name appears repeatedly in mission and provincial records. It is shown on Narváez' Plano of 1830. The Parke-Custer map of 1855 shows Rancho Semi, Semi Pass and Rio Semi (for Calleguas Creek). The spelling Simi is restored on Goddard's map. According to Kroeber, the name is from the "Ventura dialect Chumash Shimiyi or Shimii, a place or village." When the post office was established, January 19, 1889, it bore the impressive name Simiopolis; six months later, on July 15, the name Simi was adopted.

Simmler [San Luis Obispo]. Named for the Simmler family. John J. Simmler, a native of Alsace, came to California in 1853, opened the first hotel at San Luis Obispo, and was for many years the postmaster there.

Simmons Peak [Yosemite National Park]. Named in 1909 by R. B. Marshall for Dr. Samuel E. Simmons, of Sacramento (Farquhar).

Simons [Los Angeles]. The name developed by common usage after Walter Simons of Pasadena established a brickyard at this place in 1905.

Simpson Meadow [Kings Canyon National Park]. Probably named for S. M. Simpson, a member of the family who ran sheep here in the 1880's. It was previously known as Dougherty Meadow, for Bill and Bob Dougherty, who pastured horses there, but that name has since been applied to a meadow on the Monarch Divide. (Farquhar.)

Sims [Shasta]. Brewer relates in an entry of September 14, 1862, that his party had camped at "Mr. Sim Southern's (long be his name remembered)," whose marvelous tales earned him the reputation that "with him 'truth is stranger than fiction'" (pp. 306, 310). Simeon Fisher Southern had settled there in 1859; the railroad station, previously known as Welch Station, was named Sims in 1887. The Post Office Department uses the name Hazel Creek, given May 15, 1877, after the creek where hazelnuts grow. *See* Hazel Creek.

Sing Peak [Yosemite National Park]. R. B. Marshall named this peak in 1899, for Tie Sing, the faithful Chinese cook for the Geological Survey from 1888 to 1918 (Farquhar).

Sink. A common generic term designating the spot where a stream disappears in the ground. The most notable of California's "sinks" is Soda Sink, where the Mojave is absorbed by the sand.

Sisar: Canyon, Creek, Peak [Ventura]. The name is derived from that of a Chumash village, *Sisá,* repeatedly mentioned in the archives of Mission San Buenaventura in and after 1807. *Rancheria de Sisa* is shown on the *diseño* of the El Rincon grant (1834).

Siskiyou, sĭs'-kĭ-yōō: **Mountains, County.** *Siskiyou* was the Chinook word for 'bobtailed horse,' originally taken over from the Cree language. "This name, ludicrously enough, has been bestowed on the range of mountains separating Oregon and California, and also on a county in the latter State. The origin of this designation, as related to me by Mr. [Alexander C.] Anderson, was as follows. Mr. Archibald [Alexander] R. McLeod, a chief factor of the Hudson's Bay Company, in the year 1828, while crossing the mountains with a pack train, was overtaken by a snow storm, in which he lost most of his animals, including a noted bob-tailed race-horse. His Canadian followers, in compliment to their chief, or 'bourgeois,' named the place the Pass of the Siskiyou,—an appellation subsequently adopted as the veritable Indian name of the locality, and which thence extended to the whole range, and the adjoining district." (Gibbs, *Chinook Jargon.*) Another interpretation derives the name from the French *six cailloux,* 'six stones.' In an argument delivered in the State senate on April 14, 1852, Senator Jacob R. Snyder of San Francisco, who had been instrumental in creating the new county on March 22, 1852, maintained that the name "Six Callieux" (!) was given to a ford in Umpqua River where Michel La Framboise, in 1832, had led a party of Hudson's Bay Company trappers over six stones in the river. Neither version has been substantiated by documentary evidence, and the real origin may forever be shrouded in obscurity.

Sisquoc, sĭs-kwŏk': **River, station, Condor Sanctuary** [Santa Barbara]. The name is obviously Chumash and means, according to local tradition, 'quail.' It was given to a land grant, dated April 17, 1845. The river is shown as *Arroyo de Siquico* on a *diseño* (1846) of the Cuyama grant. The station was named when the Pacific Coast Railroad was built in 1887. The Condor Sanctuary was set aside by the Forest Service in 1937 in an effort to preserve the California condor from extinction.

Sissel Gulch [Siskiyou]. The gulch near the head of Moffett Creek was named for John

Baker Sissel. *See* Cecilville.

Sisson. *See* Shasta.

Sister Elsie Peak [Los Angeles]. The mountain was named for a nun who was in charge of an Indian orphanage near-by. It is more commonly known as Mount Lukens, named for Theodore P. Lukens, Mayor of Pasadena, who encouraged the building of a fire tower on the summit (Wheelock). *See* Lukens Lake.

Sisters. *See* Brothers.

Sites [Colusa]. Named in 1887 by C. E. Grunsky, for John H. Sites, landholder (E. Weyand).

Sitio. The Spanish word as used in land-grant cases designated one square league, but like *paraje* it was sometimes used in a general sense for 'place' or 'location.'

Six Rivers National Forest. The name for the eighteenth national forest of the State was suggested by Peter B. Kyne, San Francisco author, and was accepted by the Forest Service in December, 1946. The new forest embraces the watersheds of Smith, Klamath, Trinity, Mad, Van Duzen, and Eel rivers.

Skaggs Springs [Sonoma]. Named for William and Alexander Skaggs, who acquired in 1856 the land on which the springs are situated and built a resort in 1864. The name is shown on the von Leicht–Craven map.

Skeggs Observation Point [San Mateo]. Named for Col. Ino H. Skeggs, later Assistant State Highway Engineer, when that section of Skyline Boulevard was built in 1922.

Skeleton Peak [Death Valley National Monument]. The high peak of the Funeral Mountains was so named because its slopes are marked like ribs (*Chuckwalla*, February 15, 1907).

Skidoo [Death Valley National Monument]. Established as a mining camp by Harry Ramsey and Bob Montgomery in 1906, when the phrase "Twenty-three, skiddoo!" was at the height of its popularity.

Ski Heil Peak [Lassen Volcanic National Park]. Winter sports enthusiasts chose this name for the peak, which is the center of their activities in the park. The Geographic Board approved the name in 1937. Ski Heil! is the German and Swiss salutation among winter sportsmen.

Skookum: Rock, Gulch [Siskiyou]. The name preserves an interesting word of the Chinook jargon, the trade language of the Pacific Northwest. It is derived from the word *skukum* of the Chehalis Indians, meaning 'strong,' and designating also a 'ghost' or an 'evil spirit' (Gibbs, *Chinook Jargon*). This

language has left other traces in the geographical nomenclature of Oregon, Washington, and California. *See* Siskiyou.

Skull Cave [Lava Beds National Monument]. According to J. D. Howard, the cave was named by E. L. Hopkins in 1892, when he and three companions discovered two human skeletons in the cave as well as numerous skulls of bighorn, antelope, and goats.

Sky High Valley [Siskiyou]. The unusual depression on the south end of Marble Mountains was named Sky High Valley because it is at an altitude of over 5,500 feet (Forest Service). **Sky High** [Butte] is the name of the ridge between the Middle and Little North forks of Feather River. **Sky Forest** [San Bernardino]. The community was founded in 1928 and was so named because it is on top of a ridge more than a mile high, surrounded by a forest of pine, fir, cedar, and oak, with only the sky above it (Mary Henck). **Sky Parlor** [Sequoia National Park] is the name of a rocky formation on Chagoopah Plateau.

Slate. Good slate suitable for building purposes is found in various sections of the State, and about fifty geographic features are named for outcrops of this valuable stone. Most of these are Slate Creeks because the stone is easily recognized when laid bare by the action of running water. **Slate Castle: Canyon, Creek** [Sierra]. Near the head of this canyon is a sharp outcrop of slate-gray rock, in shape and apparent size resembling a castle (Stewart).

Slate Hot Springs [Monterey]. Named for Thomas B. Slate, who settled near by in 1868 (*WSP*, No. 338, p. 56).

Slater Canyon [Riverside]. The canyon in the Cleveland National Forest, named in 1960 in memory of Durward F. Slater, a U.S. Forest Service employee who lost his life in the Decker fire in August, 1959.

Sleepers Bend [Imperial]. The bend in the Colorado River was named by Ives in January, 1858: "While turning a bend . . . we suddenly noticed upon the summit of a little hill on the left bank a ludicrous resemblance to a sleeping figure. The outlines and proportions were startlingly faithful" (*Report*, p. 50).

Slinkards Valley [Alpine]. A. James Slinkard, who was road supervisor of Douglas County, Nevada, from 1862 to 1865, later built a road up Slinkards Creek into what became known as Slinkards Valley (Maule).

Slippery Ford [El Dorado]. "The gold days' immigrants found here near the foot of the

Lover's Leap peak a shallow stream-crossing where the waters spread out over a large flat rock." This ford "was also a dangerous one because of the precarious footing on the water-polished rock and the swift-flowing stream dashing across the smooth surface." (John W. Winkley.) A post office called Slippery Ford existed from November 21, 1861, to January 13, 1911.

Sloat [Plumas]. The Western Pacific named the station in 1910, in honor of Commodore John Drake Sloat, who in July, 1846, took possession of California for the United States.

Slough. In England the generic term was used originally for a muddy place and then for a miry place. In America, in the Middle West, it came to designate any good-sized backwater, and, in California, it took on the meaning of tidal creek, estuary, river channel. (Stewart, pp. 265 f.) The tidal channels of the San Francisco Bay district are often called sloughs, although on maps they appear either as sloughs or as creeks. The term creek is usually applied where the channel is really the lower end of a running stream. The generic term slough is also used for the channels and branches of the lower Sacramento and San Joaquin river systems, as well as for channels in the Tulare Lake section (*see* Lucerne; Mussel Slough) and other regions where similar hydrographic conditions prevail. In Los Angeles County the name is used for two swampy lakes which have no connection with the ocean or with a river: Bixby Slough and Nigger Slough north of Wilmington. The name of Nigger Slough was changed to Laguna Dominguez by order of the Board of Supervisors, March 30, 1938 (Co. Surveyor). The term is also found in the name of a settlement: **Sloughhouse** [Sacramento], named after the hotel called the Slough House, which had been built in 1850 by Jared Sheldon on Deer Creek, a branch of the Cosumnes (Rensch-Hoover, p. 317). The post office is listed in 1916.

Slover Mountain [San Bernardino]. The isolated hill at Colton is a fitting monument to Isaac Slover, a pioneer settler of the district. Slover, a Kentuckian trapper, had first come to California with Pattie's party in 1828. He came back with a group from New Mexico about 1841–1843 and settled in what is now San Bernardino County. (Bancroft, V, 722.)

Slug. The word was a favorite miners' term for coarse gold nuggets and was also used for the large gold coins of the 1850's; it is preserved in Slug Canyon [Sierra] and Slug Gulch [Placer].

Sly Park; Sly Park: Creek, House [El Dorado]. The flat twelve miles east of Placerville was named for James Sly, one of the Mormons who discovered the valley on July 5, 1848, on their trek from Sutters Fort to Salt Lake (Bigler).

Smartsville [Yuba]. Named for James Smart, who built a hotel here in 1856. The post office is listed since 1867 as Smartville.

Smedberg Lake [Yosemite National Park]. Named in 1895 by Lieutenant Harry Benson, for Lieutenant William R. Smedberg, Jr., who was on duty in the park at that time (Farquhar).

Smeltzer [Orange]. Named for D. E. Smeltzer, who discovered that the drained peat lands in this district were adapted for growing celery (Co. Hist., 1911, p. 65).

Smith, Mount [Los Angeles]. Probably named for "Bogus" Smith, a miner in San Gabriel Canyon about 1860 (S. B. Show).

Smithflat [El Dorado]. Named for Jeb Smith, a pioneer rancher. The name appears on maps since the 1880's.

Smith: Meadow, Peak [Yosemite National Park]. Named for a sheep owner who claimed the Hetch Hetchy Valley and who drove his stock into it every summer (Geographic Board, No. 30).

Smith Mountain [Death Valley National Monument]. Named by the Merriam expedition in 1891 for F. M. ("Borax") Smith, president of the Pacific Coast Borax Company, "who aided the expedition in Death Valley in every possible way" (Palmer).

Smith Mountain [Riverside, San Diego]. Named for Thomas L. ("Pegleg") Smith, a native of Kentucky, and a well-known trapper and horsethief, who was in California probably as early as 1829. Smith is said to have discovered gold to the east of the mountain that now bears his name while leading a party of trappers in 1836, but the mine was never found again.

Smith River [Del Norte]. Jedediah Smith traversed this region in May and June, 1828, and either he or the cartographer, David H. Burr, applied the name to what is now the lower Klamath River. He believed this was a separate stream and that the upper Klamath and the Rogue River were one and the same. This error appears as late as 1851 in Findlay's *Directory* (p. 347, where Findlay in the same breath accuses Wilkes of inaccuracies). George Gibbs in September, 1851, comments on the confusion over the identity of the stream: "The name of 'Smith's river,' which, as a matter of tradition, has been bandied from pillar to post, shifting from Eel to Rogue's river, has recently vibrated between a stream running into Pelican bay, and another, called by some Illinois river, and supposed to be the south fork of Rogue's river. Of the former, called by the Klamath Indians the Eenag'h-paha, or river of the Eenagh's, we received, at different times, information from those who had visited it." (Schoolcraft, III, 137.) Gibbs applied Smith's name to the hitherto nameless river *north* of the Klamath. The river appears in this location on Goddard's map of 1857. The town Smith River on Highway 101 received a post office August 12, 1863. *See* Jedediah Smith State Park.

Smokehouse: Canyon, Creek [Lake]. The affluent of Salmon Creek was noted for its heavy run of salmon; in the early days both Indians and whites had camps along the stream for smoking and drying fish. It received its present name about 1870, when some one rigged up a crude smokehouse (Mauldin).

Smugglers Cove [Santa Cruz Island]. The name was applied by the Coast Survey when the east shore of the island was surveyed in 1855–1856. It is reminiscent of Spanish and Mexican days when stringent laws against free trade made smuggling a dangerous but profitable enterprise along the coast.

Snag Lake [Lassen]. The lake received its name from the old tree snags that stand in it. About two hundred years ago a lava flow from Cinder Cone formed a dam across a preëxisting lake, flooding the timbered area now forming the lake and killing the trees. There are several other Snag Lakes, probably all named for a similar reason.

Snake. California's twenty-odd Snake Rivers, Creeks, Lakes, Gulches, and Sloughs, as compared with the two hundred or more Rattlesnake place names, indicate that prospectors and settlers paid little attention to any but the venomous serpent. Some of the streams were not named because of the presence of snakes but because of the meandering course of the stream. Mendocino County has a Snakehouse Creek.

Snelling [Merced]. A hotel was built here in the summer of 1851 by John M. Montgomery, Samuel Scott, and David W. Lewis. When the Charles V. Snelling family bought the hotel in the fall of the same year the place became known as Snelling's Ranch, and it is mentioned by this name in the *Statutes* of 1854

(p. 222). From 1855 to 1872 it was the county seat; the post office is listed as Snelling's Ranch in 1867.

Sniktaw: Meadow, Creek [Siskiyou]. Years ago a man by the name of Watkins resided on this small tributary of Scott River. When his neighbors decided to name it for him, he objected, saying he would not have such a "snick" of a creek named for him. Thereupon the stream was called Sniktaw, Watkins' name in reverse. (Schrader.) Mr. Watkins was very likely William F. Watkins, assemblyman from Siskiyou County in 1859, who wrote for the *Golden Era* and the Sacramento *Union* under the pseudonym Sniktaw.

Snow, Snowy. These words are found in the names of a number of orographic features, including a Snowball Mountain [Santa Barbara]. They have not, however, attained the same prominence in California nomenclature as the corresponding Spanish word, *nevada*. Mount Lassen was formerly known as Snow Butte, and on early American maps the name Sierra Nevada was translated as "Snowy Mountains."

Soberanes: Creek, Point [Monterey]. Named for a member of the large Soberanes family, prominent in the political life of the Monterey district during the Mexican regime. Their ancestor was probably José María Soberanes, a soldier of the Portolá expedition.

Soboba: Hot Springs, Indian Reservation [Riverside]. The name of a Luiseño village appears, with various spellings, since 1865 in the annual Reports on Indian Affairs. Kroeber gives the native form as *Sovovo* (*AAE*, VIII, 39).

Sobrante. A Spanish generic term used in connection with land grants. It refers to the overplus or surplus land of an area after the granted land has been measured and separated from the public domain. This surplus land was often made a new grant and the name *Sobrante* was attached to the specific name. The most celebrated Sobrante land-grant case in California annals is that of the New Helvetia Sobrante, granted to Sutter by Micheltorena February 5, 1845, but rejected by the U.S. Supreme Court on February 14, 1859. (Bowman.) **El Sobrante,** sồ-brän'-tẻ; **Sobrante Ridge** [Contra Costa]. When the Central Pacific was built from Berkeley to Tracy in 1878, the name Sobrante was applied to the station because it was on El Sobrante land grant, dated April 23, 1841. When the post office was established in 1945 the Spanish article "El" was added to the name.

Soda. The collective name for natural mineral waters, characteristically effervescent, is applied to more than a hundred hydrographic features, half of which are springs. In Lake, Nevada, Placer, San Bernardino, and Siskiyou counties the word appears in the names of communities. **Upper Soda Springs** [Siskiyou]. The name Soda Springs was probably already used by Hudson's Bay Company trappers who crossed the Sacramento at this spot. It is mentioned in the Pacific Railroad *Reports* and became widely known when Ross Mc-Cloud in 1857 built the famous inn and developed the springs. About 1889 the name was changed to Upper Soda Springs to distinguish it from Lower Soda Springs five miles south. (Marcelle Masson.) **Soda Springs** [Nevada]. The springs were developed by Mark Hopkins and Leland Stanford about 1870, and were known as Hopkins Springs until the post office was established March 8, 1875 (Morley). From 1867 to 1873 the station of the Central Pacific was known as Tinkers Station (Doyle). *See* Tinkers.

Solana Beach [San Diego]. The town was platted in 1923 by Colonel Ed Fletcher and given the Spanish name for 'sunny place' (Santa Fe).

Solano, sỏ-lä′-nō: **County.** The county, one of the original twenty-seven, was created February 18, 1850, and was named, at the request of Vallejo, in honor of both the apostle of South America in the 16th century, Saint Francis Solano, and his namesake, the chief of the Suisun Indians, Francisco Solano. The latter, originally called Sem-yeto, 'brave or fierce hand,' had probably received the name of the patron of Mission San Francisco Solano when he was baptized there. Of all great Franciscan friars, Saint Francis Solano probably stood next to Saint Francis of Assisi in the esteem of the missionaries of California. As many as three places were named for him by members of the Portolá expedition (Crespi, pp. 9, 92, 109, 138). On November 25, 1795, Padre Antonio Danti, in a place called San Francisco Solano, raised a cross where Mission San Jose was later set up (Arch. MSB, IV, 192 ff.). In 1823 Padre José Altimira, a young, ambitious friar at the San Francisco mission (Dolores), took up a previously discussed idea of giving up the mission in San Francisco and founding a new mission in what is now Sonoma County, which was to absorb the missions of San Francisco and San Rafael. He had the support of Governor Argüello, and on July 4, 1823, raised the cross at the site of the new mission and called it *Nuevo San Francisco,* i.e., after the old San Francisco Mission which was to be discontinued (Engelhardt, III, 178). The ecclesiastic authorities naturally did not approve of this illegal step, but after many bitter words a compromise was effected: old San Francisco as well as San Rafael remained as missions but Altimira was permitted to found the new mission, which, however, on the day of dedication, April 4, 1824, was rechristened San Francisco Solano (Bancroft, II, 504 f.). It was the last mission established on California soil. It is now usually referred to as Sonoma Mission, and Solano County alone preserves the memory of the great South American missionary.

Soldier. The names of more than ten geographic features in California include the word soldier; most of them were probably given by early settlers to places where soldiers were stationed for their protection. It is significant that most of these names are found in the northeastern counties, where complete pacification of the Indians was not achieved until about 1870. A few old mining camps bore the name because of the presence of a soldier, most likely a deserter. Soldier Meadow and Detachment Meadow at the headwaters of the San Joaquin [Madera] date back to the Army's administration of near-by Yosemite National Park (David Brower).

Soledad. The Spanish word for 'solitude' was repeatedly used for place naming in Spanish times. Not all Soledad names referred to an isolated place; some are a shortening of *Nuestra Señora de la Soledad* (Our Lady of Solitude). **Soledad,** sôl′-ê-dăd: **Valley, Canyon, Mountain** [San Diego]. The Portolá expedition crossed the valley on July 15, 1769, and named it Santa Isabel in honor of Elisabeth, Queen of Portugal, a saint of the 14th century (Crespi, p. 124). Anza records in his diary under date of January 10, 1776, that the Indian rancheria in the valley had been Christianized by the San Diego mission and was called *La Soledad.* On April 13, 1838, the name was applied to a land grant. Emory in 1846 gives Solidad [creek]; Williamson in 1853, Soledad, for a settlement at the site of present Sorrento; Coast Survey, 1874, Soledad Valley. **Soledad,** sŏl′-ê-dăd [Monterey]. The name is a folk-etymological rendering of an Indian name. "They told me that they gave it this name because in the first expedition of Portolá they asked an Indian his name and he replied, 'Soledad,' or so it sounded to them" (Font, *Compl. Diary*, pp. 287 f.). When the mission was founded, October 9, 1791, Padre Lasuén included the old term in the name: *La Mision de Nuestra Señora de la Soledad.* The post office was established and named after the mission in 1870. **Soledad,** sŏl'-ĕ-dăd: **Canyon, Pass** [Los Angeles]; **Mountain** [Kern]. The pass was discovered by Williamson in 1853. "As the existence of this pass was supposed previously to be unknown, I named it New Pass" (Pac. R.R. *Reports,* Vol. V, Pt. 1, p. 30). Blake renamed it Williamson's Pass, in honor of the discoverer. Bancroft's map of 1859 has again New Pass, but the Land Office map of 1859 relabels it La Soledad Pass, after an Indian village so named, shown on the *diseño* of Rancho San Francisco, 1838. The von Leicht–Craven map of 1874 has the present version.

Solis Canyon [Monterey]. The name of the canyon commemorates Joaquín Solís, a convict ranchero, one of the ringleaders of the revolt of 1828 at Monterey and *comandante general* after its temporary success. It is not known whether the land grant, Solis, in Santa Clara County, dated February 27, 1831, has any connection with the family name.

Solomon Canyon; Mount Solomon [Santa Barbara]. The name arose in the 1850's when the bandit Solomon Pico used the canyon as a base for his operations against the stagecoaches plying between Santa Barbara and San Luis Obispo. Solomon, a cousin of Pío Pico, governor of California, 1845–1846, is said to have taken to highway robbery as a protest against American occupation. By decision of the Geographic Board, July-Sept., 1965, Mount Solomon and the group of hills between Santa Maria and Los Alamos valleys are now called Solomon Hills.

Solromar, sŏl-rō-mär' [Ventura]. The name was selected by the Post Office Department from a list of twenty names submitted by residents. It was coined from the Spanish words *sol, oro,* and *mar* to suggest "golden sunset on the sea" (G. West). The post office is listed in 1945.

Solstice: Canyon, Creek [Los Angeles]. This astronomical term may have been used in the applied sense of "highest or farthest" for these places high in the Santa Monica Mountains, or it may have been given at the time of a solstice.

Solvang, sŏl'-văng [Santa Barbara]. The colony was founded in 1911 by the Danish-American Corporation, an organization headed by professors of the Danish college in Des Moines; the name is Danish, meaning 'sun meadow.'

Somersville [Contra Costa]. The thriving community at the time of the Mount Diablo coal boom was named for Francis Somers, one of the men who located the Black Diamond vein in 1859.

Somesbar, sōmz-bär'; **Somes Mountain** [Siskiyou]. According to local tradition, the place was named for a gold miner (D. Maginnis). The name is shown on the Land Office map of 1879 as Some's Bar and on the Mining Bureau map of 1891 as Sumner's Bar. The post office has been listed under the present name in Postal Guides since 1892.

Somis [Ventura]. A rancheria named *Somes* is mentioned in the records as early as 1795 and 1796 (PSP, XIV, 35; Prov. Recs., III, 47, 56). The name is spelled *Somes* and *Somo* by Taylor (July 24, 1863), and it was transferred with the new spelling to a Southern Pacific station when the section of the Ventura-Burbank line was built in 1899–1900.

Sonoma, sô-nō'mà: **Mission, Creek, Valley, County, Mountain,** town. The name of the Indian tribe is mentioned in 1815 in baptismal records as *Chucuines o Sonomas,* by Chamisso in 1816 as *Sonomi,* and repeatedly in Mission records of the following years. The name is doubtless derived from the Wintun word for 'nose,' which Padre Arroyo (Lengua, p. 22) gives as *sonom* (Suisun); other versions are *sonó* (Patwin) and *sūnō* (Wintu). Bowman's theory that Spaniards who found an Indian chief with a prominent protuberance applied "Chief Nose's" nickname to the village and the territory is plausible. Beeler believes that the name applied originally to a nose-shaped orographic feature (*CFQ,* V, 300 ff.; *AAE,* XXIX, 354; *WF,* XIII, 268 ff.). The interpretation 'valley of the moon' is more poetic but less authentic. Sonoma Mission, as it is commonly called, was established in 1824 and named San Francisco Solano. The town was founded by M. G. Vallejo in 1835, is recorded as Zanoma on Wilkes' map of 1841, and with the present spelling by Duflot de Mofras (1844). The post office was established November 8, 1849. Town, creek, and valley are mentioned in the *Statutes* of 1850. The county, one of the original twenty-seven, was created and named on February 18, 1850.

Sonora, sô-nôr'-à: town, **Creek, Pass** [Tuolumne]; **Peak** [Alpine]. The camp was established in the summer of 1848 by Mexican miners from the state of Sonora. It was first called Sonorian Camp to distinguish it from American Camp, as Jamestown was called at that time. When it was made the county seat, February 18, 1850, the name was changed to Stewart, for Major William E. Stewart (*Statutes*, 1850, p. 63). On April 18, 1850, the name was changed to the present form (*Statutes*, 1850, p. 263), probably as the result of local pressure.

Soquel, sō-kĕl': **Creek,** town, **Canyon, Cove, Point, Valley** [Santa Cruz]. *Rio de Zoquel,* apparently named after an Indian village, is mentioned as early as 1807 (Arch. Arz. SF, II, 60 f.). The name, spelled Soquel and Shoquel, was given to two land grants, dated November 23, 1833, and January 7, 1844. Town and creek are spelled Sauquil on Eddy's map (1854), and Shoquel on Hoffmann's map (1873), but the name of the post office, established July 5, 1857, is spelled Soquel.

Sorenson Hill [Butte]. The hill northwest of Oroville was named for Neils Sorenson, who homesteaded here about 1880 (Geographic Board, Jan.-Mar., 1965).

Sorrento [San Diego]. The townsite was laid out during the boom of 1886–1888 and named Sorrento after the Italian city, to which, however, it had no resemblance. The town did not develop, but the name was preserved in the name of the post office. (Grace Diffendorf.)

Soscol. *See* Suscol.

Sotcher. *See* Satcher.

Sotoyome [Sonoma]. *Rio de Satiyome* is mentioned by Vallejo on March 28, 1836 (Vallejo Docs., III, 347), and Mark West Creek is labeled *Sotoyome* on a *diseño* of the Molino grant. The name was given to a land grant, dated September 28, 1841, and November 12, 1844. According to Barrett (*Pomo,* p. 218), the name is derived from a place name, meaning 'the home of Soto,' i.e., of the chief of a Southern Pomo village near Healdsburg. According to Josefa Carrillo Fitch, patentee of the grant, the name consists of *sati,* 'brave,' and *yomi,* 'rancheria' (Fitch, Narración).

Soulajulle [Marin]. The name of the land grant, dated March 29, 1844, is probably derived from a Coast Miwok word. It is shown on several *diseños* with various spellings, but its meaning is unknown.

Soulsbyville [Tuolumne]. The gold deposits at this place were discovered in 1856 while the Platt Brothers were hunting for their cattle. In 1858 Benjamin Soulsby and his

sons struck even richer deposits. The place was named for them and became one of the richest gold-producing localities in the county. A post office was established July 16, 1877; the town is Historic Landmark 420.

South America, Lake [Sequoia National Park]. The name was applied in 1896 by Bolton C. Brown because the outline of the lake resembles the map of the southern continent (Farquhar).

Southampton: Bay, Shoal [San Francisco Bay]. This bay on the north shore of Carquinez Strait and the shoal southwest of Richmond were named by the Coast Survey in the 1850's for the U.S.S. *Southampton,* which led Commodore Jones' fleet to its anchorage at Benicia in the spring of 1849. The name is shown on Ringgold's General Chart of 1850.

South Dos Palos [Merced]. The post office was established about 1907, and was named after near-by Dos Palos. *See* Dos Palos.

Southerns [Shasta]. Named after Southern's Station, established on the Sacramento before 1879 by Sim F. Southern. *See* Sims.

South Fork [Humboldt]. A post office of this name was established June 19, 1861, and so named because of its situation on the South Fork of Eel River. It lasted only one year. When the Northwestern Pacific Railroad reached the place in 1910, the station was called Dyerville, after the (now vanished) town and post office across Eel River (Borden). October 17, 1933, a new post office was established with the old name.

South Fork Peak [Lassen]. The peak was so named because it is near the South Fork of Pit River.

South Gate [Los Angeles]. Named in 1918 after the South Gate Gardens on the Cudahy Ranch, which had been opened to the public in 1917. In 1923, when the city was incorporated, the shortened form was adopted. The name indicates the location south of Los Angeles.

South Guard. *See* North Guard.

South Laguna [Orange]. The resort was founded in 1926 by Lewis H. Lasley. When the post office was established in 1933 it was named Three Arches because of a picturesque rock formation. In 1934 the Post Office Department, upon petition of residents, changed the name to South Laguna because it is situated just south of the well-known city of Laguna Beach. (J. C. Lasley.)

South Pasadena [Los Angeles]. The city was laid out on the land of the Indiana Colony in 1885, by O. R. Dougherty of the South

Pasadena Land Office.

South San Francisco [San Mateo]. A subdivision on what is now Hunters Point was laid out and named South San Francisco in 1849 but failed to materialize. When the industrial settlement south of San Bruno Mountain developed, it was first called Baden after the railroad station; when the city was incorporated in 1908 the present name was suggested by William J. Martin.

Spadra [Los Angeles]. Established as a stage station in the 1850's and named after Spadra Bluffs, Arkansas, the former home of William Rubottom, first American settler in the valley and owner of the local tavern. In 1874 the name was given to the Southern Pacific station; the post office is listed in 1880.

Spanish. This adjective of nationality is comparatively rare in the toponymy of the State. It appears in probably not more than thirty place names, most of which are survivors of the mining days when the camps of the Mexicans, South Americans, and Portuguese were usually designated as "Spanish." It is preserved in the place called Spanish Ranch and the post office Spanish Creek in Plumas County, two former post offices, Spanish Flat and Spanish Diggings in El Dorado County, Spanish Peak [Fresno] and a number of hills and creeks. Half Moon Bay [San Mateo] was formerly called Spanishtown.

Spaulding, Lake [Nevada]. The reservoir was created by the South Yuba Water and Mining Company in 1892 and named for "Uncle" John Spaulding, one of its organizers, a former well-known stagecoach driver. In 1912–1913 the Pacific Gas and Electric Company built a new dam half a mile below but kept the old name.

Speckerman Mountain [Madera]. Named in the 1850's for a settler who lived at the foot of the mountain (Blanche Galloway).

Spence [Monterey]. The name was applied to the Southern Pacific station when the section from Salinas to Soledad was built in 1872 and 1873. It commemorates David Spence, grantee of the Encinal y Buena Esperanza grant, on which the station was established. Spence, a native of Scotland, came from Peru to Monterey in 1824 and became one of the most influential foreigners in California.

Spencer, Mount. *See* Evolution.

Spenceville [Nevada]. A post office was established in the 1870's and named after the Spenceville school district, which had been formed in 1868 and named for Edward Spence of Nevada City, who had donated the lumber for the school building ("The Knave," March 8, 1942).

Spiller: Creek, Lake [Yosemite National Park]. Named for J. Calvert Spiller, a topographical assistant with the Wheeler Survey, 1878–1879 (Farquhar).

Split Mountain [Kings Canyon National Park]. The peak which the Wheeler Survey had called Southeast Palisade and which for a while was known as South Palisade was renamed by Bolton C. Brown in 1895. "To the north . . . the crest rises into a huge mountain with a double summit . . . which I called Split Mountain" (*SCB*, I, 309). In Kern County there is another Split Mountain, and there are about ten Split Rocks in various sections of the State.

Spreckels [Monterey]. Named for Claus Spreckels, a native of Germany and one of the leaders in the industrial development of California, who established a sugar refinery here in 1899.

Spring. Most of the place names that include the word were applied because of the presence of an active spring; some may be transfer names, since the combination with Spring is a favorite in place naming throughout the United States. The word is included in the names of eight post offices and communities: Springdale [Los Angeles], Springfield [Tuolumne], Spring Garden [Plumas], Springs [San Luis Obispo], Springside [Contra Costa], Spring Valley [San Diego], Springville [Tulare]. It is also found frequently as the specific name for physical features; the best known of these is Spring Valley [San Mateo], the site of the reservoirs of the San Francisco water supply. The water company was not named after the valley but vice versa. The original Spring Valley was somewhere between Mason and Taylor and Washington and Broadway in what is now downtown San Francisco. When the supply from the "spring" in this valley became inadequate for the fast-growing population, the company turned to a new source and took the name along.

Sproul Grove [Humboldt]. The grove in the Prairie Creek Redwoods State Park was established in 1959 in honor of Robert G. and Ada W. Sproul. Sproul was president of the University of California, 1930-1958, and has been treasurer of the Save-the-Redwoods League for many years,

Sprowell Creek [Mendocino]. Named for brothers who settled here in the 1850's and were killed by Indians (Asbill). *See* Pipe Creek;

Bell Spring Mountain.

Spy Mountain [San Bernardino]. According to O'Neal (p. 77), it was named for a citizen of Giant Rock, suspected of being a spy in World War II.

Spyrock: Peak, post office [Mendocino]. According to local tradition, the high rock, which commands a good view of the country, was used by Indians to spy on white settlers. The name was applied to the station when the Northwestern Pacific was completed in 1915.

Squash Ann Creek [Humboldt]. This is a typical example of folk etymology. The name is a folk rendering of the Yurok Indian *Qwo' San Wroi* (Waterman, map 29). It is spelled Squashan on the Orick atlas sheet and on most other maps.

Squaw. The word, meaning 'woman,' is found, variously spelled and pronounced, in many Algonkian Indian dialects in the eastern United States: Narranganset: *eskwaw;* Delaware, *ochqueu;* Cree, *iskwew* (A. F. Chamberlain in Hodge). In its Anglicized spelling it has spread throughout North America and is accepted (though sometimes resented) by western Indians. In California the word has been loosely applied since the gold-rush days and has become a favorite term for place naming. There are very few counties in the State that do not have at least one Squaw Valley, Creek, Canyon, Hill, or Hollow. There is also a Squaw Dome [Madera], a Squaw Leap [Fresno], a Squaw Queen Creek [Plumas], a Squaw Tank [Joshua Tree National Monument], and two Squaw Tits [Humboldt, San Bernardino]. Squaw Valley [Fresno] and Squaw Creek [Placer] are settlements. **Squaw Rock** [Mendocino]. Historical Landmark 549, registered January 27, 1956. According to the Landmarks Committee, a jilted Indian girl named Sotuka took revenge by springing with a large rock upon her lover and his bride, who were sleeping below. All three were killed. **Squaw: Valley, Creek, Peak** [Placer]. The name goes back to the early mining and lumbering activities and is already recorded on Goddard's map of 1857. It has become a popular winter sports area, where the Winter Olympic Games were held in 1960. *See* Olympic Valley.

Stacy [Lassen]. The post office was established in 1914 and named for Mrs. Stacy Spoon (Mamie Dicting).

Stacy Creek [Shasta]. The tributary of Clear Creek was probably named for Thomas Stacy, a native of Kentucky, who was a resident of the county as early as 1871.

Stag. The use of this word in California place naming is much less frequent than Buck and Deer. There are only about ten places named Stag, including stately Stag Dome in Kings Canyon National Park and Stags Leap, a former post office in Napa County.

Staininger Ranch. *See* Scott.

Standard [Tuolumne]. The post office was established in 1912 and named for the Standard Lumber Company of Sonora (J. C. Rassenfoss).

Standard Canyon [Kern]. The canyon near Inyokern was named for an old settler named Standard, who had his ranch here and who died about 1960 (Wheelock).

Standish [Lassen]. The town was laid out in 1897. In 1899, H. R. T. Coffin of New York settled at the place and named it in honor of Miles Standish of Mayflower fame (F. J. Winchell).

Standish-Hickey State Park [Mendocino]. The Edward Hickey Memorial State Park, established July 21, 1950, was enlarged and renamed in 1953 when land (including the "Miles Standish Tree") was given for the park by Mr. and Mrs. S. M. Standish.

Standley State Recreation Area [Mendocino]. Created in 1944 in honor of Admiral William T. Standley, a native of the area.

Stanfield Hill [Yuba]. Named for William Stanfield, who opened, in 1856, the Stanfield House in Long Bar Township, just above the Galena House, another hotel on the old Foster Bar turnpike (Co. Hist., 1879, p. 87).

Stanford, Mount. *See* Crocker; Stanford University.

Stanford University [Santa Clara]. The university was established in 1885 by Leland Stanford (1824–1893), railroad builder, governor of California, and U.S. senator, and was named Leland Stanford Junior University by Mr. and Mrs. Stanford in memory of their son, who had died the preceding year. **Stanford, Mount** [Kings Canyon National Park]. Professor Bolton C. Brown, who made the first ascent, August, 1896, named the peak Mount Stanford for the University. He suggested as an alternate name Stanford University Peak, if the name Mount Stanford should be declared ineligible because of another peak so named in Placer County. This original Mount Stanford, which had been named by the Whitney Survey, was duly changed to Castle Peak, but in 1908 R. B. Marshall named one of the peaks surrounding Pioneer Basin, Mount Stanford, and now there are, after all, two Mount Stanfords in the State. *See* Crocker.

Stanislaus, stăn′-ĭs-lô, stăn′-ĭs-lôs: **River, County,** post office [Tuolumne]; **Peak** [Alpine]; **National Forest.** The river was discovered and named *Rio de Nuestra Señora de Guadalupe* by an expedition under Gabriel Moraga in October, 1806 (Arch. MSB, IV, 1–47). In 1827 or 1828, a neophyte, Estanislao, probably named for one of two Polish saints called Saint Stanislas, ran away from Mission San Jose and became the leader of a band of Indians in the San Joaquin Valley. Because it was feared that he was instigating a general uprising, two expeditions were sent out against him in 1829. The first accomplished nothing, but the second, under Mariano Vallejo, then *alférez* at Monterey, succeeded in breaking up the band in a bloody engagement at the *Rio de los Laquisimes.* (SP Mis. & C., II, 15 ff.) The river later came to be known by the name of the Indian leader who fought so bravely there. It is mentioned as *Rio Estanislao* in 1839 (Arch. SJ, I, 43). December 29, 1843, the name was used for a land grant, Rancheria del Rio Estanislao. Frémont used the Americanized version, Stanislaus River, in March, 1844 (*Expl. Exp.*, 1853, p. 359), and it appears on the Frémont-Preuss map of 1845. A Stanislaus City was founded at the site of Brannan's New Hope in 1849 (*Alta California,* September 27, 1849). It is now vanished, but it had a post office in 1875 and is still shown on the Land Office map of 1879 at the site of Ripon. The present-day post office Stanislaus is in Tuolumne County and was established August 17, 1911. The county was created April 1, 1854, from part of Tuolumne County. The national forest was created and named in 1897.

Stanton [Orange]. Named for its founder, Philip A. Stanton, Republican assemblyman from Los Angeles, 1903–1909. The post office is listed in 1912.

Star City Creek [Shasta]. The tributary of McCloud River preserves the name of the once prosperous Star City Mining District, which had probably been named for John B. Star, who is said to have operated a trading post there in the late 1850's (Steger).

Starr, Mount [Fresno, Inyo]. Named by the Sierra Club in memory of Walter A. Starr, Jr., a mountain climber of renown and author of the "Guide to the John Muir Trail and the High Sierra Region." The Geographic Board approved the name in 1938. The **Walter and Carmen Starr Grove** in the Humboldt Redwoods State Park was established in 1956 through the efforts of the Save-the-Redwoods League. The Walter A. Starr Grove in the Calaveras Big Trees State Park was established in 1959.

Starr King, Mount; Starr King: Lake, Meadow [Yosemite National Park]. The dome was named during the Civil War for Thomas Starr King (1824–1864), a Unitarian minister, who was influential in keeping California in the Union and who was the author of *The White Hills,* a classic on the White Mountains of New Hampshire. King and Junípero Serra were chosen to represent the State in the National Statuary Hall at Washington, D.C. The Indians had called the mountain *Tis-sa-ack,* 'cleft rock' (Bunnell, 1880, p. 212), and it was also known as South Dome before the name of the great orator became attached to it. The northeast peak of Mount Diablo, now labeled North Peak, had been named Mount King by Whitney when he, accompanied by King and others, ascended Mount Diablo on May 7, 1862 (Brewer, pp. 263, 267).

Starvation. The term was popular in early mining and exploring days when there was often danger that the grub might give out and the party be forced to hunt or forage in order to avoid starvation. More than ten canyons, creeks, and flats are still so named. There is a place called Starvout in Siskiyou County.

Starwein: Ridge, Flat [Del Norte]. An American version of a Yurok Indian place name, *Stowen* or *Stawain.*

Stateline [El Dorado]. The post office was established about 1900 and so named because it is just this side of the Nevada boundary.

Stauffer [Ventura]. Named for the Stauffer Chemical Company, which worked a borax deposit here before the commercial development of the extensive borax beds in Death Valley was begun in the 1880's.

Steamboat. The word is found in the names of no fewer than ten physical features in the State. It is interesting to observe that there were at least three different reasons for giving the name. **Steamboat Spring** [Sonoma]. "An opening in the rocks . . . through which is constantly ejected, with the noise of a number of steamers, a body of steam sufficient, could it be controlled, to propel a large amount of machinery" (Cronise, 1868, pp. 172 f.). **Steamboat Slough** [Yolo]. "When the Sacramento was first navigated fewer obstructions to navigation were encountered in Steamboat Slough than in old Sacramento River, as the other branch is called. For many years the slough was therefore the channel preferred by navigators..." (Wood's *Gazetteer*.) **Steamboat Rock** [Humboldt]. The name was given by the Coast Survey: "The upper part is white and the lower black, somewhat resembling a steamer with a low black hull and white upper works" (*Coast Pilot*, 1903, p. 95).

Steelys Fork [El Dorado]. The fork of Cosumnes River was named for Dr. J. W. Steely, who discovered and located a gold ledge here in March, 1852, and built two mills (Placerville *Democrat*, July 1, 1876). The name is misspelled Steeley Fork by the Geological Survey.

Stege, stēj [Contra Costa]. The railroad station and the school district preserve the name of Richard Stege, a native of Germany and a veteran of both the California gold rush and the British Columbia gold rush. About 1890 Stege settled in what is now part of Richmond on a large farm, where among many other activities he raised frogs commercially. Stege post office is listed in 1892.

Steinberger Slough [San Mateo]. The slough is the only reminder of the once promising town named for Baron Steinberger (*CHSQ*, XXIII, 176). It had a post office from 1853 to 1856.

Stephens Grove [Humboldt]. The grove in the Humboldt Redwoods State Park was established in 1922 in honor of Governor William D. Stephens (1917-1923). It is one of the earliest properties acquired by the State for state park purposes.

Stevens Creek [Santa Clara]. Named for Captain Elisha Stevens, of the Stevens-Murphy-Townsend party of 1844, who once owned a ranch here. The Spanish name was *Arroyo de San Jose Cupertino;* Hoffmann's map of the Bay region (1873) shows Cupertino or Stephens Creek. Stephens was apparently the original spelling of the name. *See* Cupertino.

Stevens Mountain [Del Norte]. Named by the Forest Service for Phil Stevens, who for many years drove the stage between Crescent City and Grants Pass (Co. Hist., 1953).

Stevenson Memorial State Park [Napa]. Created in 1949 and named for Robert Louis Stevenson, who in 1880 spent his honeymoon at the site of the old town of Silverado.

Stevens Peak [Alpine]. The mountain was named for J. M. Stevens, a county supervisor, who operated the stage station in near-by Hope Valley in the 1860's. The name was placed on the map by the Geological Survey when the Markleeville quadrangle was surveyed in 1889.

Stevinson [Merced]. Named for James J. Stevinson, who acquired a large parcel of land on the lower Merced in August, 1852. The post office is listed in 1908.

Stewart, Mount George [Sequoia National Park]. The mountain was named in April, 1929, at the suggestion of the Kiwanis Club of Visalia, for George W. Stewart, one of the men responsible for the creation of Sequoia National Park in 1890 (State Library).

Stewarts Point: point, post office, **Creek** [Sonoma]. When members of the Coast Survey charted this section of the coast in 1875, they called a secondary triangulation point, Point Stewart. It is possible that the point was named for Lieutenant Colonel C. S. Stewart of the Corps of Engineers, who in that year was engaged in the removal of Noonday Rock near the Farallones.

Stillwater: Creek, Plains [Shasta]. In 1853, De Witt Clinton Johnson settled at the creek and named it after his home town, Stillwater, New York. There was a post office Stillwater between 1870 and 1890. (Steger.)

Stingleys Hot Springs [Ventura]. Named for the owner, S. G. Stingley (*WSP*, No. 338, p. 63).

Stinking Canyon Creek [Shasta]. This seems to be the only Stinking name recorded on the maps. Many more are used locally. *See* Hedionda.

Stinson Beach [Marin]. Named for Nathan H. Stinson, who settled in 1866 at Point Reyes and in 1871 acquired the land which included the beach (Co. Hist., 1880, p. 426).

Stirling City [Butte]. When the Diamond Match Company erected a sawmill here in 1903, J. F. Nash, the superintendent, applied the name because he had seen the firm name Stirling Boiler Works on the boilers ordered for the mill (M. W. Hedge).

Stockton [San Joaquin]. In 1845, Charles M. Weber, next to Sutter the most noted pioneer of the interior valley, purchased from William Gulnac the Rancho del Campo de los Franceses. The settlement which developed there was appropriately called Tuleburg; but Weber applied the present name shortly after Commodore Robert F. Stockton had taken possession of California for the United States. It is recorded in the *New Helvetia Diary* under date of October 14, 1847: "... the two Nemshau boys which arrived yesterday... brought a passport from Weber in Stockton." **Fort Stockton** [San Diego]. Historic Landmark 54. The old Spanish earthworks built in 1840 were improved by

Commodore Stockton in November, 1846, and were occupied by United States military forces until September, 1848. *See* Weber Creek.

Stoil [Tulare]. The name of the station was coined from *S*tandard *Oil* Company, which once had a pumping station here (Santa Fe).

Stone, Stony. The names of more than a hundred physical features contain the descriptive term "stone" or "stony." Fully half of these are creeks, the oldest of which are probably Stony Creek and its tributary Grindstone Creek in Glenn County. The former is shown as Stone Creek on a *diseño* of about 1846. In the last hundred years the terms "rock" and "rocky" have generally been preferred in the American language in the naming of orographic features: only an occasional Stony: Butte, Hill, Peak, Point, or Top may be found on the map of California. About ten Stone Corrals designate natural rock enclosures; Stonewall Canyon, northeast of Soledad [Monterey], was named because of its steep rocky slopes. Stone and Stony occur also in the names of eight communities; some of the Stone names may have been given for families of that name. **Stony: Creek, Valley** [Monterey]. The names were translated from the Spanish: *Arroyo de las Piedras* and *Cañon de las Piedras* are shown on a *diseño* of the San Miguelito grant, 1841. *See* Piedra. **Stonyford** [Colusa]. The town of Smithville on Stony Creek was established and named by John L. Smith in 1863. In 1890 the Stony Creek Improvement Company bought the place and moved the town one-half mile to a new site called Stony Ford. (Co. Hist., 1891, p. 284.) **Stony Gorge Reservoir** [Glenn]. The artificial lake was created in 1963, when Stony Creek was impounded by the Black Butte Dam.

Stonemans Mountain [Los Angeles]. Named in 1853 by R. S. Williamson of the Pacific Railroad Survey, for Lieutenant George Stoneman, a member of the party. Stoneman (1822–1894), a native of Busti, New York, had been quartermaster of the Mormon Battalion in 1846–1847; he became a famous cavalry leader in the Civil War and later governor of California (1883–1887). **Camp Stoneman** [Contra Costa]. The San Francisco army port of embarkation in World War II was named in honor of the same officer by order of the War Department, May 28, 1942.

Stone Valley [Contra Costa]. Named for Silas Stone, an early settler in the valley (Co. Hist., 1926, p. 471).

Storrie [Plumas]. The post office was established April 26, 1926, and named for R. C. Storrie, the first postmaster and builder of the Bucks Creek Power House.

Stovepipe Wells [Death Valley National Monument]. There are two wells here with an abundance of good water, one or both of which were once protected by a stovepipe; hence the name.

Stover Mountain [Riverside]. Named for Cristobal Stover, an early cattleman and bear hunter, who had come to this region with Louis Robidoux. The Indians called the mountain *Ta-hual-tapa*, 'raven mountain.' (*Desert Magazine*, Feb., 1939.)

Straight Spring Gulch [Calaveras]. So named to distinguish it from near-by Crooked Spring Gulch.

Stratford [Kings]. The town was laid out in the spring of 1907 on the old Empire Ranch and named Stratton for William Stratton, manager of the ranch. When the Post Office Department rejected this name, the present name was substituted. (Co. Hist., 1940, pp. 177 f.)

Strathmore [Tulare]. The Balfour Guthrie Company, a Scottish corporation, laid out the town about 1908, and at the suggestion of Mrs. Hector Burness, wife of one of the officials, gave it the Scottish name Strathmore, meaning 'broad valley.' The place had formerly been called Roth Spur and Santos.

Strawberry. The most popular of all folk names derived from an edible wild fruit. There are about fifty Strawberry names on the map and many more are used locally, mainly for creeks, valleys, and flats, but occasionally also for hills, peaks, and points. The word is also found in the names of communities in El Dorado, Los Angeles, San Bernardino, Tuolumne, and Yuba counties. **Strawberry** [Tuolumne]. The place on State Highway 108 is the oldest of the still surviving Strawberry names. Although the post office was established as early as June 16, 1849, it was apparently not a mining camp. **Strawberry Valley** [Yuba]. The old mining town now on State Highway 20, was settled in 1850 and is shown on the maps as early as 1851. The post office was established July 6, 1855. According to Joseph Booth's diary, June 6, 1852, it was actually so called for the abundance of wild strawberries. The County History of 1879, p. 97, agrees with it and even mentions the namegiver, Capt. William Mock. But other sources maintain that the name was combined from those of two settlers; a deputy sheriff of the county described the Straw Berry Valley in 1856 (Charles De Long, Jan. 26, 1856). **Strawberry Valley** [El Dorado]. Two different stories agree that the place was not named for strawberries but for Mr. Berry, owner of the old roadhouse there. The details of the naming vary. Since Berry's straw mattresses were insufficiently stuffed, his customers were wont to cry: "More straw, Berry" (*Out West*, Nov., 1904). The teamsters called him "Straw" Berry because he kept their oats and barley and fed straw to the horses (Wells Drury, *To Old Hangtown or Bust*, 1912, pp. 12 f.). The premises of later Strawberry Valley Station had actually been preëmpted by Mr. I. F. Berry in May, 1858, so these stories may have their merits (Ruth Teiser, *CFQ*, V, 302). **Strawberry Peak** [Los Angeles]. Named "by some wags at Switzer's camp in 1886, from its fancied resemblance to a strawberry standing with its blossom end up; but one of them said, 'We called it Strawberry Peak because there weren't any strawberries on it.' The joke took; and that burlesque name has been commonly used by the old settlers; but the peak is waiting some worthy occasion for a worthy name." (Reid, p. 370.) **Strawberry Valley** [Shasta]. This valley and the settlement Berryvale (now Mount Shasta) were so named because wild strawberries were actually found there in abundance. **Strawberry Flat** [San Bernardino]. The place was also named for the abundance of the fruit, but since July 29, 1916, it has been known as Twin Peaks because the Post Office Department refused to add another Strawberry name to those already in existence.

Striped Mountain [Kings Canyon National Park]. "That nearest the pass is strikingly barred across its steep craggy summit with light streaks. As this is an unusually marked case of this peculiarity ... I called it Striped Mountain." (B. C. Brown, *SCB*, I, 309.) There is a Striped (formerly Curious) Butte in Inyo County and a Striped Rock in Mariposa County.

Strong Creek [Humboldt]. Named for Samuel Strong, who came to Humboldt County in 1853.

Stronghold [Modoc]. When the Great Northern built its extension into California to meet the Western Pacific in 1930, the station was named after Captain Jack's Stronghold, locally so known because in the Modoc War the Indian leader held out here against U.S.

troops from December, 1872, to April, 1873. Historic Landmark 9. *See* Lava Beds; Modoc.

Stubbs Island [Clear Lake]. The island preserves the name of Charles ("Uncle Jack") Stubbs, an English sailor who purchased a large estate on the shore of East Lake. A post office was established June 14, 1926, as Stubbs, but the name was changed to Clearlake Oaks, June 1, 1935 (Mauldin).

Styx [Riverside]. When the Santa Fe branch from Rice to Ripley was built in 1921, this station was given the name of the river of the lower world, although not even an intermittent creek is in evidence. Since the place is in the midst of the desert the location engineer might have intended to call it "Sticks," an out-of-the-way place.

Subeet [Solano]. The name of the Southern Pacific siding in the sugar-beet region was coined from the words *sugar* and *beet*.

Success Lake [Tulare]. The reservoir was formed by "successfully" damming Tule River east of Porterville (Geographic Board, Sept.-Dec., 1961).

Sucker. Of a number of places so named in mining days only Sucker Run [Butte] and Sucker Flat [Yuba] remain on modern maps. The latter was named for an early settler, named Gates, who came from Illinois, the "Sucker State" (Co. Hist., 1879, p. 84). It could not be ascertained whether the other names were applied for the same reason, or because the well-known carplike sucker fish was caught there, or because a camp was inhabited by "suckers." Respectable Californians were doubtless relieved when the Geographic Board (*Sixth Report*) changed the spelling of Sucker Flat [Placer] to Succor Flat (pron., sŭk'-ēr). The Oregonians, to be sure, had to submit at the same time to the Board's decision for Sucker Creek ("not Succor") in Malheur County.

Suey Creek, station [Santa Barbara]. Suey was the name of a land grant, dated April 6, 1837. The *diseño* of the grant is labeled *Sitio de Sue,* and an Arroyo of Suey is shown on an 1850 map of the rancho. It is probably derived from a Chumash word, but its meaning and origin are not known.

Sugarbowl Dome [Sequoia National Park]. So named because a depression, filled with snow most of the year, has the aspect of a bowl filled with sugar. There is another Sugar Bowl near Donner Summit, named for the same reason.

Sugar Hill [Modoc]. A wagon, partly loaded with sugar, on its way from Yreka to the military garrison at Fort Bidwell in the early 1870's, broke down, scattering soldiers' sugar ration all over the hillside; hence the name (W. S. Brown). It is not known whether Sugar Lake and Creek in Siskiyou County were named for a similar reason.

Sugarloaf. In former centuries sugar was not put up in bags or boxes, but was delivered in the form of a "loaf" to the grocer, who would break off pieces and sell it by the pound. So familiar was the sight of the conoidal sugar loaf that the word was applied to any object of similar form. It developed finally into a geographical generic term, applied to a mountain so shaped, and the map of the United States became dotted with thousands of "sugar loafs." California has its share of some hundred orographic features so named. When used as a descriptive generic term the name is usually spelled in two words, Sugar Loaf, but when the term is used with Hill, Mountain, Peak, and Butte it is usually spelled as one word. There is, naturally, an assortment of Sugarloaf Creeks, Lakes, and Meadows, named after a near-by Sugar Loaf. In Placer County [Colfax sheet] there is a group of peaks called Sugarloaves (*Names*, December, 1956). **Sugarloaf** [San Bernardino]. When the old Big Bear Park post office was reopened January 1, 1947, Mrs. Mary E. Hebert proposed the present name because the post office nestles (at 7,200 feet elevation) on Sugarloaf Mountain (Carmel Botkin).

Sugar Pine. The valuable tree, which grows to an imposing height and is seldom found in solid stands, has given its name to some thirty geographical features. *See* Pine. The name of the town **Sugar Pine** [Madera] owes its origin to a 200-foot-tall tree near the sawmill (Blanche Galloway).

Suisun, sŭ-soōn': **Bay, Creek, City, Valley, Hill, Point, Slough, Cutoff** [Contra Costa, Solano]. The bay was explored by Cañizares in August, 1775, and is labeled *Junta de los quatro Evangelistas* on Ayala's map. Since Cañizares reported that it contained fresh water (Eldredge, *Portolá*, p. 67), it became known as *Puerto Dulce* and is mentioned as Freshwater Bay as late as 1842 (Simpson, *Narrative*, I, 405). Abella's diary (October 28, 1811) mentions *estero de los Suisunes*, named after the Indian tribe or village on the north shore, whose name appears in records from 1807 on, with a great variety of spellings. L. A. Argüello speaks of *Bahilla de Suysun* on May 13, 1817, and *Bahia de los Suysunes* is shown on the Plano topografico de la Mision de San

Jose (about 1824). The modern spelling appears in the name of Suisun land grant, dated January 28, 1842. Suisun Valley, River [Creek], and Embarcadero [City] are mentioned in the *Statutes* of 1850 (pp. 61, 100). The meaning of the name is not known.

Sullivan Creek [Tuolumne]. The name of the creek is reminiscent of one of the richest gold deposits in the Sonora district, which was discovered by John Sullivan in 1848 and became known as Sullivan's Diggings (Buffum, 1850, p. 126). Sullivan's Creek is shown on Gibbes' map of 1852.

Sulphur. The frequent occurrence of sulphurous springs has given the State about 150 place names containing the word; most of these are Springs, but there are also Sulphur Creeks, Canyons, Gulches, Mountains, and one Sulphur Gap [Colusa]. No Sulphur Lake could be discovered.

Sultana [Tulare]. The station was called Atla when the San Francisco and San Joaquin Valley Railroad reached the place in 1898. Because of the possible confusion with Alta [Placer] the name was changed when the post office was established about 1900. The Sultana grapes grown there at that time are now largely supplanted by Thompson Seedless.

Summerland [Santa Barbara]. The town was laid out in 1888 by H. L. Williams, shortly after the section of the Southern Pacific had been built from Santa Barbara to Ventura. Although the United States was then dotted with place names containing the word "summer," the combination Summerland was unusual, if not unique, at that time.

Summers: Creek, Back Pasture [Mono]. In the 1860's Jesse Summers, a butcher, grazed cattle in the natural meadows which became known as Summers Back Pasture (Maule).

Summersville [Tuolumne]. Franklin and Elizabeth Summers settled at this place on Turnback Creek in 1854. The settlement developed after the discovery of gold in the spring of 1856. Registered as Historical Landmark 407, April 14, 1948.

Summit. When the highest point of a mountain pass is crossed by a trail, a highway, or a railroad, the name Summit is almost invariably applied. Six railroad stations in California are called Summit. The term also appears in the names of about fifty creeks, lakes, meadows, rocks, springs, etc., at or near a summit. **Summit Range** [Kern, San Bernardino] was so named because the Owenyo branch of the Southern Pacific reaches the highest point here. **Summit City** [Shasta]. The town was founded when construction of Shasta Dam was started in 1938, and was so named because it is near the summit, where Highway 299 begins its descent to the dam (Steger).

Sun, Sunny. These specific terms are included in the names of at least ten California communities. **Sunnyslope** [Los Angeles]. In 1861 Leonard J. Rose, a Pennsylvania German, acquired a portion of the Santa Anita grant and developed his famous Sunny Slope Farm, after which the Southern Pacific station was named. **Sunnyside** [San Diego]. The settlement was founded and named by J. C. Frisbie in 1876. **Sunnyvale** [Santa Clara]. The name was applied by W. E. Crossman about 1900 to the subdivision of a portion of the Pastoria de las Borregas grant (Thelma Miller). **Sunnymead** [Riverside]. The Sunnymead Orchard Tract was laid out and named in 1913. Since a Mr. Mead was one of the original owners of the land, he may have supplied the second part of the name (E. Larson). **Sunny Hills** [Orange]. The Sunny Hills Ranch Company bought the old Bastanchury citrus ranch and subdivided it in 1940 (Santa Fe). **Sun Valley** [Los Angeles]. The name of the post office, Roscoe, established January 15, 1924, was changed January 1, 1949, to the present name by vote of the people in the area. **Sun City** [Riverside]. The post office was established August 3, 1963, for the retirement community developed by the Del Webb corporation.

Sunflower Valley [Shasta]. The valley was once covered with sunflowers, the seeds of which were highly valued by the Indians. Pierson B. Reading, Indian agent after the American occupation, had to divide the area between the Yana and the Wintu so that each would receive its share of the harvest. (Steger.)

Sunol, sŭ-nōl': town, **Valley, Hills** [Alameda]. Named for Antonio Suñol, a native of Spain, who deserted the French ship *Bordelais* in 1818, and in 1839 was part owner of the Rancho El Valle de San José, on which town and valley are situated. Suñol's hospitality and his rich garden are repeatedly mentioned by early travelers. His place is shown on Duflot de Mofras's map, 1844.

Sunset. The term is found in the names of more than ten cliffs, peaks, rocks, and valleys and of five communities, the best known of which is Sunset Beach [Orange]. There are also a few Sunrise Hills, Peaks, and Valleys in the State.

Superstition Mountain [Imperial]. "While [the hill] appears to be composed entirely of sand,

there is a rocky mass below, and over this the sand plays, constantly shifting to and fro in the desert winds, and because of this instability the Indians of the region speak ill of it, hence its name" (James, I, 13).

Sur, sûr [Monterey]. The name El Sur, 'The South' (of Monterey), was applied to Juan B. Alvarado's land grant, dated July 30, 1834. In 1851 the Coast Survey applied the name Point Sur to the cape which was called in Spanish times *Morro de la Trompa* and *Punta que Parece Isla* (from the big rock extending into the ocean which looks like an island in the shape of a trumpet). The Coast Survey name has given rise to a big name cluster—Sur: Breakers, Canyon, River, Rock; Big Sur River, Little Sur River, Little Sur Creek, False Point Sur. The post office Sur was established October 30, 1889; on March 6, 1915, the pleasant-sounding name of another post office, Arbolado, was replaced by the name Big Sur.

Surf [Santa Barbara]. The post office was established June 22, 1897, and was so named because of its location near the ocean shore. **Surfside** [Orange]. The post office was established April 5, 1953.

Surprise. This term was often used by early-day explorers, surveyors, and prospectors for a place which they came upon unexpectedly. It is still found in the names of about twenty canyons, creeks, springs, lakes, and valleys. **Surprise Valley** [Modoc]. Of a number of explanations given for the origin of the name, the one given by William S. Brown seems the most plausible: "Emigrants who had just traversed the Black Rock Desert were 'surprised' as they came out of the arid sagebrush hills into the smiling valley." The name is shown on maps since about 1860. The lakes labeled Alkali Lakes on the maps are locally known as Surprise Valley Lakes. **Surprise Canyon** [Death Valley National Monument]. "The prospector was surprised when he found the lead, the mining sharks were surprised to hear of his luck, the growth of the camp was more surprising still" (J. R. Spears, New York *Sun*, Feb. 21, 1892).

Surpur Creek [Humboldt]. The name of this tributary of Klamath River is apparently derived from a former Yurok village on the opposite side of the river, given by Waterman as *Sr'pr* (map 10).

Susan River; Susanville [Lassen]. Both names were applied by Isaac Roop, pioneer of the Honey Lake district, for his daughter, Susan. The town developed around Roop's Fort and was known as Rooptown until 1857. The River is frequently mentioned in the Pacific Railroad *Reports* in the early 1850's. *See* Roops Fort.

Suscol: Creek, station [Napa]. The name of a Patwin Indian village recorded with variouS spellings in records and *diseños* since 1835. A *Corral de Soscol* is shown on a *diseño* (1838) of the Napa grant; a *Sierra des Soscol* (lower Howell Mountains), on a *diseño* of the Suisun grant. June 19, 1844, the name Suscol or Soscol was used for a lånd grant. The name appears as *Susqual* in the Indian Report of 1853 (p. 405). The creek is mentioned with the present spelling in the *Statutes* of 1850 (p. 61).

Sutil Island [Los Angeles]. The island southwest of Santa Barbara Island, formerly known as Gull Island, was named Sutil Island by the Geographic Board (1939). The *Sutil* was a ship of the Galiano expedition of 1792.

Sutro, soo´-tro: Forest, Heights; Mount Sutro [San Francisco]. Named for Adolph Sutro, a native of Germany, builder of the famous tunnel in the Comstock mines in Nevada in the 1870's, mayor of San Francisco 1894–1898. The forest was planted at his instigation in the 1880's; the heights, his estate above the Cliff House, was willed to the city for a public park. The official name of the hill is Sutro Crest (Geographic Board, April 6, 1910).

Sutter. The name of the great pioneer, John A. Sutter (*see* Glossary), is properly honored in a number of place names in the State. **Sutters Fort** [Sacramento]. In August, 1839, Sutter settled at the site of what is now the city of Sacramento, and in 1841 he began the construction of his famous fort, which soon became the terminus of the emigrant trail from Missouri. Sutter himself called his settlement *Nueva Helvetia* (shown on maps also in the English, German, French, and Latin forms), using the ancient name of Switzerland, but popular usage preferred Sutter's, Fort Sutter, Sutter's Fort, or simply the "Fort." **Sutterville** [Sacramento]. The town, now vanished, was laid out in January, 1846, by Bidwell and Hastings, and was envisioned by Sutter as the coming metropolis of the valley. The name is preserved in Sutterville Bend of the Sacramento River, Sutterville Lake, and Sutterville Road. **Sutter Buttes** [Sutter]. The dominant orographic features of the Sacramento Valley were called *Los Tres Picos* in Sutter's grant and were known to Hudson's Bay Company trappers in the early 1830's as

the Bute, or Buttes. On the maps of the 1840's and 1850's they appear as Three Buttes, Sutter's Buttes, *Los Picos de Sutter*, Prairie Buttes, Sacramento Buttes, or simply Butte or Bute Mountains. The Whitney Survey applied the name Marysville Buttes, and most maps used this name until the Geographic Board in October, 1949, chose the present name. **Sutter County.** One of the twenty-seven original counties; created and named February 18, 1850. **Sutter Island** in the Sacramento River is shown on Ringgold's General Chart of 1850 for part of Ryer Island. The Coast Survey transferred the name to what Ringgold called Schoolcraft Island, and named the channel west of it Sutter Slough. **Sutter Creek** [Amador]. The town was named after the creek, which had been locally known by that name since Sutter with his Kanakas and Indians had a mining camp there in 1849. The name of the village, township, and post office is mentioned in the Sacramento *Daily Democratic State Journal* of December 2, 1853; the town is mentioned in the *Statutes* of 1854 (p. 222). **Sutter** [Sutter]. The name of the town known as South Butte was changed to Sutter City during the boom of the 1880's. To avoid confusion with Sutter Creek the post office dropped the "City."

Sutter [Napa]. Named after the Sutter Home Winery by Mrs. E. C. Leuenberger, whose father, John Sutter, became manager of the winery in 1888 (Margaret Klausner).

Suwanee River [Sequoia National Park]. This tributary of the Kaweah River shows no resemblance to the stream in Florida and Georgia, after which it apparently was named.

Swanton [Santa Cruz]. Named for Fred W. Swanton, a leader in the development of public utilities in Santa Cruz County.

Swauger: Canyon, Creek [Mono]. A parcel of land here was patented to Samuel A. Swauger in 1880 (Maule). This name is misspelled Swager on the Bridgeport atlas sheet.

Swede Creek [Shasta]. The tributary of Cow Creek was named for H. O. Akerstrom, a native of Sweden, who settled near the mouth of the creek in January, 1854 (Steger). More than fifteen other Swede Canyons, Creeks, Gulches, mainly in northern counties, were named for Swedish or other Scandinavian settlers. Swede was the rural California designation for a Scandinavian: only two names with the adjective Danish and none with the adjective Norwegian were found on the available maps. *See* Dutch.

Sweet Brier Creek [Shasta]. So named because of the occurrence of a type of the sweetbrier rose, *Rosa eglanteria* (Steger).

Sweetland [Nevada]. Named for Henry P. Sweetland, who had a trading post here in 1852 (Doyle) and was an assemblyman in the fifth session (1854). The place is mentioned in the *Statutes* of 1854 (p. 222), and a post office is listed in 1858.

Sweetwater. The name is used chiefly for surface waters in regions where many springs and streams have "bitter" water. In the names of coastal features the term "freshwater," as contrasted to "ocean water," is ordinarily used instead. Sweetwater River [San Diego] was known as *Agua Dulce* in Spanish times, and Suisun Bay was once called *Puerto Dulce*.

Swifts Point [Glenn]. The name commemorates a colorful early character, Granville P. Swift, a native of Kentucky who came with the Kelsey party from Oregon in 1844. He took part in the Micheltorena campaign, was a leader in the Bear Flag uprising, and settled in Colusa County in 1847. In 1848–1849 he made a fortune in the mines. Swift Adobe is Historic Landmark 345.

Swiss. More than twenty physical features in various sections of the State bear witness to the presence of Swiss settlers, who have played an important role in California since Mexican times.

Switchback Peak [Sequoia National Park]. "So named because of the striking zigzag trail (now road) over its eastern slope" (Geographic Board, *Sixth Report*).

Switzer Canyon [San Diego]. The canyon was named for E. D. Switzer, a San Diego jeweler in the 1870's, whose home was here (C. Gunn).

Switzerland [San Bernardino]. Formerly known as Valley of the Moon because of the proximity of Moon Lake. About 1935 a Los Angeles investment company bought the tract, established the Saint Moritz Club, and called the place Switzerland because the mountains are somewhat suggestive of the Alps.

Sword Meadow [Alpine]. Apparently named for the crossed swords carved in a tree in the meadow to commemorate a duel between two Frenchmen in which one was killed. A letter from the fiancée of one of the contestants was found in the possession of the other. (J. H. Hall.)

Sycamore. The habitat of the western sycamore or plane tree is clearly indicated by the locations of the geographic features that bear the name. The tree thrives best in the moderate moisture and the average temperature of the southern Coast Ranges, and to a lesser degree in the Sierra foothills along the interior valleys to about latitude 40°. The name (and the tree) occur most frequently in Ventura, San Diego, Kern, and San Luis Obispo counties. No Sycamore names are found east or west of Butte and Colusa counties, none in the High Sierra, and none in the regions of the Great Basin. The oldest and northernmost name found was Sycamore River (now Battle Creek in Tehama County), mentioned by John Work, November 28, 1832, and shown on Abert's map of 1838. Since the sycamore prefers stream beds which are dry in summer, more than half of the names refer to canyons. Only one Sycamore Hill [Butte] and no Sycamore Mountain could be found on the maps because the tree rarely grows on slopes. In several places the name was transferred to settlements [Colusa, Los Angeles, San Bernardino]. In Spanish times the name *aliso* (alder) was often used for sycamore. Sycamore Canyon [Ventura] is shown as *Cañada de los Alisos* on the *diseño* of the Conejo grant, 1835. **Sycamore Grove** [San Bernardino]. One of the Mormon settlements in Cajon Canyon; registered as Historical Landmark 573, April 1, 1957.

Symbol Bridge [Lava Beds National Monument]. "I named this natural bridge in 1917 because of the red, white, and black writings on both walls, and the pictures of an Indian head and a Spanish priest with a ruffled collar on the south walls" (Howard). Symbol Cave and Painted Cave in the Monument were so named because Indian pictographs were seen on the walls.

Symmes Creek [Inyo]. The stream probably owes its name to J. W. Symmes, pioneer settler, who was county superintendent of schools, 1870–1873 and 1876–1882 (Farquhar).

Syncline Hill [San Luis Obispo]. The prominent elevation at the western edge of Carrizo Plain was designated as Syncline Hill by a decision of the Geographic Board, April 7, 1909. Syncline is a geological term applied to a fold formed by strata dipping toward a common line.

Table. There are about fifty Table Mountains and Hills in the State, as well as a number of Table Bluffs and Rocks. In the southern section the corresponding Spanish term, *mesa*, is frequently used instead. There is a Table Lake [Yosemite National Park] near a flat-topped unnamed mountain. Disregarding Beechey's name, Table Hill, for Mount Tamalpais, the oldest feature still so named is probably **Table Bluff** [Humboldt], called Punta Gorda in 1793 (*CHSQ*, X, 330), Ridge Point by the *Laura Virginia* party, Brannan Bluff by Sam Brannan, but known by the present name as early as September, 1851. **Table: Mountain** [Sequoia National Park], **Creek** [Kings Canyon National Park]. The mountain is first mentioned by the Whitney Survey and recorded as "Table" on Hoffmann's map of 1873. **Table Mountain** [Calaveras, Tuolumne]. "One of the most striking features in the topography and geology of Tuolumne County is the so-called 'Table Mountain,' a name given, throughout the State, to the flat table-like masses of basaltic lava which have been rendered so conspicuous by the erosion of the softer strata on each side, and which now exist as elevated ridges, dominating over the surrounding country, and remarkable for their picturesque beauty, but still more so on account of the important deposits of auriferous detritus which lie beneath them" (Whitney, *Geology*, I, 243). The Geological Survey in 1914 made four Table Mountains out of Whitney's one but forgot to number them although they are within a few miles of one another. The word is sometimes used as a generic term: Big Table and Kennedy Table northeast of Millerton Lake [Madera].

Taboose Pass [Kings Canyon National Park]. An edible groundnut found in Owens Valley was called *taboose* in the Paiute language (Farquhar). Kroeber was unable to identify the word but said that it is very likely Mono Shoshonean, judging from its sound. The name was formerly also applied to Division Creek, which rises not far from the pass, and to the pioneer stage station at the creek (Robinson).

Tache. The *Tache* (also spelled *Tachi, Tadji, Dachi*, etc.) are usually spoken of as a tribe of the Yokuts, dwelling north of Tulare Lake, but mission records mention only a village and a lake of that name. Padre Juan Martín, of Mission San Miguel, mentions in 1815 *una de las rancherias tulareñas llamada Tache*, 'one of the tulare villages called Tache' (Arch. MSB, VI, 85 f.). Estudillo on his map of 1819 labels Tulare Lake as *Laguna de Tache o Bubal*. Laguna de Tache was the name of two land grants, dated December 4, 1843, and December 12, 1843. On American maps Tulare Lake appears as Lake Chintache, Ton-

tache, etc., as well as Tula Lake, until the late 1850's. The etymology of the word is uncertain. *Tache* is given as an American native name of the yellow alder, and Robelo gives *tachi* as one of the Aztec names of a destructive insect (pp. 545, 657).

Taft [Kern]. The post office was established in 1909 and named for the newly elected President, William H. Taft. The branch railroad from Pentland reached the place in the same year but the station was called Moron, a name which persisted until about 1918. **Taft Point** [Yosemite National Park]. The name was given to the lookout station on the Pohono Trail by Robert B. Marshall when President Taft was in office.

Tagus, tä'-gŭs: Ranch [Tulare]. The name was applied to the station when the San Joaquin Valley line reached the place in the fall of 1872. Tagus is the English name of a river in Spain and Portugal.

Tahoe, tä'-hō, Lake; Tahoe: post office, Pines, Vista [Placer]; **Tahoe Valley, Al Tahoe** [El Dorado]; **Tahoe National Forest.** There has been much speculation about the meaning and the application of the name of the most beautiful of California's larger lakes. The lake was discovered by Frémont and Preuss on February 14, 1844: ". . . we had a beautiful view of a mountain lake at our feet, about fifteen miles in length, and so entirely surrounded by mountains that we could not discover an outlet" (*Expl. Exp.*, 1853, p. 334). On some of the maps in earlier editions of the report the lake is shown as Mountain Lake. Later, Frémont named it Lake Bonpland, in honor of Aimé Bonpland, the French botanist who had accompanied Humboldt on his great journey in South America, and it is so labeled on Preuss' map of 1848. This name would probably have stuck, had not the friends of John Bigler, governor of California from 1852 to 1856, succeeded in naming the lake in his honor, Lake Bigler (Eddy's Official Map of 1854). During the Civil War the Union sentiment objected strenuously to this name because Bigler was an outspoken secessionist, and a movement was started to restore to the lake its Washo Indian name, understood to be Tahoe and to mean 'big water.' Various persons claim the credit for having brought about the change. It seems likely, however, that Henry de Groot, John S. Hittell, and William H. Knight selected the name. At any rate, it was De Groot who explored the mountains in 1859 and suggested the Indian name of the lake, and it was Knight who placed the name Lake Tahoe on Bancroft's map of the Pacific States in 1862. This, however, did not end the controversy. An act of the Democratic legislature, approved February 10, 1870, declared that the lake "shall be known as Lake Bigler, and the same is hereby declared to be the official name of said lake, and the only name to be regarded as legal in official documents, deeds, conveyances, leases and other instruments of writing to be placed on State or county records, or used in reports made by State, county or municipal officers" (*Statutes*, 1869–1870, p. 64). The Whitney Survey (von Leicht–Craven) naturally has the name Lake Bigler, for the Survey was dependent upon the legislature, but the maps of the Land Office and of the Wheeler Survey, as well as most private maps, use the popular name exclusively. The "official" name was so completely forgotten that most Californians heard it for the first time when in 1945 (!) the legislature solemnly enacted that the lake "designated as Lake Bigler by Chapter 58 of the *Statutes* of 1869–70, is hereby designated and shall be known as Lake Tahoe" (*Statutes*, 1945, p. 2777). A post office Taho in El Dorado County is listed in 1868; Tahoe in Placer County is listed in 1880. Lake Tahoe National Forest was created in 1899, and consolidated with Yuba Forest Reserve under the present name in 1906. The meaning of the name is obviously 'water' or 'lake.' When Frémont approached the lake from the east in January, 1844, he heard his informants using the word *tah-ve*: "*Táh-ve*, a word signifying snow, we very soon learned to know, from its frequent repetition" (*Expl. Exp.*, 1854, p. 323). When De Groot formed a vocabulary of the Washo dialect in 1859, he confirmed Frémont's observation that *tah-ve* means 'snow' and added that *tah-oo* means 'water,' and *tah-oo-ee*, 'much water' (Placer Co. Hist., 1882, p. 404). When Kroeber in 1923 ran across an intelligent elderly Washo the latter upon inquiry replied promptly: "*Da'au* [or *ta'au*] means lake, any lake." From this may be safely deduced that *ta* is the Washo root for 'water' and that *tah-oo* or *ta-au* means 'lake water,' 'sheet of water,' while *tah-ve* means 'frozen water,' 'snow.'

Tahquitz, tä'-kwĭts: Peak, Canyon, Creek, Valley [Riverside]. The name is derived from *Tahquitz* (or *Tahkoosh*, or *Takwish*), the evil spirit of the Cahuilla Indians, which, according to Indian legend, dwells in the San Jacinto Mountains and manifests itself as a

meteor with a train of sparks. The name does not appear on older maps and was apparently applied when the San Jacinto quadrangle was surveyed in 1897–1898.

Tailholt. *See* White River.

Tailings Gulch [Mariposa]. The name of the ravine through which Sand Creek runs is left over from the gold-mining days. Trailings was the term used for the remnants of the ore which had been washed for gold, especially in hydraulic mining.

Tajanta [Los Angeles]. The name of the land grant, dated July 5, 1843, is probably derived from a Gabrielino word, but its meaning is unknown. On a *diseño* of the grant a group of trees is shown as *Monte de Tujunta*. On Land Office maps the name is spelled Tajauta.

Tajiguas, tá-hĭg'-wăs, tá-hē'-wăs: Creek, station [Santa Barbara]. According to Taylor, the name is derived from that of a Chumash village. *El rancho del Refugio en Tajiguas* (or *Jajiguas*) is mentioned on October 22, 1841 (Arch. SB, Juzgado, p. 33). The Southern Pacific station was named after the creek, probably at the time when the last link of the coast line was completed between 1894 and 1901. The Indian village received its name perhaps from *tayiyas*, another Chumash word for the islay or holly-leaved cherry. The padres of Mission Santa Barbara wrote in 1800: *el Yslay, o Tayiyas, que es una fruta algo parecida á la guinda*, 'a fruit which somewhat resembles the cherry' (Arch. MSB, II, 113 f.).

Talawa: Lake, Slough [Del Norte]. The western arm of Lake Earl and the channel preserve the name of the Athabascan tribe, who occupied the extreme northwest corner of the State. They are mentioned as *Tah-le-wah* and *To-le-wah* in 1853 (Schoolcraft, III, 139, 422) and, according to Waterman (p. 266), were designated as *To'lowel* by their southern neighbors, the Yuroks. A place, *Tolo'qʷ*, is shown on Waterman's map 2 where Jordan Creek enters Lake Earl, and a sea stack, *To'-loweL*, is indicated on map 31 north of Trinidad Head, in Yurok territory.

Talbert [Orange]. The post office was established about 1900 and named for James T. Talbert, a native of Kentucky and a veteran of the Civil War, who in 1898 bought land in the district known as Gospel Swamp. His sons, Samuel and Thomas, built the Talbert Drainage System by which the swampland was reclaimed. (Co. Hist., 1921, pp. 1186 f., 1560 f.)

Talc City Hills [Inyo]. The "city" of low mountains was so named because of the deposits of the mineral talc commonly known as soapstone (Geographic Board, Jan.-April, 1960).

Talega Canyon [San Diego]. Since *talega* is Spanish for 'bag' or 'sack,' the name might have been applied because of the shape of the canyon.

Tallac, Mount [El Dorado]. The mountain is shown as Crystal Peak on the maps of the Whitney Survey, but the Wheeler Survey in 1877 applied the Indian name, which means simply 'large mountain,' according to Kirchhoff (p. 278). Tallac was for many years a famous resort after "Lucky" Baldwin built his hotel, the Tallac House, at the lake shore about 1875.

Tallulah Lake [Yosemite National Park]. The name appears for the first time on the Bridgeport atlas sheet, 1911 (Farquhar). It may be a transfer name from Georgia, where it exists as a place name, or the lake may have been named for Tallulah LeConte (David Brower).

Talmage [Mendocino]. The post office is listed in 1892, but the origin of the name is not known. One Junius Talmadge, from Big River, was registered as a voter in the county in 1872, but he cannot be identified with the place.

Tamales. *See* Tomales.

Tamalpais, tăm′-ăl-pī′-ĭs, **Mount; Tamalpais Valley** [Marin]. The first recorded name given to the mountain appears as *Pico y Cerro de Reyes* on Cañizares' Plano of 1776. Another Spanish name, *Picacho Prieto* (dark peak) is mentioned as late as 1849. In 1826 Beechey applied the name Table Hill to the mountain because it looks like a flat table from the ocean off Point Reyes. For half a century it was so known to cartographers, or as Table Mountain, or Table Butte. The present name, according to Barrett (*Pomo*, p. 308) and Merriam (*Mewan Stock*, p. 355), was the Indian appellation and meant 'bay mountain.' Since, however, the southern Coast Miwok Indians were called *Tamales* by the Spaniards it seems more likely that it was the name of a village of the Tamal Indians at the foot of the mountain and meant probably 'the *Tamals* by the mountain.' *See* Tomales. The name appears repeatedly in the baptismal records of Mission Dolores but it is not certain that it refers definitely to a village: *Nabon, Tamulpais, Adulto Gualem* was baptized on March 13, 1801, and *Parbolo* [a child] *Tayapais de la Costa* on October

ber 28, 1806 (Arch. Mis., I, 123, 80). On a *diseño* (about 1842) of the Baulenes grant the name *Tamal paiz* appears near the mountain, and on November 25, 1845, the name is used for a land grant, Tamalpais or San Clemente, not confirmed by the United States. In American publications of the 1850's there appear such absurd typographical errors as Tamel Pisc Mountain, Tama el Paris, and Tannel Bume. The old name was used again by the Whitney Survey. Hoffmann, observing from Black Mountain [Santa Cruz], records in his notes on September 3, 1861: "Highest Blue Mt. (Tamal Pais) back of San Francisco." After 1866 the popular Bancroft maps used the name, and Beechey's appellation thereafter disappeared from the maps, although the Coast Survey did not drop it until 1883. Another alleged Indian name of the mountain, as given to Barrett (*Pomo*, p. 308) by an informant speaking the Southern Moquelumnan (Coast Miwok) dialect, was *Pa′-le-mŭs*. It is possible that this was the Indian version of the name *Palmas*, given to the mountain in the 1830's by Francisco de Haro, one-time *alcalde* at San Francisco, because it reminded him of a hill in Mexico. This "Indian" name in turn may have become Mount Palermo, the name which Wilkes' expedition applied to the mountain in 1841. Freeland's theory that the name is derived from *tamal*, 'west,' and *pawi*, 'mountain,' and means "west mountain" is as unconvincing as Barrett's and Merriam's "bay mountain." If the Indians around San Quentin really called their brethren at the foot of the mountain and beyond, *tamales*, 'westerners,' then the name could be interpreted as 'mountain of the westerners' but not as 'west mountain.' There is no evidence that Mount Tamalpais and Tomales Bay were Indian geographical names. The names were created by the Spaniards on the basis of the tribal name. Finally, the name Tamalpais may be a transfer name from Mexico, where there are numerous similar names of Aztec origin: Tamaulipas, etc. **Tamalpais Valley** [Marin]. The settlement at the foot of the mountain was known as Big Coyote until the post office was named Tamalpais, February 15, 1906. In 1908 Valley was added to the name.

Tamarack. There is no true tamarack (eastern larch) native in California, but the *Pinus murrayana* or lodgepole pine is often called tamarack or "tamrac," hence the confusion. A mountain and four lakes [Shasta], a peak

[Fresno], a flat [Yosemite National Park], a lake [Mono], and a number of creeks are named Tamarack because lodgepole pines grow on or near them.

Tambo [Yuba]. The Spanish American word for 'hotel' or 'inn' was applied to the Western Pacific station when the line was built in 1907.

Tanforan, tăn'-fô-răn [San Mateo]. The station on the suburban line and the race track were named for Maria and Toribio Tanforan, who acquired title to the land in 1868 (Wyatt). One Toribio Tanfaran had been grantee of a lot at the Mission Dolores in 1846.

Tanners Peak [Siskiyou]. Probably named for John Pryor Tanner, a native of Kentucky, who was registered as a miner from Sawyers Bar in 1878.

Tanquary Gulch [Shasta]. The gulch near Millville was named for O. H. P. Tanquary, who with James R. Keene operated the Buscombe Mill here in the late 1850's (Steger).

Tantrum Glade [Mendocino]. So named because a crazy mule once upset a camp there (Forest Service).

Tapia Canyon [Los Angeles]. Probably named for a member of the Tapia family, some of whom settled in the Los Angeles district before 1800.

Tapie Lake [Trinity]. The lake was named for Raymond E. Tapie, who stocked it with trout (Geographic Board, May, 1954).

Tapo: Canyon, Creek [Ventura]. In 1821 it was recorded that Rancho San Jose de Gracias y Simi extended as far north as *el Volcan de Azufre y Tapi en lengua de gentiles,* 'the sulphur volcano and Tapi in the tongue of the heathen' (Registro, p. 33). A rancho *Tapo* is mentioned June 16, 1829 (SP Mis. & C., II, 6), and two *cañadas . . . de Tapo* in July, 1834 (DSP Ben. Mil., LXXIX, 91).

Tar. *See* Asphalt.

Tara Brook [Contra Costa]. Named in 1948 by the owner of the land, Abe Doty, for his daughter Taralin ("Tara"), whose name had been taken from the novel *Gone with the Wind.*

Tartarus Lake [Lassen National Park]. This lake in Hot Spring Valley was given the name of the infernal regions in classical mythology; other places in the region have similar hellborn names, given because of the hot springs.

Tarzana [Los Angeles]. When Edgar Rice Burroughs bought the Otis estate in 1917, he bestowed upon it the name derived from his famous fictional character "Tarzan" (AGS: *Los Angeles,* p. 381). The post office is listed

in 1931.

Tassajara, tăs-à-hâr'-à. *Tasajera* is a Spanish American word designating a place where meat is cut in strips and hung in the sun to cure. The name is preserved in **Tassajara: Creek, Valley,** settlement [Alameda, Contra Costa], and **Tassajara: Creek, Hot Springs** [Monterey]. The creek in Alameda County is shown as *Arroyo de la Tasajera* on a *diseño* (1841) of Valle de San Jose. Tassajero is the spelling of the Geographic Board (*Sixth Report*), the ending corresponding to the Spanish American locative *-ero* in other names (*see* Pescadero). Common usage and the Post Office Department, however, favor the spelling Tassajara.

Taurusa. *See* Dinuba.

Taylor Canyon [Mono]. Named for "Black" Taylor, one of the discoverers of the Bodie mines, who wintered some cattle in Hot Springs Valley and was killed there by Indians (Robinson).

Taylor Meadow [Kern]. Named for Charlie Taylor, who for many years was manager of the A. Brown interests in Kernville (Crites, p. 269).

Taylorsville [Plumas]. Named for J. T. Taylor, who built the first barn, mill, and hotel there in 1852.

Taylorville [Marin]. The place, now commonly called Camp Taylor, was named for Samuel P. Taylor, who built the first paper mill on the Pacific Coast. *See* Paper Mill Creek.

Tea Bar [Siskiyou]. The name of the creek and settlement, once a mining community, on the east side of the Klamath is a folk-etymological rendering of *Ti'i*, a former Karok Indian village (Gifford).

Tea Canyon [Lake]. It is so called because of the growth of a wild herb used for making tea (Mauldin).

Tecate, tĕ-kä'-tĕ: post office, **Mountain** [San Diego]. A place called *Tecate,* probably a rancheria, is mentioned in the archives in 1830 (PSP Ben. Mil., LII, 59) and a *cañada de Tecate* on September 7, 1831 (Dep. Recs., IX, 112). On December 14, 1833, the name was used for a land grant, the territory of which was outside of the United States when the international boundary was established in 1847. Tecate Mountain is shown on Williamson's map of 1855. The post office was named after the mountain in 1913, and when the San Diego–Arizona Railroad was built in 1915 the name was applied to the station. Two possible derivations of the name seem plausible. It may contain the common Mexican name *tecats* for the species of gourd, *Cucurbita maxima,* or it may be derived from Mexican *atecate,* which Santamaría interprets as meaning "water in which the baker moistens her hands while making tortillas," but which one of Robelo's informants translates as *agua turbia,* 'muddy water' (p. 476).

Tecolote. The word is derived from Aztec *teutli,* 'bill,' and *colotl,* 'twisted' (Robelo, p. 663). In the southwestern United States and in northern Mexico the word designates small owls of various species (Bentley). It was repeatedly used for geographical names and has survived in Tecolote Valley [San Diego] and Tecolote Canyon [Santa Barbara]. The name of an *aguage corriente* (running spring) mentioned in 1817 (PSP, XX, 177) is probably the origin of the latter name. Tucolota Creek [Riverside] may be a misspelling of the same word. The *Real del Tecolote,* so called by the Moraga expedition of 1806 and mentioned by Muñoz *por la mucha abundancia de estos animales* has not survived. It was probably in what is now Merced or Mariposa County.

Tecopa [Inyo]. The old mining camp was named before 1892 by J. B. Osbourne for an old Paiute chief, who later demanded $200 for the use of his name. It is not known whether Mr. Osbourne paid, but it is a fact that Jim Slauson (of Resting Springs) paid tribute to Tecopa by sending him a plug hat every year. (Gill.) Tecopa was a very fine Indian, who once saved the people of Pahrump Valley from being killed by the Indians. (O. J. Fisk.) When the Tonopah and Tidewater Railroad was built in 1908 the station was named for the camp, and mining operations were resumed. The name is derived from *tecopet,* 'wildcat.' A picture of the Indian, plug hat and all, was published in *Desert Magazine,* September, 1943.

Tectah Creek [Humboldt]. The name is the American version of *Te'kta Wroi,* a Yurok place name probably meaning 'log creek' (Waterman, p. 239).

Tecuya: Creek, Mountain [Kern]. The names are derived from *Tokya,* the name applied by the Yokuts to the Chumash Indians, a division of whom occupied the region (Kroeber). A rancheria called *Tacui* is mentioned on July 29, 1806 (Arch. MSB, IV, 49 ff.).

Tehachapi, tĕ-hăch'-à-pĭ: **Creek, Pass, Mountains, Valley,** town [Kern]. The name was placed on a map as Tah-ee-chay-pah Pass by the Pacific Railroad Survey in 1853: "from the Indians we learned that their name for the creek was Tah-ee-chay-pah" (Pac. R.R.

Reports, Vol. V, Pt. 1, p. 19). *Ti'aci* is a root meaning 'to freeze' in Southern Paiute, which is only slightly different from the language spoken in the Tehachapi area. The ending may be the past passive participial suffix *-pi.* The meaning 'frozen' may have been applied first to the creek, which at some time was found to be frozen. (Stewart.) Frémont had crossed the pass in 1844 and called the creek Pass Creek. The name used by the Survey remained on the maps with many variants in spelling. The post office is listed as Tehichipa in 1870; the von Leicht–Craven map of 1874 has Tahichipi Pass, Creek, Valley, town. The spelling Tahichipi is used by Kroeber for the name given by the Yokuts to the region or part of it. In 1876 the Southern Pacific built the railroad through the canyon of Cache Creek, transferred the name from the old wagon route, and fixed the present spelling, which Brewer had used in his journal, June 7, 1863. The "new town" developed at the railroad station; the post office was at first about one mile away at Greenwich (named for the postmaster, P. D. Green). It is listed as Greenwich in the Postal Guides between 1880 and 1892, but appears as Tehachapi in 1898.

Tehama, tĕ-hā'-má: city, **County.** Kroeber in his *Handbook* mentions *tehama* as a Wintun village, and some reports give it as the name of an Indian tribe. E. J. Lewis' account of the naming, in the County History of 1880 (pp. 17 f.), is more plausible though not entirely convincing: "I . . . was told by some that it was the Indian name for plains, or prairie, but the Indians knew nothing about it whatever. I remember of reading in Gibbon's Rome about an Arabian town called Tehama, not far from Medina in Arabia . . . but further than that I can give no satisfactory explanation of the word 'Tehama.' But there is little in a name, and we would not be justified in wasting too much time over so small a matter." To be sure there is no Arabian town so named, but Tehama is an Arabian generic for 'hot lowlands' and is found repeatedly in geographical nomenclature in Arabia. In California the name certainly fits the topography of the location. According to Clara Hisken, the name is an Indian word and may mean 'low land' or 'shallow,' i.e., ford in the river. The town was laid out on R. H. Thomes' Saucos Rancho, and lots were offered for sale in the San Francisco *Alta California* on August 5, 1850. Since both men who were instrumental in founding

Tehama, R. H. Thomes and A. G. Toomes, had been carpenters and builders in San Francisco and Monterey (as early as 1841) it is not impossible that they derived the name from the Mexican word for 'shingle,' *tejamanil,* by lopping off the last syllable. (*WF,* VIII, No. 1.) If this could be proved, another interesting Aztec name would be added to California nomenclature: *tejamanil* is derived from *tla,* 'thing,' and *xamanilli,* 'cleft,' 'split' (Robelo, p. 666). *See* Thomes Creek; Toomes Creek. The County was created from portions of Shasta, Colusa, and Butte counties on April 9, 1856.

Tehipite, tĕ-hǐp′-ǐ-tĕ: **Valley, Dome** [Kings Canyon National Park]. The name is shown on the Tehipite atlas sheet of 1905. Nothing is known about its origin beyond the fact that it is Indian, probably Mono. Winchell's interpretation of the meaning as 'high rock' (Farquhar) sounds plausible.

Tejon, tĕ-hōn′: **Canyon, Creek, Hills** [Kern]. The name *Cañada del Tejon* (badger valley) was given to the canyon by the expedition of Lieutenant Francisco Ruiz in 1806 because a dead badger was found at its entrance (S.F. *Evening Bulletin,* June 5, 1863). On November 24, 1843, the name was applied to the land grant El Tejon. Sutter in his *Reminiscences* (p. 125), dictated in 1876, states that his men found Tejon Pass on the return march from the Micheltorena campaign, in March, 1844, and implies that the name Tejon was in use then. The pass is shown on Gibbes' map of 1852. **Tejon Pass** [Los Angeles]; **Old Fort Tejon** [Kern]. In September, 1853, R. S. Williamson, of the Pacific Railroad Survey, found the Tejon Pass too difficult and established a new route through the *Cañada de las Uvas,* over the pass that had been called *Buena Vista* by Fages in 1772. In the same month, Edward F. Beale, superintendent of Indian affairs, selected a site in the canyon for a fort and an Indian reservation. (Pac. R.R. *Reports,* Vol. V, Pt. 1, pp. 20 ff.) The new pass became known as Fort Tejon Pass; the name was abbreviated to the present form when the old route was abandoned.

Telegraph. Several elevations were so named because they were used for telegraphing by signal before the invention of the electrical apparatus. **Telegraph Hill** [San Francisco]. On July 11, 1846, a midshipman from the Portsmouth put up a signal pole here and "telegraphed" as the first message that the British frigate *Juno* had entered the harbor

(Rogers, *Montgomery,* p. 67). **Telegraph Peak** [San Bernardino]. The peak was originally called Heliograph Hill because the Geological Survey had a heliograph station there (Wheelock). There is another Telegraph Hill in Mariposa County. The two Telegraph canyons in Orange and San Diego counties were so named because a telegraph line passed through them.

Telephone. Spring [Death Valley National Monument]. In 1906, a telephone line passed through the canyon in which the spring is situated (Death Valley Survey). **Telephone Flat** [Modoc]. So named in 1917, when the new telephone line of the Forest Service was built across the flat (W. S. Brown).

Telescope: Peak, Mountains [Death Valley National Monument]. The peak was named in April, 1861, by W. T. Henderson because of the wide clear view from it. Henderson was one of the California Rangers who are credited with having killed the bandit Joaquin Murieta. Telescope District is shown on Farley's map of 1861. The mountains are mentioned in the Bendire Report (1867) and are shown on the von Leicht–Craven map (1874) west of Emigrant Canyon, on both sides of Wildrose Canyon. Now the term is applied to the section of the Panamints south of Wildrose Canyon.

Tells: Peak, Creek [El Dorado]. The places were not named for Wilhelm Tell but for a homesteader named Tell, who with several other Swiss had settled a few miles to the west of the peak about 1875. Tell's house, as well as Tells Creek and Peak, are shown on Wheeler atlas sheet 56-B. W. T. Russell, however, states that the peak was named for Ciperano Pedrini, better known as Bill Tell, early storekeeper of Garden Valley ("The Knave," July 23, 1944).

Temascal. *See* Temescal.

Tembladera, tĕm-blä-dĕr′-à [Monterey]. The name given to an area of several hundred acres of swampy land south of Castroville, covered by a dense overgrowth of vegetation; the Spanish word for 'marsh' or 'quagmire' is *tembladero.*

Temblor. In Spanish times the word *temblor,* meaning 'earthquake,' was frequently applied to a place where an earthquake had been felt. The Portolá expedition named the Santa Ana River *Rio de los Temblores* on July 28, 1769, because while encamped there they were shaken by a violent earthquake, which was repeated four times that day (Costansó, p. 17). Crespi called the place *Jesus de* *los Temblores,* but the soldiers, contrary to their custom, gave it a saint's name, Santa Ana, and this name the Anza expedition adopted seven years later. Among the surviving Temblor names is Temblor Range, a long mountain chain in Kern and San Luis Obispo counties.

Temecula, tĕ-mĕk´-ū-lá: town, **Canyon, Valley, Indian Reservation** [Riverside, San Diego]. An Indian rancheria *Temeca* is mentioned in 1797 (PSP, XV, 182), and the present spelling is found as early as 1820 (Arch. MSB, III, 179). According to Sparkman (p. 191), the Luiseño name is really *temeko;* this version too occurs in early records: *Temeco,* 1802 (Arch. MSB, VIII, 160). *Temecula* was the name of a rancho of Mission San Luis Rey in 1828 or before (Registro, p. 39). Later the name was used in the titles of several land grants, two of which, dated August 25, 1844, and May 7, 1845, were recognized by the United States. The name is spelled Temecola on Wilkes' map of 1841 and Temecula on Ord's sketch of 1849. The post office was named before 1880. The meaning of the name is unknown; Kroeber leaves open the possibility that it may contain the Luiseño word *teme-t,* 'sun.'

Temescal, tĕm´-ĕ-skăl. The word is not of California Indian origin, as is often stated, but is derived from Aztec *tema,* 'to bathe,' and *calli,* 'house' (Robelo, p. 91). The primitive sweathouses of the California Indians, one of the very few of their hygienic improvements, aroused the curiosity of the Spaniards, who applied to them the Mexican word for 'bathhouse,' *temascal.* The name has survived as the name of at least ten places, but it is now invariably spelled Temescal. **Temescal: Creek, Wash** [Riverside]. The name was preserved through the Temascal land grant of 1818 or 1819. Wilkes' map of 1841 shows a place Temascal east of Santa Ana Mountains. Brewer, in February, 1861, mentions Temescal: Indian village, sulphur springs, Overland station, and hills (pp. 39, 34, 44). **Temescal, Lake** [Alameda]. On a *diseño* of the San Antonio grant (dated August 3, 1820), *Arrollo* [arroyo] *de Temescal o Los Juchiyunes* is shown flowing toward *Loma de Temescal,* apparently the elevation later known as Emeryville Shellmound. Southwest of the arroyo, on the point from which the Oakland mole was later extended, the *Encinal* [oak grove] *del Temascal* is also shown. The name became well known, and in 1844 the landing place for the eastern Bay shore

was called *Embarcadero Temescal* (Davis, 1889, p. 98). The lake was created when William F. Boardman dammed the creek for the reservoir of the Contra Costa Water Company in 1870. **Temescal: Canyon, Creek** [Ventura, Los Angeles]. *Rancho del Temascal* is mentioned on December 16, 1834 (DSP, III, 205). On March 17, 1843, the name was given to a land grant.

Temettati Creek [San Luis Obispo]. *Monte y Arroyo de Temetall* (or *Temetatl*) are shown on a *diseño* of the Bolsa de Chamisal grant (1837). The place name is doubtless derived from the Mexican *temetate,* designating a simple curved stone used as a mortar for grinding corn, etc. The word is from Aztec *tetl,* 'stone,' and *metlatl,* 'mortar' (Robelo, p. 232). It is interesting that the spelling of the name on the Land Office map of 1879, Temeltatle, approximates the original Aztec, *temetlatl,* while the spelling of the Geological Survey is more like the modern Mexican.

Temple City [Los Angeles]. Named in 1923 for Walter P. Temple, founder of the town and president of the Temple Townsite Company (Los Angeles *Times,* Dec. 4, 1931, p. 16).

Temple Crag [Inyo]. The beautiful crag had been named Mount Alice for Mrs. Alice Ober of Big Pine, who chaperoned a party of young people on a trip to this region (Brierly). The Geographic Board (*Sixth Report*) decided in favor of the present descriptive name.

Templeton [San Luis Obispo]. Laid out by the West Coast Land Company with the coming of the railroad in 1886, and named Crocker. Because the name was changed shortly afterward to Templeton, it has been assumed that the town was named for Templeton Crocker of San Francisco, a grandson of Charles Crocker, one of the founders of the Central Pacific Railroad.

Templeton: Meadows, Mountain [Tulare]. Named for Benjamin S. Templeton, a sheepman (Farquhar).

Tenaja Canyon; El Potrero de Tenaja [Riverside, San Diego]. *La poza llamada Tinaja,* 'the well called Tinaja,' is mentioned in the Registro (pp. 44 f.), and *La Tinaja* is shown on a *diseño* of the Santa Margarita y Las Flores grant (1841). *Tinaja* is the Spanish word for a 'large earthen jar,' but the word is used here for 'water hole.' The name Las Tinajas de los Indios [Kern] is doubtless from the same source.

Tenaya, tĕ-nī´-à: **Lake, Creek, Canyon, Peak** [Yosemite National Park]. The lake was named on May 22, 1851, by the Mariposa

Battalion, upon the suggestion of L. H. Bunnell. "Looking back to the lovely little lake, where we had been encamped during the night, and watching Ten-ie-ya as he ascended to our group, I suggested to the Captain [Boling] that we name the lake after the old chief, and call it 'Lake Ten-ie-ya.' The Captain had fully recovered from his annoyance at the scene in camp, and readily consented to the name . . . he said, 'Gentlemen, I think the name an appropriate one, and shall use it in my report of the expedition. Beside this, it is rendering a kind of justice to perpetuate the name of the old chief.' . . . I called [Ten-ie-ya] up to us, and told him that we had given his name to the lake and river. At first, he seemed unable to comprehend our purpose, and pointing to the group of glistening peaks, near the head of the lake, said: 'It already has a name; we call it Py-we-ack.' Upon my telling him that we had named it Ten-ie-ya, because it was upon the shores of the lake that we had found his people, who would never return to it to live, his countenance fell and he at once left our group and joined his own family circle. His countenance as he left us indicated that he thought the naming of the lake no equivalent for the loss of his territory." (Bunnell, *Discovery,* 1880, pp. 236 f.) "As we resumed our march . . . I was more fully impressed with the appropriateness of the name for the beautiful lake. Here, probably, his people had built their last wigwams in their mountain home. From this lake we were leading the last remnant of his once dreaded tribe, to a territory from which it was designed they should never return as a people. . . . The Indian name for this lake, branch and cañon, 'Py-we-ack' is . . . now displaced by that of the old chief Ten-ie-ya" (*ibid.,* p. 238). The spelling Tenaya is used on the Hoffmann-Gardner map of 1867. The peak had been named Coliseum Peak by Joseph LeConte and his party, a name which did not last in spite of the name giver's exhortation: "We called this Coliseum Peak. So let it be called hereafter to the end of time." (*Journal,* pp. 76 f.)

Ten Lakes [Yosemite National Park]. The lakes were mentioned by Muir in 1872: "on the north side of the Hoffmann spur . . . there are ten lovely lakelets lying near together in one general hollow, like eggs in a nest" (Muir, *Mountains of California,* 1894, p. 100).

Ten Mile River. *See* Mile.

Tennant [Siskiyou]. The post office was established about 1922 and named for an official

of the Long Bell Lumber Company (G. F. Boyle).

Tennessee: Point, Cove, Valley [Marin]. So named because the steamer *Tennessee* was wrecked offshore in 1853. The Coast Survey named the point and the cove; the county map of 1873 shows the name for the valley.

Tent Meadow [Kings Canyon National Park]. A large block of granite, seen from a distance, resembles a white tent; hence the name (Farquhar).

Tepusquet, tĕp'-ŭs-kĕ: Creek, Peak [Santa Barbara]. *Arroyo de Tepusque* and *Sitio de Tepusque* are shown on *diseños*. On one map the name is misspelled *Tepusquet,* and in this form it was applied to the land grant, dated April 6, 1837. *Tepuzque,* from Aztec *tepuztli,* is a Mexican term for 'copper.' The term designated a coin of low value in the early times of Spanish occupation (Robelo, p. 363).

Tequepis, tĕk'-ĕ-pĭs: Canyon [Santa Barbara]. A *Rancheria de Tequeps* is mentioned in October, 1798 (Arch. MSB, VIII, 164) and in later documents. In 1837 the name appears as Tequepis for a land grant, and the canyon is shown on a *diseño* of the grant as *Cañada de Tequepis.* The name may originally have been a Chumash place name, although it has more the ring of an Aztec word.

Tequesquite, tĕk-ĕs-kĕ'-tĕ: Slough [San Benito]. The name was preserved through the Llano de Tequesquite grant, dated October 10, 1835. *Sanjon del Tequesquite* is shown on a *diseño,* and in 1861 John Gilroy testified in the Juristac case that this "ditch" is now called the Pajaro [River]. *Tequesquite* is a Mexican word derived from Aztec *tetl,* 'rock,' and *quixquitl,* 'efflorescent' (Robelo, p. 363), i.e., 'saltpeter.' Muñoz wrote on September 25, 1806 (Arch. MSB, IV, 1 ff.), that the pastures near San Joaquin River have patches of *tesquesquite.* **Tequesquite Arroyo** [Riverside]. The arroyo was doubtless so named because in hot weather "white alkali" appeared here like patches of snow (Loye Miller).

Terminal Island [Los Angeles]. This was probably the *Isla Raza de Buena Gente* of Palacios' chart of the bay (Wagner, p. 418). In American times it became known as Rattlesnake Island and was so designated by the Coast Survey until 1911. After the Los Angeles Terminal Railway had built a line from the city to the island it became known as Terminal Island and is so shown on the Official Railway Map of 1900.

Terminous [San Joaquin]. The place was established about 1900 by John Dougherty, and because it was at the end of the road that ran into the delta region he wished to call it Terminus. In the application to the Post Office Department the name was erroneously spelled with an "o," and this version was adopted. (Amy Boynton.)

Termo [Lassen]. When the Nevada-California-Oregon Railroad reached the place in 1900, the general manager applied the name to the station just because he had a liking for station names which ended in "o" (Myrick).

Terra Bella [Tulare]. The Latin word for 'land' and the Spanish word for 'beautiful' were combined to form the name applied to the station when the Southern Pacific branch from Exeter to Famoso was built in 1889. The name was applied in the spring, when the country is covered by a carpet of beautiful wildflowers (W. W. Hastings).

Terwah Creek [Del Norte]. *Turwer*, or *Tr'wr*, was the name of a Yurok campsite on the downstream flank of a long, wide point of land (Waterman, pp. 208, 235). On October 12, 1857, Lieutenant George Crook established a fort here and named it Fort Ter-Waw, after the Indian campsite (F. B. Rogers, *CHSQ*, XXVI, 1). It appears on the von Leicht–Craven map as Fort Terwah. The spelling used by the Geological Survey on the Preston Peak atlas sheet is Turwar. Historical Landmark 544, however, has restored the original spelling: Fort Ter-Waw.

Tesla [Alameda]. The name still appears on maps and recalls the thriving town named in 1898, in honor of Nicola Tesla, famous Austrian-American inventor. Plans were projected at that time to build an electric power plant at the local coal mines to supply power to Oakland (Still).

Teutonia Peak [San Bernardino]. Named after the Teutonia (now known as Dutch Silver) Mine on the northeast slope of the mountain. The mine had been named by a prospector, "Charlie" Toegel, a native of Germany. (Gill.)

Texas Spring [Death Valley National Monument]. Probably named for Charles Bennett, nicknamed "Texas" or "Bellerin Teck," who started Furnace Creek Ranch in 1870 (Death Valley Survey). **Texas Springs** [Shasta] was also named for a settler nicknamed "Texas." A number of physical features bearing the name were, however, named by miners or settlers after their home state.

Tharps Rock [Sequoia National Park]. Named for Hale D. Tharp (1828–1912), a native of Michigan who settled in the Three Rivers region in 1856 and was the first white man to explore this part of the High Sierra (Farquhar).

Thatcher: Butte, Creek [Mendocino]. Named for three brothers who camped in the vicinity while hunting deer in the winter of 1855–1856. In the spring, two of the brothers were killed by Indians; the third had gone to the Sacramento Valley for supplies. (Forest Service.)

Thermal [Riverside]. The name was applied to the station, before 1888, because of the extreme heat in the Salton Sea basin (Southern Pacific).

Thermalito: town, Forebay, Afterbay [Butte]. The name is apparently of artificial coinage, meaning something like "little hot spring," from the Greek word *thermae*, "hot springs, hot baths." The town had a post office from 1895 to 1920. The two sheets of water were created when the Oroville dam project was constructed in the 1960's and were given the euphonious name of the town

Thibau, tē'-bō: Creek [Inyo]. The stream was named for a French family who in the 1890's lived where the old country road crossed the creek. The name is sometimes spelled as pronounced, Tebo. (Robinson.)

Thimble. There are several peaks and hills so named because of their shape. The two highest and best-known Thimble Peaks are in Alpine and Inyo counties.

Thing Valley [San Diego]. In the early days the valley was called Hollister Valley for the man who raised sheep there. When Damon Thing bought the valley about 1870 and developed a cattle ranch there, it became known as Thing Valley. (C. F. Emery.)

Thomes Creek [Tehama]. The stream, spelled Toms Creek on Eddy's map of 1854 and Thoms and Thomes on later maps, emerged as Thomas Creek when the Geological Survey mapped the Vina quadrangle. The name commemorates Robert H. Thomes, a native of Maine, who came to California in 1841, worked in partnership with A. G. Toomes as a carpenter in San Francisco and Monterey, and in 1847 settled on his Rancho Los Saucos, through which the creek flows. His partner was grantee of the rancho on the opposite side of the Sacramento. *See* Toomes Creek; Tehama.

Thompson, Mount [Kings Canyon National Park]; **Thompson Ridge** [Inyo]. The peak was named by R. B. Marshall, for Almon H.

Thompson (1839–1906), who was associated with J. W. Powell in the exploration of the Colorado River, 1870–1878, and was geographer of the Geological Survey, 1882–1906 (Farquhar).

Thompson Peak [Alpine]. Named for John A. Thompson (or Thomson), a native of Norway, known popularly as "Snowshoe Thompson." From 1853 to 1876 he carried mail across the High Sierra from Placerville to Carson Valley; in the winter he used skis, then often called Norwegian snowshoes.

Thompson Peak [Trinity]. In the 1870's Packer Thompson climbed the peak on a dare and chiseled his name on the summit (J. D. Beebe). When the peak was used as a triangulation point the Geological Survey accepted the name.

Thornton [San Joaquin]. Arthur Thornton, a native of Scotland, established his New Hope Ranch here about 1855. The place was known as New Hope until the Western Pacific built across the property in 1907 and named the station for the owner of the land. *See* New-hope Landing.

Thorn: post office, **Valley** [Humboldt]. The valley was named because of the abundance of the native white-flowering thornbush (Laura Mahan). The post office at the settlement was in existence between 1888 and 1923 and was reëstablished February 16, 1951. There is a Thorn railroad station near Oro Grande in San Bernardino County, and a high mountain, Thorn Point, in Los Padres National Forest, probably named for its shape.

Thousand. This number is used in geographical nomenclature as a convenient expression for "many." Among the best-known features in California designated in this manner are: Thousand Island Lake [Madera], Thousand Lakes Primitive Area [Shasta], Thousand Oaks [Ventura], Thousand Palms [Riverside], Thousand Palms Canyon [San Diego], Thousand Springs [Shasta]

Thousand Palms. *See* Palms.

Three Arch Bay [Orange]. The name was suggested by the three natural rock arches.

Three Brothers [Yosemite National Park]. A group of three rocky peaks, named by members of the Mariposa Battalion because Chief Tenaya's three sons were captured near by. Several fanciful Indian names and interpretations are cited by Farquhar.

Three Rivers [Tulare]. The post office was established in 1878 and so named because the town is near the junction of three forks of Kaweah River.

Three Sirens [Kings Canyon National Park]. The mountain with three peaks was so named because of its location near Scylla and Charybdis, from Homer's *Odyssey*.

Throop, trōop: **Peak** [Los Angeles]. Named for Amos G. Throop, who in 1891 founded Throop University at Pasadena, now California Institute of Technology. The mountain is also known as North Baldy Peak. (Forest Service.)

Thumb, The [Inyo]. Windsor B. Putnam named the peak when he made the first ascent on December 12, 1921. The shape of the mountain resembles somewhat the end of the thumb. It is sometimes called East Palisade.

Thunder Mountain [Sequoia National Park]. Named by George R. Davis, of the Geological Survey, when he made the first ascent in August, 1905, to establish a bench mark on the summit (Farquhar). **Thunder Mountain** [Calaveras]. The name of the peak near Railroad Flat is a translation of an Indian name, according to a letter of June 29, 1872, by Phil Schuhmacher of the Whitney Survey (Davidson Papers). A Thunder Mountain in San Bernardino County is listed in the Geographic Board Decisions, Jan.-Mar., 1965. *See* Dunderberg.

Thurston Lake [Lake]. Apparently named for Charles Edwin Thurston, a native of New York, a sheepherder at Lower Lake in 1867.

Tia Juana, tē'-á wä'-ná: **River** [San Diego]. The name of a *parage,* probably of Indian origin, is spelled *Tiajuan* in 1829 (Dep. Recs., VII, 62), and appears with similar spellings in later records. Even in Spanish times it was changed by folk-etymological process to *Tia Juana,* 'Aunt Jane' (Dep. Recs., XIII, 52). The river is shown as *Arroyo de tijuan* on a *diseño* of the unconfirmed Milijo grant (1833). The name on the Mexican side of the border is now Tijuana, but the Geographic Board (*Sixth Report*) decided in favor of the time-honored Tia Juana for the stream, and for the town now known as San Ysidro.

Tiburon, tĭb'-ú-rŏn: **Point, Peninsula,** town [Marin]. *Punta de Tiburon* (shark's point) is mentioned in José Sánchez' diary on July 6, 1823 (SP Sac., XI, 47). The name appears again on Beechey's map of 1826 and on a *diseño* of Corte de Madera del Presidio land grant (1834). The early charts of the Coast Survey leave the point nameless, but a Tiburn (!) Point is shown on Hoffmann's Bay map of 1873. The name, properly spelled, was applied to the post office about 1885.

Tice Valley [Contra Costa]. Named for James and Andrew Tice, who owned Rancho El Sobrante de San Ramon, now the site of Saranap and Rossmoor.

Tick. A canyon in Los Angeles County and several other features in the State were probably so named because the surveyors were annoyed by the parasite. *See* Garrapata.

Tico [Ventura]. Probably named for Fernando Tico, who was grantee of Ojai rancho in 1837.

Tie Canyon [Death Valley National Monument]. About 1925, some 120,000 old railroad ties were purchased from the abandoned Tonopah and Tidewater Railroad to provide fuel for the eighteen fireplaces in Scotty's Castle. They were stacked in a near-by gorge, which became known as Tie Canyon. (Randall Henderson, *Desert Magazine*, September 1952, p. 8).

Tiefort Mountains [San Bernardino]. Tiefort is an old German family name as well as a German place name, but no connection with the name of the mountain range could be found. The theory of C. B. McCoy that the name goes back to Tie Foot, a Ute Indian chief who operated in the region with his band, molesting the travellers on the old Mormon Trail, sounds like folk-etymology, but is not impossible (Arda Haenszel) .

Tierra. The Spanish word for 'land' or 'earth' is repeatedly found in California place names. Corral de Tierra was the name of a land grant in Monterey County, dated April 10, 1836, and of two grants in San Mateo County, dated October 5, 1839, and October 16, 1839; it was also the alternate name of the San Pedro grant [San Mateo], dated January 26, 1839. The grant which included part of the lands of Mission Santa Clara (November 28, 1845) was called Tierra Alta (high land). In modern geography the term is found in Tierra Buena, 'good land' [Colusa]; Tierra Blanca [white] Mountains [San Diego]; Tierra Redonda [round] Mountain [San Luis Obispo]; Tierra Rejada, 'irrigated land' [Ventura]. **Tierra Buena** [Sutter]. The name of the settlement was changed from Terra Buena to the more logical version by the Geographic Board, May, 1954. **Tierra del Sol** [San Diego]. The name of the old post office Hipass was changed to the Spanish name, meaning 'Sunland,' August 20, 1956.

Tijera [Los Angeles]. Cienega o Paso de la Tijera, 'marsh or ford of the drainage channel,' is the name of a land grant, dated February 23, 1823, and May 12, 1843. The name is preserved in La Tijera, a station of the Los Angeles post office.

Tilden: Lake, Canyon, Creek [Yosemite National Park]. On Hoffmann's map of 1873 the lake appears as Lake Nina, named for Hoffmann's sister-in-law, Nina F. Browne. The present name appears on McClure's map of 1895. (Farquhar.) No explanation for the origin of the name has been given. The Tilden names are close to the Tiltill names, and Tilden Lake Trail is just a continuation of Tiltill Trail. A common origin of the two names is not impossible.

Tilden Park [Alameda and Contra Costa]. Named in 1937 by the East Bay Regional Park Board, in honor of Major Charles Lee Tilden, leader of the movement to create the regional parks (R. E. Walpole).

Tiltill: Creek, Mountain, Valley [Yosemite National Park]. The name does not appear on older maps and was probably not applied until the Dardanelles and Yosemite quadrangles were surveyed between 1891 and 1896. Since the creek was a branch of Rancheria Creek before the creation of Hetch Hetchy Reservoir, it is possible that Tiltill was the name of an Indian rancheria near the confluence of the creeks with Tuolumne River.

Timber. The word is found in the names of some twenty physical features, including Timbered Mountain in Modoc County. This term and its companion term "wooded" are applied particularly when there are some bald features near by. **Timber: Cove, Gulch** [Sonoma] were so named in the 1850's when the cove was used as a lumber-shipping point (Co. Hist., 1877, p. 100). *See* Madera.

Timbuctoo [Yuba]. Historic Landmark 320 preserves the name of the prosperous mining town of the 1850's. It is not certain whether a Negro miner dubbed "Timbuctoo," or the popular song ("for he was a man from Timbuctoo") inspired the name. According to Drury (p. 497), the first white miners "found a blackamoor busy with pick and pan, smiling a golden smile, and their ready fancy fixed on Timbuctoo as the name for the new camp."

Timms: Landing, Point [Los Angeles]. The names commemorate A. W. Timm, an early pioneer of San Pedro, who died in 1888. Historic Landmark 384. Avalon Bay on Santa Catalina Island was popularly known as Timms Cove.

Tin. Although tin ore has been found in varying amounts in several localities in the State, the name has been applied sparingly. Tin Mine Canyon and Creek are found in Riverside County and Tin Mountain in Death Valley National Monument.

Tinaquaic [Santa Barbara]. The name of the land grant, dated May 16, 1837, is of Chumash Indian origin: *Rancheria de Tinoqui* is mentioned in 1790 (PSP Ben. Mil., IX, 6). *Arroyo de Tinaquaic* is shown on a *diseño* of the grant.

Tin Cup Gulch [Shasta]. The miners who worked here once claimed that their daily find was as much gold as would fill a tin cup (Steger), hence the name.

Tinemaha, Mount; Tinemaha: Creek, Reservoir [Inyo]. The peak was known by this name to the early prospectors and cattlemen of Owens Valley and was named for a legendary Paiute chief, Tinemaha or Tinemakar, brother of Winnedumah. *See* Winnedumah.

Tinkers: Defeat, Knob [Placer]. J. A. Tinker was "a rough, hard-driving, hard-drinking teamster" who hauled freight between Soda Springs and the mines on Forest Hill Divide. From 1867 to 1873 Soda Springs Station was known as Tinkers Station. The name "Tinkers Defeat" was applied to a hairpin curve of the Soda Springs Road, because one day, so the story goes, the teamster's load, drawn by eight horses, came to grief at this place ("The Knave," May 10, 1953). The knob was named for him with humorous reference to his nose (Doyle). According to a directory of 1867, James A. Tinker was the owner of the Tinker and Fenton Hotel on Donnor Lake road.

Tioga, tī-ō'-gȧ: **Pass, Road** [Yosemite National Park], **Peak, Crest, Lake** [Mono]. The Iroquois name, meaning 'where it forks,' has been preserved in counties and rivers in Pennsylvania and New York and in a number of town names. It was transferred to California when the Tioga Consolidated Mine was registered at Bodie, March 14, 1878. In 1880 there was another Tioga Mine near Mount Dana. The famous road was built in 1882 and 1883 but was abandoned in 1884 because of financial failure. In 1915 it was bought by private subscription and donated to the government. (Farquhar.)

Tionesta, tī-ō-nĕs'-tȧ [Modoc]. Named in 1931 by J. R. Shaw, of the Shaw Lumber Company, after Tionesta Forest in Pennsylvania.

Tippecanoe [San Bernardino]. William H. Harrison's sobriquet, which refers to his victory over the Indians at Tippecanoe River, Indiana, on November 7, 1811, was a moderately popular place name, especially after the campaign of 1840 when the country resounded with the Whig battle cry: "Tippecanoe and Tyler too!" The name was applied to the Pacific Electric station about 1908.

Tipton [Tulare]. The name was applied by the Southern Pacific when the Tulare-Delano section was built between July, 1872, and July, 1873. The name of the English town in the county of Stafford had already become a popular place name in the eastern United States.

Tip Top. The name is found for several orographic features. Tip Top Mountain [San Bernardino] is appropriately applied to the highest peak of a ridge, but Tip Top Ridge east of Crannell [Humboldt] seems to be a misnomer in view of the higher elevations east and north of it.

Tish-Tang-a-Tang Creek [Humboldt]. According to Goddard, the name is the American rendering of *Djictañadiñ*, a Hupa village at the mouth of the creek (*AAE*, I, 12). According to W. E. Hotelling, it is a descriptive name, meaning 'a neck of land projecting into the river.' The name is pronounced tĭsh-tŏng-ä-tĭng, and the Forest Service is attemping to change the spelling accordingly.

Tissaack. *See* Half Dome.

Tit. It is a common custom in the western states to designate an elevation shaped like a woman's breast as Tit or Teat. The name is ordinarily used only in local speech and is seldom found on maps. *See* Squaw; Two Teats; Pecho.

Titanothere Canyon [Death Valley National Monument]. Applied in 1936 by the National Park Service because the fossil bones of a titanothere were found there (Death Valley Survey).

Titus Canyon [Death Valley National Monument]. Named for Morris Titus, a mining engineer, who perished in this canyon while on a prospecting tour in 1905.

Tobias Peak [Tulare]. Named in 1884 by John and Tobe Minter, in memory of their father, Tobias Minter, who homesteaded a meadow at the base of the mountain (R. J. Beard).

Tocaloma [Marin]. According to testimony in the Los Baulenes land-grant case in 1862, the stream called San Geronimo (now Lagunitas Creek) was also known by its Indian name *Tokelalume*. This name probably designated originally a Coast Miwok village: *lume* from *yome*, 'place,' a locative which may also be in the name Petaluma. A post office, Tocaloma, existed from April 27, 1891, to September 30, 1919. According to Kroeber, the word *tokoloma,* in Central Sierra Miwok, means 'land salamander.'

Todd: Valley, Creek [Placer]. Named for Dr. F. Walton Todd, according to Doyle a cousin of Abraham Lincoln's wife. Dr. Todd opened a store there in June, 1849. Todd's Valley Diggings are mentioned in the Sacramento *Daily Transcript,* April 19, 1851, and Todd's is shown on Gibbes' map of 1852.

Todos Santos y San Antonio [Santa Barbara] is the name of a land grant, dated August 28, 1841. A *cañada nombrada Todos Santos* (valley named All Saints) is mentioned on July 25, 1834 (DSP Ben. Mil., LXXIX, 106), and *Cajon de Todos Santos* (probably Harris Canyon) is shown on a *diseño* of 1840. *Todos Santos* was used elsewhere as a place name but does not seem to have survived. *See* Concord; San Antonio.

Toiyabe National Forest. The name Toiyabe is derived from an Indian word said to mean 'black mountain' or 'big mountain.' Toiyabe Mountains are recorded in 1867; in 1908 the forest reserve in Nevada was named after the mountains. The name became a California place name in 1946 when the northern part of Mono National Forest was incorporated into Toiyabe National Forest. The Geographic Board had decided for the spelling Toyabe in 1908, but later reversed its decision to conform with local usage.

Tokopah Valley [Sequoia National Park]. The upper valley of the Marble Fork of Kaweah River was named by former Superintendent John R. White and Colonel George W. Stewart. According to the latter, *toko'pah* means 'high.' (Farquhar.) Since *pah* is the Shoshonean generic for 'water,' the meaning may be 'high water,' possibly referring to the near-by lakes.

Tolay Creek [Sonoma]. The tidal channel was named after Tolay Lake, now drained. Padre José Altimira records in his diary under date of June 27, 1823: *Laguna de Tolay asi llamada del capitan de los Indios,* 'Tolay Lake so called for the chief of the Indians' (Arch. Arz. SF, Vol. IV, Pt. 2, p. 28).

Tolenas, tȯ-lĕ'-năs: **Creek,** town [Solano]. The *Tolenas* and *Tolenos* are mentioned in the records of baptisms of Indians at Mission San Francisco Solano in 1824 and later. March 4, 1840, the name appears in the Tolenas grant. In 1850 José Berreyesa testified in the land-grant case that the creek was named after the Indian [River Patwin] village on its banks (*WF,* VI, 373).

Tollhouse [Fresno]. In stagecoach days toll was collected at this point on the road which led to the Saver and Thorne mines. When the county took over the road, the toll was abolished but the name was kept. (M. H. Yancey.) **Toll House** [Napa], **Toll Gate Creek** [Plumas], and **Tollgate Canyon** [Fresno] also recall the days when building of toll roads was a profitable business. In Nevada County there is a Tollhouse Lake northwest of Donner Pass.

Tolowa. *See* Talawa.

Toluca Lake [Los Angeles]. North Hollywood was called Toluca when the town was founded in 1888. Toluca post office is listed from May 26, 1893, to October 17, 1906. The name is probably a transfer name from Mexico, where the old Aztec name is preserved in the name of the city of Toluca, southwest of Mexico City.

Tom, Mount [Inyo]. Thomas Clark, a resident of the now vanished town of Owensville, is credited with having made, in the 1860's, the first ascent of the peak, which was subsequently named for him (Farquhar).

Tomales, tȯ-mä'-lĕs: **Bay, Bluff, Creek, Point,** town [Marin]. The bay was discovered by Vizcaíno's expedition in January, 1603, and under the assumption that it was a river was named *Rio grande de [San] Sebastian* (Wagner, p. 419). It was later known to navigators and cartographers by a variety of names. *Tamales* as a place name is mentioned on September 26, 1819; Padre Amorós of Mission San Rafael reports that he had baptized about a hundred natives, *todos de un rumbo llamado* los Tamales [these words are underscored in the MS], *que son unos esteros que comunican con el mar de la Bodega,* 'all from the rhumb [direction, region] called the Tamales, which are several estuaries which communicate with the ocean at Bodega' (Arch. Arz. SF, Vol. III, Pt. 2, p. 112). The name, spelled both Tamales and Tomales, appears in the titles of three land grants: Punta de los Reyes or Cañada de Tamales, March 17, 1836, and June 8, 1839; Tomales y Baulenes, March 18, 1836; Bolsa de Tomales, June 12, 1846. The tip of the peninsula formed by the bay is called Point Tomales by Tyson in 1850 (p. 18), and Tomales Point on Gibbes' map of 1852. The town was settled by John Keys and Alexander Noble in 1850, and Tomales post office was established April 12, 1854 (Co. Hist., 1880, pp. 406, 408). Tomales Bay, Creek, Point, and the settlement are shown on

Eddy's map. The geographical names (including Mount Tamalpais) were given because the features were in the territory of the Tamal Indians. The name of these Indians appears in the baptismal records of Mission Dolores as early as 1801 (Arch. Mis., I, 80 ff.). They are mentioned by Chamisso in 1816 with the *Suysum* (Suisun) and the *Numpali* (Olompali), all of whom speak the same language (*Rurik,* p. 88). According to Barrett (*Pomo,* p. 308), and Merriam (*Mewan Stock,* p. 355), the tribal name was derived from the Coast Miwok word *támal* (or *tam'-mal*), 'bay.' There is no conclusive evidence to support this theory, and the name may actually be an Indian adaptation of the Mexican term *tamal.* Crespi (pp. 221, 232 f.) reports that the Portolá expeditions in October and November received from the Indians living on the San Francisco peninsula "tamales made of black seeds," and Serra writes in 1775: "The heathen of this port [San Francisco] ... make a sort of *tamal* from the seeds of the wild grasses ... They are very savory ..." (Palou, *Vida ... Junípero Serra,* chap. xlv). It is quite possible that the names *tamales* and *tamaleños,* in the sense of 'makers of tamales,' were first applied to Indians of the San Francisco Bay region and later were limited to the natives of what is now Marin County. A third theory is advanced by Lucy Freeland de Angulo: *Tamal* is a Miwok word for 'west,' and *Tamal* or *Tamaleños* were simply 'the westerners,' i.e., the people living along the coast. *See* Pinole; Tamalpais.

Tombstone, The [Fresno]. The shape of the mountain on the South Fork of San Joaquin River suggested the name, which was probably applied by the Geological Survey when the Mount Goddard quadrangle was mapped, 1907–1909. The name occurs in Tombstone Mountain [Shasta], where marble is found, in Tombstone Ridge and Creek in Fresno County on the Middle Fork of Kings River, and probably elsewhere in local usage.

Tom Creek [Modoc]. Named for Tom Cantrell, who settled here with his brothers in the 1870's (Irma Laird).

Tom Dye Rock [Lake]. Tom Dye, a resident of Middletown, who had killed a man in 1878, used this rock as his hide-out before giving himself up (Mauldin).

Tomka Valley [San Diego]. According to an Indian story, the place was named by Nahachish, the Temecula chief: "When he came to where Mendelhall lives now, the people

were eating. He had a good meal there and called the place Tumka." (*AAE,* VIII, 152.)

Tomki Creek [Mendocino]. "Tomki comes from *mto'm-kai,* the Pomo name of Little Lake valley, but has been applied by the whites to an entirely different creek and valley than the one intended by the Indians. The Huchnom name of Tomki creek is *kilīmī'l.*" (Barrett, *Pomo,* p. 259.)

Tom Martin: Creek, Peak [Siskiyou]. Probably named for a member of an Indian family that lived in the district (G. D. Gleason).

Toomes Creek [Tehama]. Named for Albert G. Toomes, a native of Missouri, who came to California in 1841 and was grantee of the Rio de los Molinos grant, through which the stream flows. The rancho is shown as Rancho de Toomes on Bidwell's 1844 map. *See* Thomes Creek.

Toowa Range [Tulare]. The name, of unknown origin, is shown on the Olancha atlas sheet of 1907 but apparently not on older maps. A similar name, Toolwass, in Kern County, is listed for a post office in 1898. A connection between the two names is indicated; both are in western Shoshonean territory but in different dialectical divisions.

Top. This generic term is used frequently for round- or broad-topped orographic features which stand out in a range of mountains or hills. Most elevations called "Top" are found in the Sierra Nevada and the Coast Ranges of central California, between Sierra and San Luis Obispo counties. About one-third of them are Round Tops; another favorite combination is Bald Top; Monterey County has a Quail Top and a San Martin Top, Plumas County a Lava Top, Fresno County a Long Top, Madera County a Redtop, and Calaveras County a plain Mountain Top.

Topanga: Canyon, post office, **Beach, Park** [Los Angeles]. The name of the canyon was preserved through the Topanga Malibu land grant, dated July 12, 1805. It is a Gabrielino Shoshonean place designation as indicated by the locative ending *-nga* (Kroeber). *Serro* [*Cerro*] *de topango* is mentioned in 1833 (Carrillo Docs., p. 70), and *Punta de Topanga* is shown on a *diseño* of the Boca de Santa Monica grant (1839).

Topatopa: Bluff, Mountains [Ventura]. Named after a rancheria of Chumash Indians near Ojai, also given as *Topotopow* and *Si-toptopo* (Kroeber). The inscription *Top Top* is shown on a *diseño* (1840 or 1841) of the Ojai grant. According to W. S. Brown, *topa topa* in local Indian speech means 'many gophers' (probably from Spanish *topo,* 'mole').

Topaz: Lake, post office [Mono]. The post office was established on the Kirman and Rickey Ranch about 1885 and was named after the artificial lake which was probably so named to indicate the clearness of the water.

Tophet Springs [Lassen National Park]. The Hebrew word of uncertain meaning, often used to designate 'hell' or a place likened to it, was applied to the hot springs three miles southwest of Mount Lassen, for obvious reasons. *See* Bumpass Hell.

Topock [San Bernardino]. According to *Desert Magazine* (Jan., 1941), the name is derived from the Mohave Indian *ahatopok,* meaning 'bridge,' and refers here to the Santa Fe bridge across the Colorado. The place was formerly called Red Rock, or Mellen for Jack Mellen, captain of a river steamboat.

Topo Creek [Monterey, San Benito]. The Spanish word for 'mole' (or 'gopher') was applied to the stream about 1865, presumably be-cause of the many burrowing rodents (E. W. Palmtag).

Tormey [Contra Costa]. Named for John Tormey and his brother Patrick, who in 1867 bought a part of the Pinole grant (Co. Hist., 1882, pp. 682 f.).

Toro. The Spanish word for 'bull' was fre-quently applied to places and has survived in several counties in the southern half of the State. **Toro,** tôr'-ō, **Creek; Mount Toro** [Monterey]. A place called *El Toro Rabon* (the bobtailed bull) is mentioned by Font on March 10, 1776 (*Compl. Diary,* p. 289), and appears repeatedly as *El Toro* in documents of the following decade. The *diseño* (1834) of the land grant El Toro shows an *Arroyo del Toro,* which is now Toro Creek. The place El Toro is shown on Wilkes' map of 1841. The mountain was apparently named by the Whitney Survey (Hoffmann's map, 1873). **El Toro** [Orange]. A *parage del Toro* is mentioned in a decree, dated July 12, 1838 (DSP Ang., II, 18). It was 'so called "because there was a nice tame bull there . . ." (Boscana, p. 217). The old name was revived for the post office in 1888, when the Post Office Department declined to ac-cept the proposed name Aliso because of its similarity to Alviso. It was spelled Eltoro until 1905, when it was officially changed to the present form upon the insistence of Eldredge. The name is also found in Santa Clara, San Luis Obispo, Riverside, and Santa Barbara counties, but in some instances may have been applied in American times.

Torquay [San Mateo]. Probably named after the famous watering place in Devonshire, England (Wyatt). Torqua Springs on Santa Catalina Island may have been named for the same reason.

Torquemada, Mount [Santa Catalina Island]. The peak west of Catalina Harbor was prob-ably named for Juan de Torquemada, whose *Monarchia Indiana* (Madrid, 1615) contained Father Antonio de la Ascension's account of the Vizcaíno expedition, which named Santa Catalina Island (S. K. Gally).

Torrance [Los Angeles]. Planned as a model city by Frederick Law Olmsted, the great landscape architect, and named in 1911 by the owner, Jared S. Torrance, a financier and philanthropist (Santa Fe).

Torrey Pines Park [San Diego]. The grove was set aside as a reserve to protect the rare pine, identified in 1850 and named *Pinus torrey-ana* for Professor John Torrey (1796–1873) of Columbia University (Drury).

Tortuga, tôr-tōō'-gȧ [Imperial]. The Spanish name for 'turtle' or 'tortoise' was applied shortly before 1900 to the Southern Pacific station on the Yuma division. There is a Canada Tortuga in Santa Barbara County.

Tower Peak [Yosemite National Park]. The Whitney Survey named that peak after the first ascent was made by Charles F. Hoffmann and his party in 1870. The name Castle Peak had been given to it more than ten years before by George H. Goddard, but was trans-ferred by mistake to a rounded peak about eighteen miles away.

Towle [Placer]. The name was applied to the Southern Pacific station in the 1880's. It is shown as Towles on the Mining Bureau map of 1892. Allen and George Towle were early lumbermen on the Dutch Flat divide (Co. Hist., 1924, p. 194).

Towne Pass [Inyo]. Named in 1860 by Darwin French for Captain Towne, a member of a party that crossed Death Valley in 1849. It is mentioned in the Sacramento *Daily Union,* July 31, 1861, as Town's Pass, and this form is shown in Wheeler's atlas (sheet 65-D). The pass is sometimes called Townes or Town-send Pass.

Townsend Flat [Shasta]. Named for Nathan A. Townsend, who developed mining claims near Briggsville and built the Townsend Dam and Ditch in the 1850's (Steger).

Townsend Pass. *See* Towne Pass.

Township. Although the word is no longer a current geographical term in California, it is used in the U.S. surveys of public lands as the name of a territorial unit comprising thirty-six sections of one square mile each. In California there are three township base lines and meridians: Mount Diablo, San Bernardino, and Humboldt. Each township has a double number: the township number (T) north and south of the base line, and the range number (R) east and west of the meridian.

Toyon, toi'-ŏn. The name of the beautiful shrub, also known as Christmas berry and California holly, is used for the names of a number of places, including two communities [Calaveras and Shasta]. Since the name is neither Aztec nor Spanish, a California Indian origin is indicated, although its etymology is entirely unknown. An *Arroyo de los Tollones* is shown on a *diseño* of Rancho Cañada de los Osos y Pecho y Yslai [San Luis Obispo]. A connection with a Chumash name for the islay or holly-leaved cherry, *tayiyas*, is not impossible. *See* Tajiguas.

Trabuco, trá-bū'-kō: **Canyon, Creek, Peak** [Orange]. The name, meaning 'blunderbuss,' was given to the place by soldiers of the Portolá expedition in July, 1769, "because at this place, where there is a small arroyo, they lost a blunderbuss" (Font, *Compl. Diary*, p. 188). *Sierra del Trabuco,* the Santa Ana Mountains southeast of Santa Ana, is mentioned by Font on December 30, 1775. The name *El Trabuco* for a *paraje,* for the creek, and for the peak is found repeatedly in Spanish and Mexican documents. On July 31, 1841, the name was applied to a land grant. *Arroyo del Trabuco* is shown on a *diseño* of Rancho de la Nacion, 1843.

Tracy [San Joaquin]. When the Southern Pacific line from Berkeley reached the place on September 8, 1878, the station was named for Lathrop J. Tracy, an official of the railroad.

Traer Agua Canyon [San Bernardino]. The name indicates the aridity of the box canyon. The Spanish phrase means 'to carry water.'

Tragedy Springs [El Dorado]. **Tragedy Creek** [Amador]. Bigler records on July 20, 1848, that they had buried three of their scouts murdered by Indians, Daniel Browett, Ezrah Allen, Henderson Cox. They had gone in advance of the party of Mormons in search for a pass and were killed probably on June 27th. "We called this place Tragedy Springs."

Trampa Canyon. *See* Las Trampas.

Tranca. The Spanish word for 'bar' was often used in the plural to designate a barrier put up for protection. **Las Trancas,** erected about 1841 by the Vallejos at the head of the tide-water on Napa River to prevent cattle from crossing at low tide, was a well-known landmark before the gold rush. The name Trancas y Jalapa was given to a part of Salvador Vallejo's grant, dated September 21, 1838. Paso de las Trancas was the alternate name of the Yajome grant [Napa], dated March 16, 1841. Agua Puerca y las Trancas grant [Santa Cruz] is dated October 31, 1843. In the Santa Monica Mountains [Los Angeles] there is a Trancas Creek, and west of Dume Point [Los Angeles] there is a Trancas Canyon. **Los Trancos Creek** [Santa Clara]. On a map of the Corte de Madera grant this creek appears as Strancos Creek, apparently a corruption of the original name.

Tranquility [Fresno]. This soothing name, which was used in several places in the East, was applied to the station by the Southern Pacific when the Ingle-Hardwick branch was built in 1912. The name of the post office, listed in 1912, is spelled with a double "l."

Tranquillon Mountain [Santa Barbara]. The prominent landfall for making Point Arguello was used by the Coast Survey as a triangulation station and simply called Arguello after the point. In 1873 the present local name was applied by William Eimbeck of the Coast Survey. "Arguello station is a misnomer; it is not at Arguello Point, and is on a mountain the name of which (Indian) is Tranquillon (Tran-quel-yon), and the pronunciation of which would have one think it was Spanish, but it is not" (Lawson, March 28, 1883).

Trap Creek [Shasta]. The tributary of Pit River was probably so named because the Indians had fish traps in it (Steger). A connection with the "traps" which gave the name to Pit River is possible.

Traver [Tulare]. Founded in 1884 and named for Charles Traver, of Sacramento, who was interested in a land- and canal-development project there.

Travertine: Rock [Imperial], **Spring** [Death Valley National Monument]. These were so named because of the incrustation of travertine, a crystalline calcium carbonate formed by deposition from the waters of the spring. Other features in the desert regions which are covered with travertine are sometimes called "Coral"; for instance, Coral Reef, south of Indio.

Treasure Island [San Francisco Bay]. The name was applied to the 400-acre artificial island built by U.S. Army engineers in San Francisco Bay and used by the 1939–1940 Golden Gate International Exposition. "The name was selected in the autumn of 1936 because it perfectly expressed a glamorous, beautiful, almost fabulous island that would present the treasures of the world during the 1939 World's Fair. It was no direct attempt to capitalize upon Robert Louis Stevenson, although the fact that he had made 'Treasure Island' a household word was a factor in their choice." (W. L. Wright.)

Treasure Lakes [Inyo]. The "treasure" consists of golden trout which were planted in the lakes. The name was approved by the Geographic Board in 1938.

Trench Canyon [Mono]. A narrow canyon named in 1884 by I. C. Russell of the Geological Survey (Maule).

Tres Ojos de Agua [Santa Cruz]. The name, meaning 'three springs,' was given to a land grant before March 18, 1844.

Tres Pinos, trĕs pē'-nŏs: town, **Creek** [San Benito]. The name of the town was not applied because of the presence of 'three pines'; it is a transfer name from a near-by community. It was originally given to the settlement on the Cienega de los Paicines grant, probably because there were three pines at the site. Lapham & Taylor's map of 1856 shows, doubtless from a mistake of the map maker, two places called Tres Pinos, neither in the right location. Goddard's map of 1860 shows the name at the site of modern Paicines. It is mentioned by Brewer on July 21, 1861, as a ranch fifteen miles from San Juan (p. 135), i.e., exactly the distance from San Juan to Paicines. When the plan for a railroad from Gilroy via Pacheco Pass to San Joaquin Valley was projected, the name Tres Pinos was appropriated by the Southern Pacific for the station, which was reached August 12, 1873, and which remained the terminus of the uncompleted line. Tres Pinos post office is shown on Hoffmann's map, and the locality formerly called Tres Pinos appears as Los Paicines Rancho House. Both Paicines and Tres Pinos are listed as post offices in 1880. Tres Pinos Creek is shown as *Arroyo del puerto del Rosario* on a *diseño,* and as Arroyo del Rosario on American maps until the Mining Bureau map of 1891 applied to it the new name. *See* Paicines.

Trevarno [Alameda]. Named after the home of George Bickford in Cornwall, England, by the Coast Manufacturing and Supply Company, which made the safety fuses invented by William Bickford, George's father.

Tri-Dam [Stanislaus]. The fifty-two million dollar irrigation project on the Stanislaus River was constructed by the Oakdale Irrigation District, and the South San Joaquin Irrigation District in conjunction with the P. G. and E., and was dedicated June 15, 1957. It was named for the three principal dams, the Donnells, the Beardsley, and the Goodwin dams. The idea of the irrigation water system in the primitive fashion goes back to the 1850's and was renewed several times. *See* Donnells Reservoir and Goodwin Dam.

Trimmer Spring [Fresno]. Named in memory of Morris Trimmer, the first settler and owner of the place (Co. Hist., 1956).

Trinidad, trĭn'-ĭ-dăd: **Bay, Head,** town, **Harbor** [Humboldt]. The Bruno de Hezeta expedition entered the bay on June 10, 1775. They took possession on the eleventh and named it *Puerto de la Trinidad* because it was Trinity Sunday (Wagner, p. 419). The name appears on most maps: Vancouver, Humboldt, Wilkes, Duflot de Mofras. The town was founded in 1850. Both Trinidad Bay and City are shown on the Coast Survey chart of 1850. Another Trinidad City near Red Bluff is recorded on Gibbes' map. The name was repeatedly used in place naming in Spanish times.

Trinity: River, County, Center, Mountains, Bally, Alps, National Forest. The name Trinity River owes its origin to an error. In late Mexican and early American times Trinidad Bay was constantly in the minds of the people, who assumed that it ranked next to San Diego and San Francisco bays as the third great California port. When Pierson B. Reading came upon the river in 1845, he gave it the name Trinity, the English version of Trinidad, in the mistaken belief that the stream entered Trinidad Bay. The name gained wide popularity after Reading discovered gold at Reading's Bar [Trinity] in July, 1848. Trinity Mountains are mentioned in 1850. The county, one of the original twenty-seven, was named on February 18, 1850; Trinity Center was settled by miners from San Francisco in 1850; the post office is listed in 1858. Trinity National Forest, comprising areas in Humboldt, Shasta, Tehama, and Trinity counties, was created and named in 1905. Trinity Alps is the name of a post office in Trinity County; it is also the generally accepted name for the mountains north of Weaverville. Trinity River was known to the Klamath Indians as *Hoopah*

(Schoolcraft, III, 139). *See* Bally; Humboldt Bay; Trinidad.

Triunfo, trī-ŭn'-fo: town, **Canyon, Pass** [Ventura]. The Portolá expedition camped probably in what is now Potrero Valley on January 13, 1770, and Crespi called the valley *El triunfo del Dulcisimo Nombre de Jesus* (The triumph of the sweet name of Jesus). Next day Crespi called an Indian rancheria in what is now Russell Valley *El triunfo de Jesus*. The abbreviated form El Triunfo appears in mission and land-grant papers. The settlement is shown on maps since the early 1850's. A post office with the name Triumfo was established August 27, 1915; the name was changed to the proper spelling April 21, 1917.

Trojan Peak [Inyo]. The peak southeast of Mount Tyndall was named in honor of the athletic teams of the University of Southern California (Geographic Board, May, 1954).

Trona [San Bernardino]. The name was applied to the post office, March 27, 1914, and to the railroad terminal from Searles to the lake bed in 1916. In 1908 Alfred de Ropp, a German engineer from the Russian Baltic provinces, succeeded in making soda and potash from the brine of Searles Lake. The product was called trona. De Ropp's company is the nucleus of the famous American Potash Chemical Corporation.

Trout. Among California place names given for species of fish, Trout stands next to Salmon in popularity. There are more than twenty-five Trout Creeks and a few Trout Buttes, Camps, and Meadows. *See* Golden Trout; Treasure Lakes.

Troy. Since 1789, when Troy in the State of New York was named, the name of the ancient city of Troy has always been a favorite American place name; it is represented in California by a Southern Pacific station in Placer County and a Santa Fe station in San Bernardino County.

Truckee: River, Pass, town [Placer, Nevada]. An account based on the recollections of Moses Schallenberger, a member of the Stevens-Murphy-Townsend party, tells the story of naming Truckee River (San Jose *Pioneer*, Mar. 15, Apr. 15, 1893): "Finally [near Humboldt Sink], an old Indian was found, called Truckee, with whom ... Greenwood talked by means of signs diagrams [*sic*] drawn on the ground. From him it was learned that fifty or sixty miles to the west there was a river that flowed easterly from the mountains. [Three of them explored ahead with Truckee and found the river. On some day early in October, 1844,] they reached the river which they named the Truckee, in honor of the old Indian chief, who had piloted them to it." An article in the Sacramento *Bee* of August 26, 1880, adds a touch of piquancy to Schallenberger's account: "In traversing this region, the Indian told them of a rapid river that flowed from one great lake to another. The party did not reach this river as soon as they expected, and they began to look upon 'Truckee's river' as a river of the mind ... When at last they reached the stream ... they had already named it. From 'Truckee's river' to 'the Truckee' was a transition natural and easy." The names seem to have been generally used after 1846 for the river and the pass, sometimes spelled Truckey or Truchy, but Frémont's name Salmon Trout River appears on Bancroft's map as late as 1858. It is interesting to note that the Spanish word for 'trout,' *trucha*, pronounced by the frontiersman, trōō'-chĭ, should so closely resemble the name Truckee and its spelling variant Truchy. It is quite possible that Frémont, when he heard the name, believed that the Spaniards had named the lake for the fish, and translated it into English. Donner Lake was known as Truckee Lake until the Whitney Survey changed the name. The town came into existence when the Central Pacific surveyed the route across the pass in 1863–1864; it was first called Coburn Station for the owner of the saloon there. After the fire of 1868 the station was renamed after the river.

Trumble Lake [Mono]. The land adjacent to the lake was patented in 1880 to John S. Trumble. The name is misspelled Trumbull on the Bridgeport atlas sheet. (Maule.)

Tub Spring [Trinity]. So named because of a barrel sawed in two and set in the spring (C. D. Willburn).

Tucho [Monterey]. A piece of land called *El Tucho* is mentioned on February 21, 1833 (Arch. Mont., VII, 56), and a rancho *El Tucho* on March 19, 1840 (Docs. Hist. Cal., I, 413), and later. The name appears to have been quite important: it was given to two confirmed land grants, dated June 21, 1841, and December 4, 1843, and appears in eight other land-grant cases. The etymology of the word is not known. The root *toch* or *tuch*, from Aztec *tochtli* or *tuchtli*, 'rabbit,' is repeatedly found in Mexican geographical names (Robelo, pp. 384 ff.), but it does not seem that the word itself was ever used instead of *conejo* for 'rabbit.' Since the name is spelled *El Tuche* in at least one source (Docs. Hist. Cal., III, 94), another derivation from a Mexican word is not impossible: *tuche* is from *tupchi,* the name of a tree called *amolillo* (Peñafiel, II, 299). A connection with Spanish *tocho,* 'pole,' 'iron bar,' is just as uncertain.

Tucker Flat [El Dorado]. Named for a stockman who took up land at the Upper Truckee River and built a road to the pass through which U. S. Highway 50 now crosses the range (E. F. Smith).

Tucker Mountain [Tulare]. Named for a homesteader on the east side of the mountain (A. L. Dickey).

Tucki Mountain [Death Valley National Monument]. The peak is not labeled on older maps. It is called Tucki or Sheep Mountain by Mendenhall in 1909. According to local tradition, *tucki* is the Shoshonean word for sheep. (Death Valley Survey.)

Tucolota Creek. *See* Tecolote.

Tujunga, tŭ-hŭng'-gȧ: **Creek, Valley, Wash,** town [Los Angeles]. An Indian rancheria, *Tuyunga,* is mentioned in August, 1795 (Arch. MSB, II, 12 ff.). *La Sierra llamada* [called] *Tujunga* is recorded in 1822 (*ibid.,* III, 237) , and *un arroyo . . . conocido con el nombre de* [known by the name of] *Tujunga* on July 25, 1834 (DSP Ben. Mil., LXXIX, 88). The name was given to a land grant, dated December 5, 1840. The post office, first spelled phonetically, Tuhunga, is listed in 1887. *Ti'anga* means 'mountain range' in Southern Paiute, and Tujunga may be derived from a similar word in the Gabrielino dialect, which is related to Southern Paiute (Stewart).

Tulainyo, tōō'-lȧ-ĭn'-yō: **Lake** [Sequoia National Park]. The name was coined in 1917 by R. B. Marshall because the lake almost touches the boundary of Tulare and Inyo counties (David Brower).

Tule; Tulare. The common cattail, the bulrush, and any similar reed are called *tule;* the place where *tule* grows is called a *tular.* These terms have developed in California into distinctive geographical names. In Texas the word *tules* is applied more loosely "to several species of yucca, and to certain kinds of reeds not identified" (Bentley), and there are a few Tule place names in the Southwest. Nowhere else in the United States, however, has the term become as important in place naming as in California. The word is derived from Aztec *tullin* or *tollin,* the root of which

is not known; it designates the cattail or similar plants with sword-like leaves, as shown by the Aztec symbol: From the beginnings of Spanish colonization the word was used descriptively. Today the names Tule, Tulare, and the diminutive Tularcitos, are used as specific terms in more than fifty place names, chiefly with Lake, Lagoon, Slough, Creek, but also with Peak, Mountain, and Hill. Tuleburg was a former and very appropriate name for Stockton. The name Tule is pronounced tōō'-lê; ,the pronunciation of Tulare is not fixed: tōō-lâr'-ê, tōō-lâr'. **Tulare: Lake** [Kings], **Basin, County,** city; **Tule: River, River Indian Reservation** [Tulare]. Before its reclamation much of San Joaquin Valley was marshland covered by a luxurious growth of reeds. The first man to see the valley in the wet season was probably Fages in 1772. He called it the *Llano de San Francisco* and described it as a great plain, "a labyrinth of lakes and tulares" (*CHSQ,* X, 218 f.). On March 4, 1776, while crossing the Cuesta Pass north of San Luis Obispo, Font speaks of *los tulares* as though it were an established name: "another range which we kept on our right [Mount Diablo Range], and behind which are the tulares" (*Compl. Diary,* p. 274). San Joaquin Valley or parts of it are repeatedly mentioned in later records as *Valle de los Tulares* and *Llano del Tular,* and Narváez' map of 1830 shows *Cienegas* [marshes] *ó Tulares* in the valley. After Smith's and Wilkes' explorations the name became restricted to the lower part of the valley. Most American maps record one or two Tule Lakes, the identity of which is often uncertain because of the peculiar hydrographic conditions in the basin. The Indian name of what is now Tulare Lake was *Chintache* (Wilkes, V, 157; map, 1841). *See* Tache. The Frémont-Preuss map of 1848 calls it *Laguna de los Tulares,* and other early American maps use this name or the old Indian name with various spellings. The name Tulare Lake is recorded in the *Statutes* of 1855 (p. 162) but was current before that date. Tule River had been called *Rio de San Pedro* by an expedition in April, 1806 (Arch. MSB, IV, 1 ff.), and appears as Tule River or San Pedro on Derby's map of 1850. Tulare County was created and named on April 20, 1852. When the Indian Reservation was set aside it was named after Tule River, on which it was first established. It is commonly called Monache Reservation. *See* Monache. The city came into existence when the Southern Pacific reached the place in 1872 and named the station after the lake. **Tularcitos: Creek, Ridge** [Monterey]. *Cañada de los Tularcitos* is recorded in 1822 (Arch. MSB, III, 296) and a place called *Tularcitos* is mentioned, together with *Laureles* and *Chupines,* in a report of 1828 (Registro, pp. 11 ff.). On January 8, 1831, the name was given to a land grant. This name is derived from a chain of small ponds, which are infested with tules and which are the source of Tularcitos Creek, main tributary of Carmel River (W. I. Wilson). Another Tularcitos grant [Santa Clara], dated October 4, 1821, does not seem to have left further traces in modern geographical nomenclature **Tule Lake** [Siskiyou]. This was apparently the lake named in 1846 by Frémont for his friend Barnwell Rhett. At any rate, it appears on most maps as Rhett Lake until about 1900. Von Leicht–Craven (1874) have Tule or Rhett Lake, and the former is now the generally accepted name. Tulelake post office was named after the lake about 1900. The disease tularemia was so named because it was first identified in Tulare County; it has nothing to do with tulares as such.

Tuledad: Canyon, Creek [Modoc, Lassen]. Named for Tuledad Matney, early-day frontiersman and later farmer and stockman, who ran cattle and horses here (W. S. Brown to O. M. Evans).

Tulucay, tōōl′-ŭ-kā: Creek [Napa]. The name was preserved through the Tulucay land grant, dated October 26, 1841. According to Barrett (*Pomo,* p. 293), the name is derived from *tŭ′lŭka,* 'red,' and the names *Tulkays* and *Ulucas* were applied to inhabitants of a Patwin village. The name *Toluca* (or *Joluca*) is mentioned in the records of Mission San Francisco Solano, and *Tular* (place where tules grow) is shown on a *diseño* of the grant; these may have some connection with the name.

Tumco [Imperial]. The name was coined in 1910 from the name of The United Mines Company. It is now a ghost town, although it once claimed 1,000 inhabitants. The original name was Hedges. (*Desert Magazine,* Sept., 1940).

Tumey Gulch [Fresno, San Benito]. Since the name was formerly spelled Toomey, it is possible that the gulch was named for William Maloy Toomey of Kentucky, listed in the *Great Register* of 1878.

Tune Creek [Shasta]. The tributary of McCloud River has a Wintu Indian name meaning

'the end' (Steger).

Tunemah: Trail, Lake, Pass, Peak [Kings Canyon National Park]. "The sheepherders frequenting that part of the country employed Chinese cooks. Owing to the roughness of the path they gave vent to their disgust by numerous Chinese imprecations. Gradually the most prominent settled itself on to the trail and it became known as 'Tunemah!' " (Elesa M. Gremke in *Sunset Magazine,* VI, 139.) The other features were named when the Tehipite and Mount Goddard quadrangles were surveyed in the 1900's.

Tungsten Hills [Inyo]. In 1913 valuable tungsten deposits were discovered west of Bishop. Adolph Knopf, Professor at Yale University, suggested the name in his report in U. S. Geological Survey *Bull.* 640-L.

Tunitas Creek [San Mateo]. *Arroyo de las Tunitas* is shown on the *diseños* (about 1839) of the San Gregorio and Cañada Verde grants. *Tunita,* the diminutive of *tuna,* the Spanish word for the fruit of the prickly pear cactus, is applied to the plant sometimes called "beach apple" (Sanchez).

Tunnabora Peak [Sequoia National Park]. The first ascent was made by George R. Davis of the Geological Survey, in August, 1905 (Farquhar). As the name does not appear on earlier maps, Davis probably applied it upon the basis of local information. The peak is at the edge of Shoshonean Koso or Panamint territory.

Tuolumne, tōō-ŏl′-ŭ-mĕ: River, County, town, Canyon, Meadows, Falls, Peak, Pass. The name is from that of Indians who once lived on the banks of Stanislaus River, probably somewhere west of modern Knights Ferry. This location would indicate that they were a branch of the Central Miwok. They were mentioned as *Taulámne* (also spelled *Tahualamne*) in Padre Muñoz' diary (1806) and as *Taualames* by Padre Viader on October 23, 1810 (Arch. MSB, IV, 85 ff.). The river is shown by Frémont and Preuss on their map of 1845, labeled *Rio de los Merced* by mistake; on their map of 1848 it appears as *Rio de los Towalumnes.* The modern spelling was used on Derby's 1849 map, and for the county, one of the original twenty-seven, when it was created and named, February 18, 1850; until 1860 various spelling variants are found on maps. Tuolumne Canyon and Meadows were named by the Whitney Survey; the falls are shown on Hoffmann's map, and the peak on Wheeler's atlas sheet 56-D. A Tuolumne City, founded in 1850 about three miles from the mouth of the river, was short-lived. The present town had its nucleus in Summerville, named for Franklin Summers, who settled there in the fall of 1854. To avoid confusion with Somersville in Contra Costa County, the Post Office Department changed the name to Carters, for C. H. Carter, a pioneer merchant. In 1899 the station of the Sierra Railroad was named Tuolumne; the post office is listed in 1904. According to Vallejo's *Report*, the name is a "corruption of the Indian word 'talmalamne,' which signifies cluster of stone wigwams." Although these Indians had no "stone wigwams," they lived, as stated in Muñoz' diary, in caves or recesses in the rocks. The suffix *-umne* means 'people' in the Yokuts and Miwok languages.

Tupman [Kern]. Named at a public meeting in 1920, for H. V. Tupman, from whom the Standard Oil Company purchased the land. Naval Petroleum Reserve No. 1 is situated near by in the Elk Hills. (Louise Stine.) The post office is listed in 1922.

Turlock [Stanislaus]. When the railroad reached the place in 1871, John W. Mitchell modestly declined to have the station on his property named for him and suggested the present name, after Turlough in the county of Mayo, Ireland.

Turn [Imperial]. When the Southern Pacific line from Calipatria to Sandia was built in 1923–1924, the name was given to the station because the railroad makes a sharp turn at this point.

Turnback Creek is a common western name for streams which, because of the topograpical condition, seem to "turn back." The best-known California creek so called is the one in Tuolumne County, the scene of a gold rush in 1856. According to A. H. Dexter, *Early Days in California* (Denver, 1886), p. 134, however, this creek was named because a group of white and Cherokee miners were forced to "turn back" here after an undecisive fight with the Indians.

Turner Lake [Yosemite National Park]. The lake was named for Henry Ward Turner, 1857-1937, a geologist of the U.S. Geological Survey, who pioneered some of the mapping of the park area (Geographic Board, May-Aug., 1963).

Turntable Creek [Shasta]. The creek received this name because there was a place to turn on the old road just north of the Pit River bridge (Schrader).

Turret. There are several mountains in the State so named because of their turret-like

formation. The best known are Turret Peak [Fresno] and Turret Mountain [Modoc].

Turup Creek [Del Norte]. The tributary of Klamath River bears the Americanized version of the Yurok name, *Tŭ'rip-hir Wroi*. A village, *Tŭ'rip*, was formerly at the mouth of the creek. (Waterman, map 9.) A Mount Toorup is mentioned by Cleveland Rockwell of the Coast Survey in 1878.

Tuscan Springs [Tehama]. Borax was first discovered in California in the waters of these springs, January 8, 1856, by Dr. John A. Veatch, who named them Tuscan Springs, after Tuscany, Italy, an important source of borax. The springs had formerly been called Lick Springs.

Tustin [Orange]. Established in 1867 and named for its founder, Columbus Tustin.

Tuttle [Merced]. The Santa Fe named the station for R. H. Tuttle, superintendent at Fresno, shortly after it had purchased the line in 1900 (Santa Fe).

Tuttle Creek [Inyo]. Named for Lyman Tuttle, who was the recorder of Russ Mining District in 1862, one of the organizers of Inyo County in 1866, and county surveyor, 1866–1872 (Robinson).

Tuttletown [Tuolumne]. The town, Historic Landmark 124, bears the name of Judge Anson H. Tuttle, who built the first log cabin in 1848 and became the first judge of the county. Some called the town Tuttleville; others, Mormon Gulch, for the Mormons who began mining there in 1848.

Twain [Plumas]. According to local tradition, the Western Pacific station was named in 1907 in memory of Mark Twain (R. Batha).

Twain-Harte [Tuolumne]. The mountain resort was named in 1924 by Katurah F. Wood for the great writers of the California scene, Mark Twain and Bret Harte (A. L. Nevins).

Tweedy Lake [Los Angeles]. The lake west of Elizabeth Lake was named for Robert Tweedy, a homesteader and the original owner (J. Hindman).

Twenty Mule Team Canyon [Inyo]. The name was applied by the Pacific Coast Borax Company to commemorate the famous twenty-mule teams, which had been used for hauling borax before the railroad was built in 1915.

Twentynine Palms. *See* Palm.

Twin. It has long been customary to designate two geographic features resembling each other as Twins. California has about two hundred places so named, chiefly Twin Peaks and Twin Lakes, but also numerous Twin Rocks, Meadows, Buttes, Sisters, Springs, and

Sloughs. Sometimes each Twin has been given a special designation for the purpose of distinguishing it from its companion: Upper and Lower Twin Lake [Lassen National Park], Big and Small Twin Lake [San Luis Obispo], Big and Little Twin Gulch [Tuolumne]. Occasionally Twins is used as a generic for orographic features: The Twins, Liebre Twins [Kern]. The modifying adjective is also included in the names of a number of communities: Twin Bridges [El Dorado], Twin Buttes [Tulare], Twin Cities [Sacramento], Twin Lakes [Santa Cruz], Twin Oaks [San Diego], Twin Peaks [San Bernardino], Twin Rocks [Mendocino]. **Twin Peaks** [San Francisco]. The popular descriptive name of the prominent landmark did not come into general use until about 1890. In Spanish times the name was *Las Papas*, 'the potatoes'; on Beechey's map (1828) and on some other non-Spanish maps the peaks are labeled *Paps*, but the charts of the Coast Survey have *Las Papas*. Another Spanish name, *Los Pechos de la Chola*, 'the breasts of the Indian girl,' probably owes its origin to American romanticism. Kirchhoff (p. 14) in 1885 gives Twin Sisters as the commonly used name. **Twin Peaks** [San Bernardino]. *See* Strawberry Flat.

Two Rock [Sonoma]. The name can be traced to Mexican times when the two big rocks were a prominent landmark called *Dos Piedras*. They are shown on several *diseños* of the 1840's. When John Schwobeda settled there before 1854 he kept the Spanish name, which is shown on Eddy's map and as late as 1873 on Hoffmann's map of the Bay region. When a post office was established on Schwobeda's farm on July 17, 1857, the name was translated to Two Rocks. In 1874 it is listed as Two Rock, and this version was adopted when the post office was reëstablished in 1915. Both Dos Piedras and Two Rock are shown on the Sebastopol atlas sheet.

Two Teats [Mono, Madera]. On older maps the two peaks San Joaquin Mountain and Two Teats appear as two breast-shaped elevations. However, the mountain now called Two Teats has actually two protrusions, one pointing east, the other west (Genny Schumacher).

Tyndall, Mount [Sequoia National Park]. The name honors John Tyndall (1820–1893), well-known British scientist and Alpinist. It was given by Clarence King and Richard Cotter, of the Whitney Survey, who made the first ascent in July, 1864. "I rang my hammer upon the topmost rock; we grasped hands, and I reverently named the grand peak Mount Tyndall" (King, *Mountaineering*, 1872, p. 75).

Tzabaco [Sonoma]. A land grant, dated October 14, 1843, was given this name, but the meaning and reason for its application are not known.

Ubehebe, ū-bē-hē'-bē: **Peak, Crater** [Death Valley National Monument]. The name is mentioned in the 1870's as the name of a mine, and it appears again as the name of a camp east of the peak during the boom of 1906–1907. The words *ube hebe* may be Shoshonean but their meaning is not known. They have been translated as 'basket in the rock' or 'basket in the sand'; such terms, however, were not used by Indians.

Uhlen Valley [Nevada]. The name became well known when the new route of Highway 40 was built across the Sierra in the 1960's. It was apparently named for an early pioneer whose identity could not be established.

Ukiah, ū-kī'-à: **Valley**, city [Mendocino]. The name is recorded on Duflot de Mofras's map of 1844 as *Jukiusme*, obviously applying to the Indians north of Clear Lake. On May 24, 1845, the root of the name appears in the *expediente* of a land grant as *Yokaya* and *Llokaya*. According to Barrett (*Pomo*, p. 168), the name consists of the two Central Pomo words, *yō*, 'south,' and *ka'ia*, 'valley.' However, Gibbs, who visited the village in 1851, spells the name *Yu-kai* and gives no meaning (Schoolcraft, III, 421). A more plausible interpretation is 'deep valley'; this meaning, confirmed by local Indians, is truly descriptive, whereas 'south valley' is not (G. E. Ward). The first white settler was Samuel Lowry in 1856, and in the same year Judge J. B. Lamar applied the present name to the settlement. The valley was first known as Parker Valley, but appears in 1858 under the name Ukiah in *Hutchings' Illustrated California Magazine* (III, 148). According to Kroeber, an Indian village called *Yokaia* existed south-southeast of Ukiah until recent times.

Ukonom Creek [Siskiyou]. The name of the tributary of Klamath River is an American rendering of Karok *Yukhnam* (Kroeber).

Ulatis Creek [Solano]. The *Ululato* Indians are mentioned by Chamisso in 1816 (*Rurik*, p. 89) as living north of the Suisun. They formed a division of the Patwin and are repeatedly mentioned, with various spellings, in mission records. The stream is shown as *Arrollo de Ululatos* on a *diseño* of the Capay grant. The present spelling was determined by a decision of the Geographic Board of April 1, 1908.

Ulistac [Santa Clara]. The name of a land grant dated May 19, 1845. It is from a Costanoan place name, as indicated by the locative case ending *-tac; uli, uri* is the word for 'head' or 'hair' (Kroeber).

Ulpinos [Solano]. Los Ulpinos was the name of the land grant conveyed to John Bidwell, provisionally on July 26, 1844, and definitively on November 20, 1844. The name is derived from that of the Indian tribe on the west side of the Sacramento just above its junction with the San Joaquin, mentioned as *nacion Julpones* on January 31, 1796 (PSP, XIV, 15), and with various spellings in later years.

Umunhum, Mount [Santa Clara]. The name is doubtless of Costanoan origin but the meaning is not known. The peak is shown as *Picacho de Umenhum* and *Umurhum* on C. S. Lyman's maps of the New Almaden Mine (1848). Hoffmann in his notes spells the name Unuhum on August 10, 1861, corrects it to Umunhum on the 20th, and records the pronunciation on the 26th: oomoonoom. Brewer in his Notes gives a similar version on September 6, 1861: oomoonoon. Since *u'mun, umanu,* and *umuni* are recorded as meaning 'hummingbird' in southern Costanoan, Beeler suggests that the name may mean 'resting place of the hummingbird.' In Santa Clara Indian mythology the hummingbird, the coyote, and the eagle are the creators of the world (*WF* XIII, 274 f.).

Un Bully. *See* Bally.

Uncle Sam. The colloquial name for the United States was a favorite name for mines and is preserved in Uncle Sam Mountain in the Santa Lucia Range [Monterey]. *See* Konocti.

Unicorn Peak [Yosemite National Park]. Named by the Whitney Survey in 1863 because the peak resembles the horn of the mythical animal: "A very prominent peak, with a peculiar horn-shaped outline, was called 'Unicorn Peak'" (Whitney, *Geology*, I, 427).

Union. Of the many idealistic and patriotic names for places in the United States, Union is the most popular. As the struggle for upholding the Union in the middle of the 19th century increased in intensity, the number of Unions, Uniontowns, and Unionvilles multiplied, especially in states where the Union

was in danger, as Kansas and Missouri. In California it was a favorite name for mining towns; only one of these, however, has survived: Union Hill [Nevada]. Today the name is found for communities or railroad stations in Napa, San Luis Obispo, San Mateo, and Santa Barbara counties, as well as for several topographical features. Union City [Alameda] has been recorded since 1851 and is probably the oldest Union name.

Universal City [Los Angeles]. The post office was established April 24, 1915, and named after the Universal Pictures Company, which was organized the same year (R. W. Gracey).

University Peak [Kings Canyon National Park]. In 1890 Joseph N. LeConte named the peak north of Kearsarge Pass in honor of the University of California. On July 12, 1896, he transferred the name to the present University Peak when he and his party made the first ascent. (Farquhar.) *See* Gould, Mount.

Unnamed Wash [Imperial]. Nameless features are often so designated by surveyors in their reports, but the army engineers who edited the Picacho Peak atlas sheet in 1943 did something unique when they created the name "Unnamed Wash."

Upland [San Bernardino]. Named in 1902 by the county board of supervisors at the request of the citizens. The original tract, opened in 1887 by the Bedford brothers, had been called Magnolia Villa, and later became identified with North Ontario. The elevation is slightly higher than that of Ontario.

Upper Lake [Lake]. The post office was established before 1867 and was named Upper Clear Lake because of its proximity to the northern shore of Clear Lake. The name was changed to the present form in 1880.

Urbita, ûr-bē'-tà: Springs [San Bernardino]. The name, coined from the Latin word *urbs* (city) and the Spanish diminutive ending, *-ita,* to suggest the meaning 'little city,' was given to a settlement near by before 1899. When the springs were developed, Dr. S. C. Bogart named the place Urbita Springs Park. From 1926 to 1930 the name was Pickering Mineral Hot Springs (for the owner, Ernest Pickering), and since 1930 it has been Urbita Springs. (Helen Luce.)

Usal, ū'-sôl: Creek, Rock, Mountain, town [Mendocino]. Apparently the name Usal is derived from the Pomo word *yoshol,* containing the stem *yo,* 'south' (Kroeber). Usal Mountain is mentioned by John Rockwell of the Coast Survey in 1878. The community came into existence when Robert Dollar formed the Usal Redwood Company and built one of his early mills there (Borden).

Usona, ū-sō′-nȧ [Mariposa]. When the post office was to be established in 1913, the residents met at a public meeting and decided to name their community after the United States of North America, using the initial letters. This rather ingenious way of creating a new euphonious name has remained unique, as far as gazetteers and postal guide tell the story. According to Stewart (p. 173), it was once proposed as a name for the United States.

Utopian colonies. Since the times of the gold rush repeated economic experiments with coöperative and religious and socialistic colonies were made in the State. Some of the coöperative undertakings, like Anaheim and Fresno, were very successful after their initial coöperative phase had passed; all the utopian colonies failed after a short existence. For the names of such colonies which remained as place names, see Colony, Kaweah, Llano. Robert V. Hine has treated the stories of the colonies in *California's Utopian Colonies*, 1953.

Uvas Creek [Santa Clara]. The name was preserved through the name of the land grant, Cañada de las Uvas, dated June 14, 1842. The word *uvas*, 'grapes,' was frequently used in Spanish times for places where wild grapes were found. Grapevine Canyon [Kern] was once *Cañada de las Uvas*. The name Uva for a Southern Pacific station in Fresno County is a modern application. Harter in Sutter County was formerly called Las Uvas. *See* Harter.

Vaca Canyon [Contra Costa]. Vaca [cow] Creek is shown on a plat of Rancho Pinole, 1865.

Vacaville; Vaca: Valley, Mountains [Napa, Solano]. These places perpetuate the name of the Vaca family, who came to California from New Mexico in 1841. Juan Manuel Vaca was co-grantee of the Los Putos or Lihuaytos grant, dated August 30, 1845, on which the town is situated. The plat of the town was filed in December, 1851, and the township was created and named November 1, 1852. Vaca Valley and Mountains are mentioned in the *Statutes* of 1855.

Vade [El Dorado]. The post office was established September 3, 1912, and named for a resident of Phillips whose name was Nevada, nicknamed "Vade" (Burt Perkins) . *See* Little Norway.

Vallecito. The generic term *valle*, 'valley,' was frequently used in Spanish times and appears in the names of more than fifteen land grants. *See* Posita. Except for Arroyo Valle [Alameda] and the names of a few subdivisions, the term is no longer found in California toponymy. Its diminutive, however, is still actively used. **Vallecito:** station, **Wash, Mountains** [San Diego]. The little valley with several cold and warm springs was a convenient stopping place on the trail from San Diego to the Colorado. The Indian rancheria of *Hawi* was in the valley, and it is likely that San Diego Mission maintained some sort of station there. In 1846, Kearny's "Army of the West" camped here, and the place was known to the soldiers as "Vallo Citron" and "Bayou Cita" (*CHSQ*, I, 145). The proper spelling is used by Whipple on his map of 1849 and by the men of the Pacific Railroad Survey. In 1858 the name was given to a station (now Historic Landmark 304) of the Butterfield Overland Mail. **Vallecitos de San Marcos** [San Diego] is the name of a land grant, dated April 22, 1840. It is forty-five miles west of the Vallecito station. **Vallecito** [Calaveras]. Daniel and John Murphy discovered gold here in 1848; later the place became known as Murphy's Old Diggings, to distinguish it from Murphy's New Diggings, now the town of Murphys (J. A. Smith). The new name, spelled Vallicito, is mentioned in the *Statutes* of 1854 (p. 222), and the post office as established as Vallicita, August 17, 1854. By this name the place was known for almost a century, until the Post Office Department restored the original Spanish spelling on October 1, 1940. **Vallecitos: Creek,** valley, settlement [San Benito]. Vallecitos Canyon is mentioned in Hoffmann's notes of July, 1861. By decision of March 6, 1912, the valley is officially called Vallecitos without the generic, although common usage continues to call it the equivalent of "Little Valley Valley."

Valle de San Jose [Alameda]. The name of a land grant dated February 23, 1839. The generic term is preserved in Arroyo Valle. *See* Arroyo Sanitarium; Vallecito. For Valle de San Jose [San Diego] *see* San Jose.

Vallejo, vȧ-lā′-ō: city, **Heights, Hill** [Solano]. The city was laid out in 1850 by Mariano G. Vallejo on his land and was the capital of the State in 1851 and 1852. It is said that Vallejo had wanted to bestow the name Eureka upon the prospective capital, but the maps of 1850 show the name Vallejo, and on March 13, 1851, this name was made official. *See* Glossary.

Valley. The word is often used as a specific term in naming towns. California has seven places so named. **Valley Ford** [Sonoma] dates back to the 1860's and was so named because the old trail crossed the Estero Americano at this point. **Valley Center** [San Diego] has been thus known since the 1870's because the settlement is situated in the center of the valley. **Valley Springs:** town, **Peak** [Calaveras]. The old mining town was known as Spring Valley because of the mineral springs in the valley of Cosgrove Creek. When the post office was established December 3, 1872, the name was changed to Valley Springs. Historic Landmark 251. **Valley Home** [Stanislaus]. The name of the German settlement Thalheim became a victim of war hysteria during the First World War, when it was replaced by the English version.

Valpe Ridge [Alameda]. Apparently named for Captain Calvin Valpey, a pioneer of 1851, or for one or more of his three sons (Still).

Valverde. *See* Verde.

Valyermo [Los Angeles]. Named in 1909 by W. C. Petchner, owner of the Valyermo Ranch. The name is a combination of two Spanish words: *val*, 'valley,' and *yermo*, 'desert.' (L. F. Noble.) The post office is listed in 1912.

Van Arsdale Lake [Mendocino]. The power reservoir was named in 1905 for W. W. Van Arsdale of San Francisco, president of the Eel River Power and Irrigation Company.

Vance Canyon [Santa Barbara]. Named for J. N. Vance, who in 1868 settled on Willow Creek, "otherwise called Vance Cañon" (Co. Hist., 1883, p. 268).

Van Damme Beach State Park [Mendocino]. Named for Charles Van Damme, whose gift of beach and other land was included in the park, formed in 1934 (E. P. Hanson).

Vanderbilt [San Bernardino]. The mining district was so named with the hope that it would prove as rich as the Vanderbilt fortune (Myrick). A post office was established February 1, 1893.

Vandever, Mount [Tulare]. The name commemorates the man who in 1890 introduced the bills in Congress establishing Yosemite, Sequoia, and General Grant national parks. William Vandever (1817–1893) was a brevet major general in the Civil War and represented the sixth district of California in Congress from 1887 to 1891. (Farquhar.)

Van Duzen River [Humboldt, Trinity]. The name Van Dusen's Fork (of the Eel River)

was given to the stream in January, 1850, by the Gregg party, for one of its members. It appears on Blake's map of 1853 as Vandusen's Fork. The "Fork" was changed to "River" by popular usage and adopted by the Geological Survey and Geographic Board.

Van Norden. *See* Norden.

Van Nuys [Los Angeles]. The post office was established in 1912, and named for Isaac N. Van Nuys, son-in-law of Isaac Lankershim, with whom he was associated in 1876 in the first successful cultivation of wheat on a large scale in southern California.

Vaquero. The Spanish word for 'cowboy' is commonly used throughout the southwestern United States, particularly in referring to Mexican cowboys (Bentley). It is found in California nomenclature as the name for several places and is generally pronounced vȧ-kâr'-ō. **Cañada de los Vaqueros** [Contra Costa, Alameda] was a land grant, dated February 29, 1844. In the mouth of the people the rancho became known by its syncopated form "The Vasco," a name still in use (Still).

Vasquez: **Canyon, Rocks** [Los Angeles]. So named because the notorious bandit Tiburcio Vasquez, who was hanged in San Jose in 1875, had his hideout among the rocks of "Robbers Roost" (Drury). The local pronunciation of the name is vȧs-kwĕz'. **Vasquez Monolith** [Pinnacles National Monument] constitutes the roof of the largest "cave" in the covered canyon. It was named in 1934, at the time of the first ascent, in the belief that this cave was another of the hideouts. (David Brower). There is a Vasquez Creek north of Nipomo in San Luis Obispo County, but it is not known if it was also named for the notorious outlaw.

Veeder, Mount [Napa, Sonoma]. Named for the Rev. Peter V. Veeder, who was minister of the Presbyterian church in Napa from about 1858 to 1861, president of the City College in San Francisco from 1861 until 1871, and later professor of physics and astronomy at the imperial university in Tokyo (State Library).

Vega [Monterey]. The Southern Pacific station was named when the line from Gilroy to Watsonville was opened, November 27, 1871. The name is derived from the name of the land grant Vega del Rio del Pajaro (plain of the Pajaro River), dated April 17, 1820, and June 14, 1833.

Venado [Sonoma]. The post office was established in 1921, and given this Spanish name for 'deer.' In the 1890's there was a post office by the same name in Colusa County; this name still appears on some maps as Venada. The name is found in other parts of the State. There was a post office named El Venado in Los Angeles County between May 8, 1914, and December 15, 1917.

Venice [Los Angeles]. Designed and built in 1904 by Abbot Kinney on a part of his Ocean Park Tract, with a system of canals (now filled) for thoroughfares, in imitation of Venice, Italy.

Ventana: Cone, Double Cone, Creek [Monterey]. The Spanish name for 'window' was applied because of a window-like opening in one of the hills.

Ventucopa [Santa Barbara]. The post office was established in 1926 at a point between Ventura and Maricopa. It was named at the suggestion of Dean ("Dinty") Parady, a resident, who coined the name from the names of these two places: *Ventu*ra, Mari*copa* (L. L. Curyea).

Ventura, vĕn-tûr′-à: city, **River, County**. In his instructions of September 15, 1768, José de Gálvez, inspector general, directed Padre Serra to name a mission between San Diego and Monterey in honor of San Buenaventura (Engelhardt, II, 7). The saint so honored was a learned doctor and prelate of the Franciscan Order of the 13th century. The mission was not founded until March 31, 1782, at the site called *La Asuncion de Nuestra Señora* by Crespi on August 14, 1769. The river appears as *Rio S. Buenaventura* on Narváez′ Plano of 1830. An attempt to found a town near the mission in 1848 was not successful, but a post office was established and named after the mission in 1861. The county was created from part of Santa Barbara County on March 22, 1872, and was given the euphonious abbreviated name Ventura. In 1891, upon petition of the residents, the Post Office Department changed the post-office name to Ventura. "Much mail and express matter designed for this office found its way to San Bernardino, and vice versa. Then the name was too long to write and too difficult for strangers to pronounce." (Y. A. Storke, Co. Hist., 1891, p. 230.) The new name was generally accepted, although the Southern Pacific did not change the name of the station until 1900. In 1905, Zoeth Eldredge, in his campaign to restore Spanish names, wrote the following obituary to the old name: "And now comes the Post Office Department, which is the most potent destroyer of all. I have spoken before of the injury done the people of San Buenaventura. They cling to that name and use it among themselves. But they

are doomed. Mapmakers, from the Director of the Geological Survey to the publisher of a pocket guide following the lead of the post office, call the place Ventura, and the historic name will be lost." (S.F. *Chronicle*, April 10, 1905.) The name of the river appears in its abbreviated form on most maps after 1895.

Ventura Rocks [Monterey]. The name of the rocks off Point Sur may be reminiscent of Buenaventura River, as the Salinas was once called. *See* Buenaventura River.

Vera, Lake [Nevada]. The lake is a power reservoir, built in 1909 and named for the daughter of Eugene de Sabla, the promoter of the project.

Verde. The Spanish adjective for 'green' was commonly used in place naming and occurs in the names of two land grants, Cañada Verde y Arroyo de la Purisima [San Mateo], dated March 25, 1838, and June 10, 1839, and Cañada Larga o Verde [Ventura], dated January 30, 1841. The word is still found in modern place names: Loma Verde [Los Angeles], Verde Canyon [Marin]; sometimes in combinations coined by Americans: Anaverde Valley [Los Angeles], Valverde [Riverside]. **Verdemont** [San Bernardino]. This name, coined from *verde* and *monte,* was applied to the Santa Fe station after the line from Barstow to San Bernardino was built in 1883.

Verdi Peak [Sierra]. The mountain is labeled Crystal Peak on the Mining Bureau map of 1891. The present name was probably applied by the Geological Survey, after the station across the Nevada line, which had been named for the Italian composer, Giuseppe Verdi.

Verdugo, vûr-dōō′-gō: **Canyon, Mountains, City, Wash** [Los Angeles]. The name commemorates the Verdugo family. José María Verdugo, a corporal of the San Diego company, who had served in the mission guard at San Gabriel, was grantee of one of the first land grants, dated October 20, 1784, and January 12, 1798. The name Rancho de los Verdugos is repeatedly mentioned in documents and appears on Narváez′ Plano of 1830 as Berdugo. The modern town was laid out by Harry Fowler in 1925, but Verdugo Park is shown on the maps of the 1910's as the terminal of a local railroad. The mountains are shown as *Sierra de los Berdugos* on a *diseño* of La Cañada grant (1843); and Sierra or Cañada de los Verdugos was the name of an unconfirmed grant of 1846.

Vergeles [Monterey, San Benito]. When José J.

Gómez was placed in possession of his two grants, which were designated by various names and dated August 2, 1834, and August 28, 1835, he requested that the name of the combined grants be changed to Los Vergeles (Bowman Index). *Vergel* is the Spanish word for 'flower and fruit garden.'

Vermilion Valley [Fresno]. The name was applied by T. S. Solomons and Leigh Bierce in September, 1894 (Farquhar). The word is quite commonly used for naming features which by nature have a bright orange-red hue, or which appear so in the evening sun. The lake in the valley is now called Feather Lake and no longer Vermilion Lake. The latter name was transferred to a small lake near-by.

Vernal Fall [Yosemite National Park]. Dr. L. H. Bunnell of the Mariposa Battalion applied the name, derived from the Latin word for 'spring,' because "the cool, moist air and the newly-springing Kentucky blue-grass at the Vernal, with the sun shining through the spray as in an April shower, suggested the *sensation* of spring . . ." (*Discovery*, 1880, p. 205). According to Brewer, the Indian name was *Tasayac* and meant 'shower of crystals'—doubtless an American interpretation (Notes, June 18, 1863).

Vernalis [San Joaquin]. The Latin word meaning 'pertaining to spring' was applied to the Southern Pacific station when the line from Tracy to Newman was built in 1887.

Vernon [Los Angeles]. Post office and station were known as Vernondale, for Captain George R. Vernon, who rose from the ranks during the Civil War and became a settler of the district after 1871. The abbreviated form was used when the city was incorporated in 1905.

Verona [Sutter]. The town was laid out in 1849, on property purchased from Sutter, and given the familiar American place name, Vernon. The post office was discontinued in the 1880's. When it was reëstablished about 1906 a new name had to be chosen because in the meantime a Vernon post office had been opened in Stanislaus County.

Versteeg, Mount [Sequoia National Park]. The mountain southeast of Mount Tyndall was named in 1964 in memory of Chester Versteeg, businessman, author, and public-spirited citizen, who died in 1963.

Vestal [Tulare]. The California Edison Company built the substation here in 1919 and named it for the virgin priestesses who tended the sacred fire of Vesta, the Roman goddess

of the hearth (Mary Sharp).

Vesuvius, Mount [Los Angeles]. In 1893 fireworks were displayed every Saturday night at 9 o'clock on the summit, ending with a miniature representation of Mount Vesuvius (Reid, p. 369); hence the name.

Vetter, Mount [Los Angeles]. Named for Victor P. Vetter, district ranger, Angeles National Forest (Forest Service).

Viboras, vē'-bô-răs: Creek [San Benito]. The name is shown on maps of San Benito County and is derived from *Arroyo de las Viboras* (the rattlesnakes), the name by which it was known in Mexican times and later (J. P. Davis).

Vicente: Point, Creek [Los Angeles]. The point was named November 24, 1793, by Vancouver, for Padre Vicente Santa María of Mission San Buenaventura. The name appears on Duflot de Mofras's map of 1844; it was adopted by the Coast Survey in 1852 but was spelled Vincente until recently.

Vichy Springs [Mendocino]. The springs were named before 1890 because their waters are similar to those in Vichy, France.

Victor [San Joaquin]. Named in 1908 by the Southern Pacific for Victor Morden, whose father, A. E. Morden, was instrumental in securing the station. The post office is listed in 1924.

Victorville, Victor Valley [San Bernardino]. The station was named Victor in 1885 for J. N. Victor, construction superintendent of the California Southern Railroad from 1881 to 1888. At the request of the Post Office Department the name was changed in 1901 to Victorville, in order to avoid confusion with Victor, Colorado.

Vidal [San Bernardino]. Founded in 1907 by Hansen Brownell and named for his son-in-law, whose name was Vidal (Santa Fe).

Vidette, East, West; Vidette Creek [Kings Canyon National Park]. "Two of these promontories, standing guard, as it were, the one at the entrance to the valley and the other just within it, form a striking pair, and we named them Videttes" (C. B. Bradley in *SCB*, II, 272). The usual spelling of the word is "vedette," and the meaning is 'a mounted sentry placed in advance of an outpost.'

Vieja, Mission [Los Angeles]. After Mission San Gabriel was built on its present site the original mission building, five miles away, was called Mision Vieja, 'old mission.' Historic Landmark 161. The adjectives *viejo* and *vieja* were often used in Spanish times in the same sense as Americans apply the word "old" in geographical nomenclature.

Viejas, vē'-ăs: **Valley, Creek, Indian Reservation, Mountain** [San Diego]. *Valle de las Viejas* is shown on a *diseño* of the Cuyamaca grant, 1845. The name was given to a land grant, dated May 1, 1846, but rejected by the United States on December 26, 1854. According to an often-repeated story, a Spanish expedition called an Indian village *Valle de las Viejas,* 'valley of the Old Women,' because at their approach the natives fled, leaving behind only the old women.

Villa. *See* Pueblo.

Villa Park [Orange]. The original name of the town, Mountain View, was changed to Villa Park when the post office was established about 1890, because there was already a Mountain View post office, in Santa Clara County (Co. Hist., 1911, p. 65).

Vina. The Spanish name *viña* for 'vineyard' was often used in Spanish times, especially in connection with the missions, most of which had at least one vineyard. La Viña was the name of an unconfirmed grant in San Luis Obispo County, dated January 4, 1842. The word has also been used for place naming in American times, albeit without the tilde and with a variety of pronunciations: Vina, vī'-nà [Tehama], listed in 1880 as a post office on Leland Stanford's once famous vineyard; La Vina, věn'-yä [Los Angeles]; Las Vinas, vě'-nàs [San Joaquin]; Canada de la Vina [Santa Barbara] was mentioned as *Arroyo de la Viña* in 1839 (Arch. SB, Juzgado, p. 5).

Vincent Gulch [Los Angeles]. Named by the Forest Service for Charles (Tom) Vincent, a pioneer miner and hunter (S. B. Show).

Vine. Because of the extensive grape culture in California the word "vine" has been repeatedly used in place names. The best known are Vineburg [Sonoma], Vineyard [Los Angeles], Vine Hill [Contra Costa]. There is a Vino, 'wine,' in Fresno County. *See* Vina.

Vinton [Plumas]. The name of the old post office Summit was changed on February 16, 1897, to the present name, for Vinton Bowen, daughter of Henry Bowen of the Sierra Valleys Railway (Myrick).

Viola [Shasta]. Named by B. F. Loomis for his mother, Viola Loomis. Loomis filed a homestead here in 1888 and later built the Viola Hotel. (Steger.)

Violin Canyon. *See* Fiddletown.

Virgilia [Plumas]. Named by the Western Pacific for Virgilia Bogue, daughter of Virgil G. Bogue, and queen of the Portolá celebration in 1909 (Drury). The post office is listed in 1929. *See* Bogue.

Virgin. Ten-odd creeks in various parts of the State and a spring in Death Valley were probably all so named because of their pure water. *See* Las Virgenes; Ribbon Fall.

Virginia. During the gold rush a number of mines, towns, and physical features were named by miners from Virginia. The name of Virginia Creek [Mono] goes back to "early days." It is shown on Hoffmann's map of 1873. It is not known whether Virginia Lake in Yosemite belongs to the same group or whether it was named, like many other mountain lakes, for a lady friend of a surveyor. Red Peak in Yosemite was changed to Virginia Peak by the Geographic Board in 1932 upon recommendation of the Park Service, because there is another, better-known Red Peak in the park.

Visalia [Tulare]. "On the 1st of November, [Nathaniel] Vise and O'Neil located and surveyed a new town called Visalia, in the finest section of that county" (S.F. *Alta California,* Dec. 11, 1852). The town was probably named after Visalia, Kentucky, which in turn had been named about 1820 for a relative of "Nat." After the county seat was moved from Woodsville to Visalia, the supervisors, on December 21, 1853, changed the name to Buena Vista. In February, 1854, the name was changed back to Visalia at the insistence of the residents. (Mitchell.)

Visitation: Valley, Point [San Francisco, San Mateo]. A cattle ranch of the San Francisco Presidio, *la Visitacion,* is mentioned in 1798 (SP Mis. & C., I, 74). Jacob P. Leese in 1839 was authorized to build houses in the place named *La Visitacion* (Prov. Recs., X, 12), and on July 31, 1841, the Cañada de Guadalupe, la Visitacion y Rodeo Viejo was granted to him. The place names, originally given for the Visitation of the Virgin Mary to Saint Elisabeth, were spelled Visitacion but were gradually Americanized, and the Geographic Board decided for Visitation (*Sixth Report*). In March, 1949, the Board revised the earlier decision and decided for the Spanish spelling. All names, including the school and the street in San Francisco, are pronounced like the American word "visitation." *See* Brisbane.

Vista. The Spanish name for 'view' was occasionally used for place naming in Spanish times (*see* Buena Vista), but most names which include the word are modern applications. Besides the popular combination Buena Vista, the word is found as the generic or specific part of many other combinations, often without regard to Spanish usage: Vista del Mar, Vista del Valle [Los Angeles], Vista Grande [San Mateo], Vista Robles [Butte], Alta Vista [Sonoma], Sierra Vista [Merced], Valle Vista [Contra Costa and Riverside]. The name is especially popular in San Diego County, which has a Vista de Malpais (a view of the Borrego Badlands), Chula Vista, Monte Vista, Sunny Vista, and a plain Vista.

Vizcaino, vĭs-kä-ē′-nō, **Cape; Vizcaino: Dome, Seavalley** [Mendocino]. The name of the explorer (see Glossary) appears first on Malaspina's chart for what Wagner believes was Punta Gorda (p. 523). On Humboldt's map (1811), C. Vizcayno is shown at latitude 40°, about halfway between Punta Gorda and the present location of Cape Vizcaino. Duflot de Mofras (1844) identifies the name with the present cape. The charts of the Coast Survey do not show the name until about 1900.

Vogelsang: Peak, Lake, Pass, Camp [Yosemite National Park]. The name was given to the peak in 1907 by H. C. Benson, for Charles A. Vogelsang, for many years executive officer of the State Fish and Game Commission (C. A. Vogelsang to F. P. Farquhar). Although named for a man, the name is singularly fitting to the beautiful place, as it means in older German 'a meadow in which birds sing.'

Volcano, Volcanic. There are about twelve peaks so named, including an imposing Knob in Madera and a Ridge in Fresno County. A group of Volcanic Lakes [Fresno], as well as Volcano Lake [Sierra], Volcano Canyon [Placer], and Volcano Falls [Tulare], are named after near-by craters. **Volcano** [Amador]. The miners called the place "The Volcano." "Bayard Taylor [1850], in his travels, speaks of several craters near, but no one else has ever seen them—they probably exist only in the poet's imagination" (Brewer, p. 435). "This marble or limestone is much broken up, and contains many caves, and chimney-like openings, from which the first explorers presumed that it had been the seat of an active volcano, at some time, and hence the name" (Bancroft Scrapbooks, I, 89). The name appears in Bowen's *Post-Office Guide* of 1851. An earlier name was Soldier's Gulch because some discharged soldiers of Stevenson's New York Volunteers mined there in 1848. Historic Landmark 29. **Volcanoville** [El Dorado]. The place north of Georgetown was an important gold-mining town. It was so named because a near-by mountain seemed to be an extinct volcano and

the miners had to work through lava cement. The place is still recorded on the Placerville atlas sheet and it had a post office until 1953.

Vollmer Peak [Alameda]. The peak formerly known as Baldy was named in 1940, by the East Bay Regional Park Board, for August Vollmer, of Berkeley, well-known authority on criminology, who had served as a member of the park board since its organization (R. E. Walpole).

Volta [Merced]. The town was laid out and named by the Volta Improvement Company in 1890; the post office is listed in 1892. The name probably was derived from the name of the great Italian electrical inventor.

Volunteer Peak [Yosemite National Park]. Replaces the former name, Regulation Peak, which was given by Lieutenant H. C. Benson in 1895 and transferred by mistake to another peak by the Geological Survey (Farquhar).

Von Schmidt Line. The maps of the Forest Service and some other maps record the old California-Nevada boundary line, established 1872–1873. See Glossary.

Vontrigger Spring [San Bernardino]. The spring at the eastern end of the New York Mountains was named for Erick Vontrigger, who made some mining locations and camped at the spring in the 1870's (O. J. Fisk).

Vultee Field [Los Angeles]. Established in 1942 and named for the Vultee Aircraft Corporation.

Waddell Creek [San Mateo, Santa Cruz]. Named for William Waddell, of Kentucky, who came to California in 1851 and built a sawmill at the creek in 1862. He was killed by a bear in 1875. (Hoover, p. 588.) The stream had been named *Cañada de San Luis Beltran* by Crespi of the Portolá expedition, October 20, 1769, and the valley was called *Cañada de la Salud* (valley of health) when the sick members of the party miraculously recovered after resting there two days.

Waddington [Humboldt]. The post office was established about 1890 and named for Alexander Waddington, a native of England, who came to California in 1867.

Wages Creek. See Weges.

Wahguyhe, wä′-gī: **Peak** [Death Valley National Monument]. The name was mentioned by Mendenhall in 1909 (*WSP*, No. 224, pp. 88 f.) and is still in use. It is doubtless a name of Shoshonean origin, but its meaning is not known. The root is probably the same as in Wahtoke.

Wahtoke: Creek, town, **Park** [Fresno]. A Yokuts

or Shoshonean "tribe" is mentioned in 1857 as *Wattokes,* high up on Kings River, and in 1861 as *Wartokes,* in the Fresno Reservation (Hodge, p. 922). The stem appears to be the Yokuts *watak,* 'pine nut' (Kroeber). The stream is shown on the Land Office map of 1859 as Wahtohe Creek. The present spelling is used by J. N. LeConte on the Kings-Kern sheet of his Sierra map, 1899–1904. The name was applied to the station when the Santa Fe built the branch line in 1910–1911.

Walalla Mountain. *See* Gualala.

Waldo [Marin]. A Waldo Street appears on the map of the Sausalito Land and Ferry Company, filed April 26, 1869. The station was named Waldo in 1891 (G. H. Harlan). Since many of the streets were named after towns and one was named Eugene Street, it is quite possible that Waldo Street was named after Waldo, Oregon. The Oregon town was named for William Waldo, who had been of service to the people of the community and who was Whig candidate for governor of California in 1853 (McArthur).

Wales Lake [Sequoia National Park]. The name for the lake northwest of Mount Whitney was proposed by the Sierra Club in 1925, in memory of Frederick H. Wales, a native of Massachusetts, veteran of the Civil War, and for many years a minister, editor, and farmer in Tulare County (Farquhar).

Walker Creek [Glenn]. Named for Jeff Walker, a sheepherder in the early 1850's (Co. Hist., 1918, p. 202).

Walker Creek [Inyo]. Named for Gus Walker, a native of Germany, who came to the San Joaquin Valley in 1859, helped in the survey of the valley, and settled in the Olancha district as a farmer in 1864 (Robinson).

Walker: Lake, Creek [Mono]. The lake northeast of Mono Pass was named for William J. Walker, who settled on the land adjoining the lake in 1880 (Maule). The name is often erroneously connected with Joseph R. Walker.

Walker: Pass [Kern], **River** [Mono]. Joseph R. Walker, of Tennessee, was one of the great pathfinders of the American West. The first time he crossed the pass which bears his name was on his return from the famous expedition of 1833 from Great Salt Lake to Monterey, on which he saw Yosemite Valley. Frémont suggested the name in his journal on March 24, 1844: "This pass, reported to be good, was discovered by Mr. Joseph Walker . . . whose name it might, therefore, appropriately bear" (*Memoirs,* I, 354). Walker was

Frémont's guide on the latter's third expedition (1845–1846), and Frémont named the river (and the lake in the State of Nevada) for him.

Wallace [Calaveras]. The place was named for an unidentified man by David S. Burson, the founder of the town (Frances Bishop). The post office was established January 1, 1883.

Wallace, Mount. *See* Evolution.

Wallace: Lake, Creek [Sequoia National Park]. The lake northwest of Mount Whitney was named in 1925, at the suggestion of the Sierra Club, for Judge William B. Wallace, a well-known pioneer mountaineer in the Kings, Kern, and Kaweah regions. Wallace came to Tulare County in 1876, where he later served for many years as judge of the superior court. (Farquhar.)

Walnut. About ten features in the State are named after the most widely cultivated species of the nut family. Some of the names are translations of the Spanish name *Nogales,* given to places where the native black walnut was found. **Walnut Creek** [Contra Costa]. A translation from the Spanish name of the creek recorded as *Arroyo de los Nogales* (creek of the walnuts) by Padre Viader on August 16, 1810 (Arch. MSB, IV). The stream is called *Arroyo de las Nueces* (creek of the nuts) on July 22, 1834 (Legis. Recs., II, 162), and this is the name of a land grant, dated July 11, 1834. The town was named after the creek when the post office was established in the 1860's. **Walnut Grove** [Sacramento]. The place was settled by "woodchoppers" as early as 1850, but the present name was not applied until the early 1860's when the post office was established. **Walnut** [Los Angeles]. The Southern Pacific station was called Lemon until 1912, when the present name was applied. The change was probably made because shortly before 1912 "lemon" came to be used in the slang sense and made the name humorous. There is a Walnut Creek about five miles north of the town. The Geological Survey on the 1941 edition of the Pomona atlas sheet sticks to the long-vanished Lemon.

Walong [Kern]. The name of W. A. Long, a Southern Pacific trainmaster, contracted to form the name Walong, was applied to a siding on the Tehachapi slope in 1876 (Santa Fe).

Walsh Station [Sacramento]. Named by the Post Office Department in 1875 for J. M. Walsh, the town's first storekeeper and postmaster (Co. Hist., 1890, pp. 202, 212).

Walteria [Los Angeles]. The community was named for Captain Walters, who built the Walters Hotel in the early part of the 20th century (R. S. Sleeth). The post office was established September 18, 1926.

Wamelo Rock [Madera]. The name appears on Hoffmann's map of 1873 and was probably applied by the Whitney Survey. In 1875 Muir stated that the granite dome was called Wamello by the Indians (Farquhar). It is shown as Fresno Dome on the Mariposa atlas sheet.

Wanda Lake [Kings Canyon National Park]. Named by R. B. Marshall of the Geological Survey, for Mrs. Wanda Hanna, daughter of John Muir (Farquhar).

Ward: Mountain, Tunnel [Fresno]. Named for Dr. George C. Ward, who directed construction of the hydroelectric plant in the Sierra Nevada. Approved by the Geographic Board in 1935.

War Eagle Field [Los Angeles]. On March 3, 1942, Major C. C. Moseley bestowed the symbolic name upon the airfield, which was established as a training center for American and British pilots.

Warm Springs [Alameda]. The post office at the site was listed as Harrisburgh from 1867 to 1880. The new name was taken from the warm springs which are two miles northeast on Agua Caliente (warm water) Creek; the "new" Warm Springs are on Agua Fria (cold water) Creek.—There are a number of other Warm Springs in the State, including two settlements [Lassen and Los Angeles].

Warner Mountains [Modoc]. Named in memory of Captain William H. Warner, who was killed by Indians at the foot of this range, just south of the Oregon line, on September 26, 1849. Warner was in command of a reconnaissance party in search of a route across the mountains. Warner Valley in Oregon is named for the same man (cf. McArthur, *Oregon Geographic Names*).

Warner Springs; Warners: Ranch, Pass [San Diego]. Named for Jonathan Trumbull (Juan José) Warner, who arrived in California in 1831, became a Mexican citizen, and was granted the Rancho Agua Caliente or Valle de San Jose in 1844. The rancheria at the springs was called *Hakupin* or *Jacopin*, (probably 'hot water') by the Diegueño Indians, and *Kupa* by the Cahuilla Indians. Warners Ranch is Historic Landmark 311; it was to the early immigrant who came via the southern route what Sutters Fort was for the immigrant who entered California via the central route.

Warren, Mount [Mono]. The name was applied by the Whitney Survey before 1867 for Gouverneur K. Warren, a member of the Pacific Railroad Survey and a distinguished Union general in the Civil War (Farquhar).

Warren Grove [Humboldt]. The grove in the Prairie Creek Redwoods State Park was established in 1954 in honor of Earl Warren, governor of California (1943-1953) and Chief Justice of the U.S. Supreme Court.

Wasco [Kern]. The Santa Fe station was established in 1898 and named Dewey, in honor of the admiral's victory in Manila Bay, May 1, 1898. When it was learned that a place named Dewey already existed in the State, William Bonham, one of the oldest settlers, was asked to select a new name. He chose Wasco after his home county in Oregon, which had been named for an Indian tribe. (A. D. Jackman.)

Wash. In England a "wash" designates a piece of ground washed by the action of the sea or a river (Knox). In western America the term is generally used for the dry bed of an intermittent stream, but in the desert regions of California it is applied to a creek bed which is dry most of the time.

Washapie Mountains [Tulare]. Named after one of the Indian villages in adjacent Drum Valley (A. L. Dickey).

Washboard, The [Fresno]. So named because the contours make the northeast slope of Kettleman Hills look like a washboard.

Washburn Lake [Yosemite National Park]. Named by Lieutenant N. F. McClure in 1895 for Albert H. Washburn, of Wawona (Farquhar).

Washington. The State naturally has a number of places named directly or indirectly in honor of the Father of the Country, including the old mining town of Washington [Nevada] and Washington Column [Yosemite National Park]. In former years there were many more: Washington Corners [Alameda] is now Irvington, and Washingtonville [Sierra] is Downieville. **Washington Peak** [Del Norte] is named after the Washington Ranch situated at its foot; **Washington Lake** (euphonious for Slough) in the Yolo Basin was named after the town now called Broderick.

Washingtons Flat [Del Norte] is named for a pioneer hunter and trapper, George Washington, who was killed there by a landslide.

Washoe; Washoe Creek [Sonoma]. The Washo (or Washoe) Indians have left no trace of their name in their old habitat, the Lake

Tahoe region. The places in Sonoma County were probably not named directly for the Indian tribe but after the Washoe mines, which were developed after 1859.

Wasioja, wä-sĕ-ō′-ä [Santa Barbara]. The post office (discontinued in 1933) was established in 1894 and named after Wasioja, Minnesota, the former home of a resident (Margaret B. Richardson).

Wassamma Creek [Madera]. Named after the Southern Miwok village on its bank (Merriam, *Mewan Stock*, p. 346). *See* Ahwahnee.

Watchorn Basin [Los Angeles]. The basin in Los Angeles harbor was named about 1912 for Robert Watchorn, an official of the Outer Harbor Dock and Wharf Company operating in that area (Co. Surveyor).

Waterford [Stanislaus]. When the Stockton-Merced branch was built in 1890 the name was given to the Southern Pacific station because it was near a much-used ford through Tuolumne River. Waterford is a famous old city of Ireland, and the name is quite common as an American place name.

Waterhouse Peak [El Dorado]. The peak was named by the Forest Service in memory of Clark Waterhouse, who had been in charge of the Angora Lookout and lost his life in World War I (E. F. Smith).

Waterloo. The British-Prussian victory over Napoleon in 1815 at Waterloo made the name a favorite for places in America before the Civil War. The place in San Joaquin County, however, owes its name to an actual fight over a land title in the early 1860's, although it is not clear from the reports which party met its Waterloo. The post office is listed in 1867.

Waterman, Mount [Los Angeles]. According to tradition in the Forest Service, the mountain was named for Robert Waterman, from 1904 to 1908 a ranger in the old San Gabriel Timberland Reserve. The original name was Lady Waterman Mount because Mrs. Robert Waterman was the first woman to climb it (Wheelock).

Waterman Canyon [San Bernardino]. When the road was built in the 1880's, Dr. Ben Barton and his associates named the canyon after the famous Waterman silver mine. The mine was owned by Robert W. Waterman, of San Bernardino, who was governor of California from 1887 to 1891. It is not known whether Waterman post office [Amador] was named for the same man.

Waterman Park [Solano]. The post office, listed in 1945, preserves the name of Robert H. Waterman, the famous clipper-ship captain. *See* Fairfield.

Waterwheel Falls [Yosemite National Park]. "The water here encounters shelves of rocks projecting from the river bottom which cause enormous arcs of water to be thrown into the air, some rising 20 feet" (Doyle).

Watkins, Mount [Yosemite National Park]. The Indian name of the mountain was *Waijau,* meaning perhaps 'Pine Mountain.' The new name was affixed, probably in the 'sixties, for Carleton E. Watkins, an early photographer of Yosemite, whose picture of Mirror Lake reflecting the mountain was especially popular. (Farquhar.)

Watson [Los Angeles]. Established as a station of the San Pedro line of the Pacific Electric Railway in 1904 and so named because it was on that part of Rancho San Pedro which was allotted in 1885 to Maria Dominguez de Watson (Co. Library).

Watson Gulch [Shasta]. Named after Watson Diggings, which had been named for a miner from Oregon who is credited with having taken the first wagon and ox team over Trinity Divide in 1849 (Steger).

Watsonville [Santa Cruz]. The town was laid out in 1852 on a part of Rancho Bolsa del Pajaro by D. S. Gregory and Judge John H. Watson, owners of the land, and was named for the latter. The post office is listed in 1854.
Watsonville Junction [Monterey]. The earlier name Pajaro (*see* Pajaro River), which had been given to the station when the railroad was built in 1871, was changed by the Southern Pacific in 1912.

Watterson Canyon [Inyo]. Named for George Watterson, a native of the Isle of Man, who operated a small mine in the canyon on the north side of the road (Robinson).

Watts [Los Angeles]. The district, which gained widespread notoriety because of the Negro riots in 1965, was named for C. H. Watts, a Pasadena realtor around 1900. He had a large ranch at this place. According to the Los Angeles *Times,* October 10, 1965, it was originally called Mud Town and it was annexed to Los Angeles in 1926. (Brother Henry.)

Watts Valley [Fresno]. Named for C. B. Watts, who settled in the valley formerly known as Popes Valley (Co. Hist., 1933, p. 48).

Waucoba: Canyon, Mountain [Inyo]. The name is Paiute for the bull pine, a local slur name for various species of pine of inferior quality but valuable to the Indians, who appreciated the seeds and not the timber.

C. D. Walcott, former director of the Geological Survey, gave this name, spelled Waucobi, to the ancient lake, the remnant of which is Owens Lake in Owens Valley (Chalfant, *Inyo*, 1922, p. 3).

Waugh Lake [Mono]. Created by the construction of a dam in 1918 and named for E. J. Waugh, chief construction engineer of the Nevada-California and Southern Sierras power companies (W. L. Huber to F. P. Farquhar).

Waukell: Creek, Flat [Del Norte]. The name is an Americanization of the Yurok name *Wo'kel* for a village and a creek (Waterman, map 9).

Waukena [Tulare]. The town was laid out by a development company in 1886. It is not certain whether the name is of Indian origin or whether it is Joaquin spelled phonetically and given a feminine ending.

Wawona [Yosemite National Park]. The cabin which Galen Clark built there in 1857 was first known as Clark's Station and, when Edwin Moore acquired half-interest in 1869, as Clark and Moore's. In 1875 the Washburn brothers bought the place and changed the name to Wawona. According to Powers (p. 398), the name is the local Indian word for 'big tree': "The California big tree is also in a manner sacred to them, and they call it *woh-woh'-nau*, a word formed in imitation of the hoot of the owl, which is the guardian spirit and deity of this great monarch of the forest. It is productive of bad luck to fell this tree, or to mock or shoot the owl, or even to shoot in his presence. Bethel states that they have often, in earlier years, tried to persuade him not to cut them down—pity they could not have succeeded!—and that when they see a teamster going along the road with a wagonload of lumber made from these trees, they will cry out after him, and tell him the owl will visit him with evil luck."

Weaver Bally. *See* Bally.

Weaverville; Weaver Creek [Trinity]. The place was called Weavertown or Weaverville for George Weaver, a prospector, who built the first cabin, in 1850. It is mentioned as Weaverville in the San Francisco *Alta California* of May 1, 1852.

Webber: Lake, Peak [Sierra]. The former Little Truckee Lake received its present name from David Gould Webber, who bought the surrounding land for a stock range in 1852. His place of residence is mentioned as Webber's Station in Brewer's Notes, November, 1861.

Weber Creek [El Dorado]. The only place name which commemorates one of the most notable pioneers of central California. Charles M. Weber, a native of Homburg, Germany, and the founder of the city of Stockton, came to California with the Bartleson party in 1841. In 1848 he mined successfully at the creek, calling his camp Weberville. Weber Creek is mentioned by Colonel Richard B. Mason on August 17, 1848. On modern maps the name of the creek is misspelled Webber. Weber Point in Stockton is Historic Landmark 165.

Wedding Cake [Trinity]. The elevation was so named about 1870 by James King and his bride on their wedding trip because, through their rose-colored glasses, it looked like a huge old-fashioned wedding cake (J. D. Beebe).

Wedertz Flats [Mono]. Named for Louis Wedertz, a pioneer, who owned the land adjacent to the flats (Maule).

Weed [Siskiyou]. Named in 1900 for Abner Weed, founder of the Weed Lumber Company. Weed, a native of Maine, was present at Lee's surrender at Appomattox, came to California in 1869, was for many years county supervisor, and from 1907 to 1909 was a State senator.

Weed Patch [Kern]. The place was so named because of a luxuriant growth of weeds caused by subirrigation. *See* Algoso; Patch.

Weges Creek [Mendocino]. The stream north of Westport was named for Alfred Weges, who settled here in 1864 (Co. Hist., 1914, p. 117). The name is spelled Wages on some maps.

Weimar, wē'-mär [Placer]. When the post office was established in 1886, the Post Office Department rejected the name of the railroad station, New England Mills, because it was too long. Mary E. Mitchell, the postmaster, and the residents decided to call the place in memory of "old Weimah," a colorful chief of the "Oleepas" in the 1850's. His mark X and the name "Weima" appear in a document published in the *Placer Times* on May 27, 1850. Since this spelling was apparently unknown in the 1880's, the name of the post office was spelled, though not pronounced, like that of the German city of Goethe and Schiller. Weimar Hill [Nevada], mentioned by Browne in 1869 (p. 115), may also have been named for the Indian.

Weisel, wī'-sĕl [Riverside]. Named by the Santa Fe for Peter J. Weisel, owner of the silica plant to which a spur was built in 1927 (G. A. Van Valin).

Weitchpec [Humboldt]. The Weitspek are mentioned as a separate language group by Gibbs in 1851 (Schoolcraft, III, 422). Since they dwelt, and still dwell, at the confluence of Klamath and Trinity rivers, the interpretation 'meeting of the waters' sounds plausible. According to Waterman (p. 257), the Indian name is *Wĕ'itspūs* and refers specifically to a small spring just to one side of the present Indian village. Waterman found the same name, translated as 'confluence,' for a point projecting into the estuary of Klamath River (p. 232). In 1859 a post office was established at the white settlement opposite the Indian village and was called Weitchpec.

Weldon [Kern]. Named for William Weldon, a stockman of the 1850's (R. Palmer).

Wells Peak [Mono]. The name was applied by the Geographic Board at the suggestion of the Forest Service, in memory of John C. Wells, supervisor of Mono National Forest, 1901–1922.

Wells Peak [Yosemite National Park]. Named by R. B. Marshall in the 1890's for Lieutenant Rush S. Wells, a native of New Mexico (Farquhar).

Wendel [Lassen]. The station was named about 1905 by Thomas Moran, president of the Nevada-California-Oregon Railroad, for a friend whose first name was Wendel (A. C. Riesenman). The post office is listed in 1915.

Wengler [Shasta]. The post office was established about 1900 and named for E. M. Wengler, part owner of the Wengler & Buick mill and first postmaster (Steger).

Weott [Humboldt]. Weott is an Americanization of Wiyot, the name of the Humboldt Bay Indians. "The name given to this people by their neighbors is Wee-yot, and Eel River is known by the same" (Gibbs, 1851, in Schoolcraft, III, 127). A village *Weyo* is shown by Waterman (map 2) just south of Buhne Point. Weott post office is listed in 1926.

West Butte [Sutter]. When the post office was established in 1867 it was so named because of the location of the settlement on the west side of the Sutter Buttes.

Westend [San Bernardino]. The name was changed in 1919 from Hanksite by F. M. ("Borax") Smith, president of the West End Consolidated Mining Company. The post office was established October 11, 1919.

Westfalls Meadow [Yosemite National Park]. Named for a German family who had a homestead near the junction of the Mariposa and old Mono trails. Shown on the Hoffmann-Gardner map of 1867.

Westgard Pass [Inyo]. A toll road was built across the pass by Scott Broder in 1873 and the route is still known as Toll Road. About 1913, A. L. Westgard of the American Automobile Association crossed the pass in search of the best transcontinental route, and the Good Roads Club of Inyo County named the pass for him. (Brierly.)

Westley [Stanislaus]. Named by the citizens in 1888, in memory of John Westley Van Benschoten, a butcher who came with Frémont in 1846, served in the Mexican War, and settled on the San Joaquin in 1850 (W. W. Coz).

Westminster [Orange]. Named in the 1870's by the Rev. L. P. Weber, who founded a colony here for people sympathetic with the ideals of the Presbyterian Church as laid down in the Westminster Assembly (1643–1649). It is one of the oldest settlements in the county.

Westmorland [Imperial]. Local sources maintain that the place was named by the developers in 1910 to call attention to *more land* to the *west* in Irrigation District No. 8, and not after a Westmorland "back East," or after the county in England.

Weston Meadow [Tulare]. Named for Austin Weston, of Visalia, who made this mountain meadow his headquarters for summer stock grazing (Farquhar).

West Point [Calaveras]. An old mining town, called Indian Gulch in 1852 and West Point in 1854. It is mentioned in *Hutchings' Illustrated California Magazine* of 1859 (p. 490).

Westport [Mendocino]. The place was called Beal's Landing for some time, for the first settler, Samuel Beal. "In 1877 James T. Rodgers began the construction of a chute, and to him belongs the honor of giving to the place its present name, he being from Eastport, Maine, naturally called the new town, Westport" (Co. Hist., 1880, p. 470).

Westwood [Lassen]. In 1913 when the Red River Lumber Company of Minnesota began extensive operations in northern California its officials called the headquarters Westwood, probably because the company already had eastern holdings. The Southern Pacific reached the place the following year and applied the name to the station.—Several other places in the State bear this name; among these are Westwood and Westwood Village [Los Angeles].

Wether Ridge [Sonoma]. No other feature in the State seems to have been named for the wether. The highest peak of the ridge is

Buck Mountain!

Whale, Whaler. The once important industry of whaling has left its imprint on names of coastal features in all parts of the world. Along the California coast are three Whale Rocks, one Whaleboat Rock, one Whalers Rock, two Whaler Islands, and one Whalers Knoll. Whaleman Harbor [San Mateo] was probably named for a man named Whaleman. *See* Ballena. **Whaleback** [Kings Canyon National Park]. The shape of the mountain which extends for three miles along Cloud Canyon suggested the name, which was probably applied when the Geological Survey mapped the Tehipite quadrangle in 1903.

Wheatland [Yuba]. When the railroad was built from Sacramento to Marysville in 1867, the name was applied to the station because it was in a wheat-growing district. The post office is listed in 1867.

Wheaton Dam [Stanislaus]. Named for M. A. Wheaton, who purchased the dam and water rights on the Tuolumne River in 1855 (S. P. Elias, *Stories of Stanislaus*, 1924, p. 20).

Wheeler. The State has four orographic features so named: **Crest** [Inyo, Mono], **Peak** [Mono], **Ridge** [Kern], **Peak** [Tuolumne]. The peak was probably named for some unidentified army officer (Farquhar); the other three may have been named for George M. Wheeler (*see* Glossary). By decision of June 7, 1911, the Geographic Board designated the chain west of Round Valley as Wheeler Ridge. The Geological Survey has disregarded this decision on both editions of the Mount Goddard atlas sheet and continues to call it Wheeler Crest. None of the features are shown in the Wheeler Atlas. Kern County has a post office called Wheeler Ridge. Wheeler Springs [Ventura] obviously has no connection with the great army engineer.

Whipple: Mountains, Well, Wash [San Bernardino]. In 1858 Lieutenant Ives named a mountain for Lieutenant Amiel W. Whipple, a member of the Mexican Boundary Commission and of the Pacific Railroad Survey: "The Needles and a high peak of the Monument range, which I have called Mount Whipple, are the most conspicuous landmarks, and designate points where the river enters and leaves Chemehuevis valley" (Ives, 1861, Pt. I, p. 60). The von Leicht–Craven map shows the highest peak of this range as Mount Whipple. When the Geological Survey mapped the Parker quadrangle in 1902–1903, it applied the name to the great mountain mass in the bend of the Colorado, which includes Monument Range, a fitting monument to the man who played an important role in the scientific delineation and recording of the geography of California and who later was one of the Union generals killed at Chancellorsville. The old name is preserved in Monument Peak.

Whiskey. In the nomenclature of the State this liquor is represented more often than all other alcoholic beverages combined. There are about fifty Whiskey names, applied to all types of features, from a butte [Siskiyou] to a run [Placer]. Various reasons have been given for the application of the name: a mule stumbled and dropped a barrel of the amber liquid in a creek; a moonshine still was operated in a secluded gulch; the miners at a certain place could consume a barrel a day; the drinking of the water of a spring made a person "rattle-weeded"; etc. The many mining towns named Whiskey naturally changed their names when the country became self-conscious and respectable. **Whiskeytown:** post office, **Reservoir** [Shasta]. The place developed as a gold-mining camp in the early 1850's. It was named after the stream on which it was located. A post office, Whiskey Creek, was established February 18, 1856, and lasted until 1864. When it was reëstablished January 6, 1881, it bore successively more "respectable" names: Blair, Stella, Schilling, until July 1, 1952, when the alcoholic name was restored. Whiskeytown Reservoir was built in 1963. *See* Schilling.

White. Next to black and red, this is the adjective of color used most frequently in place naming. More than a hundred places are called White. Two-thirds of these are orographic features; among them are more than twenty White Rocks and about fifteen White Mountains. Although there are many Black Buttes, there is apparently not a single White Butte. The chief reasons for naming elevations White are the color or absence of color in the rock formation, or the covering of snow, or the deposits of guano. A number of White Rivers, Creeks, Lakes, etc., owe their name to white rock formations, or to the milky appearance of the water. The adjective often refers not to the feature or place itself but rather to the specific term: White Horse and White Wolf, White Oaks and White Pines, White House Landing, White Cabin Creek, White Mans Ravine, White Chief Mountain. About ten communities have White in some form or combination. Whites Bridge [Fresno], White Hill [Marin], and doubtless other places and features were named for a person or persons named White. **White Mountains** [Mono]. White Mountain Peak was known to the Mono Indians as *Tos-toya,* from *toso,* 'light-colored rock,' and *toya,* 'mountain' (Robinson). "White Mountain peak is named from the appearance of its summit which seems to be composed of this rock [dolomite], often mistaken for snow, and which is found in great quantities at its base" (Hanks, *Report,* p. 178). Whitney, in 1864, believed that snow actually had given the name to the mountain: "There is a high peak called the 'White Mountain,' which is doubtless 14,000 feet or more in elevation, as it has . . . snow on its southern side, . . . [which] never entirely disappears." In 1917 the Geological Survey transferred the name to Montgomery Peak. **White-house Creek** [San Mateo, Santa Cruz]. The stream received its name from a white house, built in 1857 or before by Isaac Graham. It is said that this house served as a landmark to navigators until the growing trees obscured it (Hoover, pp. 411 f.). **White River** [Tulare]. The place was originally called Tailholt because (according to the most convincing of several stories) a miner had nailed a cow's tail on his cabin door to serve as a handle. When a post office was about to be established in the 1860's, Levi Mitchell, who thought that Tailholt would not make a very good name, substituted the name White River, after the river on which the mining camp was situated (Annie Mitchell). **White Horse: Valley, Reservoir,** post office [Modoc]. According to local tradition, surveyors named the valley about 1870 because they saw wild white horses there (Co. Library). The post office is listed in 1930. **White Water** [Riverside]. The post office was established in 1926 and named after the river, which in turn received its name because of its milky appearance, caused by deep fine sand. The name was earlier applied to a ranch east of the spot where the river disappears in the sand (Co. Hist., 1912, p. 215). Palm Springs railroad station was formerly called White Water. **White Pines** [Calaveras]. The post office, listed in 1941, was named because of the presence of a species of white pine. **White Plains** [Mendocino]. The plains between Fort Bragg and Mendocino City were so named because the topsoil is highly charged with alkaline salts and appears white in many places. This peculiar soil condition causes the dwarf cypress to develop in miniature and other conifers to grow in dwarf form.

Whitesboro [Mendocino]. Named in 1876 for Lorenzo E. White, the principal owner of the Salmon Creek Mill Company (Borden). A post office was established October 11, 1881.

Whites Bridge [Fresno]. The name was applied to the railroad station for James R. White, a Fresno pioneer, who built the bridge there (Co. Hist., 1919, p. 279). The station is on the Southern Pacific section between Newman and Fresno, which was completed in 1892.

White Wolf [Yosemite National Park]. According to Paden-Schlichtmann (p. 153), in the 1850's two cattlemen, Diedrich and Heinrich Meyer, were pursuing horsethieves, when they came upon a temporary Indian encampment and named the place for the chief of the Indian band, "White Wolf."

Whitlow [Humboldt]. The post office was established May 21, 1927, and named for Al Whitlow, a licensed surveyor (Virginia Wolf).

Whitmore [Shasta]. Named for Simon H. Whitmore, a blacksmith, at whose instigation a post office was established in 1883 (Steger).

Whitney, Mount [San Diego]. This mountain took its name from an eccentric old character who had a homestead on the west side of the mountain (Charles Kelley).

Whitney, Mount; Whitney: Pass, Creek, Meadow, Portal [Sequoia National Park, Inyo]. Josiah Dwight Whitney, chief of the State Geological Survey, 1860 to 1874, had forbidden his subordinates to name for him what is now Mount Hamilton. In July, 1864, Whitney's four chief assistants, Brewer, Hoffmann, Gardiner, and King, beheld from Mount Brewer what they rightly assumed to be the culminating peak of the Sierra Nevada. On this occasion they stood upon their privilege as discoverers and named it in honor of their chief. Clarence King in 1871 climbed the peak now known as Mount Langley, a few miles south, supposing it to be Mount Whitney. His error was discovered by others two years later. He hastened to the scene, but before he could get there John Lucas, Charles D. Begole, and A. H. Johnson, all of Inyo County, made the first ascent on August 18, 1873. There was an attempt to name it Fisherman's Peak in their honor, but the name Mount Whitney was firmly established by 1881 when the summit was occupied by Professor S. P. Langley for observations on solar heat. (For a detailed account consult Farquhar, *Place Names.*)

Whittemore Grove [Humboldt]. Dedicated September 21, 1929, and named for Harris Whittemore, a philanthropist and pioneer in reforestation.

Whittier [Los Angeles]. Founded in 1887 by the Pickering Land and Water Company, an organization of Quakers, and named at the suggestion of Micajah D. Johnson, in honor of a fellow Quaker, John Greenleaf Whittier (1807–1892), poet and reformer.

Wible Orchard [Kern]. The station was named after S. W. Wible's orchard when the Southern Pacific line from Bakersfield to McKittrick was built in 1895. Simon W. Wible, a native of Pennsylvania, came to California in 1852. In 1872 he took up a homestead, and later he became superintendent for Miller & Lux. He was one of the notable pioneers of the county. (Emily Easton.)

Wickiup, wĭk'-ĭ-ŭp. The word, of Algonkian origin, designating the rude hut of the nomadic Indian tribes of the Southwest, is found as a place name for a tributary of Tujunga Creek [Los Angeles] and for a place near Viola [Shasta].

Widow Reed Creek [Marin]. The cumbersome name *Arroyo Corte Madera del Presidio* (Hoffmann's map of the Bay region, 1873) was replaced by the Geological Survey, when they named the stream in memory of the wife of John Reed (Read, or Reid), who in 1834 built here the first sawmill in the country.

Wilbur Springs [Colusa]. Named about 1868 for a Mr. Wilbur who owned the resort.

Wilcox: Springs, Peak [Shasta]. Named for the Wilcox family which has had a homestead here since 1872. Charles W. Wilcox came to San Francisco in 1851. (Steger.)

Wildcat. More than fifty features in the State, mainly canyons, creeks, and mountains, are named Wildcat. Most of these were named because wildcats, of which California has several species, were seen, encountered, or killed there. Some names, however, may have been derived from the applied sense of the word, namely, a designation for an unsound scheme. *See* Gatos; Red Dog.

Wildman Meadow [Kings Canyon National Park]. "About 1881 Brother Jeff and I camped there with a band of sheep. After dark we were startled by a lot of unearthly yells like someone in distress. After spending a large part of the night we were unable to locate anyone and finally concluded that it must have been a wild man, and so named the meadow. Later we found the noise was caused by a peculiar looking owl." (Frank Lewis to F. P. Farquhar.)

Wildomar [Riverside]. In 1883, when the old Rancho Laguna was subdivided, Margaret Collier Graham coined the name from the given names of the new owners: *Wil*liam Collier, *Do*nald and *Mar*garet Graham (Helen Wishart). *See* Elsinore.

Wildrose: Spring, Canyon [Inyo]. The spring was named in 1860 by Dr. S. G. George and the party with him, who were searching for the "lost" Gunsight Lode (Hanks, *Report* p. 34). *See* Rose.

Wildwood. The descriptive term is found in the names of three communities in Trinity, Shasta, and Sonoma counties. **Wildwood Canyon** [San Bernardino] was originally called Hog Canyon.

Wilfred Canyon [Inyo]. Named for Wilfred Watterson, who in his younger days ran sheep successfully in that locality, and in his later days, until 1927, was an unsuccessful banker at Bishop (Robinson).

Williams [Alpine]. The name became attached to the place because Billy Williams settled at Red Lake "in the early days" (L. T. Price).

Williams [Colusa]. Named for W. H. Williams, who laid out the town in 1876. The post office is listed in 1880.

Williams Butte [Mono]. Named for Thomas Williams, who was granted a patent to the adjacent land in 1882 (Maule).

Williams Grove [Humboldt]. The State Forestry Board, in 1922, named the grove for Solon H. Williams, a former chairman of the board (Drury).

Williamson, Mount [Inyo]. Named in 1864 by Clarence King of the Whitney Survey for Robert S. Williamson of the Pacific Railroad Survey. *See* Glossary.

Williams Reservoir [Modoc]. Constructed and named about 1910 by Curtis J. Williams, a local rancher (Co. Library).

Willis Hole [Del Norte, Siskiyou]. According to a decision of the Geographic Board, 1965, the bog, 19 miles southeast of Gasquet, is named for the renowned botanist, Willis Jepson, but not Willis Jepson Hole, as the Decision List No. 6503 of the Geographic Board expressly states.

Willits: town, Creek, Valley [Mendocino]. The post office was established in the late 1870's and was named for Hiram Willits, who had settled in the district in 1857. The name is shown on the Land Office map of 1879 and is listed in the Postal Guide of 1880.

Willow. The willow has always been extremely popular for place naming because its presence usually denotes running water. In California there are about twenty species, widely distributed in the State. The maps show more than two hundred Willow Creeks, and more than one hundred Willow: Springs, Sloughs, Lakes, and Valleys. Willow is also repeatedly found with the rare generic Glen and once, in Humboldt County, with the even rarer generic Brook. There are also a number of Lone Willow Creeks and a Five Willows Springs [San Luis Obispo]. The name is a favorite for communities and post offices: Willow Ranch [Modoc], listed as a post office in 1880, Willowbrook [Los Angeles], Willow Creek [Humboldt], Willow Springs [Kern], and several others. **Willows** [Glenn]. "There was but one watering place in the plains south of Stony Creek. That was a willow pond, from which the present town of Willows took its name." (De Jarnatt and Crane, *Colusa County*, 1887, p. 11.) The town was laid out in 1876; the post office was listed as Willow from 1880 to 1917. *See* Sauce.

Will Rogers Beach State Park [Los Angeles]. Established in 1930 and named in memory of the famous actor. His home was made a state park in 1944.

Will Thrall Peak [Los Angeles]. The peak was named in memory of William H. Thrall, an early advocate of conservation, who had died in 1963 (Geographic Board, May-Aug., 1963).

Wilmer Lake [Yosemite National Park]. Named by R. B. Marshall, for Wilmer Seavey, daughter of Clyde L. Seavey (Farquhar). By decision of the Geographic Board the name was changed in 1964 (May-Aug.) to Wilma, which was apparently the name of the girl.

Wilmington [Los Angeles]. Named by Phineas Banning, one of the leaders in the early development of Los Angeles, after his birthplace in Delaware. It had been the terminal of the U.S. mail stage line since 1858 and was known as New San Pedro or Newtown until 1863. *See* Banning.

Wilseyville [Calaveras]. The post office was established September 16, 1947, and named for Lawrence A. Wilsey, an official of the American Forest Products Company, which has a subsidiary here (Marjorie Dietz).

Wilsie [Imperial]. Named for W. E. Wilsie, a farmer, who came to the Imperial Valley in 1901 (*Desert Magazine*, July, 1939). The name was applied to the station about 1917, when the San Diego and Arizona Eastern Railroad was under construction.

Wilson [Sutter]. Probably named for George W. Wilson, a merchant in Marysville, who owned a large grain farm near by about 1900 (Co. Library).

Wilson, Mount [Los Angeles]. Named for Benjamin D. ("Don Benito") Wilson, who built a burro trail up the mountain in 1864. Wilson, one of the best-known of the American settlers in southern California after 1841, was the first mayor of Los Angeles under United States rule. He was the grandfather of the late General George S. Patton.

Wilson Creek [Yosemite National Park]. Named by Lieutenant H. C. Benson for his friend Mountford Wilson, of San Francisco (Farquhar).

Wilton [Sacramento]. The station of the Central California Traction line was named for the owner of the land, Seth A. Wilton, dairy and poultry rancher, who had lived in Sacramento County since 1887 (Co. Hist., 1923, p. 311). The post office is listed in 1915.

Winchell, Mount [Kings Canyon National Park]. The name honors Alexander Winchell (1824–1891), for many years professor of geology at the University of Michigan. His cousin, Elisha C. Winchell, had given the name in 1868 to the present Lookout Point, overlooking Kings River Canyon. In 1879 the latter's son, Lilbourne A. Winchell, bestowed the same name upon a peak south of the Palisades. The Geological Survey transferred the name to a peak north of North Palisade, where it now rests. (Farquhar.)

Winchester [Riverside]. Named for one of the owners of the land when it was subdivided in 1886 (Santa Fe).

Window Cliff [Tulare]. "These cliffs are perforated with a window-like opening at the head of a gorge dropping into Kern Canyon, through which inspiring views of the [Sequoia National] park may be obtained" (Geographic Board, *Sixth Report*). *See* Ventana.

Windsor: town, **Creek** [Sonoma]. The post office was established August 31, 1855, and was named at the suggestion of Hiram Lewis, a native of England, presumably after Windsor Castle. The place had previously been known as Poor Man's Flat.

Windy Gap. *See* Wingate Pass.

Winemas Chimneys [Lava Beds National Monument]. Winema was the daughter of the chief of a small tribe at the outlet of Upper Klamath Lake. She married a white man, Frank Riddle, before the Modoc War and acted as interpreter for General Canby. (Howard.)

Winfield Scott, Fort [San Francisco]. The fort was under construction from 1854 to 1876, and was named in 1882 in memory of General Winfield Scott, Commander-in-Chief of the U.S. Army, 1841 to 1861. *See* Fort Point.

Wingate: Pass, Wash [San Bernardino]. When Lieutenant Bendire crossed the Panamint Mountains through this pass in 1867, he may have named it in memory of Major Benjamin Wingate, who died in 1862 of wounds received in the battle of Valverde, New Mexico. Wheeler records on atlas sheet 65 a Windy Gap at the west side of the pass, possibly because he misread Bendire's notes. This name was used more frequently, but the Geological Survey in 1915 decided for Wingate (Searles Lake atlas sheet).

Winnedumah [Inyo]. The name of the remarkable eighty-foot-high granite monolith commemorates Winnedumah, a Paiute medicine man, who, according to an often-repeated Indian legend, was turned into this pillar while he was invoking the help of the "great spirit" during a battle with Digger Indians. The monolith is also known as Paiute Monument. *See* Tinemaha.

Winnemucca Lake [Alpine]. The local name is Roundtop Lake, after Roundtop Peak, under which the lake nestles. The map name was perhaps given to the lake by a lucky fisherman from Nevada (where Winnemucca Lake is named for the eminent Paiute chief), and was recorded on the Markleeville atlas sheet of 1936. (Maule.)

Winnetka [Los Angeles]. The post office, established April 1, 1947, was probably named after Winnetka, Illinois. The place was formerly known as Weeks Poultry Community.

Winnibulli. *See* Bally.

Winston Ridge [Los Angeles]. Named for L. C. Winston, a Pasadena banker, who died in a blizzard while on a hunting trip in the mountains in 1900 (S. B. Show).

Winterhaven [Imperial]. The town which developed on the homestead of "Don Diego" Yeager, a pioneer of 1857, is entirely surrounded by the Yuma Indian Reservation. When a post office was to be established in 1916, a group of women, enjoying a card party when the temperature reportedly was 120° in the shade, chose the name Winterhaven, which they considered fitting. (T. J. Worthington.)

Winters [Yolo]. The town developed when the Southern Pacific built the line from Elmira to Madison in 1875. It was named for Theodore W. Winters, who donated half the land for the town.

Wintersburg [Orange]. When the Southern

Pacific extension was built to Huntington Beach in 1897, the station was named for Henry Winters, specialist in celery culture, who donated the right of way and part of the townsite (Co. Hist., 1921, pp. 873 f.).

Winters Peak [Inyo]. The peak in the Funeral Mountains was named for Aaron Winters, who had discovered borax deposits in Death Valley in 1881 (Geographic Board, Sept.-Dec., 1961).

Winton [Merced]. The old Winn (or Wynn) Ranch was subdivided by the Coöperative Land and Trust Company in 1910, and the new town was called Windfield. When the railroad station was established in 1911 the Santa Fe requested a change, and N. D. Chamberlain suggested the new name, apparently for Edgar Winton, one of the surveyors who laid out the town.

Wintun: Glacier, Butte [Siskiyou]. The southeast glacier of Mount Shasta and the butte southwest of the mountain were doubtless named for the Wintun Indians; both names are spelled Wintoon on modern maps. The butte, however, is generally known as Black Butte, a name which was made official by a decision of the Geographic Board of June 6, 1934.

Wishon: Dam, Lake, post office [Madera]. The post office was established November 12, 1923, and named for A. Emory Wishon, of the San Joaquin Light and Power Corporation, later vice-president and general manager of the Pacific Gas and Electric Company. The dam was built between 1955-1958.

Witch Creek [San Diego]. The tributary of Santa Ysabel Creek was so named because its Indian name sounded to early settlers like the Spanish *hechicera*, meaning 'witch' (Co. Library).

Wittawaket Creek [Shasta]. The name of the tributary of McCloud River is derived from Wintu Indian *Wittawaket*, 'the creek that turns around' (Steger).

Wittenberg, Mount [Marin]. The mountain was not named after Prince Hamlet's alma mater, but for a man named Wittenberg who had a ranch there (J. C. Oglesby).

Witter Springs [Lake]. Named in 1871 for Dr. Dexter Witter, who bought the land in partnership with W. P. Radcliff from Benjamin Burke, the discoverer of the springs in 1870. The post office was established as Witter's Springs, March 7, 1873; reëstablished as Witter on June 7, 1901, and changed to the present name on May 5, 1913.

Wofford Heights [Kern]. The post office was established May 16, 1953, and named after the community founded by I. L. Wofford (Helen Hight).

Wohlford, Lake [San Diego]. Named in 1924 by the Escondido Mutual Water Company for one of its officers, A. W. Wohlford, an Escondido banker and citrus grower. The lake was formerly known as Lake Escondido. (Co. Hist., 1936, pp. 145, 344, 399.)

Wolfskill: Camp, Canyon, Creek, Falls [Los Angeles]. The names commemorate one of the most notable pioneers of southern California. William Wolfskill, a native of Kentucky, came to California over the Old Spanish Trail in 1831, settled in Los Angeles in 1836, and became one of the leading pioneers of California's greatest industry, fruit-growing. **Wolfskill** [Solano]. In 1842 he was granted the Rio de los Putos grant. His brothers John and Sarchel managed the rancho, and later two other brothers, Malthus and Milton, also settled on the vast estate. The place is shown as Wolfskills on Gibbes' map (1852), but as Wolfs Hill on Eddy's map (1854).

Wolverton Creek [Sequoia National Park]. Named for James Wolverton, of Three Rivers, hunter, trapper, and veteran of the Union Army, who named the General Sherman Tree in 1879 (Farquhar).

Wood. The combination of the word Wood with a generic name is a favorite for American place names. California has at least twelve communities so named, including Woodacre [Marin], Woodcrest [Riverside], Woodlake and Woodville [Tulare], Woodside [San Mateo]. **Woodland** [Yolo]. The place was settled before 1855 by Henry Wyckoff, who opened a trading post there. When the post office was established in 1859, it was named Woodland, at the suggestion of Major F. S. Freeman, who had bought Wyckoff's store.

Wood, Mount [Mono]. Named in 1894 by Lieutenant N. F. McClure, for Captain Abram E. Wood, veteran of the Civil War, acting superintendent of Yosemite National Park 1891–1893 (Farquhar).

Woodall Creek [Shasta]. George Woodall was one of the owners of the Dry Mill at Shingletown, and his sons later gardened at the stream which now bears the pioneer family's name (Steger).

Woodbridge [San Joaquin]. In 1852 Jeremiah H. Woods began operating a ferry across the river, and the settlement which developed there became known as Woods' Ferry. In 1859 a bridge was built, and the name of the place was changed to Woodbridge. The post office is listed in 1857 as Wood's Ferry, with J. Woods as postmaster. The sites of the ferry and of the bridge are Historic Landmarks (163 and 358).

Wooden Valley [Napa]. The valley, a part of Rancho Chimiles, was formerly called Corral Valley but became known by the present name when John Wooden purchased the land in 1850 (D. T. Davis).

Woodfords [Alpine]. Known first as Carey's Mill, for John Carey, who established a sawmill here in 1853 or 1854. When Daniel Woodford became owner of the mill in 1869 the name was changed to Woodfords, and this name was adopted by the Post Office Department. (Maule.)

Woodland. *See* Wood.

Woodleaf [Yuba]. James Wood purchased the Barker Ranch in 1858, and the settlement which developed there became known as Woodville. When the post office was established about 1900 the name was changed to Woodleaf in order to avoid confusion with Woodville in Tulare County.

Woodman: Creek, Hill [Shasta]. Named for the brothers L. C. and George Woodman, who settled on Little Cow Creek in 1852 (Steger).

Woods: Creek, Crossing [Tuolumne]. Named for an early miner whose claim was on the North Fork of the Tuolumne, some eight miles southeast of Jamestown. The name Woods is recorded on Derby's map of 1849.

Woods: Creek, Lake [Kings Canyon National Park]. Named by J. N. LeConte, for Robert M. Woods, a sheepman of the Kings River region, who spent many summers from 1871 to 1900 in the Sierra (Farquhar).

Woodside [San Mateo]. According to the County History, 1883, the place was named after a lumber camp as early as 1849. The post office was established April 18, 1854.

Woodson Bridge Recreation Area [Tehama]. The property was purchased by the State in 1959 and was named after the bridge across the Sacramento River, named for Warren Woodson.

Woodson Mountain [San Diego]. Named for Dr. Marshall Clay Woodson, who had 320 acres of land at the base of the mountain in the 1890's (J. Davidson).

Woodworth, Mount [Kings Canyon National Park]. Named about 1888 for Benjamin R. Woodworth, who lived for a time in Fresno and was with a camping party in Simpson Meadow when the peak was named (Farquhar).

Woody [Kern]. Named for Sparrell W. Woody, a pioneer rancher of the 1860's.

Workman Hill [Los Angeles]. The name of the elevation commemorates William ("Julian") Workman, a native of England who came to California in 1841, and who in 1845 was cograntee of La Puente grant, on which the hill is situated.

Worthla Creek [Del Norte]. The name of the tributary of Klamath River is an Americanization of the Yurok name for the stream, which Waterman renders as *Wr'Lri Wroi* (map 9).

Wouk Grove [Humboldt]. The Abe Wouk Memorial Grove in the Grizzly Creek State Park was named in 1966 by the Save-the-Redwoods League in memory of the son of Herman Wouk, well-known American novelist.

Wounded Knee Mountain. *See* Broken Rib Mountain.

Wragg: Canyon, Creek [Napa]. The canyon opening into the lower end of Berryessa Valley was named for the first settler in the vicinity, whose name was Wragg (D. T. Davis).

Wright Chimneys [Lava Beds National Monument]. Named in memory of Ben Wright, whose party was massacred by Indians, April 26, 1873, in the Modoc War.

Wright: Lakes, Creek [Sequoia National Park]. The name was proposed by the Sierra Club in 1925 for James W. A. Wright, who had accompanied W. B. Wallace and F. H. Wales on a trip to Kern River and Mount Whitney in 1881. A mountain on the Great Western Divide was named for him in 1881, but the name never became current. (Farquhar.)

Wrights [Santa Clara]. A station on the Los Gatos–Santa Cruz railroad, named in 1880 for John V. Wright, son of James R. Wright, a pioneer of the region (Hoover, p. 532).

Wrightwood [San Bernardino]. The old Circle C Ranch was made a residential community about 1924 and was named for the subdivider, a Mr. Wright. The post office is listed in 1929.

Wyandotte: Creek, town [Butte]. Named for a party of Wyandot Indians from Kansas who prospected in the vicinity in 1850 (Co. Hist., 1882, p. 266). The Wyandott Mining Company had been organized in 1849 by William Walker, a Wyandot, who was later (1853) provisional governor of Nebraska (Bruff, p. 608). The name is found also in Los Angeles

and San Joaquin counties.

Wyeth [Tulare]. An interesting and unique name, derived from the term "wye," the joining of two railroad tracks to form the letter Y. The name was applied to the junction in 1913–1914 when the Santa Fe built the section from Cutler to connect the Minkler-Exeter line with the Reedley-Visalia line (Santa Fe). In the decades of great railroad expansion, stations near this type of junction often were given the word "Wye" as the generic part of the name. Napa Wye [Napa] seems to be the only survivor.

Wyman Creek [Inyo]. Named for Dan Wyman, who came to the White Mountains in 1861 seeking placer mines (Chalfant, *Inyo*, 1933, p. 143).

Wynne, Mount [Kings Canyon National Park]. Named in memory of Sedman W. Wynne, former supervisor of Sequoia National Forest, who lost his life while on duty (Geographic Board, *Sixth Report*).

Ximeno, hĭ-mä'-nō [Los Angeles]. Although initial Spanish "j" often appeared as "x," this place near Long Beach is the only California community listed under **X**. The name may preserve the memory of Manuel Jimeno Casarin. *See* Jimeno [Yolo].

Yager, yä'-gēr: **Creek,** settlement [Humboldt]. The name for the stream is mentioned in October, 1858, in connection with Indian attacks, and was doubtless given for one of the enterprising settlers who found the rich grazing lands suitable for stock raising.

Yajome [Napa]. The name of a land grant dated March 16, 1841, also spelled Llajome. Yajome Creek is mentioned by Pablo de la Guerra on January 4, 1850 (California Senate *Journal*, 1st sess., p. 415), but the name has not survived. The ending *-jome* or *-jomi* means 'place' in Southern Pomo and Coast Miwok (*see* Caslamayomi, Sotoyome), but the Yajome grant seems to be in Wappo territory.

Yaney Canyon [Mono]. The canyon is called Huntoon Valley on the maps of the Wheeler Survey (1877), but it was later named for the owner of the sawmill, a Mr. Yaney (Maule, p. 9).

Yankee. Next to Germans, who were invariably called Dutch, the Americans from east of the Mississippi and north of the Ohio seemed to be the only people who became known by a nickname. Numerous topographic features as well as some settlements still bear the name Yankee. Most, if not all, of these names go back to the periods of the gold rush when California had numerous

Yankee Jack, John, Jim, Maid, Girl, Doodle, etc. mines and camps; there was even a Wild Yankee Hill. **Yankee Jims** [Placer] is probably the best-known surviving settlement bearing the appellation. It had a post office from 1852 to 1940. According to the *Directory of Placer County*, 1861, pp. 12 f., the character known as "Yankee Jim" was a Sydneyite whose name was Robinson. He built a corral for stolen horses at this place and was hanged in 1852. **Yankee Hill** [Tuolumne] was another famed mining camp of the 1850's and seems to have been named for a Mr. Hill nicknamed "Yankee." There are different stories about the identity of the gentleman. **Yankee Hill** [Butte]. The post office established with this name October 19, 1856, lasted almost a century.

Yaqui Camp [Calaveras]. The place on Willow Creek was named for the Yaqui Indians who came from Mexico after the discovery of gold (*Las Calaveras*, July, 1957).

Ybarra Canyon [Los Angeles]. Probably named for a member of the Ybarra (or Ibarra) family, some of whom settled in the Los Angeles district as early as 1814.

Ycatapom Peak [Shasta]. According to local tradition *Ycatapom* is a Wintun Indian place name meaning "where the big chief lives" (Schrader).

Ycotti Creek [Shasta]. The tributary of McCloud River was named for an old Indian medicine man who lived three miles above Baird. The name should have been spelled Y-car-ne. (Steger.)

Ydalpom, wī-dăl'-pŏm [Shasta]. The place is at the site of the old Indian village (Steger). It is a Wintu place name, composed of *wai*, 'north,' *dal*, possibly 'lying,' and *pom*, 'place' (Kroeber).

Yeguas. The Spanish word for 'mares' was used more often for place names than *caballos*, 'horses.' It has survived in Yeguas Mountain [Kern, San Luis Obispo] and Las Yeguas Canyon [Santa Barbara]. *See* Cavallo; Mare.

Yellow Jacket Creek [Trinity]. Named for an Indian family by that name, owners of a claim of 160 acres in the Trinity National Forest. A near-by claim is listed in the name of Sally Jacket. (K. Smith.)

Yeomet Creek [Amador]. The mining town at the forks of Cosumnes River and Big Indian Creek was probably named for an Indian rancheria. When it was still in El Dorado County it had a post office, misspelled Yornet, from 1854 to 1861.

Yerba Buena Island [San Francisco Bay]. *Yerba buena*, 'good herb,' is the Spanish designation for the sweet-scented creeper, *Micromeria chamissonis*, named by the English botanist Bentham for Adelbert von Chamisso, the botanist of the first Kotzebue expedition. The herb was found by Font near Mountain Lake in San Francisco in March, 1776 (*Compl. Diary*, p. 333). By 1792 it had become a place name: on November 14, 1792, the *comandante del puerto* (at San Francisco Bay) reported the arrival of Vancouver, who had anchored at a *parage que llamamos la Yerba buena*, 'place which we call Yerba Buena' (SP Sac., I, 116). The cove which was used as an anchorage by later navigators and near which Richardson and Leese built their houses in 1835 and 1836, as well as the settlement which developed around these houses, was called Yerba Buena until March 10, 1847. *See* San Francisco. Yerba Buena Island, which now alone preserves the old name, was called *Isla de Alcatraces* on Ayala's map of 1775, but it is mentioned as *la Ysla de la Yerba Buena* as early as 1795 (Arch. MSB, II, 33). In American times it became known as Goat Island because it was populated with hundreds of goats in the 1840's. *See* Goat. By act of the legislature in June, 1931, the old Spanish name was restored.—The name Yerba Buena was applied to a land grant in Santa Clara County, dated November 25, 1833, and February 24, 1840. There is a Yerba Buena Creek in San Luis Obispo County, and Rand McNally's Gazetteer lists a place, Yerba Buena, in Ventura County.

Yermo, yĕr'-mō: town, **Valley** [San Bernardino]. When the San Pedro, Los Angeles, and Salt Lake Railroad (now the Union Pacific) was built in 1904–1905, the station was called Otis. When the post office was established about 1908, the name was changed to Yermo (Spanish, 'desert'), a very appropriate name.

Yettem, yĕt'-ĕm [Tulare]. In 1902 the Rev. Mr. Jenanyan applied the Armenian word for 'paradise' to the Armenian settlement. The railroad station now called Calgro was called Yettem from 1910 to 1936. *See* Cal-.

Ygnacio Valley [Contra Costa]. The name for the region north of Walnut Creek appears as Ignasio Valley on Hoffmann's map of the Bay region (1873), and is mentioned with the present spelling in the County History of 1878. The proximity to Martinez Ridge seems to indicate that the valley was named for Ygnacio Martínez. *See* Martinez.

Yokaya. *See* Ukiah.

Yokohl: Creek, Valley [Tulare]. The names in

the Blue Ridge country were derived from *Yokol* or *Yokod,* the name of a Yokuts tribe. The meaning is not known. (Kroeber.)

Yolano [Solano]. The name of the Sacramento Northern station was coined from *Yolo* and *Solano.*

Yolla Bolly. *See* Bally.

Yolo, yō'-lō: **County,** town, **Basin.** According to Vallejo's *Report,* the name is a "corruption of the Indian word 'Yoloy,' signifying a place abounding with rushes (*tular*), with which the Indians composed the term 'Toloy-toy,' Rushtown (Pueblo del Tule), situated on the western shore of the river Sacramento." Kroeber does not accept this explanation of the word; he states that *Yodoi* was the name of a Patwin village at the site of Knights Landing (*AAE,* XXIX, 261). Barrett was informed that there had been a chief named Yodo (*Pomo,* p. 294). A *Rancho del Ioleo* or *Rancho de Dioleo* is shown on the south side of Cache Creek on Bidwell's map of 1844. It is coincidental that a captain of a rancheria at Tomales Bay in 1810 bore the name Yolo (PSP, XIX, 278). The county, one of the original twenty-seven, was created and named on February 18, 1850. Yolo post office was established Feb. 3, 1853. The place was formerly called Cacheville. *See* Cache.

Yontockett [Del Norte]. The name of the school district seems to preserve the name of an Athabascan Tolowa village, but the meaning of the name is unknown (Kroeber).

Yorba Linda, yôr'-bá lĭn'-dá [Orange]. This place preserves the name of one of the oldest pioneer families of southern California, whose ancestor, Antonio Yorba, was one of Fages' Catalonian volunteers in 1769. It is situated on the Cañon de Santa Ana grant of Bernardo Yorba, the son of Antonio. The name Yorba is shown on Narváez' map of 1830 and on Duflot de Mofras's map of 1844. Yorba post office is listed in 1880. About 1913 real-estate promoters coined the new name from *Yorba* and near-by *Olinda.*

Yorkville [Mendocino]. When the post office was established about 1870 and a name was to be chosen, the settlers could not decide which of the two pioneer families should be honored. The Hiatts and the Yorks were equally prominent and prolific, and it was finally decided to end the controversy by a contest between the heads of the families, the nature of which history does not disclose. Richard H. York—who had come from Tennessee—won, and Elijah M. Hiatt received the postmastership as a consolation

prize. (F. L. McAbee.)

Yosemite, yō-sĕm'-ĭ-tĕ: **Valley, Falls, Creek, National Park.** The valley was first seen but not named by the Walker party in 1833. *See* Walker Pass. Edwin Sherman (*CHSQ,* XXIII, 368) claimed discovery of the valley in the spring of 1850, naming it "The Devil's Cellar." In March, 1851, it was entered by the Mariposa Battalion and named at the suggestion of L. H. Bunnell. "I then proposed 'that we give the valley the name of Yo-sem-i-ty, as it was suggestive, euphonious, and certainly *American;* that by so doing, the name of the tribe of Indians which we met leaving their homes in this valley, perhaps never to return, would be perpetuated'... upon a *viva voce* vote being taken, it was almost unanimously adopted" (Bunnell, 1880, pp. 61 f.). In 1852 Lieutenant Tredwell Moore replaced the final *y* by an *e,* and this version was adopted for the publications and maps of the Whitney Survey. The derivation and etymology of the name has been a subject of considerable controversy. Bunnell states that the name is a rendering of the Indian word for a 'full-grown grizzly bear,' and this interpretation has been generally accepted by anthropologists. According to Powers (pp. 361 f.), the Indians on the Stanislaus and north of it called the grizzly bear *u-zu'-mai-ti,* and with slight phonetic variations the word was heard in the territory as far as the South Fork of the Merced, i.e., throughout the old habitat of the Valley Miwok Indians. In 1810 Padre Viader mentions the *Jusmites* somewhere north of Stanislaus River (Arch. MSB, IV, 85), and on the Plano topografico de la Mision de San Jose a Christian Indian village *Josmites* is shown at the approximate site of modern Stockton. There is little doubt that this name contains the same root, namely, the Miwok word for 'grizzly bear.' For the name in Yosemite Valley, Lucy Freeland de Angulo suggests this origin: *yos* (or *yosh*), 'to kill'; *a,* an agentive suffix like the English "er"; *miti,* a collective plural suffix. The meaning then would be 'the killers' or 'a band of killers.' According to Barrett (*Myths,* p. 28), the name consists of *yō'he,* 'to kill,' and *miūtī'ya,* 'people.' (For a detailed discussion of other theories and versions, cf. Farquhar, *Place Names.*) Since the Indians living in Yosemite Valley called their village and the valley itself *A-wa'-ni* (Powers, p. 361), it follows that the name rendered by Bunnell as *Yosemity* was the name applied to the *Awani* by Indians living outside the valley. The conclusion then is almost inescapable that the Miwok word designated both 'killer' and 'grizzly,' and that the *Awani* were called "killers" or "grizzlies" by the other Indians because of their lawless character. (But *see* Beeler in *Names*, III, 185). According to J. H. Pratt (*Century*, XXXXI, December, 1890, p. 193) the Indian trouble and the necessity of sending the Mariposa Battalion did not originate with the "lawless" *Awani*. Around New Year's Day 1851, six peaceful Indians came to trade at Coulter's camp when a "drunken ruffian from Texas, without any reasonable cause, stabbed to the heart the chief of the party." Thereupon the Indians killed the attacker and two nights later stole sixteen mules from the corral. The *Jusmites* of Padre Viader and the *Josemites* of the Plano . . . de San Jose, whose names contain obviously the same root, did not dwell in the Yosemite Valley but belonged to the now extinct division of the Valley Miwok. Yet it is possible that they moved or were driven into the Valley sometime between 1825 and 1850, and that their original name has no relation to the words for grizzlies or killers. The name Yo Semite Valley was officially used when Congress by act of June 30, 1864, granted the Valley to the State of California as a recreational reserve. The national park was created by act of Congress of October 1, 1890, and the name was given by John W. Noble, Secretary of the Interior. March 3, 1905, the legislature receded Yosemite Valley to the United States, and on June 11, 1906, it became a part of Yosemite National Park. The name is found elsewhere in the State: Yosemite Incline [Nevada], Yosemite Lake [Merced].

You Bet [Nevada]. According to the County History of 1880 (p. 71), augmented by local tradition, the name originated in 1857 when Lazarus Beard, the saloonkeeper, was discussing a name for the settlement with two of his customers. Since Beard was providing free whiskey, one customer, hoping to prolong the discussion, suggested jokingly that "You bet," the saloonkeeper's favorite phrase, would make a good name. To the customer's chagrin Mr. Beard immediately accepted the suggestion, the discussion was ended, and the place was called You Bet.

Young, Mount [Sequoia National Park]. The Rev. F. H. Wales climbed the mountain on September 7, 1881, and named it for Charles A. Young (1834–1908), professor of astronomy at Princeton.

Young Lake [Yosemite National Park]. Named for General Samuel B. M. Young (1840–1924), who was acting superintendent of Yosemite National Park in 1896. General Young was a veteran of the Civil and Spanish-American wars and of many Indian campaigns, and in 1903–1904 was Chief of Staff of the U.S. Army. (Farquhar.)

Youngstown [San Joaquin]. A group of settlers, led by their pastor, the Rev. J. O. Boden, named the place in 1903 after Youngstown, Pennsylvania, their former home (Wallace Smith, p. 433).

Yountville [Napa]. Named for George C. Yount, of North Carolina, who came to California with the Wolfskill party in 1831 and in 1836 was grantee of Rancho Caymus, on which the town is situated. The name Yountville is shown on a map of the grant in 1860. The name of the settlement was formerly Sebastopol.

Yreka, wī-rē'-ká: city, **Creek** [Siskiyou]. The city started as a mining camp in the summer of 1851 and was first called Thompson's Dry Diggings and later Shasta Butte City. The name was changed by the legislature on March 22, 1852, when Siskiyou County was established: "The County Seat of said County shall be located at Shasta Butte City, and shall be known by the name of Yreka" (*Statutes*, 1852, p. 233). The name is derived from the Shasta name, *Wy-e-kah*, for Mount Shasta (Gibbs, in Schoolcraft, III, 165). Since *wai* is the Wintu word for 'north,' the name may mean 'north mountain.' In the 1920's the Indians north of Lassen Peak called Mount Shasta *Wi'ke* (Merriam, *Pit River*). The name is recorded with various spellings: Gibbes' map of 1852 has Wyreka. "It was intended the county seat should bear the name of I-eka, the Indian name of Mount Shasta, but by mistake the name of Wyreka was substituted and the error continued, with the exception of dropping the letter W, thought to be superfluous" (Yreka *Journal*, July 12, 1876).

Ysidora [San Diego]. When the railroad to Fallbrook was built in 1882, this name was given to a station on the Santa Margarita rancho. It was doubtless named for the sister of Andrés and Pío Pico, Ysidora Forster, whose husband, John Forster, had purchased the rancho in 1864.

Yuba, yōō'-bá: **River, City, County**. The river was discovered by Jedediah Smith on March 14, 1828, and given the Indian name *Henneet*. When Sutter came to the valley he named the stream *Yubu* after the Maidu village (spelled *Yubu, Yupu, Jubu* by early settlers) near the confluence of Yuba and Feather rivers. "The tribe I found at, and which still remains at the old rancheria at Yuba City, informed me that the name of their tribe was Yubu (pronounced Yuboo). As this tribe lived opposite the mouth of the river from which your county takes its name, I gave that river the name Yubu, which it has ever since borne." (Marysville *Herald*, August 13, 1850.) *Rio de los Yubas* is shown on several *diseños*. The often-repeated statement that the river was originally called *Rio de las Uvas*, 'river of the grapes,' is not supported by evidence. December 22, 1844, the name Yuba was applied to a land grant, which was later rejected by the Supreme Court. Yuba City was laid out and named after the river in August, 1849. The county, one of the original twenty-seven, was created and named on February 18, 1850. In 1950 the Geographic Board abolished the confusing names (Little North Fork of Middle Fork of North Fork!) of the numerous branches of Yuba River by naming the three main streams North, Middle, and South Yuba River and giving individual names to the minor branches.

Yucaipa, yōō-kī'-pȧ: **Creek, Valley,** town [San Bernardino]. The name is mentioned on October 15, 1841 (Arch. LA, II, 118 f.). It is derived from the Guachama (Serrano Shoshonean) dialect and means 'wet or marshy land' (O. J. Fisk). *Pah* is the Shoshonean term for 'water.'

Yucca: Creek, Mountain, Ridge [Sequoia National Park]. These were doubtless named for the species of yucca which grows there in abundance (David Brower). **Yucca Valley** [San Bernardino]. The post office was established November 15, 1945, and was so named because of the abundance of *Yucca brevifolia*, the Joshua tree. There are other places in the southern counties named after one of several species of *Yucca*. *See* Joshua, Palmdale.

Yuha: Well, Plain, Basin, Desert [Imperial]. The name does not appear on older maps and its meaning and origin are unknown. Since it is in Yuman territory the same root is indicated. The well is probably the one called *Santa Rosa de las Lajas* by Anza on March 8, 1774.

Yuhwamai [San Diego]. The Shoshonean-Luiseño Indian word meaning 'muddy place' was applied to the location by Nahachish, the Temecula chief: "He went on and came to Rincon. It was muddy there and he called it Yohama." (*AAE*, VIII, 152.)

Yulupa: Creek, station [Sonoma]. The name *Yulupa* is found on various *diseños* and probably designated an Indian village, possibly the one spelled *Jalapi* in the records of Mission San Francisco Solano in 1824. Jalapa is the name of a part of the Napa grant. In the *expedientes* of an unconfirmed land grant the name is spelled *Yulupa, Ulupa,* and *Julupa* (Bowman Index).

Yuma. The name of a strong Indian tribe which occupied the region on both sides of the Colorado River with Fort Yuma as the approximate center. The name was apparently first recorded by Kino in the latter part of the 17th century (*Kino*, I, 194). In the fall of 1849, Whipple made a careful study of the tribe and reported: "The term 'Yuma' signifies 'sons of the river,' and is applied only to those born upon the banks of the Rio Colorado" (*Extract*, p. 16). For spelling variants and other possible meanings cf. Hodge, *Handbook*. **Fort Yuma** was established and named by Heintzelman in November, 1850. **Fort Yuma Indian Reservation** was established in 1863 and named after the Fort.

Zabriskie Point [Death Valley National Monument]. Named for Christian B. Zabriskie, who came to Death Valley in 1889 as a representative of the Pacific Coast Borax Company and later became its executive head. The name Zabriskie was also applied to a station of the Tonopah and Tidewater Railroad.

Zaca: Lake, Peak, town; **La Zaca Creek** [Santa Barbara]. The name *Saca* mentioned by Padre Zalvidea on July 20, 1806 (Arch. MSB, IV, 49–68), refers to an Indian village or its chief. In 1838 the name, spelled Saca and La Zaca, was applied to a rancho, granted to an Indian named Antonio. It is probably a Chumash Indian word spelled to resemble the Spanish *saca*, 'sack.' According to Isobel Field, Robert Louis Stevenson's stepdaughter, its meaning is 'peace' or 'quiet place.' The name does not seem to appear on early maps but was apparently rescued by members of the Whitney Survey. The von Leicht–Craven map of 1874 shows Zaca Creek.

Zamora: station, **Creek,** post office [Yolo]. The Southern Pacific station was called Blacks until 1910, when the name was changed to Zamora, the name of a province and city in Spain. The post office is listed in 1916.

Zanita Point [Yosemite National Park]. The point was so named because the heroine of

Maria Teresa Yelverton's novel (1872), Zanita, hurled herself from this point into Merced River. (Cf. Farquhar, *Place Names*, p. 119.)

Zanja, Zanjon. The Spanish words for 'ditch,' 'drain,' 'channel,' were often used in place naming in Spanish times and have survived in several places. On Estudillo's map of 1819 the two channels connecting Tulare and Buenavista lakes are labeled Zanjon; the straight lines outlining the channels seem to indicate that they were man-made. The name appears in the titles of four land grants, usually spelled Sanjon, in Monterey, Merced, Fresno, and Sacramento counties. The San Rafael grant [Los Angeles] was first called La Zanja. *See* Verdugo. **Zanja Cota Creek** [Santa Barbara]. *La zanja que llaman de Cota*, 'the channel which is called Cota's,' is mentioned on June 17, 1795 (PSP, XIII, 28), and repeatedly in later years. The specific name refers probably to a member of the Cota family. On the Lompoc atlas sheet the stream is labeled Santa Cota, and on that of the Corps of Engineers, Santa Cora. **Zanja: Creek, Peak** [San Bernardino]. The stream which runs through Redlands was dug by Mission Indians in 1819 to divert water from Mill Creek. The name is still spelled the Spanish way but is usually pronounced săn'-kȧ (or săng'-kȧ). The peak was doubtless named after the stream in American times. (G. W. Beattie.) From 1917 to 1920 there was a Zanja post office, and The Zanja at Bryn Mawr, the first irrigation ditch in the county, is now Historic Landmark 43. **Sanjon de los Alisos** [Alameda] is one of the channels through which Alameda Creek discharges into San Francisco Bay; it is shown on *diseños* and on the Hayward atlas sheet.

Zapato. The name is found for several creeks in southern counties. *Zapato* is the Spanish word for 'shoe'; some of the names, however, may be derived from the sapote tree, which was introduced into California about 1810. *Zapote* is Mexican from Aztec *tzapotl*. In Fresno County there is a Zapoto Chino Creek and Canyon east of Coalinga.

Zayante Creek [Santa Cruz]. A *parage llamado Sayanta*, 'place called Sayanta,' is mentioned

in July, 1834 (Legis. Recs., II, 151), and the stream appears as *Rio* or *Arrollo de Sayante* on several *diseños*. July 21, 1834, the name was applied to land grants. According to an Indian informant, Zayante is an Indian proper name (Co. Hist., 1892, p. 46).

Zem-Zem Creek [Napa]. The stream is named after the Zem-Zem Ranch, which is still so named. In 1867 J. C. Owen acquired the property, developed the sulphur spring, and gave his ranch the mythical name Zem-Zem, said to mean 'healing waters.' (D. T. Davis.) The name is spelled Zim-Zim on the Morgan Valley atlas sheet. Zem Zem Springs [Los Angeles] were also named for the 'healing waters.'

Zenia [Trinity]. The name was applied in 1900 by George Croyden, the first postmaster, for a girl of that name (Albert Burgess).

Zinfandel [Napa]. The place on Highway 128 was named before 1900, when the Zinfandel grape was the most important product of the region.

Zmudowski Beach State Park [Monterey]. On October 10, 1952, the Park Commission changed the name of the old Pajaro River Park in recognition of the generous contributions of the Zmudowski family.

Zumwalt Meadow [Kings Canyon National Park]. Named for its former owner, Daniel K. Zumwalt (1845–1904), who was active in the movement to preserve the Big Trees (Farquhar). Zumwalt was the attorney for the Southern Pacific Railroad and was instrumental in creating the Sequoia and Grant National Parks (Oscar Berland).

Zuniga: Shoal, Point [San Diego]. The name *Barros [Bajos] de Zuñiga* for the shoal in the outer San Diego harbor is shown on Pantoja's Plano of 1782 (Wagner, No. 687). The name was probably given for José Zúñiga, a lieutenant in the San Diego company from 1781 to 1793. The name for the point appears in Vancouver's atlas (1798).

Zurich [Inyo]. The station of the narrow-gauge railroad was first given the name Alvord, but about 1913 this was changed to Zurich to avoid confusion with another station. The Alpine-like scenery a few miles to the west suggested the name of the Swiss city.

Glossary and Bibliography

A COMBINED bibliography and glossary was considered more practical and more convenient for the user of this book than separate lists of manuscripts, maps, books, contributors, and technical expressions.

The bibliographical material in this section contains items which are repeatedly cited in the text and special items not cited in the text which are not ordinarily found in the reference department of the libraries. Well-known general reference books like the Encyclopedia Americana, the Dictionary of American Biography, the Army and Navy registers, Lippincott's, Rand McNally's, and Thomas' gazetteers, general dictionaries, etc., are not listed here although they were used in preparing this Dictionary. Manuscripts or books which are cited only a few times are also omitted, but enough of the titles of such works is given in the text to identify the source easily. ("Text" means, of course, the name entries, pages 3–355.)

Each source is listed in the Glossary and Bibliography with a key word (or with some other convenient abbreviation), and this key word is given in the text as a reference. It was not considered necessary to give the page numbers of references in works which have an alphabetical arrangement or a comprehensive index, or when (in diaries) the passage can be easily identified by the date cited. For maps the key word is ordinarily the name of the man who made the map and (or) was responsible for the names on it. No consistency could be maintained, because frequently only the publisher of the map is known.

The name of a person given in parentheses in the text indicates that the information, or most of it, was received from this informant. It does not mean that he is responsible for the wording of the entry, unless quotation marks are used. Individuals who contributed repeatedly are listed and identified in this section.

Many manuscripts, maps, and books exist in different versions or editions. An attempt has been made to refer only to the version listed in this bibliography, but since the work on this book extended over a period of several years it is not impossible that there will be some discrepancies.

Any attempt to give all the sources of all the items in this book would clutter it with professional paraphernalia which would be of little value to the scholar and would be a nuisance to the general reader. Hence, references to authorities in the text have been limited; they are given, first, where all or most of the information has been taken from one single source; second, where I could not decide one way or the other on a controversial question; third, where I preferred to leave the responsibility for a statement to the source; fourth, where the first mentioning of the name or its variant is cited; fifth, where a direct quotation from a source is given. A complete bibliography and a copy of the manuscript with additional references are deposited with the Bancroft Library (at the University of California) in Berkeley, the State Library in Sacramento, and the Huntington Library in San Marino, where they may be consulted.

AAE. *University of California Publications in American Archaeology and Ethnology* (University of California Press, 1903–).

Abbot. Henry Larcom Abbot, a lieutenant of topographical engineers, assisted Lieutenant Williamson in making the railroad survey from the Sacramento Valley to the Columbia River in 1855. His report, which is in Vol. VI, Pt. 1, of the Pacific Railroad *Reports,* includes (pp. 127–129) "Route from Shasta Valley ... to Fort Reading; Explored by Williamson ... in 1851." *See* Pac. R.R. Reports; Williamson; and (in text) Abbot, Mount.

Abella. Padre Ramón Abella (1764–1842) served

at Mission Dolores from 1798 to 1819 and participated in explorations of the lower Sacramento and San Joaquin rivers in 1811 and 1817. His *diario* of the 1811 expedition is in the Archivo de la Mision de Santa Barbara, IV, 101–134.

Abert's Map. *See* Hood's Map.

Adams. Ramon F. Adams, *Western Words: A Dictionary of the Range, Cow Camp and Trail* (University of Oklahoma Press, 1944).

AGN. Archivo General de la Nación (Mexico City).

AGS. The American Guide Series, prepared by the U. S. Work Projects Administration.

Alviso Docs. Documentos para la historia de California: Archivo de la familia Alviso, 1817–1850 (original MSS, Bancroft Library).

Anza. Juan Bautista de Anza opened up the route from the province of Sonora, Mexico, to San Gabriel in 1774, and in 1775 brought the first colonists to Nueva California. His diaries from January 8 to May 27, 1774, are in Herbert E. Bolton, *Anza's California Expeditions* (5 vols.; University of California Press, 1930), II, 1–243; that from October 23, 1775, to June 1, 1776, is in III, 1–200. *See* Garcés; Palou; Font.

APCH:P. Academy of Pacific Coast History: *Publications.* The four volumes of the series were published by the University of California Press between 1909 and 1919.

Arbuckle. The reference indicates that the information was received from Clyde Arbuckle, secretary of the San Jose Historic Landmarks Commission, or that it was taken from Clyde Arbuckle and Roscoe D. Wyatt, *Historic Names, Persons and Places in Santa Clara County* (San Jose Chamber of Commerce, 1948).

Arch. Arz. SF. Archivo del Arzobispado de San Francisco: Cartas de los Misioneros de California, 1772–1849 (5 vols. in 3; transcripts and extracts, Bancroft Library).

Archivo de California. Documents formerly in the United States Surveyor General's Office, San Francisco, destroyed in the fire of 1906 (transcripts, Bancroft Library). This includes Archives of California, Miscellany; Dep. Recs.; DSP; DSP Ang.; DSP Ben.; DSP Ben. C & T; DSP Ben. CH; DSP Ben. Mil.; DSP Ben. P & J; DSP Mont.; Legis. Recs.; Prov. Recs.; PSP; PSP Ben. Mil.; PSP Pres.; SP Mis. & C; SP Sac.

Arch. LA. Archives of Los Angeles, Miscellaneous Papers, 1821–1850 (5 vols.; transcripts and extracts, Bancroft Library).

Arch. Mis. Archivo de las Misiones, 1769–1825

(1 vol.; original MSS, Bancroft Library).

Arch. Mis. S. Buen. Archivo de la Mision de San Buenaventura (2 vols.; transcripts, Bancroft Library).

Arch. Mont. Archives of Monterey County, Miscellaneous Documents (16 vols. in 1; transcripts and extracts, Bancroft Library).

Arch. MPC. Archivo de la Mision de la Purisima Concepcion (transcripts, Bancroft Library).

Arch. MSB. Archivo de la Mision de Santa Barbara, 1768–1836 (12 vols.; transcripts, Bancroft Library).

Arch. SB. Archivo de la Mision de Santa Barbara; Libros de Mision, 1782–1853 (abstracts, Bancroft Library).

Arch. SB, Juzgado. Archivo de Santa Barbara, Oficios del Juzgado de Primera Instancia, 1839–1849, 1852–1853 (abstracts and copies, Bancroft Library).

Arch. SJ. San Jose Archives, 1796–1849 (6 vols. and loose papers in office of City Clerk, San Jose, in 1 vol.; transcripts and extracts, Bancroft Library).

Argüello's Diary. The diary of Luis Antonio Argüello, commander of an expedition into the Sacramento Valley in October–November, 1821 (original MS, Bancroft Library). Padre Blas Ordaz chronicled the same expedition; in his diary (transcript, Arch. MSB, IV, 169–190) the spelling of some place names differs from Argüello's.

Arrowsmith's Map. Aaron Arrowsmith, *Chart of the World . . .*, April 1, 1790. Wagner, No. 744.

Arroyo. Padre Felipe Arroyo de la Cuesta collected vocabularies of several central California Indian dialects. MSS, *Lengua de California* and *Lecciones de Indios* in Bancroft Library.

Asbill. Frank Asbill, a descendant of early Missourian settlers in eastern Mendocino County, supplied information about a number of place names of the region.

Ashton. William E. Ashton, "Presidential Place Name Covers," in *Weekly Philatelic Gossip,* January 12, 1952, June 25, 1955.

Athabascan. Several groups of this most widespread linguistic family of North American Indians dwelt in the northwest corner of the State. The Tolowa, the Hupa, and the Mattole have left traces in geographical names. The name is also spelled Athapascan.

Atlas Sheet. An atlas sheet is a section of the topographical atlas of the United States covering one of the many thousands of quadrangles into which the Geological Survey has divided the country. Unless otherwise stated the reference is to a sheet published by the U.S. Geological Survey. *See* Helm Index.

Audubon. John Woodhouse Audubon, son of the great American ornithologist, was in California from September, 1849, to May, 1850. His diary is of great interest for early mining towns. The references are to *Audubon's Western Journal: 1849–1850* (Cleveland: Arthur H. Clark Co., 1906).

Ayala. *Plano del Puerto de San Francisco . . . 1775.* Based upon Juan Manuel de Ayala's survey and drawn by José de Cañizares; reproduced in H. E. Bolton, *Anza's California Expeditions*, I, opp. p. 385, and in Bolton, ed., *Historical Memoirs . . . Palou*, IV, opp. p. 40. Wagner, No. 640. This is the first chart of San Francisco Bay; some of the place names on it are still in use. Ayala was commander of the first official survey of the bay, but most of the responsibility for it fell to Cañizares.

Aztec. Aztecs is the current conventional term used for the Nahua tribes, who lived in Mexico at the time of the Spanish conquest. Many words, including geographical terms, were taken from their language into Mexican Spanish and thus found their way into California geography.

Bailey. G. E. Bailey, "History and Origin of California Names and Places." A number of articles published in the *Overland Monthly* (San Francisco) from July to December, 1904.

Baker's Map. George H. Baker, *Map of the Mining Region, of California, 1856* (Sacramento: E. L. Barber). Wheat, No. 289.

Bancroft. H. H. Bancroft, *History of California* (7 vols. [Vols. XVIII to XXIV of his *Works*]; San Francisco, 1884–1890). Contains rich factual material. The "Pioneer Register and Index," in Vols. II–V, includes biographical sketches of many persons mentioned in this Dictionary. **Bancroft Scrapbooks.** Materials collected in the preparation of Bancroft's Pacific States handbooks (1860–1864). Vols. I to XVII: California Counties. **Bancroft Scraps.** Collection of clippings in 113 vols.

Bancroft's Maps. For several decades after 1858 H. H. Bancroft & Co., San Francisco, published periodically nicely engraved maps of the State, which were very popular and to some extent influential in fixing place names.

Barnes. Will C. Barnes, "Arizona Place Names," University of Arizona *Bulletin*, VI, No. 1 (January 1, 1935). One of the best of our state surveys, written by a man who had the great advantage of gathering his information "in the field."

Barrett, Miwok. "The Geography and Dialects of the Miwok Indians," *AAE*, VI, 333–368. **Barrett, Myths.** "Myths of the Southern Sierra Miwok," *AAE*, XVI, 1–28. **Barrett, Pomo.** "The Ethno-Geography of the Pomo and Neighboring Indians," *AAE*, VI, 1–332. These three important contributions were written by Samuel A. Barrett.

Beattie. George W. Beattie, *Heritage of the Valley: San Bernardino's First Century* (Pasadena: San Pasqual Press, 1939).

Beckwith. Lieutenant E. G. Beckwith, Third Artillery, "Report of Explorations for a Route for the Pacific Railroad . . . Forty-first Parallel . . . 1854," Pacific R.R. *Reports*, Vol. II, [Pt. 2].

Beechey. *Narrative of a Voyage to the Pacific . . . under the Command of Captain F. W. Beechey . . . in the Years 1825, 26, 27, 28.* The references are to the original 8ᵛᵒ edition in two volumes (London, 1831). Chapters i and ii of the second volume give an account of the stay in California. A number of important names in the San Francisco Bay district (some of them misspelled) were fixed by Beechey. His map of "The Harbour of San Francisco, Nueva California . . . 1827 & 8," the first map of the bay to be fairly accurate, is reproduced in *An Account of a Visit to California 1826–'27*, edited by Edith M. Coulter, printed by the Grabhorn Press, San Francisco, for the Book Club of California, 1941.

Beeler. Madison S. Beeler, author of several articles on Indian place names in California published in *Names* and *Western Folklore*.

Belcher. Sir Edward Belcher, *Narrative of a Voyage round the World . . . during the Years 1836–1842 . . .* (2 vols.; London, 1843).

Belden. L. Burr Belden, historian and contributor to the San Bernardino *Sun-Telegram*.

Bendire Report. The report made by Lieutenant Charles Bendire of his expedition of 1867 has been misplaced in the archives of the War Department.

Bentley. Harold W. Bentley, *A Dictionary of Spanish Terms in English . . .* (Columbia University Press, 1932). A helpful book, especially for Spanish words current in the southwestern United States.

Bidwell. John Bidwell (1819–1900), a native of New York, arrived in California in 1841 and was Sutter's most faithful assistant before the gold rush. In 1849 he acquired the Arroyo Chico rancho and became the leader in the development of Butte County. In later years he was congressman, general of the California militia, and in 1892 presidential candidate on the Prohibition ticket. The references are to *Echoes of the Past . . .* , published in Chico shortly after his death and repeatedly reprinted. His map of 1844, Mapa del Valle del Sacramento (MS in California State Library; Wheat, No. 15), is the first known map of the Sacramento Valley showing the Mexican grants and rivers in detail. "On my return from Red Bluff in March, 1843, I made a map of the upper Sacramento Valley on which most of the streams were laid down, and they have since borne the names then given them" (Butte County History, 1877).

Bigler. Henry William Bigler, Diary of a Mormon in California. The Bancroft version is published in *Bigler's Chronicle of the West,* by Erwin G. Gudde (University of California Press, 1962).

Bieber. Ralph P. Bieber, ed., *Southern Trails to California in 1849* (Glendale: Arthur H. Clark Co., 1937).

Blake. William P. Blake was the geologist of the Pacific Railroad Survey, 1853–1854. His report and map are published in Vol. V, Pt. 2, of the Pacific Railroad *Reports.* In it are several maps, including *Geological Map of a Part of . . . California Explored in 1853;* on this a number of place names are recorded for the first time.

Blue Book. The reference is to the *California Blue Book and State Roster,* published (usually biennially) by the California secretary of state since 1891.

Bodega. Juan Francisco de la Bodega y Quadra, as commander of the schooner *Sonora* of the Hezeta expedition of 1775, made an important voyage up the coast as far as Alaska and named a number of places, including Bodega Bay. For an account of his discoveries and for two of his maps cf. Wagner (chap. xxv; Plates XXXVII, XXXIX).

Boggs. The reference is to Mae Hélène Bacon Boggs, *My Playhouse Was a Concord Coach . . .* (Oakland, 1942). An "anthology of newspaper clippings and documents" from 1839 to 1888; contains excellent reproductions of a number of valuable maps and several lists of post offices of the 1850's.

Bolton. The indispensable critical editions of the diaries and reports of the Anza and Portolá expeditions by the eminent historian Herbert E. Bolton are listed under Anza, Crespi, Font, and Palou. His edition of Kino's *Memoir* is listed under Kino. **Span. Expl.** refers to *Spanish Exploration in the Southwest, 1542–1706* (New York: Scribners, 1916).

Bonnycastle. R. H. Bonnycastle, *Spanish America . . .* (London, 1818). The references are to the map.

Borden. Stanley T. Borden supplied many names in the northern counties, especially those that derived from the lumber industry.

Borthwick. J. D. Borthwick, *The Gold Hunters* (New York, 1917). This popular account was first printed in 1857 under the title *Three Years in California;* it has appeared in several other editions. Borthwick was in California in 1851.

Boscana. The reference is to an interesting account of the Indians of Mission San Juan Capistrano by Padre Gerónimo Boscana, who served at the mission from 1814 to 1826 and wrote the MS while there. It was translated into English and first published in Alfred Robinson, *Life in California* (1846), and has frequently been reprinted. The edition used is *Chinigchinich,* edited by Phil Townsend Hanna and published by the Fine Arts Press, Santa Ana, in 1933.

Boundary Commission. *See* Nevada Boundary Survey.

Bowen's Guide. *See* Postal Guide.

Bowman. The reference indicates that the item was contributed by J. N. Bowman of Berkeley. **Bowman Index.** Index of California Private Land Grants and Private Land Grant Papers and Cases (MS). This monumental work on one of the most important phases of California's political, legal, and economic history is compiled from the land-grant documents in the U.S. District Court, San Francisco; the National Archives, Washington, D.C.; the State Archives, Sacramento; the U.S. Public Survey Office, Glendale; government published documents; and various county archives. The names and dates of land grants given in this Dictionary are taken from it. Until the Bowman Index appears in print, the Ogden Hoffman Index in *Report of Land Cases* (San Francisco, 1862), and the lists of land grants given in the reports and on the maps of the Land Office, must serve for general reference. *See* Land Grant. Bowman's article "The Names of the California Missions," was published in HSSC:*Q*, XXXIX, 351 ff.

Bowman's Map. Amos Bowman, *Map of Georgetown Divide . . .* (San Francisco, 1873). *See* von Leicht–Hoffmann.

Brannan. Samuel Brannan, in 1846, brought a party of Mormons from New York to settle in California. He played an important role in California history during and after the gold rush. The quotation concerning the naming of Calistoga is taken from Reva Scott's *Samuel Brannan and the Golden Fleece* (New York: Macmillan, 1944) with the permission of the publishers, The Macmillan Company.

Brewer. *Up and Down California in 1860–1864: The Journal of William H. Brewer,* edited by Francis P. Farquhar (Yale University Press, 1930). **Notes.** Brewer's field notes 1861–1864. Sixteen MS notebooks in Bancroft Library. His diaries and correspondence in that library were also checked. *See* Brewer, Mount, in the text.

Brierly. A. A. Brierly, Inyo County surveyor, supplied information on a large number of place names in his county.

Briggs Map. Henry Briggs, *The North Part of America,* 1625. Wagner, No. 295; Plate XXIII.

Brown, A. K. The reference refers to Allan K. Brown, "San Mateo County Place Names" (*Names* XII, pp. 154-184) , or to Professor Brown's more extensive manuscript with the same title.

Brown, T. P. The reference is to Thomas P. Brown's interesting column "What's in a Name," published from July, 1942, to October, 1943, in *The Headlight,* the monthly publication of the Western Pacific Railroad.

Brown, W. S. William S. Brown, formerly of the U.S. Forest Service, has collected valuable information from rangers and settlers on place names in the national forests.

Browne. J. Ross Browne, *Report on the Mineral Resources of the States and Territories West of the Rocky Mountains* (Washington: Government Printing Office, 1868). This was issued also as 40th Cong., 2d sess. (1867), House Ex. Doc. No. 202.

Bruff. *Gold Rush: The Journals and Other Papers of J. Goldsborough Bruff,* edited by Georgia Willis Read and Ruth Gaines (2 vols.; Columbia University Press, 1944). The work is an important source for the period of California history from April, 1849, to July, 1851.

Bryant. Edwin Bryant, *What I Saw in California* . . . (New York, 1849).

Buffum. E. Gould Buffum, *Six Months in the Gold Mines* . . . (London, 1850).

Buie. The reference with a date refers to Earl E. Buie's column in the San Bernardino *Daily Sun.*

Bunnell. Lafayette Houghton Bunnell, *Discovery of the Yosemite and the Indian War of 1851* . . . Quotations refer to the Chicago edi-

tion of 1880. Bunnell was a member of the Mariposa Battalion, which discovered Yosemite Valley. He is responsible for retaining some of the Indian names in the valley, including Yosemite itself. For a biographical sketch consult Farquhar under "Bunnell Point."

Burr's Map. David H. Burr's map of 1839 is based in part on Jedediah Smith's notes, or on a map made by Smith but not now extant. Burr's map is reproduced in Maurice S. Sullivan, *The Travels of Jedediah Smith. See* Sullivan.

Butler's Map. B. F. Butler, *Map of the State of California* (San Francisco, 1851). Wheat, No. 185.

Cabrillo. Juan Rodríguez Cabrillo, a Portuguese navigator in Spanish service, was commander of the first expedition to sail along the coast of California (1542) and to apply names to coastal features. None of the names survived. *See,* in the text, Mugu, Sierra Nevada, San Martin, Cabrillo; and, in the Glossary, Ferrer. Although his surname was Rodríguez, we follow the common practice in listing him under "Cabrillo."

Cahuilla. *See* Coachella in text.

California Blue Book. *See* Blue Book.

Cañizares. José de Cañizares, *Plano del Puerto de San Francisco* (1776). Wagner No. 653. Cañizares, as first pilot under Ayala, made the first official survey (1775) of San Francisco Bay (*see* Ayala) and made further explorations in 1776.

Carrillo Docs. Domingo Carrillo, Documentos para la Historia de California (transcripts, Bancroft Library).

Cary's Map. John Cary's map of North America was published in London in 1806.

Castro Docs. Documentos para la historia de California, 1821–1850, . . . Manuel Castro (2 vols.; originals, Bancroft Library).

Cermeño. *See* Rodríguez Cermeño.

CFQ. *California Folklore Quarterly,* published by the University of California Press for the California Folklore Society beginning in 1941. In 1947 the name was changed to *Western Folklore.*

Chalfant. Willie Arthur Chalfant, for many years editor and publisher of the *Inyo Register,* is the best authority on the old names of Inyo County and Death Valley. **Inyo.** *The Story of Inyo* (Chicago, 1922). **Death Valley.** *Death Valley—The Facts* (Stanford University Press, 1930, 1936). **Tales.** *Tales of the Pioneers* (Stanford University Press, 1942).

Chamisso. Adelbert von Chamisso, a German·

botanist and poet, of French extraction, was the botanist of the first Kotzebue expedition, 1815–1818. In 1816 he collected and described what is now California's state flower, commonly known as the golden poppy, and named it *Eschscholtzia californica* for Johann F. Eschscholtz, the zoölogist of the expedition. *See* Kotzebue; Rurik.

Chapman. Charles E. Chapman, *A History of California: The Spanish Period* (New York: Macmillan, 1939).

Chase. J. Smeaton Chase was an observant traveler in California who related his experiences in three interesting books published by the Houghton Mifflin Company: *Yosemite Trails* ... (1911); *California Coast Trails* ... (1913); *California Desert Trails* ... (1919).

Chemehuevi. *See* Chemehuevi in text.

Chinook Jargon. The trade language used in the American Northwest as far south as the Klamath River. The references are to George Gibbs, *A Dictionary of the Chinook Jargon* (New York, 1863).

CHSQ. *California Historical Society Quarterly,* published since 1922 in San Francisco.

Chuckwalla. *Death Valley Chuck-walla.* Greenwater, Calif. Jan. 1 - June, 1907.

Chumash. The Chumash Indians in San Luis Obispo and Santa Barbara counties have left more names on the California map than any other linguistic group, except the Wintun.

Cleland. Robert Glass Cleland, *A History of California: The American Period* (New York: Macmillan, 1927).

Coast Pilot. This invaluable book for navigation on the Pacific Coast was first published by George Davidson under the titles, *Directory of the Pacific Coast* (1858 and 1862) and *Coast Pilot of California, Oregon, and Washington* (1869 and 1889). Since 1903 it has been published at irregular intervals by the Coast Survey. The older editions are a valuable source of information concerning names along the coast.

Coast Survey. The U.S. Coast Survey, since 1878 officially designated as Coast and Geodetic Survey, commenced the charting of the Pacific Coast in 1850, and is in general responsible for many names along the coast, including the retention, translation, or hybridization of previously existing names. The names applied to certain points sometimes differ in the various publications of the Survey. A reference with a date but not a page number refers to the charts at the end of the annual *Reports;* with a page number it refers

to the *Report* itself. **Coast Survey Gazetteer.** *Geographic Names in the Coastal Areas of California, Oregon, and Washington.* Compiled by personnel of the Work Projects Administration in Philadelphia, 1939–1940. A very helpful list of all the place names which appear on the charts of the Survey. It could serve as a model for similar gazetteers. *See* Davidson; Coast Pilot.

Co. Hist. The annals of most, if not all, California counties at some time or other have been recorded in a county history. Some of these volumes not only contain valuable information about local history but also are important sources for the origin of place names. The references cited in the text may be found in the following list, in which the year, the publisher, and (when known) the author or editor are indicated.

Alameda. 1876: *The Centennial Year Book,* by William Halley (Oakland: W. Halley). 1878: *Official ... Atlas Map* (Oakland: Thompson & West). 1883: (Oakland: M. W. Wood). 1928: By Frank C. Merritt (Chicago: S. J. Clarke Pub. Co.). 1932: *The Romance of Oakland* ... by Roy C. Beckman (Oakland: Landis & Kelsey).

Amador. 1881: [By Jesse D. Mason] (Oakland: Thompson & West). 1927: Ed. by Mrs. J. L. Sargent (Jackson: Amador County Federation of Women's Clubs).

Butte. 1877: *Butte Co. ... Illustrations* ... (Oakland: Smith & Elliott). 1882: By Harry L. Wells and W. L. Chambers (San Francisco: H. L. Wells). 1918: By George C. Mansfield (Los Angeles: Historic Record Co.).

Calaveras. 1892: *See* Merced below.

Colusa. 1880: *Illustrations* ... [by W. S. Green] (San Francisco: Elliott & Moore). 1891: By Justus H. Rogers (Orland). 1918: By Charles Davis McComish and Mrs. Rebecca T. Lambert (Los Angeles: Historic Record Co.). Also contains history of Glenn County.

Contra Costa. 1878: *Illustrations* ... (Oakland: Smith & Elliott). 1882: Preface signed by J. P. Munro-Fraser (San Francisco: W. A. Slocum & Co.). 1917: Ed. by F. J. Hulaniski (Berkeley: Elms Pub. Co.). 1926: (Los Angeles: Historic Record Co.). 1940: By Mae Fisher Purcell (Berkeley: Gillick Press).

Del Norte. 1881: By A. J. Bledsoe (Eureka: Wyman & Co.). 1953: By Esther Ruth Smith (Oakland: Holmes Book Company).

El Dorado. 1883: *Historical Souvenir* ... (Oakland: Paolo Sioli). 1915: *California's El Dorado* ... by Herman Daniel Jerrett (Sacramento: Press of J. Anderson).

Fresno. 1882: (San Francisco: Wallace W. Elliott & Co.). 1892: *A Memorial and Biographical History* ... (Chicago: Lewis Pub. Co.). Also contains history of Tulare and Kern counties. 1919: By Paul E. Vandor (Los Angeles: Historic Record Co.). 1933: By Lilbourne Alsip Winchell (Fresno: A. H.

Cawston). 1941: *The Fresno County Blue Book,* by Ben R. Walker (Fresno: A. H. Cawston). 1946: *Fresno Community Book,* ed. by Ben R. Walker (Fresno: A. H. Cawston). 1956: *Fresno County Centennial Almanac* (Fresno: Centennial Committee).

Glenn. 1918: *See* Colusa above.

Humboldt. 1882: (San Francisco: Wallace W. Elliott & Co.). 1890: [By Lillie E. Hamm] (Eureka: Daily Humboldt Standard). 1915: By Leigh H. Irvine (Los Angeles: Historic Record Co.).

Imperial. 1918: Ed. by F. C. Farr (Berkeley: Elms and Franks). 1931: *See* Tout.

Inyo. *See* Chalfant.

Kern. 1883: (San Francisco: Wallace W. Elliott & Co.). 1892: *See* Fresno above. 1914: By Wallace M. Morgan (Los Angeles: Historic Record Co.). 1929: By Thelma B. Miller (Chicago: S. J. Clarke Pub. Co.). 1934: *See* Comfort.

Kings. 1913: *See* Tulare below. 1940: By Robert R. Brown and J. E. Richmond (Hanford: A. H. Cawston).

Lake. 1873: *See* Napa below. 1881: *See* Napa below. 1914: *See* Mendocino below.

Lassen. 1882: *See* Plumas below. 1916: *Fairfield's Pioneer History* . . . by Asa M. Fairfield (San Francisco: H. S. Crocker Co.).

Los Angeles. 1876: *An Historical Sketch* . . . by J. J. Warner, Benjamin Hayes, and J. P. Widney (Los Angeles: L. Lewin & Co.). 1880: [By John Albert Wilson] (Oakland: Thompson & West). 1889: *An Illustrated History* . . . (Chicago: Lewis Pub. Co.). 1890: *See* San Diego below. 1908: [L. A.] *Ingersoll's Century History, Santa Monica Bay Cities* . . . (Los Angeles). 1920: *History of Pomona Valley* . . . (Los Angeles: Historic Record Co.). Also contains history of part of San Bernardino County. 1923: Ed. by John Steven McGroarty (Chicago and New York: American Historical Society). 1939: *Know Los Angeles County,* by William J. Dunkerley (Los Angeles County Board of Supervisors).

1962-1965: *The Historical Volume and Reference Works.* Ed. by Robert P. Studer (5 vols.; Los Angeles: Historical Publishers, 1962-1965).

Marin. 1880: Preface signed by J. P. Munro-Fraser (San Francisco: Alley, Bowen & Co.).

Mariposa. 1892: *See* Merced below.

Mendocino. 1873: *See* Napa below. 1880: [By Lyman L. Palmer] (San Francisco: Alley, Bowen & Co.). 1914: By Aurelius O. Carpenter and Percy H. Millberry (Los Angeles: Historic Record Co.). Also contains history of Lake County.

Merced. 1881: (San Francisco: Elliott & Moore). 1892: *A Memorial and Biographical History of the Counties of Merced, Stanislaus, Calaveras, Tuolumne and Mariposa* (Chicago: Lewis Pub. Co.). 1925: By John Outcalt (Los Angeles: Historic Record Co.).

Monterey. 1881: (San Francisco: Elliott & Moore). Also contains history of San Benito County. 1903: *See* Santa Cruz below. 1910: By J. M. Guinn (Los Angeles: Historic Record Co.). Also contains history of San Benito County.

Napa. 1873: *Historical* . . . *Sketch Book of Napa, Sonoma, Lake and Mendocino* . . . by C. A. Menefee (Napa City: Reporter Pub. House). 1881:

Preface signed by Lyman L. Palmer (San Francisco: Slocum, Bowen & Co.). Also contains history of Lake County. 1901: Introduction signed by W. F. Wallace (Oakland: Enquirer Print). 1912: *See* Solano below.

Nevada. 1867: *Bean's History* . . . comp. by Edwin F. Bean (Nevada: Daily Gazette Book and Job Office). 1880: [By Harry Laurenz Wells] (Oakland: Thompson & West). 1924: *See* Placer below.

Orange. 1890: *See* San Diego below. 1911: Ed. by Samuel Armor (Los Angeles: Historic Record Co.). 1921: Revised edition of the preceding.

Placer. 1882: [Ed. by Myron Angel] (Oakland: Thompson & West). 1924: By W. B. Lardner and M. J. Brock (Los Angeles: Historic Record Co.). Also contains history of Nevada County.

Plumas. 1882: *Illustrated History of Plumas, Lassen & Sierra Counties* (San Francisco: Fariss & Smith).

Riverside. 1912: By Elmer Wallace Holmes (Los Angeles: Historic Record Co.). 1922: *See* San Bernardino below. 1935: *History of Riverside City and County,* by John Raymond Gabbert (Riverside: Record Pub. Co.).

Sacramento. 1880: [Ed. by George F. Wright] (Oakland: Thompson & West). 1890: *An Illustrated History* . . . by Hon. Win. J. Davis (Chicago: Lewis Pub. Co.). 1913: By William L. Willis (Los Angeles: Historic Record Co.). 1923: Ed. by G. Walter Reed (Los Angeles: Historic Record Co.). 1931: *History of the* . . . *Valley,* by J. W. Wooldridge (Chicago: Pioneer Historical Pub. Co.).

San Benito. 1881: *See* Monterey above. 1903: *See* Santa Cruz below. 1910: *See* Monterey above.

San Bernardino. 1883: (San Francisco: Wallace W. Elliott & Co.). 1890: *See* San Diego below. 1904: *Ingersoll's Century Annals* . . . by Luther A. Ingersoll (Los Angeles). 1920: *History of Pomona Valley* (Los Angeles: Historic Record Co.). 1922: Ed. by John Brown (Madison, Wis.: Western Historical Association). Also contains history of Riverside County, edited by James Boyd.

San Diego. 1888: *The City and County* . . . [By Theodore Strong Van Dyke] (San Diego: Leberthon & Taylor). 1890: *An Illustrated History of Southern California* . . . (Chicago: Lewis Pub. Co.). Also contains history of San Bernardino, Los Angeles, and Orange counties. 1922: *City of San Diego and San Diego County,* by Clarence Alan McGrew (Chicago and New York: American Historical Society). 1936: Ed. by Carl H. Heilbron (San Diego: San Diego Press Club).

San Joaquin. 1879: [By F. T. Gilbert] (Oakland: Thompson & West). 1890: *An Illustrated History* . . . (Chicago: Lewis Pub. Co.). 1923: By George H. Tinkham (Los Angeles: Historic Record Co.).

San Luis Obispo. 1883: (Oakland: Thompson & West). 1891: *See* Santa Barbara below. 1903: *See* Santa Cruz below. 1917: By Mrs. Annie L. Morrison and John H. Haydon (Los Angeles: Historic Record Co.).

San Mateo. 1878: *Moore & De Pue's Illustrated History* . . . (San Francisco: G. T. Brown & Co.). 1883: (San Francisco: B. F. Alley). 1916: By Philip W. Alexander and Charles P. Hamm (Burlingame: Burlingame Pub. Co.). 1946: *See* Stanger.

Santa Barbara. 1883: (Oakland: Thompson & West). Also contains history of Ventura County. 1891:

A Memorial . . . History of the Counties of Santa Barbara, San Luis Obispo and Ventura . . . by Mrs. Yda Addis Storke (Chicago: Lewis Pub. Co.). 1939: Ed. by Owen H. O'Neill (Santa Barbara: H. M. Meier).

Santa Clara. 1876: *Historical Atlas Map . . .* (San Francisco: Thompsòn & West). 1881: Preface signed by J. P. Munro-Fraser (San Francisco: Alley, Bowen & Co.). 1888: *See* Foote. 1922: By Eugene T. Sawyer (Los Angeles: Historic Record Co.).

Santa Cruz. 1879: *Santa Cruz County . . . with Historical Sketch* (San Francisco: Wallace W. Elliott & Co.). 1892: By E. S. Harrison (San Francisco: Pacific Press Pub. Co.). 1903: *History of the State . . . and Biographical Record of Santa Cruz, San Benito, Monterey and San Luis Obispo Counties,* by J. M. Guinn (Chicago: Chapman Pub. Co.). 1911: By Edward Martin (Los Angeles: Historic Record Co.).

Shasta. 1949: *Shasta County California, a History,* by Rosena A. Giles (Oakland: Biobooks).

Sierra. 1882: *See* Plumas above.

Siskiyou. 1881: By Harry Laurenz Wells (Oakland: D. J. Stewart & Co.).

Solano. 1878: *Historical Atlas Map . . .* (San Francisco: Thompson & West). 1879: (San Francisco: Wood, Alley & Co.). 1912: By Tom Gregory (Los Angeles: Historic Record Co.). Also contains history of Napa County.

Sonoma. 1873: *See* Napa above. 1877: *Historical Atlas Map . . .* (Oakland: Thos. H. Thompson & Co.). 1879: *Historical Sketch . . .* by Robert A. Thompson (San Francisco: A. L. Bancroft & Co.). 1880: (San Francisco: Alley, Bowen & Co.). 1911: By Tom Gregory (Los Angeles: Historic Record Co.). 1937: By Ernest Latimer Finley (Santa Rosa: Press Democrat Pub. Co.).

Stanislaus. 1881: (San Francisco: Elliott & Moore). 1892: *See* Merced above. 1921: By George H. Tinkham (Los Angeles: Historic Record Co.).

Sutter. 1879: (Oakland: Thompson & West). 1924: *See* Yuba below.

Tehama. 1880: *Tehama County . . . Illustrations . . . with Historical Sketch* (San Francisco: Elliott & Moore).

Trinity. 1858: *The Annals . . .* by Isaac Cox (San Francisco: Commercial Book and Job Steam Printing); reprinted in Eugene, Ore., 1940.

Tulare. 1883: (San Francisco: W. W. Elliott & Co.). 1888: *Business Directory and Historical . . . Hand-Book . . .* (Tulare City: Pillsbury & Ellsworth). 1892: *See* Fresno above. 1913: By Eugene L. Menefee and Fred A. Dodge (Los Angeles: Historic Record Co.). Also contains history of Kings County.

Tuolumne. 1882: [Comp. by Herbert O. Lang] (San Francisco: B. F. Alley). 1892: *See* Merced above.

Ventura. 1883: *See* Santa Barbara above. 1891: *See* Santa Barbara above.

Yolo. 1879: *The Illustrated Atlas and History . . .* (San Francisco: De Pue & Co.). 1913: By Tom Gregory (Los Angeles: Historic Record Co.). 1940: Ed. by William O. Russell (Woodland).

Yuba. 1879: By William H. Chamberlain and Harry L. Wells (Oakland: Thompson & West). 1924: By Peter J. Delay (Los Angeles: Historic Record Co.).

Also contains history of Sutter County.

Co. Library; Co. Surveyor. The reference indicates that the information was received from the county librarian or the county surveyor.

Comfort. Herbert G. Comfort, *Where Rolls the Kern: A History of Kern County, California* (Moorpark: Enterprise Press, 1934).

Cordua. Theodor Cordua settled at the site of present-day Marysville in 1841 and called his farm Neu Mecklenburg, after his home province in Germany. The references are to *The Memoirs of Theodor Cordua,* reprinted from *CHSQ,* XII, No. 4.

Costanoan. The habitat of the Costanoan Indians was in the Coast and Diablo ranges between Suisun Bay and central Monterey County.

Costansó. Miguel Costansó was an engineer attached to the Portolá expedition. The references are to "The Portolá Expedition of 1769–1770; Diary of Miguel Costansó," edited by Frederick J. Teggart, published (in both Spanish and English) in APCH:*P,* II, 161–327. **Costansó's Map.** *Carta reducida del Oceano Asiático ó Mar del Súr,* 1771. Reproduced in Wagner, Plate XXXIII. The earliest version is dated October 30, 1770.

Coues, New Light. Elliott Coues, ed., *New Light on the Early History of the Greater North West . . .* (New York: F. P. Harper, 1897). The journals of Alexander Henry and David Thompson of the Northwest Company. **Coues, Trail.** *On the Trail of a Spanish Pioneer . . . Francisco Garcés . . . 1775–1776* (New York: F. P. Harper, 1900). A well-edited account of Padre Garcés' travels. *See* Garcés.

Coulter. John Coulter, *Adventures on the Western Coast of South America and the Interior of California . . .* (2 vols.; London, 1847).

Coulter's Map. *Upper California to Illustrate the Paper by Dr. Coulter* (London, 1835). Wheat No. 8. The map accompanies Dr. Thomas Coulter's "Notes on Upper California" printed in the *Journal of the Royal Geographical Society of London,* V (1835), 59 ff.

Coy, Counties. Owen C. Coy, *California County Boundaries . . .* (Berkeley: California Historical Survey Commission, 1923). **Coy, Humboldt.** *The Humboldt Bay Region 1850–1875* (Los Angeles: California State Historical Association, 1929).

Craigie. William Alexander Craigie, ed., *A Dictionary of American English on Historical Principles* (4 vols.; Chicago, 1936–1944).

Crespi. Padre Juan Crespi was the chronicler of the Portolá expedition of 1769–1770. He probably placed more names on the map of California than any other person in Spanish times. The references are to Herbert E. Bolton's *Fray Juan Crespi* . . . (University of California Press, 1927), which contains Crespi's diary of the Portolá expedition. This diary is also in Palou's *Historical Memoirs of New California*, IV, 109–260 (*see* Palou). Crespi's diary of the Fages expedition of 1772 from Monterey to the San Francisco Bay region is in Bolton's *Fray Juan Crespi*, pp. 277–303.

Crites. Arthur S. Crites, *Pioneer Days in Kern County* (Los Angeles, 1951).

Cronise. Titus Fey Cronise, *The Natural Wealth of California* . . . (San Francisco, 1868).

Cutter. Donald C. Cutter has translated and edited the accounts of the Moraga expedition of 1808 and of the Malaspina expedition of 1791.

Dakin, Paisano. Susanna Bryant Dakin, *A Scotch Paisano: Hugo Reid's Life in California, 1832–1852* (University of California Press, 1939). In Appendix B are reprinted Reid's "Letters on the Los Angeles County Indians," first published in the Los Angeles *Star* in 1852.

Dalrymple. *Plan of Port St. Francisco* (1789) and *Plan of Port San Francisco in New Albion* (1790) and *Chart of the West-Coast of California* (1790), published by Alexander Dalrymple from Spanish sources. These maps were recently reproduced in the *Pacific Historical Review*, Vol. XVI, No. 4 (1947). The references in this Dictionary, however, are to Davidson's copies.

Dana. Richard Henry Dana, Jr., *Two Years Before the Mast: A Personal Narrative*. The references are to the Houghton Mifflin edition of 1911. Dana was in California in 1834–1835; the first edition of his classical account was published in New York in 1840.

Davidson. George Davidson (1825–1911), a native of Nottingham, England, and of Scottish ancestry, was for many years California's leading scientist in the fields of astronomy, geodesy, and geography. In 1850 he was a member of the first party sent by the U.S. Coast Survey to chart the Pacific Coast, and from 1868 to 1895 he was in charge of the Coast Survey on the west coast. His work was naturally of great importance for the nomenclature of our coastal features. Unless otherwise stated, his name refers to his papers and correspondence, now in the possession of the University of California. **Humboldt Bay.**

"The Discovery of Humboldt Bay," Geographical Society of the Pacific, *Proceedings*, II (1891), No. 2. *See* Coast Pilot; Coast Survey.

Davis, D. T. The information was received from D. T. Davis, of the faculty of Napa Junior College.

Davis, H. P. The information was received from H. P. Davis, of Nevada City.

Davis, W. H. William Heath Davis, *Sixty Years in California* . . . (San Francisco, 1889).

Death Valley Guide. Federal Writers Project, California, *Death Valley, a Guide* (Boston: Houghton Mifflin, 1939. American Guide Series).

Death Valley Survey. Death Valley National Monument: Place Name Survey (typewritten MS). An excellent regional study of geographical names by officials of the national monument: former superintendent J. R. White, present superintendent T. R. Goodwin, former ranger H. D. Curry, and former naturalist E. C. Alberts. T. S. Palmer's *Place Names of the Death Valley Region*, based to a large extent on this survey, was not received until this Dictionary was in print.

Delano. Alonzo Delano (1802–1878) wrote, under the pen name "Old Block," numerous satires, letters, travelogues, and human-interest stories depicting the times of the gold rush. Unless otherwise stated, the reference is to his *Pen-Knife Sketches or Chips of the Old Block* as republished by the Grabhorn Press (San Francisco, 1934). The book was first published in Sacramento in 1853.

De Long. " 'California's Bantam Cock.' The Journals of Charles E. De Long, 1854-1863." Ed. by Carl I. Wheat. In *CHSQ*, VIII, IX, X.

Dep. Recs. Departmental Records, 1822–1845 (14 vols. in 4). *See* Archivo de California.

Derby. Lieutenant George H. Derby of the Topographical Engineers (known in literature as John Phoenix) was engaged in California exploration in 1849 and 1850. His map of 1849 cited in this Dictionary is entitled *Sketch of General Riley's Route through the Mining Districts* (Wheat, No. 79); that of 1850, *Reconnaissance of the Tulares Valley*. Derby's maps are reproduced in *CHSQ*, XI, opp. pp. 99, 102, 247.

Desert Magazine. A well-edited periodical, published monthly since 1937 in El Centro.

Dictionary Etymologist. *See* Etymology.

Diseño. *Diseños* were the maps or plats of Spanish and Mexican land grants which usually accompanied the petition for the grant. For many grants there are a number of *diseños*.

Many *diseños* in the land-grant records of the U.S. District Court in San Francisco, some in the National Archives in Washington, D.C., and some in the State archives in Sacramento were examined. These maps are of the greatest importance as sources for Indian and Spanish names. *See* Bowman Index; Expediente; Land Grant.

Disturnell. John Disturnell, *Mapa de los Estados Unidos de Mejico* ... (New York, 1847). This was the reference map used in the negotiations of the Treaty of Guadalupe Hidalgo of 1848. Wheat, No. 33.

Docs. Hist. Cal. Documentos para la historia de California, 1770–1875 (4 vols.; originals in Bancroft Library).

Douglas. Gazetteer of the Mountains of the State of California, Preliminary (incomplete) edition, compiled by Edward M. Douglas (mimeographed; Washington, 1929). A list of the orographic features as far as they had been put on the topographical atlas of the Geological Survey in 1929.

Doyle. The extensive file of California place names collected for many years by the late Thomas B. Doyle of San Francisco.

Drury. When the name is followed by a page number, the reference is to Aubrey Drury, *California: An Intimate Guide* (New York: Harpers, 1939); when the name alone is given, the information was received directly from the author.

DSP. Departmental State Papers, 1821–1846 (20 vols. in 7). *See* Archivo de California.

DSP Ang. Departmental State Papers, Angeles, 1825–1847 (12 vols. in 4). *See* Archivo de California.

DSP Ben. Departmental State Papers, Benicia, 1821–1846 (5 vols. in 2). *See* Archivo de California.

DSP Ben. C & T. Departmental State Papers, Benicia, Commissary and Treasury, 1825–1842 (5 vols. in 1). *See* Archivo de California.

DSP Ben. CH. Departmental State Papers, Benicia, Custom House, 1816–1848 (8 vols. in 1). *See* Archivo de California.

DSP Ben. Mil. Departmental State Papers, Benicia, Military, 1772–1846 (36 vols., numbered LIII to LXXXVIII, in 3, continued from PSP Ben. Mil.). *See* Archivo de California.

DSP Ben. P & J. Departmental State Papers, Benicia, prefecturas y juzgados, 1828–1846 (6 vols. in 1). *See* Archivo de California.

DSP Mont. Departmental State Papers, Monterey, 1777–1845 (8 vols. in 1). *See* Archivo de California.

DSP San Jose. Departmental State Papers, San Jose (7 vols. in 2; transcripts, Bancroft Library).

Duflot de Mofras. Eugène Duflot de Mofras, attaché of the French legation in Mexico, visited California and Oregon in 1841–1842, charged by the French government to report upon the conditions of these territories. His reports, based on Humboldt's studies, on his own research in Mexico, and on direct observation were published in 1844 in Paris under the title: *Exploration du Territoire de l'Orégon, des Californies et de la Mer Vermeille* ... *1840, 1841, et 1842* (2 vols. and atlas). His name and a page number refer to the book. His great map, faulty in many details, is nevertheless a milestone in western American cartography. *Plan* plus a number refers to the maps of smaller areas included in the atlas, *Plan* 16 being *Port de San Francisco dans la Haute Californie* and *Entrée du Port de San Francisco*.

Dumke. Glenn S. Dumke, *The Boom of the Eighties in Southern California* (San Marino: Huntington Library, 1944).

Durán. Padre Narcisco Durán (1776–1846) served at Mission San Jose from 1806 to 1833, and with Padre Abella accompanied Luis Argüello up the lower Sacramento and San Joaquin rivers in May, 1817. His diary of this expedition, edited by Charles E. Chapman, "Expedition on the Sacramento and San Joaquin Rivers in 1817" (both in Spanish and in English), is in APCH:*P*, II, 329–349.

Eddy's Map. *Approved & Declared to be the Official Map of the State of California by an Act of the Legislature Passed March 25th 1853*. Compiled by W. M. Eddy, State Surveyor General (New York: J. H. Colton, 1854). (Wheat, No. 257.) This map has been much maligned, and Eddy has been accused of improvising his geography and toponymy (see the scathing criticism in the *Rep. Sur. Gen., 1856*, pp. 45, 236–237). The adverse criticism, however, was directed at the map probably because of its somewhat bombastic title. It is a good map, certainly not worse than most other maps before Goddard's. An excellent German map, reproduced in *Zeitschrift für Allgemeine Erdkunde*, Neue Folge, I, 208 (Berlin, 1856), is called Eddy's map, but differs considerably from the original because it has used additional sources.

Egli. J. J. Egli, *Nomina Geographica* (2d ed.; Leipzig, 1893). This work deals with the origin and etymology of more than 42,000 geographical names in all parts of the world.

Eld. Midshipman Henry Eld was a member of Lieutenant Emmons' detachment of the Wilkes expedition on its return from the Willamette Valley to San Francisco in 1841. His diary and sketches are in the possession of Yale University and are being prepared for publication. *See* Wilkes.

Eldredge. Zoeth Skinner Eldredge is the author of several books on California history. In 1905 he carried on a somewhat hysterical campaign to restore Spanish place names. Supported by George Davidson, he prevailed upon the Post Office Department to change the spelling of a number of names, including a few that were not Spanish at all. He published a *History of California* in five volumes (New York: Century History Company, 1915). **Eldredge, Portolá** refers to his *The March of Portolá and the Discovery of the Bay of San Francisco* . . . (San Francisco, 1909).

Emmons. Lieutenant George Falconer Emmons was in command of a detachment of Wilkes' expedition, exploring the interior from Columbia River to San Francisco in 1841. *See* Eld; Wilkes.

Emory. Major William H. Emory, . . . *Notes of a Military Reconnoissance from Fort Leavenworth . . . to San Diego . . . 1846–7* (Washington, 1848). **Report.** *Report on the Survey of the Boundary between the United States and Mexico* (2 vols.; Washington, 1857). The first volume contains the reports by Major Emory and his subordinate officers of their expeditions in 1849.

Engelhardt. Zephyrin Engelhardt, *The Missions and Missionaries of California* (4 vols.; San Francisco: J. H. Barry Company, 1908–1916). The standard work of its kind. Readers desiring more information on the missions are referred to Engelhardt's comprehensive index to his 4-volume work. Where the name of a mission is added to the name Engelhardt, the reference is to one of his monographs on missions published between 1920 and 1934.

Erman's Map. *Karte von Californien,* a map based on Russian sources, is published in J. Hoppe, *Californiens Gegenwart und Zukunft* (Berlin, 1849). Wheat, No. 96.

Estudillo Docs. Documentos para la historia de California, 1776–1850: archivo particular de familia Estudillo (2 vols.; originals, Bancroft Library).

Estudillo's Map. A sketch map of exploration in the San Joaquin Valley in 1819 from Mission San Juan Bautista to the Merced River and southward to Buena Vista Lake, by José María Estudillo; reproduced in Priestley's *Fages.* Estudillo's diary of his expedition from Monterey to the "rancherias situadas en los tulares" has been translated by A. H. Gayton as *Estudillo among the Yokuts* (University of California Press, 1936).

Etymology. The branch of philology devoted to the study of the origin, derivation, and evolution of words. **Folk Etymology.** The process of changing a strange word or phrase to make it resemble a well-known term. The Yurok Indian expression *quo' san wroi'* has become Squash Ann Creek in popular speech. **Dictionary Etymologist.** A term applied to one who looks up the meaning of an unfamiliar name in a dictionary of the language from which the name seems to have been taken. If he finds the word, he gives the translation and the foreign pronunciation. If he does not find the word, he declares the name to be a "corruption" of a similar word in the dictionary. Through the methods of a dictionary etymologist, Chiles Valley, named for the well-known pioneer Joseph R. Chiles, is interpreted as 'Red Pepper Valley' and is pronounced chē'-lās.

Expediente. In Spanish and Mexican times the legal papers dealing with the separation of a parcel of land from the public domain and the granting of it to an individual or institution were known as the *expediente.*

Fages. Pedro Fages, a lieutenant of Catalonian volunteers and one of the leaders of the Portolá expedition of 1769, was an outstanding figure in the early years of Spanish occupation, and from 1782 to 1791 was governor of the Californias. The name "Fages" alone refers to his *A Historical, Political, and Natural Description of California,* translated by Herbert I. Priestley (University of California Press, 1937) from a manuscript dated 1775. The book is of great value for California ethnology, and in it are mentioned numerous place names. Fages does not seem to have bestowed any names himself: his Article VI is headed "From the Real Blanco to a Place Without a Name in 36° 44'." **Fages' Diary.** "The Colorado River Campaign, 1781–1782: Diary of Pedro Fages," edited by Herbert I. Priestley (in both Spanish and English), is in APCH:*P,* III, 133–233. *See* Crespi.

Farley. [Minard H.] *Farley's Map of the Newly Discovered Tramontane Silver Mines in Southern California* . . . (San Francisco, 1861). Wheat, No. 318.

Farquhar. The name indicates that the information was received directly from Francis P.

Farquhar or that it was taken from the field copy of his *Place Names of the High Sierra* (San Francisco: The Sierra Club, 1926).

Fay. Albert H. Fay, *A Glossary of the Mining and Mineral Industry* (Washington, 1920). U.S. Bureau of Mines, Bulletin 95.

Ferrer. Bartolomé Ferrer (or Ferrelo) was second in command of the first known exploring expedition along the coast of California and became commander of the expedition after Cabrillo's death on January 3, 1543. *See* Cabrillo.

Ferrier. William W. Ferrier, *Berkeley, California . . .* (Berkeley, 1933).

Findlay. Alexander G. Findlay, *A Directory for the Navigation of the Pacific Ocean . . .* (London, 1851).

Fisk, O. J. The information was received from O. J. Fisk, of San Bernardino.

Fitch, Narración. Josefa Carillo de Fitch (Mrs. Henry D. Fitch), Narración (MS, Bancroft Library).

Folk Etymology. *See* Etymology.

Font. Padre Pedro Font was the chaplain of the second Anza expedition (1775–1776). His records and maps are sources of great importance for early Spanish place names. His name followed by a page number refers to his "Short Diary," written soon after his return from the expedition and translated and printed in Vol. III of Bolton's edition of *Anza's California Expeditions.* **Compl. Diary** refers to his expanded diary, Vol. IV of the same work. The references to his map are to Davidson's copy of the large map dated Tubutama, 1777. This map includes the result of the explorations of Garcés and is more nearly complete than either the one published in the *Complete Diary* or the one in Coues, *On the Trail of a Spanish Pioneer.*

Foote. Horace S. Foote, ed., *Pen Pictures from the Garden of the World or Santa Clara County, California . . .* (Chicago, 1888).

Forbes' Map. The reference is to the map and the sketches of California harbors in Alexander Forbes, *California: A History of Upper and Lower California . . .* (London, 1839). The map, drawn by John Arrowsmith, is: *The Coasts of Guatemala and Mexico, from Panama to Cape Mendocino . . .* (London, 1839). Inserted on it are a map by Captain Beechey of the *Harbour of San Francisco* and "Sketches" by Captain John Hall of: *Port Bodega; Puerto de S. Diego; Monterrey Harbour; St. Barbara Harbour; Port S. Gabriel, or S. Pedro.*

Forest Service. The reference means that the information was supplied by the U.S. Forest Service. The regional office in San Francisco and many of its supervisors and rangers cooperated splendidly.

Freeland. Lucy Freeland de Angulo has contributed information about several important Miwok names. That credited to "Freeland" with no reference to a printed source was received directly from her. She has published the results of her research in two monographs (*International Journal of American Linguistics,* XIII, and its *Memoir* No. 6).

Frémont. John Charles Frémont (1813–1890) was in California on two of his major explorations (1843–1844 and 1845–1846) and took a prominent part in the acquisition of the province. He is intimately connected with California place naming; not only was he influential in perpetuating many of the older names, but he also bestowed a number of big names, such as Golden Gate, Great Basin, Kern River, Mojave River, Owens Lake. **Expl. Exp.** or **Expedition** refers to his *Report of the Exploring Expedition to the Rocky Mountains . . . 1842, and to Oregon and North California . . . 1843–1844,* first printed as a Senate document in 1845. Unless otherwise stated, the reference is to the edition of 1853. **Geog. Memoir.** *Geographical Memoir upon Upper California . . .* 30th Cong., 1st sess. (1848), Senate Misc. Doc. No. 148. **Memoirs.** *Memoirs of My Life . . .* (Chicago and New York, 1887), Vol. I. Only one volume was published. **Frémont-Preuss Maps.** The map of 1845 is the map accompanying the *Report* mentioned above. The one of 1848, although entitled *Map of Oregon and Upper California,* includes all United States territory west of El Paso del Norte, Pikes Peak, and Fort Laramie. It was made by Charles Preuss from Frémont's surveys and from other authorities.

French. Dr. Darwin French led a party of fifteen in May, 1860, into Death Valley in search of the "lost" Gunsight Mine. They did not find the mine but left a number of place names.

Frickstad. *A Century of California Post Offices, 1848 to 1954,* compiled by Walter N. Frickstad (Oakland: Philatelic Research Society, 1955). A valuable contribution to the history and nomenclature of the State.

Gannett. Henry Gannett, *The Origin of Certain Place Names in the United States* (2d ed.; Washington, 1905). U.S. Geological Survey, Bulletin 258. *American Names: A Guide to the Origin of Place Names in the United States* (Washington: Public Affairs Press,

1947) is a literal reprint of this book, which contains too many inaccuracies (together with some good information) to be called a "guide."

Garcés. Padre Francisco Garcés came to California with the Anza expedition in 1774 and made important explorations in southern California. His accounts of his 1774 explorations are in Vol. II of Bolton's *Anza's California Expeditions*, pp. 307–392. Garcés was in California again in 1775–1776, starting with the Anza expedition but taking a different route after reaching Yuma. His account of this expedtion is in Coues, *Trail*.

Generic Name. The names of most physical features consist of a specific element and a generic element. The specific element is the actual name given: Diablo, Pit, Yosemite, etc. The generic element designates the feature: Mountain, River, National Park, etc. In the names of communities the generic parts, like burg, town, ville, are no longer considered separate elements.

Geographic, Geographical. An attempt has been made in this book to distinguish between the two terms by using the shorter form when referring to a natural feature, hence "geographic feature," "geographic landmark," and the term "geographical" when referring to the science of geography, hence "geographical name," "in a geographical sense." The Geographic Board is an exception to this rule.

Geographical Report. *See* Wheeler Survey.

Geographical Survey. *See* Wheeler Survey.

Geographic Board. A U.S. Board on Geographic Names was established on December 23, 1891, as a bureau of the Department of the Interior, for the purpose of making uniform the usage and spelling of geographical names. In 1906 its powers were extended to include the approval of new names submitted to the Board. For a number of years the bureau was known as the Geographic Board. Since the method of publishing decisions has changed from time to time, references will be found to reports and to decisions, with or without the date of publication.

Geological Survey. Unless otherwise stated, all references are to the U.S. Geological Survey, established as an office under the Department of the Interior, March 3, 1879. *See* Atlas Sheet; Quadrangle; Topographical Atlas.

Gibbes' Map. Charles Drayton Gibbes, *New Map of California* (Stockton, 1852), and Gibbes' *Map of the Southern Mines* are in J. H. Carson, *Early Recollection of the Mines*

(Stockton, 1852). Both maps are important sources for the names of mining settlements.

Gibbs. George Gibbs accompanied Colonel Redick McKee, U.S. Indian agent, on his expedition through northwestern California in the summer and fall of 1851. His "Journal" of this expedition and his "Observations on . . . Indian Dialects of Northern California" were published in Schoolcraft, III, 99 ff. and 420 ff. Both sources are important for place names in the territory traversed. Gibbs' map is in the Indian Office in Washington, D.C. A part of it was reproduced in Ernest de Massey, *A Frenchman in the Gold Rush* (San Francisco: California Historical Society, 1927). *See* Chinook Jargon; Schoolcraft.

Gifford. The name indicates that the information was received from Edward W. Gifford, professor of anthropology at the University of California.

Gill. R. Bayley Gill, of Cima, supplied information about names in the Ivanpah district.

Goddard. Pliny Earle Goddard's "Life and Culture of the Hupa" is in *AAE*, I, 1–88; his "Kato Texts," *ibid.*, V, 65–238.

Goddard's Map. George H. Goddard, *Britton and Rey's Map of the State of California* . . . (3d ed.; San Francisco, 1860). This is sometimes referred to as "Goddard (1860)." Goddard, a native of England, was one of the great engineers of the 1850's who played an important role in the geographical delineation of the State. His map, first published in 1857, is the first reliable map of California which made use of all the official and private surveys executed in the first decade of American occupation.

Goethe. C. M. Goethe, *Sierran Cabin . . . from Skyscraper . . .* (Sacramento, 1943).

Gonzáles. José González Cabrera Bueno compiled a *Navegacion especulativa, y practica* . . . (Manila, 1734), principally for the use of the Philippine galleons. The part relating to the California coast is based on the *derrotero* of the Vizcaíno expedition of 1602–1603 made by Francisco de Bolaños and Padre Antonio de la Ascensión. Bolaños had sailed along the coast with Rodríguez Cermeño in 1595. (*See* San Francisco in text.) The Portolá expedition had with them a copy of the *Navegacion*.

Great Register. A list of the names of registered voters of a county, compiled by the county clerk. The older registers often give not only the place of residence of the voter, but also his age, country or state of nativity, date of naturalization, occupation, and date of registration.

Gregg Party. A party of prospectors led by Dr. Josiah Gregg named many of the rivers between Humboldt and San Francisco bays in the winter of 1849–1850. Gregg, an outstanding explorer of western America, died from exposure at the end of the journey. *See* Wood, *Discovery*.

Grizzly Bear. A monthly magazine, published in Los Angeles since 1907 as the official organ of the Native Sons and Native Daughters of the Golden West.

Guerra Docs. Documentos para la historia de California; coleccion del Señor Capitan . . . José de la Guerra y Noriega (7 vols.; transcripts, Bancroft Library).

Guinn, J. M. Guinn, "Some California Place Names," in HSSC:*Q*, VII, 39 ff.

Hanks' Report. Henry G Hanks, "Report on the Borax Deposits of California and Nevada," published in *Third Annual Report of the State Mineralogist* (1883); and "Catalogue and Description of the Minerals of California . . . ," published in *Fourth Annual Report . . .* (1884).

Hanna. Phil Townsend Hanna, *The Dictionary of California Land Names* (Los Angeles: The Automobile Club of Southern California, 1946). Using the same sources accounts for the similarity of a number of entries in Mr. Hanna's book and this Dictionary.

Harrington. The reference indicates that the information was received from John P. Harrington, senior ethnologist of the Smithsonian Institution.

Hayes, C & R. Documentos para la Historia de California, 1826–1850. Originals, copies, and extracts from the Archives of San Diego County collected by Benjamin Hayes. C & R refers to the section called Commerce and Revenue. **Hayes Docs.** Benjamin Hayes, Documents for the History of California (transcripts, Bancroft Library). **Hayes, Mis.** Benjamin Hayes, Missions of Alta California (2 vols.; MSS, clippings, etc., Bancroft Library).

Headlight. *See* Brown, T. P.

Heintzelman. General Samuel P. Heintzelman, in 1862 commander of the Third Corps of the Union army in the Peninsula campaign, was (as a major) military commander in southern California from 1850 to 1855, then for several years commander and sub-Indian agent on the Klamath River. His name with the date 1853 refers to his report on the Yuma Indians (34th Cong., 3d sess., House Ex. Doc. No. 76); with the date 1858 it refers to his

report on the Klamath River Indians (35th Cong., 2d sess., House Ex. Doc. No. 2).

Helm Index. Mary H. Helm, "Index to Topographic Quadrangles of California," with an introduction by Olaf P. Jenkins, in *California Journal of Mines and Geology*, XLI (October, 1945), 251–360.

Henshaw. H. W. Henshaw, a member of the Bureau of American Ethnology, collected much California Indian linguistic material intermittently between 1884 and 1893. His extensive word and phrase lists of the Chumash and the Costanoan languages, edited by R. F. Heizer, are published in *Anthropological Records*, XV: 2 (University of California Press, 1955).

Hezeta. The reference is to the journey of the *Santiago*, commanded by Bruno de Hezeta, in 1775. Wagner, chapter xxv.

Hine. Robert V. Hine, *California's Utopian Colonies* (The Huntington Library, 1953).

Historic Landmarks. The movement to preserve landmarks of historical importance or interest was inaugurated originally by the Native Sons of the Golden West. Since 1931 more than four hundred of these landmarks have been registered and placed under the protection of the State Department of Natural Resources. The names of such of these landmarks as preserve otherwise obsolete names of geographic features have been included in this Dictionary. Cf. the *Reports on Registered Landmarks* issued at irregular intervals by the State Department of Natural Resources and the State Park Commission in coöperation with the California State Chamber of Commerce.

Hittell. Theodore H. Hittell, *History of California* (4 vols.; San Francisco, 1897–1898).

Hittell, Yosemite. John S. Hittell, *Yosemite: Its Wonders and Its Beauties* (San Francisco, 1868). The same author has a chapter on place names in his excellent book, *The Resources of California*.

Hodge. Frederick W. Hodge, ed., *Handbook of American Indians* (Smithsonian Institution, Bureau of American Ethnology, Bulletin 30, Washington, 1907–1910; citations in text are to the two-volume edition, Washington, 1912). The monumental authority on Indians north of Mexico.

Hoffmann. Charles F. Hoffmann, a native of Frankfurt am Main, Germany, was topographer and cartographer of the State Geological (Whitney) Survey throughout its existence (1860–1874). Hoffmann was one of the pioneers of modern topography and is responsible for the adoption of the contour line for the topographical atlas of the United States made by the U.S. Geological Survey. **Hoffmann's Map.** *Topographical Map of Central California together with a part of Nevada, 1873.* The most detailed and most reliable map of this part of the State until the issuance of the atlas sheets by the U.S. Geological Survey. Unfortunately the Whitney Survey was discontinued before the map was completed; the northwest section exists only as a sketch. **Map of the Bay Region.** *Map of the Region adjacent to the Bay of San Francisco, 1873.* **Hoffmann-Gardner Map.** *Map of a portion of the Sierra Nevada adjacent to the Yosemite Valley* from surveys made by Ch. F. Hoffmann and J. T. Gardner, 1863–1867. The three maps were publications of the Whitney Survey. **Hoffmann's Notes.** Hoffmann's field notes of 1861 are in the possession of his son, Ross Hoffmann. Unfortunately the books containing notes of subsequent years have been misplaced.

Hood's Map. *Map of the United States Territory of Oregon West of the Rocky Mountains . . .* Compiled in the Bureau of Topographical Engineers . . . under the direction of Col. J. J. Abert by Wash[ington] Hood (1838). Wheat, No. 11.

Hoover. Mildred Brooke Hoover, *Historic Spots in California* [Vol. III]: *Counties of the Coast Range* (Stanford University Press, 1937).

Howard. J. D. Howard, of Klamath Falls, Oregon, who made a thorough examination of the lava beds (now a national monument) from 1917 to 1927, supplied valuable information about the names in this region.

HSSC:P. Historical Society of Southern California: *Annual Publication,* published in Los Angeles, 1884–1934. **HSSC:Q.** Historical Society of Southern California: *Quarterly.* This, which began with Vol. XVII in 1935, is a continuation of HSSC:P. The publication is now called *Southern California Quarterly.*

Humboldt. Alexander von Humboldt, the pioneer of modern scientific exploration, has probably been honored in more geographical names in the western United States than any other man of science. Many explorers of the American West considered as a standard the methods of research employed by Humboldt in his epoch-making journey through South America (1797–1802). His essay on the kingdom of New Spain, which included the first reliable account of Upper California published in Europe, was first issued in Stuttgart in 1808. His map of Mexico was published in Paris in 1811.

Hunzicker. Lena B. Hunzicker compiled an index of San Diego County place names, the larger part of which was incorporated in the file of the State Geographic Board. Additional names from this file were received from the San Diego Public Library.

Hutchings. The publications of James M. Hutchings are of some importance as a source of California place names. **Scenes.** *Scenes of Wonder and Curiosity in California* (San Francisco, 1870). **Sierras.** *In the Heart of the Sierras* (Oakland, 1886). His often-mentioned *Illustrated California Magazine* (or *California Magazine*) was published from July, 1856, to June, 1861. *See* Hutchings, Mount, in text.

Hydrography, Hydrographic. The phase of physical geography referring to surface waters.

Indian Report. 33d Cong., spec. sess. (1853), Senate Ex. Doc. No. 4, a lengthy report of the Secretary of the Interior including correspondence from Indian agents and commissioners in California. It is valuable for many Indian and some other early names. **Indian Report** with the year added refers to the annual publication of the Commissioner of Indian Affairs.

Ives. Joseph C. Ives, "Report upon the Colorado River of the West, explored in 1857 and 1858 . . ." (Washington, 1861), 36th Cong., 1st sess., House Ex. Doc. No. 90.

James. George Wharton James, *The Wonders of the Colorado Desert (Southern California) . . .* (2 vols.; Boston: Little, Brown and Company, 1906).

Jayhawker Party. One of the parties of gold seekers who crossed Death Valley in 1849 and who are directly or indirectly responsible for a number of names in the region. The party had been organized in Illinois. *See* John G. Ellenbecker, *The Jayhawkers of Death Valley* (1938); Carl Wheat in HSSC:Q, XXII, 102 ff.

Jepson. Willis Linn Jepson, *The Silva of California* (University of California Press, 1911).

Johnston Report. "Report of the Secretary of the Interior, communicating . . . a Report of the Commissioner of Indian Affairs," 32d Cong., 1st sess., Senate Ex. Doc. No. 61. It includes communications to and from Colonel Adam Johnston, U.S. Indian agent, and others, in which names of Indian tribes and of streams on the east side of the San Joaquin Valley are mentioned.

Kazmarek. F. A. Kazmarek, *Ghost Towns and Relics of '49* (Stockton: Chamber of Commerce, 1936).

Keffer. Frank M. Keffer, *History of San Fernando Valley* ... (Glendale: Stillman Printing Company, 1934).

King. Clarence King, *Mountaineering in the Sierra Nevada* (Boston, 1872). *See* Clarence King, Mount, in text.

Kino. Eusebius Kino, a German Jesuit of Italian ancestry, from 1683 to 1711 an outstanding missionary and explorer, established the first mission in Lower California. The references are to Herbert E. Bolton's edition of *Kino's Historical Memoir of Pimería Alta* ... (2 vols.; Cleveland: Arthur H. Clark Co., 1919).

Kirchhoff. Theodor Kirchhoff, *Californische Kulturbilder* (Cassel, 1886). A very informative account of California in the 1880's by a German resident of San Francisco.

Knave, The. The reference is to "The Knave," a page in the Sunday edition of the Oakland *Tribune*, ably conducted for many years by the late Ad Schuster and now by Leonard Verbarg. John Winkley, Henry Mauldin, Rockwell Hunt, Alex Rosborough, and others have contributed to it interesting material on place names.

Kneiss. Gilbert H. Kneiss, *Bonanza Railroads* (Stanford University Press, 1944).

Knowland. Joseph R. Knowland, *California: A Landmark History* ... (Oakland: Tribune Press, 1941).

Knox, Alexander. *Glossary of Geographical and Topographical Terms* (London, 1904).

Kohl. Johann G. Kohl (1808–1878), a German geographer, was the pioneer of North American cartographical history. Unfortunately, his great cartographical work remained unfinished. Part of the text was published in the *Reports* of the Coast Survey for 1857 and 1885. His great collection is in the Library of Congress: Justin Winsor, *The Kohl Collection of Maps Relating to America* (Cambridge, 1886). *See* Coast Survey *Report*, 1855, p. 374. In official reports after 1855 the Coast Survey used the orthography of the names of coastal features established by Kohl. Some of Kohl's misspellings were not corrected until about 1900.

Kotzebue. Otto von Kotzebue, a son of the once famous German playwright, August von Kotzebue, commanded two Russian exploring expeditions round the world, 1815–1818 and 1823–1826. On both journeys he stayed in San Francisco several weeks, and his accounts, as well as those of his staffs, are sources of some value for place names. The refer-

ences to the second expedition are from *A New Voyage Round the World in the Years 1823, 24, 25, and 26* (2 vols.; London, 1830). *See* Chamisso; Rurik.

Kroeber. A. L. Kroeber has been for many years the foremost authority on California Indians. Unless otherwise stated, the information was either taken from the field copy of "California Place Names of Indian Origin" in *AAE*, Vol. XII, No. 2, or received from Mr. Kroeber directly. **Kroeber's Handbook.** *Handbook of the Indians of California* (Washington, 1925), U.S. Bureau of American Ethnology, Bulletin 78.

Lahainaluna. *Carta esférica de la costa de la Alta California* ... (Lahainaluna, Sandwich Islands: 1839). Wheat, No. 12.

Land Grant. At the time the landed aristocracy of Europe had already entered the last period of its struggle for existence against the new economic forces, California underwent a phase of unadulterated feudalism. From 1775 to the end of the Mexican regime, a class of large landholders was created by separating 666 land units from the public domain and granting these to citizens who had rendered services or who just promised to cultivate the land. Of these grants, 524 were confirmed by the United States courts, of which 517 were patented to the grantees or their legal successors. The date given in connection with a land grant is that of the *concedo* or the day on which the governor signed the concession. The name which was given to the grant had often been in existence long before this date; on the other hand, the name was sometimes applied later. The name of the grantee is given in the entry only if he was important historically or when it was needed to identify the grant. *See* Bowman Index; Diseño; Expediente.

Land Office Report and Map. Annual *Report of the* [U.S.] *Commissioner of the General Land Office*. Public Survey maps of various sections of the United States are frequently appended to the Reports. These maps have been instrumental in fixing the current form or spelling of many local names. The maps referred to are naturally those of the State of California.

Landrum. Elizabeth A. Landrum, Maps of the San Joaquin Valley up to 1860 ... (MS, School of Librarianship, University of California), which includes photostats of thirty-six of the more important maps of the southern half of the State.

Langsdorff. Georg Heinrich von Langsdorff, a

German surgeon and naturalist, accompanied the Russian "imperial inspector," Nikolai P. Rezanof, to San Francisco in April, 1806. An account of his stay there is found in Pt. 2 of his *Voyages and Travels . . . 1803, 1804, 1805, 1806, and 1807* (2 vols.; London, 1813–1814).

Larkin Papers. George P. Hammond, *ed., The Larkin Papers; Personal, Business, and Official Correspondence of Thomas Oliver Larkin, Merchant and United States Consul in California* (10 vols.; Berkeley, University of California Press, 1951-1964).

Las Calaveras. A quarterly published by the Calaveras County Historical Society. Includes articles on place names of the county.

La Pérouse. *A Voyage Round the World . . . 1785, 1786, 1787, and 1788, under the Command of J. F. G. de la Pérouse* (2 vols. and atlas; London, 1798–1799). The original edition, *Voyage autour du monde . . .* was published in Paris in 1797 in 4 vols. and an atlas. The French explorer was in Monterey in September, 1786; in chapters xi and xii he gives an interesting account of California in the early years of Spanish colonization. His maps are of some value as sources for place names.

Lassen. Peter Lassen, a native of Denmark, came to California in 1840 and worked in various places at his trade of blacksmith. In 1844 he was grantee of a land grant in what is now Tehama County. *See* Bosquejo in text. He became the outstanding pioneer of the northeastern section of California, and his memory is preserved in the names of more prominent geographic features than that of any of his fellow pioneers.

Latta. Frank F. Latta, *El Camino Viejo a Los Angeles* (Bakersfield: Kern County Historical Society, 1936).

Lawson. The information was taken from James Lawson's letters to George Davidson.

League. See entry in text.

LeConte. Both Joseph LeConte (1823–1901), a native of Georgia and professor of geology at the University of California from 1869 to 1901, and his son, J. N. LeConte, professor of engineering mechanics at the same university from 1895 to 1937, are intimately connected with place naming in the High Sierra. For a list of their maps consult Farquhar, pp. 123 f. **Journal.** Joseph LeConte, *A Journal of Ramblings through the High Sierra of California,* edited by Francis P. Farquhar (San Francisco: Sierra Club, 1930). **J. N. Le-Conte** given as a reference means that the

information was received from Mr. LeConte directly.

Legis. Recs. Legislative Records, 1822–1846 (4 vols. in 3). *See* Archivo de California.

Leland. The name indicates that the information was received from J. A. C. Leland.

Leon. Nicolas Leon, *Las Castas del Mexico Colonial* (Mexico, 1924).

Luddy. "Reminiscences by Hardscrabble [William Luddy]," Scott Valley *Advance,* August 20, 1900.

McArthur. Lewis A. McArthur, *Oregon Geographic Names* (2d ed.; Portland: Oregon Historical Society, 1944). One of the best regional place-name studies so far published.

McClure. *See* McClure Lake in the text.

McKenney's Directory. *McKenney's Pacific Coast Directory . . .* for 1878; 1880; 1882; 1883–4; 1886 (San Francisco and Oakland).

McNamar. Myrtle McNamar, *Way Back When* (Cottonwood, 1952). About Shasta and Tehama counties.

Maidu. A group of the Penutian Indian family east of the Sacramento from Lassen County to El Dorado County.

Mariposa Battalion. The unit was formed in the spring of 1851 to punish marauding Indians. The battalion discovered Yosemite Valley in March and made a second expedition in May, bestowing many place names.

Marsh, John. John Marsh, a native of Massachusetts and a graduate of Harvard University, acquired Rancho Los Meganos in 1837 and became the foremost pioneer of the Mount Diablo district. Information which he gave to explorers and surveyors led to the fixing of a number of place names.

Marshall. Robert B. Marshall, a native of Virginia, was topographer of the Geological Survey in California from 1891 to 1902, and geographer for California, Oregon, and Nevada from 1905 to 1907. He is responsible for the application of many names, especially in the High Sierra. Cf. Farquhar, p. 114.

Maslin. Prentiss Maslin, "Origin and Meaning of the Names of the Counties of California," *California Blue Book* (1907), pp. 275 ff.

Mauldin. Henry K. Mauldin, historian of Lake County, has published the stories of many place names in the Oakland *Tribune's* "The Knave" and has supplied others directly for this work.

Maule. William M. Maule, *A Contribution to the Geographic and Economic History of the Carson, Walker and Mono Basins* (San Francisco: U.S. Forest Service, 1938). An excellent local study of geography. Additional information was received directly from Mr. Maule.

Mendenhall. *See* WSP.

Menefee. C. A. Menefee, *Historical and Descriptive Sketch Book of Napa, Sonoma, Lake and Mendocino* . . . (Napa City, 1873).

Merriam. Clinton Hart Merriam (1855–1942), the well-known biologist and ethnologist, was for many years chairman of the U.S. Geographic Board. His extensive file of western United States bibliography and of California place names is in the Museum of Vertebrate Zoölogy of the University of California. **Mewan Stock.** "Distribution and Classification of the Mewan Stock of California," *American Anthropologist*, n.s., IX, 338 ff. **Pit River.** *The Classification and Distribution of the Pit River Indian Tribes of California*, Smithsonian Misc. Coll., LXXVIII, No. 3. **Expedition.** "The Death Valley Expedition," Pt. 2 (*North American Fauna* No. 7, Washington: Department of Agriculture, 1893).

Mexican Times. This phrase is used for the period from 1822 to 1846 only when it is necessary to distinguish from Spanish times in a political sense.

Miller, Guy. The information was received from Guy Miller, city historian of Palo Alto.

Miller, Loye. The information was supplied by Loye H. Miller, Professor of Biology, Emeritus, University of California, Los Angeles.

Miller & Lux. The name of this firm is often mentioned in the text, especially in connection with place names in the San Joaquin Valley, where the firm, in the 1880's, owned nearly all land for fifty miles on both sides of the San Joaquin River. Henry Miller and Charles Lux, German-born butchers, formed their famous partnership in 1856. Neither name is commemorated in a major geographic feature.

Mining Bureau Maps. *Geological Map of the State of California*, issued by the California State Mining Bureau. For physical geography and toponymy the most reliable map published between the time of the Whitney Survey and the mapping of California by the Geological Survey. Since 1882 the Mining Bureau has published annual reports under various titles.

Mitchell. Annie Mitchell, secretary of the Tulare County Historical Society, supplied information on names of Tulare County.

Miwok. A group of the Penutian Indian family, whose habitat was in the district between the Sacramento–San Joaquin Delta region and Yosemite. The dialect group in Marin County is known as Coast Miwok. The Southern

Sierra Miwok language has been treated in detail by Sylvia M. Broadbent, and that of the Lake Miwok by Catherine A. Callaghan in volumes 38 and 39 of the *UCPL*. The vocabularies of both works contain a number of place names.

Modoc. *See* Modoc in text.

Mono. *See* Mono in text.

Moraga, Gabriel. Moraga is repeatedly mentioned as the leader of land expeditions which applied a number of important names. He came to California in 1776, became a soldier, and rose to the rank of lieutenant; he died in 1823. His MS Diario de la tercera expedicion (1808) is in the Bancroft Library. Translated and edited by Donald C. Cutter, it was published by Glen Dawson in 1957. For Moraga's 1806 expedition *see* Muñoz.

Morley. The reference indicates that the information was received from S. Griswold Morley, professor of Spanish, University of California.

Mormon Battalion. The organization of a battalion of Mormon volunteers to participate in the Mexican War was one phase of the westward movement of the Latter-day Saints. The Mormon Battalion, like Stevenson's New York Volunteer Regiment, is known in history chiefly because many of its members played an important role in the gold rush and in the early American period of California.

Muir. John Muir (1838–1914), a native of Scotland, was one of the four founders of the Sierra Club and for many years was the best known of California's mountaineers. He has been honored in more California geographical names than any other person, although he himself was very conservative in bestowing names upon places. Unless otherwise stated, the reference is to *My First Summer in the Sierra* (Boston: Houghton Mifflin, 1911).

Muñoz. Padre Pedro Muñoz accompanied Gabriel Moraga on his expedition of 1806. His diary of this expedition is in the Archivo de la Mision de Santa Barbara, IV, 1–47.

Myrick. David F. Myrick of San Francisco has supplied information about a number of names not listed in the original edition.

Names. *Journal of the American Name Society*. A quarterly publication, founded by Erwin G. Gudde in 1952.

Narváez' Plano. *Plano del territorio de la alta California. . . . 1830*, by José María Narváez. Probably the most valuable of the Mexican maps, especially for the missions and other settlements. It is the first map to show the three mountain ranges, fairly correctly but not labeled. The hydrography is mainly imaginary. This MS map is reproduced in Wheat (No. 6).

Nevada Boundary Survey. An unofficial report of the Eastern Boundary Commission, to establish the California-Nevada line, was published in installments in the Sacramento *Daily Union*, in June and July, 1861. The date in connection with the reference refers to the issue of the *Union*.

New Helvetia Diary. The record of events kept at Sutter's Fort by Sutter and his clerks from September 9, 1845, to May 25, 1848. Published in 1939 by the Grabhorn Press, San Francisco, for the Society of California Pioneers.

Newmark. Harris Newmark, *Sixty Years in Southern California* (New York: Knickerbocker Press, 1916; new edition, 1926). The reminiscences of a man who lived through the development of Los Angeles from a sprawling village to a great metropolis.

Nordenskiöld. A. E. Nordenskiöld, *Facsimile-Atlas to the Early History of Cartography* (Stockholm, 1889). This work of the great Swedish explorer contains several maps valuable for early California nomenclature.

Official Railway Map. *See* Railroad Maps.

OHQ. *Oregon Historical Quarterly,* published by the Oregon Historical Society since 1900.

Old Block. *See* Delano.

O'Neal. Lulu Rasmussen O'Neal, *A Peculiar Piece of Desert: The History of California's Morongo Basin* (Los Angeles: Westernlore Press, 1957).

O'Neill. The reference means that the information was received from O. H. O'Neill. When followed by a page number, the reference is to the *History of Santa Barbara County* (Santa Barbara, 1939), of which he was the editor in chief.

Ord. Lieutenant E. O. C. Ord's reports on his reconnaissance in southern California in the fall of 1849 are found in 31st Cong., 1st sess., Senate Ex. Doc. No. 47, Pt. 1, pp. 119 ff. His *Topographical Sketch of the Los Angeles Plains & Vicinity, August, 1849,* is attached to the same document. **Ord's Map.** *Topographical Sketch of the Gold & Quicksilver District of California, July 25th, 1848,* which accompanied the President's Message to Congress, 30th Cong., 2d Sess., House Ex. Doc. No. 1. (Wheat, No. 54.)

Orography, Orographic. The phase of physical geography referring to mountains and hills.

Pac. R.R. Reports. *Reports of Explorations and Surveys to Ascertain the Most Practi-*

cable and Economical Route for a Railroad from the Mississippi River to the Pacific Ocean Made under the Direction of the Secretary of War in 1853–4 (12 vols. in 13; Washington, 1855–1869). The sections of interest for California's nomenclature are found chiefly in Vols. II, III, V, and XI (Pt. 2 of which contains many maps). The Survey not only named many features in the territory covered but also rescued a number of local Indian place names. *See* Beckwith; Blake; Parke-Custer; Whipple; Williamson.

Paden-Schlichtmann. *The Big Oak Flat Road,* by Irene D. Paden and Margaret E. Schlichtmann (San Francisco: Privately printed, 1955).

Paiute. *See* Piute in text.

Palmer. T. S. Palmer, *Place Names of the Death Valley Region in California and Nevada* (Washington: Privately printed, 1948). *See* Palmer in text.

Palou. Padre Francisco Palou was one of the outstanding missionaries and the author of several important works relating to early California history. When his name alone is cited the reference is to *Historical Memoirs of New California, by Fray Francisco Palou* edited by Herbert E. Bolton (4 vols.; University of California Press, 1926). **Vida . . . Serra.** *Relacion historica de la vida del venerable Padre Fray Junípero Serra* (Mexico, 1787). **Diary** in Bolton, *Anza,* II, 393 ff.

Pantoja y Arriaga. Juan Pantoja y Arriaga's journal of 1782 is in Archivo General de Mexico, California, Vol. 35 (typewritten copy in California Historical Society). Pantoja was pilot of the *Princesa* in the expedition of Estéban José Martínez, which brought supplies from San Blas to the presidios of California in 1782. He made several maps. One of his maps of San Diego harbor is in *CHSQ,* IX, No. 1 (March, 1930).

Paraje. *See* entry in text.

Parke. Lieutenant John G. Parke, of the Topographical Engineers, assisted Lieutenant Williamson in his surveys in California for a railroad from the Mississippi River to the Pacific Ocean. (*See* Williamson.) His reports concerning California are in Vol. VII of the Pacific Railroad *Reports.* **Parke-Custer Map.** *From San Francisco Bay to the Plains of Los Angeles from Explorations and Surveys Made . . . by Lieut. John G. Parke . . . 1854 & 55,* constructed and drawn by H. Custer. It is in Vol. XI, Pt. 2, of the Pacific Railroad *Reports.*

Parker. Horace Parker, *Anza–Borrego Desert Guide Book* (Palm Desert: Desert Magazine

Press; 1957).

Parsons. Mary E. Parsons, *The Wild Flowers of California* ... (San Francisco: Cunningham, Curtis, & Welch, 1909).

Pattie. James O. Pattie was in California with a group of trappers in 1828–1829 and published his *Personal Narrative* in Cincinnati, 1833. Cf. Bancroft, III, 162 ff.

Peñafiel. Antonio Peñafiel, *Nomenclatura geográfica de México: Etimologías de los nombres de lugar correspondientes a los principales idiomas que se hablan en la república* (3 vols. in 1; Mexico, 1897).

Pico Docs. Documentos para la historia de California: papeles originales, 1781–1850, ... collecion formado por el Mayor Don José Ramon Pico (3 vols.; MSS, Bancroft Library).

Piña, Expedicion. The reference is to the report of an expedition to the "Valle de San José" in May, 1829, by Joaquín Piña. (Original MS, Bancroft Library.)

Pinart. The French scientist Alphonse Pinart recorded, in 1878, Costanoan, Chumash, and Esselen words and phrases from surviving natives at several former missions. The vocabularies, edited by R. F. Heizer, are published in *Anthropological Records*, XV:1 (University of California Press, 1952).

Piute. *See* Piute in text.

Plano ... de San Jose. Plano topographico de la Mision de San Jose. An extraordinary little map, showing the region east of San Francisco Bay as far as the site of Stockton. It was probably made in the late 1820's, although it is dated 1824, by another hand. (MS, Bancroft Library.)

Pomo. *See* Pomo in text.

Portolá. Gaspar de Portolá, a Catalonian and captain of dragoons, in 1769 led the expedition from Old (*Baja*) California which was to found the first Spanish settlement in what is now the State of California. A detachment of this first land expedition discovered San Francisco Bay and bestowed many place names along the route, several of which are still in use. Unless otherwise indicated, the reference is to the "Diary of Gaspar de Portolá during the California Expedition of 1769–1770," edited by Donald Eugene Smith and Frederick J. Teggart (in both Spanish and English), in APCH:P, I, 31–89. *See* Costansó; Crespi; Eldredge; Fages; Vila.

Postal Guide. The dates of the establishment and naming of post offices are taken from the United States Official Postal Guide, published since 1878 by the Post Office Department. In this Dictionary, dates of post offices established before 1878 were taken from guides published by commercial firms, or from lists published in newspapers and almanacs. For some post offices we could give the exact date of their establishment; these dates were supplied by the Post Office Department years ago, when federal offices were less overworked. All the dates can now be found in Frickstad, *A Century of California Post Offices*. See Frickstad.

Powers. Stephen Powers, *Tribes of California* (Washington: Department of the Interior, 1877). Valuable for Indian nomenclature, and, until the publication of Kroeber's *Handbook of the Indians of California,* the best authority on California Indians.

Preuss. Charles Preuss, a native of Germany, was Frémont's topographer on the first two expeditions. For his maps *see* Frémont.

Prov. Recs. Provincial Records, 1775–1822 (12 vols. in 5). *See* Archivo de California.

Pseudo-Spanish. The term is used to describe the "Spanish" which is used in place naming by Americans without regard to Spanish grammar or usage. The term does not imply censure or criticism. Since there are no standards governing the application of names, a person has a perfect right to apply a name that may be ungrammatical in form but pleasing in sound.

PSP. Provincial State Papers, 1767–1822 (22 vols. in 14). *See* Archivo de California.

PSP Ben. Provincial State Papers, Benicia (2 "volumes": Part 1 of Archives of California, Miscellany).

PSP. Ben. Mil. Provincial State Papers, Benicia, Military, 1767–1822 (52 vols. in 3). *See* DSP Ben. Mil.; Archivo de California.

PSP, Pres. Provincial State Papers, Presidios (2 vols. in 1; transcripts, Bancroft Library). *See* Archivo de California.

Quadrangle. The Geological Survey, in preparing the topographical atlas, has divided the surface of the United States into squares, called quadrangles. The atlas sheet covering such a square is sometimes also called a quadrangle. For a detailed listing and discussion of the California quadrangles, consult the Helm Index.

Railroad Maps. The reference is to the maps attached to the annual reports of the principal railroad companies, particularly the Southern Pacific and the Santa Fe. **Official Railway Map** is the map formerly published by the state railroad commissioners of California.

Ramey. Earl Ramey, *The Beginnings of Marys-*

ville (San Francisco: California Historical Society, 1936).

Rancho. *See* entry in the text.

Reading's Map. A manuscript map of Sacramento Valley made in 1849 from actual observations by P. B. Reading. Original in State Library. Reproduced in Boggs, opposite p. 24. *See* Reading in text.

Registro. Registro de Sitios, Fierros y Señales . . . (Register of places, branding irons, and [ear] marks [used in Alta California]) is Pt. 2 of Archives of California, Miscellany.

Reid. Hiram A. Reid, *History of Pasadena* . . . (Pasadena, 1895). One of the few local histories in which place names are properly treated.

Rensch-Hoover. *Historic Spots in California.* This important reference work, compiled by Hero E. Rensch, Ethel G. Rensch, and Mildred Brook Hoover, was originally published by Stanford University Press in three separate volumes: *The Southern Counties* (1932) ; *Valley and Sierra Counties* (1933) ; *Counties of the Coast Range* (1937). A revised edition in one volume, edited by Ruth Teiser, appeared in 1948; and a third revision, edited by William N. Abeloe, was published in 1966. The citations in this dictionary refer to the original volumes.

Rep. Sur. Gen. *Annual* [sometimes *Biennial,* or *Statistical*] *Report of the Surveyor-General of the State of California,* published by the State. The early reports, especially that of 1856, are sources of value for names in certain sections of the State.

Ringgold. Lieutenant-Commandant Cadwalader Ringgold was captain of the *Porpoise,* of the Wilkes expedition. In August and September, 1841, he was in command of a detachment which explored the Sacramento Valley. Sutter and Marsh supplied him with the names of a number of important places (American, Feather, Cosumnes, Mokelumne rivers, Mount Diablo, etc.), which then became definitely established. The charts referred to are in *A Series of Charts, with Sailing Directions* . . . , published in Washington in 1851. These charts, based on Ringgold's surveys of 1850, are important sources for geographical names of the San Francisco Bay district. The General Chart is *General Chart Embracing Surveys of* [various waters inland from the Golden Gate as far as Sacramento and Stockton].

Ritchie. Robert Welles Ritchie, *The Hell-Roarin' Forty-Niners* (New York: J. H. Sears, 1928).

Robelo. Cecilio A. Robelo, *Diccionario de Aztequismos* . . . (Cuernavaca, Mexico, 1904). The standard work of its kind.

Robinson. The name without initials refers to Douglas Robinson, who prepared a valuable compilation of names in Inyo National Forest, a typewritten copy of which was placed at our disposal by the U.S. Forest Service.

Robinson, W. W. *Ranchos Become Cities* (Pasadena: San Pasqual Press, 1939).

Rockwell. The reference is to names used by John Rockwell, of the Coast Survey, in his reports.

Rodriguez, Sebastian. Two diaries, April 2 to May 6, and May 26 to June 22, 1826, record expeditions to capture runaway Indians from San Miguel and San Juan Bautista. MSS, Bancroft Library, Cowan Collection.

Rodríguez Cermeño. Sebastián Rodríguez Cermeño, a pilot sent out by the viceroy of New Spain, made a reconnaissance along the coast in 1595 as far north as 42° in the interest of the Philippine galleons, which frequently came to grief in returning from Manila to Acapulco.

Rogers. Fred Blackburn Rogers, *Montgomery and the Portsmouth* (San Francisco: J. Howell, 1958). Where the name is given alone, the information was supplied by Colonel Rogers directly.

Rowntree. Lester Rowntree, *Flowering Shrubs of California* (Stanford University Press, 1939).

Rurik. August C. Mahr, ed., *The Visit of the "Rurik" to San Francisco in 1816* (Stanford University Press, 1932). The book presents in convenient form translations of extracts from the reports and diaries of the members of the first Kotzebue expedition, which was in San Francisco Bay from October 2 to November 1, 1816. *See* Chamisso; Kotzebue.

Russell. Carl Parcher Russell, *One Hundred Years in Yosemite* . . . (University of California Press, 1947).

Sanchez. Nellie van de Grift Sanchez, *Spanish and Indian Place Names of California* (San Francisco: Robertson, 1914; third ed., 1930). Some good information behind a thick veil of sentimentality.

San Diego Arch. *See* Hayes, C & R.

Santa Fe. The reference is to "History of the Santa Fe Coast Lines," a compilation by the Atchison, Topeka & Santa Fe Railway system, a typewritten copy of which was placed at my disposal through the kindness of Lee Lyles and E. G. Ryder.

Santamaría. Francisco J. Santamaría, *Diccio-*

nario General de Americanismos (3 vols.; Mexico: Pedro Robredo, 1942).

SCB. The *Sierra Club Bulletin,* published since 1893 in San Francisco.

Schaeffer. L. M. Schaeffer, *Sketches of Travel in South America, Mexico, California* (New York, 1860).

Schoolcraft. Henry R. Schoolcraft, *Archives of Aboriginal Knowledge* (6 vols.; Philadelphia, 1860). Vol. III of this imposing work contains George Gibbs' "Journal" and "Observations" and other articles with valuable information on Indian place names in California. *See* Gibbs.

Schrader. The information was received from George Schrader, of Shasta National Forest.

Schulz. *Stories of Lassen's Place Names,* by Paul E. Schulz (Mineral, Calif.: Loomis Museum Association, 1949). A satisfactory regional study done "in the field."

Scott, Reva. *See* Brannan.

SCP:P. Society of California Pioneers, *Publication,* published annually, in San Francisco, since 1941. **SCP:Q.** *Quarterly* of the Society of California Pioneers, published from 1924 to 1933, in San Francisco.

Serra. *See* Junipero Serra Peak in text.

Shafer. "The Pronunciation of Spanish Place Names in California," *American Speech,* December, 1942. A list of the current pronunciation of 165 names.

Shastan. *See* Shasta in text.

Sherman. H. L. Sherman, comp., *A History of Newport Beach* (Los Angeles, 1931). An excellent monograph on the development of a modern California community.

Shoshonean. *See* Shoshone in text.

Simpson. Sir George Simpson, *Narrative of a Journey round the World . . . 1841 and 1842* (2 vols.; London, 1847).

Sitio. *See* entry in the text.

Smith, Jedediah. Smith was leader, in 1826, of the first party of white men to enter California after crossing the deserts west of the Rocky Mountains, and in 1827 was the first to cross the Sierra Nevada, which he did from west to east. He gave names to many features in the State, particularly on his second trip in 1827–1828, none of which seem to have survived. However, the name of the great trail blazer is commemorated in Smith River. **Smith, Travels.** *See* Sullivan.

Smith, Wallace. *Garden of the Sun* (Los Angeles: Lymanhouse, 3rd ed., 1956).

Solomons. Theodore S. Solomons, born in 1870 in San Francisco, was an explorer of the High Sierra and a man of many accomplishments.

In the 1890's he named the peaks of the Evolution Group and numerous other features in the Sierra Nevada.

Southern California Quarterly. *See* HSSC:P.

Southern Pacific. Information about railroad stations was received from the office of the Southern Pacific Company in San Francisco.

Spanish Times. The phrase is used in the book to designate the period from 1769 to 1846, when Spanish was the official language of what is now the State of California. When used in a political sense, it designates the period from 1769 to 1822, before California became a Mexican province.

Sparkman. Philip S. Sparkman, "The Culture of the Luiseño Indians" (*AAE*, VIII, 187–234).

SP Ben. Misc. State Papers, Benicia, Miscellaneous, 1773–1829 (Pt. 4 of Archives of California, Miscellany).

Specific Name. *See* Generic Name.

SP Mis. State Papers, Missions, 1785–1846 (11 vols. in 2.; transcripts, Bancroft Library).

SP Mis. & C. State Papers, Missions and Colonization, 1787–1845 (2 vols.). *See* Archivo de California.

SP Sac. State Papers, Sacramento, 1770–1845 (19 vols. in 3). *See* Archivo de California.

Stanger. F. M. Stanger, *Peninsula Community Book* (San Mateo: A. H. Cawston, 1947).

State Library. The reference indicates that the item was taken from the nomenclature file of the California State Library in Sacramento.

State Surveyor General. *See* Surveyor General.

Statutes. The Statutes of California published by the State since 1850 contain many references to place names, including the official naming of places by act of the legislature.

Steger. Gertrude A. Steger, *Place Names of Shasta County* (Redding, 1945). One of the few satisfactory regional studies in California. The reference indicates that the information was taken from this book or was supplied by Mrs. Steger directly. A revised edition of her book was edited by Helen H. Jones (Glendale: La Siesta Press, 1966).

Stephens-Murphy-Townsend Party. *See* Stevens Murphy-Townsend Party.

Stephenson. Terry E. Stephenson, "Names of Places in Orange County," *Orange County History Series,* I (Santa Ana, 1931), 45 f., II (1932), 107 ff. The name Stephenson without a page number indicates that Mr. Stephenson supplied the information to the State Geographic Board.

Stevens-Murphy-Townsend Party. The party was led by Elisha Stevens and consisted of about 50 persons. They came to California in 1844 via Fort Hall and Humboldt River and were the first party to bring wagons across the Sierra Nevada to Sutters Fort.

Stevenson's Volunteers. The regiment of New York Volunteers under the command of Jonathan D. Stevenson came round the Horn to California, arriving in March and April, 1847. It was too late to participate in military operations, but many of its members became outstanding pioneers, and their names are frequently mentioned in this book.

Stewart. The name Stewart followed by a page number refers to George R. Stewart, *Names on the Land* (New York: Random House, 1945). The name alone indicates that the information was received from Professor Stewart directly.

Still. Elmer G. Still, "Livermore History Highlights," Livermore *Herald*, October and November, 1936. Excellent sketches on place names by the city clerk of Livermore.

Sullivan. Maurice S. Sullivan, *The Travels of Jedediah Smith* ... (Santa Ana: The Fine Arts Press, 1934). This contains a transcript of Smith's journal of his second trip to California (1827) and reproduces David H. Burr's map of 1839 which shows Smith's routes.

Surveyor General. The chief geodetic officer of the State, as well as the surveyor sent by the federal government in connection with land-grant cases and the public surveys, bore this title in California after 1851. If preceded by "U.S." the reference is to the federal officer, whose reports were published in the *Report of the Commissioner of the General Land Office;* otherwise the reference is to the *Annual Report* of the state officer, published as a document of the State Assembly. The report of the State officer, particularly for the year 1855, published in 1856, contains valuable information about place names.

Sutter. John A. Sutter (1803–1880), born in Kandern, Germany, of Swiss lineage, was the first settler in the Sacramento Valley, in 1839. In the years before the discovery of gold he was perhaps the most important and most colorful character in California. He applied a number of names and suggested others to Emmons and Ringgold. The references are to the Reminiscences dictated by Sutter to Bancroft in 1876 (MS, Bancroft Library). *See* New Helvetia Diary.

Tanner. H. S. Tanner, *A Map of the United States of Mexico* ... (3d edition, 1846). Wheat, No. 32. A fair map, based on Wilkes' and Frémont's reports.

Tassin. J. B. Tassin, *A Newly Constructed ... Map of the State of California* (San Francisco, 1851). Wheat, No. 208.

Tautology, Tautological. A philological expression for the repetition of the same term in a different form or in a different language. Thus: Picacho Peak [Imperial] is literally 'Peak Peak,' since *picacho* is a Spanish word for 'peak.'

Taylor. "The Indianology of California," published by Alexander S. Taylor in four series in the *California Farmer and Journal of Useful Sciences,* between February 22, 1860, and October 30, 1863.

Taylor, Bayard. Unless otherwise stated, the reference is to the 1855 edition of Taylor's *El Dorado, or Adventures in the Path of Empire.*

Tinkham. George H. Tinkham, "From the Pages of Time—20 Years Ago," Stockton *Daily Record,* January 28 to April 6, 1935.

Topographical Atlas. The preparation of a topographical atlas of the United States is one of the major activities of the Geological Survey. *See* Atlas Sheet; Helm Index; Quadrangle.

Toponymy. The term designates the geographical names of a certain region or of a certain language.

Tout. Otis B. Tout, *The First Thirty Years ... History of Imperial Valley* ... (San Diego, 1931).

Towendolly. The reference is to Grant Towendolly, folklorist and etymologist of the Wintu Indians. His information on place names of the Shasta region was communicated through the courtesy of George Schrader and Gertrude Steger.

Township. *See* entry in the text.

Trask's Map and **Topogr. Map** refer to *Map of the State of California* and *Topographical Map of the Mineral Districts of California* ..., both published in 1853, and both reproduced in Wheat (Nos. 246, 247). **Trask, Report** refers to *Report on the Geology* ... by Dr. John B. Trask. California State Assembly Document No. 9, 1854, and Senate Document No. 14, 1855. Trask was a member of the Mexican Boundary Survey and the first geologist of the State of California.

Triangulation. A surveyor's term for the process of determining the triangles into which any portion of the surface of the earth is divided in trigonometrical survey.

Tyson. Philip T. Tyson, *Geology and Industrial Resources of California ... Including the Reports of Lieuts. Talbot, Ord, Derby and*

Williamson, of Their Explorations in California and Oregon (Baltimore, 1851). This, the first scientific report after the discovery of gold, based on personal investigations in 1849, was first published in 31st Cong., 1st sess. (1850), Senate Ex. Doc. No. 47. Among the maps accompanying it are Tyson's *Geological Reconnoissances in California* (cited in text as Tyson, 1850) and Williamson's map of Warner's route. *See* Williamson.

UCPH. *University of California Publications in History* (University of California Press, 1911–).

UCPL. *University of California Publications in Linguistics* (University of California Press, 1940–). The many volumes of Indian texts contain a number of Indian place names.

Vallejo. Mariano Guadalupe Vallejo (1807–1890), a native of Monterey, was after 1835 military commander and director of colonization at the northern frontier, and in 1836 was appointed *comandante general* of Alta California. He played an important role in the last decade of Mexican rule and continued his political career after California had become part of the Union. **Vallejo Docs.** Documentos para la historia de California, 1713–1851 (36 vols.; originals, Bancroft Library). **Vallejo's Report.** At the time of the creation of the original counties in the winter of 1849–1850, Vallejo was chairman of the "Select Committee [of the State Senate] on the Derivation and Definition of the Names of the Several Counties of the State of California." His report was first published as an appendix to the Senate Report, 1850, and was republished at irregular intervals in the editions of the *Blue Book*. In the 1958 edition, Vallejo's and Maslin's articles on the names of the counties of California were replaced by a new account written by Erwin G. Gudde.

Vancouver. George Vancouver visited California three times between 1792 and 1794 while in command of a British exploring expedition. He was the first non-Spanish navigator after Francis Drake to bestow names on features along the coast, most of which have survived. The references are to *A Voyage of Discovery to the North Pacific Ocean and round the World* . . . and to the atlas accompanying this report. Unless otherwise stated, the six-volume edition published in London in 1801 has been used.

Venegas. Miguel Venegas, *A Natural and Civil History of California*, translated from the original Spanish (2 vols.; London, 1759). This was first published in Madrid in 1757.

Viader. Transcripts of Padre José Viader's diaries of two expeditions that he made to the San Joaquin River in August and October, 1810, are in Arch. MSB, IV, 73–94.

Vila. "The Portolá Expedition of 1769–1770: Diary of Vicente Vila," edited by Robert S. Rose (in both Spanish and English), is in APCH: *P*, pp. 1–119.

Vischer. Eduard Vischer, "A Trip to the Mining Regions in the Spring of 1859," in *CHSQ*, XI.

Vizcaíno. Sebastian Vizcaíno was in command of a Spanish expedition (1602–1603) sent north by the viceroy of New Spain to find a port where the galleons returning from the Philippines could stop in case of distress. Vizcaíno discovered and named Monterey Bay and recommended it as a suitable port of refuge. The expedition, however, remained the last for a long time, and it was not until 1769 that Portolá was instructed to find the harbor of Monterey. Vizcaíno's voyage is of great interest to the student of place names because the navigator, for the sake of prestige, endowed many important coastal features with names, even those which had been named previously. Since no other navigator followed to replace Vizcaíno's names, most of these have survived to the present day. Father Antonio de la Ascensión's account of Vizcaíno's voyage, translated and edited by H. R. Wagner, is in *CHSQ*, VII, 295 ff., and VIII, 26 ff.

Von Leicht–Craven. *Map of California and Nevada.* Drawn by F. v. Leicht and A. Craven, 1873. The reference is to the edition of 1874, revised by Hoffmann and Craven, and issued by the University of California. It is the official map of the Whitney Survey and was for many years the best map of the entire State.

Von Leicht–Hoffmann. Ferdinand von Leicht and J. D. Hoffmann, *Topographical Map of Lake Tahoe* . . . It bears the date 1874 but was copyrighted in 1873. Bowman's map of 1873 has in general the same nomenclature. The von Leicht–Hoffmann map is obviously based on an original survey, but it is uncertain whether it is responsible for new names which appeared at the same time on the Bowman map. *See* Bowman's map.

Von Schmidt Boundary Map. *Map of the Eastern Boundary of the State of California,* based on A. W. von Schmidt's survey for the U.S. General Land Office, to establish the California-Nevada boundary in 1872–1873.

Von Schmidt's line south of Lake Tahoe has since been corrected. Von Schmidt (1821–1906), a German from the Baltic provinces, was one of the most prominent of the pioneer civil engineers after 1850. Besides the boundary survey his greatest achievements were the initiation of San Francisco's water-supply system and the spectacular removal of Blossom Rock.

Von Schmidt–Gibbs. *Map of California and Nevada,* by Julius von Schmidt and C. C. Gibbs, 1869.

Wagner. Henry Raup Wagner has been for many years the leading authority on the geographical history of the northwest coast of America and has published the results of his research in numerous monographs and articles. Unless otherwise stated, the reference is to his *Cartography of the Northwest Coast of America to the Year 1800* (University of California Press, 1937). This monumental work was published in two volumes, but its pages are numbered consecutively. *No.* refers to the "List of Maps" (pp. 273 ff.); *Pl.,* to the maps reproduced in Vol. I. **Wagner, Saints' Names.** Henry R. Wagner, "Saints' Names in California," HSSC:*Q,* XXIX (1947), 49 ff.

Wappo. A group of Indians around Mount St. Helena, probably belonging to the Yukian family. A vocabulary, including a number of Indian place names, of the almost extinct dialect was published by Jesse O. Sawyer in vol. 43 of *UCPL.*

Warren's Map. *Map of the Territory of the United States from the Mississippi to the Pacific Ocean* [1857], compiled, from explorations and other data, by Lieutenant G. K. Warren, 1854–1857, the general map of the Pacific R.R. *Reports* in Vol. XI, Pt. 2.

Washo. The Washo Indians' habitat was around Lake Tahoe; the name of the lake was taken from their language.

Waterman. T. T. Waterman, "Yurok Geography," *AAE,* XVI, 177 ff. One of the best studies of local Indian names.

Weight. Harold O. Weight, *Lost Mines of Death Valley* (Twentynine Palms: Calico Press, 1953).

Westways. The publication of the Automobile Club of Southern California has repeatedly published articles on California geographical names, thanks to the interest of its late editor, Phil Townsend Hanna.

WF. *Western Folklore,* published by the University of California Press for the California Folklore Society. Formerly *California Folklore Quarterly.*

Wheat. Carl I. Wheat, *The Maps of the California Gold Region, 1848–1857* (San Francisco, 1942). A beautiful product of the Grabhorn Press, containing information and reproductions of maps not easily accessible. Wheat's great historical-cartographical work, *Mapping the Transmississippi West,* 1540-1861, 5 vols., in 6, was published by the San Francisco Institute of Historical Cartography, 1957-1963.

Wheeler Survey. *Report upon United States Geographical Surveys West of the One Hundredth Meridian* (Washington, 1889). The survey was made between 1869 and 1873 by Lieutenant George M. Wheeler, Corps of Engineers, U.S.A. Vol. I, *Geographical Report,* contains valuable information about names in certain sections of the State. Appendix F, "Memoir upon the Voyages . . . ," includes reproductions of old maps with notes by J. G. Kohl. **Wheeler Atlas.** *Topographical Atlas Projected to Illustrate Geographical Explorations and Surveys West of the 100th Meridian* by Geo. M. Wheeler. The work is important for east-central and southern California, sections for which the detailed maps of the Whitney Survey were not published.

Wheelock. Walt Wheelock, owner of La Siesta Press in Glendale, California, supplied information on a large number of names from his intimate knowledge of the geography of the state.

Whipple. Amiel W. Whipple, who, as a major general, died of wounds received in the battle of Chancellorsville, May 4, 1863, was a lieutenant of the U.S. Topographical Engineers engaged in California exploration in 1849 and again in 1853–1854. **Extract.** The reference is to the "Extract from a Journal of an Expedition from San Diego, California to the Rio Colorado . . ." (31st Cong., 2d sess., Senate Ex. Doc. No. 19). **Report.** The reference is to Whipple's report in the Pacific Railroad *Reports,* Vol. III. **Whipple-Ives Map.** Map 2 of the Pacific Railroad *Reports,* Vol. XI: *From the Rio Grande to the Pacific Ocean.* **Whipple's Sketch** is published in 31st Cong., 1st sess., Senate Ex. Doc. No. 34 (1850). Cf. Grant Foreman, ed., *A Pathfinder of the Southwest . . . A. W. Whipple* (University of Oklahoma Press, 1941).

Whitney. Josiah D. Whitney (1819–1896) was director of the State Geological Survey from 1860 to 1874. He and his assistants are responsible for the naming of many physical features, especially in the mountainous regions of the State. *See* Brewer, Hoffmann,

King, in this section, and Whitney, Mount in the text. **Geology, I** refers to the first volume of the report of progress of the Survey published by authority of the Legislature of California, 1865. **Yosemite Book,** with the year, refers to Whitney's *The Yosemite Guide Book.* Cf. Edwin F. Brewster, *Life and Letters of Josiah Dwight Whitney* (Boston: Houghton Mifflin, 1909). For the maps of the Whitney Survey, *see* Hoffmann; von Leicht–Craven. Some of the correspondence and field notes of members of the Survey are deposited in the Bancroft Library.

Wilkes. *Narrative of the United States Exploring Expedition . . . 1838 . . . 1842,* by Charles Wilkes, U.S.N., commander of the expedition (5 vols.; Philadelphia, 1845). The first United States expedition to explore the interior of California, 1841. Its reports and maps are of great value for the history of the geographical delineation of California. The section dealing with California comprises chapters v and vi of Volume V; this volume includes Wilkes' *Map of Upper California . . . 1841.* The map gives a fair picture of the location of rivers of the great valley and of the Sierra Nevada.

Williamson. Lieutenant R. S. Williamson of the U.S. Topographical Engineers was assistant to Captain W. H. Warner in 1849, and in 1853 was a member of the Pacific Railroad Survey. His map of 1849 (Wheat, No. 182), sketching Warner's route, is in Tyson, *Geology;* his *Report* is in Pacific Railroad *Reports,* Vol. V, Pt. 1. His map of 1853 (Wheat, No. 250) and the Williamson-Abbot map (1855) (Wheat, No. 272) are in Vol. XI, Pt. 2, of the Pacific Railroad *Reports.*

Winchell. Lilbourne A. Winchell, a native of Sacramento, was one of the outstanding explorers of the High Sierra after 1879 and is responsible for the names of a number of features.

Windle. Ernest Windle, *Windle's History of Santa Catalina Island . . .* (2d ed.; Avalon, 1940).

Wintun. The Wintun Indians, a large group of the Penutian family, had their habitat along the entire length of Sacramento River from Siskiyou County to Suisun Bay. They are divided into three dialect groups: the Wintu, the Central Wintun, and the Patwin. The Wintun have left a distinct mark in place names, especially in Shasta, Tehama, and Trinity counties. *See* Bally in text.

Wistar. *Autobiography of Isaac Jones Wistar: 1827–1905* (2 vols.; Philadelphia, 1914).

Wolfe. Twenty-six folders of notes and scraps on California history, collected by Linnie Marsh Wolfe. Deposited in the Bancroft Library by R. E. Wolfe in 1947.

Wood, Discovery. L. K. Wood, "Discovery of Humboldt Bay." Society of California Pioneers: *Quarterly,* March, 1932. *See* Gregg party.

Wood's Gazetteer. B. D. Wood, *Gazetteer of Surface Waters of California.* U.S. Geological Survey, Water-Supply Papers 295–297 (Washington, 1912–1913). A list of all lakes and streams, based on the topographical atlas, the Land Office map, and the official county maps.

Work, John. *Fur Brigade to the Bonaventura: John Work's California Expedition, 1832–1833, for the Hudson's Bay Company,* edited by Alice B. Maloney (San Francisco: California Historical Society, 1945).

Workman. Boyle Workman, *The City That Grew* (Los Angeles: Southland Publishing Co., 1936).

WSP. The reference is to the Water-Supply Papers published by the U.S. Geological Survey. No. 224 is Walter C. Mendenhall, *Some Desert Watering Places in Southeastern California and Southwestern Nevada* (Washington, 1909); No. 225, Mendenhall, *Ground Waters of the Indio Region, California Desert* (1909); Nos. 295–297, *see* Wood's Gazetteer; No. 338, Gerald A. Waring, *Springs of California* (1915).

Wyatt. Roscoe D. Wyatt, *Names and Places . . . in San Mateo County* (Redwood City: San Mateo County Title Co., 1936). *See* Arbuckle.

Wynn, Marcia Rittenhouse, *Desert Bonanza* (Glendale: Clark Company, 1963).

Yokuts. The Yokuts Indians inhabited the San Joaquin and Tulare valleys. A number of names in their own territory and in that of their eastern neighbors are of Yokuts origin.

Yuki. A division of the linguistic family of Yukian Indians in Mendocino County.

Yuman. *See* Yuma in text.

Yurok. A division of the widespread linguistic family of Algonkin Indians. Their habitat was in Humboldt and Del Norte counties. Their geography has been carefully studied. *See* Waterman.

Zalvidea. Padre José María Zalvidea's diary of an expedition from Santa Barbara to the interior valley, July 19 to August 14, 1806, is in Arch. MSB, IV, 49–68. Anastasio Cabrillo's account of the same expedition is in the San Francisco *Evening Bulletin,* June 5, 1865.

Key to Pronunciation

Pronunciations indicated are locally current pronunciations of California place names and do not necessarily (in fact, rarely do) agree with the pronunciations in the foreign languages from which these names are derived. The key follows essentially the Guide to Pronunciation in Webster's *Collegiate Dictionary*. A hyphen (-) indicates the separation of a name into syllables. An accent (′) indicates the main stress.

ā, as in āle, fāte, lā′bor, chām′ber
å, as in chå-ot′ic, få-tal′i-ty, du′pli-cåte
â, as in câre, pâr′ent, com-pâre′, âir
ă, as in ădd, ăm, făt, ăc-cept′
ă̇, as in ăc-count′, in′fănt, guid′ănce
ä, as in fär, fä′ther, älms, pälm
à, as in àsk, gràss, dànce, stàff, pàth
a̧, as in so′fa̧, i-de′a̧, a̧-bound′, di′a̧-dem
ē, as in ēve, mēte, se-rēne′, hē′li-om′-e-ter
ẹ, as in hẹre, fẹar, wẹird, deer (dẹr)
ė, as in ė-vent′, dė-pend′, crė-ate′
ĕ, as in ĕnd, ĕx-cuse′, ĕf-face′
ĕ̇, as in si′lĕ̇nt, pru′dĕ̇nce, nov′ĕ̇l
ȩ̄, as in mak′ȩ̄r, pȩ̄r-vert′, in′fȩ̄r-ence
ī, as in īce, sīght, in-spīre′, ī-de′a, bī-ol′o-gy
ĭ, as in ĭll, ad-mĭt′, hab′ĭt, pity (pĭt′ĭ)
ĭ̇, as in char′ĭ̇-ty, pos′sĭ̇-ble, dĭ̇-rect′, A′prĭ̇l
ō, as in ōld, nōte, bōld, he′rō, cal′i-cō
ȯ, as in ȯ-bey′, tȯ-bac′co, a-nat′ȯ-my
ô, as in ôrb, lôrd, ôr-dain′; law (lô), bought (bôt), caught
    (kôt), all (ôl)
ŏ, as in ŏdd, nŏt, tŏr′rid, fŏr′est, pŏs-ter′i-ty
ŏ̇, as in cŏ̇n-ṇect′, ŏ̇c-cur′, co′lŏ̇n, cŏ̇m-bine′
oi, as in oil, nois′y, a-void′
o͞o, as in fo͞od, mo͞on; rude (ro͞od), ru-mor (ro͞o′mer)
o͝o, as in fo͝ot, wo͝ol; put (po͝ot), pull (po͝ol)
ou, as in out, thou, de-vour′
ū, as in cūbe, pūre, dū′ty, hū′man
u̇, as in u̇-nite′, for′-mu̇-late, hu̇-mane′
û, as in ûrn, fûrl, con-cûr′; her (hûr), fern (fûrn)
ŭ, as in ŭp, tŭb, stŭd′y, ŭn′der
ŭ̇, as in cir′cŭ̇s, da′tŭ̇m, cir′cŭ̇m-stance

g (always hard), as in go, guard, ghost
j, as in joke; also for soft g, as in gem
ks for x, as in vex
z, as in zone; also for soft s, as in is
zh for z, as in az′ure; for s as in pleas′ure; for si as in
    vi′sion; for g as in rouge
th, as in thick
t̶h̶, as in thus

[401]

Reference List

Obsolete, alternate, secondary, and variant names mentioned in the text and not otherwise alphabetized are listed below. Names in bold type refer to the entries in the main text under which these names may be found.

Abert, Mount. **Kaweah Peaks**
Acelanus. **Acalanes**
Achedomas. **Algodones**
Agalia. **Eagle Canyon**
Agua Caliente [Napa]. **Calistoga**
Agua Caliente [Riverside].**Palm Springs**
Agua Dulce [San Diego]. **Sweetwater River**
Ahanga, Arroyo de. **Aguanga Valley**
A'hwai. **Ojai**
Alcatraces, Isla de. **Alcatraz Island; Yerba Buena Island**
Algootoon. **Algodones**
Alila. **Earlimart**
Allens Camp. **Caliente**
Almejas, Punta de las. **Mussel; Pedro Point**
Alones, Point. **Abalone**
Alta California. **California**
Alvord [Inyo]. **Zurich**
A-mac-há-vès. **Mojave**
Amargo. **Boron**
Ambre. **Alhambre Valley**
American Camp. **Jamestown**
Anajup. **Anacapa Islands**
Angel Custodio, Punta del. **Pedro Point**
Animas, Rio de las. **Mojave River**
Anna Herman Island. **Paoha Island**
Annaly Valley. **Analy Valley**
Ansares, Llano de los. **Goose Lake**
Anyapah. **Anacapa Islands**
Apex. **Escondido**
Arbolado. **Sur**
Arena, Barra de. **Delgada, Point; Arena, Point**
Arenoso, Arroyo. **Arena, Point**
Armuyosa Desert. **Death Valley**
Ascension. **Asuncion**
Ashuksha-vit; Asuksa-gna. **Azusa**
Asientic Häbî. **Needles**
Asperin Butte. **Aspen**
Asphalto. **McKittrick**
Assumpcion, La. **Asuncion; Natividad**
Asuncion de Nuestra Señora, La. **San Buenaventura; Ventura**
Asylum. **Patton**

Atla. **Sultana**
Atwell Island. **Alpaugh**
Aujai. **Ojai**
Aulinta. **Abalone**
Aulon, Point. **Abalone; Lovers Point**
Auras, Canada de las. **Feliz**
Aux-um-ne. **Merced River**
Avellanos de Nuestra Señora del Pilar, Los. **Hazel**
Avendale. **Avenal**
Avichi, Arroyo de. **Arichi**
Avie Quah-la-Altwa. **Pilot Knob**
Awani. **Ahwahnee**
Awa'ya. **Mirror Lake**
Ayiis. **Eyese Creek**
Azuncsabit. **Azusa**

Bache, Mount. **Loma Prieta**
Bailarin, El. **Rincon Point**
Baile de las Indias. **Graciosa Ridge**
Ba-ka-wha. **Eel River**
Balboa Palisades. **Corona del Mar**
Baldy [Alameda]. **Vollmer Peak**
Balenas, Puerto. **Ballena**
Ballenas, Punta de las [San Mateo]. **Pigeon Point; Ballena**
Balley. **Bally**
Baranca Colorado. **Red Bank Creek**
Barnwell. **Manvel**
Bautismos, Cañada de los. **Cristianitos Canyon**
Bawly. **Bally**
Bay City [Orange]. **Seal Beach**
Bay Island [Orange]. **Modjeska Island**
Bayou Cita. **Vallecito**
Bay Point. **Chicago**
Beals Landing. **Westport**
Bean Hollow Lake. **Lucerne, Lake**
Bear River House [Placer]. **Applegate**
Beeler, Point. **Bihler Landing**
Bellows Butte. **Liberty Cap**
Be-loh-kai. **Potter Valley**
Belota. **Bellota**
Benderes Cañon. **Bendire Canyon**
Bengal. **Bolo**
Benton Mills. **Bagby**
Berdugos, Sierra de los. **Verdugo Mountains**
Berlin. **Genevra**
Berry. **Baker**

Berryvale. **Strawberry Valley** [Shasta]
Beulah. **Mineral King**
Biedeman, Mount [Mono]. **Biderman**
Big Bar [Butte]. **Pulga**
Big Bar [Calaveras]. **Mokelumne Hill**
Big Bear Park [San Bernardino]. **Sugarloaf**
Big Bird Lake. **Dollar Lake**
Big Coyote [Marin]. **Tamalpais Valley**
Bigler, Lake. **Tahoe**
Big Meadows [Mono]. **Bridgeport**
Big Meadows [Plumas]. **Prattville**
Big Meadows Reservoir. **Almanor, Lake**
Big Moody Creek. **Campbell Creek** [Santa Clara]
Big Valley City. **Nubieber**
Black Peak [Madera]. **Madera Peak**
Black Point Harbor [Sonoma]. **Bihler Landing**
Blacks. **Zamora**
Blair. **Whiskeytown**
Blue Mountain [San Francisco]. **Davidson, Mount**
Bodey. **Bodie**
Bo-hem-bolly. **Bally**
Bokmans Prairie. **Fieldbrook**
Bolanos Bay. **Bolinas Bay**
Bolbones, Sierra de los. **Diablo, Mount**
Bo-lem-poi-yok. **Bally; Shasta**
Bo-li Chu-ip. **Bully Choop**
Bombay. **Bolo**
Bonaventura. **Buenaventura**
Bonaventura River. **Sacramento River**
Bonete, Punta. **Bonita Point**
Bonpland, Lake. **Tahoe, Lake**
Boston Ranch. **Hurleton**
Bottileas. **Jackson**
Bourri. **Buriburi Ridge**
Bowlder. **Boulder**
Braly Mountain. **Brawley Peaks**
Brazos del Rio. **Rio Vista**
Bridgeport [Solano]. **Cordelia**
Bristol. **Bolo**
Bronco. **Floriston**
Brown [Kern]. **Mount Owen**
Browns Lake. **Lakeview**
Brownsville [Humboldt]. **Samoa**
Bryant. **Orinda**
Buena Esperanza, Rio Grande de. **Colorado River**
Buena Gente, Isla Raza de. **Terminal Island**
Buena Guia, Rio de. **Colorado River**
Buenaventura River. **Sacramento River**
Buena Vista [Tulare]. **Visalia**
Buena Vista Pass. **Tejon Pass**
Buenos Ayres, Arroyo; Portezuela de. **Corrall Hollow**
Buli. **Bally**

Bullet Chup. **Bally**
Bullwinkel. **Crannell**
Buque, El. **Bouquet Canyon**
Burneyville. **Riverbank**
Buscombe. **Millville**
Bute Mountains. **Sutter Buttes**
Butte Mills. **Magalia**
Butteville. **Edgewood**

Caballada, Arroyo de. **Cavallo Point**
Caballo, Punta de. **Cavallo Point**
Cabarker. **El Centro**
Cabeza de Milligan. **Mulligan Hill**
Cabezone. **Cabazon**
Caguenga. **Cahuenga**
Cagüilla. **Cahuilla**
Cahuia; Cahwia. **Kaweah**
Calaguasa; Calahuasa. **Santa Ynez**
Calajomanas. **Bale**
Caldwells Upper Store. **Nevada City**
California, Punta de la. **Ballena**
California National Forest. **Mendocino National Forest**
California Range. **Sierra Nevada**
Caligolman. **Carne Humana**
Cameros Valley. **Carneros Valley**
Campaña, Arroyo de la. **Battle Creek**
Campana, Cañada de. **Bell Canyon**
Campana, La. **Picacho Peak**
Camp Baldy. **Mount Baldy**
Camp Carmel. **Camp Steffani**
Campinis Campgrounds. **Camp Inis**
Campo Aleman. **Anaheim**
Camp Stephani. **Camp Steffani**
Camp Taylor. **Taylorville**
Cane Creek. **Carrizo Creek**
Cañon Mountain [Kern]. **Breckenridge Mountain**
Capa. **Capay**
Capay, Rio de [Glenn]. **Grindstone Creek**
Careys Mill. **Woodfords**
Carisal; Cariso. **Carrizo Creek**
Carizal. **Carrizo Creek**
Carmelita, Ensenada de la. **Richardson Bay**
Carmen, Isla del. **Brooks Island**
Carmen Lake. **Kirman**
Cash Creek. **Cache Creek**
Casitec. **Castaic**
Casmaria. **Casmalia**
Castec; Casteque. **Castaic**
Castle Peak [Yosemite N. P.]. **Tower Peak**
Castle Rock [Shasta]. **Castella**
Castoria. **French Camp**
Catuculu, Valle de. **Catacula**
Caxa. **Cojo**
Cayegua; Cayegues. **Calleguas**
Cemetery Hill. **Radio Hill**

Centerville Butte [Modoc]. **Opahwah Butte**
Centreville. **Centerville**
Cepsey. **Sespe**
Cerro Alto [San Luis Obispo]. **Hollister Peak**
Cespai River. **Sespe Creek**
Chachanegtac. **Coches**
Charley Haupt Creek. **Haupt Creek**
Chasta; Chasty. **Shasta**
Chauciles, Rancheria de los. **Chowchilla**
Chausila, Rancheria de. **Chowchilla**
Chay-o-poo-ya-päh. **Canebrake Creek**
Chelame Pass. **Cholame**
Chelone, Mount. **Chalone Mountain**
Chibidame. **Cole Creek**
Chileo; Chilleo. **Chilao**
Chillian Bar. **Chile, Chili**
Chilnoialny Creek. **Chilnaulna Creek**
Chintache. **Tache; Tulare Lake**
Cho-ko-nip'-o-deh. **Royal Arches**
Choloma Creek. **Cholame Creek**
Chopines, Arroyo de. **Chupines**
Choual Mountain. **Chual, Mount**
Chrysopylae. **Golden Gate**
Churntown. **Churn Creek**
Cierbo, Canada de. **Ciervo**
Cipreses, Punta de. **Cypress, Point**
Circle City. **Corona**
City of the Angels. **Los Angeles**
City Reservation, The. **Alum Rock Park**
Ciudad de los Angelos. **Los Angeles**
Clairville. **Geyserville**
Claminitt. **Klamath**
Clammitte. **Klamath**
Clarke City. **Greenfield**
Clarks Station. **Clark, Mount**
Clear Creek Hot Springs. **Hobo Hot Springs**
Clear Lake Villas. **Nice**
Clifton. **Del Rey**
Clinton. **Brooklyn Basin**
Coahuila. **Cahuilla**
Coaling Station. **Coalinga**
Coallomi. **Collayomi Valley**
Coburn Station. **Truckee**
Cochenitos. **Coches**
Cohuila. **Cahuilla**
Cole Creek [Amador]. **Cold Creek**
Colijolmanoc. **Carne Humana**
Coliseum Peak. **Tenaya Peak**
College Terrace. **Palo Alto**
Collis. **Kerman**
Collote, Arrollo de. **Coyote**
Colluma. **Coloma**
Colouse; Coloussas; Colusi. **Colusa**
Comstock. **Orland**
Conchilla Valley. **Coachella**
Cone Creek. **Kern-Kaweah River**
Cone Mountain [Siskiyou]. **Black Butte**

Conns Creek. **Asbill Creek**
Conversion, Punta de la. **Mugu**
Copéh. **Capay**
Corall. **Corral**
Corcoran, Mount. **Langley, Mount**
Cordero Valley [San Diego]. **McGonigle Canyon**
Corduas Rancho. **Marysville**
Corral Valley [Napa]. **Wooden Valley**
Corte Madera del Presidio, Arroyo. **Widow Reed Creek**
Coru; Corusies. **Colusa**
Corvallis. **Norwalk**
Cosmenes River. **Cosumnes River**
Cosomes, Rio. **Cosumnes River**
Cossomenes. **Cosumnes**
Cotineva. **Rockport; Cottaneva**
Cottonwood [Siskiyou]. **Henley**
Cottonwood Creek [Mendocino]. **Cottaneva**
County Line. **Cerrito**
Coutolanezes. **Coutolenc**
Covell. **Easton**
Covertsburg. **Red Bluff**
Cowell [San Joaquin]. **Manteca**
Cowier Creek. **Kaweah**
Cowles. **Santee**
Cow Wells. **Garlock**
Coxo. **Cojo**
Craggy Peak [Siskiyou]. **Bolivar Lookout**
Cramer. **Milo**
Cramville. **Highland; East Highlands**
Cranes Creek. **Parker Creek**
Crocker [San Luis Obispo]. **Templeton**
Cross Mountain. **Breckenridge Mountain**
Crystal Lake [Siskiyou]. **Medicine Lake**
Crystal Peak [El Dorado]. **Tallac, Mount**
Crystal Springs [Napa]. **Sanitarium**
Cuaguillomic. **Collayomi**
Cucapa. **Cocopah**
Cuchuil. **Cahuilla**
Cuesta de los Gatos. **Santa Cruz Mountains**
Cuiapaipa; Cuyapaipe. **Guyapipe**
Cullama. **Cuyama**
Cullamac. **Cuyamaca**
Culloma. **Coloma**
Curious Butte. **Striped Mountain**

Dark Hole, The. **Hole**
Davidson City. **Dominguez**
Davies Mill. **Graeagle**
Dead Mule Spring. **Mule**
Delight Spring; Delightful Spring. **Daylight Spring**
Delirium Tremens. **Alpha**
Dentville. **Knights Ferry**
Derby, Lake. **Honey Lake**
Desert Lake [Kern]. **Koehn Lake**

Desert Springs [San Bernardino]. **Pinon Hills**
De Silvas Island. **Belvedere**
Destruction River. **Sacramento River**
Devair. **Ryan**
Devils Castle [Shasta]. **Castle Crags State Park**
Devils Cellar, The. **Yosemite**
Devils Mount. **Saint Helena, Mount**
Dewey. **Wasco**
Dewing Park. **Saranap**
Dickson. **Dixon**
Dioleo, Rancho de. **Yolo**
Djictañadiñ. **Tish-Tang-a-Tang Creek**
Doheny Park. **Capistrano Beach**
Dome, The. **Balloon Dome**
Dom Pedro. **Don Pedro**
Don Gaspar, Bahia de. **Drakes Bay**
Donnel. **Bellota**
Dorris Bridge; Dorrisville. **Alturas**
Dos Rancherias. **Dos Pueblos**
Dougherty Meadow. **Simpson Meadow**
Doughertys Station. **Dublin**
Drapersville. **Kingsburg**
Drennan. **Earp**
Drunken Indian. **Indian**
Dry Diggings [El Dorado]. **Placerville**
Duffields Valley. **Pickel Meadow**
Dutch Corners. **Ducor; Newman**
Du Vrees Creek. **Islay**
Dyerville. **South Fork** [Humboldt]
Dyke Ridge. **Monarch Divide**

East Monterey. **Seaside**
East Riverside. **Highgrove**
Edgar Station. **Beaumont**
Edson. **Essex**
Eenag'h-paha. **Smith River**
Elftman. **Dominguez**
Elk Cove. **Alcove Canyon**
Elkhorn Station. **Burrel**
Elmdale. **Denair**
Elmwood Colony. **Denair**
Eltoro. **Toro**
El Venado. **Venado**
Encapa Islands. **Anacapa Islands**
Encinal del Temescal. **Oakland; Temescal**
Enecapa. **Anacapa Islands**
Eneeapah. **Anacapa Islands**
Esken. **Esquon**
Esperanza [Yolo]. **Esparto**
Esque, Rancheria. **Esquon**
Estanislao, Rio. **Stanislaus River**
Etengvo Wumoma. **Elsinore**
Eureka [Nevada]. **Graniteville**

Fallsvale. **Forest Falls; Fall River**
Falsa Vela. **Anacapa Islands**
False Bay [San Diego]. **Mission Bay**

Fanita. **Santee**
Feather Lake [Fresno]. **Vermilion Valley**
Firmin, Point. **Fermin, Point**
First Garrote. **Groveland; Second Garrote**
Fish Creek Mountain. **Grinnell Peak**
Fishpond. **Barstow**
Flugge, Rancho de. **Boga**
Forbestown. **Lakeport**
Forestville [Humboldt]. **Scotia**
Forks-of-the-Roads. **Altaville**
Forks. The. **Downieville**
Forlorn Hope. **Hopeton**
Forrestville. **Forestville**
Fortunas, Cabo de. **Arena, Point; False Cape**
Fortune. **Fortuna**
Four Brothers. **Ship**
Four Creeks. **Kaweah River**
Frances, Mount. **Liberty Cap**
Frances River. **Kaweah River**
Francisca. **Benicia**
Francisco Draco, Puerto Sr. **Drakes Bay**
Franklin City. **Schilling**
Frazier's Station. **Carlsbad**
Frayles, Los. **Farallon Islands**
Freeze Out. **Ione**
French Bar [Stanislaus]. **La Grange**
Frijoles, Arroyo de los. **Bean Hollow Lake; Lucerne, Lake**
Front. **Mount Owen**
Fuegos, Bahia de los. **San Pedro Bay**
Fulton Sulphur Springs. **Santa Fe Springs**
Fumos, Bahia de los. **San Pedro Bay**

Galero, Cabo de. **Conception, Point**
Ganogeh. **Canoga Park**
Garrotte. **Groveland; Second Garrote**
Gawalali. **Gualala**
Geneva. **Planada**
Gente Barbuda, Isla de. **Santa Cruz Island**
Gentiles, Laguna de los. **Caslamayomi**
Georgetown [Sacramento]. **Franklin**
Georgia Gap. **Georges Gap**
Germanos, Los. **Juristac**
Glacier Pass. **Sawtooth Pass**
Golden Rock. **Red Rock**
Golden Valley. **Cuddeback Lake**
Golgones, Sierra de. **Diablo, Mount**
Gottville. **Klamath River**
Gouge Eye. **Pleasant Grove**
Governador Creek. **Gobernadora Canyon**
Grandview Terrace. **Black Point**
Great Dome. **Balloon Dome**
Green Flat [Tuolumne]. **Relief Valley**
Greenland. **Furnace Creek Ranch**
Greenwich. **Tehachapi**
Growlersburg. **Georgetown**
Grullas, Laguna de las. **Crane**

Guachingo. **Guachama; San Bernardino**
Guadalupe, Rio de Nuestra Señora de. **Stanis-**
   laus River; Guadalupe River
Guajaimeie; Guajaumere. **Guajome**
Guaslay. **Cuaslui Creek**
Guasna. **Huasna River**
Gubernadora, Canada. **Gobernadora Canyon**
Guijarros, Punta de los. **Ballast Point**
Guinado. **Quinado Canyon**
Guntleys. **Christine**
Gurley Creek. **Gerle Creek**
Grafton. **Knights Landing**
Gwins Peak. **Liberty Cap**

Ha-bee-co-la-la. **Pilot Knob**
Hah Weal Asientic. **Colorado River**
Hakupin. **Warner Springs**
Halam. **Jalama**
Half Potato Hill. **Potato Hill**
Halleck [San Bernardino]. **Oro Grande**
Hambre. **Alhambra**
Hamook Häbî, **Mojave**
Hangtown Crossing. **Mills** [Sacramento]
Hanksite. **Westend**
Hansonville. **Rackerby**
Hardscrabble [Amador]. **Ione**
Harina, Arroyo de la. **San Lorenzo Creek**
Harper. **Costa Mesa**
Harrills Mill. **Millville**
Harrisburgh. **Warm Springs**
Haselbusch. **Hazelbusch**
Haslinding. **Horse Linto Creek**
Has-lintah. **Horse Linto Creek**
Hatchatchie. **Hetch Hetchy**
Hat'-te we'-we. **Hat Creek**
Haway Creek. **Haiwee Creek**
Haywood. **Hayward**
Heaton Station. **Cisco**
Hedges. **Tumco**
Helegä' ä Wroi. **Halagow Creek**
Helen, Mount. **Saint Helena, Mount**
Heliograph Hill. **Telegraph Peak**
Helisma. **Burson**
Hellen, Mount. **Saint Helena, Mount**
Hell-Out-For-Noon. **Alpha**
Heneet. **Yuba**
Hennerville Peak. **Hunewill**
Henry, Mount [Napa]. **Saint John Mountain**
Henry, Mount [Sequoia N. P.]. **Kaweah Peaks**
Hermann, Rancho de. **German** [Sonoma]
Hernandez Spring. **Resting Spring**
Hiampum. **Hyampom**
Hicks. **Hodge**
Hicksville. **Ione**
Hildreth's Diggings. **Columbia**
Hill, The. **Mokelumne Hill**
Hills Ferry. **Newman**

Hipass. **High; Tierra del Sol**
Hitchens Spring. **Jayhawker Spring**
Hoan'kut. **Honcut**
Hog Canyon [San Bernardino]. **Wildwood**
   Canyon
Hog Root. **Alpaugh**
Hollister Valley [San Diego]. **Thing Valley**
Holom. **Olompali**
Holton. **Holtville**
Honolulu. **Klamath**
Ho'-ome'R Wroi. **Ha Amar Creek**
Ho' opeu; Ho' päu. **Hoppow Creek**
Horestimba, Arroyo de. **Orestimba Creek**
Horsethief Bend. **Bend**
Hot Sigler Springs. **Seigler Springs**
Hot Spring Valley. **Drakesbad**
Howards. **Occidental**
Howells. **Cosumnes**
Hoya, La. **Jolla**
Huilic Noma. **Carne Humana**
Humbug. **North Bloomfield**
Huntoon Valley. **Yaney Valley**
Hupa. **Hoopa**
Hurumpa; Hurupa. **Jurupa**
Hu'-tci. **Huichica**

Ignasio Valley [Contra Costa]. **Ygnacio Valley**
Imperial Junction. **Niland**
Inconstant River. **Mojave River**
Indiana Colony. **Pasadena**
Indian Gulch [Calaveras]. **West Point**
Indios, Cañada de los. **Black Star Canyon**
Inglewood Rancho. **Lennox**
Injerto, Arroyo del. **San Ramon Creek**
Ioleo, Rancho del. **Yolo**
Iomosa. **Alta Loma; Hermosa**
Irma. **Island Mountain**
Irving. **Irvington**
Isaac Walton Grove. **Izaak Walton, Mount**
Isla Plana. **Mare Island**
Islar Creek. **Islay**
Ivawatch. **Avawatz**

Jacayme. **San Luis Rey**
Jackson, Mount. **Shasta, Mount**
Jacom. **Jacumba**
Jacopin. **Agua Caliente Creek** [San Diego];
   Warner Springs
Jaguara. **San Jacinto**
Jajiguas. **Tajiguas**
Jalapi. **Yulupa**
Jalchedunes. **Algodones**
Jamatayune. **Samagatuma**
Jamocha. **Jamacha**
Japatai. **Japatul**
Javill. **Colorado River**
Jedediah Mountain. **Jedediah Smith**

Jefferson. **Lennox**
Jepson Hole. **Willis Hole**
Jesus de los Temblores, Rio de. **Santa Ana River; Temblor**
Jesus Maria, Rio de. **Cache Creek**
Jimtown. **Jamestown**
Joburg. **Johannesburg**
Johnson, Mount [Yosemite N.P.]. **Lewis, Mount**
Johnsons River. **San Gabriel River**
Johnstown. **Johnsville**
Jollabollas. **Bally**
Joluca. **Tulucay**
Jonata. **San Carlos de Jonata**
Jonathan Rock. **Brother Jonathan Rock**
Jone: City, Valley. **Ione**
Jones Butte. **Dutschke Hill**
Joseph, Mount. **Lassen Peak**
Josmites. **Yosemite**
Joya, La. **Jolla**
Juan Rodriguez Island. **San Miguel**
Jubaville. **Marysville**
Jubu. **Yuba**
Juichama; Juichuneas. **Cachuma**
Jukiusme. **Ukiah**
Julupa. **Yulupa**
Junta de los quatro Evangelistas. **Suisun Bay**

Kachitule. **Cache Creek**
Kah Shoh. **Clear Lake** [Lake]
Kah-wee-ya. **Kaweah River**
Kalawpa. **Saddle; Saddleback**
Karkin. **Carquinez**
Karquines. **Carquinez**
Ka-sha-reh. **Elk River**
Kas-lin-ta. **Horse Linto Creek**
Karsebalo. **Bally**
Kendalls City. **Boonville**
Kent Canyon. **Quinado Canyon**
Kenwood [San Bernardino]. **Devore**
Ke'pel. **Capell Creek** [Humboldt]
Ketinelbe. **Kittinelbe**
Ketten Chow Valley. **Hetten; Ketten**
Keys, Point. **Reyes, Point**
Keyser Gulch. **Kaiser** [Fresno]
Khartoum. **Hartoum**
Kilīmī'l. **Tomki Creek**
Kimki harasa. **San Clemente**
Kilbeck. **Chubbuck**
Kings Peak. **Disaster Peak**
Kings River. **Centerville** [Fresno]
Kings River Canal. **Main Canal**
Kinto Creek. **Quinto Creek**
Kittleman. **Kettleman**
Klink. **Ivanhoe**
Kno'ktai. **Konocti, Mount**
Kolijolmanok. **Bale; Carne Humana**

Komacho. **Comptche**
Kongsberg. **Silver Creek**
Konigsberg. **Silver Creek**
Kori, **Arcata**
Kosmit. **Cosmit**
Kotati. **Cotati**
Kupa. **Warner Springs**

La Costa. **Ponto**
Laddville. **Livermore**
Ladoga. **Lodoga**
Laguna, Lake [Riverside]. **Elsinore**
Laguna, Point [Ventura]. **Mugu, Point**
Laguna; Laguna Grande. **Clear Lake** [Lake]
Laguna Grande [San Mateo]. **Raimundo**
Laguna Larga. **Guadalupe Lake**
Laguna Merced Military Reservation. **Funston, Fort**
Lagunita [Los Angeles]. **Bixby Slough**
Lake Fork. **Kings River**
Lambert Dome. **Lembert Dome**
Langville. **Capay**
Laquisimes, Rio de los. **Stanislaus River**
Laribee; Lariby. **Larabee**
Lassens Horn. **Cape Horn; Fandango Pass**
Latache. **Lemoore**
Latona. **Redding**
Lawson Peak. **Lassen Peak**
Leastalk. **Ivanpah**
Le Beck. **Lebec**
Leckler Canyon. **Lechler Canyon**
Le Conte, Mount. **Kaweah**
Ledro. **Lerdo**
Le-Hamite. **Indian Canyon**
Leland. **Orland**
Leodocia. **Red Bluff**
Les Fourcades. **Mokelumne Hill**
Lewis. **Mococo**
Liberty Settlement. **Riverdale**
Lick Springs. **Tuscan Springs**
Lime Point Military Reservation. **Baker, Fort**
Limpia Concepcion, Punta de la. **Concepcion, Point**
Limu; Limun. **Santa Cruz Island**
Linden [Tulare]. **Denlin**
Linn, Mount. **Hayfork Bally** under **Bally**
Little North Fork of Middle Fork of North Fork of Yuba River. **Empire Creek**
Little Pine. **Independence** [Inyo]
Little Truckee Lake. **Webber Lake**
Live Oaks [Sacramento]. **Michigan Bar**
Llagas, Arroyo de las. **Las Yeguas Canyon**
Llajome. **Yajome**
Llokaya. **Ukiah**
Llorones, Ensenada de los. **Mission: Creek, Rock**
Lobo, El. **Lion**

Loma Alta, Laguna de. **Mountain**
Lone Valley. **Ione Valley**
Lordsburg. **La Verne**
Los Angeles Island; Isla de los Angeles. **Angel Island**
Lost Valley [Fresno]. **Blaney Meadows**
Louisville. **Greenwood**
Lovitos, Arroyo de. **Lobitos**
Low Divide. **Altaville**
Lower Otay Dam. **Savage Dam; Otay**
Loya. **Sentinel Dome**
Lugonia. **Redlands; Lugo** [San Bernardino]
Lungyotuckoya. **Ribbon Fall**
Lutfenholts Creek. **Luffenholtz Creek**

McAlpine. **Calpine**
McCarthysville. **Saratoga**
McClure, Mount. **Maclure, Mount**
McDairmids Prairie. **Metropolitan**
McGills. **Miguel**
Machado. **Elsinore**
Mac-há-vès. **Mojave**
Macho Creek. **Mocho, Arroyo**
McKee, Mount. **Konocti**
McLeans River. **Clearwater Creek**
McLeans Spring. **Jayhawker Well**
McLeod's Fork. **McCloud River**
McLoud River. **McCloud River**
Maclure Fork [Yosemite N. P.]. **Lewis Creek**
Maddox. **Robbins**
Magnolia. **Inyokern**
Magnolia Villa. **Upland**
Mahews. **Mayhew**
Malacomes. **Mayacmas; Saint Helena, Mount**
Malaga [Los Angeles]. **Malibu**
Malico; Maligo. **Malibu**
Mallacomes. **Saint Helena, Mount; Mayacmas Mountains**
Maniz, Rancho de. **Muniz**
Man Ridge. **Mann Ridge**
Margarita. **Ranch House**
Marinera, Isla de la. **Marin**
Marin Meadows. **Hamilton Field**
Marion. **Reseda**
Maristul. **Moristul**
Markleville. **Cloverdale**
Maronga. **Morongo**
Martin Station. **Neponset**
Martinville. **Glenwood**
Martires, Arroyo de los. **Mojave River**
Mason. **Glendale**
Matadera, Arroyo de. **Madera Creek**
Mē-ah-nee. **Miami Mountain**
Mecklenburg. **Marysville**
Mellen. **Topock**
Meloneys Diggings. **Melones**
Merced, Rio de los. **Tuolumne River**

Meridian District. **Bostonia**
Me'rip Wroi. **Mareep Creek**
Mescaltitlan. **Mescal Island**
Mesitas, Las. **Anacapa Islands**
Meskua. **Moscow**
Messerville. **Junction City**
Messina. **Highland; East Highlands**
Mezesville. **Redwood City**
Micks Bay. **Meeks Bay**
Middle Branch of the South Fork of the San Joaquin River. **Evolution Creek**
Middle Point. **Franklin Point**
Mill Creek [Mono]. **Lundy**
Mill Valley Junction. **Almonte**
Miyakma. **Mayacmas**
Mocosin Creek. **Moccasin Creek**
Modena. **El Modena**
Mogneles River. **Mokelumne River**
Mohawa. **Mojave**
Mohr Station. **Bethany**
Moigne Mountain. **Pinto Peak**
Mokellemos. **Mokelumne River**
Mokesumne; Mokosumne. **Cosumnes**
Mok Hill. **Mokelumne Hill**
Moleta. **Red Rock**
Molinos, Arroyo de. **Mill Creek**
Monica, Sierra de la. **Santa Monica**
Monte Diablo Creek. **Convict Creek**
Montoro. **Montara**
Montosa, Cañada. **Montara**
Moores Station. **Riverton**
Moquelumne. **Mokelumne**
Moraine, Mount. **Barton Peak**
Morgan's Cove. **Hospital Cove**
Mormon Gulch. **Tuttletown**
Moron. **Taft**
Morro Twin. **Hollister Peak**
Morse's Landing. **Moss Landing**
Mortmere. **Mortmar**
Mound City. **Loma Linda**
Mountain View [Butte]. **Dogtown**
Mountain View [Orange]. **Villa Park**
Mount Aukum (post office) . **Aukum**
Moyacino, Mount. **Saint Helena, Mount**
Mto'm-kai. **Tomki Creek**
Mud Springs [El Dorado]. **El Dorado**
Mud Springs [Los Angeles]. **San Dimas**
Muguelemnes. **Mokelumne**
Munchville. **Capay**
Mureku. **Moorek**
Muristul. **Moristul**
Murphys Old Diggings. **Vallecito; Murphys**
Muscle Creek. **Mussel Slough**
Muscupiavit. **Cajon**
Musketo Creek. **Mosquito**
Mutistul. **Moristul**
Muwu. **Mugu**

Najague. **Nojogui**
Nanaguanui. **San Rafael** [Marin]
Nataqua, Territory of. **Roops Fort**
Natividad de Nuestra Señora, La. **Osos, Los**
Navy Point. **Army Point**
Neals Rancho. **Esquon**
Nebo, Mount. **Bismarck Knob**
Negro Bar. **Folsom**
Neuil, Lomaria de. **Niguel Hill**
Newapkshi. **Goose Lake**
Newburg. **Fort Dick**
New Haven. **Alvarado**
New Idria. **Idria**
New Jerusalem. **El Rio**
Newmark. **Montebello**
New Mecklenburg. **Marysville**
New Orleans Bar. **Orleans**
New Owenyo. **Owenyo**
New Pass. **Soledad Pass**
Newport [Solano]. **Collinsville**
New Redwood Canyon. **Canyon**
New River City. **Denny**
New San Pedro. **Wilmington**
New Town. **Nubieber**
Newtown. **Wilmington**
New Years Point. **Ano Nuevo**
Nicalque. **Santa Rosa Island**
Nicholaus. **Nicolaus**
Nichols Peak [Kern]. **Nicoll Peak**
Nigger Slough. **Dominguez**
Niguili. **Niguel Hill**
Nihail. **Niguel Hill**
Nina, Lake. **Tilden Lake**
Nippen. **Nipton**
Nogales, Arroyo de los [Contra Costa]. **Walnut Creek**
No'htskum. **Natchka Creek**
Nohxtska. **Natchka Creek**
Nombadjara. **Pope Creek**
Nomopeoits. **Old Woman Mountains**
Norse Butte. **Norris Butte**
Norte, Rio del. **Colorado River**
Northam. **Buena Park**
North Baldy. **Baden-Powell, Mount; Baldy**
North Baldy Peak [Los Angeles]. **Throop Peak**
North Branch of the South Fork of the San Joaquin River. **Piute Creek** [Fresno]
North Fork [Humboldt]. **Korbel**
North Fork Dry Diggings. **Auburn**
North Fork of Fresno River. **Miami Creek**
North Fork of the North Fork of Yuba River. **Lavezzola Creek**
North Los Angeles. **Northridge**
Notoma. **Natoma**
Nottingham. **Livermore**
Noua Albion. **New Albion**
Nova Albion. **New Albion**

Novarro. **Navarro**
No'-yo-bida. **Noyo River**
Noza Creek. **Battle Creek**
Nuestra Señora de Altagracia. **Conejo**
Nuestra Señora de los Angeles de Porciuncula. **Los Angeles**
Nuestra Señora del Rosario de la Marinera, Bahia de. **Marin**
Nueva California. **California**
Nueva Helvetia. **New Helvetia**
Nuevo San Francisco. **Solano**
Num-mel-be-le-sas-pom. **Eddy, Mount**

Obed. **Bell**
Ocean Park Heights. **Mar Vista**
Ocean View. **Albany**
O-co-ya Creek. **Poso Creek**
Ohjia. **Otay**
O'ho Wroi. **Ahpah**
O'hpo. **Ahpah**
Ojo Caliente. **Caliente**
Ojotska, Rio. **American River**
O-la'-mah. **Olema**
Old Beach. **Niland**
Old Canal. **Main Canal**
Old Creek [San Luis Obispo]. **Oat**
Old Fort. **Roops Fort**
Old Jerusalem. **Jerusalem**
Old Newport. **New**
Old Saddleback [Orange]. **Santiago Peak**
Oleta. **Fiddletown**
Olimpali. **Olompali**
Olom. **Olompali**
Omega" Wroi. **Omagaar Creek**
Ondo, Arroyo. **Hondo**
One-Horse Town. **Horsetown; Mule**
One Mule Town. **Mule**
Oo-moo'-chah. **Omochumnes**
Ore'qw. **Orick**
Orestiñoc, Arroyito de. **Orestimba Creek**
Oro, Isla del. **Marin**
Oroflamme. **Oriflamme**
Oroysom. **Mission San Jose**
O'segen Wroi. **Ossagon Creek**
O'Shean's View. **Albany**
Osito. **Osos, Cañada de los**
Osnito, Arroyo del. **Hospital Creek**
Ospital. **Hospital Creek**
Otis, **Yermo**
Ottitiewa. **Fort Jones**
Owens Ferry. **La Grange**
Owensmouth. **Canoga Park**

Paauw. **Palomar Mountain**
Pablo, Rancho de. **Johnsons Ranch**
Pacheco [Marin]. **Ignacio**
Pacheta. **Owens Lake**

Pacific Congress Springs. **Congress Springs**
Padding River. **Pudding Creek**
Paguay. **Poway**
Pah-wah'-te. **Magnesia Spring Canyon**
Paines Creek. **Paynes Creek**
Pait Valley. **Pate Valley**
Pa'le-mus. **Tamalpais**
Palermo, Mount. **Tamalpais, Mount**
Palmas, Mount. **Tamalpais, Mount**
Palmenthal, **Palmdale**
Paloma, Cañada. **Guejito y Canada de Palo-
mea**
Palos Colorados. **Redwood**
Palos Verdes, Cañada de. **Bixby Slough**
Pamoosa. **Moosa**
Pamusi. **Moosa**
Panasquitas. **Los Penasquitos**
Papas, Las. **Potato; Twin Peaks**
Paps. **Twin Peaks**
Parker Valley. **Ukiah Valley**
Parkinson, Mount. **Parker Mountain**
Pasajero, Arroyo. **Gatos**
Pa-sa-wei-weikit. **Backbone Creek**
Pasines, Cienega de los. **Paicines**
Paso de los Americanos, El. **American River**
Pass Creek. **Paso; Tehachapi**
Passing Island. **San Nicolas Island**
Paterson. **Cherokee**
Pa-til-le-ma. **Glacier Point**
Pasiluvra. **Persido Bar**
Pawai. **Poway**
Paxaros, Rio de los. **Pajaro River**
Pearson Springs. **Saratoga Springs** [Lake]
Pechos de la Chola, Los. **Twin Peaks; Pecho**
Pedregoso. **Santa Barbara Mission**
Pedro Nales. **Pedernales, Point**
Pe'gwi. **Freshwater Lagoon**
Peh-tsik. **Klamath**
Pences. **Pentz**
Peninsular Island. **Belvedere**
Penole; Penoli. **Pinole**
Peñon de la Campana. **Picacho**
Peralta, Lake [Alameda]. **Merritt, Lake**
Peru, Rio. **Piru River**
Petes, Las. **Pitas Point**
Petrolia [Orange]. **Olinda**
Pewipwi. **San Bernardino Peak**
Picacho Prieto [Marin]. **Tamalpais, Mount**
Pichanga; Picha Awanga. **Pechanga; Aguanga**
Pickering Mineral Hot Springs. **Urbita Springs**
Pickle Meadow. **Pickel Meadow**
Picture City. **Agoura**
Piedra Pintada, La. **Painted**
Pilot River [Alpine]. **Carson River**
Pine Grove [Sonoma]. **Sebastopol**
Pino. **Loomis**
Pi-pi-yu-na. **Kaweah**

Piro Creek. **Piru Creek**
Pit Lake [Modoc]. **Goose Lake; Pit River**
Pitos, Los. **Pitas Point**
Pitts Lake [Modoc]. **Goose Lake; Pit River**
Pitts River. **Pit River**
Pleasonton. **Pleasanton**
Pleyto. **Pleito**
Plumas, Rancho de las [Butte and Sutter].
Boga
Pocitas, Las. **Posita**
Poh-lik. **Klamath**
Pohono. **Bridalveil Fall**
Point of Rocks. **Helendale**
Pokagama. **Klamathon**
Pokerville. **Plymouth**
Pollasky. **Friant**
Pollock Bridge. **Loftus**
Polo Peak. **Jackson**
Poncho Rico Creek. **Pancho Rico Creek**
Ponga'. **Santa Catalina**
Poor Man's Flat. **Windsor**
Popes Valley [Fresno]. **Watts Valley**
Porciuncula, La. **Kern River**
Porciuncula, Nuestra Señora de los Angeles
de. **Los Angeles**
Port Harford. **San Luis Obispo**
Portuguee [Shasta]. **Portuguese Flat**
Posé Flat. **Poso Flat**
Poso de Chane, Arroyo. **Gatos**
Post Office Springs [Inyo]. **Ballarat; Post Of-
fice**
Po-sun-co-la. **Kern River**
Potiquimi. **Mark West Creek**
Pots. **Devils Mush Pot Cave**
Precipice Peak. **Cotter, Mount**
Princeton [Mariposa]. **Mount Bullion**
Promontory. **Pedernales, Point**
Puckerville. **Plymouth**
Puentes, Arroyo de las [Santa Cruz]. **Cojo**
Puerto Anegado. **Mission Bay**
Puerto Dulce. **Suisun Bay**
Puerto Dulce, Boca del. **Freshwater Lagoon;
Carquinez**
Puerto Falso. **Mission Bay**
Puerto Zuelo Lagunitas. **Lagunitas**
Punta Falsa de Año Nuevo. **Ano Nuevo**
Purisima River, La. **Santa Ynez River**
Pusher. **Dunsmuir**
Puta-to. **Putah Creek**
Putnams. **Independence** [Inyo]
Putos, Rio de. **Putah Creek**
Pyramid Point. **Lobos, Point; Pyramid**
Py-we-ah; Py-we-ack. **Pywiack Creek; Tenaya,
Lake**

Qual-a-wa-loo. **Humboldt Bay**
Quate; Quati. **Cuate**

Queermack. **Cuyamaca**
Quercus Creek. **Kirker Creek**
Quimby. **Denny**
Quintin, Punta de. **San Quentin**
Qui-Quai-mungo Range. **San Gabriel Range**
Quito, Arroyo. **Campbell Creek** [Santa Clara]
Quivira. **California; New Albion**
Qwo' San Wroi. **Squash Ann Creek**

Raliez Valley. **Reliez Valley**
Ramola. **Romoland**
Rampart Pass. **Siberian Pass**
Randolph. **Sablon**
Rattlesnake Butte [Modoc]. **Opahwah Butte**
Rattlesnake Island. **Terminal Island**
Raymundo, Cañada de. **Raimundo**
Read. **Mill Valley**
Rech-wa. **Requa**
Red Bank Creek [Butte, Yuba]. **Honcut Creek**
Red Mountain [Kings Canyon N. P.]. **Pinchot, Mount**
Red Rock [San Bernardino]. **Topock**
Reeds Springs. **Santa Catarina Springs**
Reesley Valley. **Reliez Valley**
Reina de los Angeles. **Los Angeles**
Re' kwoi. **Requa**
Reyes, Pico y Cerro de. **Tamalpais, Mount**
Reyes, Rio de. **Kings River**
Rhett Lake. **Tule Lake**
Riceville. **Corning**
Rich Dry Diggings. **Auburn**
Richfield [Orange]. **Atwood**
Richland. **Orange; Richvale**
Rickeyville. **Ione**
Ridge Point. **Table Bluff**
Rio Grande de Buena Esperanza. **Colorado River**
Rittgers Creek. **Richter Creek**
Riverbank [Yolo]. **Bryte**
Riverdale [Los Angeles]. **Glendale**
River Dell. **Rio Dell**
River of the Lake. **Kings River**
Robinsons. **Melones**
Rocky Island. **Brooks Island**
Rodriguez, Rancho de. **Jacinto**
Romanzov, Port. **Bodega**
Rooptown. **Susanville; Roops Fort**
Root. **Alpaugh**
Rootville. **Millerton Lake**
Rosario, Arroyo del. **Tres Pinos Creek**
Rosario, Bahia del. **Marin**
Rosaville. **Cambria**
Roscoe. **Sun Valley**
Rosena. **Fontana**
Roth Spur. **Strathmore**
Roussillon Bay. **Avalon Bay**
Ruch Ranch. **Carrville**

Ruso, Rio. **Russian River**
Russelsville. **Parkfield**
Russian River (town). **Healdsburg**
Rust. **Cerrito**

Saca. **Zaca**
Sacalanes. **Acalanes**
Saddleback Mountain [Shasta]. **Bass Mountain**
Saint James, Islands of. **Farallon Islands**
Saint Jose, Mount. **Lassen Peak**
Saint Joseph, Mount [Lassen]. **Lassen Peak**
Saint Luke, Islas de. **Channel Islands**
Salmon Bend. **Colusa**
Salud, Cañada de la. **Waddell Creek**
Samuel Soda Springs. **Grigsby Soda Springs**
San Alexos, Cañada de. **San Elijo Valley**
San Ambrosia, Isla de. **Santa Rosa Island**
San Amidio. **San Emigdio**
San Antonio (town). **Brooklyn Basin**
San Antonio, Cerrito de. **Cerrito, El**
San Antonio, Rio de. **Salinas River**
San Apollinares. **Cristianitos Canyon**
San Benvenuto. **Osos, Cañada de los**
San Bernardo, Rio de. **Santa Ynez River**
San Bernardo Island. **San Miguel Island**
San Buenaventura, Rio de. **Salinas River**
San Campistrano. **San Juan Capistrano**
San Cayetan, Arroyo de. **Cayetano Creek**
San Clemente, Rio de. **Alameda**
San Daniel, Laguna Grande de. **Guadalupe Lake; Laguna, Punta de la**
Sand Cut. **Aromas**
Sanders Bend. **Bend**
San Dieguillo. **San Dieguito**
San Francisco: Rio de; Llano de. **San Joaquin River; Sacramento River; Tule River**
San Gabriel, Rio de. **Hondo; Kaweah**
San Gabriel de Amuscopiabit, Caxon de. **Cajon**
San Geronimo, Arroyo. **Paper Mill Creek; Lagunitas Creek; San Geronimo Creek**
Sangre, Isla de la. **Bloody Island**
San Jacinto Hot Springs. **Gilman Hot Springs**
San Jacinto Plains. **Perris Valley**
San Jacome de la Marca. **Jamacha**
San Joaquin de la Laguna. **Santa Barbara**
San Jose, Punta de. **Fort Point**
San José Cupertino, Arroyo de. **Stevens Creek; Cupertino**
San Jose de Alvarado. **Alvarado**
San Josef o Cantil Blanco, Punta de. **Fort Point**
San Juan, Rio. **Calaveras River**
San Juan Bautista, Mount [Contra Costa]. **Diablo, Mount**

San Juan by the Sea. **Serra**

San Juan Capistrano el Viejo [San Diego]. **San Luis Rey**

Sankypoco. **San Carpoforo Creek**

San Ladislao. **Buchon, Point**

San Lucas, Isla de. **Santa Rosa Island; San Miguel Island**

San Luis [Santa Barbara]. **Gaviota**

San Luis Beltran, Cañada de. **Waddell Creek**

San Marcos, Sierra de. **Sierra Nevada**

San Martin, Sierras de. **Santa Lucia Range**

San Pablo [Imperial]. **Pilot Knob**

San Pablo [Kern]. **Castaic**

San Pedro, Bahia de. **Monterey Bay**

San Pedro, Rio de. **Tule River**

San Philipe, Rio de. **San Felipe Creek**

San Salvador de Horta, Arroyo de. **San Lorenzo Creek**

San Salvador Island. **Santa Catalina**

San Sebastian, Cabo Blanco de. **Saint George, Point**

San Sebastian, Isla de. **Santa Cruz Island**

San Sebastian, Rio Grande de. **Tomales Bay**

Santa Catalina de Bononia de los Encinos. **Encino Park**

Santa Clara de Monte Falco. **Rincon Point** [Ventura]

Santa Conefundis. **Pitas Point**

Santa Cora Creek. **Zanja Cota Creek**

Santa Cota Creek. **Zanja Cota Creek**

Santa Delfina, Rio de. **Salinas River**

Santa Humiliana, Cañada de. **San Carpoforo Creek**

Santa Margarita de Cortona. **Mescal Island; Santa Margarita**

Santa Margarita de los Peñasquitos. **Peñasquitos**

Santa Praxedis de los Rosales. **Flores; Rose**

Santa Rosa [San Luis Obispo]. **Cambria**

Santa Rosa de las Lajas. **Yuha**

Santa Teresa, Rancheria de. **Cojo**

Santiago, Rio de. **Poso Creek**

Santos. **Strathmore**

Santos Reyes, Rio de los. **Kings River**

Santo Tomas, Islotes de. **Anacapa Islands**

San Ygnacio, Rio de. **Russian River**

Saratoga Creek. **Campbell Creek** [Santa Clara]

Sastise River. **Shasta River**

Sasty River. **Shasta River**

Satiyome. **Sotoyome**

Sauquil. **Soquel**

Saver Peak. **Shaver Lake**

Sayante, Rio de. **Zayante Creek**

Scho-ko-ni. **Royal Arches**

Schoolcraft Island. **Sutter Island**

School House Station. **Colma**

Schumann Canyon. **Shuman Canyon**

Sciad Creek. **Seiad Creek**

Scodie Mountain. **Kiavah Mountain; Scodie Canyon**

Scorpion Hills. **Escorpion**

Secuan. **Sequan**

Sek-pe. **Sespe**

Semi Pass. **Simi Hills**

Senel. **Sanel Mountain**

Sentinel Rock [Alpine]. **Jeff Davis Peak**

Sequoya. **Canyon; Sequoia**

Shabaikai. **Russian River**

Shanel. **Sanel Mountain**

Sheep Island. **Brooks Island**

Sheep Mountain. **Langley, Mount; Tucki Mountain**

Shellville. **Schellville**

Shoal Point. **Richmond Point**

Shoquel. **Soquel**

Shore Acres. **Manhattan Beach**

Sibleyville. **Dinuba**

Siegler Springs; Sigler Springs. **Seigler Springs**

Sierra Azul. **Blue; Azul**

Sierra Verde de Pinos. **Pinos; Santa Cruz Mountains**

Siffords. **Drakesbad**

Silver Lakes [Alpine]. **Kinney Lakes**

Simiopolis. **Simi**

Sims [Sacramento]. **Runyon**

Siquico, Arroyo de. **Sisquoc River**

Sir Francis Drake Bay. **Drakes Bay**

Sisson. **Shasta**

Si-top-topo. **Topatopa**

Skinner Grove. **Atwell Grove**

Slabtown. **Cambria**

Slaughters Bar. **Goodyears Bar**

Slavianka. **Russian River**

Slide. **Fortuna**

Slumgullion. **Carson Hill** [Calaveras]

Smith Mountain [San Diego]. **Palomar Mountain**

Smiths Landing. **Antioch**

Smiths Neck. **Loyalton**

Smithson Springs. **Pinon Hills**

Smithville. **Stonyford**

Socouan. **Sequan**

Soldiers Gulch. **Volcano**

Solid Comfort. **Lokoya**

Solomons Hole. **Moaning Cave**

Somerset. **Bellflower**

Somes, Somo [Ventura]. **Somis**

Sonoma, Bahia de [Contra Costa]. **San Pablo Bay**

Sorass Lake. **Dry Lake**

Sotcher Lake. **Satcher Lake**

Sovovo. **Soboba**

South Butte. **Sutter**

South Clearwater. **Hynes**

South Cucamonga. **Guasti**

South Dome. **Starr King, Mount; Sentinel Dome; Half Dome**

Southeast Palisade. **Split Mountain**

South Fork; South Fork Mountain [Modoc]. **Likely**

South Gable Promontory. **Harvard, Mount**

South Riverside. **Corona**

Spanish Corral. **Ophir**

Spottiswood. **Famoso**

Spring Valley [Calaveras]. **Valley Springs**

Springville. **Fortuna**

Squashan Creek. **Squash Ann Creek**

Squaw Village. **Olympic Valley; Squaw**

Sr'pr. **Surpur Creek**

Stagg. **Ludlow**

Staininger Ranch. **Scott**

Stalder. **Mira Loma**

Starve-Out. **Grenada**

Stawain. **Starwein**

Stella. **Whiskeytown**

Stephens Creek. **Stevens Creek; Cupertino**

Stevens, Point. **Richmond, Point**

Stewart. **Sonora**

Stoney Peak. **Freaner Peak**

Stony Creek Forest Reserve. **Mendocino National Forest**

Stowen. **Starwein**

Strancos Creek. **Tranca**

Stratton. **Stratford**

Strawberry Valley [Siskiyou]. **Shasta**

Sue. **Suey Creek**

Sugarloaf [Orange]. **Pleasants Peak**

Summer Home. **Balch Park**

Summit [Plumas]. **Vinton**

Summit [Riverside]. **Beaumont**

Summit City [Alpine]. **Jeff Davis**

Summit Peak. **Ina Coolbrith, Mount**

Sumners Bar. **Somesbar**

Susqual. **Suscol**

Suysunes, Bahia de los. **Suisun Bay**

Swager. **Swauger**

Swauger [Humboldt]. **Loleta**

Sweet Pizzlewig Creek. **Pizzlewig Creek**

Sycamore [Fresno]. **Herndon**

Taa-bo-tah. **Anderson Valley**

Tacui. **Tecuya**

Tah-ee-chay-pah Pass. **Tehachapi Pass**

Tahichipi Pass. **Tehachapi Pass**

Tah-le-wah. **Talawa**

Ta-hual-tapa. **Stover Mountain**

Ta'i. **Palomar Mountain**

Tail Canyon. **Jail Canyon**

Tailholt. **White River**

Tajauta. **Tajante**

Tarro, El. **Jarro**

Tarup Creek. **Turup Creek**

Tasayac. **Vernal Fall**

Tebo. **Thibau**

Tecabala. **Bally**

Te'kta Wroi. **Tectah Creek**

Temeltatle Creek. **Temettati Creek**

Temescal, Encinal de. **Encina; Oakland**

Temetall; Temetatl. **Temettati Creek**

Ten-ie-ya Lake. **Tenaya, Lake**

Termination Valley. **Eureka Valley**

Terra Buena. **Tierra Buena**

Thalheim. **Valley Home**

Tharps Peak. **Alta Peak; Tharps Rock**

Thompsons Dry Diggings. **Yreka**

Thoms Creek. **Thomes Creek**

Three Arches. **South Laguna**

Three Buttes. **Sutter Buttes**

Tichos. **San Luis Obispo**

Ti'i. **Tea Bar**

Tijuan, Arroyo de. **Tia Juana River**

Tinaja, La. **Tenaja Canyon**

Tinoqui, Rancheria de. **Tinaquaic**

Tissaack. **Half Dome; Starr King, Mount**

Tixlimi; Tixlini. **San Luis Obispo**

Tizon, Rio del. **Colorado River**

Tlamath. **Klamath**

Toadtown. **Johnstonville**

To-bi-pa. **Capell Valley**

Todos Santos. **Concord**

Todos Santos, Puerto de. **Cojo**

Tokelalume. **Tocaloma**

To-ko-ya. **North Dome**

To-le-wah. **Talawa**

Tollones, Arroyo de los. **Toyon**

Toluca. **Tulucay Creek**

Toms Creek. **Thomes Creek**

Tontache, Lake. **Tulare Lake; Tache**

Tool-lool-lo-we-ack; Toololuwack. **Illilouette Canyon**

Toolwass. **Toowa Range**

Toorup, Mount. **Turup Creek**

Topotopow. **Topatopa Bluff**

Top Top. **Topatopa**

Tos-toya. **White Mountains**

Tote-ack-ah-noo-la. **El Capitan**

Tewalumnes, Rio de los. **Tuolumne River**

Toyabe National Forest. **Toiyabe National Forest**

Truchy River. **Truckee River**

Tuhunga. **Tujunga**

Tujunta, Monte de. **Tajanta**

Tululowehäck. **Illilouette Canyon**

Tuolumne Valley. **Hetch Hetchy Valley**

Tu'rip. **Turup Creek**

Turwar Creek. **Terwah Creek**

Turwer. **Terwah Creek**

Tuxedo, The. **Mount Hermon**

Twenty-Mile House. **Cromberg**

Ululatos, Arrollo de. **Ulatis Creek**
Ulupa. **Yulupa**
Umalibo. **Malibu**
Uncah Pah. **Colorado River**
Uncle Sam [Lake]. **Kelseyville**
Uniontown [El Dorado]. **Lotus**
University Park. **Palo Alto**
Urebure. **Buriburi Ridge**

Vaca. **Elmira**
Valale, Arroyo. **Gualala**
Vallejo Mills. **Niles**
Valley of California. **Great Central Valley**
Valley of the Moon. **Sonoma Valley; Switzer-**
land
Vallicito. **Vallecito**
Vallo Citron. **Vallecito**
Vasco, The. **Vaqueros, Canada de los**
Venados, Arroyo de los. **Deer Creek**
Vernon [Sutter]. **Verona**
Vigia, Cerro de la. **Lavigia Hill**
Villa de Branciforte. **Branciforte Creek;**
Pueblo; San Cruz
Vincente. **Vicente**
Violin City. **Fiddletown**
Virginia Mills. **Berry Creek**
Vivoras, Las. **Oso Flaco**
Vodega. **Bodega**
Volcano Creek [Tulare]. **Golden Trout Creek**

Wages Creek. **Weges Creek**
Waijau. **Watkins, Mount**
Wa-kal'-la. **Merced River**
Wakopee. **Owens River**
Walalla. **Gualala**
Wal Hollow. **Gualala**
Walloupa [Nevada]. **Guadalupe**
Walters. **Mecca**
Wash [Plumas]. **Clio**
Wasna, Rio. **Huasna River**
Water. **Newberry**
Waterman Junction. **Barstow**
Webber Creek. **Weber Creek**
Weeks Poultry Community. **Winnetka**
Wee-yot. **Eel River**
Wĕ'itspūs. **Weitchpec**
Welch Station. **Sims**
Welchs Store. **Plainsburg**
Wendling. **Navarro**
Wene'me. **Hueneme**
Wenok. **Guenoc**
Wenot. **Los Angeles**
West Lodi. **Kingdon**
Weyo. **Weott**
Whalers Harbor. **Ballena; Richardson Bay**

Wheatville. **Kingsburg**
Wheelock. **Fort Jones**
Whiskey Creek [Shasta]. **Schilling; Whiskey-**
town
Whiskey Flat [Kern]. **Kernville**
Whiskey Hill [Santa Cruz]. **Freedom**
White Horse [Siskiyou]. **Kinyon**
White Mountain [Lassen N. P.]. **Reading Peak**
White Mountain Peak. **Montgomery Peak;**
White Mountains
Whitmores Ferry. **Kingston** [King]
Whitney Creek [Tulare]. **Golden Trout**
Creek
Whitton. **Planada**
Wi'ke. **Yreka; Shasta**
Wikyo. **Palomar Mountain**
Wild River. **American River**
Willard Valley. **Cuddeback Lake**
Williamsons Pass. **Soledad Pass**
Willis Jepson Hole. **Willis Hole**
Willow Springs [Borrega State Park]. **Santa**
Catarina Springs
Wilma Lake. **Wilmer Lake**
Wi'lok-yomi. **Guilicos**
Wim-mel-che. **Kings River**
Windfield. **Winton**
Wineville. **Mira Loma**
Winimem. **Bally**
Wintoon. **Wintun**
Wishi Honopi. **Hanaupah Canyon**
Wo'kel. **Waukell**
Wolfs Hill. **Wolfskill**
Woods Dry Diggings. **Auburn**
Woods Ferry. **Woodbridge**
Woodville. **Woodleaf**
Woosterville. **Ione**
Wr'LriWroi. **Worthla Creek**
Wy-e-ka. **Yreka; Shasta**
Wynema. **Hueneme**

Xamacha. **Jamacha**
Xaslindiñ. **Horse Linto Creek**

Yabit. **Los Angeles**
Yachicumé. **Calaveras River**
Yalloballey. **Bally; Linn, Mount**
Ya-loo. **Feather River**
Yamnonalit. **Santa Barbara**
Yankee Jim's Divide. **Divide, The**
Yarro, El. **Jarro**
Yodoi. **Yolo**
Yohama. **Yuhwamai**
Yokaia; Yokaya. **Ukiah**
Yo-la Bo-li. **Bally**
Yornet Creek. **Yeomet Creek**
Yoteh. **Murderers Gulch**
Yo-wy-we. **Nevada Fall**

Yslais, Arroyo de los. **Islay**
Yu-kai. **Ukiah**
Yukhnam. **Ukonom Creek**
Yupu. **Yuba**

Zanja Onda. **Honda** [Los Angeles]

Zanjapoco; Zanjapojo. **San Carpoforo Creek**
Zanoma. **Sonoma**
Zelzah. **Northridge**
Zim-Zim Creek. **Zem-Zem Creek**
Zoquel, Rio de. **Soquel Creek**